PassKey EA Review Complete: Individuals, Businesses and Representation

IRS Enrolled Agent Exam Study Guide 2017-2018 Edition

PassKey
Learning Systems

Richard Gramkow, EA
Christy Pinheiro, EA, ABA®
Kolleen Wells, EA
Joel Busch, CPA, JD

Editor: Joel Busch, CPA, JD

This study guide is designed for test-takers who will take their exams in the 2017-2018 EA Exam testing window (May 1, 2017, to February 28, 2018).

PassKey EA Review, Complete: Individuals, Businesses, and Representation, IRS Enrolled Agent Exam Study Guide 2017-2018 Edition

ISBN: 978-0-9986118-4-6

First Printing. 2017.

PassKey EA Review® is a U.S. Registered Trademark

www.PassKeyPublications.com

Online study: www.passkeylearningsystems.com

Table of Contents

Recent Praise for the PassKey EA Review Series

(Real customers, real names, public testimonials)

PassKey was the only study aid that I used

Stephen J Woodard, CFP, CLU, ChFC

The guides were an invaluable resource. They were concise and covered the subject matter succinctly with spot-on end of chapter questions that were very similar to what I encountered on the exams.

I passed all three parts.

Robbie Cantoron

I passed all three parts of the EA exam using this book, which is why I'll give it five stars... There are many tax laws I've learned about by studying this book that I haven't encountered yet preparing returns, so I did end up learning a lot. The trick is to focus, (after reading the material), on the multiple choice questions at the end of each chapter and their solutions: this is how you'll apply and practice what you've learned and really learn the details.

This review is the best on the market.

Yaw Asiante-Asamoah

I passed on all three parts on one attempt. The questions in the Review and Workbook are similar to the real exams. I got a big raise and my bonus went up at my seasonal job. It's worth the money, trust me.

This book helped me pass.

Kenichi Mochizukion

I used the PassKey workbook after studying PassKey textbook. The example questions cover all the topics and require good understanding to answer, so it was very helpful to reveal my weak areas prior to the exam.

Wonderful!

Ana Lavallee

PassKey was all I needed to pass the three tests to become an EA in just three months. The books are easy to read and understand. Thank you!

Outstanding!

Derrell L. Chastain

Outstanding! Helped me pass the EA exam...I used all three books!

Highly recommend these materials

Tosha H. Knelangeon

Using only this book and the workbook, I passed all three EA exams on my first try. I highly recommend these materials. As long as you put in the time to read and study all the information provided, you should be well-prepared.

Very useful, I passed 1st and 2nd exams by reading only PassKey!

Shixiong Feng

Very useful, I passed the 1st and 2nd exams by only reading the PassKey EA Review. If you are willing to spend some time to read the whole book thoroughly, then this book is the only thing you need to pass the EA exams.

Worked like a charm!

Brian Lang (New York, New York)

I passed on my first try.

Excellent explanations!

Janet Briggs

The best thing about these books is that each answer has a comprehensive explanation about why the answer is correct. I passed all three EA exams on the first attempt.

I passed!

Ismail Osman

The book is excellent to pass the EA exam. I passed Part 1 on my first attempt. These are great study resources. I love PassKey!

Amazing!

Sopio Svanishvilion

PassKey helped me pass all three parts of the Enrolled Agent exam. They are a "must have" if you want to pass your EA exams.

Almost like the real EA exam!

Charlotte Ennusah

The questions in the book are almost like the questions on the real exams. I recommend this book for everyone who wants to spend less time getting their EA license.

PassKey is the way to go!

Alaina Crowell

I passed all three SEEs on the first try in ten weeks! Each unit is explained so clearly, and I was completely prepared for each SEE. Wonderful books.

Five Stars

Jane Marquiss

Wonderful books; I passed the first time! Thanks for these wonderful books!

Introduction

Congratulations on taking the first step toward becoming an enrolled agent, a widely respected professional tax designation. The Internal Revenue Service licenses enrolled agents, known as EAs after candidates pass a competency exam testing their knowledge of federal tax law. As an enrolled agent, you will have the same representation rights as a CPA, with the ability to represent taxpayers in IRS audits and appeals—an EA's rights are unlimited before all levels and offices of the IRS.

The PassKey study guide series is designed to help you study for the EA exam, which is formally called the *IRS Special Enrollment Examination* or *"SEE."*

EA Exam Basics

The EA exam consists of three parts, which candidates may schedule separately and take in any order they wish. The computerized exam covers all aspects of federal tax law, with Part 1 testing the taxation of individuals; Part 2 testing the taxation of businesses; and Part 3 testing representation, practice, and procedures.

Each part of the EA exam features 100 multiple choice questions, with no written answers required. The exam may include some experimental questions that are not scored. You will not know which of the questions count toward your score and which do not.

Computerized EA Exam Format
Part 1: Individual Taxation-100 questions
Part 2: Business Taxation-100 questions
Part 3: Representation, Practice, and Procedures-100 questions

You will have 3.5 hours to complete each part of the exam. The actual seat time is four hours, which allows time for a pre-exam tutorial and a post-exam survey. An on-screen timer counts down the amount of time you have to finish.

The testing company Prometric exclusively administers the EA exam at thousands of testing centers across the United States and in certain other countries. You can find valuable information and register online at ***www.prometric.com/SEE***.

Testing Center Procedures

The testing center is designed to be a secure environment. The following are procedures you will need to follow on test day:

1. Check in about a half-hour before your appointment time, and bring a current government-issued ID with a photo and signature. If you do not have a valid ID, you will be turned away and will have to pay for a new exam appointment. Refunds will not be issued by Prometric if you forget to bring proper ID with you.
2. The EA exam is a closed-book test, so you are not allowed to bring any notes or reference materials into the testing room. The center supplies sound-blocking headphones if you want to use them.
3. No food, water, or other beverages are allowed in the testing room.
4. You will be given scratch paper and a pencil to use, which will be collected after the exam.
5. You will be able to use an onscreen calculator during the exam, or Prometric will provide you with a handheld calculator. You cannot bring your own calculator into the examination room.
6. Before entering the testing room, you will be scanned with a metal detector wand.

7. You will need to sign in and out every time you leave the testing room. Bathroom breaks are permitted, but the test timer will continue to count down.
8. You are not allowed to talk or communicate with other test-takers in the exam room. Prometric continuously monitors the testing via video, physical walk-throughs, and an observation window.

> **Important Note:** Violation of any of these procedures may result in the disqualification of your exam. In cases of cheating, the IRS says candidates are subject to consequences that include civil and criminal penalties.

Exam-takers who require special accommodations under the Americans with Disabilities Act (ADA) must contact Prometric at 888-226-9406 to obtain an accommodation request form. The test is administered in English; a language barrier is not considered a disability.

Exam Content

Each May, using questions based on the prior calendar year's tax law, the IRS introduces multiple new versions of each part of the EA exam. If you fail a particular part of the exam and need to retake it, do not expect to see the identical questions the next time.

Prometric's website includes broad content outlines for each exam part. When you study, make sure you are familiar with the items listed, which are covered in detail in your PassKey guides. The IRS no longer releases test questions and answers from prior exams, although questions from older exams (pre-2005) are still available on the IRS website for review. Be aware that tax law changes every year, so be familiar with recent updates and do not rely too heavily on these earlier questions and answers.

Your PassKey study guides present an overview of all the major areas of federal taxation that enrolled agents typically encounter in their practices and are likely to appear on the exam. Although our guides are designed to be comprehensive, we suggest you also review IRS publications and try to learn as much as you can about tax law in general, so you are well-equipped to take the exam.

In addition to this study guide, we highly recommend that all exam candidates read:

- **Publication 17, *Your Federal Income Tax*** (for Part 1 of the exam), and
- **Circular 230, *Regulations Governing the Practice of Attorneys, Certified Public Accountants, Enrolled Agents, Enrolled Actuaries, and Appraisers before the Internal Revenue Service*** (for Part 3 of the exam).

You may download these publications for free from the IRS website.

> **Note:** Some exam candidates take *Part 3: Representation, Practice, and Procedures* first rather than taking the tests in order, since the material in Part 3 is considered less complex. However, test-takers should know that several questions pertaining to taxation of *Individuals* (Part 1) and *Businesses* (Part 2) are often included on the Part 3 exam.

Exam Strategy

Each multiple choice question has four answer choices. There are several different question formats, and examples of each format are featured in your PassKey study guides. During the exam, you should read each question thoroughly to understand exactly what is being asked. Be particularly careful when the question uses language such as "not" or "except."

If you are unsure of an answer, you may mark it for review and return to it later. Try to eliminate clearly wrong answers from the four possible choices to narrow your odds of selecting the right answer. But be sure to answer every question, even if you have to guess because all answers left incomplete will be marked as incorrect. Each question is weighted equally.

Format One-Direct Question
Which of the following entities are required to file Form 709, *United States Gift Tax Return*? A. An individual B. An estate or trust C. A corporation D. All of the above
Format Two-Incomplete Sentence
Supplemental wages do not include payments for: A. Accumulated sick leave B. Nondeductible moving expenses C. Vacation pay D. Travel reimbursements paid at the federal government's per diem rate
Format Three-All of the Following Except
There are five tests which must be met for you to claim an exemption for a dependent. Which of the following is not a requirement? A. Citizen or Resident Test B. Member of Household or Relationship Test C. Disability Test D. Joint Return Test

There may also be a limited number of questions that have four choices, with three incorrect statements or facts and only one with a correct statement or fact, which you would select as the right answer.

With 3.5 hours allotted for each part of the exam, you have slightly more than two minutes per question. Try to answer the questions you are sure about quickly, so you can devote more time to those that include calculations or that you are unsure about. Remember the clock does not stop for bathroom breaks, so allocate your time wisely.

To familiarize yourself with the computerized testing format, you may take a tutorial on the Prometric website. However, the tutorial only illustrates what the test screens look like; it does not allow you to revisit questions you have left open or marked for review, as you can do during the actual exam.

Scoring Methods

The EA exam is not graded on a curve, and the IRS does not reveal either a percentage of correct answers needed to pass or a predetermined pass rate. Each question on the exam is worth one point. The IRS determines scaled scores by calculating the number of questions answered correctly from the total number of questions in the exam and converting to a scale that ranges from 40 to 130. The IRS has set the scaled passing score at 105, which corresponds to the minimum level of knowledge deemed acceptable for EAs.

After you finish your exam and submit your answers, you will exit the testing room, and a Prometric staff member will print results showing whether you passed or failed. Test results are automatically shared with the IRS, so you do not need to submit them yourself. Test scores are confidential and will be revealed only to you and the IRS.

If you pass, your printed results will show a passing designation but not your actual score. The printout also will not indicate which specific questions you answered correctly or incorrectly.

If you fail, you will receive a scaled score, so you will be able to see how close you are to the minimum score of 105.

You will also receive the following diagnostic information to help you know which subject areas to concentrate on when studying to retake the exam:

- *Level 1: Area of weakness where additional study is necessary. It is important for you to focus on this domain as you prepare to take the test again. You may want to consider taking a course or participating actively in a study group on this topic.*
- *Level 2: Might need additional study.*
- *Level 3: Clearly demonstrated an understanding of the subject area.*

These diagnostic indicators correspond to various sections of each part of the exam.

If necessary, you may take each part of the exam up to four times during the testing window between May 1 and February 28. You will need to re-register with Prometric and pay fees each new time you take an exam part.

You may carry over passing scores for individual parts of the exam up to two years from the date you took them.

Pass Rates

The yearly pass rates for the SEE vary by exam. In the prior year testing period, the highest pass rate was for Part 3, with a nearly 90% success rate. Just over 80% of test-takers passed Part 1.

The pass rate for Part 2 was much lower, averaging about 60%. Prometric notes that it can be misleading to compare pass rates for the various exams because the same individuals do not take each one. The number of candidates who take Part 1 is nearly double the number of candidates taking either Part 2 or Part 3.

Applying for Enrollment

Once you have passed all three parts of the EA exam, you can apply to become an enrolled agent. The process includes an IRS review of your tax compliance history. Failure to timely file or pay personal income taxes can be grounds for denial of enrollment. The IRS's Return Preparer Office will review the circumstances of each case and make determinations on an individual basis. You may not practice as an EA until the IRS approves your application and issues you an enrollment card, a process that takes up to 60 days or more.

Successfully passing the EA exam can launch you into a fulfilling and lucrative new career. The exam requires intense preparation and diligence, but with the help of PassKey's comprehensive *EA Review*, you will have the tools you need to learn how to become an enrolled agent.

We wish you much success.

Ten Steps for the IRS EA Exam

STEP 1: Learn

Learn more about the enrolled agent designation and explore the career opportunities that await you after passing your EA exam. In addition to preparing income tax returns for clients, EAs can represent individuals and businesses before the IRS, just as attorneys and CPAs do. A college degree or professional tax background is not required to take the EA exam. Many people who use the PassKey study guides have had no prior experience preparing tax returns, but go on to rewarding new professional careers.

STEP 2: Gather Information

Gather more information before you launch into your studies. The IRS publishes basic information about becoming an EA on its website (*www.irs.gov/Tax-Professionals/Enrolled-Agents*). You will also find valuable information about the exam itself on the Prometric testing website at www.prometric.com/see. Be sure to download the *Candidate Information Bulletin*, which takes you step-by-step through the registration and testing process.

STEP 3: Obtain a PTIN

PTIN stands for *Preparer Tax Identification Number*. Before you can register for your EA exam, you must obtain a PTIN from the IRS. The PTIN sign-up system can be found at www.irs.gov/ptin. You will need to create an account, provide personal information, and pay a required fee. Since tax return information is used to authenticate your identity, you should use a previous year's individual tax return if you're applying for a PTIN and you filed your tax return in the past eight weeks. It takes about 15 minutes to sign up online and receive your PTIN. Candidates who choose to use the paper Form W-12, *IRS Paid Preparer Tax Identification Number (PTIN) Application and Renewal*, will have to wait about four to six weeks to have their PTINs processed. Foreign-based candidates without a Social Security number are also required to have a PTIN in order to register to take the exam; they will need to submit additional paperwork with their Form W-12.

STEP 4: Register with Prometric

Once you have your PTIN, you may register for your exam on the Prometric website by creating an account to set up your user ID and password. You must also complete Form 2587, *Application for Special Enrollment Examination*.

STEP 5: Schedule Your Test

After creating an account, you can complete the registration process by clicking on "Scheduling". Your exam appointment must be scheduled within one year from the date of registration. You can choose a test site, time, and date that are convenient for you. Prometric has test centers in most major metropolitan areas of the United States, as well as in many other countries.

You may schedule as little as two days in advance—space permitting—through the website or by calling 800-306-3926 Monday through Friday. Be aware that the website and the phone line show different inventories of available times and dates, so you may want to check both for your preferred testing dates. The testing fee is nonrefundable. Once you've scheduled, you'll receive a confirmation number. Keep it for your records because you'll need it to reschedule, cancel, or change your appointment.

STEP 6: Adopt a Study Plan

Focus on one exam part at a time, and adopt a study plan that covers each unit of your PassKey guides. You'll need to develop your own individualized study program. The period of time you'll need to prepare for each exam is truly unique to you, based on how much prior tax preparation experience you have and your current level of tax knowledge; how well you understand and retain the information you read; and how much time you have to study for each test. For those without prior tax experience, a good rule of thumb is to study at least 60 hours for each of the three exam sections. *Part 2: Businesses* may require additional study preparation, as evidenced by the lower pass rates. One thing is true for all candidates: for each of the tests, start studying well in advance of your scheduled exam date.

STEP 7: Get Plenty of Rest and Good Nutrition

Get plenty of rest, exercise, and good nutrition prior to the EA exam. You'll want to be at your best on exam day.

STEP 8: Test Day

Be sure to arrive early at the test site. Prometric advises arriving at least 30 minutes before your scheduled exam time. If you miss your appointment and are not allowed to take the test, you'll forfeit your fee and have to pay for a new appointment. Remember to bring a government-issued ID with your name, photo, and signature. Your first and last name must exactly match the first and last name you used to register for the exam.

STEP 9: During the Exam

This is when your hard work finally pays off. Focus and don't worry if you don't know the answer to every question, but make sure you use your time well. Give your best answer to every question. All questions left blank will be marked as wrong.

STEP 10: Congratulations. You Passed!

After celebrating your success, you need to apply for your EA designation. The quickest way is by filling out Form 23, *Application for Enrollment to Practice before the Internal Revenue Service*, on the IRS website. You may also pay online. Once your application is approved, you'll be issued an enrollment card, and you'll be official—a brand new enrolled agent!

PART 1: INDIVIDUALS

Essential Tax Law Updates for Individuals
Part One

Here is a quick summary of some of the important tax figures for the current enrolled agent exam cycle (May 1, 2017, to February 28, 2018):

Income Tax Return Filing Deadline: April 18, 2017

> **Note:** The normal filing deadline for individual taxpayers is April 15. The deadline is extended because the Emancipation Day, a holiday in Washington, D.C., will be observed on Monday, April 17, pushing the nation's filing deadline to April 18.

Personal Exemption Amount: $4,050

2016 Personal Exemption Phaseout Thresholds:
- Single: $259,400 -$381,900.
- Head of Household: $285,350 -$407,850
- Married Filing Jointly or Qualifying Widow(er): $311,300 - $433,800.
- Married Filing Separately: $155,650 - $216,900

2016 Standard Deduction Amounts:
- Single or married filing separately: $6,300
- Married filing jointly or Qualifying widower: $12,600
- Head of household: $9,300
- The additional standard deduction for people who have reached age 65 (or who are blind) is:
  - $1,250 for married taxpayers or
  - $1,550 for unmarried taxpayers.

Gross Income Filing Thresholds for U.S. Citizens and U.S. Residents:
- Single: $10,350 (65 or older $11,900)
- Married Filing Jointly: $20,700,
  - 65 or older (one spouse) $21,950;
  - 65 or older (both spouses): $23,200
- Head of Household: $13,350 (65 or older $14,900)
- Married Filing Separately (any age): $4,050
- Qualifying Widow(er) with dependent child: $16,650 (65 or older $17,900)
- Any taxpayer with self-employment income of $400 or more in any taxable year must file a return.

2016 Mileage Rates:
- Business: 54¢ per mile
- Charitable purposes: 14¢ per mile
- Medical and moving: 19¢ per mile

2016 Retirement Contribution Limits:

- Roth and traditional IRAs: $5,500, (catch-up contribution of $1,000 for taxpayers age 50 or older).
- 401(k), 403(b): $18,000, (catch-up contribution of $6,000 for taxpayers age 50 or older).
- Maximum contribution for defined contribution plans is $53,000.
- SIMPLE 401k or SIMPLE IRA contributions limit: $12,500 (catch-up contribution of $3,000 for taxpayers age 50 or older)

2016 Social Security Taxable Wage Base: $118,500
FUTA Wage Base: The FUTA tax rate is 6% on the first $7000 paid to each employee.
Medicare Taxable Wage Base: No limit

2016 Health Savings Accounts (HSAs) Annual Contribution Limits:

- HSA for self-only coverage: $3,350
- HSA for family coverage: $6,750

2016 Estate and Gift Tax Exclusion Amount: $5.45 million per individual
Annual Exclusion for Gifts: $14,000
Non-Citizen Marital Threshold for Gift Tax: $148,000
Top rate on qualified dividends and long-term gains for individuals: 20%

2016 Education Credits and Deductions:

- American Opportunity Credit: $2,500 per student (up to 40% refundable)
- Lifetime Learning Credit: $2,000 per return
- Coverdell Education Savings Account (amount per beneficiary): $2,000
- Tuition and fees deduction: $4,000 (this deduction is set to expire in 2017)
- Student loan interest deduction: $2,500

2016 Maximum Earned Income Tax Credit (EITC):

- $6,269 with three or more qualifying children
- $5,572 with two qualifying children
- $3,373 with one qualifying child
- $506 with no qualifying children

Investment income must be $3,400 or less for the year in order to qualify for the EITC.

2016 Earned Income Tax Credit (EITC) Phaseout Ranges:
To be eligible for the EITC, the taxpayer must have earned income less than:

- $14,880 ($20,430 if MFJ) with no qualifying child
- $39,296 ($44,846 if MFJ) with one qualifying child
- $44,648 ($50,198 if MFJ) with two qualifying children
- $47,955 ($53,505 if MFJ) with three or more qualifying children

2016 Foreign Earned Income and Housing Exclusions:

- Maximum foreign earned income exclusion: $101,300
- Base housing amount: $16,208

2016 Maximum Credit Amounts:

- Adoption Credit: $13,460 per child
- Child Tax Credit: $1,000 per child (unchanged from the previous year)
- Credit for Child and Dependent Care Expenses: $3,000 (one child); $6,000 (two or more)
- Retirement Savings Contributions Credit (Saver's Credit): up to $2,000 ($4,000 if married filing jointly)

Withholding Threshold for "Nanny Tax" or Household Employees: $2,000

"Kiddie Tax" Unearned Income Threshold: All unearned income over $2,100 is taxed at the parents' tax rate.

2016 AMT Exemption Amount

- $53,900 for Single or HOH
- $83,800 for Married Filing Jointly or Qualifying Widow(er)
- $41,900 for Married Filing Separately

Section 179 Deduction

- The $500,000 deduction limit and $2 million reduction threshold were made permanent and also indexed for inflation (there is a $2,010,000 reduction threshold for 2016).
- The special allowance for depreciable software was made permanent in 2016
- Section 179 is now allowed for certain air conditioning and heating units
- The Section 179 election can be revoked (but once revoked, it becomes irrevocable)
- The $250,000 cap attributable to Qualified Leasehold Improvement Property has been removed for 2016, allowing a full $500K deduction for qualifying property.

Bonus Depreciation: 50% Bonus depreciation has been extended. The PATH ACT also introduced a gradual reduction from 50% in 2015-2017, to 40% in 2018, and to 30% in 2019, followed by a complete phase-out of the deduction in 2019.

2016 Affordable Care Act (Obamacare) Penalty: 2.5% of household AGI or a maximum of $2,085 ($695 per adult, $347.50 per child) for those who do not purchase qualifying health insurance and do not qualify for an exclusion. However, on Jan. 20, 2017, an executive order signed by newly-elected President Trump directed federal agencies to exercise authority and discretion available to them to reduce potential burden to taxpayers. Consistent with that, the IRS has decided to make changes that would continue to allow electronic and paper returns to be accepted for processing in instances where a taxpayer doesn't indicate their health coverage status. At the time of this book's printing, the IRS would accept a taxpayer's return even if they do not respond to the Health Coverage question. However, legislative provisions of the ACA law were still in force at the beginning of 2017, and taxpayers remain required to follow the law and pay what they may owe.

Accelerated Filing Dates for Certain Information Returns: the PATH Act changed the government copy due date for Forms W-2, Form W-3, and Form 1099-MISC to January 31. This new deadline applies to paper filers as well as e-filed forms. This change only affects Forms 1099 that report nonemployee compensation. The filing deadline for other forms in the 1099 series remains unchanged.

Tax Credit Timing: The PATH Act requires that the IRS cannot send out certain refunds (specifically the EITC and the Additional Child Tax Credit) until February 15, 2017. This affects all 2016 tax returns claiming these refundable credits.

Permanent Tax Law Extensions

- **Educator expense deduction** (the Teacher Credit): The $250 deduction for certain expenses of elementary and secondary school teachers was made permanent and is now also indexed for inflation
- **Sales tax deduction:** The deduction of state and local general sales taxes was made permanent.
- Certain tax-free distributions from IRAs for charitable purposes.
- Beneficial rules for contributions of capital gain real property (real estate) made for conservation purposes are now permanent.

Temporary Extensions (Extended through 2016, set to expire in 2017)

- Energy Credits
- Qualified Principal Residence Debt exclusion
- Mortgage insurance premiums deduction
- Tuition and fees deduction

Section 179 Deduction in 2016

- $500,000 limit and $2 million reduction threshold were made permanent and also indexed for inflation ($2,010,000 reduction threshold for 2016, indexed for inflation)
- Special allowance for depreciable software made permanent
- Section 179 is now allowed for certain air conditioning and heating units
- The election can be revoked (but once revoked, it becomes irrevocable)

Tax Exemptions for American Medalists: Olympic and Paralympic athletes may now exclude the value of their medals and prize money.

Credit disallowance: There are new 2 and 10-year bans for disregarding the Child Tax Credit and American Opportunity Credit rules. In 2016, if a taxpayer claims these credits and is later determined to be ineligible for them, a ban may be imposed on the taxpayer from claiming these credits on future returns.

Truncated SSNs on Form W-2: Effective in tax year 2016, the PATH Act extends IRS authority to require truncated Social Security Numbers on Form W-2.

New FBAR filing deadline: FBARs (FinCen Form 114) will now be due on April 15, with a with a maximum 6-month extension to October 15. Previously, a taxpayer could not request an extension to file the FBAR, and the FBAR was due June 30.

Increase in Failure to File Penalty: The Trade Facilitation and Enforcement Act of 2015 increases the penalty for failing to file a tax return in 2016. The higher penalty applies to individual returns filed in 2017, for the 2016 tax season. The increased failure-file penalty is the lesser of $205 (up from $135) or 100% of the amount of tax owed.

Electronic Filing PIN No Longer Valid: The Electronic Filing PIN, an IRS-generated PIN used to verify a taxpayer's signature on a self-prepared, e-filed tax return, is no longer available. To validate a signature on an electronic return, the taxpayer must now use their prior-year adjusted gross income (AGI) or their prior-year self-select PIN. There were no changes to Practitioner PIN Method.

Form 1098-T Required: A taxpayer must have received a Form 1098-T from an eligible educational institution in order to claim the Tuition and Fees Deduction, American Opportunity Credit, or the Lifetime Learning Credit.

21st Century Cures Act: Signed by President Obama in December 2016, this health bill grants small businesses regulatory relief for employers who wish to offer insurance reimbursements to their employees. Employer reimbursements under this type of Health Reimbursement Arrangement may not exceed $4,950 for the employee (or $10,000 for family coverage).

Sharing Economy: In August 2016, the IRS launched a new online resource center that offers taxpayer guidance called the Sharing Economy Tax Center.

Definition of Marriage: The IRS issued final regulations in September 2016 regarding the definition of marriage after the landmark case of *Obergefell v. Hodges*. These regulations state that a marriage of two individuals is recognized for federal tax purposes if the marriage is recognized by the state, possession or territory of the United States in which the marriage is entered into, regardless of where the couple is living. This clarifies the law to include common law marriage as well as marriages performed in a foreign country.

Waiver of the 60-day time limit on IRA rollovers: Starting in August, 2016, Rev. Proc. 2016-47 allows eligible taxpayers can now qualify for a waiver of the 60-day rollover limit and avoid possible early distribution taxes. Taxpayers will submit the self-certification to their plan administrator or an IRA trustee (NOT to the IRS). In the past, taxpayers who failed to meet the rollover time limit could only obtain a waiver by requesting a private letter ruling from the IRS.

New ITIN Rules: All ITINs issued before 2013 will now expire, unless renewed. Application procedures have also changed. There are now three ways to apply for an ITIN. A taxpayer may use Form W-7, or apply in person with an IRS-authorized Certified Acceptance Agent or make an appointment at a designed IRS Taxpayer Assistance Center.

- Older ITINs will expire if not renewed (any ITIN issued before 2013)
- Newer ITINs will expire if not used for three years or more, unless they are renewed
- Form W-7 has been revised as of September 2016
- The IRS will no longer accept passports of dependents as stand-alone documents that lack a date of entry into the United States.

New IRS Acceptance Agent 2016 Program Changes

- The ITIN Acceptance Agent Certification process changes in 2016
- ITIN Acceptance Agent Applications are now accepted year round
- The IRS is actively recruiting IRS acceptance agents

Form 1098 Changes: The IRS Form 1098, Mortgage Interest Statement, now must include the beginning mortgage balance and the property address (not just the mailing address of the mortgage-holder).

Defending Public Safety Employees' Retirement Act: This new law expands the exemption from the 10% early withdrawal penalty tax on early distributions to qualified public safety employees from defined contribution governmental plans. This law is effective for distributions made in 2016.

Unit 1: Tax Returns for Individuals

More Reading:
Publication 17, *Your Federal Income Tax*
Publication 501, *Exemptions, Standard Deduction, and Filing Information*
Publication 971, *Innocent Spouse Relief*
Publication 519, *U.S. Tax Guide for Aliens*
Publication 552, *Recordkeeping for Individuals*
Publication 54, Tax Guide for U.S. Citizens and Resident Aliens Abroad

Overview of EA Exam Part 1: Individuals

For Part 1 of the enrolled agent exam, you will be expected to know a broad range of information about preparing tax returns for individual taxpayers. This information includes the basics of filing status, requirements, and due dates; taxable and nontaxable income; deductions, credits, and adjustments to income; determining the basis of property; figuring capital gains and losses; rental income; retirement income; estate and gift taxes, and much more. We begin with the preliminary work tax return preparers are expected to do in order to prepare accurate tax returns.

Use of Prior Year Returns

When enrolled agents and other tax professionals prepare tax returns for clients, they are expected to perform due diligence in collecting, verifying, and gathering taxpayer data. A preparer is also expected to review prior year tax returns for compliance, accuracy, and completeness. A preparer is required by law to notify a taxpayer of an error or omission on a prior year tax return and the consequences of not correcting the error or omission. However, a preparer is not required to correct the error. The use of prior year returns can help prevent major mathematical errors and alert a preparer to issues specific to a particular client.

In reviewing prior year tax returns, a preparer needs to determine whether there are items that affect the current year's return, including the following:

- Carryovers
- Net operating losses
- Credit for prior year minimum tax (Form 8801)
- Depreciation

Taxpayer Biographical Information

The following information is required to prepare an accurate tax return:

- Legal name
- Date of birth
- Marital status
- Residency status and/or citizenship
- Dependents
- Taxpayer identification number

The IRS requires each individual listed on a federal income tax return to have a valid taxpayer identification number (TIN). That includes the taxpayer, his or her spouse (if married), and any dependents. The types of TINs are:

- Social Security number (SSN)
- Individual taxpayer identification number (ITIN)
- Adoption taxpayer identification number (ATIN)

Note: A taxpayer's personal information is considered highly sensitive and confidential. A preparer who wrongfully discloses taxpayer information could face civil and criminal charges.

A taxpayer who cannot obtain an SSN must apply for an ITIN if he files a U.S. tax return or is listed on a tax return as a spouse or dependent.

ITIN Applications and Renewals

Taxpayers who are ineligible for a Social Security Number must request an ITIN. These taxpayers must file Form W-7, *Application for IRS Individual Taxpayer Identification Number*, and supply documentation that establishes their foreign status and true identity. For example, an ITIN would be required when a soldier marries a foreign spouse and wishes to file jointly. In order to file a joint return, the couple would need to request an ITIN for the foreign spouse.

Starting in 2017, there are now three ways to apply for an ITIN.

- Using Form W-7, or
- Using an IRS-authorized Certified Acceptance Agent or
- In person at a designed IRS Taxpayer Assistance Center.

Also starting in 2017, all ITINs issued before 2013 will now expire unless they are renewed. New ITIN procedures include:

- Enhanced documentation for new Individual Taxpayer Identification Numbers (ITINs)
- Older ITINs will expire if not renewed
- Newer ITINs will expire if not used within three years
- Form W-7 has been revised (as of September 2016)
- The IRS will no longer accept passports of dependents as stand-alone documents that lack a date of entry into the United States.

New ITIN Application Procedures: When a taxpayer applies for an ITIN, his Form W-7 must include original documentation such as passports and birth certificates, or certified copies of these documents from the issuing agency. Notarized copies are no longer accepted.

Example: Laurie is a U.S. citizen with a Social Security number. Laurie lives and works in Mexico. Later in the year, she marries Roman, a citizen of Mexico, who has a daughter from a prior marriage. Laurie decides to file jointly with Roman in 2016 and claim her stepdaughter as a dependent. In order to do so, they must request ITINs for Roman and his daughter.

Note: The issuance of an ITIN does not affect an individual's immigration status or give the taxpayer the right to work in the United States. A taxpayer with an ITIN is not eligible to receive Social Security benefits or the Earned Income Tax Credit. ITINs are for federal tax reporting only, and are not intended to serve any other purpose.

Adoption Taxpayer Identification Number (ATIN)

ATINs are specifically designed for adopted children who are not yet eligible for a Social Security Number. For an adopted child who does not yet have an SSN, a taxpayer may request an ATIN if:

- The child is placed in the taxpayer's home for legal adoption.

- The adoption is a domestic adoption, or the adoption is a legal foreign adoption and the child has a permanent resident alien card or certificate of citizenship.
- The taxpayer cannot obtain the child's existing SSN even though he has made a reasonable attempt to obtain it from the birth parents, the placement agency, and other persons.
- The taxpayer cannot obtain an SSN for other reasons, such as the adoption not yet being final.

An ATIN cannot be used to obtain the Earned Income Tax Credit.

Special Rule for a Deceased Child

If a child is born and dies within the same tax year and is not granted an SSN, the taxpayer may still claim that child as a dependent.

Example: Alice gave birth to a son on October 1, 2016. The baby had health problems and died three days later. He was issued a death certificate and a birth certificate, but not an SSN. Alice can claim her son as a qualifying child in 2016. Alice must paper-file her return in order to claim her deceased son as a dependent. Her son will be considered a "qualifying child" for tax purposes, even though the child only lived a short time.

The tax return must be filed on paper with a copy of the birth certificate or a hospital medical record attached. The birth certificate must show that the child was born alive, as a stillborn infant does not qualify. The taxpayer would enter "DIED" in the space for the dependent's Social Security number on the tax return.

Recordkeeping Requirements for Individuals

Whether a paid tax return preparer is involved or not, a taxpayer is responsible for keeping copies of tax returns and maintaining other records for as long as they may be needed for the administration of any provision of the Internal Revenue Code.

Generally, a taxpayer should keep copies of tax returns and supporting documentation for at least three years from the date the returns were filed or the date they were due, whichever is later.

The IRS does not require taxpayers to keep records in any particular way, but says individuals need good records for the following purposes:

Identify sources of income: Taxpayers receive money or property from a variety of sources. Individuals need this information to separate business from nonbusiness income and taxable from nontaxable income.

Keep track of expenses: Tracking expenses as they occur helps taxpayers identify expenses that can be used to claim deductions.

Keep track of the basis of property: Taxpayers need to retain records showing the original cost or other basis of property they own and any improvements made to them.

Support items reported on tax returns: If the IRS has questions about items on a return, a taxpayer should have records to substantiate those items. In an IRS audit, the burden of proof is on the taxpayer to prove their expenses in order to deduct them.

Prepare tax returns: Good records help taxpayers and their preparers file accurate returns more quickly.

Note: Even if a tax professional prepares and signs an individual's tax return, the taxpayer is ultimately responsible for the accuracy of its contents.

The IRS allows taxpayers to maintain records in any way that will help determine the correct tax. Electronic records are acceptable, as long as a taxpayer can reproduce the records in a legible and readable format. Basic records that all taxpayers should keep include items related to:

- **Income:** Forms W-2, Forms 1099, bank statements, brokerage statements, Schedules K-1.
- **Expenses:** Sales slips, invoices, receipts, canceled checks or other proof of payment, written communications from qualified charities, Forms 1098 to support mortgage interest and real estate taxes paid.
- **Home purchase and sale:** Closing statements, HUD statements, purchase and sales invoices, proof of payment, insurance records, receipts for improvement costs.
- **Investments:** Brokerage statements, mutual fund statements, Forms 1099, Forms 2439.

Basic Tax Forms for Individuals

Form 1040EZ: Form 1040EZ is the simplest tax return form. The one-page form is designed for single and joint filers with no dependents or large deductions. It shows the taxpayer's filing status, income, adjusted gross income, standard deduction, taxable income, tax, Earned Income Tax Credit, amount owed or refund, and signature. A taxpayer may use Form 1040EZ only if:

- Taxable income is below $100,000, and interest income is $1,500 or less.
- The only income is from wages, salaries, tips, unemployment compensation, Alaska Permanent Fund dividends, taxable scholarships and fellowship grants, and taxable interest.
- Their filing status is single or married filing jointly.
- The taxpayer is under age 65 and not blind.
- The taxpayer is not claiming any dependents.
- The taxpayer claims no adjustments to income and no credits other than the Earned Income Tax Credit.

Form 1040A: Form 1040A is a two-page form. Taxable income must be less than $100,000, and there can be no self-employment income. A taxpayer may not itemize deductions when using Form 1040A and is limited to certain adjustments to income and credits.

Form 1040: Form 1040, also called the "long form", is designed to report all types of income, deductions, and credits. Taxpayers who cannot use Form 1040EZ or Form 1040A must use Form 1040. Common reasons a taxpayer must use Form 1040 include:

- Taxable income exceeds $100,000.
- He wants to itemize his deductions.
- He is reporting self-employment income.
- He is reporting income from the sale of property (such as the sale of stock or rental property).

Form 1040NR: Form 1040NR is used by nonresident aliens to report their U.S. source income. The IRS defines an alien as any individual who is not a U.S. citizen or U.S. national. A nonresident alien is an alien who has not passed the green card test or the substantial presence test. Form 1040NR is used by investors overseas, as well as nonresident taxpayers who earn money while in the U.S. The 1040NR is not used by U.S. citizens or U.S. residents.

Example: Cisco is a worldwide boxing champion and a legal citizen and resident of Panama. Cisco receives a non-immigrant visa to fight in a boxing match in the U.S., where he earns $500,000 for the fight. He only remains in the U.S. for six days. After his boxing appearance, he returns to Panama. Cisco is not eligible for an SSN and must request an ITIN to report his U.S. income. Without the ITIN, he would be subject to automatic backup withholding on his U.S. earnings. Cisco's accountant correctly reports his income and tax on Form 1040NR. Cisco does not have to report his worldwide income on his Form 1040NR, only the income he earned in the United States.

Form 1040X, *Amended U.S. Individual Income Tax Return*: This form is used to correct a previously filed Form 1040, 1040A, or 1040NR. It is also used to change amounts previously adjusted by the IRS, make a claim for a carryback due to a loss or unused credit, correct a liability for the additional Medicare Tax, or make certain elections after the prescribed deadline. Amended returns cannot be filed electronically.

Federal Income Tax Rates

An individual's federal taxable income is taxed at progressive rates in the United States. The more taxable income a taxpayer has, the higher the percentage of that income he pays in taxes. The IRS groups individuals by ranges of their taxable income level, or *brackets*, and applies increasing tax rates at each successive level.

For tax year 2016, there are seven tax brackets for individuals: 10%, 15%, 25%, 28%, 33%, 35%, and 39.6%. Each year, the IRS adjusts the income ranges for inflation and issues tax tables that show how much tax is owed for specific amounts of taxable income, depending upon a taxpayer's filing status.

For example, in 2016 a single taxpayer with $9,275 of taxable income would be in the 10% tax bracket. If he had $50,000 of taxable income, he would be in the 25% tax bracket, while a taxpayer with more than $500,000 of taxable income would be in the highest tax bracket of 39.6%.

2016 Federal Tax Rates

Rate	Single Filers	MFJ or Qualifying Widower	Head of Household	MFS
10%	$0 to $9,275	$0 to $18,550	$0 to $13,250	$0 to $9,275
15%	$9,275 to $37,650	$18,550 to $75,300	$13,250 to $50,400	$9,276 to $37,650
25%	$37,650 to $91,150	$75,300 to $151,900	$50,400 to $130,150	$37,651 to $75,950
28%	$91,150 to $190,150	$151,900 to $231,450	$130,150 to $210,800	$75,951 to $115,725
33%	$190,150 to $413,350	$231,450 to $413,350	$210,800 to $413,350	$115,726 to $206,675
35%	$413,350 to $415,050	$413,350 to $466,950	$413,350 to $441,000	$206,676 to $233,475
39.60%	$415,050+	$466,950+	$441,000+	$233,476+

However, this does not mean that a taxpayer in the highest income range owes tax at 39.6% on all of their taxable income. The applicable tax rate for each successive bracket applies only to the additional amounts of taxable income that fall within that bracket.

Example: Cora is single and had $39,000 of taxable income for 2016. For the first $9,275 she is taxed at a 10% rate. For the next segment of her taxable income, from $9,275 to $37,650, she is taxed at a 15% rate. Only for the remaining $1,350, from $37,650 to $39,000, she is taxed at 25%, which is referred to as her marginal tax rate.

In addition to the regular tax in the United States, there is a parallel tax called the alternative minimum tax (AMT). A taxpayer must pay either the regular tax or the AMT, depending on whichever amounts to the greater tax. The AMT is covered in detail later.

Tax Return Due Dates and Extensions

The regular due date for individual tax returns is April 15; if April 15 falls on a Saturday, Sunday, or legal holiday, the due date is delayed until the next business day. For the 2016 tax year, a federal holiday in Washington D.C. pushes the normal filing deadline to April 18, 2017.

If a taxpayer cannot file his tax return by the due date, he may request an extension by filing Form 4868, *Application for Automatic Extension of Time to File*, which may be filed electronically. An extension grants a taxpayer an additional six months to file his individual tax return.

For the 2016 tax year, extended individual tax returns are due by October 16, 2017 (the normal extended due date is October 15).

Note: Although an extension gives a taxpayer extra time to *file* his return, it does not extend the time to *pay* any tax due. A taxpayer will owe interest on any amount that is not paid by the regular filing deadline, plus a late payment penalty if he has not paid at least 100% of the prior year's tax or 90% of the current year tax. Taxpayers are expected to estimate and pay the amount of tax due by the filing deadline.

The IRS will accept a postmark as proof of a timely-filed return. For example, if a tax return is postmarked on April 15 but does not arrive at an IRS service center until April 23, the IRS will accept the tax return as having been filed on time. In cases where a tax return is filed close to the deadline, it is advisable for a taxpayer to pay for proof of mailing or certified mail. This is also called the "mailbox rule".

E-filed tax returns are given an "electronic postmark" to indicate the day they are transmitted.

Filing Deadline Exceptions

Federal Disaster Areas: Taxpayers in federally-declared disaster areas are often granted extensions to file and pay their income taxes and to make estimated tax payments. The IRS may also abate interest and any late filing or late payment penalties that apply to taxpayers in these disaster areas.

This tax relief generally includes individuals and businesses located in a disaster area, those whose tax records are located in a disaster area, and relief workers.

June 15 Deadlines: Three groups of taxpayers are granted an automatic two-month extension to file and pay any tax due:

- Nonresident aliens who have income that is not subject to U.S. withholding.

- U.S. citizens or legal U.S. residents who are living outside the United States or Puerto Rico and their main place of business is outside the U.S. or Puerto Rico.
- Taxpayers on active military service duty outside the U.S.

A citizen or resident alien living abroad must attach a statement to his tax return explaining which situation qualifies him for the special two-month extension. Even if he is allowed an extension, the taxpayer will have to pay interest on any tax not paid by the regular tax deadline of April 15.

Taxpayers Out of the Country: A taxpayer who is out of the country can request an additional discretionary two-month extension of time to file his tax return, beyond the regular six-month extension of October 15. For calendar-year taxpayers, the "additional" extension date would be December 15.

To request this extension, a taxpayer must send the IRS a letter explaining the reason why he needs the additional two-month period of time to file. There is no specific form for this additional extension.[1] Unless the request is denied, the taxpayer will not receive a response from the IRS.

Special Rules for Combat Zones: The deadline for filing a tax return or a claim for refund, and the deadline for payment of tax owed, are automatically extended for any service member, Red Cross personnel, accredited correspondent, or contracted civilian serving in a combat zone. These taxpayers have their tax deadlines suspended from the day they started serving in the combat zone until 180 days after they leave the combat zone. These deadline extensions also apply to the spouses of armed services members serving in combat zones.

Example: Dimitri is a U.S. Marine who has served in a combat zone since March 1, so he is entitled to extra time to file and pay his taxes. The 46 days between the date he entered the combat zone and the April 15 filing deadline are added to the normal extension period of 180 days, so he has a 226-day extension period after he leaves the combat zone. IRS deadlines for assessment and collection are also suspended during any period that a US servicemember is in a combat zone.

Penalties and Interest

The IRS can assess a penalty on individual taxpayers who fail to file, fail to pay, or both. The failure-to-file penalty is generally greater than the failure-to-pay penalty. If someone is unable to pay all the taxes he owes, he is better off filing on time and paying as much as he can, as the IRS will consider payment options with individual taxpayers.

Failure-to-File Penalty: The penalty for filing late is usually 5% of the unpaid taxes for each month or part of a month that a return is late. The penalty is based on the tax that is not paid by the due date, without regard to extensions. The penalty will not exceed 25% of a taxpayer's unpaid taxes.

If both the failure-to-file penalty and the failure-to-pay penalty apply in any month, the 5% failure-to-file penalty is reduced by the failure-to-pay penalty.

[1] See IRS Publication 54, *Tax Guide for U.S. Citizens and Resident Aliens Abroad*, for more information about extended deadlines. Publication 54 discusses four extensions: an automatic 2-month extension, an automatic 6-month extension, an additional extension for taxpayers out of the country, and an extension of time to meet certain tests.

Note: The Trade Facilitation and Enforcement Act of 2015 increases the penalty for failing to file a tax return in 2016. The higher penalty applies to individual returns filed in 2017. The increased failure-file penalty is the lesser of $205 (up from $135) or 100% of the amount of tax owed.

If a taxpayer is owed a tax refund, he will not be assessed a failure-to-file penalty.

Failure-to-Pay Penalty: If a taxpayer does not pay his taxes by the due date, he could be subject to a failure-to-pay penalty of ½ of 1% (0.5%) of unpaid taxes for each month or part of a month after the due date that the taxes are not paid. This penalty can be as much as 25% of a taxpayer's unpaid taxes. The failure-to-pay penalty rate increases to a full 1% per month for any tax that remains unpaid the day after a demand for immediate payment is issued, or ten days after notice of intent to levy certain assets is issued.

Interest on the Amount Due: In addition to filing penalties, the taxpayer will also be charged interest on the amount due. Generally, interest accrues on any unpaid tax from the due date of the return until the date of payment in full. The interest rate is determined quarterly and is the federal short-term rate plus 3 percent. Interest compounds daily.

Relief from Joint Tax Liability

In certain cases, a spouse can be relieved of the tax, interest, and penalties on a joint return. When spouses file a joint return, they are both legally responsible for the entire tax liability. However, a taxpayer can file a claim for spousal relief under three different grounds:

- Innocent Spouse Relief
- Separation of Liability Relief
- Equitable Relief

Innocent Spouse Relief: This is when a joint return has understated tax liability due to erroneous items attributable to a taxpayer's spouse or former spouse. Erroneous items include income received by a spouse that is omitted from the return. Deductions, credits, and property basis are also erroneous items if they are incorrectly reported on the joint return.

To be considered an innocent spouse, the taxpayer must establish that he or she did not know (or have reason to know) that there was an understated tax liability at the time of signing the joint return. The taxpayer must request relief within two years after the date on which the IRS begins collection activity.

Separation of Liability Relief: The above restrictions also apply to separation of liability relief. In this case, however, the taxpayer must no longer be married to, or must be legally separated from, his or her spouse, or must be widowed or have lived apart for at least 12 months from the spouse with whom the joint return was filed.

The understated tax, plus interest and penalties, would be allocated to the taxpayer based on the amount for which he or she is responsible.

Equitable Relief: If a taxpayer does not qualify for the first two types of relief, he or she may be eligible for equitable relief. The IRS will review the facts and circumstances of the taxpayer's case and determine whether it would be unfair to hold the taxpayer liable for the understated tax.

Unlike the other two forms of relief, equitable relief may also be granted for an underpaid tax, meaning it was properly reported on a tax return but not paid. Further, in some cases, the spouse requesting relief may have known about the understated or underpaid tax, but did not challenge the treatment for fear of his or her spouse's retaliation.

The taxpayer has up to ten years to request equitable relief under certain circumstances. Form 8857, *Request for Innocent Spouse Relief*, is used to request all three types of relief.

Example: Nataly is a victim of domestic violence who now lives apart from her husband. When she signed her joint return, she knew her husband was underreporting income from his business but was afraid of what would happen if she refused to sign. After the IRS discovered the understated tax, Nataly filed for equitable relief and was able to document her history of spousal abuse using affidavits from family members and other proof. The IRS granted her request for relief of her portion of the understated tax, penalties, and interest.

Injured Spouse Claims

An "injured spouse" claim has a similar-sounding name but is completely different than "innocent spouse" relief. To be considered an injured spouse, a taxpayer must meet the following criteria:

- Have filed a joint return
- Have paid federal income tax or claimed a refundable tax credit
- All or part of the taxpayer's refund was, or is expected to be, applied to his or her spouse's past financial obligations
- Not be responsible for the debt

A spouse who believes that he is entitled to a portion of the refund on a joint return can file Form 8379, *Injured Spouse Allocation.*

Example: Ron filed a joint return with his wife, Valerie, who had delinquent student loans. Valerie incurred the student loan debt before she was married. Ron files Form 8379 to request his portion of their tax refund as an injured spouse. The IRS will retain Valerie's portion of the couple's tax refund to offset her debt, but will allow Ron to obtain his portion of the refund.

Refunds Claims and Amended Returns

In order to claim a refund, a taxpayer must generally file an amended tax return (Form 1040X) within three years from the date the return was originally due or two years from the date the tax was paid, whichever is later. [2] If a claim is not filed within the applicable period, a taxpayer generally will not be entitled to a refund. However, if the taxpayer files an extension and filed his original return prior to the October 15 extension deadline, the three-year period begins on the date that the taxpayer originally filed his return. Amended returns (Form 1040X) cannot be filed electronically. They must be filed on paper. If a taxpayer is entitled to a refund, he cannot request a direct deposit on Form 1040X.

Example: Don has not filed a tax return for a long time, and now he wants to file several years of delinquent tax returns: 2011 through 2016. Don files the returns and realizes that he was entitled to refunds for each year. If he files all the back tax returns by April 18, 2017, he will receive refunds for his 2013-2016 tax returns. His refunds for 2011 and 2012, however, have expired. He will not receive a refund for those years.

[2] If the taxpayer had an extension to file (for example, until October 15), but the taxpayer filed earlier and the IRS received it July 1, the return is considered filed on July 1 (Form 1040X instructions).

Example: Oleg made estimated tax payments of $1,000 and requested an extension to file his 2013 income tax return. He filed his 2013 return timely, before the extended due date of October 15, 2014. When he filed his return on September 7, 2014, he paid an additional $200 tax due. Oleg later finds an error on the return. Three years after the extended due date, he files an amended return on September 7, 2017, and claims a refund of $700.

Example: Goldie prepared her own 2013 tax return and filed it after the deadline, on July 12, 2014. She did not request an extension, so the return was delinquent when she filed it. She later discovered that she had forgotten to claim the Earned Income Tax Credit. Approximately three years later, she files an amended return on July 10, 2017. Goldie's refund claim is denied because she filed her original return past the due date *without* a valid extension. Therefore, her amended return was not filed timely.

Extended Statute for Claiming Refunds

In some cases, a request for a tax refund will be honored past the normal deadline. These special cases involve:

- A bad debt from a worthless security (up to seven years prior)
- A payment or accrual of foreign tax
- A net operating loss carryback
- A carryback of certain tax credits
- Exceptions for military personnel
- Taxpayers in federally-declared disaster areas
- Taxpayers who have been affected by a terroristic or military action

Time periods for claiming a refund are also extended when a taxpayer is "financially disabled". This usually requires that the taxpayer be mentally or physically disabled to the point that he is unable to manage his financial affairs.

Example: Roger has been helping his elderly mother, Mabel, file her tax returns for the last several years. Over time, she has become forgetful of things. In 2016, Roger discovers a large file in his mother's home filled with old brokerage statements. Several of the brokerage statements show losses from worthless securities, dating back many years. Mabel had been putting the statements away because she believed that they were unimportant. Mabel's Form 1099-B from 2010 shows a significant loss from worthless stock (over $10,000 in losses that were never reported). Even though the brokerage statement is six years old, Mabel is still allowed to amend her 2010 tax return in order to claim the stock losses. That is because the IRS allows up to seven years to amend a tax return for losses from worthless securities. Mabel can file a Form 1040X in order to claim the losses and still receive a refund under this extended statute.

Statute of Limitations for IRS Assessment and Collection

The IRS is generally required to assess tax or audit a taxpayer's return within three years after the return is filed or, if filed early, the due date of the return. If a taxpayer files his tax return late, the IRS has three years from the later of:

- The due date of the return, or
- The date the return was actually filed.
- If a taxpayer never files a return, there is no deadline for assessment of tax.

- If the taxpayer files a fraudulent tax return, there is no deadline for IRS assessment or collection.

The statute of limitations for IRS collection is ten years from the date tax is assessed, as long as there is no evidence of fraud. The ten-year period begins to run on the date of the tax assessment, not on the date of filing. So, for example, if the taxpayer owes when they file their tax return, the IRS will send a bill. The bill is the assessment.

The IRS assigns a collection statute expiration date, or "CSED", to every delinquent taxpayer account. Once the CSED expires, the IRS loses its right to seize assets or make payment demands. Certain events can extend the amount of time the IRS has to collect.

The IRS has six years to assess tax on a return if a "substantial understatement" is identified, meaning that gross income was understated by more than 25%.[3]

Example: Karolyn filed her 2013 tax return on February 27, 2014. The three-year statute period for audit began April 15, 2014, and ends on April 15, 2017. After that date, the IRS must be able to prove fraud or a substantial understatement of gross income to audit the tax return.
Example: Harold has always filed his tax returns in a timely manner. Five years ago, Harold was self-employed and did not understand how to manage his money or pay estimated taxes. He had a large tax bill from that year. Harold still filed his tax return on time and correctly reported the amount due, with the intention of making payments. The IRS issued its assessment and sent Harold a bill for $24,000 (the amount that Harold owes, plus penalties and interest). Harold requested an installment agreement and began making monthly payments towards his tax debt. Shortly thereafter, Harold had a terrible car accident and became completely disabled. He no longer has the means to work or pay the bill. The IRS has five years left to collect on the debt, and after that, the statute for collection expires. Although the interest and penalties will continue to accrue, if Harold does not have any assets or any means to pay the bill, he will likely be deemed "uncollectible".

Estimated Taxes

The federal income tax is a "pay-as-you-go" tax, meaning a taxpayer must pay taxes as he earns or receives income throughout the year.

If a taxpayer earns income that is not subject to withholding, such as self-employment income, rents, and alimony, or if his taxes withheld are insufficient to cover his tax liability, he may be required to make quarterly estimated tax payments. Estimated tax is used to pay income tax as well as self-employment tax and alternative minimum tax.

Safe Harbor Rule: Taxpayers can avoid making estimated tax payments by ensuring they have enough tax withheld from their income. A taxpayer must generally make estimated tax payments if:

- He expects to owe at least $1,000 in tax (after subtracting withholding and tax credits)
- He expects the total amount of withholding and tax credits to be less than the smaller of:
    - 100% of the tax liability on his prior year return
    - 90% of the tax liability on his current year return

[3] IRC Sect. 6501(e)(1)(A)(i).

Example: Gerald earned $95,000 in 2016 and paid $8,200 in tax. Although he expects his income to increase in 2017, he will not be assessed a penalty for underpayment of estimated taxes, provided he pays at least $8,200 in estimated tax during the year (100% of the tax liability on his prior year return).

A taxpayer will not face an underpayment penalty if the total tax liability on his return (minus the amounts of tax credits or paid through withholding) is under $1,000.

Example: Dominique has a full-time job as a secretary. She also earns money part-time as a self-employed manicurist. In 2016, she did not make estimated payments. However, Dominique made sure to increase her withholding at her regular job in order to cover any amounts that she would have to pay on her self-employment earnings. When she files her tax return, she discovers that she still owes $750. Although she is responsible for paying the tax that is owed, she will not owe an underpayment penalty because the total tax liability is less than $1,000.

A U.S. citizen or U.S. resident is not required to make estimated tax payments if he had zero tax liability in the prior year.

Example: Cassius, age 25 and single, earned $2,700 before he was laid off in 2015, and received $1,500 in unemployment compensation afterward. He did not have to pay income tax because his gross income was less than the filing requirement. In 2016, Cassius began working as a self-employed plumber but made no estimated tax payments during the year. Even though he owed $3,000 in tax at the end of the year, Cassius does not owe the underpayment penalty for 2016 because he had zero tax liability in the prior year.

If a taxpayer wishes to change his withholding amounts from his wages, he must use Form W-4, *Employee's Withholding Allowance Certificate*, and submit the form to his employer.

Safe Harbor Rule for Higher-Income Taxpayers: If the taxpayer's 2016 adjusted gross income was more than $150,000 ($75,000 if MFS), the taxpayer must pay the *smaller of* 90% of their expected tax for 2017 or 110% of the tax shown on their 2016 return to avoid an estimated tax penalty.

Estimated Tax Due Dates for Individuals

The year is divided into four payment periods for estimated taxes, each with a specific payment due date. If the due date falls on a Saturday, Sunday, or legal holiday, the due date is the next business day. A taxpayer must complete Form 1040-ES, *Estimated Tax for Individuals*, to pay his estimated tax.

If a payment is mailed, the date of the U.S. postmark is considered the date of payment.

First Payment Due: April 15
Second Payment Due: June 15
Third Payment Due: September 15
Fourth Payment Due: January 15 (of the following year)

Estimated Taxes for Farmers and Fishermen

Special rules apply to the payment of estimated tax by qualified farmers and fishermen. If at least two-thirds of the taxpayer's gross income in the current year comes from (or in the prior year came from) farming or fishing activities, the following rules apply:

- The taxpayer does not have to pay estimated tax if he files his return and pays all tax owed by the first day of the third month after the end of his tax year (usually March 1).
- The taxpayer does not have to pay estimated tax if his current year income tax withholding is at least two-thirds (.6667) of the total tax liability on his current tax return or 100% of the total tax liability on his prior year return.
- If the taxpayer must pay estimated tax, he is required to make only one estimated tax payment (called the "required annual payment") by the fifteenth day after the end of his tax year (usually January 15).

For this special tax treatment, qualified farming income includes gross farming income on Schedule F, gross farming rental income, gains from the sale of livestock, and crop shares for the use of a farmer's land. This rule also applies to qualified fishermen.

Note: This special estimated tax rule also applies to a person's share of gross income from partnerships and S corporations where the majority of its income is derived from farming or fishing. This safe harbor for estimated payments does not apply to C Corporations, however, regardless of the type of business activity.

Example: Jay is a self-employed owner of a commercial fishing vessel. All of his income is from commercial fishing, so he is not required to pay quarterly estimated taxes. Jay's records are incomplete, so he asks his tax accountant to file an extension on his behalf. Since Jay will be unable to file his tax return by March 1, 2017, his accountant notifies Jay that he is required to make a single payment of estimated taxes by January 15, 2017.

Example: Karla earns 100% of her income from growing organic strawberries. She is a qualified farmer and reports her business income on Schedule F. She is not required to pay quarterly estimated taxes. Karla filed her tax return on February 20, 2017, and enclosed a check for her entire balance due of $4,900. Since she filed before the March 1, 2017, deadline, she will not be subject to any penalty.

Note: If a qualified farmer (or fisherman) files their 2016 Form 1040 by March 1, 2017, and pays all the tax they owe at that time, they do not need to make any estimated tax payments in the previous year. This rule does not apply to any other business activity—it only applies to farmers and fishermen.

Backup Withholding

There are times an entity is required to withhold certain amounts from a payment and remit the amounts to the IRS. For example, the IRS requires backup withholding if a taxpayer's name and Social Security number on Form W-9, *Request for Taxpayer Identification Number and Certification*, does not match its records.

Example: Wesley owns a number of investments through Top Finances Corporation. In 2016, the IRS notifies Top Finances that Wesley's Social Security number is incorrect. Top Finances notifies Wesley by mail that the company needs his correct Social Security number, or it will have to start backup withholding on his investment income. Wesley ignores the notice and never bothers to update his SSN. Top Finances must begin backup withholding on Wesley's investment income.

The IRS will sometimes require backup withholding if a taxpayer has a delinquent tax debt, or if he fails to report all his interest, dividends, and other income. Payments subject to backup withholding may include wages, interest, dividends, rents, royalties, and payments to independent contractors for services.

Note: The backup withholding rate for 2016 is 28% for all U.S. citizens and legal U.S. residents.

Under backup withholding rules, a business or bank must withhold taxes from a payment if:

- The individual did not provide the payor with a valid taxpayer identification number.
- The IRS notified the payer that the TIN or SSN is incorrect.
- The IRS notified the payor to start withholding on interest and dividends because the payee failed to report income in prior years.
- The payee failed to certify that he was not subject to backup withholding for underreporting of interest and dividends.

Unit 1: Study Questions

(Test yourself first, then check the correct answers at the end of this quiz.)

1. Which of the following is not a requirement for a spouse to be eligible for innocent spouse relief?

A. When the taxpayer signed the return, he or she did not know, and had no reason to know, that there was an understatement of tax.
B. The taxpayer must have filed as either MFJ or MFS.
C. The return had an understatement of tax directly related to the spouse's erroneous items.
D. The facts and circumstances show that it would be unfair for the IRS to hold the taxpayer liable for the understatement.

2. Catherine files an extension request (Form 4868), which allows her an additional six months to file her tax return. When she finally prepares her return, she realizes that she owes a substantial amount of tax. She pays the tax when she files the return, which she does before the extended due date. Which penalties, if any, will Catherine be likely to owe?

A. She will owe interest on the amount owed and a late payment penalty.
B. She will owe interest on the amount owed and a late filing penalty.
C. She will owe interest on the amount owed, a late payment penalty, and a late filing penalty.
D. She will not owe any penalties because she filed before the extended due date and paid the taxes owed with the return.

3. Isla files as single and has no refundable credits. She is not self-employed. Based on the figures below, is she required to pay estimated tax in the current year?

AGI for prior tax year	$73,700
Total tax on prior year return	9,224
Anticipated AGI for current year	82,800
Total current year estimated tax liability	11,270
Tax expected to be withheld in current year	$10,250

A. Yes, she is required to make estimated tax payments.
B. No, she is not required to make estimated tax payments.
C. She is not required to make estimated tax payments because she does not have self-employment income.
D. None of the above is correct.

4. Generally, how long should taxpayers keep the supporting documentation for their tax returns?

A. Four years from the date the return was filed, or the return was due, whichever is later.
B. Three years from the date the return was filed, or the return was due, whichever is later.
C. Two years from the date the return was filed, or the return was due, whichever is later.
D. Ten years from the date the return was filed, or the return was due, whichever is later.

5. Ricky files his 2016 tax return on February 15, 2017. He has a balance due of $800 on the return. How long can he wait to pay the amount owed and not incur a penalty?

A. He will owe a late payment penalty unless he pays his tax liability when he files his return.
B. He has until the due date of the return (not including extensions) to pay the amount owed and not pay a penalty.
C. He has until the due date of the return (including extensions) to pay the amount owed and not pay a penalty.
D. He does not have to pay the amount due by a certain date because it is less than the safe harbor amount of $1,000.

6. Which of the following taxpayers is required to have an individual taxpayer identification number (ITIN)?

A. A nonresident alien with a Social Security number which moves outside the U.S.
B. A nonresident alien who must file a return and is not eligible for a valid Social Security number.
C. Anyone who does not have a Social Security number.
D. All nonresident and resident aliens.

7. Clark's 2013 tax return was due April 15, 2014. He filed it on March 2, 2014. Later, Clark discovered that he is eligible for an education credit that will result in a refund. He neglected to take this credit on his 2013 return. What is the latest date that Clark can amend his 2013 tax return in order to receive a refund?

A. April 15, 2016
B. April 18, 2017
C. March 2, 2017
D. March 2, 2016

8. The current backup withholding rate for U.S. taxpayers is:

A. 0%
B. 13.5%
C. 25%
D. 28%

9. Cynthia is divorced, files as head of household, and has two dependents. Cynthia is a citizen of Canada and a legal U.S. Resident (green card holder). She earned $43,000 in 2016 and plans to itemize her deductions. Which tax form should Cynthia use?

A. Form 1040.
B. Form 1040A.
C. Form 1040EZ.
D. Form 1040NR.

10. All of the statements about estimated tax payments are correct except:

A. An individual whose only income is from self-employment will generally have to pay estimated payments.
B. If insufficient tax is paid through withholding, estimated payments may be necessary.
C. Estimated tax payments are required when the amount of taxes withheld is greater than the overall tax liability.
D. Estimated tax is used to pay not only income tax, but self-employment tax and alternative minimum tax as well.

11. Which of the following is not an acceptable reason for extending the statute of limitations for claiming a refund past the normal deadline?

A. A bad debt from a worthless security.
B. Living in a federally-declared disaster area.
C. Exceptions for military personnel.
D. Living outside the country for three years.

12. If a taxpayer files his tax return more than 60 days after the due date or extended due date, what is the minimum penalty he will face?

A. A minimum of 25% of his unpaid taxes.
B. A minimum of 5% of his unpaid taxes.
C. The smaller of $205 or 100% of the unpaid tax.
D. The greater of $135 or 100% of the unpaid tax.

13. Which of the following documents will be accepted as valid means of identification for a taxpayer applying for an ITIN?

A. Notarized copies of birth certificates and passports.
B. Original birth certificates and passports.
C. Certified copies of birth certificates and passports.
D. Both B and C.

14. Dottie is a U.S. resident who paid estimated tax in 2015 totaling $2,500. In 2016, she closed her business as a self-employed florist and is now unemployed. Dottie expects to have zero tax liability in 2016. Which of the following statements is correct?

A. She is still required to make estimated tax payments in 2016.
B. She is not required to make estimated tax payments in 2016.
C. She must pay a minimum of $2,500 in estimated tax payments in 2016, or she will be subject to a failure-to-pay penalty.
D. She must make a minimum of $2,250 (90% × $2,500) in estimated tax payments in 2016, or she will be subject to an underpayment penalty.

15. What is the statute of limitations for an IRS assessment on a tax return from which more than 25% of the taxpayer's gross income was omitted?

A. There is no statute of limitations on a return in which gross income was omitted.
B. Three years from the date the return was filed, or the return was due, whichever is later.
C. Six years from the date the return was filed.
D. Ten years from the date the return was filed.

16. Rochelle is a United States citizen who lives in England. She owes $5,000 of tax for 2016. Which of the following statements is correct regarding her filing and payment requirements?

A. She must file and pay her taxes by April 18, 2017.
B. She is allowed an automatic two-month extension to file her tax return, but she must pay her taxes by April 18, 2017.
C. She is allowed an automatic two-month extension to file and pay her taxes, but she must attach a statement to her return explaining why she qualifies for the extension.
D. If she files by June 15, 2017, she will not owe any additional interest on her tax liability.

17. Sally and Albert file a joint return. Their tax refund will be applied toward Albert's unpaid child support obligations from an earlier relationship. To request her portion of their refund, Sally should file:

A. As an innocent spouse.
B. As a damaged spouse.
C. As an injured spouse.
D. For equitable relief.

18. Forrest is single and earned $200,000 as a self-employed software consultant during the current year. Under the estimated tax safe harbor rules for high-income taxpayers, he can avoid an underpayment penalty if he pays _________ of his prior year tax liability:

A. $1,000
B. 90%
C. 100%
D. 110%

Unit 1: Quiz Answers

1. The answer is B. Innocent spouse relief is available only for a spouse who has filed *jointly* and is therefore legally liable for the understatement of tax. Therefore, a taxpayer who filed MFS wouldn't qualify. To qualify for innocent spouse relief, the taxpayer must meet all of the following conditions:

- The taxpayer filed a joint return that has an understatement of tax directly related to the spouse's erroneous items.
- The taxpayer establishes that, at the time of signing the joint return, he or she did not know, and had no reason to know, that there was an understatement of tax.
- Taking into account all the facts and circumstances, it would be unfair for the IRS to hold the taxpayer liable for the understatement.

In order to apply for innocent spouse relief, a taxpayer must submit Form 8857, *Request for Innocent Spouse Relief*, and sign it under penalty of perjury.

2. The answer is A. Even though she files Form 4868, Catherine may owe interest and a late payment penalty on the amount owed if she does not pay the tax due by the regular due date. However, she will not be assessed a late filing penalty (failure-to-file) because she filed her tax return before the extended due date.

3. The answer is B. Isla does not need to pay estimated tax because she expects her income tax withholding in the current year ($10,250) to be greater than both, 90% of the tax to be shown on her current year return ($11,270 × 90% = $10,143) and 100% of her prior year tax liability ($9,224). Therefore, Isla qualifies for the safe harbor rule and is not required to make estimated tax payments. A taxpayer is not required to pay estimated tax if:

- The taxpayer had no tax liability in the prior year,
- The taxpayer was a U.S. citizen or resident alien, and
- The prior tax year covered a 12-month period.

A taxpayer also does not have to pay estimated tax if she pays enough through withholding so that the tax due on the return is less than $1,000. In most cases, a taxpayer must pay estimated tax if she expects withholding (plus any refundable credits) to be less than the smaller of:

- 90% of the tax to be shown on the current year tax return, or
- 100% of the tax shown on the prior year tax return.

4. The answer is B. Taxpayers should keep the supporting documentation for their tax returns for at least three years from the date the return was filed or three years from the date the return was due, whichever is later. This includes applicable worksheets, receipts, and other forms.

5. The answer is B. Ricky has until the original due date of the return (not including extensions) to pay the amount owed and not incur a penalty. Taxpayers should submit their payment of taxes due on or before April 15 (or the next business day if April 15 falls on a Saturday, a Sunday, or a legal holiday). For the 2016 tax year, taxpayers have until April 18, 2017, to pay the amount he owes.

6. The answer is B. If a taxpayer must file a U.S. tax return or is listed on a tax return as a spouse or dependent and is not eligible for a Social Security number, he must apply for an ITIN.

7. The answer is B. If Clark has his amended return postmarked on or before April 18, 2017, it will be within the three-year limit, and the return will be accepted. If the amended return is postmarked after that date, it will fall outside the three-year statute of limitations, and he will not receive the refund. In order to claim a refund, the amended return must be filed the later of three years from the date the return was due or two years from the date the tax was paid.

8. The answer is D. The current backup withholding rate is 28%. The IRS may require backup withholding if a taxpayer has a delinquent tax debt; if he fails to report all his interest, dividends, and other income; or if his Social Security number does not match records provided to the IRS.

9. The answer is A. Since Cynthia plans to itemize her deductions, she must file Form 1040. She cannot use a Form 1040A or a Form 1040EZ. Form 1040NR is only for nonresident taxpayers. With few exceptions, green card holders are taxed as US Citizens and do not file Form 1040NR. Nonresidents cannot file as Head of Household or take any dependency exemptions.

10. The answer is C. If a taxpayer's withholding exceeds his tax liability, no estimated payments would be required. The taxpayer would receive a refund of the overpaid tax when he files his tax return.

11. The answer is D. Living outside the country is not a valid reason to extend the statute of limitations for claiming a refund. In some cases, a request for a tax refund will be honored past the normal three-year deadline. Exceptions exist for military personnel, individuals who are financially disabled, taxpayers who live in federally-declared disaster areas, and taxpayers who have bad debts from worthless securities.

12. The answer is C. The minimum penalty is $205 or 100% of the unpaid tax (whichever is less) for a taxpayer who files his return more than 60 days late. This is an increase from the previous year. The higher penalty applies to individual returns filed in 2017, (for the 2016 tax season). The increased failure-file penalty is now the lesser of $205 (up from $135) or 100% of the amount of tax owed.

13. The answer is D. Only original documents of birth certificates and passports are accepted, or documents that have been certified by the original issuing agency. Notarized documents are no longer accepted.

14. The answer is B. A taxpayer is not required to pay estimated tax if she expects to have zero tax liability for the current tax year.

15. The answer is C. If a taxpayer omitted more than 25% of his gross income on his return, the IRS has up to six years to assess a deficiency.

16. The answer is C. A U.S. citizen or resident alien living outside the United States has an automatic two-month extension to file and pay her taxes. The same is true for members of the military who are serving outside the U.S. Rochelle must attach a statement to her tax return explaining why she qualifies for the extension. She will still owe interest on the tax that was due on April 18, 2017, if she does not pay the amount due by that date.

17. The answer is C. Sally should file a claim as an injured spouse to request her portion of their tax refund. She would do so by filing Form 8379, *Injured Spouse Allocation.* If the request is granted, the IRS will retain her husband's portion of their tax refund to offset his unpaid child support but will allow Sally to obtain her portion of the refund. In contrast, innocent spouse relief is when tax has been incorrectly reported on a joint return, and one spouse is relieved of the obligation to pay the other spouse's portion of the tax liability.

18. The answer is D. To avoid an underpayment penalty, Forrest must pay the smaller of:

- 110% of his prior year tax liability or
- 90% of his expected tax for the current year.

This estimated tax safe harbor rule applies to higher-income taxpayers with adjusted gross income of more than $150,000 ($75,000 if filing a married filing separately return).

Unit 2: Taxpayer Filing Status and Residency

For additional information read:
Publication 17, *Your Federal Income Tax*
Publication 501, *Exemptions, Standard Deduction, and Filing Information*
Publication 54, *Tax Guide for U.S. Citizens and Resident Aliens Abroad*
Publication 519, *U.S. Tax Guide for Aliens*

The IRS uses a taxpayer's filing status to determine filing requirements, standard deductions, eligibility for certain credits, and the amounts of tax owed. There are five filing statuses, with rules governing each, including special rules for annulled marriages and widow(er)s with dependent children.

In general, a taxpayer's filing status depends first on whether he or she is married or unmarried as of the last day of the year. For federal tax purposes, a marriage was traditionally defined as a legal union between a man and a woman as husband and wife.

For tax years 2013 and beyond, a marriage between same-sex spouses is also recognized as a legal union, as long as the marriage was performed in a domestic or foreign jurisdiction that recognizes the validity of same-sex marriage.[4]

Then, on June 26, 2015, in the landmark case *Obergefell vs. Hodges*, the U.S. Supreme Court held in a 5 to 4 decision that the Fourteenth Amendment requires a state to license a marriage between two people of the same sex, and to recognize a marriage between two people of the same sex when their marriage was lawfully licensed and performed out-of-state, or in another country.

This new ruling made the law uniform for legally married same-sex couples in all 50 states and the District of Columbia. However, individuals who have entered into a registered domestic partnership, civil union, or other similar relationship that is not considered a marriage under state law are not considered married for federal tax purposes.

Study Alert: Expect to be tested on the concept of same-sex marriage on the EA Exam. Remember that registered domestic partners or those in civil unions are NOT considered "married" for federal tax purposes, and you may see a question on the exam regarding this current tax law issue.

Single

A taxpayer is single for the entire tax year if, on the last day of the tax year, he or she was:

- Unmarried
- Legally separated or divorced, or
- Widowed (and not remarried during the year). However, special rules apply to widowed taxpayers. We will cover those rules later.

Example: Kenneth and Jennifer legally divorced on December 31, 2016. They do not have any dependents. They cannot file either as married filing jointly or married filing separately for 2016. Instead, each must file as "single" for 2016.

Married Filing Jointly (MFJ)

The married filing jointly status typically provides more tax benefits than filing a separate return. On a joint return, spouses report all of their combined income, allowable expenses, exemptions, and deductions. Spouses can file a joint return even if only one spouse had

[4] Revenue Ruling 2013-17 was issued in response to the Supreme Court case, *Windsor vs. United States*, in which the court ruled that the Defense of Marriage Act (DOMA) was unconstitutional under the equal protection clause and held that federal law must recognize a same-sex marriage that was valid under applicable state law. Under that ruling, the state where the marriage ceremony was performed determined whether it was recognized as legal under federal law.

income. Both spouses must agree to sign the return, and both are responsible for any tax owed, even if all the income was earned by only one spouse. A subsequent divorce usually does not relieve either spouse of the liability associated with the original joint return (see exceptions related to innocent spouse relief, covered earlier). Taxpayers can file jointly if they are married as of December 31 and:

- Live together as husband and wife or as a legally married same-sex couple
- Live together in a common law marriage recognized in the state where they now reside or in the state where the common law marriage began
- Live apart but are not legally separated or divorced[5]
- Are separated under an interlocutory (not final) divorce decree

In addition, a widowed taxpayer may use the married filing jointly status and file jointly with his deceased spouse if his spouse died during the year and he or she has not remarried as of the end of the year. A U.S. resident or U.S. citizen who is married to a nonresident alien can elect to file a joint return as long as both spouses agree to be taxed on their worldwide income.

Note: Federal law does not allow Registered Domestic Partners to file a joint return. This rule also applies to civil unions.[6] The IRS *does* recognize common-law marriages. Currently, the only states that recognize common law marriage are Alabama, Colorado, the District of Columbia, Iowa, Kansas, Montana, Rhode Island, South Carolina, Texas and Utah.

Married Filing Separately (MFS)

The MFS status is for taxpayers who are married and either:

- Choose to file separate returns, or
- Do not agree to file a joint return.

If one spouse chooses to file MFS, the other is forced to do the same, since a joint return must be signed by both spouses.

Example: Jerry and Danielle have always filed jointly in the past. However, Danielle has chosen to separate her finances from her husband this year, even though they are living together. Jerry wants to file jointly with Danielle, but she has refused. Danielle files her tax return using married filing separately as her filing status; therefore, Jerry is forced to file MFS as well.

The MFS filing status means the two spouses report their own income, exemptions, credits, and deductions on separate returns, even if one spouse had no income. This filing status may benefit a taxpayer who wants to be responsible only for his own tax, or if it results in less tax than filing a joint return. Typically, however, a married couple will pay more tax on a combined basis when filing separately than they would by filing jointly.

Specific features of the MFS filing status include the following:

- The tax rates are generally higher at the same levels of taxable income than those applicable to MFJ.
- The exemption amount for the alternative minimum tax is half that allowed on a joint return.
- Various credits, including the Earned Income Tax Credit, the Premium Tax Credit, and those for child care, education, adoption, and retirement savings, are either not allowed or are much more limited than on a joint return.
- The capital loss deduction is limited to $1,500, half that allowed on a joint return.
- The standard deduction is half the amount allowed on a joint return and cannot be claimed if the taxpayer's spouse itemizes deductions.

---

[5]State law governs whether a taxpayer is married or legally separated under a divorce or separate maintenance decree. In certain states, a legally separated couple may agree to file jointly or as married filing separately, or they may be required to do so until a divorce becomes final.

[6] See Revenue Ruling 2013-17.

Example: Dinesh and Maya keep their finances separate and choose to file MFS. Dinesh plans to itemize his casualty losses, so Maya is forced to either itemize her deductions or claim a standard deduction of zero.

One common reason a taxpayer may choose the MFS filing status is to avoid an offset of his refund against his current spouse's outstanding prior debt.

This might include delinquent child support or student loans, or a tax liability a spouse incurred before the marriage.

Example: Tom and Judith were married in 2016. Tom owes delinquent taxes from a prior year. Judith chooses to file separately from Tom, so her refund will not be offset by his overdue tax debt. If they were to file jointly, their entire refund might be retained in order to pay the debt.

Amending Filing Status from MFS

There are rules for when married taxpayers are allowed to change their filing status for a given year's return.

Taxpayers generally cannot change from a joint return to a separate return *after the due date* of the return. For example, if a married couple filed their joint 2016 tax return on March 13, 2017, and subsequently decided they wanted to file separately instead, they would have only until April 18, 2017, to file amended returns using the MFS filing status (the due date of the original return).

An exception allows a personal representative for a deceased taxpayer to change from a joint return elected by the surviving spouse to a separate return for the decedent, for up to a year after the filing deadline.

Example: Kurt and Susan have always filed jointly. Susan dies suddenly in 2016, and her last will names Harriet, her daughter from a previous marriage, as the executor of her estate. Kurt files a joint return with Susan for tax year 2016, but Harriet, as the executor, decides that it would be better for Susan's estate if her tax return were filed MFS. Harriet files an amended return claiming MFS status for Susan, and signs the return as the executor.

To change from separate returns to a joint return, taxpayers must file an amended return using Form 1040X and may do so at any time within three years from the due date of the separate returns (not including extensions).

Same-Sex Spouses

Same-sex spouses who are legally married must file as either married filing jointly or married filing separately. They do not have the choice to file as single. However, be aware that civil unions and registered domestic partnerships are not legally considered "marriages" for IRS purposes.

Registered domestic partners (or partners in a civil union) may not file a federal return using a married filing separately or jointly filing status. Therefore, these taxpayers are not married for federal tax purposes.

Example: Curtis and Antonio are registered domestic partners in the state of California. They consult Marilynn, an EA, who prepares their tax returns. Curtis and Antonio wish to file jointly. However, registered domestic partners are not married under state law. Therefore, they must file as Single for Federal tax purposes.

Head of Household (HOH)

A taxpayer who qualifies to file as head of household will usually have a lower tax rate than the rates for single or MFS, and will receive a higher standard deduction.

The head of household status is available to taxpayers who meet all three of the following requirements:

- The taxpayer must be single, divorced, legally separated, or "considered unmarried" on the last day of the year.
- The taxpayer must have paid more than half the cost of keeping up a home for the year.
- The taxpayer must have had a qualifying person living in his home for more than half the year. There are exceptions for temporary absences, such as school, or for a qualifying parent, who does not have to live with the taxpayer. This would include hospitalization and stays in a nursing home.

"Considered Unmarried" for HOH Status

There are some instances where a taxpayer can be considered unmarried (for tax purposes only). To be "considered unmarried" on the last day of the tax year, a taxpayer must meet all of the following conditions:

- File a separate return from the other spouse.
- Pay more than half the cost of keeping up a home for the tax year.
- Not live with his spouse in the home during the last six months of the tax year.
- Maintain the home as the main residence of a qualifying child, stepchild, or foster child for more than half the year.
- Be able to claim an exemption for the child (although there is an exception for divorced parents, explained later).

For the purpose of determining this filing status, valid household expenses used to calculate whether a taxpayer is paying more than half the cost of maintaining a home include:

- Rent, mortgage interest, property taxes
- Home insurance, repairs, utilities
- Food eaten in the home

Valid expenses do not include clothing, education, medical treatment, vacations, life insurance, or transportation. Welfare payments are not considered amounts that the taxpayer provides to maintain a home.

For purposes of the head of household status, a "qualifying person" is defined as:

- A qualifying child,
- A married child who can be claimed as a dependent, or
- A dependent parent.

The qualifying person for HOH filing status must generally be related to the taxpayer either by blood, adoption, or marriage. However, a foster child also qualifies if the child was legally placed in the home by a government agency.

A taxpayer's qualifying person may include the taxpayer's child or stepchild, sibling or stepsibling, or a descendant of any of these. For example, a niece or nephew, stepbrother or stepsister, or grandchild may all be eligible as qualifying persons for the HOH filing status.[7]

Example: Lewis's unmarried daughter, Araceli, lived with him all year. Araceli turned 18 at the end of the year. She does not have a job, did not provide any of her own support, and cannot be claimed as a dependent by anyone else. As a result, Araceli is Lewis's qualifying child. Lewis may use the HOH filing status.

An unrelated individual may still be considered a "qualifying relative" for a dependency exemption, but will not be a qualifying person for the HOH filing status.[8]

---

[7] A taxpayer cannot file as head of household if the taxpayer's only dependent is his or her Registered Domestic Partner.

[8] The rules for qualifying children and relatives will be covered in detail in the next unit, *Personal and Dependency Exemptions.*

Special Rules for HOH Status

Divorced or Noncustodial Parents: A taxpayer can file as HOH and not claim the qualifying child as their dependent. This happens most often with divorced parents. This is because the head of household filing status applies to the taxpayer who maintains the main home of a qualifying child.

However, a custodial parent may choose to release the dependency exemption to a noncustodial parent. In this scenario, the custodial parent would claim head of household filing status, while the noncustodial parent would claim the dependency exemption.

Example: George and Elizabeth have been divorced for five years. They have a 12-year-old daughter named Rebecca who lives with her mother during the week and only sees her father on weekends. Therefore, Elizabeth is considered the custodial parent. They agree, however, to allow George to claim the dependency exemption for Rebecca on his tax return. In 2016, George correctly files as single and claims Rebecca as his dependent. Elizabeth may still file as HOH if she otherwise qualifies, but she will not claim the dependency exemption for Rebecca.

The "considered unmarried" rules apply in determining who can claim a child for dependency and HOH purposes. A couple, even if not formally separated or divorced, must live apart for *more than half the year* in order for either spouse to claim HOH status.

Example: Luke and Pauline separated in February 2016 and lived apart for the rest of the year. They do not have a written separation agreement and are not yet divorced. Their six-year-old daughter, Kennedy, lived with Luke all year, and he paid more than half the cost of keeping up the home. Luke files a separate tax return and claims Kennedy as a dependent because he is the custodial parent. Luke can also claim head of household status for 2016. Although Luke is still legally married, he can file as HOH because he meets all the requirements to be "considered unmarried".

Example: Janine and Richard separated on July 10, 2016, but were not yet divorced at the end of the year. They have one minor child, Madeline, age eight. Even though Janine lived with Madeline and supported her for the remainder of the year, Janine does not qualify for HOH filing status because she and Richard did not live apart for the last six months of the year.

Death or Birth during the Year: A taxpayer may still file as head of household if the qualifying child is born or dies during the year. The taxpayer must have provided more than half of the cost of keeping up a home that was the child's main home while he was alive.

Example: Velma gives birth to a son in September 2016 who dies within two months of his birth. She can claim him on her tax return as a qualifying child even though he only lived a short while.

Dependent Parents: If a taxpayer's qualifying person is a dependent parent, the taxpayer can file as HOH even if the parent does not live with the taxpayer.

The taxpayer must pay more than half the cost of keeping up a home that was the parent's main home for the entire year. This rule also applies to a parent in a rest home. A qualifying "parent" may be a stepparent, in-law, or grandparent who is related to the taxpayer by blood, marriage, or adoption.

Example: Sharon is 54 years old and single. She pays the monthly bill for Shasta Pines Retirement Homes, where her 78-year-old mother lives. Sharon's mother has lived at Shasta Pines for two years and has no income. Since Sharon pays more than half of the cost of her mother's living expenses, Sharon qualifies for head of household filing status.

Example: Tina is single and fully financially supports her mother, Rue, who lives in her own apartment. Rue dies suddenly on May 2, 2016. Tina can claim her mother as a dependent and file as HOH for 2016, even though Rue was not alive for the whole year.

Nonresident Alien Spouses: A taxpayer, who is married to a nonresident alien spouse, may elect to file as HOH by "disregarding" the nonresident alien spouse. This is a unique rule that only applies to taxpayers who are married to nonresidents.

This is true even if both spouses lived together throughout the year. The taxpayer must not elect to treat the spouse as a resident and he must have a qualifying child (or other qualifying dependent, such as a parent) to qualify for the HOH status.

Example: Two years ago, Tim, a U.S. citizen, met and married Mina, a nonresident alien who is a citizen and resident of Greenland. The couple lived together in Greenland while Tim was on sabbatical from his university teaching position. They have a son who was born in 2016. Mina does not wish to file jointly with Tim and does not wish to make the election to be treated as a U.S. resident. Tim can file as head of household, even though he and Mina lived together all year because Mina is a nonresident alien.

Annulments

Annulment is a legal procedure for declaring a marriage null and void. If a taxpayer obtains a court decree of annulment that holds no valid marriage ever existed, the couple is considered unmarried even if they filed joint returns for earlier years.

Unlike divorce, an annulment is retroactive. Taxpayers who have annulled their marriage must file amended returns (Form 1040X) claiming single (or head of household status, if applicable) for all the tax years affected by the annulment that are not closed by the statute of limitations.

Example: Sara and Robert were granted an annulment on October 31, 2016. They were married for two years. Robert has sole custody of one son from a prior relationship. For 2016, Sara must file as single and must amend the prior two years' tax returns to single as well. Robert must also amend his joint returns. If he otherwise qualifies, Robert can amend his returns to head of household filing status.

Qualifying Widow(er) With a Dependent Child

Qualifying widow(er) with a dependent child is the least common filing status. A qualifying widow(er) receives the same standard deduction as married taxpayers who file jointly. In the year of the spouse's death, a taxpayer can generally file a joint return.

However, if a surviving spouse remarries before the end of the year, the married filing separately status must be used for the decedent's final return.

Example: Marian and her husband, Lou, have an infant son. Lou dies suddenly of a heart attack on February 1, 2016. Marian remarries on December 10, 2016. Since she remarried in the same year her former husband died, she no longer qualifies for the joint return filing status with her deceased husband. However, Marian does qualify to file jointly with her new spouse. Therefore, Lou's filing status for his final tax return in 2016 must be MFS.

For each of the two years following the year of the spouse's death, the surviving spouse can use the qualifying widow(er) filing status if he has a qualifying dependent and does not remarry. After two years, the taxpayer's filing status converts to single or HOH, depending upon which status applies. For example, if a taxpayer's spouse died in 2015 and he did not remarry, the taxpayer could use the qualifying widow(er) filing status for 2016 and 2017 if he has a qualifying dependent.

Example: Barbara's husband died on July 3, 2015. She has one dependent child who is ten years old. Barbara does not remarry. Therefore, Barbara's filing status for 2015 is MFJ (the last year her husband was alive). In 2016 and 2017, she can file as a "qualifying widow with a dependent child", which is a more favorable filing status than single or HOH. In 2018, she would file as HOH, assuming she remains single and does not remarry.

To be eligible for the qualifying widow(er) filing status, the taxpayer normally must:

- Not have remarried before the end of the year.
- Have been eligible to file a joint return for the year the spouse died; it does not matter if a joint return was actually filed.
- Have a qualifying child for the year. A qualifying child can be a child or stepchild, but does not include a foster child for the purposes of this filing status.
- Have furnished over half the cost of keeping up the qualifying child's home for the entire year.

Note: A taxpayer's marital status on the last day of the year (December 31) determines their marital status for the entire year, for tax purposes.

Determining Residency for Tax Purposes

In order to file an accurate tax return, a taxpayer must determine whether he is considered a *resident* or a *nonresident*. There are multiple types of tax residency.

For IRS purposes, an "alien" is an individual who is not a U.S. citizen. Aliens are further classified as nonresident aliens and resident aliens. Residency status is important because these taxpayers are taxed in different ways:

- **Resident aliens** are generally taxed on their worldwide income, the same as U.S. citizens.
- **Nonresident aliens** are taxed only on their income from sources within the United States and on certain income connected with the conduct of a trade or business in the U.S.
- **Dual status aliens** are both nonresident and resident aliens during the same tax year, with different rules applying for the part of the year a taxpayer is a U.S. resident and the part of the year he is a nonresident.

Residency for IRS purposes is not the same as legal immigration status. An individual may be considered a U.S. resident for tax purposes based upon the time he spends in the United States, regardless of immigration status.

A nonresident alien could be someone who lives outside the U.S. and simply invests in U.S. property or stocks and is therefore required to file a tax return to correctly report his earnings.

Example: Chloe Jones is a folk singer and a popular recording artist in her home country of Australia. Chloe comes to the U.S. on tour, playing a variety of different venues during the month of April. Afterwards she returns to her home country. Chloe is not a U.S. resident for tax purposes. However, she is required to report her U.S. source income. Chloe's accountant files a Form 1040NR to report the income that she earned while she was touring in the U.S. She will only report and be taxed on her U.S. source income.

Tax Residency through Marriage

A nonresident alien who does not meet the substantial presence test and does not have a green card may still elect to be treated as a resident for tax purposes if he is married to a U.S. citizen or resident. This election can be made only if:

- At the end of the year, one spouse is a nonresident alien, and the other is a U.S. citizen or resident, and
- Both spouses agree to file a joint return and to treat the nonresident alien as a resident alien for the entire tax year.

Example: Lola and Bruno are married, and both are nonresident aliens at the beginning of the year. In February, Bruno becomes a legal U.S. resident alien and obtains a green card and a Social Security number. Lola and Bruno may both choose to be treated as resident aliens for tax purposes by attaching a statement to their joint return. Lola is not eligible for a Social Security number, so she must apply for an ITIN. Lola and Bruno must file a joint return for the year they make the election, but they can file either joint or separate returns for later years.

Example: Mei, a citizen of South Korea, is in the U.S. as a graduate student on an F-1 visa status. She has resided continuously in the U.S. since arriving on August 15, 2011. She was in the U.S. all of 2016. Because international students are exempt from the substantial presence test for five years, Mei became a resident alien for federal income tax purposes in 2016. Mei is married to Quon, who lives in South Korea and is a nonresident alien. Mei and Quon can both elect to be treated as U.S. residents for tax purposes on a jointly filed return.

Tax Residency Tests

If a taxpayer is an alien, he is considered a nonresident alien for tax purposes unless he meets at least one of two tests: the *green card* test or the *substantial presence* test.

Green Card Test

An alien taxpayer is automatically considered a U.S. resident if he is a "lawful permanent resident[9]" of the United States at any time during the tax year. A taxpayer generally has this status if he is a lawful immigrant and has been issued an alien registration card, also known as a "green card".

An alien who has been present in the U.S. any time during a calendar year as a lawful permanent resident may opt to be treated as a resident alien for the entire calendar year.

Substantial Presence Test

An alien taxpayer without a green card is considered a U.S. resident for tax purposes only if he meets the substantial presence test for the calendar year. To meet this test, he must be physically present in the United States for at least:

- 31 days during the current tax year (2016), and
- 183 days during the three-year period that includes the current year (2016) and the two years immediately preceding the current year.

For purposes of the 183-day requirement, all the days present in the current year (2016) are counted, along with:

- 1/3 of the days present in the previous year (i.e., 2015), and
- 1/6 of the days present in the second year before the current year (i.e., 2014).

[9] Image provided by Department of Homeland Security, U.S. Citizenship and Immigration Services Verification Division.

Note: If an individual meets the requirements of the substantial presence test, he is considered for federal tax purposes a resident alien of the United States, even though he may be an undocumented immigrant.

Numerous exceptions are considered when counting days for the substantial presence test. Days in the United States are not counted if the alien taxpayer:

- Regularly commutes to work in the U.S. from a residence in Canada or Mexico, generally more than 75% of the workdays during the applicable working period (this is deemed a "closer connection to home country").
- Is present in the U.S. as a crew member of a foreign vessel.
- Is unable to leave because of a medical condition that arose while in the United States.
- Is a professional athlete in the U.S. to compete in a charitable sports event. These athletes exclude only the days in which they actually competed in the sports event, but do not exclude days used for practice, travel, or promotional events.
- Is an exempt individual. Exempt individuals include aliens who are:
    - Foreign government-related individuals in the U.S. temporarily, (such as foreign diplomats).
    - Teachers on temporary visas.
    - Visiting Scholars or researchers. Scholars are exempt for two years.
    - Students on temporary visas who do not intend to reside permanently in the U.S. Students are exempt from the substantial presence test for five years.

If the taxpayer does not meet either the green card test or the substantial presence test, he is considered a nonresident alien for tax purposes and is subject to U.S. income tax only on his U.S. source income.

Study Tip: You should memorize details of the substantial presence test for the EA exam, including the 183-day requirement and exceptions to the rule.

Example: Juliana is a Brazilian citizen who was physically present in the United States for 15 days in each of the years 2014, 2015, and 2016. She is not a green card holder. Juliana earned $32,000 in 2016 as a Portuguese translator for the U.S. government. Since the total days she was present in the U.S. for the three-year period do not meet the substantial presence test, Juliana is not considered a resident for tax purposes for 2016 and her earnings are taxed as a nonresident. Juliana is required to file Form 1040NR, *U.S. Nonresident Alien Income Tax Return*.

Example: Chow is a Chinese citizen and a renowned scientist. Chow was invited to the US to teach an advanced course at Yale University. Even though Chow is physically present in the United States for the entire tax year, he is not considered a resident for tax purposes, because he is a visiting scholar. Chow is required to file Form 1040NR, *U.S. Nonresident Alien Income Tax Return* to report his U.S. earnings.

Students: Most international students and scholars fall under the status of nonresident aliens. An international student is anyone who is temporarily in the U.S. on an F, J, M, or Q visa. Immediate family members of a student, including spouses and unmarried children under age 21 who reside with the student, are also considered students for tax purposes.

Any part of a calendar year in which the student is present in the U.S. counts as a full year.

Example: Nayan first came to the U.S. in 2010 from India as an F-1 student at a university. She studied in the U.S. until the end of 2011 and then returned home. She re-entered the U.S. as a J-1 student in 2016 in order to attend graduate school. For federal income tax purposes, Nayan is a nonresident alien because she has been in the U.S. for less than five years as a student.

Dual Status Aliens: A taxpayer is considered a dual-status alien when he has been both a resident alien and a nonresident alien in the same tax year. The most common dual-status tax years are the years of arrival and departure.

A taxpayer's status on the last day of the year determines whether he is a resident alien or a nonresident alien for the tax year. For the part of each year, the taxpayer is a nonresident alien, he is taxed only on his U.S. source income. For the part of each year, the taxpayer is a resident alien, he is taxed on his worldwide income. This applies even if the income was earned earlier in the year while the taxpayer was a nonresident alien, but was received after he became a resident for tax purposes.

Example: Abbas legally became a U.S. resident for tax purposes on January 1, 2016. On January 15, 2016, he received $2,000 of income for contract work he did the previous year. Even though the income was earned while he was a nonresident alien, it was received after he became a resident. This income is reported and taxed on Form 1040, not on Form 1040NR.

Tax Treaties

The United States has income tax treaties with a number of foreign countries. Under these treaties, residents of foreign countries may be taxed at reduced rates, or be exempt from U.S. income taxes on certain items of income they receive from U.S. source income. These reduced rates and exemptions vary among countries and specific items of income.

Treaty provisions generally are reciprocal. Therefore, a U.S. citizen or resident who receives income from a treaty country and who is subject to taxes imposed by foreign countries may be entitled to certain credits, deductions, exemptions, and reductions in the rate of taxes of those foreign countries.

Income received by a nonresident alien that is effectively connected with a trade or business in the United States is, after allowable deductions, taxed at the rates that apply to U.S. citizens and residents. Withholding would be made at the highest applicable rate.

Note: For nonresident aliens, income or gains from U.S. sources is generally subject to backup **withholding at 30%**, unless a lower treaty rate applies. The backup withholding rate for U.S. citizens and U.S. residents is a flat 28% rate.

2016 Filing Requirements

Not every person is required to file a tax return. A taxpayer is required to file a tax return if his 2016 gross income exceeds the combined total of the standard deduction and personal exemption amounts. The IRS defines gross income as all income a taxpayer received in the form of money, goods, property, and services that are not exempt from tax. Sometimes, a taxpayer is required to file a tax return even though none of his income is taxable.

Note: "Earned income" includes all the taxable income a taxpayer receives from working, such as wages, salaries, tips, and other employee compensation. Earned income also includes self-employment earnings that a taxpayer earns by owning a business or farm. Most other types of income are considered **unearned income**, including interest income, dividends, capital gains, retirement income, inheritances, and prizes.

The 2016 filing requirement thresholds, expressed as levels of gross income, are as follows:

Gross Income Filing Thresholds

- Single: $10,350 (65 or older $11,900)
- Married Filing Jointly: $20,700,
    - 65 or older (one spouse) $21,950;
    - 65 or older (both spouses): $23,200
- Head of Household: $13,350 (65 or older $14,900)
- Married Filing Separately (any age): $4,050
- Qualifying Widow(er) with dependent child: $16,650 (65 or older $17,900)
- Any taxpayer with self-employment income of $400 or more in any taxable year must file a return.

- A taxpayer who earned $108.28 or more as a church employee. For the purposes of this rule, a "church employee" is an employee of a church or religious organization that has a certificate in effect electing an exemption from employer social security and Medicare taxes. [10]

Example: Adrienne and Marvin are married and plan to file jointly. Adrienne is 63 and had gross income of $12,225 for the year. Marvin is 66 and had gross income of $7,500 for the year. Since their combined gross income was $19,725, they are not required to file a tax return. The filing requirement threshold for joint filers when one spouse is 65 or older is $21,950 in 2016.

Example: Rita is 66, married, and had $9,500 of wage income in 2016. Her husband, Roger, also 66, had $8,700 in wage income. They have no dependents. Normally, Roger and Rita would not have a filing requirement because their gross income is under the filing threshold for joint filers age 65 and over. However, Rita wants to file separately from her husband. She is therefore required to file a tax return because the filing threshold for MFS taxpayers of any age is $4,050 in 2016. Roger must also file a tax return because his filing status is MFS by default. Roger cannot choose to file jointly with his wife unless she agrees, since both spouses are required to sign a joint return.

Example: Laurel is 36, single, and had gross income of $17,500 last year. She does not have any children. She is required to file a tax return since her income was more than $10,350 in 2016. She will use the single filing status.

Filing Requirements for Self-Employed Taxpayers

There are different requirements for taxpayers who are self-employed. Generally, a taxpayer is required to file a tax return if he has net self-employment earnings of $400 or more.

Note: Do not confuse the filing threshold amount for self-employed taxpayers with the filing requirement for information returns (most notably, Form 1099-MISC, *Miscellaneous Income).* Form 1099-MISC is used to report a number of different types of payments, but it is most commonly used to report payments to an independent contractor who is paid at least $600 during the year.

Dependent Filing Requirements

All dependent children who earn more than $6,300 of earned income in 2016 must file an income tax return. The threshold is much lower for unearned income (investment income). When unearned income exceeds $1,050 in 2016, a tax return must be filed for the dependent. A dependent's standard deduction is calculated differently. In 2016, it normally equals the larger of:

- $1,050 (of unearned income, such as interest or dividends) or
- Their earned income plus $350, with a maximum standard deduction of $6,300.

Example: Cesar is a 16-year-old high school student who is claimed as a dependent on his parents' tax return. He worked as a pizza delivery boy ten hours a week and earned $3,200 of wages in 2016. He also had $1,100 of interest income from a certificate of deposit that his grandmother gave him last Christmas. Cesar is required to file a tax return because his unearned income exceeds $1,050. If Cesar did not have any interest income, he would not be required to file a return. The investment income is what triggers his filing requirement.

[10] For the purposes of this rule, a "church employee" does not include a minister, a member of a religious order, or a Christian Science practitioner.

Example: Annette is 17 and is claimed as a dependent on her mother's tax return. Working at an ice cream parlor during the school year, Annette earned a total of $6,600 in wages in 2016. She had no other income. Annette must file a tax return because her total earned income is more than $6,300. Her mother can still claim her as a dependent.

Example: Marc is 20, single, and a full-time college student. Marc's parents claim him on their joint tax return. He received $200 of interest income and earned $4,750 of wages from a part-time job. Marc's total income of $4,950 is below the gross income filing threshold for dependents. His investment income is also below the filing requirement. Marc is not required to file a tax return in 2016.

Even if a taxpayer is not legally required to file a tax return, he should do so if he is eligible to receive a refund. A taxpayer should file a tax return if he:

- Had income tax withheld from his pay,
- Made estimated tax payments or had prior year overpayments,
- Qualifies for the Earned Income Tax Credit, or
- Qualifies for any other refundable tax credits.

Example: Holly is single, has a young son, and qualifies for HOH filing status. In 2016, she earns $11,000 of wages and $700 of self-employment income from cleaning houses. Although Holly makes less than the filing threshold for the HOH filing status, she must file a tax return because her earnings from self-employment exceed $400. Even if Holly did not have self-employment earnings, she should still file a tax return, because she likely qualifies for the Earned Income Tax Credit. The EITC is a refundable credit which could give Holly a refund.

Additional Filing Requirements

Sometimes a taxpayer is required to file a tax return even if the gross income threshold is not met, such as in the previous example of self-employment earnings of $400 or more. Other examples include the following:

- Church employees who are exempt from employers' Social Security and Medicare taxes and have wages above $108.28.
- If the taxpayer owes Social Security tax or Medicare tax on tips not reported to his employer.
- If the taxpayer must pay the alternative minimum tax.
- If the taxpayer owes additional tax in connection with a qualified plan, an IRA, a health savings account, or other tax-favored health plan.
- If the taxpayer received a Medicare Advantage MSA, Archer MSA, or health savings account distribution.
- If the taxpayer owes household employment taxes for a household worker, such as a nanny.
- If the taxpayer must recapture an education credit, investment credit, or other credit.
- If the taxpayer received advance payments of the Premium Tax Credit for himself, his spouse, or a dependent who enrolled in coverage through the Health Insurance Marketplace.

Unit 2: Study Questions

(Test yourself first, then check the correct answers at the end of this quiz.)

1. Seven years ago, Vladimir and Pablo were legally joined in a civil union in the state of Vermont. They now live in California. What is the correct statement about their filing status for 2016?

A. Vladimir and Pablo must file jointly.
B. A civil union of same-sex spouses in Vermont is not recognized in California, so they must file joint federal returns and separate state returns.
C. Vladimir and Pablo have the choice to file as single, married filing jointly, or married filing separately.
D. Civil unions are not recognized as legal marriages for IRS purposes. Vladimir and Pablo must file as single for federal tax purposes.

2. Dana's husband died on January 14, 2016. She has one dependent son who is eight years old. She did not remarry. What is the most beneficial filing status for Dana to use for 2016?

A. Married filing jointly.
B. Single.
C. Qualifying widow(er).
D. Head of household.

3. Madison and Todd are not married and do not live together, but they have a two-year-old daughter named Amanda. Madison and her daughter lived together all year while Todd lived alone in his own apartment. Madison earned $13,000 working as a clothing store clerk. Todd earned $48,000 managing a hardware store. He paid over half the cost of Madison's apartment for rent and utilities, where his daughter Amanda lives. He also gave Madison child support and extra money for groceries. Todd does not support any other family member. Which of the following statements is correct?

A. Todd can file as head of household.
B. Madison can file as head of household.
C. Todd and Madison can file jointly.
D. Neither can claim head of household filing status.

4. Helen, age 65, and Norman, age 72, were married in 2016. They have no dependents. Helen had gross income of $2,000, and Norman had gross income of $28,000 for the year. Norman wants to file jointly, but Helen wants to file separately. Which of the following statements is correct?

A. Norman is required to file a tax return using the MFS status. Helen is not required to file a return.
B. Norman may still file jointly with Helen and sign on her behalf, as long as he notifies her in writing.
C. Norman and Helen are both required to file tax returns, and they must both file MFS.
D. Norman and Helen may both file as single.

5. Annie's husband, Enzo, has neither a green card nor a visa. He was physically present in the United States for 150 days in each of the years 2014, 2015, and 2016. Is Enzo a resident alien under the substantial presence test?

A. Yes, he is a resident alien for tax purposes.
B. No, he is a nonresident alien for tax purposes.
C. Enzo is a nonresident alien for tax purposes, but he may elect to file as a resident with his spouse.
D. None of the above is correct.

6. Trinity, age 22, is single and a full-time college student who is claimed as a dependent on her father's tax return. In 2016, Trinity earned $7,350 of wages from her part-time job as an administrative assistant. She had no other income. Is she required to file a tax return?

A. Yes.
B. No.
C. Trinity is only required to file a tax return if she is a full-time student.
D. Trinity should file a return because she will receive a refund, but she is not required to file.

7. Clarence takes care of his ten-year-old grandson. How long must his grandson live in Clarence's home in order for Clarence to qualify for head of household status?

A. At least three months.
B. More than half the year.
C. The entire year.
D. More than 12 months.

8. Zora is a citizen of Russia who is granted a green card while abroad and comes to the U.S. to work as an engineer. Zora arrives in the U.S. on November 1, 2016. She earns a total of $26,000 of U.S. wages in November and December. Which of the following statements is correct?

A. She is not required to file a U.S. tax return.
B. She is required to file a U.S. tax return, and she must file using Form 1040NR.
C. She is required to file a U.S. tax return, and she must file her return using Form 1040, 1040A or 1040EZ.
D. She is not required to file a U.S. tax return in 2016, but she will be required to file a return in 2017.

9. When may a taxpayer amend a joint tax return from "married filing jointly" to "married filing separately" after the original filing deadline?

A. Never.
B. Only within the statute of limitations for filing amended returns.
C. Only when a marriage has been annulled.
D. An estate's personal representative may amend a joint return elected by the surviving spouse to a separate return for the decedent.

10. Kathy's marriage was annulled on February 25, 2016. She was married to her husband in 2014 and filed jointly with him in 2014 and 2015. She has not yet filed her 2016 tax return. Kathy has no dependents. Which of the following statements is correct?

A. She must file amended returns, claiming single filing status for all open years affected by the annulment. She will file single for the current tax year.
B. She is not required to file amended returns. She can file jointly with her husband in 2016 because she was still married for part of the year.
C. She is not required to file amended returns. She must file as married filing separately on her 2016 return.
D. She is not required to file amended returns. She must file as single on her 2016 return.

11. A U.S. resident or citizen who is married to a nonresident alien can file a joint return as long as both spouses:

A. Sign the return and agree to be taxed on their worldwide income.
B. Are living overseas.
C. Have valid Social Security numbers.
D. Are physically present in the United States.

12. Huang is a student temporarily in the U.S. on an F-1 Visa. You are his tax preparer and you are trying to determine residency for tax purposes. Huang was present in the U.S. all year. How long is he exempt from the substantial presence test?

A. One year.
B. Three years.
C. Five years.
D. There is no exemption to the substantial presence test.

13. Which of the following statements is correct regarding the head of household filing status?

A. The taxpayer must be unmarried in order to qualify for head of household filing status.
B. The taxpayer's spouse must live in the home during the tax year.
C. The taxpayer's dependent parent does not have to live with the taxpayer in order to qualify for head of household filing status.
D. The taxpayer must have paid roughly half of the cost of keeping up the house for the entire year.

14. The married filing separately (MFS) status is for taxpayers who:

A. Are legally divorced on the last day of the year.
B. Are married and choose to file separate returns.
C. Are unmarried, but engaged to be married.
D. Are unmarried, but have a dependent child.

15. Victor is 39 years old and has lived apart from his wife, Eleanor, since February 1, 2016. Their divorce was not yet final at the end of 2016, and they were not legally separated under a separate maintenance decree. They have two minor children. Since they split up, one child has lived with Victor and the other with Eleanor. Victor provides all of the support for the minor child living with him. Eleanor refuses to file jointly with Victor in 2016. The most beneficial filing status that Victor qualifies for is:

A. Married filing separately.
B. Single.
C. Head of household.
D. Married filing jointly.

16. Lisa and Stuart were married. Stuart died in 2015. Lisa has not remarried, and she has one dependent child. Which filing status should Lisa use for her 2016 tax return?

A. Single.
B. Married filing jointly.
C. Head of household.
D. Qualifying widow with a dependent child.

17. Mary and Troy are married and lived together all year. Mary earned $7,000 in 2016, and Troy earned $42,000. Mary wants to file a joint return, but Troy refuses to file with Mary and instead files a separate return on his own. Which of the following statements is correct?

A. Mary can file a joint amended tax return and e-file it if Troy refuses to provide a signature.
B. Mary and Troy must both file separate returns.
C. Mary can file as single because Troy refuses to sign a joint return.
D. Mary does not have a filing requirement because her income is below the filing threshold.

18. Which dependent relative may qualify a taxpayer for head of household filing status?

A. An adult stepdaughter who lives in her own apartment who is supported by the taxpayer.
B. A cousin who lives with the taxpayer all year.
C. A parent who lives in his own home and not with the taxpayer.
D. An adopted child who lived with the taxpayer for five months of the tax year.

19. All of the following individuals are required to file an income tax return except:

A. A taxpayer who owes household employment tax for a nanny.
B. A church employee who is exempt from payroll taxes and who earned $106 of wages in 2016.
C. A 54-year-old qualifying widower who earned $18,000 in 2016.
D. A single taxpayer who earned $6,500 in 2016 and who owes excise tax on withdrawals from a health savings account.

20. Kylie is an 18-year-old senior in her last year of high school. She worked as a grocery store bagger on weekends and earned $1,400 in wages during 2016. She also received $2,300 for a winning scratch-off lottery ticket. Her parents claim her as a dependent on their tax return. Does Kylie have to file her own return?

A. Yes, because of the amount of her unearned income.
B. Yes, because of the combined amount of her unearned and earned income.
C. No, because her earned income is below the threshold for a dependent.
D. No, because it is illegal for a high school student to play the lottery.

21. Ezequiel and Angela are married, but they choose to file separate returns for 2016 because the IRS is investigating Ezequiel for a previous tax issue. Ezequiel and Angela file their MFS returns on time. A few months after filing their separate returns, the investigation is over, and Ezequiel's previous tax issue has been resolved. He then wishes to file amended returns and file jointly with his wife in order to claim the Earned Income Tax Credit. Which of the following statements is correct?

A. Ezequiel is prohibited from changing his filing status in order to claim this credit.
B. Ezequiel and Angela can amend their MFS tax returns to MFJ in order to claim the credit.
C. Ezequiel and Angela can amend their MFS tax returns to MFJ, but they cannot claim the credit.
D. Angela cannot file jointly with Ezequiel after she has already filed a separate tax return.

22. Louisa legally separated from her husband during 2016. They have a 9-year-old son. Which of the following would prevent Louisa from filing as head of household?

A. Louisa has maintained a separate residence from her husband since March 1, 2016.
B. Her son's principal home is with Louisa.
C. Louisa's parents assisted her with 40% of the household costs.
D. Her son lived with Louisa from July 3, 2016, to December 31, 2016.

23. Carol and Raul were married four years ago and had no children. They split up in 2015 but did not file for divorce. Although they lived apart during all of 2016, they are neither divorced nor legally separated. Which of the following filing statuses can they use?

A. Single or married filing separately.
B. Married filing jointly or married filing separately.
C. Married filing separately or head of household.
D. Single or qualifying widow(er).

24. Alexandra's younger brother, Sebastian, is 18 and lived with friends in January and February of 2016. From March through July of 2016, he lived with his sister Alexandra. On August 1, Sebastian moved back in with his friends and stayed with them the rest of the year. However, since Sebastian did not have a job, Alexandra gave him money every month and provided the majority of his financial support for the remainder of the year. Alexandra has no other dependents. Which of the following statements is correct?

A. Alexandra can file as head of household.
B. Alexandra can file jointly with Sebastian.
C. Alexandra cannot file as head of household.
D. Sebastian can file as head of household.

25. Taxpayers are considered to be married for the entire year if:

A. One spouse dies during the year and the surviving spouse does not remarry.
B. The spouses are legally separated under a separate maintenance decree.
C. The spouses are divorced on December 31 of the tax year.
D. The spouses had their marriage annulled on December 31 of the tax year.

26. Janet and Harry are married and file jointly. During 2016, Janet turned 67, and Harry turned 66. Janet's gross income was $19,000, and Harry's gross income from self-employment was $620. Harry had no other income. Based on this information, which of the following statements is correct?

A. Janet and Harry are not required to file tax returns.
B. Janet and Harry are required to file tax returns.
C. Only Janet is required to file a tax return.
D. Only Harry is required to file a tax return.

27. Which of the following dependency relationships would not qualify a taxpayer to claim qualifying widow(er) as their filing status after the death of a spouse?

A. A biological child
B. A foster child
C. An adopted child
D. A step-child

Unit 2: Answers

1. The answer is D. Same-sex marriage is now legal in all 50 states and the District of Columbia. However, for federal tax purposes, civil unions are not treated as legal marriages. Civil unions offer same-sex couples some of the same benefits of marriage under state law, but they are not recognized as "marriages" for federal tax purposes. The IRS recognizes a marriage of same-sex spouses that was validly entered into in a domestic or foreign jurisdiction whose laws recognize same-sex marriage. Therefore, Vladimir and Pablo must file as single.

2. The answer is A. If a taxpayer's spouse died during the year, the taxpayer is considered married for the whole year and can file as MFJ. Therefore, Dana should file a joint return for 2016.

3. The answer is D. Todd provided over half the cost of maintaining a home for Madison and Amanda, but he cannot file as head of household since Amanda did not live with him for more than half the year. Madison cannot file as HOH either because she did not provide more than one-half the cost of keeping up the home for her daughter. However, either Todd or Madison may still claim Amanda as a dependent.

4. The answer is A. Since Norman and Helen are married, they can file either jointly or separately. If Helen does not agree to file jointly with Norman, Norman must file MFS. The filing requirement threshold for married filing separately is $4,000. Norman is required to file a return because his gross income exceeded this threshold. Helen is not required to file a tax return because her gross income in 2016 was $2,000, below the MFS filing requirement threshold.

5. The answer is A. Enzo meets the substantial presence test and is considered a resident alien for tax purposes. He is considered to have been present in the United States for a total of 225 days. The full 150 days are counted for 2016; 50 days for 2015 (1/3 of 150); and 25 days for 2014 (1/6 of 150).

6. The answer is A. A single dependent whose earned income was more than $6,300 in 2016 must file a return.

7. The answer is B. A relative must have lived with the taxpayer more than half the year (over six months) and be the taxpayer's dependent. A taxpayer's dependent parent is an exception and does not have to live with the taxpayer.

8. The answer is C. Zora is required to file a U.S. tax return in 2016, and she must file using Form 1040, Form 1040A, or Form 1040EZ. Zora is a green card holder, and therefore she is treated as a U.S. resident for tax purposes, regardless of how much time she has been present in the United States. As a resident alien, Zora will be taxed on income from worldwide sources, including any income she earned while she was in Russia.

9. The answer is D. An executor for a deceased taxpayer can amend a joint return to an MFS return up to one year after the filing deadline. This is the only exception to a rule that generally prevents a taxpayer from amending his married filing jointly return to a married filing separately return past the filing deadline.

10. The answer is A. Kathy must file amended tax returns. She cannot file jointly with her former husband in 2016. If a couple obtains a court decree of annulment, the taxpayer must file amended returns (Form 1040X) claiming single or head of household status for all tax years affected by the annulment that are not closed by the statute of limitations for filing an amended tax return.

11. The answer is A. A U.S. resident or citizen who is married to a nonresident alien can elect to file a joint return as long as both spouses sign the return and agree to be taxed on their worldwide income. A Social Security number is not required, because a nonresident spouse that is ineligible for an SSN may request an ITIN.

12. The answer is C. In determining residency status for tax purposes, students temporarily in the U.S. on an F, J, M, or Q visa are exempt from the substantial presence test for five years. In addition, an individual who is in either of the following categories is temporarily exempt from counting days toward the substantial presence test:

- Teacher or trainee: This includes any non-immigrant temporarily present in the U.S. on a J or Q visa who is not a student. The definition includes physicians, au pairs, short-term scholars, summer camp workers, and cultural exchange visitors temporarily present in the U.S.
- Closer connection to home country: This includes individuals who have a tax home in a foreign country and have a closer connection to that country than they do the U.S.

13. The answer is C. A dependent parent does not have to live with a taxpayer in order for the taxpayer to elect the head of household filing status. This special rule applies to parents who are related to the taxpayer by blood, marriage, or adoption if the taxpayer pays more than half of the qualifying parent's household costs. Answer "A" is incorrect because a married person can still qualify for head of household if they are "considered unmarried" for tax purposes. A married person can be "considered unmarried" in certain circumstances if they live apart from their spouse and can file as head of household.

14. The answer is B. The married filing separately (MFS) status is for taxpayers who are married and either:

- Choose to file separate returns, or
- Do not agree to file a joint return.

15. The answer is C. Victor qualifies for head of household filing status because he can be "considered unmarried" for tax purposes. His child lived with him for more than six months, he did not live with his spouse the last half of the year, and he paid more than half the cost of keeping up a home for the year for a qualifying child. Couples who are living apart but not yet divorced or legally separated are allowed to file jointly, but both spouses must agree to do so. Therefore, since Eleanor refuses to file jointly with Victor, the most beneficial filing status is head of household.

16. The answer is D. In 2016, Lisa is eligible for "qualifying widow(er) with dependent child" filing status. Lisa and Stuart qualified to file MFJ in 2015, the year he died, with Lisa signing the tax return as a surviving spouse. The year of death is the last year for which a taxpayer can file MFJ. For each of the two years following the year of the spouse's death, the surviving spouse can use the qualifying widow status, if she has a qualifying dependent and does not remarry.

17. The answer is B. Married couples must agree to file jointly. If one spouse does not agree to file jointly, they are individually subject to the MFS filing threshold. In this case, both spouses are required to file tax returns because both are above the applicable earnings threshold for MFS.

18. The answer is C. A parent is the only dependent relative who does not have to live with the taxpayer in order for the taxpayer to claim head of household status. In order to file for head of household, the "qualifying person" must be one of the following: a birth child, adopted child, grandchild, stepchild, foster child, brother, sister, half-brother, half-sister, stepbrother, stepsister, or a descendant of any of those. A cousin does not qualify because they do not meet the relationship test. The adopted child in answer "D" does not qualify because the child lived with the taxpayer for less than ½ the year.

19. The answer is B. Church employees who are exempt from Social Security and Medicare taxes and have wages of $108.28 or more for the year are required to file a tax return. In answer B, the church employee's wages were below that threshold. In all of the other answers, the taxpayer would be required to file a return.

20. The answer is A. Kylie has to file a tax return because of the amount of her unearned income: the $2,300 lottery prize. A dependent with unearned income of more than $1,050 in 2016 is required to file a tax return. Her earned income—$1,400—was not high enough to trigger a filing requirement, but the lottery winnings (unearned income) do trigger a filing requirement. Answer "D" is incorrect because most U.S. states allow 18-year olds to play the state lottery.

21. The answer is B. Ezequiel and Angela are allowed to amend their separate returns to a joint return in order to claim the credit. If a taxpayer files a separate return, he may elect to amend the filing status to married filing jointly at any time within three years from the due date of the original return (not including any extensions). However, the same does not hold true in reverse. Once a taxpayer files a joint return, he cannot choose to file a separate return for that year after the due date of the return (with a rare exception for deceased taxpayers).

22. The answer is D. For Louisa to file as head of household, her home must have been the main home of her qualifying child for more than half the tax year (over six months). Since her son started living with her in July, he would not have been in the household sufficient time to qualify her for this filing status.

23. The answer is B. As long as they are married and are neither divorced nor legally separated, Carol and Raul can file a joint return or file separately. They cannot file as single.

24. The answer is C. Alexandra cannot claim head of household status because Sebastian lived with her for only five months, which is less than half the year.

25. The answer is A. Taxpayers are considered married for the entire year if:

- They were married on the last day of the tax year, or
- One spouse died during the year, and the surviving spouse has not remarried as of the end of the year.

26. The answer is B. Janet and Harry must both file tax returns. Normally, Janet and Harry would not be required to file because their combined gross income was less than the filing requirement in 2016, and they are both over 65 (this threshold applies if both spouses are 65 or over and they are filing jointly). However, because Harry's self-employment income exceeds $400, he is required to file. Further, if Janet did not wish to file a joint return with Harry, she would nevertheless be required to file separately because her income exceeds the applicable threshold of $4,050 for MFS filers. Whether they choose to file jointly or separately, both are required to file tax returns for 2016.

27. The answer is B. To be eligible for the qualifying widow(er) filing status, the taxpayer normally must have a dependent child. For the purposes of this filing status, a qualifying child can be a child, adopted child, or stepchild, but does not include a foster child. Adopted children are always treated as biological children for tax law purposes.

Unit 3: Personal and Dependency Exemptions

For additional information read:
Publication 501, *Exemptions, Standard Deduction, and Filing Information*
Publication 504, *Divorced or Separated Individuals*
Publication 519, *US Tax Guide for Aliens*

Exemptions are like tax deductions, as they reduce taxable income. Exemption amounts are indexed for inflation and are generally updated every year. For tax year 2016, the exemption amount is $4,050 per person. Taxpayers may qualify to claim two kinds of exemptions:

- **Personal exemptions,** which taxpayers claim for themselves.
- **Dependency exemptions,** which taxpayers claim for their dependents.

Only one exemption is allowed per person.

Married Couples: On a joint tax return, a married couple is allowed two personal exemptions, one for each spouse. Also, on a joint return, one spouse is never considered the dependent of the other spouse.

Example: Jenny married Rick in April of 2016. Jenny and Rick can claim two personal exemptions on their jointly filed return. Because they are married, they cannot claim each other as a dependent.

Example: Cyrus and Mandy are married with three young children. They file jointly. In this scenario, they would be able to claim five exemptions: two personal exemptions (one each for Cyrus and Mandy) and three dependency exemptions (one exemption for each of their three children). This would be a total of $20,250 in exemptions that they could claim on their tax return ($4,050 per person X 5= $20,250).

If a married couple files separate returns, each spouse can claim a personal exemption for himself or herself. However, if a spouse files a separate return, the taxpayer can claim an exemption for his spouse only if that spouse had no gross income, is not filing a return, and could not be claimed as the dependent of another taxpayer.

A taxpayer who is divorced at the end of the tax year cannot claim an exemption for a former spouse. If a taxpayer's spouse dies during the year and the surviving spouse does not remarry before the end of the year, he can claim an exemption for the deceased spouse on a jointly filed return.

Example: Barrett's wife died in 2016. He did not remarry. Barrett can claim personal exemptions for himself and his deceased wife on their jointly filed return for 2016. Therefore, his tax return would have two exemptions ($4,050 X 2), and Barrett would sign the return as a surviving spouse.

A taxpayer can claim one dependency exemption for each qualified dependent. Examples of dependents include a child, stepchild, brother, sister, or parent.

Example: Hao and Binh are married and have four dependent children. On their jointly filed return, they can claim a total of six exemptions: four dependency exemptions for their children and two personal exemptions for themselves.

Personal Exemption Phaseout

Personal and dependency exemptions are phased out or eliminated for taxpayers with adjusted gross income above specified thresholds. For an individual subject to this limitation, the total exemption amount that can be claimed is reduced by 2% for each $2,500 increment by which his AGI exceeds the applicable threshold. In 2016, the phase-out will occur over the following income ranges:

Filing Status	Phaseout Begins	Phaseout Ends[11]
Single	$259,400	$381,900
Head of Household	$285,350	$407,850
MFJ or Qualifying Widow(er)	$311,300	$433,800
MFS	$155,650	$216,900

Note: In 2016, exemptions are fully phased out once AGI reaches $381,900 for single filers. For joint filers, the phaseout occurs when AGI reaches $433,800. When taxpayers reach these thresholds, they cannot claim any exemptions—they are completely phased out. These phaseout thresholds are adjusted for inflation each year.

Tests for Dependency

In order to determine if a taxpayer can claim a dependency exemption for another person, there are three main tests:

- Dependent taxpayer
- Joint return
- Citizenship or residency

Test #1. Dependent Taxpayer Test

If a taxpayer can claim another person as a dependent, even if the taxpayer does not do so, the dependent cannot take a personal exemption on his own tax return or claim another person as a dependent, even if he has a qualifying child or qualifying relative.

Thus, there is only one personal exemption that applies to a person who qualifies as a dependent, whether he files his own return or is listed as a dependent on someone else's return.

Example: Eva is a 17-year-old single mother who has an infant son. Eva lives with her parents and has a part-time job, but she does not make enough money to support herself or her infant son. Eva is claimed as a dependent by her parents, so she cannot claim an exemption for herself, and she is prohibited from claiming her infant son as a dependent on her own tax return.

Sometimes an individual meets the rules to be a qualifying dependent of more than one person. Regardless, only one person can claim an individual as a dependent on his tax return.

Example: Dan and Linda are unmarried and live together with their daughter, Savannah. Savannah is a qualifying child for both Dan and Linda, but only one of them can claim her as a dependent on their tax return.

Test #2. Joint Return Test

If a married individual files a joint return, he normally cannot be claimed as a dependent by another taxpayer.

Example: Ellen is 18 years old and had no income in 2016. She got married on December 1, 2016, to Rex, who is 22 years old. Ellen's new husband earned $26,700 during 2016, and they file jointly, claiming two personal exemptions on their tax return. Ellen's father supported her throughout the year and even paid for their wedding. However, her father cannot claim Ellen as his dependent because she is filing jointly with her new husband.

[11] Rev. Proc. 2015-53

There is one narrow exemption to this test. The joint return test *does not apply* if the joint return is filed by the dependent only to claim a refund and neither spouse would have a tax liability, even if they filed separate returns.

Example: Greg and Taylor are both 19 years old and married. They live with Taylor's mother, Michelle. In 2016, Greg earned $2,800 from a part-time job. That was the only income that either Greg or his wife earned all year. Neither Greg nor Taylor is required to file a tax return, but they file a joint return to obtain a refund of the taxes that were withheld from Greg's wages. As the exception to the joint return test applies, Michelle can claim exemptions for both Greg and Taylor on her tax return, as long as Greg and Taylor did not claim the exemptions for themselves and all the other tests for dependency are met.

Test #3. Citizenship or Residency Test

The dependent must be a citizen or resident of the United States, or a citizen or resident of Canada or Mexico (with an exception for foreign-born adopted children).

Example: Maurice is a Canadian Citizen and a legal U.S. Resident (green card holder). He provides all of the financial support for his two children, ages 6 and 12, who are also Canadian citizens. His children live in Canada with Maurice's sister. Maurice can still claim his children as dependents, even though they are not U.S. Citizens or U.S. residents. This is because of the special exception that allows for residents and citizens of Canada and Mexico to be claimed as dependents.

Dependency Relationships

A taxpayer cannot claim a person as a dependent unless that person is either his **qualifying child** or his **qualifying relative**. There are very specific tests to identify the difference between the two.

Note: Both "qualifying children" and "qualifying relatives" must meet all of the general dependency requirements already specified: the dependent taxpayer, joint return, and citizenship or residency tests.

Tests for a Qualifying Child

The tests for a "qualifying child" are more stringent than the tests for a "qualifying relative". Having a qualifying child entitles a taxpayer to claim a dependency exemption as well as numerous tax credits, including the Earned Income Tax Credit and the Child Tax Credit. Having a qualifying relative, on the other hand, does not qualify a taxpayer for these credits.

There are five tests for a qualifying child:

- Relationship
- Age
- Residency
- Support
- Tie-breaker (for a qualifying child of more than one person)

Test #1. Relationship Test

The qualifying child must be related to the taxpayer by blood, marriage, or legal adoption. Qualifying children include:

- A child, stepchild, or adopted child
- A sibling or stepsibling
- A descendant of one of the above (such as a grandchild, niece, or nephew)
- An eligible foster child

Test #2. Age Test

In order to be a qualifying child, the dependent must be:

- Under the age of 19 at the end of the tax year, or
- Under the age of 24 at the end of the tax year and a full-time student, or
- Permanently and totally disabled at any time during the year, regardless of age.

A child is considered a full-time student if he attends a qualified educational institution full-time for at least five months during the year.

Note: For the purposes of the age test, in order to qualify as a student, the taxpayer's child must be enrolled in the number of hours or courses the school considers full-time during some part of at least five months of the year.

A child who is claimed as a dependent must be younger than the taxpayer who is claiming him, except in the case of dependents who are disabled. For taxpayers filing jointly, the child must be younger than one spouse listed on the return but does not have to be younger than both spouses.

Example: Owen and Sydney are 22 years old, married, and file jointly. Sydney's 23-year-old step-brother, Parker, is a full-time student and lives with Owen and Sydney, who provide all of his support. Parker is not disabled. Owen and Sydney are both younger than Parker. Therefore, Parker is not their qualifying child, even though he is a full-time student.

Example: Lucius, age 34, and Paige, age 20, are married and file jointly. Paige's 21-year-old brother, Jason, is a full-time student, is single, and lives with Lucius and Paige. They provide all of Jason's support. In this case, Lucius and Paige can claim Jason as a qualifying child on their joint tax return because he is a full-time student and is younger than Lucius.

Example: Andrew is 45 years old and totally disabled. Karen, his 37-year-old sister, provides all of Andrew's support and cares for him in her home, where he lives with her full-time. Despite Andrew's age, he is considered a qualifying child and a dependent for tax purposes because he is completely disabled. Karen can claim Andrew as her qualifying child, and she can also file as head of household.

Test #3. Residency Test

A qualifying child must live with the taxpayer for more than half the tax year (over six months). Exceptions apply for children of divorced parents, kidnapped children, children who were born or died during the year,[12] and temporary absences, (such as for summer camp or a missionary trip).

A temporary absence includes illness, college, vacation, military service, and incarceration in a juvenile facility. It must be reasonable to assume that the child will return to the home after the temporary absence.

Example: Scott is unmarried and lives with his 10-year-old son, Elijah. Scott provides all of Elijah's support. In 2016, Elijah became very ill and was hospitalized for seven months. Elijah is still considered Scott's qualifying child because the hospitalization counts as a temporary absence from home. Scott can claim Elijah as his qualifying child, and he can also file as head of household.

Example: Marty's nine-year-old granddaughter, Quinn, lives with him for five months of the year, with her mother for three months, and with her aunt for four months. Quinn is not Marty's qualifying child because the residency test is not met. However, she may be Marty's qualifying relative if other tests are met.

---

[12] A taxpayer cannot claim an exemption for a stillborn child. The child must be born alive, even if he lived only for a short time.

Test #4. Support Test

A qualifying child cannot provide more than one-half of his own support. A full-time student does not take scholarships (whether taxable or nontaxable) into account when calculating the support test.

Example: Douglas and Andrea file jointly. They have a daughter named Isabella, age 26. She earned $4,000 in wages before she was laid off in March and moved back in with her parents. Douglas and Andrea provided the majority of Isabella's support for the rest of the year. Isabella got a new job in December and moved out. She is not a qualifying child for federal tax purposes. Isabella meets the support test, as well as the residency test. However, she does not meet the age test.

Example: Kevin has a 19-year-old daughter named Tiffany. Kevin provided $5,000 toward his daughter's support for the year. Tiffany also has a part-time job and provided $13,000 of her own support. Therefore, Tiffany provided over half of her own support for the year. Tiffany does not pass the support test, and consequently, she is not Kevin's qualifying child. Tiffany can file a tax return as single and claim her own exemption.

Example: Penelope, age 12, had a small role in a television series. She earned $30,000 as a child actor, but her parents put the money in a trust fund for her. She lived at home with her parents all year. Penelope meets the support test since her earnings were not used for her own support. She meets the tests for a qualifying child, so she can be claimed as a dependent by her parents.

Note: The definition of **support** includes only income actually used for living expenses. For example, if a child earns income that is saved to a bank account rather than spent on the child's living expenses, the amounts are not included in the support test.

Payments received from a child placement agency for the support of a foster child are considered support provided by the agency, rather than support provided by the child.

Example: Gina is a foster parent who provided $3,500 toward her 10-year-old foster son's support for the year. The state of Nevada provided $6,000, which was considered support provided by the state, not by the child. Gina's foster child did not provide more than half of his own support for the year. Therefore, Gina can claim her foster son as a qualifying child.

Test #5. Tie-Breaker Test

Only one person can claim a qualifying child, even if the child qualifies for more than one person. If more than one taxpayer could claim the same child under the normal dependency exemption rules, the tie-breaker rules apply, meaning the child is treated as a qualifying child in the following sequence:

- By the child's parents, if they file a joint return
- If only one of the taxpayers is the child's parent, by that parent
- By the parent with whom the child lived the longest during the year
- By the parent with the highest AGI, if the child lived with each parent for the same length of time during the tax year
- By the taxpayer with the highest AGI, if neither of the child's parents can claim the child as a qualifying child
- By a taxpayer with a higher AGI than either of the child's parents who can also claim the child as a qualifying child, but does not

Example: Sophia is single and has a three-year-old son named Preston. They live with Sophia's father, Theodore (the child's grandfather). Sophia claims Preston as her qualifying child, which means the child may not be the qualifying child of Theodore, the grandfather.

Example: Penny and her sister, Rosa, live together. Their seven-year-old niece, Brianna, lived with her aunts all year while Brianna's mother was incarcerated. Penny's AGI is $12,600. Rosa's AGI is $19,000. Brianna is a qualifying child of both Penny and Rosa because she meets the relationship, age, residency, and joint return tests for both aunts. However, Rosa has the primary right to claim Brianna as her qualifying child because her AGI is higher than Penny's.

Note: The tie breaker test only applies when two people attempt to claim the same child. In cases where the parents are in agreement, there is no tie-breaker test.

Qualifying Relative

A person who is not a qualifying child may still qualify as a dependent under the rules for qualifying relatives. Even an individual who is not a family member can be a qualifying relative. Unlike a qualifying child, a qualifying relative can be any age. To be claimed as a qualifying relative, the dependent must meet the following four tests:

- Not a qualifying child
- Member of household or relationship
- Gross income
- Support

Test #1. Not a Qualifying Child Test

If a child is already a qualifying child for any taxpayer, he cannot also be a qualifying relative of another taxpayer.

Test #2. Member of Household or Relationship Test

A dependent who is not related to the taxpayer normally must have lived with the taxpayer the entire tax year in order to meet the member of household or relationship test. However, a family member who is related to the taxpayer in any of the following ways does not have to live with the taxpayer to meet this test:

- A child, stepchild, foster child, or descendant of any of them (for example, a grandchild)
- A sibling, stepsibling, or half sibling
- A parent, grandparent, stepparent, or other direct ancestor (but not a foster parent)
- A niece or nephew, son-in-law, daughter-in-law, father-in-law, mother-in-law, brother-in-law, or sister-in-law

Example: Ernie's 12-year-old nephew, Josh, lived with him for three months in 2016. For the rest of the year, Josh lived with his mother, Melody, in another state. Melody is Ernie's 32-year-old sister. Even though Josh and Melody lived in another state, Ernie still provided all of their financial support. Josh is not Ernie's qualifying child because he did not live with Ernie for more than half the year and therefore does not meet the residency test. However, Josh does meet the requirements to be Ernie's qualifying relative.

Note: For the relationship test, "family members" do not include *cousins*, who are treated as unrelated persons. A cousin must live with the taxpayer for the entire year and also meet the gross income test in order to qualify as a dependent, and even then, a cousin cannot be a qualifying child—only a qualifying relative.

Any relationship that is established by marriage does not end as a result of death or divorce. For example, if a taxpayer supports his mother-in-law, he can continue to claim her as a dependent even if he and his ex-spouse are divorced or if he becomes widowed.

Example: Mia and Caleb have always financially supported Mia's elderly mother, Gertrude, and claimed her as their dependent on their jointly filed returns. In 2014, Mia died and Caleb becomes a widower. Caleb remarries in 2016, but he continues to support his late wife's mother. Caleb can still claim Gertrude on his tax returns, even though he has remarried.

Example: Thomas lived all year with his girlfriend, Ava, and her two children in his home. Their cohabitation does not violate local laws. Ava does not work and is not required to file a 2016 tax return. Ava and her two children are not related to Thomas as family members, but they may be qualifying relatives if they meet all the other tests.

Test #3. Gross Income Test

A qualifying relative cannot earn more than the personal exemption amount, which is $4,050 in 2016. Please note that there is no "gross income test" for a qualifying child—only for a qualifying relative.

Test #4. Support Test

In order to claim an individual as a qualifying relative, the taxpayer must provide more than half of the dependent's total support during the year. Support includes amounts from Social Security and welfare payments, even if that support is non-taxable. Support does not include amounts received from nontaxable scholarships.

Support can include the fair market value of lodging.

Example: Harry's mother, Penny, received $2,400 in social security benefits and $300 in interest during 2016. Penny paid $2,000 for food and lodging and $400 for recreation. She put the $300 in interest in a savings account. Even though Harry's mother received a total of $2,700 ($2,400 + $300), she spent only $2,400 ($2,000 + $400) for her own support. If Harry spends more than $2,400 for her support and no other support was received, he would have provided more than half of his mother's support, and would be able to claim her as a qualifying relative.

Rules for Divorced and Separated Parents

Generally, to claim a child as a dependent, the child must live with the taxpayer for more than half the year. However, special rules apply if the dependent is supported by parents who are divorced or separated, or who live apart.

In most cases, the child is the qualifying child of the custodial parent. However, a custodial parent may allow the noncustodial parent to claim the dependency exemption. The noncustodial parent must attach Form 8332, *Release/Revocation of Release of Claim to Exemption for Child by Custodial Parent*, to his tax return to claim the dependency exemption.

A child may be treated as the qualifying child of the noncustodial parent if all the following conditions apply:

- The parents are divorced or legally separated, or if they lived apart at all times during the last six months of the year.
- The child received over half of his support for the year from the parents (multiple support agreement rules do not apply in this case).
- The child is in the custody of one (or both) parents.
- The custodial parent signs a written declaration (Form 8332 or a similar statement) that he will not claim the child as a dependent for the year and the noncustodial parent attaches this declaration to his return.

This rule is an exception to the normal residency test for a qualifying child. It does not apply to determination of head of household filing status or to eligibility for the Earned Income Tax Credit. These benefits can be claimed only by the custodial parent, even if the noncustodial parent claims the dependency exemption. If a divorce decree does not specify which parent is the custodial parent or which parent receives the dependency exemption, the exemption goes to the parent who has physical custody for the majority of the year.

Example: Gary and Frieda are divorced and have one child. Frieda is the custodial parent, but she agrees to release the dependency exemption to Gary by signing Form 8332. Gary files as single and claims his son as his dependent. Frieda may still file as head of household, even though she does not claim the dependency exemption for her son because she maintained the home where he lived for most of the year.

Example: Alexis and Nathan are divorced. They have one child named Dylan. In 2016, Dylan lived with Alexis for 300 nights and with Nathan for 65 nights. Therefore, for federal tax purposes, Alexis is the custodial parent and has the right to claim Dylan as her qualifying child. However, Alexis may choose to release the exemption to Nathan by signing Form 8332.

If the child lived with each parent for an equal number of nights during the year, the custodial parent is deemed to be the parent with the higher adjusted gross income.

The custodial parent can revoke a release of exemption for a child using Part III of Form 8332. A copy of the revocation must be attached to the tax return for each year the child is claimed after the revocation.

Multiple Support Agreements

A *multiple support agreement* is when two or more people jointly provide for a person's support. This happens commonly when adult children are taking care of their parents. In order for the dependency exemption to apply under a multiple support agreement, family members together must pay more than half of the person's total support, but no one member individually may pay more than half.

In addition, the taxpayer who claims the dependent must provide more than 10% of the person's support. Only one family member can claim the dependency exemption in a single year. Different qualifying family members can claim the dependency exemption in other years.

Example: Benjamin, Matthew, and Pamela are siblings who support their disabled mother, Abigail. Abigail is 83 and lives with Benjamin. In 2016, Abigail receives 20% of her financial support from Social Security, 40% from Matthew, 30% from Benjamin, and 10% from Pamela. Under the IRS rules for multiple support agreements, either Matthew or Benjamin can take the exemption for their mother if the other signs a statement agreeing not to do so. Pamela cannot claim the dependency exemption because she does not provide more than 10% of the support for her mother.

Example: Graciela and Pilar are sisters who help financially support their 64-year-old father, Alonso. Each pays approximately 20% of his care in a residential facility for elderly people. The remaining 60% is paid for by a wealthy friend who is not related to Alonso. Because more than half of Alonso's support is provided by someone unrelated who cannot claim an exemption for him, no one can claim the dependency exemption.

Unit 3: Study Questions

(Test yourself first, then check the correct answers at the end of this quiz.)

1. Tony and Isabelle provide the sole support of all the following individuals (all are U.S. citizens, but none live with them, file a tax return, or have any taxable income):

- Jennie, Tony's grandmother
- Julie, Isabelle's stepmother
- Jonathan, father of Tony's first wife
- Timothy, Isabelle's cousin

How many exemptions may Tony and Isabelle claim on their joint return?

A. Three.
B. Four.
C. Five.
D. Six.

2. Dina has three children: Luther, Tim, and Mary. Each child contributes toward her support. Luther and Tim each provide 45%, and Mary provides 10%. Which of Dina's children would be eligible to claim a dependency exemption for her in 2016 under a multiple support agreement?

A. Luther or Tim.
B. Both Luther and Tim may claim an exemption for Dina.
C. Luther, Tim, or Mary.
D. None of the three are eligible to claim the dependency exemption because no one child provided more than half of his or her mother's support.

3. All of the following statements are correct about the rules of exemptions except:

A. One spouse is never considered the dependent of the other spouse.
B. A divorced spouse cannot claim an exemption for his former spouse.
C. A taxpayer may take any personal exemption he is entitled to, regardless of adjusted gross income.
D. Exemption amounts are updated for inflation and are generally adjusted annually.

4. Giovanni and Lucia are married and classified as nonresident aliens for U.S. tax purposes. How many exemptions would they qualify for when they file their U.S. tax return(s)?

A. None.
B. One each on returns filed separately.
C. One each on a joint return.
D. It depends how many dependents they have.

5. Alyssa is 19 years old and a full-time student who is claimed as a dependent on her parents' tax return. Over the summer, she worked in a clothing boutique and earned $7,000. Alyssa wants to file a tax return to report her wage income and receive a refund. How many exemptions may she claim on her tax return?

A. Zero.
B. One.
C. Two.
D. Three.

6. Roy is a client who tells you that his wife died in February 2016. Based on this information, Roy can claim:

A. Only the personal exemption for himself.
B. Only the personal exemption for his wife.
C. Personal exemptions for both himself and his wife.
D. A personal exemption for himself and a partial exemption for his wife, prorated based on the number of months she lived during the year.

7. John provides the sole support for his mother. To claim her as a dependent on his Form 1040, John's mother must be a resident or citizen of which of the following countries?

A. The United States.
B. Mexico.
C. Canada.
D. Any of the above.

8. Amber lives with Chad, her 16-year-old son. She provided $5,100 toward his support for the year. Chad also has a part-time job and provided $12,900 toward his own support. Can Amber claim her son as a dependent?

A. Yes, she can claim her son as a qualifying child, because he is a minor.
B. Yes, she can claim Chad as a qualifying relative.
C. No, Chad provided more than half of his own support for the year. Therefore, he is neither Amber's qualifying child nor her qualifying relative.
D. None of the above.

9. Dani and Ted divorced years ago. They have six-year-old twins who live with Dani. Her AGI is $41,000, and Ted's AGI is $48,000. Although Dani is the custodial parent, their divorce decree states that Ted can claim the children on his tax return. However, Dani refuses to sign Form 8332. Which of the following statements is correct?

A. Ted can claim one child as a dependent.
B. Ted and Dani can each claim the children as dependents on their respective tax returns.
C. Since Dani is the custodial parent and refuses to sign Form 8332, Ted cannot claim either child.
D. Neither Dani nor Ted can claim the children as dependents.

10. Joseph, 52, is a single father who lives with an adopted son named Wyatt who has Down syndrome. Wyatt is 32 years old and permanently disabled. Wyatt had $800 of interest income and $5,000 of wages from a part-time job in 2016. Joseph provided $25,000 toward Wyatt's support. Which of the following statements is correct?

A. Joseph can file as head of household, with Wyatt as his qualifying child.
B. Joseph does not qualify for head of household, but he could still claim Wyatt as his qualifying relative because Wyatt does not meet the age test for a qualifying child.
C. Joseph can file as head of household, with Wyatt as his qualifying relative.
D. Joseph must file as single, and he cannot claim Wyatt because of the amount of Wyatt's income.

11. Personal and dependency exemptions are phased out:

A. For higher income taxpayers.
B. For all taxpayers who itemize deductions.
C. For all taxpayers with AGI over $100,000.
D. For all nonresident aliens.

12. Cheryl is 46 and unmarried. Her nephew, Bradley, lived with her all year and turned 18 years old on December 28, 2016. Bradley did not provide more than half of his own support. He had $4,200 of income from wages and $1,000 of investment income. Which of the following statements is correct?

A. Bradley is Cheryl's qualifying child.
B. Bradley is not a qualifying child; however, Cheryl can claim him as a qualifying relative.
C. Bradley is not a qualifying child or qualifying relative because he had income that exceeded the personal exemption amount.
D. Cheryl can claim Bradley only if he is a full-time student since he is no longer a minor child.

13. Terrence is single and 18 years old. He works a part-time job at night and goes to school full-time. His total income for 2016 was $10,500. Terrence lives with his parents, who provided the majority of his support. His parents are claiming him as a dependent on their tax return. Which of the following statements is correct?

A. Terrence is not required to file his own return.
B. Terrence's parents cannot claim him as a dependent because he earned more than the standard deduction amount for 2016.
C. Terrence is required to file his own return, and he can also take an exemption for himself.
D. His parents can claim Terrence as their qualifying child. He is required to file a tax return, but he cannot claim a personal exemption for himself.

14. Haley is 22 and a full-time college student. During the year, she lived at home with her parents for four months and lived in the college dorms for the remainder of the year. She worked part-time and earned $6,000, but that income did not amount to half of her total support. Can Haley's parents still claim her as a dependent?

A. No, because Haley earned more than the personal exemption amount.
B. No, because Haley did not live with her parents for more than half the year, and she does not meet the age test.
C. Yes, her parents can claim her as a qualifying child.
D. Yes, her parents can claim her as a dependent, but only as a qualifying relative.

15. Ursula and her son live together. Dave is 34 years old, not disabled, and has a part-time job. Ursula provides more than half of Dave's support. Ursula can claim Dave as a qualifying relative, as long as he does not earn ______ or more in 2016.

A. $1,050
B. $3,500
C. $4,950
D. $4,050

16. Ingrid and Bill file for divorce. Ingrid has one son from a prior marriage named Greg, age 15. After the divorce is final, Ingrid develops a drug problem and disappears. In 2016, Greg lives for nine months with his former stepfather, Bill, who provides all of Greg's support. Which of the following statements is correct?

A. Bill can claim Greg as his qualifying child.
B. Bill can claim Greg as his dependent but not as a qualifying child because the divorce dissolved any legal relationship between them.
C. Bill cannot claim Greg as his dependent because they are not related persons.
D. Only Ingrid can claim Greg as her dependent.

17. Sean's wife, Jackie, died in 2016. Sean did not remarry during the year, and he has one dependent child who is 16 years old. Based on this information, how many exemptions can Sean claim on his 2016 tax return?

A. Only the personal exemption for himself.
B. Only the personal exemption for himself and the dependency exemption for his son.
C. Exemptions for himself, his son, and his deceased wife.
D. A personal exemption for himself and a partial exemption for his deceased wife.

Unit 3: Answers

1. The answer is C. They may take three dependency exemptions on their tax return, and two personal exemptions for themselves (3+2 =5 total exemptions). Tony and Isabelle may take dependency exemptions for all the dependents listed, except for Timothy, since he is Isabelle's cousin. Timothy would have to live with Tony and Isabelle all year for them to claim him as their dependent. Parents (or grandparents, in-laws, stepparents, etc.) do not have to live with a taxpayer to qualify as dependents. Tony can claim Jonathan, because Jonathan was once his father-in-law, and relationships that are established by marriage do not end with death or divorce.

2. The answer is A. Only Luther, or Tim is eligible to claim the exemption under a multiple support agreement in 2016. Answer B is incorrect because only a single taxpayer can claim the exemption in a tax year. Mary is not eligible because she does not provide more than 10% of her mother's support.

3. The answer is C. At certain higher income levels, exemptions are phased out completely. The thresholds for phase-outs are determined by a taxpayer's filing status and AGI.

4. The answer is B. As nonresident aliens, each would qualify for only one personal exemption, and they would be required to file separate tax returns. They would not be able to claim exemptions for their dependents.

5. The answer is A. Since Alyssa is claimed as a dependent on her parents' tax return, she cannot claim an exemption for herself. Therefore, her total number of exemptions is zero. Regardless, she can still file a tax return in order to claim a refund.

6. The answer is C. In 2016, Roy can claim a personal exemption for his deceased wife and a personal exemption for himself. A taxpayer whose spouse dies during the year can file jointly (MFJ) in the year of death.

7. The answer is D. A dependent must be a citizen or resident alien of the United States, Canada, or Mexico.

8. The answer is C. Chad provided more than half of his own support for the year, so he is not Amber's qualifying child or her qualifying relative. To meet the support test, the child cannot have provided more than half of his own support for the year.

9. The answer is C. Without Form 8332, *Release/Revocation of Release of Claim to Exemption for Child by Custodial Parent,* signed and attached to the return, the IRS will not recognize the dependency exemption claimed by a noncustodial parent, regardless of what the divorce decree states. If a divorce decree does not specify which parent is the custodial parent or which parent receives the dependency exemption, the exemption automatically goes to the parent who has physical custody for the majority of the year.

10. The answer is A. Even though Wyatt is over the normal age threshold for a qualifying child; he is considered a qualifying child for purposes of the dependency exemption and head of household filing status. This is because Wyatt is permanently disabled and Joseph provides his financial support and care. The normal age thresholds for "qualifying children" do not apply in the case of permanently disabled individuals.

11. The answer is A. Personal and dependency exemptions are phased out or eliminated for taxpayers with adjusted gross income above specified thresholds. For taxpayers subject to this limitation, the total exemption amount that can be claimed is reduced by 2% for each $2,500 increment by which AGI exceeds the applicable threshold. For married couples filing jointly, exemptions are fully phased out once their AGI reaches $433,800; for a single filer, exemptions are fully phased out when AGI reaches $381,900.

12. The answer is A. Bradley is Cheryl's qualifying child because he meets the age test, support test, and relationship test. Also, because Bradley is single, he is a qualifying person for Cheryl to claim head of household filing status. Bradley is not required to be a full-time student because any child under the age of 19 at the end of the tax year will be treated as a qualifying child if all the other tests are met. Bradley is only 18 years old and therefore passes the age test.

13. The answer is D. His parents can claim him as their qualifying child because Terrence is under the age of 19 and does not provide more than half of his own support. He is required to file a tax return, but he cannot claim an exemption for himself. The gross income test only applies to a qualifying relative, not to a qualifying child.

14. The answer is C. Haley meets all the qualifying child tests: the relationship test; the age test (because she is under 24 and a full-time student); the residency test (because the time spent at college is a legitimate temporary absence); and the support test (because she did not provide over half of her own support). Therefore, her parents can claim her as a dependent.

15. The answer is D. Dave cannot be a qualifying child because he does not meet the age test, but he can be claimed as a qualifying relative. The 2016 limit for gross income for qualifying relatives is $4,050. Therefore, if Dave earns less than during the year, his mother can claim him as a dependent on her tax return.

16. The answer is A. A qualifying child must be related to the taxpayer by blood, marriage, or legal adoption. A step relationship formed by a legal marriage is not dissolved by divorce or death. Since Greg did not live with his mother, but did live with his stepfather, Bill, for more than half the year, Bill is considered the custodial parent for tax purposes, and he can claim his stepson as a qualifying child.

17. The answer is C. Sean can claim three exemptions on his tax return. Because they were married at the time of Jackie's death, Sean may file a joint return in the year of her death and claim a personal exemption for his deceased wife, along with a personal exemption for himself. He can also claim a dependency exemption for his son.

Unit 4: Taxable and Nontaxable Income

For additional information read:

Publication 525, *Taxable and Nontaxable Income*

Publication 15-B, *Employer's Tax Guide to Fringe Benefits*

Publication 3, *Armed Forces' Tax Guide*

The Internal Revenue Code (IRC) describes types of income that are taxable and nontaxable. Over the course of the next few units, we will cover the most common types of both. In this unit, we focus on various forms of employee compensation, but we start with a look at broader concepts regarding the taxability of income.

Federal tax law sets forth that all income is taxable unless it is specifically excluded. "exclusion" is not the same as a deduction, and it is important to understand the distinction because many deductions are phased out as a taxpayer's gross income increases. Excluded income, on the other hand, retains its character without regard to the amount of the taxpayer's gross income.

Most types of excluded income do not have to be reported on a tax return.

Example: Monte is a popular recording artist who made more than $600,000 of taxable income last year. Because of his high income, many deductions are phased out for Monte. However, in 2016, Monte is involved in an auto accident and sustains major injuries. Monte sues the other driver and receives an insurance settlement of $95,000. The settlement is excluded from his gross income because compensation for physical injuries is not taxable to the recipient, regardless of his taxable income level.

Calculating Taxable Income

For a taxpayer to figure out how much tax he owes, he first needs to determine his **gross income**.

Definition: **Gross income** is all income a taxpayer receives in the form of money, goods, property, and services that are not exempt from tax. In addition to wages, salaries, commissions, tips, and self-employment income, gross income includes other forms of compensation, such as interest, dividends, capital gains, taxable fringe benefits, and stock options.

Next, the taxpayer calculates his **adjusted gross income (AGI)** by subtracting from gross income certain specific deductions or adjustments. These deductions include IRA contributions, certain expenses for self-employed individuals, alimony payments, and moving expenses. The amount of a taxpayer's AGI is important because it helps determine eligibility for certain deductions and credits.

Finally, the taxpayer calculates his **taxable income** by subtracting additional deductions (standard or itemized) and exemptions from AGI.

Earned Income vs. Unearned Income

Earned income such as wages, salaries, tips, professional fees, or self-employment income is received for services performed. *Unearned income* includes interest, dividends, retirement income, alimony, and disability benefits. Earned income is generally subject to Social Security and Medicare taxes (also called FICA taxes). Investment income and other unearned income are generally not subject to FICA taxes.

The amount of taxable income is used to determine the taxpayer's gross income tax liability before applicable credits. The table below is a simplified example of how to calculate income tax.

How to Calculate Taxable Income and Tax Liability

Start with gross income

Subtract adjustments to income ("above the line" deductions)

= Adjusted gross income (AGI)

Subtract greater of itemized deductions or standard deduction

Subtract personal and dependency exemptions

= Taxable income

× Tax rate

= Gross tax liability

Subtract credits

= Net tax liability or refund receivable (based on amount of pre-paid tax, if any)

Constructive Receipt of Income

The doctrine of constructive receipt requires that cash-basis taxpayers be taxed on income when it becomes available and is not subject to substantial limitations or restrictions, regardless of whether it is actually in their physical possession. Income received by an agent for a taxpayer is constructively received in the year the agent receives it.

Example: Jerrald is a landlord who owns several rental properties. On December 30, 2016, a customer delivers to Jerrald's payment lock-box a $500 check for repairing a plumbing leak. Jerrald does not collect the customer deposits in the lock-box on the 30th and leaves town later that day to celebrate New Year's Eve. Jerrald does not take physical possession of the check until January 5, 2017, the same day he deposits the check in his bank account. He is considered to have constructive receipt in 2016 and must include the $500 of gross income on his 2016 tax return because the check was available to Jerrald at that time without any substantial limitations or restrictions.

Note: Most individuals are cash-basis taxpayers who report income when it is actually or constructively received during the tax year. This concept of constructive receipt would not apply to accrual-basis taxpayers who recognize income when it is earned rather than when it is received. We will cover accrual basis taxpayers in Book 2.

Funds must be available without substantial limitations under the constructive receipt rules. If there are significant restrictions on the income, or if the income is not accessible to the taxpayer, it is not considered to have been constructively received.

Income is also not considered to have been constructively received if a taxpayer declines it, as in the case of a prize or an award.

Example: Kathryn won front-row concert tickets valued at $1,200 from a local radio station. Kathryn would be required to pay taxes based on the fair market value of the tickets. However, on the day of the concert, the radio station does not receive the tickets in time from the promoter, and Kathryn is not able to attend the concert. Since she never received the proceeds, the prize is not taxable to her because she never had constructive receipt of it.

Definition: The IRS defines **fair market value** (FMV) in this way: The price at which a property would change hands between a buyer and a seller when both have reasonable knowledge of all the necessary facts and neither is being forced to buy or sell. If parties with adverse interests place a value on property in an arm's-length transaction, that is strong evidence of FMV. If there is a stated price for services, this price is treated as the FMV unless there is evidence to the contrary.

Claim of Right Doctrine

Under the claim of right doctrine, income received without restriction (over which the taxpayer has complete control) must be reported in the year received, even if there is a possibility it may have to be repaid in a later year.

If there is a dispute and income is later repaid, the repayment is deductible in the year repaid. As a result, the taxpayer is not required to amend his reported gross income for the earlier year.

Example: In 2016, Courtney sells a painting in her art gallery for $25,000. She properly includes $25,000 in her gross income and pays taxes on the income for the 2016 tax year. On March 2, 2017, the customer discovers the painting is a forgery and returns it for a full refund of $25,000. Since Courtney pays back the $25,000 in 2017, she is entitled to deduct the amount from her gross income in 2017. She does not have to amend her 2016 tax return.

Worker Classification

For federal tax purposes, the IRS classifies workers in two broad categories: employees or independent contractors. These workers are taxed in different ways, and it is critical for businesses to identify the correct classification for each individual to whom it makes payments for services. In general, a business must withhold and remit income taxes, Social Security and Medicare taxes, and pay unemployment tax on salaries and wages paid to an employee. A business generally does not have to withhold or pay taxes on payments to independent contractors.

Self-Employed Taxpayers

Self-employment income is earned by taxpayers who work for themselves. A taxpayer who has self-employment income of $400 or more in a year must file a tax return and report the earnings to the IRS.

Taxpayers who are independent contractors usually receive Forms 1099-MISC from their business clients showing the income they were paid. The amounts from the Forms 1099-MISC, along with any other business income payments, are reported by most self-employed individuals on Schedule C, *Profit or Loss from Business*, of Form 1040.

Self-employed farmers or fishermen report their earnings on Schedule F, *Profit or Loss from Farming,* of Form 1040. Self-employment income also includes:

- Income of ministers, priests, and rabbis for the performance of services such as baptisms and marriages.
- The distributive share of trade or business income allocated by a partnership to its general partners or by a limited liability company to its members. The income is reported on IRS Schedule K-1 (Form 1065).

A taxpayer does not have to conduct regular full-time business activities in order to be considered self-employed. A taxpayer may have a side business in addition to a regular job, and this is also considered self-employment.

Example: James earned $45,000 as a full-time employee for Regal Roofing. He also advertises general handyman services online. During the year, James did several handyman side-jobs on the weekends for clients. James received payments of $9,000 from several different individuals for his handyman work. He did not receive Forms 1099-MISC for the $9,000 (because they were individuals who are not required to issue Forms 1099-MISC), but he must report these payments as self-employment income on Schedule C.

Example: Jennie runs a popular taco truck with her brother, Colin. They both split profits and losses equally, and they work together as a partnership. They correctly file Form 1065, *U.S. Return of Partnership Income*, to report the gross income from the taco stand. Jennie and Colin both receive a Schedule K-1 from the partnership every year. Jennie and Colin must each report their distributive share of income from the taco stand on their respective Forms 1040, Schedule E (Part 2). The income is considered self-employment income and is subject to self-employment tax.

FICA Tax (Payroll Taxes)

The Federal Insurance Contributions Act (FICA) tax includes two separate taxes: one is Social Security tax and the other is Medicare tax. The current rate for Social Security is 6.2% for the employer and 6.2% for the employee, or 12.4% total. The current rate for Medicare is 1.45% for the employer and 1.45% for the employee, or 2.9% total.

The combined FICA tax rate for 2016 is 15.3% and applies up to $118,500 of a taxpayer's combined earned income, including wages, tips, and net earnings from self-employment. If the taxpayer's combined earned income exceeds $118,500, a rate of 2.9%, representing only the Medicare portion, applies to any excess earnings over $118,500. There is no cap on earnings subject to the 2.9% Medicare tax.

An additional Medicare surtax of 0.9% is applied to wages and self-employment income above certain thresholds.[13]

Note: The 7.65% tax rate is the combined rate for Social Security and Medicare. The Social Security portion (also called "OASDI") is 6.2% on earnings up to the applicable taxable maximum amount ($118,500 in 2016). *Remember:* the Medicare portion is 1.45% on *all* earned income. There is no yearly maximum for Medicare tax.

Self-Employment Tax

Self-employment tax (SE tax) is imposed on self-employed individuals in a manner similar to the Social Security and Medicare taxes that apply to wage earners. Self-employed individuals are responsible for paying the entire amount of Social Security and Medicare taxes applicable to their net earnings from self-employment.

If a taxpayer has wages in addition to self-employment earnings, the Social Security tax on the wages is paid first.

Example: Haywood is a self-employed graphic designer. After deducting all his expenses, he reports $120,000 in net self-employment income on Schedule C. Haywood will pay $14,694 (12.4% X $118,500 [the maximum threshold]) for the social security part of the self-employment tax in 2016. This is the maximum Social Security tax he will pay for 2016, even if he has other sources of income. He also owes 2.9% Medicare tax on the gross amount (2.9% X $120,000 = $3,480). Haywood's total self-employment tax for 2016 is $18,174 ($3,480 Medicare tax + $14,694 Social Security tax).

There are two adjustments related to the self-employment tax that reduce overall taxes for a taxpayer with self-employment income.

- First, the taxpayer's net earnings from self-employment are reduced by 7.65%. Just as the employer's share of Social Security tax is not considered wages to the employee, this reduction removes a corresponding amount from the net earnings before the SE tax is calculated.
- Second, the taxpayer can deduct the employer-equivalent portion of his self-employment tax in determining his adjusted gross income.

[13] The Additional Medicare Tax applies to wages, railroad retirement (RRTA) compensation, and self-employment income over certain thresholds.

Self-employment tax is calculated on IRS Schedule SE.

More Than One Business: If a taxpayer owns more than one business, he must net the profit or loss from each business to determine the total earnings subject to SE tax. However, married taxpayers cannot combine their income or loss from self-employment to determine their individual earnings subject to SE tax.

Example: Tanner is a sole proprietor who owns a barbershop. He has $19,000 of net income in 2016. His wife, Erin, has a candle-making business, which has overall losses of ($12,000) in 2016. Tanner must pay self-employment tax on $19,000, regardless of how he and Erin choose to file. That is because married couples cannot offset each other's income from self-employment, even if they file jointly, for self-employment tax purposes. The income of each business is allocated to each individual.

Example: Darren is a single taxpayer who is a sole proprietor with two small businesses, a computer repair shop and a car wash business that he runs only during the summer months. The computer business has net income of $50,000 in 2016, while the car wash has a net loss of $23,000 in 2016. Darren only has to pay self-employment tax on $27,000 ($50,000 - $23,000) of income because he may net the income and losses from both his businesses.

Employee Compensation

Wages, salaries, bonuses, tips, and commissions are compensation received by employees for services performed. This compensation is taxable income to the employee and a deductible expense for the employer. Employers are required by January 31 to issue Forms W-2, which show the amounts of wages paid to employees for the previous year.

Employers are required by law to withhold Social Security and Medicare taxes from an employee's wages. If the employer fails to withhold these taxes, the employee is required to file Form 8919, *Uncollected Social Security and Medicare Tax on Wages.*

Note: If a taxpayer has more than one employer and his total compensation is over the $118,500 Social Security base limit for 2016, too much Social Security tax may have been withheld. In this case, a taxpayer can claim the excess as a credit against his income tax. If he files Form 1040, he would enter the excess amount on line 71.

Advance Wages: If an employee receives advance wages, commissions, or other earnings, he must recognize the income in the year it is constructively received, regardless of whether he has earned the income. If the employee is later required to pay back a portion of the earnings, the amount would be deducted from his taxable wages at that time.

Example: Maddox requests a modest salary advance of $1,200 on December 18, 2016, so he can take a two-week vacation. His employer gives him the check on December 20, 2016. Maddox must recognize the income on his 2016 tax return, even though he will not actually "earn" the money until 2017 when he returns from his vacation.

Supplemental Wages

Supplemental wages are compensation paid to an employee in addition to his regular pay. These amounts are listed on the employee's Form W-2 and are taxable just like regular wages, even if the pay is not actually for work performed. Vacation pay and sick pay are examples of supplemental wages that are taxable just like any other wage income, even though the employee has not technically "worked" for the income. Supplemental wages may also include:

- Bonuses, commissions, prizes
- Severance pay, back pay, and holiday pay
- Payment for nondeductible moving expenses

Garnished Wages

An employee may have his wages garnished for various reasons, such as when he owes child support, back taxes due, or other debts. Regardless of the amounts garnished from the employee's paycheck, the full amount of his gross wages must be included in his taxable wages at year-end.

Example: Holden's employer garnishes part of his salary for back child support. Since the amount would have normally been included in Holden's paycheck, he must recognize the income as if he had received it himself.

Property in Lieu of Wages

An employee who receives property for services performed must generally recognize the fair market value of the property when it is received as taxable income. However, if an employee receives stock or other property that is restricted, the property is not included in income until it is available to the employee without restriction.

Example: Barry's company gives him 500 shares of stock, valued at $5,000. He cannot sell or otherwise use the shares for five years. If Barry quits his job, he forfeits the shares. He does not have to recognize the stock as income in the year he receives it because the stock is subject to substantial restrictions. Barry will report it as taxable income when the restrictions lapse and he gains complete control over the stock.

Tip Income

Tips received by food servers, baggage handlers, hairdressers, and others for performing services are taxable income. An individual who receives $20 or more per month in tips must report the tip income to his employer. An employee who receives less than $20 per month in tips while working one job does not have to report the tip income to his employer. Tips of less than $20 per month are exempt from Social Security and Medicare taxes, but are still subject to federal income tax.

Example: Lydia works two jobs, as an administrative assistant during the week and as a bartender on the weekends. She reports her tip income from the bartending job of $3,000 to her employer. Her Forms W-2 show wage income of $21,000 (admin) and $8,250 (bartender). Lydia must report $29,250, the total amount earned at both jobs, on her Form 1040. Since she reported the tip income to her employer, her bartending tips are already included on her Form W-2 for that job.

An employee who does not report all of his tips to his employer generally must report the tips and related Social Security and Medicare taxes on his Form 1040. Form 4137, *Social Security and Medicare Tax on Unreported Tip Income,* is used to compute the additional tax.

Noncash tips (for example, concert tickets or other items) do not have to be reported to the employer, but they must be reported and included in the taxpayer's income at their fair market value.

Taxpayers who are self-employed and receive tips must include their tip income in gross receipts on Schedule C.

Taxable Fringe Benefits for Employees

Employers often offer fringe benefits to employees; common fringe benefits include health insurance, retirement plans, and parking passes.

Although most employee fringe benefits are nontaxable, some benefits must be reported on the employee's Form W-2 and included in his taxable income. Examples of taxable fringe benefits include:

- Off-site athletic facilities and health club memberships
- The value of employer-provided life insurance over $50,000

- Any cash benefit or benefits in the form of a credit card or gift card
- Season tickets to sporting events, although single tickets can be excluded in certain cases
- Transportation benefits, if the value of a benefit for any month is more than a specified nontaxable limit[14]
- Employer-provided vehicles, if they are used for personal purposes

Example: Tanning Town Inc. owns a tropical resort that its employees may use free of charge. Becker visits the resort with his family for two weeks. The fair market value of the stay is $5,000. Even though Becker paid nothing for the trip, the $5,000 FMV of the vacation must be included in his taxable wages.

Example: Great American Bank pays for country club memberships for all its top executives. Membership costs $8,000 a year per person. Bank executives use the club to entertain prospective clients and investors. Even though the club membership is used for business purposes, this type of fringe benefit is taxable compensation to the employees. Great American Bank must include the full amount of the club membership ($8,000) in an employee's wages.

Nontaxable Fringe Benefits for Employees

Most fringe benefits are not taxable and may be excluded from an employee's income. For example, the value of accident or health plan coverage provided by an employer is not included in an employee's income. The following are explanations of some common types of nontaxable employee fringe benefits.

Retirement Plans

Employer contributions on behalf of their employees' qualified retirement plans are not taxable to the employees when they are made. However, when an employee receives distributions from a retirement plan, the amounts received are taxable income.

Retirement plans may also allow employees to contribute part of their pretax compensation to the plan. This type of contribution is called an elective deferral and is excluded from taxable compensation for income tax purposes, but is subject to Social Security and Medicare taxes.[15]

Cafeteria Plans

A cafeteria plan provides employees an opportunity to receive certain benefits on a pretax basis. Participants in a cafeteria plan must be permitted to choose from at least one taxable benefit (such as cash) and one qualified (nontaxable) benefit. Qualified benefits include:

- Accident, dental, vision, and medical benefits (but not Archer medical savings accounts or long-term care insurance).
- Health care flexible spending accounts (FSA, as opposed to a health savings account that a taxpayer may establish and fund on his own. An employee who is covered by an FSA generally cannot make contributions to an HSA).
- Adoption assistance.
- Dependent care assistance.

Employee contributions are usually deducted based upon salary reduction agreements.

Salary reduction contributions are not considered actually or constructively received by the employee and therefore are not considered to be taxable wages. Thus, they are generally not subject to income tax withholding, or to FICA (Social Security and Medicare taxes) or FUTA

---

[14] The non-taxable benefit for both mass transit and parking for 2016 was $255 per month. Any expense over that amount is included in the employee's taxable income as wages.

[15] The tax provisions of retirement plans are covered in detail later.

(unemployment tax). An employer may choose to make benefits available to employees, their spouses, and dependents.

Flexible Spending Arrangement (FSA): An FSA is a form of cafeteria plan benefit that reimburses employees for expenses incurred for certain qualified benefits, such as health benefits. The benefits are subject to annual maximum limits and have traditionally been subject to an annual "use-or-lose" rule, with a short (two-and-a-half-months) grace period after year-end to use any remaining balance.

In 2016, employee salary reduction contributions to a health care FSA are capped at $2,550.

Note: Both employer and employee may contribute to an employee's health FSA, but contributions from all sources combined must not exceed the annual limit ($2,550 in 2016).

If a taxpayer over-contributes to their health care FSA, the taxpayer must pay income tax, plus a 6% excise tax, on any excess contributions and related earnings for each tax year the excess contributions remain in the account. In order to avoid the excise tax on excess contributions, the taxpayer must remove the year's excess contributions and related investment earnings before the last day to file federal income taxes for the pertinent tax year, generally April 15.

Example: Huey has a health care FSA at his current job. In 2016, he contributes the maximum of $2,550 to his account. In November, he switches jobs and mistakenly contributes to the HSA that his new employer offers him. At the end of 2016, Huey has contributed a total of $4,500 to both accounts. He has an excess contribution for 2016. If Huey does not withdraw the excess contribution by the filing deadline (April 18, 2017), he will be subject to a 6% excise tax, as well as income tax, on the excess contribution and any related investment earnings. These penalties will continue year after year, until the excess contribution is corrected.

Up to $500 of unused FSA money per account may be carried over to the following year. An employer must choose between either the grace period or the carryover option.

Adoption Assistance in a "Cafeteria Plan": An employee can exclude amounts paid or reimbursed by an employer under a qualified adoption assistance program ($13,460 for 2016).

Dependent Care Assistance: An employee can exclude up to $5,000 in 2016 ($2,500 if MFS) of benefits received under a qualified dependent care assistance program each year. Amounts paid directly to the taxpayer or to a daycare provider qualify for exclusion.

Highly Compensated Employees (HCEs)

A cafeteria plan cannot have rules that favor eligibility for highly compensated employees to participate, contribute, or benefit from a cafeteria plan. If a benefit plan favors HCEs, the value of their benefits become taxable. This is to discourage companies from offering excellent tax-free benefits to their top executives while ignoring the needs of lower-paid employees. For purposes of a cafeteria plan, an HCE is any of the following:

- An officer;
- A shareholder who owns more than 5% of the voting power or value of all classes of the employer's stock;
- An employee who is highly compensated based on the facts and circumstances; or
- A spouse or dependent of a person described above.

Employer-provided benefits also cannot favor "key employees".

In 2016, a key employee is defined as:

- An officer[16] having annual pay exceeding $170,000.
- An employee who for 2016 is either one of the following:

[16] For larger companies, the maximum number of officers that are counted towards this particular testing is 50 (or if there are fewer than 50, the greater of: three officers, or 10-percent of the total number of officers).

- A more than 5% owner of the business.
- A 1% owner of the business whose annual pay exceeds $150,000.

Example: Fengrew Inc. is a C corporation with 300 employees, 25 of whom are considered highly compensated employees. Fengrew's cafeteria plan and its benefits are available to all full-time employees; therefore, the discrimination rules do not apply, and the employees' benefits are not taxable.

A plan is considered to have favored HCEs if more than 25% of all the benefits are given to HCEs.

Other Types of Employee Fringe Benefits

Educational Assistance: An employer can offer employees educational assistance for the cost of tuition, fees, books, supplies, and equipment. The payments may be for either undergraduate or graduate-level courses, and do not have to be work-related.

In 2016, $5,250 in educational assistance may be excluded per year per employee. If an employer pays more than $5,250, the excess is generally taxed as wages to the employee.[17]

The cost of courses involving sports, games, or hobbies is not covered, unless they are related to the business or are required as part of a degree program. The cost of lodging, meals, and transportation is also not included.

Tuition Reduction: An educational organization can exclude the value of a qualified undergraduate tuition reduction to an employee, his spouse, or a dependent child. A tuition reduction is "qualified" only if the taxpayer receives it from, and uses it at, an eligible educational institution. Graduate education only qualifies if it is for the education of a graduate student who performs teaching or research activities for the educational organization.

Example: Deborah is a graduate teaching assistant at Northern Arizona University. As part of her employment agreement with the college, Deborah is offered a 50% tuition waiver, reducing the cost of her own graduate tuition at the school. The normal graduate tuition cost is $14,000 per year. Because of the tuition waiver, Deborah only pays $7,000. The tuition reduction is not taxable to Deborah.

Meals and Lodging: An employer may exclude the value of meals and lodging provided to employees if they are provided:

- On the employer's business premises, and
- For the employer's convenience.

For lodging, there is an additional rule: it must be required as a condition of employment. Lodging can be provided for the taxpayer, his spouse, and the taxpayer's dependents and still not be taxable.

Example: Dominick is a project supervisor for Franklin Construction. He is provided free hotel lodging at remote job sites, where he is required to stay on-site for months while timber is cleared and the grounds are prepared for construction projects. The value of the lodging and meals is excluded from his income because it is primarily for his employer's convenience.

The exclusion from taxation does not apply if the employee can choose to receive additional pay instead of lodging. Meals may be provided to employees for the convenience of the employer on the employer's business premises for a number of reasons, such as when:

- Police officers and firefighters need to be on call for emergencies during the meal period
- The nature of the business requires short meal periods
- Eating facilities are not available in areas near the workplace

[17] There is an exception for job-related education. If the education is directly job related, amounts in excess of the $5,250 limit may qualify for exclusion as a working condition fringe benefit.

- Meals are furnished immediately after working hours because the employee's duties prevented him from obtaining a meal during working hours

Example: Paramedic Transport Inc., regularly provides meals to employees during working hours so that paramedics are available for emergency calls during the meal. The employees are not allowed to take regular lunches because of the nature of their employment. The value of the free meals is therefore excludable from the employees' wages, and the employer is allowed to deduct the cost of the meals as a business expense.

Meals furnished to restaurant employees before, during, or after work hours are also considered furnished for the employer's convenience and are not taxable to the employee.

Transportation: Employers may provide transportation benefits to their employees up to certain amounts without having to include the benefits in the employees' taxable income. Qualified transportation benefits include transit passes, paid parking, and a ride in a commuter highway vehicle between the employee's home and workplace. In 2016, employees may exclude from taxable income:

- $255 per month in combined commuter highway vehicle transportation and transit passes, and
- $255 per month in parking benefits.

An employer can also reimburse an employee up to $20 per month for reasonable expenses incurred when using a bicycle to commute to work.

Example: Joe is employed by a lumber company. He drives an employer-provided pickup truck, hauling equipment on job sites and delivering lumber to customers. He also gets to take the truck home in the evenings. In 2016, Joe drives the truck 20,000 miles, of which 4,000, or 20%, are personal miles (4,000/20,000 = 20%). The truck has an annual lease value of $4,100. Personal use is therefore valued at $820 and is included in Joe's wages.

Example: Clementine was offered a lucrative new job in New York City as a computer programmer. As part of her employment contract, she negotiates a parking space for her car. Her new employer agrees to pay the cost of the space at the garage across the street from her work. Monthly parking is quite expensive in New York City, and the monthly parking fee at the garage is $550. Since this amount exceeds the allowable limit for parking fringe benefits, a portion of the parking costs will be taxable to Clementine as wages. In 2016, the allowable transportation benefit for parking is $255. Therefore, an additional $295 ($550-$255) would be taxable to Clementine each month. This amount would be deductible by the employer as regular wages and subject to employment taxes for both the employer and the employee.

Note: The use of a company car for commuting purposes or other personal use is a taxable benefit. Therefore, the value of the vehicle's use for either of these purposes is considered taxable wages to the employee.

Cell Phones: The value of the business use of an employer-provided cell phone may be excluded from an employee's income to the extent that, if the employee paid for its use, the payment would be deductible. There must be substantial "noncompensatory" reasons for the use of a phone that relate to the employer's business.

Legitimate reasons include the employer's need to contact the employee in the event of work-related emergencies and the employee's need to be available to speak with clients when away from the office. If a cell phone is provided simply to promote goodwill, to boost an employee's morale, or to attract a prospective employee, the value of the cell phone must be added to the employee's wages.

No-Additional-Cost Services: Nontaxable fringe benefits also include services provided to employees that do not impose any substantial additional cost to the employer because the employer already offers those services in the ordinary course of doing business. Employees do not need to include these no-additional-cost services in their income.

Typically, no-additional-cost services are excess capacity services, such as unused airline seat tickets for airline employees or open hotel rooms for hotel employees.

Example: Bella is a flight attendant with Jet Way Airlines. She is allowed to fly for free on stand-by flights when there is an extra seat. This fringe benefit is allowed at no additional cost to the employer and is therefore nontaxable to the employee.

If an employee is provided with the free or low-cost use of a health club on the employer's premises, the value is not included in the employee's compensation. The gym must be used primarily by employees, their spouses, and their dependent children. However, if the employer pays for a fitness program or use of a facility at an off-site location, the value of the program is included in the employee's compensation.

Group-term Life Insurance Coverage: Up to $50,000 of life insurance coverage may be provided as a nontaxable benefit to an employee. The cost of insurance coverage on policies that exceed $50,000 is a taxable benefit.

Moving Expense Reimbursements: Reimbursements of moving expenses, if paid under an accountable plan for expenses that would otherwise have been deductible by the employee, generally are not taxable to the employee.

Definition: An "accountable" plan is an employee reimbursement allowance arrangement or a method for reimbursing employees for business expenses that complies with IRS regulations.

Employee Achievement Awards: Employers may generally exclude from an employee's taxable wages the value of awards given for length of service or safety achievement. The tax-free amount is limited to the following:

- $400 for awards that are not qualified plan awards. A qualified plan award is one that does not discriminate in favor of highly compensated employees.
- $1,600 for all awards, whether or not they are qualified plan awards.

The exclusion for employee awards does not apply to awards of cash, gift cards, or items such as vacations or tickets to sporting events.

Employee Discounts: Employers may exclude the value of employee discounts from wages up to the following limits:

- For services, a 20% discount of the price charged to nonemployee customers.
- For merchandise, the company's gross profit percentage multiplied by the price nonemployee customers pay.

De Minimis (Minimal) Benefits: This is a property or service an employer provides that has so little value that accounting for it would be impractical. Examples of de minimis benefits include the following:

- Occasional personal use of a company copying machine
- Holiday gifts with a low fair market value
- Beverages such as coffee or soft drinks for employees

Cash and gift cards are not excludable as de minimis benefits unless they are for occasional meal money or transportation fare.

Reimbursement of Employee Business Expenses

When a business reimburses its employees for certain business expenses, such as meals and travel, reimbursements are not taxable income if employees meet all of the following requirements of an accountable plan:

- Have incurred the expenses while performing services as employees
- Adequately account for travel, meal, entertainment, and lodging
- Provide evidence of their employee business expenses, such as receipts or other records
- Return any excess reimbursement within a reasonable period of time

Under an accountable plan, a business may advance money to employees; the cash advance must be reasonably calculated to equal the anticipated expenses, and it must be advanced within a reasonable period of time. If any expenses reimbursed under this arrangement are not substantiated, they are considered taxable income for the employee.

Example: Viviane runs a tax preparation business. She advances $250 to her employee, Mel, so that he can become a notary. Mel spends $90 on a notary course and then another $100 to take the notary exam. Mel returns the unused funds ($60), as well as copies of his receipts to Viviane. The expenses are qualified expenses under an accountable plan, so the amounts paid are not taxable income for Mel, and still deductible as business expenses by Viviane.

Qualifying expenses for travel are excludable from an employee's income if they are incurred for temporary travel on business away from the area of the employee's tax home. Travel expenses paid in connection with an indefinite work assignment cannot be excluded from income. Any work assignment in excess of one year is considered "indefinite." Travel expense reimbursements include:

- Costs of travel to and from the business destination (such as flights and mileage reimbursements)
- Transportation costs while at the business destination (such as taxi fares and shuttles)
- Lodging, meals, and incidental expenses
- Cleaning, laundry, and other miscellaneous expenses

Example: Woody works for a travel agency in Detroit. He flies to Seattle to conduct business for an entire week. His employer pays the cost of transportation to and from Seattle, as well as lodging and meals while there. The reimbursements for substantiated travel expenses are excluded from Woody's income.

Taxation of Clergy Members

There are special rules regarding the taxation of clergy members, defined as individuals who are ordained, commissioned, or licensed by a religious body or church denomination. A clergy member's salary is reported on Form W-2 and is taxable. Offerings and fees received for performing marriages, baptisms, and funerals must also be reported as self-employment income on Schedule C.

Housing Allowance: A clergy member who receives a housing allowance may exclude the allowance from gross income to the extent it is used to pay the expenses of providing a home. The exclusion for housing is limited to the lesser of:

- Fair market rental value (including utilities), or
- The actual cost to provide the home.

The housing allowance cannot exceed reasonable pay and must be used for housing in the year it is received. Salary, other fees, and housing allowances must be included in income for purposes of determining self-employment tax. Even if a minister is considered an employee, churches cannot withhold Social Security and Medicare taxes from his wages. They are treated as self-employed for purposes of these taxes.

Example: William is an ordained minister who receives $32,000 of salary in 2016. He receives an additional $4,000 for performing marriages and baptisms. His housing allowance is $500 per month, for a total of $6,000 per year, and is excluded from his gross income. William must report the $32,000 as salary and the $4,000 as self-employment income. The $6,000 housing allowance is subject to self-employment tax, but not to income tax.

Example: Abby is a full-time ordained minister. Her church allows her to use a cottage that has a rental value of $5,000. She is paid a salary of $12,000, and her church does not withhold Social Security or Medicare taxes. Her income for self-employment tax purposes is $17,000.

A clergy member may apply for an exemption from self-employment tax if he is conscientiously opposed to public insurance because of his religious principles. If the exemption is granted, the clergy member will not pay Social Security or Medicare taxes on his earnings, and he will not receive credit toward those benefits in retirement.

If a clergy member is a member of a religious order that has taken a vow of poverty, he is exempt from paying SE tax on his earnings for qualified services. The earnings are tax-free because they are considered the income of the religious order, rather than of the individual clergy member.

Combat Pay and Veterans' Benefits

Wages earned by military personnel are generally taxable. However, there are a number of special rules for military personnel regarding taxable income.

Combat zone wages (combat pay) are not taxable income. Hazardous duty pay is also excludable for certain military personnel. Enlisted personnel who serve in a combat zone for any part of a month may exclude their pay from tax. For officers, pay is excluded up to a certain amount, depending on the branch of service.

Example: Lee is a Navy pilot who served in a combat zone from January 1, 2016, to November 3, 2016. He is only required to report his income for December 2016, because all of the other income is excluded from taxation as combat zone pay. Even though Lee only served three days in November in a combat zone, his income for the entire month of November is excluded.

Similarly, veterans' benefits paid by the Department of Veterans Affairs to a veteran or his family are not taxable if they are for education (the G.I. Bill), training, disability compensation, work therapy, dependent care assistance, or other benefits or pension payments given to the veteran because of disability.

Disability Payments

Disability retirement benefits are taxable as wages if a taxpayer retired on disability before reaching the minimum retirement age. Once the taxpayer reaches retirement age, the payments are no longer taxable as wages. They are then taxable as pension income.

As a general rule, long term disability payments from an insurance policy are excluded from income if the *taxpayer* pays the premiums for the policy. If an *employer* pays the premiums, the employee must report the payments as taxable income. If both an employee and his employer have paid premiums for a disability policy, only the employer's portion of the disability payments would be reported as taxable income.

Disability Insurance Premiums	Taxability of Benefits
Employer pays 100%	100% taxable
Employer pays a portion and employee pays balance with post-tax dollars	Yes, the taxable percentage is based on the premiums paid by the employer
Employer pays portion and employee pays balance with pre-tax dollars	100% taxable
Employee pays 100% with post-tax dollars	Not taxable
Employee pays 100% with pre-tax dollars	100% taxable

Example: Hortense becomes disabled in 2016 and begins to receive a long-term disability benefit of $4,200 a month. The original insurance policy was paid for by both her employer and herself. Before Hortense became disabled, her employer paid 80% of the disability insurance premiums. Hortense paid the remaining premium amount (20%) with post-tax dollars. In this case, because the employer paid 80% of the policy premiums, then 80% of the benefits received would be taxable to Hortense. This means that $3,360 ($4,200 x 80%) would be taxable. The remaining benefits $840 (20% X $4,200) would not be taxable since Hortense paid that portion of the insurance premium with her own post-tax dollars.

Note: Do not confuse sick pay with disability pay. Sick leave is always taxable as wages, just like vacation pay and holiday pay.

Worker's compensation paid to a taxpayer under a worker's compensation act or other statute is always exempt from tax. Veteran's disability benefits (also called *VA Disability Compensation*) are exempt from taxation if the veteran was terminated through separation or discharged under honorable conditions.

Life Insurance Payments and Payouts

Life insurance payouts generally are not taxable to a beneficiary if the payment was the result of the death of the insured. This is true even if the proceeds were paid under an accident or health insurance policy. However, interest income received as a result of life insurance proceeds is usually taxable. Further, if a taxpayer surrenders a life insurance policy for cash, he must generally include in income any proceeds that are more than the cost of the policy.[18]

Sometimes, a taxpayer will choose to receive life insurance proceeds in installments rather than as a lump sum. In this case, part of the installment generally includes interest income. If a taxpayer receives life insurance proceeds in installments (also called a life insurance annuity), he can exclude part of each installment from his income. To determine the excluded part, the amount held by the insurance company (generally the total lump sum payable at the death of the insured person) is divided by the number of installments to be paid. The taxpayer would include any amount over this excluded portion as taxable interest income.

Example: Libby's brother died in 2016, and she is the sole beneficiary of his life insurance. The face amount of the policy is $75,000. Rather than take a lump sum payment, Libby chooses to receive 120 monthly installments of $1,000 each. The excluded part of each installment is $625 ($75,000 ÷ 120), or $7,500 for an entire year. The rest of each payment, $375 a month (or $4,500 for an entire year), is taxable interest income to Libby.

[18] There are limited exceptions when the policy holder is deemed to be terminally or chronically ill.

Unit 4: Study Questions

(Test yourself first, then check the correct answers at the end of this quiz.)

1. Debby broke her leg in a car accident in 2016 and was unable to work for three months. She received an accident settlement of $13,000 from her insurance company. During this time, she also received $7,500 of sick pay from her employer. In addition, she received $5,000 from the accident policy she had purchased herself. How much of this income is taxable to Debby?

A. $5,000
B. $7,500
C. $12,500
D. $18,000

2. Income was constructively received in 2016 in each of the following situations *except*:

A. Wages were deposited in the taxpayer's bank account on December 26, 2016, but were not withdrawn by the taxpayer until January 8, 2017.
B. A taxpayer was informed his check for services rendered was available on December 15, 2016. The taxpayer did not pick up the check until January 30, 2017.
C. A taxpayer received a check by mail on December 31, 2016, but did not deposit the check until January 5, 2017.
D. A taxpayer's home was sold on December 28, 2016. The payment was not received by the taxpayer until January 2, 2017, when the escrow company released the funds.

3. Lavina received the following income and fringe benefits in 2016:

Wages	$30,000
End-of-the-year bonus	2,000
Parking pass per month	90
Employer contributions to her 401(k) plan	900
FMV of free use of a gym on the employer's premises	500

How much income must Lavina report on her 2016 tax return?

A. $30,000
B. $32,000
C. $32,500
D. $34,480

4. Which of the following tip income is exempt from federal income tax?

A. Tips of less than $20 per month.
B. Noncash tips.
C. Tips not reported to the employer.
D. All tips are taxable.

5. Bartholomew is a naval officer who was injured while serving in a combat zone. He was later awarded Veterans Affairs (VA) disability benefits. How are these payments reported on Bartholomew's tax return?

A. 100% of the disability benefits may be excluded from income.
B. Up to 50% of the disability benefits may be excluded from income.
C. 100% of the disability benefits may be excluded from income for enlisted personnel, but not for officers.
D. The disability benefits are taxable.

6. Which of the following fringe benefits is taxable (or partially taxable) to the employee?

A. Health insurance covered 100% by the employer.
B. An employer-provided company car that is used for commuting.
C. Group-term life insurance coverage of $50,000.
D. Employer contributions to an employee's 401(k) plan.

7. What is adjusted gross income?

A. The sum of all sources of taxable income that the taxpayer receives during the year.
B. The amount of earned income a taxpayer receives during the year.
C. Another term for taxable income.
D. Gross income minus certain allowable deductions or adjustments, calculated before exemptions and the standard deduction or itemized deductions are taken.

8. Self-employment income does not include:

A. Income of ministers, priests, and rabbis for the performance of services such as baptisms and marriages.
B. The share of partnership ordinary income allocated to general partners on Schedule K-1.
C. Wages earned by a temporary employee.
D. Payments to independent contractors.

9. Foster owns a restaurant. He furnishes his daytime waitress, Alida, two meals during each workday. Foster encourages (but does not require) Alida to have her breakfast on the business premises before starting work so she can help him answer phones. She is required to have her lunch on the premises. How should Foster treat this fringe benefit to Alida?

A. None of Alida's meals at the restaurant are taxable.
B. All of Alida's meals at the restaurant are taxable.
C. Alida's lunch is not taxable, but her breakfast is.
D. Alida's meals are taxed at a flat rate of 15%.

10. Orrin is an ordained minister in the Evangelical Church of Chicago. He owns his home, and his monthly house payment is $900. His monthly utilities total $150. The fair rental value in his neighborhood is $1,000. Orrin receives a housing allowance from his church in the amount of $950 per month. What amount of his housing allowance would he include in his gross income?

A. $0
B. $100 per month
C. $150 per month
D. $950 per month

11. Which of the following types of fringe benefits are deductible by an employer but not taxable to the employee?

A. De minimis fringe benefit.
B. Use of an employer's apartment, vacation home, or boat.
C. Membership in a country club or athletic facility.
D. A gift card.

12. Salvador is an enlisted soldier in the U.S. Army who served in a combat zone from January 30, 2016, to September 2, 2016. He returned to the United States and received his regular duty pay for the remainder of the year. How many months of his income are taxable in 2016?

A. Zero. All the income is tax-free.
B. Three months are subject to tax.
C. Four months are subject to tax.
D. Twelve months are subject to tax.

13. Which of the following fringe benefits provided by the employer will result in taxable income to the employee?

A. A cell phone used by a salesperson to talk to clients while on the road.
B. Reimbursements paid by the employers for qualified business travel expenses.
C. Use of a company van for daily commuting.
D. Occasional personal use of an office copy machine.

14. Marco is employed as an accountant by a large firm. When he travels for his audit work, he submits his travel receipts for reimbursement by his firm, which has an accountable plan for its employees. Which of the following statements is correct about accountable plans?

A. The reimbursed amounts are not taxable to Marco.
B. Marco may still deduct his travel expenses on his tax return.
C. His employer cannot deduct the travel expenses, even though Marco was reimbursed in full.
D. Reimbursed expenses are taxable to the employee, and the employer can also deduct the expenses as they would any other current expense.

15. Faye was the beneficiary on her mother's life insurance policy. Her mother died on December 12, 2016. Faye received the following payments on January 31, 2017:

- $160,000 death benefit from her mother's life insurance policy
- $175 of interest income on the life insurance proceeds

What is the proper treatment of these payments?

A. The insurance benefit and interest income are both taxable in 2016, since that is the year that the policy holder died.
B. The insurance benefit and interest income are both taxable to Faye in 2017.
C. Only the $175 of interest income is taxable in 2017. The life insurance proceeds are not taxable.
D. None of these payments are taxable to Faye. Instead, they are taxable to her mother's estate.

16. Of the following, only ____________ is not taxable income:

A. A holiday bonus.
B. Overtime pay.
C. Vacation pay.
D. A travel reimbursement.

17. Brendan is a flight attendant who earned wages of $30,000 in 2016. The airline provided free transportation on standby from his home in Little Rock to the airline's hub in Charlotte. The fair market value of the commuting flights was $5,000. Brendan also received advances under an accountable plan of $10,000 for overnight travel, but only spent $6,000. He returned the excess ($4,000) to his employer. Brendan was injured on the job and received worker's compensation of $4,000. What amount must he include in gross income?

A. $30,000
B. $34,000
C. $35,000
D. $37,000

18. Orval and Rae are married and both are self-employed. Orval owns a business that has a $9,750 net profit in 2016. His wife, Rae, has an overall business loss of ($11,100) for 2016. They both file Schedules C to report their self-employment income. Which of the following statements is correct?

A. On their joint return, they will not have to pay self-employment tax, because the losses from Rae's business will offset Orval's income.
B. They can file MFS and offset each other's self-employment tax.
C. Orval must pay self-employment tax on $9,750, regardless of his wife's income or losses.
D. If they choose to file separate returns, they may split the profits and losses equally between their two businesses.

19. Elaine is a cash-basis taxpayer and sells cosmetics on commission. On December 25, 2016, Elaine receives $10,000 of income from commissions, plus an advance of $1,000 for future commissions in 2017. She also receives $200 of expense reimbursements from her employer after turning in her receipts as part of an accountable plan. How much income should Elaine report on her 2016 tax return?

A. $0
B. $11,000
C. $11,200
D. $10,200

Unit 4: Answers

1. The answer is B. Only Debby's sick pay is taxable as wages. Sick pay from an employer is taxable as wages and is therefore included in Debby's gross income. Settlements for personal injuries from an accident are not taxable. If a taxpayer pays the full cost of an accident insurance plan, the benefits for personal injury or illness are not included in income. If the employer pays the cost of an accident insurance plan, the amounts are taxable to the employee.

2. The answer is D. A taxpayer does not need physical possession of income in order to have constructive receipt. However, income is not considered constructively received if the taxpayer cannot access the funds because of restrictions. Since the taxpayer's control of the receipt of the funds in the escrow account was substantially limited until the transaction had closed, the taxpayer did not constructively receive the income until the following year.

3. The answer is B. Only the wages and the bonus are taxable ($30,000 + $2,000). The parking pass is a nontaxable transportation benefit, and the employer contributions are not taxable until Lavina withdraws the money from her retirement account. Lavina does not have to report the use of the gym, because it is on the employer's premises and therefore not taxable.

4. The answer is D. All tip income is subject to federal income tax, whether cash or noncash. An individual who receives less than $20 per month of tips while working one job does not have to report the tip income to his employer, but the income is still subject to federal income tax and must be reported on the taxpayer's Form 1040.

5. The answer is A. All of the disability benefits are excluded from taxable income. VA disability compensation is exempt from taxation if the veteran was terminated through separation or discharged under honorable conditions. The VA does not issue Form W-2, Form 1099-R, or any other tax-related document for veterans' disability benefits.

6. The answer is B. An employer-provided company car would be partially taxable if it was used for personal driving. The value of the personal use of the automobile must be added to the employee's wages. These valuation rules are covered in IRS Publication 15-B, *Employer's Tax Guide to Fringe Benefits*.

7. The answer is D. Adjusted gross income (AGI) is gross income (the sum of all income subject to taxation that the taxpayer receives during the year) minus certain allowable deductions or adjustments. AGI is calculated before exemptions, and the standard deduction or itemized deductions are taken.

8. The answer is C. Wage income is never considered self-employment income. The other examples listed are all types of self-employment income and subject to self-employment tax on Form 1040.

9. The answer is A. Meals furnished to Alida are not taxable because they are for the convenience of the employer. Meals that employers furnish to a restaurant employee during, immediately before or after the employee's working hours are considered furnished for the employer's convenience. Since Alida is a waitress who works during the normal breakfast and lunch periods, Foster can exclude from her wages the value of those meals. If Foster allowed Alida to have meals without charge on her days off, the value of those meals would be included in her wages.

10. The answer is A. Clergy members may exclude from gross income for income tax purposes, but not for self-employment tax purposes, the rental value of a home, or a rental allowance to the extent the allowance is used to provide a home, even if deductions are taken for home expenses paid with the allowance.

11. The answer is A. A de minimis fringe benefit is deductible by the employer but is not taxable to the employee. The IRS defines a de minimis benefit in this way: a benefit that, considering its value and the frequency with which it is provided, is so small as to make accounting for it unreasonable or impractical. For example, a de minimis fringe benefit might include occasional snacks, coffee, or doughnuts provided in a company's breakroom. The items in the other choices would be taxable to the employee.

12. The answer is B. If a taxpayer serves in a combat zone as an enlisted person for *any part* of a month, all of his pay received for military service that month is excluded from gross income. Since Salvador served for a few days in September, as well as January, all the income for those months is excluded as combat pay. Only October through December would be taxable.

13. The answer is C. Use of a company vehicle for commuting is not a qualified fringe benefit. Commuting expenses are not deductible. Use of a company van after normal working hours is personal use and not business use, so it would result in taxable income to the employee. The cell phone, reimbursements for business travel, and the occasional personal use of an office copy machine are noncash fringe benefits that are not taxable.

14. The answer is A. Under an accountable plan, employee reimbursements are not included in the employee's income. The employer can deduct the expenses as current expenses on its tax return. The employee is not required to be taxed on any amounts received in accordance with the terms of a qualified accountable plan; however, the employee cannot deduct any employment-related expenses that have been reimbursed to him by his employer.

15. The answer is C. Life insurance proceeds are not taxable to the recipient. Interest earned on life insurance proceeds is taxable. Faye must report the interest income in the year she receives it.

16. The answer is D. Travel reimbursements, if paid through an accountable plan, are not included in an employee's wages.

17. The answer is A. Brendan only has to include his wages on his tax return. The free flights offered on standby to airline personnel are considered no-additional-cost services and are not taxable to the employee. Reimbursements under an accountable plan and amounts paid for workers' compensation are nontaxable. Since Brendan returned the unspent amounts to his employer, the travel reimbursements qualify under an accountable plan, and the amounts spent are not taxable to him.

18. The answer is C. Orval must pay self-employment tax on his earnings, regardless of how he and Rae choose to file. Taxpayers cannot combine both spouses' income or loss to determine their earnings subject to SE tax. However, if a taxpayer has more than one business, he must combine the net profit or loss from each to determine the total earnings subject to SE tax.

19. The answer is B. Elaine's commissions must be included in gross income, as well as advance payments in anticipation of future services ($10,000 + $1,000 =$11,000). The expense reimbursements from an accountable plan ($200) would not be included in her taxable income.

Unit 5: Interest and Dividend Income

For additional information read:

Publication 550, *Investment Income and Expenses*

FS Publication 51, *Using Savings Bonds for Education*

Taxpayers who lend or deposit cash or invest in securities such as stocks, bonds, and mutual funds may earn income from interest, dividends, and capital appreciation. This unit covers interest and dividend income. Other types of income from investments, such as capital gains resulting from sales, are covered later.

Interest Income

Interest is a form of income that may be earned from deposits, such as in bank and money market accounts, notes receivable, and investments in instruments such as bonds. Some interest income is taxable, and some is not.

Certain distributions, commonly referred to as dividends, are actually reported as taxable interest income. These include "dividends" on deposits or share accounts in cooperative banks, credit unions, domestic savings and loan associations, and mutual savings banks. A taxpayer can also have taxable interest from certificates of deposits (CDs) and other deferred interest accounts.

Interest income is generally reported to the taxpayer on Form 1099-INT by the financial institution or other payor if the amount of interest is $10 or more for the year. Even if a taxpayer does not receive Form 1099-INT from a payor, all taxable interest income must be reported. If taxable interest income exceeds $1,500, the taxpayer cannot file Form 1040EZ and must report the interest on Schedule B, *Interest and Ordinary Dividends*, and file Form 1040 or Form 1040A.

Example: Leona has five savings accounts in different banks. The total amount of interest earned from the accounts is $1,950. Leona will receive five Forms 1099-INT. She must list each payor and amount on Schedule B and file it with her tax return.

Example: Ina has two savings accounts. In 2016, she earns $6 in interest from the first savings account and $8 in interest from the second account. Because the amounts are below the reporting threshold, she does not receive a Form 1099-INT from either bank. The interest is still taxable income and must be reported on her return, assuming that she has a filing requirement for the year.

Interest on U.S. Treasury Bills, Notes, and Bonds

Interest on U.S. obligations, such as U.S. Treasury bills, notes, and bonds issued by any agency of the United States, is normally taxable for federal income tax purposes.

The **Series EE bond** is the most common type of U.S. savings bond. These bonds are issued at a discount, and the difference between the purchase price and the amount received when the bonds are later redeemed (or "cashed in") is interest income.

Series I bonds are issued at face value with a maturity period of 30 years. The face value and accrued interest are payable at maturity.

Individual taxpayers can generally report interest income from a Series EE or Series I savings bond either:

- When the bond matures or is redeemed (whichever occurs first), or
- Each year as the bond's redemption value increases.

However, a taxpayer must use the same reporting method for all the Series EE and Series I bonds he owns. When a taxpayer redeems savings bonds, he should receive a Form 1099-INT from the bank or other payer. To exclude interest earnings on Series EE and Series I bonds, a taxpayer must be at least 24 years old before the bond's issue date.

Series HH U.S. savings bonds are issued at face value and pay interest twice a year. Taxpayers must report the interest in the year it is paid.

Interest earned on other U.S. obligations, such as U.S. Treasury bills, notes, and bonds, is taxable when it is received.

Interest on Educational Savings Bonds

Taxpayers may purchase and eventually redeem certain Series EE or I bonds on a tax-free basis to pay qualified higher education expenses. The expenses must be for the taxpayer, his spouse, or dependents for whom an exemption is claimed.

The taxpayer must use both the principal and interest to pay for qualified education expenses. If the amount of savings bonds cashed during the year exceeds the amount of qualified educational expenses paid during the year, the amount of excludable interest is reduced.

Example: Molly is a full-time college student. She redeemed several education savings bonds in 2016 to pay for her college expenses. The total bond proceeds were $10,000 ($8,000 principal and $2,000 in interest). Molly's qualified educational expenses were only $8,000. She used the remaining $2,000 to make a down payment on a new car. Therefore, since Molly used only 80% of the bond proceeds for qualified expenses, she can only exclude 80% of the bond interest. The excludable portion would equal $1,600 (80% x $2,000 bond interest = $1,600). She would pay tax on the remaining $400 of bond interest.

Married taxpayers who file separately (MFS) do not qualify for the education savings bond interest exclusion. If a taxpayer cashes an education savings bond during the year, and then files MFS, all the interest would be taxable, regardless of whether or not the taxpayer had qualifying education expenses. For the purposes of this exclusion, qualified educational expenses include:

- College tuition and fees (such as lab fees and other required course expenses), except for expenses for any course or other education program involving sports, games, or hobbies that are not part of a degree program.
- Expenses paid for any course required as part of a degree or certificate program.
- The costs of room and board, as well as books, are not eligible expenses for this exclusion.

The amount of qualified expenses is reduced by the amount of any scholarships, fellowships, employer-provided educational assistance, and other forms of tuition reduction. The exclusion is calculated and reported on Form 8815, *Exclusion of Interest from Series EE and I U.S. Savings Bonds Issued After 1989*. There are certain rules that must be followed in order for the educational exclusion to qualify:

- The bonds must be purchased by the owner. They cannot be a gift.
- Qualified higher education expenses must be reduced by certain tax-free benefits received and by expenses used to claim the American Opportunity and Lifetime Learning credits.
- The total interest received may be excluded only if the combined amounts of the principal and the interest received do not exceed the taxpayer's qualified higher education expenses.

Note: The costs of required textbooks are not qualified expenses for the purposes of the savings bond interest exclusion.[19] However, the cost of required textbooks *is* a qualified educational expense for the purposes of the Lifetime Learning Credit and the American Opportunity Credit.

Gift for Opening a Bank Account: If a taxpayer receives noncash gifts or services for making deposits or for opening an account in a savings institution, the value of the gift may have to be reported as interest. For deposits of less than $5,000, gifts or services valued at more than $10 must be reported as interest. For deposits of $5,000 or more, gifts or services valued at more than $20 must be reported as interest. The value of the gift is determined by the financial institution.

A cash bonus for opening a new checking or credit card account is also taxable interest. Similarly, reward points or airline miles that a bank offers as a gift to customers who open new accounts are taxable. However, cash back and reward points earned on credit and debit card purchases are not taxable interest income.

Interest Earned on a Certificate of Deposit

Interest earned on a certificate of deposit (CD) is generally taxable when the taxpayer receives it or is entitled to receive it without paying a substantial penalty.

The interest a taxpayer pays on funds borrowed from a financial institution to meet the minimum deposit required for a CD, and the interest a taxpayer earns on the CD are two separate items. The taxpayer must include the total interest earned on the CD in income. If the taxpayer itemizes deductions, he can deduct the interest paid as investment interest, up to the amount of net investment income.

Example: Sienna wanted to invest in a $10,000 six-month CD. She deposited $5,000 of her own money in a CD with a bank and borrowed an additional $5,000 from the same bank to make up the $10,000 minimum deposit required to buy the six-month CD. The certificate of deposit earned $575 at maturity in 2016, but Sienna actually received a net amount of $265 for the year after taking into account the $310 of interest paid to the bank. This represented the $575 Sienna earned on the CD, minus $310 interest charged on the $5,000 loan. The bank gives Sienna a Form 1099-INT for 2016 showing the $575 interest she earned. The bank also gives Sienna a statement showing that she paid $310 in investment interest during the year. Sienna must include the total interest amount that she earned, $575, in her gross income for 2016. She can deduct the interest expense of $310 only if she itemizes deductions on Schedule A.

Tax-Exempt Interest

Interest earned on debt obligations of state and local governments (also commonly called *muni bonds* or *municipal bonds*) is generally exempt from federal income tax, but may be subject to income taxes by state and local governments. However, interest on federally-guaranteed state and local obligations is generally taxable. In addition, even if interest on an obligation is nontaxable, the taxpayer may need to report a capital gain or loss when the investment is sold.

The taxpayer's Form(s) 1099-INT may include both taxable and tax-exempt interest. Tax-exempt interest must be reported on Form 1040, even though it is not taxable.

Dividend Income

A dividend is a distribution of cash, stock, or other property from a corporation or a mutual fund. The payor will generally use Form 1099-DIV to report dividend income to taxpayers. If a taxpayer does not receive Form 1099-DIV from a payor, he must still report all taxable dividend income.

[19] For more information on educational savings bonds, see FS Publication 0051, *Using Savings Bonds for Education*.

Generally, if a taxpayer's total dividend income is more than $1,500, it must be reported on Schedule B, *Interest and Ordinary Dividends*. Otherwise, it can be reported directly on Form 1040 or 1040A. Dividends are not subject to employment taxes.

Ordinary Dividends: Ordinary dividends are corporate distributions in cash (as opposed to property or stock shares) that are paid to shareholders out of earnings and profits. Unless they are qualified dividends, they are taxed at ordinary income rates rather than at lower long-term capital gain rates. Ordinary dividends are reported on Box 1a of Form 1099-DIV.

Nondividend Distributions: Distributions that are not paid out of earnings and profits are nondividend distributions. They are considered a recovery or return of capital and therefore are generally not taxable. However, these distributions reduce the taxpayer's basis in the stock of the corporation. Once the basis is reduced to zero, any additional distributions are capital gains and are taxed as such. Nondividend distributions are reported on Box 3 of Form 1099-DIV.

Qualified Dividends: Qualified dividends are reported to the taxpayer on box 1b of Form 1099-DIV. These are ordinary dividends that are given preferred tax treatment as long-term capital gains if specific criteria are met.

2016 Tax Rate on Qualified Dividends	
Tax Bracket (Ordinary Income)	Tax Rate (Qualified Dividends)
10%, 15% brackets	0%
25%, 28%, 33%, 35% brackets	15%
39.6% bracket	20%

In order for the dividends to qualify for these preferred tax rates, the following are the two most common requirements that must be met:

- The dividends must be paid by a U.S. corporation or a qualified foreign corporation,[20] and
- The taxpayer generally must have held the stock for more than 60 days during the 121-day period that begins 60 days before the ex-dividend date.

When figuring the holding period for qualified dividends, the taxpayer may count the number of days he held the stock and include the day he disposed of the stock. The date the taxpayer acquires the stock is not included in the holding period. A longer holding period may apply for dividends paid on preferred stock.

Example: Israel bought 5,000 shares of Moonshine Corporation stock on July 9, 2016. Moonshine paid a cash dividend of 10 cents per share. The ex-dividend date was July 17, 2016. Israel's Form 1099-DIV from Moonshine shows $500 in dividends. However, Israel sold the 5,000 shares on August 12, 2016. Israel held his shares of Moonshine for only 34 days of the 121-day required holding period (34 days from July 17, 2016, to August 12, 2016), which began on May 18, 2016 (60 days before the ex-dividend date), and ended on September 15, 2016. Israel has no qualified dividends from Moonshine because he held the stock for less than the required 61 days. He does not qualify for the preferred tax treatment that is given to qualified dividends. Instead, his dividends will be taxed as ordinary income.

Definition: The **ex-dividend date** is the date a shareholder will no longer be entitled to receive the most recently declared dividend (typically the day following the record date).

Mutual Fund Distributions

A taxpayer who receives mutual fund distributions during the year should also receive Form 1099-DIV identifying the types of distributions received. Mutual fund distributions are

[20] A "qualified foreign corporation" for the purposes of this rule is generally a foreign corporation whose stock is traded on a U.S. stock exchange or if a tax treaty between the U.S. and the foreign country of the corporation allows for qualified dividend status.

reported based upon the character of the income source and may include ordinary dividends, qualified dividends, capital gain distributions, exempt-interest dividends, and nondividend distributions.

Capital gain distributions from a mutual fund are always treated as long-term, regardless of the actual period the mutual fund investment is held. Distributions from a mutual fund investing in tax-exempt securities are tax-exempt interest and retain their tax-exempt character for the payee. Even so, the taxpayer must report them on his tax return.

If a mutual fund or Real Estate Investment Trust (REIT) declares a dividend payable to shareholders in October, November, or December, but actually pays the dividend during January of the following year, the shareholder is considered to have received the dividend on December 31 of the prior tax year and must report the dividend in the year it was declared. Mutual fund distributions may be reported on Form 1040 or Form 1040A. This is a special rule that applies only to this type of dividend.

Stock Dividends

A stock dividend is a distribution of stock, rather than money, by a corporation to its own shareholders. A stock dividend is generally not a taxable event and does not affect the shareholder's income in the year of distribution, because he is not actually receiving any money and all shareholders increase their total number of shares pro rata.

When a stock dividend is granted, the total basis of the shareholder's stock is not affected, but the basis of individual shares is adjusted by the inclusion of the newly-issued shares.

Example: Razor Ball Corporation declares a year-end stock dividend. Scarlett is a shareholder in Razor Ball, and prior to the stock dividend she owns 100 shares. Her basis in the shares is $5,000, or $50 per share. Scarlett receives a stock dividend of 100 shares. After the dividend, Scarlett owns 200 shares. Her overall basis in the shares does not change (it is still $5,000), but her new basis in each individual share is $25 per share ($5,000/200 = $25 per share). Scarlett does not have any taxable income as a result of the stock dividend.

If a shareholder has the option to receive cash instead of stock, the stock dividend is taxable in the year it is distributed. The recipient of the stock must include the FMV of the newly-issued stock in his gross income, and that same amount is the basis of the shares received.

Example: The Arch Corporation declares a year-end stock dividend and gives its shareholders the option of receiving cash instead of stock. Therefore, the stock dividend becomes a taxable event. Prior to the dividend, Dale owns 1,000 shares in Arch Co., and his basis in the shares is $10,000, or $10 per share. Dale decides to take the stock instead of cash and receives an additional 100 shares. The FMV of the stock at the time of the distribution is $15 per share. Dale must recognize $1,500 of income ($15 FMV × 100 shares = $1,500), which also is his basis in the new shares.

Dividend Reinvestment Plans (DRIP): A dividend reinvestment plan allows a taxpayer to use dividends to purchase more shares of stock in a corporation instead of receiving dividends in cash. If the taxpayer uses his dividends to buy more stock at a price equal to its fair market value, he must still report the dividends as income.

Some plans also allow taxpayers to invest cash to buy shares of stock at a price less than fair market value. In this case, the taxpayer must report as dividend income the difference between the cash he invests and the FMV of the stock he purchases.

Example: Lois owns 100 shares of Barclift Corporation, which is currently trading at $50 a share on the open market. Through Barclift's DRIP, Lois buys 50 additional shares at a price of $40 per share. She must report $500 as dividend income ($10 per share difference between FMV and purchase price multiplied by 50 shares).

Constructive Distributions

Certain transactions between a corporation and its shareholders may be regarded as constructive distributions. They may be considered dividends or nondividend distributions and may be taxable to the shareholders. Examples of constructive distributions include:

- **Payment of personal expenses:** If a corporation pays personal expenses on behalf of an employee-shareholder, the amounts should be classified as a distribution, rather than expenses of the corporation.
- **Unreasonable compensation:** If a corporation pays an employee-shareholder an unreasonably high salary considering the services actually performed, the excessive part of the salary may be treated as a distribution.
- **Unreasonable rents:** If a corporation rents property from a shareholder and the rent is unreasonably higher than the shareholder would charge an unrelated party for the use of the property, the excessive part of the rent may be treated as a distribution. Conversely, if a corporation rents property *to* a shareholder and the rent is unreasonably low, the discounted portion of the rent could be treated as a distribution as well.
- **Cancellation of a shareholder's debt:** If a corporation cancels a shareholder's debt without repayment by the shareholder, the amount canceled may be treated as a distribution.
- **Property transfers for less than FMV:** If a corporation transfers or sells property to a shareholder for less than its FMV, the excess may be treated as a distribution.
- **Below market or interest-free loans**: If a corporation gives a loan to a shareholder on an interest-free basis or at a rate below the applicable federal rate, the uncharged interest may be treated as a distribution.

Example: Maureen's father owns 95% of Fallon Orthotics Corporation, and she and her siblings own the remaining 5%. Maureen performs secretarial duties on a part-time basis for the corporation and is paid a salary of $700,000 a year. The corporation also pays for various personal expenses Maureen incurs, such as monthly payments on the car she uses to commute to work. The IRS would likely consider Maureen's salary as unreasonably high based on the nature of her duties, meaning that a portion of the salary and the personal expenses would be reclassified as constructive distributions.

Unit 5: Study Questions

(Test yourself first, then check the correct answers at the end of this quiz.)

1. A taxpayer must generally have held stock for ________________ in order for his dividend income to be considered qualified dividends.

A. More than 30 days during the 121-day period that begins 60 days before the ex-dividend date.
B. More than 60 days during the 121-day period that begins 60 days before the ex-dividend date.
C. More than 120 days.
D. More than one year.

2. Which of the following dividends are reported as interest income on a taxpayer's return?

A. Stock dividends.
B. Dividends earned on deposits in credit unions.
C. Preferred dividends.
D. Qualified dividends.

3. Six years ago, Derrick bought a U.S. Series EE savings bond and decided to report the interest earned each year until maturity. This year, he bought another Series EE savings bond. How should Derrick report the interest on this new bond?

A. He must wait until the second bond matures to report all the interest earned at that time.
B. He must report the interest earned each year until maturity.
C. He can use either method to report interest earned, as long as he makes the election on a timely filed return.
D. This type of interest is now exempt from federal income tax.

4. Alec received a Form 1099-DIV from his brokerage firm showing that he earned $1,200 of ordinary dividends in 2016. He received no other dividends during the year. How should this income be handled on Alec's tax return?

A. He must report the dividend income on Schedule B, but it is not taxable.
B. He must report the dividend income on Schedule B. It is taxable as ordinary income.
C. He can report the dividend income on page one of his Form 1040. It is taxable as ordinary income.
D. He does not have to report the dividend income until he sells the stock from the corporations that distributed the dividends.

5. Nondividend distributions are:

A. Considered a return of capital.
B. Never taxable.
C. Always taxable as ordinary income.
D. Both A and B.

6. Anand opened a savings account at his local bank and deposited $800. He received a $15 calculator as a gift for opening the account, and he earned $20 of interest in 2016. Anand also received $100 of municipal bond interest in his mutual funds account. How much taxable interest income must Anand report on his Form 1040?

A. $15
B. $20
C. $35
D. $135

7. Robert is a 5% employee-shareholder of a family-owned corporation. Which of the following would the IRS likely classify as a constructive distribution?

A. Use of a company copy machine for making occasional personal copies.
B. Payment of Robert's monthly gym membership by the corporation.
C. Dental benefits paid by the corporation through a cafeteria plan.
D. All of the above.

8. Toni files as head of household and has modified AGI of $72,000 in 2016. She owns a Series EE savings bond, which she purchased as an investment to help pay for her daughter Holland's education. She redeems the bond in 2016 and immediately uses all the funds to pay college tuition expenses for Holland. Toni claims Holland as a dependent. The bond's interest is reported on:

A. Toni's tax return, and it is 100% taxable.
B. Holland's tax return and it is 100% taxable.
C. Toni's tax return, and it is exempt from taxes.
D. Nowhere. It is not taxable and not required to be reported, as long as Toni uses all the funds to pay for qualified higher education costs.

9. All of the following statements about stock dividends are correct except:

A. When a stock dividend is granted, the basis of the stockholder's existing shares is adjusted to reflect issuance of the new shares.
B. A stock dividend occurs when a corporation distributes stock to its own shareholders.
C. A taxpayer generally recognizes income only when he sells the stock received in a stock dividend distribution.
D. A stock dividend is never taxable if a taxpayer has the choice to receive cash instead of stock.

10. Miguel deposited $4,000 of his own funds and also borrowed $12,000 from the bank to buy a six-month certificate of deposit for $16,000. The certificate earned $375 at maturity in 2016, and Miguel received $175, which represented the $375 he earned minus $200 of interest charged on the $12,000 loan. The bank gives Miguel a Form 1099-INT showing the $375 interest he earned. The bank also gives him a statement showing that he paid $200 of interest. How should Miguel report these amounts on his tax return?

A. He should report $175 of interest income.
B. He should report $375 of interest income. The $200 of interest he paid to the bank is not deductible.
C. He should report $375 of interest income and can deduct $200 on his Schedule A, subject to the net investment income limit.
D. He does not have to report any income from this transaction.

11. Araceli received $500 of interest from bonds issued by the state of New Jersey. How should she report this on her Form 1040?

A. It must be reported on her tax return, but it is not taxable income.
B. It must be reported as interest income, and it is 100% taxable.
C. She does not have to report the bond interest.
D. She must report the interest on her state tax return, but it does not have to be reported on her federal return.

12. Kent invested in a mutual fund in 2016. The fund declared a dividend, and Kent earned $19. He did not receive a Form 1099-DIV for the amount, and he did not withdraw the money from his mutual fund. Kent sold his investment in the mutual fund on January 2, 2017. Which of the following statements is correct?

A. The dividend is not reportable in 2016 because Kent did not receive the money yet.
B. The dividend is not reportable in 2016 because Kent did not receive a 1099-DIV.
C. The dividend is taxable and must be reported in 2016.
D. The dividend is taxable and must be reported in 2017.

13. Marcelo opened a savings account at his local bank and deposited $800. The account earned $20 interest in 2016. On his credit card account, Marcelo received $100 worth of reward points for charging $10,000 of purchases, which he used to pay a portion of his credit card bill. How much interest income must Marcelo report on his Form 1040?

A. $20
B. $75
C. $120
D. $900

14. All of the following statements about dividends are correct *except*:

A. A taxpayer will pay a higher tax rate on an ordinary dividend than on a qualified dividend.
B. A taxpayer will pay a higher tax rate on a qualified dividend than on an ordinary dividend.
C. The ex-dividend date is the date a shareholder will no longer be entitled to receive the most recently declared dividend (normally right after the record date).
D. When figuring the holding period for qualified dividends, the taxpayer may count the number of days he held the stock (starting the day after the stock was acquired) and include the day he disposed of the stock.

15. Constance is using educational savings bonds to help pay her college expenses. Which of the following is a qualified expense for the educational savings bond exclusion?

A. College tuition.
B. Room and board.
C. Required textbooks.
D. Student health fees.

Unit 5: Answers

1. The answer is B. A taxpayer must generally have held stock for more than 60 days during the 121-day period that begins 60 days before the ex-dividend date. The ex-dividend date is the date a shareholder will no longer be entitled to receive the most recently declared dividend. When figuring the holding period for qualified dividends, the taxpayer may count the number of days he held the stock and include the day he disposed of the stock. The date the taxpayer acquires the stock is not included in the holding period. A longer holding period may apply for dividends paid on preferred stock.

2. The answer is B. The dividends earned on deposits in credit unions are reported and taxed as interest income.

3. The answer is B. Savings bond owners must use the same interest-reporting method for all the Series EE and Series I bonds they own.

4. The answer is C. Ordinary dividends are taxable as ordinary income in the year they are earned. Only amounts over $1,500 must be reported on Schedule B, so Alec can report the $1,200 of dividend income directly on page one of his Form 1040.

5. The answer is A. Nondividend distributions are not paid out of a corporation's earnings and profits. They are considered a recovery or return of capital and therefore are generally not taxable. However, these distributions reduce the taxpayer's basis. Once basis is reduced to zero, any additional distributions are taxed as capital gains.

6. The answer is C. A gift for opening a bank account is normally taxed as interest income. If no other interest is credited to Anand during the year, the Form 1099-INT he receives will include the fair market value of the calculator and show a total of $35 of interest for the year. The $100 of municipal bond interest is not taxable for federal tax purposes, but it must be reported on the return.

7. The answer is B. The payment of personal expenses on behalf of an employee-shareholder is treated as a constructive distribution. In this case, the payment of his monthly gym membership is likely to be reclassified as a taxable dividend to Robert or a nondividend distribution, depending upon whether the corporation has earnings and profits. Choice C is incorrect because dental and medical benefits paid by an employer are an allowable employee benefit. Answer A is incorrect because the use of a company copier is an allowable de minimis fringe benefit. See Publication 5137, *Fringe Benefit Guide,* for more information.

8. The answer is C. As the buyer and owner of the bond, Toni reports the interest on her tax return, but excludes the interest from her taxable income because she used the funds to pay for qualified higher education expenses for her dependent daughter in the same year.

9. The answer is D. If a taxpayer is given a choice between receiving cash or stock, a stock dividend is taxable in the year it is distributed.

10. The answer is C. Miguel must include the total amount of interest earned, $375, in his income. If he itemizes deductions on Schedule A, he can deduct $200 of interest expense, subject to the net investment income limit. He may not report the investment income and expenses on a net basis.

11. The answer is A. Interest earned on state and local bonds (muni bonds) are generally tax-exempt at the federal level. Although the interest is not taxable, it must still be reported on the taxpayer's federal return. Note that these bonds may be taxable at the state and local level, even if they are not taxable at the federal level.

12. The answer is C. Kent earned the dividends in 2016, and whether or not he received a 1099-DIV is irrelevant. Mutual fund dividends are taxable <u>in the year declared</u> regardless of whether the taxpayer withdraws the dividends or reinvests them, so Kent must report the earnings in 2016.

13. The answer is A. If no other interest is credited to Marcelo during the year, the Form 1099-INT he receives will show $20 of interest for the year. The IRS does not count reward points or cash back from a credit card as taxable interest income, so Marcelo does not have to report the $100 or pay tax on it.

14. The answer is B. Ordinary dividends are taxed at higher ordinary income rates than qualified dividends. If certain conditions are met, qualified dividends are given preferred tax treatment. Qualified dividends must have been paid by a U.S. corporation or a qualified foreign corporation, and the taxpayer generally must have held the stock for more than 60 days during the 121-day period that begins 60 days before the ex-dividend date.

15. The answer is A. The savings bond education tax exclusion permits qualified taxpayers to exclude from their gross income all or part of the interest paid upon the redemption of eligible Series EE and I Bonds. Eligible educational expenses include tuition and required fees. The costs of room and board, as well as books, are not eligible expenses.

Unit 6: Basis of Assets

For additional information read:
Publication 551, *Basis of Assets*
Publication 544, *Sales and Other Dispositions of Assets*

The tax treatment of an asset varies based on whether the asset is personal-use, business property, or investment property. When an asset is sold, the difference between the asset's basis and the selling price may be a taxable gain or loss. Sometimes, when an asset is disposed of or sold, no gain or loss is recognized until a later date. In order to correctly calculate gains and losses, you must first understand the concept of basis.

Study Note: Understanding basis and how it is applied to various types of property is critical to your success in passing Part 1 *and* Part 2 of the EA exam. You will be expected to calculate basis in multiple questions.

The initial basis of an asset is usually its cost. However, there are instances in which basis is determined based upon the fair market value of the asset when acquired by the taxpayer, rather than its cost, typically when property is acquired by inheritance and sometimes by gift. The cost basis of an asset may include:

- Sales taxes charged during the purchase
- Freight-in charges and shipping fees
- Installation costs and testing fees
- Delinquent real estate taxes that are paid by the buyer of a property
- Legal and accounting fees to transfer an asset

Example: Raoul purchases a new car for $15,000. The sales tax on the vehicle is $1,200. He also pays a delivery charge to have the car shipped from another dealership to his home. The freight charge is $210. Therefore, Raoul's basis in the vehicle is $16,410 ($15,000 + $1,200 + $210).

Example: Hilda is a self-employed writer. She purchases a new printer for her home office. The printer costs $540, with an additional $34 for sales tax. Therefore, Hilda's basis in the item is $574 ($540 + $34).

In order to correctly report a taxable gain or loss related to disposition of an asset, a taxpayer needs to identify:

- The asset's basis or adjusted basis:
  - As described above, the initial basis of an asset is usually its purchase cost, including certain ancillary charges.
  - Adjusted basis includes the original basis plus any increases or decreases resulting from events, transactions, or tax benefits that occur after the original purchase or acquisition by the taxpayer (such as subsequent improvements, depreciation deductions, casualty losses, rebates, and insurance reimbursements).
- The asset's holding period:
  - Short-term property is held one year or less.
  - Long-term property is held <u>more</u> than one year (at least a year, plus one day).
- The proceeds from the sale.

Example: Brian buys a house for $120,000. The following year, he paves the driveway, which costs $6,000. Brian's adjusted basis in the home is now $126,000 ($120,000 original cost + $6,000 for major improvements).

Depreciation

Depreciation is an income tax deduction that allows a business to recover the cost or basis of property used in the business over time. It is an annual allowance for the wear and tear, deterioration, or obsolescence of assets. The amount allowed as an annual depreciation deduction is intended to roughly approximate the reduction in the value of assets as they age. Property ceases to be depreciable when the business has fully recovered the property's cost, or when the taxpayer sells or retires it from service, whichever happens first.

Some types of property, such as land, cannot be depreciated. Most other types of tangible property, such as buildings, machinery, vehicles, furniture, and equipment, are depreciable.

Study Note: Depreciation is an important business concept, so it is tested most often on *Part 2: Businesses* of the EA exam. For Part 1 of the EA exam, test-takers must understand depreciation primarily in the context of rental property.

Basis of Real Property (Real Estate)

The basis of real estate usually includes a number of costs in addition to the purchase price. If a taxpayer purchases real property (such as land or a building), certain fees and other expenses are included in the cost basis. They may include real estate taxes the seller owed at the time of the purchase if the real estate taxes were paid by the buyer.

Example: Tara sells Lawrence a home for $100,000. She had fallen behind on her property tax payments, so Lawrence agrees to pay $3,500 of delinquent real estate taxes as a condition of the sale. Because a taxpayer is not allowed to deduct property taxes that are not his legal responsibility, Lawrence must add the property taxes paid to his basis. His basis in the home is $103,500 ($100,000 + $3,500).

If a property is constructed rather than purchased, the basis of the property includes the expenses of construction. This includes the cost of payments to contractors, building materials, and inspection fees.

Demolition costs and other costs related to the preparation of land prior to construction must be added to the basis of the land, rather than to any buildings constructed on it later.

Example: Wanda pays $50,000 for an empty lot where she plans to build her home. She also pays $2,800 for the removal of tree stumps and $6,700 to demolish an existing concrete foundation on the lot. These costs must be added to the basis of the land, not to the basis of the house. Therefore, Wanda's basis in the land is $59,500 ($50,000 + $2,800 + $6,700).

Settlement Costs: Generally, a taxpayer must include settlement costs for the purchase of property in his basis. The following fees are some of the closing costs that can be included in a property's basis:

- Abstract fees
- Charges for installing utilities
- Legal fees (including title search and preparation of the deed)
- Recording fees

- Surveys
- Transfer taxes
- Owner's title insurance

Also included in a property's basis are any amounts the seller legally owes that the buyer agrees to pay, such as recording or mortgage fees, charges for improvements or repairs, and sales commissions. A taxpayer cannot include fees incidental to getting a loan in the basis of the property financed with proceeds from the loan.

Basis of Securities

A taxpayer's basis in securities (such as stocks or bonds) is usually the purchase price plus any additional costs (e.g., brokers' commissions).

When a taxpayer sells securities, his investment broker should provide Form 1099-B, *Proceeds from Broker and Barter Exchange Transactions,* by January 31 following the end of the tax year, showing the proceeds of the sale. The IRS also receives a copy of Form 1099-B. If Form 1099-B does not identify a taxpayer's basis, the taxpayer must keep track of this information. If a taxpayer cannot provide evidence of his basis in an asset sold, the IRS may deem the basis to be zero.

A taxpayer may own more than one block of shares in a particular company's stock. Each block may differ from the others in its holding period (long-term or short-term), its basis, or both. When directing a broker to sell stock, a taxpayer may specify which block, or part of a block, to sell; this is called *specific identification*. The specific identification method requires good recordkeeping; however, it simplifies the determination of the holding period and the basis of stock sold, and gives the taxpayer better control over the recognition of taxable income and losses when selling part of an investment.

If the taxpayer cannot identify a specific block at the time of sale, shares sold are treated as coming from the earliest block purchased. This method is called First In, First Out (FIFO).

Example: Amber buys two blocks of 400 shares of stock (800 shares total). She buys 400 on May 1, 2013, for $11,200, and an additional 400 shares two months later for $11,600. On September 10, 2016, she sells 400 shares for $11,500 without specifying which block of shares she is selling. The sold shares are therefore treated as coming from the earliest block purchased (those purchased in May 2013). Since the basis and holding period defaults to the original block of shares, Amber realizes a long-term capital gain of $300 ($11,500 - $11,200).

Note: The IRS requires stockbrokers and mutual fund companies to report the basis for most stock purchased. The reporting is made to investors and to the IRS. You must understand how to calculate the basis of securities because this subject is tested frequently on Part 1 of the exam.

Events that occur after the purchase of stock can require adjustments (increases or decreases) to the basis per individual share.

For example, the original basis per share can be changed by events such as stock dividends and stock splits. Stock dividends and stock splits usually are not taxable events. However, a stock dividend may be taxable when shareholders have the option to receive cash or other property instead of stock.

- **Stock dividends** are additional shares a company grants to its shareholders in lieu of paying cash dividends. These additional shares increase the number of shares owned by an individual shareholder, so his original basis is spread over more shares, which decreases the basis per individual share. The total basis of all the shares remains the same.
- A **stock split** is similar to a stock dividend and occurs when a company issues additional shares of stock for every existing share an investor holds. Stock splits are a way for a company to lower the market price of its stock. For example, in a 2-for-1 stock split, a corporation issues one share of stock for every share outstanding. This decreases a shareholder's basis per individual share by half. An original basis of $200 for 100 shares becomes $200 for 200 shares in a 2-for-1 stock split. However, the total basis in the stock remains the same even though the basis per share decreases.

Example: Sean buys 100 shares of WinPro Corp. for $50 per share. His cost basis is $50 × 100 shares or $5,000. In 2016, WinPro declares a 2-for-1 stock split, and Sean receives 100 additional shares of stock. Therefore, his new basis in each individual stock is $25 = ($5,000 ÷ [100+100]). His total basis in the shares remains $5,000.

Example: Tia bought 50 shares of stock of Yates Corp. in 2008 for $10 a share. In 2009, Tia bought another 200 shares of Yates Corp. for $11 a share. In 2011, she bought an additional 100 shares for $9 a share. In 2016, she sells 130 shares. She cannot identify the exact shares she sold, so she must use the stock FIFO method to determine the basis of the shares that she sold. Tia calculates her stock basis as follows:

Shares purchased:

Year Purchased	# of shares	Cost per share	Total cost
2007	50	$10	$500
2008	200	$11	$2,200
2010	100	$9	$900
Total shares:	**350**		

The basis of the stock sold is figured as follows:

50 shares (50 × $10) of stock bought in 2008	$500
80 shares (80 × $11) of stock bought in 2009	$880
Total basis of stock sold in 2016	**$1,380**

Example: Victoria pays $1,050 for 100 shares of stock, plus a broker's commission of $50. Her basis in the 100 shares is $1,100 ($1,050 original cost + $50 broker's commission), or $11 per share ($1,100/100). Victoria later receives ten additional shares of stock as a stock dividend. Her $1,100 basis must be spread over 110 shares (100 original shares plus the ten-share stock dividend). Her basis per share decreases to $10 ($1,100/110).

Stock Options

A taxpayer may purchase options to buy or sell property, such as stocks or commodities, through an exchange or in the open market. He may realize a gain or loss from the sale or trade of an option itself, or he may exercise the option to buy or sell the underlying property and realize a gain or loss from disposition of that property.

In addition, companies may grant options to their employees, as compensation for their service and as an incentive that allows them to purchase the company's stock at a later date. If an employee receives stock options, he may have income when the options are granted, when he exercises them (to buy the company's stock), or when he sells or otherwise disposes of the options or the stock. In general, there are two types of stock options:

- **Incentive Stock Options (ISOs)**
- **Nonqualified Stock Options (NSOs)**

These options are treated very differently for tax purposes. In most cases, incentive stock options (ISOs) provide more a favorable tax treatment than nonqualified stock options (NSOs). In the next section, we will cover these two types of options and their taxable effect on individual taxpayers.

Note: For Part 1 of the EA Exam, you must understand the concept of stock options from the perspective of the individual taxpayer *receiving* the options. For Part 2 of the EA Exam, you must understand stock options from the point of view of the corporation *issuing* the stock options.

The nature, timing and amount of income depend on whether the options are considered to be *statutory* or *nonstatutory* options.

Statutory Stock Options

There are two types of statutory stock options:

- **Incentive Stock Options (ISOs)** allow employees to purchase stock at a pre-established price (exercise price) that may be below the actual market price on the date of exercise.
- Stock options granted under **Employee Stock Purchase Plans (ESPPs)**.

For either of these types of options, the taxpayer must normally be an employee of the company granting the option, or a related company, at all times during the period beginning on the date the option is granted and ending three months before the option is exercised.

The tax advantage of a statutory stock option is that income is not reported when the option is granted or when it is exercised. Income is only reported once the stock is ultimately sold.

However, the bargain element of an ISO, representing the difference between the exercise price and the market value of the stock on the exercise date, is considered a tax preference item for purposes of the alternative minimum tax. The employee's basis in the stock is the actual amount paid at exercise plus any amounts paid for the option itself or in connection with the exercise of it. Thus, the employee may have taxable income or a deductible loss when he sells the stock he bought by exercising the option. The income or loss will generally be treated as capital gain or loss if the employee:

- Does not sell the stock until two years after the date of the grant of the option, and
- The stock is held by the employee for at least one year after the option is exercised. Otherwise, all or a portion may be treated as ordinary income or loss.[21]

Example: The Bodysculpt Fitness Corporation has an employee stock purchase plan (ESPP). The option price is the lower of the stock price at the time the option is granted or at the time the option is exercised. The value of the stock when the option was granted was $25. Bodysculpt Fitness deducts $5 from Morgan's pay every week for 48 weeks (total = $240 [$5 × 48]). The value of the stock when the option is exercised is $20. Morgan receives 12 shares of Bodysculpt stock ($240 ÷ $20). Her holding period for all 12 shares begins the day after the option is exercised, even though the money used to purchase the shares was deducted from her pay on many different days. Morgan's basis in each share is $20.

Nonstatutory Stock Options

A nonstatutory or nonqualified stock option (NQSO) also allows an employee to purchase stock at a pre-established exercise price.

If the option is actively traded on an established market or its FMV is otherwise readily determinable, the employee must recognize compensation income, either at the date of grant, if there are no restrictions that affect its value to the employee, or at a later date when any restrictions no longer apply.

Note: A major difference between ISOs (Incentive Stock Options) and NQSOs (Nonqualified Stock Options) is that, with NQSOs, the difference between the strike price[22] and market price is included on the employee's Form W-2 in the year granted (the amounts are usually reported on Form W-2, Box 14 as code V). The ordinary income for ISOs isn't reported until the option is exercised.

Example: Patricia works for a company that grants her a nonstatutory stock option to buy 1,000 shares of stock at $5 per share. At the date of the grant, the stock is trading at $7.50 per share, and there are no restrictions on Patricia's ability to exercise the option or sell the shares, so she must recognize $2,500 of ordinary income (equal to the discount of $2.50 per share for each of the 1,000 shares). In year five, Patricia exercises her options and purchases 1,000 shares of stock at $5 per share. The ordinary income would be included in her Form W-2 in Box 14 (Code V). The stock is now worth $20 per share, and she sells all 1,000 shares at that price. She recognizes $12,500 as capital gain, the difference between the selling price ($20,000) and her basis in the stock of $7,500 (purchase price of $5,000 for the stock plus the gain of $2,500 recognized when her stock options were granted).

If the option's FMV is not readily determinable at the date of grant, the difference between the exercise price and the market value of the stock on the exercise date must be recognized as ordinary income in the year the option is exercised.

An employee's basis in stock is the market value of the stock at the time of grant or exercise plus any amount paid for the option itself.

[21] IRC Section 422(a)

[22] The "strike price" is the price at which the option holder can purchase the underlying security.

Example: Basil works for a company that grants employees Incentive stock options. In 2016, Basil has the opportunity to buy 1,000 shares of company stock at $2 per share. The stock is not sold on the open market,[23] and its fair market value cannot be readily determined. Basil does not recognize income at the time the stock is granted. A few years later, the company has an initial public offering, and its stock sells for $10 per share. Basil exercises his stock options and purchases 1,000 shares of stock at $2 per share. Basil must recognize $8,000 as ordinary income.

Basis Other Than Cost

The following are examples of situations in which an asset's basis is determined by something other than purchase cost.

Property in Exchange for Services: If a taxpayer receives property in payment for services, he must include the property's FMV in income, and this becomes his basis in the property. If two people agree on a cost for services beforehand, the agreed-upon cost may be used to establish the amount included as income and as the asset's basis.

Example: Cassidy is a CPA who prepares tax returns for a long-time client named Katie. Katie loses her job and cannot pay Cassidy's bill, which totals $400. Katie offers Cassidy an antique vase in lieu of paying her invoice. The fair market value of the vase is approximately $525. Cassidy agrees to accept the vase as full payment on Katie's delinquent invoice. Cassidy's basis in the vase is $400, the amount of the invoice that was agreed upon by both parties.

Basis After Casualty Loss: If a taxpayer has a casualty loss, he increases the basis in the property by the amount spent on repairs that restore the property to its pre-casualty condition. However, he must also decrease the basis of the property by any related insurance proceeds.

Example: Ira paid $5,000 for a car several years ago. It was damaged in a flood, so he spends $3,000 to repair it. He does not have flood insurance on the car. Therefore, his new basis in the car is $8,000 ($5,000 + $3,000).

Basis After Mortgage Assumption: If a taxpayer buys property and assumes an existing mortgage on it, the taxpayer's basis includes the amount paid for the property plus the amount owed on the mortgage. The basis also includes the settlement fees and closing costs paid to buy the property. However, fees and costs for obtaining a loan on the property (points) are not included in a property's basis.

Example: Sondra buys a building for $20,000 cash and also assumes an existing mortgage of $80,000 on it. Therefore, her basis is $100,000.

Basis of Property Transferred from a Spouse: The basis of property transferred by a spouse (or former spouse if the transfer is due to divorce) is the same as the spouse's adjusted basis. Generally, there is no gain or loss recognized on the transfer of property between spouses (or between former spouses if the transfer is because of divorce). This rule applies even if the transfer was in exchange for cash, the release of marital rights, the assumption of liabilities, or other considerations.

[23] Incentive stock options (ISOs) are a type of employee stock option that can be granted only to employees. ISOs are also sometimes referred to as incentive share options or Qualified Stock Options by the IRS.

Example: Before they divorced, Margot and Zachary jointly owned a home that had a basis of $50,000 and an FMV of $250,000. When they divorced last year, Margot transferred her entire interest in the home to Zachary as part of their property settlement. Zachary's basis in the home is the same as their original joint basis of $50,000.

Basis of Inherited Property

The basis of inherited property is generally the FMV of the property on the date of the decedent's death, regardless of what the deceased person paid for the property. This means that if the property is sold by the beneficiary, gain will be calculated based on the change in value from the date of death.

This usually results in a beneficial tax situation for anyone who inherits property because the taxpayer generally gets an increased or "stepped up" basis. However, there are cases in which this rule can work against taxpayers. Although the value of most property such as stocks, collectibles, and bonds increases over time, there are also instances in which a property's value drops. This creates a "stepped down" basis.

Although the basis of an estate for estate tax purposes is usually determined on the date of death, a special rule allows the personal representative of the estate to elect a different valuation date of six months after the date of death. This is known as the alternate valuation date.

To elect the alternate valuation date, the estate's value and related estate tax must be less than they would have been on the date of the taxpayer's death. If the alternate valuation date has been elected for the estate, the basis for inherited assets is normally the fair market value of the assets six months after the date of death.

However, if any assets are received from the estate less than six months after the date of death, the basis in these inherited assets is the fair market value as of the date the asset was distributed to the heir.

Example #1: Sasha's uncle bought 300 shares of stock many years ago for $500. Sasha inherited the stock when her uncle died. On the date of his death, the stock was valued at $9,000, so Sasha's basis is $9,000. She later sells the stock for $11,000. She has a gain of $2,000 ($11,000 - $9,000).

Example #2: With the same facts, if Sasha were to sell the stock for $8,000, she would have a loss of $1,000 ($9,000 - $8,000).

Example #3: Sasha's aunt also bought 100 shares of stock many years ago for $10,000. Sasha inherited the stock when her aunt died. On the date of her aunt's death, the value of the stock was $500, meaning Sasha's basis in the stock is stepped down for tax purposes to $500. She later sells the stock for $500. She cannot report a loss on the stock.

If a federal estate tax return (Form 706) is not filed for the deceased taxpayer, the basis in the beneficiary's inherited property is the FMV value at the date of death, and the alternate valuation date does not apply.

Basis of Gifted Property

The basis of property received as a gift is determined differently than property that is purchased. The taxpayer must know the donor's adjusted basis in the property when it was gifted, its fair market value on the date of the gift, and the amount of gift tax the donor paid on it, if any.

Generally, the basis of gifted property for the donee is equal to the donor's adjusted basis. This is called a "transferred basis". For example, if a taxpayer gives his son a car and the taxpayer's basis in the car is $2,000, the basis of the vehicle remains $2,000 for the son. The holding period of the gift would also transfer to the donee.

Example: Alicia's father gives her 50 shares of stock that he purchased ten years ago. Her father has an adjusted basis in the stock of $500. Alicia's basis in the stock, for purposes of determining gain on any future sale, is also $500 (this is a "transferred basis"). Alicia is also considered to have "held" the stock for ten years, the same amount of time that her father held the stock.

In situations where the fair market value of the property on the date of the gift is less than the transferred basis, the donee's basis for gain is the transferred basis. However, if the donee reports a loss on the sale of gifted property, his basis is the lower of the transferred basis or the FMV of gifted property on the date of the gift.

The sale of gifted property can also result in no gain or loss. This happens when the sale proceeds are greater than the gift's FMV but less than the transferred basis.

Example: Benny's Aunt Roberta bought 100 shares of IBM stock when it was at $92 per share. Roberta's basis for the 100 shares is $9,200. Roberta gives the stock to Benny when it is selling at $70 and has an FMV of $7,000. In this case, Benny has a dual basis in the stock. He has one basis for purposes of determining a gain, and a different basis for determining a loss. Here are three separate scenarios that help illustrate how the gain or loss would be calculated when Benny sells the gifted stock:

Scenario #1: If Benny sells the stock for more than his aunt's basis, he will use her basis to determine his amount of gain. For example, if he sells the stock for $11,000, he will report a gain of $1,800 ($11,000 - $9,200).

Scenario #2: If Benny sells the stock for less than the FMV of the stock at the time of the gift ($7,000 in the example), he will use as his basis the FMV at the time of the gift to determine the amount of his loss. For example, if the stock continues to decline and Benny eventually sells it for $4,500, he can report a loss of $2,500 ($7,000 - $4,500).

Scenario #3: If Benny sells the stock for an amount between the FMV and the donor's basis, no gain or loss will be recognized. For example, if Benny sells the stock for $8,000, there will be no gain or loss on the transaction (his basis will be deemed to be $8,000, the same as his sales price).

Unit 6: Study Questions

(Test yourself first, then check the correct answers at the end of this quiz.)

1. Stephen purchases a truck for $15,000 to use in his carpentry business. He pays $5,000 in cash and finances the remaining $10,000 with a five-year loan. He also pays taxes and delivery costs of $1,300 and $250 to install a protective bedliner. What is Stephen's basis for depreciation of the truck?

A. $6,550
B. $10,000
C. $16,550
D. $16,300

2. On June 1, 2016, Pham Software Corporation granted 500 Incentive Stock Options to one of their executives, Wesley. The stock had an option price of $25. On December 31, 2016, Wesley exercised all of his options when the market price per share was $50. What is the basis of his stock and how much should be included on his Form W-2 as income for 2016?

A. Basis $12,500; income $0
B. Basis $0; income $0
C. Basis $12,500; income $12,500
D. Basis $12,500; income $25,000

3. Which of the following is not added to the basis of a property?

A. Legal and accounting fees.
B. Points on a loan.
C. Sales tax.
D. Freight-in charges.

4. The basis of inherited property is generally:

A. The adjusted basis to the decedent.
B. The fair market value of the property on the date of the decedent's death.
C. The purchase price that the decedent paid.
D. Determined nine months after the death of the decedent.

5. On February 11, 2016, Henry bought 1,000 shares of stock for $4 per share and paid an additional $70 for his broker's commission. What is Henry's basis in the stock?

A. $1,000
B. $4,000
C. $4,070
D. None of the above

6. Mackenzie purchases an empty lot at auction for $50,000. She pays $15,000 in cash and finances the remaining $35,000 with a bank loan. The lot has a $4,000 lien against it for unpaid property taxes, which she also agrees to pay. Which of the following statements is correct?

A. Her basis in the property is $50,000, and she can deduct the property taxes on her Schedule A as property taxes paid.
B. Her basis in the property is $19,000.
C. Her basis in the property is $54,000.
D. Her basis in the property is $46,000.

7. On January 3, 2016, Brigit purchased 1,000 shares of stock at a cost of $5,100, including the broker's commission. On August 14, 2016, she sold 500 shares for $3,300. What is the adjusted basis of the stock she sold?

A. $5,100
B. $2,550
C. $3,300
D. $3,255

8. Which statement is not correct about the basis of assets?

A. The basis of an asset is always equal to its cost.
B. The basis of purchased stocks or bonds is the acquisition price plus any additional costs, such as brokers' commissions.
C. The adjusted basis of a property must be determined before figuring gain or loss on the sale or exchange of the property.
D. The cost basis of an asset includes sales tax and other expenses connected with the purchase.

9. Two years ago, Arnold paid $1,050 for 100 shares of Kirkner Corporation stock, plus a broker's commission of $50. During the year, Arnold received ten additional shares of Kirkner stock as a nontaxable stock dividend. What is the adjusted basis of Arnold's stock at the end of the year?

A. $9 per share
B. $10 per share
C. $11 per share
D. $25 per share

10. Julian owned one share of common stock that he bought for $45. The corporation distributed two new shares of common stock for each share held. Julian then had three shares of common stock. What is Julian's basis for each share?

A. $5
B. $45
C. $15
D. $135

11. If a taxpayer cannot determine his basis in a property and the property is sold, the IRS will deem the basis to be:

A. Zero.
B. Fair market value.
C. Actual cost.
D. Average cost.

12. During the year, Clementine bought 52 total shares of GRE Corporation for $624. That cost included a $40 broker commission. Later, in the year, GRE Corporation issued a 2-for-1 stock split. What is her basis per share after the split?

A. $12 per share
B. $6 per share
C. $24 per share
D. $26 per share

13. Which of the following must be added to the basis of a property, rather than deducted as a current expense on a taxpayer's return?

A. Casualty loss.
B. The cost of demolishing a building.
C. Personal property tax based on the value of a car.
D. Investment interest expense.

14. David wishes to sell a home that he inherited from his mother last year. His mother had paid $45,000 for the home ten years ago. She put a new roof on the property two years ago at a cost of $10,500. The fair market value of the home on the date of his mother's death was $120,000. An estate tax return was not required for his mother's estate, and the alternate valuation date was not elected. What is David's basis in the home?

A. $45,000
B. $55,500
C. $34,500
D. $120,000

15. Esteban installs artificial turf at a client's home and bills the client $1,500. After the installation, his client, Alice, receives a foreclosure notice and is unable to pay Esteban's bill. Alice has a golden-doodle show dog that just had puppies. The FMV of each puppy is $1,800. Esteban loves animals and decides to take one of the puppies as full payment on Alice's delinquent bill. What is Esteban's basis in his new dog?

A. $0
B. $300
C. $1,500
D. $1,800

16. On April 1, 2016, Miletech Corporation granted 1,000 Nonqualified Stock Options to Gary, (an employee). The exercise price on the shares was $23 per share. On December 31, 2016, Gary exercised all of his options when the market price per share was $43. What is the basis of his stock, and what amount should be included on Gary's Form W-2 as wage income in 2016?

A. Basis $23,000; income $0
B. Basis $43,000; income $20,000
C. Basis $0; income $0
D. None of the above

17. Flora gave Clifford a rental property. She had purchased the property ten years ago for $120,000 and claimed $18,000 in depreciation. The fair market value of the rental house on the day of transfer was $144,000. Assuming no gift tax was paid, what is Clifford's basis in the property?

A. $102,000
B. $120,000
C. $126,000
D. $144,000

18. Claire owned two shares of common stock. She bought one for $30 in 2008 and the other for $45 in 2011. In 2016, the corporation distributed two new shares of common stock for each share held. Claire had six shares after the distribution. How is the basis allocated between these six shares?

A. All six shares now have a basis of $12.50.
B. Three shares have a basis of $10 each and three have a basis of $15 each.
C. The shares are valued at $45 each.
D. None of the above.

19. Which of the following does not decrease the basis of an asset?

A. Depreciation.
B. Manufacturers' rebates.
C. Theft losses.
D. Assessments for local improvements.

20. Becky owns a piece of land she purchased several years ago for $25,000. The land is now worth $75,000. During the year, she borrows $50,000 from the bank to improve the property. She uses $46,000 of the loan to demolish an existing foundation on the property and clear it for construction, which will begin next year. What is Becky's basis in the land after the demolition is completed?

A. $0
B. $30,000
C. $71,000
D. $75,000

Unit 6: Answers

1. The answer is C. Stephen's basis in the truck includes the cost of acquiring the property (including any taxes associated with the purchase and delivery charges) and preparing it for use (in this case, installing the bedliner). Therefore, his basis is as follows: (\$15,000 + \$1,300 + \$250) = \$16,550. Any funds that are borrowed to pay for an asset are included in the basis.

2. The answer is A. For Incentive Stock Options (ISOs), the basis in the stock is the actual price per share paid upon exercise of the options. In this case, the executive's basis is 500 × \$25 = \$12,500. The bargain element attributable to the difference between the exercise price and the value at the date of exercise ([\$50 - \$25] × 500 shares = \$12,500) is not recognized by the taxpayer until the stock is sold. However, the taxpayer may need to make an adjustment for alternative minimum tax (AMT) purposes for the bargain element. When the stock is sold, income will be recognized for the difference between his basis and the net proceeds of the sale. Note that the rules are different for Incentive Stock Options (ISOs) and Nonqualified Stock Options (NSOs). They are treated very differently for tax purposes.

3. The answer is B. Points related to a loan used to acquire property may be deductible in the year they are paid or amortizable over the term of the loan. They are not added to the basis of the property.

4. The answer is B. The basis of inherited property is generally the FMV of the property on the date of the decedent's death, regardless of what the deceased person paid for the property.

5. The answer is C. Henry's basis in the stock is \$4,070 ([1,000 × \$4] = \$4,000 + \$70).

6. The answer is C. Mackenzie's basis is determined as follows: (\$50,000 + \$4,000 = \$54,000). She cannot deduct the delinquent property taxes on her Schedule A. Any obligations of the seller assumed by the buyer increase the basis of the asset and are not currently deductible. Since Mackenzie did not owe the property taxes, but she still agreed to pay them, she must add the property tax to the basis of the property.

7. The answer is B. Brigit's original basis in the total stock was \$5,100, which is \$5.10 per share, so her basis in the 500 shares she sold is 500 × \$5.10, or \$2,550.

8. The answer is A. In many situations, the initial basis of an asset is its cost, including any sales tax or brokers' commissions paid. However, there are many other times when cost cannot be used to determine basis, such as when an asset is inherited or received as a gift.

9. The answer is B. Arnold's original basis per share was \$11 ([\$1,050 + \$50 broker's commission = \$1,100] ÷ 100). After the stock dividend, his \$1,100 basis must be spread over 110 shares (100 original shares plus the additional 10 shares). Therefore, if Arnold's basis in the stock was \$1,100 for 100 shares, the ten additional shares mean Arnold's basis per share decreased to \$10 per share (\$1,100 ÷ 110).

10. The answer is C. Julian's basis in each share is \$15 (\$45 ÷ 3). If a taxpayer receives a nontaxable stock dividend, he divides the adjusted basis of the stock by the total number of shares of stock (old and new). The result is the taxpayer's basis for each share of stock.

11. The answer is A. In order to compute gain or loss on a sale, a taxpayer must determine his basis in the property sold. If he cannot determine his basis in the property, the IRS will deem the basis to be zero.

12. The answer is B. The stock is $6 per share after the stock split. Figure the answer as follows:

Initial purchase: 52 shares=$624 ($40 broker commission already included in the price)
2-for-1 stock split doubles the shares to 104 total shares, so $624 (original basis) ÷ 104 shares = **$6 per share**.

13. The answer is B. Demolition costs are not deductible. They must be added to the basis of the land on which the building was located.

14. The answer is D. David's basis in the home is $120,000, the FMV on the date of his mother's death. Heirs can generally use a stepped-up basis for inherited property, regardless of what the deceased person actually paid for the asset. The basis of inherited property is generally the FMV of the property on the date of the decedent's death. When the property is ultimately sold, the beneficiary's gain or loss will be calculated based on the change in value from the date of death.

15. The answer is C. If a taxpayer receives property as payment for services, he must include the property's FMV in income, and this becomes his basis. However, if the two parties agree on a cost beforehand, the IRS will usually accept the agreed-upon cost as the asset's basis.

16. The answer is B. The options were issued at an exercise price of $23, which means that $20,000 ($43 - $23 = $20 × 1,000), representing the difference between his exercise price and the stock's value at exercise, must be included in his W-2 for 2016. The basis of the stock would be the value on December 31, 2016 ($43,000), which includes the amount paid for the stock ($23,000) and the amount of taxable income recognized ($20,000). When the stock is later sold, the taxpayer would recognize gain or loss equal to the difference between his sales proceeds and his $43,000 basis in the stock. Note that the rules are different for Incentive Stock Options (ISOs) and Nonqualified Stock Options (NSOs). They are treated very differently for tax purposes.

17. The answer is A. The basis of gifted property for the donee is generally equal to the donor's adjusted basis, which is called a transferred basis. ($120,000 minus $18,000 depreciation = $102,000). If the fair market value of the property on the date of the gift is less than the transferred basis, the donee's basis for gain is the transferred basis. However, if the donee reports a loss on the sale of gifted property, his basis is the lower of the transferred basis or the FMV of gifted property on the date of the gift.

18. The answer is B. The shares now are valued as follows: three with a basis of $10 each ($30 ÷ 3), and three with a basis of $15 each ($45 ÷ 3). If a taxpayer receives a nontaxable stock dividend, she must divide the adjusted basis of the old stock by the number of shares of old and new stock. The result is the taxpayer's basis for each share of stock.

19. The answer is D. The basis of property must be increased for tax assessments the taxpayer is required to pay in order to finance local improvements, such as paving roads and building ditches. Basis is decreased for depreciation deductions and manufacturers' rebates received, and when the taxpayer incurs theft or other casualty losses.

20. The answer is C. Becky's basis in the land is calculated as follows: $25,000 (cost basis) + $46,000 (demolition costs) = $71,000. The loan amount is irrelevant because the act of borrowing does not increase basis; the amount spent on the improvement of the property increases its basis.

Unit 7: Capital Gains and Losses

For additional information read:
Publication 550, *Investment Income and Expenses*
Publication 523, *Selling Your Home*
Publication 544, *Sales and Other Dispositions of Assets*

Many of the items a taxpayer owns and uses for personal or investment purposes are capital assets. The net gains that result from their disposition may be subject to tax at favorable capital gains tax rates. Examples include:

- A main home or vacation home
- Furniture, a car, or a boat
- Antiques
- Stocks, bonds, and mutual funds (except when held for sale by a professional securities dealer)

Note: Losses from the sale of personal-use property, such as a main home, furniture, or jewelry, are not deductible.

Note: Do not confuse "personal-use property" with "personal property". "Personal property" is a legal term that is used by the IRS as well as legal and accounting professionals. The legal definition of "personal property" describes assets *other* than real estate, land, or buildings.

Example: Liam owns a station wagon that he uses to commute to work, run errands, and take on weekend ski trips. He purchased the car four years ago for $21,000. In 2016, he sells the car for $13,000. Liam cannot claim a loss from the sale of the car since it is his personal-use vehicle.

Example: Mason sold his personal computer to his friend for $750. Mason paid $5,000 for the computer five years ago. Mason used the computer to play games, surf the Internet, and pay bills on-line. He did not use the computer for business. Mason cannot deduct a loss on the sale of his personal computer.

Example: Priscilla collects antique coins as a hobby. She is not a professional coin dealer. Two years ago, Priscilla purchased an antique Roman coin at an estate sale for $50. In 2016, she is offered $1,000 for the coin, and she promptly sells it. Priscilla has a taxable capital gain that she must report on her tax return.

Although losses on personal-use property are not deductible, the gains on the sale of personal-use property may be taxable, subject to certain exclusions.

The applicable capital gains tax rate depends on the holding period, the type of asset, and the taxpayer's ordinary income tax bracket.

Noncapital Assets

Assets held for business-use or created by a taxpayer for purposes of earning revenue (author's writings, copyrights, inventory, etc.) are considered noncapital assets. Gains and losses from the sale of business property are reported on Form 4797, *Sales of Business Property*, and in the case of individual taxpayers, the amounts flow through to Form 1040, Schedule D, *Capital Gains and Losses.*

Example: Tony is the sole proprietor of a health club. In 2016, he sells used fitness equipment to make room for new equipment. Since the equipment was business property, Tony reports the sale on Form 4797. Also during the year, Tony sells some stock at a substantial profit. He has a capital gain on the stock that he reports on Schedule D.

The following assets are noncapital assets:

- Inventory or any similar property held for sale to customers
- Depreciable property used in a business, even if it is fully depreciated
- Real property used in a trade or business, such as a commercial building or a residential rental
- Self-produced copyrights, transcripts, manuscripts, drawings, photographs, or artistic compositions
- Accounts receivable or notes receivable acquired by a business
- Stocks and bonds held by professional securities dealers
- Business supplies
- Commodities and derivative financial instruments

Unlike capital assets, the costs of many noncapital assets may be deducted as business expenses when they are sold.

Example: Michael is a self-employed fisherman who reports his income and expenses on Schedule F. In 2016, he sells some of his commercial fishing equipment. The fishing equipment is a noncapital asset, and the sale must be reported on Form 4797, *Sales of Business Property*. Also during the year, Michael sells his vacation home at a substantial loss. Unlike the fishing equipment, the vacation home is a capital asset, but since it is personal-use property, he cannot deduct the loss.

Holding Period (Short-Term or Long-Term)

When a taxpayer disposes of investment property, his holding period affects the tax treatment of his capital gain or loss. This is important because long-term capital gains are taxed at lower rates than short-term gains.

If a taxpayer holds investment property for more than one year, any capital gain or loss is long-term capital gain or loss. If a taxpayer holds investment property for one year or less, any capital gain or loss is short-term capital gain or loss.

Long-term = <u>more</u> than one year (at least a year and a day)
Short-term = one year or less

To determine how long a taxpayer has held an investment property, he must begin counting on the date after the day he acquires the property. The day the taxpayer disposes of the property is part of the holding period.

Example: Nicky bought 50 shares of stock on February 5, 2015, for $10,000. She sells all the shares on February 5, 2016, for $20,500. Nicky's holding period is not more than one year, and so she has a short-term capital gain of $10,500. The short-term gain is taxed at ordinary income tax rates. If Nicky had waited one more day, she would have received long-term capital gain treatment on her gain, and been taxed at a lower rate.

Example: Stuart bought 100 shares of stock on October 1, 2015, for $1,200. To determine his holding period, Stuart must start counting his holding period on October 2, 2015 (the day *after* the purchase). He sells all the stock on October 2, 2016, for $2,850. Stuart's holding period has been more than one year, and therefore, he will recognize a long-term capital gain of $1,650 in 2016 ($2,850 - $1,200).

Stock shares acquired as a result of a nontaxable stock dividend or stock-split have the same holding period as the original shares owned.

Example: On September 10, 2014, Nathan bought 500 shares of Felton Software stock for $1,500, including his broker's commission. On June 6, 2016, Felton Software distributes a 2% nontaxable stock dividend (10 additional shares). Three days later, Nathan sells all his Felton Software stock for $2,030. Although Nathan owned the 10 shares he received as a nontaxable stock dividend for only three days, a long-term holding period applies to all of his shares in the stock. Because he bought the stock for $1,500 and then sold it for $2,030 more than a year later, Nathan has a long-term capital gain of $530 on the sale of the 510 shares.

The holding period for a gift is treated differently than the holding period for purchased property. If a taxpayer receives a gift of property, his holding period normally includes the donor's holding period. This concept is known as *tacking on* the holding period.

Example: Florence gives her niece, Marian, an acre of land. At the time of the gift, the land had an FMV of $23,000. Florence's adjusted basis in the land was $20,000. Florence held the property for six months. Marian holds the land for another seven months. Neither held the property for over a year. Regardless, Marian may "tack on" her holding period to her aunt's holding period. Therefore, if Marian were to sell the property, she would have a long-term capital gain or loss, because jointly they held the property for 13 months or more than one year.

If a taxpayer inherits property, he is considered to have held the property long-term, regardless of how long he actually held it.

Determining Capital Gain or Loss

A taxpayer determines gain or loss on a sale or trade of stock or property by comparing the amount realized with the adjusted basis of the property.

Example: Corbin receives Form 1099-B showing a net sales price of $1,200 on the sale of 600 shares of LeGrand Corporation. He bought the stock six years ago and sold it on September 25, 2016. His basis in LeGrand, including commissions paid, is $1,455. He will report a $255 loss on Schedule D.

A disposition of stock, and the related income or loss must be reported in the year of sale, regardless of when the taxpayer receives the proceeds. Capital losses are netted against capital gains.

A taxpayer can deduct up to $3,000 ($1,500 for MFS) of net capital losses against ordinary income in a tax year. Unused losses in excess of this limit are carried over to later years. The carryover losses are combined with gains and losses that occur in the next year.

Amounts carried over retain their character as either long-term or short-term and are reported on Schedule D. Thus, a long-term capital loss carried over to the next tax year will reduce that year's long-term capital gains before it reduces that year's short-term capital gains.

Example: Nadine purchased 50 shares of Hanson stock five years ago for $5,000. Two years ago, she purchased 750 shares of Sherwin stock for $8,200. In 2016, Nadine sells all her stock. Her Hanson stock sells for $2,000, and her Sherwin stock sells for $13,000. Nadine's gain and loss are both long-term because she held both stocks for more than one year. Her long-term loss and long-term gain are netted against each other, resulting in a net long-term capital gain, as follows:

Stock	Basis	Sale Price	Gain (Loss)
Hanson	$5,000	$2,000	($3,000)
Sherwin	$8,200	$13,000	$4,800
Net Long-term Capital Gain			**$1,800**

Example: Arthur purchased stock three years ago for $16,000. The stock declines in value, and he sells it in 2016 for $12,000. Arthur has a $4,000 long-term capital loss on the stock sale. He also has $60,000 of wages in 2016. He can claim $3,000 of his long-term capital loss against his ordinary income, thereby lowering his gross income to $57,000 ($60,000 - $3,000). The remainder of the long-term capital loss ($1,000) must be carried forward to the following tax year.

Note: Married taxpayers are actually at a disadvantage when deducting capital losses. On a joint return, the capital loss limit is $3,000, which is the same limit for single taxpayers. MFS filers only get half of that (a $1,500 capital loss limit).

Example: Judy and Paul are married and file separate returns (MFS). In 2016, Judy sells some stock and incurs a $5,000 capital loss. Paul also sells some stock and has a $12,500 capital gain. Judy can only claim $1,500 of her loss on her tax return because she is filing MFS. Paul must pay tax on the entire gain on his separate tax return.

A capital loss can be carried over indefinitely during the taxpayer's life. However, once a taxpayer dies, the capital losses not used on the final return cannot be carried over to a beneficiary or an heir. Capital losses always belong to the decedent. Any capital loss carryovers that are not used on the taxpayer's final return are essentially lost.

Worthless Securities

A taxpayer may choose to "abandon" a security that has lost its entire value in order to take advantage of the loss for tax purposes rather than retaining ownership. Stocks, stock rights, and bonds (other than those held for sale by a securities dealer) that became worthless during the tax year are treated as though they were sold for zero dollars on the last day of the tax year. To abandon a worthless security, a taxpayer must permanently surrender all rights to it and receive no consideration in exchange.

Example: Reginald owned 500 shares of WorldCom stock. The company files for bankruptcy and the bankruptcy court extinguishes all rights of the former shareholders. Reginald learns of the bankruptcy court's decision in December 2016. Rather than wait for a formal notice from the court, he chooses to abandon his WorldCom securities, knowing that his shares are essentially worthless. He takes a capital loss on his 2016 tax return, reflecting the value of his worthless shares as "zero."

A loss from worthless securities receives special tax treatment. Unlike other losses, a taxpayer is allowed to amend a tax return for up to seven years in order to claim a loss from worthless securities. This is more than double the usual three-year statute of limitations for amending returns.

Capital Gains from Mutual Funds

A mutual fund is a regulated investment company generally created by pooling funds of investors to allow them to take advantage of a diversity of investments and professional management. Two different types of transactions may result in taxable capital gains reporting by a taxpayer who invests in mutual funds.

First, profits resulting from investments made by the fund itself are reported to its own shareholders as capital gain distributions on Form 1099-DIV. The capital gain distributions are always taxed at long-term capital gains tax rates, without regard to how long a taxpayer has owned shares in the mutual fund.

In addition, if a taxpayer disposes of shares that represent all or a portion of his investment in the mutual fund itself, Form 1099-B will be issued. The taxable gain or loss that results from the sale or exchange of the taxpayer's shares in the mutual fund is reported on Form 1040, Schedule D. Brokers are now required to include the basis of mutual funds on Form 1099-B.

Wash Sales

A wash sale occurs when an investor sells a security to claim a capital loss, only to repurchase it again very soon thereafter. A taxpayer cannot deduct a loss on the sale of an investment if an identical investment was purchased within 30 days before or after the sale.

A wash sale is considered to have occurred when a taxpayer sells a security and, within 30 days:

- Buys the identical security,
- Acquires a substantially identical security in a taxable trade, or
- Acquires a contract or option to buy the identical security.

If a taxpayer's loss is disallowed because of the wash sale rules, he must add the disallowed loss to the basis of the new stock or securities.

The result is an increase in the taxpayer's basis in the new stock or securities. This adjustment postpones the loss deduction until the disposition of the new stock or securities.[24]

It is considered a wash sale if a taxpayer sells stock and his spouse then repurchases identical stock within 30 days, even if the spouses file separate tax returns.

Example: Carlos sells 800 shares of Granger Corporation stock on December 4, 2016, resulting in a loss of $3,200. He regrets selling the stock, so on January 2, 2017, he repurchases 800 shares of Granger stock on the open market. Because of the IRS wash sale rules, all of the $3,200 loss is disallowed, and he must add the disallowed loss to the basis of the newly-purchased shares. He cannot take the loss until he finally sells the repurchased shares at some later time.

For purposes of the wash sale rules, securities of one corporation are not considered identical to securities of another corporation. This means that a person can sell shares in one

[24] Wash sale rules do not apply to trades of commodity futures contracts and foreign currencies. The rules also do not apply to dealers in stocks or securities.

corporation and then purchase shares in a different corporation and this will not trigger a wash sale. Similarly, preferred stock of a corporation is not considered identical to the common stock of the same corporation.

Home Sale Gain or Loss

The following are used to figure the gain or loss on the sale of a home:

- Selling price
- Amount realized
- Basis
- Adjusted basis

Selling Price: The selling price is the total amount the taxpayer received for his main home. It includes money, all notes, mortgages, or other debts taken over by the buyer as part of the sale, and the fair market value of any other property or services that the seller received. Real estate sales proceeds are reported on Form 1099-S, *Proceeds From Real Estate Transactions*. If a taxpayer does not receive a Form 1099-S, he must rely upon sale documents and other records.

Amount Realized: The amount realized is the selling price minus selling expenses, which include commissions, advertising fees, legal fees, and loan charges paid by the seller, such as points.

Basis: The basis in a home is determined by how the taxpayer obtained the home. For example, if a taxpayer purchases a home, the basis is the cost of the home. If a taxpayer builds a home, the basis is the building cost plus the cost of land. If a taxpayer receives a home through inheritance or gift, the basis is either its FMV or the decedent's or donor's adjusted basis.

Example: Eve is single. She sells her home for $350,000. She purchased the home 20 years ago for $50,000 and had lived in it continuously since then. She pays $4,000 in seller's fees to sell the home. Her amount realized in the sale is $346,000 ($350,000 - $4,000 = $346,000). Her basis is subtracted from her amount realized in order to figure her gain: ($346,000 - $50,000 basis) = $296,000.

If the taxpayer inherited the home, the basis is generally its FMV on the date of the decedent's death, or the later alternate valuation date chosen by the representative for the estate.

Adjusted Basis: The adjusted basis is the taxpayer's basis in the home increased or decreased by certain amounts. Increases include additions or improvements to the home that have a useful life of more than one year. Repairs that simply maintain a home in good condition are not considered improvements and should not be added to the basis of the property. Decreases to basis include deductible casualty losses, credits, and product rebates. Depreciation reduces basis for business assets, such as rental property, but is never taken on personal-use property.

Formula for figuring adjusted basis:
Basis + Increases - Decreases = Adjusted Basis

Example: Immanuel purchased his home ten years ago for $125,000. In 2016, he added another bathroom to the property at a cost of $25,000. Immanuel's adjusted basis in the home is therefore $150,000 ($125,000 purchase price + $25,000 addition).

If the amount realized on the sale of a home is less than the adjusted basis, the difference is a loss. A loss on the sale of a primary residence can never be deducted.

If the amount realized is more than the adjusted basis of the property, the difference is a gain. As described in detail later, the taxpayer may be able to exclude all or part of the gain. If not excluded and the taxpayer owns a home for one year or less, the gain is reported as a short-term capital gain. If the taxpayer owns the home for more than one year, the gain is reported as a long-term capital gain.

There are special rules regarding the sale of a taxpayer's primary residence. We will go over those rules later, in the chapter dedicated to nonrecognition property transactions (Unit 8).

Related Party Transaction Rules

Special rules apply to related party transactions, which are between two parties who are joined by a special relationship. If a taxpayer sells an asset to a close family member or to a business entity that the taxpayer controls, he may not receive all the benefits of the capital gains tax rates, and he may not be able to deduct his losses. The rules were made to prevent related persons and entities from shuffling assets back and forth and taking improper losses.

50% Control Rule: If a taxpayer controls more than 50% of a corporation or partnership, any property transactions between the taxpayer and the business are subject to related party transaction rules.

In general, a loss on the sale of property between related parties is not deductible. When the property is later sold to an unrelated party, gain is recognized only to the extent it is more than the disallowed loss. If the property is later sold at a loss, the loss that was disallowed to the related party cannot be recognized. If a taxpayer sells or trades property at a loss (other than in the complete liquidation of a corporation), the loss is not deductible if the transaction is between the taxpayer and the following related parties:

- Members of immediate family, including a spouse, siblings, ancestors, or descendants (children, grandchildren, etc.).
- A partnership or corporation that the taxpayer controls. A taxpayer "controls" an entity when he has more than 50% ownership in it. This also includes partial ownership by other family members.
- A tax-exempt or charitable organization controlled by the taxpayer or a member of his family.
- Losses on sales between certain closely related trusts or business entities controlled by the same owners.

Note: For purposes of this rule, the following are not considered related parties: uncles, aunts, nephews, nieces, cousins, stepchildren, stepparents, in-laws, and ex-spouses.

Example: Vicky purchases stock from her father for $8,600. Her father's basis in the stock is $11,000. Vicky later sells the stock on the open market for $6,900. Her recognized loss is $1,700 (her $8,600 basis minus $6,900). Vicky cannot deduct the loss that was disallowed to her father.

Example: Aida buys stock from her brother, Clyde, for $7,600. Clyde's cost basis in the stock is $10,000. He cannot deduct the loss of $2,400 because of the related party transaction rules. Later, Aida sells the same stock on the open market for $10,500, realizing a gain of $2,900. Aida's reportable gain is $500 (the $2,900 gain minus the $2,400 loss not allowed to her brother).

Example: Tran sells 100 shares of stock to her step-brother, Thai. She recognizes a $3,000 capital loss on the transaction. Since a step-brother is not considered a related party for IRS purposes, she is allowed to take the loss on her tax return.

In the case of a related party transaction, if a taxpayer sells multiple pieces of property and some are at a gain while others are at a loss, the gains will generally be taxable while the losses cannot be used to offset the gains.

Installment Sales

An installment sale is a sale of property in which at least one payment is expected to be received after the tax year in which the sale occurs. If a taxpayer sells property and receives payments over multiple years, he may use the installment method in order to defer tax by only reporting a portion of his gain as each installment is received.

A taxpayer's gain, or gross profit, is the amount by which the selling price exceeds the adjusted basis in the property sold. A gross profit percentage is calculated by dividing the gross profit from the sale by the selling price.

Study Note: Test-takers may be required to determine gross profit percentage on an installment sale for either Part 1 or Part 2 of the EA exam.

Each payment received on an installment sale typically consists of the following three parts:

- Interest income
- Return of the adjusted basis in the property
- Gain on the sale (determined by applying the gross profit percentage to the amount of the payment received minus the interest portion)

In each year the taxpayer receives a payment, he must report the interest income and the portion that relates to his gain on the sale. The taxpayer does not include in income the part that is the return of his basis in the property. A taxpayer would normally calculate his installment sale income using the following formula: (next)

Calculating Gross Profit Percentage

1. Enter the selling price for the property: ________________
2. Enter the adjusted basis for the property: ________________
3. Enter the selling expenses: ________________________
4. Enter any depreciation recapture: ____________________
5. Add lines 2, 3, and 4. This is the adjusted basis for installment sale purposes: __________
6. Subtract line 5 from line 1. This is the gross profit: ________________. (If zero or less, there is no gain, and a taxpayer would not use the installment method.)
7. Divide line 6 by line 1. This is the gross profit percentage: ____________________
8. Multiply line 7 by amount of the current year installment payment (exclusive of interest income). This is the installment gain recognizable for the year: _____________

Definition: When a taxpayer disposes of certain types of property that have been depreciated, the property may be subject to **depreciation recapture**, which requires that the taxpayer report all or a portion of the prior depreciation deductions as ordinary income in the year of the sale.

Example: In 2016, Chloe sells an empty lot with a basis of $40,000 for $100,000. Her gross profit is $60,000 ($100,000 - $40,000) for a gross profit percentage of 60%. She receives a $20,000 down payment and the buyer's note for $80,000. In 2016, Chloe must report $12,000 gain allocated from the down payment she received. The note provides for four annual payments of $20,000 each, plus 8% interest, beginning in 2017. Exclusive of the interest income, she must report $12,000 of her installment gain for each $20,000 payment received ($20,000 × .60 = $12,000).

The selling price includes the cash and any other property to be received from the buyer, any existing mortgage or debt the buyer pays or assumes, and any selling expenses the buyer pays.

However, if the buyer assumes or pays off a mortgage or other debt on the property sold, the calculation of gross profit percentage is affected. The mortgage assumption is considered a recovery of basis in the year of sale and is subtracted before calculating the gross profit percentage, except to the extent that it exceeds the adjusted basis of the property for installment sale purposes.

In contrast, if the property is sold to a buyer who holds a mortgage on it and the mortgage is canceled rather than assumed, the cancellation is treated as a payment received in the year of the sale and is not subtracted in calculating the gross profit percentage.

Example: Ernesto sells property in an installment sale for $6,000. His gross profit is $1,500. The gross profit percentage on the sale is 25% ($1,500 ÷ $6,000). After subtracting interest, Ernesto reports 25% of each payment, including the down payment, as installment sale income in the year received. The remainder of each payment is the tax-free return of the property's basis.

If installment payments are made according to a schedule other than what was originally agreed, income is recognized according to the actual payments received. However, if the parties subsequently agree to adjust the selling price, the gross profit percentage must be recalculated, and income from future installments must be recognized based upon the adjusted gross profit.

If a taxpayer decides not to use the installment method, he must report all the gain in the year of the sale. Installment sale rules do not apply to property that is sold at a loss.

The installment method cannot be used for publicly traded securities, such as stocks and bonds. A taxpayer must report gain on the sale of securities in the year of the sale, regardless of whether the proceeds are received in the following year.

Example: Dillon owns 500 shares of stock, which he sells at a gain on December 29, 2016. Dillon does not receive the proceeds until January 15, 2017. Dillon is required to report the capital gain on the sale of the stock on his 2016 tax return. He cannot delay reporting the gain, and the sale is not considered an installment sale.

Installment sales to related persons are generally allowed. However, if a taxpayer sells property to a related person who then sells or disposes of the property within two years of the original sale, the taxpayer will lose the benefit of installment sale reporting.

Example: Lou sells a plot of land to his daughter, Melanie. The sale price is $25,000, and Lou realizes a profit on the sale of $10,000. Melanie agrees to pay in five installments of $5,000. A year later, Melanie decides she no longer wants the property and she sells the land to another person. Lou must report the entire profit of $10,000 on the sale, even though he may not have received all the installment payments. The installment sale method is disallowed on the related party sale because the property was disposed of during the two-year holding period.

Installment sales are reported on Form 6252, *Installment Sale Income*, which is attached to Form 1040. A taxpayer may also be required to complete Schedule D or Form 4797.

Reporting Asset Sales

Capital gains and losses are typically reported on these two forms:

- Schedule D, *Capital Gains and Losses*, and
- Form 8949, *Sales and Other Dispositions of Capital Assets.*

Taxpayers who must file Form 8949 and Schedule D will not be able to use either the 1040A or the 1040EZ form; they must file Form 1040.

Schedule D is used to report gain or loss on the sale of investment property and most capital gain (or loss) transactions. However, before the taxpayer can calculate their net gain or loss on Schedule D, he may also have to complete Form 8949, *Sales and Other Dispositions of Capital Assets.* Form 8949 reports the details about each stock trade the taxpayer makes during the year.

The totals from certain transactions can be reported directly on Schedule D without needing to report them on Form 8949. A taxpayer can skip filing Form 8949 if both of the following are true:

- He received a Form 1099-B that shows basis was reported to the IRS and does not show a nondeductible wash sale loss in box 5, and
- He does not need to make any adjustments to the basis or type of gain or loss (short-term or long-term) reported on Form 1099-B, or to his gain or loss.

Example: Eugene receives a Form 1099-B reporting the sale of stock he had held for five years. It shows gross proceeds of $8,000 and cost basis of $3,000. Box 6b is checked, meaning that his basis was reported to the IRS. Eugene does not need to make any adjustments to the amounts reported on Form 1099-B. He does not report the amounts on Form 8949. Instead, he enters the amounts directly onto his Schedule D.

There are two parts to Form 8949. The first is for short-term assets, and the second part is for long-term assets. Form 8949 is used to report the following:

- The sale or exchange of capital assets
- Gains from involuntary conversions (other than from casualty or theft)
- Nonbusiness bad debts and worthless securities

The information reported on Form 8949 describes all sales and exchanges of capital assets, including stocks, bonds, and mutual funds. This form must be filed along with Schedule D, which contains the summary of all capital gains and losses.

Unit 7: Study Questions

(Test yourself first, then check the correct answers at the end of this quiz.)

1. Lily bought shares in the Vanest Mutual Fund in 2013 for $8 a share. Since then, she received the following nondividend distributions:

- 2013: $2 per share
- 2014: $2 per share
- 2015: $3 per share
- 2016: $3 per share

What is Lily's basis in the stock and what amount of gain, if any, must she report in 2016?

A. $0 basis; $6 gain.
B. $14 basis; $0 gain.
C. $0 basis; $2 gain.
D. $8 basis; $3 gain.

2. What is the maximum number of years a taxpayer can carry over an unused capital loss?

A. One year.
B. Two years.
C. Five years.
D. As many years as required to utilize the entire deduction.

3. Five years ago, Marsha bought 100 shares of stock. Her sale date was March 10, 2016. Marsha's original cost for the stock was $10,110, plus an additional $35 of broker's fees. When she sold the stock, she received gross proceeds of $8,859. What is the net gain or loss from this transaction?

A. $1,286 long-term capital loss.
B. $1,286 short-term capital loss.
C. $1,251 long-term capital loss.
D. $1,251 long-term capital gain.

4. Which of the following losses is deductible?

A. A loss on the sale of a primary residence.
B. A loss on the sale of a vacation home.
C. A loss on the sale of a personal-use mobile home.
D. A loss on the sale of rental property.

5. Oliver operates an electronics repair business as a sole proprietorship. In 2016, Oliver sold property that was acquired for use in the business for $15,000. The purchase price of the property was $12,000, and Oliver had claimed depreciation of $3,000 related to the property. He accepted a down payment of $5,000 from the buyer, along with a note requiring additional payments of $2,500 plus interest in each of the next four years. Based upon the information provided, what amount of taxable income will result in 2016 if Oliver uses the installment method to report the sale of this property?

A. Capital gain of $5,000 and ordinary income of $1,000.
B. Capital gain of $1,000 and ordinary income of $3,000.
C. Capital gain of $2,000.
D. Capital gain of $1,000 and ordinary income of $1,000.

6. Nikhil's adjusted basis in 500 shares of Edico Corporation was $2,550. He owned the shares for three months. If he sold 500 shares for $3,300, what is the resulting gain or loss?

A. $750 short-term gain.
B. $700 short-term gain.
C. $750 long-term gain.
D. $750 long-term loss.

7. Ruben bought 100 shares of stock on October 1, 2015, when the share price was $26. He sold the stock for $20 a share on October 1, 2016. How should this trade be reported, and what is the nature of Ruben's gain or loss?

A. Short-term capital loss of $600.
B. Long-term capital loss of $600.
C. This is a wash sale, and there is no gain or loss.
D. Short-term capital loss of $500.

8. When trying to determine the holding period for investment property, which of the following is important?

A. The cost of the property.
B. In the case of gifted property, the amount of the gift.
C. The date of acquisition.
D. The amount realized in the transaction.

9. Gianna purchased 200 shares of stock on January 26, 2016, for $1,000. She sold all the shares on December 31, 2016, for $2,500. On January 9, 2017, the shares were delivered and payment was submitted to Gianna's account. How should this sale be reported?

A. $1,500 long-term gain on her 2016 return.
B. $1,500 short-term gain on her 2016 return.
C. $1,500 long-term gain on her 2017 return.
D. $1,500 short-term gain on her 2017 return.

10. Fred bought ten shares of Jixi Corporation stock on May 2, 2015. He sold them for a $7,000 loss on May 2, 2016. He has no other capital gains or losses. He also has $20,000 of wage income. How must Fred treat this transaction on his tax return?

A. He can deduct the $7,000 as a long-term capital loss on his 2016 return.
B. He can deduct the $7,000 as a short-term capital loss on his 2016 return.
C. He can deduct $3,000 as a short-term capital loss to offset his wage income on his 2016 return. The remaining amount, $4,000, must be carried over to future tax years.
D. He cannot deduct any of the capital loss; it must be carried over to future tax years.

11. Norma sells an empty lot with an adjusted basis of $20,000. Her buyer assumes an existing mortgage on the property of $15,000 and agrees to pay Norma $10,000, with a cash down payment of $2,000 and then $2,000 every year (plus 12% interest) in each of the next four years. What is Norma's gross profit and gross profit percentage on the installment sale?

A. The gross profit is $5,000, and the gross profit percentage is 20%.
B. The gross profit is $10,000, and the gross profit percentage is 100%.
C. The gross profit is $15,000, and the gross profit percentage is 20%.
D. The gross profit is $5,000, and the gross profit percentage is 50%.

12. Mario purchased his home five years ago for $150,000. He sold it at a loss for $115,000 in 2016. Which of the following statements is correct?

A. If he itemizes deductions, Mario can claim a loss of $35,000 on his 2016 tax return.
B. Mario can claim a loss of $3,000 in 2016, but must carry over the remainder to future years until the loss is completely deducted.
C. Mario can claim a loss of $35,000 because the home sale was an involuntary conversion.
D. Mario cannot claim a loss for the sale of his home.

13. Tahir purchased 100 shares in Foresthill Mutual Fund in April 2016 for $750. He received a capital gain distribution of $120 in 2016. The $120 was reported to him on Form 1099-DIV. How should this be reported on his tax return?

A. He must reduce his stock's basis by $120.
B. He must report the $120 as interest income.
C. He must report the $120 as a long-term capital gain.
D. He must report the $120 as a short-term capital gain.

14. Melissa purchased 1,000 shares of Devil Foods Company stock in 2012 at $10 per share. She sold 900 shares on January 15, 2016, at $9 per share, resulting in a $900 loss. Melissa's husband, Alex, purchased 900 shares of Devil Foods Company stock on February 10, 2016. Alex and Melissa keep their finances separate and will file MFS in 2016. Which of the following statements is correct?

A. Melissa can deduct the $900 capital loss on her tax return.
B. Melissa has a wash sale, and her loss is not deductible.
C. Alex can deduct the loss on his separate tax return.
D. None of the above.

15. Phil and Sharon owned a vacation home for 14 months before selling it for $254,000. Their adjusted basis in the home was $232,000, and they incurred $12,500 of selling expenses. Prior to the sale, they did not rent the home. What is the nature and amount of their gain?

A. $22,000 long-term capital gain.
B. $9,500 long-term capital gain.
C. $9,500 short-term capital gain.
D. $34,500 long-term capital gain.

16. Conrad purchased Blue-Chip Corporation stock in 2010 and sold it in 2016. Also in 2016, he traded in a copy machine that he used in his business since 2009 for a new model. On December 15, 2016, Conrad's mother gave him 35 shares of Energy Corporation stock that she had held for five years, and the fair market value of the stock was more than her basis in the stock at the time of the gift. Conrad sold the gifted stock two weeks after he received it from his mother. What is the holding period for all these assets?

A. All are short-term.
B. Blue-Chip stock and copy machine are long-term, and Energy Corporation stock is short-term.
C. All the stocks are long-term; the copy machine is short-term.
D. All are long-term.

17. Consuela purchased 1,000 shares of Hometown Mutual Fund on February 15, 2012, for $15 per share. On January 31, 2016, she sold all her shares for $3.75 per share. She also earned $45,000 of wages in 2016. She has no other transactions during the year. How should this transaction be reported on her tax return?

A. She has a capital loss of $11,250 that she can deduct against her wage income.
B. She must carry over the losses to a future tax year and offset future capital gains.
C. She can deduct a $3,000 capital loss on her 2016 tax return and the remainder of the losses will carry forward to subsequent years.
D. She can deduct a $5,000 capital loss on her 2016 tax return and the remainder of the losses will carry forward to subsequent years.

18. Noah bought two blocks (each of 400 shares) of Acme Corporation stock. He purchased the first block in April 2009 for $1,200 and the second block in March 2016 for $1,600. In June of 2016, he sold 400 shares for $1,500 but is unable to specify which block of stocks he sold. Noah's stock sale results in a:

A. Short-term loss of $100.
B. Short-term gain of $300.
C. Long-term loss of $100.
D. Long-term gain of $300.

19. Colin purchased 100 shares of Entertainment Digital Media stock for $1,000 on December 1, 2015. He sold these shares for $750 on December 22, 2016. Colin has seller's remorse, and on January 19, 2017, he repurchases 100 shares of Entertainment Digital for $800. Which of the following statements is correct?

A. Colin can report a $250 capital loss in 2016.
B. Colin can report a loss in 2016 and a taxable gain in 2017.
C. Colin cannot deduct his stock loss of $250 and must add the disallowed loss to his basis.
D. Colin can report a $250 capital loss in 2017.

20. All of the statements are correct about related party transactions except:

A. If a taxpayer controls more than 50% of a corporation or partnership, any property transactions between the taxpayer and business would be subject to the related party transaction rules.
B. Typically, a loss on the sale of property between related parties is not deductible.
C. The related party transaction rules apply to step-parents and step-siblings.
D. Related party transaction rules are designed to prevent improper deductions between two parties joined by a special relationship.

Unit 7: Answers

1. The answer is C. The first $8 of nondividend distributions per share reduces Lily's basis to zero. In 2016, the final $2 of nondividend distribution must be reported as capital gain.

2. The answer is D. Unused capital losses may be carried over indefinitely until they are utilized. There is no limit to how many years the taxpayer can claim the losses.

3. The answer is A. The answer is calculated as follows: The original basis is increased by the broker's commission. Therefore, Marsha's adjusted basis is $10,145 ($10,110 + $35). The gross proceeds from the sale are $8,859, which is subtracted from the basis, resulting in a long-term capital loss of $1,286 ($8,859 - $10,145) because she held the stock for more than one year.

4. The answer is D. Losses on the sale of personal-use property, including a loss on the sale of a primary residence or a vacation home, are not deductible. Only losses associated with business property and investment property (such as stocks and bonds or rental property) are deductible.

5. The answer is B. The amount of depreciation deducted for the property ($3,000) is recaptured and reported in 2016 as ordinary income. This amount is added back to the adjusted basis of $9,000 to determine the adjusted basis for the installment sale ($12,000). This amount is subtracted from the total proceeds of the sale ($15,000) to determine the gross profit of $3,000, which derives a gross profit percentage of 20%. This percentage is applied to the portion of proceeds received in 2016 ($5,000) to determine the amount of capital gain recognizable this year.

Original purchase price	$12,000
Minus depreciation deductions	(3,000)
Adjusted basis at date of sale	9,000
Depreciation recapture	3,000
Adjusted basis for installment sale	(12,000)
Proceeds of sale	15,000
Gross profit percentage	20%
Proceeds in 2016	5,000
Capital gain to be recognized	**$1,000**

6. The answer is A. The sales price is $750 more than the adjusted basis of the shares. The gain is short-term since Nikhil did not own the shares for more than one year.

7. The answer is A. Ruben has a short-term capital loss of $600 = (100 shares × $26) - (100 shares × $20). Ruben's holding period was not more than one year, which means that the loss must be treated as short-term. To determine holding period, begin counting on the day after the date the taxpayer acquires the property.

8. The answer is C. To determine the holding period; a taxpayer must begin counting on the day *after* the acquisition date. If a taxpayer's holding period is not more than one year, the taxpayer will have a short-term gain or loss. The amount realized in the transaction has no bearing on the holding period.

9. The answer is B. The sale and income must be reported in the year the security is sold, regardless of when the proceeds were received. She held the shares for less than one year, so Gianna has a short-term gain that must be reported on her 2016 tax return.

10. The answer is C. Fred has a short-term capital loss because he did not hold the stock for more than one year. He can deduct $3,000 of the loss in 2016, netting against his wage income. The remaining amount, $4,000, must be carried over to future tax years. A capital loss carryover retains its character as either long-term or short-term.

11. The answer is D. Norma's gross profit is $5,000, and the gross profit percentage is 50%. Her selling price is $25,000 ($2,000 down payment + $8,000 to be paid over four years + $15,000 for buyer's assumption of mortgage). Therefore, Norma's gross profit is $5,000 ($25,000 – $20,000 adjusted basis). If the entire selling price were payable in cash, her gross profit percentage would have been 20% ($5,000/$25,000). However, if a buyer assumes or pays off a mortgage or other debt on a property, the calculation of the installment sale gross profit percentage is affected. The mortgage assumption is subtracted before calculating the gross profit percentage, except to the extent that it exceeds the adjusted basis of the property for installment sale purposes, to derive what the IRS calls "contract price," rather than selling price. The mortgage assumption is considered a recovery of the seller's basis in the year of sale. Although the mortgage assumption is considered a payment, none of the gross profit is recognized in connection with the assumption. Instead, in this case, the contract price is considered to be $10,000 ($25,000 selling price - $15,000 mortgage assumption). Therefore, Norma's gross profit percentage is 50% ($5,000 ÷ $10,000). Norma must report half of each payment received as gain from the sale. She must also report all interest received as ordinary income.

12. The answer is D. Losses on the sale of personal-use property, including residences, are never deductible.

13. The answer is C. Mutual funds frequently distribute capital gains to shareholders. Capital gain distributions for mutual funds are always taxed as long-term capital gains, no matter how long a taxpayer has actually held the mutual fund shares.

14. The answer is B. The loss is disallowed. Melissa has a wash sale because her spouse repurchased identical securities within 30 days. It does not matter if they file separate returns. If a taxpayer sells stock and her spouse then repurchases identical stock within 30 days, the taxpayer has a wash sale. The fact that the taxpayers file MFS is irrelevant—the wash sale rules still apply.

15. The answer is B. The sale of a second home is a taxable event. Since Phil and Sharon owned the property for longer than one year, their gain is long-term. The gain is calculated as follows:

Sale price	$254,000
Minus selling expenses	(12,500)
Net proceeds	241,500
Minus adjusted basis in the property	(232,000)
Taxable gain on the sale	**$9,500**

16. The answer is D. All the property is long-term property. Generally, if a taxpayer holds investment property for more than one year, any gain or loss is a long-term gain or loss. If the taxpayer holds a property for one year or less, any gain or loss is a short-term gain or loss. However, if a taxpayer receives a gift of property, his holding period includes the donor's holding period if the fair market value of the gift was more than the donor's basis. Since Conrad's mother had held the stock for a few years, Conrad's disposition would receive long-term treatment.

17. The answer is C. Consuela cannot deduct all her stock losses in the current year. She can claim a $3,000 capital loss on her 2016 tax return and the remainder of the losses will carry forward to subsequent years.

18. The answer is D. Noah realized a long-term gain of $300 because the basis and holding period would automatically default to the oldest block of shares. A FIFO method is used if the taxpayer cannot specifically identify the shares sold.

19. The answer is C. Because Colin bought substantially identical stock, this is considered a wash sale and he cannot deduct his loss of $250 on the sale. Instead, he must add the disallowed loss to the cost of the new stock to obtain his adjusted basis in the new stock.

20. The answer is C. Related party transaction rules do not apply to uncles, aunts, nieces, nephews, cousins, stepchildren, stepparents, or in-laws.

Unit 8: Nonrecognition Property Transactions

For additional information read:
Publication 544, *Sales and Other Dispositions of Assets*
Publication 523, *Selling Your Home*

For some transactions in which a taxpayer sells or exchanges property, gains may be nontaxable, partially taxable, or deferred. Three of the most common types of nonrecognition transactions involve:

- **Sale of a main home** (section 121, excluded gain)
- **Like-kind exchanges** (section 1031 exchange)
- **Involuntary conversions** (section 1033 exchange)

Note: For Part 1 of the EA Exam, you will be tested primarily on the sale of a main home, involuntary conversions of personal-use property, and like-kind exchanges of residential rental property (Form 1040, Schedule E). For Part 2 of the EA exam, you will be tested on nonrecognition property transactions, but exclusively with business or rental property.

Sale of Main Home (Section 121)

In many cases, a taxpayer may exclude the gain from the sale of a main home. Up to $250,000 of gain may be excluded by single filers and up to $500,000 by joint filers. Generally, if the taxpayer can exclude all of the gain, it is not even necessary to report the sale. However, if part of the gain is taxable, the sale must be reported on Schedule D. Gain from the sale of a home that is not the taxpayer's main home must be reported as income.

The section 121 exclusion applies only to a "main home" and not to rental properties, vacation homes, or second homes. A taxpayer's main home is the residence where he lives most of the time. It does not have to be a traditional house. The main home can be a house, houseboat, mobile home, cooperative apartment, or condominium. To qualify as a home, it must have sleeping, kitchen, and bathroom facilities.

Example: Wayne owns and lives in a house in Detroit. He also owns a lake cottage, which he uses only during the summer. The house in Detroit is his main home; the lake cottage is not. Wayne sells the lake cottage and has $100,000 of gain. The gain cannot be excluded because the cottage is not his main home. He must pay tax on the entire gain.

If the home was used for business purposes or as rental property, the gain is reported on Form 4797, *Sales of Business Property.* If a taxpayer took depreciation deductions because he used his home as a rental or for other business purposes, he cannot exclude the part of the gain equal to any deductible depreciation. Section 121 applies only to the nonbusiness portion of a home.

Example: Erica lives in one-half of a duplex she owns and lets her daughter live in the other unit of the duplex rent-free. She purchased the duplex ten years ago for $200,000. In 2016, Erica sells the duplex for $340,000, a gain of $140,000. Since only half of the duplex counts as her main home, Erica may exclude only half of the gain ($70,000). She must report the other $70,000 as long-term capital gain.

Eligibility Requirements for Section 121

To be eligible for the section 121 exclusion, a taxpayer must:

- Have sold his main home
- Meet ownership and use tests
- Not have excluded gain in the two years prior to the current sale of a home

Ownership and Use Tests: During the five-year period ending on the date of the sale, the taxpayer must have:

- Owned the home for at least two years (the ownership test), and
- Lived in the home as his main home for at least two years (the use test).

Example: For the past six years, Lindsay lived with her parents in the home her parents owned. On September 1, 2015, she bought the house from her parents. She continued to live there until December 14, 2016, when she sold it because she wanted a bigger house. Lindsay does not meet the requirements for exclusion. Although she *lived* in the property as her main home for more than two years, she did not *own* it for the required two years. Therefore, she does not meet both the ownership and use tests.

A taxpayer meets the tests if he owned and lived in the property as his main home for either 24 full months or 730 days (365 × 2) during the five-year period.

Example: Irene bought a house in September 2011. After living there for ten months, she moved in with her boyfriend and kept her house vacant. They broke up and she moved back into her own house in 2015. She lived there for 16 months until she sold it in September 2016. Irene meets the ownership and use tests because, during the five-year period ending on the date of sale, she owned the house for four years and lived in the house a total of 26 months.

Note: The required two years of ownership and use do not have to be continuous. Further, ownership and use tests can be met during different two-year periods.

Short, temporary absences, even if the property is rented during those absences, are still counted as periods of use. Short absences include vacations and other seasonal absences. Longer breaks, such as a one-year sabbatical, are not included.

Example: In 2008, Carter began living in an apartment he rented. The apartment was converted to a condominium, which he purchased on December 1, 2013. In 2014, Carter became seriously ill, and on April 14 of that year, he moved into his daughter's home. On July 10, 2016, while still living in his daughter's home, Carter sold his condo. He can exclude all the gain on the sale because he meets the ownership and use tests. His five-year "lookback" period is from July 11, 2011, to July 10, 2016 (the date he actually sold the condo). He *owned* the condo from December 1, 2013, until July 10, 2016 (more than two years). He lived there from 2008 until April 14, 2014 (more than two years), so he would qualify to exclude all the gain, even though his ownership and use periods do not always overlap.

Example: Katarina bought her home on February 1, 2013. Each year, she left her home for a four-month vacation in Ecuador. Katarina sold the house on March 1, 2016. She may exclude up to $250,000 of gain. Her vacations are considered short temporary absences and are counted toward her periods of use.

Different Rules for Married Homeowners

The ownership and use tests are applied differently to married homeowners. Married homeowners can exclude gain of up to $500,000 if they meet all of the following conditions:

- They file a joint return.
- Either spouse meets the ownership test (only one is required to own the home).
- Both spouses meet the use test.
- Neither spouse has excluded gain in the two years before the current sale of the home.

If they do not satisfy these requirements, the couple cannot claim the maximum $500,000 exclusion.

Example: Leigh owns her home and has lived in it continuously for the last seven years. She meets William and marries him in September 2016. They move in together, but William doesn't like Leigh's house, and he convinces her to sell it a few months later. Leigh sells the home on December 10, 2016, and has $350,000 of gain. Leigh meets the ownership and use tests, but William does not meet the use test because he only lived in the house for a few months. Leigh can exclude up to $250,000 of gain on her 2016 tax return, whether she files MFJ or MFS. The $500,000 exclusion for joint returns does not apply.

Example: Robert owns a home that he has lived in continuously for five years. In June 2013, he marries Annabel. She moves in, and they both live in the house together until December 1, 2016, when the house is sold. Robert meets the ownership test and the use test. Annabel does not own the home because Robert is listed as the sole owner of the property. However, she meets the "use test" because she lived in the home for at least two years. Therefore, on a jointly filed return, they can claim the maximum $500,000 exclusion.

Legally married same-sex spouses are eligible for the maximum $500,000 exclusion from gain on their jointly-filed returns.

Example: Brandon and Max were legally married in Vermont two years ago. In 2016, they sell the house they had co-owned and lived in together for ten years. The house sold for $575,000 more than they paid for it. Brandon and Max may receive the maximum $500,000 exclusion for married couples when they file jointly in 2016. The remaining $75,000 of gain is taxable as long-term capital gain.

Unrelated Individuals: An unmarried couple or other taxpayers who own a home and live together may take the $250,000 exclusion individually on their separate returns if they meet the use and ownership tests.

Example: Greta and Carolyn are sisters. They are both widowed in 2016 and decided to purchase a home and live together. If they later sell the home, the ownership and use tests would apply to them individually. Each could claim an exclusion of up to $250,000 for her portion of the sale on her individual return.

Deceased Spouse: When a taxpayer's spouse dies, the taxpayer is considered to have owned and lived in a home during any period of time that the spouse owned and lived in it as a main home (provided that the taxpayer did not remarry before the date of sale). In effect, the holding period of the deceased spouse is tacked on for surviving spouses. As a result, the surviving spouse may exclude up to $500,000 of gain even if he sells the home within two years from the date of death of the deceased spouse.

Example: Alice owned and lived in her home for seven years. She married Stanley in April 2016, and he moved into the home with her. Alice died six months later, and Stanley inherited the property. He did not remarry. Stanley decides to sell the home on December 1, 2016. Even though he did not own or live in the house for two years, he meets the test requirements because his period of ownership and use includes the period that Alice owned and used the property before her death. Stanley may exclude up to $500,000 of the gain under the special rule that applies to deceased spouses.

Note: This "special rule" also applies to a home that is transferred by a spouse in a divorce. The receiving spouse is considered to have owned the home during any period of time that the transferor owned it.

Military Personnel Exception: Members of the armed forces are often required to move and might have difficulty meeting the tests for ownership and use within the five-year period prior to the sale of a home. The five-year period can be suspended for up to ten years for military and Foreign Service personnel, Peace Corps workers, and intelligence officers that are on official extended duty. This provides the taxpayer a better opportunity to meet the two-year use test even if he and/or his spouse did not actually live in the home during the normal five-year period required of other taxpayers.

Disability Exception: There is an exception to the use test if, during the five-year period before the sale of the home, a taxpayer becomes physically or mentally unable to care for himself, but he has owned and lived in the home for at least one year. The taxpayer is considered to have lived in the home during any time that he is forced to live in a licensed facility, including a nursing home. The taxpayer must still meet the two-year ownership test.

Reduced Exclusions

A taxpayer who owned and used a home for less than two years (and therefore does not meet the ownership and use tests) or who has used the home sale exclusion within the prior two-year period may be able to claim a reduced exclusion under certain conditions.

This may apply if a home sale has occurred primarily because of "unforeseen circumstances" during the taxpayer's period of use and ownership. Unforeseen circumstances include the following:

- Death, divorce, or legal separation.
- Certain health reasons related to care for the taxpayer, a spouse, a child, or certain other related persons. The related person does not have to be a dependent in order for the reduced exclusion to apply.
- Unemployment or a job change. The job-related exclusion applies if a new job is at least 50 miles farther from the old home than was the former place of employment. If there was no former place of employment, the distance between the new place of employment and the old home must be at least 50 miles.
- Multiple births resulting from the same pregnancy.
- Damage to the residence resulting from a disaster, an act of war, or terrorism.
- Involuntary conversion of the property.

The circumstances may involve the taxpayer, his spouse, a co-owner, or a member of the taxpayer's household. The IRS also has the discretion to deem other circumstances as unforeseen.

Example: Justin purchased his new home in Mississippi in June 2015, but he lost his job shortly after he moved in. He found a new job in North Carolina and sold his house in April 2016. Because the distance between Justin's new place of employment and his former home is at least 50 miles, the sale satisfies the distance requirement. Justin's sale of his home is due to a change in place of employment, and he is entitled to claim a reduced exclusion on his gain from the sale.

Calculating the Reduced Exclusion

The reduced exclusion amount equals the full $250,000 (or $500,000 for married couples filing jointly) multiplied by a fraction. The numerator is the shorter of:

- The period the taxpayer owned and used the home as a principal residence during the five-year period ending on the sale date, or
- The period between the last sale for which the taxpayer claimed the exclusion and the sale date for the home currently being sold.

The denominator is two years or the equivalent in months or days. Thus, the amount of the reduced exclusion is figured by multiplying the full exclusion amount by the number of days or months the taxpayer owned and used the property, and dividing by either 730 days or 24 months.

Example: Sabrina, a single taxpayer, lived in her principal residence for one full year (365 days) before selling it at a $400,000 gain in 2016. She qualifies for the reduced exclusion because she is pregnant with triplets (multiple births exclusion). Sabrina can exclude $125,000 of gain ($250,000 × [365 ÷ 730]).

Example: Carrie purchased her home on January 1, 2016, for $350,000. Her mother is diagnosed with cancer, and Carrie must move to care for her. Even though Carrie does not claim her mother as a dependent, the move still qualifies as an unforeseen circumstance. Carrie sells her home on May 1, 2016, for $430,000, realizing a gain of $80,000. She qualifies for the reduced exclusion, so part of her gain is nontaxable. She owned and occupied the home for 121 days (January 1 to May 1). She may exclude $41,438 ($250,000 × [121 days ÷ 730 (365 X 2 years)]). Therefore, Carrie's taxable gain is $38,562 ($80,000 - $41,438). This amount is a short-term capital gain since she owned the house for less than one year.

Land Sales: If a taxpayer sells the land on which his main home is located but not the house itself, he cannot exclude the gain. Similarly, the sale of a vacant plot of land with no house on it does not qualify for the section 121 exclusion.

Example: Theresa purchased an empty lot in 2013 for $90,000, planning to build her dream home. Construction was delayed and her house was never completed. In December 2016, Theresa sells the land for $150,000. She owned the property for more than a year, so she has $60,000 of long-term capital gain. None of the gain can be excluded from income because there is no residence on the property. Section 121 only applies to homes, not to empty land.

If a taxpayer sells a vacant lot that is adjacent to his main home, he may be able to exclude the gain from the sale under certain circumstances. Gain from the sale of vacant land that was used in connection with a principal residence may be excluded if the land sale occurs within two years before or after the sale of the home. The sale of the land and the sale of the home are treated as one sale for purposes of the exclusion.

Like-Kind Exchanges (Section 1031 Exchange)

A section 1031 *like-kind exchange* occurs when a taxpayer exchanges business or investment property for similar property. If the exchange qualifies under section 1031, the taxpayer does not recognize any resulting gain and cannot deduct any losses until he later disposes of the property received. To qualify for nonrecognition treatment, the exchange must meet all of the following conditions:

- The property must be held for investment or for productive use in a business. Property held for personal use, such as a personal residence, does not qualify.
- The property must not be "held primarily for sale" (such as inventory).
- There must be an actual exchange of two or more assets or properties (the exchange of cash for property is treated as a sale, not as an exchange).
- For instances in which a property is transferred in exchange for like-kind property to be received later (known as a deferred exchange), the property to be received must be identified in writing (or actually received) within 45 days after the date of transfer of the property given up.

Further, the replacement property in a deferred exchange must be received by the earlier of:

- The 180th day after the date on which the property given up was transferred, or
- The due date, including extensions, of the tax return for the year in which the transfer of that property occurs. The IRS is very strict about these deadlines.

Taxpayers report like-kind exchanges on Form 8824, *Like-Kind Exchanges*.

Qualifying Exchanges: To qualify under section 1031, an exchange must involve like-kind property, such as the trade of real property for real property or personal property for personal property.

Definition: The accounting term **"personal property"** does not refer to items used for personal use but rather to assets used in a business that is not classified as real property (real estate).

An exchange of real property generally qualifies more easily as like-kind, regardless of how each property is used or whether each property is improved or unimproved. For instance, the exchange of a building for farmland would qualify, as would the exchange of an apartment complex for an office building. However, the exchange of factory machinery (personal property) for a factory building (real property) is not a qualifying exchange.

In contrast, an exchange of personal property must involve items that are at least similar enough to both be categorized within one of several asset classes established by the IRS. For example, the exchange of a panel truck for a pickup truck may qualify as a trade of like-kind property, but the exchange of a pickup truck for a semi-truck likely would not.

Example: Casey exchanges a private jet with an adjusted basis of $400,000 for an office building valued at $375,000. The exchange of personal property (an airplane) for real property (the building) does not qualify for section 1031 treatment, so gain (or loss) must be recognized on this transaction.

Nonqualifying Exchanges: The exchange of equipment or business assets that are used within the United States for similar items used outside the United States would not be considered an exchange of qualifying like-kind property. Similarly, real estate within the United States and real estate outside the United States is not "like" property, and an exchange would not qualify for section 1031 treatment.

Other exchanges that do not qualify for section 1031 treatment include the following types of property:

- Livestock of different sexes
- Securities, bonds, stocks, currency, or notes
- Partnership interests

Taxable Exchanges: If a taxpayer receives property in exchange for other property that is not similar or related in use to the property exchanged, he may need to recognize gain if the fair market value of the property received is greater than the adjusted basis of the property exchanged. His basis in the property received is generally its FMV at the time of the exchange.

Example: Tyler trades an empty lot with an adjusted basis of $10,000 for an SUV to use in his pest control business. The SUV's fair market value is $15,000. Since the exchange does not qualify for section 1031 treatment, Tyler must report $5,000 of capital gain. The SUV's basis is $15,000.

Boot: Although the Internal Revenue Code itself does not use the term "boot," it is frequently used to describe cash or other property added to an exchange in order to compensate for a difference in the values of properties traded.

An exchange that includes "boot" may still be valid under section 1031, but the taxpayer who receives boot may have to recognize taxable gain to the extent of the cash and the FMV of unlike property received. The amount considered boot would be reduced by qualified costs paid in connection with the transaction.

Example: Sloan wishes to exchange his rental property in a 1031 exchange. The relinquished rental property has an FMV of $60,000 and an adjusted basis of $30,000. The replacement property Sloan receives has an FMV of $50,000, and he also receives $10,000 of cash as part of the exchange. Sloan, therefore, has a gain of $30,000 on the exchange (combined value of $60,000 received minus his basis of $30,000 in the property exchanged). He is required to pay tax on only $10,000, the cash (boot) received in the exchange. The rest of his gain is deferred until he disposes of the property at a later date.

When an exchange involves property that is subject to a liability, assumption of the liability is treated as if it was a transfer of cash and thus considered boot by the party who is relieved of the liability. If each property in an exchange is transferred subject to a liability, a taxpayer is treated as having received boot only if he is relieved of a greater liability than the liability he assumes.

Basis of Property Received in a Like-Kind Exchange

The basis of the property received is generally the adjusted basis of the property transferred.

Example: Judy has a rental house with an adjusted basis of $70,000. In 2016, she trades the rental house for an empty lot with an FMV of $150,000. Judy's basis in the lot is $70,000, equal to the adjusted basis of the property she exchanged.

If a taxpayer trades property and also pays money as part of the exchange, the basis of the property received is the basis of the property given up, increased by any additional money paid.

Example: Jorge trades a plot of land with an adjusted basis of $30,000 for a different plot of land in another town with an FMV of $70,500. He pays an additional $4,000 of cash. Jorge's basis in the new land is $34,000: his $30,000 basis in the old land plus the $4,000 cash.

Example: Peyton bought a new diesel truck for use in her catering business. She received a credit of $13,600 for trading in her old truck and also paid $43,000 of cash. The old truck cost $50,000 two years ago, and Peyton had taken depreciation deductions of $39,500 on it. She has a $3,100 gain on the exchange ($13,600 trade-in allowance minus her $10,500 adjusted basis for the old truck), but recognition of the gain is postponed under the rules for like-kind exchanges.

If a taxpayer receives boot in connection with an exchange and recognizes gain, the basis of the property received is equal to the basis of the property given up plus the amount of gain recognized.

Example: Cole exchanges a tractor with an adjusted basis of $50,000 for a harvester with an FMV of $60,000. He receives cash of $10,000 in connection with the exchange and must recognize gain to the extent of the boot received. His basis in the harvester is $60,000 ($50,000 basis in the old tractor plus $10,000 recognized gain).

Related Party Transactions

Like-kind exchanges are allowed between related parties. However, if either party disposes of the property within two years after a 1031 exchange, the exchange is disqualified from nonrecognition treatment; any gain or loss that was deferred in the original transaction must be recognized in the year the disposition occurs. For purposes of this rule, a related person includes a close family member (such as a spouse, sibling, parent, or child). It also includes a corporation or partnership in which a taxpayer holds ownership or interests of more than 50%.

The two-year holding period rule does not apply:

- If one of the parties involved in the exchange dies
- If the property is subsequently converted in an involuntary exchange (such as a fire)
- If it can be established to the satisfaction of the IRS that the exchange and subsequent disposition were not done mainly for tax avoidance purposes

The IRS gives close scrutiny to exchanges between related parties because they can be used by taxpayers to evade taxes on gains.

Involuntary Conversions (Section 1033)

An involuntary conversion occurs when a taxpayer's property is lost, damaged, or destroyed, and the taxpayer receives an award, insurance money, or some other type of payment, as a result of:

- Casualty, disaster, or theft,
- Condemnation (or threat of condemnation).

Involuntary conversions can occur with business property as well as personal-use property, but the rules differ for each. Gain or loss from an involuntary conversion is usually recognized for tax purposes unless the property is a main home. A taxpayer reports the gain or deducts the loss in the year the gain or loss is realized. A taxpayer cannot deduct a loss from an involuntary conversion of personal-use property unless the loss resulted from a casualty or theft.

However, under section 1033, a taxpayer can elect to defer reporting gain on an involuntary conversion if he receives proceeds from insurance or another source and invests in property that is similar to the converted property.

Example: A hurricane destroys Denise's residential rental property that had an adjusted basis of $50,000. The insurance company gives Denise a check for $100,000, which is the FMV of the home. Denise buys a replacement rental property six months later for $100,000. Her gain on the involuntary conversion is $50,000 ($100,000 insurance settlement minus her $50,000 basis). However, Denise does not have to recognize any taxable gain because she reinvested all her insurance proceeds in another, similar property under a qualified 1033 exchange.

Replacement Period: The replacement period for an involuntary conversion generally ends two years after the end of the first tax year in which any part of the gain is realized.

Real property that is held for investment or used in a trade or business is allowed a three-year replacement period. The replacement period is four years for livestock that is involuntarily converted because of weather-related conditions.

Example: Barney owns a drywall repair business. On September 1, 2016, a flood destroys a storage shed filled with his supplies. Barney's insurance company reimburses him for the loss on October 26, 2016. He has until December 31, 2018 (two years) to replace the shed and supplies using the insurance proceeds. Barney is not required to report the insurance proceeds on his 2016 tax return. If he reinvests all the proceeds in a replacement property, he will not have any taxable gain.

Example: Lane and Candace are married and file jointly. They paid $100,000 for their home ten years ago. They receive an insurance payment of $700,000 after their home is destroyed in a mudslide, for a $600,000 gain on the conversion. They may exclude $500,000 of the gain under section 121, leaving $100,000 as taxable long-term capital gain. If they reinvest the insurance proceeds in a new home, under the rules for involuntary conversions, they may defer the remainder of the gain. If they choose not to reinvest the insurance proceeds, then they will be required to pay capital gains on $100,000.

If a main home is damaged or destroyed and is in a federally-declared disaster area, the replacement period is extended to four years. A five-year replacement period has been applied to certain extreme disaster areas, but only if the replacement property is purchased in the same area.

Property Type	Replacement Period
Most property except those noted below	Two years
Real property (real estate) that is held for investment or business use, such as residential rentals and office buildings	Three years
Sale of livestock due to weather-related conditions	Four years
Main home in federally-declared disaster area	Four to five years

If a taxpayer reinvests in replacement property similar to the converted property, the replacement property's basis is the same as the converted property's basis on the date of the conversion, subject to the following adjustments:

The basis is **decreased** by the following:

- Any loss a taxpayer recognizes on the involuntary conversion
- Any money a taxpayer receives that he does not spend on similar property

The basis is **increased** by the following:

- Any gain a taxpayer recognizes on the involuntary conversion
- Any additional costs of acquiring the replacement property

Example: Franco owns an apartment building in Texas with a basis of $250,000. He receives an insurance settlement of $400,000 after the building is destroyed by a tornado. A year later, Franco purchases another apartment building in Wisconsin for $380,000. Franco's realized gain on the involuntary conversion is $150,000 ($400,000 - $250,000 basis). He must recognize $20,000 of gain because he received an insurance payment of $400,000 but only spent $380,000 on the replacement property ($400,000 - $380,000). His basis in the new property is $250,000, which is calculated as the cost of the new property in Wisconsin minus the deferred gain ($380,000 - $130,000 = $250,000). If Franco had used all the insurance proceeds and invested it in the new property, he would not have to report any taxable gain.

Example: Paula paid $100,000 for a rental property five years ago. After factoring in her depreciation deductions, her adjusted basis in the property is $75,000 at the beginning of 2016. The property is insured for $300,000 and is destroyed by fire in June 2016. On December 15, 2016, Paula receives a $300,000 payment from her insurance company. Paula reinvests all the insurance proceeds, plus $5,000 more of her own savings, into a new rental property. She qualifies to defer all of her gain. Her basis in the new property is $80,000 ($75,000 + $5,000 of her additional investment).

Condemnations

A condemnation is a type of involuntary conversion. Condemnation is the process by which private property is taken from its owner for public use. The property may be taken by the government or by a private organization that has the legal power to seize it.

The owner generally receives a condemnation award (money or property) in exchange for the property that is taken. A condemnation is like a forced sale, with the owner being the seller and the government or other third party being the buyer.

Example: The local government informs Trevor that his farmland is being condemned to create a public park. Although Trevor does not want to sell his land, the government forces the sale and issues a condemnation award to Trevor, paying him the property's fair market value of $400,000. Trevor's basis in the farmland was $80,000. Trevor decides not to purchase replacement farmland. Therefore, he has a taxable event, and he must recognize $320,000 as income ($400,000 - $80,000 = $320,000). However, if Trevor were to purchase replacement property with the condemnation award, he would have a nontaxable section 1033 exchange.

Amounts taken out of a condemnation award to pay debts on the property are considered paid to the taxpayer and are included in the amount of the award.

Example: The state condemned Nhan's property in order to build a light rail system. The court award was set at $200,000. The state paid him only $148,000 because it paid $50,000 to his mortgage company and $2,000 in accrued real estate taxes. Nhan is considered to have received the entire $200,000 as a condemnation award.

The time period for replacing condemned property is the same as other qualified section 1033 exchanges, two years after the end of the first tax year in which any part of the gain on the condemnation is realized. For real property held for business use or investment, the replacement period is three years instead of two.

Example: Joel owns a pool hall. In February 2016, the building is condemned by the city because asbestos is discovered in the ceiling. He receives his condemnation award from his insurance company in May 2016. He has until December 31, 2019, to replace the condemned pool hall with a similar building. This is because the pool hall is business-related real estate, so Joel has three full years to reinvest the proceeds.

Condemnation of a Main Home: If a taxpayer has a gain because his main home is condemned, he can generally exclude the gain as if he had sold the home under the section 121 exclusion. Single filers can exclude up to $250,000 of the gain and joint filers up to $500,000. Any excess gains above these amounts may be potentially excludable under section 1033.

Unit 8: Study Questions

(Test yourself first, then check the correct answers at the end of this quiz.)

1. Christy exchanged a rental duplex with an adjusted basis of $160,000 for a rental house. The fair market value of the rental house she received was $200,000. She also received $10,000 of cash and paid $5,000 of exchange expenses. What is her recognized (taxable) gain on the transaction, if any?

A. $0
B. $5,000
C. $10,000
D. $45,000

2. Isaiah has lived in and owned his home for 15 months when he decides to move in with his girlfriend, so he sells his home for $285,000. His adjusted basis in the home is $160,000. What is the amount and nature of his taxable gain on the sale?

A. $0
B. $35,000 long-term capital gain.
C. $125,000 long-term capital gain.
D. $125,000 short-term capital gain.

3. Heather is single and bought her first home five years ago for $350,000. She lived continuously in the house until she sold it in 2016 for $620,000. Which of the following statements is correct?

A. She may exclude $250,000 of gain and report the remaining amount as a long-term capital gain.
B. She may exclude the entire gain. There is no amount that needs to be reported.
C. She may not exclude the gain.
D. She may exclude $250,000 of gain. The remaining amount must be reported as a short-term capital gain.

4. Which of the following transactions cannot qualify for a section 1031 like-kind exchange?

A. An exchange of a building in Manhattan for 20 acres of empty farmland.
B. An exchange of an apartment building in New Mexico for an office building in Alaska.
C. An exchange of a business computer for a business printer.
D. An exchange of inventory for different inventory.

5. Bob and Grace were married in January 2010. They purchased their first home together in March 2010 for $150,000. In February 2016, Bob and Grace legally separated, and the court granted Grace ownership of the home as part of the divorce settlement. The divorce became final in June 2016, and the fair market value of the home was $370,000 when ownership was transferred to Grace. She sells the house on December 23, 2016, for $480,000. What is Grace's taxable gain in the transaction?

A. $0
B. $80,000
C. $120,000
D. $210,000

6. Which of the following would not be an acceptable "unforeseen circumstance" for a taxpayer to take a reduced exclusion on the sale of his primary residence?

A. The home is condemned by the city.
B. A legal separation.
C. The birth of twin girls.
D. Moving to another state to be closer to grown children.

7. Lucille owns a home in the Vail ski area. She stays at the ski home most weekends and spends the entire months of December, January, and February there. When she is not at the ski home, she lives in a four-room apartment that she rents in Denver. What is Lucille's main home for purposes of the section 121 exclusion?

A. Her ski home in Vail.
B. Her apartment in Denver.
C. She is considered a transient for tax purposes.
D. None of the above.

8. Bailey exchanges his residential rental property with an adjusted basis of $50,000 and an FMV of $80,000 for a different rental property with an FMV of $70,000. What is Bailey's basis in the new property?

A. $50,000
B. $70,000
C. $80,000
D. $100,000

9. Aiden exchanges a residential rental property in Las Vegas with a basis of $100,000 for an investment property in Miami Beach valued at $220,000. Aiden also received $15,000 of cash boot in the exchange. What is Aiden's taxable gain on the exchange, if any, and what is his basis of the new property in Miami Beach?

A. Taxable gain: $15,000; basis: $115,000.
B. Taxable gain: $0; basis: $235,000.
C. Taxable gain: $15,000; basis: $135,000.
D. Taxable gain: $15,000; basis: $220,000.

10. Geoff sold his main home in 2016 at a $29,000 gain. He meets the ownership and use tests to exclude the gain from his income. However, he used one room of the home for business in 2014 and 2015. His records show he claimed $3,000 of depreciation for a home office. What is Geoff's taxable gain on the sale, if any?

A. $0
B. $1,000
C. $2,000
D. $3,000

11. A tornado destroyed Bryant's home on July 15, 2016. He wants to replace the home using a section 1033 exchange for involuntary conversions. What is the latest that Bryant can replace the property in order to defer any gain from his insurance reimbursement that was paid to him on August 23, 2016?

A. December 31, 2018
B. July 15, 2017
C. August 23, 2018
D. December 31, 2017

12. Jonah exchanged an empty lot that he held for investment for a rental building. The original cost of the empty lot was $16,000, and he had made $10,000 of improvements (such as permanent fencing) prior to the exchange. The fair market value of the rental building at the time of the exchange was $36,000. Jonah did not recognize any gain from the exchange. What is his basis in the new property?

A. $10,000
B. $16,000
C. $26,000
D. $36,000

13. Mitchell and Kay are married and file jointly. They owned and used their house as their main home for 15 months. Mitchell got a new job in another state, and they sold their home. What is the maximum amount they can exclude from income under the rules regarding a reduced exclusion?

A. $22,727
B. $250,000
C. $312,500
D. $500,000

14. Allen is a flight instructor. He trades in a small plane (adjusted basis $300,000) for another, larger plane (FMV $750,000) and pays $60,000 of cash in addition. He uses the plane 100% in his flight instruction business. What is his basis in the new plane?

A. $300,000
B. $360,000
C. $690,000
D. $750,000

15. Gino bought a house for $189,000 in July 2012. He lived there continuously for 13 months and then moved in with his girlfriend. They later separated, and Gino moved back into his own house and lived there for 12 months until he sold it in July 2016 for $220,000. What is the amount and nature of his gain?

A. Gino has no taxable gain because the sale qualifies for section 121 exclusion.
B. $31,000 long-term capital gain.
C. $31,000 short-term capital gain.
D. $30,000 long-term capital gain.

16. Katherine owns a yacht that she rents out for parties. Her purchase price was $150,000. A typhoon destroys the yacht in 2016. Katherine collects $175,000 from her insurance company and promptly reinvests all the proceeds in a larger, new yacht, which costs her $201,000. What is her basis in the new yacht?

A. $175,000
B. $176,000
C. $201,000
D. $226,000

17. Annalise sold her primary residence in Utah and moved to Iowa. She had purchased the house in 2001 for $200,000, and she sold it in 2016 for $550,000, net of selling expenses. During the time she lived in the house, she paid $25,000 for major improvements and $15,000 for general repairs. Assuming that Annalise utilizes the maximum available exclusion, what amount would she report as taxable gain?

A. $0
B. $60,000
C. $75,000
D. $100,000

18. Christian owned an office building with an adjusted basis of $400,000. The building was destroyed by a fire in 2016, and Christian received an insurance reimbursement of $600,000. He purchases a new office building for $450,000 and invests the rest of the insurance proceeds in stocks. Which of the following statements is correct?

A. He has $200,000 of taxable gain he must recognize on his tax return.
B. He has $150,000 of taxable gain he must recognize on his tax return.
C. He does not have a taxable gain.
D. He has $50,000 of taxable gain he must recognize on his tax return.

19. Shane and Phyllis moved after living in their home for 292 days because Phyllis became pregnant with triplets and they needed a larger home. The gain on the sale of the home is $260,000. Since they lived there for less than two years but meet one of the exceptions, what is the actual amount of their reduced exclusion? (Two years = 730 days).

A. $60,000
B. $200,000
C. $260,000
D. $500,000

20. Clayton trades farm land with an adjusted basis of $44,000 for a tractor with a fair market value of $77,000. What is the basis of the tractor and how much taxable gain, if any, must Clayton report?

A. $0 gain; $33,000 basis
B. $0 gain; $77,000 basis
C. $33,000 gain; $44,000 basis
D. $33,000 gain; $77,000 basis

Unit 8: Answers

1. The answer is B. Although the total gain on the transaction is $45,000, the recognized gain is only $5,000. The answer is calculated as follows:

FMV of like-kind property received	$200,000
Cash	10,000
Total received	210,000
Subtract: Exchange expenses paid	(5,000)
Amount realized	205,000
Subtract: Adjusted basis of property transferred	(160,000)
Realized Gain	$45,000
Cash received (boot)	$10,000
Subtract: Exchange expenses paid	(5,000)
Recognized (taxable) gain	**$5,000**

2. The answer is C. His gain is $125,000, the result of subtracting the adjusted basis in the home from the amount realized ($285,000 - $160,000 = $125,000). Since he does not meet the ownership or use tests or qualify for a reduced exclusion, he cannot exclude any of his gain under section 121, (because he hasn't lived in the house for 2 out of the last 5 years). He owned the property for more than a year, so the gain is taxed as a long-term capital gain.

3. The answer is A. As a single taxpayer; Heather may exclude a maximum gain amount of $250,000 from the sale of her home. Her gain is $270,000 ($620,000 - $350,000). Her taxable gain is $20,000 ($270,000 gain - $250,000 exclusion), which must be reported as a long-term capital gain.

4. The answer is D. Inventory never qualifies for like-kind exchange treatment. The property must not be held "primarily for sale", such as merchandise, retail stock, or inventory. Generally, real property exchanges will qualify for like-kind treatment, even though the properties themselves might be dissimilar. Business computers and printers are in the same asset class, so that exchange is valid.

5. The answer is B. Grace meets the ownership and use tests, and the basis in the property remains the same. Property transfers related to a divorce are nontaxable, and the FMV of the property at the time of the divorce has no bearing on the taxable outcome. Since she owned the property for longer than one year, the taxable portion of Grace's gain would be reported as a long-term capital gain. The gain is calculated as follows:

Original cost	$150,000
Sale price	480,000
Total realized gain	330,000
Section 121 exclusion	-250,000
Taxable gain	$80,000

6. The answer is D. The move to be closer to grown children would not qualify. All of the following events would be qualifying events in order to claim a reduced exclusion from a premature sale:

- A divorce or legal separation
- A pregnancy resulting in multiple births or serious health issues
- The home is sold after being seized or condemned
- A move due to a new job or new employment

If any of these exceptions apply, the taxpayer may figure a reduced exclusion based on the number of days he owned and lived in the residence.

7. The answer is B. Lucille's main home is her rental apartment in Denver because she lives there most of the time. If she were to sell the ski home, she would not qualify for the section 121 exclusion on the sale because it is a vacation home and not her primary residence.

8. The answer is A. His basis in the new property is the same as the basis of the property given up: $50,000.

9. The answer is A. Aiden's total gain on the exchange is $135,000 ($220,000 value of new property + $15,000 cash - $100,000 basis in the old property). However, only the cash boot received is taxable. Aiden's basis in the new building is $115,000 (the original basis in the property he gave up plus the gain recognized as a result of the boot received).

10. The answer is D. Geoff can exclude $26,000 ($29,000 - $3,000) of his gain. He has a taxable gain of $3,000. He must report the depreciation recapture as ordinary income. If a taxpayer took depreciation deductions because he used his home for business purposes or as a rental property, he cannot exclude the part of the gain equal to any depreciation allowed as a deduction.

11. The answer is A. Bryant must acquire qualifying replacement property by December 31, 2018 (*two* years from the *end* of the tax year during which any part of the gain is realized.) Since Bryant received the reimbursement check in 2016, he has 2 years from December 31, 2016, to acquire replacement property. Different types of property have different replacement periods. For example, if Bryant's main home had been located in a federally-declared disaster area, he could have had four years to replace the property.

12. The answer is C. The basis in the new building is the same as his basis in the empty lot. The $10,000 spent on improvements is added to the $16,000 cost, so the adjusted basis of the relinquished empty lot was $26,000. Therefore, this is his basis in the new property, as well. The fair market value is irrelevant in this calculation.

13. The answer is C. A reduced exclusion is available, even though the taxpayers did not live in the home for two full years. They qualify for a reduced exclusion because they are moving for a change in Mitchell's employment. Their maximum reduced exclusion is $312,500 ($500,000 × [15 months/24 months]). The reduced exclusion applies when the premature sale is primarily due to a move for employment in a new location.

14. The answer is B. Allen's basis is $360,000: the $300,000 basis of the old plane plus the $60,000 cash paid. The fair market value of the property has no bearing on Allen's basis in the new property.

15. The answer is A. This sale qualifies for section 121 treatment. Gino meets the ownership and use tests because, during the five-year period ending on the date of sale, he owned the house for three years and lived in it for a total of 25 months (over 2 years). The gain is not taxable and does not need to be reported.

16. The answer is B. Since Katherine purchased replacement property, the basis of the replacement property is the cost of the new yacht ($201,000) minus her deferred gain ($25,000), or $176,000. The deferred gain of $25,000 is calculated as follows: Insurance proceeds of $175,000 minus the cost of the old yacht of $150,000. Alternatively, the basis of the replacement property could be determined as follows: Basis of the old yacht ($150,000) plus cash paid in excess of insurance proceeds ($201,000 - $175,000 = $26,000).

17. The answer is C. Annalise's adjusted basis in the house would be the total of her original purchase price of $200,000 and the $25,000 cost of improvements. The cost of repairs would not be considered in determining her adjusted basis. Therefore, her gain on the sale would be $325,000, or the excess of her net proceeds over her adjusted basis. Since she met the requirements for ownership and use of the house as her primary residence, she qualifies for the maximum exclusion of $250,000 available to a single taxpayer, and the taxable portion of her gain would be $75,000.

Purchase price of house	$200,000
Cost of improvements	25,000
Adjusted basis	225,000
Net proceeds of sale	**$550,000**
Gain on sale	325,000
Exclusion for single taxpayer	(250,000)
Taxable gain	**$75,000**

18. The answer is B. Christian's realized gain is $200,000 ($600,000 - $400,000) and his taxable gain is $150,000. He purchased another building for $450,000, so he may defer $50,000 of the gain under section 1033 for involuntary conversions. The remainder of the gain, $150,000 ($600,000 - $450,000), must be recognized because he did not reinvest the remaining proceeds in like-kind property. If Christian had reinvested all the proceeds in the new building, his entire gain would have been deferred.

19. The answer is B. The couple has a reduced exclusion of $200,000 (292/730 multiplied by the $500,000 maximum exclusion available for married taxpayers). The remaining $60,000 would be considered taxable capital gain income and would be reported on Schedule D. This move qualifies for the reduced exclusion because multiple births from the same pregnancy are considered an unforeseen circumstance.

20. The answer is D. This is a taxable exchange of property that is not similar. Clayton must report $33,000 of gain, the difference between the adjusted basis of the farmland and the FMV of the tractor ($77,000 minus $44,000). The basis of property received in a taxable exchange is generally its FMV at the time of the exchange.

Unit 9: Rental and Royalty Income

For additional information read:
Publication 527, *Residential Rental Property*
Publication 946, *How to Depreciate Property*
Publication 525, *Taxable and Nontaxable Income*

Rental income is any payment received for the use or occupation of property. In most cases, taxpayers must include amounts received as rent in their gross income.

Property owners can deduct the expenses of managing, conserving, and maintaining their rental properties. Common rental expenses include:

- Mortgage interest and property taxes
- Maintenance, repairs, and cleaning fees
- Advertising
- Utilities
- Insurance
- Depreciation

Advance Rent: Taxpayers must report rental income when it is constructively received, i.e. available without restrictions. This includes advance rent, which is any amount received before the period that it covers. Thus, a taxpayer must include advance rent in income in the year he receives it, regardless of the period covered or the accounting method used.

Example: Gene rents out a duplex. On December 20, 2016, his tenant pays two months of rent in advance for January and February because she is leaving town on vacation. Gene cannot delay reporting of the income. He must report all the advance rent as taxable income in 2016 (when he received it), not in 2017.

Lease Cancellation: If a tenant pays to cancel a lease, the amount received for the cancellation is rental income. The payment is included in the year received regardless of the taxpayer's accounting method.

Security Deposits: A security deposit is not considered income upon initial receipt if the deposit is refundable to the tenant at the end of the lease. However, if the taxpayer keeps the security deposit because the tenant did not live up to the terms of the lease or because he damaged property, the deposit amount is recognized as income in the year it is forfeited by the tenant.

Insurance Premiums Paid in Advance: If a cash-basis taxpayer pays an insurance premium for more than one year in advance, he can deduct only the part of the premium payment that applies to that year. He cannot deduct the total premium in the year he pays it.

Local Benefit Taxes: In most cases, a taxpayer cannot deduct charges for local taxes that increase the value of a rental property, such as assessments for streets, sidewalks, or water and sewer systems. These charges are nondepreciable capital expenditures that must be added to the basis of the property. Only taxes to maintain or repair such infrastructure, or to pay interest charges related to financing its construction, can be deducted.

Property or Services in Lieu of Rent: If a taxpayer receives property or services as payment for rent instead of cash, the fair market value must be recognized as rental income. If the tenant and landlord agree in advance to a price, the agreed-upon price is deemed the fair market value unless there is evidence to the contrary.

Example: Beth owns an apartment complex. Beth's tenant, Chris, is a professional chimney sweep. Chris offers to clean all of Beth's chimneys in her apartment building instead of paying three months' rent in cash. Beth accepts Chris's offer. Beth must recognize income for the amount Chris would have paid for three months' rent. However, Beth can deduct that same amount as a business expense for maintenance of the property.

If a tenant pays expenses on behalf of the landlord, the landlord must recognize the payments as rental income. The landlord can deduct the expenses as rental expenses.

Example: Rosetta owns an apartment building. While she is out of town, the furnace in the apartment building breaks down. Kerry, Rosetta's tenant, pays for the emergency repairs out-of-pocket and deducts the furnace repair bill from his rent payment. Rosetta must recognize as rental income both the actual amount of rent received in cash from Kerry and the amount he paid for the repairs. Rosetta can deduct the cost of the furnace repair as a rental expense.

Vacant Property: A taxpayer cannot deduct any loss of rental income for the period a property is vacant. However, if the taxpayer is actively trying to rent the property, he can deduct ordinary and necessary expenses as soon as the property is made available for rent.

Example: Rodrigo purchased a rental property and made the property available for rent on March 1, 2016, by advertising it in the local newspaper. He found a tenant who moved in on June 1, 2016. Even though the rental was unoccupied from March through May, Rodrigo can still deduct the mortgage interest and other expenses related to the property during that period, because the property was available and advertised to rent.

Depreciation of Rental Property: A taxpayer begins to claim deductions for depreciation of a rental property when he places it in service for the production of income. Rental property is considered "placed in service" when it is ready and available for rent. Depreciation ends when a taxpayer has either fully recovered his cost or other basis, or when the property is retired from service, whichever happens first.

Three basic factors determine how much depreciation a taxpayer can deduct:

- Basis
- Recovery period for the property
- Depreciation method used, including certain conventions

The cost of land is never depreciated because land does not wear out, become obsolete, or get used up. For a personal residence that is later converted to rental property, the depreciable basis is the lower of:

- The taxpayer's adjusted basis in the property, or
- The fair market value of the property at the time of conversion.

Most residential rental buildings are depreciated over 27.5 years, and nonresidential buildings are generally depreciated over 39 years.

Example: In 2016, Shannon buys a rental property for $200,000. It has an assessed value of $160,000, of which $136,000 is for the house, and $24,000 is for the land. Shannon can allocate 85% ($136,000 ÷ $160,000) of the purchase price to the house and 15% ($24,000 ÷ $160,000) of the purchase price to the land. Therefore, her basis in the house is $170,000 (85% of $200,000) and her basis in the land is $30,000 (15% of $200,000). Shannon may use $170,000 as her basis for depreciation on the property.

Example: A residential rental building with a cost basis of $137,500 would generate depreciation of $5,000 per year ($137,500/27.5 years).

Example: Five years ago, Lance purchased a home for $180,000. On the date of purchase, the assessed value of the land was $30,000. After living in the home for five years, Lance converted it to a rental property on April 1, 2016. Since land is not depreciable, Lance includes only the cost of the house when calculating his basis for depreciation. The allocated cost of the house is $150,000 ($180,000 - $30,000). In 2016, the county assessor's office assigned the home an FMV of $185,000, of which $40,000 was for land and $145,000 for the house. The basis for depreciation of the house is the FMV on the date of conversion ($145,000) because it is less than Lance's allocated cost ($150,000). Lance uses $145,000 to calculate depreciation, which is reported on Schedule E, *Supplemental Income and Loss (From rental real estate, royalties, partnerships, S corporations, estates, trusts, REMICs, etc.).*

Repairs vs. Improvements to Rental Property

A taxpayer can currently deduct the cost of repairs to rental property, but cannot currently deduct the cost of improvements. Instead, the taxpayer must recover the cost of an improvement by taking depreciation deductions over its applicable recovery period.

A repair generally keeps an asset or property in good working condition, but does not add to the value of the asset or substantially prolong its life. Repainting, fixing leaks, and replacing broken windows are examples of repairs.

Example #1: Keith owns a rental home. A baseball broke a window, so he replaced it with an upgraded model, an insulated double-pane window that helps control heating and cooling costs. Even though this window is a substantial upgrade from the previous one, it is still considered a repair, because the old window was broken and needed to be replaced. If Keith were to replace all the windows in the house, the upgrade would be considered an improvement, and he would be required to capitalize the cost and claim depreciation deductions over a period of years.

Example #2: Keith also replaces the entire roof at the cost of $17,000. This is considered a substantial improvement, and the cost of the roof must be depreciated over time rather than deducted against current income.

Note: In September 2013, the IRS released its final tangible property regulations, a highly complex set of rules governing repairs and capitalization that affect all taxpayers who use tangible property in their businesses. These rules change the way businesses treat expenditures for tangible property. For the EA exam, most of the specific details of these regulations will likely not be tested. However, you should have a general understanding of the concept that a business may recover the costs of property either through current deductions or through periodic depreciation deductions for items required to be capitalized.

Under a safe harbor rule of the tangible property regulations,[25] materials and supplies costing no more than $2,500[26] are generally deductible in the year they are used or consumed.

[25] The tangible property regulations are covered in more detail in Book 2, *Businesses*. For Part 1 of the exam, you may have to know how these new regulations apply to rental property.

An improvement is anything that results in the betterment of a property, restoration of a property, or adaptation of a property to a new or different use. Examples include:

- Additions of an extra bedroom, bathroom, deck, or garage
- The installation of a new roof
- Installation of central air conditioning, new plumbing, wall-to-wall carpeting, or upgraded wiring
- Construction of a retaining wall, fence, or swimming pool

Example: Glenna owns a rental property. In 2016, she spent $8,000 to replace the carpet, $6,540 to pave the driveway, and $175 to repair a couple of broken gutters. Only the gutter repair ($175) can be expensed on her 2016 tax return. The costs of the new carpet and the new driveway must be capitalized and depreciated over time.

The capitalized cost of an improvement is depreciated separately from the original cost of the asset or property that is being improved.

Rental Rules

The tax treatment of rental income, expenses, and losses depends on several factors: whether a taxpayer is a real estate professional or actively manages a property; whether there is any personal use of the rental property, and if so, whether the dwelling is considered a home; and whether the rental activity is for profit. We will briefly review the rules related to each of these situations next.

The Special $25,000 Loss Allowance for Rental Activity

The deductibility of losses from passive activities is limited, and a taxpayer usually cannot deduct losses from passive activities to offset his nonpassive income (such as wages). In general, a trade or business activity is considered a passive activity if the taxpayer does not *materially participate* in it. A taxpayer materially participates in an activity if he is involved in the operation of that activity on a regular, continuous, and substantial basis.

Generally, losses from passive activities that exceed income from passive activities in the same year are disallowed. The disallowed losses are carried forward to the next taxable year and can be used to offset future income from passive activities.

The passive activity loss rules for taxpayers involved in rental activities are an exception, as most rental activities are considered passive activities, even if the taxpayer does materially participate in them. However, when a taxpayer *actively participates* in a rental real estate activity, he may be able to deduct up to $25,000 of losses against his nonpassive income. It should be noted that active participation is a different, and less stringent, standard than material participation.

Note: Active participation is not the same thing as material participation. Material participation is a much stricter standard. For example, the owner of a rental property will generally be treated as actively participating if he makes management decisions such as approving new tenants, deciding rental contracts, approving repairs, and other similar management decisions.

[26] Effective for taxable years beginning on or after January 1, 2016, the Internal Revenue Service in Notice 2015-82 increased the de minimis safe harbor threshold from $500 to $2,500 per invoice or item for taxpayers without applicable financial statements.

In order to actively participate, a taxpayer must own at least 10% of the rental property and must make management decisions in a significant and bona fide way, such as approving new tenants and establishing the rental terms.

Example: Theodore owns a residential rental property in San Diego, California. He also lives in San Diego and has a regular job that he works full time. Theodore actively manages his rental by choosing his own tenants, hiring workers to do any required repairs, and collecting the rent. Theodore is actively participating in this rental activity.

Note: If the IRS determines a taxpayer has not actively participated, rental losses are not currently deductible, and he is not eligible for the special $25,000 loss allowance.

Example: Toni owns a rental property in Hawaii. She lives in Nevada. Toni hired a management company to manage the property and screen new tenants. The management company handles all the repairs and collects the rent. The management company charges a fee for its services and then remits the net proceeds to Toni monthly. It has been several years since Toni has visited the property. Toni is not actively participating in this rental activity. She is not eligible for the special $25,000 loss allowance.

The full $25,000 loss allowance is available for taxpayers, whether single or MFJ, whose modified adjusted gross income (MAGI) is $100,000 or less. If a taxpayer is married and files a separate return, but lived apart from his spouse for the entire tax year, the taxpayer's special allowance for rental losses cannot exceed $12,500; this full allowance would be available if his MAGI is $50,000 or less. However, if the taxpayer lived with his spouse at any time during the year and is filing MFS, the taxpayer cannot use any of his passive rental losses to offset nonpassive income.

Rental losses that cannot be deducted due to the limitations described above can be carried forward indefinitely and used in subsequent years, subject to the same limitations.

Example: Philip and Susanne own a residential rental property that they manage themselves. In 2016, they have wages of $98,000 and a rental loss of $26,800. Because they meet both the active participation and the MAGI tests, they are allowed to deduct $25,000 of the rental loss as an offset to their nonpassive income (wages). The remaining amount over the $25,000 limit ($1,800) that cannot be deducted in the current year is carried forward and may be used in the following year.

For every $2 by which a taxpayer's MAGI exceeds $100,000, the allowance is reduced by $1. If MAGI is $150,000 or more (or $75,000 or more if married filing separately), the $25,000 allowance is fully phased out.

Example: Hal and Lorena file jointly and have MAGI of $140,000. They have $25,000 of losses from the residential rental property that they actively manage. Because they actively manage the property, they potentially qualify to deduct up to $25,000 of losses against their nonpassive income. However, because their joint income is over $100,000, they are subject to the phase-out. Therefore, Hal and Lorena's deduction for rental losses is reduced by $20,000 (0.5 × ($140,000 - $100,000). They can deduct $5,000 ($25,000 - $20,000) against their nonpassive income. The additional $20,000 of losses is carried forward to the following year.

Definition: MAGI is a taxpayer's adjusted gross income with certain deductions added back in. These may include IRA contributions, rental losses, student loan interest, and qualified tuition expenses, among others. A taxpayer's MAGI is used as a basis for determining whether he qualifies for certain tax deductions.

Example: Kendrick owns a rental property in San Francisco. He actively participates in the rental activity. In the previous tax year, he incurred $9,000 in losses on his rental. Kendrick's modified adjusted gross income was $150,000 in that year. Because of his income threshold, Kendrick's rental losses are suspended, and he is not allowed to deduct any rental losses. The following year, (2016) Kendrick had $5,000 in losses from his rental activity. However, he also changed jobs in the middle of the year, and now his AGI is lower. In 2016, Kendrick's AGI is $85,000, so his rental losses are now allowable. His suspended rental losses from the prior year ($9,000) and his current year losses ($5,000) will be allowed on his 2016 tax return, for a total deduction of $14,000.

Exception for Real Estate Professionals

If a taxpayer qualifies as a real estate professional, losses from rental real estate activities in which he materially participates are not considered passive activity losses and are fully deductible.[27] If the tests for material participation are not met, rental losses are considered passive and are normally deductible only up to $25,000, based upon the passive activity rules outlined previously.

In most instances, if a property owner provides only basic services to tenants, such as trash collection, he reports rental income and expenses on Schedule E, Form 1040. It is not subject to self-employment tax.

In contrast, owners of property who provide significant services to the renter, such as maid cleaning and housekeeping services, are generally required to report revenue and expenses related to the property on Schedule C, *Profit of Loss from Business,* and any net profit is subject to self-employment tax. The most common examples of taxpayers who report their rental activities on Schedule C, instead of on Schedule E, are hotel owners and motel operators.

Example: Joseph owns two residential rental properties and provides basic services to his tenants. He manages them and collects rents. He also has a full-time job as a restaurant manager. He is not a real estate professional. Joseph must report his rental income and losses on Schedule E. His rental income is considered passive activity income, and it is not subject to self-employment tax.

Example: Sabi owns a small motel in downtown Cincinnati. Sabi does not offer long-term rentals. The hotel offers full maid service, cleaning, and breakfast daily. Since she provides "significant services" as a motel owner, the income would be treated as self-employment income, rather than rental income. Sabi would report her income on Schedule C.

[27] The determination of whether someone is a "real estate professional" is based on a number of factors. In general, a taxpayer qualifies as a real estate professional if he performs more than 750 hours of services during the taxable year in real property trades or businesses in which he materially participates and more than one-half of the total personal services performed in trades or businesses by the taxpayer during the year are performed in real property trades or businesses in which the taxpayer materially participates.

Not Rented for Profit

A taxpayer who does not rent his property to make a profit can deduct rental expenses only up to the amount of his rental income. The IRS calls this a "not-for-profit rental." He cannot deduct a loss or carry forward to the next year any rental expenses that are more than his rental income for the year. The taxpayer reports the rental income on Form 1040; if he itemizes deductions, he can deduct expenses for mortgage interest and real estate taxes on Schedule A. He can also report his other rental expenses as miscellaneous itemized deductions on Schedule A, but the deductibility is subject to the 2% floor.

The IRS will presume a taxpayer is renting property to make a profit if his rental income is greater than his rental expenses for at least three out of five years.

If a taxpayer is just starting his rental activity and does not have three years showing a profit, he can elect to postpone the determination of whether the rental is for profit by filing Form 5213, *Election to Postpone Determination as to Whether the Presumption Applies that an Activity is Engaged in for Profit.* This gives the taxpayer five years to determine whether his rental is for profit or not for profit.

Renting Part of Property

A taxpayer who rents part of a property must divide certain expenses between the part of the property used for rental purposes and the part used for personal purposes, as though there were actually two separate pieces of property. Expenses related to the part of the property used for rental purposes can be deducted as rental expenses on Schedule E. This includes a portion of expenses that normally are nondeductible personal expenses, such as painting the outside of a house. If an expense applies to both rental use and personal use, such as a heating bill for the entire house, the taxpayer must divide the expense between the two. The two most common methods for dividing such expenses are based on:

- The number of rooms in the house, and
- The square footage of the house.

Example: Pablo rents out a bedroom in his house. The room is 12 × 15 feet or 180 square feet. Pablo's entire house, including this room, is 1,800 square feet. Pablo can deduct as a rental expense 10% of any expense that must be divided between rental use and personal use. Pablo's 2016 heating bills for the entire house totaled $600, and therefore $60 ($600 × .10) can be considered a deductible rental expense. The balance, $540, is a personal expense that Pablo cannot deduct.

A common situation involves a duplex in which the landlord lives in one side and rents out the other. Certain expenses, like mortgage interest and real estate taxes, apply to the entire property and must be split to determine rental and personal expenses.

Example: Gillian owns a duplex with two units of the same size. She lives in one side and rents out the other. In 2016, Gillian paid $12,000 of mortgage interest and $4,000 of real estate taxes for the entire property. Gillian can deduct $6,000 of mortgage interest and $2,000 of real estate taxes on Schedule E. She can claim the other $6,000 of mortgage interest and $2,000 of real estate taxes attributable to her personal use on Schedule A as itemized deductions.

If a taxpayer owns a partial interest in rental property, he can deduct expenses paid according to the percentage of ownership.

Personal Use of Dwelling Unit

When a taxpayer has a residence (whether a main home or a second home) that is used personally at certain times and rented out at other times, he must divide his expenses between rental use and personal use. Rental expenses generally will be no more than a taxpayer's total expenses multiplied by the following fraction: the denominator is the total number of days the dwelling is used, and the numerator is the total number of days actually rented at a fair rental price.

Any day the unit is rented at a fair rental price is a day of rental use. Any day the unit is available for rent but not actually rented is not a day of rental use.

Example: Carol owns a vacation home in Hawaii that she rented for 90 days in January, February, and March. She can deduct the rental expenses on Schedule E only for those 90 days. However, she can deduct expenses for mortgage interest and real estate taxes for the other 275 days of the year on her Schedule A.

If a taxpayer uses a property for both rental and personal purposes, the tax treatment of expenses depends on whether his personal use is considered to be usage as a "home". It is considered usage as a home if he uses the property for personal purposes during the year for more than the greater of fourteen days, or 10% of the total days it is rented at a fair rental price. Days of personal use are counted when:

- A member of the taxpayer's family uses the property without paying a fair rental price.
- Anyone uses the property at less than fair rental price.
- Use of the property is donated to a charitable organization.

However, any day the taxpayer spends working on repairs and maintaining the property is not counted as personal use, even if his family is also staying there.

Example: Mike owns a mountain cabin at Lake Tahoe that was used as follows in 2016: He rented it for 60 days during the ski season, spent a week at the cabin cleaning and making repairs before the rental period began, and donated a week of rental use to a local charity. In apportioning expenses:

- 7/67 days would be treated as personal use (for use by the charity); expenses such as mortgage interest and property taxes would be deductible in this ratio on Schedule A.
- The remaining 60/67 days would be treated as rental use, and this fraction of total expenses incurred would be deductible on Schedule E.
- The seven days cleaning and making repairs would not count as either personal or rental use for purposes of allocating expenses.

Mike's cabin is not considered a "home" because his personal use was less than 14 days and less than 10% of the total days it was rented.

Renting a dwelling unit that is also used by the taxpayer for personal purposes during the year is not considered a passive activity. If a taxpayer's rental expenses are more than his rental income, he cannot use the excess expenses to offset income from other sources. However, excess deductions may be carried forward to the next year and treated as rental expenses for the same property, subject to the same limits.

Example: Jack owns a condo on Hilton Head Island. He uses it as a personal residence four months out of the year and rents it out to tenants the rest of the year. Jack's rental income is $8,000 in 2016, and his rental expenses are $10,000. Jack cannot deduct the full $10,000 of rental expenses, but he can carry over the remaining $2,000 and deduct that amount from future rental income on the condo.

Minimal Rental Use (15 Day Rule)

If a taxpayer rents a main home or vacation home for fewer than 15 days, he does not have to recognize any of the income as taxable. He also cannot deduct any rental expenses. This is called the "15-day rule."

Example: Brynn owns a condo on the Gulf Coast which is her personal residence. While she was away on vacation, she rented her condo for 11 days, charging $100 per day for a total of $1,100. She also had $320 of rental expenses during that time. Brynn does not report any of the income or expenses based on the exception for minimal rental use.

Converting to Rental Use: If a taxpayer changes a main home or second home to rental use at any time other than the beginning of a tax year, he must divide his expenses between rental use and personal use. He can deduct as rental expenses only the portion that is for the part of the year the property was used or held for rental purposes.

For depreciation purposes, the property is treated as being placed in service on the conversion date. When a taxpayer converts property held for personal use to rental use, the basis for depreciation will be the lesser of fair market value or his adjusted basis on the date of conversion.

Royalty Income

Like rental income, royalty income is reported on line 17 of Form 1040. Royalties from copyrights, patents, and oil, gas, and mineral properties are taxable as ordinary income.

In many cases, a taxpayer reports details of royalties on Schedule E, *Supplemental Income and Loss*. However, self-employed writers, musicians, and inventors report income on Schedule C, *Profit or Loss from Business,* and are subject to self-employment tax.

Example: In 2016, Don's brother died. Don inherited a copyright from his brother, who had written an instruction manual for woodworking. Don then leased the copyrighted material to schools and colleges for their use. Since he had not created the copyright himself, Don will report the royalty income on Schedule E.

Royalties from copyrights on literary, musical, or artistic works, or from patents on inventions, are paid to a taxpayer for the right to use his work over a specified period of time. Royalties are often based on the number of units sold, such as the number of books, tickets to a performance, or machines sold.

Example: Marisa is the self-employed author of a popular series of books for young children. She receives royalties from her publisher based on the number of books she has sold over a certain period of time. Marisa must report these royalties as taxable income on her Schedule C.

A taxpayer is required to issue Form 1099-MISC, *Miscellaneous Income,* to each person to whom he has paid at least $10 of royalties for the year.

Unit 9: Study Questions

(Test yourself first, then check the correct answers at the end of this quiz.)

1. Ian signs a three-year lease to rent a building he owns. In December 2016, he receives $12,000 for the first year's rent and $12,000 as rent for the last year of the lease. He also receives a $1,500 security deposit that is refundable at the end of the lease. How much rental income must Ian include in his 2016 tax return?

A. $1,500
B. $12,000
C. $24,000
D. $25,500

2. In 2016, Jane is single and has $40,000 of wages, $2,000 of passive activity income from a limited partnership, and $3,500 of passive activity loss from a rental real estate activity in which she actively participated. Which of the following statements is correct?

A. The first $2,000 of Jane's $3,500 passive loss offsets her passive income. Jane can deduct the remaining $1,500 loss to reduce taxation of her wages.
B. Jane cannot deduct the passive loss to reduce taxation of her wages.
C. Jane cannot offset the rental loss against the passive income from the partnership because it is not the same type of passive activity.
D. Jane must carry over her loss to the subsequent tax year.

3. Rosemary's home is used exclusively as her residence all year, except for 13 days. During this time, Rosemary rents her home to alumni while the local college has its homecoming celebration. She made $3,000 of rental income and had $500 of rental expenses during this 13 day period. Which of the following statements is correct?

A. All of the rental income may be excluded.
B. Rosemary can exclude only $2,500 of the rental income.
C. Rosemary can deduct her rental expenses when she reports her rental income on Schedule E.
D. Rosemary must recognize all $3,000 of rental income, and she can deduct the $500 in expenses on Schedule E.

4. Pam ordered a heating, ventilating, and air conditioning (HVAC) unit for her rental property on November 15, 2016. It was delivered on December 28, 2016, and was installed and ready for use on January 2, 2017. She paid for the unit using a credit card and paid off the card on February 2, 2017. In which month should the HVAC unit be considered placed in service for depreciation purposes?

A. November 2016
B. December 2016
C. January 2017
D. February 2017

5. Reba converted her primary residence to rental use during the year. Her original cost was $189,000, of which $13,200 was allocated to the land and $175,800 was to the house. On the date of the conversion, the property had a fair market value of $158,000, of which $11,000 was allocable to the land and $147,000 to the house. What is Reba's basis for depreciation on Schedule E?

A. $147,000
B. $189,000
C. $175,800
D. $158,000

6. Nicklaus decides to convert his residence to rental property. He moves out of his home in May 2016 and starts renting it on June 1, 2016. He has $12,000 of mortgage interest for the year. How should Nicklaus report his mortgage interest expense?

A. Report the entire $12,000 on Schedule E.
B. Report the entire $12,000 on Schedule A.
C. Report $7,000 on Schedule E as interest expense and $5,000 on Schedule A as mortgage interest.
D. Report $8,000 on Schedule E as interest expense and $4,000 on Schedule A as mortgage interest.

7. Which of the following costs related to rental property should be classified as a capital improvement and depreciated rather than being expensed currently?

A. Replacing an entire deck.
B. Repairing a broken toilet.
C. Painting the family room.
D. Patching a hole in the wall.

8. Which of the following describes depreciation?

A. A business expense that applies only to rental properties.
B. An improvement to an asset that must be capitalized.
C. A common type of accounting method used by most partnerships.
D. An annual tax deduction that accounts for the reduction in the value of an asset as it ages.

9. Tina owns a residential rental house. Last year, she paid $968 to repair a broken window. The cost of the labor was $468, and the cost of the replacement window was $500. She replaced the broken window with a premium energy-saving window. What is the correct treatment of this expense?

A. She cannot deduct the cost since it was an improvement; she must add it to the basis of the property.
B. She can deduct $468 as a rental expense on Schedule E (the labor cost). The cost of the actual window ($500) must be capitalized and depreciated.
C. She can deduct the entire $968 as a rental expense on Schedule E.
D. She can deduct $968 on Schedule A as an itemized deduction.

10. In 2016, Travis and Brittany moved to Florida. They decided to rent their house in California instead of selling it. They had purchased the home five years ago for $500,000 and had paid $80,000 for various improvements through the years. The purchase price of $500,000 was attributable to fair market values of $100,000 for the land and $400,000 for the house. Their new tenant paid a refundable security deposit of $6,000 and moved in on July 1, 2016. The FMV of the property on July 1 was $525,000, comprised of $105,000 for the land and $420,000 for the house. The tenant then paid rent of $3,000 each month from July through December of 2016. Travis and Brittany incurred the following expenses in 2016 related to the house:

- Mortgage interest: $10,000
- Property taxes: $10,000
- Casualty insurance: $1,000

In addition, they paid $500 for repairs during December. Exclusive of depreciation expense, what was Travis and Brittany's taxable rental income?

A. $1,500
B. $7,000
C. $7,250
D. $13,000

11. Based upon the information in the previous question, what is the amount of basis on which depreciation should be calculated for the rental period?

A. $400,000
B. $480,000
C. $580,000
D. $420,000

12. Matt and Diane are legally separated and have lived in separate residences for three years. They file separate tax returns (MFS). They own a rental property jointly, actively participate in the rental activity, and share income and losses equally. The rental property had $30,000 of losses during the year. Matt has wage income of $48,000 in 2016. He has no other items of income or loss. What is the maximum amount of rental losses that Matt can claim on his separate return?

A. $0
B. $12,500
C. $15,000
D. $25,000

13. All of the following statements about not-for-profit rentals are correct except:

A. Rental losses cannot be carried forward to the next year.
B. A taxpayer with a not-for-profit rental can deduct rental expenses only up to the amount of his rental income.
C. Profit is determined when rental income is greater than rental expenses for four out of five years.
D. A taxpayer with a new rental may elect to postpone the determination of whether the activity is for profit or not for profit for five years.

Unit 9: Answers

1. The answer is C. Ian must include $24,000 in his income in the first year. He must recognize all the advance rent as income in the year of receipt. The security deposit does not have to be recognized as income because it is refundable to the tenant.

2. The answer is A. Jane can use $2,000 of her rental loss to offset the passive activity income from the limited partnership. The remaining $1,500 loss can be offset against her $40,000 of wages. A taxpayer can deduct up to $25,000 per year of losses for rental real estate activities in which she actively participates, so long as their modified AGI does not exceed a certain amount. This special allowance is an exception to the general rule disallowing losses in excess of income from passive activities against non-passive income.

3. The answer is A. All the rental income may be excluded under the "15-day rule." The home is primarily for personal use, and a rental period of less than 15 days is disregarded, which means the IRS does not consider it a rental. The rental income is not taxable, but the rental expenses (such as utilities or maintenance costs) are not deductible.

4. The answer is C. Depreciation begins on the placed-in-service date when an asset becomes available for use. Typically, the placed-in-service date and the purchase date are the same, but that is not always necessarily the case. Since Pam did not have the HVAC unit ready for use until January 2, 2017, she must wait until 2017 to begin depreciating the unit. The fact that the unit was paid for with a credit card is irrelevant (it is treated the same as if it was paid by check or cash).

5. The answer is A. When a taxpayer converts property held for personal use to rental use (for example, the rental of a former home), the basis for depreciation will be the lesser of fair market value or adjusted basis on the date of conversion. The basis for depreciation on the house is its fair market value on the date of the conversion ($147,000) because the FMV on the date of conversion is less than the amount of her original cost that was allocable to the house ($175,800).

6. The answer is C. Nicklaus must allocate his expenses between personal use and rental use. He can deduct as rental expenses seven-twelfths (7/12) of annual expenses, such as taxes and insurance. Starting in June, he can deduct as rental expenses the amounts he paid for items generally billed monthly, such as utilities. When figuring depreciation, he should treat the property as placed in service on June 1.

7. The answer is A. The replacement of the deck would be considered a depreciable improvement. The other choices are repairs and may be deducted as current expenses.

8. The answer is D. Depreciation is an income tax deduction that allows a business to recover the cost or basis of property it uses over time. It is an annual allowance for the wear and tear, deterioration, or obsolescence of assets.

9. The answer is C. Generally, the expenses of renting a property, such as maintenance, insurance, taxes, and interest, can be deducted from rental income. This cost is a repair, not an improvement because the window was broken. If all the windows had been replaced with energy-efficient windows, the cost would have been considered an improvement and added to the property's basis.

10. The answer is B. They must report six months of rental income at $3,000 per month, or $18,000, but the security deposit of $6,000 is refundable and therefore not recognized as income in 2016. They can deduct 6/12 of the amounts incurred for mortgage interest, property taxes, and casualty insurance, or $10,500, plus the $500 cost of repairs while the house was rented. Thus, their reportable net rental income before considering depreciation would be $7,000.

Taxable rental income:	
Six months of rent (at $3,000)	$18,000
Minus deductible expenses:	
Mortgage interest (for six months)	5,000
Property taxes (for six months)	5,000
Casualty insurance (for six months)	500
Repair cost	500
Expenses before depreciation	(11,000)
Rental income before depreciation	**$7,000**

11. The answer is D. The basis for depreciation is the lesser of fair market value or the taxpayer's adjusted basis on the date the property was converted to rental use. The adjusted basis of the house on July 1, 2016, was $480,000 (original cost of $400,000 plus improvements of $80,000), but the FMV of $420,000 on the same date was lower. The basis of the land is not subject to depreciation and not included in the calculation.

Adjusted basis of house:	
Cost	$400,000
Improvements	80,000
Total adjusted basis	480,000
FMV on July 1, 2016	**$420,000**

12. The answer is B. Matt is allowed to claim a maximum of $12,500 of losses on his separately filed return. If a taxpayer actively participated in a passive rental real estate activity that produced a loss, he can deduct the loss to offset his nonpassive income, up to $25,000. However, married persons filing separate returns who lived apart during the year are each allowed a maximum of $12,500 for losses from passive real estate activities. Married persons who file separate returns but lived together during the year are not allowed to take losses on rental real estate activity. Instead, the losses are suspended and must be carried over until the property produces income, or the property is disposed of.

13. The answer is C. The determination of whether a rental is for profit or not for profit is made when rental income exceeds rental expenses for three out of five years, not for four out of five years.

Unit 10: Other Taxable Income

For additional information read:
Publication 525, *Taxable and Nontaxable Income*
Publication 4681, *Canceled Debts, Foreclosures, Repossessions, & Abandonments*
Publication 504, *Divorced or Separated Individuals*

In this unit, we discuss a number of other types of taxable income that must be reported on Form 1040.

Taxable Recoveries

A recovery is a return of an amount a taxpayer deducted or took a credit for in an earlier year. The most common recoveries are refunds, reimbursements, and rebates of deductions itemized on Schedule A. A taxpayer must include a recovery in income in the year he receives it, to the extent the deduction or credit reduced his tax in the earlier year.

Example: In the prior year, Perla paid $2,700 for medical expenses. She subtracted $2,500, which was 10% of her adjusted gross income, to determine her medical expense deduction of $200. In 2016, Perla's medical insurance reimbursed $500 of her prior year medical expenses. The only portion of the $500 reimbursement she must include in her income for 2016 is $200, the amount she actually deducted.

State and local income tax refunds are reported as taxable income in the year received only if the taxpayer itemized deductions in the prior year in which those taxes were overpaid. The payer should send Form 1099-G, *Certain Government Payments*, to the taxpayer by January 31, and also send a copy to the IRS.

Example: Wally claimed the standard deduction on his prior year federal tax return. In 2016, he received a refund of $600 for state income taxes he paid during the prior year. The state tax refund is not taxable in 2016, as Wally received no federal tax benefit from his state tax payments because he did not itemize deductions in the previous year.

Refunds of federal income taxes are not included in a taxpayer's income because they are never allowed as a deduction.

Alimony Received

Alimony is taxable income to the recipient and deductible by the payer. In contrast, child support is not taxable income to the receiver and not deductible by the payer because it is viewed as a payment a parent makes simply to support his or her own child.

Alimony *received* is taxable income to the payee and reported on line 11 of Form 1040. Alimony *paid* is an adjustment to income for the payor. The payor does not have to itemize in order to deduct alimony payments made.

Example: Mark and Sibba are divorced. Their divorce decree requires Mark to pay Sibba $200 per month as child support and $150 per month as alimony. Mark makes all of his child support and alimony payments on time. Therefore, in 2016, he can deduct $1,800 ($150 × 12 months) as alimony paid, and Sibba must report $1,800 as alimony received as taxable income. The amount paid as child support, $2,400 ($200 × 12), is not deductible by Mark and is not reported as income by Sibba.

The alimony paid is listed on the first page of Form 1040 on line 31a. Form 1040A or Form 1040EZ cannot be used by a taxpayer who takes a deduction for alimony.

If a divorce agreement specifies payments of both alimony and child support and only partial payments are made by the payer, the partial payments are considered child support until that obligation is fully paid. Any additional amounts paid are then treated as alimony.

Example: Elsa and Jessie are divorced. Their divorce decree requires Jessie pay Elsa $2,000 a month ($24,000 [$2,000 × 12] a year) as child support and $1,500 a month ($18,000 [$1,500 × 12] a year) as alimony. Jessie falls behind on his payments and pays only $36,000 during 2016. In this case, the first $24,000 paid is considered child support and only the remaining amount of $12,000 ($36,000 - $24,000) is considered alimony. Jessie can deduct $12,000 as alimony paid. Elsa must report $12,000 as alimony income received.

If an alimony payment is subject to reduction based on a contingency relating to a child (e.g., attaining a certain age, marrying), the amount subject to reduction is treated as child support. If alimony payments continue after the receiving spouse dies, they will automatically be considered child support, not alimony. In order for a payment to qualify as alimony:

- The divorce agreement may not include a clause indicating that the payment is something else (such as child support or repayment of a loan).
- If the spouses are legally separated, they cannot live together when the alimony payments are made, or the IRS will not consider the payments to be alimony.
- The payor must have no liability to make any payment (in cash or property) after the death of the former spouse.

Alimony does not include:

- Payments that are a former spouse's share of income from community property
- Payments to keep up the payer's property
- Free use of the payer's property
- Noncash property settlements

Note: Property settlements are simply a division of property and are not treated as alimony. In general, property transferred to an ex-spouse as part of a divorce proceeding is not a taxable event.

Example: Olga and Phillip divorce in 2016. As part of their divorce agreement, Olga must transfer a portion of her IRA account to Phillip. The IRA transfer is properly outlined in their property settlement agreement. On October 1, 2016, their divorce becomes final. Two days later, the IRA transfer is completed, and $12,000 is transferred directly from Olga's IRA to Phillip's IRA. The transfer is considered a division of marital assets and is not alimony. It is also not subject to an early withdrawal penalty.

Payments made to a third party can be considered alimony in some cases. For example, if, under the terms of a divorce agreement, a spouse pays the medical bills of his ex-wife, a cash payment to the hospital can count as alimony. For a jointly owned home, half of the mortgage payments and real estate taxes may be deducted as alimony, assuming the divorce decree or separation agreement requires a taxpayer to pay these expenses for his ex-spouse. The ex-spouse must include the payments as alimony received.

Government Benefits

Most government welfare benefits, including food stamps, heating assistance programs, and non-federal assistance benefits from states or local agencies are exempt from federal taxation. Worker's compensation, which provides wage replacement and medical benefits to injured workers, is not taxable income. In contrast, unemployment compensation is taxable.

Example: Wilma was laid off from her job in 2016. She received $300 a week of unemployment compensation for 26 weeks. When she was unable to find another job, she began receiving benefits from her state's WIC program, which provided vouchers for food for her and her toddler. The unemployment compensation would be taxable income, but the welfare (WIC) benefits would not be taxable.

Social Security Income

Social Security income is reported to the taxpayer on Form SSA-1099, and these benefits are taxable in certain cases, depending upon a taxpayer's income and the amount of benefits received for the year. To determine if any percentage of his Social Security benefits is taxable, a taxpayer must compare the base threshold amount for his filing status with the total of:

- One-half of his benefits, plus
- All of his other income, including tax-exempt interest.

If the sum is less than the base amount for his filing status, none of the Social Security is taxable. If the sum is more than the base amount for his filing status, a percentage of the Social Security is taxable.

Base Amounts for Calculating Taxability of Social Security
MFJ: $32,000
Single, HOH, QW, or MFS (and lived apart from his/her spouse all year): $25,000
MFS (if lived with spouse at any time during the year): $0

The taxpayer calculates the taxable portion on a worksheet in the *Instructions for Form 1040*, or Publication 915, *Social Security and Equivalent Railroad Retirement Benefits.* The taxable portion of Social Security benefits is never more than 85% and, in most cases, is less than 50%. Spouses who file jointly must combine their incomes and Social Security benefits when figuring the taxable portion of their benefits, even if one spouse did not receive any benefits.

Example: Bo and Yvonne are both over 65. They file jointly, and both received Social Security benefits during 2016. At the end of the year, Bo received a Form SSA-1099 showing net benefits of $7,500. Yvonne received a Form SSA-1099 showing net benefits of $3,500. Bo also received wages of $20,000 and taxable interest income of $500. He did not have any tax-exempt interest.

1. Total Social Security benefits		$11,000
2. Enter one-half of SS		$5,500
3. Enter taxable interest and wages	$20,500	
4. Sum ($5,500 + $20,500)	$26,000	

Bo and Yvonne's benefits are not taxable for 2016 because the total above is not more than the base amount ($32,000) for married filing jointly.

Other Income (Line 21)

"Other income" includes items that do not have separately identified lines on Form 1040. This line is the catch-all for all other types of taxable income that is not reportable on another schedule or area of Form 1040. Examples, which we cover in detail next, include:

- Gambling winnings
- Cancellation of debt income
- Hobby income
- Certain types of court awards
- Prizes and awards
- Taxable distributions from a Coverdell education savings account or a qualified tuition program if they are more than the qualified higher education expenses for a designated beneficiary

Note: Remember, taxpayers are required to report all taxable income, whether or not the taxpayer receives a document from the payer reporting the amount paid.

Gambling Winnings

Gambling income may include winnings from lotteries, raffles, horse races, and casinos. Gambling winnings should be reported to a taxpayer on Form W-2G if he wins:

- $600 or more from gambling
- $1,200 or more from bingo or slot machines
- $1,500 or more from keno
- Any amounts subject to federal income tax withholding

A taxpayer must report and pay tax on all gambling winnings, regardless of whether he receives a Form W-2G. Gambling losses are deductible on Schedule A as a miscellaneous deduction that is not subject to the 2% limit, but the deduction is limited to the amount of gambling winnings.

Example: Yolanda had $1,000 of gambling winnings and $3,000 of gambling losses in 2016. Her deduction for gambling losses cannot exceed $1,000, the amount of her gambling winnings. In order to claim the deduction for her losses, Yolanda must itemize and list her gambling losses on Schedule A, Form 1040.

The taxpayer must keep an accurate diary or similar record of gambling winnings and losses, along with tickets, receipts, canceled checks, and other documentation. He is not required to include these supporting records with his tax return, but they should be retained in case of an audit.

Cancellation of Debt Income

Generally, if a taxpayer's debt is canceled or forgiven, the taxpayer must include the debt forgiveness or cancellation of debt (COD) in his gross income. If a lender cancels a debt and issues Form 1099-C, the lender will indicate on the form if the borrower was personally liable for repayment of the debt. The tax impact depends on the type of debt: whether the loan is recourse or nonrecourse. A recourse debt holds the borrower personally liable. All other debt is considered nonrecourse.

Cancellation of debt may include any indebtedness for which a taxpayer is personally liable or which attaches to the taxpayer's property, such as an auto loan, credit card debt, mortgage, or home equity loan.

Note: A nonrecourse loan does not allow the lender to pursue anything other than the collateral. For example, if a borrower defaults on a nonrecourse home loan, the bank can only foreclose on the home. The bank cannot take further legal action to collect the money owed on the debt. Whether a debt is recourse or nonrecourse may vary from state to state, depending on state law. If a lender forecloses on property subject to a recourse debt and cancels the portion of the debt in excess of the FMV of the property, the canceled portion is treated as ordinary income. This amount must be included in gross income unless it qualifies for an exception or exclusion.[28]

If the debt is a nonbusiness debt, the canceled debt amount is reported as "other income" on line 21 of a taxpayer's Form 1040. The taxpayer must generally report two transactions:

1. The cancellation of debt income
2. Gain or loss on the sale or repossession, generally equal to the difference between the FMV of the property at the time of the foreclosure and the taxpayer's adjusted basis in the property

If a personal asset such as a vehicle is repossessed, the repossession is treated as a sale for tax purposes, and a gain or loss must be computed. A loss related to a personal asset would be nondeductible.

Example: Zach lost his sailboat because he could no longer make his payments. At the time of repossession, he owed a balance of $170,000 to the lender, and the FMV of the sailboat was $140,000. Zach is personally liable for the debt (recourse loan), so the abandonment is treated as a sale. The "selling price" from the repossession is $140,000, and Zach must recognize $30,000 in debt forgiveness income ($170,000 - $140,000).

Example: Doreen bought a new car for $15,000. She made a $2,000 down payment and borrowed the remaining $13,000 from her bank. Doreen is personally liable for the car loan (recourse debt). The bank repossessed her car because she stopped making payments. The balance due on the loan at the time of the repossession was $10,000. The FMV of the car when repossessed was only $9,000. Since repossession is treated as a sale for tax purposes, the gain or loss must be computed. Doreen compares the amount realized ($9,000) with her adjusted basis ($15,000) to determine that she has a $6,000 nondeductible loss. She also has ordinary income from cancellation of debt. That income is $1,000 ($10,000 canceled debt – $9,000 FMV). Doreen must report the canceled debt as income on line 21 of her Form 1040.

Definition: A **nonrecourse debt** is a type of loan that is secured by collateral in which the borrower does not have personal liability for the loan. The most common type of nonrecourse debt is a home mortgage.

Many home mortgages are nonrecourse. This means that if the borrower defaults, the lender can seize the home, but cannot seek out the borrower for any further compensation, even if the FMV of the home does not cover the remaining loan balance. If the taxpayer

[28] There is no taxable income from a canceled debt if it is intended as a gift (for example, if a taxpayer owes his parents money, but they choose to forgive the debt).

abandons property that secures debt for which the taxpayer is not personally liable (a nonrecourse loan), the abandonment is treated as a sale or exchange.

If a loan is nonrecourse and the borrower does not retain the asset, the borrower does not have to recognize cancellation of debt income. However, there is a deemed sales price based on the amount of the nonrecourse loan at the time of the abandonment or foreclosure.

A taxpayer may question the taxability of canceled debt because it can apply in a tax year in which cash is not received. In a situation where property is surrendered or repossessed, such as a foreclosure, the taxpayer may feel that by giving up the property, he should be relieved from any further obligation.

Example: Felix lost his home to foreclosure because he lost his job and could no longer make his mortgage payments. At the time of the foreclosure, Felix owed a balance of $170,000 to his mortgage lender, and the fair market value of the home was $140,000. The mortgage is a nonrecourse loan. Since Felix is not personally liable for the debt (nonrecourse loan), Felix abandons the property, and the bank forecloses. The abandonment is treated as a sale (for tax purposes) and the "selling price" would be $170,000, which is the balance of the loan.

Example: Phoebe borrows $10,000 to take a vacation and defaults on the loan after paying back only $2,000. She has the ability to pay back the loan but chooses not to. The lender writes off the remaining balance of the loan instead of pursuing Phoebe for the balance of the loan. Therefore, there is a cancellation of debt of $8,000, which is taxable income to Phoebe.

Non-Taxable Canceled Debt

There are several circumstances in which canceled debt is not taxable.

Insolvency: A taxpayer is insolvent when his total debts are more than the FMV of his total assets. If a taxpayer is insolvent when the debt is canceled, the canceled debt is not taxable, but only to the extent of the insolvency (i.e., by how much his debts exceed his assets). For this purpose, the taxpayer's assets include the value of everything he owns, including pensions and retirement accounts.

Example: In 2016, Darla had $5,000 of credit card debt, which she did not pay. The bank decided to cancel the entire $5,000 credit card balance. She received a Form 1099-C from her credit card company showing canceled debt of $5,000. Immediately before the cancellation, Darla's total liabilities were $15,000 and the FMV of her total assets was $7,000. Therefore, at the time the debt was canceled, Darla was insolvent to the extent of $8,000 ($15,000 total liabilities minus $7,000 FMV of her total assets). Darla can exclude the entire $5,000 canceled debt from income.

Bankruptcy: Debts discharged through bankruptcy court in a Title 11 bankruptcy case are not considered taxable income. The taxpayer must attach Form 982, *Reduction of Tax Attributes Due to Discharge of Indebtedness,* to his federal income tax return to report debt canceled in bankruptcy.

Home Mortgage Debt: Normally, when a bank forecloses on a home and sells it for less than the borrower's outstanding mortgage, the bank forgives the unpaid mortgage debt, and the canceled debt is taxable income to the homeowner. However, a taxpayer may exclude income realized as a result of loan modification or foreclosure of a taxpayer's principal residence. The principal residence is the home where the taxpayer ordinarily lives most of the time. This exclusion does not apply to second homes or vacation homes. Further, the exclusion does not apply unless it is directly related to a decline in the home's value or the taxpayer's financial condition. This provision for exclusion of home mortgage debt from a primary residence was extended by the PATH Act.

Qualified principal residence indebtedness (QPRI) is a mortgage secured by a taxpayer's principal residence that was taken out to buy, build, or substantially improve that residence and may also include debt from refinancing. QPRI cannot be more than the cost of the home plus improvements. The maximum amount that can be treated as QPRI is $2 million ($1 million if MFS).

If only part of a loan is qualified principal residence indebtedness, the exclusion from income for QPRI applies only to the extent the amount canceled exceeds the amount of the loan that is not QPRI.

However, the remaining part of the loan may qualify for a different exclusion (such as the exclusion for insolvency).

Example: Ken incurred a mortgage debt of $800,000 when he purchased his home for $880,000. He made a down payment of $80,000 and financed the rest through his bank. When the FMV of the property was $1 million, Ken refinanced the debt for $850,000. At the time of the refinancing, the balance of the original loan was $740,000. Ken used the $110,000 he obtained from the refinancing ($850,000 minus $740,000) to buy a luxury car and take a vacation to the Bahamas. Two years after the refinancing, Ken lost his job. Ken's home declined in value to $750,000. Based on Ken's circumstances, the lender agreed to a short sale of the property for $735,000, and cancellation of the remaining $115,000 of the $850,000 debt. Ken can exclude only $5,000 of the canceled debt from his income using the exclusion for canceled QPRI ($115,000 canceled debt minus the $110,000 amount of the debt that was not QPRI). Ken must include the remaining $110,000 of canceled debt in income.

The taxpayer must report the amount of debt forgiven on his return by completing Form 982, *Reduction of Tax Attributes Due to Discharge of Indebtedness.*

Example: Adam's home is subject to a $320,000 recourse mortgage. Adam's mortgage lender forecloses on the home in January 2016. The residence is later sold by the bank for $280,000 in December 2016. Adam has $40,000 of income from discharge of indebtedness and can claim the exclusion by filing Form 982 with his 2016 tax return.

Cancellation of Student Loans: Certain student loans contain a provision that all or part of the debt incurred to attend a qualified educational institution will be canceled if the student later works for a specified period of time in certain professions. The canceled debt does not have to be recognized as income on a taxpayer's return.

Example: Tatum is a medical student completing her residency. In return for forgiveness of her student loans, she agrees to work for four years as a pediatrician in a state program in Minnesota that serves rural and poor communities. The canceled debt does not have to be recognized as income.

Qualified Farm Indebtedness: If a taxpayer incurred the canceled debt in a farming business, it is generally not considered taxable income.

Canceled Debt that is Otherwise Deductible: If a taxpayer uses the cash method of accounting, he should not recognize canceled debt income if payment of the debt would have otherwise been a deductible expense.

Example: Jiao is a self-employed interior designer. A CPA firm agrees to file her business tax return and bill her at a later date. Jiao receives $2,200 of tax preparation and bookkeeping services for her business on credit. Later, Jiao loses a major account and has trouble paying her debts, so her CPA forgives the amount she owes. Jiao does not include the canceled debt in her gross income because payment of the debt would have been deductible as a business expense had it been paid.

Hobby Income

A hobby is an activity typically undertaken primarily for pleasure. Even though it may produce income, a hobby is not considered a business because it is not carried on to make a profit.

The IRS presumes that an activity is "carried on for a profit" if it makes a profit during at least three of the last five tax years, including the current year. However, determination of whether an activity is a hobby or a business is determined by a number of factors, including an analysis of the following:

- Does the effort put into the activity indicate an intention to make a profit?
- Does the taxpayer depend on income from the activity?
- If there are losses, are they due to circumstances beyond the taxpayer's control, or did they occur in the start-up phase of the business?
- Has the taxpayer changed methods of operation to improve profitability?
- Does the taxpayer or his advisors have the knowledge needed to carry on the activity as a successful business?
- Has the taxpayer made a profit in similar activities in the past?
- Does the activity make a profit in some years?
- Can the taxpayer expect to make a profit in the future from the appreciation of assets used in the activity?

Income from a hobby is taxable and reported on Form 1040 line 21. Hobby income is generally not subject to self-employment tax, and the use of losses from a hobby to offset income is limited. Expenses related to a hobby activity are deductible, but only up to the amount of hobby income. Hobby expenses must be itemized on Schedule A. If a taxpayer does not have enough expenses to itemize, then the hobby expenses are not deductible. Also, any expenses that exceed hobby income are not deductible.

Example: Chester breeds aquarium fish as a hobby. Twice a year, he goes to an Exotic Fish convention and sells some of his fish. Although he makes money on occasion, he mainly does this activity for pleasure. Chester plans to continue attending the conventions whether he makes money or not. Therefore, the income is hobby income. The convention costs are hobby expenses and deductible only up to the amount of his hobby income.

Court Awards and Damages

Court awards for compensation for lost wages or profits are generally taxable as ordinary income, as are punitive damages.

Compensatory damages for personal physical injury or physical sickness are not taxable income, whether they are from a settlement or from an actual court award.

Example: Felix was injured in a car accident in 2016. His legs were broken, and he suffered other serious physical injuries. He received an insurance settlement for his injuries totaling $950,000. This is nontaxable income because it is payment for a physical injury.

Damages received for emotional distress due to physical injury or sickness are treated the same way as damages for physical injury or sickness, so they are not included in income.

If emotional distress is not due to a physical injury (for example, an employment lawsuit in which a taxpayer suffers emotional distress for injury to reputation), the proceeds are taxable, except for any damages received for medical care due to that emotional distress. Emotional distress includes physical symptoms such as headaches, insomnia, and stomach disorders.

Example: Kristina won a court award for emotional distress caused by unlawful discrimination. The emotional distress resulted in her hospitalization for a nervous breakdown. The court awarded Kristina damages of $100,000, including $20,000 to refund the cost of her medical care for the nervous breakdown. In this case, $80,000 ($100,000 - $20,000) would be considered a taxable court award. The $20,000 of damages for her medical care would not be taxable.

Civil damages, restitution or other monetary awards that the taxpayer received as compensation for a wrongful incarceration are not taxable.

Example: Reuben was wrongfully convicted of murder and later released after spending almost 15 years in prison. Reuben was awarded $50,000 per year of wrongful imprisonment. None of the award is taxable income to Reuben.

Prizes and Awards

Prizes and awards are usually taxable and are reported on line 21. If the prize or award is in the form of property rather than cash, the fair market value of the property is treated as the taxable amount. The winner may avoid taxation of the award by rejecting the prize. The taxpayer may also avoid taxation by having the payer directly transfer the prize to a charity or other nonprofit organization.

Example: A national education association chooses Jerry, a college instructor, as its teacher of the year. He is awarded $3,000, but he does not accept the prize. Instead, Jerry directs the association to transfer his winnings to a college scholarship fund. Jerry never receives a check or has control over the funds; therefore, the award is not taxable to him.

Employee awards for safety, length-of-service, or achievements are generally not taxable to the employee unless they exceed specified limits.[29]

[29] Employee awards are covered in greater detail in Book 2, *Businesses*, because they are a common employee fringe benefit. Fringe benefits are generally tested on Part 2 of the EA exam.

Educational Assistance

Many types of educational assistance are tax-free if they meet certain requirements.

Scholarships and Fellowships: A scholarship is an amount paid to an undergraduate or graduate student to pursue studies. A fellowship is an amount paid to an individual to pursue research. A scholarship or fellowship is excluded from income only if:

- The taxpayer is a degree candidate at an eligible educational institution that has been nationally accredited.
- It does not exceed qualified educational expenses.
- It is not designated for other purposes, such as room and board.
- It does not represent payment for teaching, research, or other services.

Qualified educational expenses include tuition, required fees, and course-related expenses such as books.

Example: Aubrey is a graduate student who received a scholarship of $3,000. Under its terms, she must serve as a part-time teaching assistant. From the $3,000 scholarship, she receives $1,250 for teaching, which is listed as income on her Form W-2. She had expenses of more than $5,000 for tuition and course-related books. Aubrey may exclude $1,750 of the scholarship funds from income, but the $1,250 is taxable and must be included in her gross income.

An athletic scholarship is tax-free only if it meets the requirements described above.

Pell Grants: A Pell Grant is a need-based grant that is treated as a scholarship for tax purposes. It is tax-free to the extent it is used for qualified educational expenses during the specified grant period.

Payment to Service Academy Cadets or Midshipmen: An appointment to a United States military academy is not a scholarship or fellowship. Cadets and midshipmen receive free tuition and room and board, which is nontaxable. However, they also get government pay while at the military academy; these amounts are taxable income.

Veterans' Educational Benefits: Veterans' benefits for education are tax-free if administered by the Department of Veterans Affairs.

Example: Moises served in Afghanistan and has since returned to college. He receives two education benefits under the GI bill: a $1,534 monthly basic housing allowance and $3,840 tuition paid directly to his college. Neither of these benefits is taxable to Moises, and he is not required to report them on his tax return.

Section 529 Plans

Qualified Tuition Programs: QTPs, also known as section 529 plans, are established and maintained by states or educational institutions. These plans allow a taxpayer to either prepay a student's qualified educational expenses at an eligible educational institution or contribute to an account that will be used to pay future expenses. The amounts contributed to a section 529 plan are not deductible for federal tax purposes.

Eligible institutions include virtually all accredited colleges, universities, vocational schools, and other postsecondary educational institutions. Qualified expenses include tuition, fees, books, computer equipment and software, and room and board for any time the beneficiary is enrolled in college. A beneficiary may be anyone the taxpayer designates: himself, a child, a grandchild, or an unrelated person.

Distributions from a 529 plan are reported to the taxpayer on Form 1099-Q. The part of a distribution representing the amount paid or contributed to the plan is not included in income.

The beneficiary also generally does not have to include in taxable income any earnings distributed from a 529 plan if the total distribution is less than or equal to a student's qualified education expenses (after reduction of the latter by other tax-free education assistance received during the year).

If the total distribution is greater than a student's adjusted qualified expenses, an allocable portion of the earnings is taxable. In this type of taxable distribution, an additional tax of 10% generally applies on the amount included in income.

Example: Seven years ago, Emma's parents opened an account for her with a Qualified Tuition Program maintained by the state of Virginia. Over the years, they contributed $22,000 to the account. The total balance in the account was $33,000 on the date the distribution was made. In September 2016, Emma enrolled in college and had $10,000 of qualified education expenses for the rest of the year. She paid her college expenses from the following sources:

- QTP distribution: $7,500
- Partial tuition scholarship (tax-free): $4,000
- Gift from her parents: $1,000

Emma must reduce her qualified educational expenses by the tax-free scholarship ($10,000 minus $4,000), so she has $6,000 of adjusted qualified educational expenses. Since that amount is less than the QTP distribution, part of the earnings shown on Form 1099-Q is taxable and would be reported on Line 21 of Form 1040.

Any amount distributed from a 529 plan is not taxable if it is rolled over to another 529 plan for the use of the same beneficiary or for a member of the beneficiary's family. The amount must be paid to another educational account within 60 days after the date of distribution.

Example: Yasir still had $3,000 left in his 529 plan after he graduated from college. He wanted to help his younger sister, who was still in high school. Within 60 days after distribution of the remaining portion of his 529 plan, he contributed the money to his sister's 529 plan, so the distribution was not taxable to him or his sister.

Starting in 2016, the definition of "qualified higher education expenses" for distributions from 529 accounts now includes the purchases of computer equipment and technology.

Coverdell Education Savings Accounts (ESAs)

A Coverdell ESA is a trust or custodial account set up to pay qualified elementary, secondary, or higher education expenses for a designated beneficiary. In order to contribute to an ESA, the contributor's MAGI must be below $110,000 in 2016 ($220,000 if married filing jointly). Contributions must be in cash (not property) and must be made by the due date of the contributor's tax return (not including extensions). There is no limit to the number of accounts that can be established for a beneficiary; however, the total contribution to all accounts on behalf of a beneficiary in any year cannot exceed $2,000, no matter how many accounts are established.

All contributions that exceed $2,000 for a single beneficiary in a taxable year will be treated as excess contributions. There will be a 6% excise tax if the excess contributions and earnings on them are not withdrawn from the child's accounts before June 1 of the following tax year. Any earnings withdrawn as part of a corrective distribution are taxable in the year of the excess contribution, even if the distribution occurs in the following year.

Note: The penalty for excess contributions is imposed on the *beneficiary* of the account (usually a minor child), and not on the person who over-contributed to the account. The excise tax must be reported on the child's income tax return, using IRS Form 5329, *Additional Taxes on Qualified Plans (Including IRAs) and Other Tax-Favored Accounts.* This rule seems contrary to common sense, but the penalty is imposed on the child, not the child's parents, or the contributor of the excess funds.

Contributions must be made before the beneficiary reaches age 18 unless the beneficiary is special-needs. Contributions to a Coverdell are not deductible. The beneficiary needs to withdraw the balance from the account before age 30.

If there is a balance in the ESA when the beneficiary reaches age 30, it must be distributed within 30 days. The beneficiary can also choose to transfer the ESA to another beneficiary (such as a younger sibling or another family member) in order to avoid the tax. If the beneficiary is special-needs, the Coverdell account can continue in existence (without transfer to another beneficiary) after the beneficiary turns 30.

Example: Three Coverdell ESAs were set up for Lindsay when she was born: one by her parents, one by her grandparents, and one by her great-uncle. In 2016, her grandparents contribute $1,500 to Lindsay's account. The most her parents and great-uncle can contribute is a combined $500, because the maximum contribution per year for a single beneficiary is $2,000.

Example: Francis earned a full scholarship to Stanford University. He enrolled when he was 19, and had a Coverdell ESA with $52,000. Since his tuition was already paid by his scholarship, Francis only used the ESA for books and required lab fees. Francis graduated college four years later, and had only used a total of $9,000 from his Coverdell. Rather than withdrawing the money and paying the 10% tax, Francis transferred the Coverdell to his younger sister, who is 17 and still in high school. His sister can use the remaining amounts in the Coverdell for her own future college expenses.

The beneficiary of a Coverdell account can receive distributions to pay qualified education expenses that are tax-free if the amount of the distributions does not exceed the beneficiary's adjusted qualified education expenses. If a distribution does exceed the beneficiary's qualified education expenses, a portion of the earnings is taxable and is reported as "other income" on line 21 of Form 1040. An additional penalty tax of 10% applies to distributions that are not used for qualifying expenses.

If a beneficiary receives distributions from both a 529 plan and a Coverdell ESA in the same year and the total distributions exceed the beneficiary's adjusted qualified education expenses for that year, the expenses must be allocated between the distributions from each account. The total expenses must also be reduced by any amounts used in claiming an American Opportunity or Lifetime Learning Credit for that year.

Miscellaneous Line 21 Income Items

Other types of income that are taxable to the recipient and reported on line 21 include the following:

- Strike benefits
- Jury duty pay (when it is not turned over to the employee's employer and deducted as an adjustment to income)
- Fees paid by an estate to a personal representative/executor
- Gifts or gratuities received by a host or hostess of a party or event where sales are made

Example: Kathleen hosts a cooking party for 15 friends, which includes a live demonstration by a Pampered Chef consultant. At the end of the evening, the women order $1,000 worth of cookware and other products from the consultant. Kathleen receives a gift of $215 of products for hosting the party, which she must report as income at its fair market value.

Bartering Income

Bartering is an exchange of property or services, usually without an exchange of cash. Barter may take place on an informal, one-on-one basis between individuals and businesses, or it may occur on a third-party basis through a barter exchange company. Taxpayers may barter for a variety of goods and services: computer services for auto repairs, or dental work for carpet cleaning, for example. The FMV of the goods or services exchanged must be reported as income by each party in the year of the exchange. If the parties have agreed ahead of time as to the value of services exchanged, the agreed-upon value will be accepted as the fair market value.

Example: Brayden builds custom kitchen cabinets. Annemarie is a veterinarian. Brayden builds new cabinets for Annemarie's kitchen, and Annemarie performs hip dysplasia surgery on Brayden's German shepherd. They agree in advance that the cost for the kitchen cabinets and the surgery is $2,500. They each must report $2,500 of income on their tax returns.

Bartering income from business services is reported on Schedule C or Schedule F if the taxpayers are self-employed.

A barter exchange is an organization that serves as a third party to coordinate barter transactions between members of the organization. Members contract with each other to exchange property or services. The barter exchange provides a record of the fair market value of all income a member receives from transactions on Form 1099-B, *Proceeds from Broker and Barter Exchange Transactions.*

Summary: Taxable vs. Nontaxable Income

TAXABLE INCOME	NONTAXABLE INCOME
Wages, salaries, tips, bonuses, vacation pay, severance pay, commissions	Most employer-provided fringe benefits
Interest on bank and money market accounts; CDs; dividends; Treasury bonds	Interest on most state and local bonds
Gains from sales of property, stocks and bonds, stock options, etc.	Life insurance proceeds
Fees paid to an estate's executor	Gifts and inheritances
Alimony	Child support
Social Security benefits (above the base amount and limited to 85% of benefits)	Welfare payments, food stamps, other forms of public assistance
Court awards for punitive damages and lost wages	Compensation or court awards for physical injury or illness, and awards for wrongful incarceration
Unemployment compensation; strike benefits	Worker's compensation
Barter and hobby income	Combat pay and certain veteran's benefits
Certain distributions from Coverdell savings accounts or qualified tuition programs	Scholarships, Pell grants, employer-provided educational assistance
Cancellation of debt income (unless excludable)	Canceled debt from a primary residence, bankruptcy, or insolvency
Gambling winnings; most prizes and awards	Certain employee awards for safety, achievement, or service

Unit 10: Study Questions

(Test yourself first, then check the correct answers at the end of this quiz.)

1. Penelope is under 18 and has two Coverdell accounts. One was set up by her grandparents, and the other was set up by her mother. Penelope received $3,200 in total contributions in her Coverdell accounts in 2016. Which of the following statements is true?

A. The contributions are tax deductible and can remain in the accounts until Penelope reaches 30 years of age.
B. Penelope has an excess contribution of $1,200. The excess contribution must be withdrawn, or it will be subject to an excise tax.
C. Penelope must invest the proceeds in a traditional IRA.
D. Penelope has an excess contribution of $200. She can transfer this excess contribution to another beneficiary.

2. In which of the following instances is canceled debt not excluded from income?

A. Mortgage debt of a rental property in foreclosure.
B. Insolvency.
C. Bankruptcy.
D. Debt as part of a farming business.

3. Under Cary's divorce decree, he must pay his ex-wife, Eugenia, $30,000 of alimony per year. The decree also requires that Cary pays child support of $12,000 per year. The payments will stop after 15 years. However, if Eugenia dies before the end of the 15-year period, Cary must still pay Eugenia's estate the difference between $450,000 ($30,000 annually × 15 years) and the total amount paid up to that time. Eugenia dies at the end of the tenth year, and Cary must pay her estate an additional $150,000 ($450,000 – $300,000). How are the payments that occurred after Eugenia's death characterized for tax purposes?

A. Child support.
B. Alimony.
C. Other income.
D. Taxable income.

4. Alexander, age 64, is single and retired. He earned the following income in 2016. To determine if any of his Social Security is taxable, Alexander should compare how much of his income to the $25,000 base amount?

Part-time job	$8,000
Bank interest	5,000
Social Security	11,000
Taxable pension	6,000
Total	**$30,000**

A. $11,000
B. $24,500
C. $25,000
D. $30,000

5. Karly is trying to get her finances in order. During the year, she negotiated a settlement with her credit card company, to which she owed a delinquent debt. She owed $10,000 on her credit card. As part of the negotiation, the credit card company agreed to accept a $2,500 settlement as payment in full. Karly was not insolvent and not in bankruptcy when the debt was canceled. What amount should be reported as "other income" on Karly's Form 1040, line 21?

A. $0
B. $10,000
C. $2,500
D. $7,500

6. Isabella had $9,000 of gambling winnings during the year. She also incurred $15,000 of gambling losses. How should these transactions be reported on her tax return?

A. The $9,000 of winnings are reported as income, and the $15,000 of losses are reported as an adjustment to income on Form 1040.
B. The $9,000 of winnings are reported as income, and the $15,000 of losses are reported as an itemized deduction subject to the 2% limit on Schedule A.
C. The $9,000 of winnings are reported as income, and $9,000 of losses are reported as an itemized deduction not subject to the 2% limit on Schedule A.
D. The $9,000 of winnings are reported as income, but the gambling losses are not deductible.

7. Ed received $32,000 of wages in 2016. He also won a prize from his homeowner's association for developing a new water conservation plan. The prize was free landscaping service for a year, valued at $600. Ed also received $7,000 in child support and $2,000 in alimony from his ex-wife. Ed has full custody of his children. What is Ed's taxable income (before deductions and adjustments) for 2016?

A. $32,000
B. $32,600
C. $34,600
D. $39,600

8. Expenses related to a hobby activity are deductible, but only up to the amount of:

A. Taxable income.
B. Ordinary income.
C. Passive income.
D. Hobby income.

9. In 2016, Mina was discharged from her liability to repay $10,000 of credit card debt. The lender reported the discharged debt on Form 1099-C. Immediately prior to the debt cancellation, Mina had liabilities of $15,000 and the fair market value of her assets was $2,000. What portion of the canceled debt must Mina include in income?

A. $10,000
B. $3,000
C. $5,000
D. $0

10. Beth and Clifton's divorce decree requires Clifton to pay Beth $250 per month of child support and $1,500 per month of alimony. Clifton makes all of his child support and alimony payments on time during 2016. How much of these payments is Beth required to report as taxable income on her 2016 return?

A. $0
B. $1,500
C. $18,000
D. $21,000

11. Archer is a former National Football League cornerback. In 2016, he is awarded a sizable settlement in a class action lawsuit for concussion injuries. The settlement will be paid in installments over a period of ten years. How should Archer report the damages he is awarded on his income tax return?

A. He must include the entire amount of his settlement in his gross income for 2016.
B. He must include in his gross income only the portion of the settlement paid to him each year when it is received.
C. He must report the settlement on his tax return, but it is not taxable income.
D. He may exclude the payments from his gross income.

12. Ginny had the following income in 2016:

Source	**Amounts**
Wages	$14,000
Interest	125
Gambling winnings	1,000
Gambling losses	2,000
Discrimination lawsuit settlement	10,000
Child support payments	1,000
Food stamp benefits	5,000

How much gross income must Ginny report on her tax return?

A. $14,125
B. $15,125
C. $25,125
D. $30,000

13. Which of the following is not taxable income to the recipient?

A. Long-term disability payments from a policy paid by the recipient's employer.
B. Bartering income.
C. Gains from the sale of stock.
D. $25,000 of group-term life insurance coverage provided by an employer.

14. Jean received the following income: wages, interest, child support, alimony, inheritance, worker's compensation, and lottery winnings. What amount of her income is taxable?

Source	Amounts
Wages	$13,000
Interest	15
Child support	6,000
Alimony	2,000
Inheritance	10,000
Worker's compensation	1,000
Lottery winnings	5,000

A. $13,015
B. $16,015
C. $20,015
D. $30,015

15. Paulo, 72, experiences age-related discrimination on his job and sues his company. After he files the lawsuit, he is physically attacked by the company owner, who breaks Paulo's arm. The court awards Paulo the following amounts:

- $4,000 for emotional distress attributable to the age discrimination and resulting lawsuit
- $10,000 for loss of wages
- $35,000 for physical injury related to the assault
- $16,000 reimbursement for medical expenses

How much of this award is taxable to Paulo?

A. $4,000
B. $10,000
C. $14,000
D. $49,000

16. During 2016, Anaya received payments of $20,000 for alimony and $15,000 for child support. Based upon the terms of her divorce settlement, her ex-spouse was also required to pay $14,000 of mortgage payments for the house they owned jointly. What portion of the amounts above must Anaya include in income?

A. $27,000
B. $34,000
C. $35,000
D. $49,000

17. Sven and Samantha filed jointly and received the following income in 2016. How much income should be reported on their joint return?

- W-2 income for Samantha for wages of $40,000.
- W-2 for Samantha for $2,000, the value of a trip she won to the Bahamas. She is planning to take the trip in the following year.
- Court settlement of $10,000 paid to Sven from a car accident for serious injuries he suffered.
- $4,000 child support for Samantha's son from a previous marriage.

A. $40,000
B. $42,000
C. $46,000
D. $52,000

18. Which of the following would be considered taxable income to the recipient?

A. Life insurance proceeds paid to a beneficiary.
B. Adoption expense reimbursements.
C. Unemployment compensation.
D. Worker's compensation benefits.

19. Bart had a $15,000 loan from his credit union but stopped making payments. The credit union determined that the legal fees to collect might be higher than the amount Bart owed, so it canceled the remaining amount of $5,000 due on the loan. Bart did not file for bankruptcy, nor is he insolvent. How much income must he include from the debt cancellation?

A. $0
B. $5,000
C. $10,000
D. $15,000

20. Hank received Social Security in 2016 totaling $11,724. Also in 2016, Hank sold all of his stock and moved into senior housing. He received $31,896 of taxable income from the stock sale. What is the maximum taxable amount of Hank's Social Security benefits?

A. $31,896
B. $20,172
C. $11,724
D. $9,965

21. Brent, a dermatologist, agreed to exchange services with a handyman, Tevin. Brent removed a mole for Tevin and Tevin fixed Brent's running toilet in his medical office. Brent generally charges $200 for mole removal, and Tevin generally charges $150 to fix a toilet. They agreed in advance that the fee would be $150. They did not exchange cash. How much income must Brent recognize for this barter transaction?

A. $50
B. $150
C. $200
D. $250

Unit 10: Answers

1. The answer is B. Penelope has an excess contribution of $1,200. The excess contribution must be withdrawn by June 1 of the next tax year, or it will be subject to an excise tax of 6%, plus 6% of any interest or profits derived from the excess contribution. The maximum contribution to a Coverdell is $2,000 per year per beneficiary, regardless of how many accounts the beneficiary has. Any *earnings* withdrawn as part of a corrective distribution are taxable in the year of the excess contribution, even if the corrective distribution occurs in the following year.

2. The answer is A. Foreclosure of a rental property does not qualify for exclusion of canceled debt income. A taxpayer may exclude income realized as a loan modification or foreclosure of a taxpayer's principal residence. Canceled debt related to rental property, other business property, second homes, and vacation homes does not qualify.

3. The answer is A. For tax purposes; alimony cannot continue after the death of the receiving spouse. Since the payments are required even after Eugenia's death, none of the annual payments are considered alimony for tax purposes. The payments are considered "disguised child support" and cannot be deducted by Cary as alimony.

4. The answer is B. In order to figure out the taxable portion of Social Security, the taxpayer's total income, including tax-exempt interest, must be compared to the base amount for his filing status, which is $25,000. The amount of income that should be compared to the $25,000 base amount is calculated as follows:

Part-time job	$8,000
Interest	5,000
½ of Social Security	5,500
Taxable pension	6,000
Total	**$24,500**

Alexander does not have to pay tax on his Social Security. His income plus one-half of Social Security is less than the applicable base amount ($25,000). However, he is still required to file a tax return, because his overall income exceeds the minimum filing requirement.

5. The answer is D. Karly would report $7,500 in cancelled debt income ($10,000 - $2,500) on line 21 of her Form 1040.

6. The answer is C. The $9,000 of winnings are reported as income, and $9,000 of the losses are reported on Schedule A as an itemized deduction not subject to the 2% floor. The amount of losses deducted may not exceed gambling winnings.

7. The answer is C. The wages and the prize are both taxable income. Child support is not taxable to the receiver, nor deductible by the payer. The alimony is taxable to Ed and deductible by his ex-wife. The answer is calculated as follows: ($32,000 + $600 + $2,000) = $34,600.

8. The answer is D. Expenses related to a hobby activity are deductible, but only up to the amount of hobby income. Hobby expenses are only deductible on Schedule A as an itemized deduction. If a taxpayer does not itemize, he cannot deduct hobby expenses.

9. The answer is D. The amount of Mina's assets immediately prior to the debt cancellation exceeded the amount of debt that was discharged. Therefore, the entire amount of the debt cancellation can be excluded from income.

Liabilities	$15,000
Fair market value of assets	(2,000)
Amount of insolvency	13,000
Amount of debt cancellation	**$10,000**

10. The answer is C. Alimony is taxable income to the recipient and deductible by the payer. Therefore, Clifton can deduct $18,000 ($1,500 × 12 months) as alimony paid, and Beth must report $18,000 as alimony received. The amount paid as child support, $3,000 ($250 × 12), is not deductible by Clifton and is not reported as income by Beth.

11. The answer is D. Gross income does not include the amount of damages received due to physical injuries or sickness, regardless of whether the damages are paid as lump sums or as periodic payments.

12. The answer is C. The wages, interest income, gambling income, and settlement from a discrimination lawsuit must all be reported ($14,000 + $125 + $1,000 + $10,000 = $25,125). The child support payments and the food stamp benefits are not taxable. The gambling losses do not affect the inclusion of the gambling income within gross income. However, if Ginny chooses to itemize deductions, her gambling losses may be deducted on Schedule A to the extent of her gambling income. If Ginny does not itemize, the gambling losses are not deductible.

13. The answer is D. An employer may provide up to $50,000 of life insurance coverage as a nontaxable benefit to an employee. The value of any insurance coverage that exceeds $50,000 is a taxable benefit. All of the other items are taxable.

14. The answer is C. The wages, interest, alimony, and lottery winnings are taxable income ($13,000 + $15 + $2,000 + $5,000 = $20,015). Child support, inheritances, and worker's compensation are nontaxable income.

15. The answer is C. The amounts for loss of wages and emotional distress are taxable as ordinary income ($4,000 + $10,000 = $14,000). Damages for emotional distress that is not due to physical injury or sickness are usually taxable (as in this case where the distress was attributed to the job discrimination and lawsuit). The damages awarded for physical injury are not taxable.

16. The answer is A. Anaya must report the cash alimony payments and one-half of the mortgage payments as taxable alimony ($20,000 + $7,000). The child support payments are not taxable.

17. The answer is B. The answer is $42,000 ($40,000 wages + $2,000 prize). Samantha must recognize the prize even though she has not taken the trip because she had constructive receipt of the winnings. The accident settlement and the child support payments are not taxable.

18. The answer is C. Unemployment compensation is taxable income.

19. The answer is B. Bart's inability to pay his debt is not a result of bankruptcy or insolvency, so he must include the full amount of the canceled debt ($5,000) in his gross income.

20. The answer is D. The maximum amount that is ever taxable on net Social Security benefits is 85%, which in Hank's case is $9,965.

21. The answer is B. Brent must include $150 in income. He can also deduct the cost of the repair ($150) if it qualifies as a business expense. If a taxpayer exchanges services with another person and both have agreed ahead of time on the value of those services, that value will be accepted as fair market value unless the value can be shown to be otherwise.

Unit 11: Adjustments to Gross Income

For additional information read:

Publication 529, *Miscellaneous Deductions*

Publication 535, *Business Expenses*

Publication 521, *Moving Expenses*

Publication 970, *Tax Benefits for Education*

Publication 590-A, *Contributions to Individual Retirement Arrangements*

An "adjustment to income" reduces taxable income and thus the amount of tax owed. They are reported on page 1 of Form 1040.

Adjustments are subtracted from gross income in order to derive adjusted gross income (AGI), whereas itemized deductions and the standard deduction are subtracted from AGI. Because adjustments are taken before AGI is calculated, they are designated as "above-the-line" deductions.

Adjustments are beneficial because they not only reduce taxable income, but a lower AGI may increase a taxpayer's eligibility for certain credits and deductions and the amounts that he can claim. Unlike "below-the-line" deductions, adjustments are not added back when calculating the alternative minimum tax.

Adjusted Gross Income

Adjustments to Income

Line	Description	Box	Amount
23	Educator expenses	23	
24	Certain business expenses of reservists, performing artists, and fee-basis government officials. Attach Form 2106 or 2106-EZ	24	
25	Health savings account deduction. Attach Form 8889	25	
26	Moving expenses. Attach Form 3903	26	
27	Deductible part of self-employment tax. Attach Schedule SE	27	
28	Self-employed SEP, SIMPLE, and qualified plans	28	
29	Self-employed health insurance deduction	29	
30	Penalty on early withdrawal of savings	30	
31a	Alimony paid b Recipient's SSN ▶	31a	
32	IRA deduction	32	
33	Student loan interest deduction	33	
34	Tuition and fees. Attach Form 8917	34	
35	Domestic production activities deduction. Attach Form 8903	35	
36	Add lines 23 through 35		
37	Subtract line 36 from line 22. This is your **adjusted gross income** ▶		

Note: Form 1040 (the "long form") is needed for most tax deductions and adjustments; Form 1040-EZ cannot be used. Form 1040A can be used if a taxpayer is reporting only the following adjustments to income: educator expenses, traditional IRA deduction, student loan interest deduction, and tuition and fees deduction.

Common Adjustments to Gross Income

There are many types of adjustments to gross income, and we will cover the most common ones in this unit. These are the adjustments listed in the order they are reported on Form 1040:

- Educator expenses (Line 23)
- Certain business expenses of reservists, performing artists, and fee-basis government officials (Line 24)
- Health savings account deduction (Line 25)

- Moving expenses (Line 26)
- Deductible part of self-employment tax (Line 27)
- Self-employed SEP, SIMPLE, and qualified plans (Line 28)
- Self-employed health insurance deduction (Line 29)
- Penalty on early withdrawal of savings (Line 30)
- Alimony paid (Line 31a)
- IRA deduction (Line 32)
- Student loan interest deduction (Line 33)
- Tuition and fees (Line 34)
- Domestic production activities deduction (Line 35)
- Write-in adjustments (Line 36)
    - Archer MSA deduction
    - Jury duty pay remitted to an employer
    - Repayment of unemployment benefits
    - Other adjustments

Line 23: Educator Expense Deduction

An eligible educator is allowed to deduct up to $250 of unreimbursed expenses for books, supplies, computer equipment (including related software and services), other equipment, and supplementary materials used in the classroom.

Since this is an adjustment to income, teachers can deduct these expenses even if they do not itemize deductions. The PATH Act permanently extended the above-the-line deduction for eligible educators' classroom expenses. For courses in health and physical education, expenses are deductible only if they are related to athletics. Nonathletic supplies for physical education and expenses related to health courses do not qualify. Materials used for homeschooling cannot be deducted.

An eligible educator must work at least 900 hours a school year in a school that provides elementary or secondary education (K-12). College instructors do not qualify. For the purposes of this credit, an "educator" includes a:

- Teacher or instructor
- Counselor
- Principal
- Teacher's aide

Example: Devina is a third-grade teacher who worked 1,600 hours during the tax year. She spent $262 on supplies for her students. Of that amount, $212 was for educational software. The other $50 was for supplies for a unit she teaches on health. Only the $212 is a qualified expense that she can deduct.

On a joint tax return, if both taxpayers are eligible, they each may take the deduction, up to a maximum of $500. Any expenses that exceed the adjustment to income may be deducted as unreimbursed employee expenses on Schedule A, subject to the 2%-of-AGI limit.

Line 24: Certain Business Expenses of Reservists, Performing Artists, and Fee-Basis Government Officials

Certain employees are allowed to claim specified work-related expenses as an adjustment to income, rather than as a deduction on Schedule A. This adjustment applies only to reservists (members of the reserve component of the Armed Forces of the United States, National Guard, or the Reserve Corps of the Public Health Service); qualified performing artists; and state or local government officials who are compensated on a fee basis.

Line 25: Health Savings Account Deduction (HSAs)

A health savings account (HSA) allows a taxpayer to save funds intended to pay for health care expenses on a tax-preferred basis. The HSA contributions are deductible as an adjustment to income. The taxpayer can take tax-free withdrawals from the HSA to pay for his qualifying medical expenses.

An HSA must be established exclusively to pay medical expenses for the taxpayer, his spouse, and his dependents. HSA accounts are usually set up with a bank, an insurance company, or through an employer. To qualify, the taxpayer:

- Must not be enrolled in Medicare.
- Cannot be claimed as a dependent on anyone else's tax return.
- Must be covered under a high deductible health plan and have no other health coverage, other than for a specific disease or illness; a fixed amount for a certain time period of hospitalization; or liabilities incurred under worker's compensation laws or tort liabilities.

An employee and his employer are both allowed to contribute to the employee's HSA in the same year. If an employer makes an HSA contribution on behalf of an employee, it is excluded from the employee's income and is not subject to income or payroll taxes.

For 2016, taxpayers can contribute up to $3,350 for an individual and $6,750 for a family (in 2016, the limits for a family contribution were increased, but the single contribution limits stayed the same). HSA holders who are age 55 and older get to save an extra $1,000 as a catch-up contribution. Any excess contributions over these limits are subject to a 6% penalty.

2016 Health Savings Account (HSA) Contribution Limits

Taxpayer	Minimum Deductible	Maximum Out-of-Pocket	Contribution Limit	55 and Over
Single	$1,300	$6,550	$3,350	+$1,000
Family	$2,600	$13,100	$6,650	+$1,000

Allowable medical expenses are those that would generally qualify for purposes of the deduction for medical and dental expenses and which are not paid or reimbursed by the taxpayer's high deductible health plan. Withdrawals from an HSA for purposes other than payment of allowable medical expenses are subject to income tax. They may also be subject to a 20% penalty, except in the following instances:

- When a taxpayer turns age 65 or older
- When a taxpayer becomes disabled
- When a taxpayer dies

Example: Teddy is 67, single, and has an HSA through his employer. In 2016, his car breaks down and he doesn't have the funds to repair it. Teddy withdraws $2,000 from his HSA to pay for the car repairs. Since he did not use the funds to pay for qualifying medical expenses, the entire withdrawal is subject to income tax. However, Teddy avoids the 20% additional penalty tax because he is over 65.

A taxpayer will receive Form 5498-SA from the HSA trustee showing the amount of contributions for the year. The deduction for an HSA is reported on Form 8889, *Health Savings Accounts*.

To claim the HSA deduction for a particular year, the HSA contributions must be made on or before that year's tax filing date (without extensions). For 2016, HSA contributions must be made on or before the 2016 tax year filing deadline (April 18, 2017).

Line 26: Moving Expenses

If a taxpayer moves due to a change of job or business location, he can deduct qualifying moving expenses that his employer does not reimburse. Moving expenses are reported on Form 3903, Moving Expenses. To qualify for the moving expense deduction, the taxpayer must satisfy these tests:

- The move must be related to work or business, and
- The taxpayer must meet the tests for time and distance.

Time Test: This test is different for employees than for those who are self-employed. For employees, moving costs are deductible only if the taxpayer works full-time at the new work location for at least 39 weeks in the first 12 months. For joint filers, only one spouse has to qualify for the time test in order to deduct moving expenses.

Self-employed taxpayers must work full-time for at least 39 weeks in the first 12 months at the new location, and at least 78 weeks within the first 24 months at the new location. For this test, any combination of full-time work as an employee or as a self-employed person qualifies.

Example: Randy quit his job and moved from Missouri to Georgia to begin a full-time job as a mechanic for Custom Motorcycles. He worked at the motorcycle shop 40 hours each week. Shortly after his move, Randy also opened a part-time motorcycle repair business from his home garage. Because Randy's principal place of business is Custom Motorcycles, he satisfies the time test by meeting the 39-week test as an employee. However, if Randy is unable to satisfy the requirements of the 39-week test during the 12-month period, he may instead be able to satisfy the 78-week test because he also works as a self-employed person.

If a taxpayer fails to meet the time test, he must report the moving expenses as "other income" in a later tax year or amend the tax return on which the moving expenses were claimed.

Exceptions to the Time Test: A taxpayer does not have to meet the time test and may still deduct moving expenses if any of the following applies:

- The taxpayer is in the armed forces and moved because of a change of station.
- The taxpayer's main job location was outside the United States, and he moved back to the United States because he retired from his position.
- A taxpayer is the surviving widow(er) of a person whose main job location at the time of death was outside the United States.
- The taxpayer's job at the new location ends because of death or disability.
- The taxpayer is transferred or laid off for a reason other than willful misconduct.

Example: Darrell's company transfers him from New York to Tennessee, and he deducts his moving expenses. Darrell expects to continue his full-time employment in Tennessee and does not expect it to be a temporary move. A few months later, his employer goes bankrupt and closes the entire Tennessee division. Darrell is laid off. He does not have to satisfy the time test.

Example: Shelby moves from Michigan to Ohio for a new job as a building manager. Six months after she starts the job, she dies. On Shelby's final tax return, her executor can deduct her moving expenses since the job ended due to her death.

Exceptions for Seasonal Work and Temporary Absences: For purposes of the moving expense deduction, if a taxpayer's trade or business is seasonal, the off-season weeks when no work is available may still be counted as weeks during which he worked full-time. In order to qualify, the off-season must be less than six months, and the taxpayer must work full-time before and after the off-season.

Example: Chelsea moves from North Dakota to Jackson Hole, Wyoming for a job at a ski resort. She works full-time during the ski season and is off for five months during the summer. Chelsea may still count this time as full-time work since her employment is expected to be seasonal.

A taxpayer is still considered to be employed on a full-time basis during any week he is temporarily absent from work because of illness, labor strikes, natural disasters, or similar causes.

Distance Test: Under the distance test, the new job must be at least 50 miles farther from the taxpayer's old home than the old job location was from the taxpayer's old home. If the taxpayer had no previous workplace, the new job must be at least 50 miles from the old home.

This means that if a taxpayer starts a job for the first time, the place of work must be at least 50 miles from his former home to meet the distance test. The location of the taxpayer's new home doesn't factor into the equation.

Example: Gael graduated college in 2016 and was immediately offered a new job. Gael has always lived with his parents in Dallas, TX. His new job is located in Fort Worth, which is 33 miles away. Gael moves to Fort Worth in 2016 and starts his new job. He does not qualify for the moving expense deduction because he does not meet the distance test.

Example: Abe moved to a new city and took a job as an attorney in a different law firm. His old job was six miles from his former home. Therefore, in order to deduct his moving expenses, his new job location must be at least 56 miles from that former home. Abe calculates the distance between his new job and his old home and discovers that it is 58 miles. Abe's moving expenses are deductible.

A taxpayer who starts a first job or returns to full-time work after a long absence can also qualify for the deduction. Moving expenses incurred within one year of the date the taxpayer first reported to work at the new location can generally be deducted. There is no requirement that the job be in the same field. If a taxpayer does not move within one year of the date he begins the new job; the moving expenses are not deductible unless he can prove that circumstances prevented moving within that period. Failing to sell a former home, for example, would not be an adequate reason. Members of the armed forces moving because of a permanent change of station or a military order are not required to meet the distance test or the time test.

Qualifying Moving Expenses: Expenses that qualify for the moving expense deduction include:

- The cost of packing and moving household effects and family members.
- Storage costs (only while in transit and for up to 30 days after the day of the move).
- The cost of connecting or disconnecting utilities required because a taxpayer is moving his household goods, appliances, or personal effects.
- The cost of shipping a car or a pet to a new home.
- Travel expenses (including lodging, but not meals) for one trip per person. Family members are not required to travel together.

Actual car expenses such as gas and oil are tax deductible if accurate records are kept, or a taxpayer can use the standard mileage rate instead (19 cents per mile driven for moving purposes in 2016). Parking fees and tolls are also tax deductible, but general car repairs, maintenance, insurance, and depreciation of a taxpayer's car are not deductible moving expenses.

Example: Ethan and Jackie are married and file jointly. In February 2016, Ethan and Jackie moved from Rhode Island to Alabama where Ethan was starting a new job. He drove the family car to Alabama, a trip of 1,100 miles. His actual expenses were $281 for gas, plus $40 for tolls and $150 for lodging, for a total of $471. One week later, Jackie flew from Rhode Island to Alabama. Her only expense was a $400 plane ticket. The couple's moving expense deduction is $871 (Ethan's $471 + Jackie's $400).

Nondeductible Moving Expenses: Moving expenses that cannot be deducted include:

- Pre-move house-hunting expenses
- Temporary living expenses
- Meals while traveling
- Expenses of buying or selling a home, home improvements to help sell a home, or a loss on a home sale
- Real estate taxes
- Car tags and driver's license renewal fees
- Storage charges except those incurred in transit or for a foreign move

Employer-Reimbursed Moving Expenses: When an employer reimburses a taxpayer for deductible moving expenses, the reimbursement is excluded from taxable income. However, if an employer reimburses an employee for nondeductible expenses (such as the expense incurred from breaking a lease), the reimbursement is taxable as wages and must be included on the employee's Form W-2.

Example: Gabriel was offered a job at XelCorp Engineering. He agreed to accept the offer if XelCorp paid all his moving expenses. The cost of his professional movers was $9,600, which the company paid. This amount is deductible by XelCorp as a business expense and not taxable to Gabriel since it is a deductible moving expense. XelCorp also reimbursed Gabriel for a $7,500 loss on the sale of his home. Because this is reimbursement of a nondeductible expense, it is taxable and must be included on Gabriel's Form W-2. The $7,500 is deductible to XelCorp, but it is categorized as a wage expense and therefore subject to payroll tax.

Line 27: Deductible Part of Self-Employment Tax

A self-employed taxpayer can subtract from income 50% of self-employment tax, equal to the amount of Social Security and Medicare taxes that an employer normally pays for an employee, which is excluded from an employee's income. The deduction is figured on Schedule SE. A self-employed taxpayer cannot deduct one-half of the additional Medicare tax on earned income.[30]

Line 28: Self-Employed Retirement Plans

Self-employed individuals can deduct contributions to the following types of retirement plans:

- Simplified Employee Pension (SEP) plans
- Savings Incentive Match Plan for Employees (SIMPLE) plans
- Qualified plans

A taxpayer must have self-employment income in order to contribute to his own plan.[31] However, a self-employed taxpayer does not need to show a profit on Schedule C in order to contribute to an employee's retirement plan.

Example: Tony is a self-employed kickboxing instructor. He has a full-time receptionist named Francine that works in his training gym. In 2016, Tony makes a large fitness equipment purchase for his training gym. The fitness equipment qualifies for accelerated section 179 expensing. As a result, Tony reduces his taxable income to zero for the year. He cannot contribute to a retirement plan because he has no taxable income on his Schedule C. However, Tony is still allowed to contribute to Francine's retirement plan.

[30] The additional Medicare tax and other provisions of the Affordable Care Act are covered later.

[31] SEP, SIMPLE, and qualified retirement plans are primarily tested on the businesses section of the EA exam (Part 2), so they are covered primarily in Book 2 of the PassKey EA Review.

Line 29: Self-Employed Health Insurance Deduction

A self-employed taxpayer may be able to deduct up to 100% of his health insurance premiums as an adjustment to income. Premiums paid by the taxpayer for his spouse and dependents under age 27 at the end of the year are also deductible. However, the deduction is limited to the net profit or other earned income from the business under which the health coverage is arranged, minus the deductions on Lines 27 and 28 of Form 1040. The taxpayer must either:

- Be self-employed and have a net profit for the year;
- Be a partner with net earnings from self-employment; or
- Have received wages from an S corporation in which he was a more-than-2% shareholder.

Long-term care insurance is also considered health insurance for purposes of this deduction. The policy can be in the name of the business or in the name of the business owner.

A self-employed taxpayer may not take the deduction if either he or his spouse (if MFJ) is eligible to participate in an employer-sponsored and subsidized health insurance plan, even if they decline coverage.

Line 30: Penalty on Early Withdrawal of Savings

If a taxpayer withdraws money from a certificate of deposit (CD) or other time-deposit savings account prior to maturity, he usually incurs a penalty for early withdrawal. This penalty is charged by the bank or other financial institution and withheld from a taxpayer's proceeds.

Taxpayers can take an adjustment to income for early withdrawal penalties. The penalties are reported on a taxpayer's Form 1099-INT, *Interest Income*, or on Form 1099-OID, *Original Issue Discount*, which lists interest income as well as the penalty amount.

Example: Early in 2016, Gloria invested in a $15,000 one-year certificate of deposit. In November, she had an unexpected medical expense and had to liquidate the CD. She paid a penalty of three months' interest, which totaled $150. Gloria can claim the penalty ($150) as an adjustment to income.

Note: Don't be confused by this concept! It is frequently tested. Only the penalty for early withdrawal from a timed deposit (a certificate of deposit) is tax deductible. The penalty for early withdrawal from an IRA or a retirement plan is never deductible.

Line 31a: Alimony Paid

As described in the preceding unit, alimony received is taxable income. Alimony paid is generally treated as the mirror image and is a deductible expense that is claimed on Page 1 of Form 1040.

By definition, Alimony is a payment to a former spouse under a divorce or separation instrument. The payments do not have to be made directly to the ex-spouse. For example, payments made on behalf of the ex-spouse for expenses such as medical bills, housing costs, and other expenses can also qualify as alimony. Voluntary payments not required by a divorce decree or separation instrument do not qualify as alimony.

Example: Yvette's divorce settlement requires that she pay her ex-husband $16,000 a year. Per the divorce agreement, she also must pay his ongoing medical expenses. In 2016, her ex-husband had $9,500 of medical expenses. She can deduct the full amount ($25,500) as an adjustment to income because it is required by her divorce agreement.

Example: Under the terms of Anthony's divorce decree, he must pay his ex-wife $12,600 in 2016. As a favor, he also makes $2,400 in payments to cover part of her vehicle lease so she can keep steady employment. Anthony can claim the $12,600 as an adjustment to income. He cannot count the lease payments because they were not required by the divorce agreement.

Line 32: IRA Deduction

An individual retirement arrangement (IRA) offers tax advantages for setting aside money for retirement. Some taxpayers can claim a deduction for the amounts contributed to a traditional IRA as an adjustment to gross income.

Amounts that do not qualify for deduction include:

- Contributions to a Roth IRA
- Contributions to a traditional IRA that are nondeductible because the taxpayer and/or spouse is covered by an employer-sponsored retirement plan and modified adjusted gross income (MAGI) exceeds certain limits
- Contributions that apply to the previous tax year
- Rollover contributions

Deductions are allowed in full for contributions to a traditional IRA by a taxpayer (and spouse, if married) who is not covered by a retirement plan at work. If the taxpayer (and/or spouse) is covered by a retirement plan at work, deductions are phased out at certain income levels.[32]

Line 33: Student Loan Interest Deduction

Generally, personal interest (other than mortgage interest) is not deductible. However, interest on a qualified student loan is deductible. A qualified student loan is a loan used solely to pay qualified higher education expenses for the taxpayer, his spouse, or his dependents. A taxpayer can claim the deduction for 2016 if:

- He paid interest on a qualified student loan on which he was legally obligated.
- His filing status is not married filing separately.
- Neither he (nor his spouse, if filing jointly) can be claimed as a dependent on someone else's return.

The maximum deduction for student loan interest in 2016 is $2,500. A phaseout applies for taxpayers with modified adjusted gross income (MAGI) exceeding $65,000 ($130,000 MFJ). The deduction is completely phased out for taxpayers with modified adjusted gross income (MAGI) of $80,000 or more ($160,000 for MFJ). Taxpayers who file MFS are not allowed to take a deduction for student loan interest.

Example: Veronica and her husband file jointly. Their modified adjusted gross income is $168,000. She completed her doctorate and paid $3,400 of student loan interest in 2016. Due to their high income, they cannot deduct any of their student loan interest as an adjustment to income.

In order for student loan interest to qualify, the student must have been enrolled at least half-time in a higher education program leading to a degree, certificate, or other recognized educational credential. A student who used the loan to take classes for other purposes does not qualify.

Example: Peter graduated from a technical college where he had been enrolled full-time in a certificate program for automotive repair. Peter may take the student loan interest deduction.

A student loan is not eligible if it is from certain related persons (such as family members or certain corporations, partnerships, or trusts). Loans from an employer plan also do not qualify. The student loan interest deduction limit is per return, not per student. For example, if a taxpayer has three children and pays $2,000 in student loan interest for each of them, the

[32] The rules regarding IRA contributions, distributions (withdrawals), and rollovers are covered in detail later, in a dedicated unit for retirement plans.

maximum deduction is still only $2,500. Qualified higher education expenses are costs of attending an eligible educational institution, including graduate schools, such as:

- Tuition and fees
- Room and board
- Books, supplies, and equipment
- Other necessary school-related expenses, such as transportation

Qualified expenses must be reduced by the amounts of tax-free items used to pay them, such as the following:

- Employer-provided educational assistance benefits
- Tax-free withdrawals from a Coverdell Education Savings Account
- U.S. savings bond interest already excluded from income
- Tax-free scholarships and fellowships
- Veterans' educational assistance benefits
- Any other nontaxable payments (except gifts or inheritances) received for educational expenses

Example: In 2016, Eva's college tuition expenses are $7,200. She also receives a gift of $1,000 from her aunt and $1,000 of her veterans' G.I. Bill. Therefore, Eva's qualified higher education expenses are $6,200 because veterans' assistance benefits must be subtracted. The gift from her aunt does not have to be subtracted.

Lenders are required to send the taxpayer Form 1098-E, *Student Loan Interest*, when the amount of interest paid is at least $600 or more.

Summary: Student Loan Interest Deduction

Maximum deduction	$2,500 per tax return, per year.
Loan qualifications	The student loan: • Must have been taken out solely to pay qualified education expenses, and • Cannot be from a related person or made under a qualified employer plan.
Student qualifications	The student must be the taxpayer, a spouse, or a dependent, and must be enrolled at least half-time in a degree program when the loan was incurred.
Time limit	The taxpayer can deduct interest paid during the remaining period of the student loan.
MAGI phaseout ranges	Single: $65,000-$80,000; MFJ: $130,000-$160,000. MFS does not qualify to take this deduction, regardless of income threshold.

Line 34: Tuition and Fees

Taxpayers can deduct qualified tuition and related higher education expenses paid for academic periods beginning in 2016 and the first three months of 2017.[33] For example, if a taxpayer paid $1,500 in December 2016 for qualified tuition for the spring semester that begins in January 2017, the taxpayer would be able to deduct that $1,500 on their 2016 return.

The Tuition and Fees Deduction is up to $4,000 for qualifying tuition and fees paid for a qualified student (the taxpayer, a spouse, or a dependent). The deduction is reduced to $2,000 for taxpayers with income between the income phaseout thresholds. The phaseout begins at

[33] At the time of this book's printing, the Tuition and Fees Deduction is set to expire on December 31, 2016, and has not been extended for 2017.

$65,000 ($130,000 for MFJ). A taxpayer whose modified adjusted gross income is greater than $80,000 ($160,000 for joint filers) cannot claim the tuition and fees deduction.

Qualified education expenses include: tuition, fees, and other required course materials. Qualified expenses do *not* include:

- Room and board, medical expenses (including student health fees), transportation, or other personal expenses
- Course-related books, supplies, equipment, and nonacademic activities and fees, unless they are *required* as a condition of enrollment
- Any course or other education involving sports, games, or hobbies, or any noncredit course

A taxpayer cannot claim the tuition and fees deduction based on expenses that have already been paid with a tax-free scholarship, fellowship, grant, or education savings account.

Note: The expenses that qualify for the tuition and fees deduction are more limited than the expenses that qualify for the student loan interest deduction. Generally, for the tuition and fees deduction, qualified education expenses are only amounts paid for tuition expenses at an eligible college or vocational institution

Restrictions: A taxpayer filing MFS cannot take the tuition and fees deduction. If a taxpayer is claimed as a dependent on someone else's return, he cannot take the deduction for himself. Nonresident aliens also do not qualify for this deduction.

A taxpayer cannot claim the tuition and fees deduction and an education credit for the same student. A taxpayer who is eligible to claim the American Opportunity Credit or Lifetime Learning Credit is allowed to figure his return both ways and choose the deduction resulting in the lowest tax.

Line 35: Domestic Production Activities Deduction

The domestic production activities deduction is a tax deduction available to manufacturing businesses that have employees in the United States. The deduction is designed to stimulate domestic production. A sole proprietor could qualify for this deduction if his business has employees and pays wages,[34] although it is rare.

Line 36: Other Adjustments

Line 36 of Form 1040 is reserved for more obscure deductions. This line on the form allows the taxpayer to manually indicate what type of adjustment is being taken. Some of the miscellaneous adjustments that may be entered on line 36 include deductions to an Archer MSA; jury duty pay remitted to an employer; and repayment of unemployment benefits.

[34] The DPAD is covered more thoroughly in Part *2: Businesses*.

Unit 11: Study Questions

(Test yourself first, then check the correct answers at the end of this quiz.)

1. Kyle is 26 and has an HSA. He becomes permanently disabled in 2016 due to an auto accident. Which of the following statements is correct?

A. He may withdraw money from his HSA for nonmedical expenses, but the withdrawals will be subject to income tax and also an additional penalty of 20%.
B. He may withdraw money from his HSA for nonmedical expenses. The withdrawals will be subject to income tax, but will not be subject to a penalty.
C. He may not take nonmedical distributions from his account.
D. He must be at least 65 to take nonmedical distributions from an HSA.

2. Deborah was self-employed in 2016 and had self-employment tax of $4,896. Which of the following statements is correct?

A. She can deduct 100% of the self-employment tax she paid on Schedule C.
B. She can deduct 50% of the self-employment tax she paid on Schedule C.
C. She can deduct 50% of the self-employment tax she paid as an adjustment to income on Form 1040.
D. She cannot deduct self-employment tax.

3. Jermaine and Anna have MAGI of $45,000. They are married and file a joint return. Two years ago, they took out a loan so their daughter, Miranda, could earn her degree. Miranda is their dependent. In 2016, they paid $3,000 of student loan interest. How much student loan interest can Jermaine and Anna deduct on their tax return?

A. $0
B. $1,000
C. $2,500
D. $3,000

4. All of the following statements are correct about the educator expense deduction except:

A. A school counselor may qualify.
B. A part-time teacher may qualify.
C. A school principal may qualify.
D. A college instructor may qualify.

5. Under his divorce decree, Rick must pay the medical expenses of his former spouse, Linda. In January 2016, Rick sends a check totaling $4,000 directly to General Medical Hospital in order to pay for Linda's emergency surgery. Which of the following statements is correct?

A. This payment qualifies as alimony, and Linda must include the $4,000 as income on her return.
B. This payment does not qualify as alimony, but Rick can claim a deduction for the medical expenses on his return.
C. Linda must include the $4,000 as income on her return, but Rick cannot deduct the expense as alimony because it was paid to a third party.
D. None of the above.

6. Dave and Bea file jointly. In March 2016, they move from Arizona to Connecticut, where Dave is starting a new job. Dave drives his car to Hartford. His expenses are $400 for gas, $40 for bridge tolls, $150 for lodging, and $70 for meals. One week later, Bea quits her job and drives to Hartford to join her husband. Bea's expenses are $500 for gas, $40 for tolls, $35 for parking, $100 for lodging, and $25 for meals. A week later, they pay $600 to ship their pet, a miniature horse, to Connecticut. How much can they deduct for moving expenses?

A. $590
B. $1,265
C. $1,865
D. $1,960

7. Chuck and Mallory are married and file jointly. Chuck is self-employed, and his net profit was $50,000 in 2016. They pay $700 per month for health insurance coverage. Mallory was a homemaker until she started working for a construction company in early February. Mallory and Chuck became eligible to participate in her employer's health plan on March 1, 2016, but they did not want to switch insurance providers, so Mallory declined her employer's coverage. Which of the following statements is correct?

A. They can deduct $700 for both January and February, and $350 per month for each of the last ten months of the year, as self-employed health insurance premiums on Chuck's Schedule C.
B. They can deduct $1,400 in self-employed health insurance premiums, which is for January and February, the two months they were not eligible to participate in an employer plan.
C. They can deduct 100% of their health insurance premiums because they declined the employer coverage.
D. They can deduct 50% of their health insurance premiums on Chuck's Schedule C.

8. Years ago, Sammy took out a student loan for $90,000 to help pay his college tuition. He graduated and began making payments on his student loan in 2016. Sammy made 12 payments in 2016, which included $1,600 of interest and $2,000 of principal. How much is Sammy's student loan interest deduction?

A. $1,600
B. $2,000
C. $2,500
D. $2,600

9. Marshall lost his job last year and withdrew money from a number of accounts. He paid the following penalties:

Penalty for early withdrawal from a CD	$100
Penalty for early withdrawal from a traditional IRA	200
Late penalty for not paying his rent on time	50

What amount can Marshall deduct as an adjustment to income on his Form 1040?

A. $0
B. $100
C. $200
D. $250

10. Lynn was offered a position in another city. Her new employer reimburses her for the $9,500 loss on the sale of her home because of the move. How should this reimbursement be treated?

A. The employer can reimburse Lynn and make the payment nontaxable through an accountable plan if properly documented.
B. Because this is a reimbursement of a nondeductible expense, it is treated as wages and must be included on Lynn's Form W-2.
C. The reimbursement is tax-exempt because it is a qualified moving expense.
D. The expense is nontaxable as long as Lynn's employer makes the payment directly to her mortgage lender.

11. Bruce makes an excess contribution to his HSA by accidentally contributing over the maximum allowable amount. What is the penalty on excess contributions if Bruce does not correct the problem?

A. No penalty.
B. 6% penalty.
C. 10% penalty.
D. 20% penalty.

12. An adjustment to income is considered the most beneficial type of deduction because:

A. It favors taxpayers who choose to itemize their deductions.
B. It is simpler to figure out qualifying expenses for adjustments to income than it is other deductions.
C. It lowers a taxpayer's adjusted gross income, and thus can affect the amounts of certain credits and deductions he may be able to claim.
D. There is no significant difference between an adjustment to income and other tax deductions.

13. Emilio is a sophomore at his state university, working on his degree in anthropology. In 2016, he paid $3,000 of tuition and $10,000 to live in optional on-campus housing. In addition to tuition, he is required to pay a fee of $300 to the university for the rental of the equipment he uses in his anthropology program. What amount of qualifying expenses does he have for purposes of the tuition and fees deduction?

A. $3,000
B. $3,300
C. $13,000
D. $13,300

14. Drew borrowed $15,000 from his sister to pay for college. He signed a notarized loan statement and is making regular payments of $500 per month, including 10% interest. In 2016, he paid $1,400 of student loan interest. Which of the following statements is correct?

A. Drew can deduct all the interest as qualified student loan interest.
B. Drew can deduct $2,500 of the interest as qualified student loan interest.
C. Drew cannot deduct the interest.
D. Drew can deduct $6,000 ($500 × 12 months) as qualified student interest.

15. Jasmine is a part-time art teacher at an elementary school. She spends $185 on qualified expenses for her art students and $75 on materials for a health course that she also teaches. She worked 440 hours as an educator during the tax year. How much can she deduct in educator expenses as an adjustment to income?

A. $0
B. $185
C. $250
D. $260

16. George paid $14,000 of alimony to his ex-wife during the year. Which of the following statements is correct?

A. He can deduct alimony only if he itemizes deductions on his tax return.
B. The deduction for alimony is entered on Schedule A as an itemized deduction.
C. He can deduct alimony paid, even if he does not itemize deductions.
D. He can deduct alimony paid on Form 1040A.

17. Two full-time teachers who are married and file jointly can deduct a maximum of ________ in educator expenses:

A. $100
B. $250
C. $500
D. $750

18. Chase is moving for a new job. He has the following expenses:

Moving truck rental	$500
Moving family and pets	300
Storage unit while moving	200
Breaking his existing apartment lease	400
Pre-move house-hunting	500

Assuming that Chase passes all the required tests, what is his allowable moving expense deduction?

A. $500
B. $800
C. $1,000
D. $1,900

19. Which of the following qualifies as a deductible education expense for the tuition and fees deduction?

A. College club dues.
B. Student health fees.
C. Room and board.
D. Student activity fees required as a condition for enrollment.

20. Marina is a software specialist who works and lives in Boston. A company offers her a new job in Raleigh, North Carolina, more than 700 miles away. As part of the offer, she negotiates a deal to work part-time for the first six months. Marina's husband is a stay-at-home father to the couple's two young children. The family makes the move from Boston to Raleigh, and Marina begins work at her new job. Does she meet both the time and distance tests in order to deduct her moving expenses as an adjustment to income?

A. No, she does not meet the distance test.
B. No, she does not meet the time test or distance test.
C. She meets the distance test, but not the time test.
D. Marina meets both tests and is able to deduct her moving expenses.

21. Carlie had an HSA account set up with her employer that had \$3,000 in the account at the end of the year. She then quit her job in late December and withdrew all the funds from her HSA. She did not use the \$3,000 for qualifying medical expenses. What is the consequence of this action?

A. Nothing; taxpayers are allowed to withdraw from their HSA accounts at any time.
B. Nonmedical withdrawals from an HSA are prohibited and will result in a forfeiture of the funds.
C. Withdrawals from an HSA for non-eligible expenses are subject to income tax and a 20% penalty.
D. Withdrawals from an HSA for non-eligible expenses are subject to income tax and a 6% penalty.

Unit 11: Answers

1. The answer is B. Withdrawals for nonmedical expenses from an HSA are allowed, but are subject to income tax. Nonmedical distributions are also subject to an additional penalty tax of 20%, except when the taxpayer has turned 65, become disabled, or died. Kyle has become permanently disabled, in which case his HSA withdrawals are not subject to penalty.

2. The answer is C. Deborah can deduct 50% of the self-employment tax she paid as an adjustment to income on page 1 of her Form 1040.

3. The answer is C. The maximum deduction for student loan interest is $2,500. The deduction is limited to the lesser of $2,500 or the amount of interest actually paid. It doesn't matter how many qualifying student loans there are; the maximum is $2,500 per tax return (not per taxpayer).

4. The answer is D. College instructors do not qualify. An eligible educator must work 900 hours a year in a school that provides elementary or secondary education (K-12). Part-time teachers qualify, if they meet the yearly teachers requirement for hours worked. The term educator includes instructors, counselors, principals, and aides.

5. The answer is A. The payment may be treated as alimony for tax purposes because the medical payments are a condition of the divorce agreement. Payments to a third party on behalf of an ex-spouse under the terms of a divorce instrument can be alimony, if they qualify. These include payments for a spouse's medical expenses, housing costs (rent and utilities), taxes, and tuition. The payments are treated by the ex-spouse as if they were received directly, and included as income.

6. The answer is C. The cost of both trips is deductible. However, the cost of meals is not deductible. The costs of travel, transportation, and lodging are all deductible. The costs of moving personal items and pets are deductible. The answer is figured as follows:

Dave's deductible expenses: $400 + $40 + $150 = $590
Bea's deductible expenses: $500 + $40 + $35 + $100 = $675
Cost of shipping horse: $600
Total deductible expenses: $590 + $675 + $600 = $1,865

If a married couple files jointly, either spouse can qualify for the full-time work test. Family members are not required to travel together.

7. The answer is B. Chuck and Mallory can deduct only $1,400 ($700 X two months) of self-employed health insurance for the months that they were ineligible to participate in an employer plan. No deduction is allowed for self-employed health insurance for any month that the taxpayer has the *option* to participate in an employer-sponsored and subsidized plan. This is true even if the taxpayer declines the coverage. A self-employed taxpayer can deduct 100% of health insurance premiums as an adjustment to income, but only if neither he nor his spouse was eligible to participate in an employer health plan.

8. The answer is A. Only the interest is deductible. A payment toward the principal on the loan is not a deductible expense. Student loan interest is interest a taxpayer paid during the year on a qualified student loan. It includes both required and voluntary interest payments.

9. The answer is B. Early withdrawal penalties are deductible if made from a time deposit account, such as a certificate of deposit. The other types of penalties are not deductible.

10. The answer is B. Expenses of buying or selling a home (including closing costs, mortgage fees, and points) are never deductible as moving expenses. If an employer pays or reimburses expenses, the amounts are treated as taxable compensation and must be reported as wages on Lynn's Form W-2.

11. The answer is B. A 6% penalty applies to excess contributions to a health savings account. Excess contributions made by an employer must be included in an employee's gross income. Excess contributions to an HSA are not deductible.

12. The answer is C. Adjustments are deducted from gross income to derive adjusted gross income (AGI), and itemized and standard deductions are subtracted from AGI. The amount of a taxpayer's AGI is important, as it can affect his eligibility for certain deductions and the amounts that he can claim. For example, certain items are phased out at specified levels of AGI, and some itemized deductions must exceed specified percentages of AGI in order to be deductible. In addition, itemized deductions may be subject to the alternative minimum tax, or may total less than the taxpayer's applicable standard deduction.

13. The answer is B. The rental fee ($300) and the tuition costs ($3,000) qualify for the tuition and fees deduction, which Emilio can claim as an adjustment to income. Because the equipment rental fee must be paid to the university and is a requirement for enrollment and attendance, it is a qualified expense. Student-activity fees and expenses for course-related books, supplies, and equipment can be included in qualified educational expenses if the fees and expenses paid to the institution are required. The housing is not a qualified educational expense.

14. The answer is C. Interest paid to a family member is not qualified interest for purposes of the student loan interest deduction. Related persons include a spouse, brothers and sisters, half-brothers and half-sisters, ancestors (parents, grandparents, etc.), and lineal descendants (children, grandchildren, etc.).

15. The answer is A. Because Jasmine worked only 440 hours as an educator during the tax year, she cannot deduct her educator expenses as an adjustment to income. An educator must have at least 900 hours of qualified employment during the school year to take this deduction as an adjustment to income.

16. The answer is C. George can deduct alimony paid, even if he does not itemize deductions. He must file Form 1040 and enter the amount of alimony paid as an adjustment to income.

17. The answer is C. On a jointly filed tax return, if both taxpayers are teachers, they both may take the deduction, up to a maximum of $500 ($250 each).

18. The answer is C. The cost of breaking a lease is not a deductible moving expense. House-hunting before a move is also not deductible. Therefore, Chase can deduct $1,000 ($500 for a moving truck + $300 for moving his family and pets + $200 for a storage unit).

19. The answer is D. Only the student activity fees qualify for the tuition and fees deduction. Deductions are not allowed for room and board and other basic expenses of going to college, other than required tuition and fees. Student activity fees, course-related books, supplies, and equipment may be deductible only if they are required by the institution as a condition of enrollment.

20. The answer is C. Marina is not able to deduct her moving expenses. She meets the distance test because her old home in Boston is more than 50 miles from her new office in Raleigh. However, to meet the time test, she must work full-time for a period of at least 39 weeks in the first 12 months. Since she is only working part-time for six months, this does not fulfill the requirements of the time test. A spouse does not need to be employed for a MFJ couple to deduct moving expenses.

21. The answer is C. Withdrawals from an HSA for non-eligible expenses are allowed, but the withdrawal is subject to a 20% penalty, in addition to regular income tax.

Unit 12: Standard Deduction & Itemized Deductions

For additional information read:
Publication 502, *Medical and Dental Expenses*
Publication 600, *State and Local General Sales Taxes*
Publication 936, *Home Mortgage Interest Deduction*
Publication 526, *Charitable Contributions*
IRS Publication 1771, *Charitable Contributions–Substantiation and Disclosure Requirements*

A taxpayer generally may choose either to claim a standard deduction amount or to itemize deductions. The choice should be based on which option results in a lower tax liability.

The standard deduction is a specific dollar amount that reduces the amount of income on which a taxpayer is taxed. Using the standard deduction eliminates the need for a taxpayer to itemize his actual allowable deductions, such as medical expenses, charitable contributions, or state and local taxes. The standard deduction amounts are based on a taxpayer's filing status and are adjusted every year for inflation.

Filing Status	2016 Standard Deduction
Single	$6,300
Head of Household	$9,300
Married Filing Separately	$6,300
Married Filing Jointly	$12,600
Qualifying Widow(er)	$12,600
Dependent Standard Deduction	$1,050

Depending on the option selected, either the applicable standard deduction amount or the taxpayer's total itemized deductions is subtracted from his adjusted gross income.

An additional standard deduction is available to taxpayers who, at the end of the year, are:

- 65 or older, and/or
- Blind or partially blind.

The additional standard deduction amount in these cases is $1,250 per taxpayer for married filers and $1,550 for single or head of household filers. A taxpayer who is *both* blind and 65 or older may take the basic standard deduction and additional standard deduction amounts for both age and blindness.

Additional Standard Deduction Amounts-2016	
Taxpayers who are age 65 and/or blind	
Filing Status	Additional Amount Allowable
Single, HOH	$ 1,550
MFS, MFJ, QW	$ 1,250

Note: For filing purposes, a taxpayer is considered to be age 65 in tax year 2016 if they were 65 on December 31, 2016, or if they turned 65 on January 1, 2017.

The additional amount for blindness is allowed if the taxpayer is blind on the last day of the tax year, even if he was not blind the rest of the year. A taxpayer must obtain a statement from an eye doctor indicating that:

- The taxpayer cannot see better than 20/200 in the better eye, even when corrected with eyeglasses, or
- The taxpayer's field of vision is not more than 20 degrees (the taxpayer has disabled peripheral vision).

Example: Wade, 46, and Christine, 33, file jointly. Neither is blind. They decide not to itemize their deductions. Their standard deduction is $12,600 in 2016.

Example: Gilbert, age 52, and Lisa, age 51, are married and do not itemize deductions. Because they file jointly, their base standard deduction is $12,600 in 2016. Lisa is also blind, so she can claim an additional standard deduction amount of $1,250. Therefore, the total standard deduction of their joint return is $13,850 ($12,600 + $1,250) in 2016.

The standard deduction for a deceased taxpayer is the same as if the taxpayer had lived the entire year, with one exception: If the taxpayer died *before* his actual sixty-fifth birthday, the higher standard deduction for being 65 does not apply.

Example: Richard is single and died on November 1, 2016. He would have been 65 if he had reached his birthday on December 18, 2016. He does not qualify for a higher standard deduction because he died before his sixty-fifth birthday, even though it would have happened during the 2016 tax year. His standard deduction is $6,300 on his final income tax return, which must be filed by his executor before April 18, 2017.

Standard Deduction for Certain Dependents

The standard deduction for a dependent which can be claimed on another person's return is limited to the greater of:

- $1,050, or
- The dependent's earned income (such as wages) plus $350, but not more than the regular standard deduction amount. For a single person, this is generally $6,300 in 2016. However, the standard deduction amount can be higher if the dependent is 65 or older and/or blind.

Example: Amy is 19, single, and legally blind. She is claimed as a dependent on her parents' 2016 return. Amy has interest income of $1,300 and wages from a part-time job of $2,900. Because she is claimed as a dependent, Amy's base amount for the standard deduction is $3,250 ($2,900 wages + $350). Because she is also blind, she is also allowed an additional standard deduction amount of $1,550. Her standard deduction is $4,800 ($2,900 + $350 + $1,550).

Example: Georgia is single, 22, and a college student with a part-time job. Her parents support her, so they claim her as a dependent on their 2016 tax return. Georgia files a return and takes the standard deduction, but she does not claim her own exemption (because her parents are claiming her as a dependent). She has wages of $780 from her part-time job, and taxes withheld from her wages totaling $35. Her standard deduction is $1,130 ($780 wages + $350).

Itemized Deductions

Itemized deductions may be taken instead of the standard deduction; they allow taxpayers to reduce their taxable income based on specific personal expenses. If a taxpayer's total itemized deductions are greater than his applicable standard deduction amount, they will normally result in lower taxable income and a lower tax liability. In most cases, a taxpayer may choose whether to claim itemized deductions or the standard deduction, depending on which is more beneficial. However, taxpayers are *required* to itemize in the following cases:

- If married and filing separately and one spouse itemizes, the other spouse also must itemize.[35]
- If the taxpayer is a nonresident or dual-status alien (who is not married to a U.S. citizen or resident).
- If the taxpayer files a tax return for a period of less than 12 months due to a change in accounting methods.

If a taxpayer itemizes deductions, he must complete and file Schedule A along with his Form 1040. We will review the specific requirements for various itemized deductions in this and the next unit.

Limitation on Itemized Deductions (the Pease Limitation)

The "Pease Limitation" is named after Congressman Donald Pease, who originally introduced the legislation. This provision limits the amount of itemized deductions for taxpayers in higher income brackets.

The limitation reduces the total amount of a higher-income taxpayer's itemized deductions by the lesser of:

- 3% of the amount by which the taxpayer's AGI exceeds a specific threshold, or
- 80% of the total amount of the otherwise allowable itemized deductions.

The Pease Limitation only affects certain tax deductions. The limitation does not apply to the following itemized deductions:

- Medical expenses
- Investment interest expense
- Casualty or theft losses
- Gambling losses

Itemized Deduction AGI Threshold Amounts

2016 Pease Limitation	
Filing Status	AGI Phaseout Ranges
MFS	$155,650 to $216,900
Single	$259,400 to $381,900
HOH	$285,350 to $407,850
MFJ, QW	$311,300 to $433,800

The limitation applies to all other itemized deductions, including charitable contributions; mortgage interest; state, local, and property taxes; and miscellaneous itemized deductions. The Pease Limitation does not apply under the AMT.

[35] This rule only applies when *both* spouses are filing MFS. If one spouse is MFS, but the other spouse qualifies for HOH filing status (Head of Household), then the spouses are not forced to itemize, and they may choose the standard deduction if they wish.

Example: For tax year 2016 Andrew and Pauline are filing jointly. Their adjusted gross income is $325,500. Their itemized deductions on Schedule A are as follows:

Property taxes:	$17,900
Mortgage interest paid:	$45,000
Investment interest expense:	$41,000
Charitable gifts:	$21,000
Job search expenses:	$17,240
Total *before* applying Pease Limitation:	$142,140

Andrew and Pauline's investment interest expense deduction ($41,000) isn't subject to the overall limit on itemized deductions. They use the Itemized Deductions Worksheet in the Schedule A (Form 1040) instructions to figure their overall limit. Of their $142,140 total itemized deductions, they can deduct only $141,714 ($142,140 - $426). They enter $141,714 on Schedule A (Form 1040), line 29.[36]

Medical and Dental Expenses

Medical and dental expenses (other than self-employed health insurance premiums) are deductible only if a taxpayer itemizes deductions. Further, most taxpayers can deduct only the amount of unreimbursed medical expenses that exceeds 10% of adjusted gross income.[37]

Example: Tracy, age 53, had unreimbursed medical expenses totaling $2,500 in 2016. Her AGI was $40,000. Tracy cannot deduct any of her medical expenses on Schedule A because they are not more than 10% of her AGI ($40,000 × .10 = $4,000).

Example: Manuel, age 46, paid $12,000 in out-of-pocket expenses for knee surgery in 2016. His AGI was $100,000. The amount of medical expenses in excess of $10,000 (AGI of $100,000 × 10% limitation), or $2,000, is allowed as an itemized deduction on Schedule A.

Special Rules for Taxpayers 65 and Over: Only through 2016, a taxpayer (and spouse, if married) age 65 or over can deduct the amount of unreimbursed medical expenses that exceeds 7.5% of AGI, rather than 10%. The 7.5% floor also would apply if *either* spouse reaches age 65 by the end of the tax year.[38] A change in the applicable AGI percentage can occur because of marriage, divorce, or annulment.

Example: Meredith, age 59, and Rudy, age 66, had unreimbursed medical expenses of $8,000 in 2016. Their AGI was $70,000. Because Rudy is older than 65, they may use the 7.5%-of-AGI threshold and deduct $2,750 on their Schedule A, the amount in excess of the 7.5% floor ($70,000 × .75 = $5,250). The 7.5% limitation applies to all their medical expenses, regardless of which spouse incurred them.

[36] Example adapted from Publication 17, chapter 29.

[37] The change from the original 7.5% medical expenses threshold to 10% was introduced in 2014 as part of the Affordable Healthcare Act and applies until the end of 2016.

[38] The floor for medical expenses is 10% for all taxpayers, regardless of age, after December 31, 2016.

Example: Neil, age 61, is married to Cora, age 66. Their unreimbursed medical expenses total 9% of their AGI. They can deduct the amount that exceeds the 7.5% floor because Cora is over age 65. However, on November 2, 2016, Neil and Cora divorce. Now they must both file as single for 2016. Neil, who is age 61, now can deduct only the amount of his unreimbursed medical expenses that exceeds 10% of his AGI, while Cora may continue to use the 7.5% floor.

Note: The special 7.5% threshold for taxpayers 65 and older is only temporary—starting in 2017, regardless of age, all taxpayers will be subject to a 10%-of-AGI limit for medical expenses.

Qualifying Medical Expenses

A taxpayer may only deduct medical expenses they paid during the year, regardless of when the services were provided. Qualified medical expenses include expenses paid for:

- The taxpayer or the taxpayer's spouse
- Dependents (the individual must have been a dependent at the time the medical services were provided or at the time the expenses were paid). However, there is an exception to this rule for children of divorced or separated parents.

A taxpayer can deduct medical expenses paid on behalf of an adopted child, even before the adoption is final. A taxpayer can also deduct medical expenses paid for a dependent parent. All the standard rules for a dependency exemption apply, so the dependent parent does not have to live with the taxpayer to qualify.

Note: If a child of divorced or separated parents is claimed as a dependent on either parent's return, each parent can deduct medical expenses they individually paid for the child. This is true even if the other parent claims the child's dependency exemption. Basically, it doesn't matter which parent claims the child—the medical expenses are deductible for the parent that pays them.

Example: Julie pays all the medical expenses for her father, age 62, who is her dependent, but does not live with her. The medical expenses are deductible on Julie's tax return as an itemized deduction to the extent they exceed the 10% threshold.

Example: Raymond and Carmen are divorced. Their son, Colby, lives primarily with Carmen, who claims him as a dependent on her tax return. Carmen also deducts Colby's annual medical and dental bills, including orthodontia expenses for his braces. However, in April, Colby falls on the playground and fractures his arm. The out-of-pocket expenses for Colby's broken arm are $5,500. Colby's father, Raymond, pays for the emergency room visit and the expenses related to the injury, and Raymond can deduct the expenses on Schedule A, even though he does not claim his son as a dependent.

Qualifying medical expenses include the costs of diagnosis, cure, mitigation, treatment, or prevention of disease, and the costs of medical (but not cosmetic) treatments. They include the costs of:

- Medically necessary equipment, supplies, and diagnostic devices
- Dental and vision care
- Transportation to obtain medical care
- Qualified long-term care insurance

Deductible medical expenses include:

- Fees paid to doctors, dentists, surgeons, chiropractors, psychiatrists, psychologists, and nontraditional medical practitioners
- In-patient hospital care or nursing home services, including the cost of meals and lodging charged by the hospital or nursing home
- Acupuncture treatments
- Lactation supplies
- Treatment at centers for alcohol or drug addiction, participation in smoking-cessation programs, and prescription drugs to alleviate nicotine withdrawal
- Weight-loss programs prescribed by a physician (but not diet food items)
- Insulin and prescription drugs (but prescription drugs brought in or shipped from a different country are generally not deductible)
- Admission and transportation to a medical conference relating to a chronic disease (but the costs of meals and lodging while attending the conference are not deductible)
- Veterinary care when it relates to the care of animals trained to assist persons who are visually-impaired, hearing-impaired, or disabled.

Example: Olaf is a Gulf War Veteran. Olaf is recovering from severe Post-Traumatic Stress Disorder. Olaf's physician recommends that he obtain a service dog to help aid him with his recovery. The doctor gives Olaf a written physician's statement explaining the recommendation. With the help of a Veteran's support group, Olaf obtains a trained service dog in 2016. The dog's veterinary costs are deductible medical expenses on Olaf's individual tax return.

Note: Medical expenses must be primarily to alleviate or prevent a physical or mental defect or illness. Medical expenses do not include expenses that are merely beneficial to general health, such as vitamins, spa treatments, gym memberships, or vacations. In addition, the cost of over-the-counter medications cannot be deducted.

Medical Insurance: If a taxpayer receives insurance reimbursement for medical care expenses, those amounts are not deductible. Qualifying medical expenses include medical insurance and long-term care insurance premiums that the taxpayer paid with after-tax dollars. A taxpayer cannot deduct insurance premiums paid by an employer-sponsored plan unless the premiums are included in Box 1 of his Form W-2.

Note: The value of a taxpayer's annual health care coverage is reported on Form W-2. The amount includes the portions paid by both the employer and the employee. Although this amount is reported on Form W-2, it does not mean the amount is taxable; it is for informational purposes only. This is a recent requirement of the Affordable Care Act.

Payments for medical expenses out of a health savings account (HSA) are not deductible, but contributions to HSAs may be deducted as an adjustment to gross income.

Long-Term Care Services: A taxpayer may include limited amounts paid for qualified long-term care services and insurance premiums in his medical expense deductions.

Long-term care services include necessary diagnostic, preventive, therapeutic, rehabilitative, maintenance, and personal care services that are required by a chronically-ill individual and provided under a plan of care by a licensed doctor.

The deductibility of costs of qualified long-term care premiums is limited by the age of the taxpayer. The expenses generally cannot include costs that would be reimbursed under Medicare.

2016 Long Term Care Premiums - Deductibility	
Age	**Maximum deduction for the year**
Age 40 or under	$390
Over 40 but not more than 50	$730
Over 50 but not more than 60	$1,460
Over 60 but not more than 70	$3,900
Over 70 years of age	$4,870

The limits on deductible long-term care premiums are per individual, not per tax return. For example, a married couple over age 70 could deduct up to **$9,740** ($4,870 X 2 persons) on a joint return in 2016.

Other Medical Expenses: If a taxpayer or a dependent is in a nursing home and the primary reason for being there is medically related, the entire cost, including meals and lodging, is a medical expense.

A taxpayer can deduct legal fees necessary to authorize treatment for a mental illness. However, legal fees for the management of a guardianship estate or for conducting the affairs of a person being treated are not deductible as medical expenses.

Medical Expenses of Deceased Taxpayers: In addition to expenses paid before a taxpayer's death, his survivor or personal representative can elect to treat medical expenses paid by the estate within one year after his death as if the taxpayer had paid when the medical services were provided.

Example: Anne had heart surgery in November 2016 and incurred $20,000 of medical bills. When she died on December 2, 2016, her 2016 medical bills had not yet been paid. The executor of Anne's estate is her son, Benny. Benny pays his late mother's outstanding medical bills on February 3, 2017. As the executor, Benny may elect to deduct Anne's final medical expenses on her 2016 tax return (her final tax return), even though the medical expenses were not paid by him until 2017. This special election only applies to deceased taxpayers.

Cosmetic Surgery: Cosmetic surgery is only deductible if it is used to correct a defect or disease. A cosmetic procedure simply for the enhancement of someone's physical appearance is not a deductible medical expense.

Example: Bethany undergoes a mastectomy to remove her breasts as part of treatment for cancer. A cosmetic surgeon later reconstructs her breasts to correct a deformity that is directly related to cancer. The cost of the cosmetic surgery is deductible as a medical expense because the surgery corrects an earlier defect or disease.

Medically-Related Transportation, Meals, and Lodging: Vehicle mileage may be deducted if transportation is for medical reasons, such as trips to and from doctors' appointments. If a taxpayer uses his own car for medical transportation, he can deduct actual out-of-pocket expenses for gas and other expenses, or he can deduct the standard mileage rate for medical expenses, which is 19 cents per mile in 2016. A taxpayer can also deduct the costs of taxis, buses, trains, planes, or ambulances, as well as tolls and parking fees.

A taxpayer can deduct the cost of meals and lodging at a hospital or similar institution if the principal reason for being there is to receive medical care. The care must be provided by a doctor, hospital, or medical care facility, and there must not be any significant element of personal pleasure or recreation.

Capital Improvements for Medical Reasons: Capital improvements such as home improvements are usually not deductible. However, a home improvement may qualify as a deductible expense if its main purpose is to provide medical care to the taxpayer or to dependent family members.

The deduction for capital improvements is limited to the excess of the actual cost of the improvements over the related increase in the fair market value of the home. Home improvements that qualify as deductible medical expenses may include:

- Wheelchair ramps
- Lowering of kitchen cabinets
- Railings and support bars
- Elevators
- Special lift equipment

Tenants can deduct the entire cost of disability-related improvements since they are not the owners of the property.

Example: Lonnie, age 61, has a heart condition. He cannot easily climb stairs or get into a bathtub. On his doctor's advice, he pays for the installation of a special sit-in bathtub and a stair lift in his rented house. The landlord did not pay any of the cost. Lonnie can deduct the entire amount as a medical expense, subject to the 10% threshold.

Deductible Taxes

Taxpayers can deduct certain taxes if they itemize deductions. To be deductible, a tax must have been imposed on the taxpayer and paid by the taxpayer during the tax year. Deductible taxes include:

- State, local, and foreign income taxes
- State and local sales taxes
- Real estate taxes
- Personal property taxes

State and Local Taxes: Taxpayers are allowed to deduct either *sales/use* taxes or state and local *income* taxes, depending on which provides the larger deduction, but not both. Income taxes paid include taxes withheld from salaries and wages, amounts paid for prior years, and estimated tax payments.

Real Estate Taxes: State, local, or foreign real estate taxes based on the assessed value of the taxpayer's real property (such as a house or land) are deductible. If the taxes are paid from a mortgage escrow account, the taxpayer can deduct only the amount actually paid out of the escrow account during the year to the taxing authority.

Note: Foreign real estate taxes are deductible on Schedule A. The property does not have to be located in the United States for the real estate tax to be deductible.

Some real estate taxes are not deductible, including taxes imposed to finance improvements to property, such as assessments for streets, sidewalks, and sewer lines. In addition, itemized charges for services and homeowner's association fees are not deductible.

Example: Genevieve makes the following payments: state income tax, $2,000; real estate taxes, $900; local benefit tax for improving the sewer system, $75; homeowner's association fee, $250. Her total deductible taxes are $2,900 ($2,000 + $900 = $2,900). The $75 local benefit tax and the $250 homeowner's association fee are not deductible.

If a property is sold, the real estate taxes are prorated between the buyer and the seller according to the number of days that each owned the property, and adjustments are charged or credited on the settlement statement depending upon which party is responsible for paying the taxing authority. **Escrow accounts:** If a portion of the taxpayer's monthly mortgage payment goes into an escrow account, and periodically the lender pays the real estate taxes out of the account to the local government, the taxpayer is only allowed to deduct the amount that was actually paid out of the escrow account during the year to the taxing authority.

Foreign Income Taxes: Generally, a taxpayer can choose between claiming the Foreign Tax Credit or claiming an itemized deduction on Schedule A for income taxes paid to a foreign country, depending on which option results in the lowest tax. The rules regarding which foreign taxes qualify for either the credit or the deduction are covered later.

Personal Property Taxes (DMV Fees): Personal property taxes are deductible if they are:

- Charged on personal property, including cars, boats, or items used in a business, such as equipment and furniture;
- Based on the value of the property; and
- Charged on a yearly basis, even if collected more or less than once a year.

Example: Patty receives an annual registration notice for her car from the California Department of Motor Vehicles. The bill is broken down as follows:

- Registration: $25
- Vehicle license fee: $58
- Weight fee: $32
- County fee: $13
- Owner responsibility fee: $15

The notice states that the vehicle license fee is based on the car's value. Only the vehicle license fee is tax deductible on Schedule A.

Deductible Interest

Taxpayers are allowed to deduct certain types of interest. Qualified interest payments are deductible as itemized deductions on Form 1040, Schedule A. Deductible interest includes:

- Home mortgage interest
- Points on a mortgage loan
- Mortgage insurance premiums
- Investment interest expense

Home Mortgage Interest

Home mortgage interest is paid on a loan secured by a taxpayer's home. The loan may be a mortgage, a second mortgage, a home equity loan, or a line of credit. A taxpayer is allowed to deduct the interest related to a primary residence and a second home. Under current laws, taxpayers may deduct interest on the loan balance of up to $1 million of home acquisition debt secured by a qualified primary or secondary residence.

Example: Kenji has a $150,000 mortgage on his main home where he lives. He also has a $75,000 mortgage on a beach cottage in North Carolina and a $90,000 mortgage on a condo in Utah. Kenji can deduct the mortgage interest on his main home and on the condo, but he cannot deduct the mortgage interest on the cottage because the deduction is limited to two homes.

A second home can include any other residence a taxpayer owns and treats as a home, but the taxpayer does not have to actually use the second home during the year in order to deduct the mortgage interest paid on the related loan.

Note: Although a taxpayer can deduct real estate taxes on more than two properties, he cannot deduct mortgage interest on more than two homes.

An empty lot does not qualify for the mortgage interest deduction. If a taxpayer builds a house that becomes a qualified home when ready for occupancy, he can deduct mortgage interest for a period of up to 24 months from when construction begins. A taxpayer can deduct late charges on a mortgage loan as mortgage interest.

Example: Reese owns his home and pays his mortgage on a monthly basis. In 2016, he falls behind on his mortgage payments and sends in his payment late on two occasions. The mortgage company charges Reese a $35 fee for each late payment. The late fees are deductible as mortgage interest.

Mortgage Deduction Limits

If all of the taxpayer's mortgages fit into one or more of the following three categories, he can deduct all of the interest:

- Mortgages obtained on or before October 13, 1987 (grandfathered debt).
- Mortgages obtained after October 13, 1987, to buy, build, or improve a home (called home acquisition debt), but only if these mortgages plus any grandfathered debt total **<u>$1 million</u>** ($500,000 if MFS) or less.
- Mortgages obtained after October 13, 1987, for purposes other than to buy, build, or improve the home (called home equity debt, or home equity lines of credit), but only if these mortgages are $100,000 or less.

If one or more of the taxpayer's mortgages does not fit in at least one of these categories, his interest deductions will be limited.

Example: Shirley has a mortgage of $800,000 against her primary residence and another of $500,000 against a vacation home. Both loans were used solely to acquire the homes. The loan amounts add up to $1.3 million. Since the total loan amounts exceed the $1 million limit for home acquisition debt, Shirley's mortgage interest deduction is limited.

Home Equity Lines of Credit (Special Rules)

The interest paid on home equity debt related to a main home and a second home is deductible, in most cases. Taxpayers can generally deduct interest paid on the first $100,000 of a home equity loan. The home equity debt limit is reduced to $50,000 for taxpayers who are married filing separately. A taxpayer can deduct the interest on home equity debt, subject to the limits described above, no matter how he uses the proceeds.

Example: Jeremy and Ashley obtained two home equity loans totaling $90,000. They used the loans to pay off gambling debts, credit card payments, and medical expenses. The couple can deduct the interest on their home equity loans because the total does not exceed $100,000.

If the home equity line is used to improve the home, then the interest is deductible up to the one million dollar limit. Remember, the amount of deductible mortgage interest on an equity loan depends primarily on what the loan is used for.

If a taxpayer borrows $250,000 in a home equity line of credit, and all of the loan proceeds are used to substantially improve the home, then the entire amount would be considered a qualifying loan for the mortgage interest deduction. In that case, the mortgage interest would be deductible up until the $1 million limit.

Example: Noah owns his own home. He decides to borrow a $150,000 home equity line in order to consolidate his credit card debt and buy a new car. Only the interest on the first $100,000 of the loan is deductible. The interest on the remaining $50,000 of the loan is not deductible as mortgage interest.

Example: Griselda owns her home. In 2016, she decides to add an extra bedroom, a new bathroom, and she installs a new pool. The bedroom addition cost $66,000, the new bathroom cost $22,000, and the new pool cost $29,000, for a total cost of $117,000. Griselda applies for a home equity line of credit to finance the improvements. Since the home equity loan was used entirely to improve the property, all of the interest is deductible as mortgage interest, even though the loan amount exceeds $100,000.

Example: Carla purchased her home ten years ago and paid cash. Its fair market value is now $80,000. She did not have a mortgage until last year, when she took out a $45,000 home equity loan, secured by her home, to pay for her daughter's college tuition. This loan is home equity debt. Since it is less than the $100,000 limit, the mortgage interest on the equity line is deductible.

Equity Loans Exceeding Fair Market Value

If the home equity line is used for something other than home improvements, and the amount of the home equity loan exceeds the fair market value of the home,[39] a portion of the interest will be disallowed, even if the equity line does not exceed $100,000.

The taxpayer must calculate the percentage of deductible interest based on a percentage.[40]

---

[39] Lenders traditionally refuse to lend more money than a home's fair market value. Although it is now uncommon for a bank to lend a borrower more than a home's value, it was common for lenders to offer 125% of a home's value as an equity line of credit, before the housing crisis of 2007-2008. This issue is still covered in IRS Publication 17, so you must understand it.

[40] Internal Revenue Code Section 163(h)(3) provides additional guidance for the limitations on the home mortgage interest deduction.

Example: Kody bought his home five years ago. Its FMV is now $110,000, and the current balance on his original mortgage is $95,000. His bank offers him a home equity loan with borrowings up to 125% of the FMV of the home. To consolidate some of his other debts, Kody takes out a new $42,500 home equity loan ([125% × $110,000] – $95,000). Kody's home equity loan exceeds the FMV of the home minus the balance of his home acquisition debt ($110,000 - $95,000 = $15,000). Therefore, his deductible mortgage interest relating to the home equity loan is limited to the interest on $15,000.

Points and Other Prepaid Mortgage Interest

Points are interest charges a borrower pays up-front to obtain a loan. Points generally represent prepaid interest a borrower pays at closing in order to obtain a lower interest rate. Points may also be called loan origination fees, including VA and FHA fees, maximum loan charges, premium charges, loan discount points, or prepaid interest.

Loan fees paid for specific services, such as home appraisal fees, document preparation fees, VA funding fees, or notary fees are not interest and are not deductible. In order to deduct points, the following requirements must be met:

- The mortgage must be secured by the taxpayer's main home, and the mortgage must have been used to buy, build, or improve the home.
- The points must not be an excessive or unusual amount for the local area.
- The points paid must not be more than the amount of unborrowed funds.
- The points must be computed as a percentage of the loan principal, and they must be listed on the settlement statement.

If all these requirements are met, the taxpayer can deduct points in connection with the acquisition or construction of the home either in the year paid or over the life of the loan. Tax law treats "purchase" mortgage points differently from "refinance" mortgage points. Points paid to refinance a mortgage are generally not fully deductible in the year paid and must be deducted over the life of the loan unless the proceeds are used to improve a main home. A second home or vacation home would not qualify for this exception.

Example: Abby refinanced her home in January 2016. She did not use the proceeds of the loan to improve the home. Instead, she used the loan proceeds to pay off other bills. She paid $1,500 in points for a 15-year refinance of her existing mortgage. She is entitled to deduct only $100 per year on her Schedule A ($1,500 ÷ 15 years).

Mortgage Insurance Premiums

A taxpayer can deduct qualified mortgage insurance[41] premiums (also called PMI) for coverage related to home mortgages after 2006. The deduction for mortgage insurance premiums is phased out for higher-income taxpayers.

2016 Mortgage Insurance Phaseout Ranges	
Single, MFJ, QW	$100,000 - $109,000
MFS	$50,000 - $54,500

[41] A lender may require mortgage insurance to protect itself in case a borrower defaults. Mortgage insurance protects the lender, not the borrower, and it generally allows the homebuyer to make a smaller down payment than would otherwise be required.

A taxpayer cannot deduct any mortgage insurance premiums if the AGI on their return exceeds $109,000 ($54,500 if married filing separately).

Form 1098: If a taxpayer paid more than $600 during the year for mortgage interest (including points and mortgage insurance premiums) in connection with any single mortgage, the amounts should be reported to the taxpayer on Form 1098, *Mortgage Interest Statement,* by the financial institution that received the payments.

Investment Interest Expense

When a taxpayer borrows money to buy property held for investment, interest he pays on that borrowed money is investment interest expense and may be deductible. The amount of investment interest expense a taxpayer can deduct each year is limited to the amount of net investment income earned. However, he can carry forward any disallowed investment interest expense to the next year.

Example: Mariko borrows money from a bank to buy $3,000 worth of short-term bonds. The bonds mature during the year, and Mariko makes $400 of investment interest income. She also has $210 in investment interest expense, which she paid on the loan originally taken out to buy the bonds. Mariko must report the full amount of $400 as investment interest income. She can deduct the $210 of investment interest expense on Schedule A.

Example: Jackson borrows money from a bank in order to buy $10,000 worth of U.S. gold coins. During the year, the coins lose value, and he has no investment income. Jackson paid $326 of investment interest expense on the loan he used to buy the coins. He may not take a deduction for the investment interest expense because he has no investment income, but he may carry over to the next tax year the investment interest expense he could not deduct.

The deductible amount of investment interest expense and any disallowed amount that may be carried over to the following year are calculated on Form 4952, *Investment Interest Expense Deduction.*

A taxpayer cannot deduct interest related to passive activities or incurred to produce tax-exempt income (such as state and local bonds that generate tax-exempt interest income) as investment interest expense.

Nondeductible Interest and Investment Expenses: The following expenses cannot be deducted:

- Interest on personal loans, such as car loans
- Fees for credit cards and finance charges for nonbusiness credit card purchases
- Loan fees for services needed to get a loan
- Interest on a debt the taxpayer is not legally obligated to pay
- Service charges
- Interest to purchase or carry tax-exempt securities
- Late payment charges paid to a public utility
- Expenses relating to stockholders' meetings or investment-related seminars
- Interest expenses from single-premium life insurance and annuity contracts
- Interest incurred from borrowing against an insurance policy
- Short-sale expenses
- Fines and penalties paid to any government entity for violations of the law

Example: José and Blanca file a joint return. During the year, they paid:

1. $3,180 of home mortgage interest reported to them on Form 1098
2. $400 of credit card interest
3. $1,500 to the home mortgage lender for an appraisal fee
4. $2,000 of interest on a car loan

José and Blanca can deduct only their home mortgage interest ($3,180). None of the other charges are allowable as a tax deduction.

Charitable Contributions

Taxpayers who itemize deductions can deduct certain charitable contributions to qualified organizations. Taxpayers may contribute cash, property (such as clothing and furniture), securities, or other assets. A taxpayer can deduct a contribution only in the year it is actually made. A donation charged to a credit card before the end of 2016 counts for 2016, even if the credit card bill is not paid until the following year. A donation made by check counts for 2016 if the donor mails it in 2016, even if the charity cashes the check in the following year.

In order to claim deductions for noncash donations, the donated items must be in good condition. In most cases, the taxpayer will be able to claim a deduction for the fair market value of the contribution (generally what someone would be willing to pay at a garage sale or thrift store). No deduction is allowed for items that are in poor or unusable condition. Deductible contributions may include:

- Unreimbursed expenses that relate directly to the services the taxpayer provided for the organization.
- The amount of a contribution in excess of the fair market value of items received, such as merchandise and tickets to a charity ball or a sporting event.
- Transportation expenses, including bus fare, parking fees, tolls, and either the actual cost of gas and oil or a standard mileage deduction of 14 cents per mile in 2016.

Volunteer Expenses: A taxpayer cannot deduct a monetary value for the hours he spends volunteering. However, taxpayers are allowed to deduct out-of-pocket costs related to their volunteer work for qualifying organizations.

A taxpayer can deduct expenses incurred while traveling to perform services for a charitable organization only if there is no significant element of personal pleasure in the travel. However, a deduction will not be denied simply because the taxpayer enjoys providing the services. The taxpayer can take a charitable contribution deduction for the expenses if he is on-duty in a genuine and substantial way throughout the trip.

Example: Emily is an attorney who donates time to her local church for its legal needs. In 2016, she spent ten hours drafting legal documents for the church, which is a qualified religious organization. She also had $200 of out-of-pocket expenses because she purchased a new printer for the church. The printer was delivered directly to the church rectory for its use. Emily can take a charitable deduction for $200, the amount she spent on behalf of her church. She cannot deduct the value of her time.

Example: Francine regularly volunteers at her local animal shelter, a qualified animal rescue organization. She uses her own car to travel to and from the shelter. She is not reimbursed for mileage. Francine also fosters kittens on behalf of the shelter. She pays for cat food for the foster kittens and other supplies out-of-pocket. She receives an annual statement from the animal shelter substantiating her donations. Francine can deduct her mileage and her unreimbursed expenses as a charitable contribution, but cannot deduct the value of her time.

Exchange Students: A taxpayer can deduct some expenses paid for a foreign or American student who is living with him. The student must be sponsored by a qualifying organization, not be related to the taxpayer, and be part of a program to provide educational opportunities.

Example: The Jensen family hosts a high school student from Portugal in their home for nine months during 2016. The exchange student is sponsored by AFS; Intercultural Programs USA, a qualifying organization. The Jensens can deduct up to $50 a month in expenses while the student lives with them.

Nonqualifying Organizations: Not all nonprofit organizations qualify as charitable organizations for purposes of donors being able to claim tax deductions. An organization may qualify for nonprofit status so that its own activities are not subject to income tax, but this designation does not automatically provide qualification for purposes of deductible contributions. The following are examples of items that do not qualify as deductible charitable contributions:

- Gifts to civic leagues, social and sports clubs, and Chambers of Commerce
- Gifts to groups run for personal profit
- Gifts to political groups, candidates, or political organizations
- Gifts to homeowner's associations
- Donations made directly to individuals
- The cost of raffle, bingo, or lottery tickets, even if the raffle is part of a qualified organization's fundraiser
- Dues paid to country clubs or similar groups
- Gifts and dues to labor unions (although union dues may be deductible on Schedule A as a miscellaneous itemized deduction)
- Blood donated to a blood bank or to the Red Cross
- Any part of a contribution that benefits the taxpayer, such as the FMV of a meal eaten at a charity dinner

Example: Renee paid the Chamber of Commerce a $30 entry fee to run in a 10K race it was sponsoring on behalf of a cancer-related charity. The Chamber is not a qualifying charitable organization, so none of Renee's entry fee is tax deductible as a charitable contribution. If the race had been organized by the charity itself, part of her entry fee might have been deductible.

Example: Bill goes to a church fundraiser that includes a bingo game. Bill spends $200 on bingo cards but does not win anything. Even though the $200 went directly to the church, the cost of the bingo game is not considered a charitable gift and is therefore not deductible.

Substantiation Requirements for Charitable Gifts

There are strict recordkeeping requirements for taxpayers who claim deductions for charitable contributions, depending upon the nature and amounts. The IRS imposes recordkeeping and substantiation rules on donors and disclosure requirements on the charities themselves. Here are the basic rules for ALL charitable gifts:

- At a minimum, the donor must have at least a bank record **or** a written receipt (or written acknowledgment) from a charity for **any** cash contribution before the donor can claim a charitable deduction.
- The *donor* is responsible for obtaining a written receipt from a charity for any single contribution of $250 or more before he can claim a charitable deduction.
- Charitable organizations are required to provide a written disclosure to a donor who receives goods or services in exchange for a single payment in excess of $75.[42]

Rules for Cash Donations

Cash Donations of LESS than $250: Cash contributions include those paid by cash, check, debit card, credit card, or payroll deduction. If the value of an individual donation is less than $250, the taxpayer must keep a reliable written record, such as the following:

- A bank, credit union, or credit card statement that shows the name of the qualified organization, the date of the contribution, and the amount of the contribution.
- A receipt (or a letter or other written communication) from the qualified organization showing its name, the date of the contribution, and the amount of the contribution.
- For payroll deductions, a pay stub or Form W-2, plus a pledge card or other document showing the name of the qualified organization.
- For text donations, a telephone bill, as long as it shows the name of the qualified organization, the date of the contribution, and the amount given.

A donor should not attach the acknowledgment or receipt to his tax return, but must retain it to substantiate the contribution.

Example: Gary donates $25 per month to the Humane Society. Gary always pays by check, and he keeps the canceled check as a record of his contribution. This is a valid method of recordkeeping for donations under $250. He does not need to have an additional receipt from the organization to substantiate his deduction.

Cash Donations of $250 or MORE: For cash donations of $250 or more, the taxpayer must have a receipt or written acknowledgment from the organization that includes:

- The amount of cash the taxpayer contributed.
- The date of the contribution.
- Whether the qualified organization gave any goods or services as a result of the contribution (other than certain token items and membership benefits). The absence of this simple statement by a charity has led to court cases in which major cash contributions have been challenged, and in some cases, disallowed.
- If applicable, a description and a good faith estimate of the value of goods or services provided by the organization as a result of the contribution.

[42] See Publication 1771, *Charitable Contributions Substantiation and Disclosure Requirements*

The taxpayer must obtain the receipt on or before:

- The date the taxpayer files his tax return for the year he makes the donation, or
- The due date, including extensions, for filing the return.

If the donation is via payroll deduction, any amount of $250 or more must be substantiated with a pay stub or W-2, and a statement about whether goods or services were given by the qualified organization.

Note: A single annual statement from the charitable organization may be used to substantiate multiple contributions of $250 or more.

Rules for Noncash Donations (Gifts of Property)

Noncash Contributions of Less than $250: For each contribution of less than $250, the taxpayer must obtain a receipt from the receiving organization and keep a list of the items donated.

Example: Gary donated ten dress shirts to Goodwill during the year. He made a list of the items he donated and received a receipt from the organization when he dropped off his donation. In Gary's town, Goodwill sells dress shirts in their thrift shops for about $5 each. Based on the thrift store's valuation of his donation, Gary has made a charitable donation of $50.

Noncash Donations between $250 and $500: For each contribution of at least $250, but not exceeding $500, the taxpayer must have the same documentation as described above for noncash contributions less than $250. In addition, the organization's written acknowledgment must state whether the taxpayer received any goods or services in return and included a description and a good faith estimate of the fair market value of any such items.

Noncash Donations Over $500: If a taxpayer's total deduction for all noncash contributions for the year is more than $500, he must also file Form 8283**,** *Noncash Charitable Contributions.*

Noncash Donations Over $5,000: If any single donation or a group of similar items is valued at more than $5,000, a qualified appraiser is required to make a written appraisal of the donated property. The taxpayer must also complete Form 8283, Section B, and attach it to his tax return. He generally does not have to attach the appraisal itself, but must retain a copy for his records. For donations of artwork valued at more than $20,000, or property valued at more than $500,000, the appraisal itself must be included with the tax return.

Special Rules for Donated Vehicles

Special rules apply to any donation of vehicles, including boats and airplanes. If the taxpayer claims a deduction of more than $500, he can only deduct the smaller of:

- The gross proceeds from the sale of the item by the charity, or
- The fair market value on the date of the contribution.

The charitable organization should provide Form 1098-C, *Contributions of Motor Vehicles, Boats, and Airplanes*, which shows the gross proceeds from the sale of the vehicle donated. If the taxpayer does not attach Form 1098-C, the maximum deduction that can be taken for the donation is $500. Vehicles not in working condition may have zero donation value.

Example: Kevin donates his used motorcycle to his church fundraiser. The FMV of the motorcycle is $2,500. The church sells the motorcycle 60 days later for $1,700 and sends Kevin a Form 1098-C. He can deduct only $1,700 on his Schedule A (the smaller of the FMV or the gross proceeds from the sale) and must attach a copy of the Form 1098-C to his tax return.

Two exceptions apply to the rules regarding vehicle donations:

- If the charity keeps the vehicle for its own use, the taxpayer can generally deduct the vehicle's FMV.
- If the charity gives or sells the vehicle directly to a needy person, the taxpayer can generally deduct the vehicle's FMV.

Deductible Contribution Limits

A taxpayer cannot deduct aggregate charitable contributions that exceed 50% of his adjusted gross income. For example, if a taxpayer had $100,000 of adjusted gross income in 2016, the maximum charitable contributions he could deduct would be $50,000 (50% of AGI). Contributions must be paid in cash or other property before the close of the tax year in order to be deductible. There are three major AGI limits:

- **The 50% limit** (this applies to most donations)
- **The 30% limit** (this applies to certain organizations and certain types of gifts)
- **The 20% limit** (this applies specifically to gifts of capital gain property to certain nonprofits)

Any amounts disallowed as a result of this limit could be carried forward to future years. Be aware that the 50% limit applies to *most* charitable contributions. The **50%-of-AGI contribution limit** applies to contributions made to:

- Churches, synagogues, and similar religious organizations,
- Hospitals,
- Most schools,
- State or federal government units, and
- Nonprofits organized solely for charitable, religious, educational, scientific, or literary purposes or for the prevention of cruelty to children or animals.

Certain organizations that foster national or international amateur sports competition also qualify (examples include the Olympics, Special Olympics, and the Paralympic Games).

Example: Pandora likes to volunteer and donate to her local animal shelter. In 2016, her AGI for the year was $30,000. She has money saved in her bank account, and she makes a large donation of $18,000 to the shelter. Her maximum charitable deduction for the year would be $15,000 (50% of her $30,000 AGI). Her disallowed contribution, $3,000 ($15,000 allowable deduction -$18,000 donation), would be carried over to the following year and can be used on a future return.

A taxpayer's deductible contributions to certain other types of nonprofit organizations are limited to either 30% or 20% of his AGI.

The **30% limit** applies to organizations that include the following:

- Veterans organizations
- Fraternal societies (such as the Knights of Columbus or Elks)
- Nonprofit cemeteries

In addition, a **separate 30% limit** applies in the following cases:

- Gifts for use by the charitable organization (such as the donation of a refrigerator the organization uses for itself)
- Gifts of appreciated property (also called capital gain property)

The **20% limit** applies to contributions of capital gain property to organizations subject to the 30% limit.

Example: Howard's adjusted gross income is $50,000. During the year, he gave appreciated stocks with an FMV of $15,000 to his church, which is a 50% limit organization. Howard also gave $10,000 cash to a veteran's organization. The $10,000 gift is subject to the 30% limit based on the nature of the organization. The $15,000 gift of appreciated property is subject to the separate 30% limit. However, both gifts are fully deductible by Howard, because neither is more than the 30% limit that applies ($15,000 in each case), and together they are not more than the 50% limit of Howard's AGI ($50,000 × 50% = $25,000).

Charitable Contribution Carryovers: To the extent a taxpayer's deductions for contributions are limited, they may be carried over to subsequent years. However, the carryover period is generally limited to five years. Any carryover amounts that cannot be deducted within five years due to the AGI limits are lost.

Any contributions made by the taxpayer and carried over to future years retain their original character. For example, contributions made to a 30% organization continue to be subject to the 30%-of-AGI limit.

Special Rules for Conservation Easements

Many taxpayers choose to donate real estate to their favorite charities. Special rules apply to conservation easements. Conservation easements are gifts of real property (real estate) that are specifically for conservation purposes. There are very unique rules that apply to charitable gifts of this type. Unlike other capital gain property, if the real property has appreciated in value, the charitable deduction is not limited to 30% of adjusted gross income.

In 2016, the charitable deduction allowed for conservation property is 50% of adjusted gross income, regardless of whether or not the property has appreciated. There is also a separate, higher allowance that applies specifically to farmers and ranchers.[43]

The carryforward period for a donor to take tax deductions for a conservation agreement is fifteen years, rather than the usual five years for other types of charitable gifts.

Example: In 2016, Gerald decides to make a donation of property to The Nature Conservancy. Gerald donates 500 acres of land with the intent to preserve the area for fishing and wildlife. Gerald purchased the land twenty years ago for $1,000,000. The land has appreciated in value. Gerald obtains a qualified appraisal of the property, stating that the land has a current fair market value of $1,400,000. In 2016, Gerald's AGI is $400,000. Because of the special threshold that applies to conservation easements, Gerald will be able to take a charitable deduction of up to 50% of his $400,000 AGI. Therefore, his $1,400,000 gift permits a deduction of $200,000 ($400,000 AGI X 50% =$200,000) in 2016 and charitable carryforward of $1,200,000 that he can use in future years to offset his taxable income. If Gerald had been a qualified farmer or rancher, he would have been able to deduct up to 100% of his AGI for the year, for a full $400,000 deduction on Schedule A.

[43] The PATH Act created numerous incentives for charitable contributions of capital gain real property that is set aside for conservation purposes.

Unit 12: Study Questions

(Please test yourself first, and then check the correct answers at the end of this quiz.)

1. Vera and Jack are married and file jointly. They contributed $15,000 of cash to their synagogue during 2016. They also donated $3,000 to a private foundation that is a nonprofit cemetery organization to which a 30% contribution limit applies. Their adjusted gross income for 2016 was $30,000. Vera and Jack's deductible contributions for 2016 and carryover to the next year are:

A. An allowable charitable deduction of $18,000, with zero carryover to next year.
B. An allowable charitable deduction of $15,000, with a $2,100 carryover to next year.
C. An allowable charitable deduction of $7,500, with a $2,100 carryover to next year.
D. An allowable charitable deduction of $15,000, with a $3,000 carryover to next year.

2. Angie and Sheldon, both age 41, file a joint return and claim their two children as dependents. They have adjusted gross income of $68,400. In 2016, the family accumulated $6,620 of unreimbursed medical and dental expenses that included the following:

Prescription medications filled in the U.S.	$2,300
Prescription medications ordered and shipped from another country	320
Prescription contact lenses for Angie	400
Teeth whitening procedure by Angie's dentist and custom bleach trays	600
Smoking cessation program for Sheldon	3,000

What amount can they deduct for their medical expenses?

A. $6,020
B. $5,700
C. $3,020
D. $0

3. Which of the following taxes can taxpayers deduct on Schedule A?

A. Federal income tax.
B. Real estate tax.
C. Taxes on alcohol and tobacco.
D. Foreign sales taxes.

4. Christopher and Ariel file a joint return. During the year, they paid:

Home mortgage interest	$5,000
Credit card interest	600
Auto loan interest	4,000
Loan interest on an empty lot that was purchased to build a second home	3,000

What amount can they report as deductible mortgage interest?

A. $0
B. $5,000
C. $8,000
D. $8,600

5. Which of the following taxpayers must either itemize deductions or claim zero as their deduction?

A. Mindy, who files a joint return with her husband.
B. Leslie, who is single, claims two dependents, and files Form 1040.
C. Pearl, whose itemized deductions are more than the standard deduction.
D. Gabe, whose wife files a separate return and itemizes her deductions.

6. Amelia donates $430 in cash to her church. Which of the following is required on the receipt to substantiate the donation correctly for IRS recordkeeping requirements?

A. The reason for the contribution.
B. Amelia's home address.
C. The amount of the donation.
D. Amelia's method of payment.

7. Which of the following home improvements cannot be deducted as an itemized medical expense?

A. The cost of installing porch lifts and other forms of lifts.
B. The cost of lowering cabinets to accommodate a disability.
C. The cost of making doorways wider to accommodate a wheelchair.
D. An elevator that costs $4,000 and adds $5,000 to the FMV of the home.

8. Which of the following contains none of the deductions subject the reduction of total itemized deductions for certain higher income taxpayers (the Pease Limitation)?

A. Gambling losses, investment interest expense, and medical expenses.
B. Charitable contributions, employee business expenses, and medical expenses.
C. Charitable contributions, theft losses, and the mortgage interest deduction.
D. Miscellaneous itemized deductions, casualty losses, and real estate taxes.

9. Which of the following taxes can taxpayers deduct on Schedule A?

A. Local sales taxes.
B. Fines for speeding.
C. Social Security taxes.
D. Homeowner's association fees.

10. Justin, age 37, had the following medical expenses in 2016:

- Contributions to health savings account (HSA): $6,000
- Treatment of a broken leg: $9,000 (of which $8,000 was reimbursed by his insurance)
- Doctor-prescribed back brace: $1,900
- Child care while in the hospital: $200

What is his medical expense deduction before limitation based on the 10%-of-AGI threshold?

A. $1,900
B. $2,900
C. $7,900
D. $8,900

11. Which of the following taxpayers is required to itemize deductions and cannot take the standard deduction?

A. Sophie, who has one dependent child.
B. Andrea, who wants to deduct the alimony she paid to her ex-husband.
C. Gabrielle, whose itemized deductions are more than the standard deduction.
D. Samir, who is a nonresident alien.

12. For a tax to be deductible, all of the following must be correct except:

A. The tax must be imposed during the tax year.
B. The taxpayer must be legally liable for the tax.
C. The tax must be paid during the tax year.
D. The tax must be paid by the taxpayer.

13. All of the following factors determine the amount of a taxpayer's standard deduction except:

A. The taxpayer's filing status.
B. The taxpayer's adjusted gross income.
C. Whether the taxpayer is 65 or older, or blind.
D. Whether the taxpayer can be claimed as a dependent.

14. Iris is single and has the following income and expenses:

Wages	$70,000
Net investment interest income	3,000
Mortgage interest	24,000
Investment interest expense	5,000
Personal credit card interest	3,400
Car loan interest	1,200
Late fees on her mortgage	50

What is Iris's total allowable deduction for interest expense on her Schedule A?

A. $24,000
B. $27,000
C. $27,050
D. $32,400

15. Thomas donates to his church multiple times during the year. Which one of the donations listed below will require a qualified appraisal before the contribution can be deducted on his return?

A. A cash donation of $1,000.
B. A donation of antique furniture valued at $5,500.
C. A donation of appreciated stock with a fair market value of $12,500.
D. A donation of a motorcycle valued at $450.

16. Herschel and Angeline will file separate tax returns in 201
+9606. Herschel plans to itemize his medical expenses, therefore, _____.

A. They will have to file jointly.
B. Angeline must take the standard deduction.
C. Angeline must either itemize her deductions or claim a zero standard deduction.
D. Angeline may choose to itemize or take the standard deduction.

17. Kiara donates her used car to a qualified charity. She bought it three years ago for $15,000. A used car guide shows the FMV for this type of car is $5,000. Kiara's friend, Buck, offered her $4,500 for the car a week ago. Kiara receives Form 1098-C from the organization showing the car was sold for $1,900. How much is Kiara's charitable deduction?

A. $15,000
B. $5,000
C. $4,500
D. $1,900

18. Harold, age 65, and his wife Marie, age 59, incurred the following medical expenses:

Physician and hospital fees	$10,000
Dental and orthodontic fees	5,000
Medical and dental insurance premiums	12,000
Prescription eyeglasses and contact lenses	1,000
Health club dues	1,000
Prescription medications	3,000
Nonprescription medicines	1,000
Pre-cancerous mole removal at doctor's office	805

The insurance premiums were paid through Harold's employer-sponsored health insurance plan and were not reported as income in box 1 of his Form W-2. Harold and Marie had adjusted gross income of $100,000 in 2016. What is the amount of their medical expense deduction?

A. $9,805
B. $12,305
C. $19,805
D. $33,805

19. Oscar donated a leather coat to a thrift store operated by his church. He paid $450 for the coat three years ago. Similar coats in the thrift store sell for $50. What is Oscar's charitable deduction?

A. $0
B. $50
C. $400
D. $450

20. Which of the following taxes is not deductible on Schedule A?

A. Property taxes paid on a vacation home.
B. Special assessments to improve the sidewalks.
C. Property taxes based on a vehicle's value.
D. Property taxes paid on a home in Mexico.

21. Don owns three homes and has an AGI of $128,000 in 2016. His primary residence is in Chicago. He also owns a mountain cabin in Lake Tahoe and a small condo in Las Vegas, which he uses several times a year. In 2016, Don did not use the cabin, and it sat empty all year. He pays property tax and mortgage interest on all three properties.

Home Location	Mortgage Interest	Property Tax
Main Home in Chicago	$18,500	$7,500
Cabin in Tahoe	$5,200	$2,800
Condo in Las Vegas	$4,500	$1,950

Based on the information above, which of the following statements is correct?

A. Only the mortgage interest and property tax on his main home in Chicago are deductible. Don has a mortgage interest deduction of $18,500 and a property tax deduction of $7,500.
B. The mortgage interest and property tax on both his main home and the cabin are deductible. The mortgage interest and the property tax on the third property, the condo in Las Vegas, are not deductible. Therefore, Don has a mortgage interest deduction of $23,700 and a property tax deduction of $10,300.
C. The mortgage interest and property tax on all three homes are deductible. Therefore, Don has a mortgage interest deduction of $28,200 and a property tax deduction of $12,250.
D. Only the mortgage interest on the first two properties is deductible. The property tax on all three homes is deductible. Therefore, Don has a mortgage interest deduction of $23,700 and a property tax deduction of $12,250.

22. In 2016, Martin donates $3,900 of cash and contributes a painting with a fair market value of $16,000 to his church. Martin has a basis of $5,000 in the painting. He also donates $4,000 of cash to his local chamber of commerce. His AGI for the year is $45,000. What is the maximum amount he can deduct for charitable contributions for the year?

A. $9,000
B. $17,400
C. $22,500
D. $25,000

23. Carroll, age 66, and his wife, Ellen, age 59, file jointly. Which of the following statements is correct regarding their qualified medical expenses, if they itemize deductions?

A. They can deduct 7.5% of their qualified medical expenses if they itemize their deductions.
B. They can deduct 10% of their qualified medical expenses if they itemize deductions.
C. They can deduct only the amount by which their total medical expenses for the year exceed 7.5% of adjusted gross income.
D. They can deduct only the amount by which their total medical expenses for the year exceed 10% of adjusted gross income.

24. Xavier, age 29, paid medical expenses of $6,200 during the year. His AGI is $46,000 in 2016. Taking into account the AGI limit, how much can Xavier deduct on his Schedule A?

A. $0
B. $620
C. $1,600
D. $6,200

25. Julio spent the entire day attending his human rights organization's regional meeting as a delegate. He spent $250 on a plane ticket to the meeting and $25 on materials for the meeting. In the evening, Julio went to the theater with two other meeting attendees. He spent $50 on movie tickets. The charity did not reimburse Julio for any of his costs. How much can he deduct as a charitable expense?

A. $0
B. $250
C. $275
D. $125

26. Bowen donated to all of the following nonprofit organizations in 2016. What is his allowable deduction for charitable gifts on Schedule A?

Organization	**Amount**
Methodist Church	$100
County animal shelter	120
Salvation Army	75
American Red Cross	25
Democratic party	50
Chamber of Commerce	300
Total contributions	**$670**

A. $320
B. $370
C. $220
D. $670

Unit 12: Answers

1. The answer is D. Vera and Jack cannot deduct more than $15,000, which is 50% of their income of $30,000. The remaining amount must be carried forward to a future tax year. The carryforward period is five years for most charitable deductions.

2. The answer is D. Angie and Sheldon cannot deduct any of their medical expenses. Only the portion of total medical expenses that exceeds 10% of the taxpayer's AGI is deductible. The total of Angie and Sheldon's medical expenses, $6,620, is less than $6,840 ($68,400 × 10%). Further, of the items listed, only the smoking cessation program, the contact lenses, and the prescription medications filled in the United States are qualified medical expenses. Prescription medications shipped from other countries are ineligible. The teeth whitening procedure would be considered a cosmetic enhancement and would not be a qualified medical expense, whether performed by a dentist or not.

3. The answer is B. Only the real estate taxes are deductible. Taxpayers can deduct real estate tax on Schedule A as an itemized deduction.

4. The answer is B. Only their home mortgage interest ($5,000) is deductible as interest on Schedule A. The other types of interest are all personal interest, which is not deductible. Interest paid on a plot of land is not deductible as mortgage interest, even if the taxpayer later decides to build a home on the property. Only the interest secured by an actual home (not land) is deductible as mortgage interest.

5. The answer is D. A married taxpayer who files separately and whose spouse itemizes deductions must either itemize his deductions or claim zero as his deduction. He is not permitted to utilize the standard deduction.

6. The answer is C. A taxpayer can claim a deduction for a contribution of $250 or more only if she has a receipt or acknowledgment from a qualified organization. The receipt must include:

- The amount of cash contributed
- Whether the qualified organization gave the taxpayer any goods or services in return
- If applicable, a description and good faith estimate of the value of any goods or services provided in return by the organization

A receipt must also show the date of the donation and the name of the organization that was paid.

7. The answer is D. The deduction for capital improvements is limited to the excess of the actual cost of the improvements over the increase in the fair market value of the home. Since the increase in fair market value of the home exceeds the cost of the improvements, none of the cost can be deducted as a medical expense.

8. The answer is A. The limitation on itemized deductions does not apply to deductions for medical expenses, investment interest expense, casualty or theft losses, and allowable gambling losses. The following itemized deductions are limited for higher-income taxpayers:

- Charitable contributions,
- Mortgage interest,
- State, local, and property taxes, and
- Miscellaneous itemized deductions (answer continued).

It reduces the total amount of otherwise allowable itemized deductions by 3% of the amount by which the taxpayer's AGI exceeds specific thresholds. The limitation cannot be more than 80% of the otherwise allowable itemized deductions.

9. The answer is A. A taxpayer has the option of claiming state and local sales taxes as an itemized deduction on Schedule A instead of claiming state and local income taxes. A taxpayer cannot claim both. The other expenses listed are not deductible on Schedule A.

10. The answer is B. His medical expense deduction before limitation is $2,900 ($1,900 + $1,000). The child care cost is not deductible, even though it was incurred while Justin was obtaining medical care. The amount reimbursed by insurance is not deductible. Contributions to an HSA may be claimed as an adjustment to gross income, but not as a medical expense deduction. Payments for medical expenses out of an HSA are not deductible.

11. The answer is D. A nonresident or dual-status alien (who is not married to a U.S. citizen or resident) must itemize deductions. He cannot use the standard deduction. The other taxpayers listed are not required to itemize their deductions, but may elect to do so if they wish.

12. The answer is A. Taxpayers can deduct tax imposed during a prior year, as long as the taxes were paid during the current tax year.

13. The answer is B. The standard deduction amount is based on the taxpayer's filing and dependent status, and whether the taxpayer is blind or at least 65 years old. It is not based on a taxpayer's income.

14. The answer is C. The answer is calculated as follows: $24,000 + $3,000 + $50 = $27,050. The deduction for investment interest expense is limited to net investment income ($5,000 - $3,000). The excess amount of interest expense must be carried over to the next tax year and may be used to offset net investment income in future tax years. Late fees paid on a qualifying mortgage are deductible as interest. The credit card interest and car loan interest are not deductible.

15. The answer is B. The IRS requires a taxpayer to obtain a written appraisal by a qualified appraiser for any noncash contribution of more than $5,000. The antique furniture would require a qualified written appraisal before the taxpayer could deduct the donation on his tax return. The taxpayer must complete Form 8283 and attach it to his tax return. Thomas must retain a copy of the appraisal for his own records, but in most cases, does not have to attach the appraisal with his tax return. Answer A is incorrect because a cash donation does not require an appraisal. Answer C is incorrect because the donation of stock or other securities does not require an appraisal. A donation of a vehicle valued at less than $500 does not require an appraisal or any other type of documentation beyond a written acknowledgment from the organization.

16. The answer is C. Since they are both filing MFS, Angeline is forced to either itemize her deductions or claim a zero standard deduction. A taxpayer whose spouse itemizes deductions must either itemize deductions or claim zero as the standard deduction. This only applies in situations when both taxpayers are filing MFS. If one spouse qualifies for Head of Household filing status, then neither spouse would be forced to itemize.

17. The answer is D. Kiara can deduct $1,900 for her donation. She is allowed to take the lesser of the car's FMV or the amount for which the charity was able to sell the car. Since the charity sold the car for only $1,900, that is the amount of the donation, regardless of any other estimates of its value.

18. The answer is B. The insurance premiums are not deductible because they were paid through an employer health insurance plan and were not reported in box 1 of Form W-2. Neither club dues nor nonprescription medicines (except insulin) are deductible. The deductible costs listed total $19,100. Deductibility of the resulting total of $19,820 is limited to the amount in excess of 7.5% of adjusted gross income (because Harold is 65 or over), which is $7,500, so their medical expense deduction calculated on Schedule A would be $12,305.

Calculation for Deductible Medical Expenses		
Physician and hospital fees		$10,000
Dental and orthodontic fees		5,000
Eyeglasses and contact lenses		1,000
Prescription medications		3,000
Pre-cancerous mole removal at doctor's office		805
Total deductible expenses		**$19,805**
Adjusted gross income	$100,000	
7.5% deduction limit	($7,500)	
Applying the limitation	($19,805 - $7,500) =$12,305	
Allowable Medical expense deduction on Schedule A	**$12,305**	

19. The answer is B. Oscar's donation is limited to $50. Generally, the FMV of used clothing and household goods is far less than original cost. For used clothing, a taxpayer should claim as the value the price that a buyer typically would pay in a thrift shop or at a garage sale.

20. The answer is B. The assessment to improve sidewalks is not deductible. Many local governments impose taxes that finance improvements to property, such as assessments for streets, sidewalks, and sewer lines. These taxes cannot be deducted, but rather must be added to the basis of the taxpayer's property.

21. The answer is D. The mortgage interest and property tax on both, his main home in Chicago and the cabin, are deductible. The property tax on all the homes is deductible. The mortgage interest on a second home is deductible, even if the taxpayer did not use the home during the year. A taxpayer may deduct mortgage interest on up to two homes. There is no limitation on the deduction for property tax, so a taxpayer may deduct property tax on more than two homes. The answer is calculated as follows:

Home Location	Mortgage Interest	Property Tax
Main Home in Chicago	$18,500	$7,500
Cabin in Tahoe	5,200	2,800
Condo in Las Vegas	Not Deductible	1,950
Totals	**$23,700**	**$12,250**

22. The answer is B. The contribution to the Chamber of Commerce is not deductible. The cash contribution to his church is fully deductible. However, charitable gifts of appreciated property, such as Martin's painting, are subject to a maximum deduction of 30% of the taxpayer's adjusted gross income. Martin calculates his charitable contribution as follows:

(AGI of $45,000 × 30%) =	$13,500
Cash contribution to the church	3,900
Total allowable deduction in 2016	**$17,400**
Carryover = $2,500 ($16,000 FMV- $13,500 30% AGI Limitation)	

Martin must carry over $2,500 to the following year. There is a five-year carryover period for any excess charitable contribution deductions.

23. The answer is C. Since one spouse (Carroll) is over 65, and they file jointly, both taxpayers may deduct the medical expenses that exceed 7.5% of their AGI. A different threshold applies to taxpayers who are under 65. A taxpayer who is under the age of 65 can only deduct medical expenses for the year that exceed 10% of their adjusted gross income.

24. The answer is C. Xavier can deduct only $1,600 of his medical expenses because that is the amount that exceeds 10% of his AGI ($46,000 AGI × 10% = $4,600), the applicable threshold. So his allowable medical expenses are figured as follows:

Total medical expenses for the year	$6,200
AGI of $46,000 × 10% limitation	(4,600)
Total allowable medical deduction in 2016	**$1,600**

25. The answer is C. Julio's charitable contribution is $275 ($250 plane ticket + $25 materials= $275). He can claim his travel and meeting expenses as charitable contributions because they are directly related to his charitable activities. However, he cannot claim the cost of the evening at the theater, as that is a personal entertainment expense.

26. The answer is A. The contributions to the political organization and the Chamber of Commerce are not deductible on Schedule A. Bowen's allowable deduction is calculated as follows: $100 + $120 + $75 + $25 = $320.

Unit 13: Other Itemized Deductions

For additional information read:
Publication 587, *Business Use of Your Home*
Publication 547, *Casualties, Disasters, and Thefts*
Publication 529, *Miscellaneous Deductions*

There are a number of less common itemized deductions that are lumped together as "miscellaneous itemized deductions". Although these deductions are less frequently used than the more common deductions on Schedule A, you can still expect to see questions about them on Part 1 of the EA Exam. In addition to the deductions described in the previous unit, taxpayers may claim the following:

- Personal casualty and/or theft losses
- Miscellaneous expenses subject to the 2%-of-AGI limit
- Miscellaneous expenses **not** subject to the 2%-of-AGI limit

Casualty and Theft Losses

In this unit, we will cover personal casualty and theft losses.[44] A "casualty loss" is the damage, destruction, or loss of property resulting from an identifiable event that is sudden, unexpected, or unusual.

Casualty losses can include the damage caused by natural disasters, as well as financial losses from theft and other crimes. Other examples include a car accident, house fire, earthquake, flood, theft, act of vandalism, or act of terrorism. Losses that do not meet this definition and are thus not deductible include:

- Damage done by pets
- Progressive deterioration, such as the following:
  - Termite or moth damage[45]
  - Damage or destruction of trees and plants by a fungus, disease, or pests
  - Loss of property caused by drought
  - Damage to a water heater that bursts
  - Steady weakening of a building due to wind and weather conditions
- A car accident if the taxpayer's willful act or negligence caused it
- Arson if committed by or on behalf of the taxpayer
- Accidental breakage of china, dishes, or other items during regular use
- Losses in real estate value from market fluctuations
- Losses in the value of an IRA account
- Lost property, unless it is the result of a sudden, unexpected, and unusual event

Example: A car door accidentally slams on Julia's hand, breaking the setting of her diamond ring. The diamond falls from the ring and is never found. The loss is deductible as a casualty because it is the result of an identifiable event that is sudden, unexpected, or unusual.[46]

In order to deduct a casualty or theft loss, the taxpayer must be able to prove:

- The type of casualty loss (car accident, fire, storm, etc.) and the date of occurrence

[44] Casualty losses are treated differently depending on whether the loss occurred to business property, investment property, or personal-use property. In this unit, we cover primarily casualty losses from personal-use property and investment property. Casualty losses from business and investment property will be covered in Book 2, *Businesses*.

[45] Note: there are several court cases where the taxpayer has been allowed (in certain situations) to deduct termite damage as a qualifying casualty event, but the IRS continues to hold their position that termite damage and other insect damage is not an allowable casualty loss. For the EA exam, you must answer questions based on the IRS' current position on a tax issue, regardless of any pending or past litigation that may have occurred.

[46] This example is taken from IRS Publication 547, *Casualties, Disasters, and Thefts.*

- That the taxpayer was the legal owner of the property, or legally liable for the damage (such as leased property when the lessee is responsible for damage)
- Whether the loss was subject to any insurance reimbursement

Example: Gregory rents a car from Reliable Rentals. He declines the optional insurance coverage and signs a contract stating he will be responsible for any damage. The rental car is stolen, and Gregory must reimburse Reliable Rentals for the cost of the car. His car insurance does not have rental car coverage, so he is liable for the full amount. Gregory can deduct the loss as a casualty loss, subject to the applicable rules.

Casualty losses are deductible only for actual damage to a property. Payments for the cost of cleaning up or making repairs are not part of a casualty loss itself, but generally may be used as a measure in determining a decrease in the FMV of a property. When calculating a decrease in the FMV of a property, a taxpayer may not consider the following:

- The replacement cost of stolen or destroyed property
- An item's sentimental value
- Related expenses such as the cost of temporary housing or a rental car
- A decline in market value of property near a casualty area

Example: Don purchased an antique vase at a garage sale for $600. Later, he discovered the vase was a rare collectible and its FMV was $20,000. He told a bunch of his friends, and then the vase was stolen from his home two months later. His casualty loss is limited to the $600 he paid for it, which is his basis in the vase. Don cannot claim a casualty loss deduction for $20,000, the actual value of the item.

Example: Nicole purchased a condo for $200,000. Two months later, a hurricane destroyed five properties on her block. Although her property was undamaged by the hurricane, a later appraisal showed that properties within a five-mile radius had declined 15% in fair market value because people were afraid to purchase homes in "hurricane territory." The reduction in her home's FMV is not a deductible casualty loss.

Casualty losses are subject to the "single event rule." This means that events closely related in origin are considered a single event. For example, it is a single casualty when the damage comes from two or more closely related causes, such as wind and flood damage from the same storm. A single casualty may also damage two or more pieces of property, such as a hailstorm that damages both a taxpayer's home and his car parked in the driveway.

Reporting a Casualty Loss or Gain

A taxpayer must complete Form 4684, *Casualties and Thefts*, to report a gain or loss resulting from a casualty or theft. The net deductible amount can be claimed by an individual taxpayer only if he itemizes deductions. A loss on personal use (nonbusiness) property is subject to certain limits (described next). It is calculated on Form 4684 and reported on Schedule A.

If an insurance reimbursement for a casualty loss exceeds the taxpayer's basis in the property, he will have a gain that may need to be reported. However, reporting the gain on damaged, destroyed, or stolen property can be postponed if the insurance reimbursement is spent to restore the property or to purchase similar property within a specified period of time.

Example: Forty years ago, Albert bought a vacation cottage for $18,000. A storm destroyed the cottage, now valued at $250,000. Albert received $146,000 from his insurance company. He had a gain of $128,000 ($146,000 – $18,000 basis). Albert spent the full amount of $146,000 to rebuild his cottage. Since he used the insurance proceeds to rebuild his cottage, he can postpone reporting or recognizing the gain until the cottage is sold.

The replacement period begins on the date the property was damaged, destroyed, or stolen, and ends two years after the close of the first tax year in which any part of the gain is realized.

For a main home or its contents located in a federally-declared disaster area, the replacement period is generally four years rather than two. For disaster area losses, taxpayers may choose to deduct the loss on the previous year's tax return, rather than in the year the disaster loss occurred. This may result in a lower tax for that year, often producing or increasing a cash refund.

Nonbusiness Casualty Loss Limits

A taxpayer can deduct casualty and theft losses related to personal-use property only to the extent they exceed two separate limits:

$100 Rule: First, each separate casualty or theft loss is deductible only to the extent that it exceeds $100. It does not matter how many pieces of property are damaged, destroyed, or stolen in a single event; the taxpayer has to reduce his total loss for each event by $100.

Example: During the winter, a hurricane came through Colleen's town. The hurricane caused extensive damage to her car and her house. This event would be considered a single casualty, even though multiple pieces of property were damaged. Colleen must calculate all her losses from this event, and reduce the loss by $100.

Example: Nahor has a $750 deductible on his car's collision insurance. Nahor gets into an auto accident and his car is damaged. His insurance company pays to repair all the damage minus the $750 deductible. Since the deductible is his only out-of-pocket expense, Nahor's casualty loss is based solely on his deductible. His casualty loss is $650 ($750 - $100) because the first $100 of a casualty loss on personal-use property isn't deductible.

Example: A fire damaged Rick's house in January, causing $3,000 in damage. In September, a storm damaged his house again, causing $5,000 in damage. These two disasters are considered separate events. Therefore, Rick must reduce each separate casualty loss by $100.

The 10% Rule

Second, a taxpayer can deduct the total of all casualty or theft losses during the year (after the reduction of each one by $100) only to the extent the total is more than 10% of his AGI. This rule does not apply to a net disaster loss within a federally-declared disaster area.

However, married couples filing jointly who have a loss from the same event are treated as if they were one person; the $100 limit is applied only once to each shared loss event and the 10% limit is applied to their joint AGI to determine deductibility of their aggregate losses. For losses on personal-use property, this is how the taxpayer determines his deduction:

1. Calculate the *lesser* of the FMV or adjusted basis of the item prior to the loss.
2. Subtract reimbursements from insurance (if any).
3. Subtract $100 for each event.
4. Subtract 10% of the taxpayer's AGI.

Example: Raquel bought a new leather sofa four years ago for $3,000. In April, a fire destroyed the sofa. Raquel estimates that it would now cost $5,000 to replace it. However, if she had sold the sofa before the fire, she probably would have received only $1,900 because the sofa was already four years old. Raquel's casualty loss is $1,900 (the FMV of the sofa immediately before the fire), subject to the $100 and 10% rules. Her loss is not $3,000 (her basis), and it is not $5,000 (the replacement cost). Raquel's AGI for 2016 was $15,000. Her deductible loss is calculated as follows: $1,900 loss minus $100 = $1,800. 10% of her AGI is $1,500. Her deductible casualty loss is, therefore, $300, the amount by which $1,800 exceeds $1,500.

Example: Inga's house was burglarized on July 1, 2016. Her total theft losses were $20,000. Her homeowner's insurance reimbursed $18,000 of her loss. Therefore, Inga's remaining casualty loss after the insurance reimbursement was $2,000 ($20,000 loss - $18,000 insurance reimbursement). Inga's AGI for 2016 is $29,500. In order to figure her deductible loss, she must first apply the $100 rule and then the 10% of AGI rule. Inga's theft loss deduction is figured as follows:

Casualty Loss Calculation	
Loss after insurance	$2,000
Subtract $100	($100)
Loss after "$100 rule"	$1,900
Subtract 10% x $29,500 AGI	($2,950)
Allowable theft loss deduction	**$0**

Inga does not have a deductible theft loss deduction because her loss after applying the $100 rule ($1,900) is less than 10% of her AGI ($2,950). The loss is disallowed due to the 10% of AGI rule that applies to nonbusiness casualty losses.

Insurance Reimbursements

Taxpayers can deduct qualified casualty and theft losses to their homes, household items, and vehicles. However, if the property is covered by insurance, a taxpayer cannot deduct a loss unless he files a claim for reimbursement. If the taxpayer decides not to file an insurance claim but has a deductible, he can claim the amount of the insurance deductible as his loss, since that amount would not have been covered by the policy anyway.

Example: A small fire causes $8,000 in damage to Maria's home. She does not want her homeowner's insurance premium to go up, so she declines to file a claim and pays to repair the fire damage out-of-pocket. Maria cannot deduct the full amount of the loss because she did not file an insurance claim. However, she can deduct the amount of her insurance deductible, subject to the $100 and 10%-of-AGI limitations. This is because she would have had to pay the deductible whether she filed a claim or not.

A taxpayer does not have to reduce his casualty loss by insurance payments received to cover living expenses in the following situations:

- When a taxpayer loses use of his main home because of a casualty.
- When government authorities do not allow a taxpayer access to his main home because of a casualty or a threat of one.

If the insurance payments are more than the temporary increase in his living expenses, a taxpayer must generally include the excess in his income. However, if the casualty occurs in a federally-declared disaster area, the excess insurance payments are not taxable.

The taxable part of the insurance payment should be included in income for the year the taxpayer gains use of his main home, or in a later year when the taxable part of the insurance payment is received.

Example: A tornado damages Olivia's main home in January 2016. After repairs were made, she moved back into her home in September 2016. She received insurance payments that were $1,500 more than the temporary increase in her living expenses. Olivia includes this amount in income on her 2016 Form 1040. In January 2017, she receives a final insurance payment of $500 to cover any remaining living expenses that she incurred in the previous year. She must include the final insurance payment on her 2017 tax return.

Theft Losses

A theft loss may be deducted in the year the theft is discovered, regardless of when it actually occurred. The taking of property must be illegal under the law of the state where it occurred, and it must have been done with criminal intent. Qualifying theft losses include those resulting from blackmail, burglary, embezzlement, extortion, kidnapping for ransom, larceny, robbery, and mail fraud. A taxpayer is not required to show that someone was convicted of theft.

If a taxpayer takes a deduction for stolen property and authorities later recover the property, he must report the recovery as income in the year the property is recovered, but only to the extent of the amount that actually reduced his tax in an earlier year.

Insurance Cost: The cost of insurance or other protection is not deductible as a casualty loss, but it is deductible as a business expense by business taxpayers.

Example: Jordan pays for renter's insurance to cover the furniture and appliances in his main home from theft or other disaster losses. Jordan cannot deduct the cost of the renter's insurance as a casualty loss.

Example: Danny is a self-employed mechanic and owns a small auto shop. He pays for business property insurance to protect his equipment from casualty and theft. Since the insurance covers his business property, the cost of the insurance is deductible as an expense on his Schedule C.

Miscellaneous Expenses Subject to the 2% Limit

Certain miscellaneous expenses, including unreimbursed employee expenses, are deductible on Schedule A to the extent they exceed 2% of a taxpayer's AGI. The taxpayer must figure their allowable deduction by subtracting 2% of their adjusted gross income from the total amount of these expenses.

Unreimbursed Employee Business Expenses

An employee can deduct certain work-related expenses as itemized deductions. These expenses are first reported on Form 2106, *Employee Business Expenses*, and the amount is transferred to Schedule A. The taxpayer can deduct only unreimbursed employee expenses that are:

- Paid or incurred during the tax year,
- For carrying on the business of being an employee, and
- "Ordinary and necessary."

An expense does not have to be required to be deductible. However, it must be a common expense that would be accepted in the taxpayer's trade or profession. The following are examples of unreimbursed employee expenses that may be deductible:

- Business bad debts of an employee
- Business liability insurance premiums
- Malpractice insurance
- Depreciation on an asset the employer requires for work
- Dues to professional societies or to a chamber of commerce
- Subscriptions to professional journals
- Expenses of looking for a new job in the taxpayer's present occupation
- Licenses and regulatory fees
- Union dues
- Work clothes and uniforms (if required and not suitable for everyday use)
- Tools and supplies used for work
- Passport for a business trip
- Work-related education
- Travel, transportation, meals, and lodging related to the taxpayer's work

Unreimbursed Meal and Entertainment Expenses

An employee can deduct unreimbursed business-related meals and entertainment expenses he incurred for entertaining a client, customer, or another employee. The deduction for business meals and entertainment is generally limited to 50% of the unreimbursed cost. The taxpayer must apply the 50% limit before including the expenses on Schedule A (and applying the 2%-of-AGI limit). The taxpayer can deduct meals and entertainment expenses only if they meet the following tests:

- The main purpose of the meal or entertainment was the active conduct of business,
- The taxpayer conducted business during the entertainment period, and
- The taxpayer had more than a general expectation of some other specific business benefit at a future time.

Employee Travel Expenses: A taxpayer cannot deduct commuting expenses, which are expenses incurred when an employee travels from his home to his main workplace. However, there are numerous instances where an employee can deduct mileage or other travel expenses relating to his employment. Deductible employee travel expenses may include those related to:

- Going from one work location to another in the course of business.
- Visiting clients or customers.
- Going to a business meeting away from the regular workplace.
- Traveling from a first job to a second job in the same day.
- Going from the taxpayer's home to a temporary workplace.

Any amounts reimbursed by an employer are not deductible by the employee.

Example: Andy's AGI is $45,000. He works as a salesman for a radio station, selling advertising to local businesses. He frequently travels to the businesses in order to talk to the owners in person and encourage them to purchase more radio advertising. Andy's employer (the radio station) does not reimburse Andy for his mileage. In 2016, Andy has $1,100 in miscellaneous deductible work-related expenses. In order to figure his deductible expenses, he must first determine the 2%-of-AGI limit (2% × $45,000 = $900). He can therefore deduct only $200 of those expenses ($1,100 - $900 = $200).

Tax Home and Work Location

A taxpayer's tax home is his principal place of work, regardless of where he actually lives. A taxpayer's tax home is used to determine if travel expenses are deductible. Travel and meal expenses are considered deductible if the taxpayer is traveling away from his tax home, which is determined based on the following two factors:

- The travel is away from the general area or vicinity of the taxpayer's tax home.
- The trip is long enough or far enough away that a taxpayer cannot reasonably be expected to complete the roundtrip without sleep or rest.

Example: Seville is a truck driver who lives in Tucson, Arizona with his family. He is employed by a trucking firm that has its main terminal in Phoenix. At the end of his long trucking runs, Seville returns to the terminal in Phoenix and spends one night there before returning home. Seville cannot deduct any expenses he has for meals and lodging in Phoenix or the cost of traveling from Phoenix to Tucson. This is because Phoenix is Seville's tax home.

When a taxpayer is traveling away from his tax home, he can deduct ordinary and necessary expenses incurred while traveling on business, such as:

- The cost of getting to a business destination (air, rail, bus, car, ferry, etc.)
- Meals and lodging while away from home (the deduction for business meals is generally limited to 50% of the unreimbursed cost)
- Taxi fares

- Dry cleaning and laundry
- Use of a car while at the business location
- Computer rental fees
- Baggage charges, including shipping samples and display materials to the destination
- Tips on eligible expenses

Special Department of Transportation Rules: Certain taxpayers subject to the Department of Transportation's "hours of service" limits can deduct 80% of meal expenses while traveling away from their tax home. These workers include the following:

- Certain air transportation workers such as pilots, crew, and mechanics regulated by the Federal Aviation Administration
- Interstate truck operators and bus drivers regulated by the Department of Transportation
- Certain railroad employees such as engineers and conductors regulated by the Federal Railroad Administration
- Certain merchant mariners regulated by the Coast Guard

Temporary Work Assignments

There are special rules for temporary work assignments that are expected to last for one year or less. When a taxpayer is working away from his main place of business, and the job assignment is temporary, his tax home does not change. The taxpayer can deduct his travel expenses because the job assignment is of a temporary nature, and therefore, the travel is considered business-related.

However, travel expenses paid in connection with an indefinite work assignment are not deductible. Any work assignment longer than one year is considered indefinite. A taxpayer cannot deduct travel expenses at a work location if it is realistically expected that he will work there for more than one year.

Example: Terry is a construction worker who lives and works primarily in Los Angeles. Because of a shortage of jobs, he agrees to work at a construction site in Fresno for ten months. Since the job lasts less than one year, the Fresno job is considered temporary, and Terry's tax home is still in Los Angeles. Therefore, his travel expenses, including meals and lodging, are deductible while traveling between his temporary place of work and his tax home in Los Angeles.

Special Rule for Military Members

Members of the armed forces on a permanent duty assignment overseas are not considered to be traveling away from home. Therefore, they cannot deduct their travel expenses for meals and lodging while on permanent duty assignment.

Convention Travel

A taxpayer can deduct the cost of travel and attendance to conventions in the U.S. or the "North American area," including Canada and Mexico.[47] For conventions outside of the North American area, travel expenses are normally not deductible unless the convention is directly related to the business of the taxpayer (or the employer of the taxpayer) and it is as reasonable for the convention to be held outside of the "North American area" than inside the area.

For cruises, there is a $2,000 annual cap on deductions or $4,000 if both spouses went on qualifying cruise ship conventions and they file jointly. The IRS imposes strict substantiation requirements on taxpayers who claim this deduction. A deduction is not allowed for conventions focused exclusively on investments or financial planning.

[47] The IRS maintains a list of these countries, many of which are tourist destinations and not normally associated with the "North American area." Examples include Aruba, Jamaica, Costa Rica, Barbados, Bermuda, Panama, the Marshall Islands, and the Netherlands Antilles (Revenue Ruling 2016--16).

Home Office Deduction

If a taxpayer uses a portion of his home regularly and exclusively for business purposes, he may be able to deduct a portion of the operating expenses and depreciation of the home. In order to qualify as a home office, the space must be used exclusively and regularly:

- As the taxpayer's principal place of business, or
- As a place to meet with patients or clients in the normal course of business, or
- In the case of a separate structure not attached to the home, in connection with the trade or business.

The regular and exclusive use must be for the convenience of the employer, and not just helpful to the employee's job. The home office deduction is calculated based on the percentage of the home that is used for business. A taxpayer can use any reasonable method to compute business percentage, but the most common methods are to:

- Divide the square footage of the home used for business by the total square footage of the home, or
- Divide the number of rooms used for business by the total number of rooms in the home (if all rooms in the home are about the same size).

Taxpayers cannot deduct expenses for any portion of the year during which there was no business use of the home.

Example: Lillian is a part-time medical transcriptionist with a qualified home office. The entire square footage of her home is 1,200 square feet. Her home office is 240 square feet, so her home office percentage is 20% (240 ÷ 1,200) of the total area of her home. Her business percentage is 20%.

Simplified Home Office Deduction

The IRS has recently developed a simplified option for taxpayers who claim the home office deduction. The criteria for who qualifies remain the same, but the calculation and recordkeeping requirements have been simplified. Highlights of this simplified deduction include:

- A deduction of $5 per square foot for the space in the home that is used for business, with a maximum allowable square footage of 300 square feet (for a maximum deduction of $1,500)
- No depreciation deduction or recapture of depreciation upon sale of the home
- Home-related itemized deductions, such as for mortgage interest and real estate taxes, may be claimed in full on Schedule A, without allocation of portions to the home office space

Each year, a taxpayer must choose whether to elect the simplified method or the regular method for calculating the home office deduction. If he chooses the regular method after having used the simplified method, depreciation is calculated using an optional depreciation table for the property.

Job Search Expenses

A taxpayer can deduct job search expenses in the same occupation. Expenses can be deducted even if the taxpayer does not find a new job. If the job search qualifies, the taxpayer can deduct the costs of using an employment agency or career counselor, of traveling to interviews, and of printing and mailing resumes. The following expenses are not deductible:

- Job search expenses for a new occupation
- Living expenses incurred during a period of unemployment between the end of a job and the next period of employment
- Job search expenses incurred by a taxpayer looking for a job for the first time

Job-Related Education

The cost of courses designed to maintain or improve the skills needed for a taxpayer's present job (or required by his employer or the law) is deductible as an employee business expense. The education must meet at least one of the following tests:

- The education must maintain or improve skills required for the taxpayer's current line of work.
- The education must be required by law or by the taxpayer's employer as a condition of his employment.

If a taxpayer has a regular job and enrolls in work-related education courses on a temporary basis, he can also deduct the round-trip costs of transportation between his home and school. This is true regardless of the location of the school, the distance traveled, or whether the taxpayer attends school on non-work days.

In some cases, a taxpayer may be able to take an education credit for his education expenses and may choose between the credit and the miscellaneous itemized deduction, depending upon which produces a lower tax.

Note: A taxpayer cannot deduct the cost of travel that in itself constitutes a form of education. For example, an individual who works as a Chinese-English interpreter cannot deduct the costs of a personal vacation to China, simply because it might benefit his language skills.

Uniforms

The cost of uniforms and other special work clothes required by an employer can be deducted as a work-related expense. The uniforms must not be suitable for everyday use. The taxpayer can also deduct the cost of upkeep, including laundry and dry cleaning bills.

Examples of employees who can deduct the cost of their uniforms include delivery workers, firefighters, health care workers, law enforcement officers, letter carriers, professional athletes, and transportation workers.

Musicians and entertainers can deduct the cost of theatrical clothing and accessories that are not suitable for everyday wear. An employee can also deduct the cost of protective clothing, such as safety shoes or boots, safety glasses, hard hats, and work gloves. Full-time active-duty military personnel cannot deduct the cost of their uniforms. However, they may be able to deduct the cost of insignia, shoulder boards, and related items.

Gifts to Clients

A taxpayer can deduct no more than $25 for business gifts he gives to a single client or customer during the tax year. A gift to a member of the customer's family is generally considered a gift to the customer himself. If both a taxpayer and his spouse give gifts, they are treated as one taxpayer, even if they have separate businesses. Incidental costs such as packaging and shipping expenses are generally not included in determining the cost of a gift for purposes of the $25 limit.

Example: Noelle tutors students to prepare them for their SAT exams. She gives eight students dictionaries in December to thank them for their business. Each gift is worth $29. Noelle can deduct $200 on her tax return ($25 × 8 = $200).

Investment Expenses

Investment expenses directly connected with the production of investment income are allowed as a deduction. Examples include investment counseling fees and the rental of a safe deposit box to keep investment documents.

Hobby Expenses

An activity is considered a hobby rather than a business when it is not carried on to make a profit. Expenses related to a hobby are deductible, but only up to the amount of hobby income.

Example: In 2016, Sadie earned $2,000 from selling her quilts at craft shows and had $5,000 in expenses. For Sadie, the vast majority of the quilts that she made were for pleasure, and she never had any intent to make a profit selling them. She would be able to claim $2,000 of these expenses, the amount equal to her hobby income. However, her deduction is further limited to the amount by which this item and any other applicable miscellaneous deductions exceed 2% of her AGI. Sadie's AGI was $40,000 in 2016, and she had no other miscellaneous itemized deductions to report. Therefore, her deductible hobby expenses are limited to $1,200 ($2,000 - $800 [2% × $40,000 AGI]).

Deductible Legal Fees

Most legal expenses are not deductible by individual taxpayers because they are considered personal expenses. But some legal expenses are deductible if they are incurred when a taxpayer is attempting to produce or collect taxable income, such as legal advice related to collecting alimony or earning investments.

To be deductible, tax advice fees must be separately stated on an attorney's bill. A taxpayer can deduct fees for legal advice on federal, state, and local taxes of all types, including income, estate, gift, and property taxes, even if the advice is related to a divorce.

Example: The lawyer handling Ben's divorce consults another law firm, which handles only tax matters, to obtain information on how Ben's divorce will affect his taxes in the future. Since Ben consulted with the second law firm specifically to discuss tax issues, he can deduct the part of the fee paid to the second firm and separately stated on his bill as an itemized deduction, subject to the 2% limit.

Example: Jenna pays an attorney $4,500 for handling her divorce. This fee is not deductible. She pays an additional $1,500 fee for services to collect alimony that her former husband refuses to pay. Jenna can deduct the fee for collecting alimony ($1,500), subject to the 2% limit if it is separately stated on the attorney's bill.

Tax Preparation Fees

A taxpayer may generally deduct tax preparation fees in the year he pays them. Deductible fees include the cost of tax preparation software and tax publications and any fee the taxpayer paid for electronic filing of his return. A taxpayer can also deduct fees paid to appraisers, actuaries, and accountants for services in determining the correct tax.

Miscellaneous Deductions Not Subject to the 2% Limit

There are some miscellaneous expenses that a taxpayer can deduct on Schedule A, without regard to the 2% limit. These expenses include:

Gambling losses to the extent of gambling winnings: The full amount of a taxpayer's gambling winnings is reported on line 21 of his Form 1040. Gambling losses are deducted on Schedule A, up to the total amount of gambling winnings. Taxpayers must have kept a written record of their losses. Gambling losses in excess of winnings are not deductible.

Example: Jason likes to gamble at the blackjack tables at his local casino. In 2016, he wins $6,200 playing blackjack but has $9,500 in gambling losses. He is required to report the full amount of the winnings on Form 1040. His deduction for gambling losses is limited to $6,200 on Schedule A. He cannot write off the remaining $3,300 in losses. He also cannot or carry the losses forward to future years. If Jason chooses not to itemize his deductions, then none of his gambling losses would be deductible.

Work-related expenses for individuals with a disability: These are expenses that enable a disabled person to work, such as special equipment or attendant care services at his workplace.

Example: Erin has a visual disability. She requires a large screen magnifier in order to see well enough to perform her work. Erin purchased her screen magnifier for $550. She can deduct its cost as an itemized deduction not subject to the 2% floor.

Amortizable premium on taxable bonds: If the amount a taxpayer pays for a bond is greater than its stated principal amount, the excess is called a bond premium. Annual amortization of the premium is treated as a miscellaneous itemized deduction not subject to the 2% limit.

Casualty or theft losses from income-producing property: A taxpayer can deduct a casualty or theft loss as a miscellaneous itemized deduction, not subject to the 2% limit if the damaged or stolen property was income-producing property (meaning property held for investment, such as stocks, bonds, gold, silver, vacant lots, and works of art).

Estate tax on income in respect of a decedent: Income in respect of a decedent (IRD) is income owed to a decedent at the time he died. If a decedent's estate has paid federal estate taxes on IRD assets, a beneficiary may be able to claim an IRD tax deduction, not subject to the 2% floor.

Deductions for Nonresident Aliens

Specific limitations on deductions apply to nonresident aliens who are required to file Form 1040NR. They cannot claim the standard deduction. Further, except for personal exemptions and certain itemized deductions, they can claim deductions only to the extent they are connected with income related to their U.S. trade or business. The following itemized deductions are allowed:

- State and local income taxes
- Qualifying charitable contributions to U.S. nonprofit organizations
- Casualty and theft losses
- Miscellaneous itemized deductions

Itemized deductions related to mortgage interest are not allowed.

Bad Debt Deductions

There are two kinds of bad debts: **business bad debt** and **nonbusiness bad debt**. If a taxpayer cannot collect money owed to him, he may have a bad debt. To deduct a bad debt, the taxpayer must have a basis in it: The taxpayer must have already included the amount in income or must have already loaned out the cash.

Note: Unlike the other deductions discussed in this and the prior unit, bad debt deductions usually are not itemized on Schedule A. Deductible business bad debts are generally reported on an individual taxpayer's Schedule C (or other corresponding schedule such as Schedule E or F, depending on the type of business). Business bad debts incurred by an employee are a rare exception and may be deductible as miscellaneous itemized deductions, subject to the 2% limit. Deductible nonbusiness bad debts are reported on Schedule D.

Business Bad Debts

A business bad debt is a loss from the worthlessness of a debt that either was created or acquired in operating a trade or business or was closely related to the business when it became partly or totally worthless. Business bad debts are typically the result of credit sales to customers, but they can also be the result of loans to suppliers, clients, employees, or distributors. Goods and services customers have not paid for are shown in the business's books as either accounts receivable or notes receivable.

If the business is unable to collect any part of these accounts or notes receivable, the uncollectible part is a business bad debt. However, the business can take a bad debt deduction for these accounts and notes receivable only if the amount owed was included in gross income either for the year the deduction is claimed or for a prior year.

Thus, a business that uses the cash method of accounting would normally report income when payment is received and would not usually have a bad debt deduction for amounts owed that are not received because those amounts would not previously have been included in income.

Nonbusiness Bad Debts

All other bad debts are classified as "nonbusiness" bad debts. In order to be deductible, a nonbusiness bad debt must:

- **Be totally worthless:** A partly worthless nonbusiness debt cannot be deducted.
- **Be genuine:** A debt is genuine if it arises from a debtor-creditor relationship based on a valid and enforceable obligation to repay a fixed or determinable sum of money. There must be a profit motive in order for the loan to qualify as a true debtor-creditor relationship. If a taxpayer lends money to a relative or friend with the understanding that it will not be repaid, it is considered a gift and not a loan. Unless a taxpayer has documentation that proves otherwise, the IRS generally considers loans to relatives or friends to be gifts. For example, when minor children borrow from their parents, there is no genuine debt, and bad debt cannot be deducted.
- **Have basis to the taxpayer:** The taxpayer must have already included the amount in income or loaned out cash. Thus, a cash method taxpayer generally cannot take a bad debt deduction for unpaid salaries, wages, rents, fees, interest, dividends, and similar items.
- **Be claimed only in the year the debt becomes worthless:** The taxpayer does not have to wait until a debt is due to determine it is worthless, if there is proof that the debt is already worthless (for example, if the debtor has all of his debts completely discharged through bankruptcy). A debt becomes worthless when there is no longer any chance that the amount owed will be paid.

It is not necessary to go to court if it can otherwise be demonstrated that a debt would be uncollectible. However, the taxpayer must document that he has taken reasonable steps to collect the debt. Bankruptcy of a debtor is generally good evidence of the worthlessness of a debt.

Example: In January 2016, Stephanie loans her friend, Jed, $14,000 to buy a car. Jed signs a note and promises to pay the entire debt back with interest by December 31, 2016. Jed has a stroke in June 2016 and cannot pay his debts, so he files for bankruptcy. The bankruptcy court notifies all creditors that no amounts will be paid to Jed's creditors. Stephanie does not have to wait until the debt comes due. Jed's bankruptcy means the loan has become worthless since there is no longer any chance the amount owed will be paid. Stephanie can deduct the nonbusiness bad debt.

A legitimate nonbusiness bad debt is reported as a short-term capital loss on Form 8949, *Sales and Other Dispositions of Capital Assets,* and Schedule D. It is subject to the capital loss limit of $3,000 per year, or $1,500 if the taxpayer files MFS. The taxpayer must include a detailed bad debt statement with a description of the debt, the amount, and the date it became due; the name of the debtor; the efforts made to collect the debt; and the reason the debt is worthless.

Nondeductible Expenses

The IRS has a lengthy list of expenses that individual taxpayers cannot deduct.[48] These are just a sample of personal expenses the IRS lists as nondeductible:

- Lunch with coworkers or meals while working late
- Country club dues, athletic club fees, and gym memberships
- Residential telephone lines and home security systems
- Home repairs, insurance, and rent
- Losses from the sale of a home, furniture, or a personal car
- Brokers' commissions
- Burial or funeral expenses, including the cost of cemetery lots
- Fees and licenses, such as car license or registration costs (except certain portions that may be considered deductible property taxes), marriage licenses, and dog tags
- Fines and penalties for breaking the law, such as parking tickets
- Life and disability insurance premiums
- Investment-related seminars
- Lost or misplaced cash or property
- Political contributions
- Expenses of attending stockholders' meetings
- Voluntary unemployment benefit fund contributions
- Adoption expenses (although a taxpayer may be able to claim a credit)
- Travel expenses for another individual
- Interest on a personal credit card
- Expenses of earning or collecting tax-exempt income

Example: Nirali received taxable interest income of $2,400 and tax-exempt interest of $600 during 2016. In connection with this income, she had total investment expenses of $250 for the year. She cannot specifically identify the amounts of individual expense items that relate to each type of interest income. Therefore, 80% ($2,400/$3,000) of the expense is allocated to the taxable interest income and 20% ($600/$3,000) is for the tax-exempt interest. Subject to the 2% limit, she can deduct expenses of $200 (80% of $250).

[48] A basic rule is that most personal, living, or family expenses are not deductible.

Unit 13: Study Questions

(Test yourself first, then check the correct answers at the end of this quiz.)

1. Brady's toolshed caught fire in 2016. The shed is not attached to his primary residence. The shed is completely destroyed and the equipment inside the shed is also badly damaged. Brady estimates the property damage at $6,000. He fixes the damage himself, so he does not file an insurance claim. Brady pays $3,000 for the cost of the materials and estimates the value of his labor to be $2,800. His insurance company has a $1,000 deductible for any casualty loss claim filed. What is Brady's deductible casualty loss before any deductions or income limitations?

A. $0
B. $1,000
C. $5,800
D. $6,000

2. Marissa works as a tax preparer. In 2016, her employer requires preparers to take several courses in order to keep their current positions. Marissa incurred the following expenses when she took these courses:

Required supplies	$100
Tuition	550
Required books	120
Credit card interest from paying tuition	50
Bus passes to and from school	65
Total business related educational expenses	**$885**

What is Marissa's deductible work-related educational expense on her Schedule A *before* applying the 2% limitation?

A. $550
B. $670
C. $835
D. $885

3. All of the following miscellaneous itemized deductions are subject to the 2% of AGI limit except:

A. Tax preparation fees.
B. Malpractice insurance.
C. Baggage fees during a business trip.
D. Gambling losses to the extent of gambling winnings.

4. Stanton is a salesman in Oregon who attends a four-day convention for his industry in Las Vegas. He has the following expenses that are not reimbursed by his employer:

Roundtrip airfare	$400
Airline baggage fee	25
Car rental	125
Hotel	650
Business meals	300
Entertaining prospective clients	120

What amount can Stanton deduct on his Schedule A, before applying the 2%-of-AGI floor?

A. $1,200
B. $1,410
C. $1,500
D. $1,620

5. Alfred lives in Baltimore where he has a seasonal job for eight months each year and earns $25,000. He works the other four months in Miami, also at a seasonal job, and earns $9,000. Where is Alfred's tax home?

A. Miami.
B. Baltimore.
C. Alfred is a transient for tax purposes.
D. Alfred has no tax home.

6. Kim uses her home office while she works as a translator for an online company. She meets the requirements for deducting expenses for the business use of her home. Her home office is 480 square feet, and her home is 2,400 square feet. She chooses not to use the simplified option for calculation. What is Kim's business use percentage in order to figure her allowable deduction?

A. 5%
B. 10%
C. 15%
D. 20%

7. Monique is an attorney who reports the income from her practice on the accrual basis. In 2016, she receives $2,000 from the settlement of a bankruptcy case of a former client who owed her $15,000. What amount of bad debt deduction can Monique claim?

A. $15,000
B. $13,000
C. $2,000
D. None, because she uses the accrual basis.

8. Connor is deaf. He purchased a special device to use at work so he can identify when his phone rings. He paid for the device out-of-pocket, and his employer did not reimburse him. How should Connor report this on his tax return?

A. Connor can deduct the purchase as an itemized deduction, not subject to the 2% floor.
B. Connor can deduct the purchase as an itemized deduction, subject to the 2% floor.
C. Connor cannot deduct the purchase because he is not totally disabled.
D. Connor cannot deduct the purchase because he is not self-employed.

9. Enrique and Crystal had adjusted gross income of $75,000 in 2016 and incurred the following miscellaneous expenses:

Homeowner's association dues	$1,000
Fine from homeowner's association for violation of bylaws	100
Loss from burglary of their home	9,000
Tax preparation fees	250

Based upon the information provided, what is the amount of expenses they can deduct for 2016?

A. $1,750
B. $10,250
C. $1,350
D. $1,400

10. Which of the following is deductible as an employee business expense?

A. Employer-reimbursed expenses under a tuition reimbursement (nontaxable) program.
B. Taking classes that maintain or improve skills needed in the taxpayer's present work.
C. Taking classes that are required by a taxpayer's employer or the law to keep his present salary or job.
D. Both B and C.

11. Eli purchased a used car for $11,000 in 2016. He did not purchase auto insurance, and three months later he totaled his car in an auto accident. The car's FMV on the date of the accident was $10,000. He was able to sell the damaged car to a salvage yard for $300. Eli's AGI for 2016 was $50,000. What is Eli's deductible casualty loss on Schedule A?

A. $0
B. $4,200
C. $4,600
D. $9,700

12. Joshua's adjusted gross income was $20,000 in 2016, and he had the following expenses:

Tax preparation fee	$100
Safe deposit box rental to store bonds	75
Life insurance premiums	600
Home security system	175
Loss on sale of personal vehicle	(1,800)
Investment journals and newsletters	250
Investment advisory fees	200
Attorney fees for preparation of a will	1,000

What is the amount of Joshua's total qualified miscellaneous itemized expenses (before the application of the AGI limitation)?

A. $2,400
B. $1,225
C. $800
D. $625

13. All of the following may be claimed as miscellaneous itemized deductions except:

A. Unreimbursed commuting expenses to and from work.
B. Union dues.
C. Expenses of looking for a new job in the same career field.
D. Work-related expenses for individuals with a disability.

14. Patrice's antique Persian rug was damaged by a new puppy. Patrice estimates the loss at $4,500. Her AGI for the year is $30,000. How much of the casualty loss can she deduct?

A. $0
B. $4,500
C. $4,400
D. $1,400

15. Isaac's home was damaged by a tornado. He had $90,000 worth of damage, but $80,000 was reimbursed by his insurance company. Isaac's employer had a disaster relief fund for its employees. Isaac received $4,000 from the fund and spent the entire amount on repairs to his home. What is Isaac's deductible casualty loss before applying the deduction limits?

A. $0
B. $4,000
C. $6,000
D. $10,000

16. Hosanna is working on a temporary work assignment in another city. She is not sure how long the assignment will last. She travels overnight every week. So far, the work assignment has lasted 11 months in 2016, and Hosanna has incurred $800 of travel expenses and $300 of meal expenses. What is her deductible expense for this activity in 2016?

A. $0
B. $800
C. $950
D. $1,100

17. Using the simplified option to calculate a home office deduction, the maximum area that can be taken is:

A. 100 square feet
B. 250 square feet
C. 300 square feet
D. 500 square feet

18. All of the following may be claimed as miscellaneous itemized deductions except:

A. Funeral expenses.
B. Union dues.
C. Laundry costs for work uniforms.
D. Investment expenses.

19. Simon's AGI is $75,000. Therefore, the first___________ of miscellaneous employee work-related expenses is not deductible.

A. $1,000
B. $1,500
C. $5,625
D. $7,500

20. Which of the following types of destruction could create a potentially deductible casualty loss?

A. Dry rot
B. Terrorist attack
C. Termite damage
D. Carpet beetles

21. If a taxpayer's main home is destroyed in a flood and the area is later declared a federally-declared disaster area, how long would he typically have to purchase replacement property?

A. Two years.
B. Three years.
C. Four years.
D. Ten years.

22. Roberto is a nonresident alien who files Form 1040NR. Which of the following is he not allowed to claim as an itemized deduction on his income tax return?

A. A loss on a stolen laptop and audiovisual equipment used in his business in the U.S.
B. A charitable deduction to the American Cancer Society.
C. Mortgage interest on his main home.
D. Amounts paid for his state income tax.

23. Sandy has the following income and losses in 2016:

Wages	$45,000
Gambling winnings	10,000
Gambling losses	(13,000)
Attorney fees for a divorce	1,500

How should these transactions be treated on her tax return?

A. She should report $55,000 of income and $10,000 of miscellaneous itemized deductions on Schedule A, not subject to the 2% floor.
B. She should report $53,000 of income and $13,000 of miscellaneous itemized deductions on Schedule A, subject to the 2% floor.
C. She should report $55,000 of income and $13,000 of miscellaneous itemized deductions on Schedule A, subject to the 2% floor.
D. She should report $45,000 of income and $14,500 of miscellaneous itemized deductions on Schedule A, not subject to the 2% floor.

24. Brooke had adjusted gross income of $20,000 in 2016. Her home sustained damage from a storm, and she incurred a loss of $3,000. Her home insurance policy had a deductible of $2,500 for this type of loss, so she elected not to file a claim. Based upon the information provided, what is the amount of casualty loss Brooke can deduct for the year, after the application of the $100 and 10% of AGI limitations?

A. $400
B. $900
C. $2,000
D. $3,000

25. Ali is a single taxpayer who has AGI of $100,000 in 2016. He loaned $8,000 to his friend Phoebe in 2011 and Phoebe has not yet repaid him. What amount of bad debt deduction can Ali claim?

A. $1,500
B. $3,000
C. $8,000
D. $0

26. During the year, Leon paid $350 to have his tax return prepared. He also paid union dues of $450 and paid an attorney $3,000 to draft his will. What are Leon's total miscellaneous itemized deductions on his Schedule A before the 2% limitation?

A. $350
B. $450
C. $800
D. $3,800

27. All of the following statements are correct except:

A. A taxpayer can deduct job-related expenses, subject to the 2%-of-AGI limit.
B. Job search costs, such as the use of an employment agency, are deductible expenses.
C. The job search does not have to result in a new job for the taxpayer in order for his expenses to be deductible.
D. A taxpayer can deduct expenses related to the search for a job in a new occupation.

28. Marilyn won the lottery and then made personal loans to several friends. Each loan was a true debtor-creditor relationship but not business related. She could not collect on many of these loans. How does Marilyn report these transactions?

A. The losses from the uncollectible loans are not deductible since they were personal loans.
B. The losses are deductible as nonbusiness bad debts on Schedule D.
C. The losses are deductible as a business expense on Schedule C.
D. The losses are deductible on Schedule A as casualty losses.

29. Which of the following is an allowable miscellaneous deduction, subject to the 2%-of-AGI limit?

A. Veterinarian expenses for a family pet that is not a service animal.
B. Casualty loss for $50 cash that a dependent daughter lost at a shopping mall.
C. Cost of takeout meals for a live-in girlfriend.
D. Expenses related to earning taxable interest.

30. Wes had a fire in his garage that destroyed his car and two antique desks. He had recently bought the car for $30,000. The FMV of the car just before the fire was $27,500. Its FMV after the fire was $500 (scrap value). He had purchased the desks for $2,500, and their FMV just before the fire was $5,000. Wes's insurance company reimbursed him a total of $24,000. Wes's AGI in 2016 was $70,000. What is his casualty loss deduction?

A. $0
B. $3,500
C. $1,000
D. $900

31. Addison is a real estate agent who sold seven homes to seven buyers in 2016. She likes giving each of her clients a gift after closing. Addison purchases an $80 gift basket for each customer. She can deduct a total of _________ for the gifts as a business expense.

A. $0
B. $25
C. $175
D. $560

32. Hector works as part of the crew on an Amtrak train. He regularly travels away from his tax home on long train trips. In 2016, he incurs $3,760 of unreimbursed meal expenses during his business travels. Before application of the 2% threshold, how much can Hector deduct on his Schedule A?

A. $1,880
B. $2,820
C. $3,008
D. $3,760

33. Which of the following expenses are all itemized deductions subject to the 2%-of-AGI limitation?

A. Home office expense, hobby expenses, educator expenses.
B. Donation to a qualified charity, gambling losses, business-related entertainment expenses.
C. Cost of safety goggles required for work, tax preparation fees, dues to a professional society.
D. Impairment-related work expenses of a disabled employee, legal fee to collect alimony, union dues.

Unit 13: Answers

1. The answer is B. If a taxpayer's property is covered by insurance and the taxpayer declines to file an insurance claim, the eligible casualty losses are limited to the amount that is not normally covered by insurance, such as the amount of an insurance deductible.

2. The answer is C. Marissa can deduct all the costs as work-related educational expenses except the credit card interest, which is a personal expense and not deductible.

3. The answer is D. Gambling losses, to the extent of gambling winnings, are not subject to the 2%-of-AGI limit.

4. The answer is B. Stanton can deduct 100% of the air fare, baggage fee, car rental fee, and hotel costs as unreimbursed employee expenses, before applying the 2%-of-AGI floor. However, he can deduct only 50% of the business meals and entertainment expenses, for a total of $1,410 ($400 + $25 + $125 + $650 + $150 meals + $60 entertainment).

5. The answer is B. Baltimore is Alfred's main place of work because he spends most of his time and earns most of his income there. Therefore, Baltimore is Alfred's tax home for IRS purposes.

6. The answer is D. Kim uses 20% of her home for business, as her office is 20% (480 ÷ 2,400) of the total area of her home.

7. The answer is B. Monique can claim the difference between the $15,000 owed to her (and previously reported as accrual-basis income when earned) and the $2,000 received in the bankruptcy settlement as a business bad debt deduction. The former client's bankruptcy provides evidence to support the worthlessness of the remaining amount owed to Harriet.

8. The answer is A. Connor can deduct the expenses for the special device as an impairment-related work expense. If a taxpayer has a physical or mental disability that limits employment, he can deduct the expense as a miscellaneous itemized deduction, not subject to the 2%-of-AGI floor.

9. The answer is D. Neither the homeowner's association dues, nor the fine are deductible. The tax preparation fees did not exceed 2% of adjusted gross income, and therefore are not deductible. The amount of the burglary loss, minus $100, that exceeds 10% of adjusted gross income is deductible as a casualty loss.

Loss from theft	$9,000
Minus $100 threshold	(100)
Loss after $100 limit	8,900
Adjusted gross income	75,000
Multiply by 10% limit	7,500
Casualty loss deduction ($8,900 - $7,500)	**$1,400**

10. The answer is D. A taxpayer can deduct the costs of qualifying work-related education as employee business expenses. Amounts that are reimbursed by an employer cannot be deducted by the taxpayer.

11. The answer is C. Eli's deductible casualty loss on Schedule A is $4,600. This is a nonbusiness casualty loss, so Eli must first reduce his loss by $100 and then by 10% of his AGI. Although his basis in the car is $11,000, he must use the FMV to determine his loss because it is lower.

FMV	$10,000
Insurance	0
Salvage value	(300)
Statutory reduction	(100)
10% of AGI	(5,000)
Deductible loss	**$4,600**

12. The answer is D. The expenses deductible as miscellaneous itemized expenses are the income tax preparation fee ($100); the safe deposit box rental ($75); the investment journals and newsletters ($250); and the investment advisory fees ($200). His total deduction before application of the 2% floor is $625.

13. The answer is A. The expense of commuting to and from work is not deductible.

14. The answer is A. A casualty loss is not deductible if the damage is neither unexpected nor unusual, such as when it is caused by a family pet.

15. The answer is C. Isaac's casualty loss before applying the deduction limits is $6,000. Isaac must reduce his loss ($90,000) by the $80,000 insurance proceeds and the $4,000 he received from his employer.

16. The answer is A. Hosanna cannot deduct any of the expenses, because travel expenses paid in connection with an indefinite work assignment are not deductible.

17. The answer is C. If a taxpayer chooses the simplified option for calculating the home office deduction, the maximum allowable area is 300 square feet at $5 per foot, for a maximum deduction of $1,500.

18. The answer is A. Funeral expenses are not deductible as a miscellaneous itemized deduction. All of the other expenses listed are deductible as itemized deductions on Schedule A.

19. The answer is B. Simon's employee work-related expenses are subject to a limit, based upon 2% of adjusted gross income. Therefore, Simon must calculate his deduction on Schedule A by first subtracting 2% of his AGI ($75,000 × .02 = $1,500) from the total amount of these expenses.

20. The answer is B. A loss due to a terrorist attack would qualify as a casualty loss. A "casualty loss" is the damage, destruction, or loss of property resulting from an identifiable event that is sudden, unexpected, or unusual. Loss of property due to progressive deterioration isn't deductible as a casualty loss.

21. The answer is C. For most casualty losses; taxpayers have two years to purchase a replacement for damaged or destroyed property. However, in the case of most federally-declared disaster areas, the period is four years. In certain extreme cases, the replacement period is extended to five years.

22. The answer is C. Nonresident aliens are limited as to the types of itemized deductions they can claim. Among other restrictions, they are not allowed to claim the deduction for mortgage interest.

23. The answer is A. The full amount of income ($45,000 + $10,000 = $55,000) must be reported on Form 1040. The gambling losses are deductible on Schedule A, but only up to the amount of gambling winnings. Gambling losses are not subject to the 2% of income limitation. Attorney fees for a divorce are not deductible, but separate legal advice related to collecting alimony is deductible.

24. The answer is A. Because the property was covered by insurance and Brooke did not file a claim, the casualty loss deduction is limited to the amount of the insurance deductible, as this amount would have been her out-of-pocket cost if a claim had been filed. This amount is further subject to a reduction of $100 and limited to the net amount that exceeds 10% of adjusted gross income.

Loss from storm	$3,000
Limited to amount of deductible	2,500
Minus $100	(100)
Net loss	2,400
Adjusted gross income	20,000
Multiply by 10% limit	2,000
Casualty loss deduction ($2,400 - $2,000)	**$400**

25. The answer is D. Based on the information presented; it appears unlikely that Ali would be able to claim a nonbusiness bad debt deduction. In order to do so, he would need to be able to demonstrate that: 1) he had a debtor-creditor relationship with Phoebe that included a valid and enforceable obligation for her to repay the loan; 2) he had taken reasonable steps to collect the debt; and 3) the debt was totally worthless.

26. The answer is C. The attorney's fee for drafting the will is not deductible. The tax preparation fees and union dues are deductible, but are subject to the 2%-of-AGI floor.

27. The answer is D. For job search expenses to be deductible, they must relate to the taxpayer's current occupation. A taxpayer cannot deduct expenses if they are connected with the search for a job in a new field. A taxpayer who starts a first job or who returns to full-time work after a long absence can also qualify for the deduction.

28. The answer is B. Nonbusiness bad debts are reported as short-term capital losses on Schedule D. They are subject to the capital loss limit of $3,000 per year.

29. The answer is D. Expenses related to earning or collecting tax-exempt income are not deductible; however, the expenses of earning taxable interest are. The other items listed are personal or family expenses that are not deductible.

30. The answer is A. Wes does not have a deductible casualty loss. Since the fair market value of the car was lower than its cost, it is used as the starting point to determine his loss. Net of the salvage value, he had a loss of $27,000 on the car. His loss on the desks is limited to his original cost since it was lower than FMV. Thus he had total losses of $29,500 before the insurance reimbursement, and a net loss of $5,500. After subtracting the $100 deduction, he had potentially deductible losses of $5,400. However, his deduction is limited to the amount of the losses that exceeds 10% of his AGI, or $7,000 (see calculation, next).

Calculations	**Car**	**Desks**
Basis for the casualty loss	$27,000	$2,500
Insurance reimbursement		24,000
Net loss after insurance reimbursement ($29,500 - $24,000)		5,500
Subtract $100		5,400
AGI × 10% ($70,000 × 10%)		7,000
Allowable casualty loss		**$0**

31. The answer is C. Addison can deduct $25 for each of the presents because there is an annual limit of $25 per gift per customer. Her total deduction would be (7 × $25 = $175).

32. The answer is C. Hector is an employee who falls under the special Department of Transportation hours of service rules, meaning he can deduct 80% of his unreimbursed meal expenses ($3,760 × .80 = $3,008), rather than the normal 50%.

33. The answer is C. This is the only answer where all three items are subject to the 2%-of-AGI floor. In answer A, educator expenses are an adjustment to income. In answer B, charitable donations are not a miscellaneous deduction, and gambling losses are a miscellaneous deduction not subject to the 2% floor. In answer D, impairment-related work expenses of a disabled employee are a miscellaneous deduction not subject to the 2% floor.

Unit 14: Tax Credits

For additional information read:
Publication 972, *Child Tax Credit*
Publication 503, *Child and Dependent Care Expenses*
Publication 596, *Earned Income Credit*
Publication 970, *Tax Benefits for Education*

A tax credit directly reduces a taxpayer's liability on a dollar-for-dollar basis, which means it is usually more valuable than a tax deduction of the same dollar amount that only reduces the amount of taxable income. Various types of tax credits are either refundable or nonrefundable.

Note: New due diligence requirements apply to Tax Preparers who prepare returns claiming the Earned Income Tax Credit (EITC), the Child Tax Credit (CTC), and the American Opportunity Tax Credit (AOTC). Starting with the 2016 tax year, preparers must complete Form 8867, *Paid Preparer's Due Diligence Checklist,* for each EITC, CTC/ACTC or AOTC claim they prepare. This new requirement is covered in more detail in Book 3, *Representation.*

Nonrefundable Tax Credits

A nonrefundable tax credit reduces a taxpayer's liability for the year to zero but not beyond that, so any remaining credit is not refunded to the taxpayer. Among the most common nonrefundable tax credits are:

- Foreign Tax Credit (covered later)
- Credit for Child and Dependent Care Expenses
- Child Tax Credit
- Adoption Credit
- American Opportunity Credit (partially refundable)
- Lifetime Learning Credit
- Retirement Savings Contributions Credit
- Residential energy credits

Credits cannot be claimed if the taxpayer is filing Form 1040EZ.

Refundable Tax Credits

A refundable tax credit can reduce a taxpayer's liability to zero and also generate a refund to the taxpayer for the amount by which the credit exceeds the amount of tax he would otherwise owe. Refundable tax credits include the following:

- Additional Child Tax Credit
- Earned Income Tax Credit[49]
- Premium Tax Credit (related to the Affordable Care Act, covered later)
- American Opportunity Tax Credit (partially refundable)

Child and Dependent Care Credit

The Child and Dependent Care Credit allows a taxpayer a credit for a percentage of child care expenses for children under age 13 and for disabled dependents of any age. This is a nonrefundable credit for child care expenses that allow taxpayers to work or to seek work. The credit offsets regular tax and the alternative minimum tax.

---

[49] Note: The Protecting Americans from Tax Hikes Act prevents retroactive claims of the Earned Income Tax Credit, the Child Tax Credit, and the American Opportunity Credit for any individual that did not have a valid ITIN or SSN for the taxable year. In the past, a taxpayer was allowed to amend their return in order to claim these credits retroactively after a valid taxpayer identification number was issued.

The credit ranges from 20% to 35% of qualifying expenses, depending on a taxpayer's income. For 2016, the limit on qualifying expenses is $3,000 for one child and $6,000 for two or more children. If a taxpayer receives a reimbursement under a flexible spending account, the amount is treated as being pre-tax, and the taxpayer must deduct the reimbursed amount from his qualified expenses to determine the credit. A taxpayer must pass five eligibility tests to qualify for the Credit for Child and Dependent Care Expenses:

- Qualifying person test
- Earned income test
- Work-related expense test
- Joint return test
- Provider identification test

Test #1. Qualifying Person Test

For purposes of the Child and Dependent Care Credit, a "qualifying person" is:

- A dependent child under the age of 13 (at the time the care was provided)
- A spouse who is physically or mentally unable to care for himself
- Any other disabled person who is unable to care for himself and that the taxpayer either claims as a dependent or could claim if not for certain specified circumstances

Example: Rocky paid someone to care for his disabled wife, Janet, so he could work. Janet requires an in-home care aide. Rocky also paid to have someone prepare meals and babysit his 12-year-old daughter, Tamara. Both Janet and Tamara are qualifying persons for the Dependent Care credit.

Test #2. Earned Income Test

Both the taxpayer and his spouse, if married, must have earned income during the year to qualify for this credit. This generally means both spouses must work. The credit is not available to MFS filers. In the event one spouse does not have earned income, for purposes of this test the taxpayer's spouse is treated as having earned income for any month he is:

- A full-time student, or
- Disabled.

For any month that a spouse has no actual earned income, but has deemed earned income because they were a full-time student or disabled, the amount of deemed earned income by that non-working spouse is $250 per month if the couple has a pre-qualifying individual for this credit; or $500 per month if the taxpayer has two or more dependents.

Example: Jessica and Quincy are married. Quincy worked as a custodian in 2016. Jessica attended school full-time from January 1 to June 30. She was unemployed during the summer and did not attend school the rest of the year. Jessica is treated as having earned income for the six months she attended school full-time.

The amount of work-related expenses to figure the credit cannot be more than:

- The taxpayer's earned income for the year, if he is single at the end of the year, or
- The smaller of his or his spouse's earned income for the year if he is married at the end of the year.

Test #3. Work-Related Expense Test

Child and dependent care expenses must be work-related to qualify for this credit, meaning a taxpayer must be working or searching for work. Expenses incurred so that a spouse may do volunteer work or take care of personal business, or so that a married couple can go on a "date night" do not qualify.

Example: Patsy is a stay-at-home mom who volunteers several hours a week for a local autism information hotline. Her husband works full-time as a maintenance worker. They pay a babysitter to stay with their daughter during the hours Patsy volunteers. The couple does not qualify for the credit because the babysitting expense is not work-related. Since Patsy does not have a job, is not disabled, and is not a full-time student, the child care expenses are ineligible.

Example: Darcy's four-year-old son attends a daycare center while she works three days a week. The daycare charges $150 for three days a week and $250 for five days a week. Sometimes Darcy pays the extra money so she can run errands on her days off. This extra charge is not a qualifying expense. Darcy's deductible expenses are limited to $150 a week, the amount of her work-related daycare expense.

The following kinds of expenses qualify for the credit:

- Education: Preschool or other programs below the level of kindergarten; before or after-school care for a child in kindergarten or above
- Care outside the home for a child under 13 or in a care center for a disabled dependent
- Transportation for a care provider to take a qualifying person to or from a place where care is provided
- Fees and deposits paid to an agency or preschool to acquire child care
- Household services, if they are at least partly for the well-being and protection of a qualifying person

Example: Roger's 10-year-old child attends a private school. In addition to paying for tuition, Roger pays an extra fee for before and after-school care so he can be at work during his scheduled hours. Roger can count the cost of the before and after-school program when figuring the credit but cannot count the cost of tuition.

Example: Maura is single and her elderly mother, Edna, is her dependent. Edna is completely disabled and must be in an adult daycare. Maura pays $8,000 per year for Edna to be in the adult daycare. Maura may take the credit because Edna is disabled and incapable of self-care.

Examples of child care expenses that do not qualify include:

- Tuition costs for children in kindergarten and above
- Summer school or tutoring programs
- The cost of sending a child to an overnight camp (but day camps generally do qualify)
- The cost of transportation not provided by a care provider
- A forfeited deposit to a daycare center (since it is not for care and therefore not a work-related expense)

Example: Ellie is divorced and has custody of her 12-year-old daughter, Destiny, who takes care of herself after school. In August, Ellie spends $2,000 to send Destiny to an overnight camp for two weeks. She also sends Destiny to a Girl Scout day camp for a week in July while Ellie is working. The cost of the Girl Scout camp is $75. Ellie may only count the $75 toward the credit because the cost of sending a child to an overnight camp is not considered a work-related expense. Next summer, when Destiny turns 13, she will no longer be a qualifying child under the rules for this credit.

Care expenses do not include amounts paid for food, clothing, education, or entertainment. Small amounts paid for these items, however, can be included if they are incidental and cannot be separated from the cost of care.

Example: Krista takes her three-year-old child to a nursery school that provides lunch and activities as part of its program. The meals are included in the overall cost of care, and they are not itemized on her bill. Krista can count the total cost when she figures the credit.

Payments for child care will not qualify for the credit if made to a family member who is either:

- The taxpayer's own child under age 19
- Any other dependent listed on the taxpayer's tax return

Taxpayers may combine costs for multiple dependents. For example, if a taxpayer pays daycare expenses for three qualifying children, the $6,000 limit on qualifying expenses does not need to be divided equally among them.

Example: Alec has three children. His qualifying daycare expenses are $2,300 for his first child; $2,800 for his second child; and $900 for his third child. Alec can use the total amount, $6,000, when figuring his credit.

Example: Diego and Valeria both work and have three children. They have $2,000 of daycare expenses for their first child; $3,000 for their second child; and $4,000 for their third child. Although their total child care expenses are $9,000, they may use only the first $6,000 as their basis for the credit.

Example: Lori is a single mother with a five-year-old son. She takes him to daycare five days per week so she can work. Lori makes $46,000 of wages and spends $5,200 per year on daycare. The maximum amount of qualifying expenses she can claim for the credit is $3,000 since she only has one qualifying child, even though her actual expenses exceed that amount.

Test #4. Joint Return Test

The joint return test specifies that married couples who wish to take the credit must file jointly. However, a married taxpayer can be "considered unmarried" for tax purposes if he qualifies for head of household filing status. With divorced or separated taxpayers, only the custodial parent is allowed to claim the credit.

Test #5. Provider Identification Test

This test requires that taxpayers provide the name, address, and taxpayer identification number of the person or organization who provided the care for the child or dependent. If a daycare provider refuses to supply its taxpayer identification information, the taxpayer may still claim the credit.

He must report whatever information he has (such as the provider's name and address) and attach a statement to Form 2441, *Child and Dependent Care Expenses,* explaining the provider's refusal to supply the information.

Child Tax Credit

Taxpayers with income below certain threshold amounts can claim the Child Tax Credit for each qualifying child under the age of 17. This is a nonrefundable credit of up to $1,000 per qualifying child. A taxpayer whose tax liability is zero cannot take the Child Tax Credit because there is no tax to reduce. However, he may be able to take the Additional Child Tax Credit, which is refundable.

The Child Tax Credit is reduced if the taxpayer's modified adjusted gross income is above certain thresholds.

In 2016, the phaseout threshold is $55,000 for married couples filing separately; $75,000 for single, head of household, and qualifying widow(er). The phaseout is $110,000 for couples filing jointly. For each $1,000 (or fraction thereof) of income above the phaseout threshold, the child tax credit is reduced by $50. In addition, the Child Tax Credit is limited to the amounts of regular income tax and any alternative minimum tax owed.

Example: Clint files as head of household and has three children who qualify for the Child Tax Credit. His MAGI is $54,000, and his tax liability is $4,680. Clint is eligible to take the full credit of $1,000 per child ($3,000) because his MAGI is less than $75,000 and his tax liability is greater than $3,000.

Example: Cordell and Roxana file jointly and have two children who qualify for the Child Tax Credit. Their MAGI is $86,000, and their tax liability is $954. Even though their MAGI is less than the threshold limit of $110,000, they can claim only $954, reducing their tax to zero. Since their tax liability is zero, Cordell and Roxana cannot claim the maximum Child Tax Credit of $1,000 per child, but they may be eligible for the Additional Child Tax Credit, which is a refundable credit.

Definition of a Qualifying Child: To be eligible to claim the Child Tax Credit, the taxpayer must have at least one qualifying child. To qualify, the child must:

- Be claimed as the taxpayer's dependent.
- Meet the relationship test: be the son, daughter, adopted child, stepchild, foster child, brother, sister, stepbrother, stepsister, or descendant of any of them (for example, a grandchild, niece, or nephew).
- Meet the age criterion: be under age 17 at the end of the year.
- Not have provided over half of his own support.
- Have lived with the taxpayer for more than six months of the tax year.[50]
- Be a U.S. citizen, a U.S. national, or a resident of the U.S. However, foreign-born adopted children qualify if they lived with the taxpayer all year, even if the adoption is not yet final.[51]

Example: Edward's son, Jeff, turned 17 on December 31, 2016. He is a U.S. citizen and has a valid Social Security number. According to the Child Tax Credit rules, he is not a qualifying child for this credit because he was not *under* age 17 at the end of the year. Disability has no effect on the eligibility for this credit.

Example: Laura's adopted son, Nash, is 14. He is a U.S. citizen and lived with Laura for the entire tax year. Laura provided all of her son's support. Nash is a qualifying child for the Child Tax Credit because he was under age 17 at the end of the tax year; he meets the relationship requirement; he lived with Laura for more than six months of the year, and Laura provided his support.

Additional Child Tax Credit

The Additional Child Tax Credit is available for certain individuals who do not qualify for the full amount of the nonrefundable Child Tax Credit. In order to claim the Additional Child Tax Credit, a taxpayer must be able to claim the Child Tax Credit, even if he does not qualify for the full amount.

Since the Additional Child Tax Credit is refundable, it can produce a refund even if the taxpayer does not owe any tax. The Additional Child Tax Credit allows eligible taxpayers to claim up to $1,000 for each qualifying child after subtracting the allowable amount of Child Tax Credit. For taxpayers with earned income over $3,000, the credit is based on the lesser of:

- 15% of the taxpayer's taxable earned income that is more than $3,000, or
- The amount of unused Child Tax Credit (caused when tax liability is less than the allowed credit).

[50] There are special rules for children of divorced or separated parents, as well as children of parents who never married. In some cases the noncustodial parent may be entitled to claim the dependency exemption for a child and thus the Child Tax Credit and Additional Child Tax Credit. In addition, there is an exception for an infant who is born during the tax year and has not lived long enough to meet the six-month requirement.

[51] Remember, retroactive claims of the child tax credit are now prohibited. The PATH Act prohibits retroactively claiming the child tax credit by amending a return (or filing an original return if the taxpayer failed to file) for any prior year in which the individual or a qualifying child for whom the credit is claimed did not have a valid ITIN.

Example: May and Dimitri have two dependent children, MAGI of $66,000, and owe tax of $850. Because their tax liability is less than the full amount of the Child Tax Credit, they may be able to take the Additional Child Tax Credit of up to $1,150 ($2,000 for two children- $850 their tax liability).

Schedule 8812, *Child Tax Credit*, is used to report both the Child Tax Credit and the refundable Additional Child Tax Credit.

A taxpayer can no longer claim the additional child tax credit if he files Form 2555, *Foreign Earned Income Exclusion*.

Adoption Credit

In 2016, a nonrefundable credit of up to $13,460 per child can be taken for qualified expenses paid to adopt a child. For a special needs child, the maximum credit amount is allowed even if the taxpayer does not have any adoption expenses.

If a taxpayer receives employer-provided adoption benefits that are excluded from income, he may still be able to take the Adoption Credit. However, the exclusion and the credit cannot be claimed for the same expenses, and any allowable exclusion must be claimed before any allowable credit.

The exclusion is limited to the same dollar amount as the credit. The phase-out ranges are the same for all taxpayers, regardless of filing status (in 2016, the phase-out range is $201,920-$241,920). Married taxpayers generally must file jointly to claim either the credit or the exclusion.

Although the Adoption Credit is nonrefundable, any unused credit may be carried forward for up to five years. Qualified adoption expenses are directly related to the adoption of a child. These include:

- Adoption fees and court costs
- Attorney fees
- Travel expenses related to the adoption, including meals and lodging
- Re-adoption expenses to adopt a foreign child

Qualified adoption expenses do not include:

- Illegal adoption expenses
- A surrogate parenting arrangement
- Adoption of a spouse's child[52]

An eligible child is:

- Under 18 years old, or
- Physically or mentally disabled, regardless of age.

Special Needs Child: A taxpayer can claim the full credit for a special needs child regardless of actual expenses paid or incurred. For the purposes of this rule, a special needs child must be a United States citizen or U.S. resident when the adoption begins.[53]

Further, one of the following must apply:

- The state has determined the child cannot or should not be returned to his parents' home, or
- The state has determined the child will not be adopted unless assistance is provided to the adoptive parents.

[52] Although a taxpayer cannot deduct adoption expenses to adopt a spouses' child, qualified adoption expenses *does* include expenses paid by a registered domestic partner to adopt his or her partner's child, as long as those expenses otherwise qualify for the credit.

[53] Foreign children aren't considered to have special needs for purposes of the adoption credit.

In making the determination about special needs, a state may take into account the following factors: a child's ethnic background and age; whether he is a member of a minority or sibling group; and whether he has a physical, mental, or emotional handicap.

Example: Noel and Cassie adopt a special needs child, and the adoption is finalized in 2016. Their actual adoption expenses are $7,500. They are allowed to claim the full $13,460 credit in 2016 because they adopted a special needs child. Their actual tax liability is 8,000, so the adoption credit will reduce their tax liability in 2016 to zero. They can carryforward any unused adoption credit for up to five years.

Unsuccessful Adoptions: A taxpayer who has attempted to adopt a child in the U.S. and been unsuccessful is still eligible for the credit or exclusion from taxable income for employer-provided adoption assistance payments. Eligible expenses may include those related to unsuccessful attempts to adopt as well as an adoption attempt that is ultimately successful. However, if the eligible child is from a foreign country, the taxpayer cannot take the credit or exclusion unless the adoption becomes final. A foreign child is defined as a child who was not a citizen or resident of the United States at the time the adoption effort began.

Timing of Payment: For a domestic adoption, qualified expenses paid before the year in which the adoption becomes final may be claimed in the year after the expenses were paid. Once the adoption becomes final (or if it is unsuccessful), the taxpayer can claim the expenses in the year paid. For a foreign adoption, expenses paid before or during the year of finality are allowable in that year.

Education Credits

Two education credits are available based on qualified expenses a taxpayer pays for postsecondary education:

- American Opportunity Tax Credit (also called the AOC or AOTC)
- Lifetime Learning Credit[54]

Certain general rules apply to both of these credits, in addition to specific rules for each. A taxpayer may take education credits for himself, his spouse, and his dependents who attended an eligible educational institution during the tax year.

Eligible educational institutions include colleges, universities, vocational schools, and community colleges. Taxpayers can claim payments that are prepaid for an academic period that begins in the first three months of the next calendar year.

Example: Tom paid $1,500 in December 2016 for college tuition for the spring semester that begins in January 2017. Tom can claim $1,500 of education credits on his 2016 return, even though he will not start college until 2017.

A taxpayer cannot claim education credits if he:

- Can be claimed as a dependent on someone else's tax return
- Files MFS
- Has adjusted gross income above the phaseout limit for his filing status
- Has a spouse who was a nonresident alien for any part of the tax year[55]

To claim the credit for a dependent's education expenses, the taxpayer must claim the dependent on his return, but he does not necessarily have to pay for all of the dependent's

[54] If a taxpayer does not qualify for either of these education credits, he may still qualify for the Tuition and Fees Deduction (as an adjustment to income), which can reduce the amount of taxable income by up to $4,000. A taxpayer must choose to take either the tax credit(s) or the deduction, and should consider which provides the greatest tax benefit.

[55] This rule does not apply if the nonresident spouse elects to be treated as a resident alien for tax purposes.

qualified education expenses. If a taxpayer does not claim an exemption for a dependent who is an eligible student, the student may be able to claim an education credit on his own return.

Example: Cathy has a 19-year-old son named Trent who is a full-time college student. Trent's grandmother paid his tuition directly to the college. For purposes of claiming an education credit, either Cathy or Trent is treated as receiving the money as a gift and paying for the qualified tuition and related expenses. If Cathy claims Trent as a dependent, she can claim an education credit. Alternatively, if Trent claims an exemption for himself on his own return and his mother does not, he can claim the credit.

If a taxpayer has education expenses for more than one student, he may be eligible to take the American Opportunity Credit for one student and the Lifetime Learning Credit for another student on the same tax return.

Example: Reed is 49 and pays college expenses for himself and his dependent daughter, Ivy, age 18. Reed is attending graduate school to earn a doctorate degree. Reed qualifies for the Lifetime Learning Credit. Ivy is an undergraduate and qualifies for the American Opportunity Credit. Reed can take both credits on his tax return for each eligible student, Ivy and himself.

Example: Elias is a college senior studying to be a dentist. This year, in addition to tuition, he pays a fee to the university for the rental of the dental equipment he is required to use in the program. Elias's equipment rental fee is a qualified education expense.

Form 8863 is used to figure and claim both education credits. Qualified education expenses are tuition and related expenses, such as books and other course materials required as a condition of enrollment.

Any course of instruction or other education involving sports, games, or hobbies is not a qualifying expense unless the course is part of the student's degree program (or if taken to improve job skills, in the case of the Lifetime Learning Credit). Qualified education expenses must be reduced by the amount of any tax-free educational assistance received, such as Pell grants, tax-free portions of scholarships, and employer-provided educational assistance. Education expenses that do not qualify include:

- Room and board
- Any medical expenses, including health insurance or student health fees, even if charged by the college
- Other insurance costs
- Transportation costs
- Personal, living, or family expenses

Tuition expenses are reported to the student on Form 1098-T, *Tuition Statement*, issued by the school.

Example: Faith received Form 1098-T from the college she attends. It shows that her tuition was $9,500 and that she received a $1,500 tax-free scholarship. Her maximum qualifying expenses for the education credit are $8,000 ($9,500 - $1,500).

Example: Jacqueline paid $3,000 for tuition and $5,000 for room and board at her university. She was also awarded a $2,000 tax-free scholarship and a $4,000 student loan. To qualify for an education credit, she must first subtract the tax-free scholarship from her tuition, her only qualified expense. A student loan is not considered tax-free educational assistance because it must be paid back. To calculate her education credit, Jacqueline has $1,000 of qualified expenses ($3,000 tuition - $2,000 scholarship).

American Opportunity Tax Credit (AOTC /AOC)

The American Opportunity Tax Credit (AOTC) allows taxpayers to claim a credit of up to $2,500 based on qualified tuition and related expenses paid for each eligible student. The credit covers 100% of the first $2,000 and 25% of the second $2,000 of eligible expenses per student. Qualified expenses include tuition and required fees, books, supplies, equipment, and other *required* course materials (but not room and board).

Unlike other education credits and deductions, the American Opportunity Credit is partially refundable. Up to 40% of the credit is refundable, which means the taxpayer can receive up to $1,000 even if no taxes are owed. The credit is not refundable if the student is subject to the "kiddie tax" rules. Requirements for the AOC are as follows:

- **Degree requirement:** The student must be enrolled in a program that leads to a degree, certificate, or other recognized educational credential.
- **Workload:** For at least one academic period of the year, the student must carry at least half of the normal full-time workload for his course of study.
- **No felony drug conviction:** The student must be free of any felony conviction for possessing or distributing a controlled substance.
- **Four years of postsecondary education:** The credit can be claimed only for expenses related to a student's postsecondary education and only for the first four years.

For 2016, the AOTC phases out for joint filers with modified adjusted gross income between $160,000-$180,000, and between $80,000-$90,000 for taxpayers filing as single, head of household, or qualifying widow(er).

If a student does not meet all of the conditions for the American Opportunity Credit, he may still be able to take the Lifetime Learning Credit.

Lifetime Learning Credit

The Lifetime Learning Credit is a nonrefundable tax credit of 20% of qualified tuition, fees and any amounts paid directly to the educational institution for required books, supplies and equipment, up to $10,000, paid during the tax year. The maximum credit is $2,000 per tax return, not per student. A family's maximum credit is the same regardless of the number of qualified students. The requirements for the Lifetime Learning Credit differ from those for the AOTC as follows:

- **No workload requirement:** A student is eligible no matter how many or how few courses he takes.
- **Non-degree courses eligible:** A student qualifies if he is simply taking a course to acquire or improve job skills.
- **All levels of postsecondary education:** A student may be an undergraduate, graduate, or professional degree candidate.
- **Unlimited number of years:** There is no limit on the number of years for which the credit can be claimed for each student.
- **Felony drug convictions permissible:** A student can be convicted for a felony drug conviction and still qualify.

Example: Roland attends Creek Community College after spending six months in prison for a felony cocaine conviction. He paid $4,400 for the course of study, which included tuition, equipment, and books required for the course. The school requires that students pay for books and equipment when registering for courses. The entire $4,400 is an eligible educational expense under the Lifetime Learning Credit. Although he meets all the other requirements for the American Opportunity Credit, Roland does not qualify for the AOC because he has a felony drug conviction. He may claim the Lifetime Learning Credit instead.

Example: Lai works full-time and takes one course a month at night school. Some of the courses are not for credit, but she is taking them to advance her career. She is not pursuing a degree. The education expenses qualify for the Lifetime Learning Credit, but not for the American Opportunity Credit.

For 2016, the Lifetime Learning Credit is phased out for single filers with modified adjusted gross income between $55,000 and $65,000. For joint filers, the phase-out is between $111,000 and $131,000 of MAGI. If the taxpayer's MAGI is over $65,000 ($131,000 for joint filers), they cannot claim the credit.

Earned Income Tax Credit

The Earned Income Tax Credit (EITC), also known as the Earned Income Credit (EIC), is a fully refundable federal income tax credit for lower-income people who work and have earned income and adjusted gross income under certain thresholds. There are very strict rules and income guidelines for the EITC. To claim the EITC, a taxpayer must meet all of the following tests:

- Have a Social Security number that is valid for employment. Any qualifying child must also have a valid SSN.
- Have earned income from wages, combat pay, or self-employment.
- Not have investment income that exceeds $3,400 in 2016.
- Not file as MFS.
- Not be claimed as a dependent by another taxpayer.
- Be a U.S. citizen or legal resident all year (a nonresident alien married to a U.S. citizen or resident alien filing jointly can still qualify).

Qualifying Income for the EITC: Only earned income, such as wages, tips, union strike benefits, and net earnings from self-employment, qualifies for the EITC. For EITC purposes, "earned income" does not include the following income:

- Social Security benefits
- Workfare payments
- Alimony or child support
- Pensions or annuities
- Unemployment benefits
- Inmate wages, including amounts paid while in work release programs
- Income from investments, rental activities, or other passive sources.

Example: Malika earns $11,500 in wages during 2016. Her wages would qualify her for the Earned Income Tax Credit, but she also has $4,000 of investment income during the year, from a certificate of deposit that she inherited from her grandmother. A taxpayer with $3,400 or more of investment income in 2016 does not qualify for the EITC, regardless of her earnings. So Malika would not qualify for the EITC in 2016 due to her investment income.

Income that is excluded from tax is generally not considered earned income for the EITC. Nontaxable combat pay is an exception. A taxpayer can choose to include their nontaxable combat pay in their earned income if it gives them a better tax result.

Taxpayers without Qualifying Children

Low-income taxpayers without children may qualify for the EITC in certain cases, but the rules are stricter, and the amount of the credit is lower. A taxpayer with a qualifying child can claim the EITC without any age limitations, but a taxpayer *without* a child can only claim the EITC if all of the following tests are met:

- Must be at least age 25 but under 65 at the end of the year (if married, either spouse can meet the age test)
- Must live in the United States for more than half the year
- Must not qualify as a dependent of another person
- Cannot file Form 2555 (related to foreign earned income exclusion[56])

[56] A taxpayer who elects not to exclude foreign income from his gross income may still be eligible for the EITC.

Qualifying Children for EITC Purposes

The definition of a "qualifying child" for purposes of the EITC is stricter than it is for the dependency exemption. The taxpayer's qualifying child must meet all the following tests:

- **Relationship test**
- **Age test**
- **Joint return test**
- **Residency test**

Relationship Test: The child must be related to the taxpayer in one of the following ways:

- Son, daughter, stepchild, eligible foster child, adopted child, or descendant of any of them (for example, a grandchild), or
- Brother, sister, half-brother, half-sister, stepbrother, stepsister, or descendant of any of them (for example, a niece or nephew).

Example: Rusty is 27 and supports his younger sister, Colleen, who is 16. He has taken care of her since their parents died five years ago. Colleen is Rusty's qualifying child for purposes of the Earned Income Tax Credit.

An adopted child is generally treated as the taxpayer's own child. However, special rules apply for foreign adoptions. Any qualifying child listed on Schedule EITC also must have a valid SSN. Since an ATIN is not sufficient, then a taxpayer with an ATIN is not a qualifying child for EITC purposes. A foster child must be placed in the taxpayer's home by an authorized placement agency or by court order in order to be eligible.

Age Test: To qualify for the EITC, the child must be:

- Age 18 or younger,
- A full-time student age 23 or younger, or
- Any age, if permanently disabled.

In addition, the qualifying child must be younger than the taxpayer claiming him, unless the child (dependent) is permanently disabled.

Example: Garth, age 45, supports his older brother, Jeremiah, age 56. Jeremiah, who is mentally challenged and permanently disabled, lives with Garth. In this case, Jeremiah meets the criteria to be Garth's qualifying child for purposes of the EITC.

Joint Return Test: The qualifying child (dependent) cannot file a joint return with a spouse, except to claim a refund.

Example: Margaret's 18-year-old son and his 18-year-old wife had $800 of interest income and no other income. Neither is required to file a tax return. Taxes were taken out of their interest income due to backup withholding, so they file a joint return to get a refund of the taxes withheld. The exception to the joint return test applies, so Margaret's son may still be her qualifying child if all the other tests are met.

Residency Test: The child must have lived with the taxpayer in the United States for more than half the year. For purposes of the EITC, U.S. military personnel stationed outside the United States on extended active duty are considered to live in the U.S. during that duty period, so their children meet the residency test. This means that only a custodial parent can claim the EITC.

A child who was born or died during the year meets the residency test for the entire year if the child lived with the taxpayer the entire time he was alive in 2016.

Example: Gwynne gave birth to a baby girl in March. The infant died one month later. The child is still a qualifying child for purposes of the EITC because she meets the other tests for age and relationship.

Earned Income and AGI Limits

Both the taxpayer's earned income and his adjusted gross income must be less than the following limits:

Filing Status	Qualifying Children Claimed			
	Zero	One	Two	Three or more
Single, HOH, or QW	$14,880	$39,296	$44,648	$47,955
MFJ*	$20,430	$44,846	$50,198	$53,505

*MFS filers do not qualify to take the EITC, so they are not listed on this table.

Example: Graham is single and his AGI is $39,600. He has one qualifying child. Graham cannot claim the EITC because his AGI exceeds the income threshold for single filers with one child.

EITC Fraud and Penalties: If the IRS audits a taxpayer's return and disallows all or part of the EITC, the taxpayer:

- Must pay back the amount in error with interest;
- May need to file Form 8862, *Information to Claim Earned Income Credit after Disallowance*;
- Cannot claim the EITC for the next two years if the IRS determines the error is because of reckless or intentional disregard of the rules; or
- Cannot claim the EITC for the next ten years if the IRS determines the error is because of fraud.

Note: Paid tax preparers face significant due diligence requirements in preparing EITC claims for their clients. Preparers must use Form 8867, *Paid Preparer's Earned Income Credit Checklist,* to determine eligibility for every EITC claim, EVERY SINGLE YEAR. The four-page, five-part form is required for each client who is claiming the EITC each year. The preparer must attach the checklist to the tax return of any client who is claiming the EITC. A preparer who fails to meet his EITC due diligence requirements is subject to a preparer penalty per failure. Due diligence requirements for EITC claims are covered in more detail in Book 3, *Representation.*

Retirement Savings Contributions Credit

Qualified individuals are allowed a nonrefundable credit of up to $1,000 ($2,000 MFJ) for eligible contributions to an IRA or an employer-sponsored retirement plan. The amount of the credit is the eligible contribution multiplied by the applicable credit rate, which is based on filing status and AGI.

Note: On past exams, the IRS has also referred to this credit as the "Saver's Credit". Either term may be used on the EA exam, since both terms are currently used on the IRS website as well as IRS publications.

To be eligible for the Retirement Savings Contributions Credit, a taxpayer must be at least 18 years old and must not be a full-time student or be claimed as a dependent on another person's return. AGI for 2016 must not be more than:

- $61,500 for married filing jointly.
- $46,125 for head of household.
- $30,750 for single, married filing separately, or qualifying widow(er).

Example: Truman is 24 and earns $35,000 during the year. He is single and contributes $3,000 to his 401(k) plan at work. Truman is not eligible for the credit because his income exceeds the threshold limit for single filers.

Eligible contributions include those to both traditional IRAs and Roth IRAs, elective deferrals to 401(k) or other qualified employer-sponsored retirement plans, and voluntary employee contributions to other qualified retirement plans.

Most workers who contribute to traditional IRAs already deduct all or part of their contributions. The Saver's Credit is in addition to these deductions.

When figuring the credit, a taxpayer generally must subtract the amount of distributions received from his retirement plans, in the two years before the year the credit is claimed; the year the credit is claimed; and the period after the end of the credit year but before the due date, including extensions, for filing the return for the credit year.

The Saver's Credit amount can be as low as 10% or as high as 50% of a maximum annual contribution of $2,000 per person, depending on filing status and AGI.

Also note that foreign income cannot be included in the taxpayer's adjusted gross income for the purposes of calculating this credit.

Residential Energy Credits

A number of tax credits for residential energy efficiency expired at the end of 2016, but are still valid for the 2016 tax season. These tax credits apply to equipment purchases made in 2016.[57]

Residential Energy Efficiency Property Credit

This credit applies to solar, wind, geothermal and fuel-cell technology. A credit is available for property that is used in the taxpayer's principal residence and a second home. The credit for fuel-cell equipment only qualifies if it is installed in the taxpayer's main home. The credit is equal to 30% of the cost of the equipment, including installation. Rental properties do not qualify for this credit. The following property is included:

- Geothermal Heat Pumps
- Small Wind Turbines (Residential)
- Solar Energy Systems[58]
- Fuel Cells (Residential Fuel Cell and Micro-turbine Systems)

There is no maximum credit threshold for qualifying solar, wind, and geothermal equipment, but the maximum credit for fuel cells is $500 for each half-kilowatt of power capacity, or $1000 for each kilowatt.

Nonbusiness Energy Property Tax Credit

For this credit, only equipment and property that meets technical efficiency standards set by the Department of Energy qualifies. The credit is 10% of cost up to $500, or a specific amount from $50-$300. For this credit, the IRS distinguishes between two kinds of property. The first is "residential energy property costs." It includes:

- Stoves that use biomass fuel
- Air source heat pumps
- Air conditioning units
- Natural gas, propane or oil furnaces and fans
- Insulation, Roofs
- Water heaters (non-solar)
- Windows, doors & skylights

The second type of property is referred to as "qualified energy efficiency improvements," and includes, home insulation, exterior doors, exterior windows and skylights, and certain roofing materials. This credit is extremely limited. It is a maximum of $500 for all years combined, from 2006 to the present. These credits do not apply to new construction or rental property. Of that $500 limit, a maximum of $200 can be allocated for energy-efficient windows. Energy credits are reported on Form 5695, *Residential Energy Credits*.

[57] The tax credit for home solar Photovoltaics and water heating systems does not expire until 2021.

[58] The credit is not available for solar panels that are used exclusively to heat swimming pools or hot tubs.

Unit 14: Study Questions

(Test yourself first, then check the correct answers at the end of this quiz.)

1. Gail's earned income from wages is $7,000 in 2016. She has interest income of $3,500. She is single and has a valid Social Security number. She does not have any dependents. Which of the following statements is correct?

A. Gail qualifies for the Earned Income Tax Credit.
B. Gail does not qualify for the Earned Income Tax Credit.
C. Gail qualifies for the Earned Income Tax Credit and the Child Tax Credit.
D. Gail qualifies for the Child Tax Credit.

2. Orlando is a university senior studying to be an optometrist. Which of the following expenses is a qualifying expense for the American Opportunity Tax Credit?

A. The rental of the vision equipment he is required to use to enroll in this program.
B. Student health fees.
C. Room and board.
D. A physical education course not related to his degree program.

3. Which of the following individuals could be a qualifying child for the Child Tax Credit?

A. An 18-year-old dependent who is a full-time student.
B. A six-year-old nephew who lived with the taxpayer for seven months.
C. A child actor who is 15 years old and provides over half of his own support.
D. A foster child who has lived with the taxpayer for four months.

4. Which of the following expenses is not a qualified expense for purposes of the Adoption Credit?

A. Court costs.
B. Re-adoption expenses to adopt a foreign child.
C. Attorney fees for a surrogate arrangement.
D. Travel expenses.

5. Beatrice has three dependent children, ages 10, 12, and 18, who live with her. Assuming she meets the other criteria, what is the maximum Child Tax Credit she can claim on her 2016 tax return?

A. $0
B. $1,000
C. $2,000
D. $3,000

6. Which of the following individuals is eligible for the American Opportunity Credit?

A. Garrett, who is enrolled full-time as a postgraduate student pursuing a master's degree in biology after having completed a four-year undergraduate degree.
B. Lucy, who is taking a ceramics class at a community college for fun.
C. Doug, who is a full-time undergraduate student and was convicted of a felony for distributing marijuana.
D. Beth, who is pursuing a degree in computer science degree and who attended classes the entire school year.

7. In 2016, John and Hannah adopt a special needs child who is completely disabled. Their adoption expenses are $7,000, and their travel expenses related to the adoption are $1,200. Their modified AGI for 2016 is $175,000. What is their maximum Adoption Credit in 2016?

A. $7,000
B. $8,200
C. $13,460
D. $0

8. Noah, 29, decides to go to college for the first time. Which of the following will disqualify him from taking the Lifetime Learning Credit?

A. Noah is not seeking a degree, and is only taking two courses to improve his job skills.
B. Noah is pursuing a graduate degree.
C. Noah is attending school less than half-time.
D. Noah is already claiming the tuition and fees deduction.

9. Rocco has three kids in college. They are all his dependents:

- Cosima, age 21, a college sophomore working on her first bachelor's degree
- Marico, age 19, a college freshman working on his first bachelor's degree
- Kasha, age 23, a graduate student, working on her first master's degree. Kasha had a four-year bachelor's degree from the same college

Based on the above scenario, what is the maximum amount in American Opportunity Credits (AOC) Rocco can claim on his tax return?

A. $2,500
B. $6,000
C. $5,000
D. $7,500

10. All of the listed expenses are deductible for the Lifetime Learning Credit except:

A. Required books.
B. On-campus childcare in order to attend class.
C. Tuition.
D. Required fees.

11. The American Opportunity Credit has a maximum credit of up to ____________.

A. $2,500 credit per eligible student
B. $2,000 credit per eligible student
C. $2,500 credit per tax return
D. $4,000 credit per eligible student

12. Samira and Rishi are married and file jointly. Their daughter, Chetana, was enrolled full-time in college for all of 2016. Samira and Rishi obtained a loan in 2016 and used the proceeds to pay for Chetana's tuition and related fees for 2016. They repaid the loan in 2017. When will they be entitled to claim an education credit?

A. They cannot claim an education credit.
B. 2016.
C. 2017.
D. Either 2016 or 2017.

13. Edwin is a professional bookkeeper. He takes an accounting course at the local community college to improve his work-related skills. Edwin is not a degree candidate. Which educational credit does he qualify for?

A. The American Opportunity Credit.
B. The College Saver's Credit.
C. The Lifetime Learning Credit.
D. The General Education Credit.

14. To qualify for the Earned Income Tax Credit, which of the following statements is correct?

A. The taxpayer must have a dependent child.
B. The taxpayer must be a U.S. citizen or legal U.S. resident all year.
C. The taxpayer's filing status can be MFS or MFJ.
D. The taxpayer's only income can be from Social Security benefits.

15. Nina pays for daycare costs for the following individuals so she can work. Each is a qualifying individual for purposes of the Child and Dependent Care Credit except:

A. Nina's husband, who is totally disabled.
B. Nina's son, age 13, who is Nina's dependent.
C. Nina's nephew, age 12, who is also Nina's dependent.
D. Nina's niece, who is 35, lived with her all year and is completely disabled.

16. Zoe attends college full-time, pursuing an undergraduate degree in business. Because she changed majors in her junior year, she is now in her fifth year of college. She has a $4,000 Pell grant for 2016, and her parents have claimed the American Opportunity Credit for Zoe the past four years. What amount can they claim for the AOC in 2016 based upon the following expenses for Zoe?

Tuition	$15,000
Room and board	12,000
Required Student Health Fees	1,000

A. $0
B. $2,500
C. $2,000
D. $11,000

17. Vincent has two kids in graduate school. His wife, Olivia, also attends a doctorate program at a local university. Vincent and his wife file jointly. What is the maximum amount of the Lifetime Learning Credit that Vincent can claim on his 2016 return?

A. $2,000 per student (up to a maximum of $4,000 per tax return)
B. $2,500 per student.
C. $6,000 maximum ($2,000 per qualifying student).
D. $2,000 per tax return.

18. For purposes of the EITC, the following type of income is considered earned income:

A. Alimony.
B. Interest and dividends.
C. Capital gains
D. Household employee income reported on Form W-2.

19. Generally, which is most beneficial to taxpayers when it comes to reducing income tax liability: a nonrefundable credit, a refundable credit, or a deduction?

A. A nonrefundable credit.
B. A refundable credit.
C. A deduction.
D. All are equally beneficial in reducing income tax liability.

20. Which of the following education tax benefits listed below is refundable?

A. The Tuition and Fees Deduction
B. The American Opportunity Credit
C. The Lifetime Learning Credit
D. Student Loan Interest Deduction

21. Couples who file jointly may be eligible to claim up to ___________ per year for contributions to an IRA under the Retirement Savings Contributions Credit?

A. $500
B. $1,000
C. $2,000
D. $5,000

22. Which of the following filing conditions would prevent an individual from qualifying for the Earned Income Tax Credit?

A. MFS filing status.
B. A taxpayer with nontaxable combat pay.
C. Investment income of $3,100.
D. A taxpayer who is 68 years old with one qualifying child.

23. All of the following are qualified expenses for purposes of the Child and Dependent Care Credit except:

A. A $500 payment to a grandparent for child care while the taxpayer is employed.
B. A $300 payment to a daycare center while the taxpayer is looking for employment.
C. A $500 child care expense while the taxpayer obtains medical care.
D. A $600 adult daycare expense for a disabled spouse while the taxpayer works.

24. Orrin was audited in 2016, and the IRS determined that he claimed the Earned Income Tax Credit erroneously due to reckless disregard of the EITC rules. For how many years is Orrin prohibited from claiming the EITC?

A. None.
B. Two years.
C. Five years.
D. Ten years.

25. Which of the following statements is correct regarding a paid preparer's EITC due diligence requirements?

A. He is subject to a $50 penalty for each failure to meet his due diligence requirements.
B. He is required to complete Form 8867, the EITC checklist, for every client who is claiming the Earned Income Tax Credit. The preparer must retain a copy for his records and make it available to the IRS upon request.
C. He is required to complete and attach Form 8867, the EITC checklist, to the tax return of every client who is claiming the Earned Income Tax Credit.
D. He is required to complete and attach Form 8867, the EITC checklist, to the tax return of every client, regardless of whether the taxpayer is claiming the Earned Income Tax Credit.

26. Which of the following credits are refundable for 2016?

A. Lifetime Learning Credit.
B. The Residential Energy Credit.
C. The Additional Child Tax Credit.
D. The Dependent Care Credit.

27. Scott is 43 and unmarried. Scott's half-brother, Alexander, turned 16 on December 30, 2016. Alexander lived with Scott all year, and he is a U.S. citizen. Scott claimed Alexander as a dependent on his return. Which of the following statements is correct?

A. Alexander is a qualifying child for the Child Tax Credit.
B. Alexander is not a qualifying child for the Child Tax Credit because he is too old to be eligible.
C. Alexander is not a qualifying child for the Child Tax Credit because siblings do not qualify.
D. Alexander only qualifies for the Child Tax Credit if he is a full-time student.

Unit 14: Answers

1. The answer is B. Gail does not qualify for the Earned Income Tax Credit because her investment income exceeds $3,400 in 2016. She does not qualify for the Child Tax Credit because she does not have a qualifying child.

2. The answer is A. Because Orlando's equipment rental fee must be paid to the university as a condition for enrollment, it is considered a qualified related expense. For AOTC purposes, "qualified education expenses" do not include insurance or medical expenses (such as student health fees), room and board, transportation, or similar personal, living, or family expenses, or any course of instruction or other education involving sports, games, or hobbies, unless the course is part of the student's degree program.

3. The answer is B. A nephew who lived with the taxpayer for seven months may qualify. In order to qualify for the Child Tax Credit, the taxpayer must have a qualifying child who lived with him for more than six months and who is under the age of 17. The child cannot have provided more than half of his own support.

4. The answer is C. Expenses related to a surrogate arrangement are not a qualified adoption expense. Qualified adoption expenses are expenses directly related to the legal adoption of an eligible child. These expenses include adoption fees, court costs, attorney fees, travel expenses (including amounts spent for meals and lodging) while away from home, and re-adoption expenses to adopt a foreign child.

5. The answer is C. Beatrice can claim $2,000 as a maximum credit, or $1,000 for each qualifying child. For purposes of this credit, she only has two qualifying children, because one of her dependents is already over 17 and therefore no longer eligible for the credit.

6. The answer is D. Beth is eligible for the American Opportunity Credit because she is pursuing a degree and is enrolled at least half-time for at least one academic period during 2016. Courses that do not lead to a degree, certificate or other recognized credential do not qualify for the AOC. Students with felony drug convictions are ineligible for this credit.

7. The answer is C. John and Hannah can take the full Adoption Credit of $13,460 in 2016 because they adopted a special needs child. Under a special rule for taxpayers who adopt special needs children, the maximum Adoption Credit is allowed, even if the taxpayer has a lesser amount of adoption expenses.

8. The answer is D. A taxpayer cannot take an education credit and the tuition and fees deduction for the same student.

9. The answer is C. The American Opportunity Tax Credit is worth up to $2,500 per student. Rocco can potentially claim $5,000 in AOC credits on his tax return ($2,500 each for Cosima and Marico). Cosima and Marico would be qualifying students for AOC purposes because they are working on their first undergraduate degree. Kasha would not qualify, because she is working on a graduate degree after having completed a four-year undergraduate degree. The American Opportunity Credit is only available for four years of postsecondary school.

10. The answer is B. Child care is not a qualifying education expense, even if the child care is offered on-campus. For purposes of the Lifetime Learning Credit, qualified education expenses are tuition and certain related expenses required for enrollment or attendance at an eligible educational institution.

11. The answer is A. The American Opportunity Tax Credit is worth up to $2,500 per eligible student. The maximum credit equals 100% of the first $2,000 and 25% of the next $2,000 of qualified expenses.

12. The answer is B. Samira and Rishi are eligible to claim an education credit for 2016. The credit should be claimed for the year in which the taxpayer paid the expenses, not the year in which the loan is repaid.

13. The answer is C. Edwin qualifies for the Lifetime Learning Credit. He does not qualify for the American Opportunity Credit because he is not a degree candidate and because his course does not meet the requirements. The "College Saver's Credit" and the "General Education Credit" do not exist.

14. The answer is B. The taxpayer must be a U.S. citizen or legal resident all year. A taxpayer cannot claim the EITC if his filing status is MFS. Taxpayers do not need to have a dependent child in order to qualify for the Earned Income Tax Credit. However, the amount of the credit is greatly increased if the taxpayer has a qualifying child. A taxpayer must have earned income to qualify for the EITC; Social Security benefits do not qualify.

15. The answer is B. Nina's son does not qualify because he is over the age limit for the credit. To qualify for the Child and Dependent Care Credit, the dependent must be *under* the age of 13 or completely disabled.

16. The answer is A. Zoe does not qualify for the AOC because she is in her fifth year of college and her parents have already claimed the credit the prior four years. If she had been eligible for the credit, she would have had $11,000 of qualifying expenses. Room and board and student health fees are not qualifying expenses for the AOC, and the qualifying tuition cost must be reduced by any tax-free scholarships, such as the Pell grant. The AOC is a maximum credit of $2,500 per student (100% of the first $2,000 of eligible expenses and 25% of the next $2,000). Zoe qualifies for the Lifetime Learning Credit.

17. The answer is D. The maximum credit is $2,000 per tax return. The credit is allowed for 20% of the first $10,000 of qualified tuition and fees paid during the year. The credit is per tax return, not per student, so only a maximum of $2,000 can be claimed each year, no matter how many qualifying students a taxpayer may have.

18. The answer is D. Household employee income is considered earned income because it is a type of wages. Alimony, workfare payments, and interest and dividends are not considered earned income for purposes of the EITC.

19. The answer is B. A refundable credit, such as the Earned Income Tax Credit, is not limited by an individual's tax liability. The taxpayer can receive a refund even if he has zero tax liability.

20. The answer is B. Up to 40% of the American Opportunity Credit (up to $1,000) is refundable, meaning that the taxpayer can receive a refund even if they have zero tax liability.

21. The answer is C. Married couples who file jointly are allowed a nonrefundable credit of up to $2,000 for eligible contributions to an IRA or an employer-sponsored retirement plan. The credit is $1,000 per year for single filers.

22. The answer is A. Taxpayers cannot claim the EITC if they file Married Filing Separately. All the other choices would not disqualify a taxpayer from claiming EITC. Combat pay is considered qualifying income for EITC purposes. The investment income threshold for EITC in 2016 is $3,400. A taxpayer who is 68 years old may be eligible for EITC if they have a qualifying child.

23. The answer is C. Child care costs to obtain medical care are not a deductible expense. Deductible costs must be work-related and for a child under 13, a disabled dependent, or a disabled spouse of any age. Child care costs incurred so that the taxpayer can volunteer, obtain medical care, run errands, or do other personal businesses do not qualify.

24. The answer is B. Orrin cannot claim the EITC for two tax years. There are restrictions on EITC claims by taxpayers for whom a previous claim was denied or reduced due to any reason other than a math or clerical error. If a taxpayer was determined to have claimed the EITC due to reckless or intentional disregard of the EITC rules, he cannot claim the EITC for two tax years. If the error was due to fraud, the taxpayer cannot claim the EITC for ten tax years.

25. The answer is C. As part of his due diligence requirements, a paid preparer must complete and attach Form 8867, *Paid Preparer's Earned Income Credit Checklist*, to the tax return of every client who is claiming the EITC. The checklist is a four-page form with questions the preparer must ask to determine client eligibility for the credit. A preparer faces a $500 fine for each failure to meet the EITC due diligence standards.

26. The answer is C. The Additional Child Tax Credit is refundable, meaning it can result in a refund even if a taxpayer does not owe tax.

27. The answer is A. Alexander is a qualifying child for the Child Tax Credit because he was under age 17 at the end of 2016. Siblings can be qualifying children for purposes of this credit, and half-siblings are treated the same as full siblings for tax purposes.

Unit 15: Affordable Care Act Tax for Individuals

For additional information read:

Publication 5187, *Health Care Law: What's New for Individuals & Families*

Publication 974, *Premium Tax Credit*

The Affordable Care Act (ACA)[59] contains over 20 new taxes or tax increases that are, (or will be), administered by the IRS. The law requires most U.S. citizens and residents to have qualifying health insurance or to pay a penalty for not doing so. In recent years, a universal mandate, known as the *individual shared responsibility provision*, took effect.

Note: In this unit, we provide an overview of the key ACA tax provisions you should understand for the EA exam. The ACA is extremely complex, and its provisions affect taxpayers in many different ways depending upon their individual situations. Parts of the ACA remain unsettled, with judicial and congressional challenges to some provisions and executive branch delays to others.[60]

Large employers also have annual reporting responsibilities concerning what health insurance they offered to their full-time employees. In this book, we will cover the ACA from the taxpayer's perspective. The ACA from the employer's perspective is covered in detail in Book 2, *Businesses*.

Important Forms for the ACA

In order to simplify reporting, the IRS has created a new group of forms to help handle some of the requirements of the ACA. If the taxpayer is covered by health insurance, he will most likely receive one of the forms listed below. The taxpayer must use the information from these statements when preparing his taxes. The forms are provided to different groups of people.

- **Form 1095-A**, *Health Insurance Marketplace Statement:* This form is for individuals who enroll in Marketplace[61] coverage. This form reports basic information about the insurance company that issued the taxpayer's policy, the exchange where he enrolled, and document coverage for each month.
- **Form 1095-B,** *Health Coverage:* This is for people whose insurance comes from a source other than the Marketplace.
- **Form 1095-C,** *Employer-Provided Health Insurance Offer and Coverage*: Individuals who work for applicable large employers will get this form (employees will also get this form if they enroll in self-insured coverage provided by an applicable large employer).

In December 2016, the IRS issued a notice delaying the reporting requirement for Forms 1095.[62] The due date for furnishing to individuals the 2016 Form 1095-B, *Health Coverage,* was extended from January 31, 2017, to March 2, 2017. [63] The due date for furnishing to individuals the 2016 Form 1095-C, *Employer-Provided Health Insurance Offer and Coverage,* has changed from January 31, 2017, to March 2, 2017.

---

[59]Although commonly known as Obamacare, the actual name of the health care law is the "Patient Protection and Affordable Care Act," often shortened to the Affordable Care Act or ACA.

[60] In January, 2017, U.S. Senate approved a budget resolution that sets the stage for broad swaths of the Affordable Care Act to be repealed. At the time of this book's printing, no formal repeal of the ACA has yet taken place, although changes to the law are expected for 2017.

[61] The "Marketplace", also called the "Health Insurance Marketplace," is an online resource where taxpayers can learn about their health coverage options.

[62] IRS Notice 2016-70

[63] The due date for filing with the IRS the 2016 Form 1094-B, *Transmittal of Health Coverage Information Returns,* and Form 1095-B, *Health Coverage,* remains unchanged. The due date is February 28, 2017; if filing electronically, the due date is March 31, 2017.

Some taxpayers will receive multiple forms in the same year. For example, if a taxpayer purchased health insurance through the Marketplace and then started a new job in the middle of the year that offered health coverage, depending on how the taxpayer's employer-sponsored insurance is set up, he may receive both Forms 1095-B and 1095-C on a single, combined form.

Minimum Essential Coverage

Under the Affordable Care Act, each individual must have qualifying health care coverage, known as *minimum essential coverage*, for each month of the year. This requirement applies to individuals of all ages. Coverage that qualifies includes:

- Employer-sponsored coverage, including self-insured plans, COBRA, and retiree coverage
- Coverage purchased in either federal or state health insurance Marketplaces (also known as exchanges)
- Medicare Part A and Medicare Advantage plans
- Most Medicaid coverage
- Certain types of veterans health coverage and most types of TRICARE coverage

Coverage that provides only limited benefits generally does not qualify as minimum essential coverage. For example, this includes stand-alone dental and vision insurance plans, accident or disability income insurance plans, worker's compensation insurance, and Medicaid family planning services.

An estimated three-quarters of taxpayers have qualifying health care coverage in 2016. They must self-report their coverage by checking the box on page 2 of Form 1040. Taxpayers are not required to send in proof of health care coverage to the IRS when filing their tax returns.

Example: Rosalia, age 58, had health insurance through her employer for every month of 2016. Her husband, Benito, age 67, had Medicare coverage for all of 2016. On their joint return, they check the box attesting that they had full-year insurance coverage. They have fulfilled their "shared responsibility" of the Affordable Care Act, and will not owe a penalty to the IRS.

Health Coverage Exemptions

There are multiple coverage exemptions that will excuse an individual from the requirement to have minimum essential health insurance coverage. A taxpayer must apply to the Health Insurance Marketplace for certain types of exemptions. If an exemption is approved by the Health Insurance Marketplace, the taxpayer will receive an *exemption certificate number* (ECN), which must be entered into most software programs in order to e-file.

Form 8965, *Health Coverage Exemptions*, is the form used for reporting ACA Exemptions. Below are all health coverage exemptions for the 2016 tax year.

Income-Related Exemptions

- **Affordability exception:** Taxpayers who do not have access to coverage considered affordable based on their projected household income may be exempt from paying penalties. In this case, if the lowest-priced coverage available to the taxpayer, either through a Marketplace or job-based plan, would exceed 8.13% of household income in 2016, then the taxpayer is exempted from the penalty.
- **No filing requirement:** If the taxpayer doesn't have to file a tax return because his income is below the filing requirement, then he is exempted from the penalty.

Health Coverage-Related Exemptions

- **Short-Term Coverage Gap:** The taxpayer was uninsured for less than three consecutive months of the year. A taxpayer with a coverage gap of 3 months or more is not exempt for any of those months.
- **State Did Not Expand Medicaid:** The taxpayer lived in a state that didn't expand its Medicaid program, but the taxpayer would have qualified if it had. In order to qualify for this exemption, the taxpayer would need to provide a copy of his Medicaid denial of eligibility notice.

Example: Andres was covered by Medicaid until April 23, 2016. He started a new job, and his employer-sponsored health coverage started on June 1, 2016. Andres is eligible for the short coverage gap exemption because he was without coverage for less than three months.

Group Membership Exemptions

- **Recognized Tribe:** The taxpayer is a member of a federally-recognized tribe or eligible for services through an Indian Health Services provider.
- **Health Sharing Ministries:** The taxpayer is a member of a recognized health care sharing ministry.
- **Religious Objections:** The taxpayer is a member of a recognized religious sect with religious objections to insurance, including Social Security and Medicare.

Other Allowable Exemptions

- **Incarceration:** Taxpayers who are in jail, prison, or another correctional facility.
- **Citizens Living Abroad/Some Noncitizens:**
    - U.S. citizens or residents who spent at least 330 days outside of the U.S. during a 12-month period.
    - U.S. citizens who are bona fide residents of a foreign country
    - Certain resident aliens who are citizens of a foreign country that has an income tax treaty with the U.S.
    - Taxpayers who are not legally present in the U.S. (undocumented aliens)
- **Acceptable Hardships:** If the taxpayer experienced one of these listed hardships an exemption may potentially be granted:
    - The taxpayer was homeless.
    - The taxpayer was evicted or was facing eviction or foreclosure.
    - The taxpayer received a shut-off notice from a utility company.
    - The taxpayer experienced domestic violence.
    - The taxpayer experienced the death of a close family member.
    - The taxpayer experienced a fire, flood, or other natural or human-caused disaster that caused substantial damage to his property.
    - The taxpayer filed for bankruptcy.
    - The taxpayer had medical expenses that resulted in substantial debt.
    - The taxpayer experienced unexpected increases in necessary expenses due to caring for an ill, disabled, or aging family member.
    - The taxpayer expects to claim as a dependent a child who has been denied coverage for Medicaid, and another person is required by court order to give medical support to the child. In this case, the taxpayer doesn't have to pay the penalty for the child.
    - As a result of an eligibility appeals decision, a taxpayer is eligible for enrollment in a qualified health plan (QHP) through the Marketplace, lower

costs on his monthly premiums, or cost-sharing reductions for a time period when he was not enrolled in health insurance through the Marketplace.

- The taxpayer's individual insurance plan was cancelled during the year, and the taxpayer believes that other Marketplace plans are unaffordable.

Example: Jody is single. Her gross income for 2016 was $9,800. She did not purchase health insurance, but she is exempt from the individual shared responsibility provision because her income is below the filing threshold for filing a return. She does not file a tax return, and she is not required to file Form 8965 since she is automatically exempt from the penalty.

Example: Jonathan and his four children live in Wyoming, a state that did not expand Medicaid under ACA. Their household income is below 138% of the federal poverty line. They do not have qualified health coverage. When Jonathan files his tax return, he attaches Form 8965 and claims an exemption to the individual shared responsibility provision. Jonathan will not owe a penalty for failing to have minimum essential coverage.

Note: There's no "hardship" exemption based only on employment status. So if a taxpayer becomes unemployed during the year, that in itself is not considered a valid hardship. However, several exemptions apply to people with low income.

Penalties: The Shared Responsibility Payment

If a taxpayer (or any of his dependents) does not have minimum essential coverage for each month of the year and does not qualify for an exemption, he will face a penalty called the *shared responsibility payment* (SRP) when he files his tax return.[64]

Example: Cory and Maryanne are married and have two dependent children under age 18. For half of the year, no member of their family had minimum essential coverage, and no one qualified for an exemption. Cory and Maryanne must calculate the shared responsibility payment for the six months of the year they did not have qualified health coverage.

For 2016, the annual Shared Responsibility Payment is the *greater* of:

- 2.5% of household income, or
- $695 per adult and $347.50 per child, up to a family maximum of $2,085.

The maximum penalty in 2016 is $2,085 per family. The Shared Responsibility Payment is capped at the national average premium for a bronze-level qualified health plan available through the Marketplace that would cover everyone in the tax household who does not have coverage or qualify for an exemption.

A taxpayer calculates the amount due for the shared responsibility payment by using the instructions to Form 8965. The payment is reported on page 2 of Form 1040 in the "other taxes" section.

Note: The IRS is specifically prohibited from using enforcement actions such as liens and levies to collect an SRP that a taxpayer does not pay. However, if a taxpayer is due a refund, the IRS may offset the liability by subtracting the SRP amount from his current or future refund.

Premium Tax Credit

The Premium Tax Credit is a new refundable federal tax credit to help eligible taxpayers pay for health insurance premiums. The credit is based on a taxpayer's income and is only available for taxpayers who purchased their insurance through a federal or state exchange. The

[64] On Jan. 20, 2017, an executive order signed by newly elected president Donald Trump directed federal agencies to exercise authority to reduce potential burden of the ACA. On February 3, 2017, the IRS disabled the e-file error related to the Annual Shared Responsibility Payment and will currently not reject an e-filed return that leaves the box unchecked or otherwise does not have either the appropriate penalty computed on Line 61 or have an exemption included with the return. At the time of this book's printing, the current legislative provisions of the ACA law are still in force, and taxpayers remain required to follow the law and pay what they may owe.

amount of the Premium Tax Credit is based on a sliding scale, so the higher the household income, the lower the amount of the credit. To be eligible for a Premium Tax Credit, a taxpayer must generally meet all of the following requirements:

- Purchase health insurance through the Marketplace.
- Be a U.S. citizen or legal U.S. resident.
- Be unable to get coverage from an employer or the government.
- Not be claimed as a dependent on anyone else's tax return.
- If married, the couple must generally file a joint tax return.[65] In general, taxpayers who file separate returns will not qualify for the credit.
- The taxpayer must meet certain household income requirements. Household income must be at least 100%, but not more than 400%, of the federal poverty line for the family size. For purposes of the Premium Tax Credit, a taxpayer's household income is the total of the taxpayer's modified adjusted gross income (MAGI), the taxpayer's spouse's MAGI (if filing jointly) and the MAGI of all dependents required to file a federal income tax return.

Example: Don and Luna are married and file jointly. They have two dependent children. Luna works part-time and does not receive health insurance through her employer. Don was unemployed for several months during 2016 before starting a new job in April. His employer-sponsored health insurance started May 1, 2016. From January through April, the family purchased health insurance through the federal exchange. Assuming they meet the income guidelines, Don and Luna can claim the Premium Tax Credit for the four months that they had Marketplace coverage.

Advance Premium Tax Credit Payments

When a taxpayer first applies for a Marketplace plan, the amount of the credit is estimated using information the taxpayer provides about family size and projected household income. Since it can be difficult to know exactly how much income a taxpayer will earn in a given year and family circumstances can change during the year, the actual amount of the credit can vary from the estimated amount.

When enrolling in a plan, a taxpayer must choose whether to have some or all of the benefit of the expected credit paid in advance to his insurance company or wait to claim all of the benefits on his tax return. A taxpayer who chose advance credit payments must file a tax return, regardless of whether he meets any other filing requirements, in order to reconcile the advance credit payments with the actual Premium Tax Credit earned. This reconciliation is calculated on Form 8962. If the credit allowed is less than the advance credit payments received, normally the difference will be subtracted from the taxpayer's refund or added to his balance due.

Example: Antoine is self-employed, and his income varies from year to year. When he enrolled in a health insurance plan through his state exchange, he estimated his 2016 earnings based on his prior year income. He learned he was eligible for the Premium Tax Credit, which he chose to take in full as advance credit payments. Antoine's business did well in 2016, and he made substantially more money than he expected, meaning his actual household income did not meet the guidelines for the Premium Tax Credit. He reconciles the advance credit payment amounts on Form 8962 and discovers he received a benefit of $1,000 in payments for which he is no longer eligible. Antoine is not owed a refund, so he must enter $1,000 on the excess advance premium tax credit repayment line of his Form 1040. That amount is added to his overall tax liability.

[65] In the case of married taxpayers who file separately, certain eligibility exceptions to the Premium Tax Credit apply, such as for domestic abuse or spousal abandonment.

Note: The Premium Tax Credit is refundable. If the amount of the credit is more than the amount of the tax liability of the return, a taxpayer may receive the difference as a refund. If no tax is owed, a taxpayer can receive the full amount of the credit as a refund.

Changes in family size due to marriage, divorce, birth, or adoption can affect the amount of the credit.

A taxpayer is supposed to report changes in circumstances to the Marketplace so the amount of the advance credit payments can be recalculated during the year. A taxpayer should also report changes in eligibility for government-sponsored or employee-sponsored health coverage, a move to a new address, an increase or decrease in the number of dependents, and other factors that may affect eligibility for the Premium Tax Credit.

Although the IRS is restricted in its ability to collect the shared responsibility payment, the agency may use full collection actions, including levies and liens, against a taxpayer who does not repay excess advance premium tax credits.

Net Investment Income Tax (NIIT)

The Affordable Care Act imposes a net investment income tax on higher-income taxpayers; it applies to individuals, estates, and trusts.[66] For individuals, a 3.8% tax is imposed on the lesser of:

- The individual's net investment income for the year, or
- Any excess of the individual's modified adjusted gross income for the tax year over the following thresholds:

Filing Status	Threshold Amount
MFJ or QW	$250,000
MFS	$125,000
Single or HOH	$200,000

These threshold amounts are not indexed for inflation. The NIIT is imposed only on U.S. citizens and resident aliens; nonresident aliens are not subject to the NIIT. Net investment income that is subject to the tax includes:

- Interest, unless it is otherwise tax-exempt
- Dividends
- Capital gains
- Rental and royalty income
- Non-qualified annuities
- Income from businesses involved in trading of financial instruments or commodities
- Income from businesses that are passive activities for the taxpayer

Net investment income does not include wages, self-employment income, Social Security benefits, veterans' benefits, unemployment compensation, alimony payments, or distributions from IRAs or certain qualified retirement plans.

The NIIT does not apply to any gains excluded from gross income for regular income tax purposes. Additionally, net investment income does not include any gain on the sale of a personal residence excluded from gross income (Section 121 exclusion).

Example: Trey is single and earned a salary of $175,000 in 2016. He also had $15,000 of income from dividends and capital gains, for MAGI of $190,000. This amount is less than the $200,000 threshold for single filers, so Trey is not subject to the Net Investment Income Tax.

[66] The net investment income tax first went into effect in 2013.

Example: Leanna is single and earned a salary of $175,000 in 2016. She also received $80,000 of dividend income, for a total MAGI of $255,000, which exceeds the threshold for single filers by $55,000. The Net Investment Income Tax is based on the lesser of $55,000 (the amount by which her MAGI exceeds the threshold for single filers) or $80,000 (her "net investment income"). Leanne owes NIIT of $2,090 ($55,000 × 3.8% = $2,090).

To the extent that gains are not otherwise offset by capital losses, the following are common examples of items included in computing net investment income:

- Gains from the sale of stocks, bonds, and mutual funds
- Capital gain distributions from mutual funds
- Gains from the sale of investment real estate
- Gains from the sale of interests in partnerships and S corporations, to the extent the partner or shareholder was a passive owner

Example: Reza and Zari are married and file jointly. They sell the main home that they have lived in for five years for $1.8 million and realize a gain of $850,000 on the sale. They may exclude $500,000 under section 121, so their gain subject to regular income tax is $350,000. They also have $75,000 of net investment income from other sources, for a total of $425,000. Their MAGI is $525,000, which exceeds the MFJ threshold amount of $250,000 by $275,000. They are subject to the NIIT on the lesser of $425,000 (NII) or $275,000 (the amount of excess MAGI). Reza and Zari owe NIIT of $10,450 ($275,000 × 3.8% = $10,450).

A gain from the sale of a second home that is not a primary residence would not be eligible for section 121 exclusion and therefore would be fully subject to the NIIT. Federal income tax credits generally may be used to offset net investment income.

Investment interest expense, investment advisory and brokerage fees, expenses related to rental and royalty income, and tax preparation fees can also be deducted to determine gross investment income, which is used to arrive at net investment income.

The NIIT is subject to estimated tax provisions, so taxpayers may need to adjust their withholding or estimated payments to avoid underpayment penalties. Employers are not required to withhold the tax from an employee's wages. The tax is computed on Form 8960, *Net Investment Tax: Individuals, Estates, and Trusts.*

Additional Medicare Tax

The Affordable Care Act imposes an additional Medicare tax[67] of 0.9% that applies to a taxpayer's earned income. An employer is required to withhold the additional Medicare tax if an employee is paid more than $200,000, regardless of an employee's filing status or whether the employee has wages paid by another employer. There is no employer share of the additional Medicare tax. Self-employed taxpayers cannot deduct one-half of the 0.9% additional Medicare tax. The additional Medicare tax is computed on Form 8959, *Additional Medicare Tax.* The tax is assessed on earned income in excess of the following thresholds:

Filing Status	Threshold Amount
MFJ	$250,000
MFS	$125,000
Single, HOH, or QW	$200,000

The thresholds are not adjusted for inflation. A taxpayer's earned income (including wages, taxable fringe benefits, bonuses, tips, commissions, and self-employment income) that is

[67] The additional Medicare tax first went into effect in 2013.

subject to regular Medicare tax is also subject to the additional Medicare tax to the extent it exceeds the applicable threshold amount for his filing status.

Example: Norma is single. She earns $350,000 in wages during 2016. The additional 0.9% tax will be calculated on her earnings above $200,000. This means that $150,000 will be subject to additional Medicare tax ($350,000 wages - $200,000 threshold amount). She will pay $1,350 in additional Medicare tax on her 2016 tax return ($150,000 x 0.9% = $1,350). This additional tax is withheld from Norma's wages automatically by her employer.

A taxpayer may be subject to the additional Medicare tax even if amounts are not withheld from his wages.

Example: Steven is single and earned $145,000 of salary in 2016. Because his earnings are below the $200,000 threshold for single filers, his company did not withhold any amount for the additional Medicare tax. He also had $85,000 of self-employment income from selling custom watercolor paintings he created. Steven's total earned income is $230,000. He would be required to pay additional Medicare tax on the $30,000 of earned income that exceeds the $200,000 threshold. Steven would owe $270 in additional Medicare tax on his 2016 income tax return ($30,000 × 0.9% = $270). He must calculate the tax and attach Form 8959, *Additional Medicare Tax*, to his tax return.

Example: Steven gets married on December 31, 2016, to Elaine, who earned wages of $7,000 during the year. Because they are married as of the last day of the year and file jointly, their threshold for the additional Medicare tax is $250,000. Their combined earned income is $237,000, below the $250,000 threshold for MFJ. Steven and Elaine do not owe the additional Medicare Tax.

If an employer withholds amounts for an employee who earns more than $200,000, but the employee and his spouse's combined earnings are less than the $250,000 MFJ threshold, they can apply the overpayment against any other type of tax that may be owed on their income tax return.

Example: Quan and Kim are married and file jointly. Quan earned $120,000 of salary in 2016, and Kim earned $190,000. Their employers do not withhold amounts for the additional Medicare tax because neither has earnings above $200,000. However, their combined earned income is $310,000, which is above the $250,000 threshold for joint filers by $60,000. Quan and Kim will owe $540 of additional Medicare tax on their 2016 income tax return ($60,000 × 0.9% = $540). They must calculate the tax and attach Form 8959, *Additional Medicare Tax*, to their tax return.

Unit 15: Study Questions

(Test yourself first, then check the correct answers at the end of this quiz.)

1. Laverne had Minimum Essential Coverage (MEC) all year. On which form would she report her qualifying coverage?

A. Form 1040, Other Taxes.
B. Form 8965.
C. Form 1095-A.
D. Form 1095-B.

2. Terry and Lulu are married but choose to file separately because of Terry's past-due child support. Their household income for 2016 is at 200% of the federal poverty line. They enroll in the federal Marketplace for health coverage, which they had for 2016. Which of the following statements is correct?

A. They are not eligible for the Premium Tax Credit because their household income is too high.
B. They are not eligible for the Premium Tax Credit because of their filing status.
C. They are not eligible for the Premium Tax Credit and will owe a shared responsibility payment.
D. They are eligible for the Premium Tax Credit.

3. Which of the following taxpayers would be subject to the additional Medicare tax in 2016?

A. Randy, who files as HOH and earned $180,000 of wages and $50,000 of investment income.
B. Kerrie, who is single and earned $196,000 of compensation, fringe benefits, and bonuses.
C. Liz, who files separately from her husband and earned $140,000 of wages.
D. None of the above.

4. Which of the following taxpayers would not be subject to the net investment income tax (NIIT)?

A. An estate.
B. A nonresident alien.
C. A trust.
D. An individual with only rental income in 2016.

5. In 2016, Suzanne had health insurance through her employer for every month of the year. She does not receive Form 1095-B from her employer. All of the following statements are correct except:

A. Suzanne must attach proof of her insurance coverage when she files her income tax return.
B. Suzanne will not owe the individual shared responsibility payment.
C. Suzanne's employer is required to provide Form 1095-B to employees by March 31.
D. Suzanne is not eligible for the Premium Tax Credit.

6. Which of the following individuals would be eligible for the Premium Tax Credit, assuming he met applicable income guidelines?

A. A taxpayer who had minimum essential coverage through his employer.
B. A taxpayer who was enrolled for two months through the federal Marketplace.
C. A taxpayer who received Medicaid coverage for 12 months of the year.
D. All of the above are eligible for the PTC.

7. The additional Medicare tax is:

A. 0.9% on a taxpayer's earned income above a certain threshold.
B. 3.8% on a taxpayer's earned income above a certain threshold.
C. 0.9% on a taxpayer's investment income above a certain threshold.
D. 3.8% on a taxpayer's investment income above a certain threshold.

8. Which of the following does not qualify as minimum essential coverage under the Affordable Care Act?

A. COBRA.
B. Coverage purchased through a state Marketplace.
C. Medicare
D. Worker's compensation insurance.

9. Milka is single. She has the following income in 2016:

- $73,000 interest income
- $200,000 gain from selling her main home that she had lived in and owned for seven years
- $245,000 MAGI

Calculate Milka's net investment income tax, if any, for 2016:

A. $0
B. $1,710
C. $2,774
D. $10,374

10. The Premium Tax Credit is:

A. Nonrefundable.
B. Refundable.
C. Available to all taxpayers with essential minimum coverage.
D. Available to all taxpayers with essential minimum coverage who purchased insurance through the federal Marketplace (but not from a state exchange).

11. Which of the following is a correct statement about the net investment income tax?

A. The tax is 3.8% of the excess of MAGI over a threshold amount.
B. The tax is 3.8% of net investment income.
C. The tax is 3.8% of the greater of net investment income or the excess of MAGI over a threshold amount.
D. The tax is 3.8% of the lesser of net investment income or the excess of MAGI over a threshold amount.

12. The IRS may take the following actions to collect the shared responsibility payment from a taxpayer:

A. Offsetting his tax refund.
B. Offsetting his tax refund and putting a lien on his property.
C. Offsetting his tax refund, putting a lien on his property, and levying his property.
D. None of the above is allowed.

13. Kyong enrolled in the federal Marketplace for 2016 in order to obtain health insurance. She estimated her household income for the year, qualified for the Premium Tax Credit, and chose to have half of the expected credit paid in advance to her insurance company. What must Kyong do when she files her income tax return?

A. She must repay half of the credit that she received in advance.
B. She will not owe any additional amount but may be eligible for a larger amount of the credit.
C. She must reconcile the advance premium tax credit payments with the actual Premium Tax Credit that she calculates on Form 8962. Any excess amount will be counted as household income and used to project her credit for the next year.
D. She must reconcile the advance premium tax credit payments with the actual Premium Tax Credit she calculates on Form 8962. She may receive a refund, or she may have to repay any excess advance premium tax credit payments, depending on her individual situation.

14. Adrienne and Bill are married and file jointly. Adrienne has $133,000 of self-employment income. Bill earned $184,000 in wages. Compute the amount of their additional Medicare tax, if any.

A. $2,853
B. $1,053
C. $603
D. They do not owe the additional Medicare tax.

Unit 15: Answers

1. The answer is A. Taxpayers who have Minimum Essential Coverage all year will indicate this on Form 1040, page 2, by checking the box in the "Other Taxes" section. Answer B is incorrect because coverage exemptions are reported on Form 8965. Answers C and D are incorrect because these forms are used by the Marketplace and employers, not individual taxpayers.

2. The answer is B. Terry and Lulu have minimum essential coverage because they purchased health insurance through the federal exchange and had it for each month of the year. However, they are not eligible for the Premium Health Credit because they file separate returns. Unless one of a limited number of exceptions applies, a married couple cannot claim the credit unless they file jointly.

3. The answer is C. The additional Medicare tax is applied to MFS taxpayers whose earned income exceeds $125,000 in 2016. Liz will owe an additional .9% tax on the $15,000 of earned income that exceeds the $125,000 threshold ($15,000 × .009 = $135 additional Medicare tax).

4. The answer is B. A nonresident alien would not be subject to the net investment income tax. The net investment income tax applies to individuals, estates, and trusts. Only U.S. citizens and U.S. residents are subject to the tax.

5. The answer is A. Because Suzanne had employer-sponsored health coverage for all 12 months of 2016, she has fulfilled her obligations under the Affordable Care Act and does not owe the shared responsibility payment. She must check the box for "full-year coverage" on page 2 of Form 1040, but she is not required to send in proof to the IRS when she files her return. She must retain documentation of her coverage, as she would any other records needed to substantiate items on her tax return.

6. The answer is B. To be eligible for the Premium Tax Credit, a taxpayer, his spouse, or his dependents must have been enrolled in either the federal Marketplace or a state exchange at some point during the year. A taxpayer enrolled in an employer-sponsored plan, including retiree coverage, is not eligible for the Premium Tax Credit, even if the plan is unaffordable. A taxpayer who received coverage through Medicaid or other government health plans outside of the Marketplace is not eligible for the PTC.

7. The answer is A. The additional Medicare tax applies to 0.9% of a taxpayer's earned income above a threshold based on his filing status. For single, head of household, and qualifying widow(er) filers, the threshold is $200,000. For married couples filing jointly, the amount is $250,000. For married couples filing separately, the amount is $125,000.

8. The answer is D. Worker's compensation insurance, and other plans that offer only limited benefits, do not fulfill the minimum essential coverage requirements. Employer-sponsored plans, including self-insured, COBRA, and retiree plans, generally offer qualifying coverage. All plans purchased through a federal or state exchange also qualify as minimum essential coverage, so Medicare, Medi-Cal, and Medicaid would all qualify.

9. The answer is B. The NIIT applies to the lesser of Milka's investment income ($73,000) or her MAGI above the threshold for her filing status, which is $200,000 for a single filer ($245,000 MAGI - $200,000 threshold = $45,000). Thus, her NIIT is calculated as follows: $45,000 × 3.8% = $1,710. The $200,000 gain from selling her home is excluded from taxation under section 121 and is therefore not part of the calculation for the NIIT.

10. The answer is B. The Premium Tax Credit is refundable, meaning that a taxpayer may be able to receive the full amount of credit as a refund, assuming he has no other tax liability. The PTC is available only to a taxpayer, his spouse, or his dependents who had health coverage through a federal or state exchange for all or part of the year.

11. The answer is D. For individuals; the net investment income tax is 3.8% of the lesser of net investment income, or the excess of modified adjusted gross income over a threshold amount. For example, the threshold for spouses filing joint returns is $250,000; the threshold is $200,000 for single filers.

12. The answer is A. The IRS is not allowed to take any enforced collection measures to collect a taxpayer's liability related to the shared responsibility payment. However, if a taxpayer is owed a tax refund, it can be used to offset the unpaid SRP. In contrast, the IRS is not restricted in the collection methods it may use against a taxpayer who does not repay excess advance premium tax credits. Both liens and levies are allowed to collect excess advance premium tax credit payments.

13. The answer is D. Any taxpayer who claims the Premium Tax Credit (whether advance credit payments were made or not) must file a tax return and include Form 8962, *Premium Tax Credit* (PTC). Kyong must do a monthly calculation to determine the actual amount of her PTC, which must then be reconciled with the advance premium tax credits paid to her insurer to lower her premium payments. Kyong must enter the amount of any excess advance premium tax credit payments made on her behalf on her return and normally repay the excess. If there were no excess advance premium tax credit payments and the amount of the PTC is more than the amount of her tax liability, she may receive the difference as a refund.

14. The answer is C. Their combined compensation is $317,000, which is $67,000 above the applicable threshold of $250,000 for joint filers. Their additional Medicare tax is $603 ($67,000 × 0.9%).

Unit 16: Additional Taxes and Credits

More Reading:
Publication 54, *Tax Guide for U.S. Citizens and Resident Aliens Abroad*
Publication 519, *U.S. Tax Guide for Aliens*
Publication 514, *Foreign Tax Credit for Individuals*
Tax Topic 556, *Alternative Minimum Tax*
Publication 929, *Tax Rules for Children and Dependents*

In this unit, we cover a variety of other taxes and credits, including the taxation and reporting of foreign income, the "nanny tax," and the "kiddie tax." We start with a look at the alternative minimum tax (AMT).

Alternative Minimum Tax

As described in the preceding units, federal tax law provides special treatment for certain types of income and allows deductions and credits for certain types of expenses. These tax benefits can significantly reduce the regular income tax liabilities for some taxpayers. The AMT limits the extent to which these tax benefits can be used to reduce the total amount of income tax paid by higher-income taxpayers. Congress adopted the AMT in 1969 in an attempt to ensure that individuals and corporations pay at least a minimum amount of tax.[68]

When calculating the AMT, many common items considered in the computation of the regular income tax liability are either adjusted downward or eliminated entirely. These include personal exemptions; the standard deduction or certain itemized deductions, such as state, local, and foreign taxes; miscellaneous itemized deductions subject to the 2% floor; investment interest expense; and mortgage interest on home equity debt if the loan was not used to buy or improve the home. In addition, the benefits of the following tax preference items must be eliminated when calculating the AMT:

- Depletion
- Excess intangible drilling costs
- Interest on private activity bonds
- Accelerated depreciation on property placed in service before 1987
- Exclusion of gain on qualified small business stock

The AMT is a parallel tax system, with every taxpayer responsible for paying the higher of the regular tax or a calculated tentative minimum tax. The AMT is the excess of the tentative minimum tax over the regular income tax. Thus, the AMT is owed only if the tentative minimum tax is greater than the regular tax.

In general, the tentative minimum tax is computed by:

1. Starting with AGI minus itemized deductions, if any, for regular tax purposes,
2. Eliminating or reducing certain adjustments and preferences (the exclusions, deductions, and credits that are allowed in computing the regular tax, such as those mentioned above), to derive alternative minimum taxable income (AMTI),
3. Subtracting the AMT exemption amount,
4. Multiplying the amount computed in (3) by the applicable AMT rate, and
5. Subtracting the AMT Foreign Tax Credit.

The AMT exemption in step 3 is an amount that is deducted from alternative minimum taxable income before calculating the tentative minimum tax. The exemption phases out after a taxpayer's AMTI reaches a certain level, which is based on his filing status.

---

[68] The American Taxpayer Relief Act of 2012 included provisions for the AMT to be permanently indexed for inflation, meaning the income threshold for an individual to be subject to the AMT will rise automatically each year.

2016 AMT Phaseout Ranges			
Filing Status	AMT Exemption Amount	Excess Taxable Income (AMTI)	AMT Phaseout Income Level
MFJ, QW	$53,900	$186,300	$119,700
Single	$83,800	$186,300	$159,700
MFS	$41,900	$93,150	$79,850

Most tax preparation software will automatically compute whether a taxpayer owes the AMT. A taxpayer who prepares his own return without using software may need to complete Form 6251, *Alternative Minimum Tax-Individuals*, to determine whether he owes the AMT.

If a taxpayer received or claimed any of the following items in the tax year, he is required to complete, but may not necessarily need to file, Form 6251:

- Accelerated depreciation
- Stock received through incentive stock options that were not sold in the same year
- Tax-exempt interest from private activity bonds
- Intangible drilling, circulation, research, experimental, or mining costs
- Amortization of pollution-control facilities or depletion
- Income (or loss) from tax-shelter farm activities or passive activities
- Interest from long-term contracts not figured using the percentage of completion-method
- Mortgage interest that is not used to buy, build, or substantially improve a home
- Investment interest expense reported on Form 4952
- Net operating loss deduction
- Alternative minimum tax adjustments from an estate, trust, electing large partnership, or cooperative
- Section 1202 exclusion (gains from qualifying Small Business Stock)
- Any general business credit in Part 1 on Form 3800
- Empowerment zone and renewal community employment credit
- Qualified electric vehicle credit
- Alternative fuel vehicle refueling property credit
- Credit for prior year minimum tax

Credit for Prior Year Minimum Tax

A nonrefundable credit may be available to individuals, estates, and trusts for alternative minimum tax paid in prior years to the extent that a taxpayer's regular tax in the current year is greater than his tentative minimum tax. If applicable, the credit is calculated on Form 8801, *Credit for Prior Year Minimum Tax – Individuals, Estates, and Trusts*.

The AMT is caused by two types of adjustments and preferences: exclusion items and deferral items. Exclusion items are those that affect only a single tax year and therefore cause a permanent difference between regular taxable income and alternative minimum taxable income (AMTI). AMT adjustments/preferences that are exclusion items and are not used to determine the minimum tax credit are as follows:

- Personal exemption
- Standard deduction
- Itemized deductions
- Percentage depletion
- Certain tax-exempt interest
- Exclusion of gain from qualified small business stock

For individual taxpayers, an example of an exclusion item is the deduction for state and local income taxes. These taxes are never deductible for AMT purposes, and they are added back into AGI in the calculation of AMTI in the year they are paid.

Deferral items are adjustment and preference items, such as depreciation, that affect more than one tax year. Because they affect the difference between regular taxable income and AMTI in multiple tax years, they generally do not cause a permanent difference in taxable income over time.

The minimum tax credit is allowed only for the portion of AMT caused by deferral items, which may generate credit for future years.

Example: Leland and Erika are married and file jointly. They had an AMT liability in the previous year after they exercised incentive stock options. They use Form 8801 to calculate how much of their AMT was related to that and other deferral items and discover they have a $1,500 credit carryforward. Their regular tax in 2016 is $4,000, and their tentative minimum tax is $3,000. They can use $1,000 of the minimum tax credit carryforward to reduce their regular tax, but they cannot reduce it below the tentative minimum tax amount. The balance of $500 can be carried forward.

Kiddie Tax on Investment Income

Years ago, wealthy families could transfer investments to their minor children and save tax dollars because the investment income would be taxed at the children's lower rates. Congress closed this tax loophole, and now investment income earned by dependent children may be taxed at the parent's rate. This law became known as the "kiddie tax".

The kiddie tax does not apply to earned income (such as wages); it applies only to investment income, such as interest, dividends, and capital gains distributions. Part of a child's investment income may be taxed at the parent's marginal tax rate if:

- The child's investment income is more than $2,100 (in 2016).
- The child is under age 18 or a full-time college student under age 24.
- The child is required to file a tax return for the tax year.
- At least one of the child's parents was alive at the end of the year.
- The child does not file a joint return for the tax year.

Parents can avoid paying the kiddie tax only if the child is age 18 or older and has enough earned income to provide greater than half of his own support. In that case, the tax would be based on the child's tax rate and not the parent's.

The kiddie tax only applies when a dependent child's investment income exceeds $2,100 in 2016. The first $1,050 in investment income is tax-free; the second $1,050 is taxed at the child's marginal rate. All of the child's investment income in excess of $2,100 is then taxed at the parent's tax rate. A taxpayer can report and pay the kiddie tax in either of two ways:

- The parents may include the child's investment income on their tax return (using Form 8814, *Parent's Election to Report Child's Interest and Dividends*), or
- The child may file a separate tax return (using Form 8615, *Tax for Certain Children Who Have Unearned Income*).

The tax on the child's income will be the same either way, unless an exception to the kiddie tax rules applies. A child's investment income is subject to the net investment income tax, which is calculated using only the child's income and not the parent's. However, the NIIT applies only if the child's net investment income exceeds the $200,000 threshold for single filers. This scenario would be very rare.

Example: Bill and Donna have a 15-year-old son named Jack. In 2016, Jack has $2,500 of interest income from a CD his grandfather gave him. He does not have any other taxable income. The first $1,050 of investment income is not taxable. The next $1,050 is taxed at the 10% income tax rate, which is Jack's marginal rate. The remainder, $400, is taxed at his parents' marginal rate.

Example: Kendra is 16 years old. She has a number of investments that she inherited when her parents died three years ago. Kendra lived with her grandmother, Edna, all year. Kendra has $5,600 in investment income during the year. Kendra is not subject to the kiddie tax rules because she does not have a living parent. In this case, Kendra would not be required to file Form 8615, and Kendra's grandmother would not have to file Form 8814, even if Edna claims her granddaughter as a dependent on her tax return.

Nanny Tax (Tax on Household Employees)

A taxpayer who has household employees may need to pay employment taxes. This obligation is commonly referred to as the "nanny tax," or the tax on Household Employees.

Example: Daniel hires Candy to babysit his three children and do housework in his home. Daniel sets Candy's schedule and gives specific direction about household and child care duties. Daniel also provides all the equipment and supplies Candy needs to do her work. Candy is Daniel's household employee, and subject to the nanny tax rules.

If a taxpayer pays a household employee cash wages (including amounts paid by check, money order, etc.) of $2,000 or more in 2016, he must withhold the employee's share of Social Security and Medicare taxes, and remit them along with the employer's matching share, for a total of 15.3%, unless he chooses to pay both the employer's and employee's shares. If the amount of wages paid to an employee during the year is less than this threshold, no Social Security or Medicare taxes are owed.

Note: An employer is not required to withhold income tax from a household employee's wages. However, income tax may be withheld at the employee's request. Even if the employer is not required to pay FICA (Social Security and Medicare) taxes, the employee's wages may be subject to income tax.

If a taxpayer pays wages of $1,000 or more[69] to a household employee in any quarter, he must also pay federal unemployment tax. The tax applies to the first $7,000 of wages per employee. The maximum FUTA tax rate is 6.0%, but credits reduce this rate to 0.6% in most cases.

A worker is the taxpayer's employee if the taxpayer can control not only what work is done, but how it is done, regardless of whether the work is full-time or part-time; the employee is paid on an hourly, daily, weekly, or per job basis; or the employee is hired through an agency. Examples of household employees include babysitters, housekeepers, private nurses, yard workers, and drivers.

A self-employed worker, such as a daycare provider who cares for several children from different families in her own home, is not considered a household employee.

Example: Christopher hires Robby to do weekly yard maintenance and cut his grass. Robby runs a lawn care business and provides gardening services to many other clients. Robby also advertises his business in the local newspaper. Robby provides his own tools and supplies. Robby is self-employed and not considered Christopher's household employee.

[69] This FUTA tax threshold is different for other types of employees. In 2016, the FUTA tax reporting threshold is $1,000 in wages in any calendar quarter for household employees and farmworkers. The threshold is $1,500 or more (in any calendar quarter) for all other employees.

Example: Abner is a widowed single taxpayer with infant twin boys. Abner hires Tabitha to take care of his twin boys while he is at work. Tabitha usually works Monday through Friday, 9 AM to 6 PM. She is an experienced nanny, and she also cleans Abner's home during the day. Tabitha is a household employee. Abner is required to file payroll returns as well as Schedule H with his Form 1040.

A taxpayer who is required to pay Social Security and Medicare taxes or federal unemployment taxes for household employees, or who withholds income tax for them, must file Schedule H, *Household Employment Taxes,* with his Form 1040. The taxpayer will need an employer identification number (EIN) to file Schedule H. He also must file Form W-2, *Wage and Tax Statement,* and furnish a copy of the form to the employee.

A taxpayer who is an employer of household employees may need to increase the federal income tax withheld from his pay or pension or make estimated tax payments in order to avoid an estimated tax penalty resulting from his liability for employment taxes in connection with household employees, as shown on Schedule H. The taxpayer has several options. He can:

- Increase his federal income tax withheld by giving his employer a new Form W-4
- Increase his federal income tax withheld by giving the payor of his pension a new Form W4-P, *Withholding Certificate for Pension or Annuity Payments*
- Make estimated tax payments by filing Form 1040-ES, *Estimated Tax for Individuals*

Estimated taxes must be withheld or paid as the tax liability is incurred, so a taxpayer cannot wait until he files his tax return (and Schedule H) to pay household taxes owed.

Wages paid to a taxpayer's spouse, parent, or child under the age of 21 are exempt from the nanny tax rules.

Example: Paula hires her mother, Rose, to take care of her children during the week. In this case, since Paula has hired her mother, the payments are exempt from the nanny tax rules. No Social Security and Medicare taxes will be owed by either Paula or her mother. No Federal Unemployment Tax (FUTA) would be owed. However, Rose would owe income tax on the amounts that she earned.

A taxpayer cannot claim a dependency exemption for a household employee such as a nanny, even if the employee lives with the taxpayer.

First-Time Homebuyer Credit Repayment

First-time homebuyers who claimed a special tax credit in 2008 are required to repay a portion of the funds received over a 15-year period. The First-Time Homebuyer Credit took the form of a loan in 2008. For example, a homebuyer who claimed the maximum credit of $7,500 must repay $500 per year as an additional tax. The amount is entered on line 60b on Form 1040. A taxpayer who claimed the credit and sells a home purchased in 2008 must complete Form 5405, *First-Time Homebuyer Credit and Repayment of the Credit*. The repayment is limited to the amount of gain on the sale if the sale is to an unrelated taxpayer. The credit was also available in 2009 and 2010 but has since expired. A taxpayer who purchased his home and received the credit in either 2009 or 2010 does not have to repay the credit unless he sold the home within a three-year period following the purchase.

Example: Alexa purchased her home in 2008 and claimed the full amount of the First-Time Homebuyer Credit. She still lives in the home and uses it as her main residence. She is required to pay back her credit in equal yearly installments of $500 over a period of 15 years. When she files her 2015 tax return, the repayment is listed on her Form 1040 as an additional tax.

Foreign Income and Taxes

Generally, all income of U.S. citizens and U.S. resident aliens is subject to tax by the United States, regardless of where the individual lives and even if the income is earned outside the United States. "Foreign earned income" is income received for services performed in a foreign country while the taxpayer's tax home is also in a foreign country. It does not matter whether the income is paid by a U.S. employer or a foreign employer.

Example: Brenda and Sonny are married and file jointly. In 2016, they were both employed in Peru, with Brenda earning $80,000 and Sonny earning $26,000. Each qualifies for the foreign earned income exclusion. Brenda also has $6,000 of work-related expenses. She cannot deduct any of her expenses because she is already excluding all of her income from taxation by taking the foreign earned income exclusion.

Foreign Earned Income Exclusion: If a taxpayer is eligible for the foreign earned income exclusion, his income up to a certain threshold is not taxed. For 2016, the maximum foreign earned income exclusion is $101,300.

If married taxpayers file jointly and both individuals live and work abroad, each can claim the foreign earned income exclusion, for a total exclusion amount of $202,600.

Nonresident aliens do not qualify for the foreign earned income exclusion. A taxpayer must be either a U.S. citizen or a legal resident alien of the United States who lives and works abroad and must pass one of two tests in order to claim the exclusion:

- **Bona Fide Residence Test:** A U.S. citizen or U.S. resident alien who is a bona fide resident of a foreign country for an uninterrupted period that includes an entire tax year.
- **The Physical Presence Test:** A U.S. citizen or U.S. resident alien who is physically present in a foreign country or countries for at least 330 full days during 12 consecutive months. A taxpayer may qualify under the physical presence test, and the income may span a period of multiple tax years. If so, the taxpayer must prorate the foreign earned income exclusion based on the number of days spent in the foreign country.

Note: The exclusion does not apply to the wages and salaries of members of the Armed Forces and civilian employees of the U.S. government.

The foreign earned income exclusion is calculated using Form 2555, *Foreign Earned Income,* which must be attached to Form 1040. If a choice is made to exclude foreign earned income, the choice remains in effect for subsequent years, unless revoked.

Foreign Housing Exclusion or Deduction: In addition to the foreign earned income exclusion, a taxpayer can claim an exclusion (or a deduction) for foreign housing costs. The maximum foreign housing exclusion for 2016 is $16,208, or $44.28 per day (16% of the maximum foreign earned income exclusion at $101,300).

The housing exclusion applies only to amounts paid by an employer, while the housing deduction applies only to amounts paid with self-employment earnings. Qualified housing expenses include reasonable expenses paid for housing in a foreign country. Only housing expenses for the part of the year that the taxpayer actually qualified for the foreign earned income exclusion are considered.

Example: Sergio is a U.S. citizen who lived in Vietnam all of 2016 and was employed by a Vietnamese company as an advertising consultant. He lived rent-free in an apartment provided by his employer. Sergio received a salary of $95,000, and the fair rental value of his housing was $12,000, for a total of $107,000 of earned income. He qualifies for the foreign earned income exclusion and the foreign housing exclusion.

Foreign Income Taxes: Generally, income taxes paid to a foreign country can be deducted as an itemized deduction on Schedule A or as a credit against U.S. income tax. A taxpayer can choose between these options and use whichever one results in the lowest tax.

Foreign Tax Credit: U.S. citizens and resident aliens are eligible for the Foreign Tax Credit, which is designed to relieve taxpayers of the double taxation burden that occurs when their foreign source income is taxed by both the U.S. and a foreign country. Nonresident aliens are not eligible. Four tests must be met to qualify for the credit:

- The tax must be imposed on the taxpayer.
- The taxpayer must have paid or accrued (if an accrual basis taxpayer) the tax.
- The tax must be a legal and actual foreign tax liability.
- The tax must be an income tax.

Although taxpayers can choose between taking the deduction or the credit for all foreign taxes paid, in most cases, it is to their advantage to take the Foreign Tax Credit, since a credit directly reduces tax liability. A taxpayer cannot claim both, the deduction and the tax credit on the same return, but may alternate years, taking a credit in one year and a deduction in the next year.

Taxpayers also cannot claim the Foreign Tax Credit for taxes paid on any income that has already been excluded using the foreign earned income exclusion or the foreign housing exclusion. Unlike the foreign earned income exclusion, which applies only to income that is earned while a taxpayer is living and working abroad, the Foreign Tax Credit applies to any type of foreign income, including investment income. Foreign tax paid may be reported to the taxpayer by a financial institution on Form 1099-INT or Form 1099-DIV.

Taxpayers can claim the credit on Form 1040 if, among other conditions, all foreign income is specified passive category income and total taxes paid do not exceed $300 ($600 MFJ). If the tax paid exceeds $300 ($600 MFJ), the taxpayer must file Form 1116, *Foreign Tax Credit*, to claim the credit.

Example: Yusuf and Fatima are married and file jointly. They own a number of foreign stocks, and their Form 1099-DIV shows foreign tax paid of $590. The couple is not required to complete Form 1116 because their foreign taxes are less than $600.

Example: Colette is a U.S. citizen who is also a shareholder of a French corporation. She receives $700 of income from the French corporation. The French government imposes a 10% tax ($70) on Colette's earnings. She must include the gross earnings ($700) in her income. The $70 of tax withheld is a qualified foreign tax for purposes of the Foreign Tax Credit.

Certain taxes do not qualify for the Foreign Tax Credit, including interest or penalties paid to a foreign country, taxes imposed by countries involved with international terrorism, and taxes on foreign oil or gas extraction income.

Note: Currently, the foreign tax credit does not apply to any tax paid to Syria, Sudan, North Korea or Iran. These countries are sanctioned by the U.S.

The Foreign Tax Credit is nonrefundable, but the taxpayer is allowed a one-year carryback and a ten-year carryforward of any unused credit amount.

Fixed, Determinable, Annual, or Periodic (FDAP) Income

Fixed, Determinable, Annual, or Periodic (FDAP) income applies to foreign persons earning income in the U.S. FDAP income consists primarily of passive investment income, including interest, dividends, rents, royalties, pensions, and annuities. Deductions are not allowed against FDAP income, and it is taxed at a flat 30% rate or a lower rate if there is a tax treaty between the U.S. and the taxpayer's country of residency.

This 30% or lower rate only applies if the FDAP income or gains from U.S. sources are not "effectively connected" with a taxpayer's U.S. trade or business. A nonresident alien who receives income that is effectively connected with his trade or business in the United States is taxed at the rates that apply to U.S. citizens and residents. The IRS definition of FDAP includes all passive investment income except:

- Gains derived from the sale of real or personal property

- Items of income excluded from gross income, regardless of the U.S. or foreign status of the income's owner, such as tax-exempt municipal bond interest and qualified scholarship income

Compensation for personal services performed in the United States can also be FDAP income. If a nonresident alien receives income for personal services performed partly in the U.S. and partly outside the U.S., he must allocate the income based on the number of days where the services were performed.

Example: Alain, a citizen, and resident of Canada, is employed as a professional hockey player by a U.S. hockey team. He received $200,000 in compensation for 120 days of play during 2016: 75 days in the U.S. and 45 days in Canada. The amount of U.S. source income is $125,000 ([75 days of play in the US ÷ 120 total days =.625] × $200,000).

Unit 16: Study Questions

(Test yourself first, then check the correct answers at the end of this quiz.)

1. Ahmed is a citizen and resident of Iran, a country that does not have a tax treaty with the United States. Ahmed is not a U.S. citizen or U.S. resident, but he owns several rental properties and other investments in the U.S. that produce passive investment income. His FDAP income is taxable at a flat __________ rate.

A. 25%
B. 28%
C. 30%
D. 35%

2. Colton is 22, a full-time college student, and is claimed as a dependent on his parents' tax return. He also has a part-time job at a local mall. Colton has $210 of dividend income in 2016. What is the maximum amount of wages Colton can earn in 2016 without triggering the kiddie tax?

A. $350
B. $2,100
C. $6,200
D. No maximum.

3. Ella hired a part-time nanny to work in her home. She paid the nanny $1,900 of wages in 2016. Which of the following statements is correct?

A. Ella is not required to issue a Form W-2 to the nanny and does not have to report or pay Social Security and Medicare taxes on the nanny's wages.
B. The income is not taxable to the nanny.
C. No reporting is required by either party if the wages are paid in cash.
D. Ella can deduct the nanny's wages as a business expense on Schedule C.

4. All of the following statements are correct about the alternative minimum tax except:

A. Congress passed the alternative minimum tax to ensure that individuals and corporations that benefit from certain exclusions, deductions, or credits pay at least a minimum amount of tax.
B. The tentative minimum tax is figured in addition to a taxpayer's regular tax.
C. The AMT is the excess of the tentative minimum tax over the regular tax.
D. The AMT is permanently indexed for inflation.

5. In 2016, when does an employer have to withhold and pay Social Security and Medicare taxes for a household employee?

A. When the taxpayer pays any employee for household services.
B. When the taxpayer pays a household employee $1,000 or more of wages a year.
C. When the taxpayer pays a household employee $2,000 or more of wages a year.
D. When the taxpayer pays his 20-year-old daughter to care for her younger siblings.

6. Natalie is a U.S. citizen who lives and works in Australia, which is her tax home. She does not maintain a residence in the U.S. In 2016, she received the following income:

- Annuity income from a U.S. investment: $12,500
- Taxable interest: $2,000
- Wages: $90,000

Natalie wants to take the foreign earned income exclusion on her individual tax return. What is the total amount of qualifying foreign earned income that Natalie can report on her Form 2555?

A. $101,300
B. $99,200
C. $92,000
D. $90,000

7. Which of the following taxpayers would not be eligible for the Credit for the Prior Year Minimum Tax by filing Form 8801?

A. An S corporation.
B. A trust.
C. An estate.
D. An individual.

8. Which of the following statements is correct regarding the Foreign Tax Credit?

A. The Foreign Tax Credit is a refundable credit.
B. The Foreign Tax Credit is available to U.S. citizens and nonresident aliens.
C. Taxpayers may choose to take a deduction for foreign taxes paid, rather claim than the Foreign Tax Credit.
D. Taxpayers can claim both a deduction and a tax credit for foreign taxes paid, provided the taxes were paid to different countries.

9. In determining a taxpayer's credit for prior year minimum tax, which of the following would not be considered?

A. Depreciation.
B. Mortgage interest.
C. Incentive stock options.
D. None of the above is considered in determining the credit for prior year minimum tax.

10. The Foreign Tax Credit applies to:

A. Taxpayers who have paid foreign taxes to a foreign country on foreign-sourced income and are subject to U.S. tax on the same income.
B. Taxpayers who have paid U.S. taxes while living and working abroad.
C. Taxpayers who have paid U.S. taxes while living and working abroad and who are subject to U.S. tax on their worldwide income.
D. Nonresident aliens who have paid foreign taxes to a foreign country on foreign-sourced income and are subject to U.S. tax on the same income.

Unit 16: Answers

1. The answer is C. Ahmed will be taxed at a flat 30% rate on his FDAP (Fixed, Determinable, Annual, or Periodical) income. A 30% (or lower treaty) tax rate applies to FDAP income or gains from U.S. sources, but only if they are not effectively connected with a taxpayer's U.S. trade or business. FDAP income consists primarily of passive investment income, including interest, dividends, rents, royalties, pensions, and annuities. FDAP income is all income except:

- Gains derived from the sale of real or personal property.
- Items of income excluded from gross income, without regard to the U.S. or foreign status of the owner of the income, such as tax-exempt municipal bond interest and qualified scholarship income.

2. The answer is D. The kiddie tax only applies to investment income, not to wages. Therefore, Colton's wage income will not be subject to the kiddie tax. Under the provisions of the kiddie tax, unearned income that is in excess of $2,100 will be taxed at the parent's marginal rate.

3. The answer is A. Ella is not required to issue a Form W-2 to the nanny, and does not have to report or pay Social Security and Medicare taxes on the nanny's wages. If an employer pays a household employee wages of less than $2,000 in 2016, the employer is not required to report or pay Social Security and Medicare taxes on that employee's wages. However, employers who withhold federal income taxes from their employee's wages must issue a Form W-2. Regardless of whether Form W-2 is issued, the nanny must report the income on Form 1040.

4. The answer is B. The tentative minimum tax is calculated separately from the regular tax. The AMT is owed only if the tentative minimum tax is greater than the regular tax.

5. The answer is C. In 2016; the nanny tax applies when a taxpayer pays a household employee $2,000 or more of wages a year.

6. The answer is D. U.S. citizens, and resident aliens who live abroad are taxed on their worldwide income. However, they may qualify to exclude a portion of their foreign earnings (up to $101,300 for 2016). A qualifying individual with qualifying income may elect to exclude foreign earned income, and this exclusion applies only if a tax return is filed and the income is reported. Natalie has $104,500 of gross income, but only her wages ($90,000) would qualify for the foreign earned income exclusion.

7. The answer is A. Only individuals, estates, and trusts are eligible to claim the Credit for the Prior Year Minimum Tax by filing Form 8801. The credit is calculated differently for corporations, which use a different form and set of instructions to determine whether they are eligible for the credit.

8. The answer is C. Taxpayers have the option to claim an itemized deduction for foreign taxes paid on Schedule A. They may choose either the deduction or the credit, whichever gives them the lowest tax. Taxpayers cannot claim both the deduction and a tax credit on the same return.

9. The answer is B. Itemized deductions, such as mortgage interest, are exclusion items not used to determine the minimum tax credit. Other exclusion items include personal exemptions and the standard deduction. Items such as depreciation are deferral items and are used to calculate the credit.

10. The answer is A. The Foreign Tax Credit applies to taxpayers who have paid foreign taxes to a foreign country on foreign-sourced income and are subject to U.S. tax on the same income.

Unit 17: Retirement Accounts

More Reading:
Publication 590, *Individual Retirement Arrangements (IRAs)*
Publication 575, *Pension and Annuity Income*
Publication 560, *Retirement Plans for Small Business*

There are a variety of retirement accounts individuals can establish for themselves and retirement plans that can be established by employers and self-employed individuals.

In this unit, we primarily cover traditional individual retirement arrangements (traditional IRAs) and Roth IRAs, as they are tested heavily on Part 1 of the EA exam. We will also briefly address other types of retirement plans. Form 1099-R, *Distributions From Pensions, Annuities, Retirement or Profit-Sharing Plans, IRAs, Insurance Contracts, etc.*, is used to report distributions of $10 or more from a retirement plan or an IRA.

Traditional IRA: Amounts in a traditional IRA, including contributions and earnings, are generally not taxed until they are distributed. Typically, a taxpayer can deduct his traditional IRA contributions as an adjustment to gross income. However, the adjustment can be phased out at higher income levels.

Roth IRA: Contributions to a Roth IRA are paid with after-tax income and are not deductible. In contrast to a traditional IRA, withdrawals from a Roth IRA are generally not taxed. Income limits apply in determining who is eligible to participate in a Roth IRA.

A taxpayer cannot claim an adjustment for a deductible IRA contribution on Form 1040EZ; he must use Form 1040 or Form 1040A.

Note: The rules regarding IRAs and retirement plans apply to same-sex spouses who are legally married in any state.[70] A same-sex spouse is entitled to all spousal benefits and protections provided to heterosexual spouses from traditional IRAs, Roth IRAs, and qualified retirement plans. However, these rules do *not* apply to domestic partnerships and civil unions.

2016 IRA Contribution Limits

The limits for contributions to an IRA in 2016 are the lesser of qualifying taxable compensation (as described below) or the following amounts:

- **$5,500** per taxpayer (**$6,500** if age 50 or older)
- Taxpayers filing MFJ (even if only one had compensation): **$11,000** (or **$13,000** if both spouses are age 50 or older)

This yearly IRA contribution limit does not apply to:

- Rollover contributions (rolling over from one IRA account to another)
- Qualified reservist repayments[71]

Traditional IRA Rules

To make contributions to a traditional IRA:

- The taxpayer must be under age 70½ at the end of the year.
- The taxpayer must have qualifying taxable compensation, such as wages, salaries, commissions, tips, bonuses, or self-employment income.

[70] In June 2015, the landmark U.S. Supreme Court ruling *Obergefell v. Hodges* legalized same-sex marriage in every state.

[71] If a taxpayer was a reservist in the Armed Forces and was called to active duty, the taxpayer can contribute (repay) any IRA amounts equal to any qualified reservist distributions received. The taxpayer can make these repayment contributions even if the payments would cause the total yearly contributions to exceed the general limit on IRA contributions.

If either the taxpayer or his spouse is covered by an employer plan and his income is too high, his deductible IRA contribution will be phased out.

For purposes of making an IRA contribution, taxable alimony (but not child support payments) counts as qualifying compensation. This allows taxpayers to build retirement savings in IRAs even if they rely on alimony income for support. Nontaxable combat pay also qualifies as compensation for this purpose.

Example: Stan is an Army medic serving in a combat zone for all of 2016. Although none of his combat pay is taxable, it is still considered qualifying compensation for purposes of an IRA contribution. He is allowed to contribute to a Roth or Traditional IRA if he wishes.

Compensation for purposes of contributing to an IRA does not include:

- Rental income
- Dividend and interest income
- Pension or annuity income
- Deferred compensation
- Prize winnings or gambling income
- Items (except for nontaxable combat pay) that are excluded from income, such as foreign earned income and excludable foreign housing costs

Example: Larry is 54 and wants to contribute to his traditional IRA. He received $10,000 of rental income; $8,000 of interest income; and $3,000 of wages from a part-time job. The rental and interest income are not considered for purposes of determining his IRA contribution. Therefore, the maximum he can contribute to his traditional IRA is $3,000, the amount of his wages.

Note: A taxpayer can never contribute more than he has earned for the year. Minors who want to start contributing to an IRA must abide by limits based on their own taxable income, *not* the income of their parents.

Example: Penelope is 17 years old and has a part-time job. She is claimed as a dependent on her parent's return. She earns $4,300 in wages during 2016. She also has $3,500 in dividend income from stocks that she inherited from her grandmother. Penelope may contribute to an IRA in 2016 because she has earned income. Her IRA contribution would be limited to $4,300, the amount of her wages. The investment income is not qualifying compensation for IRA purposes.

IRAs cannot be owned jointly. Therefore, each spouse must have their own IRA account. However, a married couple filing jointly may contribute to each of their IRA accounts, even if only one taxpayer has qualifying compensation.

Example: Joaquin, 49, and Meg, 51, are married and file jointly. Joaquin works as a paramedic and makes $46,000 per year. Meg is a homemaker and has no taxable income. Even though Meg has no qualifying compensation, they may contribute to her IRA account. Their combined maximum contribution for 2016 is $12,000. Joaquin may contribute $5,500 to his IRA, and Meg may contribute $6,500 to her IRA because she is over 50 years old. This special rule only applies if the taxpayers file jointly.

If married taxpayers choose to file separately, they must consider only their own qualifying compensation for IRA contribution purposes.

Example: Greg is 35, works full-time, and earned $55,000 in wages during the year. His wife, Lila, is 34 and earned $3,600 in 2016. They choose to file MFS. Therefore, Lila is limited to a $3,600 IRA contribution, the amount of her qualifying compensation. Greg may contribute the full $5,500 to his own IRA account.

Contributions can be made to a traditional IRA at any time on or before the due date of the return (not including extensions). For the 2016 tax year, a taxpayer may make an IRA contribution up until April 18, 2017. This makes an IRA contribution a rare opportunity for late-stage tax planning because it can occur after the tax year has already ended.

A taxpayer can even file his return claiming a traditional IRA contribution before the contribution is actually made. However, if a contribution is reported on the taxpayer's return, but it is not made by the deadline, the taxpayer must file an amended return.

Example: Paul files his 2016 tax return on March 5, 2017, and claims a $4,000 deduction for an IRA contribution on the return. Paul may wait as late as April 18, 2017, the due date of the return, to make the IRA contribution.

If a person's only qualifying compensation for the year is from self-employment and the self-employment activity generates a loss for that year, he would not be able to contribute to an IRA. However, if the taxpayer has wages in addition to self-employment income, a loss from self-employment would not be subtracted from the wages when figuring total "qualifying" compensation income for purposes of determining his IRA contribution.

Example: Marcy is 45 and earns $10,000 of wages working part-time for a library. She also works as a self-employed photographer, but her photography business has a net loss of $5,400 for the year. Even though Marcy's *net* income for 2016 is only $4,600 ($10,000 wages – $5,400 loss from self-employment), her qualifying compensation for purposes of an IRA contribution is still $10,000, the amount of her wages. This means that Marcy can make a full IRA contribution of $5,500 in 2016, assuming she has the funds to do so.

For married taxpayers filing a joint return, the combined IRA contributions cannot exceed their combined qualifying compensation.

Example: Elliott and June are both age 49 and married. Elliott has $23,000 of passive rental income for the year. June has $13,000 of pension income and $7,000 of wages. Only June's wages count as qualifying compensation for purposes of an IRA contribution. If they file jointly, they can contribute a maximum of $7,000 to their IRAs. One of them can contribute up to the maximum annual amount ($5,500), and the other can contribute up to $1,500 (equal to the remaining amount of June's qualifying compensation), or they could split the $7,000 in another manner.

Deductibility of Traditional IRA Contributions

A taxpayer may not be able to deduct all of his traditional IRA contributions. Deductibility is based on income, filing status, and whether the taxpayer or his spouse is covered by an employer retirement plan at work. A taxpayer is permitted to contribute to a traditional IRA regardless of whether he or his spouse is covered by an employer retirement plan; however, the deductible portion of the contribution may be limited. If a taxpayer exceeds the income limits for making a fully deductible contribution to a traditional IRA, the excess portion can still be made as a nondeductible or after-tax contribution. Regardless of whether a portion of the contribution is nondeductible, the related earnings will grow on a tax-deferred basis.

Taxpayer (and Spouse) Not Covered by an Employer Plan: If neither the taxpayer nor his spouse is covered by an employer plan, there is no limitation on the deductibility of either of their traditional IRA contributions, other than as stated above. Thus, either can deduct the smaller of:

- $5,500 ($6,500 if 50 or older) or $11,000 ($13,000 if 50 or older) if filing MFJ, or
- 100% of qualifying compensation.

If a taxpayer makes nondeductible contributions to a traditional IRA, he must attach Form 8606, *Nondeductible IRAs.* Form 8606 reflects a taxpayer's cumulative nondeductible contributions, which is his tax basis in the IRA. If a taxpayer does not report nondeductible contributions properly, all future withdrawals from the IRA will be taxable unless the taxpayer can prove, with satisfactory evidence, that nondeductible contributions were made.

Example: Tamara is single and earned $95,000 in 2016. She is covered by a retirement plan at work, but she still wants to contribute to a traditional IRA. She is phased out for the deduction because her MAGI exceeds the threshold for single filers covered by an employer plan. If she contributes to a traditional IRA in 2016, she must file Form 8606 to report her nondeductible contribution. She is still allowed to contribute to a traditional IRA, but the amounts would not be deductible on her Form 1040.

Taxpayer (or Spouse) Covered by an Employer Plan

If either a taxpayer or his spouse, or both, is covered by (participates in) an employer retirement plan, the tax-deductible contribution to a traditional IRA is phased out at the following levels of modified adjusted gross income (MAGI):

Phase-outs when Taxpayer (or Spouse) is Covered by an Employer Plan

Filing Status	MAGI Range	Allowable Deduction
Single, HOH, or MFS (did not live with spouse*)	$61,000 or less	A full deduction.
	more than $61,000 but less than $71,000	A partial deduction.
	$71,000 or more	No deduction.
MFJ (for the covered spouse*), QW	$98,000 or less	A full deduction.
	More than $98,000 but less than $118,000	A partial deduction.
	$118,000 or more	No deduction.
MFS (lived with spouse*)	less than $10,000	A partial deduction.
	$10,000 or more	No deduction.

If neither spouse is a participant in an employer retirement plan, their IRA contributions are fully deductible.

***Note #1:** If the taxpayer files MFS but did not live with their spouse during the year, the IRA deduction is determined under the "Single" filing status.

***Note #2**: If filing as MFJ and only one spouse is covered by a retirement plan, then for the non-covered spouse: a full deduction is allowed at MAGI of $184,000 or less; a partial deduction for more than $184,000 but less than $194,000; and no deduction at $194,000 or more.

If neither spouse is a participant in an employer-sponsored retirement plan, their IRA contributions are fully deductible.

Married taxpayers who file MFS generally have a much lower phaseout range than those with any other filing status. However, if a taxpayer files a separate return and *did not live* with his spouse at any time during the year, the taxpayer is treated as "single" for IRA contribution purposes.

Example: Don, age 43, and his wife are not legally divorced, but they have lived in separate residences for the past three years. In 2016, Don earns $40,000 and files MFS. He is covered by an employer retirement plan, but is nevertheless allowed to deduct his full IRA contribution of $5,500. This is because he did not live with his spouse at any time during the year, and therefore is not subject to the lower IRA phaseout limits that normally apply to MFS filers.

Splitting IRA Contributions Between Multiple Accounts

A person may have IRA accounts with multiple financial institutions and may split his annual contributions between accounts; his aggregate contributions for the year are subject to the limits described above.

Further, a taxpayer may choose to split his contributions between a traditional IRA and a Roth IRA; again, his combined contributions are subject to the maximum annual contribution limits outlined before.

Example: In 2016, Leo has $3,200 in wages and $14,000 in rental income. He does not have any other earnings in 2016. His maximum IRA contribution is limited to $3,200 (the amount of his earned income). Leo decides to split his IRA contributions between a traditional IRA and a Roth IRA. He contributes $2,200 to a traditional IRA and $1,000 to a Roth IRA. The most Leo will be able to deduct as an adjustment to income is the $2,200 contribution to his traditional IRA. Roth IRA contributions are never deductible.

Example: Alan is 32. He has a traditional IRA through his bank and a Roth IRA through his stockbroker. Alan wants to contribute to both accounts. Alan can contribute to both of his retirement accounts, but the combined contributions for 2016 cannot exceed $5,500, the annual maximum. Alan decides to contribute $3,000 to his Roth IRA and $2,500 to his traditional IRA.

Example: Naomi, 25, has $3,000 of interest income and no other income in 2016. Naomi marries Carl during the year. Carl has taxable wages of $34,000, and he plans to contribute $5,500 to his traditional IRA. If he and Naomi file a joint return, each can contribute $5,500 to a traditional IRA. Naomi, who has no qualifying compensation, can use Carl's compensation, reduced by the amount of his IRA contribution ($34,000 – $5,500 = $28,500), to determine her maximum contribution to a traditional IRA.

Required Minimum Distributions (RMDs)

A person cannot keep funds in a traditional IRA account indefinitely. When the account owner reaches 70½ years of age, the funds must be distributed in annual required minimum distributions (RMDs).

The first RMD payment can be delayed until April 1 of the year following the year the taxpayer turns 70½. The distribution for each subsequent year must be made by December 31. The amount of each RMD is based on IRS tables.[72]

Failure to take an RMD can result in a penalty tax equal to 50% of the amount the taxpayer should have withdrawn, but did not. He must file Form 5329, *Additional Taxes on Qualified Plans*, to report the excise tax that applies as a result of the failure to take the RMD.

Example: Dinah reaches age 70½ in 2016. Her first RMD must be distributed to her by April 1, 2017, in order to avoid the 50% excise tax. At the end of the year, her IRA account balance was $79,500. The applicable distribution period per the IRS tables for someone her age (71) on that date is 26.5 years. Her required minimum distribution for 2016 is $3,000 ($79,500 ÷ 26.5).

Required Minimum Distributions also apply to inherited IRAs. With an inherited IRA, the beneficiary generally needs to take annual distributions no matter what age he is. The same rule about taking a Required Minimum Distribution still applies. The beneficiary of the inherited IRA must begin withdrawing no later than December 31 of following year after the IRA owner died.

Example: Judy dies May 1, 2016. Judy's only son, Russell, is the sole beneficiary of Judy's IRA account. Russell must begin withdrawing an RMD no later than December 31, 2017, the year after his mother's death. This rule applies no matter how old Russell is.

Note: RMDs are not required if the beneficiary of an inherited IRA is a surviving spouse under 70½ years of age, and the spouse simply does a spousal rollover into his or her own IRA.

[72] An RMD is calculated by dividing the balance of the IRA account by a life expectancy factor that the IRS publishes in tables within Publication 590, *Individual Retirement Arrangements (IRAs).*

Example: Ulysses, age 72, and Layla, age 61, are married. Both spouses have traditional IRA accounts. Ulysses began taking required distributions from his traditional IRA in the previous year. However, in 2016, Ulysses dies, and his wife inherits his IRA account. Rather than take a distribution from her late husband's account, Layla decides to do a spousal rollover of the entire account balance into her own IRA. The rollover is not a taxable event. Layla is not required to take any minimum distributions from the account until she reaches age 70½.

Taxability of Distributions

Distributions from a traditional IRA are generally taxable in the year they are received, subject to the following exceptions:

- Rollovers to another retirement plan or account (other than conversions to a Roth IRA, as discussed below)
- Qualified charitable distributions
- Tax-free withdrawal of contributions
- Distributions of nondeductible contributions

Qualified Charitable Distributions (QCD)

A taxpayer who is 70½ or older may choose to make a qualified charitable distribution (QCD)[73] of up to $100,000 ($200,000 for MFJ) from his IRA to qualified charitable organizations. In order to qualify, the funds must come out of the taxpayer's IRA by the deadline for minimum distributions, (generally December 31).

The IRA trustee must make the distribution directly to the qualified charity (the taxpayer cannot request a distribution and then donate the money later). Likewise, any tax withholdings on behalf of the owner from an IRA distribution cannot qualify as QCDs.

Example: Blanche regularly donates to the Red Cross. In 2017, Blanche turns 71. Instead of taking a minimum distribution from her IRA, she contacts her IRA trustee and requests to make a Qualified Charitable Contribution directly to the charity. The QCD counts towards her current year's RMD, as long as the funds are withdrawn from the IRA by December 31.

10% Penalty on Early Distributions

A taxpayer may withdraw funds at any time from a traditional IRA account. However, distributions before age 59½ will generally be subject to an extra 10% tax, in addition to normal income tax on the amount distributed. There are some exceptions to the general rule for early distributions. An individual may not have to pay the additional 10% tax in the following situations:

- To the extent the taxpayer has unreimbursed medical expenses that exceed 10% (or 7.5% if age 65 or older) of adjusted gross income.
- The distributions do not exceed the cost of the taxpayer's medical insurance while unemployed.
- The taxpayer becomes disabled.
- The distributions are not more than qualified higher education expenses.
- The distributions are used to buy, build, or rebuild a first home (up to $10,000).
- The distributions are used to pay the IRS due to a levy.
- Made as part of a series of substantially equal periodic payments for the life of the taxpayer.
- The distributions are made to a qualified reservist (an individual called up to active duty).

---

[73] The PATH Act made the QCD election permanent.

Even though distributions in these situations will not be subject to the additional 10% tax, they will be subject to income tax at the taxpayer's normal rates. Distributions that are properly rolled over into another retirement plan or account (other than conversions to a Roth IRA) are generally not subject to either income tax or the 10% additional penalty.

Example: Lauren, age 39, takes a $5,000 distribution from her traditional IRA account. She does not meet any of the exceptions to the 10% additional penalty tax, so the $5,000 is an early distribution. Lauren must include the $5,000 in her gross income and pay income tax on it. In addition, she must pay a 10% penalty tax of $500 (10% × $5,000).

Roth IRA Vs Traditional IRA

Unlike a traditional IRA, none of the contributions to a Roth IRA are deductible, but the entire balance is generally tax-free at the time of withdrawal. However, distributions generally cannot be made until after a five-year holding period and after the taxpayer has reached age 59½. Further, income limits apply, which means high-income earners may be prohibited from contributing to Roth IRAs.

Whether or not a taxpayer can make a Roth IRA contribution depends on his filing status and modified adjusted gross income (MAGI). In 2016, the following income limits apply to Roth IRAs:

Filing Status	Roth IRA phaseout ranges
Single, HOH filers[74]	$117,000–$132,000
MFJ and QW filers	$184,000–$194,000
MFS (lived with spouse)	$0–$10,000

In general, a taxpayer cannot contribute to a Roth IRA if his income is above the phaseout thresholds. However, a "backdoor" Roth IRA is still possible in 2016. By this method, the taxpayer simply opens a traditional IRA, makes a contribution, and then converts the funds to a Roth in the same year. We will cover IRA conversions in more detail later.

The major differences between a Roth IRA and a traditional IRA are as follows:

- Contributions to a Roth IRA are not deductible by the taxpayer, and participation in an employer plan has no effect on the taxpayer's contribution limits.
- There are no required minimum distributions from a Roth IRA. No distributions are required until a Roth IRA owner dies.
- Unlike traditional IRAs, contributions to a Roth IRA can be made by individuals of any age, even those who are over the age of 70½.

IRA Rollovers

A rollover is a transfer from one retirement plan or account to another retirement plan or account. If executed properly, most rollovers are nontaxable events. However, taxpayers can also choose to convert a traditional IRA into a Roth IRA. In this case, the conversion will result in taxation of any previously untaxed amounts in the traditional IRA.

Beginning in 2016, a taxpayer can make only one rollover from an IRA to another IRA in any 12-month period, regardless of the number of IRAs the taxpayer owns.[75] There are two exceptions to this rule:

- Trustee-to-trustee transfers between IRAs are not limited
- Rollovers from traditional to Roth IRAs ("backdoor conversions") are not limited

[74] This phaseout range also applies to MFS taxpayers who did not live with their spouses at any time during the year.
[75] Internal Revenue Bulletin: 2014-16

Rollover Rules

If a taxpayer receives an IRA distribution and wishes to make a nontaxable rollover, he must complete the transaction by the 60th day following the day he receives the distribution.[76]

> **Example:** Adam quits his old job on September 1, 2016. On September 14, 2016, Adam begins a new job. He has an existing IRA account, and he decides to transfer the balance of his traditional IRA account to his new employer's retirement plan. Adam receives a distribution from his IRA of $50,000 in cash and $50,000 in stock. On October 9, 2016, he rolls over the entire amount of $100,000 into his new employer's plan. Because the transaction is completed within 60 days, it is completely nontaxable. The rollover must be reported on Form 1040.

If a taxpayer sells the distributed property (such as stocks distributed from an IRA) and rolls over all the proceeds into another traditional IRA or qualified retirement plan within the required time frame, no gain or loss is recognized. The sale proceeds (including any increase in value) are treated as part of the distribution and are not included in the taxpayer's gross income.

If a taxpayer receives both property and cash in a rollover distribution, he can roll over part or all of the property, part or all of the cash, or any combination of the two he chooses. He can also sell the property and roll over the proceeds into a traditional IRA.

But he cannot keep the property and substitute his own funds for property he receives.

> **Example:** Billy receives a distribution from his employer's plan of $20,000 cash and $30,000 worth of stock. He decides to keep the stock. He can roll over the $20,000 cash received, but he cannot substitute an additional $30,000 in cash in place of the stock and treat this amount as if it had also been rolled over.

A taxable distribution paid from an employer-sponsored retirement plan is subject to mandatory tax withholding of 20%, even if the taxpayer intends to roll it over. If the taxpayer does roll it over and wants to defer tax on the entire taxable portion, he will be forced to add funds from other sources equal to the amount of tax withheld.

In order to avoid this mandatory withholding, a taxpayer may request a "direct rollover". The distribution is then made directly from the custodian for the employer-sponsored plan to the custodian for the employee's IRA or his new employer's retirement plan. Under this option, the 20% mandatory withholding does not apply.

Rollover after the Death of an IRA Owner

Following the death of an IRA owner, the IRA usually passes to a beneficiary. There are very different rules if the beneficiary is a surviving spouse, versus any other type of beneficiary (such as a child or a sibling).

After the death of a traditional IRA's owner, a surviving spouse has two options: he or she can elect to treat the IRA as being his own by changing the ownership designation, or roll over the IRA balance to his own IRA account or certain other types of retirement plans.

> **Example:** Allison, 42, and Lorenzo, 53, are married. Allison dies suddenly in 2016, and at the time of her death, she has $83,000 in her traditional IRA account. Lorenzo chooses to roll over the entire $83,000 into his own IRA account, thereby avoiding taxation on the income until he retires and starts taking distributions.

For any beneficiary other than a surviving spouse, there are a number of factors that determine the period over which amounts remaining in an IRA upon the owner's death would be payable. These include whether the owner died on or before the date he was required to

[76] Starting in August, 2016, Rev. Proc. 2016-47 allows eligible taxpayers can now qualify for a waiver of the 60-day rollover limit and avoid possible early distribution taxes. Taxpayers will submit the self-certification to their plan administrator or an IRA trustee (NOT to the IRS). In the past, taxpayers who failed to meet the rollover time limit could only obtain a waiver by requesting a private letter ruling from the IRS.

begin taking distributions, whether the beneficiary is an individual (or the owner's estate), and the life expectancies of the owner and the beneficiary in the year of death. If a Roth IRA owner dies and the sole beneficiary is the spouse, he can delay distributions until the owner would have reached 70½ or treat the IRA as his own.

For other beneficiaries, the account balance must generally be distributed by the end of the fifth calendar year after the owner's death, or be paid as an annuity over the beneficiary's life expectancy beginning the year following the year of death.

Example: Delores, who was single and had no children, died in 2016. At the time of her death, Delores had a traditional IRA worth $42,000. The beneficiary of her IRA is her brother, Dean, age 42. Although he cannot roll over the IRA since he is not Delores's spouse, Dean can choose how he receives the IRA proceeds. Dean can choose a lump sum distribution, a five-year distribution, or a "stretch" IRA payout (an annuity paid over time). No matter what type of distribution Dean selects, the amounts will be subject to income tax. However, the 10% early withdrawal penalty is waived for a beneficiary of an IRA when the original IRA owner has died.

Conversion of a Traditional IRA to a Roth IRA

In the past, taxpayers in higher income brackets were unable to contribute to a Roth IRA. They were also unable to convert from a traditional IRA to a Roth IRA. The IRS rules changed several years ago, and there is no longer an income threshold on IRA conversions. High-income taxpayers can convert to a Roth as long as they pay the appropriate tax on the conversion. This is frequently called a "backdoor conversion."

There is no 10% early withdrawal penalty if the funds from the traditional IRA are deposited into a Roth IRA within 60 days. If a taxpayer wishes to convert all or a portion of his traditional IRA to a Roth IRA, he is required to pay income taxes on the amount of pre-tax (deductible) contributions converted, as well as the growth in value resulting from earnings on those contributions. After the funds are converted to a Roth IRA, additional earnings are tax-free, and distributions are generally not subject to tax.

Example: Nancy converts her traditional IRA to a Roth IRA in 2016. The traditional IRA has a balance of $100,000. The entire balance represents deductible contributions and earnings that have not previously been taxed. She reports the amount of the balance that was converted to a Roth IRA as taxable income in 2016.

A Roth conversion is reported on Form 8606, *Nondeductible IRAs*. An inherited traditional IRA is generally not eligible to be converted to a Roth IRA unless it is inherited directly from a spouse. Non-spousal beneficiaries (for example, a child who inherits a traditional IRA from a deceased parent) are not allowed to convert a traditional IRA to a Roth IRA.

Recharacterization

A taxpayer may undo or reverse a rollover or conversion of one type of IRA to a different type of IRA through a *recharacterization.* Essentially, by recharacterizing an IRA, it is as if the conversion or rollover never occurred.

A recharacterization can only be done through a trustee, and it must be completed by October 15 of the year after the taxpayer made the initial conversion. The deadline applies even if the taxpayer did not request an extension to file his return, and filed his return on or before the filing deadline. If a taxpayer recharacterizes a contribution, he must do all three of the following:

- Include in the transfer any net income allocable to the contribution. If there was a loss, the net income might be a negative amount.
- Report the recharacterization on the tax return for the year during which the contribution was made.

- Treat the contribution as having been made to the second IRA on the date that it was actually made to the first IRA.

A taxpayer must report an IRA recharacterization on Form 8606, *Nondeductible IRAs.*

Example: On June 1, 2016, Andrew converts his traditional IRA to a Roth IRA. However, his investments perform poorly, and his account loses value after the conversion. Because he does not want to pay tax on the value of the converted funds, he decides to recharacterize the conversion and move the funds back to a traditional IRA. On January 10, 2017, Andrew opens a traditional IRA with the same trustee and instructs the trustee of the Roth IRA to make a trustee-to-trustee transfer of the Roth conversion contribution to the new traditional IRA. Due to the recharacterization, Andrew has no taxable income from the conversion to report for 2016.

Traditional IRA vs. Roth IRA

Issue	Traditional IRA	Roth IRA
Age limit	A person over 70½ cannot contribute.	No age limit for contributions.
2016 Contribution Limits	The lesser of $5,500 (or $6,500 if age 50 or older by the end of the year) and qualifying taxable compensation.	Same.
Deductibility of contributions	Generally deductible.	No. Contributions to a Roth IRA are never deductible.
Filing requirements	No filing requirement unless nondeductible contributions are made. Nondeductible contributions must be reported on Form 8606.	Filing requirement related to conversion of a traditional IRA to a Roth IRA. None related to contributions made directly to a Roth IRA.
Mandatory distributions	RMDs by April 1 of the year following the year a taxpayer reaches age 70½.	There are no required distributions unless the IRA owner dies.
How distributions are taxed	Distributions from a traditional IRA are taxed as ordinary income.	Distributions from a Roth IRA are generally not taxed.
Income limits	Phaseout of deductibility is based upon AGI if taxpayer and/or spouse are covered by an employer plan.	There are income limits for contributions, but conversions of a traditional IRA to a Roth IRA are still allowable.

Excise Tax on Excess Contributions

If a taxpayer accidentally contributes more to his IRA than is allowed for the year, the excess contribution is subject to a 6% excise tax. Contributions made to a traditional IRA in the year a taxpayer reaches age 70½ are also considered excess contributions. However, the IRS will allow a taxpayer to correct an excess contribution if certain rules are followed.

If he makes a contribution that exceeds the annual maximum or his qualifying compensation, the excess contribution and all related earnings must be withdrawn from the IRA before the due date (*including* extensions) of the tax return for that year. If a taxpayer corrects the excess contribution within this period, the 6% penalty will apply only to the amounts earned on the excess contribution. The taxpayer must also report the earnings on the excess contribution as taxable income for the year in which the withdrawal is made. For each year that the excess amounts remain in the IRA, the taxpayer must pay the 6% tax. However, this tax can never exceed 6% of the value of the taxpayer's IRA at the end of the tax year.

Note: A taxpayer cannot apply an excess contribution to an earlier year even if the taxpayer contributed less than the maximum amount allowable for an earlier year. However, the taxpayer is allowed to apply an excess contribution to a later year if the contributions for that later year are less than the maximum allowable for that year.

Example: Betsy, age 62, is self-employed and owns several rental properties. She contributes $5,500 to her traditional IRA in December 2016. She files for an extension to prepare her tax return. When she finally gives her records to her accountant, he discovers that Betsy's taxable income from self-employment is only $4,500 and her rental income is $38,000. Only the self-employment income counts as compensation for purposes of contributing to her IRA, so Betsy has inadvertently made an excess contribution of $1,000. Betsy must withdraw the excess contribution and any earnings on it by the extended due date of her return or face an excise tax of 6% on both.

Example: In 2016, Jonas is 49 years old and single. His wages for the year are $52,000. He has two IRA accounts, and he contributes $3,000 to each account in 2016. Jonas has accidentally made an excess contribution of $500 ($6,000 total IRA contributions - $5,500 2016 limit). The excess contributions earned $5 interest in 2016 and $6 interest in 2017. Jonas does not realize his mistake, and he does not withdraw the $500 in excess contribution or the interest it earned by the due date of his return. Since he doesn't discover the error until after his filing deadline, now Jonas is liable for an excise tax on his excess contributions. He figures the additional tax on Form 5329. To avoid the excise tax for 2017, he can correct the excess amount by allocating the $500 to the next year, or he can withdraw it from the account.

Prohibited Transactions

Generally, a prohibited transaction is the "improper use" of an IRA by the owner, a beneficiary, or a disqualified person (typically a fiduciary or family member). Prohibited transactions related to an IRA include:

- Borrowing money from it
- Using it as security for a loan
- Buying property for personal use with IRA funds
- Personally borrowing money from the IRA
- Selling, leasing, or exchanging property to the account
- Accepting unreasonable compensation for managing property or assets held by the IRA
- Granting account fiduciaries to obtain, use, or borrow against account assets for their own gain
- Transferring plan assets, lending money, or providing goods and services to "disqualified persons," usually a close family member, or a business that a close family member owns and controls.

For the purposes of the prohibited transaction rules, "family members" includes the taxpayer's spouse, parents, grandparents, children; and grandchildren and spouses of the taxpayer's children and grandchildren. Family members do not include in-laws, cousins, friends, aunts, uncles, siblings, and step-siblings.

Example: Jada uses her traditional IRA as collateral for an auto loan. This is a prohibited transaction.

Although occurrences of prohibited transactions are rare, the consequences can be catastrophic. If a prohibited transaction occurs at any time during the year, normally the account ceases to be treated as an IRA and its assets are treated as if having been wholly distributed on the first day of the year. However, in situations where an IRA account, or a portion of an IRA account, is used as a security for a loan, only the amount used as security for the loan is treated as a distribution from the IRA as of the first day of the year that the loan was made, but the IRA continues to exist. If the total fair market value as of that date is more than the taxpayer's basis in the IRA, the excess amount is reportable as taxable income. It may also be subject to the additional 10% penalty on early distributions.

Example: The fair market value of Noah's traditional IRA was $300,000 as of January 1, 2016. He had previously made $200,000 of nondeductible contributions to his IRA, so that was his basis in the account. On June 1, Noah, age 40, borrowed $150,000 from his IRA to purchase himself a vacation home. This is a prohibited transaction, and Noah's entire IRA account will no longer be treated as an IRA. Since the FMV of the IRA on the first day of the year, $300,000, is greater than Noah's basis, $200,000, the excess amount of $100,000 is reported as taxable income. Noah would also be subject to the additional 10% penalty for withdrawing funds before the age of 59½.

Note: Prohibited transactions are rare occurrences, and they generally only occur when a taxpayer has a "self-directed" IRA. A self-directed IRA is a type of account that offers a taxpayer the ability to use his retirement funds to make almost any type of investment without requiring a financial institution or another custodian.

Example: Paul is 52 and has $180,000 in his traditional IRA. His daughter, Lanie, wants to buy a home for $140,000 but does not have sufficient funds. As a result, Paul lends his daughter $140,000 from in his self-directed IRA to buy the home. This is a prohibited transaction. For Paul, the IRA is deemed immediately disqualified as of January 1, 2016 (the year in which the prohibited transaction occurred). The entire amount of the IRA is deemed distributed in 2016, and an early withdrawal penalty of 10% would also apply to the entire amount of the IRA ($180,000).

Prohibited IRA Investments

Almost any type of investment is permissible inside an IRA, including stocks, bonds, and real estate. However, there are some investments that are prohibited. For example, the law does not permit IRA funds to be invested in life insurance or collectibles. If the taxpayer invests in any of these using IRA funds, it is treated as a prohibited transaction. The following investments are prohibited:

- Collectibles such as artwork, rugs, and antiques
- Precious metals, coins, and gemstones (exceptions exist for U.S. coins and bullion)
- S corporation stock
- Insurance contracts

There is a narrow exception for investments in gold and silver coins minted by the U.S. Treasury Department. Investments in certain gold, silver, palladium, and platinum bullion are also allowable.

Retirement Plans for Businesses

Retirement plans for businesses include Simplified Employee Pension (SEP) plans, Savings Incentive Match Plan for Employees (SIMPLE) plans and qualified plans. The term "qualified" refers to certain IRS requirements that the plan and the employer must adhere to in order to obtain tax-favored status. SEP and SIMPLE plans must also meet certain requirements but are much less complex than those that apply to qualified plans.

Study Note: Business retirement plans are covered in greater detail, and from the employer's perspective, in *PassKey EA Review Book 2: Businesses*, as much of the related information is tested on Part 2 of the EA exam. In Part 1 of the exam, you will need to understand the employee's perspective with regards to retirement plans. For Part 2, you must understand retirement plans from the employer's perspective.

If retirement plans are structured and administered properly, businesses can deduct contributions they make on behalf of their employees or, if self-employed, themselves. Both the contributions and the earnings are generally tax-free until distribution. Further, some plans also allow employees to make contributions, most commonly in pre-tax dollars (so that a portion of their salaries are not taxed until the amounts are later distributed to them by the plan).

SEP Plans: SEPs provide a simplified method for employers to make contributions to a retirement plan for themselves and their employees. Instead of setting up a profit-sharing plan with a trust, an employer can adopt a SEP agreement and make contributions directly to individual SEP-IRA accounts (similar to a traditional IRA as described previously) for himself and each eligible employee. A SEP plan is funded exclusively by employer contributions; employee contributions are not permitted.

SIMPLE Plans: An employer can generally set up a SIMPLE plan if the business has 100 or fewer employees who received at least $5,000 of compensation during the preceding year. Under a SIMPLE plan, employees can choose to make salary reduction contributions rather than receiving these amounts as part of their regular pay. An employer can contribute matching or nonelective contributions. A SIMPLE plan can be structured in one of two ways: using SIMPLE IRAs (again, similar to traditional IRAs as described previously) or as a SIMPLE 401(k) plan (similar to the qualified 401(k) plans described below).

Qualified Retirement Plans

There are two basic kinds of qualified retirement plans: defined contribution plans and defined benefit plans, and different rules apply to each. An employer is allowed to have more than one type of qualified plan, but contributions cannot exceed annual limits. Contributions for self-employed taxpayers are limited to 100% of compensation. If the business does not have any income for the year, no contribution can be made.

All qualified plans are subject to federal regulation under the Employee Retirement Income Security Act (ERISA). The federal government does not require an employer to establish a retirement plan, but it provides minimum federal standards for qualified plans.

Defined Benefit Plans

A defined benefit plan, often called a traditional pension plan, promises a specified benefit amount or annuity for each participant after retirement. Benefits are typically based on formulas that consider the participant's years of service with the employer and his earnings history.

The federal government and most state and local governments provide defined benefit plans for their employees. However, fewer businesses now offer defined benefit plans because they are costly to administer and inflexible.

The benefits promised by many defined benefit plans are protected by federal insurance. Contributions to a defined benefit plan are not optional. Contributions are typically based on actuarial calculations that estimate the amounts necessary to pay benefits in the future.

Defined Contribution Plans

A defined contribution plan provides an individual account for each participant in the plan depending upon how the plan is structured. It provides benefits to each participant based on the amounts contributed to the participant's account, along with subsequent investment income or losses, and, in some instances, allocations of forfeitures among participant accounts.

The participants, the employer, or both may contribute to the individual participant accounts. Examples of defined contribution plans include profit-sharing plans, 401(k) plans, 403(b) plans, and 457 plans.

Depending upon how a qualified plan is structured, salary reduction/elective deferral contributions are employee contributions based on a percentage of the employee's compensation and are generally made on a pre-tax basis.

This limitation applies to the aggregate amounts of contributions to any qualified plans, SEPs, and SIMPLE plans in which the individual participates during the year. However, the contribution cannot exceed the amount of the employee's compensation. Depending on the individual plan, the employer may provide matching contributions for employees who make elective deferrals.

Example: Jon earns $80,000 per year as an insurance executive. He participates in his company's profit-sharing 401(k) plan. He contributes 3% of his pre-tax wages to the plan in 2016, or $2,400 ($80,000 × .03). Jon's company contributes a matching 3% to his individual 401(k) account.

Distributions: Distributions to participants may be made either on a periodic basis, such as annuity payments or as a lump sum. As is the case with distributions from traditional IRA accounts (as well as SEP and SIMPLE plans), distributions generally are not permitted prior to when the participant retires or otherwise terminates employment, dies, becomes disabled, or reaches age 59½.

Earlier distributions are generally subject to an additional 10% penalty tax.

Required minimum distributions from defined contribution plans must generally begin by April 1 of the year following the calendar year when the taxpayer retires, or the year in which the taxpayer reaches age 70½, whichever comes later.

Example: In 2016, Jon retires at age 63 after working 35 years at an insurance company. He would have been required to take distributions by April 1 of the year following the calendar year in which he reaches age 70½. However, he chooses to begin taking distributions from his 401(k) account in the same year he retires.

Note: For purposes of the net investment income tax, net investment income does not include distributions from a qualified retirement plan, such as a 401(k), or from traditional or Roth IRAs. However, these distributions are taken into account when determining the modified adjusted gross income threshold.

Restricted Loans from Qualified Plans

Unlike traditional IRAs and Roth IRAs, distributions from a qualified plan are generally restricted. This means that a taxpayer cannot withdraw from the account whenever he chooses. Generally, distributions of elective deferrals cannot be made until one of the following occurs:

- The taxpayer dies, becomes disabled, or has a severance from employment.
- The plan terminates, and no successor defined contribution plan is established or maintained by the employer.
- The taxpayer reaches age 59½ or incurs a financial hardship.

However, some borrowing is allowed. A qualified plan may allow its participants to borrow specified portions of their individual account balances, subject to certain restrictions. A loan can generally be no more than the lesser of $50,000, or the greater of $10,000 or 50% of the vested portion of the participant's account balance. If a loan is not repaid according to the specified payment terms, it may be considered a taxable distribution. This may apply if a participant terminates employment with the employer that sponsors the plan.

Hardship Distributions

A 401(k) plan may allow participants to receive hardship distributions because of an immediate and heavy financial need, such as sudden medical or funeral expenses.

Hardship distributions are limited to the amount of the employee's elective deferrals and generally do not include any income earned on the deferred amounts. The amount of the distribution may include amounts necessary to pay taxes or penalties anticipated to result from the distribution, including the 10% penalty levied on early distributions.

> **Example:** Kendra's home is in foreclosure, and she is in immediate danger of being evicted. She requests a hardship distribution from her 401(k), which is granted. Since she is under age 59½, Kendra would likely have to pay the 10% early distribution penalty.

Unit 17: Study Questions

(Test yourself first, then check the correct answers at the end of this quiz.)

1. Frank, 72, and Sue, 61, are married and file jointly. In 2016, Frank earned wages of $30,000, and Sue earned $5,000. If Frank and Sue file jointly, how much can they contribute to their traditional IRAs?

A. $5,500
B. $6,500
C. $11,500
D. $13,000

2. An excess contribution to an IRA is subject to tax. Which of the following statements is correct?

A. The taxpayer will not have to pay the 6% tax on the excess contribution if he withdraws the excess contribution and any earnings on the excess contribution before the due date of the tax return for the applicable year, including extensions.
B. The 6% tax is due on both the excess contribution and any earnings on the excess contribution, even if the taxpayer withdraws the excess contribution from the account.
C. A taxpayer will not have to pay the 6% tax on the excess contribution if he withdraws the excess contribution and any earnings on the excess contribution before the due date of the tax return for the year, not including extensions.
D. A taxpayer will not have to pay the 6% on earnings on the excess contribution if he is disabled.

3. Contributions to a traditional IRA can be deducted for a given tax year if they are made:

A. Any time during the year or by the due date of the return, not including extensions.
B. Any time during the year or by the due date of the return, including extensions.
C. By December 31.
D. Any time during the year, but only while the taxpayer is employed.

4. Which of the following statements is correct regarding loans from a qualified plan?

A. Loans from a qualified plan are never permitted.
B. Loans are permitted up to the full amount of the employee's contributions to the qualified plan.
C. Loans are permitted, but generally cannot exceed $50,000, or the greater of $10,000 or 50% of the vested portion of the employee's account balance.
D. Loans are permitted, but only under specific and defined circumstances of hardship.

5. Elizabeth and Landon are age 62, married, and lived together all year. They both work and each has a traditional IRA. In 2016, Landon earned $4,000 of wages and received $11,000 of annuity income. Elizabeth earned $52,000. They prefer to file separately. If they file separate returns, what is the maximum that Landon can contribute to his IRA?

A. $1,000
B. $4,000
C. $5,500
D. $6,500

6. Lucas, an unmarried college student working part-time, earns $3,500 in 2016. He also receives $500 of interest income and $4,000 from his parents to help pay tuition. What is his maximum IRA contribution in 2016?

A. $0
B. $3,500
C. $5,500
D. $6,500

7. Kristin, 42, is a full-time graduate student with $1,200 of wages. She marries Adniel, 50, during the year. Omar has taxable compensation of $46,000 in 2016. What is the maximum they can contribute to their traditional IRA accounts in 2016 if they file jointly?

A. $1,200
B. $6,700
C. $11,000
D. $12,000

8. Penny, age 48, and William, age 49, are married and file jointly. Both are self-employed and report their business income on Schedule C. William's business has $9,900 in profits during the year. His wife, Penny, has an overall business loss of ($3,100) for 2016. Penny also earned $3,000 in wages from a seasonal job. What is their maximum allowable IRA contribution for 2016?

A. They are allowed to contribute $5,500 each.
B. William can contribute $5,500. Penny can only contribute $3,000.
C. William can contribute $5,500. Penny can only contribute $4,400.
D. William can contribute $5,500. Penny cannot contribute to her IRA, because she has an overall loss for the year.

9. Steve, age 36 and single, is in the Marines. He has the following income in 2016:

Nontaxable combat pay	$30,500
Regular wages	2,100
Interest income	4,600

What is the maximum amount that Steve can contribute to a traditional IRA?

A. $2,100
B. $4,600
C. $5,500
D. $6,500

10. Rafael, 40, earns $26,000 in wages during the year. Although he is allowed to contribute up to $5,500 to his IRA, he only has enough cash to contribute $2,500. On May 30, 2017, Rafael expects to receive a big commission bonus, and he wishes to make a catch-up contribution for 2016. Rafael filed a timely extension for his tax return, so his federal return isn't due until October 15, 2017. Which of the following statements is correct?

A. Rafael can contribute an additional $3,000 in May 2017 for the 2016 tax year as long as he files his tax return by the extended due date.
B. Rafael cannot contribute an additional $3,000 for the 2016 tax year after the normal filing deadline.
C. Rafael can contribute an additional $3,000 in May 2017 for the 2016 tax year only if he files his return by April 18, 2017.
D. Rafael cannot make a 2016 contribution to his IRA after December 31, 2016.

11. When does the IRS require the owner of a Roth IRA to start taking withdrawals?

A. After the death of the IRA owner.
B. At age 59½.
C. At age 70½.
D. Never.

12. Which of the following statements is correct?

A. A taxpayer can convert a traditional IRA to a Roth IRA. The transaction is tax-free.
B. A taxpayer can convert a traditional IRA to a Roth IRA. Any applicable tax must be paid on the conversion.
C. A taxpayer can rollover a traditional IRA to a Roth IRA only if his income is under $100,000.
D. A taxpayer cannot convert a traditional IRA to a Roth IRA.

13. Miguel is 37. In 2016, he contributed $1,500 to a Roth IRA. He also wants to contribute the allowable maximum to a traditional IRA account. What is the maximum he can contribute to a traditional IRA in 2016, assuming he had sufficient qualifying compensation?

A. $0
B. $3,000
C. $4,000
D. $5,000

14. Undoing or reversing an IRA is called a:

A. Conversion.
B. Rollover.
C. Recharacterization.
D. Distribution.

15. Jody is single, age 51, and has the following compensation in 2016:

Annuity income	$1,600
Wages	3,000
Alimony	2,300
Interest income	3,000
Rental income	6,000

What is the maximum amount that Jody can contribute to her traditional IRA in 2016?

A. $3,000
B. $5,500
C. $5,300
D. $6,500

16. Which of the following distributions from a traditional IRA is subject to an additional 10% penalty?

A. Distributions made prior to age 59½.
B. Distributions made after age 70½.
C. Distributions made to an unrelated beneficiary after the IRA owner's death.
D. Distributions made due to an IRS levy.

17. Shari received a distribution in 2016 from her IRA and wanted to roll it over to an IRA with another bank. How long does she have to complete the rollover in order to avoid income tax on the distribution?

A. 30 days.
B. 60 days.
C. Until the end of the year.
D. Until the due date of her return.

18. Which of the following is considered an excess contribution to an IRA?

A. A contribution to a traditional IRA by a taxpayer in the year he has reached age 70½.
B. A rollover to a Roth IRA.
C. A contribution to a Roth IRA by a taxpayer who is age 75.
D. A contribution made by a taxpayer who only has alimony income.

19. Megan, age 36, is married and files jointly her spouse. She contributes $5,500 to a traditional IRA, and she is also a participant in her employer's retirement plan. She and her husband had modified adjusted gross income of $195,000 in 2016. Which of the following is correct regarding her IRA contribution?

A. It is fully deductible.
B. It is partially deductible.
C. It is not deductible.
D. She would be subject to a 6% excise penalty if she contributed to an IRA.

Unit 17: Answers

1. The answer is B. Only Sue can contribute to a traditional IRA. Frank cannot contribute because he is over 70½ years old. However, Sue is over 50 and can utilize Frank's qualifying compensation in order to contribute the maximum of $6,500 to her IRA.

2. The answer is A. The taxpayer will not have to pay the 6% tax on the excess contribution if the excess contribution and any earnings are withdrawn by the due date of his return, including extensions. If a taxpayer corrects the excess contribution in time, the 6% penalty will apply only to the earnings on the excess contribution.

3. The answer is A. A taxpayer cannot deduct a contribution to an IRA after the due date of his tax return, even if he files for an extension. IRA contributions for 2016 must be made by April 18, 2017.

4. The answer is C. Depending on its terms; a qualified plan may allow a participant to borrow funds from his account balance. A loan can be no more than the lesser of:

- $50,000, or
- The greater of $10,000 or 50% of the vested portion of the participant's account balance.

5. The answer is B. Since Landon is married and lived with his wife during the year but is filing separately, he can contribute no more than $4,000, the amount of his only qualifying compensation for IRA purposes.

6. The answer is B. His IRA contribution for 2016 is limited to $3,500, the total amount of his wages. The interest income and the gifted money from his parents are not qualifying compensation for IRA purposes.

7. The answer is D. They can contribute $12,000 if they file jointly. Kristin can contribute $5,500, and Adniel can contribute $6,500 because he is 50. Even though Kristin only has $1,200 of compensation, she can use her husband's compensation to determine her maximum contribution.

8. The answer is A. On a jointly filed return; they are both allowed to contribute and deduct the maximum allowable for their age bracket ($5,500 in 2016). William and Penny use their combined income to figure their maximum allowable IRA contribution in 2016. Even though Penny has an overall loss for the year, she does not have to offset her Schedule C losses from her wages when determining her allowable IRA contribution. The answer is figured as follows:

Qualifying Compensation: William: $9,900 + Penny: $3,000 = $12,800

If they file jointly, they can each contribute $5,500 ($5,500 X 2 = $11,000, which is less than the amount of their qualifying compensation).

9. The answer is C. Steve may contribute $5,500, the maximum contribution allowed for his age, because a taxpayer may elect to treat nontaxable combat pay as qualifying compensation for IRA purposes. The interest income is not considered compensation.

10. The answer is B. Rafael cannot contribute an additional $3,000 after April 18, 2017, the due date for filing 2016 tax returns, regardless of whether he files an extension. If contributions to a traditional IRA for the year were less than the limit, a taxpayer cannot contribute more after the original due date of the tax return to make up the difference. If Rafael wants to make an additional contribution for 2016, he must do it by the *normal* filing deadline, regardless of whether he files an extension or not.

11. The answer is A. Unlike traditional IRAs, Roth IRAs do not require withdrawals until after the death of the owner.

12. The answer is B. A taxpayer may convert his traditional IRA to a Roth IRA. If a taxpayer wishes to convert all or a portion of his traditional IRA to a Roth IRA, he is required to pay income taxes on the amount of pre-tax (deductible) contributions converted, as well as the growth in value resulting from earnings on those contributions. After the funds are converted to a Roth IRA, additional earnings are tax-free, and distributions are generally not subject to tax. However, penalties apply if the taxpayer withdraws from the Roth IRA within five years of the conversion. The conversion is reported on Form 8606, *Nondeductible IRAs*.

13. The answer is C. Assuming Miguel has sufficient qualifying compensation; he could contribute $4,000. The 2016 maximum for contributions to *all types* of IRAs is $5,500 per taxpayer (for taxpayers under 50). Taxpayers are allowed to have different types of IRA accounts, but the maximum contribution limits apply to their total contributions for the year.

14. The answer is C. When a taxpayer reverses a rollover or conversion of one type of IRA to a different type of IRA, it is called a recharacterization. A recharacterization can only be done through a trustee, and it must be completed by October 15 of the year after the year in which the taxpayer made the initial conversion. By recharacterizing an IRA, it is as if the conversion or rollover never occurred.

15. The answer is C. Her maximum contribution for 2016 is $5,300. Only Jody's wage income of $3,000 and the $2,300 of alimony qualify as compensation for purposes of an IRA contribution. The annuity income, rental income, and interest income do not qualify.

16. The answer is A. Distributions made prior to age 59½ are subject to a 10% early withdrawal penalty, if no exception applies. Some exceptions that allow early distributions from an IRA, as well as from qualified retirement plans, include the following:

- Distributions made to a beneficiary or estate after death
- Distributions made because of permanent disability
- Distributions to the extent of medical expenses (medical expenses that exceed 10%, or 7.5% for those age 65 and older, of adjusted gross income), whether or not the taxpayer itemizes deductions for the year
- Distributions made due to an IRS levy

The distributions listed above are not subject to the early distribution penalty, but they are subject to income tax at the taxpayer's normal tax rates.

17. The answer is B. Shari has 60 days to complete the rollover. If she does not complete the rollover within 60 days, the distribution is subject to income tax in 2016.

18. The answer is A. A taxpayer's contributions to a traditional IRA in the year he reaches age 70½ (and any later years) are considered excess contributions. An excess contribution and any earnings on it are subject to an additional 6% tax if the taxpayer does not withdraw the contribution and the earnings by the due date of the tax return, including extensions.

19. The answer is C. Contributions to a traditional IRA by an MFJ taxpayer who participates in an employer-sponsored retirement plan are allowed, but their deductibility is phased out at higher income thresholds. When MAGI reaches $194,000 (for joint filers) in 2016, the traditional IRA contribution is not deductible. If a taxpayer makes nondeductible contributions to a traditional IRA, she must attach Form 8606, *Nondeductible IRAs*, to her tax return.

Unit 18: FBARS and Foreign Financial Accounts

More Reading:
IRS FBAR Reference Guide
Reporting of Foreign Financial Accounts on the Electronic FBAR (IRS Webinar)
Instructions for FinCEN Form 114
Instructions for Form 3520

In this chapter, we will discuss foreign financial reporting requirements for U.S. taxpayers. The subject of foreign financial reporting is extremely complex, and the IRS continues to issue guidance on how taxpayers and tax professionals should approach this difficult topic. In past EA Exams, the issue of foreign financial reporting was not tested. However, it is possible that the IRS will begin to test on this important topic during the current testing cycle.

A person who holds a foreign financial account may have a reporting obligation even when the account produces no taxable income, and even if the person does not have an individual income tax filing requirement. For the purposes of foreign financial reporting requirements, a "United States person" includes U.S. citizens, U.S. residents, and U.S. entities. There are four major forms used for reporting foreign bank accounts, foreign assets, and foreign gifts. These are:

- The FBAR (Form 114, *Report of Foreign Bank and Financial Accounts*)
- Form 8938, *Statement of Specified Foreign Financial Assets*
- Schedule B, *Interest and Ordinary Dividends (Part III)*
- Form 3520, *Annual Return to Report Transactions with Foreign Trusts and Receipt of Certain Foreign Gifts*

Federal law requires that U.S. persons report all worldwide income, including income from foreign trusts and foreign bank accounts. In many cases, these taxpayers need to complete Schedule B and attach it to their tax return. Certain taxpayers may also have to fill out and attach Form 8938, *Statement of Foreign Financial Assets*. Form 3520 is used to report certain foreign gifts and bequests. Schedule B, Form 3520, and Form 8938 are filed together with a taxpayer's annual Form 1040.

The FBAR filing requirement, however, is considered a separate filing requirement than filing a regular tax return. FBARs are not filed with the IRS. These forms are filed directly with the Financial Crimes Enforcement Network (FinCEN), which is a division of the U.S. Treasury Department. The IRS is responsible for FBAR enforcement. Generally, records of accounts required to be reported on the FBAR should be kept for five years from the due date of the report, which is the year *following* the calendar year being reported.

FBARs in General

The term "FBAR" refers to Form 114, *Report of Foreign Bank and Financial Accounts*. In 2003, the Department of the U.S. Treasury delegated enforcement authority regarding the FBAR to the Internal Revenue Service (IRS). With regards to FBAR filings, the IRS is responsible for:

- Investigating possible civil violations,
- Assessing and collecting civil penalties, and
- Issuing administrative rulings.

The FBAR must be filed electronically and is only available online through the BSA E-Filing System.[77] Taxpayers cannot paper-file FBAR returns. A U.S. taxpayer is required to file an FBAR if:

- The person had a financial interest in, or signature authority over, at least one financial account located outside of the United States, and
- The *aggregate* value of all foreign financial accounts exceeded $10,000 (U.S. dollars) at any time during the calendar year reported.[78]

The IRS defines "signature authority" as the authority of an individual or individuals to control the disposition of assets held in a foreign financial account by direct communication with the bank or other financial institution.

Note: The recently enacted *Surface Transportation Act* changed the standard FBAR due date to April 15 beginning with the 2016 tax year.[79] Filers failing to meet the FBAR annual due date of April 15 are allowed an automatic extension to October 15. In prior years, no extensions were permitted.

The FBAR is due by April 15th of the year following the year in which the account holder meets the $10,000 threshold.

Example: Joel is a U.S. citizen. Joel's parents are citizens of Canada and live in Canada. Joel has signature authority on his elderly parents' accounts in Canada, but he has never written a check or made any withdrawals from his parents' bank account. The bank account balance reaches $10,000 for the first time in 2016. Joel is required to file an FBAR by April 18, 2017. Whether or not his signature authority is ever exercised is irrelevant to the FBAR filing requirement.

All FBAR forms are required to be filed electronically with the Treasury Department's Financial Crimes Enforcement Network (FinCEN); they are not filed as part of a tax return.

FBAR Penalties

The Treasury Department reports that FBAR filings have surged in recent years, with filings exceeding one million per year. The consequences of failure to timely file an FBAR can be severe. Both civil penalties and criminal sanctions can be imposed.

By law, civil penalties could be up to $10,000 per year for a "non-willful" failure to file. A "willful" failure could result in the greater of $100,000 or 50% of the balance in an unreported foreign account per year for up to six years. Criminal penalties may include a fine of up to $250,000 and five years in prison.

However, the IRS recently issued guidance[80] on penalties for failing to file an FBAR that caps the maximum percentage of the penalty. In most cases, the total penalty amount for all years under examination will be limited to 50% of the highest aggregate balance of all unreported foreign financial accounts during the years under examination.

---

[77] The BSA E-Filing System is a U.S. Treasury website, and is used for online filing of FBAR returns. The website also supports electronic filing of Bank Secrecy Act (BSA) forms through a secure network.

[78] Accounts are converted to U.S. currency based on the exchange rate as of the end of the calendar year, applied to the highest balance in the account during the year, even if the highest balance in the foreign account was sometime before the end of the year.

[79] The due date for FBAR filings for foreign financial accounts maintained during calendar year 2016 is April 18, 2017, consistent with the Federal income tax due date.

[80] May 13, 2015, *Interim Guidance for Report of Foreign Bank and Financial Accounts (FBAR) Penalties,* Department of the Treasury.

The guidance also establishes procedures and documentation requirements for IRS examiners conducting examinations related to FBAR penalties.

Offshore Voluntary Disclosure Program (OVDP)

The IRS's Offshore Voluntary Disclosure Program (OVDP) offers taxpayers with undisclosed income from offshore accounts a way to disclose foreign accounts and possibly face reduced penalties and avoid criminal prosecution. Streamlined compliance procedures are also in effect. The IRS has FBAR submission procedures for taxpayers who do not need to use either OVDP or the streamlined procedures to report undisclosed income from offshore accounts. A taxpayer may avoid penalties for filing a delinquent FBAR if he:

- Has not filed a required FinCEN Form 114, *Report of Foreign Bank and Financial Accounts* (FBAR),
- Is not under a civil examination or criminal investigation by the IRS, and
- Has not already been contacted by the IRS about the delinquent FBARs.

The taxpayer should file the delinquent FBAR reports electronically, including a statement explaining why he is filing late. The IRS will not impose a penalty for failure to file the delinquent reports if the taxpayer properly reported and paid all tax on the income from the foreign financial accounts that are reported on the FBARs.

Example: Ursula is a citizen of Spain and a legal U.S. resident. She travels frequently to her home country and maintains a bank account there with an average balance of $20,000. She is required to file an FBAR to report this foreign account. For tax year 2016, Ursula must file her FBAR by April 18, 2017.

Because foreign financial institutions may not be subject to the same reporting requirements as financial institutions located within the United States, the FBAR is designed to help the U.S. government identify persons or entities that use offshore accounts to hide income or illicit funds.

Example: Alberto is a legal U.S. resident who has a bank account in Mexico. In prior years, the value of his foreign bank account totaled approximately $7,500. Therefore, Alberto did not have an FBAR requirement. However, in 2016, Alberto decides that he wants to build a vacation home in Mexico. He transfers $18,000 to his Mexican bank account on January 10, 2016, in order to begin construction on his new residence. Although he later withdraws all the funds, he is still required to file an FBAR. Alberto must file his FBAR by April 18, 2017, because the aggregate value of his foreign accounts reached $10,000 in 2016. However, he is not required to file Form 8938 (to be discussed later), because the value of his foreign assets is below the required thresholds.

Note: A safe deposit box at a foreign financial institution is not considered a financial account for reporting purposes.

Form 3520: Reporting Foreign Gifts and Bequests

U.S. individuals who received large gifts or bequests from certain foreign persons may be required to file Form 3520, *Annual Return to Report Transactions with Foreign Trusts and Receipt of Certain Foreign Gifts.* A foreign person is defined as a nonresident alien individual or a foreign corporation, partnership, or estate. In 2016, a U.S. person must file Form 3520,

Annual Return to Report Transactions with Foreign Trusts and Receipt of Certain Foreign Gifts, if he receives:

- Gifts or bequests valued at more than $100,000 from a nonresident alien individual or foreign estate, or
- Gifts valued at more than $15,671 in 2016 from foreign corporations or foreign partnerships.

Form 3520 is considered an "information return," not a tax return, because foreign gifts or bequests are not subject to income tax. However, failure to file a required Form 3520 can result in steep penalties. The penalty for reporting a foreign gift late is $10,000 or 35% of its value. However, no penalty applies if the failure to report was due to reasonable cause and not willful neglect. The taxpayer is required to report a gift or bequest on Form 3520 when he constructively receives it. A taxpayer must aggregate gifts received from related parties.

Example: Josephine is a US citizen that has many relatives living in Canada. In 2016, Josephine received $60,000 from her Canadian grandfather and $50,000 from her Canadian brother. Josephine must report the gifts because the total is more than $100,000. She is required to report them in Part IV of Form 3520. Gifts from foreign trusts must be treated as trust distributions and reported in Part III of Form 3520.

Example: Ginny is a U.S. citizen who lives and works in the United States. Ginny's grandmother, Claudette, is a French citizen. In January 2016, Claudette dies and leaves Ginny a large inheritance of $250,000. After her grandmother's estate is settled by the executor, Ginny receives the inheritance via wire transfer on March 1, 2016. Since Ginny constructively received the funds in 2016, her Form 3520 is due on April 18, 2017.

Taxpayers file Form 3520 separately from their income tax return. The due date for filing Form 3520 is the same as the due date for filing an annual income tax return (generally April 15), including extensions.

Note: A "foreign gift" to a U.S. person does not include amounts paid for qualified tuition or medical payments made on behalf of the U.S. person.

Example: Jason is a U.S. citizen attending college in the United States. His aunt, Judith, is a citizen of Australia. Judith offers to pay her nephew's tuition. She makes a payment directly to Jason's college. There are no filing requirements for this foreign gift.

Form 8938: Statement of Specified Foreign Financial Assets

Generally, taxpayers who hold foreign financial assets with an aggregate value that exceeds $50,000 ($100,000 MFJ) on the last day of the tax year, or that exceeds $75,000 ($150,000 MFJ) at any time during the tax year, must also file Form 8938, *Statement of Specified Foreign Financial Assets,* with their tax returns. This is a separate filing requirement in addition to the FBAR filing requirements.

However, a taxpayer who is not required to file a return for the year does not need to file Form 8938, even if the value of his specified foreign assets is greater than one of the reporting thresholds.

Example: Eloise is a U.S. citizen and resident with funds deposited in three different foreign banks. As of December 31, 2016, bank account #1 had $5,000; bank account #2 had $3,000; and bank account #3 had $2,500. Eloise is required to electronically file an FBAR by April 18, 2017, because the aggregate value of her accounts is more than $10,000. However, she is not required to file Form 8938, because the value of her offshore assets is below the required thresholds.

Schedule B, Reporting Foreign Accounts and Trusts

Schedule B is used to report interest and dividend income received during the tax year. However, the last part of Schedule B (Part III) is used by taxpayers who have financial accounts in foreign countries. This section of the form is where the taxpayer must disclose any foreign bank or investment accounts and whether or not the taxpayer received any distributions from a foreign trust.

The reporting requirements for these taxpayers have increased significantly in recent years as part of FATCA, which refers to the Foreign Account Tax Compliance Act. The law addresses tax noncompliance by U.S. taxpayers with foreign accounts by focusing on reporting by these taxpayers and by foreign financial institutions.

In general, federal law requires U.S. citizens and resident aliens to report any worldwide income, including income from foreign trusts and foreign bank and securities accounts. In most cases, affected taxpayers need to complete and attach Schedule B to their tax returns. Part III of Schedule B asks about the existence of foreign accounts, such as bank and securities accounts, and generally requires U.S. citizens to report the country in which each account is located.

On Part III, Schedule B, a taxpayer must check yes or no to the question of whether he had at any time during the year a financial interest in or signature authority over a financial account. A taxpayer who had a financial interest in a foreign account should check the "yes" box even if he is not required to file FinCEN Form 114, *Report of Foreign Bank and Financial Accounts* (FBAR).

A financial account includes securities, brokerage, savings, checking, deposit, time deposit, or other accounts that are maintained with a financial institution. A financial account also includes a commodity futures or options account, an insurance policy with a cash value (such as a whole life policy), an annuity policy with a cash value, and shares in a mutual fund.

Example: Patty has an uncle who is a Greek citizen. In 2016, her uncle died, and Patty inherited $200,000 in foreign bearer bonds from her uncle. The bonds are held outside of a regular bank account. Patty is required to report the value of the bonds on Form 8938, even if she did not cash them out.

A financial account is considered to be located in a foreign country if the account is *physically located outside* of the United States. This includes accounts maintained with a branch of a U.S. bank if it is physically located outside the United States. However, a branch of a foreign bank is not a foreign account if it is physically located in the United States.

Note: The potential penalties for willful failure to file an FBAR are huge. These penalties might include criminal prosecution as well as large civil penalties.

Example: Ricky directly holds shares of a U.S.-based mutual fund. The mutual fund invests solely in foreign stocks. Since the foreign stocks are held in a mutual fund, Ricky does not need to report his ownership in the mutual fund or the holdings of the mutual fund.

Differences Between the FBAR vs. Form 8938

Data	FBAR	Form 8938
Who must file?	U.S. persons, which includes U.S. citizens, resident aliens, trusts, estates, and domestic entities.	Specified individuals, which includes U.S. citizens, resident aliens, and certain nonresident aliens. This form does not apply to entities.
Reporting thresholds	$10,000 held in any foreign bank at any time during the calendar year.	$50,000 on the last day of the tax year or $75,000 at any time during the tax year.
When does the taxpayer have "an interest" in an account or asset?	Financial interest in an applicable foreign account, or signature authority on an applicable foreign account.	Any income, gains, losses, deductions, credits, gross proceeds, or distributions from holding or disposing of the account or asset that are (or would be required to be) reported, included, or otherwise reflected on the taxpayer's return.
What is Reported?	The maximum value of financial accounts.	The maximum value of specified foreign financial assets.
How are values determined and reported?	Converted to U.S. dollars using the end of the calendar year exchange rate and report in U.S. dollars.	Fair market value of the asset in U.S. dollars.
Due Date	Due by April 15 (extensions allowed).	The same due date as the taxpayer's individual return, including extensions.
Filing Procedures	File electronically through FinCEN's BSA E-Filing System. The FBAR is not filed with a federal tax return.	File with income tax return (Form 1040).
Penalties	Willful non-filing: up to the greater of $100,000 or 50% of account balances; Non-willful: up to $10,000; criminal penalties may also apply.	Up to $10,000 for failure to disclose, and an additional $10,000 for every 30 days of non-filing after IRS notice of a failure to disclose, up to a potential maximum penalty of $60,000; criminal penalties may also apply.

Unit 18: Study Questions

(Test yourself first, then check the correct answers at the end of this quiz.)

1. Which form are taxpayers required to submit with their individual tax return if they hold foreign financial assets with an aggregate value that exceeds $50,000 ($100,000 MFJ) on the last day of the tax year?

A. Form 8938.
B. Form 1040 G.
C. Schedule L.
D. FBAR.

2. Part ______ of the Schedule B is completed by taxpayers who have financial accounts in foreign countries.

A. Part I.
B. Part II.
C. Part III.
D. Schedule B is not used for this purpose.

3. Which of the following documents is completed to report foreign bank and financial accounts?

A. Schedule B.
B. Form 1116.
C. Form 2555.
D. FinCen 114.

4. Generally, U.S. citizens, resident aliens, and certain nonresident aliens must report specified foreign financial assets _________ if the aggregate value of those assets exceeds certain thresholds.

A. Form 1040.
B. FinCen 114.
C. Form 8938.
D. Form 9465.

5. Regarding the FBAR reporting requirement, the IRS issued guidance on penalties for failing to file the FBAR that caps the maximum percentage of the penalty. In most cases, the total penalty amount for all years under examination will be limited to _______ of the highest aggregate balance of all unreported foreign financial accounts during the years under investigation.

A. 50%
B. 75%
C. 25%
D. 10%

6. As a general rule, how long should taxpayers keep records related to an FBAR filing?

A. 3 years.
B. 5 years.
C. 7 years.
D. 10 years.

7. Louise is a U.S. citizen with funds deposited in three different Canadian banks. At the end of the tax year, bank account #1 had $5,500; account #2 had $3,250; and account #3 had $2,200. Is she required to file an FBAR, and if so, when is the due date?

A. No, each bank account has less than $10,000, so she is not required to file an FBAR.
B. Yes, Louise is required to file an FBAR by April 18, 2017.
C. Yes, Louise is required to file an FBAR by October 30, 2017.
D. Yes, Louise is required to file an FBAR as well as a Form 8938 by April 18, 2017.

8. Jim, a U.S. citizen who lives in Iowa, has a bank account located in Austria. He opened the account several years ago to send money to his mother, who is a citizen of Austria. He has signature authority on the account but does not withdraw money from it or collect any of the interest income on the account. On December 31, 2016, the account has a balance of $23,000. He otherwise does not have a U.S. filing requirement or any tax liability for the year. What is Jim's reporting requirement for this account?

A. He is not required to file returns since he does not have a filing requirement or owe U.S. tax.
B. He must file Form 8938, *Statement of Specified Foreign Financial Assets*, with the IRS when he files his tax return.
C. He must file an FBAR, *Report of Foreign Bank and Financial Accounts*, with the Treasury Department.
D. He must file an FBAR, *Report of Foreign Bank and Financial Accounts*, with the Treasury Department, and file Form 8938, *Statement of Specified Foreign Financial Assets*, with the IRS when he files his tax return.

9. A U.S. person who receives a gift or bequest valued at more than ___________ from a nonresident alien or foreign estate must file an information return with the IRS.

A. $10,000
B. $25,000
C. $50,000
D. $100,000

10. Which of the following is a NOT considered United States person for the purposes of filing an FBAR?

A. A United States citizen who lives in Israel.
B. A U.S. Resident who lives in Russia.
C. A nonresident alien with U.S. investments.
D. A U.S. consular officer that lives and works overseas in a U.S. embassy.

Unit 18: Answers

1. The answer is A. Generally, taxpayers who hold foreign financial assets with an aggregate value that exceeds $50,000 ($100,000 MFJ) on the last day of the tax year, or that exceeds $75,000 ($150,000 MFJ) at any time during the tax year, must file Form 8938 with their returns. The FBAR is not included with the income tax return.

2. The answer is C. Part III of the Schedule B is completed by taxpayers who have financial accounts in foreign countries.

3. The answer is D. The FinCen 114 (FBAR) is the form used to report foreign bank accounts and foreign financial accounts.

4. The answer is C. U.S. citizens, resident aliens, and certain nonresident aliens must report specified foreign financial assets on the Form 8938 if the aggregate value of those assets exceeds certain thresholds.

5. The answer is A. In most cases, the total penalty amount for all years under examination will be limited to 50% of the highest aggregate balance of all unreported foreign financial accounts during the years under investigation.

6. The answer is B. Generally, records of accounts required to be reported on the FBAR should be kept for five years from the due date of the report, which is the year *following* the calendar year being reported.

7. The answer is B. The taxpayer is required to electronically file an FBAR by April 18, 2017, because the aggregate value of her accounts is more than $10,000. However, she is not required to file Form 8938, because the value of her offshore assets is below the required thresholds.

8. The answer is C. There are two separate reporting requirements for taxpayers who hold certain types of foreign assets or who have certain amounts of funds in foreign bank accounts. An FBAR generally must be filed with the Treasury Department if a taxpayer has more than $10,000 in offshore bank accounts. Taxpayers also must file a statement with the IRS if they hold foreign financial assets with an aggregate value that exceeds $50,000 ($100,000 MFJ) on the last day of the tax year, or that exceeds $75,000 ($150,000 MFJ) at any time during the tax year. In Jim's case, since the funds in his foreign account total $23,000, he is only required to file an FBAR. He is required to file the FBAR, even if he earns no money from the account and owes no U.S. tax.

9. The answer is D. Form 3520, *Annual Return to Report Transactions with Foreign Trusts and Receipt of Certain Foreign Gifts*, is an information return, not a tax return, because foreign gifts or bequests are not subject to income tax. In 2016, a U.S. person must file Form 3520 if he receives:

- Gifts or bequests valued at more than $100,000 from a nonresident alien individual or foreign estate, or
- Gifts valued at more than $15,671 from a foreign corporation or foreign partnership.

An individual who fails to file a required Form 3520 could be subject to steep penalties.

10. The answer is C. Nonresident aliens are not subject to the FBAR filing requirement. All of the following are subject to the FBAR filing requirement if they hold foreign bank accounts or applicable foreign assets.

- A citizen or resident of the United States
- A domestic entity
- A domestic corporation
- A domestic estate or trust

Unit 19: Estate and Gift Taxes

More Reading:
Publication 559, *Survivors, Executors, and Administrators*
Publication 950, *Introduction to Estate and Gift Taxes*
Instructions for Form 1041
Instructions for Form 706
Instructions for Form 709

Estates in General

An estate is a separate legal entity created when a taxpayer dies. The estate tax is a tax on the transfer of assets or property from an individual's estate to his beneficiaries after his death. The estate filing threshold for 2016 is $5,450,000.

Note: For Part 1 of the EA exam, you will be required to understand how estate and gift taxes affect individual taxpayers, especially the living beneficiaries of those estates. For Part 2 of the exam, you will be tested on the tax treatment of estates and trusts as legal entities. It is possible that questions will overlap, and therefore we cover the concept of estate taxation from various perspectives.

After a person dies, a personal representative, such as an executor, or an administrator appointed by a court, will typically manage the estate and settle the decedent's financial affairs. If there is no executor or administrator, another person with possession of the decedent's property may act as the personal representative. If a probate court proceeding is necessary, the judge will appoint an executor if one is not named in the decedent's will.

Note: The executor or "personal representative" must include fees paid to them from an estate in their gross income. If the executor is not in the trade or business of being an executor (for instance, the executor is a friend or family member of the deceased), these fees are reported on the executor's individual Form 1040, line 21. If the executor is in the "trade or business" of being an executor, they would report the fees received from the estate as self-employment income on Schedule C.

After a taxpayer dies, the following tax returns may need to be filed:

- **Form 1040:** Final income tax return for the decedent (for income received before death).
- **Form 1041**, *U.S. Income Tax Return for Estates and Trusts*: Fiduciary income tax returns for the estate for the period of its administration.
- **Form 706**, *United States Estate (and Generation-Skipping Transfer) Tax Return*: If the gross estate, based on the fair market value of its assets, exceeds the applicable threshold. This return is used to report tax on the taxable estate (the gross estate minus certain deductions).

Either the personal representative or a paid preparer must sign each required return. The personal representative is also responsible for determining any estate tax liability before the estate's assets are distributed to beneficiaries.

The tax liability for an estate attaches to the assets of the estate itself. If the assets are distributed to the beneficiaries before the taxes are paid, the beneficiaries may be held liable for the tax debt, up to the value of the assets distributed.

Final Income Tax Return (Form 1040)

The taxpayer's final income tax return is filed on the same form that would have been used if the taxpayer were still alive, but "deceased" is written after the taxpayer's name. The filing deadline is April 15 of the year following the taxpayer's death, the same deadline that applies for individual income tax returns.

The personal representative must file the final individual income tax return of the decedent for the year of death and any returns not filed for preceding years. If an individual died after the close of a tax year, but before the return for that year was filed, the return for that year will not be the final return. The return for that year will be a regular return, and the personal representative must file it.

Example: Milly dies on February 28, 2017. At the time of her death, she had not yet filed her prior year tax return. She earned $71,000 of wages in 2016. She also earned $16,000 of wages between January 1, 2017, and her death on February 28, 2017. Therefore, Milly's 2016 and 2017 tax returns must be filed by her representative or executor. The 2017 return will be her final individual tax return.

Example: James was unmarried when he died on April 20, 2016. His only daughter, Lillian, was named as the executor of his estate. James earned wages in 2016 before his death, so a final tax return is required for 2016. Lillian asks her accountant to help prepare her father's final Form 1040, which will include all the taxable income that James received before his death. The accountant also helps Lillian with the valuation of her father's estate. After determining the fair market value of all her father's assets, her accountant concludes that James' gross estate is valued at approximately $7 million on the date of his death. As this exceeds the filing threshold for 2016, an estate tax return (Form 706) is also required to be filed, and Lillian is responsible for filing both returns.

On a decedent's final tax return, the rules for personal exemptions and deductions are the same as those that apply for any individual taxpayer. The full amount of the applicable personal exemption may be claimed on the final tax return, regardless of how long the taxpayer was alive during the year.

Income in Respect of a Decedent (IRD)

Income in respect of a decedent (IRD) is any taxable income that was earned but not received by the decedent by the time of death. IRD is not taxed on the final return of the deceased taxpayer. IRD is reported on the tax return of the person (or entity) that receives the income. This could be the estate, in which case it would be reported on Form 1041, as described below. Otherwise, it could be the surviving spouse or another beneficiary, such as a child. IRD retains the same tax nature that would have applied if the deceased taxpayer were still alive. For example, if the income would have been short-term capital gain, it is taxed the same way to the beneficiary. IRD can come from various sources, including:

- Unpaid salary, wages, or bonuses
- Distributions from traditional IRAs and employer-provided retirement plans
- Deferred compensation benefits
- Accrued but unpaid interest, dividends, and rent
- Accounts receivable of a sole proprietor

Example: Carlos was owed $15,000 of wages when he died. The check for these wages was not remitted by his employer until three weeks later and was received by his daughter and sole beneficiary, Rosalie. The wages are considered IRD, and Rosalie must recognize the $15,000 as ordinary income, the same tax treatment that would have applied for Carlos.

Example: Beverly died on April 30. At the time of her death, she was owed (but had not yet received) $1,500 of interest on bonds and $2,000 of rental income. Beverly's beneficiary will include $3,500 of IRD in gross income when the interest and rent are received. The income retains its character as interest income and passive activity rental income.

IRD is included in the decedent's estate and may be subject to estate tax. If it is received by a beneficiary and subject to income tax on the beneficiary's return, the beneficiary may take a deduction for estate tax paid on the IRD.

This deduction is taken as a miscellaneous itemized deduction on Schedule A and is not subject to the 2% floor.

Form 1041, Tax Return for Estates and Trusts

An estate is a taxable legal entity that exists from the time of an individual's death until all assets have been distributed to the decedent's beneficiaries. As investment assets will usually continue to earn income after a taxpayer has died, this income, such as rents, dividends and interest, must be reported. Form 1041 is a fiduciary return used to report the following items for a domestic decedent's estate, trust, or bankruptcy estate:

- Current income and deductions, including gains and losses from disposition of the entity's property, and excluding certain items such as tax-exempt interest (collectively, *distributable net income* or DNI);
- A deduction for income either held for future distribution or distributed currently to the beneficiaries (income distribution deduction) that are limited to DNI; and
- Any income tax liability.

Current income would include IRD if it was received by the estate rather than by specific beneficiaries. Expenses of administering the estate can be deducted either from the estate's income on Form 1041 in determining its income tax, or from the gross estate on Form 706 in determining the estate tax liability, but cannot be claimed for both purposes.

Schedule K-1 is used to report any income that is distributed or distributable to each beneficiary and is filed with Form 1041, with a copy also given to the beneficiary.

Estates are allowed some of the same tax credits that are allowed to individuals. The credits are generally allocated between the estate and the beneficiaries. However, estates are not allowed the Credit for the Elderly or the Disabled, the Child Tax Credit, or the Earned Income Tax Credit.

Note: Just like individual taxpayers, estates and certain trusts are subject to the Net Investment Income Tax (an additional tax of 3.8% on net investment income). The provisions for this tax are generally similar to those for individuals, and it must be reported on Form 8960, *Net Investment Tax: Individuals, Estates, and Trusts.*

The due date for Form 1041 is the fifteenth day of the fourth month following the end of the entity's tax year, but is subject to an automatic extension of five-and-one-half months if Form 7004 is filed. The tax year may be either a calendar or a fiscal year for an estate, subject to the election made at the time the first return is filed. Trusts must generally use a fiscal year. An election will be made on the first return as to the accounting method (cash, accrual, or other) of reporting the estate's income.

Form 1041 must be filed for any domestic estate that has gross income for the tax year of $600 or more or a beneficiary who is a nonresident alien (with any amount of income).

The Estate Tax

Estate tax may apply to the decedent's taxable estate, which is the gross estate minus any allowable deductions. In 2016, an estate valued at less than $5,450,000 would generally not be taxable or have a filing requirement.

Gross Estate: The gross estate is based upon the fair market value of the decedent's property, which is not necessarily equal to his cost, and includes:

- The FMV of all tangible and intangible property owned partially or outright by the decedent at the time of death

- Life insurance proceeds payable to the estate or, for policies owned by the decedent, payable to the heirs
- The value of certain annuities or survivor benefits payable to the heirs
- The value of certain property that was transferred within three years before the decedent's death

The gross estate does not include property owned solely by the decedent's spouse or other individuals. Lifetime gifts that are complete (so that no control over the gifts was retained) are not included in the gross estate.

Deductions from the Gross Estate: Once the gross estate has been calculated, certain deductions (and in special circumstances, reductions to value) are allowed to determine the taxable estate. Deductions may include:

- Funeral expenses paid out of the estate
- Estate administrative expenses, if not deducted on Form 1041
- Debts owed at the time of death
- The marital deduction (generally, the value of property that passes from the estate to a surviving spouse)
- The charitable deduction (generally, the value of property that passes from the estate to qualifying charities)
- The state death tax deduction (generally, any inheritance or estate taxes paid to any state)

The following items are not deductible from the gross estate:

- Federal estate taxes paid
- Alimony paid after the taxpayer's death; these payments are treated as distributions to a beneficiary

Property taxes are deductible only if they accrue under state law prior to the decedent's death.

Special Rule for Medical Expenses

Debts not paid before death, including medical expenses subsequently paid on behalf of the decedent, are liabilities that can be deducted from the gross estate on the estate tax return. However, if medical expenses for the decedent are paid out of the estate during the one-year period beginning with the day after death, the personal representative can alternatively elect to treat all or part of the expenses as paid by the decedent at the time they were incurred, and deduct them on the decedent's final tax return (1040).

Example: Frances, age 76, died on June 1, 2016, after a long battle with cancer. She incurred $42,000 of medical expenses, half during 2015 (the prior year) and half during 2016. The estate's executor paid the entire outstanding $42,000 bill in August 2016. He elects to file an amended return for Frances for 2015, claiming $21,000 as a medical expense deduction. The remaining $21,000 will be deducted on Frances' final income tax return, subject to the same limit. The medical expenses cannot also be claimed on the federal estate tax return.

The Marital Deduction

Transfers from one spouse to the other are typically tax-free. The marital deduction allows spouses to transfer an unlimited amount of property to one another during their lifetimes or at death without being subject to estate or gift taxes.

To receive an unlimited deduction, the spouse receiving the assets must be a U.S. citizen and a legal spouse, and must have outright ownership of the assets. The unlimited marital deduction is generally not allowed if the transferee spouse is not a U.S. citizen (even if the spouse is a legal resident of the United States).

Example: Walt and Martha are married, and both are U.S. citizens. Walt dies and leaves his wife, Martha, all his assets, which total $15 million on the date of his death. The transfer is tax-free to Martha because of the unlimited marital deduction. Martha's estate may or may not owe tax when she dies, but the transfer of assets to a surviving spouse is generally a nontaxable event, provided that the surviving spouse is a U.S. citizen.

Note: If the receiving spouse is not a U.S. citizen, assets transferred tax-free are limited to an annual exclusion amount. Non-citizen spouses can only receive $148,000 in 2016. This is true even if the spouse is a legal U.S. resident (a green card holder); it is one of the rare instances where U.S. citizens are taxed differently than legal U.S. residents.

The Estate Tax Return (Form 706)

An estate tax return is filed using Form 706, *United States Estate (and Generation-Skipping Transfer) Tax Return.* This return is due nine months after the death of the decedent. A six-month extension is allowed.

After the taxable estate is computed, it is added to the value of lifetime taxable gifts. The applicable estate tax rate is applied to derive a tentative tax, from which any gift taxes paid or payable are subtracted to determine the gross estate tax. The maximum estate tax rate is 40% in 2016. However, all or a portion of the gross estate tax may be eliminated after applying the Basic Exclusion Amount.

This Basic Exclusion Amount is adjusted for inflation each year and may be used to reduce or eliminate gift and/or estate taxes. The exclusion is $5,450,000 in 2016. Most taxpayers never use the lifetime exclusion amount, and less than 1% of taxpayers are affected by the estate tax.

There is a special rule that applies to widows and widowers. A surviving spouse can add any unused exclusion of his deceased spouse who died most recently to his own estate tax return. This enables them together to transfer up to $10.9 million tax-free. This is also known as "portability."

Deceased Spousal Unused Exclusion (DSUE)

This is the unused portion of the decedent's predeceased spouse's basic exclusion (the amount that was not used to offset gift or estate tax liabilities). A portability election must be made to claim the DSUE on behalf of the surviving spouse's estate. This election can be made automatically by timely completion and filing of Form 706 for the estate of the predeceased spouse. Portability is not automatic. This means that the executor, usually a surviving spouse, will need to transfer the unused exclusion to the surviving spouse. This is done by filing an estate tax return. The estate tax return is required when the first spouse dies, even if no tax is owed. This return is due nine months after the death of the first spouse. A six-month extension is allowed.

Example: Matt died in early 2016 and left a gross estate valued at $9 million. His assets transferred to his wife, Leslie (who is a U.S. citizen), and none were taxed because of the unlimited marital deduction. Thus, none of the $5.45 million basic exclusion amount available to Matt's estate was used (and none had been used to offset gift tax liabilities during his lifetime). Leslie then died later the same year. Assuming Form 706 was timely filed for Matt's estate and Leslie had not used any of her basic exclusion amount, Matt's unused basic exclusion is added to Leslie's basic exclusion, for a total exclusion amount of $10.9 million. If Leslie's estate is valued at less than $10.9 million, the full amount can be excluded, and no estate tax will be owed.

Example: Marlene died in 2016 and left an estate valued at $3 million. She had not previously used any of her basic exclusion amount to avoid paying gift taxes, so the entire exclusion amount of $5.45 million is available to her estate. As this amount exceeds the estate's value, no estate tax is owed, and an estate tax return does not need to be filed.

Inheritances

For federal income tax purposes, cash inheritances are generally not taxable to the beneficiary, although the beneficiary may be responsible for if there is a related estate tax liability that has not been satisfied.

> **Example:** Hamid's aunt died and left him $100,000 cash in her will. Hamid does not owe any federal tax on the inheritance.

Distributions of retirement plan benefits or distributions from taxable IRA accounts to the decedent's beneficiaries are generally subject to income tax when received.

The decedent's surviving spouse may be able to defer taxation by rolling over the assets of a taxable IRA to another IRA or to a qualified plan.

Qualified distributions from a Roth IRA or of previously nondeductible contributions to a traditional IRA are generally not taxable.

> **Example:** Josepha dies and leaves her entire estate to her son, Lucas. At the time of her death, she had a significant cash balance in her bank account as well as several rental properties. The estate has a filing requirement, but Lucas ignores his accountant's advice and simply withdraws all the money from his late mother's bank account. He also sells all the rental properties and takes the money in order to take several lavish trips. Although inheritances are generally not taxable to the beneficiary, the fact that Lucas took possession of his mother's assets without filing her required estate tax return or satisfying the estate tax liability would make him directly responsible for the tax. The IRS can come after Lucas in order to satisfy the estate's debts.

Basis of Estate Property

Although cash inheritances are not subject to federal income tax, money received from the sale of inherited property may be taxable. The basis of property inherited from a decedent is generally one of the following:

- The FMV of the property on the date of death
- The FMV on an alternate valuation date, if elected by the personal representative
- The value under a special-use valuation method for real property used in farming or another closely-held business, if elected by the personal representative
- The decedent's adjusted basis in land to the extent of the value excluded from the taxable estate as a qualified conservation easement

> **Example:** Jared is the executor of his father's estate. His father's will directs that the estate be split equally between Jared and his four siblings. Their father dies on June 1, 2016, and Jared does not elect the alternate valuation date. The fair market value of his father's residence on the date of death is $500,000. In December 2016, the siblings agree to sell their late father's home for $550,000. Collectively, they must report a gain of $50,000 ($550,000 sale price minus $500,000 adjusted basis).

Alternate Valuation Date: If elected, the alternate valuation date is six months after the date of death. The estate value and related estate tax must be less than they would have been on the date of the taxpayer's death. However, for any assets distributed to a beneficiary after death, but prior to six months after death, the basis for these assets is the fair market value as of the date of distribution.

Jointly Owned Property: Property that is jointly owned by a decedent and another person will be included in full in the decedent's gross estate unless it can be shown that the other person originally owned or otherwise contributed to the purchase price. The surviving owner's new basis of property that was jointly owned must be calculated.

To do so, the surviving owner's original basis in the property is added to the value of the part of the property included in the decedent's estate. Any deductions for depreciation allowed to the surviving owner for his portion of the property are subtracted from the sum.

If property is jointly held between a husband and wife as tenants by the entirety, or as joint tenants with the right of survivorship (if they were the only joint tenants), one-half of the property's value is included in the gross estate, and there is a step-up in basis for that one-half. The other half is stated at the surviving spouse's cost basis, net of any deductions for depreciation allowed to the surviving spouse on that half. If the decedent holds property in a community property state, half of the value of the community property will be included in the gross estate of the decedent, but the entire value of the community property will receive a step-up in basis.

Example: Chen and Xia, brother and sister, owned rental property they purchased for $60,000 as joint tenants with right of survivorship. Chen paid $30,000 of the purchase price (for 50% ownership of the property), and Xia also paid $30,000 (for 50% ownership of the property). Under local law, each had a half interest in the income from the property and shared expenses equally. When Chen died, the FMV of the property was $100,000. Depreciation deductions allowed before his death were $20,000. Xia's original basis was $30,000. Upon Chen's death, she acquired his one-half share of the property and her basis in this portion of the property is stepped up to $50,000 (.50 × $100,000), resulting in a basis of $80,000 ($50,000 + $30,000 = $80,000). After subtracting her half of the depreciation deductions taken, Xia's adjusted basis in the property after Chen's death is $70,000 ($80,000 - $10,000).

Generation-Skipping Transfer Tax (GST)

In the past, wealthy families used various strategies to transfer wealth and assets to their grandchildren and other descendants. In response to this, Congress created the generation-skipping transfer tax, also known the GST, to close this tax loophole.

The generation-skipping transfer tax (GST) may apply to gifts during a taxpayer's lifetime or transfers occurring after his death, called bequests, made to "skip persons". A skip person is usually a grandchild, but it also applies to those who are more than 37½ years younger than the person making the gift or bequest. The most common scenario is when a taxpayer makes a gift to a grandchild.

The GST is assessed when the property transfer is made, including instances in which property is transferred from a trust. The GST is based on the amounts transferred to skip persons, after subtracting the allocated portions of the donor's available GST exemption. In 2016, the GST exemption is the same as the estate tax basic exclusion amount, and the GST tax rate is set at the maximum estate tax rate of 40%.

The GST is imposed separately and in addition to the estate and gift taxes.

Example: Patrick sets up a trust that names his adult daughter, Helene, as the sole beneficiary of the trust. In January 2016, Patrick dies, and the trust passes to Helene. However, later in the year, Helene also dies, and the trust passes to her children (Patrick's grandchildren). Patrick's grandchildren are skip persons for purposes of the GST, and the trust's property may now be subject to the GST.

Any payments for tuition or medical expenses on behalf of a skip person that are made directly to an educational or medical institution are exempt from gift tax and GST.

Example: Gordon wants to help support his grandchildren, but he tries to make sure that his gifts are not subject to gift tax, GST, or estate tax. In 2016, he pays his grandchild's college tuition in full and writes a check directly to the college for $25,000. Since the amounts were paid directly to the college, there is no tax consequence for this gift, and no additional reporting is required.

The Gift Tax

The gift tax may apply to the transfer of property by one individual to another, whether the donor intends the transfer to be a gift or not. Gift tax is imposed on the donor, not the receiver, of the property. However, under special arrangements, the donee may agree to pay the tax instead of the donor.

As discussed previously, an individual taxpayer's liability for estate tax and gift tax is subject to a combined basic exclusion amount ($5.45 million in 2016), and the use of any portion of this exclusion amount to reduce payment of gift taxes during the taxpayer's lifetime will reduce the amount available upon death to reduce applicable estate taxes. The following gifts are not taxable:

- Gifts to an individual that do not exceed the annual exclusion amount. In 2016, the gift exclusion amount is $14,000 per donee.
- Tuition or medical expenses paid directly to the educational or medical institution for someone else.
- Unlimited gifts to a spouse, as long as the spouse is a U.S. citizen.
- Gifts to a political organization for its use.
- Gifts to a qualifying charity.
- A parent's support for a minor child. This may include support required as part of a legal obligation, such as by a divorce decree.

Gift taxes are reported on Form 709, *United States Gift (and Generation-Skipping Transfer) Tax Return*. Form 709 must be filed if:

- A taxpayer gives more than the annual exclusion amount to at least one individual (except to a U. S. citizen spouse).[81]
- A taxpayer "splits gifts" with a spouse.
- A taxpayer gives a future interest to anyone other than a U.S. citizen spouse.

If a gift tax return is required to be filed, Form 709 is generally due by April 15 of the following year. However, if the donor dies during the year, the filing deadline may be the due date for his estate tax return. Taxpayers who extend the filing of Form 1040 for six months using Form 4868 are deemed to have extended their gift tax returns, if no gift tax is due with the extension.

If the taxpayer does not extend their individual return, the gift tax return can be extended separately by using Form 8892, *Application for Automatic Extension of Time to File Form 709 and/or Payment of Gift/Generation-Skipping Transfer Tax*.

Definitions: A gift is considered a **present interest** if the donee has all immediate rights to the use, possession, and enjoyment of the property or income from the property. A gift is considered a **future interest** if the donee's rights to the use, possession, and enjoyment of the property or income from the property will not begin until some future date. Future interests include reversions, remainders, and other similar interests or estates. A gift of a future interest cannot be excluded under the annual exclusion ($14,000 per donee in 2016).

Example: Dion is 26, and Earlene is his mother. Earlene gives her son, Dion, a gift of $14,000 of cash during the year. She also pays his college tuition, totaling $21,000, and writes the check directly to the college. Earlene also pays for Dion's medical bills by issuing the check directly to his doctor's office. None of these gifts are taxable, and no gift tax return is required.

Example: Dave is single. In 2016, Dave gives his best friend Gary $18,000 to help start his first business. The money is not a loan, so Dave is required to file a gift tax return since the amount exceeds the $14,000 annual exclusion amount.

[81] For 2016, the exclusion from tax on a gift to a spouse who is <u>not</u> a U.S. citizen is $148,000.

Applying the Applicable Credit to Gift Tax: After a taxpayer determines which of his gifts are taxable, he must calculate the amount of gift tax on the total taxable gifts and apply the applicable credit for the year.

Gift Splitting by Married Couples

Both the basic exclusion amount and the annual exclusion amount apply separately to each spouse, and each spouse must separately file a gift tax return if he or she made reportable gifts during the year. However, if a married couple or either spouse makes a gift to another person, the gift can be considered as being one-half from one spouse and one-half from the other spouse. This concept is known as *gift splitting.*

Gift splitting allows a married couple to give up to $28,000 (in 2016) to a single individual without making a taxable gift. Both spouses must consent to split the gift.

Example: Ronnie and his wife, Margie, agree to split gifts of cash. Ronnie gives a friend $21,000, and Margie gives her niece $18,000. Although each gift is more than the annual exclusion amount of $14,000, they can use gift splitting to avoid making a taxable gift to each donee. In each case, because one-half of the split gift is not more than the annual exclusion amount, it is not taxable. A gift tax return is required.

Example: Felicia gives her cousin, Jessie, $24,000. Felicia elects to split the gift with her husband, Ralph, and Ralph is treated as if he gave Jessie half the amount, or $12,000. Assuming they make no other gifts to Jessie during the year, the entire $24,000 gift is tax-free. However, a gift tax return is required.

If a married couple splits a gift, each spouse must generally file his or her own individual gift tax return. However, certain exceptions may apply that allow for only one spouse to file a return if the other spouse signifies consent on the donor spouse's Form 709.

Basis of Property Received as a Gift

For purposes of determining gain or loss on a subsequent disposition of property received as a gift, a taxpayer must consider:

- The gift's adjusted basis to the donor just before it was given to the taxpayer,
- The gift's FMV at the time it was given to the taxpayer, and
- Any gift tax actually paid on appreciation of the property's value while held by the donor (as opposed to gift tax offset by the donor's applicable credit amount).

If the FMV of the gift was equal to or greater than the donor's adjusted basis in the gift right before the transfer, the donee's basis will be the donor's basis (transferred basis), adjusted for any gift tax paid on the donor's appreciation. If the FMV of the gift was less than the donor's adjusted basis in the gift right before the transfer:

- When the donee sells the property received as a gift, he calculates gain based upon the donor's adjusted basis.
- If the donee sells property at a loss, the taxpayer's basis would be the FMV at the time of the gift.
- If the donee sells the property at a price higher than the FMV at the time of the gift, but lower than the donor's adjusted basis at the time of the gift, the basis at the time of the sale will be the sales price, resulting in no gain or loss on the sale.

Example: In 2016, Peggy received a gift of property from her uncle with an FMV of $50,000. Her uncle's adjusted basis was $20,000. For gift tax purposes, the amount of the gift was $36,000 ($50,000 minus the $14,000 annual exclusion). Peggy's uncle paid gift tax of $7,000. However, that amount is adjusted to $5,833 ($30,000 ÷ $36,000 = .83 × $7,000) to account for the gift tax paid on appreciation of the property's value. Peggy's basis is $25,833 (the donor's adjusted basis plus gift tax paid on the donor's appreciation).

Example: Edward's father gives him 20 shares of stock that are currently worth $900. Edward's father has an adjusted basis in the stock of $500. Edward's basis in the stock is also $500.

Example: Belinda receives an acre of land as a gift from her brother. Her brother's adjusted basis in the land is $50,000, and its FMV on the date of the gift is $40,000. A couple of years later, Belinda sells the gifted land for $35,000. Since she sold the property at a loss, her basis in the land is $40,000, because it is the lower of her brother's adjusted basis and the FMV at the date of the gift.

Generally, the value of a gift is its fair market value on the date of the gift. However, the value of the gift may be less than its fair market value to the extent that the donee gives the donor something in return.

Example: Daniel sells his son, Nicolas, a house well below market value. Nicolas only pays $10,000 for the house. In 2016, the fair market value of the house is $90,000. Therefore, Daniel has made a gift to his son of $80,000 ($90,000 - $10,000 = $80,000). Daniel is required to file a gift tax return because the gift exceeds the $14,000 threshold for 2016.

The Unified Credit

The gross estate tax is reduced by the *applicable credit*, also referred to as the *unified credit*. For the 2016 tax year, the unified credit exclusion is $5.45 million per taxpayer. The annual gift tax exclusion is $14,000. The unified credit is the combination of the lifetime gift tax exclusion and estate tax exclusion.

Just as with the basic exclusion amount, any portion of the applicable credit amount used to avoid payment of gift taxes reduces the amount of credit available in later years that can be used to offset gift or estate taxes.

For example, if a taxpayer exceeds the annual gift tax exclusion amount in any year, the taxpayer can choose to either pay the tax on the excess or take advantage of the unified credit to avoid paying the tax.

Note: For taxable gifts, each taxpayer has an aggregate lifetime exemption before any out-of-pocket gift tax is due. For example, a taxpayer can give away up to $5.45 million during their lifetime above the annual $14,000 exclusion and still avoid paying any gift tax.

Example: Faye, who was single, died in 2016 and left an estate valued at $20 million. During her lifetime, she had used $1 million of her basic exclusion to offset payments of gift tax. That reduces the amount her estate may exclude to $4.45 million, which is then subtracted from her $20 million taxable estate. That leaves a total of $15.55 million to be taxed at the estate tax rate.

The due date for Form 706 is nine months after the decedent's date of death. An automatic six-month extension may be requested. However, the tax is due by the due date and interest is accrued on any amounts owed that are not paid at that time.

The assessment period for estate tax is three years after the due date for a timely filed estate tax return. The assessment period is four years for transfers from an estate.

Unit 19: Study Questions

(Test yourself first, then check the correct answers at the end of this quiz.)

1. Carl was divorced. He died in 2016, with a gross estate valued at $10,300,000. The estate also had the following activity:

Funeral and burial expenses	$42,000
Outstanding debt to a friend	200,000
Alimony paid to his ex-wife	75,000
State estate tax paid	25,000
Federal estate tax paid	125,000
FMV of land designated for donation to the American Humane Society	500,000

What is the total amount of the items listed that can be deducted from Carl's gross estate to determine the taxable estate?

A. $767,000
B. $892,000
C. $925,000
D. $967,000

2. In 2016, Jeffrey gives $25,000 to his girlfriend, Rachel. Which of the following statements is correct?

A. The first $14,000 of the gift is not subject to the gift tax, but the remainder is subject to gift tax, and Rachel is responsible for paying it.
B. Rachel is required to file a gift tax return and pay tax on the entire gift.
C. Jeffrey is required to file a gift tax return, Form 709.
D. Jeffrey may choose to report the gift tax on Form 1040, Schedule A.

3. Eileen's aunt gives her a gift of a remainder interest on her estate. Eileen will have full use of the estate after her aunt dies. Which is the correct statement about this gift?

A. Eileen can use the annual gift tax exclusion for this gift in 2016.
B. The gift is considered a present interest.
C. Eileen must pay estate tax on the gift in 2016.
D. Eileen cannot use the annual gift tax exclusion for this gift.

4. Max dies on May 1, 2016, and leaves his entire estate to his wife, Jeanne, a U.S. citizen. The estate is valued at $50 million. What amount of tax must Jeanne pay on her husband's estate in 2016?

A. $0
B. $5.45 million
C. $20 million
D. Unable to calculate because it depends on the amount of applicable credit.

5. Shawn, a single taxpayer, has never been required to file a gift tax return. In 2016, Shawn gave the following gifts:

- Tuition paid directly to a state university for an unrelated person: $18,000
- Payment to General Hospital for his brother's medical bills: $14,500
- Cash donations paid to his city's homeless shelter, a qualified 501(c)(3) organization: $50,000
- Political gift paid to the Libertarian Party (not a qualified 501(c)(3) charity): $15,000

Is Shawn required to file a gift tax return for 2016?

A. No.
B. Yes, because the donation to the political party is not an excludable gift.
C. Yes, because each of the gifts exceeded $14,000.
D. Yes, because the political gift is a reportable transaction.

6. Which of the following is not income in respect of a decedent?

A. Wages earned before death but still unpaid at the time of death.
B. Vacation time paid after death.
C. Taxable IRAs and retirement plans.
D. A royalty check that was received before death but not cashed.

7. When is an estate tax return due?

A. Four months after the close of the taxable year.
B. Six months after the close of the calendar year.
C. Nine months after the date of death.
D. Twelve months after the date of death.

8. Phil is unmarried and died in 2016. At the time of his death, he had assets of $4 million and owed debts of $500,000. He also had life insurance policies in place that paid $1 million to his only child. He had not used any of his basic exclusion amount during his lifetime. Based upon the information provided, what is the taxable amount of Phil's estate that must be reported on Form 706?

A. $0
B. $4 million
C. $4.5 million
D. $5 million

9. In general, who is responsible for paying gift tax?

A. The estate.
B. The donor.
C. The receiver of the gift.
D. The executor.

10. Delia's estate has funeral expenses for the cost of her burial. How should the executor deduct these costs?

A. Funeral expenses are an itemized deduction on Form 1040.
B. Funeral expenses are deducted on Form 1041.
C. Funeral expenses are deducted on Form 706.
D. Funeral expenses cannot be deducted as an expense.

11. Duncan died in 2015. Following his death, the executor of his estate paid the following bills. Which of these is not an allowable deduction in determining Duncan's taxable estate?

A. Administration expenses.
B. State inheritance taxes.
C. Charitable contributions.
D. Alimony paid after the taxpayer's death.

12. Alana had gifts totaling $28,000 in 2016 that were subject to gift tax. When is her gift tax return due?

A. March 15, 2017
B. April 18, 2017
C. October 15, 2017
D. September 15, 2017

13. Mandy was single. She died in 2016, and her executor did not elect the alternate valuation date. Given the following information, determine the value of Mandy's gross estate (all amounts listed are FMV at the date of her death):

- Household goods and personal effects: $25,000
- Antiques and collectibles: $300,000
- Certificates of deposit: $30,000
- Mortgage receivable on sale of property: $500,000
- Income tax refund due from Mandy's individual tax return: $6,000

A. $355,000
B. $361,000
C. $855,000
D. $861,000

14. Which of the following statements concerning the deceased spousal unused exclusion (DSUE) is correct?

A. The DSUE allows an unlimited estate tax deduction for a surviving spouse and his or her children.
B. The predeceased spouse must have died from natural causes.
C. The maximum DSUE available for a spouse who dies in 2016 is $14,000.
D. A portability election must be made by filing Form 706.

15. Emma's father dies during the year. Emma is the sole beneficiary of her father's traditional IRA. Emma is 46 years old when she takes possession of her father's IRA. Which of the following statements is correct about the distributions from the inherited IRA account?

A. Emma can avoid taxation by rolling over the assets of the IRA to another IRA or to a qualified plan.
B. The distributions are taxable to Emma, but not subject to an early withdrawal penalty.
C. Any tax on the distributions must be paid from her father's estate.
D. The distributions are taxable to Emma, and also subject to an early withdrawal penalty because Emma is younger than 59½.

16. Sandy and Matthew are married and have combined assets of $10 million. On May 10, 2016, Sandy dies. The FMV of Sandy's estate is $3.5 million on the date of her death. Matthew is the executor of his wife's estate and her sole heir. Since the value of Sandy's estate was below $5.45 million threshold, Matthew decides not to file an estate tax return, and he declines to take the portability election. What future impact does this have on Matthew, the surviving spouse?

A. There is no taxable effect on Matthew in this scenario.
B. Since Matthew declined to file an estate tax return, he did not elect portability. There will be estate tax due upon Matthew's death, assuming that the value of his assets does not decline, and there will be no deductions for estate tax purposes.
C. Matthew will owe tax in 2016 on his individual return from his inheritance.
D. Sandy's estate will owe estate tax in 2016. Her estate tax return must be filed by the executor.

17. The executor of Ophelia's estate is her sister, Elise. Elise decides to make a distribution of 100% of the estate's assets before paying the estate's income tax liability. Which of the following statements is correct?

A. The beneficiaries of the estate can be held liable for the payment of the liability, even if the liability exceeds the value of the estate assets.
B. No one can be held liable for the tax if the assets have been distributed.
C. The beneficiaries can be held liable for the tax debt, up to the value of the assets distributed.
D. None of the above.

18. Dustin pays $15,000 of college tuition for his niece, Delia, directly to her college. Which of the following statements is correct?

A. The gift is taxable, and Delia must report the gift tax on her individual tax return.
B. The gift is not taxable, but Dustin must file a gift tax return.
C. The gift is taxable, and Dustin must file a gift tax return.
D. The gift is not taxable, and no gift tax return is required.

19. Which of the following items is not an allowable deduction from the gross estate?

A. Debts owed at the time of death.
B. Medical expenses.
C. Funeral expenses.
D. Federal estate tax.

20. Bert and Sybil owned business property that they purchased for $100,000. They were joint tenants with right of survivorship. Each paid one-half of the purchase price. They took depreciation deductions prior to Sybil's death of $40,000. Under local law, each had a one-half interest in the income from the property. At the time of Sybil's death, the fair market value of the property was $200,000, one-half of which is includible in Sybil's estate. What is Bert's basis in the property after Sybil's death?

A. $80,000
B. $100,000
C. $130,000
D. $200,000

21. In which case must a gift tax return be filed?

A. A married couple gives a gift of $14,000 to an unrelated person.
B. A married couple gives a gift of $15,000 to a related person.
C. A single individual gives a gift of $4,000 to an unrelated person.
D. A wife gives a gift of $20,000 to her husband who is a U.S. citizen

22. All of the following gifts are excluded from the determination of the gift tax except:

A. A gift made to a political organization for its own use.
B. A cash gift given to a nonresident alien spouse of a U.S. citizen.
C. A medical bill paid directly to a hospital on behalf of a relative.
D. A gift made to a qualifying charity.

23. Janna is the executor for her father's estate. He died on November 5, 2016. Which of the following dates may she elect to use as an alternate valuation date for his estate?

A. January 1, 2017
B. April 15, 2018
C. May 5, 2017
D. October 15, 2017

24. Which of the following statements is incorrect regarding a married couple that uses gift splitting?

A. They must file a joint gift tax return along with their annual return (Form 1040).
B. They can give a gift of up to $28,000 to a single individual without using any of their basic exclusion amounts to avoid paying gift tax.
C. They must file gift tax returns even if no gift tax is owed.
D. Each must consent to split gifts.

25. Ida died in 2016. Which of the following assets would not be included in the calculation of her gross estate?

A. Life insurance proceeds payable to Ida's children.
B. The value of property transferred to Ida's son five years before her death.
C. The value of property owned jointly by Ida and her spouse.
D. The value of Ida's traditional IRA.

26. Cash inheritances are generally:

A. Taxable to the beneficiary.
B. Taxable for federal tax purposes, but not for state tax purposes.
C. Taxable in amounts over $2.5 million.
D. Not taxable to the beneficiary.

27. A taxpayer dies on May 4, 2016. Assuming that Form 706 needs to be filed for his estate, when is his estate tax due?

A. November 4, 2017
B. January 1, 2017
C. February 4, 2017
D. April 15, 2017

28. During 2016, prior to his death in December, Herman gave $30,000 to each of his two granddaughters. He also paid $80,000 directly to Birchland College for their college tuition costs. When Herman died, how much of his basic exclusion amount would he have used up as a result of these gifts?

A. $60,000
B. $140,000
C. $32,000
D. $112,000

29. Leighton received 100 shares of stock as an inheritance from her brother, who died on January 6, 2016. Her brother's adjusted basis in the stock was $14,750. The stock's fair market value on the date of her brother's death was $22,200. The executor of the estate elects the alternate valuation date for valuing the gross estate. Six months later, on July 6, 2016, the stock's fair market value was $23,100. Leighton finally received the stock on August 26, 2016, when its fair market value was $23,500. She sold the stock a week later for $23,450. What is Leighton's basis in the inherited stock?

A. $23,100
B. $23,500
C. $22,200
D. $14,750

Unit 19: Answers

1. The answer is A. Once the gross estate has been calculated, certain deductions (and in special circumstances, reductions to value) are allowed to determine the taxable estate. Federal estate taxes and alimony paid after the taxpayer's death are not deductible from the gross estate. Alimony payments are treated as distributions to a beneficiary and are therefore not included in the calculation of the taxable estate. The answer is calculated as follows: $42,000 funeral expenses + $200,000 outstanding debt + $25,000 state estate tax paid + $500,000 charitable gift of land = $767,000 allowable deductions.

2. The answer is C. Jeffrey is required to file a gift tax return. Gift tax is paid by the donor, not the recipient, of the gift. The first $14,000 of the gift is not subject to gift tax because of the annual exclusion. The remaining $11,000 is a taxable gift and must be reported on Form 709.

3. The answer is D. A gift of a future interest cannot be excluded under the annual exclusion ($14,000 per person in 2016). A gift is considered a present interest if the donee has all immediate rights to the use, possession, and enjoyment of the property or income from the property. A gift is considered a future interest if the donee's rights to the use, possession, and enjoyment of the property or income from the property will not begin until some future date. Future interests include reversions, remainders, and other similar interests or estates.

4. The answer is A. Jeanne will owe no estate taxes related to the value of Max's estate. The marital deduction allows for the transfer of an unlimited value of property from one spouse to another during his lifetime or from his estate after death without being subject to gift or estate taxes. To qualify for this unlimited deduction, the spouse receiving the assets must be a U.S. citizen and a legal spouse, and must have outright ownership of the assets.

5. The answer is A. None of the gifts are taxable, and no reporting is required. Tuition or medical expenses paid for someone directly to an educational or medical institution are not counted as taxable gifts. Nor are gifts to a political organization for its own use or gifts to a qualified charity.

6. The answer is D. Since the royalty check was received before the taxpayer died, it is not considered IRD income. Income in respect of a decedent is taxable income earned but not received by the decedent by the time of death. The fact that the royalty check was not cashed has no bearing on the nature of the income, and it should be reported as taxable income on the decedent's final income tax return (Form 1040).

7. The answer is C. Estate tax returns are due nine months from the date of death, although the executor may request an extension of time to file.

8. The answer is A. After calculating allowable deductions from the gross estate, Phil's net estate is valued at $4.5 million. This amount is less than the basic exclusion amount of $5.45 million for 2016, so no estate tax is applicable in this case. Also, because the gross value of the estate was less than $5.45 million an estate tax return is not required to be filed.

Assets	$4,000,000
Minus liabilities	(500,000)
Life insurance proceeds	1,000,000
Net Estate	**$4,500,000**

9. The answer is B. The donor is generally responsible for paying gift tax.

10. The answer is C. No deduction for funeral expenses can be taken on Form 1041 or Form 1040. Funeral expenses may be claimed only as a deduction from the gross estate on Form 706.

11. The answer is D. Alimony paid after a taxpayer's death is not deductible from the gross estate. It is considered a distribution to a beneficiary. Deductions from the gross estate are allowed for:

- Funeral expenses paid out of the estate and administration expenses for the estate
- Debts owed at the time of death
- The marital deduction, charitable deduction, and state death tax deduction

12. The answer is B. Alana would be required to file her gift tax return by April 18, 2017, the filing deadline for individual returns. Gift tax returns are typically due on April 15 of the following calendar year (the filing deadline), and payment of the tax is also due then, although the filing may be subject to a six-month extension. If the donor died during the year, the filing deadline is the due date for his estate tax return.

13. The answer is D. All of the property listed is included in determination of the gross estate. The gross estate is based upon the fair market value of the decedent's property, which is not necessarily equal to her cost, and includes:

- The FMV of all tangible and intangible property owned partially or outright by the decedent at the time of death
- Life insurance proceeds payable to the estate or, for policies owned by the decedent, payable to the heirs
- The value of certain annuities or survivor benefits payable to the heirs
- The value of certain property that was transferred within three years before the decedent's death

The gross estate does not include property owned solely by the decedent's spouse or other individuals. Lifetime gifts that are complete (so that no control over the gifts was retained) are not included in the gross estate.

14. The answer is D. The portability election allows a surviving spouse's estate the right to use a deceased spousal unused exclusion (DSUE), which is the remaining unused portion of the previously deceased spouse's basic exclusion amount. In 2016, an individual can leave $5.45 million estate tax-free at death. The portability election must be made by filing an estate tax return for the deceased spouse, even if no estate tax is owed.

15. The answer is B. The IRA distributions are taxable to Emma, but not subject to a penalty. Distributions of retirement plan benefits or distributions from taxable IRA accounts to a decedent's beneficiaries are generally subject to income tax when received. The decedent's surviving spouse may be able to defer taxation by rolling over the assets of a taxable IRA to another IRA or to a qualified plan. However, a child or other beneficiary is not allowed this same treatment. Qualified distributions from a Roth IRA or of previously nondeductible contributions to a traditional IRA are generally not taxable.

16. The answer is B. Since Matthew declined to file an estate tax return, he did not elect portability. No estate tax is due after Sandy's death because the value of her estate is below the exclusion amount. However, all her assets passed to her surviving spouse. Matthew's estate is now in excess of the annual exclusion amount. Assuming there is no change in the value of Matthew's assets and no applicable deductions upon his passing, there will be estate tax due upon his death. He could have avoided this scenario if he had filed an estate tax return and elected portability.

17. The answer is C. The tax liability for an estate attaches to the assets of the estate itself. If the assets are distributed to the beneficiaries before the taxes are paid, the beneficiaries can be held liable for the tax debt, up to the value of the assets distributed.

18. The answer is D. Tuition or medical expenses paid directly to a medical or educational institution for someone else are not included in the calculation of taxable gifts, and there is no reporting requirement.

19. The answer is D. Federal estate tax is not deductible from the gross estate. The other items listed are allowable deductions from the gross estate. The decedent's unpaid medical expenses represent liabilities that can be deducted from the gross estate. Alternatively, if the expenses are paid by the estate during the one-year period beginning with the day after death, the personal representative can elect to treat all or part of the expenses as paid by the decedent at the time they were incurred, and deduct them on the decedent's final tax return (1040).

20. The answer is B. When they purchased the property, Bert's basis was $50,000 ($100,000 × .50. He was allowed half of the depreciation ($40,000 ÷ 2 = $20,000), which decreased his basis to $30,000. When Bert acquired the property in its entirety after Sybil's death, the fair market value of the portion owned by Sybil was included, based on the stepped-up basis of $200,000. The one-half portion representing Sybil's interest ($200,000 × .50 = $100,000) is added to Bert's basis for a final basis of $130,000.

21. The answer is B. In order to make a gift to one individual in excess of the annual exclusion of $14,000 and avoid using any of their basic exclusion amounts; a married couple can use gift splitting. Gift splitting allows married couples to give up to $28,000 to a person without making a taxable gift ($14,000 from each spouse), but they each must consent to the gift, and each may be required to file a gift tax return. Alternatively, the gift of $15,000 could be considered to have been from only one spouse (without using gift splitting); that spouse would need to file a gift tax return because the gift exceeds the annual exclusion of $14,000. Gifts to a spouse generally do not require a return to be filed, unless the spouse is not a U.S. citizen.

22. The answer is B. Although a full marital deduction is allowed for a spouse who is a U.S. citizen, a transfer of property to a noncitizen spouse is limited to $148,000 in 2016, and the excess amount would be subject to gift tax.

23. The answer is C. An estate is normally valued on the date of the decedent's death. However, an executor may elect an alternate valuation date for an estate, which would be six months after the date of death. The estate value and related estate tax must be less than they would have been on the date of the taxpayer's death.

24. The answer is A. If a married couple splits a gift, each spouse must generally file his or her own individual gift tax return. Couples cannot file a joint gift return. However, certain exceptions allow for only one spouse to file a return if the other spouse signifies consent on the donor spouse's Form 709.

25. The answer is B. The value of property transferred to Ida's son five years before her death would not be included in her gross estate. A taxpayer's gross estate includes the following:

- The FMV of all tangible and intangible property owned partially or outright by the decedent at the time of death
- Life insurance proceeds payable to the estate or, for policies owned by the decedent, payable to the heirs or beneficiaries
- The value of certain annuities or survivor benefits payable to the heirs or beneficiaries

- The value of certain property transferred within three years before the taxpayer's death (not five years, as stated in answer B)

26. The answer is D. For federal income tax purposes, cash inheritances are generally not taxable to the beneficiary, although the beneficiary may be responsible for a related estate tax liability that has not been satisfied.

27. The answer is C. If required to be filed, Form 706, *United States Estate (and Generation-Skipping Transfer) Tax Return,* must be filed nine months after the date of a decedent's death. The estate tax would be owed at this time. An executor may request a six-month extension to file Form 706, but the tax would still be owed on the earlier date.

28. The answer is C. Each granddaughter's cash gift of $30,000 would have been reduced by the annual exclusion amount of $14,000, and a portion of Herman's basic exclusion amount would have been used to avoid payment of gift tax on the excess amount of $16,000. Thus, he used a total of $16,000 for each granddaughter, or $32,000. Since the $80,000 was paid directly to Birchland College on behalf of the granddaughters, it was not subject to gift tax, and none of his basic exclusion amount would have been used as a result of these additional gifts. It should be noted that his cash gifts to the granddaughters would also be subject to generation-skipping tax.

29. The answer is A. The basis of property received from a decedent is generally the fair market value of the property on the date of the decedent's death. However, an executor has the option of choosing an alternate valuation date, which is six months after the date of death for valuing the gross estate. Since the alternate valuation date was elected by the executor, the Leighton's basis is the fair market value on the alternate valuation date, or $23,100.

PART 2: BUSINESSES

Essential Tax Law Updates for Businesses

Part Two

2016 Social Security Taxable Wage Base: $118,500 (unchanged from 2015). A combined tax rate of 12.4% applies up to this limit, consisting of employee and employer portions of 6.2% each. The Social Security tax rate for self-employed persons is 12.4%.

2016 Medicare Taxable Wage Base: No limit. A combined tax rate of 2.9% applies, consisting of employee and employer portions of 1.45% each. The Medicare rate for self-employed persons is 2.9%.

FUTA Wage Base: The FUTA tax rate is 6% on the first $7,000 paid to each employee.

2016 Mileage Rates:

- Business: 54¢ per mile
- Charitable purposes: 14¢ per mile
- Medical and moving: 19¢ per mile

2016 Retirement Plans:

- SIMPLE Plan maximum employee deferrals: $12,500 (age 50 and over: $15,500)
- SEP annual contribution limit maximum:
    - The lesser of 25% of compensation or $53,000
- Traditional and Roth IRA Contribution Limit: $5,500 (age 50 and over: $6,500)

2016 Traditional IRA Phase-out Based on MAGI (Participants in Employer Plans):

- Married Filing Jointly: $98,000 - $118,000
- Married Filing Separately: $0 - $10,000
- All other filing statuses: $61,000 - $71,000
- Nonparticipant married to a participant: $184,000 - $194,000

*If *neither* spouse is a participant in an employer plan, the traditional IRA contribution is fully deductible.

Roth IRA Phase-out Based on MAGI:

- Married Filing Jointly: $184,000 - $194,000
- Married Filing Separately: $0 - $10,000
- All other filing statuses: $117,000 - $132,000

*Roth conversions (the "backdoor" Roth IRA) are still allowable in tax year 2016.

401, 403, and 457 Plans:

- Maximum employee elective deferral: $18,000
- Employee catch-up contribution (age 50 or older): $6,000

- Defined contribution maximum limit from all sources: $53,000 (this maximum amount includes employee deferrals, employer contributions, and catch-up contributions).

2016 Gift and Estate Tax Thresholds:

- Estate and Gift Tax Rate 40%
- Combined Estate and Gift Tax Exclusion: $5,450,000
- Annual Gift exclusion: $14,000 (unchanged from 2015)
- Gift to non-citizen spouse: $148,000

Estates (Exemption Amounts)

- A bankruptcy estate is allowed a personal exemption of $4,050 and a standard deduction of $6,300 for tax year 2016.
- A decedent's estate is allowed a $600 exemption.

2016 Generation-Skipping Transfer (GST) Tax:

- GST Tax Rate: 40%
- GST Tax Exemption: $5,450,000

AMT Exemption for Trusts and Estates (Based on AMTI): $ 79,850 - $175,450

Section 179 Deduction

- $500,000 limit and $2 million reduction threshold were made permanent and also indexed for inflation ($2,010,000 beginning phase-out for 2016)
- Special allowance for depreciable software made permanent
- Section 179 is now allowed for certain air conditioning and heating units (for property placed in service after December 31, 2015).
- The Section 179 election can be revoked (but once revoked, it becomes irrevocable)
- Congress extended the Section 179 eligibility for qualified leasehold improvement, and the $250,000 cap attributable to Qualified leasehold improvement property has been removed for 2016.

Accelerated filing dates for information returns: Employers are now required to file all Form W -2s with the federal government by January 31, 2017. This accelerated filing date also applies to any Form 1099-MISC that shows nonemployee compensation.

Estate consistent basis reporting: New reporting rules (IRC Section 6035) now require the basis of property acquired from a decedent to be consistent with the property's basis as reported on the decedent's estate tax return. A $260 penalty applies for failure to file Form 8971 and furnish Schedules A. A new version of Form 8971, *Information Regarding Beneficiaries Acquiring Property from a Decedent*, was issued December 18, 2015, along with updated instructions.

New Safe Harbor for De Minimis Errors: Starting in 2016, the IRS has established a safe harbor from penalties for the failure to file correct information returns and for failure to furnish correct payee statements by providing that if the error is $100 or less ($25 or less in the case of errors involving tax withholding). The issuer of the statement is not required to file a corrected return unless the recipient requests one. This provision is effective for information returns and statements required to be filed after December 31, 2016.

Updated Entity Tax Return Deadlines

- Partnership and S Corporation tax returns will be due the 15th day of the third month after the end of their tax year (March 15 for calendar-year entities).
- C Corporation tax returns will be due the 15th day of the fourth month after the end of the tax year. (April 15 for calendar-year corporations). A special rule to defer the due date change for C Corporations with fiscal years that end on June 30 defers this change until December 31, 2025 (a full ten years).
- The due date for businesses furnishing to individuals/employees the Form 1095-B, Health Coverage, has changed from January 31, 2017, to March 2, 2017.
- New FBAR filing deadline: FBARS (FinCen Form 114) will now be due on April 15, with a with a maximum 6-month extension to October 15. Previously, a taxpayer could not request an extension to file the FBAR, and the FBAR was due on June 15.

New Extension Deadlines:

- Partnerships will have a longer extension period, a maximum of six months, (rather than the previous five-month extension),
- Fiduciary returns for Estates and Trusts (Form 1041) will be allowed an extension of five and a half months, two weeks longer than the previous five-month extension.
- The Form 5500 (Annual Return/Report of Employee Benefit Plan) will have a maximum automatic extension of three and half months.
- Form 990 (Return of Organization Exempt From Income Tax) will have a maximum automatic extension of six months (the previous automatic extension period was three months).
- C Corporation extensions: In 2017, the IRS decided to grant a full 6-month extension for calendar-year C corporations, under the authority of Code Sec. 6081(a) instead of the five months as stated in IRC Sect. 6081(b). The new deadline is reflected in the updated Instructions to Form 7004, which were revised on February 2, 2017.

Permanent Tax Law Extensions

- The Research Credit (IRC § 41): Small start-ups can claim $250,000 of research and development credits to offset its share of social security taxes instead of their regular income tax liability.
- The Employee Wage Credit for employees who are active duty members of the uniformed services was extended and made permanent (IRC §45P)
- The exclusion of 100% of gain on certain small business stock was made permanent (IRC § 1202)
- Military housing allowance exclusion for determining whether a tenant in certain areas is low-income (IRC § 142(d)(2)(B)(ii))
- The basis adjustment to stock of S corporations making charitable contributions of property was made permanent (IRC § 1367)

Temporary Business Extensions

- Bonus depreciation provisions extended five years (slated to expire in 2019)
    - 50% through 2017
    - 40% 2018
    - 30% 2019 (bonus depreciation is set to phase out completely in 2019)
- Expansion of election to accelerate AMT credits in lieu of Bonus Depreciation extended through 2019

Extended Business Credits

- New Markets Tax Credit
- Work Opportunity Tax Credit was renewed and expanded to include long-term unemployed individuals.

Information Return Penalties Increased

Penalties for failure to file correct information returns have increased in 2016. The penalty for failure to file or furnish a correct information return after August 1 is now $260.

Form W-2 Verification Code IRS Initiative: A Verification Code will appear on some versions of Form W-2 in a separate, labeled box. This IRS initiative is one in a series of steps to combat identity theft and refund fraud. This code only used for e-file purposes and is not entered on paper-filed returns. Omitted and incorrect W-2 Verification Codes will currently not delay the processing of a tax return.

Enhancement of Food Inventory Donations: Starting in 2016, non-corporate taxpayers are now allowed to benefit from newly increased 15% taxable income limitation of food inventory donations (IRC Section 170(e)(3)(C)). In general, the donation must be made to qualifying 501(c)(3) organizations.

TEFRA Repealed: The *Bipartisan Budget Act of 2015* included major changes to the way the IRS will audit partnerships. The budget act repeals the current TEFRA partnership audit rules, replacing them with a new procedure that will make it easier for the IRS to audit partnerships. The new rules generally apply after December 31, 2017. However, partnerships may elect for these changes to apply to any partnership return filed for tax years beginning after November 2, 2015. All partnerships may elect to adopt the new rules for their 2016 tax returns (Form 1065).

21st Century Cures Act: Signed by President Obama in December, 2016, this health bill grants small businesses regulatory relief for employers who wish to offer insurance reimbursements to their employees. Employer reimbursements under this type of Health Reimbursement Arrangement may not exceed $4,950 for the employee per year (or $10,000 per year for family coverage).

Unit 1: Business Entities and Requirements

More Reading:

Publication 583, *Starting a Business and Keeping Records*

Publication 1635, *Understanding Your EIN*

Publication 334, *Tax Guide for Small Business*

Publication 1779, *Independent Contractor or Employee*

Publication 505, *Tax Withholding and Estimated Tax*

Overview of EA Exam Part 2: Businesses

For Part 2 of the enrolled agent exam, you will be expected to know a broad range of information about tax provisions that affect various types of businesses. You will need to understand the different types of businesses, including sole proprietorships, partnerships, corporations, and farming businesses, as well as trusts and estates, retirement plans, and tax-exempt organizations, and the special tax laws that apply to each.

Specifically, Part 2 of the exam is broken down into the following sections and corresponding percentages of questions:

- 45%: *Entities in general* (business entities; partnerships; corporations in general; forming a corporation; S corporations),
- 40%: *Business Financial Information* (business income; business expenses, deductions, and credits; business assets; analysis of financial records; advising the business taxpayer), and
- 15%: *Specialized Returns and Taxpayers* (trust and estate income tax; exempt organizations; retirement plans; farmers).

We start with an overview of the different types of business entities. Each has its own drawbacks, risks, and benefits. We briefly review each type below and will examine the more complex entities in greater depth in later units.

Sole Proprietorships

A sole proprietorship is not a separate legal entity. It is an unincorporated business that is owned and controlled by one person. A sole proprietorship may be a single-person business or it may have several employees, but there is only one owner who accepts all the risk and liability of the business. It is the simplest business type and also the easiest to start. An estimated 70% of businesses in the United States are sole proprietorships.

A sole proprietorship cannot be passed on to a new owner as the same business entity because, by definition, a sole proprietorship is owned and operated by a single, specific individual. If a business operated as a sole proprietorship is sold, it must be operated by the new owner as either a different sole proprietorship or as a different type of business entity through a sale of assets.

A taxpayer does not have to conduct full-time business activities to be considered self-employed. Operating a part-time business in addition to having a regular job or business may also be self-employment, and may therefore constitute a sole proprietorship.

An activity qualifies as a business if its primary purpose is for profit and if the taxpayer is involved in the activity with continuity and regularity. A hobby, which is not conducted for profit, does not qualify as a business.

Sole proprietors often receive Forms 1099-MISC from their business customers showing income they were paid.

The amounts reported on Forms 1099-MISC, along with any other business income, are reported and taxed on the taxpayer's personal income tax return. Income and expenses from the sole proprietorship are reported on Schedule C**,** *Profit or Loss from Business,* of Form 1040.

A taxpayer may use the simplified Schedule C-EZ if he:

- Had business expenses of $5,000 or less
- Did not claim any depreciation expense
- Used the cash method of accounting
- Did not have inventory at any time during the year
- Did not have a net loss from the business and had no prior year passive activity losses
- Was the sole proprietor for only one business
- Had no employees during the year
- Did not deduct expenses for business use of his home and had no depreciation or amortization to report for the year

A self-employed individual with net earnings of $400 or more from self-employment is required to pay self-employment tax by filing Schedule SE, *Self-Employment Tax*, with his Form 1040.

Example: Darius works as an independent plumbing contractor for Conway Construction Inc. Conway Construction sends Darius a Form 1099-MISC that shows he received $25,000 for contract work in 2016. He also received payments of $7,000 from several individuals for contract work he completed on their homes. Although Darius did not receive Forms 1099-MISC for the $7,000, he must include the payments as self-employment income, along with the $25,000 from Conway, on his Schedule C.

Married Couple Businesses

Often, a small business is operated by a husband and wife without incorporating or creating a formal partnership agreement. The business is usually considered a partnership, whether or not there is a formal partnership agreement.

If both spouses materially participate as the only members of a jointly owned and operated business, the business may be treated as a *qualified joint venture*. This allows them to avoid the complexity of filing a partnership return, but still allows each spouse to take credit for self-employment earnings from the business for Social Security purposes. Items of business income, gain, loss, deduction, and credit are split between the spouses in accordance with their respective interests in the business. The spouses then file separate Schedules C and separate Schedules SE. This option is available only to married taxpayers who file joint tax returns.

A qualified joint venture is available only to businesses owned and operated by spouses as co-owners and not in the name of a state law entity; spousal owners of a limited liability company or a limited partnership do not qualify.

Note: Federal tax law makes many references to laws specific to a "husband and wife." These laws also apply to same-sex spouses who were legally married.

Partnerships

A partnership is a relationship that exists between two or more taxpayers who join together to carry on a trade or business. Each person contributes money, property, labor, or skill and expects to share in the profits and losses of the business.

A partnership must file an annual information return to report the income, deductions, gains, and losses from its operations, but the partnership itself generally does not pay income tax. Instead, any profits or losses "pass through" to its partners, who are then responsible for reporting their respective shares of the partnership's income or loss on their individual returns.

Example: James and Madeline are father and daughter who operate the Hunnicutt Consulting Partnership. Each is active in the business, and each has an equal share in partnership interests and profits. The partnership must file Form 1065 to report its income and loss for the year. The partnership must also issue a Schedule K-1 to each partner. In 2016, Hunnicutt Consulting had $80,000 of net ordinary income. Since they share profits and losses equally, James and Madeline will each report $40,000 of self-employment partnership income on their individual tax returns. A taxpayer's share of Partnership income is reported on page 2 of Schedule E, *Supplemental Income and Loss (From rental real estate, royalties, partnerships, S corporations, estates, trusts, REMICs, etc.)*.

A partnership must always have at least one *general partner* whose actions legally bind the business and who is legally responsible for a partnership's debts and liabilities.

The default legal classification for a partnership is a *general partnership* where all partners are *general* partners with each partner jointly and severally liable for the debts and obligations of the partnership.

A "limited" partnership is a partnership that has at least one limited partner in addition to its general partner(s). A limited partnership allows an investor to own an interest in a business without assuming personal liability or risk beyond the amount of his investment. A *limited partner* has no obligation to contribute additional capital to the partnership, and therefore does not have an economic risk of loss for partnership liabilities.

Example: Santino wants to open a dance club. He approaches his aunt, Julia, for the funds. Julia agrees to invest in her nephew's business, but she does not want to be involved in the day-to-day running of the club. After consulting with an advisor, Santino and his aunt form a limited partnership. Per their partnership agreement, Julia is a limited partner. She is an investor in the club. She gives her nephew $250,000 to establish the club. Santino is an experienced restaurateur and nightlife expert, so he runs the club. Santino is the general partner.

A partnership can look very different depending on how it is structured; it can be anything from a small business run by a married couple to a complex business organization with hundreds of general partners and limited partners as investors. A partnership can have an unlimited number of partners.

An unincorporated organization with two or more owners is generally classified as a partnership for federal tax purposes if its members carry on a business and divide its profits. However, a joint undertaking merely to share expenses is not a partnership. For example, co-ownership of rental property is usually not considered a formal partnership unless the co-owners provide substantial services to the tenants.

Example: Anderson and Sal are cousins who own a rental property together. Each owns a 50% interest in the rental. Anderson takes care of any repairs, and Sal collects and divides the rent. They do not have any other business with each other. The co-ownership of the rental property is not considered a partnership for tax purposes. Instead, they would divide the income and expenses based on their ownership percentages, and each would report his respective share on Schedule E on his individual return.

A partnership's annual tax return is filed on Form 1065, *U.S. Return of Partnership Income.* Partners are not employees of the business, and they should not be issued a Form W-2. Instead, the partnership must furnish a copy of Schedule K-1 to each of its partners, showing the income and losses allocated to him. A partnership return must show the name and address of each partner and the partner's share of taxable income. The return must be signed by a general partner. A limited partner may not sign the return or represent a partnership before the IRS.

A **Limited Liability Partnership (LLP)** is an entity that is formed under state law by filing articles of organization as an LLP and is generally used for specific professional services, such as those offered by a law or CPA firm. Typically, an LLP allows each partner to actively participate in management affairs but still provides limited liability protection to each partner. A partner in an LLP generally would not be personally liable for the partnership debts or the malpractice of other partners (or the employees under the management of other partners) and would only be at risk for his own malpractice and his interest in the partnership's assets.[82]

Example: Leigh and Martin are CPAs in California who decide to go into business with each other. They form an LLP by registering their business with California's Secretary of State. Once they complete their registration, they open an office and begin accepting accounting clients. For tax purposes, their business will be taxed as a partnership, and they will be required to file a Form 1065 every year. In a limited liability partnership, the partners enjoy some protection against personal legal liability.

C Corporations

When forming a corporation, prospective shareholders provide money, property, or both in exchange for the issuance of the corporation's capital stock. A corporation is considered an entity separate from its shareholders and must elect a board of directors who are responsible for oversight of the company. A corporation conducts business, realizes net income or loss, and distributes profits to shareholders.

Most major companies are organized as C corporations. C corporations and S corporations (discussed below) are differentiated for tax purposes only. Legally they are both simply corporations.

A C corporation may have an unlimited number of shareholders and may be either foreign or domestic. A C corporation must file annual income tax returns on Form 1120, *U.S. Corporation Income Tax Return,* to report its net income and losses, and pay tax on its income. Its after-tax profits may also be taxable income to its shareholders when distributed as dividends, resulting in double taxation.

The corporation does not receive a tax deduction when it distributes dividends to shareholders, and shareholders cannot deduct any losses of the corporation.

A corporation generally takes the same deductions as a sole proprietorship to figure its taxable income, but is also allowed certain special deductions.

S Corporations

An S corporation is a distinct form of entity organized under applicable state law as a corporation but specially applied for with the IRS for tax purposes. For federal income tax purposes, an S corporation is generally not subject to tax; instead its income, losses, deductions, and credits are passed through to its shareholders in a manner similar to a partnership. However, the S corporation itself may be responsible for tax on certain built-in gains and passive investment income.

An S corporation is required to file an annual income tax return to report its income or loss using Form 1120S, *U.S. Tax Return for an S Corporation.* It also reports each shareholder's applicable share of income or losses on Schedules K-1. The shareholders report the pass-through income or loss on their individual tax returns. As a result, the shareholders of S corporations are generally able to avoid double federal taxation on their corporate income.

S corporations must meet the following requirements:

- Be a domestic corporation.

[82] The laws regarding LLPs and LLCs vary greatly from state-to-state. Information is generally available online through a state's secretary of state's office or the governor's office.

- Have only "permitted" shareholders (partnerships, corporations[83], and nonresident aliens are not eligible).
- Have no more than 100 shareholders.
- Have only one class of stock (voting and nonvoting stock are not considered to be separate classes of stock, as long as they have identical rights to distribution and liquidation proceeds).
- Not be an ineligible type of corporation (certain financial institutions, insurance companies, and domestic international sales corporations are not eligible for S corporation status).

Limited Liability Companies (LLC)

A limited liability company (LLC) is another type of business entity that may be formed under state law. Depending upon whether it has a single member (owner) or multiple members, it will be treated for federal tax purposes either as a part of the owner's individual (or corporate if owned 100% by a corporation) tax return (a "disregarded entity," as described further below) or as a partnership, unless it elects to be treated as a corporation. Most LLCs are taxed as partnerships. Thus, like the owners of S corporations and partnerships, the members of an LLC can avoid double taxation.

An LLC can provide the liability protection of a corporation with the tax benefits of a partnership.

Unlike a partnership, none of the members of an LLC are personally liable for its debts. If a limited liability company (LLC) is treated as a partnership for tax purposes, it must file Form 1065 annually and one of its owners must sign the return.

Personal Service Corporations (PSC)

The IRS classifies a business as a personal service corporation (PSC) if its principal activity during the prior tax year is performing personal services. Personal services include any activity performed in the fields of accounting, actuarial science, architecture, consulting, engineering, health (including veterinary services), law, and the performing arts. The majority of a PSC's stock is typically owned by employees, retired employees, or their estates.

Note: Unlike other corporations, personal service corporations are always taxed at a flat rate of 35%. An S corporation cannot be a PSC, so the PSC tax rate applies only to C corporations. If the taxpayer makes an S election and has his income directly taxed as distributions, the 35% tax rate does not apply.

Farmers and Fishermen

Farming businesses are primarily engaged in crop production, animal production, or forestry and logging. They may include stock, dairy, poultry, fish, fruit, and tree farms, as well as plantations, ranches, timber farms, and orchards. It is the nature of the activity and not the entity type that determines whether a business qualifies as a farming business.

Congress has enacted many tax laws specific to farming that provide special tax treatment and reflect the highly unpredictable nature of the business. For example, farmers have a different schedule for paying estimated taxes; they may postpone gain or income in certain cases that other businesses cannot; they can deduct a higher percentage of mileage expenses than other businesses, and they are given special tax considerations when disaster strikes.

Farming and fishing businesses operating as sole proprietorships report income and loss on Schedule F, *Profit or Loss from Farming*, of Form 1040. A farmer is typically self-employed if he operates his own farm or rents farmland from others to engage in the business of farming.

[83] There is an exception for S corporations who own 100% of another S corporation under certain circumstances, as well as an exception for 501(C)(3) organizations that are organized as corporations.

Self-employed farmers and fishermen must also complete Schedule SE to determine self-employment taxes due. A farming business may also be organized as a partnership or a corporation.

Tax-Exempt Organizations (Nonprofit Entities)

The Internal Revenue Code (IRC 501(c)(3))[84] outlines the requirements for tax-exempt organizations. They must be organized and operated exclusively for charitable, educational, or religious purposes, and none of their earnings may be used to benefit any private shareholder or individual. Nonprofit organizations may be created as corporations, trusts, or unincorporated associations, but never as partnerships or sole proprietorships.

Most organizations must request tax-exempt status by filing Form 1023, *Application for Recognition of Exemption.* However, churches, including synagogues, temples, and mosques, are treated as tax-exempt by default and do not have to apply for exemption.

An exempt organization must annually file Form 990, *Return of Organization Exempt from Income Tax,* to report its income and losses. Form 990 is usually an informational return only, but a nonprofit organization may be taxed on activities outside the scope of its tax-exempt status.

Entity Classification Election Rules

Certain business entities may choose how they will be classified for tax purposes by filing Form 8832, *Entity Classification Election*.

An LLC with a single member is classified as an entity "disregarded," or as not being separate from its owner for income tax purposes, unless the owner files Form 8832 and chooses to be taxed as a corporation. Thus, a single-owner LLC owned by an individual is treated as a sole proprietorship and the owner is subject to the tax on net earnings from self-employment if the LLC is a trade or business.

Similarly, a single-owner LLC owned by a corporation or a partnership is included in the owner's tax return as if it were a division of the corporation or partnership. A domestic LLC with at least two members is considered a partnership by default, unless it files Form 8832 and elects to be treated as a corporation.

An election to change an LLC's classification cannot take effect more than 75 days prior to the date the election is filed; nor can it take effect later than 12 months after the date the election is filed. Once a business entity makes an election to change its classification, it generally cannot change the election again within five years (60 months).

The 60-month limitation does not apply if the previous election was made by a newly formed eligible entity and was effective on the date of formation.

Example: Kelly and Ned are married and own their own business, an LLC, which is treated as a partnership for tax purposes. A few months later, they decide to change the classification and be taxed as a corporation, so they file Form 8832. At this point, if Kelly and Ned change their minds again and want their business to be classified as a partnership, they would have to wait at least 60 months (five years).

Employer Identification Number (EIN)

An employer identification number is used for reporting purposes. Unlike Social Security numbers that are assigned to individuals, EINs are assigned to business entities. A business must apply for an EIN if any of the following apply:

- The business pays employees

[84] The Internal Revenue Code is the basis of federal tax law. It is enacted by Congress in Title 26 of the United States Code.

- The business operates as a corporation, exempt organization, trust, estate, or partnership
- The business files any of these tax returns:
    - Employment
    - Excise
    - Alcohol, Tobacco, and Firearms
- The business withholds taxes paid to a nonresident alien
- The business establishes a pension, profit-sharing, or retirement plan

If a sole proprietor has no employees, he is not required to obtain an EIN. However, an EIN can be requested by a sole proprietor who simply wishes to protect his Social Security number for privacy reasons. This way, a sole proprietor can provide his EIN rather than his SSN to companies that need to issue him a Form 1099-MISC for independent contractor payments. If a sole proprietor decides to form a business entity such as a partnership or corporation, he will be required to request an EIN for each separate entity. A new EIN is required for any of the following changes:

- When a sole proprietor or partnership decides to incorporate
- When a sole proprietor takes on a partner and becomes a partnership
- When a partnership becomes a sole proprietorship (for example, when one partner dies)
- When a sole proprietor files for bankruptcy under Chapter 7 or Chapter 11
- When a taxpayer terminates one partnership and begins another partnership
- When a business establishes a pension, profit-sharing, or retirement plan

New EIN Not Required

A business does not need to apply for a new EIN in any of the following instances:

- To change the name of a business
- To change the location or add locations (stores, plants, enterprises, or branches of the same entity)
- If a sole proprietor operates multiple businesses (including stores, plants, enterprises, or branches of the same entity)

Further, a single-member limited liability company (LLC) classified as a disregarded entity may use the owner's SSN or EIN and does not need a separate EIN, unless the business is required to file employment or excise tax returns.

Taxpayers can apply for an EIN online or manually file Form SS-4, *Application for Employer Identification Number.*

Recordkeeping for Businesses

Adequate records help a taxpayer to monitor business operations, verify his income and expenses, and support expenses on his tax return. Except in a few cases, the law does not require a business to keep any specific kind of records or to use a particular recordkeeping system, so long as the system clearly shows a business's income and expenses.

The taxpayer's recordkeeping system should include a summary of business transactions, which is usually made in the taxpayer's books, such as accounting journals and ledgers. The books must show the business's gross income, as well as its deductions and credits. Additional documents must be kept to support these entries. These include sales slips, paid bills, invoices, receipts, deposit slips, canceled checks, credit card charge slips, cash register tapes, Forms 1099-MISC, invoices, mileage logs, and cell phone records.

Electronic records are acceptable so long as they provide a complete and accurate record of data that is accessible to the IRS in a legible format. They are subject to the same controls and retention guidelines as those used for the taxpayer's original hard copy books and records.

Taxpayers must keep records as long as they are needed for the administration of any provision of the Internal Revenue Code. Usually, this means the business must keep records long enough to support income and deductions until the statute of limitations for a related tax return has expired.

Definition: A **"statute of limitation"** is a time period to review and analyze tax-related issues. The Internal Revenue Code requires that the IRS must assess, refund, credit, and collect taxes within specific time limits known as the statute of limitations. When they expire, the IRS can no longer assess additional tax, allow a claim for refund by the taxpayer, or take collection action.

Generally, a taxpayer must keep records for at least three years from when a tax return was due or was filed, whichever is later. If a business has employees, it must keep all employment tax records for at least four years.

Taxpayers must keep records relating to property until the statute of limitations expires for the year in which the property is sold or otherwise disposed of. These records are needed to figure any depreciation, amortization, or depletion deductions, and to figure basis for computing gain or loss. A taxpayer may need to keep records relating to the basis of property even longer since they may be important in determining the basis of replacement property.

Business funds should be kept separate from personal funds. The IRS is more likely to audit a business and deny deductions and losses if there is no clear separation between business and personal expenses. A separate bank account for business-related transactions is advisable, with business-related bills paid from it rather than from a personal account.

Business Reporting Requirements

Businesses are subject to a number of reporting requirements, including the following:

Form 8300: When a business receives a cash payment of more than $10,000 from one transaction or from two or more related transactions, it must file Form 8300, *Report of Cash Payments Over $10,000 Received in a Trade or Business,* by the fifteenth day after the date of the cash transaction. This requirement also applies to certain other monetary instruments, such as traveler's checks, money orders, and cashier's checks.

By January 31 of the year following the reportable transaction, it must also provide to each person whose name is required to be included in Form 8300 a written statement that shows the aggregate amount of reportable cash transactions the business reported to the IRS for that person. These requirements are intended to assist in efforts to combat money laundering.

Form W-2: A business must complete and file with the Social Security Administration Forms W-2, *Wage and Tax Statement,* showing the wages paid and taxes withheld for the year for each employee. A copy of the W-2 must be given to each current and former employee who received taxable wages or salaries during the year by no later than January 31 of the following year. Employers filing 250 or more Forms W-2 must file electronically unless granted a waiver by the IRS.

Form W-9: A taxpayer uses this form to provide his correct taxpayer identification number (TIN) to any individual or entity who is required to file an information return with the IRS.

Form 1099: A business must report nonemployee compensation paid during the year to certain independent contractors that provided services by providing a Form 1099-MISC by January 31 of the following year. Specifically, the amounts that businesses are required to report on Forms 1099 include:

- Commissions, fees, and other compensation paid to a single individual when the total amount is $600 or more during the year
- Interest, rents, annuities, and income items paid to a single individual when the total amount is $600 or more

Payments to corporations are generally exempt from Form 1099 reporting requirements. Forms 1099-MISC should only be used for payments that are made in the course of a trade or business. Personal payments are not reportable.

Example: Brett hires a painter to paint his main home. The job costs $2,500. Brett is not required to report the payment to the painter because it is for his personal residence. Since it was a personal payment, Brett cannot deduct the cost on his tax return. However, the painter is still required to report the income on his personal return. The following year, Brett calls the same painter to paint the interior of his business office, which he owns. The job costs $1,000. Since the cost is a business expense, Brett is required to issue a Form 1099-MISC to the contractor.

Form W-4: When a business hires an employee, it must have the employee complete a Form W-4, *Employee's Withholding Allowance Certificate.*

Form W-4 tells the employer the employee's marital status, the number of withholding allowances the employee is claiming, and any additional amount to use when deducting federal income tax from the employee's pay. If an employee fails to complete a Form W-4, the employer must withhold federal income taxes from his wages as if he were single and claiming no withholding allowances.

Note: The PATH Act revised the filing deadline for Form W-2 and certain types of Form 1099 (those reporting nonemployee compensation must now be filed earlier). Beginning with tax year 2016, businesses will now have a single filing deadline for all Form W-2s. This is true for both employee and IRS copies, or whether filing on paper or electronically. This new IRS deadline is one month earlier than previous years. The failure-to-file penalties have also increased. The revised penalty is at least $500 per payee statement with no maximum penalty.

New Information Return Filing Deadlines for 2016		
Form Number	**Due to Recipient**	**E-file with IRS**
1099-MISC (nonemployee compensation)	January 31, 2017	January 31, 2017
1099-B, 1099-S, 1099-MISC boxes 8 or 14	February 15, 2017	February 28, 2017[85]
Other 1099, Forms W-2G (for gambling income)	January 31, 2017	March 31, 2017
Form W-2 (for employee wages)	January 31, 2017	January 31, 2017[86]

Financial Statements

Financial statements are the formal records of a business's financial activities. There are many types of financial statements, but the two most common ones used for tax reporting purposes are the income statement and the balance sheet.

Income Statement: The income statement is also called the profit and loss statement. It indicates the business's revenue, expenses, and net income or loss during a period, such as a month, quarter, or fiscal or calendar year.

Balance Sheet: The balance sheet is a summary of a business's assets, liabilities, and equity on a specific date, such as at the end of its fiscal year. A balance sheet provides a snapshot of the business's financial condition. Balance sheet accounts are carried forward from year to year, unlike income statement accounts, which are closed out at year-end and only reflect business operations within a specified period.

[85] A full list of due dates for information returns is available on the IRS website here: www.irs.gov/businesses/small-businesses-self-employed/a-guide-to-information-returns

[86] Forms W-2 (for employee wages) are required to be mailed to the recipient and e-filed with the Social Security Administration by January 31, 2017.

Employee and Worker Classification

Because businesses are responsible for withholding and/or paying income, employment, and FUTA taxes and reporting payments to independent contractors, they must accurately determine whether a person they pay is an independent contractor or an employee. A business is generally not required to withhold or pay taxes in connection with payments to independent contractors. However, it must understand the relationship that exists with each person it pays to perform services. A person performing services for a business may be:

- An independent contractor
- An employee
- A statutory employee
- A statutory nonemployee

The IRS evaluates three primary characteristics to determine the relationship between a business and workers it pays for services:

- **Behavioral Control:** Covers whether the business has a right to direct or control how the work is done.
- **Financial Control:** Covers whether the business has a right to direct or control the financial and business aspects of the worker's job. Factors include how the worker is paid, whether expenses are reimbursed, and whether tools and supplies are provided.
- **Type of Relationship:** Relates to how the worker and the business owner perceive their relationship, such as whether there are written contracts or employee-type benefits, such as vacation pay or a retirement plan.

Whether a person is classified as an employee or an independent contractor depends on the facts and circumstances of each individual case.

Example: Rich, an electrician, submits a job estimate to a housing complex for electrical work at $16 per hour for 400 hours. He is to receive $1,280 every two weeks for the next ten weeks. Rich will receive $6,400, regardless of whether he works more or less than 400 hours to complete the work. He also performs electrical installations under contracts with other companies that he obtains through ads placed online. Rich would likely be classified as an independent contractor.

Example: Donna is a salesperson employed full-time by an auto dealership. She is on duty in the showroom on certain assigned days and times. She uses lists of prospective customers that belong to the dealership. She develops leads and reports results to the sales manager. Because of her experience, she requires minimal assistance in closing and financing sales. She is paid a commission and is eligible for bonuses offered by the dealership. The business also pays the cost of her health and group-term life insurance. Donna is classified as an employee of the dealership.

If the determination of whether a worker is an employee or independent contractor is still unclear after weighing the various facts and circumstances of an individual case, Form SS-8, *Determination of Worker Status for Purposes of Federal Employment Taxes and Income Tax Withholding,* can be filed with the IRS.

The form may be filed by either the business or the worker. The IRS will review the case to officially determine the worker's status. Employers who misclassify workers as independent contractors rather than employees may face substantial tax penalties for failing to pay employment taxes and failing to file payroll tax forms.

An independent contractor is considered self-employed and pays self-employment tax if net earnings are $400 or more. He reports income on Schedule C. There is generally no tax withholding on income received as a self-employed individual, as long as he has provided his tax identification number to the payer. However, an independent contractor may be required to make quarterly estimated tax payments.

Note: If a business does not have a Social Security number or taxpayer identification number for a payee such as an independent contractor, it must withhold federal income taxes at a 28% rate. U.S. source income received by a foreign person (a nonresident alien) is subject to withholding rate of 30%.

Statutory Employees

Some workers are classified as statutory employees. They are issued Forms W-2 by their employers, but statutory employees report their wages, income, and allowable expenses on Schedule C, just like self-employed taxpayers. The difference is that statutory employees are not required to pay self-employment tax, because their employers must treat them as employees for Social Security tax purposes. Examples of statutory employees include:

- Full-time life insurance salespeople
- Traveling salespeople
- Certain commissioned truck drivers
- Directors (board members) of corporations as well as officers of nonprofit organizations
- Certain home workers who perform work on materials or goods furnished by the employer

If a person is a statutory employee, the "statutory employee" in box 13 of Form W-2 should be checked.

Statutory Nonemployees

There are two main categories of statutory nonemployees: direct sellers and licensed real estate agents. They are treated as self-employed for federal tax purposes, including income and employment taxes, if:

- Payments for their services are directly related to sales, rather than to the number of hours worked, and
- Services are performed under a written contract providing that they will not be treated as employees for federal tax purposes.

Compensation for a statutory nonemployee is reported on Form 1099-MISC. The taxpayer then reports the income on Schedule C.

Example: Adele works as a full-time real estate agent for GAG Realty Services. She visits GAG's offices at least once a day to check her mail and her messages. She manages dozens of listings and splits her real estate commissions with GAG. She does not work for any other real estate company. Adele is classified as a statutory nonemployee. GAG Realty issues Adele a Form 1099-MISC for commissions, and she files Schedule C to report her income and expenses.

Employment Taxes and Self-Employment Tax

An employer uses information from the employee's Form W-4, as well as the IRS withholding tables, to calculate how much to withhold from each wage payment. The employer must also withhold the employee's share of Social Security and Medicare taxes from wages, and pay the corresponding employer's share of each tax.

Employers must report federal income taxes withheld and employment taxes on Form 941, *Employer's Quarterly Federal Tax Return*, or Form 944, *Employer's Annual Federal Tax Return.* Businesses must also make federal tax deposits of income and employment taxes electronically, generally by using the Electronic Federal Tax Payment System (EFTPS).

In 2016, only the first $118,500 of an individual's employee compensation and/or net earnings from self-employment is subject to the Social Security tax. There is no cap on the Medicare tax.

Social Security and Medicare Taxes: 2016 Rates	
Social Security tax rate	**2016**
Employer's portion	6.2%
Employee's portion	6.2%
Total for self-employed taxpayer	12.4%
Maximum earnings subject to Social Security taxes	$118,500
Regular Medicare Tax Rate	**2016**
Employer's portion	1.45%
Employee's portion	1.45%
Total for self-employed individual	2.9%
Maximum earnings subject to Medicare taxes	No limit

An **additional** Medicare tax of 0.9% applies to an individual taxpayer's earned income that exceeds the following thresholds:

2016 "Additional" Medicare Tax Thresholds	
Filing Status	**Threshold Amount**
MFJ	$250,000
MFS	$125,000
Single, HOH, or QW	$200,000

A taxpayer's earned income (including wages, taxable fringe benefits, bonuses, tips, commissions, and self-employment income) that is subject to Medicare tax is also subject to the additional Medicare tax to the extent it exceeds the applicable threshold amount for his filing status.

An employer is required to withhold the additional Medicare tax if an employee is paid more than $200,000, regardless of an employee's filing status or whether the employee has wages paid by another employer. There is no "employer's share" of the additional Medicare tax like there is for other Social Security taxes. A taxpayer may be subject to the additional Medicare tax even if amounts are not withheld from his wages.

Self-employed Taxpayers: Self-employed taxpayers can deduct half of their SE tax in figuring their adjusted gross income. Self-employed taxpayers *cannot* deduct one-half of the 0.9% additional Medicare tax.

An individual general partner in a partnership is considered to be self-employed, and his income is subject to self-employment tax, just like a sole proprietor's. Income reported by the partnership to limited partners is considered passive activity income (and is generally not subject to self-employment tax).

Employing Family Members

The tax requirements for a business that employs family members may differ from those applicable to other employees. The rules vary depending on the family relationship and the type of business entity.

Child working for a parent: If the parent's business is one of three types (a corporation, an estate, or a partnership in which only one of the child's parents is a partner), payments for the child's services are subject to all federal taxes, including income, unemployment, Social Security, and Medicare.

If the parent's business is a sole proprietorship or a partnership in which each partner is the child's parent, payments for the child's services are subject to income tax withholding regardless of age. If the child is under 18, payments are not subject to Social Security and Medicare taxes. If the child is under 21, payments are not subject to FUTA tax.

Example: Bradford and Cherie are married partners in a restaurant that they own and operate. Their daughter, Lexie, age 15, works as a hostess at the restaurant on the weekends. Her parents pay her $10 an hour. Bradford and Cherie must withhold income tax on Lexie's earnings. However, because of her age, her income is not subject to Social Security, Medicare, and unemployment taxes.

Parent working for a child: Payments are subject to income tax, Social Security, and Medicare taxes, but not FUTA tax, regardless of the business entity type.

Spouse employed by a spouse: Payments are generally subject to income, Social Security, and Medicare taxes, but not FUTA tax. However, FUTA tax is applicable if the spouse works for a corporation or a partnership in which the employing spouse is a partner.

Example: Alma and Raymundo are married and file jointly. Alma makes $40,000 working as a teacher. Raymundo makes $230,000 as a physician for Mercy Hospital. They have no other earned income during the year. Because Raymundo's salary exceeds $200,000, Mercy Hospital is required to withhold and remit an additional 0.9% Medicare tax on the excess over the threshold of $200,000 (i.e., the applicable tax is on $30,000). The total additional Medicare tax withheld by the employer is $270 ($30,000 × 0.009). Alma and Raymundo file jointly and their combined AGI on their joint income tax return is $270,000, which is $20,000 over the threshold for joint filers (AGI $270,000 - $250,000 MFJ threshold). Therefore, their actual additional Medicare tax is $180 ($20,000 X .9%). Assuming they do not owe any other federal income taxes, interest, or penalties to which the withholding could be applied, they will receive a $90 ($270 amount withheld - $180 actual tax) refund of the additional 0.9% Medicare tax withholding.

Trust Fund Recovery Penalty (TFRP)

Trust fund taxes refer to amounts withheld from employees' wages (Social Security, Medicare, and income tax) by employers and held in trust until they are remitted to the Treasury. This penalty is also called the "100% penalty." If a business does not deposit its trust fund taxes in a timely manner, the IRS may assess a trust fund recovery penalty (TFRP). The amount of the penalty is equal to the unpaid balance of the trust fund taxes.

The TFRP may be assessed against any person who:

- Is **responsible** for collecting or paying withheld income and employment taxes, or for paying collected excise taxes, and
- **Willfully fails** to collect or pay them.

Once the IRS asserts the penalty, it can take collection action against the personal assets of anyone who is deemed a "responsible person." It is not only the executives of businesses or the top finance and accounting personnel who may be held responsible for the TFRP. A responsible person may also include a person who signs checks for the company or who otherwise has authority to spend business funds, such as a bookkeeper. For the IRS to determine that an individual willfully failed to pay the required taxes, the responsible person:

- Must have, or should have, been aware of the outstanding taxes, and

- Intentionally disregarded the law or been plainly indifferent to its requirements (no evil intent or bad motive is required).

Using available funds to pay other creditors when the business fails to pay employment taxes is an indication of willfulness.

Example: Greta ran her own accounting business and also processed the payroll for her local church. The church had four employees. Greta prepared and signed the payroll tax returns and all the checks and then gave them to the pastor to mail. The pastor did not mail the payroll tax reports or remit the payments to the IRS. Instead, he used the money to purchase a new church organ. Greta knew the pastor was misusing the funds, but did not report the information to authorities. The IRS assessed the TFRP against the pastor, the church, and Greta. Even though Greta was just the bookkeeper, she knew that the pastor was improperly handling the payroll tax funds and she did nothing about it, so the IRS can assess the TFRP against Greta.

Federal Unemployment (FUTA) Tax

A business reports and pays FUTA tax separately from federal income tax, and Social Security and Medicare taxes. FUTA tax is paid only by the employer. The standard FUTA tax rate is 6% on the first $7,000 of each employee's wages. However, the employer may receive a credit of up to 5.4% when it files Form 940, *Employer's Annual Federal Unemployment (FUTA) Tax Return*, for state unemployment taxes paid on employee wages, resulting in a net FUTA tax rate of 0.6%.

Business Entities Snapshot				
Business Type	**Sole Proprietorship**	**C Corporation**	**S Corporation**	**General Partnership**
Formation	No state filing required.	State filing required.	State filing required.	No state filing required.
Existence	Automatically dissolved upon death.	Perpetual life.	Perpetual life.	Varies from state to state.
Liability	A sole proprietor has unlimited liability because the sole proprietorship is not a separate legal entity.	Shareholders are not responsible for the debts of the corporation.	Shareholders are typically not responsible for the debts of the corporation.	General partners are liable for the debts of the partnership.
Operational Requirements	None.	Board of directors, annual meetings, and annual reporting required.	Board of directors, annual meetings, and annual reporting required.	No formal requirements.
Management	A sole proprietor has full control of management and operations.	Management reports to the directors, who are elected by the shareholders.	Management reports to the directors, who are elected by the shareholders.	Partners may have an oral or written operating agreement.
Taxation	Not a separate taxable entity. A sole proprietor pays all taxes on his/her individual return.	Taxed at the entity level. Dividends paid to owners are also taxable income for them.	Generally no tax at the entity level. Income/loss is passed through to shareholders.	Generally, no tax at the entity level. Income/loss is passed through to partners.
Pass Through?	Yes	No	Yes	Yes
Double Taxation	No	Yes	No	No
Transferability of Interest	No	Yes	Yes	Varies

Unit 1: Study Questions

(Test yourself and then check the correct answers at the end of this section.)

1. A domestic LLC with at least two members that does not file Form 8832 is automatically classified as _________ for federal income tax purposes.

A. An S corporation.
B. A partnership.
C. A qualified joint venture.
D. A personal service corporation.

2. Don and Selma are married and run a small pet grooming business together. They want to treat their business as a qualified joint venture. They live in a community property state. Which of the following statements is correct?

A. They may choose to report their qualified joint venture as a sole proprietorship on two separate Schedules C, so long as they file jointly.
B. They may choose to report their qualified joint venture as a single sole proprietorship on two separate Schedules C, so long as they file separate tax returns (MFS).
C. They must file a partnership tax return for their business activity.
D. They may file a single Schedule C, listing Don as the sole proprietor one year and Selma as the sole proprietor the next year.

3. In which of the following instances is a partnership not required to obtain a new EIN?

A. The partners decide to incorporate.
B. The partnership is taken over by one of the partners and is subsequently operated as a sole proprietorship.
C. The general partner ends the old partnership and begins a new one.
D. The partnership adds other business locations.

4. Which of the following is considered a drawback of the C corporation entity?
A. It may have many different shareholders.
B. It may have investors who are nonresident aliens.
C. Profits are subject to double taxation: once at the corporate level and again at the shareholder level when distributed as dividends.
D. It is run by a board of directors.

5. A sole proprietor may not be required to file Schedule SE if his net earnings for 2016 were:

A. Less than $400
B. $400 or more
C. Less than $5,000 but more than $400
D. More than $5,000

6. Mandy and her friend, Tammy, work together, making beaded necklaces and selling them at craft shows. They run their business jointly and attempt to make a profit, but they do not have any type of formal business agreement. They share with each other the profits or losses of the business. They received $24,900 in 2016 from selling necklaces, and they had $1,900 of expenses. Where and how is the correct way for Mandy and Tammy to report their income?

A. Split the income and report as "other income" on each taxpayer's individual Form 1040.
B. Each must report her own income and expenses on separate Schedule Cs.
C. Mandy and Tammy should calculate income and subtract expenses, and each should report the net amount as "other income" on her individual Form 1040.
D. Mandy and Tammy are working as a partnership and should report their income on Form 1065.

7. Julian is self-employed and has a small business selling used DVDs. The gross income from his business is $20,000 and his business expenses total $9,500. Which schedule must Julian complete to report his business income and expenses?

A. Schedule F.
B. Schedule C.
C. Schedule D.
D. Schedule A.

8. All of the statements are correct about the following business entities except:

A. S and C corporations may have an unlimited number of shareholders.
B. An LLC typically provides the liability protection of a corporation but the tax benefits of a partnership.
C. "Pass through" entities include LLCs, LLPs, S corporations, and partnerships.
D. A sole proprietorship bears all the liabilities and risks of a business.

9. A sole proprietor would be required to obtain a new EIN in which of the following instances?

A. If he is required to file excise tax returns
B. If he changes the name of his business
C. If he changes location
D. If he operates multiple locations

10. A personal service corporation (that is a C corporation) is always taxed at a____________ rate.

A. 15%
B. 28%
C. 35%
D. 39.6%

11. Federal law requires businesses to provide a Form 1099-MISC for each independent contractor paid at least ________ for services during a year.

A. $400
B. $500
C. $600
D. $1,000

12. Dan is a full-time life insurance salesman and a statutory employee. He receives a Form W-2 for his earnings. How should he report his income?

A. On Form 1040 as regular wage income.
B. On Schedule C, not subject to self-employment tax.
C. On Schedule C, subject to self-employment tax.
D. On Schedule K-1.

13. The IRS evaluates all of the following characteristics to assess the relationship between a business and its workers except:

A. Type of relationship.
B. Financial control.
C. Income level.
D. Behavioral control.

14. Caden, age 16, works behind the counter of a juice bar owned by his mother, a sole proprietor. Which of the following taxes, if any, should be withheld from his paycheck?

A. Income tax.
B. Income tax, Social Security and Medicare taxes.
C. Income tax, Social Security and Medicare taxes, and FUTA tax.
D. None of the above.

15. When a business receives a cash payment of more than $10,000 from a single transaction, it is required to file:

A. Form 1099-MISC
B. Form W-2
C. Form 8300
D. Form 941

16. Which of the following organizations does not require an EIN?
A. An estate.
B. A C corporation.
C. Nonprofit organizations.
D. A sole proprietorship with no employees.

17. A business that fails to pay required payroll taxes may be subject to:

A. A penalty for underpayment of estimated tax.
B. The trust fund recovery penalty.
C. A penalty for substantial valuation misstatement.
D. A penalty for gross understatement of income.

Unit 1: Answers

1. The answer is B. A domestic LLC with at least two members that does not file Form 8832 is classified as a partnership for federal income tax purposes.

2. The answer is A. They may choose to report their qualified joint venture as a sole proprietorship on two separate Schedules C, as long as they file jointly.

3. The answer is D. A partnership is not required to obtain a new EIN simply to add business locations. In all of the other circumstances, the entity would need to obtain a new EIN.

4. The answer is C. C corporations are subject to double taxation. The other statements are facts about C corporations but are not considered drawbacks.

5. The answer is A. If a taxpayer's net earnings from self-employment are less than $400, he should enter the net profit on line 12 of Form 1040 and attach Schedule C to the return. A taxpayer is not required to file Schedule SE unless he has net earnings from self-employment of $400 or more.

6. The answer is D. Mandy and Tammy are working as a partnership and should report their income and expenses on Form 1065, *U.S. Return of Partnership Income.* Each partner should receive a Schedule K-1 to report her individual share of the partnership's income on her Form 1040.

7. The answer is B. Julian must complete Schedule C to report his business income and expenses.

8. The answer is A. Only a C corporation may have an unlimited number of shareholders. An S corporation is limited to no more than 100 shareholders.

9. The answer is A. A sole proprietor who is required to file excise tax returns (or employment tax returns) must obtain an EIN. A sole proprietorship is not required to obtain a new EIN when it changes location or its business name. An individual may operate multiple businesses using the same EIN, so long as the businesses are sole proprietorships.

10. The answer is C. A personal service corporation (that is a C corporation) pays a 35% flat rate on its taxable income. The principal activity of a PSC is providing personal services to individuals or groups. PSCs are not eligible for graduated tax rates.

11. The answer is C. Federal law requires businesses to provide a Form 1099-MISC for each independent contractor paid at least $600 for services during a year. If a business makes payments to a corporation (rather than an individual), it is generally not required to issue a Form 1099-MISC.

12. The answer is B. Statutory employees are unique because they report their wages, income, and allowable expenses on Schedule C, like self-employed taxpayers. However, statutory employees are not required to pay self-employment tax because their employers treat them as employees for Social Security tax purposes.

13. The answer is C. Income level is not a factor in determining a worker's status. The main issue involves whether the employer or the worker has the right to direct or control how the work is done and to control the financial and business aspects of the job. This helps determine whether a worker should be classified as an employee or an independent contractor.

14. The answer is A. Family members who work for other family members are subject to different tax requirements. Only income tax is withheld from the paycheck of a child under age 18 who is working for a parent who is a sole proprietor.

15. The answer is C. A business must file Form 8300, *Report of Cash Payments Over $10,000 Received in a Trade or Business,* when it receives a cash payment of more than $10,000 from one transaction or from two or more related transactions.

16. The answer is D. A sole proprietorship without employees does not require an employer identification number. The other choices listed all require an EIN.

17. The answer is B. The trust fund recovery penalty applies to any person who is responsible for collecting or paying income and employment taxes, or for paying excise taxes collected, and who willfully fails to collect or pay these taxes. The amount of the penalty is equal to the unpaid balance of the trust fund taxes.

Unit 2: Accounting Periods and Methods

More Reading:
Publication 334, *Tax Guide for Small Business*
Publication 538, *Accounting Periods and Methods*

Tax Year

The tax year is an annual accounting period for reporting income and expenses. Individuals generally file their tax returns on a calendar-year basis. Certain businesses have the option to file their tax returns on either a calendar-year or a fiscal-year basis.

Calendar Tax Year: Twelve consecutive months beginning January 1 and ending December 31.

Fiscal Tax Year: Generally twelve consecutive months ending on the last day of any month except December. However, one variation of a fiscal year end does not fall on the same date each year. A 52/53-week tax year is a fiscal tax year that varies from 52 to 53 weeks but does not necessarily end on the last day of the month. For example, some businesses choose to end their fiscal year on a particular day of the week, such as the last Friday in June or the Saturday that falls closest to January 31.

Example: Paula works for the state of California. The state's budget follows a fiscal year that runs from July 1, 2016, through June 30, 2017. This is a 12-month period not ending in December. Most federal and state government organizations operate on a fiscal-year basis, as do most large corporations.

Short Tax Year: A tax year of less than 12 months. A short tax year may result in the first or last year of an entity's existence, or when an entity changes its accounting period (for example, from a fiscal year to a calendar year, or vice versa). Even if a business is not in existence for a full year, the requirements for filing the return and paying any tax liability are generally the same as if a full 12-month tax year had ended on the last day of the short tax year.

Example: Eduardo and Jared are friends who started a business partnership five years ago, each sharing equally in the profits and losses. Eduardo died on November 1, 2016; therefore, the partnership is no longer in existence. Jared decides to continue the business as a sole proprietor. Jared must request a new employer identification number since his business structure has changed. The partnership is dissolved, and a final partnership tax return must be filed for the short tax year from January 1, 2016, to November 1, 2016 (the date of Eduardo's death).

Example: Jillian formed the Rare Books Corporation on February 1, 2016. She immediately started having financial troubles and dissolved her corporation on October 31, 2016. Jillian must file a corporate return for a short tax year covering the nine-month period that Rare Books was in existence.

A business adopts a tax year when it files its first income tax return. Any business may adopt the calendar year as its tax year. A new C corporation may generally elect to use a fiscal year instead. However, the IRS may require use of the calendar year in the following instances:

- The business keeps no books.
- There is no annual accounting period.

- The present tax year does not qualify as a fiscal year.
- The Internal Revenue Code or income tax regulations require use of a calendar year.

Form 1128, *Application to Adopt, Change, or Retain a Tax Year*, is used to request a change in the tax year.

If a business files its first tax return using the calendar tax year and later changes its business structure (such as moving from a sole proprietorship to a partnership), the business must continue to use the calendar year unless it receives IRS approval or is otherwise forced to change in order to comply with the IRC.

A taxpayer's death marks the end of his final tax year as an individual taxpayer and the following day is the beginning of the first tax year for his estate.

The executor or personal representative of the estate is responsible for filing the individual's final income tax return (Form 1040), income tax returns for the estate (Form 1041), and possibly an estate tax return (Form 706).

Example: Desmond is an unmarried physician. He dies on July 1, 2016, and his son, Raleigh, is named the executor of his estate. Raleigh is responsible for filing Desmond's final individual tax return (Form 1040). The final Form 1040 covers the period from January 1 through July 1. In addition, he must file income tax returns for the estate for the period that begins on July 2 and ends when the estate's assets have been distributed. Raleigh must request an EIN for his father's estate, which is considered a separate entity for tax purposes. Desmond's assets are valued at approximately $15 million on the date of his death. Therefore, in addition to the income tax returns, an estate tax return must also be filed.

The executor chooses the estate's tax period when he files its first income tax return. Generally, the estate's first tax year is any period of 12 months or less that ends on the last day of a month. If the executor selects the last day of any month other than December, the estate has adopted a fiscal tax year.

The due date for Form 1041 is the fifteenth day of the fourth month following the end of the entity's tax year. Starting with tax year 2016, the Form 1041 extended due date is now September 30.

Required Tax Year

Partnerships, S corporations, and PSCs generally must use a "required" tax year. This means that, unless the entity can establish a legitimate business purpose for a different tax year, a partnership's "required" tax year must conform to its partners' tax years. If one or more partners with the same tax year owns a majority (more than 50%) interest in the partnership's capital and profits, the tax year of those partners is the required tax year for the partnership.

An entity does not have to use a required tax year if it receives permission from the IRS to use another permitted tax year or if it files an election under section 444 (as described further below).

Unless it can establish a business purpose for using a fiscal year, an S corporation or PSC must generally use the calendar year.

A partnership, an S corporation, or a PSC can file Form 1128, *Application to Adopt, Change, or Retain a Tax Year*, to support its business purpose for using a fiscal year. For example, a seasonal business (such as a ski resort) may elect a fiscal year based on a genuine business purpose. It is not considered a legitimate business purpose to elect a particular fiscal tax year so that partners or shareholders may defer income recognition.

Example: Quantum Partnership has two partners, both of which are C corporations. Corporation A owns a 30% partnership interest in Quantum and operates on a calendar year. Corporation B owns the remaining 70% of the partnership interest and operates on a fiscal year ending February 28.

Partners	Partnership Interest	Tax Year
Corporation A	30%	Calendar year (December 31)
Corporation B	70%	February 28 (fiscal year-end)

Since Corporation B owns a majority interest in Quantum Partnership, the partnership must file on the same tax year as Corporation B.

If there is no majority interest tax year, the partnership must use the tax year of all of the principal partners (those who have an interest of 5% or more in the partnership's capital and profits). If there is no majority interest tax year and the principal partners do not have the same tax year, the partnership must use the tax year that would result in the least aggregate deferral of income to its partners.

Example: Andrew and Bella each have a 50% interest in the Chef Supplies Partnership. Andrew uses the calendar year and Bella uses a fiscal year ending November 30. Chef Supplies must adopt a fiscal year ending November 30 because this results in the least aggregate deferral of income to the partners, as shown in the following table.

Least Aggregate Deferral Of Income

With Year End 12/31:

	Year End	Interest	Months of Deferral	Interest × Deferral
Andrew	31-December	50%	0	0
Bella	30-November	50%	11	5.5
Total Deferral				**5.5**

With Year End 11/30:

	Year End	Interest	Months of Deferral	Interest × Deferral
Andrew	31-December	50%	1	0.5
Bella	30-November	50%	0	0
Total Deferral				**0.5**

Section 444 Election

A partnership, an S corporation, or a PSC can request to use a tax year other than its required tax year by filing Form 8716, *Election to Have a Tax Year Other Than a Required Tax Year*. This is known as a section 444 election and it does not apply to any business that establishes a genuine business purpose for using a different tax year.

A partnership or an S corporation that makes this election must make certain required payments based upon the value of the tax deferral the owners receive by using a tax year different from the required tax year. A PSC that makes the election must make certain distributions to its owner-employees by December 31 of each applicable year. A business can request a section 444 election if it meets all of the following requirements:

- It is not a member of a tiered structure.
- It has not previously had a section 444 election in effect.
- It elects a year that meets the deferral period requirement.

The deferral period depends on whether the entity is using the election to retain its tax year or to adopt or change its tax year. If it intends to retain its tax year, it may only do so if the deferral period is three months or less. The deferral period is the number of months between the beginning of the retained year and the end of the first required tax year. If the entity is requesting adoption or a change to a tax year other than the required tax year, the deferral period is the number of months from the end of the new tax year to the end of the required tax year. Generally, the IRS will allow a section 444 election only if the deferral period is less than the shorter of:

- Three months, or
- The deferral period of the tax year being changed.

Example: Davidson Partnership, a newly formed partnership owned by two calendar-year partners, begins operations on December 1, 2016. Davidson wants to make a section 444 election to adopt a September 30 tax year. Davidson's deferral period for the tax year beginning December 1, 2016, is three months, the number of months between September 30 and December 31.

The section 444 election remains in effect until it is terminated. If the election is terminated, another section 444 election cannot be made for any tax year. The election also ends automatically when any of the following occurs:

- The entity changes to its required tax year.
- The entity liquidates.
- The entity becomes a member of a tiered structure.
- The IRS determines that the entity willfully failed to comply with the required payments or distributions.
- The entity is an S corporation and the S election is terminated. However, if the S corporation immediately becomes a PSC, it can continue the prior section 444 election.
- A PSC ceases to be a PSC. Again, however, if a PSC becomes an S corporation, it can continue the prior election.

Filing Due Dates for Entities

Note: The PATH Act permanently changed the due date for partnership tax returns. Starting in 2016, partnership (and S Corporation) tax returns will be due the 15th day of the third month after the end of their tax year. Therefore, a calendar year partnership tax return would be due March 15th. C corporation tax returns are now due on April 15th.

For partnerships on a fiscal year, returns are due on the fifteenth day of the third month following the end of the year. For these and other entities' returns, if the due date falls on a Saturday, Sunday, or legal holiday, it is delayed until the next business day.

If a C corporation uses the calendar year, its tax returns are due on April 15 of the following year. If the corporation is on a fiscal year, the tax return is normally due on the fifteenth day of the fourth month following the end of the tax year.

However, a corporation with a fiscal tax year ending June 30 must file by the 15th day of the 3rd month after the end of its tax year. A corporation with a short tax year ending anytime in June will be treated as if the short year ended on June 30, and must file by the 15th day of the 3rd month after the end of its tax year. In 2017, the IRS decided to grant a full 6-month extension for calendar-year C corporations, under the authority of Code Section 6081(a) instead of the five months as stated in IRC Sect. 6081(b). The new deadline is reflected in the updated Instructions to Form 7004, which were revised late, on February 2, 2017.

C corporations with tax years ending on June 30 will continue to have a due date of September 15 until tax year 2025. After Dec. 31, 2025, the regular due date for corporations with a June 30 fiscal year-end will be October 15.

Dissolving entities must file short-year tax returns. In this case, the due date would be based on the date of final dissolution.

Example: A calendar-year C corporation dissolved on July 22, 2016, and ceased all operations. Its final return is due by November 15, 2016 (the fifteenth day of the fourth month following the close of its short tax year). The return will cover the period from January 1, 2016, through July 22, 2016.

Nonprofit entities using the calendar year must file their information returns by May 15. For nonprofit entities using a fiscal year, returns are due on the fifteenth day of the fifth month following the end of the year.

Entities and individuals may request extensions of time to file their federal income tax returns.

An extension does not grant the entity additional time to pay the tax due. The tax due must be paid by the filing deadline, or the entity will be subject to interest and penalties on the amount of unpaid tax.

Study Note: For Part 2 of the EA exam, you *must* memorize filing deadlines for partnerships, C corporations, and the other entities covered in this study guide.

Entity Type (Calendar-Year entities)	Tax Year 2016 Due Date
Sole Proprietorships	April 18, 2017 (extension: October 15)
Partnerships	March 15, 2017 (extension: September 15)
C Corporations	April 18, 2017 (extension: October 15)[87]
S Corporations	March 15, 2017 (extension: September 15)
Exempt Organizations (Form 990)	May 15, 2017 (extension: November 15[88])
Form 1041 (trust and fiduciary returns)	April 15, 2017 (extension: September 30)
Employee Benefit Plans (Form 5500)	July 31, 2017 (extension: November 15)
FBAR	April 15, 2017 (automatic 6 month extension available)

Accounting Methods

An accounting method is a set of rules used to determine when and how income and expenses are reported. No single accounting method is required of all taxpayers. However, the taxpayer must use a system that reflects income and expenses, and it must be used consistently from year to year. Businesses generally report taxable income under one of the following accounting methods:

- **Cash method**
- **Accrual method**
- **Special methods** of accounting for certain items of income and expenses
- **Hybrid method** using elements of the methods above

The special methods include, for example, those related to accounting for long-term contracts, farming operations, and installment sales. Different rules apply to each accounting method.

A business owner may use different accounting methods if he has two separate and distinct businesses.

Two businesses will not be considered separate and distinct unless a separate set of books and records is maintained for each business.

Example: Blake is a self-employed enrolled agent. He prepares tax returns from January through April every year. He is also a motivational speaker who is booked for many paid engagements. He reports his tax preparation business using the accrual method and his speaking business using the cash method. He keeps separate books and records for each business. Blake may use different accounting methods because he has two separate and distinct businesses with separate sets of records.

[87] As a reminder, a C Corporation tax return is now due on the 15th day of the 4th month after the end of the corporation's tax year. However, a corporation with a fiscal tax year ending June 30 must file by the 15th day of the 3rd month after the end of its tax year. A corporation with a short tax year ending anytime in June will be treated as if the short year ended on June 30, and must file by the 15th day of the 3rd month after the end of its tax year. C corporations with tax years ending on June 30 will continue to have a due date of September 15 until tax year 2025. After Dec. 31, 2025, the regular due date for these returns will be October 15.

[88] The new extension procedure for exempt entities will be a single, automatic 6-month extension. In the past, the IRS required exempt entities to file two separate, 3-month extensions.

Cash Method

The cash method of accounting is the simplest method to use, but the IRS restricts its use to businesses of certain types and sizes. The following businesses are required to use the accrual method rather than the cash method:

- A corporation (other than an S corporation) with average annual gross receipts exceeding $5 million
- A partnership with a corporate partner (other than an S corporation) and average annual gross receipts exceeding $5 million
- Any business that carries, produces, or sells inventory, unless the business has average annual gross receipts of $1 million or less
- Any tax shelter, regardless of its size
- Any corporation with long-term contracts

Note: The most common accounting method is the **cash method**, which is used by most individuals and many small businesses. The **accrual method** is used by most large corporations and is a more accurate method of recognizing income and expenses, because it reflects when taxable income is actually earned.

An entity (other than a tax shelter) with gross receipts that do not exceed the applicable threshold described above can use the cash method. Average annual gross receipts are determined by adding the gross receipts for the current tax year and the two preceding tax years and dividing the total by three.

Gross receipts for a short tax year are annualized. An entity that fails to meet the applicable gross receipts test for any tax year is prohibited from using the cash method and must change to the accrual method, effective for the tax year in which the entity fails to meet the test.

Example: Cameron and William Davis are brothers. Years ago, they formed the Davis and Davis Beverage Corporation, a C corporation. In 2016 and its annualized gross receipts for the year are $4.2 million. The corporation may use the cash method because it has gross receipts under $5 million and does not have any inventory.

Example: Green Bay Corporation produces inventory and its gross receipts were $200,000 for 2014, $800,000 for 2015, and $1,100,000 for 2016. The company's average annual gross receipts are therefore $700,000 ([$200,000 + $800,000 + $1,100,000] ÷ 3 = $700,000). Green Bay Corporation may continue to use the cash method in upcoming years.

Example: Lundgren Company makes golf cart parts. The company carries inventory throughout the year. Lundgren's gross receipts have never exceeded $900,000. Therefore, even though it carries inventory, Lundgren may continue to use the cash method because its average annual gross receipts are less than $1 million.

A business that produces, purchases, or sells inventory and has average annual gross receipts that exceed $1 million is generally required to use the accrual method. There are exceptions for certain types of businesses.

Exceptions to the Rules Outlined Above: The following entities may always use the cash method of accounting:

- A qualified family farming corporation with gross receipts of $25 million or less

- A qualified personal service corporation (PSC)
- Self-employed artists, authors, and photographers who sell works that they have created through their own efforts
- Qualifying small business taxpayers[89]

Study note: You should memorize the basic rules of which entities can and cannot use the cash method and the accrual method for the EA exam.

Under the cash method, a taxpayer generally deducts expenses when they are paid, based upon the presumption that the expenses relate to the current tax year and that they would not be deductible if paid in advance. This means that a business generally cannot attempt to lower its taxable income by paying expenses applicable to future years. The taxpayer would instead capitalize costs paid in advance and deduct them in the years to which they apply.

However, there is an exception called the 12-month rule under which the cash-basis taxpayer is not required to capitalize amounts paid for periods that do not extend beyond the earlier of the following:

- 12 months after the benefit begins, or
- The end of the tax year after the tax year in which payment is made.

Example: Simba is a sole proprietor who rents retail space for her eyebrow threading business. She pays two years of rent in advance in order to receive a substantial discount from her landlord. She cannot use the 12-month rule because the benefit from her advance payment exceeds the 12-month time period. She must recognize the rent expense over the two-year period, regardless of which method of accounting she uses.

Example: Garrison Partnership is a calendar-year business. It pays $15,000 on July 1, 2016, for a business insurance liability policy that is effective for one year beginning on that date. The 12-month rule applies, and the full $15,000 is deductible in 2016.

Example: Sherry is a sole proprietor and pays $3,000 in 2016 for an insurance policy that is effective for three years (36 months), beginning on July 1, 2016. This payment does not qualify for the 12-month rule. Therefore, only $500 (6/36 × $3,000) is deductible in 2016, $1,000 (12/36 × $3,000) is deductible in 2017, $1,000 (12/36 × $3,000) is deductible in 2018, and the remaining $500 is deductible in 2019 when the policy expires.

Constructive Receipt of Income: Under the cash method, taxpayers report income when it is actually or "constructively" received during the tax year. Income is constructively received when the amount is credited to the taxpayer's account or made available without restriction so that the taxpayer or his agent has access to the funds. The taxpayer does not need to have physical possession of the payment. However, income is not considered to be "constructively" received if control or use of it is restricted.

[89] There is a limited exception for "qualifying small business taxpayers" with average annual gross receipts between $1 million and $10 million that may be exempt from this requirement and be allowed to use the cash method. To be eligible, a qualifying small business taxpayer's principal activity cannot be in certain industries, including manufacturing, wholesale trade, or retail trade. Its principal activity must involve the provision of services, which may include providing property (inventory) related to those services, or the fabrication or modification of personal property. For example, a business with gross receipts of $1 million whose primary business is bicycle repair but that also has a very limited inventory of bicycles for customers to use during the repair period (like a "loaner bike") might qualify for this exception.

Example: Patel Brothers Partnership operates on the cash method. Interest income is credited to Patel's bank account in December 2016, but the partners do not withdraw it until January 2017. The partnership must include the interest income in its gross income for 2016, not 2017. The partnership had ownership and control of the income in 2016, so it is taxable in the year received.

Example: Better Jail Bonds LLP is a cash-basis partnership that bills a customer on December 10, 2016. The customer sends the company a postdated check. The check is received on December 31, 2016, but cannot be deposited until the following year because it was postdated to January 2, 2017. Better Jail Bonds would include this income in gross income for 2017, since constructive receipt did not occur until then.

Accrual Method

Under the accrual method of accounting, a business generally records income when a sale occurs or income is earned, regardless of when the business gets paid. Income is generally reported when one or more of the following occurs:

- Payment is received.
- The taxpayer earns the income.
- The income is due to the taxpayer.
- Title has passed.

A business that uses the accrual method must also report costs when they are incurred, either as expenses or as capitalized assets. It does not matter when the business actually pays for the expenses. The accrual method gives a more accurate assessment of a business's financial situation than the cash method. Income earned in each period is more accurately matched against the expenses for that period, so a business gets a better picture of net profit or loss.

Example: Alliance Computer Inc. is a calendar-year, accrual-basis corporation. The business sold a computer on December 28, 2016, for $2,500 and provided the customer with a bill that same day, but did not receive payment until February 2, 2017. Ali must include the $2,500 in his 2016 income, the year the company actually earned the income, even though the related payment did not occur until the following year.

Hybrid Accounting Method

Businesses may also use a hybrid accounting method that is a combination of the cash, accrual, and perhaps other special methods, so long as the hybrid method clearly reflects income and is used consistently. However, the following restrictions apply:

- If inventory is necessary to account for income, the business must use the accrual method for purchases and sales. The cash method can be used for other income and expense items.
- If an entity uses the cash method for reporting income, it must use the cash method for reporting expenses.
- If an entity uses the accrual method for reporting expenses, it must use the accrual method for reporting income.

Changing Accounting Methods

When a business files its first tax return, it may choose any permitted accounting method. Subsequent changes, either in the overall accounting method or the treatment of a material item, generally require that the taxpayer obtain IRS approval. Prior approval is needed for:

- Changes from cash to accrual or vice versa, unless the change is required by law.
- Changes in the method used to value inventory, such as switching from LIFO to FIFO (see discussion of these methods below).
- Changes in the method of depreciation or amortization.

The taxpayer must file Form 3115, *Application for Change in Accounting Method*, to request a change in either an overall accounting method or the accounting treatment for an individual item. However, IRS consent is not required for the following:

- Making an adjustment in the useful life of a depreciable or amortizable asset (but a taxpayer cannot change the recovery period for MACRS or ACRS property)
- Correcting a math error or an error in figuring tax liability
- A change in accounting method when the change is required by tax law, such as when a business's average gross receipts exceed $5 million

Note: With the implementation of the final tangible property repair regulations, many business entities will need to file Form 3115 and request an accounting method change to comply with the new rules. The IRS issued two recent revenue procedures to update the procedures of how to change an accounting method for federal income tax purposes. Specifically, the regulations detail ways to obtain advance (non-automatic) consent and automatic consent for an accounting change.[90]

Example: Gary is a general partner in Ultimate Consumer Goods and discovers an error in the useful life of a depreciable asset. The asset should have been depreciated over 15 years rather than five. Ultimate Consumer Goods does not have to ask the IRS for permission to correct the depreciation error.

Shipping Terms and Transfer of Ownership

Certain shipping terms dictate when a taxpayer must take an item out of its inventory and recognize income from a sale. The terms indicate the point at which title (ownership) of goods transfers from seller to buyer. The three most common terms are:

1. **FOB Destination:** Title passes to the buyer at the point of destination (when the goods arrive at the buyer's location).
2. **FOB Shipping Point:** Title passes to the buyer at the point of shipment (when the goods leave the seller's premises). FOB shipping point is also called "FOB origin".
3. **C.O.D.** ("cash on delivery" or "collect on delivery"): Payment is made upon delivery and title passes at that time. For a business that sells by mail on a C.O.D basis, the merchandise is generally included in the seller's closing inventory until the buyer pays for it.

[90] The IRS recently released an additional revenue procedure to clarify and simplify the Form 3115 filing requirements for small business taxpayers. Businesses with assets totaling less than $10 million or average annual gross receipts totaling $10 million or less are permitted to make certain tangible property changes without filing Form 3115.

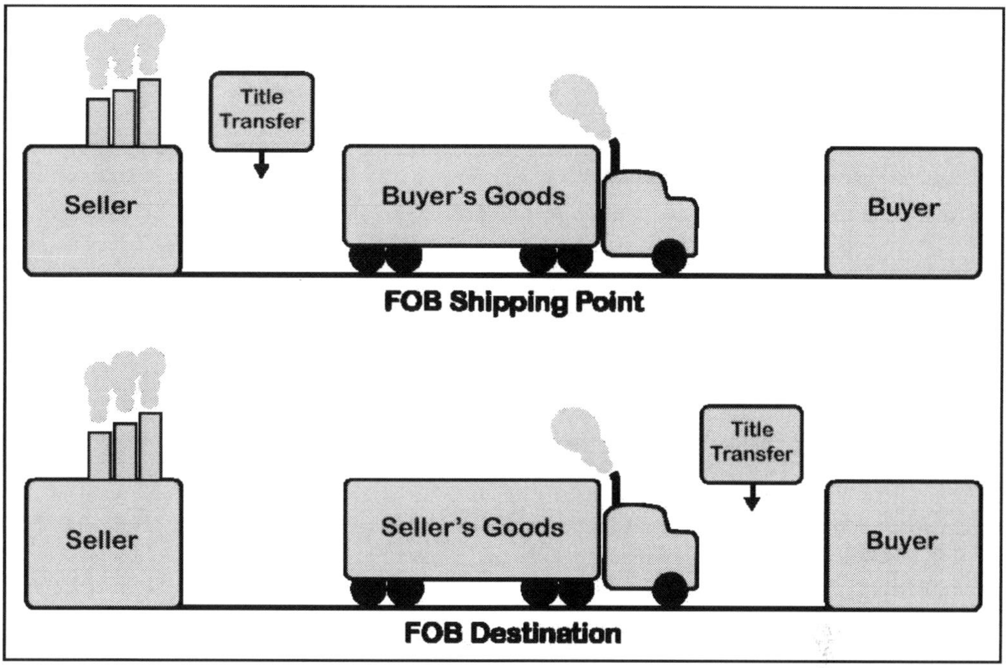

Example: Weiss Fine Furniture is a calendar-year, accrual-basis corporation that manufactures custom household furniture. It does not accrue income until the furniture has been delivered and accepted by the buyer. In 2016, the company receives an order for furniture to be custom manufactured for a total price of $20,000. Weiss ships the furniture FOB destination to the customer on December 26, 2016, but it is not delivered and accepted by the customer until January 3, 2017. Weiss will bill its customer for the $20,000 contract price and recognize the income from this sale in 2017, because the furniture had not been accepted and the title had not passed to the buyer until 2017. In this case, the method of shipping is important, because it determines in which year the business will recognize the income.

Accounting for Inventory

A business that produces or sells products must track its inventory to correctly calculate income. Businesses often make a full physical inventory count at the end of each tax year, as well as at other reasonable intervals.

The recorded inventory balances are then adjusted to agree with the actual counts. Physical inventory counts may identify irregularities such as theft, as well as damaged goods and obsolete products.

Example: Wrightwood Grocery Store takes a physical inventory once a month. During the physical inventory, store employees are required to record any damaged goods such as dented cans and ripped packaging. When the physical inventory is completed, the manager does a reconciliation to her records. She adjusts the books to reflect adjustments for shrinkage and damaged merchandise.

A taxpayer's inventory should include all of the following, if applicable:

- Merchandise or stock in trade
- Raw materials, work in process, finished products
- Supplies that physically become a part of items for sale (labels, packaging, etc.)

A taxpayer's inventory may also include:

- Purchased merchandise if title has passed to the taxpayer, even if the merchandise is still in transit or the business does not have physical possession of it for another reason
- Goods under contract for sale that have not yet been segregated and applied to the contract
- Goods out on consignment
- Goods held for sale in display rooms or booths located away from the taxpayer's place of business

The following merchandise is not included in inventory:

- Goods the business has sold, if legal title (ownership) has passed to the buyer
- Goods consigned to the taxpayer
- Goods ordered for future delivery if the business does not yet have title

Not Included in Inventory: Land, buildings, and depreciable equipment that are used in the business are never included in the calculation of inventory.

Common Inventory Methods

The value of a business's inventory is a major factor in figuring taxable income. Several common methods are used to assign costs to the items in inventory. They include the specific identification method, the average cost method, FIFO, and LIFO.

Some inventory methods are suited for specific types of businesses, while others are ideal for larger or smaller businesses.

Specific Identification Method

This method is used when it is possible to identify and match the actual cost to specific items in inventory.

It is most useful with an inventory that includes a limited number of highly specific and high-dollar items, such as custom goods or rare items like artwork or gemstones. Specific identification inventory valuation is also used for larger items such as furniture or vehicles.

This method is used when individual items can be clearly identified, such as with a serial number. The business simply accounts for each individual item as it is sold.

This method requires a detailed physical count, so that the business knows exactly how many goods remained in year-end inventory.

Example: The Classic Custom Autos dealership sells rare collectible cars. Each car is tracked individually by its vehicle identification number and its actual cost. When a car is sold, the cost is taken out of inventory. This is an example of specific identification inventory valuation.

FIFO (First-in, First-out)

The first-in, first-out (FIFO) method is a variation of the average cost method in which it is assumed that inventory items are sold in the order they are acquired or produced, with the oldest goods sold first and the newest goods sold last. This assumption would mirror the actual flow of inventory items in certain businesses, such as rotating stock in a grocery store.

The actual quantities in inventory at the end of the tax year are assigned costs based upon the cost of items of the same type that the business most recently purchased or produced. The formula for figuring inventory based on the FIFO method is as follows:

Unit Cost Per Item = (Cost/Quantity) for the most recent lot of the item that was purchased or produced

Aggregate Inventory Cost = (Unit Cost Per Item × Quantity) for each item

In an economy with rising prices (inflation), the use of FIFO will typically assign a higher value to ending inventory than other methods and thus result in reporting lower cost of sales and higher taxable income.

Example: Rabat Electronics, a cash-basis, calendar-year taxpayer, sells car audio equipment. Beginning inventory on January 1 included 300 car stereos with cost per unit of $20. On January 10, the business purchased 600 stereos at $20.10; on January 16, it purchased 400 stereos at $20.20; and on January 25, it purchased 500 stereos at $20.30. In January, the business sold 1,200 car stereos. Under FIFO, it is assumed that the oldest merchandise is sold first. Rabat Electronics had a beginning inventory of 300 stereos. Those units are assumed to have been sold first, followed by the units purchased on January 10 and January 16. Thus, the cost assigned to the units on hand at the end of January is determined as follows:

Beginning inventory	**300**
January 10 purchases	600
January 16 purchases	400
January 25 purchases	500
Total units available	1,800
Units sold	(1,200)
Units in inventory at end of January	**600**

Composition based upon FIFO assumption:

January 25 purchases	500	@ $20.30 = 10,150
Unsold portion of January 16 purchases	100	@ $20.20 = 2,020
Total inventory at end of January	600	$12,170

LIFO (Last-in, First-out)

The last-in, first-out (LIFO) method assumes that the newest inventory purchased or produced is sold first, and the oldest inventory is sold last.

Since the prices of goods, labor, and materials generally rise over time, this method will typically result in assigning a lower aggregate value to inventory on hand, higher amounts being recorded as the cost of sales, and lower taxable income.

As a result, use of the LIFO method is subject to highly complex rules governing its calculation and close scrutiny by the IRS. The formula for figuring inventory using the LIFO method is as follows:

Unit Cost Per Item = (Cost/Quantity) for the oldest lot of the item that was purchased or produced **Aggregate Inventory Cost = (Unit Cost Per Item × Quantity) for each item**

Example: Using the same background information for Rabat Electronics outlined above but using a LIFO assumption rather than FIFO, the 300 units on hand at January 1 are assumed to have a LIFO cost per unit of only $10 because Rabat has been in business for 20 years and the unit costs of its purchases have approximately doubled during that period due to inflation. Therefore, the cost assigned to the units on hand at the end of January is determined as follows:

Beginning inventory	**300**
January 10 purchases	600
January 16 purchases	400
January 25 purchases	500
Total units available	1,800
Units sold	(1,200)
Units in inventory at end of January	**600**

Composition based upon LIFO assumption:

Beginning inventory	300 @ 10.00 =	3,000
Unsold portion of January 10 purchases	300 @ 20.10 =	6,030
Total inventory at end of January	**600**	**$9,030**

In comparison to the earlier FIFO example, the aggregate cost assigned to ending inventory using LIFO would be lower. Since the income generated by Rabat in January from selling 1,200 units would be the same using either inventory method, its taxable income would be higher using FIFO instead of LIFO.

Unless a business has used the LIFO method from its inception, it must obtain permission from the IRS to change to LIFO from another method of inventory valuation. Permission is requested by filing Form 970, *Application to Use LIFO Inventory Method.*

Differences between FIFO and LIFO

Economic Climate	FIFO	LIFO
Periods of rising prices (Inflation)	(+) Higher value of inventory (-) Lower cost of goods sold	(-) Lower value of inventory (+) Higher cost of goods sold
Periods of falling prices (Deflation)	(-) Lower value of inventory (+) Higher cost of goods sold	(-) Higher value of inventory (+) Lower cost of goods sold

Average Cost Method

This method is commonly used when a business has quantities of items that are largely interchangeable rather than individually unique. It allows the business to calculate an average cost per unit without tracking the individual units as they are purchased, manufactured, or sold. The formula for figuring average inventory cost is:

Average Unit Cost = (Total Cost of Units Purchased or Manufactured)/ (Total Quantity of Units) **Aggregate Inventory Cost** = (Average Unit Cost) × (Units in Current Inventory)

Example: Anna owns a pet store. She purchases five dog leashes at $10 apiece. The following week, the price of the leashes goes up, and she purchases five more leashes at $20 apiece. Anna then sells five leashes the following week. The weighted average cost of Anna's inventory is calculated as follows:

Total cost of leashes:

(Five leashes at $10 each) = $50

(Five leashes at $20 each) = $100

<u>Total number of units = 10 leashes</u>

Weighted average = $150 / 10 = $15

The average cost per leash for the 10 leashes Anna has purchased is $15. If she applies this average cost to the five leashes unsold at the end of the week, the calculated cost of the leashes on hand would be $75 ($15 × 5 leashes).

Other Inventory Valuation Methods

In addition to the inventory accounting methods already described, the following methods, or conventions, are commonly used to assign value to inventory: cost, lower of cost or market, and retail.

Retail Method

Under the retail method, the total retail selling price of goods on hand at the end of the tax year in each department or for each class of goods is reduced to approximate cost by using an average markup expressed as a percentage of the total retail selling price. For example, if a store marks up its merchandise by 35%, that percentage would be used as a basis for estimating the cost of its current inventory.

Cost Method

All direct and indirect costs are included.

- For merchandise on hand at the beginning of the tax year, cost means the ending inventory price of the goods.
- For merchandise purchased during the year, cost means the invoice price minus appropriate discounts, plus transportation or other charges incurred in acquiring the goods. It may also include other costs that must be capitalized under the uniform capitalization rules.
- For merchandise produced during the year, cost means all direct and indirect costs, including those that have to be capitalized under the uniform capitalization rules.

A trade discount is sometimes given for volume or quantity purchases. The cost of the actual value of inventory must be reduced by trade discounts.

Lower-of-Cost or Market Method

This method may be used for inventory, such as fashion clothing, that tends to lose value quickly. The market value of each item on hand is compared with its cost and the lower of the two is used as its inventory value. Market value is typically based upon the normal selling price at the date the inventory is being valued.

If inventory is offered for sale below market in the normal course of business, inventory can be valued at the lower price, less the direct cost of disposition. This method may also be used for items that cannot be sold at normal prices or are unusable because of damage, imperfections, changes of style, odd or broken lots, or other similar causes. In these cases, items should be valued at their actual selling price minus the direct cost of disposition, even if another method is used to value the rest of the entity's inventory. However, the lower-of-cost or market method cannot be used in conjunction with the LIFO method.

The lower of cost or market method applies to the following:

- Goods purchased and on hand
- The basic elements of cost (direct materials, direct labor, and certain indirect costs) of goods being manufactured and finished goods on hand

Example: Graham makes motorcycle accessories at his machine shop. Under the lower of cost or market method, the following items would be valued at $600 in closing inventory.

Inventory Item	Cost	Market	Lower
Chrome Air Cleaners	$300	$500	$300
Custom Foot Pegs	$200	$100	$100
Chrome Drag Bars	$450	$200	$200
Total	**$950**	**$800**	**$600**

Graham must value each item in the inventory separately. He cannot value the entire inventory at cost ($950) and at market ($800) and then use the lower of the two figures.

Cost of Goods Sold (COGS)

The methods described above to determine the value of a business's ending inventory allow calculation of cost of goods sold (COGS), which is deducted from a business's gross receipts to determine its gross profit. The following expenses related to inventory sold are included in the calculation of COGS:

- The cost of products or raw materials, including freight
- Storage
- Labor costs
- Factory overhead

In a manufacturing business, labor costs allocable to the cost of goods sold include both the direct and indirect labor used in fabricating the raw material into a finished, saleable product. Other labor costs not associated with the manufacturing process, such as selling or administrative expenses, are not included in the COGS equation.

Example: In calculating COGS, American Custom Shoes includes the cost of leather and thread in the shoes it manufactures, as well as wages for the workers who produce the shoes. COGS is recorded as an expense as the company sells its finished goods.

The equation for cost of goods sold is as follows:

Beginning Inventory +

Inventory Purchases and Production Costs -

Ending Inventory =

Cost of Goods Sold

When a business incurs a casualty or theft loss of inventory, it has two options to record the loss. The business can adjust its cost of goods sold, or it can record the loss separately as a casualty or theft loss.

If the entity chooses to report a casualty loss, it must adjust opening inventory to eliminate the loss items and avoid counting the loss twice.

Example: Doggie Delights Inc. is an accrual-basis corporation that manufactures custom dog sweaters. The value of sweater inventory was $2,500 at December 31, and is $3,500 at January 31. In January, Doggie Delights has $20,000 of sales. In the same month, the corporation also has a number of expenses, including wages for the sweater designers ($5,000) and the cost of raw materials such as yarn, appliqué, and rhinestones ($3,000). The wages and the cost of the raw materials are directly related to the production of the inventory (the sweaters) and are included in the cost of goods sold calculation. Other costs not directly related to the manufacture of the sweaters, which might include items like a receptionist's salary ($1,500), telephone charges ($130), and advertising ($1,200) are also expensed, but are not part of COGS. The income statement for January would look like this:

Gross income from sales:	$20,000
COGS: ($2,500 + $5,000 + $3,000 - $3,500)	(7,000)
Gross profit	13,000
Other expenses: ($1,500 + $130 + $1,200)	(2,830)
Income for January	**$10,170**

Uniform Capitalization Rules (UNICAP)

The uniform capitalization rules (commonly referred to as UNICAP) provide detailed guidance regarding the direct costs and certain indirect costs related to the production of goods or the purchase of merchandise for resale that businesses must capitalize as part of the cost of inventory. These costs cannot be deducted when incurred. They must be capitalized and deducted later when the inventory is used or sold. Businesses subject to the uniform capitalization rules include the following:

- Retailers or wholesalers that purchase merchandise for resale,
- Manufacturers that produce real or tangible property for sale, and
- Taxpayers who construct assets for their own trade or business.

However, the uniform capitalization rules do not apply to the following taxpayers and expenditures:

- Resellers of personal property with average annual gross receipts of $10 million or less for the three prior tax years.
- Sellers of personal-use or nonbusiness property (such as a hobby activity that produces occasional income, but is not a business).
- Research and experimental expenditures.
- Marketing costs.
- Intangible drilling and development costs of oil and gas or geothermal wells.
- Property produced under a long-term contract.
- Timber raised, harvested, or grown, and the underlying land.

- Qualified creative expenses incurred as self-employed writers, photographers, or artists that are otherwise deductible on their tax returns.
- Loan originations.
- Property provided to customers in connection with providing services. It must be de minimis and not be included in inventory in the hands of the service provider.
- The costs of certain producers who use a simplified production method and whose total indirect costs are $200,000 or less.

Example: Mugshot Studios produces movies for Hollywood. Film production is subject to the UNICAP rules, so Mugshot must capitalize all of its costs, including set design, costumes, special effects, film editing, and salaries for actors and production workers. When a film is finally completed and distributed, Mugshot Studios is allowed to deduct the production costs as COGS.
Example: Creative Costumes manufactures Halloween costumes. During August, Creative Costumes purchases raw materials to produce costumes for the upcoming holiday. All the materials and shipping costs associated with the inventory must be capitalized rather than expensed. As the costumes are sold, Creative Costumes expenses the costs associated with the inventory as cost of goods sold. At the end of each month, Creative Costumes does a physical inventory count and adjusts COGS for any damaged or stolen inventory.

Unit 2: Study Questions

(Test yourself and then check the correct answers at the end of this section.)

1. Which of the following date ranges would be a permissible fiscal tax year?

A. January 1, 2016 to December 31, 2016.
B. February 2, 2016 to February 2, 2017.
C. July 1, 2016 to June 30, 2017.
D. May 1, 2016 to May 31, 2017.

2. All of the following costs must be included in inventory except:

A. The cost of shipping raw materials to the seller's factory.
B. The cost of shipping a finished product to a customer.
C. Raw materials.
D. Direct labor costs.

3. Which of the following changes in accounting method does not require prior approval from the IRS?

A. A change from FIFO to LIFO inventory valuation.
B. A change from the cash method to the accrual method.
C. A change in the overall method of figuring depreciation.
D. A correction of a math error in depreciating an asset.

4. Which of the following entities can use the cash method of accounting?

A. A family farming corporation with average gross receipts of $22 million.
B. A C corporation with average gross receipts of $50 million.
C. A tax shelter with average gross receipts of $50,000.
D. A corporation with long-term contracts and average gross receipts of $900,000.

5. Which would not be considered the end of an acceptable tax year?

A. January 31
B. April 15
C. December 31
D. The last Friday in February.

6. Which of the following entities cannot use the cash method of accounting?

A. A partnership that produces inventory for sale to customers and has $1.2 million of average annual gross receipts.
B. A C corporation without inventory that has $4.5 million of average annual gross receipts.
C. A qualified family farming corporation with $24 million of average annual gross receipts.
D. A sole proprietor with inventory and $500,000 of average annual gross receipts.

7. Under the lower of cost or market method of valuing inventory, what is the value of the inventory as a whole, based on the table below?

Item	Cost	Market
Shirts	$200	$500
Shoes	$300	$200
Shorts	$225	$150
Total	**$725**	**$850**

A. $725
B. $850
C. $750
D. $550

8. Helen is the owner of Banner Custom Sofas, a calendar-year, accrual-basis S corporation. She sells five sofas to Sonny's Interior Design on December 21, 2016, and bills Sonny's for $2,500 on that date. Sonny's pays the invoice in full on January 15, 2017. Banner would include this income in:

A. 2015
B. 2016
C. 2017
D. None of the above.

9. Vargas Cellular Corporation, a C corporation, was organized on April 1, 2016. It elected the calendar year as its tax year. When is the first tax return due for Vargas Cellular for this short tax year?

A. April 18, 2017
B. April 15, 2016
C. March 15, 2018
D. May 15, 2017

10. Which of the following activities would make a taxpayer subject to the uniform capitalization (UNICAP) rules?

A. An individual taxpayer who produces items as a hobby and occasionally sells them at a profit.
B. A taxpayer who produces property for sale to wholesale retailers.
C. A taxpayer who acquires land and holds it for investment.
D. A freelance artist who carries an inventory of artwork valued at $1.2 million.

11. Ray operates a retail clothing store using the accrual method and reports income on Schedule C, *Net Profit or Loss from Business.* He also runs a lawn care service that he operates only in the summer months. Which of the following statements is correct?

A. The lawn care business is required to use the accrual method of accounting because Ray has already elected this method for his other business, and all businesses operated by one individual must use the same method of accounting.
B. The lawn care business may use either the cash or accrual method, so long as both businesses have separate and distinct records.
C. Ray may keep one set of records for the two businesses and use different methods of accounting for them.
D. Ray must combine the income for both businesses and keep one set of record books for both.

12. Ben owns a jewelry store. All of the following transactions are examples of constructive receipt of income in 2016 *except*:

A. Ben receives a check payment in his mailbox on December 31, 2016, but does not pick-up the check from the mailbox and deposit the check in the bank until January 2, 2017.
B. Ben receives a direct deposit of funds to his bank account on December 15, 2016, but does not withdraw any of the funds until March 2017.
C. Ben receives a signed IOU from a delinquent account in November 2016. He receives payment on this account on January 10, 2017.
D. An escrow agent receives a payment on Ben's behalf that is restricted for his use. It is an advance payment for a custom ring, but he cannot access any of the funds until the ring is delivered and inspected by the buyer. On December 28, 2016, the ring is delivered and the restriction is lifted. Ben picks up the cash on January 9, 2017.

13. Chris is the owner-shareholder of Dress Down Fridays, a calendar-year S corporation. He manufactures clothing items for resale to the general public and also sells them to wholesale distributors. Chris is trying to figure out his inventory calculations in order to file his 2016 tax return. Which of the following items should be included in his year-end inventory?

A. 2,000 t-shirts out on consignment to a retailer.
B. The machinery used to manufacture the clothing.
C. An order of fabric that was in transit from a supplier, FOB destination (the title had not yet passed to Chris).
D. Shipping boxes and packaging materials for mailing the shirts out to customers.

14. Which of the following types of property are not exempt from the uniform capitalization rules?

A. Qualified expenses of a writer, photographer, or performing artist.
B. Timber and the underlying land.
C. Services provided to customers.
D. Audio recordings produced by a corporation.

15. Thomas is a cash-basis sole proprietor who reports income and loss on Schedule C. He purchased a bulk order of watches for his mail order business. The watches cost $5,000, and the related shipping cost is $350. What is the correct treatment of the shipping cost he paid for delivery of the watches?

A. Thomas may elect to deduct the $350 shipping cost on his tax return as an expense.
B. Shipping cost paid on the watches must be added to the basis of the inventory.
C. Thomas cannot deduct the shipping cost and cannot capitalize it.
D. Thomas may elect to deduct the shipping cost as an itemized deduction on Schedule A.

16. A business must adopt its first tax year by:

A. The due date (including extensions) for filing a return.
B. The due date (not including extensions) for filing a return.
C. The date the EIN is established.
D. The first time the business pays estimated payments.

17. All of the following practices are acceptable methods of accounting for inventory except:

A. The taxpayer includes in inventory only the direct costs associated with manufacturing the goods.
B. The taxpayer has a theft loss of inventory when a disgruntled employee steals substantial amounts of merchandise. The taxpayer chooses to increase his cost of goods sold to account for the stolen items and properly reports his beginning and ending inventory.
C. The taxpayer values his inventory using the lower of cost or market method, applying the method to each item in his inventory.
D. The taxpayer has two businesses, and he keeps a separate set of books for each business. He chooses to use LIFO for the first business and FIFO for the second one.

18. Soft Pillows Partnership, a bedding manufacturer, had the following expenses during the tax year:

Beginning inventory	$80,000
Ending inventory	52,500
Raw materials purchased	12,000
Manufacturing costs	80,000
Freight-in costs	550
Freight-out to customers	750

Calculate Soft Pillow's cost of goods sold (COGS) for the year:

A. $67,050
B. $120,050
C. $120,800
D. $670,800

Unit 2: Answers

1. The answer is C. A fiscal tax year is any tax year that is 12 consecutive months and ends on the last day of any month except December. Answer A is incorrect because this is a calendar year, not a fiscal year. Answer B is incorrect because a fiscal year, other than a 52-53 week year or a short tax year, must end on the last day of the month. Answer D is incorrect because it is more than 12 consecutive months.

2. The answer is B. Shipping finished products to customers is not an expense that should be included in inventory. This cost is a current expense and would be deductible when incurred, rather than capitalized as a cost of the inventory.

3. The answer is D. The correction of a math error does not require prior approval from the IRS. Consent from the IRS is not required for the following changes:

- Correction of a math error for computing tax liability or other mathematical error
- A correction in depreciable life or correction of a depreciation error
- An adjustment to an asset's useful life

4. The answer is A. A family farming corporation may use the cash method of accounting if its average annual gross receipts are $25 million or less. A C corporation with gross receipts exceeding $5 million is required to use the accrual method. A tax shelter must always use the accrual method, regardless of its gross receipts. A corporation with long-term contracts must always use the accrual method.

5. The answer is B. April 15 is the IRS due date for individual tax returns but would not be the end of a tax year, except in a rare instance in which an entity's existence terminates or an individual dies on that date. Answer A is incorrect because January 31 is the last day of the month, which qualifies as a fiscal tax year-end. Answer C is incorrect because December 31 is a calendar year-end. Answer D is incorrect because a tax year that ends on the same day of the week every year is a 52/53-week tax year, which is a legitimate type of fiscal year.

6. The answer is A. Generally, an entity cannot use the cash method if it has average annual gross receipts exceeding $5 million. However, if a company has inventory, the threshold for gross receipts is generally $1 million. A qualified family farming corporation can use the cash method if its average gross receipts do not exceed $25 million.

7. The answer is D. To value inventory using the lower of cost or market method, compare the cost and the fair market value of each of the items in inventory, and choose the lower of the two to obtain the inventory's value. The answer is calculated as follows: ($200 for shirts + $200 for shoes + $150 for shorts) = $550 inventory valuation.

8. The answer is B. The income would be included on Banner's 2016 tax return, because Banner is using the accrual method of accounting for income and expenses. Under the accrual method, income is reported in the year earned and expenses are deducted in the year incurred. Since Banner sold the sofas in 2016, the income would be reported in 2016, regardless of when payment is received.

9. The answer is A. Since the corporation chose a calendar year, its first tax return is due April 18, 2017. This short period return will cover the period from April 1, 2016, through December 31, 2016. Tax returns for C corporations are normally due on the fifteenth day of the fourth month after the end of the corporation's tax year. Because April 15, 2017 falls on a weekend and April 17, 2017 is an IRS-recognized holiday, the return is due April 18, 2017 (the first non-weekend, non-holiday).

10. The answer is B. A taxpayer is subject to the uniform capitalization rules if he produces real or personal property for use in a trade or business. Producing items for personal use or as a hobby would not be subject to the UNICAP rules. Independent (self-employed) authors, writers, and artists are exempt from the rules.

11. The answer is B. A taxpayer may use different methods of accounting for two distinct and separate businesses. Separate accounting books must be kept for each business.

12. The answer is C. According to the doctrine of constructive receipt, income is included in gross income when a person has an unqualified right to the funds. Constructive receipt must be more than just a billing, an offer, or a mere promise to pay. The amount promised to Ben as an IOU, therefore, does not have to be included in income for 2016.

13. The answer is A. Chris should include the consigned goods in his inventory, since he retains title to the goods on consignment until they are sold by the retailer. Machinery and other fixed assets used by a business are not included in its inventory. Answer "D" is incorrect because shipping supplies are typically treated as an expense, and not capitalized or added to the cost of inventory.

14. The answer is D. A corporation that produces audio recordings or films would be subject to UNICAP. Generally, the uniform capitalization rules apply to a taxpayer that produces property for use or resale in a business. A company that provides only services would not carry an inventory, so it is not subject to UNICAP. Independent (self-employed) authors, writers, and artists are exempt from the rules.

15. The answer is B. The shipping cost related to a purchase increases an asset's cost basis. If the property is merchandise bought for resale (such as inventory), the shipping cost is part of the cost of the merchandise and must be capitalized and later recovered as cost of goods sold when the watches are resold.

16. The answer is B. A business must adopt its first tax year by the due date (not including extensions) for filing a return for that year. A business adopts a tax year when it files its first income tax return.

17. The answer is A. Taxpayers must include direct and indirect costs in inventory. Taxpayers can claim a casualty or theft loss of inventory by increasing the cost of goods sold to properly report beginning and ending inventories. Taxpayers may choose to use different accounting methods for different businesses, so long as the businesses are kept separate and distinct accounting records are maintained for each.

18. The answer is B. The cost of goods sold is calculated as follows:

Beginning inventory	$80,000
Raw materials purchased	12,000
Freight-in	$550
Manufacturing costs	80,000
Ending inventory	(52,500)
COGS	**$120,050**

The cost of freight-out to customers is not included in the calculation of inventory or capitalized as COGS. It is instead deductible as a business expense (this cost is usually expensed out as postage and delivery).

Unit 3: Business Income

More Reading:
Publication 525, *Taxable and Nontaxable Income*
Publication 334, *Tax Guide for Small Business*
Publication 925, *Passive Activity and At-Risk Rules*

Gross income reportable by a business for tax purposes includes all types of income received, unless specifically exempt from taxation, in the form of money, property, or services. Sources of income for a business include the following:

- Income received for services
- Income received for manufacturing or selling merchandise
- Gains from the sale of business or investment property
- Income from the discharge of indebtedness (debt cancellation income)
- Income from an interest in an estate or trust
- Portfolio income from investments
- Fair market value of property or services received through bartering
- Rental activities and royalties

In addition to earning income that is exempt from tax, businesses may engage in transactions for which taxation of income is deferred to a later date. An example is a section 1031 exchange, which allows for deferral of income on the exchange of business or investment property. In this unit, we review the details of various types and treatments of business income.

Advance Payment for Services

An advance payment for services to be performed in a later tax year is generally taxable in the year it is receieved, even by an accrual-based taxpayer. However, if there is an agreement that the service will be completed by the end of the next tax year, recognition of the income can be delayed until the next year. The taxpayer cannot postpone the recognition of income beyond the next year.

Service Agreement: If a taxpayer receives an advance payment for a service agreement on property he sells, leases, builds, installs, or constructs, he can postpone reporting income, but only if he offers the property without a service agreement in the normal course of business. Postponement is not allowed if:

- The taxpayer will perform any part of the service after the end of the tax year immediately following the year he receives the advance payment.
- The taxpayer will perform any part of the service at any unspecified future date that may be after the end of the tax year immediately following the year he receives the advance payment.

Example: Ross is an accrual-based, calendar-year taxpayer who owns a computer repair shop. In 2016, he receives payments for one-year contracts that specify he will repair or replace certain computer components that break. Ross includes each payment evenly in gross income over a one-year period as it is earned.

Example: The Best Service Tennis Club is a calendar-year, accrual-based taxpayer that holds tennis clinics for new players. On November 1, the club receives payment for a 12-month contract for 24 one-hour clinics beginning on that date. The club gives six clinics in 2016. The club must include one-fourth (6/24) of the payment in income for 2016 and three-fourths (18/24) of the payment in 2017, even if the club does not give all of the clinics by the end of 2017.

Guarantee or Warranty: Generally, an accrual-basis taxpayer cannot postpone reporting income received under a guarantee or warranty contract.

Advance Payment for Sales

Special rules apply to including income from advance payments on agreements for the future sale of goods to customers, such as gift certificates or cards that can be redeemed later for goods. The advance payment is generally included in income in the year it is received, even by a taxpayer reporting under the accrual method.

However, there is an alternative method in which the advance payment can be included in gross receipts under the method of accounting the taxpayer uses for tax purposes or the method of accounting used for financial reporting, whichever is earlier.

Example: Tangerine Specialty Foods uses the accrual method of accounting for tax and financial reporting purposes and accounts for the sale of goods when it ships the goods. A customer purchases a $100 gift card from Tangerine's website on December 28, 2016, using a credit card. Tangerine ships the gift card to the customer on January 3, 2017. Under the alternative method of reporting income for advance payment of sales, Tangerine may recognize the $100 of gross receipts in either 2016 (the tax year in which it received the payment) or 2017 (the tax year in which it shipped the gift card).

Passive Activity Limits

Certain types of business activities are considered passive activities and are subject to passive activity limits on the deductibility of losses. The rules apply to individuals, estates, trusts (other than grantor trusts), personal service corporations, and closely held corporations.

They also apply to owners of grantor trusts, partnerships, and S corporations. Before applying the passive activity limits, a taxpayer must determine the effects of at-risk limits,[91] which apply to individuals (including partners and S corporation shareholders), estates, trusts, and certain closely held corporations.

There are two kinds of passive activities:

- Trade or business activities in which the taxpayer does not materially participate during the year. The taxpayer materially participates in an activity if he is involved in the operations of the activity on a regular, continuous, and substantial basis.
- Rental real estate activities, even if the taxpayer does materially participate, except for bona fide real estate professionals.

Study Note: There are additional exceptions related to limits on deductibility of passive losses from real estate rental activities. These exceptions are more relevant to individual taxpayers and are generally tested on Part 1 of the EA exam, rather than Part 2.

[91] At-risk limits are explained in detail in later units pertaining to the specific types of entities that may be affected.

The determination of whether a taxpayer materially participated is based upon satisfaction of at least one of several tests, including whether the taxpayer's participation in the activity:

1. Was for more than 500 hours.
2. Was substantially all the participation in the activity of all individuals for the tax year, including the participation of individuals who did not own any interest in the activity.
3. Was for more than 100 hours during the tax year, which was at least as much as any other individual for the year.
4. Included any five of the ten immediately preceding tax years.
5. Included a personal service activity in which he materially participated for any three preceding tax years.

If a taxpayer owned an activity as a limited partner, he is generally not treated as materially participating in the activity.

However, he may be treated as materially participating if he met test (1), (4), or (5) above. Further, he would not be treated as a limited partner if he were also a general partner in the partnership at all times during the partnership's tax year.

A taxpayer's participation in an activity includes his spouse's participation. A closely held corporation or a personal service corporation is treated as materially participating in an activity only if one or more shareholders who own more than 50% of the corporation materially participate in the activity.

Passive Activity Loss Limitations

Losses from passive activities that exceed the income from passive activities in a given year are generally disallowed as deductions for the current year. The taxpayer uses Form 8582, *Passive Activity Loss Limitations,* to summarize income and losses from passive activities and compute deductible losses, and Form 8582-CR, *Passive Activity Credit Limitations,* to summarize the credits from passive activities and compute the amount of passive activity credit allowed.

Disallowed passive losses are carried forward to the next taxable year. A similar rule applies to credits from passive activities. Generally, the taxpayer can deduct in full any previously disallowed passive activity losses in the year he disposes of his entire interest in the activity. Form 8582-CR may also be used to make an election to increase the basis of credit property upon disposal.

Definition: Ordinary income is income that is subject to regular tax rates, as opposed to long-term capital gain income that is generally subject to more favorable tax rates for individuals, estates and trusts.

Example: Marjorie owns a 25% interest in a partnership that runs a hair salon and a 10% interest in an S corporation that runs a yoga studio. She has no involvement in the day-to-day operation of either business; therefore, her interest in each business is considered a passive activity. In 2016, the hair salon partnership has an ordinary loss of $40,000, of which $10,000 is allocated to Marjorie because of her 25% ownership. The yoga studio business has ordinary income of $75,000, of which $7,500 is allocated to Marjorie because of her 10% ownership. As Marjorie's losses from passive activities for the year exceed her income from passive activities by $2,500 ($10,000 of loss minus $7,500 of income), deduction of the excess loss is disallowed. Marjorie may carry forward the $2,500 excess loss to the next year.

A former passive activity is an activity that was a passive activity in an earlier tax year, but is not a passive activity in the current tax year. A prior year's disallowed loss from the activity can be deducted up to the amount of current year income from the activity. Passive activity income does not include:

- Portfolio income, such as interest, dividends, annuities, and royalties not derived in the ordinary course of a trade or business, or gain or loss from the disposition of property that produces these types of income or that is held for investment.
- Personal service income. This includes salaries, wages, commissions, self-employment income from trade or business activities in which the taxpayer materially participated, deferred compensation, taxable Social Security and other retirement benefits, and payments from partnerships to partners for personal services.
- Any income from intangible property, such as a patent, copyright, or literary, musical, or artistic composition, if the taxpayer's personal efforts significantly contributed to the creation of the property.
- State, local, and foreign income tax refunds.
- Income from a covenant not to compete.
- Alaska Permanent Fund dividends.
- Cancellation of debt income, if at the time the debt is discharged, the debt is not allocated to passive activities.

Example: Alberto has a job working full-time as a firefighter. The income that he earns from his job is classified as wages, (earned income, or income from personal services). He also owns several CDs (certificate of deposit) through his local credit union. He earns interest on the CDs when they mature. The interest is classified as portfolio income.

Note: The three main categories of income are active income, passive income and portfolio income. Portfolio income includes interest, dividends, etc. Do not confuse the widely-used term "passive income" with "passive activity income". Although many of the items listed above seem passive in nature, they are by definition excluded from treatment as passive activities. This categorization of income is important because passive activity losses generally cannot be offset against active income or portfolio income (with a few exceptions).

Grouping Business Activities

A taxpayer can treat one or more trade or business or rental activities as a single activity if the activities form an appropriate economic unit for measuring gain or loss under the passive activity rules. If two activities are grouped into one larger activity, a taxpayer needs only to show material participation in the activity as a whole. If the two activities are separate, he must show material participation in each one.

Generally, when activities are grouped into appropriate economic units, they may not be regrouped in a later tax year. However, if any of the activities resulting from a grouping is not an appropriate economic unit and one of the primary purposes of the grouping is to avoid the passive activity rules, the IRS may regroup the activities.

Example: Malcolm owns a bagel shop and a movie theater at a shopping mall in Cincinnati and a bagel shop and a movie theater in Milwaukee. There may be more than one reasonable method for grouping Malcolm's activities, including the following: 1) the movie theaters and the bagel shops into one activity; 2) a separate movie theater activity and a separate bagel shop activity; 3) a Cincinnati activity and a Milwaukee activity; or 4) four separate business activities in four different cities.Malcom decides that he wants to group the bagel shops together as a single business and the movie theatres together as a single business. He reports both bagel shop's income on one Schedule C, and the income and loss from the movie theatres on another Schedule C.

Example: Roberta is a partner in Forever Young LLC, which sells skin care products to drug stores. She is also a partner in Verona Trucking. Forever Young LLC and Verona Trucking are under common control. Verona's main business is transporting goods for Forever Young, and it is the only trucking business Roberta is involved in. Roberta groups Forever Young's wholesale activity and Verona's trucking activity as a single activity.

In general, a rental activity cannot be grouped with a trade or business activity. However, they can be grouped together if the activities form an appropriate economic unit and:

- The rental activity is insubstantial in relation to the trade or business activity,
- The trade or business activity is insubstantial in relation to the rental activity, or
- Each owner of the trade or business activity has the same ownership interest in the rental activity, in which case the part of the rental activity that involves the rental of items of property for use in the trade or business activity may be grouped with the business activity.

Example: Miles and Shira are married and file jointly. Miles is the only shareholder of Eco-Clean Dry Cleaners, an S corporation. Shira is the only shareholder of Fontana Properties, an S corporation that owns a commercial office building, part of which is rented to Eco-Clean. Fontana Properties' rental business and Eco-Clean's dry cleaning business are not insubstantial in relation to each other. Since Miles and Shira file a joint return, they are treated as one taxpayer for purposes of the passive activity rules. The same ownership applies (Miles and Shira, who are a married couple) to both businesses, with the same ownership interest (100% in each). Miles and Shira may conclude that Fontana Properties' rental activity and Eco-Drycleaner's dry cleaning store form an appropriate economic unit and group them as a single business activity.

Rental Income

A business may have income from rental activity for any amounts received or accrued as payment for the use of property. Rental income may also include advance payments and deposits from renters.

Rental income earned by a sole proprietor, and related expenses, are generally reported on the following forms:

- **Schedule C**, *Profit or Loss from Business*: Used for professional real estate dealers, and by owners of hotels and boarding houses who provide significant services for tenants or guests. The services must be substantial and not simply those normally provided with the mere rental or lease of property for occupancy only. Normally services such as daily maid service will be considered a substantial service.

- **Schedule E**, *Supplemental Income and Loss (from rental real estate, royalties, partnerships, S corporations, estates, trusts, REMICs,* etc.): Used by taxpayers who are not professional real estate dealers or do not provide substantial services.

Generally, rental income earned by an individual taxpayer is not subject to employment taxes, unless the taxpayer is a professional real estate dealer. A taxpayer qualifies as a real estate dealer if he is primarily engaged in the business of selling real estate to customers. Rental income reported on Schedule C, including rent received by a real estate dealer from real estate held primarily for sale to customers, is subject to self-employment tax. Income reported on Schedule E typically is not subject to SE tax.

Example: Joe owns two residential rental properties. He manages them himself and collects rents. Joe also has a full-time job as a restaurant manager. He is not a real estate dealer. Joe should report his rental income and losses on Schedule E. His rental income is not subject to self-employment tax.

Lease cancellation payments received from a tenant are reported as income in the year received. Advance rental payments received under a lease must be recognized in the year received, regardless of which accounting method is used.

However, a security deposit is not considered income upon initial receipt, if the deposit is refundable to the tenant at the end of the lease. If the taxpayer keeps the security deposit because the tenant did not live up to the terms of the lease or because he damaged property, the deposit amount is recognized as income in the year it is forfeited by the tenant.

A taxpayer in the business of renting personal property, such as equipment, vehicles, or formal wear, includes the rental income on Schedule C. Advance payments for renting personal property must be reported in the year received.

Definition: Personal property is not the same as "personal-use" property that a taxpayer uses for personal purposes. In its most general definition, personal property includes any tangible asset other than real estate. The distinguishing factor between personal property and real property is that personal property is movable, while real property, such as land or buildings, generally remains in one location.

Investment Income

A business may earn interest or dividend income from investments or from lending money to others. A common example is when a C corporation owns stock in another corporation.

For most sole proprietors, dividend income is considered nonbusiness income and is reported directly on Form 1040. However, dividends are treated as business income by professional stockbrokers and securities dealers.

Bartering Income

Bartering occurs when a taxpayer exchanges goods or services without exchanging money. An example of bartering is a plumber doing repair work for a dentist in exchange for dental services. The fair market value of goods and services received in a barter exchange must be included in income by each party in the year received. If the parties agree in advance on the fair market value of goods and services exchanged, it may be used, absent conflicting evidence.

Definition: The IRS defines **fair market value** (FMV) as the price at which a property would change hands between a buyer and a seller when both have reasonable knowledge of all the necessary facts and neither is being forced to buy or sell.

Example: Ethan is a self-employed social media marketer. Ethan and Bryce, a house painter, are members of a barter club where members contact each other directly and bargain. In return for Ethan's marketing services, Bryce paints Ethan's business office. Ethan must report the exchange as income on Schedule C. Bryce must also include in his income the fair market value of the services Ethan provided.

Income from Canceled Debt

If a business-related debt is canceled or forgiven, other than as a gift or bequest, the business generally includes in income the amount of the cancellation of debt (COD). However, a cash-basis business is not required to realize income from a canceled debt to the extent that the payment of the debt would have led to a business deduction.

Example: Barbells Partnership is a cash-basis business. The company arranges computer repair services on credit but later has trouble paying its debts. The computer repair company forgives the repair bill. The partnership is not required to recognize the canceled debt as income because payment of the repair bill would have been deductible as a business expense anyway.

In the example above, the canceled debt of an accrual-basis business would be considered income, because a deduction for the repair expense already would have been recorded. If a taxpayer owes a debt to a seller for property he bought and the seller reduces the amount owed, the taxpayer generally does not have income from the reduction.

If the taxpayer is bankrupt or insolvent, the amount of the COD may be excluded from taxable income. If the taxpayer is not bankrupt or insolvent, the amount of the reduction is treated as a purchase price adjustment, and the buyer's basis in the property is reduced.

Additional exclusions may apply to the discharge of qualified farm indebtedness and qualified real property business indebtedness.

Taxpayers who use these exclusions are required to reduce specified tax attributes, including loss and credit carryforwards and the bases of assets, by corresponding amounts.

Business-Related Court Awards and Damages

Court awards and settlements that grant compensation for physical injuries or illness are generally excluded from taxation. Most other types of court awards and settlements are taxable income, such as:

- Damages for:
  - Patent or copyright infringement,
  - Breach of contract, or
  - Interference with business operations.
- Compensation for lost profits.
- Interest earned on any type of court award.
- Punitive damages related to business income or business activity.

Note: With respect to court awards, punitive damages may be awarded in addition to compensatory damages for actual monetary losses. Punitive damages are generally meant to "punish" the defendant for a willful or malicious act. Punitive damages are subject to income tax but are not subject to self-employment tax.

Example: Harold is a professional trucker. He was in a serious car accident during one of his long hauls. He sustained physical injuries and permanent damage to his foot, which was broken during the accident. Harold sued the truck manufacturer when it was discovered that the brakes on his semi-truck were faulty. During the trial, it was discovered that the manufacturer knew about the defect for several years, but chose not warn customers. Harold wins his case. The jury awards him $500,000 in compensatory damages for his injuries, and $2 million dollars in punitive damages. Even though Harold is self-employed, the compensatory damages are not taxable to Harold and do not need to be reported as business income, because they are compensation for his injury. The punitive damages are taxable, but not subject to self-employment tax.

Amounts Not Considered Business Income

Just as with individual taxpayers, certain types of business-related income and property transfers are not taxable or reportable. Others may be partially taxable, and in some instances the recognition of income is delayed until a later date. Examples include:

- Issuances of stock, including the sale of Treasury stock
- Most business loans (which create debt, not income)
- State and local taxes that are collected in connection with sales or the provision of services and remitted to state or local governments
- Like-kind exchanges of property
- Gain from an involuntary conversion, if the gain is reinvested properly.

Unit 3: Study Questions

(Test yourself and then check the correct answers at the end of this section.)

1. Which of the following is considered passive activity income?

A. Income from a trade or business in which a taxpayer does not materially participate.
B. Portfolio income.
C. Rental real estate income earned by a bona fide real estate professional.
D. Both B and C.

2. When is a business not required to realize income from a canceled debt?

A. Canceled debt is always taxable to a business.
B. A business does not have to recognize canceled debt income to the extent that the payment of the debt would have led to a business deduction.
C. Canceled debt is never taxable income to a business.
D. Canceled debt is taxable income for a sole proprietorship or partnership, but not for a C corporation or an S corporation.

3. The Mickelson Tool Corporation rents large tools and machinery for use in construction projects. The company always charges a refundable security deposit and a nonrefundable cleaning deposit when someone rents a machine. Mickelson Tool received the following amounts in 2016:

- Rental income: $50,000
- Security deposits: $4,050
- Cleaning deposits: $1,500

What amount should be included in the corporation's gross income?

A. $50,000
B. $51,500
C. $54,050
D. $55,550

4. Which of the following would not be considered income for tax purposes?

A. Interest earned on a court award.
B. Damages received in a lawsuit or as settlement for personal physical injuries.
C. Barter income from consulting services.
D. Legal damages awarded for copyright infringement.

5. Camille, a calendar-year, accrual-based taxpayer, owns a studio that teaches ballroom dancing. On October 1, 2016, she receives payment for a one-year contract for 96 one-hour lessons beginning on that date. She gives eight lessons in 2016 and the rest in the following year. How and when must she recognize this payment as income?

A. All income must be recognized in 2016.
B. All income may be deferred until 2017 since that is when most of the lessons are given.
C. 8/96 of the income must be recognized in 2016 and the rest, 88/96, in 2017.
D. All of the income can be split equally between 2016 and 2017.

6. A taxpayer can treat one or more trade, business, or rental activities as a single activity:

A. To avoid the passive activity loss rules.
B. By making an election each year to determine whether or not to group the activities into appropriate economic units.
C. If he does not materially participate in any of the activities.
D. If the activities form an appropriate economic unit for measuring gain or loss under the passive activity rules.

7. Which of the following statements is not correct about grouping passive activities?

A. If two activities are grouped into one larger activity, the taxpayer will need only to show material participation in the activity as a whole.
B. A taxpayer may group two or more trade or business activities if they comprise an appropriate economic unit.
C. The IRS may challenge the grouping of passive activities.
D. A rental activity cannot be grouped with a trade or business activity.

8. Harley is a real estate dealer who develops and sells real estate on a regular basis. He also owns two duplexes and an office building that he rents out because he could not sell them. He works on these rental activities full-time. How should Harley report his rental income?

A. On Schedule E.
B. On Schedule C.
C. On Schedule D.
D. Harley's rental income is not taxable because he is a real estate professional.

9. Losses from passive activities are generally deductible only up to the amount of __________ from passive activities in a given year.

A. Other losses.
B. Debt basis.
C. Capital gains.
D. Income.

10. When are advance rental payments taxable?

A. In the year they are received.
B. In the period in which they are accrued.
C. They are not taxable.
D. They are taxable when the checks are cashed.

11. Sean has an ownership stake in several businesses. He is a passive investor and did not materially participate in any of them. In 2016, he had the following results from these activities:

- Appliance repair store: $20,000 loss
- Ice cream parlor: $31,000 income
- Cupcake store: $17,500 loss

What is the tax treatment of Sean's ownership of these businesses?

A. Taxable income of $31,000 and deductible losses of $37,500.
B. Deductible loss of $6,500.
C. No taxable income in 2016; carryover of passive activity loss of $6,500 to 2017.
D. Taxable income of $31,000 in 2016; carryover of passive activity loss of $37,500 to 2017.

12. Allen's Exotic Pets, a cash-basis taxpayer, purchases $1,000 worth of legal services on credit in 2016. His business is struggling, and he is unable to pay the bill. The law firm forgives the bill in January 2017. What is the correct statement about how Allen's Exotic Pets should handle the canceled debt?

A. The company must recognize the canceled debt income in 2016.
B. The company must recognize the canceled debt income in 2017.
C. The company must recognize half the canceled debt income in 2016 and half in 2017.
D. The company does not have to recognize the canceled debt income because payment of the legal services bill would have been deductible as a business expense.

13. What is personal property?

A. Personal assets of a taxpayer.
B. Real property owned by a business taxpayer.
C. Assets that are moveable and tangible.
D. Real property owned by a nonbusiness taxpayer.

14. Which of the following is business income?

A. Like-kind exchanges of property.
B. Business loans.
C. The sale of Treasury stock.
D. A barter exchange of services between two sole proprietors.

Unit 3: Answers

1. The answer is A. Trade or business activities in which the taxpayer does not materially participate during the year are generally considered passive activities. Rental real estate activities, even if the taxpayer does materially participate, are generally considered passive activities. However, there is an exception for real estate professionals. Portfolio income, such as interest, dividends, annuities, and royalties not derived in the ordinary course of a trade or business, or gain or loss from the disposition of property that produces these types of income or that is held for investment, is not passive activity income.

2. The answer is B. Canceled debt is not taxable income for a business to the extent that payment of the debt would have led to a business deduction.

3. The answer is B. The refundable security deposits are not taxable income, because those amounts are returned to the customer if the items rented are returned in good condition. The amounts included in gross income would be the rental income and the nonrefundable cleaning deposits ($50,000 + $1,500 = $51,500).

4. The answer is B. Certain items of income are excluded from gross income. Gross income does not include most types of compensation for physical injuries.

5. The answer is C. Under the rules of advance payment for services, Camille must recognize income from the eight lessons she gives in 2016 and the rest in 2017, regardless of whether she actually has given all of the lessons by the end of 2017.

6. The answer is D. A taxpayer can treat one or more trade or business or rental activities as a single activity if the activities form an appropriate economic unit for measuring gain or loss under the passive activity rules. If two activities are grouped together, he needs only to show material participation in the activity as a whole. If the two activities are separate, he must show material participation in each one. Grouping cannot be done simply to avoid the passive activity rules, and activities generally cannot be regrouped in a later year if they were grouped into appropriate economic units.

7. The answer is D. In general, a rental activity cannot be grouped with a trade or business activity. However, they can be grouped together if the activities form an appropriate economic unit and:

- The rental activity is insubstantial to the trade or business activity,
- The trade or business activity is insubstantial in relation to the rental activity, or
- Each owner of the trade or business activity has the same ownership interest in the rental activity, in which case the part of the rental activity that involves the rental of items of property for use in the trade or business activity may be grouped with the trade or business activity.

8. The answer is B. Normally, rental income is not subject to employment taxes, and it is reported on Schedule E, *Supplemental Income and Loss*. However, as he is a real estate dealer, Harley's income from the rentals is subject to employment taxes and must be reported on Schedule SE as well as on Schedule C, *Profit or Loss for Business*.

9. The answer is D. Losses from passive activities that exceed the income from passive activities in a given year are generally disallowed. The losses may be carried forward to the next year. Only when a taxpayer materially participates in a trade or business activity are his losses not limited.

10. The answer is A. Advance rental payments received under a lease must be recognized in the year received, regardless of which accounting method is used. This means that a taxpayer who owns rental properties and receives rent in advance cannot delay recognizing the income, even if the taxpayer is on the accrual basis.

11. The answer is C. Under the passive activity limitation rules, Sean would not be able to deduct the full amount of his losses. Since he had passive activity income of $31,000 in 2016, he can offset losses up to that amount. He can carry over the remaining losses of $6,500 to the following year.

12. The answer is D. As a cash-basis taxpayer, Allen's Exotic Pets would have been able to deduct the cost of the legal services as a business expense. It is therefore not required to recognize the canceled debt income.

13. The answer is C. Personal property has a similar name, but should not be confused with "personal-use" property that a taxpayer uses for personal purposes rather than for business purposes. In a broad definition, personal property includes any asset other than real estate. Personal property is movable, unlike land and buildings that remain in one location.

14. The answer is D. A barter exchange of services between two sole proprietors would be business income. The fair market value of goods and services received in a barter exchange must be included in income by each party in the year received. If the two parties agree in advance to the fair market value of the goods or services being exchanged, the IRS will generally accept that amount as the FMV.

Unit 4: Business Expenses

More Reading:

Publication 535, *Business Expenses*

Publication 538, *Accounting Periods and Methods*

Publication 587, *Business Use of Your Home*

Publication 463, *Travel, Entertainment, Gift, and Car Expenses*

Business expenses are the costs of carrying on a trade or business, and are usually deductible if the business operates to make a profit. However, some costs must be capitalized and depreciated or amortized. This unit addresses general concepts and other types of business expenses.

A cash-basis business claims deductible business expenses in the period they are paid. Accrual businesses claim business expenses when they are incurred.

Expenses under the Accrual Method

Under the accrual method of accounting, a taxpayer generally deducts or capitalizes business expenses when both of the following apply:

- All events have occurred that fix the fact of liability, and the liability can be determined with reasonable accuracy.
- Economic performance has occurred: the property or services are provided or the property is used.

Exception for Recurring Items: Expenses for certain recurring items may be treated as incurred during the tax year even though economic performance has not occurred. In the above example, office supplies may qualify as a recurring item.

If so, the taxpayer can deduct them in 2016, even if the supplies are not delivered until 2017 when economic performance occurs. The exception for recurring items applies if all of the following requirements are met:

- The all-events test described above has been met.
- Economic performance occurs by the earlier of the following dates:
  - 8½ months after the close of the year, or
  - The date the taxpayer files a timely return, including extensions, for the year.
- The item is recurring and the taxpayer consistently treats similar items as incurred in the tax year in which the all-events test is met.
- And either:
  - The item is not material, or
  - Accruing the item in the year in which the all-events test is met results in a better match against income than accruing the item in the year of economic performance.

A new expense or an expense that is not incurred every year can be treated as recurring if the taxpayer reasonably expects to incur it regularly in the future. The exception does not apply to workers' compensation or tort liabilities.

Example: Tessa is an accrual-based, calendar-year taxpayer. She orders office supplies on December 20, 2016 and receives them two days later. She does not pay the bill for the supplies until January 10, 2017. She can deduct the expense in 2016 because all events have occurred to fix the liability, the amount of the liability can be determined, and economic performance occurred in 2016.

Deductible Business Expenses

To be deductible, a business expense must be both *ordinary* and *necessary*. An ordinary expense is one that is common and accepted in the taxpayer's industry. A necessary expense is one that is helpful and appropriate for the particular trade or business. However, an expense does not have to be indispensable to be considered necessary.

Example #1: Louisa is an enrolled agent who sends newsletters to clients with year-end tax-saving tips. The newsletters are a marketing tool for her business and would be considered ordinary and necessary. She can deduct the printing and mailing costs as a business expense.

Example #2: Louisa renovates her home office and spends $8,000 on silk designer curtains for the windows. As she does not meet with clients in her home office, an expenditure of this size would likely not be considered reasonable, and therefore would not be deductible as a business expense.

In addition to being ordinary and necessary, the following rules apply to business expenses:

- Some costs must be capitalized rather than deducted. Certain costs that would otherwise be currently deductible are allocated to the cost of producing inventory or holding it for resale. If a cost is included in inventory, it may later be deductible as a component of cost of goods sold. Other costs must be capitalized and either amortized ratably to expense or added to the basis of an asset and recovered when the asset is disposed.
- Personal, family, and living expenses generally cannot be deducted as business expenses.

Business Organizational and Start-up Costs

The costs associated with starting a business generally must be treated as capital expenditures and may not be deducted currently or amortized, subject to the exceptions described below.

The following costs related to a new business may be deductible as current expenses in 2016:

- $5,000 to organize a corporation or partnership, and
- $5,000 of start-up costs.

However, if organizational costs incurred or start-up costs incurred exceed $50,000, there is a dollar-for-dollar reduction until the current deduction for either item is eliminated.

Organizational costs or start-up costs that are not currently deductible may be amortized ratably over 180 months (15 years) on Form 4562, *Depreciation and Amortization*. The amortization period starts with the month the taxpayer begins operating the business.

Example: Bronco Corporation has start-up expenses of $51,000 in 2016. Bronco is $1,000 over the $50,000 threshold so it must reduce its deduction for start-up expenses by the amount that it is over the threshold. Bronco can deduct $4,000 of its start-up expenses ($5,000 allowable deduction minus the excess $1,000). The remaining amount of start-up expenses, $47,000 ($51,000 - $4,000 allowable deduction), must be amortized over 180 months.

Example: Clear-Water Inc. opened for business on November 1, 2016. Prior to opening, the company incurred $21,200 of start-up expenses for advertising and manager training. Since Clear-Water had less than $50,000 of start-up costs, the company can deduct the full $5,000 on its 2016 tax return, and can also claim $180 of amortization ([$21,200 - $5,000]/180 = $90 per month × 2 [two months, November and December]).

All amounts paid to investigate a business before actually creating the business are amortizable start-up costs. Amortizable start-up costs for purchasing a business include only investigative costs incurred in the course of a general search for or preliminary investigation of the business. These are costs that help you decide whether to purchase a business. Costs incurred in an actual attempt to purchase a specific business are capital expenses that cannot be amortized.

Start-up Costs

Start-up costs are amounts paid or incurred for: (a) creating an active trade or business; or (b) investigating the creation or acquisition of an active trade or business. Start-up costs include amounts paid or incurred in connection with an existing activity engaged in for profit; and for the production of income in anticipation of the activity becoming an active trade or business. Business start-up costs are incurred before a business actually begins operations. Common start-up costs include:

- An analysis or survey of potential markets
- Advertisements to announce the opening of a business (before it actually opens)
- Salaries and wages for employees who are being trained and their instructors
- Travel and other necessary costs for securing prospective distributors, suppliers, or customers
- Salaries and fees for executives and consultants, or for similar professional services

Example: Moonlight Corporation received its corporate charter on September 12, 2016. During the remainder of 2016, the company paid $15,500 for Internet and television advertising; $2,000 for training of employees; and $4,000 of consultant fees. Moonlight officially opened its doors on January 8, 2017. The company can elect to deduct $5,000 as start-up costs in the 2016 tax year, the year in which it started business. It will then amortize the remaining $16,500 over 180 months starting in January 2017.

Start-up costs do not include deductible interest, taxes, or research and experimental costs.

If a taxpayer completely disposes of a business before the end of the amortization period, he can deduct the remaining unamortized start-up costs. However, the business can deduct these deferred start-up costs only to the extent they qualify as a loss.

If an individual attempts to go into business and is unsuccessful (i.e., the business is not actually created), the costs incurred may fall into two categories:

- Costs incurred before making a decision to purchase or start a specific business, which are considered personal and thus nondeductible
- Costs incurred in an attempt to purchase or start a specific business, which are capital costs that may be claimed as a capital loss.

The cost of assets acquired in connection with an unsuccessful attempt to go into business must be capitalized and cannot be deducted or recovered until the assets are disposed.

If a corporation incurs costs related to an unsuccessful attempt to acquire or start a new business, it can deduct all of its investigatory costs as a business loss.

Example: Rocio wants to purchase a local bakery. She incurs $3,400 in legal fees as well as contract costs during the negotiation process. However, before the final contract is signed, one of the owners of the bakery changes his mind and decides that he doesn't want to sell. Rocio may deduct the costs that she incurred in connection with her attempt to purchase the business as a capital loss.

Qualifying Organizational Costs

If a taxpayer decides to form a corporation, the corporation can elect to deduct up to $5,000 of its initial organizational expenditures and amortize the remainder over a period of 180 months. Qualifying organizational costs must be:

- For the creation of a business

- Chargeable to a capital account
- For a partnership, incurred by the due date of the tax return (excluding extensions) for the year business begins
- For a corporation, incurred before the end of the first tax year in which the corporation is in business

Examples of qualifying organizational costs include:

- The cost of temporary directors
- The cost of organizational meetings
- Filing fees for a corporation (or an LLC or LLP)
- State incorporation fees for corporations
- Legal and accounting fees for setting up the business

Deductible Taxes

Businesses generally can deduct taxes in the year paid, regardless of which method of accounting the business uses. Under the accrual method, a taxpayer may ratably accrue real estate taxes.

Real Estate Taxes: In order for real estate taxes to be deductible, the taxing authority must calculate the tax based on the assessed value of the real estate. If a property is sold, the deductible portion of the real estate taxes must be allocated between the buyer and the seller according to the number of days in the property tax year that each owned the property. The seller is treated as paying the taxes up to, but not including, the date of sale. The buyer is treated as paying the taxes beginning with the date of sale.

Businesses cannot deduct taxes charged for local benefits and improvements that tend to increase the value of property. These include assessments for streets, sidewalks, water mains, sewer lines, and public parking facilities. A business must instead increase the basis of its property by the amount of the assessment.

However, a business can deduct taxes for local benefits such as maintenance, repairs, or interest charges related to capital improvements.

Example: Lawrence owns a business office on Grand Street. During the year, the city charged an assessment of $4,000 to each business on Grand Street to improve the sidewalks. Lawrence cannot deduct this assessment as a current business expense. Instead, he must increase the basis of his property by the amount of the assessment.

Example: Waterfront City converts a downtown area into an enclosed pedestrian mall. The city assesses the full cost of construction, financed with 10-year bonds, against the affected properties. The city pays the principal and interest with the annual payments made by the property owners. The assessments for construction costs are not deductible as taxes or as business expenses but are depreciable capital expenses. The part of each payment used to pay the interest on the bonds is deductible as taxes.

Personal Property Taxes: Taxes imposed by a state or local government on personal property used in a taxpayer's trade or business are deductible.

Income Taxes: Federal income taxes are never deductible. However, corporations and partnerships can deduct state and local income and franchise taxes. A self-employed individual who reports income on Schedule C can deduct state and local income taxes as an itemized deduction on Schedule A.

Example: Reiner Company is a calendar-year C corporation incorporated in Utah. Utah imposes a 5% state tax on Reiner's corporate earnings. In 2016, Reiner pays $12,000 of state income tax to Utah. This state tax would be deductible as a business expense on the corporation's federal tax return.

Sales and Use Taxes: Sales and use taxes collected by a business in connection with the sale of goods or services to its customers are remitted to the taxing authorities, and are excluded from the business's gross receipts and its deductible expenses. When a business pays sales tax in connection with the purchase of goods or services, the tax is considered a component of the cost of the item purchased. Thus, if the item is depreciable property, the sales/use tax is added to its depreciable basis. If the item is merchandise for resale or to be used in the production of inventory, the tax is capitalized as a component of inventory. If the tax is related to a currently deductible business expense, it is likewise considered part of that expense.

Excise Taxes: Excise taxes that are ordinary and necessary expenses of carrying on a trade or business are deductible. Excise taxes are taxes paid when purchases are made on a specific item, such as gasoline, or activity, such as highway usage by trucks. When paid in connection with the purchase of a specific item an excise tax is considered part of the cost of that item. Therefore, it may be deductible currently or as the item is used, or be subject to capitalization, such as when the item is used in manufacturing inventory. Under the Affordable Care Act, indoor tanning salons are subject to a 10% excise tax, which is a deductible business expense.

Business Bad Debts

Most business bad debts are a result of credit sales of goods or services to customers for which payment has not been received. These are recorded in a business's books as either accounts receivable or notes receivable. If, after a reasonable period of time, a business has tried to collect the amount due, but is unable to do so, the uncollectible part becomes a business bad debt.

A debt becomes uncollectible or worthless when there is no longer any chance the amount owed will be paid. A business does not have to wait for the debt to be due or to obtain a court judgment to show the debt is uncollectible.

A business bad debt is a loss from the worthlessness of a debt that was either:

- Created or acquired in a taxpayer's trade or business, or
- Closely related to the trade or business when it became partly or totally worthless.

To be considered closely related to a taxpayer's trade or business, the primary motive for incurring the debt must be business related.

A taxpayer can claim a business bad debt deduction only if the amount owed was previously included in his gross income. Thus, unlike an accrual-basis taxpayer, a cash-basis business does not report income until payment is actually or constructively received from a customer. Since a cash-basis business does not report any income on sales made on credit (until paid), cash-basis businesses will not have deductible business bad debts.

When a business loans money to a client, supplier, employee, or distributor for a business reason and the balance due later becomes worthless, the business can deduct the balance as a bad debt. However, the loan must have a genuine business purpose in order for this treatment to qualify.

Example: Carol is an accrual-based taxpayer who owns an eyeglass manufacturing company. One of her salesmen, Dawson, loses all his samples and asks Carol for a loan to replace them. Carol loans Dawson $3,000 to replace his eyeglass samples and sample bags. Dawson later quits his job without repaying the debt. Carol has a business-related bad debt that she can deduct as a business expense.

If a taxpayer receives property in partial settlement of a debt, the debt should be reduced by the property's FMV, which becomes the taxpayer's basis in the property. The remaining unpaid balance of the debt can be deducted as a bad debt when and if it becomes worthless.

An entity may later recover a debt that was previously written off as a bad debt deduction. If a business recovers a bad debt that was deducted in a prior year, the recovered portion must be included as income in the current year tax return. There is no need to amend the prior year tax return on which the bad debt deduction was claimed.

Insurance Expenses

The following types of business-related insurance premiums are deductible:

- Property and casualty insurance (that covers fire, storm, theft, accident, or similar losses)
- Business interruption insurance (that reimburses a business if it is temporarily shut down due to a fire or similar disaster)
- Credit insurance that covers losses from business bad debts
- Liability insurance
- Malpractice insurance
- Contributions to a state unemployment insurance fund (deductible as taxes)
- Vehicle insurance that covers vehicles used in a business (not deductible if a business uses the standard mileage rate to figure vehicle expenses)
- Group-term life insurance for employees
- Group accident, health, long-term care, and workers' compensation insurance for employees

As described earlier, if a cash-basis business pays insurance premiums in advance, it may rely upon a 12-month rule and deduct amounts paid that do not extend beyond the earlier of the following: (1) 12 months after the benefit begins, or (2) the end of the tax year after the tax year in which payment is made.

Self-Employed Health Insurance Deduction

A self-employed individual may be able to deduct premiums paid for medical and dental insurance and qualified long-term care insurance for himself, his spouse, and his dependents.

To qualify, a taxpayer must have a net profit reported on his Schedule C (Form 1040), or Schedule F; be a partner with net earnings from self-employment reported on Schedule K-1; or be a more-than-2% shareholder in an S corporation who had premiums paid or reimbursed by the corporation and reported to him as wages on Form W-2.

Note: If a partnership pays accident or health insurance premiums for its partners, it generally can deduct them as guaranteed payments to the partners. If an S corporation pays accident or health insurance premiums for its more-than-2% shareholder-employees, it generally can deduct them and must also include them in the shareholders' wages subject to federal income tax withholding. A C Corporation can deduct employee health premiums dollar-for-dollar as a regular business expense.

He cannot take the deduction for any month he was eligible to participate in any employer-subsidized health plan (including one that his spouse was eligible for), even if he or his spouse did not actually participate in the plan.

The self-employed health insurance deduction is only available to a business that has net income for the year. If the business earns no money or incurs a loss, the taxpayer does not get a deduction.

This is not the case for C corporations, however. A C corporation may fully deduct its employee health insurance premiums, even if the corporation has a loss for the year.

Example: Danny is a sole proprietor who reports income and loss on Schedule C. In 2016, he pays $12,000 for health his insurance. He had a net loss of $3,000 for the year because of a fire in his warehouse. Since he does not have any net earnings for the year, his health insurance is not deductible.

Interest Expense

A business can deduct interest paid or accrued during the tax year on debts related to a trade or business for which it is legally liable. It does not matter what type of property secures the loan. A business deducts business-related interest as follows:

- **Cash Method:** A business can deduct interest paid during the tax year. It cannot deduct a promissory note given in payment of interest because it is a promise to pay and not an actual payment.
- **Accrual Method:** A business can deduct interest that has accrued during the tax year.

A taxpayer cannot accelerate a tax deduction by paying interest in advance of when it is due. If a business uses the accrual method, it cannot deduct interest owed to a related person who uses the cash method until payment is made and the interest is includable in the gross income of that person.

If the proceeds of a loan are used for more than one purpose, the related interest must be allocated based upon the use of the proceeds, among the following:

- Personal interest
- Investment interest
- Portfolio interest
- Interest related to a trade or business

Interest charged on income tax assessed on an individual's income tax returns is not a business deduction, even if the tax is related to income from a trade or business. This interest should be treated as a business deduction only in figuring a net operating loss deduction. Penalties on underpaid deficiencies and underpaid estimated tax are not interest and are not deductible.

Rent Expense

A business can deduct expenses for renting property, including real estate, machinery, and other items used to conduct business. However, the cost of acquiring a lease is not considered rent and must be amortized over the term of the lease.

Generally, rent paid in a trade or business is deductible in the year paid or accrued. However, if a taxpayer pays rent in advance, he can deduct only the amount that applies to his use of the rented property during the tax year. The rest of the payment can be deducted only over the period to which it applies.

If a taxpayer has both business and personal use of rented property, he may only deduct the amount actually used for business. To compute the business percentage, the taxpayer must compare the portion of the property used for business to the entire property. The resulting percentage is used to figure the business portion of the rent expense.

Example: Ainsley rents a business office to use both as a personal studio for painting and as a site to run her tutoring business. Her total rental payments for the year are $11,000. The office is 1,000 square feet; she uses 800 square feet for the tutoring business and the remaining 200 square feet for her personal art studio. Therefore, she uses the office 80% for her business and 20% for personal purposes. The deductible portion of the rent expense is $8,800 (80% × $11,000).

Home Office Deduction

A self-employed taxpayer may be able to deduct certain expenses related to part of his home if the space is used regularly and exclusively for business and it is:

- The taxpayer's principal place of business, and/or
- The place used to meet with patients, clients, or customers in the normal course of business; or

- A separate structure not attached to the home that is used in connection with the business.

A taxpayer can use any reasonable method to calculate the percentage of the home that is used for business. Typically, the square footage of the home used for business is divided by the home's total square footage. Because of the exclusive use rule, a taxpayer is not allowed to deduct business expenses for any part of the home that is used for both personal and business purposes.

A self-employed taxpayer must complete Form 8829, *Expenses for Business Use of Your Home,* and then transfer the total to his Schedule C (Form 1040).

Simplified Home Office Deduction: A taxpayer may also choose to compute his home office deduction using a simplified calculation formula: a deduction of $5 per square foot is allowed for the space in the home that is used for business, up to a maximum allowable square footage of 300 square feet (for a maximum deduction of $1,500).

Example: Rick is a self-employed insurance broker with a home office he uses exclusively for business. The office measures 15 × 15, or 225 square feet. Rick deducts $1,125 ($5 × 225) using the simplified option. He does not have to calculate depreciation or prorate his utilities under the simplified method.

Under this option, a taxpayer can claim the full amount of allowable mortgage interest, real estate taxes, and casualty losses on his home as itemized deductions on Schedule A.

These deductions do not need to be allocated between personal and business use, as is required under the regular method. The simplified option does not include a deduction for depreciation.

Each year, a taxpayer may use either the simplified method or the regular method to calculate the home office deduction. If he chooses the regular method after having used the simplified method in an earlier year, depreciation is calculated using an optional depreciation table for the property.

Employee-related Business Use: The home office deduction is also available for an employee who uses part of his home for business. However, there are two additional tests that must be met:

- The business use must be for the convenience of the employer, and
- The employee must not rent any part of his home to his employer and use the rental portion to perform services as an employee for that employer.

Business Travel, Meals, and Entertainment

To be deductible for tax purposes, business expenses for travel, meals, and entertainment must be incurred while carrying on a genuine business activity. The taxpayer must be able to prove that entertainment expenses, including meals, are directly related to the conduct of business.

Adequate records must be retained to support these expenses, including receipts, bills, or canceled checks. An exception is made for expenses, other than lodging, that cost less than $75.

Travel costs with a business purpose are 100% deductible. However, if the travel includes an element of personal travel, the personal portion of the expense may not be deductible. In some instances, the personal portion may be incremental costs related to a spouse's travel. In other cases, a business must determine the nondeductible portion of an expense by multiplying it by a fraction. The numerator of the fraction is the number of personal days during the travel period and the denominator is the total number of days spent traveling.

Example: Paul flies to New Orleans on business and takes his wife with him so she can vacation there. Paul pays $190 for each airline ticket and $200 for a double hotel room. The cost of a single hotel room is $150. Paul can deduct the cost of his plane ticket and $150 for the hotel room. His wife's expenses are not deductible as a business expense.

Only 50% of the cost is deductible for business meals or entertainment incurred while:

- Traveling away from home (whether eating alone or with others) on business
- Entertaining customers at a restaurant or other location
- Attending a business convention or reception, business meeting, or business luncheon
- Obtaining deductible educational expenses, such as meals during a continuing education seminar

Taxpayers are considered "traveling away from home" if their duties require them to be away from home substantially longer than an ordinary day's work and they need to sleep or rest to meet the demands of their work.

The following related expenses are also subject to the 50% limit:

- Taxes and tips on a business meal or entertainment activity
- Cost of a room in which the business holds a dinner or cocktail party

The cost of transportation to a business meal or a business-related entertainment activity is not subject to the 50% limit.

Example: Karen is a business owner who takes a client to lunch. The total restaurant bill is $88. She also pays cab fare of $10 to get to the restaurant. Karen's deductible expense is $54:

Deductible meal expense	$88 × 50% = $44
Deductible travel expense	$10
Total deductible business expense	**$54**

Exceptions to the 50% Limit: The following meals are 100% deductible by the employer:

- Meals that are included in employees' wages as taxable compensation
- Meals that qualify as a de minimis fringe benefit, such as occasional coffee and doughnuts
- Meals that are made available to the general public as part of a promotional activity, such as a real estate broker who provides dinner to potential investors at a sales presentation
- Meals furnished to employees when the employer operates a restaurant or catering service
- Meals furnished to employees as part of a teambuilding activity
- Meals that are required by federal law to be furnished to crew members of certain commercial vessels
- Meals furnished on an oil or gas platform or drilling rig located offshore or in Alaska

Special Department of Transportation Rules (DOT)

There is also an exception for certain individuals subject to the U.S. Department of Transportation (DOT) "hours of service" limits who are traveling away from their tax home. A business is allowed to deduct 80% of employees' meal costs when DOT hours of service limits apply to the following:

- Certain air transportation workers such as pilots, crew, and mechanics regulated by the Federal Aviation Administration
- Interstate truck operators and bus drivers regulated by the Department of Transportation
- Certain railroad employees such as engineers and conductors regulated by the Federal Railroad Administration
- Certain merchant mariners regulated by the Coast Guard

Per Diem Rates for Business Travel

To ease recordkeeping requirements, a business may use a federal per diem rate as an alternative to keeping track of employees' actual expenses during business travel away from home.

Per diem is a daily allowance paid by a business to its employees for lodging, meals, and incidental expenses incurred when traveling. The allowance is in lieu of paying actual travel expenses. There is a per diem rate for combined lodging and meal costs and a per diem rate for meal costs alone. An employer may use either per diem method for reimbursing employee travel expenses. A self-employed person can only use a per diem rate for meal costs. Per diem payments not in excess of the federal rate are not included in an employee's taxable wages, if an employee submits an expense report to the employer.

The applicable per diem rates vary based on whether the travel is domestic and foreign, and also by location. For example, the per diem rate in large cities like Los Angeles and New York is higher than for smaller cities. The IRS publishes the per diem rates every year in Publication 1542, *Per Diem Rates.*

Deductible Entertainment Expenses

A business is allowed to deduct 50% of business-related entertainment expenses that are incurred for entertaining a client, customer, or employee, as long as either the directly-related test or the associated test described below is met. It is not necessary to prove that the entertainment actually resulted in business income or another business benefit.

The IRS looks at whether there is a "clear business setting" associated with the entertainment and whether there are "substantial distractions" at the location that prevent business from being conducted.

A taxpayer cannot deduct entertainment expenses that are "lavish or extravagant" under the circumstances. A taxpayer also cannot claim the cost of a meal as an entertainment expense if he is claiming the meal as a travel expense.

If a taxpayer takes a client to a special event, he cannot deduct more than 50% of the face value of the ticket, regardless of the amount paid.

Deductible Entertainment Expenses	
General rule	**Expenses to entertain a client, customer, or employee are deductible.**
Definitions	Entertainment includes any activity generally considered to provide entertainment, amusement, or recreation, and includes meals provided to a customer or client.
Tests	**Directly-related test**
	• Entertainment takes place in a clear business setting, **<u>OR</u>**
	• The main purpose of entertainment was the active conduct of business, and • The taxpayer engaged in business with the client during the entertainment period, and • The taxpayer had more than a general expectation of getting income or some other specific business benefit.
	Associated test
	• Entertainment is associated with the taxpayer's business, and
	• Entertainment occurs directly before or after a substantial business discussion.

Example: Following a day of business meetings, Erik wants to take his two best clients to a basketball game, but the tickets are sold out, so Erik pays a scalper $390 for three tickets. The face value of each ticket is $52. Erik may only use the face value of the tickets as a basis for his deduction, and he also must apply the 50% limit. Therefore, his deductible entertainment expense is $78, figured as follows:

Cost of three event tickets (face value of $52 × 3):	$156
Apply the 50% limit ($156 × 50%):	$78

Transportation Expenses

Ordinarily, expenses related to use of a vehicle for business can be deducted as transportation expenses. To claim a deduction for business use of a car or truck, business-related costs must have been incurred for one or more of the following:

- Traveling from one work location to another within the taxpayer's tax home area (generally, the tax home is the entire city or general area where the taxpayer's main place of business is located, regardless of where he actually lives).
- Visiting customers.
- Attending a business meeting away from the regular workplace.
- Traveling from home to a temporary workplace. A temporary workplace can be either within or outside the taxpayer's tax home area.

Self-employed individuals, including partners in a partnership, may choose to use either the standard mileage rate or actual car expenses in order to figure the deduction for vehicle expenses. C corporations generally cannot use the standard mileage rate. However, businesses, including C corporations, may reimburse an employee under an accountable plan for business-related use of his car using the standard mileage rate. Any amounts reimbursed in excess of the standard mileage rate are reportable on the employee's Form W-2 as wages.

Whether using the standard mileage rate or claiming actual expenses, a taxpayer must keep records that identify the vehicle and provide evidence of ownership or a lease.

Further, he should maintain a daily log showing miles traveled, destination, and business purpose to support the total business miles claimed or the business use percentage to be applied to allocate actual expenses.

Actual vehicle expenses include the costs of the following items:

- Depreciation
- Lease payments
- Registration
- Garage rent
- Repairs and maintenance
- Gas, oil, and tires
- Insurance, parking fees, and tolls

If business use of the vehicle is less than 100%, expenses must be allocated between business and personal use, and only the business use portion is deductible.

Example: Brandon uses a delivery van in his landscaping business. He has no other car, so the van is used for his personal transportation on the weekends. Brandon chooses to deduct actual costs, rather than using the standard mileage rate. Based on his records, Brandon's total vehicle expenses in 2016 are $6,252, which includes the cost of diesel fuel, oil changes, tire replacement, and repairs. Brandon uses the vehicle 75% for business, so his allowable auto expense deduction using the actual expense method is $4,689 ($6,252 × 75%).

For 2016, the standard mileage rate for business use of a vehicle is 54¢ per mile. A taxpayer who elects to use the standard rate cannot deduct actual expenses of operating a vehicle, such as gas, oil, and insurance.

However, business-related parking fees and tolls may be deducted in addition to the standard mileage rate.

A taxpayer filing Schedule C or Schedule F can deduct interest on a loan relating to the purchase of the automobile. However, an employee cannot deduct the interest on a loan relating to an automobile purchase.

A business is prohibited from using the standard mileage rate if it:

- Operates five or more cars at the same time
- Claimed a depreciation deduction using any method other than straight-line, including MACRS
- Claimed a section 179 deduction on the car
- Claimed the special depreciation allowance on the car
- Claimed actual car expenses for a car that was leased

Recordkeeping for Travel, Entertainment, and Gift Expenses				
Expense	**Amount**	**Date**	**Description**	**Business Purpose**
Travel	Record of each expense for travel, lodging, and meals.	Dates for each trip and number of days spent on business.	Destination (name of city, town, etc.)	Business purpose for the expense.
Entertainment	Cost of each separate expense.	Date of entertainment.	Location of the place of entertainment.	Business purpose for the expense.
Gifts	Cost of the gift.	Date of the gift.	Description of the gift.	Business relationship.
Transportation	Cost of each separate expense.	Date of the expense.	The business destination.	Business purpose for the expense.

Business Gifts

A business can deduct business-related gifts to clients and customers. The deductible amount is limited to $25 for amounts given to any person during the year. If a taxpayer and a spouse both give gifts, they are treated as one taxpayer for this limit, even if they have separate businesses. A gift to the spouse of a business customer or client is generally considered an indirect gift to the customer or client.

The $25 limit for business gifts does not include incidental costs such as packaging, insurance, and mailing costs, or the cost of engraving jewelry, which may be deducted separately. Related costs are considered incidental only if they do not add substantial value to a gift.

Example: Hawaii Fruit Corporation gives a large fruit and nut basket to its best customer, Dominic's Produce Company. The fruit basket costs $57, and the shipping and mailing of the basket costs $17. Hawaii Fruit Corporation can deduct $25 for the basket and $17 for the cost of mailing, for a total deduction of $42.

Example: Corinne sells greeting cards to a boutique. She gives three candy boxes to each of the store's owners to thank them for their patronage. Corinne pays $80 for each package, or $240 total. She can deduct $75 ($25 limit × 3) for the packages.

Exceptions: The following items are considered promotional and not subject to the $25 gift limit:

- An item with the business name clearly imprinted on it that costs $4 or less (examples include imprinted pens, desk sets, and plastic bags)
- Signs, display racks, or other promotional materials to be used on the business premises of the recipient

A business may also deduct gifts to employees. Noncash gifts of nominal value that are distributed to employees to promote goodwill may be excluded from taxable compensation. Gifts of greater value and of cash or cash-equivalent items such as gift cards are considered compensation.

Example: Rogan Corporation gives each of its 75 employees a $25 turkey during the holidays. The company can deduct the cost of the turkeys ($1,875 = $25 × 75). The gift is not taxable to the employee, and the fair market value of the gift is not included in the employee's wages.

Charitable Contributions as Business Expenses

Among business entities, only C corporations are permitted to deduct charitable contributions on their income tax returns. The deduction is limited to 10% of taxable income, and is explained later in the dedicated units for C Corporations.

Self-employed taxpayers cannot deduct charitable contributions as business expenses, but can claim deductions on Schedule A if they itemize deductions. Contributions made by partnerships and S corporations are reported on their respective returns as separately stated items, and may be deductible by their partners and shareholders.

Deducted or Capitalized Costs

There are certain costs that businesses may choose to either deduct currently or capitalize as an addition to the basis of a related asset. There are specific rules about the circumstances in which each type of item may be deducted, or if capitalized, how its cost may be recovered through depreciation or amortization.

Examples of costs that are generally capital in nature, but which a business may elect to deduct currently include research and experimental costs; certain intangible drilling costs; and circulation costs for publishers of newspapers and magazines.

Miscellaneous Business Expenses

Additional expenses that may be deductible by a business include the following:

- Advertising
- Credit card convenience fees
- Certain franchise or trademark fees
- Education and training for employees
- Internet-related expenses, such as domain registration fees
- Interview expense allowances for job candidates
- Outplacement services provided to employees
- Legal and accounting fees directly related to operating the business
- Tax preparation fees for business returns
- License and regulatory fees paid annually to state or local governments
- Penalties paid for late performance or nonperformance of a contract
- Repairs to business property, including the cost of labor and supplies

- Subscriptions and memberships to trade magazines and professional organizations
- Supplies and materials used during year
- Utilities, including heat, lights, power, telephone service, and water and sewage

Nondeductible Expenses

The following expenses are not allowed as business deductions:

- Political contributions, including indirect contributions such as advertising in a convention program of a political party
- Lobbying expenses for Federal or State legislation (limited lobbying for local legislation may be deductible[92])
- Dues for country clubs, golf and athletic clubs, and hotel and airline clubs, even if the club is used for business activity
- Penalties and fines paid to any governmental agency for breaking the law, such as parking tickets or fines for violating local zoning codes
- Legal and professional fees for work of a personal nature

[92] IRC Sect. 162(e)(2)

Unit 4: Study Questions

(Test yourself and then check the correct answers at the end of this section.)

1. Axel operates a computer service repair business as a sole proprietorship. He has four employees who also service customers' computers in the field. Axel drives a sedan when he visits clients, and each of his four technicians drives a van assigned to them to make their repair visits. Which of the following methods can Axel use to claim deductions for the cost of these vehicles?

A. He can use the standard mileage rate for the sedan, but must use actual expenses for the vans.
B. He must use actual expenses for all of the vehicles.
C. He must use the standard mileage rate for the sedan, but can use actual expenses for the vans.
D. He can choose to use either method.

2. Alexa is a self-employed accountant who reports income and loss on Schedule C. She goes to a continuing education seminar out-of-state and incurs the following expenses:

Seminar	$400
Train ticket	35
Restaurant meal expense	26
Taxi fare to the restaurant	10

What is her deductible expense for this event?

A. $400
B. $435
C. $458
D. $465

3. In 2016, Helton Partnership, a cash-basis partnership, borrowed $50,000 to purchase machinery. Interest of $2,500 on the loan was due in December 2016. Rather than pay the interest, the partnership refinanced the loan and the interest due into a new loan of $53,800 on December 31, 2016: the original loan amount plus the interest due and an additional $1,300 in loan origination fees. The first payment on the new loan was due January 29, 2017. How much interest is tax deductible by Helton Partnership in 2016?

A. $0
B. $2,500
C. $2,800
D. $3,800

4. Norman is an interstate truck driver subject to the Department of Transportation rules for hours of service. During 2016, he incurs $3,064 in meal expenses while on the job. What is his deductible expense for business meals?

A. $1,532
B. $2,298
C. $2,451
D. $3,064

5. Kimberly is a sole proprietor and files a Schedule C. How should she report the $2,000 of charitable contributions she made on behalf of her business in 2016?

A. The contributions may be deducted on Schedule A as an itemized deduction.
B. The contributions may be deducted on Schedule C as a business deduction.
C. The contributions may not be deducted.
D. Up to 10% of the taxpayer's charitable contributions may be deducted on Schedule C. The remaining amount must be carried over to the next taxable year.

6. Which of the following is not required in order to meet the directly-related test for entertainment expenses to be deductible?

A. Business was engaged in during the entertainment event.
B. The main purpose of the entertainment was the conduct of business.
C. There was more than just the general expectation of business benefit.
D. The entertainment resulted in profit for the business.

7. Brady owns Super Sweets Company. He gives the following business gifts to a customer:

- Glass display for Super Sweets: $500
- Coffee and tea gift basket: $50
- Twenty pens imprinted with the Super Sweets name and logo: $35
- Postage for the gift basket: $20

How much can Brady deduct on his tax return?

A. $25
B. $525
C. $580
D. $605

8. Delia, a self-employed real estate agent, traveled to a business convention by train and incurred the following expenses:

- Train ticket: $100
- Meals: $80
- Hotel room: $90
- Computer game: $50

How much is deductible as a current business expense?

A. $190
B. $230
C. $280
D. $320

9. Mountain Suppliers made a business loan to Sugarhill Corporation, a supplier, in the amount of $10,000. After paying $2,000, Sugarhill Corporation defaults on the loan. Mountain Suppliers makes a good faith attempt to collect the loan, but the debt becomes worthless. How much of this bad debt may Mountain Suppliers deduct as a business expense?

A. $0
B. $2,000
C. $8,000
D. $10,000

10. Marion operates a shoe repair shop in a building she owns. In 2016, she had the following income and expenses:

- Repairs to shop floor: $1,000
- Property tax on business assets: $2,000
- Assessment for sidewalks: $5,800
- Utilities for her store: $1,800

What is the tax treatment of the above expenditures?

A. Deduct repairs, property tax, and utilities as business expenses. The assessment must be added to the basis of the property and depreciated.
B. All of the above expenses are deductible.
C. The property tax must be deducted on Schedule A, and the rest of the expenses may be deducted as business expenses on Schedule C.
D. Only the utilities and repairs may be deducted.

11. Luxe Chocolate Corporation is a cash-basis, calendar-year business. On October 1, 2016, Luxe Chocolate pays $3,600 for a business insurance policy covering three years. The policy coverage begins October 1, 2016 and ends September 30, 2019. How does Luxe Chocolate treat the expense for its insurance policy?

A. The entire $3,600 may be deducted in 2016.
B. 2016 deduction $1,200; 2017 deduction $1,200; 2018 deduction $1,200.
C. 2016: deduction $1,500; 2017 deduction $1,200; 2018 deduction $900.
D. 2016: deduction $300; 2017 deduction $1,200; 2018 deduction $1,200; 2019 deduction $900.

12. Bob owns Jackpot Pawn Shop. He makes a business loan to a client in the amount of $5,000. Bob also loans his brother $1,000 so he can buy a car. His brother, Keith, used to work sporadically at the shop as an employee. Both of the loans are now uncollectible. How much can Bob deduct as a business bad debt expense?

A. $1,000
B. $4,000
C. $5,000
D. $6,000

13. Lily owns a dress shop. Several years ago, she correctly deducted a $10,000 business bad debt after a fabric supplier defaulted on a loan after it was properly deemed to be worthless after making good faith attempts to collect on the loan. In 2016, the fabric supplier wishes to do business with Lily again and repays $9,000 of the loan. How must Lily report this payment?

A. She must amend her prior year tax return to correct the previously reported bad debt deduction.
B. She must reflect this recovery of $9,000 as income in 2016.
C. She can deduct a loss of $1,000 on her 2016 tax return.
D. She is not required to report the $9,000 loan repayment if she is on the cash basis.

14. Maddie rents a small storage unit for her business on February 1, 2016. She is given a discount if she pays the full amount of the lease upfront, which is $1,620 for a three-year lease. What is the amount of Maddie's 2016 deductible expense for leasing the storage unit?

A. $495
B. $540
C. $560
D. $1,620

15. Mike borrowed $100,000 to purchase a machine for his business. The machine cost $90,000. The rest of the money went into Mike's bank account, and he purchased a jet ski with the money later in the year. However, the entire loan was secured by his business assets. Which of the following statements is correct?

A. Mike cannot purchase personal items with a business loan; therefore, none of the interest is deductible.
B. All of the interest is deductible, because it is secured by his business assets.
C. Only the amount of interest allocable to purchase of the business machine is deductible.
D. None of the answers is correct.

16. Garrett operates his printing business out of rented office space. He uses a truck to deliver completed jobs to customers. Which of the following statements is not correct?

A. Garrett can deduct the cost of round-trip transportation between customers and his print shop.
B. Garrett can deduct traveling costs between his home and the print shop.
C. Garrett can deduct the cost of mileage to deliver completed jobs to the post office for mailing.
D. Garrett can deduct the costs to travel to his customers who are disabled and cannot come to his shop.

17. The Castellano Partnership paid the following penalties in 2016. Which are deductible?

A. A penalty paid to the county for violating construction regulations.
B. A penalty imposed by the IRS for late filing of a Form 1065 partnership return.
C. A penalty paid to the city for violating its sign ordinance.
D. A penalty for late performance of a contract.

18. Only-a-Dollar is a retail store. It pays a combined 8.25% sales tax to local and state taxing authorities when a customer purchases its merchandise. How should Only-a-Dollar treat this sales tax expense?

A. Include the amount in its gross receipts and its deductible expenses.
B. Add the amount to the depreciable basis of property of the items sold.
C. Capitalize the cost as a component of inventory of the items sold.
D. Exclude from its gross receipts and deductible expenses the sales taxes it collects and remits them to local and state taxing authorities.

19. Which of the following costs qualify as business start-up costs?

A. State and local taxes.
B. Research and experimental costs.
C. A survey of potential markets.
D. Both B and C.

20. Devina is divorced and a sole proprietor who owns a public relations business. She has a nine-year-old son she claims as a dependent. In 2016, she paid $7,400 of premiums for medical and dental health insurance for herself and her son. She reported a net profit of $23,000 on her Schedule C for the year. Which of the following statements is correct?

A. Health premiums are no longer deductible under the Affordable Care Act.
B. She can deduct 50% of the premiums on Schedule A.
C. She can deduct 100% of the premiums as an adjustment to income.
D. She can deduct the premiums directly on Schedule C.

Unit 4: Answers

1. The answer is B. Axel is forced to use actual costs for his business-related automobile expenses. Many businesses, including self-employed individuals, but not C corporations, can choose to use either the standard mileage rate or actual vehicle expenses in order to claim deductions for the cost of vehicles used in the business. However, a business is prohibited from using the standard mileage rate if it operates five or more vehicles at the same time. Since he has four employees, plus himself, and each has their own company-provided vehicle, he has reached the five-vehicle threshold that requires the use of the actual cost method.

2. The answer is C. The answer is $458 ($400 + $35 + $10 + [26 × 50%]). Her deductible meal expenses are subject to a 50% limit, but the taxi fare, the train ticket, and the seminar are fully deductible.

3. The answer is A. The partnership is on the cash basis; therefore, it can only deduct interest actually *paid* during the year. Since the partnership did not actually pay any interest, it does not have a deductible expense. The fact that the loan was refinanced has no bearing on the deductibility of the interest.

4. The answer is C. A taxpayer who is subject to the Department of Transportation's hours of service can deduct a larger percentage of his meal expenses when traveling away from his tax home. He would multiply his meal expenses incurred while away from home on business by the DOT hours of service limit of 80% ($3,064 × .80 = $2,451).

5. The answer is A. Self-employed taxpayers can deduct these contributions on Schedule A, subject to applicable AGI limits. The contributions cannot be deducted as a business expense on Schedule C. Only C corporations can deduct charitable contributions as a business expense, subject to a limit of 10% of taxable income.

6. The answer is D. The taxpayer is not required to prove that the entertainment event actually produced a profit. The taxpayer must meet either the directly-related test or the associated test in order to deduct an entertainment expense. The directly-related test requires that business was engaged in during the entertainment event; the main purpose was the conduct of business; and there was more than just the general expectation of business benefit.

7. The answer is C. There is a $25 limit per person per tax year for business gifts; however, the cost of packaging, insuring, and mailing are not included in determining the cost of a gift for purposes of the $25 limit. Promotional items such as the display rack are also not included in the cost. Therefore, the business can deduct $580 ($500 + $25 + $35 + $20) = $580:

- Glass display: $500
- Coffee and tea basket: $25 (only $25 is deductible as a gift expense)
- 20 imprinted pens: $35
- Postage for the gift basket: $20

8. The answer is B. Delia can deduct the cost of her hotel room, one-half of her meal expense, and her train ticket to attend the convention ($100 + $90 + (80 × 50%) = $230). The cost of the computer game is a personal expense and not deductible.

9. The answer is C. A loan to a client, customer, employee, or distributor for a business reason can be deducted as a business bad debt if it becomes worthless. The amount of the loan, minus what was repaid, is the deduction on Mountain Supplier's tax return: $10,000 - $2,000 = $8,000.

10. The answer is A. The repairs, property tax, and utilities are all deductible as business expenses. The property tax is deductible as a business expense on Schedule C (rather than on Schedule A) because it is assessed on business property. Assessments for streets, sidewalks, sewer lines, and other public services generally add value to the property and must be added to the basis of the property, rather than deducted currently.

11. The answer is D. Since the advance payment covers more than 12 months (36 months), the $3,600 must be deducted ratably over the three-year period. To figure the monthly premium amount, the policy cost is divided by the coverage period: ($3,600 ÷ 36 = $100). The number of months of coverage in each tax year is then multiplied by the monthly premium:

- 2016: Deduction of $300 ($3,600 ÷ 36 × 3)
- 2017: Deduction of $1,200: ($3,600 ÷ 36 × 12)
- 2018: Deduction of $1,200 ($3,600 ÷ 36 × 12)
- 2019: Deduction of $900 ($3,600 ÷ 36 × 9)

12. The answer is C. Only the loan to the client would be deductible as a business bad debt expense. A loss related to a loan to a client, customer, employee, or distributor for a business reason can be deducted as a business bad debt. Since Keith is a related person and not a regular employee and the loan was for personal reasons, Bob cannot deduct his loss on the loan to his brother as a business bad debt.

13. The answer is B. Lily is not required to amend her prior year return to report the recovery of the bad debt. Since Lily recovered a bad debt that was deducted properly in a prior year, she should include the recovered portion as income in her current year tax return.

14. The answer is A. If a taxpayer pays rent in advance, only the amount that applies to the current year is deductible. The balance must be deducted over the period to which it applies.

Deductible lease expense for 2016:
$1,620/36 (months) = **$45 per month**
$45 × 11 months (February to December) = **$495**

15. The answer is C. Generally, interest on a business loan is fully deductible. However, debt incurred for personal reasons is not deductible as a business expense. The amount of interest attributable to the portion of loan proceeds used to purchase the business machine is deductible, but not the amount for the jet ski, which is a personal expense.

16. The answer is B. A taxpayer cannot deduct the costs of driving a car between his home and his main workplace. These costs are personal commuting expenses. The costs of driving to meet with clients or do other business-related errands are deductible.

17. The answer is D. Penalties paid for the late performance or non-performance of a contract are deductible. Penalties or fines paid to any government entity because of a violation of laws or regulations are not deductible.

18. The answer is D. As a retailer, Only-a-Dollar acts as a collection agent for the state taxing authorities. The amounts of sales tax it collects and remits to them should be excluded from its taxable gross income and deductible expenses. A business should not deduct state and local sales taxes imposed on the buyer that the business must collect and pay over to the state or local government. Also, the business should not include these sales taxes in gross receipts or sales. For more information, see IRS Publication 535.

19. The answer is C. A business can deduct up to $5,000 of start-up costs. Start-up costs are costs incurred in creating an active trade or business or investigating the creation or acquisition of an active trade or business.

20. The answer is C. A self-employed individual with a net profit for the year can deduct premiums paid for medical and dental insurance for herself, her spouse (if married), and her dependents. The deduction is not available for any month the individual (or spouse) was eligible to participate in an employer-sponsored health plan, even if she did not participate.

Unit 5: Employee Compensation & Fringe

More Reading:
Publication 535, *Business Expenses*
Publication 15-A, *Employer's Tax Guide*
Publication 15-B, *Employer's Tax Guide to Fringe Benefits*

Employee Compensation

An employer can deduct the compensation it provides its employees if all of the following tests are met:

- The payments must be ordinary and necessary expenses directly related to the trade or business.
- The amounts must be reasonable. Reasonable pay is the amount that like businesses would normally pay for the same or similar services. If the IRS determines pay is excessive, it can disallow deduction of the excess amount.
- There must be proof that services were actually performed (unless the compensation qualifies as supplemental wages, such as maternity leave, sick pay, or vacation pay).
- The expenses must have been paid or incurred during the tax year.

Supplemental wages refers to compensation paid in addition to an employee's regular salary or wages. Supplemental wages also may include the following:

- Bonuses, commissions, overtime pay and severance pay
- Taxable awards
- Taxable employee awards and prizes
- Back pay
- Retroactive pay increases
- Payments for nondeductible moving expenses

Supplemental wages are taxable to the employee just like regular wages and deductible as a wage expense by the employer.

Example: Doug is a salesman for a department store. In 2016, he earns wages of $20,000; commissions of $12,000; overtime of $5,000; and an end-of-the-year bonus of $1,000. All are taxable compensation to Doug and deductible by his employer.

Transfers of property to an employee can also be considered compensation. The fair market value of the property on the date of transfer is deductible by the business and taxable to the employee. The business would recognize a gain or loss on the transfer equal to the difference between the fair market value and its basis in the property.

In addition to deducting compensation payments to employees, a business can deduct amounts paid to independent contractors.

Employment Taxes: A business's deduction for compensation paid to employees is not reduced by the Social Security, Medicare, and income taxes it is required to withhold from them. Further, a business can deduct the amounts paid as the employer's share of Social Security and Medicare taxes, as well as state and federal unemployment and disability fund taxes.

Example: A partnership pays its secretary $18,000 a year. After withholding various taxes, the employee receives $14,500. The business also pays an additional $1,500 of employment taxes on the secretary's wages. The full $18,000 can be deducted as wages. The business can also deduct the $1,500 additional paid as taxes.

A self-employed individual can deduct one-half of his self-employment tax as a business expense in figuring adjusted gross income. This deduction only affects income tax. It does not affect net earnings from self-employment or self-employment tax.

Fringe Benefits

A fringe benefit[93] is a form of additional compensation that may be provided by a business to those who perform services, such as employees and independent contractors. There are many types of fringe benefits that employers are allowed to offer their employees on a tax-free basis.

Study Note: For Part 1 of the EA exam, you must understand fringe benefits from the employee's perspective. For Part 2, you must know how these benefits are treated from the employer's perspective.

A business must include in a recipient's taxable compensation the amount by which the value of a fringe benefit is more than the sum of the following amounts:

- Any amount the law excludes from taxation
- Any amount the recipient paid for the benefit

If the recipient of a taxable fringe benefit is an employee, the benefit is subject to employment taxes and must be reported on Form W-2. If the recipient of a taxable fringe benefit is not an employee, the benefit is not subject to employment taxes, but it may have to be reported on Form 1099-MISC for independent contractors or Schedule K-1 for partners.

Generally, nontaxable benefits are not subject to income tax withholding, Social Security and Medicare taxes, or unemployment (FUTA) tax. However, there are exceptions for certain items. For example, an S corporation shareholder with ownership of more than 2% is not considered an employee for purposes of excluding certain fringe benefits, such as accident and health benefits, and this benefit is therefore subject to income tax withholding.

Further, exclusion of an otherwise nontaxable benefit may be disallowed if there is discrimination in favor of highly compensated employees (as described later).

Cafeteria Plans

A cafeteria plan, including a flexible spending arrangement, is a written plan that provides employees an opportunity to choose between receiving at least one taxable benefit, such as cash, and one qualified (nontaxable) benefit.

Employees may generally contribute a portion of their salaries on a pre-tax basis to pay for a portion of the qualified benefits. Having a salary reduction option is typically deemed sufficient to satisfy the requirement to provide a taxable option, even though the amounts are withheld on a pre-tax basis.

The plan may make benefits available to employees, their spouses, and their dependents. Qualified benefits may include:

- Accident and health benefits (but not Archer medical savings accounts or long-term care insurance)
- Adoption assistance
- Dependent care assistance
- Group-term life insurance
- Health savings accounts (HSAs)
- Flexible spending arrangements (FSAs)

A cafeteria plan cannot include certain other types of fringe benefits, which may nevertheless be deductible by the employer and non-taxable to the employee. Some of these

[93] Fringe benefits are covered in extensive detail in IRS Publication 15-B, *Employer's Tax Guide to Fringe Benefits*.

additional items are addressed later in this unit under the heading "Other Types of Employee Fringe Benefits."

Rules for Highly Compensated Employees

If a cafeteria plan favors either "highly compensated employees" (HCEs) or "key employees" as to eligibility to participate, contributions, or benefits, the employer must include in their taxable income the value of taxable benefits they could have selected.

This is intended to discourage employers from offering tax-free benefits to their owners or highly compensated executives, while ignoring lower-paid employees. Highly compensated employees are usually limited in the amount of money they can set aside in their 401(k) plans and other retirement plans. Non-discrimination testing was put into place to ensure all employees benefit from the company retirement plan, not just executives. In order to qualify for tax-favored status, an employee benefit plan must not discriminate in favor of highly compensated employees (HCEs) and key employees.

For IRS purposes, a Highly Compensated Employee is someone who owns higher than 5% stake in a company for the current tax year or the previous year. The taxpayer is also considered a highly compensated employee if he was paid more than $120,000 for 2016.

In 2016, a **"highly compensated employee"** also includes any of the following:

- An officer of the company,
- A shareholder who owns more than 5% of the voting power or value of all classes of the company's stock,
- An employee who is highly compensated based on the facts and circumstances, or
- A family member of a person described above.[94]

Employees that are hired mid-year will not be considered highly compensated employees until the start of the following year when they are eligible to collect their entire salary. For example, an HCE hired in November 2016 would not qualify as an HCE until January 1, 2017.[95]

In the case of HCEs, ownership is just as important as the salary. For example, even if an employee's salary is $50,000, if the employee owns 5% or more of the company then that person could be classified as an HCE.

Example: Gideon Trucking Inc. maintains a 401(k) plan for its employees. Their retirement plan has 21 participants, all of them full-time employees of the company. During the year, Gideon Trucking performed a review of the of their retirement plan. Gideon Trucking discovered that Highly Compensated Employees had employer matching contributions of 7% to their 401(k) plans, and other employees had employer matching contributions of 4%. This means Gideon's employee retirement plan failed the 401(k) nondiscrimination tests. To correct the problem, Gideon Trucking made qualified nonelective contributions for their non-highly compensated employees.

A **"key employee"** is defined as any employee who, at any time during the prior year was:

- An officer whose annual compensation from the employer exceeds $170,000; or
- A 5% owner of the business; or
- An employee owning more than 1% of the business and whose compensation exceeds $150,000 for the year.

A cafeteria plan or retirement plan is considered to have favored key employees if more than 25% of all the nontaxable benefits are given to key employees.

[94] Family aggregation rules treat a spouse, child, grandparent or parent of someone who's a 5% owner, as a 5% owner. Each of these individuals is considered an HCE for the plan year.

[95] For more information, see the U.S. Department of Labor Wage and Hour Division fact sheet on highly compensated workers.

Example: Jim is the Vice President of Zenith Corporation. He makes $185,000 a year. Because that compensation is over the federal threshold, Jim is considered a highly compensated employee.

Types of Allowable Benefits

Accident and Health Benefits: Nontaxable accident or health benefits may include the following:

- Contributions to the cost of accident or health insurance, including long-term care insurance
- Contributions to a separate trust or fund that directly or through insurance provides accident or health benefits
- Contributions to Archer MSAs or health savings accounts

Adoption Assistance: An adoption assistance program provides payments or reimbursements for qualifying expenses related to adopting a child, with up to $13,460 excludable in 2016.

Dependent Care Assistance: An annual exclusion of up to $5,000 ($2,500 if MFS) may apply to benefits received by an employee under a dependent care assistance program that provides for a qualifying person's care and allows the employee to work. The exclusion cannot exceed the smaller of the earned income of either the employee or the employee's spouse.

Group-term Life Insurance Coverage: An employer can exclude the cost of up to $50,000 of group-term life insurance from the taxable wages of an insured employee. The value of insurance coverage that exceeds $50,000 is a taxable benefit and must be included in the employee's wages, after reduction for any amount the employee paid toward the insurance.

Health Savings Accounts (HSAs)

An HSA is an account owned by a company's employee or former employee. Any contributions an employer makes become the employee's property and cannot be withdrawn by the employer. Contributions to the account are used to pay current or future medical expenses of the account owner, his spouse, and any qualified dependent. The medical expenses must not be reimbursable by insurance or other sources.

In order to qualify for an HSA, the individual must be covered by a high-deductible health plan (HDHP).

No contributions can be made to an individual's HSA after he becomes enrolled in Medicare Part A or Part B. Any excess contributions to an HSA are subject to a 6% penalty tax unless corrected by the deadline (generally the HSA owner's filing due date, plus extensions).

Example: Nancy, who is single with no dependents, has always participated in an HSA offered by her employer. Nancy turns age 65 in January 2016, and promptly enrolls in Medicare. She ceases to be an eligible individual for HSA purposes when she becomes enrolled in Medicare, therefore, she is no longer eligible to participate in the HSA. She accidentally contributes $3,000 to her HSA in 2016. Nancy must correct the excess contribution before the due date of her tax return, or she will be subject to an excise tax of 6%.

An employer's contribution amount to an employee's HSA must be comparable for all employees who have comparable coverage during the same period, or there will be an excise tax equal to 35% of the amount the employer contributed to all employees' HSAs.

However, an employer is allowed to make *larger* HSA contributions for a non-highly compensated employee than for a highly compensated employee.

Contribution and Out-of-Pocket Limits for Health Savings Accounts and High-Deductible Health Plans for 2016	
HSA contribution limit (employer + employee)	Self-only: $3,350 Family: $6,750
HSA catch-up contributions (age 55 or older)*	$1,000
HDHP minimum deductibles	Self-only: $1,300 Family: $2,600
HDHP maximum out-of-pocket amounts (this amount includes deductibles, co-payments and other amounts, but *not* insurance premiums)	Self-only: $6,550 Family: $13,100
* Catch-up contributions of $1,000 for qualified individuals can be made any time during the year in which the HSA participant turns 55.	

Flexible Spending Arrangements (FSA)

An FSA is a form of cafeteria plan benefit that reimburses employees for expenses incurred for certain qualified benefits, such as child care or health benefits. The employee must substantiate his expenses, and the distributions from the FSA to the employee are tax-free.

An FSA generally cannot provide a cumulative benefit to the employee beyond the plan year. However, an employer may choose to allow an employee a grace period of up to two-and-a-half months from the end of the plan year to use his balance.

For tax year 2016, the contribution limit for health flexible spending accounts (FSAs) is $2,550. Taxpayers are allowed to carry over up to $500 of unused funds per account. Alternatively, an employer may also offer a grace period (through March 15 of the following year) to incur qualifying expenses to use up their FSA funds. At the end of the grace period, all unspent funds would be forfeited back to the employer.

A Dependent Care FSA is limited to $5,000 per calendar year, per family.

Working Condition Benefits

This exclusion from wages applies to property and services an employer provides so that the employee can perform his job. If an employer provides an employee with a product or service and the cost of it would have been allowable as a business or depreciation deduction if he paid it himself, it would be deductible to the employer and excludable from an employee's income.

Example: Gordy works as an accountant. His employer provides him with a subscription to an accounting trade journal. The subscription's cost is not included in Gordy's income because he would have been able to deduct it as a business deduction had he paid for it himself.

A common working condition benefit is an employee's use of a company car for business purposes. An employer who provides a car for an employee can exclude the amount that would be allowed as a deductible business expense if the employee paid for its use.

Alternatively, an employer may include the entire annual lease value of a car in the employee's wages and the employee can then claim any deductible business expense for the car as a potential itemized deduction on his personal income tax return.

A qualified nonpersonal-use vehicle is one that an employee is unlikely to use more than minimally for personal purposes because of its design. Examples include fire trucks, police cars, hearses, school buses, cement mixers, and tractors.

Note: Any vehicle designed to carry cargo of over 14,000 pounds is automatically qualified as a nonpersonal-use vehicle. Pickup trucks and vans of 14,000 pounds or less are also considered qualified nonpersonal vehicles if they have been specially modified for business purposes and are likely to be used only minimally for personal purposes. Modifications include being marked with permanent decals or painted with advertising logos and being fitted with certain equipment specific to the business. An example of this would be a modified utility van used by an electrician. Even if the van does not meet the 14,000 pound requirement, if the van has been modified specifically to carry tools and equipment, then it may be considered a nonpersonal-use vehicle.

An employer-provided cell phone is another common working condition benefit. There must be a substantial business reason to provide the employee a cell phone; it cannot simply be used to boost an employee's morale, to attract a prospective worker, or as a means of providing additional compensation to an employee.

Example: Evelyn is an advertising executive who frequently visits clients at their locations. She uses her employer-paid cell phone to keep in touch with clients and her own firm while she is out of her office. If Evelyn did not have a legitimate business reason for the phone, its value would be added to her wages and her firm could not deduct it as a business expense.

Accountable Plans

A business can reimburse employees for business-related expenses. There are two types of reimbursement plans:

- **Accountable Plans**: Amounts paid under an accountable plan are deductible by the employer but they are not taxable wages and are not subject to income tax withholding or payment of Social Security, Medicare, and FUTA taxes.
- **Nonaccountable Plans**: Amounts paid under a nonaccountable plan are taxable to employees as wages and are subject to all employment taxes and withholding. Generally, there are no substantiation requirements for a nonaccountable plan.

For expenses to qualify under an accountable plan, the employee must follow strict guidelines in order to have the expenses reimbursed. An accountable plan requires employees to:

- Have incurred the expenses while performing services as employees.
- Adequately account for the expenses, including travel, meals, and entertainment, within a reasonable period of time.
- Provide documentary evidence of travel, mileage, and other employee business expenses.
- Return any excess reimbursement or allowance to the employer within a reasonable period of time, if paid in advance. A cash advance must be reasonably calculated to equal the anticipated expense, and the employer must make the advance within a reasonable period of time.

Example: Maggie is a loan agent who goes to various locations to sign mortgage paperwork. In April, Maggie's employer gives her a $1,000 advance to cover her flight, hotel, and transportation on a business trip to Alaska. Maggie spends $940 on her travel expenses during the trip. When she returns, she submits her receipts to substantiate the expenses. She also pays back the excess advance to her employer. She has met the requirements of an accountable plan, and the advanced funds are not included in her taxable wages.

Example: Kim's employer gives her $1,000 a month ($12,000 total for the year) for her business expenses. Kim doesn't have to provide any proof of her expenses to her employer. Kim is being reimbursed under a nonaccountable plan. Her employer must include the $12,000 on Kim's Form W-2 as if it were wages. If Kim wants to deduct her business expenses, she must complete Form 2106.

Example: Dana is a cosmetics saleswoman for Sunshine Cosmetics. She takes two potential clients out to dinner and pays for the meal. She keeps track of her business mileage on a spreadsheet. The following week, she submits her receipts and the spreadsheet to Sunshine Cosmetics for reimbursement. Dana's employer reimburses her for the out-of-pocket expenses she incurred. This arrangement is considered an accountable plan. The reimbursement is not taxable to Dana and is deductible by the employer as a regular business expense (subject to the 50% limitation on deductibility of meal costs).

Other Types of Employee Fringe Benefits

Employee Achievement Awards: Employers may generally exclude from an employee's wages the value of awards given for length of service or safety achievement. An employer's deduction and the tax-free amount for each employee are limited each year to the following:

- $400 for awards that are not qualified plan awards.
    - $1,600 for all awards, if an employee receives both qualified and non-qualified awards during the year.

Qualified plan awards are employee achievement awards under a written plan that does not discriminate in favor of highly compensated employees.

Example: Rowell Company awards a set of golf clubs to an employee as a nonqualified plan employee achievement award. The fair market value of the golf clubs is $750. The amount included in taxable wages to the employee is $350 ($750 - $400). Rowell Company can deduct $400 as a business expense.

The exclusion for employee awards does not apply to awards of cash, gift cards, or other intangible property such as vacations or tickets to sporting events.

Athletic Facilities: The value of an employee's use of a health club or athletic facilities may be excluded from wages, but only if the facility is on premises that the employer owns or leases. If the employer pays for a gym membership or a fitness program provided to the employee at an off-site location, the value is included in the employee's compensation.

De Minimis (Minimal) Benefits: An employer may exclude the value of a de minimis benefit provided to an employee from the employee's wages. This is something an employer provides that has so little value that accounting for it would be impractical, such as coffee and doughnuts in the break room. Cash and cash equivalent items, such as gift cards or the use of a credit or debit card, are not excludable as de minimis benefits, except for occasional meal money or transportation fare.

Educational Assistance: An educational assistance program is a separate written plan that allows an employer to provide educational assistance to employees for the cost of tuition, fees, books, supplies, and equipment. The payments may be for either undergraduate or graduate-level courses, and do not have to be work-related.

In 2016, up to $5,250 of educational assistance may be excluded per year per employee. If an employer does not have an educational assistance plan or pays more than $5,250, the excess is taxed as wages to the employee unless the benefits are working condition benefits.

Tuition Reduction Benefits: An educational organization can exclude the value of a qualified undergraduate tuition reduction it provides to an employee, his or her spouse, or a dependent child. Graduate education only qualifies if it is for the education of a graduate student who performs teaching or research activities for the educational organization.

Example: At the University of Texas, students who are employed as Teaching Assistants are eligible for tuition reduction benefits. The students work directly for the college, assisting the professors. The Tuition Reduction Benefits are tax exempt, and are applied directly to the student's tuition bill, which is reduced by 70% for graduate assistants. No additional tax reporting is required.

Employee Discounts: Employers can exclude from wages the price reductions they give to employees on services or property they offer to customers in the normal course of business, up to the following limits:

- For a discount on services, 20% of the price charged nonemployee customers for the service.
- For a discount on merchandise or property, the company's gross profit percentage multiplied by the price nonemployee customers pay.

Employee Stock Options

A corporation may grant stock options to its employees, as compensation for past service and an incentive for retention, that allow them to purchase the company's stock at a later date. If an employee receives stock options, he may have income when the options are granted, when he exercises them (to buy the company's stock), or when he sells or otherwise disposes of the options or the stock. The nature, timing, and amount of the employee's taxable income and the employer's deduction for compensation expense depend on whether the options are considered to be statutory or nonstatutory options. There are two types of statutory stock options:

- **Incentive stock options (ISOs),** which allow employees to purchase stock at a pre-established price (exercise price) that may be below the market price on the date of exercise.
- **ESPPs:** These are options granted under employee stock purchase plans (ESPPs). A stock purchase plan enables employees to purchase their own company's common stock, often at a discount from the regular market price.

The tax advantage of a statutory stock option for the employee is that income is not reported when the option is granted or when it is exercised. However, the employer corporation cannot take a deduction for compensation expense. The employee does report income when he ultimately sells the stock. If he satisfies certain holding period requirements, the income is treated as capital gain. If not, it is treated as ordinary income, and the employer is entitled to a compensation deduction at that time.

Nonstatutory or "nonqualified" stock options (NSOs) also allow employees to purchase stock at a pre-established exercise price. The employee must recognize compensation income, either at the date of grant or on the exercise date, and the employer is entitled to a corresponding compensation expense deduction at the same time.

Meals and Lodging

An employer may exclude from taxable wages the value of meals and lodging it provides to employees if they are provided:

- On the employer's business premises, and
- For the employer's convenience.

For lodging, there is an additional rule: it must be required as a condition of employment. Lodging can be provided for the taxpayer, the spouse, and the taxpayer's dependents, and still not be taxable. The exclusion from taxation does not apply if the employee can choose to receive additional pay instead of lodging.

Situations in which meals may be provided to employees for the convenience of the employer on the employer's business premises include the following:

- Workers such as police officers, firefighters, and other emergency personnel need to be on call for emergencies during the meal period
- The nature of the business requires short meal periods
- Eating facilities are not available in areas near the workplace
- Meals are furnished to all employees on a regular basis, as long as meals are furnished to more than half of the employees for the convenience of the employer
- Meals are furnished immediately after working hours because the employee's duties prevented him from obtaining a meal during working hours

Meals provided to restaurant employees during, or immediately before or after work hours are also considered furnished for the employer's convenience. Meals provided to employees for the convenience of the employer are not subject to the normal 50% deductibility limit; they are 100% deductible by the employer.

Example: An employer has pizza delivered to the office at a group meeting because the business requires the meeting be kept short, and there are no alternative restaurants in the immediate area. The meal is 100% deductible by the business.

Moving Expense Reimbursements

An employer can exclude qualifying moving expense payments or reimbursements from an employee's taxable wages if they are paid under an accountable plan for expenses that would otherwise have been deductible by the employee if he had paid or incurred them without reimbursement. Deductible moving expenses include only the reasonable expenses of:

- Moving household goods and personal effects from the employee's former home to the new home, and
- Traveling, including lodging, from the former home to the new home.

Expenses for meals are not included, and the move must meet both the distance test and the time test. The distance test is met if the new job location is at least 50 miles farther from the employee's old home than the old job location was. The time test is met if the employee works at least 39 weeks during the first 12 months after arriving in the general area of the new job location.

Example: Ridge Manufacturing Inc. wants to hire Paul to lead their new marketing department. Paul lives in another state, and only agrees to accept the position if Ridge Manufacturing pays for all his moving expenses. The company agrees to pay Paul's moving expenses as a condition of his employment contract. Paul incurs $7,000 in moving expenses, consisting of $6,000 for moving his household goods, $800 for airfare at the time of the move, and $200 in meals while he is in transit. The employer reimburses Paul for all these expenses. Ridge Manufacturing must include the cost of the meals ($200) in Paul's wages, since the cost of meals is not a deductible moving expense for IRS purposes. The rest of the moving expenses would have been deductible on Paul's tax return, so those expenses are tax-free to him and deductible by his employer.

No-Additional-Cost Services

An employer can exclude from an employee's taxable income the value of a service provided to the employee if it does not create substantial additional cost for the business.

Typically, no-additional-cost services are excess capacity services, such as airline, bus, or train tickets; hotel rooms; or telephone services provided free or at a reduced price to employees working in those lines of business.

Example: Thessaly works as an airline stewardess. The airline allows their current employees to fly for free by using a standby travel program. Thessaly flies for free to Cancun. The value of her airline ticket may be excluded from her wages.

Example: Tony works as a personal trainer for Zoom Gym. Since Tony is an employee, Zoom Gym offers Tony a free gym membership and an employee discount at their apparel store inside the gym. These benefits would be tax-free to Tony because they do not create substantial additional cost for Zoom Gym.

Employee Transportation Benefits

Employers can provide transportation benefits to their employees up to certain amounts without having to include the benefit in the employee's taxable income.

Qualified transportation benefits include transit passes, qualified parking, rides in a commuter highway vehicle between the employee's home and workplace, and qualified bicycle commuting reimbursements. In 2016, employees can exclude:

- $255 per month in combined commuter highway vehicle transportation and transit passes, and
- $255 per month in parking benefits.
- $20 per month for expenses incurred when commuting to work by bicycle

Employees can receive transit passes and benefits for parking during the same month; they are not mutually exclusive. If an employer allows an employee to use a company vehicle for commuting or other personal use, the value of the vehicle's use is taxable to the employee.

Affordable Care Act for Employers (ACA)

The Affordable Care Act provisions mandating that certain employers provide health insurance for full-time workers went into effect in 2015.

Implementation of the *employer shared responsibility provisions* was delayed until 2016 for some businesses, depending on the number of full-time employees.

Employers with 50 or more employees[96] will be subject to the Employer Shared Responsibility provisions. For ACA purposes, a full-time employee is an individual employed on average at least 30 hours per week, or at least 130 hours in a calendar month. An employer that meets the 50 full-time employee threshold is referred to as an "Applicable Large Employer" or ALE.

Under the Employer Shared Responsibility provisions, if these employers do not offer affordable health coverage that provides a minimum level of coverage to their full-time employees (and their dependents), the employer may be subject to an Employer Shared Responsibility payment if at least one of its full-time employees receives a premium tax credit for purchasing individual coverage on the Health Insurance Marketplace.

The general rule is that if an employer offers group health coverage to any full-time employees, the employer must offer coverage to *all* full-time employees. The employer has the option to offer coverage to part-time employees, but is not required to do so. If an employer offers coverage to any part-time employees, then *all* the part-time employees must be offered coverage.

The ACA "employer mandate" is a requirement that all businesses with 50 or more full-time equivalent employees (FTE) provide health insurance to at least 95% of their full-time employees and dependents up to age 26.

The "employer responsibility provision" will generally apply to larger firms with at least 50 or more full-time employees starting in 2016. Small employers with 49 (or fewer) employees are not subject to the mandate.

[96] This mandate ONLY applies to employers with 50 full-time employees (or a combination of full-time and part-time employees that is the hourly equivalent to 50 full-time employees).

Unit 5: Study Questions

(Test yourself and then check the correct answers at the end of this section.)

1. An employer can exclude qualifying moving expense reimbursements from an employee's taxable wages. With regards to the tests for qualified moving expenses, the distance test is met if the new job location is at least ___________ from the employee's old home than the old job location was.

A. 50 miles farther
B. 25 miles closer
C. 60 miles farther
D. 20 miles farther

2. All of the following are fringe benefits that may be excluded from an employee's pay except:

A. Dependent care assistance of up to $5,000 a year.
B. A gift card of $25 for the holidays.
C. Moving expense reimbursements.
D. Adoption assistance.

3. The Pancake House provides the following benefits to its employees. Which of these is fully taxable to the employee?

A. Qualified group term life insurance of $50,000.
B. Educational assistance of up to $5,250.
C. A membership at the local country club with a value up to $1,200.
D. Free transit passes, up to $250 per month.

4. Heart-Wise Ambulance Services provides meals and lodging for ten paramedics at the workplace as a condition of employment because they are not allowed to leave the premises when they are on a shift. The employees eat and sleep on premises for free. Which of the following statements is correct?

A. All the costs of meals and lodging can be excluded from the employees' wages and deducted as an expense by the employer.
B. The meals and lodging are not taxable to the employee, but the employer can deduct only 50% of the meal expense.
C. The meals and lodging are taxable to the employees and deductible by the employer. The employee may then deduct the costs as employee business expenses.
D. The meals and lodging can be deducted by both the employees and the employer as business expenses.

5. All of the following are excludable from an employee's wages and deductible by the employer except:

A. An outstanding employee achievement award valued at $300.
B. Occasional snacks provided by the employer in the employee break room.
C. Employer-provided vehicles that employees may also use for personal purposes.
D. Meals furnished during work hours for the convenience of the employer.

6. Evermore Inc. reimburses employees for their business travel and transportation expenses. Which of the following is taxable to the employee?

A. Travel reimbursements made under an accountable plan.
B. Travel reimbursements made under a nonaccountable plan.
C. Parking passes at a cost of $250 per month.
D. A qualified bicycle commuting reimbursement of $20 per month.

7. Renee is a full-time employee of Right Angles Engineering, which offers its employees reimbursement through an education assistance program. In 2016, she takes graduate accounting courses and has $5,900 of tuition expenses and $300 of expenses for required books. Right Angles reimburses Renee for all the expenses. How should this reimbursement be treated?

A. All of the amounts are excluded from Renee's income, and the amounts are deductible by Right Angles as a qualified fringe benefit.
B. The first $5,250 of the educational expenses is excluded from Renee's wages as a qualified fringe benefit, and the remaining amount is taxable as wage income to her.
C. Only $5,900 (the tuition costs) of the educational expenses are excluded from the Renee's wages as a qualified fringe benefit, and the remaining amount is taxable as wage income to her. The cost of the books is not a qualified educational expense.
D. All of the reimbursement is taxable as wages to Renee because graduate courses do not qualify for reimbursement under a fringe benefit plan.

8. Which of the following benefits must be included in an employee's income?

A. Child care reimbursed under a qualified flexible spending plan.
B. Employee discounts on products.
C. A holiday gift of a $50 gas card.
D. A holiday gift of a $25 canned ham.

9. The ACA "employer mandate" applies to businesses with at least ________ full-time equivalent employees.

A. 25 or more
B. 50 or more
C. 100 or more
D. The ACA employer mandate applies to all employers.

Unit 5: Answers

1. The answer is A. An employer can exclude qualifying moving expense reimbursements from an employee's taxable wages. With regards to the tests for qualifying expenses, the distance test is met if the new job location is at least 50 miles farther from the employee's old home than the old job location was.

2. The answer is B. The value of the gift card would always be treated as cash, and would be taxable to the employee.

3. The answer is C. Employer-paid memberships at athletic facilities and country clubs are taxable benefits. A workout room or gym on the employer's premises is the exception.

4. The answer is A. Employers may exclude the value of meals and on-site lodging from an employee's wages if they are provided for the convenience of the employer. Meals provided to employees for the convenience of the employer are 100% deductible by the employer.

5. The answer is C. The value of a vehicle for personal use by an employee is a taxable benefit. If an employer provides a car for an employee's use, the amount that can be excluded as a working condition benefit is the amount that would be allowed as a deductible business expense if the employee paid for its use. There are exceptions for emergency personnel such as police officers who are required to use their emergency vehicles. Employee achievement awards may be exempt up to $1,600. Meals are exempt if either furnished for the employer's convenience or if considered de minimis, such as occasional snacks.

6. The answer is B. Travel reimbursements made under a nonaccountable plan are taxable to the employee as wages. All of the other choices would be not be taxable to the employee and classified as a fringe benefit.

7. The answer is B. Although all of the expenses are qualified educational expenses, only the first $5,250 is excluded from Renee's wages as a qualified fringe benefit, and the remaining amount is taxable as wage income to her. If an employer pays more than $5,250 for educational benefits for an employee during the year, the excess is taxed as wages.

8. The answer is C. Gifts of cash or cash equivalents such as gift cards must be included in income. Fringe benefits that may be excluded from income include employee discounts, amounts reimbursed through a qualified flexible spending plan, and de minimis holiday gifts.

9. The answer is B. The ACA "employer mandate" is a requirement that all businesses with 50 or more full-time equivalent employees (FTE) provide health insurance to at least 95% of their full-time employees and dependents up to age 26.

Unit 6: Other Deductions & Credits

More Reading:

Instructions for Form 3800, *General Business Credit*

Publication 334, *Tax Guide for Small Business*

Publication 536, *Net Operating Losses for Individuals, Estates, and Trusts*

Instructions for Form 8903, *Domestic Productions Activities Deduction*

Instructions for Form 4626, *Alternative Minimum Tax-Corporations*

In addition to the deductions already covered, businesses can reduce their taxable income through various business credits, the domestic production activities deduction and the net operating loss deduction. We start with a look at the net operating loss, which can allow a business with losses for the year to recover past tax payments or reduce future tax payments.

Net Operating Losses (NOLs)

A net operating loss (NOL) occurs when a business has tax deductions that exceed its income, resulting in negative taxable income for a tax year. C corporations NOLs are discussed later. Partnerships and S corporations generally cannot use NOLs, but their partners and shareholders may be able to use their individual share; the NOL flows through to the partners or shareholders, who can use the NOL to offset other business and non-business income.

Example: Kirill and Maxim operate a 50/50 partnership together. In 2016, the Partnership has $3,000 in overall losses. The losses are allocated to the individual partners on Schedule K-1 (Form 1065). In this case, since they have an equal partnership, Kirill and Maxim will each have $1,500 in partnership losses that they can potentially deduct on their individual returns.

For an individual, estate, or trust to have an NOL, the loss must be caused by deductions from:

- A trade or business that results in an overall loss.
- Work as an employee.
- Casualty or theft losses (personal or business-related).
- Losses from rental property.
- Moving expenses.
- A farming business.

Depending upon whether it had taxable income in prior years, a business may choose to carry back an NOL to offset prior year taxable income or to carry forward the NOL to offset taxable income in future years.

The default is to carry back an NOL for up to two years (starting with the tax year two years prior to the year that the NOL was generated). Any remaining NOL not utilized in the prior two tax years can be carried forward for up to 20 years.

Note: A net operating loss that is not used in the correct carryback and carryforward periods is lost and cannot be deducted in any other tax year.

Example: Harrison is a sole proprietor who owns a flooring business. He has no other income sources. In 2016, his business has a net operating loss of $13,000. This is the first year that his business has lost money. In 2015, Harrison's business had taxable income of $10,000 and in 2014, the business had taxable income of $25,000. Harrison may carry back $10,000 in losses to 2014 and then $3,000 in losses to 2015.

A business may elect not to carry back an NOL and only carry it forward, but this election must be made on a timely filed return. If a taxpayer fails to file a return on time and does not make the proper election, he is forced to carry back the NOL.

There are certain instances in which a business qualifies for a longer NOL carryback period. The following are exceptions to the two-year carryback rule:

- Farmers are eligible for a five-year carryback period for farming losses.
- "Qualified small businesses"[97] may carry back a loss three years if the loss is due to a federally-declared disaster.
- Net operating losses due to a casualty or theft may be carried back three years.
- Product liability losses have a ten-year carryback period. An example would be when a business sells an item that is later subject to a recall and lawsuits.

To claim a refund from an NOL, an individual taxpayer may choose to amend a prior year tax return or may use Form 1045, *Application for Tentative Refund*, to apply for a quick tax refund resulting from the carryback of an NOL.

If the taxpayer is self-employed, the net operating loss does not change the amount of self-employment tax to any of the years it is carried forward or back to. Also, if a business or individual owes interest and penalties in a prior year, the NOL carryback will not abate them.

Example: Gregory operates a farming business and files his return on Schedule F. In 2016, he has a net operating loss of $35,000. He had income of $25,000 in the prior year, so he elects to carry back his NOL in order to receive a refund of the income tax he paid. Gregory also owed self-employment taxes and an early withdrawal penalty from an IRA in 2015, but his farming NOL will not offset his prior year self-employment tax or his early withdrawal penalty. The NOL *only* reduces the income tax liability. As a farmer, Gregory would be able to carry back the NOL up to five years.

The following items are not allowed when figuring an NOL:

- Any deduction for personal exemptions.
- Capital losses in excess of capital gains.
- The exclusion of gain from the sale of qualified small business stock.
- Nonbusiness deductions in excess of nonbusiness income (hobby losses).
- A net operating loss from another year (a carryback or a carryforward).
- The domestic production activities deduction (DPAD).
- A self-employed taxpayer's contribution to a retirement plan.

Income from other sources may eliminate or reduce a net operating loss for the year. For example, if a taxpayer has income from wages, as well as a net operating loss from a small business, the wage income and the NOL will offset taxable income.

Example: Jim runs an auto detailing business as a sole proprietor. In 2016, he had an $8,000 NOL from his Schedule C business. Jim files jointly with his wife, Elaine. She has $23,000 of taxable income from wages. On their jointly filed return, Jim's net operating loss is absorbed by Elaine's $23,000 of wages, making their joint AGI $15,000 ($23,000 - $8,000 NOL).

Business Credits

A variety of tax credits are available for businesses. Credits are generally more valuable than deductions of the same amount because they are subtracted directly from a business's tax liability, dollar-for-dollar based on the amount of the applicable credit. However, most tax credits are available in limited situations, applying only to certain industries or to very specific activities.

General Business Credit

Many business credits fall under the umbrella of the general business credit (GBC). The GBC is not a single credit but is instead a combination of various individual credits. Each

[97] A "qualified small business" for purposes of this rule is a sole proprietorship or a partnership that has average annual gross receipts of $5 million or less during the three-year period ending with the tax year of the NOL.

business credit is claimed on a separate form; the credits are then reported in aggregate on Form 3800, *General Business Credit.*

If a business only claims one credit, then Form 3800 is not required. The one credit is considered the business's "general business credit" for the year. If the business claims more than one credit listed below, the business is required to file Form 3800, *General Business Credit*.

The GBC is a nonrefundable credit that is subtracted directly from tax, reducing an entity's tax liability dollar for dollar. Generally, credits cannot be claimed to the extent that they would reduce a business's tax bill below its tentative minimum tax. Further, the GBC may not offset any of a business's employment tax liabilities.

If a business is unable to use its entire GBC in the year it was earned, it can generally be carried back to the prior year and forward for up to 20 years. A business's GBC consists of its carryforward of business credits from prior years plus the total of its current year business credits.

Study Note: In addition to eligibility for and deduction of the general business credit as a whole, Prometric's online exam specifications reference the Disabled Access Credit, Investment Credit, and Small Business Healthcare Tax Credit, suggesting they are the most likely to be tested on the EA exam.

All of the following credits, with the exception of the electric vehicle credit, are part of the General Business Credit. The form used to figure each credit is also shown below. The following section also includes an overview of the more widely-claimed business credits.

- **Form 3468, Investment Credit:** This credit is actually the sum of multiple credits. The investment credit is available to businesses who engage in specific types of projects on their property. It consists of the:
    - **Rehabilitation Credit:** this credit is designed to encourage businesses to restore or preserve an older building or one that qualifies for historic status.
    - **Energy Investment Credit:** this credit is designed for businesses who use certain types of alternative energy, such as solar, wind or geothermal energy.
    - **Qualifying Advanced Coal Project Credit, Qualifying Gasification Project Credit ,** and **Qualifying Advanced Energy Project Credit:** for projects that generate electricity using coal, while also reducing carbon dioxide emissions. These credits are designed to reduce greenhouse emissions by retrofitting existing technology to make it cleaner or spurring investment in alternative energy.

  The Investment Credit allows businesses to take a deduction for a percentage of certain investment costs from their tax liability in addition to the normal allowances for depreciation. In general, a business cannot claim the Investment Credit for property that is:

    - Used mainly outside the United States;
    - Used by a governmental unit or foreign person or entity;
    - Used by a tax-exempt organization;
    - Used for lodging or in the furnishing of lodging; or
    - Any property that has already been expensed under section 179.

Note: The Investment Tax Credit has been modified by Congress a number of times over the years. The details regarding this credit are listed in the 2016 Instructions for Form 3468.

- **Form 5735, American Samoa Economic Development Credit**
- **Form 5884, Work Opportunity Credit: Work Opportunity Tax Credit (Form 5884):** The WOTC provides a credit for hiring qualified veterans and members of certain targeted

employee groups. Employers can hire eligible employees from the following target groups for WOTC.

- Unemployed Veterans (including disabled veterans)
- Temporary Assistance for Needy Families (TANF) Recipients
- Food Stamp (SNAP) Recipients
- Designated Community Residents (living in Empowerment Zones or Rural Renewal Counties)
- Vocational Rehabilitation Referred Individuals
- Ex-Felons
- Supplemental Security Income Recipients
- Summer Youth Employees (living in Empowerment Zones)
- Qualified Long-Term Unemployment Recipient (newly added in 2016)

The PATH Act retroactively reinstated and extended the Work Opportunity Credit through 2019. The WOTC amount is calculated on Form 5884 and reported on Form 3800, *General Business Credit*. Tax-exempt organizations claim the credit on Form 5884-C, *Work Opportunity Credit for Qualified Tax-Exempt Organizations Hiring Qualified Veterans,* as a credit against the employer's share of Social Security tax. The amount of the credit varies depending on the targeted group that an employee belongs to (for example, a veteran who receives food stamps or an ex-felon) and the period of unemployment before the employee is hired. In 2016, the WOTC includes a new targeted group: Qualified Long-Term Unemployment Recipient (Hired on or after January 1, 2016).

- **Form 6478, Alcohol and Cellulosic Biofuel Fuels Credit**
- **Form 6765, Credit for Increasing Research Activities**
- **Form 8586, Low-Income Housing Credit**
- **Form 8611, Recapture of Low-Income Housing Credit**
- **Form 8820, Orphan Drug Credit**
- **Form 8826, Disabled Access Credit:** This is a nonrefundable tax credit for an eligible small business that incurs expenses to provide access to persons who have disabilities. The expenses must be incurred for the business to comply with the Americans with Disabilities Act. The amount of the Disabled Access Credit is 50% of qualified expenses that exceed $250, with a maximum credit per year of $5,000. To be eligible, a business must have had gross receipts of $1 million or less or had no more than 30 full-time employees during the preceding tax year.

Example: Helene owns a small roadside diner that was originally built in 1930. To comply with current ADA regulations, she retrofitted the diner's restroom to allow wheelchair access. Qualified expenses totaled $12,000. Helene can claim the full $5,000 of the credit (50% of a maximum of $10,000 of qualified expenses).

Note: If Helene had only incurred $5,250 of qualified expenses, the first $250 of the expenses would not qualify for the credit, but the remainder would – resulting is a credit of $2,500 ($5,250 - $250) x 50% = $2,500)

- **Form 8834, Qualified Plug-in Electric and Electric Vehicle Credit**
- **Form 8835, Renewable Electricity, Refined Coal, and Indian Coal Production Credit**
- **Form 8844, Empowerment Zone and Renewal Community Employment Credit:** If a business hires qualified empowerment zone employees in 2016, the business can claim this credit for up to 20% of qualified wages, up to $15,000 per employee. Empowerment Zones are distressed urban and rural areas nationwide that are in need of revitalization. Partnerships and S corporations must file Form 8844, Empowerment Zone Employment Credit. Otherwise, the credit is reported on Form 3800, General Business Credit.

- **Form 8845, Indian Employment Credit:** The Indian Employment Credit was established to provide businesses with an incentive to hire members of Indian tribes who live on or near reservations. This credit is decreased by any Work Opportunity Credit amount claimed for the same employee.
- **Form 8846, Credit for Employer Social Security and Medicare Taxes Paid on Certain Employee Tips** This credit is equal to the employer's portion of Social Security and Medicare taxes paid on tips received by employees of restaurants and other food service establishments where tipping is customary. An employer must meet both of the following requirements to qualify for the credit:
    - Have employees who received tips from customers for serving food or beverages, and
    - Have paid employer Social Security and Medicare taxes on these tips.
    - This credit does not apply to other tipped employees, such as hairdressers, chauffeurs, or bellhops.
- **Form 8847, Credit for Contributions to Selected Community Development Corporations**
- **Form 8864, Biodiesel and Renewable Diesel Fuels Credit**
- **Form 8874, New Markets Credit:** The PATH Act extended the New Markets Credit through 2019. The credit is for businesses that make investments in low-income communities. The credit equals 39% of the qualified investment and is claimed over seven years.
- **Form 8881, Credit for Small Employer Pension Plan Startup Costs** Employers can claim a tax credit equal to 50% of the cost to set up and administer the plan, up to a maximum of $500 per year, for each of the first three years of the plan.
- **Form 8882, Credit for Employer-Provided Childcare Facilities and Services**
- **Form 8896, Low Sulfur Diesel Fuel Production Credit**
- **Form 8900, Qualified Railroad Track Maintenance Credit**
- **Form 8906, Distilled Spirits Credit**
- **Form 8908, Energy Efficient Home Credit**
- **Form 8910, Alternative Motor Vehicle Credit**
- **Form 8911, Alternative Fuel Vehicle Refueling Property Credit**
- **Form 8923, Mine Rescue Team Training Credit**

Small Business Healthcare Tax Credit (Form 8941)

The Credit for Small Employer Health Insurance Premiums is a refundable credit that was expanded as part of the Affordable Care Act. It is not grouped as part of the General Business Credit.

The credit is specifically targeted toward employers with low and moderate income workers and phases out as average annual wages increase. To be eligible for the credit, all of the following must apply:

- The employer must have fewer than 25 full-time equivalent (FTE) employees.
- Average annual wages of qualifying employees must be less than $52,000 in 2016.
- The employer must pay at least 50% of the employees' premium costs.
- The employer must offer coverage through the SHOP Marketplace in order to qualify.[98]

[98] The SHOP Marketplace is a federal government website designed for small employers who want to provide health coverage to their employees. To use the SHOP Marketplace, the business must have 50 or fewer full-time equivalent employees (FTEs).

The credit is phased out completely for employers with 25 full-time employees or those paying annual average wages of $52,000 or more.

Note: The amount of the Small Business Healthcare Tax Credit is calculated on a sliding scale. The credit is higher for smaller employers, and lower for larger businesses.

The Small Business Healthcare Tax Credit is worth up to 50% of the employer's contribution toward the employees' premium costs (up to 35% for tax-exempt employers).

The employer must pay premiums on behalf of employees enrolled in a qualified health plan offered through a Small Business Health Options Program (SHOP) Marketplace, or qualify for an exception to this requirement. The credit can be claimed for a maximum of two consecutive years.

Example: Patrick is the owner of a small watch repair business. He has twelve full-time employees, and pays $50,000 a year toward their health care premiums for coverage purchased through the SHOP marketplace. Based on the average wages of his employees, Patrick qualifies for a 15% credit, so he can claim a credit of $7,500.

Note: Unlike most other business credits, Small Business Healthcare Tax Credit is refundable. An employer must reduce its health insurance premium expense deduction by the amount of the credit. Because the credit is refundable, even if an employer has no taxable income, the business may be eligible to receive the credit as a refund.

Domestic Production Activities Deduction (DPAD)

The domestic production activities deduction (known as the DPAD, authorized by IRC section 199) is designed to stimulate domestic manufacturing and farming.

The DPAD is calculated on Form 8903, *Domestic Production Activities Deduction*. Individual taxpayers, including partners or shareholders in pass-through entities and beneficiaries of trusts and estates, claim the DPAD deduction as an adjustment to income on Form 1040. C corporations claim this deduction on Form 1120.

In 2016, the DPAD is equal to 9% of the lesser of:

- Qualified production activities income (QPAI), or
- Adjusted gross income for an individual, estate, or trust (or taxable income for all other taxpayers) determined without regard to the DPAD.

However, the deduction is also limited to 50% of Form W-2 wages paid to employees for the year. Payments made to independent contractors and reported on Form 1099-MISC are not wages and do not qualify for purposes of the DPAD.

The DPAD offers significant tax savings for qualified domestic businesses. However, unlike many other deductions, the DPAD can only be used by businesses with taxable income. The deduction cannot be carried forward or carried back. A business cannot claim the DPAD in years when the business has a tax loss.

The following activities are qualified production activities eligible for claiming the DPAD:

- Manufacturing goods in the United States.
- Selling, leasing, or licensing items that have been manufactured in the United States.
- Selling, leasing, or licensing motion pictures that have been produced in the United States (except for pornography or sexually explicit films).
- Construction of real property in the United States.
- Engineering and architectural services relating to a U.S.-based construction project.
- Software development and production in the United States.
- The production of water, natural gas, and electricity in the United States.
- The growth and processing of agricultural products and timber.

QPAI is the excess of domestic production gross receipts (DPGR) over the sum of:

- Cost of goods sold allocable to DPGR, and

- Other expenses, losses, and deductions (other than the DPAD) properly allocable to DPGR.

A business's gross receipts must be allocated between DPGR and non-DPGR, and its cost of goods sold must then be allocated to each. One of several methods must then be used to allocate other expenses, losses, and deductions. The use of certain of these methods is limited to small businesses that meet specified parameters.

Example: SkyWest Corporation manufactures building components that it sells wholesale to building contractors. All of SkyWest's manufacturing activity is in the U.S., and therefore qualifies for the DPAD. In 2016, SkyWest had QPAI of $650,000 from its manufacturing activity and taxable income (without regard to the DPAD) of $800,000. It paid $225,000 in W-2 wages to its employees. The company's DPAD deduction would therefore be the *lesser* of:

- 9% of the $650,000 of QPAI, or
- 50% of the $225,000 of wages.

Thus, SkyWest's DPAD would be $58,500 (.09 × $650,000).

Example: Raiser Ranch Inc. is a meat processor that has various slaughtering plant locations in the United States as well as two locations in Brazil. Although this type of production activity is qualified for the DPAD, only the U.S.-based production qualifies for the DPAD. Raiser Ranch must allocate its gross receipts between the factory production in the United States and the production in Brazil to calculate DPGR and non-DPGR.

Example: Funsports Corporation produces children's sports uniforms in the U.S. The company has domestic production activity income of $90,000 during the year. Wages that are allocatable to the production activity equal $38,000. Therefore, the domestic production activities deduction could potentially equal $90,000 × 9% = $8,100 (the lesser of 50% of wages or 9% of QPAI). However, Funsports Corporation purchased an expensive delivery truck in 2016, and decides to take accelerated depreciation on the truck. After applying Section 179, Funsports Corporation only has $2,000 in taxable income. Therefore, their DPAD would be limited to $2,000; the remaining amount of their taxable income.

Gross receipts from the following business types are NOT qualified production activities and therefore not eligible for the DPAD:

- Construction services that are deemed "cosmetic" in nature, such as drywall and painting.
- Leasing or licensing items to a related party.
- Selling food or beverages prepared at restaurants, bars, or similar dining establishments.
- The transmission or distribution of electricity, natural gas, or water (although the production of electricity, natural gas, or potable water in the United States is a qualified activity).
- Any advertising, product placement, customer service businesses, and other telecommunications services.
- Most service-type businesses (consultants, barbers, party planners, etc.).

Example: Yummy Corp. owns four popular buffet-style restaurants in Phoenix, Arizona. The company has gross receipts of $2 million dollars during the year, and pays out $1,250,000 in gross wages to all its employees. The corporation is not eligible for the DPAD because the sale of food or beverages is not "qualified production activity". This is true even if the company hires only U.S. workers and all their production and sales occur in the U.S.

Unit 6: Study Questions

(Test yourself and then check the correct answers at the end of this section.)

1. Lorelei is a sole proprietor who designs and sells custom jewelry direct to customers. She has three full-time employees whose wages average $16,000 in 2016. She paid the health insurance premiums for her employees who are enrolled in coverage through the SHOP marketplace. Which of the following statements is correct?

A. She does not qualify for the Small Business Health Care Tax Credit.
B. She may qualify for a credit of up to 50% of the premiums she paid for her employees.
C. She may qualify for a credit of up to 35% of the premiums she paid for her employees.
D. She may qualify for the Small Business Health Care Tax Credit for up to three years.

2. Which of the following does not qualify for the domestic production activities deduction?

A. Manufacturing goods in the United States.
B. Construction of buildings in the United States.
C. Selling food or beverages prepared at restaurants in the United States.
D. Software development in the United States.

3. Stacy owns the Peach Pit Cannery. In 2016, she renovated her cannery to comply with the Americans with Disabilities Act. The Peach Pit Cannery had gross receipts of $750,000 and spent $15,000 on disabled access upgrades. What is Stacy's current year Disabled Access Credit?

A. $2,500
B. $5,000
C. $7,500
D. $15,000

4. Bennett Corporation could not use all of its general business credits in 2016. What is the carryover period for the GBC?

A. The GBC may be carried back two years and carried forward five years.
B. The GBC may be carried back five years and carried forward 10 years.
C. The unused GBC cannot be carried over to another tax year.
D. The GBC may be carried back one year and carried forward for 20 years.

5. The Work Opportunity Tax Credit provides a credit for businesses that:

A. Provide job training for out-of-work veterans and other individuals in targeted groups.
B. Give severance to laid-off workers.
C. Invest in federal empowerment zones.
D. Hire unemployed veterans and other individuals in targeted groups.

6. Bettina owns her own photography business, and she has an NOL in the current year. She elects to carry back her losses. How long may she carry back and carry forward her NOL?

A. Back five years, forward 20 years.
B. Back two years, forward 20 years.
C. Back three years, forward 25 years.
D. Back two years, forward five years.

7. Which of the following is not part of the Investment Credit in 2016?

A. Qualifying Advanced Coal Project Credit.
B. Hydroelectric Power Credit.
C. Rehabilitation Credit.
D. Energy Investment Credit.

8. Which event would create an NOL?

A. Selling a personal-use car for a loss.
B. Selling a primary residence for a loss.
C. Casualty loss from a fire at a business location.
D. Loss from the sale of corporate stock.

9. All of the following statements are correct regarding the DPAD except:

A. The DPAD cannot be more than 25% of the wages a business pays its employees.
B. Businesses with both domestic and foreign business activity must use only their domestic income in calculating the DPAD.
C. The DPAD can be as much as 9% of a company's taxable income.
D. The DPAD is authorized by section 199 of the Internal Revenue Code.

10. Which of the following items is allowed when figuring a net operating loss?

A. Capital losses in excess of capital gains.
B. A net operating loss from another year (a carryback or a carryforward).
C. The domestic production activities deduction.
D. The loss from the theft of business property.

11. The Disabled Access Credit conforms to the applicable standards of the:

A. Architectural Standards Act.
B. U.S. Department of Labor.
C. Americans with Disabilities Act.
D. National Organization on Disability.

12. Angela is a sole proprietor who owns a busy candle-making shop. Angela's net business income is $300,000 for the year. Angela has three full-time employees. She paid her three employees a total of $118,000 of wages during the year. Based on this information, what is Angela's allowable DPAD deduction for the year?

A. She is not eligible for the DPAD because she is a sole proprietor.
B. $118,000
C. $59,000
D. $27,000

13. Alistair is a sole proprietor who files his return on Schedule C. He had the following profit and losses:

- 2013: Net profit $7,000
- 2014: Net profit $9,000
- 2015: Net profit $6,000
- 2016: Net operating loss $24,000

How should Alistair report his net operating loss on his tax return?

A. NOL carryback of $7,000 to 2013; NOL carryback of $9,000 to 2014; NOL carryback of $6,000 to 2015; NOL carryforward of $2,000 to future years.
B. NOL carryback of $9,000 to 2014; NOL carryback of $6,000 to 2015; NOL carryforward of $9,000 to future tax years.
C. NOL carryback of $6,000 to 2015, NOL carryforward of $18,000 to future tax years.
D. NOL carryforward of $24,000 to 2017.

Unit 6: Answers

1. The answer is B. Based on the information provided, Lorelei may qualify for a credit of up to 50% of the premiums she paid for her employees. The actual percentage credit is determined by the number of full-time equivalent employees and their average annual wages. Small tax-exempt employers can qualify for a credit of up to 35% of the health insurance premiums paid for their employees. The Small Business Health Care Tax Credit is refundable, is designed for small business employers with fewer than 25 low to moderate income workers, and may be claimed for two consecutive years.

2. The answer is C. Selling food or beverages prepared at restaurants in the United States is specifically disallowed for purposes of the DPAD. Most U.S.-based manufacturing qualifies for the DPAD.

3. The answer is B. The amount of the Disabled Access Credit is 50% of the qualified expenses in excess of $250, but the maximum credit per year is limited to $5,000.

4. The answer is D. Normally, businesses can carry back unused business credits one year and carry them forward for 20 years.

5. The answer is D. The WOTC offers credits to businesses who hire out-of-work veterans, as well as other individuals in eight different targeted groups.

6. The answer is B. In general, a net operating loss may be carried back to the two previous years, and the remaining loss may be carried forward to the subsequent 20 years.

7. The answer is B. The Investment Credit is the sum of five credits that are designed to spur investment in activity that reduces greenhouse emissions and rehabilitates historic property. In 2016, the Investment Credit consists of the following five credits:

- the Rehabilitation Credit,
- Energy Investment Credit,
- Qualifying Advanced Coal Project Credit,
- Qualifying Gasification Project Credit, and
- Qualifying Advanced Energy Project Credit.

8. The answer is C. Only the casualty loss is potentially deductible for purposes of the net operating loss. Losses from the sale of stock are capital losses and cannot be used to create an NOL. Losses from the sale of personal-use property or a primary residence are not deductible.

9. The answer is A. The DPAD cannot be more than 50% (not 25%) of the wages a business pays its employees. All of the other statements are correct about this business deduction designed to stimulate manufacturing and other production activities in the United States.

10. The answer is D. The losses due to the theft of business property would be allowed in figuring a net operating loss.

11. The answer is C. The Disabled Access Credit is a nonrefundable tax credit for an eligible small business that pays expenses to provide access to disabled persons. The taxpayer must pay or incur the expenses to enable the business to comply with the Americans with Disabilities Act.

12. The answer is D. Angela is entitled to a DPAD deduction based upon the *lower* of:

- 9% of her net business income or
- 50% of her qualified wages.

Therefore, her DPAD deduction is $27,000 (9% X $300,000), since the 50% of wages equals $59,000 ($118,000 X 50%), which is higher than $27,000.

13. The answer is B. Business NOLs can be carried back two years, so Alistair would have an NOL carryback of $9,000 to 2014; and NOL carryback of $6,000 to 2015; and an NOL carryforward of $9,000. Any remaining amount of an NOL must be carried forward for up to 20 years.

Unit 7: Basis of Business Assets

More Reading:
Publication 551, *Basis of Assets*
Publication 547, *Casualties, Disasters, and Thefts*
Instructions for Form 3115, *Application for Change in Accounting Method*

A business asset is any type of property used in the conduct of a trade or business: land, buildings, machinery, furniture, trucks, patents, and franchise rights are examples. Some assets are tangible, and others are intangible. Taxpayers generally must capitalize the cost of business assets, rather than deduct them in the year the cost is incurred.

In order to compute gain or loss on the sale or other disposition of an asset, a business must be able to determine its basis.

Definition: Basis is the amount of a taxpayer's investment in an asset or property for tax purposes. Understanding how to calculate basis in various contexts, including for business entities such as corporations and partnerships, is critical to an individual's success in passing *Part 2: Businesses* of the EA Exam.

The basis of property is also used to determine tax deductions for depreciation, amortization, depletion, and casualty losses. If a business cannot determine the basis of an asset, the IRS will deem it to be zero.

The basis of property is usually its cost: the amount a business pays for the asset. The cost is the amount paid in cash, notes, other property, or services. Both cash-basis and accrual-basis businesses can charge expenses on a credit card and deduct them in the year the charge is incurred, regardless of when the credit card is paid.

An asset's cost basis also may include amounts paid for the following items:

- Sales tax on the purchase
- Freight to obtain the property
- Installation and testing costs
- Excise taxes
- Legal and accounting fees to obtain property
- Revenue stamps
- Recording fees
- Real estate taxes (if assumed by the buyer)
- Settlement costs for the purchase of real estate
- The assumption of any liabilities on the property

Note that the calculation of basis generally does not include interest payments.

If a business produces real or tangible personal property for use in a trade or business, it may be subject to the uniform capitalization rules.

Note: Certain events that occur during the period of ownership may increase or decrease basis, resulting in an ***adjusted basis***. For example, the basis of property is ***increased*** by the cost of improvements that add to the value of the property. The basis of property is ***decreased*** by depreciation deductions, insurance reimbursements for casualty and theft losses, and certain other items such as rebates.

Example: Naomi pays $4,000 for a new commercial dryer for her laundromat. Naomi also pays an additional $505 for shipping and sales tax. The installation cost for the dryer is $250. These costs are all added to the purchase price, resulting in an adjusted basis of $4,755.

Basis of Real Property

Real property, often called real estate, includes land and anything built on it. Real property also includes anything growing on, or attached to land (such as trees or an existing foundation). When a taxpayer buys real property, certain fees and other expenses become part of the cost basis in the property.

Settlement Costs: Certain settlement fees and closing costs related to buying a property are added to its basis. These include abstract fees; charges for installing utility services; legal fees, including title search and preparation of the sales contract and deed; recording fees; surveys; transfer taxes; owner's title insurance; and any amounts the seller owes that the taxpayer agrees to pay, such as charges for improvements or repairs and sales commissions.

However, the following settlement fees and closing costs cannot be included in the basis of a property:

- Casualty insurance premiums
- Rent or utility costs related to occupancy of the property before closing
- Any charges for acquiring a loan, such as mortgage insurance premiums, loan assumption fees, cost of a credit report, fees for appraisal reports, fees for refinancing a mortgage, and points. Points are prepaid interest on a loan and are generally deducted as interest over the life of the loan.

Real Estate Taxes: If a taxpayer pays real estate taxes on property he buys that the seller owed, those taxes are added to the basis and cannot be deducted currently.

Assumption of Mortgage: If a taxpayer buys property with an existing mortgage, the basis includes the amount paid in cash for the property plus the amount of the mortgage assumed.

Example: The Oceanside Partnership purchases a commercial building for $200,000 of cash and assumes a mortgage on the building of $800,000. The partnership also pays $5,500 of legal fees to a real estate attorney to handle the purchase. Oceanside's basis in the building is $1,005,500 ($200,000 + $800,000 + $5,500).

Constructing Assets: If a taxpayer builds property or has assets built, the costs of construction are included in the basis. In addition to the cost of land, these may include labor and materials; architect's fees; building permit charges; payments to contractors; rental equipment; inspections; employee wages paid for the construction work; and the cost of building supplies and materials used in the construction. The value of an owner's labor (if a sole proprietor rather than an employee-owner of a corporation) or any other labor for which payment is not made is not included in the basis.

Demolition Costs: Demolition costs increase an asset's basis because they are necessary to prepare the property for use. As such, costs incurred to demolish a building are added to the basis of the land on which the building was located. The costs of clearing land for construction also must be added to the basis of the land.

Example: Tony buys a lot with a badly damaged building on it for $25,000. He demolishes the building and prepares the land for a new structure. The demolition costs $13,000. Tony's adjusted basis in the land is $38,000 ($25,000 + $13,000).

Rehabilitation Costs: Rehabilitation costs increase basis. However, any rehabilitation credits allowed for the expenses must be subtracted.

Repair vs. Improvement Rules

Improvements increase the value of a property or asset. A taxpayer is required to capitalize the cost of improvements, thus increasing the property's basis, and claim depreciation deductions over a period of years. Examples of improvements include the installation of new electric wiring, adding a new roof or central air conditioning, or renovation of a kitchen.

In contrast, a repair keeps a property in operating condition but does not add to its value or substantially prolong its life. Examples include repainting a property or replacing broken windows. Unlike improvements, the costs of repairs can be deducted currently.

Example: Douglas repairs a leaky toilet in a rental duplex. The cost of the repair may be deducted as a current expense. The following year, Douglas replaces the entire plumbing system in the duplex with new pipes and bathroom fixtures. This is an improvement that increases the value of the property. Douglas must capitalize the cost of the new plumbing, increasing the property's basis, and depreciate the cost of this improvement over its useful life.

After ten years of various temporary or proposed regulations, the IRS's final tangible property regulations took effect on January 1, 2014, but the IRS is still issuing guidance for them, even into 2017. The regulations are hundreds of pages long, extremely complex, and affect virtually every business taxpayer.[99] The IRS has since issued several notices regarding these regulations.

The regulations establish the rules governing the capitalization and expensing of physical assets that a taxpayer purchases, repairs, maintains, improves, or disposes.

The tangible property regulations apply to C corporations, S corporations, partnerships, LLCs, and individuals filing a Form 1040 with Schedule C, Schedule E, or Schedule F. Under the new regulations, an "improvement" is classified as a cost involving:

- The **betterment** of property, or
- The **restoration** of property,
- The **adaptation** of a property to a new or different use.

The regulations divide a building into nine different structural components called "building systems," such as those for plumbing, heating and air conditioning, and electrical, each of which may be a separate unit of property, in addition to the building itself. Under the new, narrower definition of an improvement, costs must be evaluated for a specific building system, and not just for the building as a whole.

For example, the cost to refurbish an elevator may "improve" the elevator, but would not be significant to the building as a whole, so under the prior rules the cost could have been deducted as a repair. Under the new rules, the cost may be significant to the elevator system as a unit of property and therefore must be capitalized.

Example: Three years ago, Curtis purchased a small apartment building for $750,000. In 2016 he spends $18,000 to fix damaged wiring in the electrical system. Under the old rules, the $18,000 cost likely would be considered a repair because it is relatively small compared to the overall cost of the building. Under the new rules, the electrical system is a separate structural component or building system. This means that the $18,000 must be compared with the cost of the electrical system alone, not the cost of the whole building. The cost is more significant in this context and thus is more likely to be deemed an improvement.

Study Note: Given the complexity of the rules and their specificity to various types of property and how it is used, it is unlikely an EA test-taker would be expected to be familiar with all the details of the repair regulations. Many experienced tax professionals are still interpreting the key changes and how they apply to their business clients. For the EA exam, it should be sufficient to have a basic grasp of the underlying concepts of expensing repairs as current deductions vs. capitalization through depreciation deductions. In this unit, we look at how improvements are categorized and at the safe harbors that the regulations carve out for expensing property. Later in the book, we discuss concepts of depreciation and amortization.

[99] The rules may require businesses to make internal changes to accounting practices and procedures for financial and tax accounting purposes. Many taxpayers will be required to file Form 3115, *Request for an Accounting Method Change,* to comply with the regulations.

Safe Harbor Rules

As the previous example illustrates, in some instances the regulations make it more difficult to classify costs as repairs and deduct them currently and thus more likely the costs will need to be capitalized. The de minimis safe harbor election does not include costs for the purchase of inventory or land. The new regulations include several safe harbor rules that allow expensing in specific instances:

1. **De Minimis Expensing Safe Harbor #1:** Businesses with an applicable financial statement (AFS)[100], may use this safe harbor to deduct amounts paid for tangible property up to $5,000 per invoice or item. The rule applies as long as the business has a written capitalization policy or procedure that provides for expensing items that cost less than specified amounts or have an economic useful life of 12 months or less.
2. **De Minimis Expensing Safe Harbor #2:** If the business does not have qualifying financial statements, it may be permitted to deduct items that cost up to $2,500 ($500 prior to 2016) per invoice or per item.[101]
3. **Small Taxpayer Safe Harbor for Real Property:** Taxpayers with gross receipts of $10 million or less can expense as repairs, rather than capitalize as improvements, amounts up to the lesser of $10,000 or 2% of the unadjusted basis of a building property, as long as the unadjusted basis is $1 million or less. This is an election the taxpayer must make on his tax return. Once made, the election is irrevocable.
4. **Routine Maintenance Safe Harbor:** This allows for deduction of routine maintenance costs that are required more than once within a ten-year period for buildings, or more than once within the applicable class life period for non-building properties.
5. **$200 *de minimis* Election for Materials and Supplies:** In addition to the safe harbor rules listed, materials and supplies (that are not inventory) may be deducted in the year the item is used or consumed in the business. "Material and supplies" are classified as:
    - Any unit of property that cost $200 or less.
    - Any unit of property that has a useful life of 12 months or less.
    - Spare parts acquired to maintain or repair a unit of property.
    - Incidental materials and supplies that are not part of inventory, used in the business, and generally not tracked (e.g., pens, paper, staplers, toner, trash baskets).

Example #1: Gruber Co. purchases 10 boxes of copy paper every month to use in its secretarial offices. The cost of the copy paper is approximately $220 per invoice. Even though the amount exceeds the $200 de minimis threshold, it is still deductible as a current expense, because the supplies are reordered every month. Thus, the copy paper has a useful life of 12 months or less, and is therefore deductible as a supplies expense.

---

[100] An "AFS" is a financial statement required to be filed with the Securities Exchange Commission (SEC), as well as other types of certified audited financial statements accompanied by a CPA report, including a financial statement provided for a loan, reporting to shareholders, or for other non-tax purposes. An AFS also includes a financial statement required to be provided to a federal or state government or agency other than the IRS or the SEC.

[101] Effective for taxable years beginning on or after January 1, 2016, the Internal Revenue Service increased the de minimis safe harbor threshold from $500 to $2,500 per invoice or item for taxpayers without applicable financial statements. In addition, the IRS will provide audit protection to eligible businesses by not challenging the use of the $2,500 threshold for tax years ending before January 1, 2016.

Example #2: In 2016, Rhonda purchases 50 scanners at a discount. The scanners cost $199 each, and they are for use by employees in her business. Each scanner is a separate unit of property. In 2016, 35 scanners are used and the remaining 15 scanners are stored for future use. The 35 scanners are deductible in 2016, and the remaining 15 will be deductible in the year they are used.

Example #3: Rhonda pays $1,200 for a box of 10 toner cartridges to use as needed for laser printers in her business. The toner cartridges represent 10 units of property for $120 each; therefore, each cartridge is deductible as materials and supplies when used. Rhonda does not have qualifying financial statements. However, she makes the de minimis safe harbor election, so she deducts the full $1,200 in the year of purchase.

Example #4: Rhonda purchases a mold to create widgets for her business. The mold costs $16,000, but it is expected to be useful for only six months, after which, a new mold must be purchased. Even though the mold is expensive, it is deductible when consumed in her business, because its useful life is less than one year.

Other Changes to Basis of Business Property

Among the items that increase the basis of property are the following:

- The cost of extending service lines to the property
- Impact fees
- Legal fees, such as the costs of defending and perfecting title
- Zoning costs

Government assessments for items such as paving roads and sidewalks increase the value of a property, and therefore must be added to the property's basis.

A business cannot deduct assessments as taxes, but can deduct charges for maintenance, repairs, or interest charges related to the improvements.

A business must decrease the basis of property by amounts that represent a recovery of the business's cost of the property. For example, rebates and casualty losses are among the items that decrease an asset's basis.

Example: Kristin buys a color copier that costs $1,200 to use in her business. The cashier at the store gave her a rebate form when she purchased the machine. She sends in a rebate receipt and receives a $100 rebate from the manufacturer. The correct way to account for this rebate is to reduce the basis of the asset to $1,100 ($1,200 - $100).

Items that reduce the basis of property also include the following:

- Deductions for amortization, depreciation, section 179, and depletion
- Nontaxable corporate distributions
- Exclusion of subsidies for energy conservation measures
- Residential energy credits, vehicle credits, and the Investment Credit
- Certain canceled debt excluded from income
- Amounts received for easements

Casualty and Theft Losses of Business Property

Deductible casualty and theft losses and related insurance reimbursements reduce the basis of property. A casualty is defined as the damage, destruction, or loss of property resulting from an identifiable event that is sudden, unexpected, or unusual.

Deductible losses related to business and income-producing property (such as rental property) are reported on Form 4684, *Casualties and Thefts*, and are deductible without regard to whether they exceed the $100 and 10% of AGI thresholds that apply for personal-use property.

Example: A fire at Ramon's home destroys his couch and coffee table, which are personal-use property, for a loss of $5,000. This loss must be reduced by $100, and Ramon can deduct the portion that exceeds 10% of his AGI. The same fire also damages a business asset, a laptop computer that he had brought home that day in order to catch up on his work. The computer is destroyed, resulting in a business casualty loss of $3,000 that is fully deductible, without having to reduce it by the $100 and 10% of AGI like the couch and coffee table.

A casualty loss is not deductible if the damage or destruction is caused by progressive deterioration due to normal wear and tear from weather conditions or insect damage.

If an entity has business property that is stolen or destroyed, the deductible loss is figured as follows:

The taxpayer's adjusted basis in the property
MINUS
Any salvage value/scrap value
MINUS
Any insurance or other reimbursement received

Theft may involve taking money or property by the following means: blackmail, burglary, embezzlement, extortion, kidnapping for ransom, larceny, and robbery. The taking of property must be illegal under the state law where it happened, and it must have been done with criminal intent.

Example: Jeff owns a shop that sells sports memorabilia. Two years ago, Jeff purchased a signed Mike Trout baseball jersey for display for $150 at an estate sale. The jersey was stolen in 2016. The FMV of the jersey was $1,000 just before it was stolen, and his insurance did not cover the loss. Jeff's deductible theft loss is $150, equal to his basis in the jersey.

Casualty losses are generally deductible only in the tax year during which the casualty occurred, even if a business does not repair or replace the damaged property until a later year. Theft losses can be deducted only in the year the business discovers the property was stolen.

Insurance Reimbursements: If a business has insurance coverage for property that is lost or damaged, it must file a claim for reimbursement or it will not be able to deduct the loss. The portion of the loss that is not reimbursable by insurance, such as a deductible, is not subject to this rule.

Example: Howard and Gayle are partners and have a gourmet food truck that is used for business purposes. Howard has an accident that causes $2,350 in damage to the truck. He and Gayle pay the repair bill out-of-pocket so their business insurance costs will not increase. The insurance policy has a $500 deductible. Because the insurance would not cover the first $500 of the loss, this amount is their deductible casualty loss. The amount of their loss in excess of $500 is not deductible because they did not file an insurance claim.

A business that has a casualty or theft loss must decrease its adjusted basis in the property by any insurance or other reimbursement it receives and by any deductible loss. A business increases its basis in the property by the amounts spent, whether with proceeds of an insurance reimbursement or otherwise, on repairs that restore the property to, or beyond, its pre-casualty condition.

Basis of Securities

The basis of stocks, bonds, and other securities is the purchase price plus any costs of purchase, such as commissions and recording or transfer fees. A taxpayer must keep track of the basis per share of all stock purchases and sales.

Example: In 2016, Yuen Corporation purchases 2,000 shares of Catalyst Corporation stock. The cost of the stock is $24,000, and Yuen Corporation pays a broker's fee of $550 on the purchase and transfer. Therefore, the basis of the stock is $24,550 ($24,000 + $550 broker's fee).

Events that occur after the purchase of the stock can require adjustments to the basis per share of stock. The original basis per share can be changed by events such as stock dividends, stock splits, and DRIP (dividend reinvestment plan) activity.

- Stock dividends involve the issuance of additional shares to current shareholders. The shareholder's total basis is unchanged but is spread over more shares, which decreases the basis per share.
- A stock split is similar to a stock dividend. For example, a two-for-one stock split increases the number of outstanding shares two-fold and decreases the value and the basis per share by half.

As with a stock dividend, the total basis remains the same after a stock split. For example, if a taxpayer has 100 shares with a cost of $50 per share, his basis is $5,000.

Assuming a two-for-one stock split, the taxpayer now has 200 shares with a basis per share of $25, which still equals a total basis of $5,000.

Example: In 2016, Hollinger Partnership purchases 100 shares of Better Electronics for $11,000. There is an additional $200 in broker's commissions, so the original basis per share is $112 ([$11,000 + $200] ÷ 100). Later in 2016, Hollinger receives 40 additional shares of Better Electronics' stock as a nontaxable stock dividend. The $11,200 basis must now be spread over 140 shares (100 original shares plus the 40-share stock dividend). The adjusted stock basis is $80 per share ($11,200 ÷ 140).

Basis Other Than Cost

There are times when the cost of an asset cannot be used as basis. In certain cases, the adjusted basis of an asset is determined using other methods. For example:

- **Property Received for Services:** If a taxpayer receives property for his services, he must include the property's FMV in income. The amount included in income is the taxpayer's basis in the property. If the services were performed for a price agreed on beforehand, this price may be used as the fair market value of the property, as long as there is no evidence to the contrary.
- **Property in Lieu of Wages:** When property is transferred in lieu of wages, the employer is entitled to deduct the property's fair market value at the time of the transfer and the same amount is taxable compensation for the employee. A gain or loss is realized if there is a difference between the fair market value and the adjusted basis of the property.
- **Bargain Purchases:** A bargain purchase is a purchase of an item for less than its fair market value. If, as compensation for services, a taxpayer buys goods or other property at less than the FMV, the difference between the purchase price and the property's FMV must be included in his income. His basis in the property is its fair market value (the purchase price plus the amount included in income).

Unit 7: Study Questions

(Test yourself and then check the correct answers at the end of this section.)

1. Reggie purchases 25 printers for use in his business. The printers cost $90 each for a total of $2,250. What is the correct statement about how he should treat this purchase?

A. He must capitalize the total expense of $2,250.
B. He can deduct $90 for the current year.
C. He can choose to expense some of the printers and capitalize others to maximize profit.
D. He can deduct the cost of each printer in the year it is used or consumed in the business.

2. Jade purchases a warehouse for her business, but it is in such bad condition that she decides to demolish it and build a new one. The demolition costs $15,600. How must Jade report this cost on her tax return?

A. The cost for the demolition is added to the basis of the land where the original demolished structure was located.
B. The demolition may be deducted on her tax return on Schedule E.
C. The demolition cost may be deducted on her tax return on Schedule C.
D. The demolition cost must be amortized over 180 months.

3. What item would not be included in an asset's basis?

A. Sales tax.
B. Installation charges.
C. Recording fees.
D. Interest paid on a loan to purchase the asset.

4. Ian buys a building. He makes a $15,000 down payment in cash. He also assumes a mortgage of $180,000 on it and pays $1,000 of title fees and $2,000 of points. What is Ian's basis in the building?

A. $15,000
B. $195,000
C. $196,000
D. $198,000

5. All of the following items decrease the basis of property except:

A. Casualty or theft loss deductions and insurance reimbursements.
B. The cost of defending a title.
C. Depreciation.
D. Amortization.

6. Alex is having financial difficulties, so he sells his office building to Cheryl, a real estate investor, who plans to use it as a business rental property. Alex was liable for $5,000 in delinquent real estate taxes on the property, which Cheryl agrees to pay. How should Cheryl treat this transaction?

A. Cheryl cannot deduct these taxes as a current expense; she must add the amount to the basis of the property.
B. Cheryl can deduct these taxes as a current expense on her Schedule A.
C. Cheryl can deduct these taxes as a current expense on her Schedule E.
D. Cheryl can deduct these taxes as a current expense on her Schedule C.

7. Anya purchases a die-cut machine for her business that costs $8,000. It has a useful life of less than a year. Under the tangible property regulations, she:

A. Must capitalize the cost of the machine.
B. Can deduct the expense during the current tax year.
C. Can deduct the expense during the next tax year.
D. Must file Form 3115 for the current tax year before she is able to deduct any business expenses.

8. Irina owns a fabric store. In 2016, she has a loss of $14,000 of business inventory due to water damage from a storm. The loss is completely covered by insurance. However, Irina will not be reimbursed by her insurance company until 2017. How should she treat this loss?

A. She should claim the entire loss as a casualty loss in 2016 and then claim the income from the insurance company reimbursement in 2017.
B. She must reduce the amount of her inventory loss in 2016. For 2017, she must include the insurance reimbursement as income.
C. She does not need to report this loss on her 2016 tax return, since she knows she will receive a reimbursement within a short period of time.
D. She must reduce her cost of goods sold in 2016 to reflect the loss and then claim the reimbursement as income in 2017.

9. How does a stock split affect the basis of securities?

A. There is no effect.
B. It increases the basis of stock.
C. It decreases the basis of stock.
D. It decreases the basis per share of stock but does not affect the total basis of the stock.

10. Under the tangible property regulations, what are the categories for determining what constitutes an "improvement" to property rather than a repair?

A. Betterment, restoration, or adaptation.
B. Prolonging life and creating value.
C. Renovation, amelioration, or restoration.
D. Enhancement and repair.

11. Franco purchases 50 shares of Canine Country stock for $3,500. He pays a broker's fee of $100. He later receives 40 additional shares of Canine Country stock as a nontaxable stock dividend. The following year, the company declares a two-for-one stock split. Calculate the total basis of Franco's Canine Country stock and his per share basis:

A. Stock basis: $3,500; per share basis: $38.88.
B. Stock basis: $3,500; per share basis: $19.44.
C. Stock basis: $3,600; per share basis: $20.
D. Stock basis: $3,600; per share basis: $40.

12. Priscilla's Pastries is a cupcake shop that operates as a sole proprietorship. In order to expand, the business bought a building for $250,000 in 2016. Priscilla, the business owner, paid the title company $13,000 in settlement fees to purchase the property. She also assumed an existing mortgage of $35,000 on the property. Legal fees of $9,500 were incurred in a title dispute with a neighbor in April 2016. The title was finally transferred to Priscilla in June 2016. Property taxes in the amount of $2,600 were incurred on the property after ownership was transferred. What is Priscilla's overall basis in the building at the end of 2016?

A. $250,000
B. $285,000
C. $307,500
D. $310,100

13. Arrowhead Model Builders is constructing a custom home. Calculate the basis of the property from the following information:

Land purchase price	$125,000
Construction loan proceeds	40,000
Points on construction loan	3,000
Tear-down of existing home	20,000
Clearing of brush	10,000
Construction workers' wages	50,000
Construction materials	300,000

A. $227,000
B. $505,000
C. $548,000
D. $545,000

14. A business does not have qualifying financial statements. Under the de minimis expensing safe harbor rule, he can deduct items that cost up to __________ per invoice or item.

A. $200
B. $500
C. $5,000
D. $2,500

15. A hailstorm damages a van owned by Marjorie, a sole proprietor who offers mobile chiropractic services. The van's basis is $25,000, and her insurance company reimburses her $4,000 for the hail damage. Marjorie decides to replace the cracked windshield at a cost of $500 and pockets the rest of the insurance money. What is the adjusted basis of her van?

A. $21,500
B. $28,500
C. $29,000
D. $19,500

16. Chan Delivery Services is having cash-flow difficulties, so it transfers a pickup truck to Bonnie, an employee, in lieu of wages. The company owes Bonnie $7,000 of wages. At the time of the transfer, the truck had a fair market value of $7,000 and an adjusted basis to Chan Delivery of $5,500. How should the company report this transaction?

A. Wage expense of $7,000.
B. Wage expense of $5,500.
C. Wage expense of $2,500.
D. Wage expense of $7,000 and gain on sale of $1,500.

17. In 2016, the Vaughn Legal Partnership provides legal services to Andrews Pawn Shop. Andrews Pawn then becomes insolvent. In lieu of payment, Vaughn Partnership accepts a set of gold coins with a fair market value of $5,000 and an electric scooter with a fair market value of $2,000 and an adjusted basis of $1,000. What amount of income must Vaughn Partnership report for this transaction?

A. $7,000
B. $6,000
C. $8,000
D. $5,000

Unit 7: Answers

1. The answer is D. The tangible property regulations include rules regarding "materials and supplies" that allow a unit of property with a cost of $200 or less to be deducted in the year it is used or consumed in the business. Each printer would be treated as a separate unit of property, so the entire amount could be deducted currently rather than capitalized.

2. The answer is A. Demolition costs or other losses related to the demolition of any building are added to the basis of the land.

3. The answer is D. Interest charges are not added to an asset's basis. Interest is a currently deductible expense.

4. The answer is C. Ian's basis is $196,000. The title fees, mortgage amount, and the down payment are added to figure the cost basis of the building. The points are not included in the basis.

5. The answer is B. The cost of defending title to a property increases its basis.

6. The answer is A. Cheryl cannot deduct the taxes as a current expense, since they are delinquent real estate taxes and the person who is legally liable for the debt is Alex. However, the taxes may be added to the property's basis and depreciated as part of her purchase price.

7. The answer is B. Under the materials and supplies rules of the tangible property regulations, a unit of property with a useful life of a year or less may be deducted rather than capitalized. Although Anya's business may be subject to the Form 3115 filing requirement as a result of the new regulations related to capitalization and repairs expense, this requirement would not affect the deductibility of other types of business expenses.

8. The answer is C. Irina expects to be fully reimbursed for her loss, so reporting it on her 2016 return is not necessary. However, if Irina's insurance company reimbursement is ultimately either more or less than her loss, she may realize an additional gain or loss. Whether a gain would be taxable will depend on how she uses the insurance proceeds.

9. The answer is D. A stock split increases the number of outstanding shares, which decreases the basis per share, but it does not change the basis of the stock as a whole.

10. The answer is A. Under the new regulations, an improvement is redefined as a cost involving a betterment of the unit of property, a restoration of the unit of property, or an adaptation of the unit of property to a new or different use.

11. The answer is C. The basis is the stock's purchase price plus the broker's fee ($3,500 + $100 = $3,600). After the stock dividend, Franco has 180 shares of stock ([50 shares + 40 shares] × 2 = 180). The stock split reduces his per share basis by half to $20 ($3,600 ÷ 180 shares of stock).

12. The answer is C. The basis is $307,500 ($250,000 + $13,000 + $35,000 + $9,500). The settlement fees, the mortgage assumed by the buyer, and the legal fees for defending the title are all included in the basis of the property. The property taxes are not included in the basis of the building because they were incurred when Priscilla was already the legal owner. Instead, the property taxes may be deducted as a current expense.

13. The answer is B. All items are added to the property's basis except for the points on the loan (an expense that is deducted over the life of the loan) and the construction loan ($125,000 + $20,000 + $10,000 + $50,000 + $300,000 = $505,000).

14. The answer is D. If a business does not have qualifying financial statements, it may be permitted to deduct items that cost up to $2,500 per invoice or per item in 2016. A business that has a written capitalization policy or procedure for expensing items can deduct amounts expensed in its financial statements that cost up to $5,000.

15. The answer is A. Marjorie must reduce the basis of her van by the portion of any insurance proceeds that are not used for repairs. Since she uses $500 of the proceeds to repair the windshield, the adjusted basis is $21,500 ($25,000 - $4,000 + $500 = $21,500).

16. The answer is D. When property is transferred in lieu of wages, the employer is entitled to deduct its fair market value at the time of the transfer. A gain or loss is realized if there is a difference between the fair market value and the adjusted basis of the property. The transfer is treated as a sale, so Chan Delivery would have to report a gain. Chan Delivery should deduct $7,000 as wage expense and report the gain on the sale of the truck, figured as follows: $7,000 - $5,500 = $1,500.

17. The answer is A. Vaughn Partnership must include the FMV of the coins ($5,000) and the FMV of the scooter ($2,000) as income. Property exchanged for services must be included as income at its fair market value.

Unit 8: Depreciation and Amortization

More Reading:
Publication 946, *How to Depreciate Property*

Depreciation is an income tax deduction that allows a taxpayer to recover the cost or other basis of certain property. It is an annual allowance for the wear and tear, deterioration, or obsolescence of the property. Most types of tangible property, such as buildings, machinery, vehicles, furniture, and equipment are depreciable. Likewise, certain intangible property, such as patents, copyrights, and computer software is depreciable or amortizable.

The costs of business assets and improvements generally must be capitalized. The capitalized cost of these asset purchases may be recognized as depreciation or amortization expense over their estimated "useful life" unless they qualify for the section 179 deduction, bonus depreciation, or certain specified safe harbor exceptions.

Definition: Useful life: In general, an asset's "useful life" is usually the period of time for which the asset will be economically useful in a business. This can vary based on a number of factors, but the IRS established asset classes for most types of property and equipment and assigns a useful life (also called a recovery period) to each asset class. This concept will be covered extensively in this unit.

Depreciation Rules

The cost of land and certain land improvements cannot be depreciated. Most other types of tangible property, such as buildings, machinery, vehicles, furniture, and equipment, are depreciable. Likewise, certain intangible property, such as patents, copyrights, and computer software, is amortizable. In order to be depreciated or amortized, an asset must meet all the following requirements:

- The taxpayer generally must own the property. However, taxpayers may depreciate capital improvements for property they lease (for example, a fence that is built on property that the business leases from another party).
- The taxpayer must use the property in business or in an income-producing activity. If a taxpayer uses the property for both business and personal use, he can only deduct an amount of depreciation based on the business-use percentage.
- The property must have a determinable useful life of more than one year.

The property ceases to be depreciable when the business has fully recovered its cost or when it sells or retires the property from service, whichever happens first.

Example: Better Produce, Inc. is a canning company that processes fruits and vegetables. In 2016, an older canning machine ceases to function properly. Better Produce has the option to purchase a new machine for $500,000, or completely rebuild its old machine, which will extend its useful life for another five years. Better Produce chooses to rebuild the machine at a cost of $125,000. Since the cost of the rebuild extended the useful life of the machine for several more years, the $125,000 cost must be capitalized and depreciated over its useful life, which is now an additional five years.

In order to properly depreciate an asset, a taxpayer must determine the following:

- The depreciable basis of the property
- The depreciation method for the property
- The class life (which is representative of the asset's useful life)
- Whether the asset is listed property
- Whether the taxpayer elects to expense any portion of the asset
- Whether the taxpayer qualifies for any bonus first-year depreciation

Definition: Depreciation is an annual allowance for the wear and tear, deterioration, or obsolescence of an asset. Tax depreciation is based on the original, historical cost of the asset and is not indexed for inflation.

Nondepreciable Assets

Certain property cannot be depreciated, including:

- Land
- Property placed in service and disposed of in the same year
- Property used only for personal use
- Property with a useful life of one year or less
- Equipment that is used to build capital improvements
- Inventory
- Section 197 intangibles such as copyrights, patents, franchises, non-compete agreements, and goodwill, which must be amortized, not depreciated

Example: Natalie is a self-employed accountant who must purchase new payroll software every year. She should not depreciate the software, but may instead deduct its entire cost as a business expense since the software has a useful life of only one year.

If an asset, such as a home or motor vehicle, has both personal and business use, only the business portion of its cost may be depreciated.

Example: Tenda is a part-time videographer. He advertises his services online and occasionally does wedding and birthday videography. In 2016, he also uses his videography equipment to record various family functions, including his son's wedding and a family reunion. He uses the videography equipment approximately 60% of the time for business, and the rest (40%) for personal use. The cost of the equipment must be allocated between business and personal use based on these percentages.

Reporting Depreciation: A taxpayer must use Form 4562, *Depreciation and Amortization* to:

- Claim deductions for depreciation and amortization;
- Make an election under section 179 to currently expense certain depreciable property; and
- Provide information on the business/investment use of automobiles and other listed property.

Depreciation begins when a taxpayer places property in service of a trade or business or for the production of income.

Example: Donald buys a machine for his business that is delivered on December 20, 2016. However, the machine is not installed and operational until January 12, 2017. It is not considered placed in service until 2017, and the first depreciation expense deduction can be claimed in 2017. If the machine had been ready and available for use when it was delivered, it would have been considered placed in service in 2016 even if it were not actually used until 2017.

Example: On June 23, Sue bought a home to use as residential rental property. She made several repairs and had it ready for rent in September. At that time, she began to advertise the home for rent in the local newspaper. Sue did not find a tenant until November 10. She can begin to depreciate the rental property in September and start taking other rental expenses because the property is considered placed in service when it is ready and available for rent.

Salvage Value (or Scrap Value): An asset cannot be depreciated below its salvage (or scrap) value. Salvage value is the asset's estimated fair market value at the end of its useful life. Salvage value is affected both by how a business uses the property and how long it uses it.

If it is the business's policy to dispose of property that is still in good operating condition, the salvage value may be relatively large. If the business's policy is to use property until it is no longer usable, its salvage value may be zero.[102]

Example: Cooper Trucking purchases a new delivery truck in 2016 for $125,000. The MACRS class life of the truck is five years. At the end of five years, Cooper Trucking estimates it will sell the used delivery truck at auction for $30,000, so it uses this amount as the salvage value. The basis of the truck is $125,000, but the basis for depreciation is $95,000 ($125,000 - $30,000), since the business expects to recover $30,000 at the end of the asset's useful life.

Depreciation Methods in General

Once a business chooses a depreciation method for an asset, the business must generally use the same method for the life of the asset.

Straight-Line Depreciation: This is the simplest method. This method lets a business deduct the same amount of depreciation each year over the useful life of the property. It is the most conservative depreciation method. To use the straight-line method, a business must first determine the asset's basis, salvage value, and estimated useful life. If the asset has a salvage value, it is subtracted from the basis. The balance is the total depreciation expense deduction the business can take over the useful life of the property.

If an asset originally cost $200, has an estimated salvage value of zero, and a five-year recovery period, the straight-line depreciation allowance would be $40 ($200 ÷ 5) each year for five years.

Straight-line Depreciation = (Cost minus Salvage Value) ÷ Useful Life

A business may switch to the straight-line method at any time during the useful life of the property without IRS consent. However, after a business changes to straight-line, it cannot change back to any other method for a period of ten years without written permission from the IRS.

Example: On April 1, 2016, the Redstone Corporation purchases an advanced computer system for $40,000. The system has a five-year life. There is no salvage value. Depreciation is calculated as follows:

Depreciation for 2016 = ($40,000 ÷ 5 years) × (9 months ÷ 12) = $6,000.

Depreciation for 2017 = ($40,000 ÷ 5 years) × (12 ÷ 12) = $8,000.

The Double-Declining Balance Method: This method uses a flat percentage depreciation rate over the life of the asset. For example, if five years is the asset's life, the double-declining balance method has a depreciation rate of (2 ÷ 5), or twice the straight-line depreciation rate. Instead of spreading the cost of the asset evenly over its life, this method expenses the asset by applying a constant rate to the declining balance of the asset, which results in declining depreciation expense each successive period.

The logic for the double-declining balance method is that there should be a greater deduction in the earlier years when the asset is more productive.

Example: For an asset that originally cost $200 and has a five-year life, double-declining balance depreciation is $80 = ([2 ÷ 5] × $200) in the first year; $48 = ([2 ÷ 5]×[$200 - $80]) in the second year; $28.80 = ([2 ÷ 5]×[$200 - $80 - $48]) in the third year; and so on.

[102] Note that salvage value is typically ignored under MACRS (IRC Sect. 168(b)); however, IRS Publication 946, *How to Depreciate Property,* still covers the important concept of salvage value. See Publication 946 for more information.

Modified Accelerated Cost Recovery System (MACRS)

Under MACRS, depreciable assets are divided into nine separate classes that dictate the number of years over which their cost will be recovered. Each MACRS class has a schedule that specifies the percentage of the asset's cost that is depreciated each year. For example, computers are depreciated over five years, and office furniture is depreciated over seven years.

The modified accelerated cost recovery system (MACRS) is the depreciation method generally used for most tangible property. Real property is depreciated using the straight-line method, with an equal amount of expense each year. Nonresidential real property, such as office buildings, shopping malls, and factories, is depreciated over a 39-year recovery period. Residential buildings, such as apartment complexes and residential rentals, are depreciated over a 27.5-year period.

The depreciation calculations allocate deductions of the asset's cost over a recovery period roughly consistent with the asset's estimated useful economic life. These are general estimates that the IRS has assigned to certain types of assets, and the true economic life of an asset might differ.

MACRS Class Life Table

Property Class	Asset Type
3-year property	Certain tractor units; race horses over two years old; qualified rent-to-own property.
5-year property	Computers; office machinery; small aircraft, automobiles, taxis, buses, and trucks; breeding cattle and dairy cattle; appliances, carpets, and furniture used in residential retail activity; certain geothermal, solar, and wind property.
7-year property	Office furniture and fixtures; agricultural machinery and equipment; any other property that does not have a designated class life.
10-year property	Vessels and water transportation equipment; trees or vines bearing fruit or nuts; single purpose agricultural or horticultural structures.
15-year property	Improvements to land such as fences, roads, and bridges; municipal wastewater treatment plants; qualified restaurant and retail improvement property; qualified leasehold improvement property.
20-year property	Certain municipal sewers; farm buildings (other than single purpose agricultural or horticultural structures).
25-year property	Certain municipal sewers; water utility property.
27.5-year property	Residential rental property, if more than 80% of its gross rental income is from dwelling units.
39-year property	Section 1250 nonresidential real property, such as office buildings, stores, and warehouses.

Section 179 Deduction

The section 179 deduction is a special allowance that allows a business to elect to take a full deduction for the cost of new or used property in the first year it is placed in service, rather than depreciating it over its useful life. To qualify for the section 179 deduction, the property must meet all the following requirements:

- It must be eligible property.
- It must be acquired for business use (and used more than 50% for business in the year placed in service).
- It must have been acquired by purchase.

- It must not have been purchased from a related party, including a spouse, ancestors, or lineal descendants.

> **Note:** The PATH Act expanded the Section 179 deduction and made the deduction permanent. Additionally, the existing Section 179 cap will be indexed for inflation in $10,000 increments for future years.

The section 179 deduction applies the eligible property when it is "placed in service." This may be different than the date of purchase. Property is considered "placed in service" when it is ready and available to use, even if the item is not being currently used. Eligible property generally includes the following:

- Tangible personal property, such as machinery and equipment
- Property contained in or attached to a building (other than structural components), such as refrigerators, grocery store counters, office equipment, printing presses, testing equipment, and signs (however, the Section 179 deduction is not available for residential rental properties)
- Gasoline storage tanks and pumps at retail service stations
- Livestock, including horses, cattle, hogs, sheep, goats, and mink and other furbearing animals
- Off-the-shelf computer software
- Single purpose agricultural or horticultural property
- Storage facilities
- Qualified real property (as described later)

This deduction does not apply to land, intangible assets (except software), inventory, property used outside the United States, or air conditioning or heating units.

The section 179 deduction may not exceed taxable business income for the year, calculated without regard to the section 179 deduction itself and certain other items. However, an amount disallowed due to this limitation may be carried over for an unlimited number of years. The deduction can be elected for individual qualifying assets, up to a maximum of $500,000 for 2016.

However, to the extent the cost of qualifying section 179 property placed in service by the taxpayer exceeds $2.01 million in 2016, the maximum deduction is reduced on a dollar-for-dollar basis, and eliminated if the total cost of qualifying property is at least $2.51 million. This is often called the Section 179 "spending cap."

For partnerships, the section 179 limits described above apply to both the partnership and to each individual partner. The partnership determines its deduction subject to these limits, and then allocates the deduction among the partners. The partner considers the amounts allocated based upon his interest in the partnership and from any other sources in relation to the same limits.

Qualified Real Property (QRP)

Businesses generally cannot deduct the costs of real property (real estate) under section 179. However, a special provision allows businesses to expense up to $500,000 in 2016 for costs of qualified real property (QRP). In the prior year, the expensing limit was $250,000 on such property but the PATH Act raised the threshold to the full section 179 limit ($500,000) beginning in 2016. This provision applies only to the following:

- Qualified leasehold improvement property
- Qualified restaurant property (such as major renovation of a restaurant building's main dining area)
- Qualified retail improvement property (such as an interior upgrade of a retail clothing store)

Example: In 2016, Armando owns pizza restaurant by becoming a franchise owner of Papa's Pizza, a popular Italian food chain. In 2016, Armando renovates the interior of the dining room by upgrading the booths and remodeling the kitchen at a cost of $260,000. He also purchases a computer for use in his business at a cost of $5,000. The initial franchise cost payable to Papa's Pizza was $25,000. Therefore, Armando has the following outlays for the year:

Computer	$5,000
Qualified real property	$260,000
Franchise contract	$25,000
Total asset purchases	**$290,000**

Since the limit for expensing QRP under section 179 is $500,000 in 2016, Armando may expense the full $260,000 of the renovation costs. He may also take the section 179 deduction for the full cost of the computer. Armando's allowable section 179 deduction is therefore limited to $265,000 ($5,000 computer + $260,000 of QRP). The cost of the franchise is not deductible under Section 179. A franchise, trademark, or trade name is a Section 197 *intangible asset*, and must be amortized over 15 years.

Trade-in Property: If a business buys qualifying property with cash and a trade-in, its depreciable basis for purposes of the section 179 deduction includes only the cash portion of the purchase price.

Example: Fickle Feet, a retail athletic shoe store, traded two wood displays with a total adjusted basis of $680 for a new glass display that cost $1,320. Fickle Feet received an $800 trade-in allowance for the old displays and paid an additional $520 of cash for the new glass display. The shop also traded a used van with an adjusted basis of $4,500 for a new van costing $9,000. Fickle Feet received a $4,800 trade-in allowance on the used van and paid $4,200 of cash for the new van. Only the portion of the new property's basis paid with cash qualifies for the section 179 deduction. Therefore, Fickle Feet's qualifying costs for the section 179 deduction are $4,720 ($520 + $4,200).

50% Bonus Depreciation

If the cost of business property cannot immediately be deducted in full as a section 179 expense, a business may elect to take bonus depreciation for certain types of new property.

This provision allows a business to write off 50% of certain property costs in the first year, with the remaining cost depreciated over the asset's useful life. Applicable section 179 deductions are generally used first, followed by bonus depreciation, unless the business has an insufficient level of taxable income.

Congress retroactively extended bonus depreciation through 2019. However, unlike Section 179, which was made permanent by the PATH Act, the bonus depreciation percentage will be gradually phased out as follows:

- 50% for through 2017
- 40% in 2018
- 30% for 2019

After 2019, bonus depreciation will be phased out completely.

Example: Murray owns an auto dismantling business. He purchases a new vehicle crushing machine for his business that costs $610,000. He claims $500,000 of the cost as a section 179 deduction. For the remaining cost of $110,000, he claims 50% bonus depreciation. The remaining $55,000 basis of the machine must be depreciated over its useful life.

The bonus depreciation allowance applies to tangible personal property with a recovery period of 20 years or less, as well as to certain buildings and leasehold improvements, office equipment, and purchased computer software. It does not apply to real property or intangible assets such as patents or copyrights.

Bonus depreciation does not apply to used or refurbished property.

Note: In order to qualify for bonus depreciation, the property must be new (unlike the requirement for section 179 deductions, which are allowed for both new and used property). Bonus depreciation is also not subject to the same $2.01 million phase-out as the section 179 deduction, so the deduction is available to much larger businesses.

Listed Property

Definition: Listed property is a specific class of depreciable property that is subject to special tax rules because it is often used for both business and personal purposes.

Listed property is certain property that is used by taxpayers in a business which is also frequently used for personal purposes. In order to avoid the abuse of depreciation deductions for certain property, congress enacted the "listed property" rules. The IRS includes the following as listed property:

- Any passenger vehicle weighing under 6,000 pounds and any other property used for transportation
- Property used for entertainment, recreation, or amusement such as photographic or video recording equipment
- Certain computers and related peripheral equipment. Computer equipment used exclusively at a business location (including a qualified home office) is not considered listed property.

If an item is used for both business and personal purposes, deductions for depreciation and section 179 are limited to the percentage of business use. Further, if business use is not more than 50%, section 179 deductions and bonus depreciation allowances are not allowed, and depreciation must be calculated using the straight-line method.

Example: In 2016, Eleanor buys and places in service a new computer that costs $4,000. She uses the computer 80% for her business and 20% for personal purposes. She can deduct $3,200 under section 179 for the business portion of the cost (80% × $4,000).

The IRS no longer categorizes cellular telephones as listed property.

Heavy Sports Utility Vehicle Exception: A taxpayer cannot elect to expense under section 179 more than $25,000 of the cost of any heavy sport-utility vehicle (SUV) and certain other vehicles placed in service during the tax year. This rule applies to vehicles weighing between 6,000 and 14,000 pounds.

This rule does not apply to certain types of vehicles, including ambulances, hearses, taxis, transport vans, shuttle vans, clearly marked emergency vehicles, and other qualified nonpersonal use vehicles.

Example: Sergey is a busy real estate broker. He purchases a luxury SUV in 2016 for $65,000. The SUV weighs 6,500 pounds, so the "Heavy Duty Sports Vehicle" exception applies. He uses the vehicle 100% for business. The first-year depreciation amount will be $49,000 ($25,000 Section 179 deduction + $20,000 bonus depreciation deduction [50% x $40,000] + $4,000 MACRS depreciation deduction [$4,000 =$20,000 ÷ 5 year MACRS class life for the SUV]).

Example: Cavalier Transport purchased a $75,000 shuttle bus in 2016. The bus weighs 7,900 pounds, seats 10 passengers, and is 100% business-use. Since this vehicle qualifies for an exception (the entire $75,000 would be fully deductible under Section 179.

Amortization

Amortization is used to deduct the cost or basis of an intangible asset over its estimated life. With the exception of off-the-shelf computer software intangible assets are not eligible for section 179 deductions. The basis of an intangible asset is usually the cost to buy or create it.

Definition: Intangible property is property that has value, but it cannot be seen or touched.

Examples of intangible assets include goodwill, patents, copyrights, trademarks, trade names, franchises, and favorable relationships with customers or suppliers that are carried over from an acquired business.

A taxpayer may amortize certain start-up costs for purchasing an active trade or business. These include only the investigative costs that help the taxpayer decide whether to purchase the business. Costs incurred in an attempt to purchase a specific business are capital costs that cannot be amortized.

Certain intangible assets, including the preceding examples, are designated as section 197 intangibles and must be amortized over a 15-year period (180 months). Another example is the cost of a covenant not to compete executed in connection with the acquisition of a trade or business. As a section 197 intangible asset, this cost would be amortized over 15 years, even though the covenant agreement may be in place for a shorter period.

Example: Heather is a podiatrist. Another podiatrist is retiring, so she is purchasing his business for $1 million. The practice has $750,000 of tangible assets, including medical equipment and office furnishings. The remainder of the purchase price ($250,000) is attributed to goodwill, which Heather must amortize over 15 years. Her goodwill deduction is $16,667 a year ($250,000 ÷ 15).

Depletion

Depletion is similar in concept to depreciation, and is the method of cost recovery for mining and agricultural activities. Depletion refers to the exhaustion of a natural resource as a result of production, such as by mining, quarrying, or cutting (of timber). Mineral property, timber, and natural gas are all examples of natural resources that are subject to the deduction for depletion.

There are two ways of figuring depletion:

- **Cost depletion**
- **Percentage depletion**

Some businesses employ cost depletion at the outset of operations when a large number of units of the deposit are extracted and sold, and then convert to percentage depletion later when percentage depletion yields a more sizable deduction.

Cost Depletion: This method allocates the cost of a natural resource over the total anticipated volume to yield cost depletion per unit (expressed in tons, barrels, etc.) A depletion deduction is then allowed each year based on the units exploited.

After a business determines the property's basis, estimates the total recoverable units, and knows the number of units sold during the tax year, it can calculate the cost depletion deduction as follows:

Divide the property's basis for depletion by estimated total recoverable units =
Rate per unit
Multiply the rate per unit by actual units sold =
Cost depletion deduction

Example: In 2016, Brian buys a timber farm, and he estimates the timber can produce 300,000 units when cut. At the time of purchase, the adjusted basis of the timber is $24,000. Brian cuts and sells 27,000 units. Brian's depletion rate for each unit is $.08 ($24,000 ÷ 300,000). His deduction for depletion in 2016 is $2,160 (27,000 × $.08).

Percentage Depletion: Under this method, a flat percentage of gross income from the property is taken as the depletion deduction. Percentage depletion may not be used for timber and its use for oil and gas properties is subject to strict limits.

To figure percentage depletion, the business multiplies a certain percentage, specified for each mineral, by gross income from the property during the year.

The percentage depletion deduction generally cannot be more than 50% (100% for oil and gas property) of taxable income from the property, calculated before the depletion deduction and the domestic production activities deduction (DPAD).

Unit 8: Study Questions

(Test yourself and then check the correct answers at the end of this section.)

1. Bonus depreciation is taken:

A. After a section 179 deduction is taken.
B. Before a section 179 deduction is taken.
C. Before section 179 and regular MACRS deductions are taken.
D. After section 179 and regular MACRS deductions are taken.

2. Friendship Dentistry bought out Andrews Brothers Dentistry. The gross sales included dental supplies, furniture, fixtures, dental equipment, and goodwill of the existing practice. The contract also included a do-not-compete clause. The contract details of the sale are listed below.

Contract Purchase Details	
Dental Supplies	$4,000
Furniture	16,500
Fixtures	10,800
Dental equipment	15,500
Goodwill	60,000
Covenant not to compete	40,000
Gross Sales Price	**$146,800**

Based on this information, what is the total dollar amount of the assets that must be amortized? How long is the required amortization period?

A. The Goodwill ($60,000) must be amortized over 60 months (5 years).
B. The Goodwill and the dental equipment ($75,500) must be amortized over 60 months (5 years).
C. The Goodwill and the covenant not to compete ($100,000) must be amortized over 180 months (15 years).
D. The entire purchase ($146,800) would be amortized as a single asset and classified as an installment sale.

3. Which of the following would not qualify for a depletion deduction?

A. Oil well.
B. Timber.
C. Diamond mine.
D. Gasoline refinery.

4. Levi owns a convenience store. He purchases two computers from his grandfather and places both in service in 2016 as part of a bona fide business transaction. The computers cost $750 each. Which of the following statements is correct?

A. Levi can claim a section 179 deduction for the computers.
B. Levi can claim regular MACRS depreciation on the computers.
C. Levi is not allowed to depreciate the computers since they were purchased from a related party. But he can claim a section 179 deduction for them.
D. Levi can claim either section 179 or bonus depreciation on the computers.

5. Which of the following types of business property qualifies for the section 179 deduction?

A. A delivery truck.
B. A business building.
C. A residential rental property.
D. A patent.

6. Mary purchases a new computer for $1,100. She uses the property 75% for her business and 25% for personal purposes. What is Mary's section 179 deduction?

A. $0
B. $275
C. $825
D. $1,100

7. Lou is a sole proprietor who buys a cell phone for $720. Based on his phone records, Lou uses the cell phone 45% for business use and 55% for personal use. What is his section 179 deduction for 2016?

A. $0
B. $324
C. $396
D. $720

8. Builder's Corporation is a calendar-year, accrual-basis corporation that specializes in constructing office buildings. Builder's bought a truck on December 1, 2016, that had to be modified for use in the business. The truck is 100% business-use. Builder's accepted delivery of the modified truck on January 10, 2017. The truck was first used for its intended purpose on February 23, 2017. Builder's paid for the truck with a certified check on March, 1, 2017. What month can Builder's start depreciating the truck?

A. December, 2016
B. January, 2017
C. February, 2017
D. March, 2017

9. Which of the following property is a business not able to depreciate?

A. Property placed in service and disposed of in the same year.
B. Fruit trees.
C. Machinery.
D. Buildings.

10. Which of the following vehicles is considered listed property for tax purposes?

A. An ambulance.
B. A passenger automobile weighing 6,000 pounds or less.
C. A taxi.
D. A marked police car.

11. In 2016, Maui Sightseeing Tours purchased a previously owned helicopter with a total cost of $2,525,000. The corporation's taxable income for 2016 was $600,000. What is the business' allowable section 179 deduction or bonus depreciation for the helicopter?

A. $0
B. $500,000 Section 179 deduction; $1,012,500 bonus depreciation
C. $600,000 Section 179 deduction; $962,500
D. $0 Section 179 deduction; $1,262,500 bonus depreciation

12. Taj is a professional DJ. In 2016, he buys and places in service professional sound-recording equipment. He pays $15,000 of cash and receives a $3,000 trade-in allowance for his used equipment. Both the old and the new video-recording equipment were used 90% for business and 10% for personal purposes. His allowable section 179 deduction is:

A. $16,200
B. $13,500
C. $12,600
D. $15,000

13. The maximum section 179 expense a business can elect to deduct for qualified real property (QRP) placed in service in 2016 is:

A. $179,000
B. $250,000
C. $500,000
D. $2 million

14. Lucy and Jessica are equal (50%) partners in a restaurant. In 2016, they purchase a new $30,000 pizza oven for the restaurant and want to take the section 179 deduction for the full cost of the oven. The partnership's ordinary income before the section 179 deduction is $25,000. There were no other qualifying section 179 purchases during the year. What is the amount of section 179 deduction that Lucy can deduct on her individual tax return?

A. $0
B. $6,000
C. $12,500
D. $15,000

15. Using MACRS, what is the recovery period for depreciating a commercial office building?

A. 20 years.
B. 25 years.
C. 27.5 years.
D. 39 years.

Unit 8: Answers

1. The answer is A. If the entire cost of business property cannot immediately be deducted as a section 179 expense, a business may elect to take bonus depreciation for certain types of new property. This provision allows a business to write off 50% of certain property costs in the first year, with the remaining cost depreciated over the asset's useful life. Applicable section 179 deductions are used first, followed by bonus depreciation, unless the business has an insufficient level of taxable income.

2. The answer is C. The cost of the Goodwill and a covenant not to compete are both section 197 intangible assets. These two assets total $100,000 of the contract price. These assets must be amortized over 15 years (180 months). The other assets listed are depreciable assets (not amortizable). They would be depreciated using MACRS.

3. The answer is D. A gasoline refinery would not qualify since its activity involves refining a product rather than the depletion of a natural resource. Depletion is the exhaustion of natural resources, such as mines, wells, and timber, as a result of production.

4. The answer is B. The computers do not qualify as section 179 property because Levi and his grandfather are related persons, meaning Levi cannot claim a section 179 deduction. However, Levi may still depreciate the computers using the MACRS depreciation schedule.

5. The answer is A. A delivery truck may qualify for Section 179 expensing. Tangible personal property, including vehicles, generally qualifies for the section 179 deduction. Except certain qualified real property (QRP), most real estate generally does not qualify for section 179 treatment. Intangible assets do not qualify for section 179 treatment.

6. The answer is C. The business part of the cost of the property is $825 (75% × $1,100).

7. The answer is A. When a taxpayer uses property for both business and nonbusiness purposes, he can elect the section 179 deduction only if he uses the property more than 50% for business in the year the asset is placed into service. Lou may nevertheless claim depreciation deductions for the business portion of the phone.

8. The answer is B. Builder's may consider the truck to have been placed in service when it is ready for its intended purpose, which was on January 10, 2016. Builder's does not actually need to use it for that purpose in order to begin depreciation, but the asset needs to be ready and available for business use.

9. The answer is A. Property placed in service and disposed of in the same year is not depreciated. Rather, it is expensed.

10. The answer is B. Regular passenger automobiles weighing 6,000 pounds or less are listed property.

11. The answer is A. The corporation is not allowed to take a Section 179 deduction for the helicopter, because its total asset purchases for the year exceed the spending cap of $2.51 million maximum business asset purchases. The helicopter purchase is also not eligible for bonus depreciation, because the helicopter was "pre-owned" (used). Unlike the Section 179 deduction, only new purchases qualify for bonus depreciation.

12. The answer is B. The section 179 deduction applies only to the amount actually paid in cash and not to the value of his trade-in allowance, and further applies only to the portion used for business purposes. Thus, the deduction is limited to 90% of $15,000, or $13,500.

13. The answer is C. In 2016, taxpayers can deduct up to $500,000 of qualified real property (QRP) under section 179. This special allowance for QRP is included within the maximum $500,000 section 179 limit.

14. The answer is C. The partnership's section 179 deduction for the $30,000 oven is limited to the partnership's income of $25,000. The deduction is split between the two partners ($25,000 × 50%) = $12,500. Section 179 is a separately stated item on a partnership tax return. Assuming she has no section 179 deductions from other sources, Lucy's deduction would be $12,500.

15. The answer is D. Commercial real property is depreciated over a 39-year recovery period.

Unit 9: Disposition of Business Assets

More Reading:
Publication 544, *Sales and Other Dispositions of Assets*

There are many different ways a business can dispose of an asset. For example, an asset can be sold, traded, exchanged, abandoned, involuntarily converted, or destroyed. The tax treatment will vary based on the type of asset and also the disposition method. A business may recognize a gain or loss for tax purposes if it:

- Sells an asset for cash
- Exchanges property for other property
- Receives payment by a tenant for the cancellation of a lease (treated as if it were a sale of the property)
- Receives property to satisfy a debt
- Abandons property
- Loses property or has damaged property as a result of casualty or theft (and if it receives a related insurance reimbursement for such a loss)

A taxpayer may fully depreciate an asset until its adjusted basis is zero, but continue to use the asset thereafter. If an asset is sold or otherwise disposed of, its adjusted basis is compared to any amounts received to determine whether there is a gain or loss.

The treatment of gains or losses reportable for tax purposes is dependent upon whether they are classified as capital gains and losses or as ordinary income (and whether the capital gains and losses are long-term or short-term). For individual taxpayers, capital gains may be subject to more favorable capital gains tax rates. To properly report the disposition of an asset, a taxpayer must determine whether it is a capital asset, a noncapital asset, or a section 1231 asset.

Gains and losses on dispositions of business assets are generally reported on Form 4797, *Sales of Business Property.*

Capital Assets versus Noncapital Assets

Capital Assets: Capital assets include personal-use assets, collectibles, and investment property such as stocks, bonds, and other securities (unless held by a professional securities dealer).

Example: Jim owns 25 mechanical toy banks, which he collects as a hobby. He is not a professional dealer. Jim's mechanical banks are considered capital assets. In 2016, he sells one of his toy banks to a friend for $1,500. He originally purchased the toy for $900. Jim must report a capital gain of $600 on the sale.

Tax law divides investment profits into different classes determined by the holding period and the type of asset. Capital losses from the sale of stocks are generally deductible (up to a certain limit), but losses from the sale of personal-use property are not deductible. We will discuss the differences in reporting and recognition of gain or loss on capital assets throughout this chapter.

Noncapital Assets

Assets that are used in a trade or business or as rental property are called "noncapital assets." These include the following:

- Inventory
- Depreciable property used in a business, even if it is fully depreciated
- Real property used in a trade or business, such as a commercial building or a residential rental

- Self-produced copyrights, transcripts, manuscripts, drawings, photographs, or artistic compositions
- Accounts receivable or notes receivable acquired by a business
- Stocks and bonds held by professional securities dealers
- Business supplies
- Commodities and derivative financial instruments

Example: In February 2016, Ines purchases a black-and-white copy machine for use in her business for $5,500. In November 2016, she decides she needs a color copier instead. Ines sells the used black-and-white copier for $3,000. The copier is a depreciable business asset, so it is treated as a noncapital asset. The loss on the sale of the copier would be deductible.

Example: Tim is a sole proprietor who files a Schedule C. Tim owns a motorcycle shop that sells expensive custom motorcycles. In 2016, his motorcycle shop burns down. The fire completely destroys ten motorcycles that he has in inventory. Since these motorcycles are business inventory, his losses are fully deductible as business losses. Tim also lost his personal motorcycle in the fire, which was parked in the shop overnight. Tim's motorcycle is a personal-use asset, therefore, this loss would not be deductible on his Schedule C. Tim may be able to claim the loss of his personal motorcycle as a casualty loss on his individual return, but only if he itemizes deductions on Schedule A. Even then, Tim can only deduct the amount of the loss that exceeds 10% of his AGI after applying the $100 reduction that applies to all personal casualty losses.

Disposition of Section 1231 Assets

Section 1231 assets include certain business (noncapital) assets that have been held for more than one year, as well as certain business and investment property disposed of in involuntary conversions.

The tax code gives special treatment to transactions involving disposition of section 1231 assets. If the taxpayer has a net loss from all section 1231 transactions, the loss is treated as ordinary loss.

If the section 1231 transactions result in a net gain, the gain is generally treated as long-term capital gain. This is a more favorable tax treatment since ordinary losses are not limited, and capital gains tax rate are more favorable than ordinary income. However, this is not the case with depreciation recapture, or with any unrecaptured section 1231 losses that had been claimed in the prior five years (also known as the "five-year lookback rule"). Both are taxed as ordinary income, as discussed below.

Example: Philip owns an antique vase that he purchased at auction two years ago. He also owns a residential rental property that he purchased three years ago and two vehicles. One is a pizza delivery van he bought five years ago, which he uses exclusively in his restaurant business. The second is his personal-use SUV that he uses for commuting and everyday errands. Phillip's assets are categorized as follows:

1. Antique vase: A capital asset, because it is a collectible
2. Residential rental property: Section 1231 (rental property held over one year)
3. Pizza delivery van: Section 1231 (business property held over one year)
4. SUV: A capital asset, because it is a personal-use vehicle

Gain or loss on the following transactions is subject to section 1231 treatment:

1. **Sale or exchange of cattle and horses:** They must be used for draft, breeding, dairy, or sporting purposes and held for 24 months or longer.
2. **Sale or exchange of other livestock:** Other livestock includes hogs, mules, sheep, goats, donkeys, and other fur-bearing animals. They must be used for draft, breeding, dairy, or sporting purposes and held for 12 months or longer. This does not include poultry. Gains

and losses from section 1231 property used in farming are reported on Form 4797, *Sales of Business Property*, which is then attached to the taxpayer's Schedule F.

3. **Sale or exchange of depreciable (or amortizable) property:** Business property that is held for more than one year. Examples include machinery and trucks, as well as amortizable section 197 intangibles, such as patents or copyrights.
4. **Sale or exchange of business real estate:** The property must be used in a business activity and held for more than one year. Examples include barns, factory buildings, and office buildings.
5. **Sale or exchange of unharvested crops:** The crops and land must be sold, exchanged, or involuntarily converted at the same time and to the same person, and the land must have been held longer than one year. Growing crops sold with a leasehold on the land, even if sold to the same person in a single transaction, are not included.

"Market livestock" are animals held for sale in the ordinary course of the taxpayer's business. These are treated as regular inventory. Once the livestock is selected or held for breeding, dairy, or draft purposes, the livestock is considered a section 1231 asset.

Example: Kevin owns a small farm where he raises goats for sale. Kevin has three pedigreed male goats that are held for breeding purposes only (as studs). His remaining goats are raised for sale and eventual slaughter. In 2016, Kevin is offered $3,900 for the sale of one of his pedigreed billy goats. Kevin accepts the offer, and reports the sale of the stud goat on Form 4797, *Sales of Business Property*. Also during the year, he sells 15 of his other goats, which he sells for $200 each, for a gross of $3,000. The other 15 goats are treated as inventory, so that sale must be reported on Schedule F as an ordinary sale.

Example: Six years ago, Mezuel Corporation purchased an industrial shredder for $10,000. The company sells the used shredder this year for $700. Mezuel had depreciated the asset down to its salvage value,[103] which was estimated at $1,000. The company has a loss of $300 on the sale of the shredder ($1,000 salvage value minus $700 sale price). The shredder is a section 1231 asset and the loss is an ordinary loss.

The Five-Year Lookback Rule for Section 1231 Assets

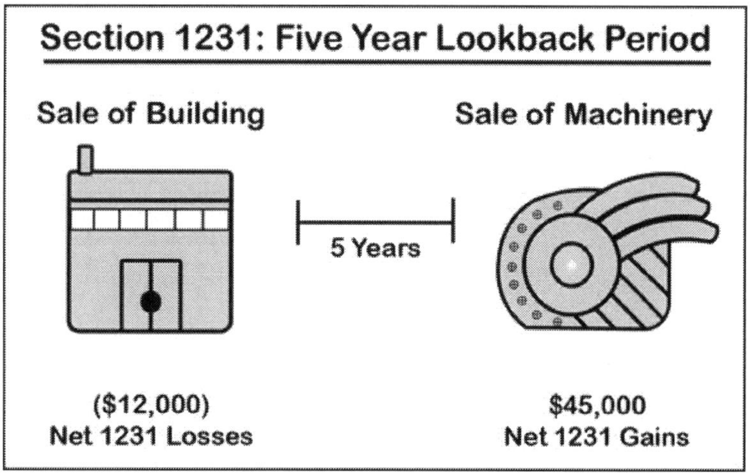

[103] Note that IRS Publication 946 states that salvage value does not apply to MACRS property. However, Publication 534, under the section that covers "Other Methods of Depreciation," the concept of salvage value is discussed and explained. The EA exam has tested on the concept of salvage value in the past.

Normally any net gains on all section 1231 transactions for the year are treated as long-term capital gains. However, if there are any net 1231 losses in the prior five tax years, these prior five-year 1231 losses change the character of the 1231 gains in the current year from long-term capital gain to ordinary income. See the extended example, next.

Extended Example: Neo Jumpers Inc. sold a piece of machinery and had $45,000 of section 1231 gains in 2016. In the five years prior to 2016, there was one year (2013) in which the corporation had net 1231 losses. In 2013, Neo Jumpers had $12,000 of net 1231 losses from the sale of a building, which the corporation deducted as an ordinary loss in 2013. Because the $12,000 of net section 1231 loss in 2013 was within the five-year lookback period prior to 2016 (in which it had a net 1231 gain of $45,000), for 2016, $12,000 of the $45,000 1231 gain will be treated as ordinary income (under the five-year lookback rule) and the remaining $32,000 will be classified as long-term capital gain.

Note: Because all of the $12,000 of net 1231 losses from 2013 were recaptured (treated as ordinary income) in 2016 under the five-year lookback rule, none of the $12,000 net 1231 loss from 2013 will have to be included in any potential five-year lookback recharacterization analysis for either the 2017 or 2018 tax years. However, had the net 1231 losses from 2013 not been fully recaptured in 2016, the remaining unrecaptured 1231 losses from 2013 would be potentially included in the five-year lookback analysis for 2017 (and for 2018 as well).

Example #2: Using the same facts as the previous example, except that if the 2013 net 1231 losses had been $60,000 instead of $12,000, then $45,000 of the $60,000 of net 1231 losses from 2013 would have recharacterized the net 1231 gains in 2016, from long-term capital gain to ordinary income. The remaining $15,000 of unrecaptured gain would be included in the five-year lookback for 2017 (and potentially 2018 as well).

Examples of section 1231 property includes: buildings, business machinery, land, natural resources (such as timber, coal, and domestic iron ore), unharvested crops, cattle, and other livestock. Section 1231 property does not include poultry, trademarks, or inventory.

Non-Section 1231 Transactions

The sale, exchange, or involuntary conversion of inventory is not a section 1231 transaction, even if the inventory has been held for more than one year. Inventory is an ordinary income asset.

Example: Harwell Company manufactures shipping containers. Harwell has owned land and a building that houses its manufacturing operations for 15 years. The land and the building are therefore section 1231 assets, because they are used in a business and have been held for more than one year. Harwell also has unsold shipping containers in inventory. Inventory is not a section 1231 asset.

The sale of a copyright or a literary, musical, or artistic composition is not a section 1231 transaction if a taxpayer's personal efforts created the property, or if it was received as a gift from a previous owner whose personal efforts created it. The sale of such property results in ordinary income.

However, an inherited copyright, however, is treated as a capital asset and receives a stepped-up basis and capital gain treatment upon disposition.

Example: Debbie is a self-employed writer who reports her income on Schedule C. She writes and publishes a popular crockpot cookbook. A few years later, Debbie sells the copyright of her manuscript to a publisher. This is not a section 1231 transaction, because the copyright was self-created, and it must be reported as ordinary income. Debbie would report the sale of her copyright on Schedule C and the amount would be subject to income tax as well as self-employment tax.

Note: Remember that any assets qualifying for Section 1231 treatment must be held long term (over one year). Short-term assets (assets held one year or less) are never given Section 1231 treatment and always produce ordinary income.

Depreciation Recapture

Depreciation recapture may be required when a business sells previously depreciated or amortized property at a gain. All or a portion of the gain attributable to depreciation that would otherwise be treated as capital gain may need to be recaptured as ordinary income. The balance of the gain in excess of the recaptured depreciation is treated as capital gain.

Example: Mort runs a dairy farm as a calendar-year sole proprietorship. In February 2014, Mort buys a tractor (five-year property) that costs $10,000. MACRS depreciation deductions for the tractor are $1,500 in 2014 and $2,550 in 2015 (based upon MACRS table for 150% declining balance depreciation using a half-year convention). Mort decides to sell the tractor in May 2016 for $7,000. The MACRS deduction in 2016 until the date of the sale is $893 (½ of $1,785). The gain on the sale of the tractor that must be treated as ordinary income is figured as follows:

Original purchase price		$10,000
MACRS depreciation deductions ($1,500 + $2,550 + $893)	(4,943)	
Adjusted basis		5,057
Amount received in the sale		7,000
Gain realized ($7,000 - $5,057)		**$1,943**

The realized gain is less than the amount of depreciation subject to recapture, so the entire amount is treated as ordinary income.

Section 1245 vs. Section 1250

In determining depreciable recapture for property sold at a gain, there is a critical distinction between two types of property: section 1245 and section 1250. For section 1245 property, any gain attributable to previous depreciation deductions is taxed as ordinary income, subject to income tax; however, the amount escapes self-employment tax, which is a notable tax benefit.

For section 1250 property, the depreciation recapture is limited to the portion of previously deducted depreciation in excess of deductions that would have been taken if computed using the straight-line method.

Section 1245 Property

This type of property includes tangible personal property, (such as office furniture and equipment) that is subject to depreciation. Section 1245 property does not include buildings and structural components. Section 1245 property includes:

1. Personal (tangible or intangible) property, or
2. Other tangible property (not including buildings) that is depreciable and that is:
    a. Used as an integral part of certain specified activities (the manufacturing, production, extraction, or communication of electrical energy, gas, water, or sewage disposal services), or
    b. A facility used for the bulk storage of fungible commodities.

Definition: A **"fungible good" or "fungible asset"** is one that is essentially interchangeable with other goods or assets of the same type, such as a specific grade of a particular commodity. Examples of highly fungible commodities are crude oil, soybeans, and wheat.

A grain silo is considered section 1245 property rather than section 1250 property, even if it is attached permanently to the land. Storage structures for oil and gas and other minerals are considered section 1245 property.

Example: Several years ago, Crystal purchased a used book-binding machine for $1,000 for her cookbook business. She has claimed $400 of depreciation on the machine. In 2016, Crystal sells the machine for $1,100. Her gain is as follows:

Sale price of the machine:	$1,100
Minus adjusted basis ($1,000 - $400):	600
Crystal's gain on the sale of the machine:	**$500**

A portion of the gain is ordinary income ($400 of depreciation recapture for section 1245 property), and the remainder of $100 is long-term capital gain.

Section 1250 Property

Section 1250 property usually consists of most other permanent structures, and land improvements of general use and purpose. Section 1250 also includes structural components, such as deck, shingles, girders, and gutters. The property must be used for business or held for investment, and not for personal-use.

Common examples of section 1250 property include residential rental property, factory buildings, barns, warehouses, and office buildings. Since buildings are generally depreciated using the straight-line method, taxpayers usually receive more favorable treatment of depreciation recapture for section 1250 property.

Example: Maeve has owned an apartment building for many years. She originally purchased the building for $2.5 million. After taking straight-line depreciation deductions, her adjusted basis in 2016 is $800,000. She sells the property in 2016 for $4.5 million. Her gain is as follows:

Sale price	$4,500,000
Minus adjusted basis	800,000
Gain on sale	**$3,700,000**

Because the building is section 1250 property and Maeve has only taken straight-line depreciation, there is no depreciation recapture, and the entire amount of the gain is treated as long-term capital gain. Had the building been depreciated using an accelerated method, as was more common prior to the adoption of the current MACRS system, a portion of the prior year's depreciation deductions might have been subject to recapture.

Installment Sales

An installment sale involves a disposition of property in which the seller receives at least a portion of the sales proceeds during a year subsequent to the year of the sale. The resulting gain is typically reported using the installment method. If a business elects out of using the installment method, it must report the entire gain in the year of the sale, even if it does not receive the remaining proceeds until later years. Each payment received on an installment sale transaction may include the following components:

- Return of the seller's adjusted basis in the property
- Gain on the sale
- Interest income (attributable to financing the sale over a period of time)

The taxpayer must calculate a gross profit percentage, representing the ratio of the gain on the sale (numerator) to the total proceeds to be paid minus any interest income (denominator). The denominator will also equal the total of the gain and the return of the seller's adjusted basis in the property. Each year, including the year of sale, the total payments received minus the portion attributable to interest is multiplied by the gross profit percentage to determine the portion of the gain that must be recognized.

Example: A business sells a machine for a price of $6,000, with a gross profit of $1,500, and it will receive payments totaling $6,000 plus interest over four years. The gross profit percentage is 25% ($1,500 ÷ $6,000). After subtracting the applicable interest portion from each payment, the business will apply the gross profit percentage to each installment, including any down payment, and report the resulting amount as installment sale income for each tax year in which it receives payments. The remainder of each payment is the tax-free return of the machine's adjusted basis.

Note: A taxpayer's gain, or gross profit, is the amount by which the selling price exceeds the adjusted basis in the property sold. The gross profit percentage is generally calculated by dividing the gross profit from the sale by the selling price. You may be required to understand how to calculate gross profit percentage for both Parts 1 and 2 of the EA exam.

The taxpayer's gain from an installment sale is reported on Form 6252, *Installment Sale Income*. If the arrangement is modified at a later date or the full amount of the sale price is not paid, the resulting gross profit on the sale may also change.

Example: In 2014, the Greenbelt Partnership sells land under an installment sale. The land has a basis of $40,000, and the sale price is $100,000. Therefore, the gross profit from the sale is $60,000 and the partnership's gross profit percentage is 60%. After signing the installment contract, the partnership received a $20,000 down payment and the buyer's note for $80,000. The note provides for four annual payments of $20,000 each, plus 8% interest, beginning in 2015. The partnership reported a gain of $12,000 on each payment it received in 2014 and 2015. In 2016, the buyer started to have financial difficulties. The Greenbelt Partnership and the buyer agreed to reduce the purchase price to $85,000. The remaining installment payments during 2016, 2017, and 2018 are reduced to $15,000 for each year. The new gross profit percentage is now 46.67%. Greenbelt will report a gain of $7,000 (46.67% of $15,000) on each of the $15,000 installments received in 2016, 2017, and 2018.

In certain circumstances, a business may be treated as having received a payment, even though it has not received cash. For example, the receipt of property or the assumption of a mortgage by the buyer may be treated as a payment. If the buyer assumes or pays off a mortgage or other debt on the property sold, the calculation of gross profit percentage is affected.

The mortgage assumption is subtracted before calculating the gross profit percentage, except to the extent that it exceeds the adjusted basis of the property for installment sale purposes. In contrast, if the property is sold to a buyer who holds a mortgage on it and the mortgage is canceled rather than assumed, the cancellation is treated as a payment received in the year of the sale and is not subtracted in calculating the gross profit percentage.

If a business reports the sale of property under the installment method, any applicable depreciation recapture under section 1245 or 1250 is taxable as ordinary income in the year of sale, even if no payments are received in that year. If the gain is more than the depreciation recapture amount, the remainder of the gain would be recognized using the installment method rules. An installment sale does not apply to:

- The sale of inventory, even if the business receives a payment after the year of sale
- Dealer sales of real or personal property in the normal course of business
- A sale that results in a loss
- The sale of stock or securities traded on an established market

Installment sales to related persons are allowed. However, if a taxpayer sells property to a related person who then sells or disposes of the property within two years of the original sale, the taxpayer will lose the benefit of installment sale reporting.

Example: Resort Properties Corporation sells a motel to a 50% shareholder of the corporation, John Palmer. The sale price of the hotel is $2 million, and Resort Properties realizes a profit on the sale of $250,000. John agrees to pay the note in five installments of $400,000. Eighteen months later, John sells the motel to another unrelated company. Resort Properties must report the entire profit of $250,000 on the sale, even though it has not received all of the installment payments. The installment sale method is disallowed on the related party sale, because the property was disposed of before the end of the two-year holding period.

Like-Kind Exchanges (Section 1031)

A section 1031 "like-kind" exchange occurs when a business or individual exchanges business or investment property for similar property. If an exchange qualifies under section 1031, the taxpayer does not pay tax currently on a resulting gain and cannot deduct a loss until the acquired property is later sold or otherwise disposed of. To qualify for nonrecognition treatment, an exchange must meet all of the following conditions:

- The property must be held for investment or for productive use in a business.
- The property must not be "held primarily for sale" (such as inventory).
- There must be an actual exchange of two or more assets or properties. The exchange of cash for property is treated as a sale, not as an exchange.

The simplest form of 1031 exchange is a simultaneous swap of one property for another. Alternatively, it may be arranged as a deferred exchange, in which the disposition of one property and the later acquisition of a replacement property are mutually dependent parts of an integrated transaction. In contrast, simply selling a property and using the proceeds to purchase another similar property is a taxable transaction.

In a deferred exchange, the property to be received must be identified in writing (or actually received) within 45 days after the date of transfer of the property given up. Further, the replacement property in a deferred exchange must be received by the earlier of:

- The 180th day after the date on which the property given up was transferred, or
- The due date, including extensions, of the tax return for the year in which the transfer of that property occurs.

A qualified intermediary must be used to facilitate a deferred exchange. This is an independent party who acquires the relinquished property and transfers it to a buyer. The intermediary holds the sales proceeds to prevent the taxpayer from having actual or constructive receipt of the funds. The intermediary then acquires the replacement property and transfers it to the taxpayer to complete the exchange within the allowable time limits.

Example: A corporation purchases a medical office building for $300,000. After four years, the fair market value of the property is $350,000. If the corporation were to sell the property, it would recognize a gain of $50,000. If the corporation instead arranges a like-kind exchange and either receives a similar property in exchange or invests the proceeds from the exchange of the building in a similar property, the taxable gain could be deferred.

Example: Otis owns a piece of land in Louisiana he wants to exchange, and he arranges a 1031 exchange transaction. When the land sale closes, his escrow company holds the proceeds. Within 45 days, Otis identifies an apartment building he wants to buy in Arkansas and negotiates a contract to buy the building. Within the required 180 days, the escrow company releases the funds he needs to close the purchase, and the exchange transaction is complete. The escrow company is considered a qualified intermediary, and Otis has successfully postponed recognition of any gain related to disposition of the original property.

Qualifying Exchanges

To qualify under section 1031, an exchange must involve like-kind property, such as the trade of real property for real property or personal property for personal property.

An exchange of real property qualifies more easily as like-kind, regardless of how each property is used or whether each property is improved or unimproved. For instance, the exchange of a building for farmland would qualify, as would the exchange of an apartment building for an office building. In contrast, the exchange of factory machinery for a factory building is not a qualifying exchange.

An exchange of personal property must involve items that are at least similar enough to both be categorized within one of several asset classes established by the IRS. For example, the exchange of a panel truck for a pickup truck may qualify as a trade of like-kind property, but the exchange of a pickup truck for a semi-truck likely would not.

The exchange of equipment or business assets that are used *within* the United States for similar items used *outside* the United States would not be considered an exchange of qualifying like-kind property.

All of the following can be exchanged as like-kind property:

- Condos, land, apartment buildings, duplexes, commercial buildings, residential rentals, and retail buildings
- A single business property exchanged for two or more properties and vice versa
- Water rights, mineral rights, oil and gas interests, copyrights, trademarks, and other intangible assets (but not partnership interests or securities)
- Livestock (but not livestock of different sexes)

Nonqualifying Exchanges

Exchanges involving the following types of property do not qualify for section 1031 exchange treatment:

- Inventory, or any property purchased for resale
- Stocks, bonds, notes, or other securities
- Real property or business property within the United States and business property outside the United States
- Exchanges of shares of corporate stock in different companies
- Exchanges of partnership interests or LLC membership interests
- A personal home or personal-use property (such as a personal car or vacation home)
- Land under development for resale
- Corporation common stock
- Livestock of different sexes[104]

Definition: Boot is a term used to describe cash or other property that is included in an exchange to compensate for a difference in the values of the like-kind properties traded.

Boot: A taxpayer who receives boot in a section 1031 exchange may have to recognize a taxable gain to the extent of the cash and the FMV of unlike property received.

Example: Stephen and Tricia decide they will exchange rental properties. Stephen's rental property is more valuable, so Tricia agrees to exchange her rental property and an additional $10,000 of cash. Therefore, Stephen must recognize $10,000 of any gain he realizes on the transaction, even if section 1031 tax deferral otherwise applies.

[104] This is a frequently-tested concept. If your exam question is about livestock specifically, then be aware that an exchange of male and female livestock is not allowable under IRC 1031. For example, a trade of "bulls" for "cows" would not be a qualifying 1031 exchange.

The taxable gain cannot exceed the amount of gain that would have been recognized if the property had been sold in a taxable transaction. The amount considered boot would be reduced by qualified costs paid in connection with the transaction.

When an exchange involves property that is subject to a liability, assumption of the liability is treated as a transfer of cash and thus considered boot for the party who is relieved of the liability. If each property in an exchange is transferred subject to a liability, a taxpayer is treated as having received boot only if he is relieved of a greater liability than the liability he assumes. This is called "debt reduction boot," and it occurs most often when a taxpayer is acquiring a less expensive or less valuable property.

Although a taxpayer may have to recognize gain on a partially taxable like-kind exchange, he would never recognize a loss. However, a loss on a like-kind exchange would affect the taxpayer's basis in the property received and the tax treatment when it is ultimately sold or disposed.

If a taxpayer receives boot in connection with an exchange and recognizes gain, the basis of the property received is equal to the basis of the property given up plus the amount of gain recognized.

Basis of Property Received in a Like-Kind Exchange: The basis of the property received is generally the adjusted basis of the property transferred.

Example: Judy has a rental house with an adjusted basis of $70,000. During the year, she trades her rental house for an undeveloped lot with an FMV of $150,000. Judy's basis in the lot is $70,000, equal to the adjusted basis of the property she exchanged.

If a taxpayer trades property and also pays money as part of the exchange, the basis of the property received is the basis of the property given up, increased by any additional money paid.

Example: Peyton pays $43,000 cash for a new diesel truck for her business. She receives a trade-in allowance of $13,600 on her old truck, which she had paid $50,000 for two years ago. She has taken depreciation deductions of $39,500 on the old vehicle. She has a $3,100 gain on the exchange ($13,600 trade-in allowance minus her $10,500 adjusted basis for the old truck), but recognition of the gain is postponed under the rules for like-kind exchanges. Her basis in the new truck is $53,500, the total of the cash paid ($43,000) and her adjusted basis of $10,500 in the old truck.

Example: Jorge trades a plot of land (adjusted basis $30,000) for a different plot of land in another town (FMV $70,500). He pays an additional $4,000 in cash. Jorge's basis in the new land is $34,000, his $30,000 basis in the old land plus the $4,000 cash.

Related Party Exchanges

Like-kind exchanges are allowed between related parties, including family members. However, if either party disposes of the property within two years after a 1031 exchange, the exchange is usually disqualified from nonrecognition treatment; any gain or loss that was deferred in the original transaction must be recognized in the year the disposition occurs. The two-year holding period rule may not apply:

- If one of the parties involved in the exchange dies
- If the property is subsequently converted in an involuntary exchange (such as a fire or a flood)
- If it can be established to the satisfaction of the IRS that the exchange and subsequent disposition were not done mainly for tax avoidance purposes

Example: Tim and Harry are brothers. Tim owns a residential rental property and Harry owns an undeveloped tract of land. On January 10, 2016, they exchange their properties. Since they are related parties, each must hold the property he acquired for at least two years or the exchange may be disallowed and treated as a sale. On March 1, 2016, Harry dies, and the rental property passes to his son, who promptly sells it. In this case, the original 1031 exchange is still valid, because the holding period rule does not apply if one of the parties in a related exchange dies before the two-year holding period expires.

For purposes of this rule, a "related person" includes:

- A close family member (siblings, spouses, ancestors, and lineal descendants).
- An entity (corporation or partnership) in which the taxpayer owns either directly or indirectly more than a 50% interest. This includes ownership by a spouse or another close family member.
- Two entities in which the same taxpayer owns directly or indirectly more than 50% of each.
- An executor and a beneficiary of an estate.
- A trust for which the taxpayer is the fiduciary and the related party is a beneficiary either of that same trust or a related trust, or is a fiduciary of a related trust.

The IRS gives close scrutiny to exchanges between related parties because they can be used by taxpayers to evade taxes on gains.

Note: for the purposes of this rule, "related parties" do not include: step-parents, step-siblings, ex-spouses, uncles, aunts, in-laws, or cousins. Remember, *half*-siblings are considered related parties. *Step*-siblings are NOT related parties.

Example: Ximena and Arturo legally divorced in March 2016. They have three children together. Their divorce was amicable. Three months after their divorce is finalized, Ximena and Arturo exchange rental properties in a Section 1031 transaction. Arturo sells his rental property sixty days later. Since their divorce was already final at on the date of the exchange, then the exchange is valid. The related party transaction rules do not include ex-spouses.

Reporting Requirements: A taxpayer who transfers property in a like-kind exchange must file Form 8824, *Like-Kind Exchanges*, with his tax return for the year of the exchange. If the exchange involves a related party, the form must also be filed for each of the following two years.

Involuntary Conversions (Section 1033)

An involuntary conversion occurs when a taxpayer's property is lost, damaged, or destroyed, for which the taxpayer may receive an award, insurance reimbursement, or some other type of payment, as a result of:

- Theft
- Disaster
- Condemnation, or threat of condemnation

A taxpayer typically reports a gain or deducts a loss in the year the gain or loss is realized. However, under section 1033, a taxpayer can defer reporting gain on an involuntary conversion if he receives proceeds from insurance or another source and invests in property similar to the converted property. The gain on the involuntary conversion is then deferred until a taxable sale or exchange of the replacement property occurs at a later date.

Replacement Periods

The replacement period for an involuntary conversion generally ends two years after the end of the first tax year in which any part of the gain on the condemnation is realized.

A three-year replacement period is allowed for real property that is held for investment, such as office buildings or residential rentals. The replacement period is four years for livestock that is involuntarily converted because of weather-related conditions. If the property is subject to an involuntary conversion in certain federally-declared disaster areas, the replacement period can be up to five years.

The replacement property must be purchased before the end of the tax year in which the replacement deadline applies. If the involuntary conversion property is not replaced within the allowed time period, an amended tax return would have to be filed for the year the involuntary conversion occurred, reporting a taxable transaction.

Usually, the taxpayer's basis in the new property will be its cost, reduced by any gain realized on the old property that was not recognized. However, the basis may be increased by any gain the taxpayer recognizes on the involuntary conversion and decreased by the following:

- Any loss the taxpayer recognizes on the involuntary conversion
- Any reimbursement he receives and does not reinvest in similar property

Example: A hurricane destroys Denise's residential rental property that has an adjusted basis of $50,000. Denise receives insurance reimbursement for $100,000, the fair market value of the property. Denise buys a replacement rental property six months later for $100,000. Her gain on the involuntary conversion is $50,000 ($100,000 insurance settlement minus her $50,000 basis). However, Denise does not have to recognize any taxable gain because she reinvested all the insurance proceeds in another, similar property.

Example: Cody is a general contractor whose business truck is destroyed in an accident. It had been partially depreciated, and its adjusted basis was $40,000. The insurance company sends a check for $55,000 to replace the truck. Two months later, Cody uses all the insurance money to purchase a replacement truck, paying an additional $2,000 out-of-pocket to purchase the new vehicle. The basis in the new truck is $42,000 ($40,000 basis of the old truck + $2,000 additional out-of-pocket cost). This does not have to be reported as a taxable transaction because it is a qualified involuntary conversion of business property.

Unit 9: Study Questions

(Please test yourself and check the correct answers at the end of this section.)

1. The Drake Partnership owned a $20,000 business machine that had been depreciated by $12,000, so the partnership's adjusted basis in it was $8,000. In 2016, the partnership sold the machine for $25,000. What is the nature of the tax treatment resulting from the sale?

A. Capital gain of $17,000.
B. Ordinary income of $12,000 and capital gain of $5,000.
C. Ordinary income of $17,000.
D. Capital gain of $12,000 and ordinary income of $5,000.

2. Which of the following dispositions of depreciable property can trigger depreciation recapture?

A. Installment sale.
B. Gift.
C. Transfer at death.
D. Section 1031 exchange where no money or unlike property is received.

3. Caraway Carwash paid $200,000 for business equipment in January 2016. They find that the equipment does not meet their needs and Caraway decides to sell the equipment for $180,000 in October 2016. Caraway had not taken any depreciation on the equipment. How should this transaction be reported?

A. Caraway has a section 1231 loss of $20,000 on the sale of the equipment. This is treated as an ordinary loss.
B. Caraway has a section 1231 loss of $20,000 on the sale of the equipment. This is treated as a capital loss.
C. This is an installment sale, with a loss of $20,000 that is treated as an ordinary loss.
D. Caraway has an ordinary loss.

4. Which of the following is not section 1245 property?

A. Computer.
B. Office building.
C. Display shelving.
D. Grain silo.

5. Which of the following property types qualifies for section 1031 like-kind exchange?

A. A personal residence.
B. Inventory property.
C. Corporation common stock.
D. An empty lot held for investment.

6. On January 10, 2016, a rental office building owned by Financial Advisory Corporation burns down. The property had an adjusted basis of $260,000, and Financial Advisory receives an insurance reimbursement of $310,000. Financial Advisory buys another rental office property for $290,000 in March 2016. What is Financial Advisory gain as a result of this transaction?

A. $0
B. $20,000
C. $30,000
D. $50,000

7. Which of the following assets is not section 1231 property?

A. Office building.
B. Unharvested crops.
C. Business asset held for less than one year.
D. Patent.

8. Jennifer operates Right Hair Salon, a sole proprietorship. In 2016, she sells all of her old salon chairs for $3,500 in order to buy new ones. She had purchased the chairs seven years ago for $15,000, and they were fully depreciated. Therefore, her basis in the chairs is zero at the time of the sale. How should she report this transaction?

A. She reports a loss of $11,500 on Schedule C.
B. She reports a gain of $3,500 on Form 4797 and Schedule C. The entire $3,500 is treated as depreciation recapture, which is subject to ordinary income tax rates.
C. She reports a gain of $3,500 on Form 4797 and Schedule C. The entire $3,500 is taxed as a long-term capital gain.
D. She is not required to report this sale.

9. Barbara exchanges an apartment building with an adjusted basis of $125,000 for a business office building. The fair market value of Barbara's old property is $500,000. The fair market value of the business office building is $475,000. What is Barbara's basis in the new building?

A. $125,000
B. $475,000
C. $500,000
D. $525,000

10. Arboreal Acres is a farming corporation. In 2016, Arboreal sells a used tractor for $25,000. The original cost of the tractor was $20,000, and it is fully depreciated. What is the tax treatment for Arboreal's sale of the tractor?

A. There is no gain or loss on the sale of the tractor.
B. Arboreal has a gain of $25,000. The first $20,000 is considered section 1245 recapture and is taxed as ordinary income. The remaining $5,000 is considered section 1231 capital gain.
C. Arboreal Acres has a gain of $25,000. The first $15,000 is considered section 1245 recapture and is taxed as ordinary income. The remaining $10,000 is considered section 1231 capital gain.
D. The entire gain is considered section 1245 recapture and will be taxed as ordinary income.

11. Which of the following property exchanges does not qualify as a like-kind exchange?

A. Exchange of an apartment building for an office building.
B. Exchange of livestock of different sexes.
C. Exchange of improved property for unimproved property.
D. Exchange of farm machinery for factory machinery.

12. Scott has a small airplane that he used in his crop-dusting business for two years. Its adjusted basis is $35,000, and its trade-in value is $45,000. He trades his old plane for a new plane that costs $200,000 and pays the dealer an additional $155,000 in cash. What is Scott's basis of the new plane?

A. $35,000
B. $155,000
C. $190,000
D. $200,000

13. The Karabell Company trades a delivery truck with an adjusted basis of $11,000 and cash of $6,000 for a new truck with a fair market value of $25,000. How much gain must Karabell recognize in this exchange, and what is its basis in the new truck?

Gain	Basis of New Truck
A. $0	$17,000
B. $0	$25,000
C. $8,000	$17,000
D. $8,000	$25,000

14. Fran and Zachary are mother and son who complete a section 1031 exchange in January 2016, properly exchanging two residential rentals. On June 29, 2016, Fran dies, and her rental property is inherited by her husband, who promptly sells it. Which of the following statements is correct?

A. Since one of the properties in the exchange has been sold before the two-year time limit for related parties, the section 1031 exchange is disallowed, and both parties (Zachary and Fran's Estate) must pay tax on the transaction.
B. The section 1031 exchange is still valid.
C. Since this was a related party exchange, the section 1031 exchange is still valid for Zachary, but Fran's estate must pay tax on the exchange because her husband disposed of the property before the two-year waiting period ended.
D. The nonrecognition treatment is lost for both parties, but Fran's husband is liable for the tax on the exchange, since he was the owner of the property when it was sold.

15. Jamal sells a duplex with an adjusted basis of $150,000. The buyer agrees to pay Jamal $300,000, with a cash down payment of $100,000 and $20,000 (plus 5% interest) in each of the next ten years. What is Jamal's gross profit and gross profit percentage on the installment sale?

A. The gross profit is $5,000, and the gross profit percentage is 50%.
B. The gross profit is $10,000, and the gross profit percentage is 100%.
C. The gross profit is $150,000, and the gross profit percentage is 50%.
D. The gross profit is $5,000, and the gross profit percentage is 100%.

16. Which of the following trades qualifies as a nontaxable like-kind exchange?

A. The exchange of a vacant lot in the city for farmland in the country.
B. The exchange of livestock of different sexes.
C. The exchange of shares of stock for units of bonds.
D. The exchange of an apartment building in New York City for an apartment building in Mexico City.

17. Angelina exchanges a laser copier used in her tax practice for a new color model. The cost of the original printer was $5,000 and she had taken $1,000 of depreciation. She exchanged her old copier as a trade-in and paid an additional $2,000 in cash to complete the exchange. What is Angelina's basis in the new machine?

A. $1,000
B. $2,000
C. $6,000
D. $7,000

18. Sergio is a self-employed carpenter who owns a compressor for use in his business. He trades the compressor (adjusted basis $3,000) for a large table saw (FMV $7,500) and pays an additional $4,000 cash to the seller in a qualified exchange. What is Sergio's basis in the saw?

A. $7,000
B. $7,500
C. $4,000
D. $3,000

19. Cecil operates an auto salvage yard as a sole proprietorship. During 2016, Cecil sold Section 1245 property (heavy equipment) that was used in the business for $100,000. The purchase price of the property was $120,000, and Cecil had claimed section 179 and depreciation deductions totaling $47,000. Based upon the information provided, what is the nature and amount of taxable income that will result from the sale of this property?

A. Capital gain of $27,000.
B. Ordinary income of $27,000.
C. No gain or loss.
D. Ordinary income of $47,000 and capital loss of $20,000.

20. Sadie owns a small gym as a sole proprietor. She sells some used fitness machines in 2016 for $65,000. She had purchased the equipment for $90,000 several years ago. She has taken $50,000 of depreciation deductions, and a section 179 deduction of $10,000. How should Sadie report the sale of these business assets?

A. Ordinary loss of $25,000.
B. Long-term capital gain of $35,000.
C. Ordinary income of $35,000.
D. Ordinary income of $10,000 and long-term capital gain of $25,000.

Unit 9: Answers

1. The answer is B. The total gain on the sale is $17,000 ($25,000 - $8,000). Because the machine is section 1245 property, the partnership must recognize ordinary income of $12,000 (to recapture depreciation deductions taken on the machine), and the remaining $5,000 ($17,000 - $12,000) is treated as a capital gain.

2. The answer is A. An installment sale can trigger recapture. If a business reports the sale of previously depreciated property using the installment method, any applicable depreciation recapture under section 1245 or 1250 is taxable as ordinary income in the year of sale.

3. The answer is D. Because the business asset was held for less than one year, the business has an ordinary loss. Assets that are purchased and disposed of in the same year are not depreciated.

4. The answer is B. Section 1245 property does not include real estate such as buildings and structural components. Storage structures such as oil and gas storage tanks, grain storage bins, and silos are not treated as buildings, but as section 1245 property.

5. The answer is D. Real property held for investment qualifies for like-kind exchange treatment. A personal residence, inventory, and common stock do not qualify under section 1031.

6. The answer is B. This transaction is treated as a Section 1033 involuntary conversion. Financial Advisory recognizes a taxable gain of $20,000 ($310,000 - $290,000), equal to the portion of the insurance reimbursement that was not reinvested in replacement property. Financial Advisory's unrecognized gain is $30,000, the difference between the $50,000 realized gain and the $20,000 recognized gain. The basis of the new property is as follows:

Cost of replacement property	$290,000
Minus gain not recognized	(30,000)
Basis of replacement property	**$260,000**

If Financial Advisory had reinvested all the insurance proceeds in a new property, the entire gain would have been deferred.

7. The answer is C. In order to qualify as section 1231 property, the property must have been held by the business for over one year.

8. The answer is B. Since the amount realized from the sale is less than Jennifer's original cost for the chairs, the entire gain of $3,500 is treated as depreciation recapture, which is subject to ordinary income tax rates (but not subject to self-employment tax). She reports the sale of the chairs on Form 4797 and Schedule C.

9. The answer is A. Generally, an exchange of real property qualifies as a nontaxable exchange under section 1031. In a nontaxable exchange situation, the FMV of the properties exchanged may have no bearing on the basis of the property received. In this case, the basis of the new property is the same as the basis of the old property ($125,000).

10. The answer is B. The first $20,000 is considered section 1245 recapture and is taxed as ordinary income. The remaining $5,000 is considered section 1231 capital gain.

11. The answer is B. The exchange of livestock of different sexes does not qualify. The exchange of real estate for real estate and the exchange of business property for similar business property are exchanges of like-kind property.

12. The answer is C. Scott's basis is $190,000 ($155,000 cash paid plus the $35,000 adjusted basis of the old plane).

13. The answer is A. This exchange qualifies as a nontaxable exchange for Karabell. Any gain on the exchange is deferred until the new asset is later disposed. The $6,000 of cash is added to the basis of the old truck to determine the basis of the new truck ($11,000 + $6,000 = $17,000).

14. The answer is B. In a related-party exchange, the nonrecognition treatment will generally be lost if either property in the exchange is disposed of within two years. However, the section 1031 exchange will still be valid if either party in the transaction dies, or if the property is subject to an involuntary conversion. In this case, the exchange is still valid, because the owner of the property (Fran) died.

15. The answer is C. Jamal's gross profit is $150,000 ($300,000 selling price - $150,000 adjusted basis), and the gross profit percentage is 50% ($150,000 ÷ $300,000). Jamal must report half of each payment received as gain from the sale. He must also report all interest received as ordinary income.

16. The answer is A. The exchange of a vacant lot for a tract of farmland qualifies for like-kind exchange treatment. Section 1031 specifically excludes exchanges of inventory; stocks, bonds, notes, or other securities; partnership interests; livestock of different sexes; and personal property used predominantly in the United States for personal property used predominantly outside the United States. Properties are like-kind if they are of the same nature or character, even if they differ in grade or quality.

17. The answer is C. The adjusted basis of the old copier was $4,000 ($5,000 - $1,000 depreciation). She paid an additional $2,000 to acquire the new machine. Therefore, the basis of the new model is $6,000 ($4,000 adjusted basis + $2,000 cash paid).

18. The answer is A. The basis of the saw is $7,000, the $3,000 basis of the old asset plus the $4,000 paid.

19. The answer is B. The disposition of the property results in a gain of $27,000, equal to the proceeds of $100,000 minus the adjusted basis of $73,000 (purchase price of $120,000 minus depreciation and section 179 deductions of $47,000). Because this was section 1245 property, the gain is characterized as ordinary income to the lesser of the actual gain or the amount of depreciation and section 179 expenses recaptured ($47,000).

Purchase price	$120,000
Minus depreciation and section 179 deductions	(47,000)
Adjusted basis at date of sale	73,000
Proceeds	100,000
Gain on sale	**$27,000**
Potential depreciation recapture (as ordinary income)	$47,000

20. The answer is C. Sadie has a gain of $35,000, equal to the difference between her sales proceeds of $65,000 and her adjusted basis of $30,000 (cost of $90,000 minus the accumulated depreciation of $60,000). Although she has had the property for more than one year, it is personal property classified as section 1245 property and therefore is subject to depreciation recapture to the extent of the entire amount of depreciation (and section 179 deductions) taken. Since this amount exceeds her gain, the entire amount of her gain will be taxed as ordinary income.

Unit 10: Partnerships in General

More Reading:
Publication 541, *Partnerships*
Instructions for Form 1065

Partnership Basics

An unincorporated business with two or more owners is generally classified as a partnership for federal tax purposes. A partnership is a pass-through entity that is generally not directly taxed on its income. Instead, income and loss are determined at the partnership level and are taxable to the individual partners. In this respect, a partnership is similar to a sole proprietorship, except that it is run by more than one person.

Unlike corporations, general partnerships do not require any formal legal documents in order to form. Partnerships that have some form of liability protections for some of the partners (such as limited partnerships and limited liability partnerships) do require formal documents – including those filed with the state. A partnership must have at least two partners and at least one of them must be a general partner. A joint undertaking merely to share expenses is not a partnership. For example, a rental property owned by two people is would generally not be classified as a business or a partnership.

Certain entities with different legal structures may be classified as partnerships for tax purposes, either based upon their election by filing Form 8832, *Entity Classification Election,* or by default, as in the case of a domestic limited liability company (LLC) with at least two members that is classified as a partnership unless it files Form 8832 and elects to be treated as a corporation. However, the following organizations are prohibited from being classified as partnerships:

- A corporation (although a corporation can be a partner in a partnership)
- A joint-stock company or joint-stock association
- An insurance company
- Certain banks
- A government entity
- An organization required to be taxed as a corporation by the IRS
- Certain foreign organizations
- Any tax-exempt (non-profit) organization
- Any real estate investment trust (REIT)
- Any organization classified as a trust or estate
- Any other organization that elects to be classified as a corporation by filing Form 8832

The Partnership Agreement

The term *partnership agreement* refers to any written document or oral agreement that bears on the underlying economic arrangement of the partners, including allocations of income, gain, loss, deductions, and credits. Examples of such documents include:

- Loan and credit agreements
- Assumption agreements
- Indemnification agreements
- Subordination agreements
- Correspondence with a lender concerning terms of a loan
- Loan guarantees

A partnership agreement can be modified during the tax year and even after the tax year has closed to include items and elections pertaining to that year's tax return. However, the partnership agreement cannot be modified after the due date for filing the partnership return for the year, not including extensions.

Example: Terry and Dawn are friends who run a cash-basis, calendar-year partnership together. They split the partnership's proceeds 50-50. In 2016, they decide to alter their partnership agreement. They have until the due date of the partnership return to change the partnership agreement. Filing for an extension does not give them additional time.

Partnership Filing Requirements

A partnership must file a tax return unless it has no activity for the year. A partnership reports its income or loss on Form 1065, which is due on the fifteenth day of the third month following the close of the tax year.

Starting with tax year 2016, the partnership tax due date has changed. Under the Surface Transportation Act, partnerships must now file their returns by the 15th day of the third month after the end of the tax year. Since most partnerships are calendar-year partnerships, their tax returns are generally due on March 15. A six-month extension is allowed, so most partnerships would have an extended due date of September 15.

The extension is requested on Form 7004, *Automatic Extension of Time to File Certain Business Income Tax, Information, and Other Returns.*

The partnership return must show the name and address of each partner and the partner's distributive share of taxable income (or loss) on Schedule K-1. The partnership is also required to furnish a copy of each partner's Schedule K-1 to the partner by the due date (including extensions) of the partnership tax return. The individual partner then reports his share of partnership income on Schedule E of Form 1040.

Example: Lovett Partnership is a calendar-year, cash-basis partnership that is required to file Form 1065 every year. The partnership has five partners and each partner receives a Schedule K-1 for his share of partnership income and losses, which are then reportable on the partners' individual tax returns. Each partner must receive his Schedule K-1 by the due date of the partnership return (or by the extended due date, if the partnership requests an extension).

The IRS requires partnerships with more than 100 partners (Schedules K-1) to file their returns electronically. If a partnership fails to do so, it may be subject to penalty unless it was unable to file electronically (e.g., because the e-filing was rejected, the return required paper attachments, etc.). The partnership return must be signed by a general partner.

The penalty for late filing Form 1065 is $195 per month, per partner, for up to 12 months. For purposes of this penalty, a fraction of a month is subject to a full month's late filing penalty. For even a small partnership, the late filing penalties can be very severe. Separate from and in addition to the late filing of a Form 1065, for each failure to furnish Schedule K-1 to a partner when due, normally a $260 penalty per each late-filed K-1 may be imposed.

Example: The Anders partnership has four partners. It files its tax return two months late with the IRS, but issues each partner their Schedule K-1 by the due date. The partnership is liable for a late filing penalty for Form 1065 of $1,560 ($195 × two months × four partners). If the partnership had provided each partner with their Schedule K-1 two months late as well, the separate Schedule K-1 late filing penalty will be $2,080 ($260 x two months x four partners).

Additional penalties may apply if the partnership fails to supply a tax identification number or fails to furnish information on tax shelters. These penalties may not be imposed if the partnership can show reasonable cause for its failure.

Partners who work in a partnership are not employees and generally do not receive wages or Forms W-2. General partners are considered to be self-employed and therefore must pay estimated payments just like other self-employed individuals. Limited partners are subject to self-employment tax only on guaranteed payments, such as salaries and professional fees for services rendered.

General Partnership vs. Limited Partnership

The two most common types of partnerships are general partnerships and limited partnerships. In a general partnership, all of the partners have unlimited liability for partnership debts. In a limited partnership, there must be at least one general partner and at least one limited partner. The limited partners have no obligation to contribute additional capital to the partnership under state law and therefore do not have an economic risk of loss related to partnership liabilities. In this respect, a limited partner is like an investor in a corporation. Limited partners generally cannot participate in the management or the day-to-day administration of the partnership.

A limited partnership (LP), and other types of partnerships with some form of liability protections, such as a limited liability partnership (LLP) and, in some states, a limited liability limited partnership (LLLP), is formed under state limited liability law. Often, the owners of limited liability partnerships offer professional services (e.g., attorneys or doctors). This entity type protects individual partners from liability for the malpractice of other partners.

Family Partnerships

Family members can form a partnership together, and frequently do. However, family members will be recognized as partners only if one of the following requirements is met:

- If capital is a material income-producing factor, the family members must have acquired their capital interests in a bona fide transaction (even if by gift or purchase from another family member), actually own the partnership interests, and actually control the interests. This means that a family member who acquires a partnership interest from another family member needs to treat the activity as a bona fide business activity.
- If capital is not a material income-producing factor, the family members must have joined together in good faith to conduct a business. They must have agreed that contributions from each entitle them to a share in the profits and that some capital or service is provided by each partner.

Capital (investment) is a material income-producing factor if a substantial part of the gross income of the business comes from the use of capital. For example, this would apply if the operation of the business requires substantial inventories or investment in a plant, machinery, or equipment.

In general, capital is not a material income-producing factor if the income of the business consists principally of fees, commissions, or other compensation for personal services performed by members or employees of the partnership.

If a family member (or any other person) receives a gift of a capital interest in a partnership in which capital is a material income-producing factor, the donee's distributive share of partnership income is subject to both of the following restrictions:

- It must be figured by reducing the partnership income by reasonable compensation for services the donor provides the partnership.
- The share attributable to donated capital must not be proportionately greater than the donor's distributive share attributable to the donor's capital.

Example: Ronald sold 50% of his business to his daughter, Cindy. The resulting partnership had a profit of $60,000. Capital is a material income-producing factor. Ronald performed services worth $24,000, which is reasonable compensation, and Cindy performed no services. The $24,000 must be allocated to Ronald as compensation. Of the remaining $36,000 of profit due to capital, at least 50%, or $18,000, must be allocated to Ronald since he owns a 50% capital interest. Cindy's share of partnership profit cannot be more than $18,000.

For purposes of determining a partner's distributive share, an interest purchased by one family member from another family member is considered a gift from the seller. The fair market value of the purchased interest is considered donated capital.

For this purpose, members of a family include only spouses, ancestors, and lineal descendants (grandchild, daughter, son, etc.).

Costs of Organizing and Starting a Partnership

The costs to organize a partnership and to start up a business are treated much like similar costs incurred by other types of businesses. As discussed previously, start-up and organizational costs can be deductible. Up to $5,000 of organizational costs and $5,000 of start-up costs can be deducted immediately in the year the partnership's active trade or business begins. Amounts that are not deducted as a current expense can be amortized ratably over a period of 180 months (15 years) starting in the month the business begins.

Businesses start losing the immediate $5,000 up-front deduction when their organizational and/or start-up costs exceed $50,000, and then must reduce the deduction dollar-for-dollar by the amount exceeding the $50,000 threshold. Therefore, if a business has more than $55,000 in either organizational or start-up costs, all of the organizational and start-up expenses (testing separately for each type) must be amortized over an 180-month period.

The election to either deduct these costs currently or to capitalize and amortize them is irrevocable and applies to all organizational and start-up costs related to the trade or business. The partnership must file Form 4562, *Depreciation and Amortization*, with its tax return to claim these deductions.

Example: Penny and Judson are business partners. They opened up Awesome Taco Truck in 2016. Before they opened for business, they paid $5,900 in radio advertising to promote it. The business can deduct $5,000 on the first-year partnership return as start-up expenses. The remaining start-up costs, $900 ($5,900 - $5,000) must be amortized over 180 months. If the business closes before the amortization period is over, the company can deduct any remaining expenses on the business' final tax return.

Special Partnership Allocations

Unlike S corporations, which must report all income and expenses in proportion to stock ownership, partnerships have more flexibility. Partnership agreements can be written to reflect special allocations of income, gain, loss, or deductions, as long as the allocations are consistent with the economic sharing arrangement among the partners.

For example, the partnership agreement may allocate all of the depreciation deductions to one partner or specify that the partners share capital, profits, and losses in different ratios.

Example: Nico and Rhoda form a partnership and open a restaurant. Nico contributes only $1,000 and Rhoda contributes $99,000. Due to Nico's previous expertise in restaurant management and his daily participation in the business, the partnership agreement provides that Nico will be allocated 20% of the restaurant's taxable income and 2% of the partnership's losses. Thus, although Nico owns only 1% in partnership capital, his profit sharing ratio is 20%. This tax allocation between Nico and Rhoda is allowed because it reflects their underlying economic arrangement.

Example: Alicia and Sandy form a partnership to run a wedding cake bakery. The bakery is opened during the year, and the partnership has ordinary income of $10,000. The partnership agreement states they will share income and losses equally (50/50). Alicia and Sandy agree that the $10,000 of income will be distributed equally between them. However, for tax purposes, they want the income to be allocated as $7,500 to Alicia and $2,500 to Sandy. The tax allocation (75/25) is not consistent with the underlying economic arrangement in their partnership agreement (50/50). Unless the partnership agreement contains other provisions that justify this allocation, it has no economic effect and must be reallocated to the partners based on their economic sharing ratio.

Example: Pandora, who has design and sewing skills, forms a partnership with Jayne, who has the money to invest in developing a clothing line. Jayne contributes $100,000 of cash to the partnership. Pandora and Jayne agree to split the business profits 20/80 until Jayne recovers her entire investment; thereafter, profits will be split 50/50. These special allocations are written into their partnership agreement.

Guaranteed Payments

A partnership may be required by the terms of its partnership agreement to make guaranteed payments to one or more partners without regard to whether the partnership has income or loss for the year. Guaranteed payments are not the same as partnership distributions. They may compensate the partner for services or for the use of capital, as if they were made to a person who is not a partner.

Guaranteed payments are generally deducted by the partnership on Form 1065 as a business expense and reported to the partner receiving the guaranteed payment on their Schedule K-1.

The partner who receives a guaranteed payment reports the full amount of the payment as ordinary income on Schedule E (Form 1040) of his individual tax return for the tax year in which the partnership's tax year ends, and also reports his distributive share of the partnership's ordinary income or loss. Guaranteed payments are not subject to income tax withholding by the partnership.

Example: Erica is a partner in the Schultz Partnership. Under the terms of her partnership agreement, she is entitled to a guaranteed payment of $10,000 per year, regardless of how profitable the partnership is. In 2016, Erica's distributive share of partnership income is 10%. Schultz Partnership has $50,000 of ordinary income after deducting Erica's guaranteed payment. She must include ordinary income of $15,000 ($10,000 guaranteed payment + $5,000 [$50,000 × 10%] for her distributive share) on her individual income tax return.

Separately Stated Items

Many of the individual components of a partnership's income or loss are calculated similarly to those of an individual. However, some deductions are not allowed at the partnership level, and certain items of income and loss must be separately stated on the tax return.

These separately stated items flow through to the partners with a specific character. For example, a partnership that makes charitable contributions must list them as a separately stated item. Each individual partner then reports his share of the charitable contributions on his Schedule A.

Each year, a partnership provides Schedules K-1 to each of its partners, indicating their respective shares of:

- **Ordinary income or loss,** and
- **Separately stated items.**

The following items must be separately stated on a partnership's return:

- Net short-term capital gains and losses
- Net long-term capital gains and losses
- Charitable contributions
- Dividends eligible for a dividends-received deduction
- Taxes paid to a foreign country
- Taxes paid to a U.S. possession (Guam, Puerto Rico, etc.)
- Section 1231 gains and losses
- Section 179 deductions and bonus depreciation
- Any tax-exempt income and expenses related to the tax-exempt income
- Investment income and related investment expenses
- Rental income, portfolio income, and related expenses
- Any recovery items, such as bad debts

Example: The Stevenson Partnership operates as an accrual-based business. The partnership's gross receipts for 2016 were $250,000. In addition, it had the following income and expenses:

Liability insurance	($5,000)
Charitable contributions	(2,000)
Continuing education	(9,000)
Rental income	25,000
Guaranteed payments to partners	(15,000)

Ordinary income for the Stevenson Partnership is figured as follows:

Gross Receipts	$250,000
Liability insurance	(5,000)
Continuing education	(9,000)
Guaranteed payments to partners	(15,000)
Ordinary income:	**$221,000**

The rental income and charitable contributions are not considered in determining ordinary income of the partnership. Instead, these are separately stated items that pass through to the partners and retain their character, just as they would for a sole proprietorship. Each individual partner receives a Schedule K-1 from the partnership, reporting his share of ordinary income or loss and each separately stated item. The partners report these amounts on their tax returns. Guaranteed payments are deductible by the partnership because they are treated like wages and are taxable to the partners who receive them.

Note: For the EA exam, you should be able to distinguish the items that are separately stated on a partnership's tax return.

Example: Barry is a 25% partner in a business with three other partners. The partnership makes $20,000 of charitable contributions in 2016 that are reported on the partnership tax return, Form 1065. As the partnership is a pass-through entity, it does not receive a tax benefit from deductible contributions. Instead, Barry's Schedule K-1 shows $5,000 as his share of the partnership's contributions, which he can potentially claim on his individual tax return.

Contributions to a Partnership

When a partnership is formed or new partners are added, the partners contribute property or cash in exchange for their partnership interests. Generally, neither the partner nor the partnership recognizes gain or loss in connection with contributions, whether made in connection with the partnership's formation or after it is operating. However, a partner's contribution can result in gain or loss recognition in the following situations:

- When property is contributed to a partnership that would be treated as an investment company if it were incorporated. A partnership is treated as an investment company if over 80% of the value of its assets is held for investment in cash or readily marketable items.
- When contributed property is distributed to a different partner within seven years of the original contribution date. The contributing partner would recognize gain on the difference between the fair market value and the adjusted basis of the property as of the contribution date. The character of the gain or loss will be the same as would have resulted if the partnership had sold the property to the distributee partner.
- When a partner contributes cash or property to a partnership and then receives a distribution of different property. In this case, the transaction may be considered a disguised sale. A disguised sale is not treated as a contribution and a subsequent distribution but as a sale of property, if:
    - The distribution would not have been made if the initial contribution had not occurred, and
    - The partner's right to the distribution does not depend on the success of partnership operations.

If a contribution and distribution occur within two years of each other, the transfers are presumed to be a sale unless the facts clearly indicate they are not. If the contribution and distribution occur more than two years apart, the transfers are presumed not to be a sale unless the facts clearly indicate they are.

Example: Alberta contributes land with a fair market value of $150,000 and a basis of $100,000 to her partnership. In the same year, the partnership distributes $100,000 of cash and marketable securities worth $50,000 to Alberta. This transaction would likely be considered a disguised sale rather than a tax-free contribution and distribution of property.

When a partner contributes property to a partnership, the partnership's basis is generally the same as the adjusted basis of the partner, including any gain recognized by the partner in connection with the contribution. The partner's holding period for the property is also carried over. For example, if a partner contributes a building with an FMV of $100,000 and a basis of $50,000, the basis of the building in the hands of the partnership would also be $50,000.

Contribution of Services

A partner can acquire an interest in a partnership as compensation for services performed or to be performed. The tax treatment depends upon whether the partner receives a capital interest or a profits interest.

If a partner receives a capital interest as compensation for services, the partner must recognize ordinary income equal to the fair market value of a partnership interest that is transferred in exchange for services. The amount is treated as a guaranteed payment and is included in the partner's gross income in the first tax year during which the partner can transfer the interest.

If a partner receives a profits interest as compensation for services, the receipt may not be taxable to the partner or the partnership, except in certain circumstances.

Example: Greer is an attorney who contributes her services to a partnership in exchange for a 10% partnership interest. It is deemed a capital interest, as the partnership agreement provides for distribution of assets to Greer in the event she withdraws from the partnership or the partnership liquidates. The fair market value of the partnership interest is $3,000. Greer is required to recognize $3,000 of ordinary income, and her basis in the partnership is $3,000. The payment is deducted by the partnership as a guaranteed payment and is taxable to Greer as ordinary income.

Basis of a Partner's Interest

A partner's basis in his partnership interest may be referred to as *outside basis*. This is in contrast to the partnership's basis in its assets, which is known as *inside basis*.

Note: Be familiar with these two terms, as the EA exam may use them in questions when test-takers are asked to determine a partner's or a partnership's basis.

Inside basis and outside basis may initially be equal in a newly-formed partnership, but certain distributions of property from the partnership, transfers of partnership interests, and other basis adjustment items may disrupt this equality. By means of an IRC section 754 election, the partnership may be able to make upward or downward adjustments to the basis of its assets in order to restore the equality between inside basis and outside basis.

The initial basis of a partnership interest is generally equal to the cash plus the adjusted basis of any property the partner contributed. The adjusted basis of a partner's partnership interest is ordinarily determined at the end of the partnership's tax year. However, if there is a sale or exchange of all or part of a partner's interest or a liquidation of his entire interest in a partnership, the adjusted basis must also be determined on the date of the transaction.

Example: Sam and Harriet form a partnership. Sam contributes a building to the partnership that has an adjusted basis of $45,000 and an FMV of $100,000. Harriet contributes $100,000 cash. The basis of Sam's partnership interest is $45,000 and the basis of Harriet's interest is $100,000.

The following items increase a partner's (outside) basis in the partnership:

- The partner's additional cash and the adjusted basis of non-cash contributions to the partnership
- The partner's increased share (or assumption of) partnership liabilities
- The partner's distributive share of taxable and nontaxable partnership income
- The partner's distributive share of the excess of the deductions for depletion over the basis of the depletable property

In addition, if a partner must recognize a gain as a result of his partnership contribution, the gain is added to the basis of his partnership interest. A partner may be required to recognize a gain when he contributes an asset to the partnership that is subject to liability (such as the contribution of a building that is subject to a mortgage), as the other partners are assuming part of his liability.

Any increase in a partner's liabilities because of his assumption of partnership liabilities is treated as if it were a contribution of cash or property to the partnership by the partner. If a partner's share of partnership liabilities increases, this increase is treated as if the partner contributed cash or property to the partnership.

A partner's (outside) basis in the partnership is decreased by the following items:

- The money and adjusted basis of property distributed to the partner by the partnership.
- The partner's distributive share of the partnership's losses (including capital losses) and the partner's distributive share of nondeductible partnership expenses (but not capital expenditures). This includes the partner's share of any section 179 expenses,

even if the partner cannot deduct the entire amount on his individual income tax return.

- The partner's deduction for depletion for any partnership oil and gas wells, up to the proportionate share of the adjusted basis of the wells allocated to the partner.

If a partner's share of partnership liabilities decreases or the partnership assumes any of the partner's individual liabilities, the amounts are treated as distributions to the partner by the partnership.

For example, if contributed property is subject to a debt and the debt is assumed by the partnership, the basis of the contributing partner's interest is reduced (but not below zero) by the portion of the liability assumed by the other partners. The partner must reduce his basis because the assumption of the liability is treated as a distribution to him. The other partners' assumption of the liability is treated as a contribution by them to the partnership.

Example: Stephanie acquired a 20% interest in a partnership by contributing a moving van that had an adjusted basis to her of $8,000 and a related $4,000 loan balance. The partnership assumed the loan. The basis of Stephanie's interest is:

Adjusted basis of contributed property	$8,000
Minus loan assumed by other partners (80% × $4,000)	($3,200)
Basis of Stephanie's partnership interest	**$4,800**

A partner's basis can never go below zero. To avoid this, a partner must recognize gain equal to the amount by which cash distributions or a decrease in his share of partnership liabilities exceeds his basis.

Example: Roy acquired a 20% interest in a partnership by contributing an asset that had an adjusted basis of $8,000 and a related $12,000 loan balance. Since his basis in the asset is less than the loan balance, the $1,600 difference between the portion of the loan assumed by the other partners, $9,600 (80% × $12,000), and his basis of $8,000 is treated as capital gain from the sale or exchange of a partnership interest. Roy's partnership basis is zero.

Partnership Loss Limitations

The amount of a partnership's loss that a partner is allowed to deduct on his tax return is dependent on the partner's basis in the partnership. In general, a partner cannot deduct losses that exceed his partnership basis. Losses disallowed due to insufficient basis are carried forward until the partner can deduct them in a later year, typically when there is sufficient basis in the partnership.

Debts incurred on behalf of the partnership can increase a partner's individual basis. For example, if a partner takes out a $50,000 loan to finance partnership operations and he personally guarantees the debt, the debt is considered part of his basis in the partnership for purposes of deducting partnership losses.

Example: Rebecca invests $1,000 in the Goldblatt Partnership in return for a 10% general partnership interest. The Goldblatt Partnership takes out a $500,000 loan and incurs $100,000 of losses during the first year. Rebecca's share of partnership liabilities would increase her basis to $51,000 ($1,000 cash investment + [$500,000 × 10%]). Rebecca's share of the loss is $10,000 ($100,000 × 10%), reducing her basis to $41,000. Rebecca is allowed to deduct the entire amount because her partnership basis included her share of the partnership's debt.

If the partner does not have any personal liability to satisfy the debt of a partnership, deductible losses may be limited by the at-risk rules.

The at-risk rules limit the deductibility of losses to the partner's basis, not including his share of any nonrecourse debt.

This means that a partner is prohibited from taking losses based on partnership liabilities unless the partner would be forced to satisfy the debt with his personal assets. This is intended to prevent abusive deductions from tax shelter activities.

A partner (or related person) is considered to have assumed a partnership liability when he is personally liable for it, and:

- The creditor knows that the liability was assumed by the partner or related person,
- The creditor can demand payment from the partner or related person, and
- No other partner or person related to a partner will bear the economic risk of loss on that liability immediately after the assumption.

Example: Gary and Santiago form a general partnership, with cash contributions of $2,000 from each. Under the partnership agreement, they share all partnership profits and losses equally. The partnership borrows an additional $10,000 and purchases equipment. Both partners are personally liable for the debt in the event it is not paid by the partnership. This debt is included in the partners' basis in the partnership. Each partner's basis would include his allocated share of the liability, or $5,000. Therefore, each partner's basis is $7,000 (initial $2,000 contribution + $5,000 share of the liability) and each of their amounts at-risk in the partnership is $7,000.

The effect of liabilities on an individual partner's basis depends mainly on two factors:

- Whether or not the liability is recourse or nonrecourse
- Whether or not the partner is a general or limited partner

A nonrecourse liability is usually secured by an asset or property, and its terms provide that the creditor has no claim against the owner of the property. At most, the creditor may have a claim against the property.

An example of this would be a mortgage loan where the lender's only recourse in case of default is to repossess the property. A partnership liability is considered a nonrecourse liability if no partner has an economic risk of loss for that liability.

Example: Reuben purchases a used van for his business, but he is unable to make the payments. The loan is a nonrecourse loan because the only action the lender can take is to repossess the vehicle. The lender repossesses the vehicle while there is still a balance on the auto loan. However, the lender cannot seek payment from Reuben for the balance of the loan.

A partner's share of nonrecourse liabilities is proportionate to his share of partnership profits. A partner's basis in a partnership interest includes the partner's share of a partnership liability only if, and to the extent, the liability:

- Creates or increases the partnership's basis in any of its assets,
- Gives rise to a current deduction to the partnership, or
- Is a nondeductible, noncapital expense of the partnership.

A partnership liability is a recourse liability when the individual partners have an economic risk of loss. A partner has an economic risk of loss to the extent that he or a related person would be obligated to make payments to a creditor in the event of a constructive liquidation.

Partners generally share recourse liabilities based on their ratios for sharing losses. A limited partner has no obligation to contribute additional capital to the partnership, and therefore does not have an economic risk of loss in the partnership's recourse liabilities. Thus, unless a limited partner guarantees a partnership liability or makes a loan to the partnership, his basis will generally not be affected by the partnership's recourse liabilities.

Unit 10: Study Questions

(Please test yourself and check the correct answers at the end of this section.)

1. Todd and Charlotte form a general partnership with cash contributions of $20,000 each. Under the partnership agreement, they share all partnership profits and losses equally. They borrow $60,000 and purchase depreciable business equipment. However, Todd has poor credit, so Charlotte is the only signer on the loan. Charlotte is required to pay the creditor if the partnership defaults, so she has an economic risk of loss related to the loan. The payments on the loan are made out of the partnership bank account. What is Charlotte's basis in the partnership, and what is Todd's basis?

A. Charlotte: $80,000, Todd: $20,000.
B. Charlotte: $60,000, Todd: $20,000.
C. Charlotte: $20,000, Todd: $20,000.
D. Charlotte: $60,000, Todd: $60,000.

2. When payments are made by a partnership to partners without regard to partnership income, these payments are called:

A. Capital gains.
B. Ordinary distributions.
C. Passive income.
D. Guaranteed payments.

3. Carolyn and Jerome form a partnership in 2016. Each contributes $5,000 for an equal partnership interest. Their partnership agreement states that they will share income and losses equally. However, Carolyn will provide accounting services to the partnership and receive a guaranteed payment each year of $21,000, regardless of the partnership's income or loss. In 2016, the partnership earns $50,000 before deducting the guaranteed payment. What is Jerome's distributive share of partnership profits for the year?

A. $0
B. $14,500
C. $22,500
D. $25,000

4. Which of the following statements is correct regarding limited partners in a partnership?

A. A limited partner has an economic liability for damages and an economic risk of loss.
B. A limited partner does not have an economic risk of loss in the partnership's recourse liabilities.
C. A limited partner does not have an economic risk of loss in the partnership's recourse liabilities; however, a limited partner may be required to contribute additional capital.
D. A limited partner is treated just like a general partner when it comes to the partnership's recourse liabilities.

5. The G&H Partnership has two partners, Gil and Hassid, who share profits and losses equally (50/50). The partnership has the following activity during the year:

Gross income from operations:	$200,000
Business expenses:	30,000
Tax-exempt interest income:	10,000
Rental income:	120,000
Charitable contributions:	4,000

What is Hassid's share of the partnership's ordinary income?

A. $85,000
B. $91,000
C. $100,000
D. $105,000

6. José and Carlos form a partnership. Each contributes $20,000 during the initial formation of the partnership. Their partnership agreement states that José will receive 35% of the distributive income and Carlos will receive 65%. In 2016, the partnership has income of $200,000. What is each partner's distributive share of the partnership profits?

A. José: $70,000, Carlos: $130,000.
B. José: $100,000, Carlos: $100,000.
C. José: $35,000, Carlos $65,000.
D. José: $77,000, Carlos $143,000.

7. Polly and Diane form P&D Partnership. Polly contributes $16,000 cash and Diane contributes equipment with a fair market value of $15,000 and an adjusted basis of $5,000. What amount should Diane report as a gain as a result of this transaction?

A. $0
B. $3,000
C. $5,000
D. $8,000

8. If a partnership requests additional time to file its return, how long will the filing deadline be extended?

A. Three months.
B. Five months.
C. Six months.
D. Nine months.

9. John, Robin, Shanette, and Theresa form a partnership. Each partner contributes $10,000 and receives an equal interest in the partnership (25%). Under the partnership agreement, they share partnership profits and losses equally. The partnership borrows $135,000 and purchases business equipment. All of the partners except for Theresa personally guarantee the liability. What is each partner's basis after this transaction?

A. Theresa's basis is zero, and the other partners each have a basis of $58,333.
B. Theresa's basis is $10,000, and the other partners each have a basis of $43,750.
C. Theresa's basis is $10,000, and the other partners each have a basis of $55,000.
D. Each partner has a basis of $43,750.

10. Which of the following is not a separately stated item on a partnership tax return?

A. Net long-term capital gains and losses.
B. Investment income.
C. Section 179 deductions and bonus depreciation.
D. Guaranteed payments.

11. D&D Pet Stores operates as an accrual-based partnership and files Form 1065 for 2016. In addition to receipts from pet food sales of $250,000, the partnership has the following items of income and expenses for 2016:

Salaries	$50,000
Insurance	5,000
Charitable contributions	5,000
Licenses	5,000
Rental income	25,000
Guaranteed payments	75,000

What is the ordinary income that D&D Pet Stores should report on its Form 1065?

A. $85,000
B. $115,000
C. $190,000
D. $210,000

12. Which of the following increases the basis of a partner's interest in a partnership?

A. A partner's share of tax-exempt interest from municipal bonds owned by the partnership.
B. A decrease in the partner's share of liabilities.
C. A distribution of $2,000 of cash to the partner.
D. A property distribution with an FMV of $5,000.

13. The Kissinger Partnership generated income and expenses as stated below. What is the amount of ordinary business income that Kissinger should report for 2016?

- Employee wages: $15,000
- Rental real estate income: $20,000
- Charitable contributions: $500
- Cost of goods sold: $10,000
- Income from cosmetics sales: $75,000

A. $65,000
B. $69,500
C. $50,000
D. $30,000

14. Daniel is a general partner in the Vrettos Partnership. During the year, Daniel personally assumes $100,000 of the partnership's liabilities. Which of the following statements regarding partnership liabilities is correct?

A. The assumption of partnership debt by Daniel is treated as a distribution of cash to Daniel, and it decreases Daniel's partnership basis.
B. The assumption of partnership debt by Daniel increases his basis.
C. Daniel cannot assume partnership liabilities.
D. Only limited partners are allowed to assume partnership liabilities.

15. Monica contributes property to a partnership for a 40% interest. The property has a fair market value of $7,000, an adjusted basis of $4,000, and a related mortgage of $1,000 that the partnership assumes. What is Monica's basis in her partnership interest?

A. $4,000
B. $3,000
C. $6,000
D. $3,400

16. Derrick is a 10% partner in Hartville Roads Partnership. According to the partnership agreement, Derrick is entitled to a fixed annual guaranteed payment of $5,000. During the year, Hartville Roads has $55,000 of ordinary income before deducting the guaranteed payment. How much partnership income should Derrick report on his individual return for this year?

A. $11,500
B. $16,000
C. $10,000
D. $5,000

17. Hatta Persian Restaurant operates as a calendar-year partnership. Hatta's two partners, Assad and Ted, share profits and losses 60% and 40%, respectively. For tax year 2016, Hatta Restaurant had the following income and expense:

- Gross sales: $270,000
- Cost of goods sold: $80,00
- Bank interest income: $2,500
- Wages paid: $50,000
- Short-term capital loss: $5,000

Compute the partnership's ordinary income and flow-through amounts to the partners and choose the correct outcome.

	Assad		Ted	
A.	Ordinary income: Short-term capital loss:	$85,000 $3,000	Ordinary income: Short-term capital loss:	$57,000 $2,000
B.	Ordinary income:	$82,500	Ordinary income:	$55,000
C.	Ordinary income: Interest income: Short-term capital loss:	$81,000 $1,500 $3,000	Ordinary income: Interest income: Short-term capital loss:	$54,000 $1,000 $2,000
D.	Ordinary income: Interest income: Short-term capital loss:	$84,000 $1,500 $3,000	Ordinary income: Interest income: Short-term capital loss:	$56,000 $1,000 $2,000

18. A partner is not considered at risk for which of the following amounts?

A. The money and adjusted basis of any property the partner contributed to a partnership's activity.
B. The partner's share of income retained by the partnership.
C. A partnership's nonrecourse liability.
D. Certain amounts borrowed by the partnership for use in the activity if the partner is personally liable for repayment.

19. Bea acquired a 30% interest in a partnership by contributing property in which she had an adjusted basis of $25,000. The property's fair market value was $50,000, and it had a $40,000 mortgage that was assumed by the partnership. What is Bea's gain or loss on the contribution of her property to the partnership?

A. $0
B. $3,000 gain
C. $12,000 gain
D. $10,000 loss

20. What is the latest that a partnership agreement can be modified and its terms be applicable to the partnership tax return during a taxable year?

A. Up until the close of the taxable year.
B. No later than the date for filing the partnership return (without extensions).
C. Up until the first day of the taxable year.
D. No later than the extended due date for filing the partnership return.

Unit 10: Answers

1. The answer is A. This loan amount is included in Charlotte's basis in the partnership because she has an economic risk of loss related to this liability. An additional $60,000 of basis in the partnership's depreciable property was created as a result of incurring this debt. Her basis in the partnership would be $80,000 ($20,000 + $60,000), while Todd's basis would be only $20,000.

2. The answer is D. Guaranteed payments are made by a partnership to a partner and determined without regard to the partnership's income. A partnership treats guaranteed payments for services, or for the use of capital, as a business expense, just as if they were made to a person who is not a partner.

3. The answer is B. The guaranteed payment must be deducted before figuring each partner's distributive share. The answer is figured as follows:

$50,000 - $21,000 = $29,000
$29,000 × 50% = $14,500

Guaranteed payments are deducted from partnership income before determining the distributive share of income or loss for each partner.

4. The answer is B. A limited partner generally has no obligation to contribute additional capital to the partnership. Therefore, absent some other factor, such as the guarantee of a partnership liability by the limited partner or the limited partner making a loan to the partnership, a limited partner generally does not have an economic risk of loss in connection with the partnership's recourse liabilities.

5. The answer is A. The rental income, tax exempt income, and charitable contributions are all separately stated items that do not affect the calculation of ordinary income. Instead, each partner's share of the separately stated items is passed through to him. The partnership's ordinary income is split evenly, so Hassid's portion is as follows:

($200,000 - $30,000) = $170,000 of ordinary income
$170,000 × 50% = **$85,000**

6. The answer is A. The profits are allocated according to the partnership agreement. José's distributive share is calculated as follows: 35% × $200,000 = $70,000. Carlos's share is calculated as follows: 65% × $200,000 = $130,000.

7. The answer is A. Usually, neither the partner nor the partnership recognizes a gain or loss when property is contributed to the partnership in exchange for a partnership interest. This applies whether a partnership is being formed or is already operating. However, if an asset is encumbered by a liability, such as a mortgage, there is a possibility that the partner will recognize a gain in connection with the contribution.

8. The answer is C. Form 7004, *Automatic Extension of Time to File Certain Business Income Tax, Information, and Other Returns*, is used by partnerships to extend their filing deadline for six months starting for the 2016 tax year. Starting with the 2016 tax year, the extended due date for a calendar-year partnership is Sept. 15, 2017.

9. The answer is C. If a partner's share of partnership liabilities increases, this increase is treated as a contribution of money by the partner to the partnership. The debt is included in the bases of the three partners who signed the personal guarantees. Since Theresa does not have an economic risk of loss for this liability, the liability does not increase her basis. The basis for each of the other partners would include his or her share of the liability ([$135,000 ÷ 3 partners] = $45,000 + $10,000 cash investment).

10. The answer is D. Guaranteed payments are deductible by the partnership because they are treated like wages and are taxable to the partners who receive them. The other items are separately stated on the partnership's Form 1065. Each individual partner receives a Schedule K-1 from the partnership, reporting his share of ordinary income or loss and each separately stated item. Separately stated items pass through to the partners and retain their character as the partners report these amounts on their individual tax returns.

11. The answer is B. All of the items listed are included in the calculation of ordinary income except the charitable contributions and the rental income, both of which must be separately stated on Form 1065. Thus, ordinary income will be $115,000 ($250,000 - $50,000 - $5,000 - $5,000 - $75,000). Like the other deductions listed, guaranteed payments to partners are treated as a deduction in determining ordinary income or loss.

12. The answer is A. Partnership income, including tax-exempt interest, increases a partner's basis in his partnership interest. All of the other items will decrease a partner's interest in a partnership.

13. The answer is C. Kissinger's ordinary income for 2016 is equal to its sales income minus the cost of goods sold and wages ($75,000 - $10,000 - $15,000 = $50,000). The income from rental real estate and the charitable contributions must be separately stated on the partnership's tax return.

14. The answer is B. The assumption of partnership debt by Daniel increases his basis. If a partner's share of partnership liabilities increases, or a partner's individual liabilities increase because he assumes partnership liabilities, it is treated as if the partner made a contribution to the partnership.

15. The answer is D. The basis of Monica's partnership interest is the adjusted basis of the property she contributes ($4,000) minus the portion of the related mortgage liability assumed by the other partners (60% × $1,000 = $600), or $3,400.

16. The answer is C. Derrick must include $10,000 of ordinary income from the partnership on his tax return. The answer is figured as follows:

1. $55,000 - $5,000 guaranteed payment = $50,000 of ordinary income
2. $50,000 × 10% = $5,000 (Derrick's share of the partnership's ordinary income)
3. ($5,000 guaranteed payment + $5,000 [$50,000 × 10%] distributive share) = **$10,000**

Guaranteed payments are determined without regard to the partnership's income. They are deducted as a business expense when figuring the partnership's ordinary income. The individual partner who receives the guaranteed payments reports the payments on Schedule E (Form 1040) as ordinary income, along with his distributive share of the partnership's ordinary income.

17. The answer is D. Interest income and short-term capital losses are separately stated items that flow through to each partner and retain their character. The other items listed are components of ordinary income, determined as follows: gross sales of $270,000, minus the cost of goods sold of $80,000 and wages of $50,000 = ordinary income of $140,000. Absent any provisions in the partnership agreement to the contrary, both ordinary income and the separately stated items would be allocated according to the 60%/40% profit-sharing arrangement.

18. The answer is C. The at-risk rules limit the deductibility of losses to the partner's basis, not including his share of any of the partnership's nonrecourse debt (except for qualified nonrecourse debt).

19. The answer is B. The basis of Bea's partnership interest should be the adjusted basis of the property contributed ($25,000) minus the portion of the mortgage liability assumed by the other partners (70% × $40,000 = $28,000). However, this would result in a basis of negative $3,000, and a partner's basis in a partnership can never go below zero. To avoid creating a negative basis, Bea must recognize a gain of $3,000.

20. The answer is B. Partners can modify their partnership agreement after the close of the tax year, but no later than the due date (without extensions) for filing the partnership return.

Unit 11: Partnership Distributions & Liquidations

More Reading:
Publication 541, *Partnerships*
Instructions for Form 1065

Partnership Distributions

A partnership is not a taxable entity; its income and losses flow through and are reported on the partners' individual tax returns. Each partner is taxed on his distributive share of income, whether or not it is actually distributed.

Partnership distributions may include the following:

- Distributions of the partnership's earnings for the current or prior years.
- A withdrawal by a partner in anticipation of the current year's earnings.
- A complete or partial liquidation of a partner's interest.
- A distribution to all partners in a complete liquidation of the partnership.

A partnership distribution is not taken into account in determining the partner's distributive share of the partnership's income or loss. If a gain or loss from the distribution is recognized by the partner, it must be reported on his return for the tax year in which the distribution is received. Cash or property withdrawn by a partner in anticipation of the current year's earnings is treated as a distribution received on the last day of the partnership's tax year.

A partner's adjusted basis in his partnership interest is decreased (but not below zero) by the cash and adjusted basis of property distributed to the partner.

Example: The adjusted basis of Angela's partnership interest is $14,000. She receives a distribution of $8,000 cash and land that has an adjusted basis to the partnership of $2,000 and a fair market value of $3,000. The distribution decreases the basis of her partnership interest to $4,000 based on the amount of the cash and the basis of the asset (land) distributed ($14,000 – [$8,000 + $2,000]). Because the distribution does not exceed the basis of her partnership interest, Angela does not recognize gain. Any gain related to the excess of the land's fair market value over its adjusted basis may be recognized if she later disposes of it.

Unless there is a complete liquidation of a partner's interest, the basis of property (other than cash) distributed to the partner is its adjusted basis to the partnership immediately before the distribution.

Example: The adjusted basis of Casey's partnership interest is $45,000. She receives a distribution of property that has an adjusted basis of $23,000 to the partnership plus $6,000 in cash. Her basis in the property is $23,000.

However, a partner cannot have a negative partnership basis. Therefore, the basis of property distributed to a partner cannot be more than the adjusted basis of his interest in the partnership, reduced by any cash received in the same transaction.

Example: The basis of Mike's partnership interest is $10,000. He receives a distribution of $4,000 cash and a parcel of land that has an adjusted basis to the partnership of $8,000. His basis in the land is limited to $6,000 ($10,000 - $4,000, the cash he receives), since the total amount cannot exceed his partnership interest. After the distribution, his partnership basis would be zero.

A partnership does not recognize any gain or loss because of distributions it makes to partners. The partnership may be able to elect to adjust the basis of its undistributed property. However, when a partnership distributes the following items, the distribution may be treated as a sale or exchange of property rather than a distribution:

- Unrealized receivables or substantially appreciated inventory items distributed in exchange for any part of the partner's interest in other partnership property, including cash
- Other property, including cash, distributed in exchange for any part of a partner's interest in unrealized receivables or substantially appreciated inventory items

This treatment does not apply to the following distributions:

- A distribution of property to the partner who contributed the same property to the partnership
- Payments made to a retiring partner or successor in interest of a deceased partner that are the partner's distributive share of partnership income or guaranteed payments

Special rules for distributed inventory: A gain or loss on a sale or exchange of unrealized receivables or inventory items a partner received in a distribution is generally treated as ordinary income or loss. However, if a partner holds the inventory (in the hands of the partnership) for at least 5 years, then sells it, the gain would be treated as a capital gain if the assets were capital assets in the hands of the partner.

Example: Marcia was a general partner in Super Deluxe Gemstones, a retail business that sold semi-precious gems that actually increase in value over time. On January 3, 2016, the store distributed and Marcia received, inventory of gemstones that had a basis of $19,000 to the partnership. Marcia kept the gemstones for her own, personal use. She sold all of the gemstones for $24,000 in December 2016. The $5,000 gain is taxed as ordinary income to Marcia, even though the gemstones were capital assets in her hands. If she had held the inventory for more than 5 years after the distribution and sold it at a gain, her gain would have been capital gain and taxed at a lower rate.[105]

If a partnership acquires a partner's debt and extinguishes the debt by distributing it to the partner, the partner will recognize capital gain or loss to the extent the fair market value of the debt differs from the basis of the debt.

The partner is treated as having satisfied the debt for its fair market value. If the issue price of the debt exceeds its FMV when distributed, the partner may have to include the excess amount in income as canceled debt.

Sale of a Partnership Interest

A partnership interest is a capital asset. As a result, a gain or loss on the sale or exchange of a partnership interest is normally treated as a capital gain or loss.[106] Gain or loss is calculated as the difference between the amount realized and the adjusted basis of the partner's interest

[105] This example is modified from an example in IRS Publication 541.

[106] An exception to this rule is if the partnership has any cash-basis unrealized receivables or inventory with a built-in-gain (otherwise known as "hot assets") at the time of the partnership sale or exchange. If so, then in accordance with IRC §751, some of the gain or loss could be classified as an ordinary gain or loss instead of entirely a capital gain or loss.

in the partnership. If the selling partner is relieved of partnership liabilities, he must include the liability relief as part of the amount realized for his interest.

Example: Selene became a partner in the Rincon Partnership by contributing cash to the formation of the partnership. The adjusted basis of her partnership interest at the end of 2016 is $20,000, which includes her $15,000 share of partnership liabilities. Selene sells her interest in the partnership for $10,000 in cash on December 31, 2016. At the time of the sale she had been credited for her share of the partnership's income for the tax year. Selene realizes $25,000 from the sale of her partnership interest ($10,000 cash payment + $15,000 liability relief). She must report $5,000 ($25,000 realized – $20,000 basis) as a capital gain.

An exchange of partnership interests does not qualify as a nontaxable exchange of like-kind property.

Liquidation of a Partnership

When a partnership dissolves or stops doing business, it is called a partnership liquidation. A partnership may dissolve when a partner dies, or when one partner drops out of the business. The basis of property received in complete liquidation of a partner's interest is the adjusted basis of the partner's interest in the partnership reduced by any cash distributed to the partner in the same transaction.

A partner's holding period for property distributed to him includes the period held by the partnership. If the property was contributed to the partnership by a partner, the holding period includes the period held by that partner also.

Example: Merle's basis in his partnership interest is $20,000. In a distribution to liquidate his entire interest, he receives a delivery truck and a utility trailer. The truck has an adjusted basis to the partnership of $15,000 and an FMV of $15,000. The trailer has an adjusted basis to the partnership of $14,000 and an FMV of $4,000. To figure his basis in each property, Merle first assigns a basis of $15,000 to the truck and $14,000 to the trailer. This leaves a $9,000 basis decrease (the $29,000 total of the assigned basis minus the $20,000 allocable partnership basis). He allocates the entire $9,000 to the trailer to reflect its unrealized depreciation. Merle's basis in the truck is $15,000, and his basis in the trailer is $5,000 ($14,000 - $9,000).

If a partnership is liquidated or dissolved with unamortized organizational or start-up expenses, the unamortized amounts can be deducted in the partnership's final tax year.

Example: The Nielson Partnership is liquidating five years after it formed. It had been amortizing $36,000 of organizational and start-up costs over 180 months. After five years, the partnership had amortized $12,000 ($36,000 ÷ 60 months). Nielsen can deduct the remaining unamortized amount of $24,000 ($36,000 - $12,000) on its final tax return.

Payments made by the partnership to a retiring partner or a deceased partner's estate or in liquidation of the interest of a retiring or deceased partner in exchange for his interest in partnership property are considered a distribution, not a distributive share or guaranteed payment that could give rise to a deduction for the partnership. A retiring or deceased partner is treated as a partner until his interest in the partnership has been completely liquidated.

In a partnership liquidation, the liquidating distributions are similar to regular distributions except that the partner may recognize a loss if the total of cash and the basis of property received is less than his basis in the partnership. A partner cannot recognize a loss on a partnership distribution unless all of the following requirements are met:

- The adjusted basis of the partner's interest in the partnership exceeds the distribution.
- The partner's entire interest in the partnership is liquidated.
- The distribution is in cash, unrealized receivables, or inventory items.

Example: The Webb-Bruner Partnership is liquidating. Donnie's adjusted basis in the partnership is $80,000. He receives a liquidating cash distribution of $60,000. As Donnie's adjusted basis of his partnership interest exceeds the distribution, he has a capital loss of $20,000 ($80,000 - $60,000).

Partnership Termination

A partnership terminates when one of the following events takes place:

- All its operations are discontinued and no part of any business, financial operation, or venture is continued by any of the partners in a partnership.
- At least 50% of the total interest in partnership capital and profits is sold or exchanged within a 12-month period, including a sale or exchange to another partner.

The partnership's tax year ends on the date of termination.

If the partnership is terminated before the end of its regular tax year, Form 1065 must be filed for the short tax year from the beginning of the tax year through the date of termination. The return is due on the fifteenth day of the third month following the date of termination.

Example: Dyer Partnership is a calendar-year partnership. It terminates and stops doing business on May 3. Its final Form 1065 for the short tax year period of January 1 through May 3 is due on August 15, the fifteenth day of the third month following the date of termination.

If a partnership is converted into an LLC classified as a partnership, the conversion does not terminate the partnership, and there is no sale, exchange, or termination of partnership interests. The partnership's tax year does not close, and the LLC can continue to use the partnership's taxpayer identification number.

Cancellation of a Partner's Debt

If a partnership terminates and one of the former partners is insolvent and cannot pay his share of the partnership's debts, the other partners may be forced to pay more than their share of the liabilities. If another partner pays any part of an insolvent partner's share of the debts, he can take a bad debt deduction.

Example: Hank and Jocelyn are 50/50 partners in a company that provides online tutoring services. The company is struggling and Hank and Jocelyn decide to discontinue the business. The partnership is terminated and it has $50,000 of liabilities to creditors after liquidating all of its assets. However, Hank has filed for personal bankruptcy and the court has declared him insolvent. Even though Jocelyn is a 50% partner, she assumes responsibility for the entire $50,000 of partnership debt, which she pays herself. She can claim a bad debt deduction in the amount of $25,000, equal to Hank's share of the debt that she personally assumed.

The cancellation of debt exclusions described earlier are applied at the partner level rather than at the partnership level. Thus, for example, an individual partner would need to be insolvent to utilize the insolvency exclusion for his share of COD income passed through from an insolvent partnership. If a partner is able to use the exclusion, he would be required to reduce specified tax attributes, including loss and credit carryforwards and the basis of assets.

Related Party Transactions

A partnership cannot deduct a loss on the sale or trade of property if the transaction is directly or indirectly between related parties. Under the related party transaction rules, an individual is considered to be the owner of a partnership interest directly or indirectly owned by his family members.

Members of a family, for this purpose, include only brothers, sisters, half-brothers, half-sisters, spouses, ancestors, parents, and lineal descendants (children, grandchildren).

For the purposes of this rule, "related parties" does not include: ex-spouses, in-laws, step-siblings, cousins, or step-parents.

Example: Freeway Partnership is owned by two brothers, Jackson and Terry. MBO Partnership is owned by two sisters, Dominica and Paulette. Dominica and Paulette are first cousins to Jackson and Terry. During the year, Freeway Partnership sells a factory building to MBO Partnership. Freeway Partnership recognizes a loss on the sale. The loss is allowable, because first cousins are not considered related parties.

Losses are not allowed from a sale or exchange of property (other than an interest in the partnership) directly or indirectly between a partnership and a person whose direct or indirect interest in the capital or profits of the partnership is more than 50%.

If a sale or exchange is between two partnerships in which the same persons directly or indirectly own more than 50% of the capital or profits interests in each partnership, no loss is allowed.

Example: George and Lynn are siblings. Lynn is a 60% partner in the BuildRite Machinery Partnership, and George is a 55% partner in the Schluter Partnership. If one partnership sells property to the other at a loss, the loss will not be allowed because the partnerships are considered related parties, because the majority ownership in both partnerships is held by two closely related family members (George and Lynn). Losses will instead be suspended until the property is eventually disposed of in a non-related party transaction.

The basis of each partner's interest in the partnership is decreased (but not below zero) by the partner's share of a disallowed loss.

If the purchaser later sells the property, only the gain realized that is greater than the loss not allowed will be taxable. If a gain from the sale of the property is not recognized because of this rule, the basis of each partner's interest in the partnership is increased by the partner's share of that gain.

Unit 11: Study Questions

(Please test yourself and check the correct answers at the end of this section.)

1. Davisville Farming Partnership sold a tractor to the Winters Partnership at a loss of $50,000. Davisville owned the tractor for only five months. Davisville is owned 30% by Marvin, 30% by Moses, and 40% by Geoff. Geoff is Marvin's brother. Winters Partnership is owned 80% by BRIG Corporation. Marvin owns 25% of the stock of BRIG Corporation and Geoff's daughter, Freya, owns the remaining 75% of BRIG's corporate stock. How much of the loss on the sale of the tractor should Davisville Farming Partnership recognize for tax purposes on their Form 1065?

A. $0
B. $3,000
C. $35,000
D. $50,000

2. The adjusted basis of Allison's partnership interest is $24,000. She receives a distribution of $9,000 cash and machinery that has an adjusted basis of $1,000 and a fair market value of $7,000. How much gain should Allison recognize on this distribution?

A. $0
B. $1,000
C. $2,000
D. $7,000

3. Nina, a partner in the Amass Partnership, receives distributions of $1,000 of cash and property worth $2,000, in which Amass has a basis of $1,500. Nina's outside basis at the time of the distributions is $20,000. The partnership has assets of $40,000 and no outstanding liabilities. The distributions are made at the end of the year, after partnership income (loss) has been recorded. How much gain should Nina recognize on the distributions and what is her basis in the property received?

A. She recognizes a gain of $500 on the property received and her basis in the property is $2,000.
B. She recognizes gain of $1,500 on the property and cash received. Her basis in the property received is $3,500.
C. She recognizes no gain on the property received. Her basis in the property received is $1,500.
D. She recognizes a gain of $1,000. Her basis in the property received is $1,500.

4. The adjusted basis of Josue's partnership interest is $10,000. He receives a distribution of $4,000 cash and a van that has an adjusted basis to the partnership of $9,000 and a fair market value of $12,000. This was not a liquidating distribution. What is Josue's basis in the van?

A. $5,000
B. $6,000
C. $12,000
D. $16,000

5. Marty is retiring from Sunnyside Partnership this year. His adjusted basis in the partnership is $50,000. He receives a distribution of $65,000 cash. How would Marty report this transaction?

A. $15,000 capital gain
B. $50,000 capital gain
C. $65,000 capital gain
D. $65,000 ordinary income

6. Bart and Ellen are equal partners in Bantam Partnership. In 2016, the partnership breaks up. Bart is insolvent, and Ellen becomes responsible for paying a portion of his partnership debt. Which of the following statements is correct?

A. Ellen cannot take a bad debt deduction for any debt that the partnership incurred.
B. Bart is not responsible for paying any of his liabilities after dissolution.
C. Ellen can take a bad debt deduction for any amount that she must pay that is not her share of the partnership debt.
D. None of the above.

7. In 2016, Laney sold her partnership interest for $45,000. Her adjusted basis at the time of the sale was $29,500, which includes her $12,500 share of partnership liabilities. When she initially invested in the partnership, she contributed $10,000 worth of equipment. There was no profit or loss at the partnership level that had not been credited at the time she sold her interest. What is the amount and nature of her income or loss from the sale of her partnership interest in 2016?

A. $7,500 ordinary loss
B. $10,000 capital gain
C. $12,500 ordinary income
D. $28,000 capital gain

8. Bill owns a 75% capital interest in the Shanahan Partnership. Bill's wife, Veronica, is a 65% owner in the Underdahl Partnership. Bill and Veronica file separate tax returns and keep all their books and records separate. Shanahan Partnership sells Underdahl Partnership a factory machine for $7,600. Shanahan's basis in the machinery is $10,000. What is Shanahan Partnership's deductible loss?

A. $0
B. $2,400
C. $7,600
D. $10,000

9. The adjusted basis of Adrian's partnership interest is $17,500. He received a distribution of $9,000 cash and a piece of land with an adjusted basis of $2,500 to the partnership and a fair market value of $4,000. What is the gain to be recognized at the time of these distributions?

A. $0
B. $1,500
C. $4,500
D. $6,000

Unit 11: Answers

1. The answer is A. A loss is not allowed from a sale or exchange of property directly or indirectly between a partnership and a person (or entity) whose direct or indirect interest in the capital or profits of the partnership is more than 50%. In this case, Marvin and Geoff own a combined interest of 70% in the Davisville Farming Partnership, and they indirectly own over 50% in the Winters Partnership. Since Marvin and Freya (who is Geoff's daughter, and a related party) own a combined interest of 85% in BRIG Corporation, their indirect interest in the Winters Partnership is 85% × 80%, or 68%. The loss on the sale of the tractor is therefore disallowed by the related party transaction rules.

2. The answer is A. Because the sum of cash and the adjusted basis of the property does not exceed the basis of her partnership interest, Allison does not recognize any gain on the distribution. Any gain on the machinery will be recognized when she sells it.

3. The answer is C. Nina recognizes no gain because the total of cash and the basis of property received does not exceed her basis in the partnership. She assumes the partnership's basis of $1,500 in the property received, and may recognize gain or loss if she later sells the property.

4. The answer is B. Josue's basis for the van is limited to $6,000 ($10,000 basis - $4,000, the cash he receives), equal to the remaining basis in his partnership interest after subtracting the cash received. After the distributions, his basis in the partnership interest is zero.

5. The answer is A. A retiring partner or the successor in interest of a deceased partner recognizes gain to the extent that any cash (and marketable securities treated as cash) distributed is more than the partner's adjusted basis in the partnership. Marty must recognize $15,000 of capital gain. This is the difference between his adjusted basis in the partnership and the amount of his distribution ($65,000 - $50,000).

6. The answer is C. If a business partnership dissolves and one of the former partners is insolvent and cannot pay his share of the partnership's debts, other partners may have to pay more than their respective shares. If a partner pays any part of the insolvent partner's share of the debts, she can take a bad debt deduction for the amount paid. Ellen is allowed to take a bad debt deduction for the liabilities she must pay that are in excess of her share of partnership liabilities.

7. The answer is D. When Laney sold her partnership interest, she was relieved of her $12,500 share of the partnership's liabilities, so her adjusted basis for purposes of calculating her gain on sale of the interest is $17,000 ($29,500 - $12,500). Thus, her gain is $28,000 (proceeds of $45,000 minus the adjusted basis of $17,000). Approached differently, the amount of liability relieved from Laney upon sale of her interest might be viewed as additional proceeds, but her gain would still be $28,000 ($45,000 + $12,500 - $29,500). As a partnership interest is a capital asset, any gain or loss recognized on the sale of the interest is typically treated as a capital gain or loss.

8. The answer is A. Shanahan Partnership's loss of $2,400 is not deductible. A loss on the sale or exchange of property between related persons is not deductible. This applies to both direct and indirect transactions. The fact that Bill and Veronica file separate tax returns does not prevent them from being related parties for purposes of this transaction.

9. The answer is A. Because the total of cash and the basis of property distributed ($9,000 + $2,500 = $11,500) does not exceed Adrian's adjusted basis of $17,500 in his partnership interest, he will recognize no gain as a result of the distribution. He assumes the partnership's adjusted basis of $2,500 in the property received, and will recognize gain or loss if he later sells this property.

Unit 12: C Corporations in General

More Reading:
Publication 542, *Corporations*
Publication 544, *Sales and Other Dispositions of Assets*
Instructions for Form 1120, *U.S. Corporation Income Tax Return*

Most major companies are organized as C corporations, which are taxed under subchapter C of the Internal Revenue Code. A C corporation can own property in its own name and it can be sued directly. The shareholders who own stock in a corporation do not own its individual assets. Individual shareholders are protected from legal liability, except in very unusual circumstances.

The IRS requires certain businesses to be taxed as corporations. The following businesses formed after 1996 are automatically treated as corporations:

- A business formed under a federal or state law that refers to it as a corporation
- A business formed under a state law that refers to it as a joint-stock company or joint-stock association
- Insurance companies
- Certain banks
- A business owned by a state or local government
- A business specifically required to be taxed as a corporation by the IRC (for example, certain publicly-traded partnerships)
- Certain foreign businesses
- Any other business that elects to be taxed as a corporation and files Form 8832, *Entity Classification Election*

Basic Concepts

Basic concepts regarding C corporations include:

1. **Perpetual life and limited liability:** A C corporation enjoys perpetual life and limited liability.
2. **Double taxation:** Earnings of a C corporation may be taxed twice: first at the corporate level and again at the shareholder level if they are distributed as dividends. Shareholders of a C corporation cannot deduct corporate losses.
3. **Shareholder meetings:** A corporation must maintain a list of all its shareholders, and generally must conduct at least one shareholder meeting per year.
4. **Organization:** A C corporation must file a charter, issue stock, and be overseen by a board of directors.
5. **Number of shareholders:** A C corporation may have a single owner-shareholder or an unlimited number of shareholders.
6. **Articles of incorporation:** A corporation's existence starts when articles of incorporation are filed with the state office that handles incorporations (usually the Secretary of State), along with any required filing fees.
7. **Liquidation:** If a C corporation liquidates, it will recognize gain or loss on the sale or distribution of its assets. Corporate shareholders then recognize gain or loss on the surrender of their stock to the corporation.
8. **Stock:** A C corporation may sell common and/or preferred stock with different voting rights.
9. **Tax-free fringe benefits:** A C corporation's shareholder-employees can receive tax-free employee fringe benefits that are deductible by the corporation as a business expense.

Filing Requirements

A domestic corporation in existence for any part of a tax year (including corporations in bankruptcy) must file an income tax return, regardless of its taxable income or activity. A C corporation files Form 1120, *U.S. Corporation Income Tax Return.* Tax-exempt organizations organized as corporations file Form 990 rather than Form 1120.

A corporation must continue to file tax returns even if there is no business activity or profits. However, it does not have to file after it has formally dissolved.

A corporation must generally file by the fifteenth day of the fourth month after the end of its tax year. Thus, a calendar-year corporation must typically file its tax return by April 15 of the following year. In 2017, the due date for calendar-year C Corporations is April 18, 2017.[107] (Prior to the 2016 tax year, the due date for calendar year C corporation returns was March 15.)

The extended due date for calendar year 1120 C corporation returns also changed, from September 15 to October 15, or six months after the due date of the return.

Note: This new due date applies to all C Corporations *except* those whose fiscal year ends on June 30. A special exception in the Surface Transportation Act will defer the due date change for C Corporations with fiscal years that end on June 30 defers the change until December 31, 2025 (a full ten years).

Example: Inman Design Corporation's tax year ends December 31, 2016. It must file its Form 1120 by April 18, 2017. If Inman Design were to file an extension, their corporate return for 2016 would be due on October 15, 2017.

Example: Strauss Motors Inc. is a domestic corporation with a fiscal year-end of June 30. Since the exception for June 30th fiscal-year corporations applies, the regular due date for the C corporation return (Form 1120) remains September 15.

Electronic filing is mandatory for C corporations with $10 million or more in assets and at least 250 or more returns of any type, including information returns such as Forms W-2 or Forms 1099.

A corporation must file Form 7004, *Automatic Extension of Time to File Certain Business Income Tax, Information, and Other Returns,* to request a six-month extension of time to file its income tax return. Form 7004 does not extend the time for paying the tax due on the return. Interest, and possibly penalties, will be charged on any part of the tax due and not paid. The interest is figured from the original due date of the return to the date of payment.

A penalty for late filing is assessed at 5% of any unpaid tax for each month the return is late, up to a maximum of 25% of the unpaid tax on the return. The late filing penalty is reduced by any late payment penalty for the same period.

The minimum late *filing* penalty for Form 1120 has increased from $135 to $205 or the amount of tax owed, whichever is smaller.[108]

The penalty for late *payment* of corporate income tax is one-half of 1% of the unpaid tax for each month that the tax is not paid, up to a maximum of 25% of the unpaid tax.

These penalties may not be imposed if the corporation shows reasonable cause for not paying or filing on time.

---

[107] Corporate tax returns to be filed in 2017 have new due dates that will impact nearly all C Corporations. Note that these new due dates do not apply to S Corporations—the due date for the Form 1120-S, *U.S. Income Tax Return for an S Corporation*, remains March 15 for calendar-year entities.

[108] The IRS has increased the minimum late filing penalty for certain returns filed more than 60 days late. In this circumstance, the minimum penalty has increased from $135 to $205 or the amount of tax owed, whichever is smaller. The increase applies to C Corporation returns required to be filed after December 31, 2015, effective immediately.

Estimated Tax Payments

Corporations are required to make estimated tax payments if they expect their tax due to be $500 or more during the taxable year. Penalties apply if estimated tax payments are not made on time. Most business entities, including corporations, are required to use the Electronic Federal Tax Payment System, (also called EFTPS), to make their estimated tax payments. Installments are due on a quarterly basis, on the fifteenth day of the fourth, sixth, ninth, and twelfth months of the corporation's taxable year. These due dates remain unchanged from the previous year.

Thus, a calendar-year corporation is required to make estimated payments on April 15, June 15, September 15, and December 15 (note that the estimated tax due dates for corporations are not the same as the estimated tax due dates for individuals).

In general, each quarterly federal tax payment is 25% of the corporation's "required annual payment", which is the lesser of two amounts:

- Current-year tax liability: 100% of the federal income tax reported on return for the current taxable year of the payment
- Prior-year safe harbor: 100% of a corporation's federal income tax reported on return for the preceding year

If a corporation later determines that it needs to revise their estimated tax liability, they will be required refigure the installment payments. In this scenario, an immediate catch-up payment should be made to reduce any penalty related to earlier installments.

There is no penalty for underpayment of estimated tax if the tax is less than $500, or if each quarterly estimated tax payment is at least 25% of the corporation's current-year tax. Penalties apply to corporate taxpayers who underpay their required quarterly payments. The penalty is for underpayment is nondeductible.

There is also no underpayment penalty if each estimated tax installment is at least 25% of the income tax on the prior year return. However, corporations without a tax liability in the preceding year cannot use the 100% prior-year safe harbor amount to determine their required estimated tax payment.

The safe harbor provision will also not apply in the following instances:

- If the prior tax year was a short year (less than 12 months)
- If the corporation did not file a return for the prior year
- If the corporation had at least $1 million of taxable income in any of the last three years

Example: Allegra Corporation had an overall business loss in the previous year, and therefore did not have a tax liability. Therefore the safe harbor provision for estimated tax payments will not apply. Allegra Corporation must accurately estimate their federal income tax liability for the current year and pay 100% of the federal income tax due on the current year tax return.

Corporate Refunds and Amended Returns

Corporations may use Form 1139, *Corporate Application for Tentative Refund,* or Form 1120X, *Amended U.S. Corporation Income Tax Return,* to apply for a refund. If a corporation does not file Form 1139, it must file Form 1120X to apply for a refund. Form 1120X must be filed within three years of the due date, including extensions, for filing the return for a year in which it sustains a loss.

If a corporation accidentally overpays its estimated tax, it may use Form 4466, *Corporation Application for Quick Refund of Overpayment of Estimated Tax,* to obtain a quick refund of its estimated tax payments. Form 4466 may be used if a corporation's overpayment is at least 10% of its anticipated tax liability and at least $500.

Corporate Taxation

Unlike a partnership or an S corporation, a C corporation is not a pass-through entity. This means that the earnings of a C corporation may be taxed twice. Corporate income is taxed when it is earned and then may be taxed again if it is distributed to shareholders as dividends. A corporation does not receive a tax deduction for the distribution of dividends to its shareholders.

A C corporation's income does not retain its character when it is distributed to shareholders. A corporation can have revenue from many different sources, including sales of products, services, and investment income. If, for example, a C corporation has rental income, it pays tax on this and any other sources of income at the corporate level. When the corporation's after-tax income is distributed to shareholders, this portion does not retain its character as rental income. It is distributed merely as a dividend.

This also applies if the corporation earns tax-exempt income. For example, a C corporation may earn tax-exempt income from investing in municipal bonds. If this income is used to make distributions to shareholders, its tax-exempt character is lost, and the distributions will be taxable dividends to the shareholders.

Example: White Paper Products, a C corporation, receives tax-exempt income from bonds. White Paper subsequently distributes income to its shareholders as taxable dividends. Even though a portion of the income was tax-exempt to White Paper, it does not retain its tax-exempt character when distributions are made to the shareholders. In contrast, in the case of an S corporation or a partnership, the income would have retained its character when it was passed through to the partners or S corporation shareholders.

Example: Jennison, Inc. is a calendar-year C corporation with twenty shareholders. After deducting business expenses, Jennison has $150,000 of taxable net income in 2016. The corporation also earns $4,000 of interest from municipal bonds. The $4,000 of tax-exempt bond interest is excluded from the corporation's taxable income. In December 2016, Jennison distributes $120,000 to its shareholders, based on their ownership stake. The company cannot take a tax deduction for the distribution. Each shareholder has an equal stake in the company, so each one receives $6,000 of dividend income ($120,000 ÷ 20 = $6,000). Each shareholder is required to recognize $6,000 of dividend income for 2016 on their individual tax returns.

Accumulated Earnings Tax

A corporation is allowed to accumulate a reasonable portion of its earnings for possible expansion or other bona fide business reasons. However, a corporation may be subject to the accumulated earnings tax if it does not distribute enough of its profits to shareholders. This tax was instituted to prevent corporations from hoarding income in order to avoid income tax on distributions for its shareholders.

Note: The **accumulated earnings tax** is levied at a rate of **20%** of the excess amount accumulated. It is not automatically applied; it is assessed only after audit. A corporation would have the opportunity to try to justify the amount of its accumulated earnings during an IRS examination.

If the accumulated earnings tax applies, interest is also assessed from the date the corporate return was originally due, without extensions.

An accumulation of $250,000 or less is generally considered reasonable for most businesses. However, for personal service corporations, the limit is $150,000. Reasonable needs of the business include the following:

- Specific, definite, and feasible plans for use of the earnings accumulation in the business.

- The amount necessary to redeem the corporation's stock included in a deceased shareholder's gross estate, if the amount does not exceed the reasonably anticipated total estate and inheritance taxes and funeral and administration expenses incurred by the shareholder's estate.

The absence of a bona fide business reason for a corporation's accumulated earnings may be indicated by many different circumstances, such as a lack of regular distributions to its shareholders or withdrawals by the shareholders classified as personal loans. Actions to expand the business generally qualify as a bona fide reason for the accumulated income.

Specific examples may include:

- The expansion of the company to a new area or a new facility.
- Acquiring another business through the purchase of stock or assets.
- Providing for reasonable estimates of product liability losses.

The fact that a corporation has an unreasonable accumulation of earnings is sufficient to establish liability for the accumulated earnings tax unless the corporation can show the earnings were not accumulated to allow its shareholders to avoid income tax.

Corporate Alternative Minimum Tax

Tax laws give special treatment to some types of income and allow special deductions and credits for some types of expenses. As these laws allow some corporations with substantial economic income to significantly reduce their regular tax liabilities, the corporate alternative minimum tax (AMT) is intended to ensure that corporations pay at least a minimum amount of tax on their income.

Note: A corporation owes AMT if its tentative minimum tax is more than its regular tax.

Small corporations are exempt from corporate AMT. Most corporations will automatically qualify for the exemption in their first year of existence. After its first year, a corporation is considered a small corporation if its average annual gross receipts for the prior three years (or portion thereof) do not exceed $7.5 million ($5 million for its first three-year period). If a corporation fails to be treated as a small corporation in any year, it will be ineligible for the AMT exemption for that year and all subsequent years.

The starting point for the determination of income for AMT purposes is the corporation's regular taxable income. Regular taxable income is modified by a series of additional computations called adjustments and preferences. Adjustments can either increase or decrease taxable income, whereas preferences are calculated on a property-by-property basis and only apply to the extent that they are positive. Adjustments include a portion of accelerated depreciation on buildings and equipment, amortization of pollution control facilities, mining exploration and development expenses, income reported under the completed contract method of accounting, and installment sales income.

Corporations use Form 4626, *Alternative Minimum Tax-Corporations*, to calculate minimum tax for AMT purposes. This calculation includes determining the *alternative tax net operating loss deduction* (ATNOLD), which is the sum of alternative tax net operating loss (ATNOL) carrybacks and carryforwards to the tax year.

The ATNOL for a loss year is the excess of the deductions allowed for figuring alternative minimum taxable income (AMTI), excluding the ATNOLD, over the income included in AMTI.

Note: The amount of the ATNOL that can be deducted when calculating AMT income generally cannot exceed 90% of AMTI. If the ATNOL exceeds this limit, it can be carried back two years or forward up to 20 years.

Corporations use Form 8827, *Credit for Prior Year Minimum Tax*, to figure the minimum tax credit, if any, for alternative minimum tax incurred in prior tax years and any minimum tax credit carryforward. A minimum AMT tax credit may be carried forward indefinitely.

Accounting Methods

Like other entities, C corporations may generally use any permissible accounting method for keeping track of income and expenses.

The "nonaccrual experience method" is a method of accounting for bad debts. If a corporation uses the accrual method of accounting and qualifies to use the nonaccrual experience method for bad debts, it is not required to accrue service-related income that it expects to be uncollectible.

Accrual-method corporations are not required to maintain accruals for certain amounts from the performance of services that, on the basis of their experience, will not be collected, if:

- The services are in the fields of health, law, engineering, architecture, accounting, actuarial science, performing arts, or consulting (personal service corporations); or
- The corporation's average annual gross receipts for the three prior tax years do not exceed $5 million.

This provision does not apply if the corporation charges interest on late payments, or if it charges customers any penalty for failure to pay an amount timely. Further, a corporation cannot use this method for amounts owed from activities such as lending money, selling goods, or acquiring receivables.

Additional Form 1120 Schedules

Corporations may be required to submit certain additional schedules along with their Form 1120. For example, Schedule L includes balance sheets of the beginning and end of the year, based on the corporation's books and records. Small corporations are not required to complete Schedule L if both assets and gross receipts are below $250K for the taxable year.

Differences in accounting rules for financial reporting (book income) and tax reporting can lead to differences in the amounts of income reported to shareholders and tax authorities. Preparation of a C corporation's income tax return includes a reconciliation of book income to taxable income.

Study Note: Be very familiar with the filing requirements for Schedules L, M-1, M-2, and M-3 for the EA exam, as detailed below.

For small corporations with less than $10 million in assets, the differences in book income and taxable income are reconciled on Schedule M-1 of Form 1120. Large corporations with more than $50 million in assets use Schedule M-3, *Net Income (Loss) Reconciliation for Corporations with Total Assets of $10 million or More*.

Example: Armington Corporation had $8 million in assets in 2016. It uses Schedule M-1 to reconcile the difference between its book and taxable income.

Example: Marcus Corporation had $50 million in assets in 2016. It must use Schedule M-3 to reconcile the difference between its book and taxable income.

A recent regulation permits corporations that have at least $10 million but less than $50 million in total assets to file Schedule M-1 in place of Schedule M-3, Parts II and III, which reconcile net income or loss per the income statement and report expense and deduction items. However, Part 1, *Financial Information and Net Income (Loss) Reconciliation*, is still required. Examples of items that would be included in the reconciliation on Schedule M-1 or Schedule M-3, if applicable, are:

- Excess of capital losses over capital gains.
- Charitable contribution carryover (the amount of charitable contributions that are disallowed for tax purposes and must be carried over to the next taxable year).
- Travel and entertainment expenses in excess of the allowable 50% limit.
- Federal income taxes paid or accrued, which are deductible for accounting purposes but not for tax purposes.

- Other expenses recorded on the books but not deductible on the return.
- Advance rental income.
- Other income subject to tax that is not included in book income.
- Tax-exempt interest income.
- Other income included on the books but not subject to tax.
- Deductions on the return not charged against book income.

A foreign corporation that is required to file Form 1120-F generally must also complete Schedule M-2.

Note: Corporations with total receipts and total assets of $250,000 or less at the end of the year are not required to file any of these additional schedules: Schedules L, M-1, M-2, or M-3. Remember this filing threshold.

Contributions of Capital

A corporation is formed initially by a transfer of money, property, or services by prospective shareholders in exchange for stock in the corporation. A transfer of assets may take place when a business that previously operated as a partnership or sole proprietorship opts to become a corporation.

Contributions to the capital of a corporation are generally not taxable transactions to the corporation, whether or not they are made by the shareholders. A shareholder will not recognize gain when a cash contribution is made for stock. This is just like when a person purchases stock on the open market for cash. The shareholder's basis in the stock is the amount of cash contributed.

However, a transfer of property, rather than cash, to a corporation may have tax consequences to both the corporation and the shareholder. For example, if a shareholder contributes property to a corporation, he generally recognizes gain and the basis of the contributed property to the corporation is the same as the basis that the shareholder had in the property, after increase for any gain that the shareholder recognized in the exchange. There is an exception, however, for situations in which property is contributed and the shareholder controls the corporation immediately after the transfer. This is called a section 351 transfer, and is explained below.

The basis of property contributed to a corporation's capital by anyone other than a shareholder is zero.

Example: The city of Omaha, Nebraska gives Enterprise Motors Corporation a plot of land as an enticement to locate its new manufacturing facility there. Enterprise Motor accounts for the property as a contribution to capital. The land has zero basis since the property was contributed by a non-shareholder.

If stock is exchanged for services, the recipient of the stock recognizes taxable income based upon fair market value of the services provided, and that amount is his basis in the stock.

Example: Justin is a web designer who provides web design services to a corporation. He agrees to accept stock as payment instead of cash. The stock is valued at $5,000. Justin must recognize ordinary income of $5,000 as payment for services he rendered to the corporation. His basis in the stock is $5,000.

Section 351: Nontaxable Corporate Transfers

If a taxpayer transfers property to a corporation in exchange for stock, and immediately afterward, the taxpayer controls the corporation, the exchange may not be taxable. This rule applies both to individuals and to entities that transfer property to a corporation. It also applies whether the corporation is being formed or is already in operation. The effect is to allow the investing shareholder to contribute assets to a corporation without immediate tax consequences, and to defer recognition of taxable gain until the stock received is later disposed. This nonrecognition rule does not apply in the following situations:

- The corporation is an investment company.
- The taxpayer transfers the property in a bankruptcy proceeding in exchange for stock that is used to pay creditors.
- The stock is received in exchange for the corporation's debt (other than a security, such as a bond) or for interest on the corporation's debt (including a security) that accrued while the taxpayer held the debt.

In order to be considered "in control" of a corporation immediately after a section 351 exchange, the transferors must own at least 80% of the total combined voting power of all classes of stock entitled to vote and at least 80% of the outstanding shares of each class of nonvoting stock.

Example: Amanda owns an office building. Her basis in the building is $100,000. She organizes a corporation when the building has a fair market value of $300,000. Amanda transfers the building to the corporation for all its authorized capital stock. No gain is recognized by Amanda or the corporation on the transfer.

Example: Aaron transfers property with a basis of $100,000 to a corporation in exchange for stock with a fair market value of $300,000. This represents only 75% of each class of stock of the corporation. The other 25% was already issued to other persons. Aaron must recognize a taxable gain of $200,000 on the transaction.

This nonrecognition rule does not apply to services that are rendered in exchange for stock. The value of stock received for services is income to the recipient.

Example: Wayne is an architect. In 2016, he transfers property worth $35,000 and provides architectural design services valued at $3,000 to a corporation in exchange for stock valued at $38,000. Right after the exchange, Wayne owns 85% of the outstanding stock. No gain is recognized on the exchange of property. However, Wayne must recognize ordinary income of $3,000 as payment for professional services he rendered to the corporation.

If, in an otherwise nontaxable exchange of property for stock, the shareholder receives money or property in exchange for the contribution of property, he would recognize gain to the extent of the money and the fair market value of property received. If the corporation assumes the shareholder's liabilities, the assumption generally is not treated as if the shareholder received money or other property, unless:

- The liabilities the corporation assumes are more than the shareholder's adjusted basis in the property transferred, in which case gain is recognized up to the difference. However, if the liabilities assumed give rise to a deduction when paid, such as a trade account payable or interest, no gain is recognized.
- There is no good business reason for the corporation to assume the liabilities, or if the main purpose in the exchange is to avoid federal income tax.

The shareholder's basis in his stock must be reduced by the amount of the liabilities assumed by the corporation.

Example: Abiah transfers machinery to a corporation in exchange for all of the corporation's outstanding stock. The machinery's FMV at the time of the transfer is $200,000. Abiah's basis in the machinery is $80,000. The machinery is encumbered by an outstanding loan of $30,000, which the corporation assumes. In this example, the section 351 exchange is valid, and no gain or loss is recognized in the transaction. Abiah's basis in the stock is $50,000 ($80,000 basis of property contributed minus the $30,000 loan that was assumed by the corporation).

Study Note: You must understand the concepts related to section 351 transfers as you may encounter multiple questions on this topic on the EA exam.

Both the corporation and certain stockholders involved in a nontaxable exchange of property for stock must attach to their income tax returns a complete statement of all facts pertinent to the exchange. This reporting requirement applies to stockholders who own 5% or more of a public company or 1% or more of a privately held company.[109]

Exclusions from Nonrecognition Treatment

This nonrecognition rule does not apply when the property transferred is of a relatively small value when compared to the value of stock already owned, and the main purpose of the transfer is to qualify for the nonrecognition of gain or loss. Property transferred will not be considered to be of small value if its FMV is at least 10% of the FMV of the stock already owned or to be received by the transferor.

If a group of transferors exchanges property for corporate stock, each transferor may not receive stock in proportion to his interest in the property transferred. However, if a disproportionate transfer takes place, it may be treated as if the stock were first received in proportion to the interests in the property and then portions were used to make gifts, pay compensation for services, or to satisfy the transferor's obligations.

If a corporation transfers its stock in satisfaction of indebtedness and the fair market value of its stock is less than the indebtedness, the corporation has income to the extent of the difference from the cancellation of indebtedness. For example, if stock is given to an individual to pay for a debt, the transfer does not qualify for nonrecognition treatment.

[109] The rules regarding section 351 exchanges also apply to S corporations.

Unit 12: Study Questions

(Please test yourself and check the correct answers at the end of this section.)

1. John transfers property worth $43,000 and renders services valued at $6,000 to a corporation in exchange for stock valued at $49,000. Right after the exchange, John owns 90% of the outstanding stock. How much income, if any, must he recognize in this transaction?

A. $0
B. $3,000
C. $6,000
D. $49,000

2. Which of these domestic business entities will be automatically taxed as a corporation?

1. A joint stock company.
2. An insurance company.
3. Any business formed under a state law that refers to it as a corporation.
4. A single member limited liability company (LLC) owned by an individual.

A. All of the above.
B. 1, 2, and 3
C. 3 only
D. 2 and 3

3. Piping Media Corporation has net income for books of $3 million in 2016. What is its net taxable income if it also has the following activity?

Federal income tax expense	$1,500,000
Travel and entertainment expenses	200,000
Tax-exempt interest income	100,000
Capital losses	47,000
Capital gains	18,000

A. $4,471,000
B. $1,529,000
C. $4,729,000
D. $4,529,000

4. Nell transfers a building with a basis of $200,000 and an FMV of $350,000 to a corporation in exchange for stock with a fair market value of $300,000. This represents 65% of the stock of the corporation. How much gain is recognized by Nell on this transaction?

A. $0 gain or loss
B. $50,000
C. $100,000
D. $150,000

5. The Design Vine Corporation has $1 million of total receipts and $6 million of assets at the end of the year. Which of these schedules is the corporation required to file?

A. Schedule L.
B. Schedule L and M-1.
C. Schedule M-3.
D. Schedule L and M-3.

6. The accumulated earnings tax is levied at a rate of _______ on accumulated taxable income.

A. 5%
B. 15%
C. 20%
D. 50%

7. Lori and Marcus each transfer property with a basis of $10,000 to a corporation in exchange for stock with a fair market value of $30,000. The total stock received by them represents 75% of the corporation's stock. The other 25% of the corporation's stock was issued earlier to Anne, an unrelated person. The taxable consequences are:

A. None, because it is a transfer of property for stock.
B. Lori and Marcus each must recognize a gain of $20,000.
C. Lori and Marcus each must recognize a gain of $30,000.
D. 80% of the transaction is recognized as a taxable gain.

8. Vihaan transferred a small warehouse with an adjusted basis of $10,000 and a fair market value of $140,000 to the Data-Tech Corporation in exchange for 100% of Data-Tech stock. The building was subject to an existing mortgage of $25,000, which Data-Tech Corporation assumed. The fair market value of the stock was $150,000. What are the amounts of Vihaan's realized gain and his recognized gain?

A. $165,000 realized gain; $15,000 recognized gain.
B. $35,000 realized gain; $15,000 recognized gain.
C. $165,000 realized gain; $25,000 recognized gain.
D. $130,000 realized gain; $15,000 recognized gain.

9. Kirsten is trying to decide whether to form an S corporation or a C corporation for her business. What are factors that may persuade her *against* using the C corporation structure?

A. Earnings of a C corporation are taxed twice (at the corporate level and at the shareholder level if they are distributed as dividends).
B. Shareholders of a C corporation cannot deduct corporate losses.
C. A corporation has limited liability.
D. Both A and B.

10. The amount of the alternative tax net operating loss (ATNOL) that can be deducted generally cannot exceed _________ of alternative minimum taxable income (AMTI).

A. 50%
B. 75%
C. 80%
D. 90%

11. To be eligible for section 351 treatment, immediately after the exchange, a taxpayer must own at least _____ of the total combined voting power of all classes or stock entitled to vote and at least ______ of the outstanding shares of each class of nonvoting stock.

A. 50% and 50%
B. 70% and 80%
C. 80% and 80%
D. 80% and 100%

12. Kathleen transferred machinery with an adjusted basis of $70,000 and a fair market value of $110,000 to the Carpenteria Corporation in exchange for 100% of Carpenteria Corporation stock and $20,000 cash. The machinery was encumbered by a loan of $25,000, which the Carpenteria Corporation assumed upon the transfer. The fair market value of the stock that Kathleen received was $75,000. What are the amounts of Kathleen's realized gain and her recognized gain?

A. $25,000 realized gain; $25,000 recognized gain.
B. $50,000 realized gain; $45,000 recognized gain.
C. $50,000 realized gain; $20,000 recognized gain.
D. $35,000 realized gain; $20,000 recognized gain.

13. BRB Corporation's fiscal year ends June 30. Not counting extensions, what is the due date for its tax return?

A. September 15
B. April 15
C. October 15
D. January 15

14. The accumulated earnings tax may be imposed on C corporations that accumulate earnings beyond the reasonable needs of their businesses. Which of the following reasons would not be an example of a reasonable accumulation?

A. The expansion of the company to a new area or a new facility.
B. Acquiring another business through the purchase of stock or other assets.
C. Allowing the shareholders to take bona fide loans from the corporation.
D. Providing for reasonable estimates of product liability losses.

15. Gorilla Pet Products, a cash-basis corporation that operates on the calendar year, is required to make estimated tax payments during the year. What are the due dates for the estimated payments?

A. April 15, June 15, September 15, and December 15.
B. January 15, March 15, June 15, September 15, and December 15.
C. March 1, June 1, September 1, and December 1.
D. None of the above is correct.

Unit 12: Answers

1. The answer is C. John recognizes ordinary income of $6,000 as payment for services he rendered to the corporation. Normally, the exchange of money or property for a controlling interest in a corporation is treated as a nontaxable exchange. However, the exchange of services for stock does not qualify for this treatment. The value of stock received in exchange for services is taxed as income to the recipient.

2. The answer is B. A single member LLC owned by an individual will be taxed as a sole proprietorship unless an election is made by filing Form 8832, *Entity Classification Election.* If a single-member LLC is owned by a C corporation, the LLC is treated as a division of the corporate shareholder for tax purposes – with the LLC's financial information included in the corporation's 1120 corporate tax return. The rest of the choices are automatically required to be taxed as corporations.

3. The answer is D. Piping Media Corporation's net taxable income would be calculated as follows:

Net income for books	$3,000,000
Plus federal income tax expense	1,500,000
Plus 50% of travel and entertainment expenses	100,000
Plus excess of capital losses over capital gains	29,000
Less tax-exempt interest income	(100,000)
Taxable income	**$4,529,000**

A corporation must generally report on either Schedule M-1 or Schedule M-3 the items that reconcile from net income (loss) on their books to taxable income reported on the return. Specific examples may include:

- Excess of capital losses over capital gains.
- Charitable contribution carryover (the amount of charitable contributions that are disallowed and must be carried over to the next taxable year).
- Travel and entertainment in excess of the allowable 50% limit.
- Federal income taxes paid or accrued, which are deductible for accounting purposes but not for tax purposes.
- Advance rental income.
- Differences in book and tax depreciation.

4. The answer is C. Nell must recognize a taxable gain of $100,000 ($300,000 FMV of stock minus $200,000 basis) on the transaction. IRC section 351 provides that no gain or loss will be recognized if property is transferred to a corporation solely in exchange for stock if, immediately after the exchange, the shareholder is in control of the corporation. However, Nell did not control the corporation after the transfer. In order to be in control of a corporation, the transferor must own, immediately after the exchange, at least 80% of the total combined voting power of all classes of stock entitled to vote and at least 80% of the outstanding shares of each class of nonvoting stock. Since Nell owns only 65% of the shares, the exchange is taxable.

5. The answer is B. Design Vine is required to file both, Schedule L, *Balance Sheets Per Books*, and Schedule M-1, *Reconciliation of Income (Loss) per Books with Income per Return,* along with its Form 1120. For small corporations with less than $10 million in assets, the differences in book and taxable income are reconciled in Schedule M-1 of Form 1120. Corporations with less than $250,000 of total receipts and total assets at the end of the year are not required to complete Schedules L, M-1, M-2, or M-3.

6. The answer is C. The accumulated earnings tax is levied at a rate of 20% of the excess amount accumulated.

7. The answer is B. They each must recognize a gain of $20,000 ($30,000 FMV of stock - $10,000 basis). If a shareholder contributes property to a corporation, he generally recognizes gain. The basis of the contributed property to the corporation is the same as the basis that the shareholder had in the property, after increase for any gain that the shareholder recognized in the exchange. There is an exception for situations in which property is contributed and the shareholder controls the corporation immediately after the transfer. In order to be considered in control of a corporation immediately after the exchange, the transferors must own at least 80% of the total combined voting power of all classes of stock entitled to vote and at least 80% of the outstanding shares of each class of nonvoting stock. In this case, Lori and Marcus do not own at least 80% of the corporation immediately afterward, so the exception does not apply.

8. The answer is A. $165,000 realized gain; $15,000 recognized gain. In situations where a shareholder contributes property for stock in a corporation and controls the corporation immediately after the transfer, he typically would not recognize gain. However, if the shareholder receives money or property in addition to the corporation's stock in exchange for his contribution of property, he would recognize gain to the extent of any money received plus the fair market value of property received. If the corporation assumes the shareholder's liabilities, the assumption generally is not treated as if the shareholder received money for this property. However, if the liabilities the corporation assumes are more than the shareholder's adjusted basis in the property transferred, gain is recognized up to the difference. In this case, Vihaan's realized gain is calculated as follows:

Fair market value of stock received	$150,000
Mortgage assumed by corporation	25,000
Total fair market value received	175,000
Adjusted basis of property	(10,000)
Realized gain	**$165,000**

Vihaan recognizes gain to the extent the mortgage assumed ($25,000) exceeds his basis in the property contributed ($10,000), or $15,000.

9. The answer is D. Earnings of a C corporation may be taxed twice: first at the corporate level and again at the shareholder level if they are distributed as dividends. Further, shareholders of a C corporation cannot deduct corporate losses. Both are drawbacks of structuring a business as a C corporation, as opposed to an S corporation or a partnership, both of which are pass-through entities. One of the main benefits of a corporation structure, including C corporations, is the limited liability it affords directors, officers, shareholders, and employees.

10. The answer is D. When calculating the alternative minimum tax, a corporation can substitute the net operating loss with the alternative tax net operating loss (ATNOL). The ATNOL for a loss year is the excess of the deductions allowed for figuring alternative minimum taxable income (AMTI), excluding the ATNOL deduction, over the income included in AMTI. The amount of the ATNOL that can be deducted when calculating AMT income generally cannot exceed 90% of AMTI. If the ATNOL exceeds this limit, it can be carried back two years or forward up to 20 years.

11. The answer is C. When a taxpayer transfers property to a corporation in exchange for stock and immediately afterward controls the corporation, the exchange may qualify for section 351 treatment. The exchange generally would not be taxable until the stock received is later disposed. To be eligible as a section 351 nontaxable exchange, the taxpayer must own, immediately after the exchange, at least 80% of the total combined voting power of all classes of stock entitled to vote and at least 80% of the outstanding shares of each class of nonvoting stock.

12. The answer is C. In situations where a shareholder contributes property for stock in a corporation and controls the corporation immediately after the transfer, the shareholder typically would not recognize gain. However, if the shareholder receives money or property *in addition* to the corporation's stock in exchange for her contribution of property, she would recognize gain to the extent of any money received plus the FMV of property received. In this case, Kathleen's realized gain is calculated as follows:

Fair market value of stock received	$75,000
Cash received	20,000
Mortgage assumed by corporation	25,000
Total fair market value received	120,000
Adjusted basis of property	(70,000)
Realized gain	**$50,000**

Kathleen recognizes gain only to the extent of the cash received ($20,000).

13. The answer is A. The due date for BRB Corporation's income tax return is September 15. A corporation must file its income tax return by the fifteenth day of the fourth month after the end of its tax year. However, C Corporations with fiscal years ending on June 30, the due date for the C corporation return remains September 15, the 15th day of the third month following the close of the fiscal year.

14. The answer is C. Allowing shareholders to draw personal loans from a corporation is not a valid reason for a corporation to accumulate earnings. In fact, this is one of the items the IRS looks for that may lead to imposing the accumulated earnings tax upon a corporation. Making loans to shareholders would allow them to access the corporation's earnings without taking taxable distributions.

15. The answer is A. Installments for corporations are due by the fifteenth day of the fourth, sixth, ninth, and twelfth months of the year. For example, a calendar-year corporation would have estimated tax due dates of April 15, June 15, September 15, and December 15.

Unit 13: Corporate Transactions

More Reading:
Publication 542, *Corporations*

The tax treatment of certain items is different for C corporations, as compared with individuals and other types of entities. C corporations are subject to their own tax rate schedules.

Corporate Capital Gains and Losses

Unlike the favorable capital gains' rates available to individuals, the capital gains of a C corporation are taxed at the same rate as its ordinary income. A corporation figures its capital gains and losses much like an individual. However, in the case of a C corporation, its capital losses are only deductible to the extent of its capital gains. A C corporation is not allowed to offset capital losses against its other income the way individuals can (up to a limit).

Note: Among the drawbacks of the C corporation structure are double taxation; the inability of shareholders to deduct corporate losses; the absence of preferential capital gains tax rates; and the limitation on deductibility of capital losses.

If a corporation has an excess capital loss, it may carry the loss back or forward to other tax years and deduct it from any net capital gains that occurred in those years. The default election is for a corporation to carry back its capital losses to the earliest of the three preceding years in which it had net capital gains; any remaining losses may be carried forward a maximum of five years.

Note: In general, a C corporation's excess capital is carried to other years in the following order:

- Three years prior to the loss year
- Two years prior to the loss year
- One year prior to the loss year
- Any loss remaining is carried forward for five years (with few exceptions).

If after carrying back a net capital loss three years and forward five years, any part of the capital loss still remains, it is lost forever, and the corporation cannot use the loss to offset any future capital gains.

A capital loss from another year cannot create or increase a net operating loss in the year to which it is carried. Further, capital losses can be carried only to years that would otherwise have had a net capital gain.

In rare instances, longer carryback and carryforward periods may be allowed. Capital losses that are a result of foreign expropriation[110] may not be carried back, but may be carried forward for ten years.

In the case of a regulated investment company (RIC), net capital losses may be carried forward eight years. When a corporation carries back or carries forward a capital loss, the loss does not retain its character as a long-term loss. All capital loss carryforwards and carrybacks are treated as short-term losses. A C corporation cannot carry back capital losses to any previous year when it was an S corporation.

[110] This is when a foreign nation takes a corporation's assets for its own use.

Example: In 2016, Chambrun Corporation, a calendar-year C corporation, has a capital gain of $3,000 and a capital loss of $9,000. The capital gain offsets some of the capital loss, leaving a net capital loss of $6,000. Chambrun treats this $6,000 as a short-term loss when carried back or forward. The corporation carries the $6,000 short-term loss back to 2015 (as it had no capital gains in any other prior year). In 2015, Chambrun had a short-term capital gain of $8,000 and a long-term capital gain of $5,000 (a total of $13,000 of capital gains). It carries back the loss and subtracts the $6,000 short-term loss (carryback) first from the net short-term gain. This results in a net capital gain of $7,000 that consists of a net short-term capital gain of $2,000 ($8,000 - $6,000) and a net long-term capital gain of $5,000, which allows the corporation to receive a refund of the income tax it paid in the prior year.

Net Operating Losses (NOLs)

A C corporation figures and deducts a net operating loss (NOL) in the same manner as an individual, an estate, or a trust, and the same carryback (normally up two years) and carryforward (up to 20 years) periods apply. A corporation can elect to forgo the carryback and just carryforward the NOL, but only on a timely filed return. A corporation figures an NOL the same way it figures taxable income. It starts with gross income and subtracts its deductions.

If its deductions are more than its gross income, the corporation has an NOL. However, the following rules apply for figuring NOLs:

- A corporation cannot increase its current year NOL by carrybacks or carryovers from other years in which it has a loss.
- A corporation cannot use the domestic production activities deduction to create or increase a current year NOL.
- A corporation can take the deduction for dividends received, without regard to the aggregate limits that normally apply.
- A corporation can figure the deduction for dividends on certain preferred stock of public utilities without limiting it to its taxable income for the year.

An NOL carryback can only be used to reduce income tax. If the corporation owes other taxes or penalties from a prior year, a carryback will not reduce the penalties.

Example: Artisan Cheese Corporation had taxable income of $30,000 in 2015. Business then slowed, and Artisan Cheese has an NOL of $20,000 in 2016. The company decides to carry back its NOL to recover a portion of the income taxes it paid in 2015. Artisan Cheese also incurred a $220 late-payment penalty in 2015 for failing to remit its estimated taxes on time. The corporation cannot recover the amount paid for the estimated tax penalty, only the amounts paid in income tax.

A C corporation with a net operating loss can file for a refund by using Form 1139 or by amending a prior year tax return using Form 1120X. If a corporation elects to waive carryback and instead carry forward its NOL, it enters the carryover on Form 1120, Schedule K. If the corporation is filing a consolidated return, it must also attach a required statement or the election will not be valid.

If a corporation reasonably expects to have a net operating loss in its current year, it may automatically extend the time for paying income tax liability for the preceding year by filing Form 1138, *Extension of Time For Payment of Taxes by a Corporation Expecting a Net Operating Loss Carryback.*

Corporate Charitable Contributions

Unlike other business entities, C corporations can deduct the amount of charitable contributions made to qualified organizations, up to 10% of taxable income. A corporation figures its taxable income for this limit without regard to the following:

- The deduction for charitable contributions

- The dividends-received deduction
- The domestic production activities deduction
- Any net operating loss carryback to the tax year
- Any capital loss carryback (but not carryforward) to the tax year

The rules regarding what qualifies as a charitable organization and required supporting documentation are the same for corporations as they are for individuals. Generally, no deduction is allowed for any charitable contribution of $250 or more unless the corporation obtains a receipt from the donee organization.

The written receipt or acknowledgment should show the amount of cash contributed or a description of the property contributed. The receipt or acknowledgment should also give a description and a good faith estimate of the value of any goods or services provided in return for the contribution, or state that no goods or services were provided in return for the contribution.

If a corporation (other than a closely held or personal service corporation) claims a deduction of more than $500 for contributions of property other than cash, a schedule describing the property and the method used to determine its fair market value must be attached to the corporation's return. In addition the corporation should keep a record of:

- The approximate date and manner of acquisition of the donated property.
- The cost or other basis of the donated property held by the donor for less than 12 months prior to contribution.
- Any donation of a used vehicle, boat, or similar property if it takes a deduction larger than $500 for the donated vehicle.

If the deduction claimed for donated property exceeds $5,000, the corporation must complete Form 8283, *Noncash Charitable Contributions,* and attach it to its tax return. However, if the corporation is a personal service corporation or a closely held corporation, it must attach Form 8283 for a claimed non-cash charitable contribution of more than $500.

A corporation must obtain a qualified appraisal for all deductions of property claimed in excess of $5,000. A qualified appraisal is not required for the donation of cash, publicly traded securities, or inventory.

A corporation using the cash method deducts contributions in the tax year they are paid. A corporation using the accrual method can deduct unpaid contributions if the board of directors authorized the contributions during the year, and the corporation pays the contributions by the due date for filing the corporation's tax return (not including extensions).

A declaration with a statement that includes the date that the board of directors adopted the resolution must accompany the return.

Example: Affiliated Finance Services, Inc. is a calendar-year, accrual-basis corporation. Affiliated Finance Services' board of directors approves a charitable contribution of $5,000 to the United Way on December 15, 2016. Affiliated Finance Services deducts the contribution on its 2016 corporate tax return. Affiliated Finance Services, Inc. does not have to pay the contribution until April 18, 2017, (the due date for filing the corporation's tax return).

A corporation can carry over charitable contributions made during the current year that exceed the 10% limit to each of the subsequent five years, subject to the same 10% limitation in each year. Any excess contributions not used within that five-year period are lost. No carryback is allowed for charitable contributions.

A corporation cannot deduct a carryover of excess contributions to the extent it increases a net operating loss carryover.

Example: Hernandez Sporting Goods has net income of $600,000 in 2016 before taking into account its charitable contributions. The corporation donated $80,000 to a qualified charity in 2016. It also has a net operating loss carryover of $100,000 from a prior year. Therefore, the corporation's charitable deduction is limited to $50,000. The allowable contribution deduction is figured as follows:

($600,000 - $100,000 = $500,000) × 10% = $50,000

The charitable contribution that is not allowed in the current tax year can be carried forward for up to five years. If Hernandez Sporting Goods does not use the remainder at the end of five years, the deduction is lost.

Example: Gromwell Corporation, a calendar-year C corporation, makes a large charitable contribution in 2016. As a result, the corporation has a carryover of excess contributions paid in 2016 and it does not use all the excess on its return. Gromwell Corporation can carry the rest over to future tax years. After five years, it can no longer carry over the excess charitable contributions and the amounts are lost.

Dividends-Received Deduction

A corporation can deduct a percentage of certain dividends received from other corporations in which it has an ownership interest.

The dividends-received deduction (DRD) is designed to reduce the consequences of double taxation. Without this deduction, corporate profits could be taxed to the corporation that earned them, then to its corporate shareholders, and then again to the individual shareholders of the parent corporation.

The DRD complements the consolidated return regulations, which allow affiliated corporations to file a single consolidated return for U.S. federal income tax purposes. It is available to C corporations but not to LLCs, S corporations, partnerships, or individuals.

If a corporation receives dividends from another corporation, it is entitled to a deduction of 70% of the dividends received, if the corporation owns less than 20% of the other corporation.

If the corporation receiving the dividend owns 20% or more of the other corporation, the deduction increases to 80% of the dividends received. If the corporation receiving the dividends owns more than 80% of the distributing corporation, it is allowed to deduct 100% of the dividends it receives. To summarize, the deduction for dividends received is based on the percentage of stock ownership in the distributing corporation:

Percentage of Stock Ownership	Dividends-Received Deduction
Less than 20%	70%
20 - 80%	80%
Greater than 80%	100%

The percentage of stock ownership is determined without regard to preferred stock.

Example: The Quincy Corporation owns 25% of Magellan Health Corporation. The Quincy Corporation has taxable income of $70,000 before taking into account its dividend income. In 2016, Quincy received $100,000 of dividends from Magellan Health. Quincy is allowed an 80% dividends-received deduction, figured as follows: $80,000 = ($100,000 × 80%). Therefore, only $20,000 of the dividends received from Magellan Health Corporation are taxable. In 2016, the Quincy Corporation's taxable net income is $90,000 ($70,000 + $20,000).

Example: JORDI Corporation owns 85% of the outstanding stock in Humboldt Corporation. In 2016, JORDI receives $250,000 of dividends from Humboldt. Because JORDI has over 80% ownership of Humboldt, it can claim the 100% dividends-received deduction and the dividends are not taxable.

If a corporation is entitled to a 100% DRD, there is no taxable income limitation, and the corporation can deduct the full amount of the dividends received. However, if a corporation is entitled to a 70% DRD, it can deduct amounts only up to 70% of its taxable income. If a corporation is entitled to an 80% DRD, it can deduct amounts only up to 80% of its taxable income. In each case, the corporation would determine taxable income without the following items:

- The DRD
- The net operating loss deduction
- The domestic production activities deduction
- Any adjustment due to the nontaxable part of an extraordinary dividend
- Any capital loss carryback to the tax year

If a corporation has an NOL for a tax year, the DRD must be figured differently. The limit of 80% (or 70%) of taxable income does not apply if use of the unlimited DRD by the receiving corporation would result in a net operating loss.

Example: Verde Eco-Products Corporation loses $25,000 from its own business operations in 2016. Verde Eco-Products also receives $100,000 of dividend income from a 20%-owned corporation. Therefore, Verde Eco-Product's taxable income in 2016 is $75,000 ($100,000 - $25,000 loss) before the DRD. If Verde Eco-Products claims the full DRD of $80,000 ($100,000 × 80%) and combines it with a loss from operations of $25,000, it will create an NOL of ($5,000). Therefore, the 80% of taxable income limit does not apply. The corporation can deduct the full $80,000 DRD.

Example: Redwood Patio Corporation has a loss of $15,000 from business operations in 2016. However, it also has dividends of $100,000 from a corporation in which it holds an interest of 50%. Therefore, Redwood's taxable income is $85,000 before applying the DRD. After claiming the DRD of $80,000 ($100,000 × 80%), its taxable income is $5,000. Because Redwood would not have an NOL after applying a full 80% DRD, its allowable DRD is limited to 80% of its taxable income (before the DRD), or $68,000 ($85,000 × 80%).

Corporations cannot take a deduction for dividends received from the following entities:

- A real estate investment trust (REIT)
- A tax-exempt corporation
- A corporation whose stock was held less than 46 days
- A corporation whose preferred stock was held less than 91 days
- Any corporation, if another corporation is under an obligation to make related payments for positions in substantially similar property

Dividends on deposits in domestic building and loan associations, credit unions, mutual savings banks, cooperative banks, and similar organizations are taxed as interest income—not dividends. They do not qualify for the DRD.

Small business investment companies can deduct 100% of the dividends received from taxable domestic corporations.

Study Note: For the EA exam, you must understand how to calculate the dividends-received deduction and how it applies to a C corporation's taxable income and net operating losses.

Related Party Transactions

Strict rules apply to related party transactions. A corporation that uses the accrual method cannot deduct business expenses and interest owed to a related person who uses the cash method until the corporation makes the related payment and the amount is included in the related person's income. These rules also deny the deduction of a loss on the sale or trade of property (other than in the complete liquidation of a corporation) between related persons.

For purposes of these rules, the following persons are considered related to a corporation:

- A corporation that is a member of the same controlled group.
- An individual who owns, directly or indirectly, more than 50% of the value of the outstanding stock of the corporation.
- A partnership, if the same persons own more than 50% of the value of the outstanding stock of the corporation and more than 50% of the partnership.
- An S corporation, if the same persons own more than 50% of the value of the outstanding stock of each corporation.
- A trust fiduciary, when the trust or its grantor owns, directly or indirectly, more than 50% of the value of the outstanding stock of the corporation.
- An employee-owner of a personal service corporation, regardless of the amount of stock owned.

In determining whether a person directly or indirectly owns any of the outstanding stock of a corporation, the following rules apply:

- Stock directly or indirectly owned by or for a corporation, partnership, estate, or trust is considered owned proportionately by or for its shareholders, partners, or beneficiaries.
- An individual is considered to own the stock that is directly or indirectly owned by or for his family. "Family" includes only brothers and sisters (including half-brothers and half-sisters), a spouse, ancestors, and lineal descendants.[111]
- An individual owning any stock in a corporation is considered to own the stock that is directly or indirectly owned by his partner.

Example: Robert is a 90% owner in Nampa Boots Corporation. His wife, Eileen, is a 55% owner of Terabyte Corporation. Robert is considered a related person for the purposes of ownership in Terabyte Corporation. Therefore, for the related-party transaction rules, Robert is also considered a 55% owner in Terabyte Corporation and Eileen is considered a 90% owner in Nampa Boots Corporation.

Closely Held Corporations

A closely held corporation generally has a small number of shareholders (often family members) and no public market for its stock. Corporate ownership and management often overlap. A corporation is considered to be closely held if both of the following apply:

- It is not a personal service corporation.
- At any time during the last half of the tax year, more than 50% of the value of its outstanding stock is, directly or indirectly, owned by or for five or fewer individuals. An individual in this case includes certain trusts and private foundations.

A closely held corporation is subject to additional limitations in compensation paid to corporate officers and the tax treatment of items such as passive activity losses and at-risk rules. The at-risk rules for closely held corporations are similar to those that apply to partners

[111] A "lineal descendant" is a person who is in direct line to the taxpayer, such as child, grandchild, great-grandchild. For the purpose of this rule, family does not include cousins, step-siblings, uncles, aunts, or in-laws. It also does not include ex-spouses.

in a partnership. These rules dictate that a closely held corporation's losses are only deductible up to the amount at risk of financial loss in connection with an activity. The amount at risk generally equals:

- The money and the adjusted basis of property contributed by the taxpayer to the activity, and
- The money borrowed for the activity.

The at-risk amount also includes the FMV of property (adjusted for any liens or encumbered mortgages) that is pledged as security or collateral for the debts of the activity. The following items increase an entity's amount at risk:

1. A contribution of additional cash (or property) to the venture.
2. Any recourse loan for which the corporation is liable for repayment.

The amount at risk is decreased by the following items:

1. An investor's withdrawal of cash or property from the activity.
2. A nonrecourse loan where the corporation is not liable for repayment.

The amount at risk cannot be decreased below zero. If this occurs, suspended losses from prior years must be reduced.

Example: Allworth Corporation is a closely held C corporation with only two shareholders: a father and son. Allworth Corp. invests $50,000 in a business venture, and also pledges the value of a factory building as collateral for a $100,000 loan that is used in the business venture. Allworth's factory building has a fair market value of $150,000. Allworth Corp.'s amount at risk in the business venture is only $100,000 [$50,000 plus the $50,000 ($150,000 - $100,000) equity in the building].

Controlled Groups

Under federal law, related companies and organizations are treated as a single group for certain tax purposes. A controlled group is a group of corporations that are related through common ownership, typically as either parent-subsidiary or brother-sister.

A controlled group is allowed a single set of graduated income tax brackets, a single exemption amount for AMT purposes, and a single accumulated earnings credit of $250,000. In each case, these amounts must be allocated among the members of the group. Members of controlled groups are also subject to the rules regarding related party transactions that may require deferral of recognition for losses or expenses incurred by one party.

A **Parent-Subsidiary Controlled Group** involves a parent corporation that owns at least 80% of the voting power of at least one other corporation (with possible additional corporations that are at least 80% owned by either the common parent or one of the subsidiary entities).

Example of a Parent-Subsidiary Controlled Group:

Ciara Corporation owns:

- 90% of the stock of Shiffrin Corporation
- 80% of the stock of Noble Holdings Corporation
- 65% of the stock of Bowes Corporation

Unrelated persons own the percentage of stock not owned by Ciara Corporation. As Ciara Corporation owns 80% or more of the stock of Shiffrin and Noble Holdings, it is the common parent of a parent-subsidiary group consisting of the three corporations. Bowes Corporation is not a member of the group because Ciara Corporation's ownership is less than 80%.

A **Brother-Sister Controlled Group** involves situations in which five or fewer individuals, estates, or trusts own 80% or more of the combined voting power for multiple corporations, and have identical common ownership within the individual corporations of at least 50%. In other words, "effective control" requires collective ownership of more than 50% of the stock of each corporation, (but only to the extent such stock ownership is identical with respect to each corporation).

Example of a Brother-Sister Controlled Group:

Kendrick Corporation and Leitzel Corporation are owned by four unrelated shareholders in the following percentages:

Shareholder	Kendrick Corp.	Leitzel Corp.
Albert	70%	30%
Benny	10%	50%
Cristobel	10%	10%
Derrick	10%	10%
Total Ownership	**100%**	**100%**

The same five (or fewer) common owners must own more than 80% of stock or some interest in all members of the controlled group. In this example, the four shareholders together own 100% of the stock of each corporation, so the first test is met. They also meet the second test of owning more than 50% of the stock of both corporations (the same four individuals, in aggregate, own at least 50% of both corporations), taking into account only the identical ownership in each corporation.

Shareholder	Identical Ownership Percentage in Both Corporations
Albert	30%
Benny	10%
Christabel	10%
Derrick	10%
Total	**60%**

Unit 13: Study Questions

(Test yourself and then check the correct answers at the end of this section.)

1. During 2016, Bernardino Fine Jewelry, a domestic C corporation, had the following income, expenses, and deductions:

Gross receipts	$95,000
Net capital gains	10,000
Business expenses (not including charitable contributions)	65,000
Charitable contribution	20,000
NOL carryover from the prior year	30,000

What is the amount of Bernardino Jewelry's allowable charitable contribution deduction for 2015?

A. $1,000
B. $3,000
C. $4,000
D. $20,000

2. Which of the following statements is correct about a controlled group of corporations?

A. Members of a controlled group are entitled to only one accumulated earnings tax credit.
B. A parent corporation and its 80% owned subsidiary would be considered members of a controlled group.
C. Members of controlled groups are subject to rules regarding related party transactions that may require deferral of recognition for losses or expenses incurred by one party.
D. All of the above.

3. James Corporation owns 50% of Nguyen Corporation's outstanding common stock. James has taxable income of $8,000, which includes dividends received of $10,000 from its investment in Nguyen Corporation. What is James Corporation's taxable income after applying the DRD?

A. $0
B. $1,600
C. $6,400
D. $8,000

4. Rosa's Fine Stationery is a cash-basis C corporation. During the year, Rosa's received $140,000 in dividends from a domestic corporation in which it owns less than 20% of the stock. Rosa's has taxable income of $180,000 during the year, before figuring the dividends-received-deduction. Based on this information, what is the dividends-received-deduction for Rosa's Fine Stationery?

A. $70,000
B. $98,000
C. $100,000
D. $126,000

5. BMD Corporation is a calendar-year corporation that uses the accrual method. What is the last day that the corporation can pay a charitable contribution and still deduct it on its 2016 tax return?

A. December 31, 2016
B. January 15, 2017
C. March 15, 2017
D. April 18, 2017

6. Acclimated Corporation owns 25% of Wilson Fine Foods Corporation. In 2016, Acclimated received $10,000 of dividends from Wilson's Fine Foods, Inc. Assuming no other limitations apply, Acclimated's dividends-received deduction is:

A. $7,000
B. $8,000
C. $2,000
D. $0

7. In 2016, Reliable Corporation made contributions totaling $20,000 to qualified charitable organizations. Due to income limitations, Reliable Time could deduct only $15,000 of the contributions on its return. Which of the following correctly states the treatment of the excess $5,000 of charitable contributions?

A. It can be carried back for two years and carried forward for 20 years.
B. It can be carried forward for 20 years.
C. It can be carried back for three years and carried forward for ten years.
D. It can be carried forward for five years. They cannot be carried back.

8. The Ababa Plastics Corporation is a calendar-year C corporation. In 2016, it has $400,000 of taxable income before consideration of the following additional items:

- Charitable contributions: $50,000
- Dividends-received deduction: $70,000
- Domestic production activities deduction: $40,000

What portion of the charitable contributions is deductible?

A. $50,000
B. $29,000
C. $40,000
D. $36,000

9. Xena Corporation is a cash-basis C corporation. In 2016, the corporation has a net short-term capital gain of $23,000 and a net long-term capital loss of $29,000. How should these capital gains and losses be treated?

A. The corporation can deduct a $6,000 long-term capital loss on its 2016 tax return.
B. The corporation can carry back the $29,000 long-term capital loss to a prior year, where it may only be deducted against long-term capital gains.
C. The corporation can carry back the $6,000 net capital loss to a prior year, where it may be deducted against short-term capital gains.
D. The corporation must carry forward the entire capital loss to the following tax year. Carryback of capital losses is not allowed.

10. Which of the following best describes a brother-sister controlled group?

A. A brother and sister each own 50% of a corporation, or a total of 100% of the corporation combined.
B. A parent corporation that owns at least 80% or more of the voting power of at least one other corporation, with at least two brothers and one sister or two sisters and one brother as owners.
C. Five or fewer individuals, estates, or trusts own 80% or more of the combined voting power for multiple corporations, and have identical common ownership within the individual corporations of at least 50%.
D. A corporation that controls at least two other corporations where a brother and sister are chief executive officers of the different corporations and each control over 50% of their respective corporations.

11. In 2016, Mansour Corporation has a $15,000 loss from its business operations. In addition, Mansour has received $100,000 of taxable dividends from a 30%-owned corporation. Therefore, its taxable income is $85,000 before applying the dividends-received deduction. What is the corporation's dividends-received deduction?

A. $15,000
B. $68,000
C. $80,000
D. $100,000

12. The Surf's Up Corporation had an NOL of $110,000. Which of the following statements is correct?

A. The corporation can forgo the carryback period and choose to carry the entire loss forward to the next 20 years.
B. The corporation is required to carry back losses for two years and then forward for 15 years.
C. The corporation can carry back losses five years and carry them forward for 25 years.
D. A corporation cannot carry back losses. It can only carry them forward.

13. Redd Beauty Products and Helena Mountain Coffee are both domestic C corporations. Redd Beauty Products owns 25% of Helena Mountain Coffee. Redd Beauty's income from its business operations in 2016 is $500,000. In addition to its business income, Redd Beauty received dividends from Helena Mountain Coffee of $145,000. What is Redd Beauty's dividends-received deduction?

A. $36,250
B. $101,500
C. $116,000
D. $145,000

14. Kendall Corporation has net income of $600,000 before its charitable contribution of $65,000. The company also has an NOL carryover of $200,000 from the prior year. What is Kendall Corporation's allowable charitable contribution?

A. $0
B. $6,500
C. $60,000
D. $40,000

Unit 13: Answers

1. The answer is A. A C corporation can deduct charitable contributions made to qualified organizations, up to 10% of taxable income. Taxable income for this purpose is determined without regard to certain items, including the charitable contribution deduction itself and any net operating loss carryback (but not carryforward) to the tax year. Therefore, Bernardino Jewelry's charitable contribution deduction would be determined as follows:

Gross receipts	$95,000
Expenses	(65,000)
Net capital gains	10,000
NOL from 2012	(30,000)
Taxable income before contribution deduction	10,000
Deduction limit at 10%	**$1,000**

2. The answer is D. A parent-subsidiary controlled group involves a parent corporation that owns at least 80% or more of the voting power of at least one other corporation. A controlled group is allowed a single set of graduated income tax brackets, a single exemption amount for AMT purposes, and a single accumulated earnings credit of $250,000. Members of controlled groups are also subject to rules regarding related party transactions that may require deferral of recognition for losses or expenses incurred by one party.

3. The answer is B. James Corporation cannot deduct the full $8,000 (80% × $10,000) dividends-received deduction that would normally apply based upon its 50% ownership, because doing so would not result in a net operating loss. The deduction is instead limited to 80% of taxable income (before applying the DRD), which is $6,400 (80% × $8,000). Taxable income after applying the IRD is $1,600 ($8,000 - $6,400).

4. The answer is B. The DRD deduction for a corporation that owns less than 20% of the stock is 70% of the dividends received ($140,000 × 70% = $98,000). The DRD is limited to taxable income unless the corporation has an NOL after considering the deduction.

5. The answer is D. The corporation can have until the due date of its tax return to pay the contribution. A corporation using the accrual method can choose to deduct unpaid contributions for the tax year if the board of directors authorizes the contribution during the tax year, and the corporation pays the contribution before the due date of the return. The due date for calendar year C Corporations is April 18, 2017.

6. The answer is B. If a corporation receiving dividends owns 20% or more of the corporation issuing the dividends, it generally qualifies for a dividends-received deduction equal to 80% of the dividends received. Therefore, Acclimated Corporation can deduct amounts up to 80% of its taxable income, calculated without regard to the DRD itself and certain other items ($10,000 × .80 = $8,000).

7. The answer is D. Reliable Corporation can carry over excess charitable contributions made during the year that result from the 10% limit on deductibility to each of the subsequent five years. Any excess charitable contributions that are not used in this five-year period are lost. A corporation cannot carry back excess charitable contributions.

8. The answer is C. The corporation's deductible charitable contributions are limited to 10% of its taxable income, before consideration of the following items:

- The deduction for charitable contributions
- The dividends-received deduction
- The domestic production activities deduction
- Any net operating loss carryback to the tax year
- Any capital loss carryback to the tax year

Qualifying contributions in excess of this limitation can be carried over for five years. In this case, $40,000 ($400,000 × 10%) would be deductible, and $10,000 would be carried over to the following year.

9. The answer is C. The corporation may carry back the $6,000 capital loss ($29,000 - $23,000) to the earliest of the three preceding years, where it may be deducted against short-term capital gains. Any remaining losses can be carried forward for up to five years. The corporation treats this $6,000 as a short-term capital loss when carried back or forward, because capital loss carrybacks and carryforwards do not retain their original character.

10. The answer is C. A brother-sister controlled group is when five or fewer individuals, estates, or trusts own 80% or more of the combined voting power for multiple corporations, and have identical common ownership within the individual corporations of at least 50%. Despite the name, the owners do not have to be related as siblings.

11. The answer is B. The corporation would not have an NOL after applying the full dividends-received deduction, so its allowable dividends-received deduction is limited to 80% of its taxable income (before applying the DRD), or $68,000 ($85,000 × 80%).

12. The answer is A. A corporation is not *required* to carry back losses. It may *elect* to forgo the carryback period, as long as the election is made on a timely filed return. Net operating losses can be carried back to the two years before the loss year and forward for up to 20 years following the loss year.

13. The answer is C. Generally, if a corporation receives dividends from another corporation in which it owns an interest of 20% to 80%, it is entitled to a deduction of 80% of the dividends received, subject to limitation based upon its taxable income without regard to the DRD and certain other items. Since Redd owns 25% of Helena, its DRD is $116,000 ($145,000 × 80%).

14. The answer is D. The corporation's charitable contribution is limited to $40,000 and is calculated as follows: ($600,000 - $200,000) × 10% = $40,000. A C corporation can claim a limited deduction for charitable contributions. The deduction is limited to 10% of taxable income, calculated before the charitable contribution, dividends-received deduction, and net operating loss or capital loss carrybacks (but not carryforwards).

Unit 14: Corporate Distributions & Liquidations

More Reading:
Publication 542, *Corporations*

Corporate Distributions

Corporate distributions or dividends occur when cash, stock, or other property is distributed to shareholders based on the shareholders' ownership of the corporation's stock. When a corporation earns profits, it may retain the profits in the business (as retained earnings) or pay all or a portion of the profits as dividends to shareholders. The amounts a corporation pays as dividends are not deductible expenses. Dividends are most commonly paid in cash. However, a dividend can take the form of stock or other property. The most common kinds of corporate distributions are:

- Ordinary dividends (either in cash or in property)
- Capital gain distributions
- Nondividend distributions
- Distributions of stock or stock rights

The FMV of distributed property becomes the shareholder's basis in the property. A distribution may be reduced by the following liabilities:

- Any liability of the corporation the shareholder assumes
- Any liability applicable to distributed property, such as mortgage debt the shareholder assumes in connection with distribution of ownership in a building

The basis of distributed property can never go below zero, no matter how much liability a shareholder assumes.

Reporting Requirements for Distributions

A corporation must furnish Form 1099-DIV, *Dividends and Distributions,* to each shareholder who receives a dividend of $10 or more during a calendar year by January 31 of the following year.

The corporation must also file copies of the Forms 1099-DIV with the IRS, along with Form 1096, *Annual Summary and Transmittal of U.S. Information Returns,* is generally due by February 28 (March 31 if filing electronically)[112] of the year following the year of the distribution.

The corporation is allowed to furnish Forms 1099-DIV to shareholders any time after April 30 of the year of the distributions if the corporation has made its final distributions for the calendar year.

Distributions from Earnings and Profits

The amount of a C corporation's earnings and profits (E&P) determines the tax treatment of corporate distributions to shareholders.

The starting point for determining corporate E&P is the corporation's taxable income. The following are the most common transactions that **increase** the amount of E&P:

- Long-term contracts reported on the completed contract method
- Intangible drilling costs deducted currently
- Mine exploration and development costs deducted currently
- Dividends-received deduction

[112] The IRS e-file deadline for information returns such as Forms 1099 is usually March 31, whereas if the corporation is filing these forms by paper, the deadline is February 28. However, the deadlines to provide the form to the recipient will vary. Starting in 2017, the federal government versions of Forms W-2 and certain 1099-MISC (those showing nonemployee compensation) are now due on or before January 31.

- Interest income on state and local bonds
- Nontaxable life insurance proceeds
- Federal income tax refunds
- Domestic production activities deduction
- Deferred gain on installment sales

The following are the most common transactions that **reduce** the amount of E&P:

- Corporate federal income taxes
- Life insurance policy premiums on a corporate officer
- Excess charitable contributions (over 10% limit)
- Expenses relating to tax-exempt income
- Excess of capital losses over capital gains
- Corporate dividends and other distributions
- Fines and penalties
- Nondeductible lobbying expenses
- Nondeductible portion of meals and entertainment

Accumulated Earnings and Profits

Accumulated earnings and profits are earnings and profits (E&P) that the corporation accumulated in a prior year and has not distributed to its shareholders. If a corporation's current year E&P are less than the total distributions made during the year, part or all of each distribution is treated as a distribution of accumulated E&P.

Note: Any part of a distribution from current-year earnings and profits or accumulated earnings and profits is reported as dividend income to the shareholder and is generally taxable as ordinary income to the shareholder rather than as capital gains.

If accumulated earnings and profits are reduced to zero, the remaining part of a distribution reduces the adjusted basis of the shareholder's stock. This is referred to as a nondividend distribution and it is not taxable to the shareholder until his basis in the stock is fully recovered. This nontaxable portion is considered to be a *return of capital* that he had previously invested in the corporation.

Definition: Return of capital refers to the return of some or all of an investor's investment in a company or partnership. Since it represents the recoupment of investment, return of capital is not considered income, but instead decreases the net value and tax basis of the investment.

If the corporation makes nondividend distributions to a shareholder that exceed the adjusted basis of his stock, the excess distribution is treated as a gain from the sale or exchange of property and is taxable to the shareholder as capital gain.

Example: Tobias is the only shareholder of Seaside Corporation, a calendar-year corporation. During the year, Seaside makes four $1,000 distributions to Tobias. At the end of the year (before subtracting distributions made during the year), the corporation has $10,000 of current year earnings and profits. Since the corporation's current year E&P ($10,000) were more than the amount of the distributions it made during the year ($4,000), all of the distributions are treated as distributions of current-year E&P. The corporation must issue Form 1099-DIV to Tobias by January 31 to report the $4,000 distributed to him as dividends. Seaside Corporation must use Form 1096, *Annual Summary and Transmittal of U.S. Information Returns*, to report this transaction to the IRS by February 28 (March 31 if filing electronically). The corporation does not deduct these dividends on its income tax return.

If nondividend distributions are made to shareholders, the corporation must report these distributions to the IRS on Form 5452, *Corporate Report of Nondividend Distributions*.

Distributions of Property

A sale or exchange of property by a corporation to a shareholder that is not a corporation may be treated as a distribution to the shareholder, to the extent the FMV of the property on the date of the sale or exchange exceeds the price he paid.

A distribution of property is also treated as if the corporation had sold the property to the shareholder. A corporation (either a C corporation or an S corporation) recognizes gain on a distribution of property to a shareholder if the FMV of the property is more than its adjusted basis.

Example: Wright Stuff Corporation distributes to a shareholder $65,000 of cash and an excavator with a $35,000 adjusted basis and a $50,000 FMV. Wright Stuff must recognize a $15,000 gain on the distribution of property because its FMV is more than its adjusted basis ($50,000 - $35,000 = $15,000).

For this purpose, the FMV is considered to be the greater of the property's actual FMV or the amount of liabilities the shareholder assumes in connection with the distribution. If the distributed property was depreciable or amortizable, the corporation may have to treat all or a portion of the gain as ordinary income from depreciation recapture.

These transactions may be taxable to the shareholder at FMV and are reported on Form 1099-DIV or Form 5452, *Corporate Report of Nondividend Distributions*. A corporation generally cannot recognize a loss on a distribution of property (i.e., where the property's FMV is less than the adjusted cost basis). However, a corporation is allowed to recognize losses when depreciated property is distributed to shareholders in complete liquidation (when the corporation ceases operations).

Stock Distributions

Stock distributions or stock dividends occur when a corporation issues additional shares of its own stock to shareholders, rather than paying a cash dividend or distributing property.

Stock rights, also known as stock options, may be distributed by a corporation to some or all of its shareholders to allow them to purchase additional shares at a set price.

Distributions by a corporation of its own stock or stock rights are tax-free to shareholders and not deductible by the corporation. However, they may be treated as taxable property distributions in rare situations, including when:

- The shareholder has the choice to receive cash or other property instead of stock or stock rights.
- The distribution gives cash or other property to some shareholders and an increase in the percentage interest in the corporation's assets or earnings and profits to other shareholders.
- The distribution is in convertible preferred stock.
- The distribution gives preferred stock to some shareholders and common stock to other shareholders.
- The distribution is paid based on ownership of preferred stock.

A corporation must capitalize, rather than deduct, the expenses of issuing a stock dividend, such as printing, postage, and any fees for listing on stock exchanges.

Constructive Distributions

A constructive distribution may occur when a corporation confers a benefit upon a shareholder. A transaction recorded by the corporation as an expense may be recategorized instead as a constructive distribution.

This would make the transaction nondeductible to the corporation and in many instances taxable to the shareholder.

Examples of constructive distributions include:

- **Payment of personal expenses:** If a corporation pays personal expenses on behalf of a shareholder, the amounts should be classified as a distribution rather than expenses of the corporation.
- **Unreasonable compensation:** If a corporation pays an employee-shareholder an unreasonably high salary considering the services actually performed, the excessive part of the salary may be treated as a distribution.
- **Unreasonable rents:** If a corporation rents property from a shareholder and the rent is unreasonably higher than the shareholder would charge an unrelated party for use of the property, the excessive part of the rent may be treated as a distribution.
- **Cancellation of a shareholder's debt:** If a corporation cancels a shareholder's debt without repayment by the shareholder, the amount canceled may be treated as a distribution.
- **Property transfers for less than FMV:** If a corporation transfers or sells property to a shareholder for less than its FMV, the excess may be treated as a distribution.
- **Below market or interest-free loans**: If a corporation gives a loan to a shareholder on an interest-free basis or at a rate below the applicable federal rate, the uncharged interest may be treated as a distribution.

Example: Jambi Corporation rents office space from a 75% shareholder, Alan, who is the sole owner of the office building. The corporation pays Alan $15,000 a month for its space. He charges other tenants $5,000 a month for offices with the same square footage. The excessive rent of $120,000 ($15,000 - $5,000 = $10,000 × 12 months) would likely be disallowed as an expense for Jambi Corporation and recharacterized as a constructive distribution to Alan.

Stock Redemptions

A stock redemption occurs when a corporation buys back its own stock from a shareholder in exchange for cash or property. The stock acquired may be canceled, retired, or held as Treasury stock.

A shareholder is required to treat the amount realized on a stock redemption as either a dividend or a sale of stock. Stock redemptions are generally treated as dividends unless certain conditions are met, as follows:

- The redemption is not equivalent to a dividend, meaning that the shareholder's proportionate interest and voting power in the corporation has been substantially reduced.
- There was a substantially disproportionate redemption of stock, meaning that the amount received by the shareholder is not in proportion to his stock ownership.
- The redemption was due to a complete termination of a shareholder's interest in the corporation.
- The redemption is of stock held by a non-corporate shareholder and was part of a partial liquidation.
- The distribution is received by an estate and does not exceed the sum of death taxes plus funeral and administration expenses to be paid by the estate.

The corporation may realize a gain from the redemption, as if property were sold at its fair market value to the shareholder. The corporation must recognize income on the distribution of depreciated property to the extent of depreciation or the amount realized (whichever is less). The corporation may not recognize a loss on a stock redemption unless:

- The redemption occurs in a complete liquidation of the corporation, or
- The redemption occurs on stock held by an estate.

Corporate Liquidations and Dissolutions

Liquidating distributions are distributions received by a shareholder during a complete or partial dissolution of a corporation. When a corporation dissolves, it redeems all of its stock in a series of distributions.

Complete liquidation occurs when the corporation ceases to be a going concern and its activities are merely for the purpose of winding up its affairs, paying its debts, and distributing any remaining balance to its shareholders.

In certain cases in which the buyer is a corporation in control of the distributing corporation, the distribution may not be taxable. A corporate dissolution or liquidation must be reported on Form 966, *Corporate Dissolution or Liquidation*, within 30 days after the resolution or plan is adopted to dissolve the corporation or liquidate any of its stock. Exempt entities are not required to file Form 966, even if they are organized as corporations.

When property is distributed in a complete liquidation, the transaction is treated as if the corporation sold the assets to a buyer at fair market value. The corporation recognizes gain or loss on the liquidation in an amount equal to the difference between the FMV and the adjusted basis of the assets distributed. A corporation is allowed to recognize losses during the liquidation, except for losses resulting from transactions with related parties.

Example: Blair Corporation distributes a building to one of its shareholders as part of a complete liquidation. The adjusted basis of the building is $750,000 and its fair market price is $400,000. Blair Corporation can recognize a loss of $350,000.

Amounts received by the shareholder in complete liquidation of a corporation are treated as full payment in exchange for the shareholder's stock. A liquidating distribution is considered a return of capital and is not taxable to the shareholder until the shareholder recovers all of his basis in the stock.

After the basis of the stock has been reduced to zero, shareholders must report any additional amounts as a capital gain. If a dissolving corporation distributes property that is subject to a liability, the gain or loss is adjusted to reflect assumption of the liability. If the liability is greater than the FMV of the property, the amount of the liability is treated as the FMV of the property. A corporation is required to provide each shareholder a Form 1099-DIV showing the amount of the liquidating distribution.

Example: Maurer Farm Equipment Corporation is going through a complete liquidation. Saul, a shareholder, receives a liquidating distribution of property (a tractor). Maurer Corporation's basis in the tractor is $3,000. The fair market value of the tractor is $13,000. However, the tractor is encumbered by a liability of $15,000 (an unpaid loan), which Saul assumes. Because the remaining loan amount is more than the FMV of the tractor, the amount of the liability is treated as the FMV. The corporation must recognize a $12,000 gain on the distribution ($15,000 loan - $3,000 basis), and Saul is treated as having received a liquidating distribution of $15,000.

A corporation must file an income tax return for the year it goes out of business, even if it has no income or business activity in that year. If the dissolution is effective on any day other than the last day of the corporation's tax year, the final tax return is due on the fifteenth day of the fourth month following the close of its short tax year.

Unit 14: Study Questions

(Test yourself and then check the correct answers at the end of this section.)

1. Ryan is a minority shareholder (1% shareholder) in PRK Corporation with a basis of $20,000 in his stock. He also has an outstanding $10,000 loan that he owes to the corporation. In 2013, Ryan has financial difficulties and defaults on the loan. PRK Corporation tries to collect for a few years, but finally cancels Ryan's debt in 2016. How should this cancellation of debt be reported?

A. The debt cancellation is treated as a $10,000 distribution to Ryan.
B. The debt cancellation is considered a return of capital to Ryan.
C. The debt cancellation is a charitable contribution to Ryan.
D. The debt cancellation is a $10,000 capital gain to Ryan.

2. Pasqual Corporation has operated on a fiscal year that runs from August 1 through September 30. However, the corporation is having financial trouble and is dissolved on February 10. When is its final tax return due?

A. April 15
B. June 15
C. June 30
D. September 15

3. Trotter Corporation distributes to a shareholder $75,000 of cash and a delivery truck with a $40,000 adjusted basis and a $60,000 FMV. What gain or loss, if any, must Trotter Corporation recognize?

A. No gain or loss is recognized in this transaction.
B. $20,000 gain
C. $40,000 gain
D. $20,000 loss

4. Three years ago, Mark purchased 100 shares of Rock Star, Inc. for $10 per share. In 2016 Rock Star completely liquidated and distributed $20,000 to Mark in exchange for all of his stock. Mark must report this distribution as:

A. $20,000 of long-term capital loss.
B. $19,000 of short-term capital gain.
C. $19,000 of long-term capital gain.
D. $19,000 of ordinary income.

5. All of the examples below are considered corporate distributions except:

A. Ordinary dividends to a shareholder.
B. Capital gain distributions to a shareholder.
C. Constructive distributions to an employee-shareholder.
D. Wage compensation to an employee-shareholder.

6. Geraldine owns 1,000 shares of Beckman Software Corporation. Her shares were all acquired three years ago, and her basis in the stock is $20,000. Beckman Software completely liquidated on November 30, 2016 and distributed $56,000 in two payments to Geraldine. She received $16,000 on December 5, 2016 and $40,000 on January 10, 2017. How much gain or loss does Geraldine recognize in 2016 and 2017?

A. $4,000 loss in 2016 and $40,000 gain in 2017.
B. $4,000 loss in 2016 and $44,000 gain in 2017.
C. No gain or loss in 2016 and $40,000 gain in 2017.
D. No gain or loss in 2016 and $36,000 gain in 2017.

7. Distributions of stock rights are generally tax-free to shareholders. Which of the following statements is not correct?

A. Even if a shareholder has a choice to receive cash instead of stock rights, so long as the shareholder chooses to receive stock rights, the distribution will be tax-free.
B. Stock rights are distributions by a corporation of rights to acquire its own stock.
C. Stock rights are sometimes called stock options.
D. Stock rights can be taxable in some circumstances.

8. The Midwestern Grain Corporation distributes property with an adjusted basis of $1,000 and a fair market value of $4,000 subject to a liability of $6,000 to Joseph, a shareholder. Joseph assumes the $6,000 liability. What is the gain or loss, if any, Midwestern Grain must recognize as a result of the distribution?

A. $1,000 loss
B. $3,000 gain
C. $5,000 gain
D. $0

9. April bought 50 shares of Briggspoint, Inc. stock five years ago for $1,000. In 2014, she received a return of capital distribution of $800. April did not include this amount in her income, but correctly reduced the basis of her stock to $200. She received another return of capital distribution of $300 in 2016. The first $200 of this amount reduced April's stock basis to zero. How should she report the remaining $100 distribution?

A. April must report $100 of long-term capital gain.
B. April does not have to report the additional return of capital.
C. April must report the $100 as ordinary income.
D. April must report any additional return of capital as a capital loss.

10. Which of the following statements about stock distributions is correct?

A. A stock distribution must be treated like a cash distribution that is taxable to the shareholder.
B. Stock distributions are usually taxable to the corporation when distributed to shareholders.
C. Stock distributions are deductible by a corporation as an expense.
D. Stock distributions are generally not taxable to shareholders and not deductible by the corporation.

11. Buffalo Corporation displays a collection of fine artwork in its main office. When the 75% shareholder retires, he is presented with his choice from the art collection. He selects a painting with a fair market value of $250,000. Buffalo Corporation's basis in the painting is $100,000. How should the transaction be reported on the Buffalo Corporation's tax return?

A. $150,000 loss
B. $150,000 distribution
C. $150,000 taxable gain
D. $250,000 taxable gain

12. When using taxable income as a starting point, which of the following transactions increases the amount of a C corporation's earnings and profits?

A. Excess of capital losses over capital gains.
B. Dividends-received deduction.
C. Life insurance premiums on a corporate officer.
D. Excess charitable contributions.

13. Millerton Software is a C corporation that was formed in 2010. At the beginning of 2016, Millerton Software had accumulated earnings and profits of $100,000. The company makes a $5,000 distribution to its 100% shareholder in the first month of each quarter (four distributions throughout the year). At the end of the year, Millerton Software had $150,000 of gross income and $140,000 of expenses from ordinary business operations. Millerton also received $5,000 in fully tax-exempt interest from state bonds. What part of the second quarter distribution is treated as a distribution of accumulated earnings and profits?

A. $1,250
B. $2,500
C. $3,750
D. $5,000

14. Six years ago, Sabine purchased 100 shares of Vitality Nature Corporation stock for $50 per share. In 2016, the corporation completely stopped operations and liquidated. After paying its outstanding liabilities, Vitality Nature distributed $10,000 of cash and appreciated property worth $90,000 to its shareholders. Sabine's portion of the distributed assets and cash was $12,000. What must she report from this liquidating distribution in 2016?

A. $0 gain
B. $3,000 capital gain
C. $7,000 capital gain
D. $10,000 capital gain

Unit 14: Answers

1. The answer is A. If a corporation cancels a shareholder's debt without repayment by the shareholder, the amount canceled is treated as a distribution to the shareholder.

2. The answer is B. A corporation must file an income tax return for the year it goes out of business, even if it has no income or business activity in that year. This is called a "short year" return. In Pasqual Corporation's case, that date is June 15 (the 15th day of the fourth month *after* the month the corporation was officially dissolved).

3. The answer is B. A corporation will recognize a gain on the distribution of property to a shareholder if the FMV of the property is more than its adjusted basis ($60,000 FMV - $40,000 adjusted basis = $20,000 gain). This is the same treatment that would apply if the property were sold for its FMV.

4. The answer is C. Mark has a $19,000 long-term capital gain. His basis in the stock was $1,000 (100 shares stock × $10), so his gain is figured as follows: ($20,000 distribution - $1,000 basis). Gain or loss recognized by shareholders on distributions in a corporate liquidation is generally determined by the difference between the total of the cash and property received by the shareholders and the basis of the stock they surrendered. The gain or loss will be long-term or short-term depending on the length of time the stock was held. Since Mark purchased the shares several years ago, his holding period exceeds one year and is therefore recognized as long-term capital gain on his return.

5. The answer is D. Salaries or wages paid to an employee-shareholder are not considered a distribution. Instead, the wages would be treated as a business expense just like wages for the corporation's other employees. The wages are deductible by the corporation and taxable to the employee-shareholder.

6. The answer is D. The liquidating distribution is not taxable until the shareholder's stock basis ($20,000) has been recovered. Geraldine recovered $16,000 of her basis in 2016 and the remaining balance of $4,000 in 2017. Her recognized gain is $36,000 ($56,000 total distribution – her $20,000 basis). She will recognize no gain or loss in 2016, but must recognize $36,000 of capital gain in 2017, because this amount exceeds her basis in the stock.

7. The answer is A. If the shareholder has an option to receive cash instead of stock rights, the distributions of stock and stock rights are taxable.

8. The answer is C. A distribution of property to a shareholder is treated as if the corporation had sold the property to the shareholder. The corporation recognizes gain on the distribution if the FMV of the property is more than its adjusted basis. The FMV is considered to be the greater of the property's actual FMV or the amount of liability the shareholder assumes in connection with the distribution. In this case, the FMV is considered to be the liability of $6,000 assumed by Joseph, so Midwestern Grain must recognize a gain of $5,000 ($6,000 – adjusted basis of $1,000).

9. The answer is A. When the basis of a shareholder's stock has been reduced to zero, the shareholder must report any additional return of capital received as a capital gain. Since April has held the stock for more than one year, the gain is reported as a long-term capital gain.

10. The answer is D. Generally, distributions of stock and stock rights are not taxable to shareholders and not deductible by the corporation.

11. The answer is C. The corporation must recognize a gain for any property distributed that has an FMV higher than its adjusted basis. This is the same treatment the corporation would receive if the property were sold for its FMV. The answer is figured as follows:

FMV of distribution	$250,000
Subtract adjusted basis	(100,000)
Recognized gain	**$150,000**

It should be noted that the FMV of $250,000 is also reported as a distribution to the shareholder, and will be his basis in the painting.

12. The answer is B. The amount of a C corporation's earnings and profits determines the tax treatment of corporate distributions to shareholders. The starting point for determining corporate E&P is the corporation's taxable income. The following are the most common transactions that increase the amount of E&P:

- Long-term contracts reported on the completed contract method
- Intangible drilling costs deducted currently
- Mine exploration and development costs deducted currently
- Dividends-received deduction
- Interest income on state and local bonds
- Nontaxable life insurance proceeds
- Federal income tax refunds
- Domestic production activities deduction
- Deferred gain on installment sales

The following are the most common transactions that reduce the amount of E&P:

- Corporate federal income taxes
- Life insurance policy premiums on a corporate officer
- Excess charitable contributions (over 10% limit)
- Expenses relating to tax-exempt income
- Excess of capital losses over capital gains
- Corporate dividends and other distributions
- Fines and penalties
- Nondeductible lobbying expenses
- Nondeductible portion of meals and entertainment

13. The answer is A. Distributions from a C corporation are deducted first from current E&P, and then from accumulated E&P. Any part of a distribution from current-year E&P or accumulated E&P is reported as dividend income to the shareholder. If a corporation's current E&P are less than the total distributions made during the year, part or all of each distribution is treated as a distribution of accumulated E&P. Since Millerton's distributions during the year ($5,000 X 4 quarterly distributions = $20,000) were more than its current-year E&P of $15,000 ($150,000 gross income- $140,000 expenses + $5,000 interest), the amount of each distribution is treated as having been paid partially from current-year E&P in the ratio of current E&P for the year to total distributions for the year ([$15,000 ÷ $20,000] × $5,000) = $3,750.The remainder of each distribution ($5,000 - $3,750 = $1,250) is treated as having been paid from accumulated E&P.

14. The answer is C. The capital gain is calculated as follows: Her basis is $5,000 ($50 × 100 shares). The excess of her portion of the distribution over her basis ($12,000 distribution - $5,000 basis) results in a $7,000 capital gain.

Unit 15: S Corporations

More Reading:
Form 1120-S Instructions
Publication 538, *Accounting Periods and Methods*

The rules governing S corporations are found in subchapter S of the Internal Revenue Code. An S corporation has similarities to both a C corporation and a partnership. Like a partnership, an S corporation is a pass-through entity and is generally not taxed on its earnings. Instead, income and losses pass through to shareholders. Like a C corporation, an S corporation enjoys liability protection that a partnership does not.

S corporations do have some drawbacks. They are less flexible than partnerships. For example, in a partnership, the partners can have different allocations for income and loss based on their partnership agreement. However, with an S Corporation, profits and losses must be passed through to the shareholders based on their percentage of stock ownership. Shareholders can't make any special agreements or arrangements for allocating profits and losses in an imbalanced manner.

There are instances in which an S corporation is forced to pay tax on its earnings. There are also restrictions on the number and types of shareholders an S corporation can have.

Electing S Corporation Status

To become an S corporation, a business must file an election on Form 2553, *Election by a Small Business Corporation.* The filing must be made within 2.5 months after the start of its tax year for the election to be effective at the beginning of the year. An election made after the first 2.5 months of the tax year becomes effective on the first day of the following tax year, unless the corporation receives IRS approval to make the election retroactive to the beginning of the tax year. Based on updated guidelines, the IRS will generally accept a late S-election if the following requirements are met:

- The entity intended to be classified as an S corporation, is an eligible entity, and failed to qualify as an S corporation solely because the election was not timely,
- The entity has reasonable cause for its failure to make the election timely,
- The entity and all shareholders reported their income consistent with an S corporation election in effect for the year the election should have been made and all subsequent years, and
- Less than three years and 75 days have passed since the effective date of the election (unless certain additional conditions are met).

If an entity does not qualify for relief under these guidelines, it may request relief through a private letter ruling.

An S corporation generally may choose to use either the cash or the accrual method of accounting.

S Corporation Requirements

The main requirements for S corporation status are:

- It must be a domestic corporation.
- It cannot have more than 100 shareholders.
- Shareholders generally must be U.S. citizens or residents, if individuals, or certain kinds of trusts, banks, estates, or certain tax-exempt corporations. Corporate shareholders and partnerships are generally excluded. However, certain tax-exempt corporations, including 501(c)(3) corporations, may be S corporation shareholders. In contrast, an S corporation is allowed to own a partnership interest or own stock in a C corporation. Nonresident aliens cannot be shareholders.

- A business must meet the definition of a small business corporation, per IRC section 1361.
- An S corporation can only have one class of stock, but that stock can be voting or nonvoting. The difference in voting rights allows one group of shareholders to retain voting control, while allowing other shareholders to benefit from corporate earnings. However, all the stock of an S corporation must possess identical rights to distribution and liquidation proceeds.
- Profits and losses must be allocated to shareholders in proportion to each one's interest in the business.
- All shareholders of an S corporation must give consent for the S election.

If the S election is made during the corporation's tax year for which it first takes effect, each individual shareholder who holds stock at any time during the part of that year before the election is made must also consent to the election. This is true even if the person may have sold or transferred his stock before the election is made.

Example: Ron, Tara, and William are all equal shareholders in a C corporation. In January 2016, William decides to retire and sells all his shares in the C corporation to Sandra, an unrelated person. In February, Ron, Tara, and Sandra vote to elect S corporation status. All the current shareholders must agree to the election. William must also agree, even though he sold all his stock before the election was made.

Example: A husband and wife own 90% of an S corporation and their son owns the remaining 10% of the stock. The son announces his marriage to a nonresident alien and he gives her one-half of his stock. The S corporation's status is revoked, because a nonresident alien cannot hold stock ownership in an S corporation.

For the 100-shareholder limit, related persons are considered one shareholder. Spouses are automatically treated as a single shareholder. A family, defined as a group of individuals descended from a common ancestor, plus spouses and former spouses of either the common ancestor or anyone lineally descended from that person, is considered a single shareholder as long as any family member elects such treatment.

When a shareholder dies, the deceased shareholder's spouse and the estate are still considered one shareholder for the shareholder limit.

However, a husband and wife cannot be considered a single shareholder if they divorce, or if the marriage is dissolved for any other reason than death. Therefore, a shareholder's divorce can potentially increase the number of shareholders to a number in excess of the 100-shareholder limit. If an S corporation fails to meet this restriction, the S election is considered terminated, and the S corporation ceases to be an S corporation and is instead taxed as a C corporation. The following entities cannot elect S corporation status:

- A bank or thrift institution that uses the reserve method of accounting for bad debts
- An insurance company
- A domestic international sales corporation (DISC)
- Any foreign entity

Filing Requirements for S Corporations

An S corporation files its tax return on Form 1120S, and allocated amounts of income, deductions, and credits pass through to individual shareholders and are reported on Schedule K-1. The return must be signed and dated by an authorized corporate officer or, in certain instances, by a fiduciary, such as a receiver, trustee, or assignee, on behalf of the corporation.

An S corporation is always required to file a tax return, regardless of income or loss. The filing requirement ends only when the corporation is dissolved. The IRS mandates electronic filing for S corporations with $10 million or more in assets that file 250 or more returns of *any* type (Forms W-2, Forms 1099, Schedules K-1) per year.

The tax return is due on the fifteenth day of the third month following the tax year end. For a calendar-year corporation, the tax return is due March 15.[113] A corporation that has dissolved must generally file by the fifteenth day of the third month after the date it dissolved.

A six-month extension of time to file can be requested using Form 7004, *Automatic Extension of Time to File Certain Business Income Tax, Information, and Other Returns*.

Shareholders of an S corporation are required to pay estimated taxes in connection with their own returns. S corporations are only required to pay estimated taxes if $500 or more of certain corporate-level taxes apply.

Required Tax Year

In general, S corporations operate on a calendar year. There are some exceptions to this rule. An S corporation must use one of the following accounting periods:

- A calendar year (Jan 1-Dec 31)
- A natural business year (a "natural business year" is a 12-month fiscal year ending at a low point of a business's activities. For example, a ski resort may have a natural business year that ends after the close of the peak snowing season).An ownership tax year (the tax year that coincides with greater than 50% ownership of the corporation)
- A fiscal year duly elected and approved by the IRS under section 444
- A 52-53 week year that ends with reference to any year listed above

An S corporation may always use a calendar year, or any other tax year for which it establishes a bona fide business purpose. A new S corporation must use Form 2553, *Election by a Small Business Corporation*, to elect a tax year. An existing S corporation that wishes to change its existing tax year may use Form 1128, *Application to Adopt, Change, or Retain a Tax Year*. However, Form 8716, *Election to Have a Tax Year Other Than a Required Tax Year*, is used to apply for a tax year change under section 444.

S Corporation Income and Expenses

As with a partnership, all the income of an S corporation must be allocated to the shareholders, even if it is not distributed. Income, gains, losses, deductions, and credits are allocated to each shareholder on a pro-rata basis, according to the number of shares of stock held by the shareholder on each day of the corporation's tax year, and retain their character when they are passed through. The shareholder then reports the items on his tax return.

Some of the items that pass through to shareholders on a pro rata basis and retain their character must be separately stated on an S corporation's tax return. These include:

- Net income or loss from rental real estate activity (rental income)
- Portfolio income or loss that include:
    - Interest income
    - Dividend income
    - Royalty income
- Capital gains or losses
- Section 1231 gain or loss
- Charitable contributions
- Section 179 expense deduction
- Foreign taxes paid or accrued
- Expenses related to portfolio income or loss

---

[113] Note that although the due date for C Corporations has changed in 2017, the due date for S Corporations remains the same as in previous years.

- Credits, including:
    - Low-income housing credit
    - Qualified rehabilitation expenses
- Investment interest expense
- Tax preference and adjustment items needed to figure a shareholder's AMT
- Nonbusiness bad debts

Unlike a C corporation, an S corporation is not eligible for a dividends-received deduction.

Example: The Oliveira Company is an S corporation with a single shareholder. In 2016, it has $100,000 of gross receipts; $40,000 wage expense to its shareholder; $15,000 of charitable contributions; $10,000 of rental losses; and $8,000 of capital gains. Its ordinary income is $60,000 ($100,000 gross receipts minus $40,000 wages). The other items are all separately stated on Form 1120S, but are not used to determine ordinary income or loss.

S Corporation Basis

To compute basis in the stock of an S corporation, a shareholder starts, just as for a C corporation, with his initial capital contribution or the initial cost of the stock purchased. However, his basis may vary based on how the stock was acquired (by purchase, gift, or inheritance). In general, a shareholder's basis in S corporation stock is determined as follows:

How Stock Acquired	How Stock Basis is Determined
Stock purchase	If the S corporation shares were purchased outright, initial basis is the cost of the shares.
S corporation capitalized	If the shares were received when the S corporation was formed under IRC §351, the basis in the stock is equal to cash invested and/or the basis of property transferred to the corporation, increased by any gain recognized on the transfer, and decreased by any boot received from the corporation (IRC §358).
Prior C corporation	Initial basis in S corporation stock is the basis in the C corporation stock at the time of conversion.
Gift	The recipient's basis in shares received by gift is generally the donor's basis (IRC §1015). Suspended passive activity losses can increase the basis of a gift (IRC §469).
Inheritance	The basis of inherited stock is its fair market value at the date of the former holder's death or, if elected, the alternate valuation date (IRC §1014).
Services rendered to the S corporation	Basis in stock received in exchange for services is measured by the stock's fair market value, rather than by the value of the services (Treas. Reg. §1.61-2).

Both the taxability of a distribution and the deductibility of a loss are dependent on a shareholder's stock basis, and normally basis is adjusted annually, on the last day of the S corporation year, in the following order:

- Increased for income items and excess depletion
- Decreased for distributions
- Decreased for nondeductible, noncapital expenses and depletion
- Decreased for items of loss and deductions

S corporation shareholders must pay taxes on their share of the corporation's current year income, regardless of whether the amounts are distributed. The shareholder's Schedule K-1 reflects the income, loss, and deductions that are allocated to him, but does not state the taxable amount of a distribution. The taxable amount of each distribution is contingent upon a shareholder's stock basis, and it is the shareholder's responsibility to track his individual basis.

Distributions from an S corporation must be paid to all shareholders on the same date as pro rata distributions based on the shareholders' individual ownership percentages.

S corporation distributions are generally not treated as dividends and not subject to income tax, except in cases where a corporation has accumulated E&P from years before it elected to become an S corporation. Distributions from an S corporation with no accumulated earnings and profits are considered a return of capital and reduce the shareholder's basis in the stock of the corporation. Distributions that exceed the shareholder's adjusted stock basis are treated as capital gains and must be reported by the shareholder on Schedule D.

Example: Lucinda is the sole shareholder of an S corporation. Her basis as of January 1, 2016, is $25,000. She receives a distribution of $28,000 in December 2016, which reduces her basis to zero. She must report the excess $3,000 as a capital gain.

The amount of an S corporation distribution is equal to the sum of cash and the fair market value of the property received by a shareholder. If an S corporation distributes appreciated property, the distribution is treated as a sale to the shareholder.

To the extent the FMV of the property exceeds the corporation's adjusted basis, the corporation would recognize gain. The gain passes through to the shareholders and increases the basis of their stock. No loss is recognized if the FMV of the distributed property is less than the corporation's basis. S corporation shareholders are required to compute both stock basis and debt basis. A shareholder's basis in S corporation stock can never be reduced below zero.

The amount of loss that is deductible on a shareholder's tax return is limited to the shareholder's at-risk basis, and is applied in the following order:

- Cash and the adjusted basis of property that the shareholder contributed to the S corporation, subject to annual adjustments as described above (adjusted stock basis), and
- Any loans the shareholder makes to the corporation or any amounts that are borrowed for use by the S corporation for which the shareholder is directly liable (debt basis).

If a shareholder has S corporation losses and deductions in excess of his adjusted stock basis and those losses and deductions are claimed based on debt basis, the debt basis of the shareholder will be reduced by the claimed losses and deductions. If an S corporation repays reduced basis debt to the shareholder, part or all of the repayment is taxable to the shareholder.

The basis adjustment rules under IRC §1367 are similar to the partnership rules. However, while a partner has a unitary basis in his partnership interest, the adjustments to the basis of stock of an S corporation are applied on a separate share basis. The following additional rules apply:

- Losses and deductions not allowable in the current year due to basis limitations are suspended. However, if nondeductible expenses exceed basis, they do not get carried forward.
- Suspended losses and deductions retain their character in subsequent years. They are carried forward indefinitely until basis is increased in subsequent years or until the shareholder permanently disposes of the stock.
- If stock is sold, suspended losses are lost. The sales price does not have an impact on the stock basis. A stock basis computation should be reviewed in the year stock is sold or disposed.
- If the current year has different types of losses and deductions that exceed the shareholder's basis, the allowable losses and deductions must be allocated pro rata based on the size of the particular loss and deduction items.

- In determining current year allowable losses, current year loss and deduction items are combined with the suspended losses and deductions carried over from the prior year, though the current year and suspended items should be separately stated.
- A shareholder only has debt basis to the extent he has personally lent money to the S corporation. A loan guarantee does not create debt basis.
- Part or all of the repayment of a reduced basis debt is taxable to the shareholder.

If an S corporation engages in rental activity or has a shareholder who does not materially participate in S corporation activities, the passive activity loss rules apply to the individual shareholders. If the passive activity loss rules apply, the shareholders' at-risk amounts must be reduced by the full amounts allowable as current deductions.

In contrast to the treatment applicable for a partnership, cancellation of debt income is applied at the entity level for corporations, including S corporations. The debtor is required to reduce specified tax attributes, including loss and credit carryforwards and the basis of assets.

Limited Taxation of S Corporations

S corporations generally are not subject to taxation since they are primarily pass-through entities. However, in certain cases, S corporations are subject to taxes. A subchapter S corporation may have to pay income tax due to:

1. Excess net passive investment income
2. Built-in gains
3. Investment credit recapture
4. LIFO recapture

None of these taxes are deductible as business expenses by the S corporation (except for the portion of any built-in gains tax allocable to ordinary income). An S corporation may also be responsible for other taxes, such as payroll taxes if it has employees, and penalties, such as late filing penalties.

Excess Net Passive Income Tax

An S corporation that had been a C corporation previously and had accumulated E&P during that period may have to pay tax at the corporate level on excess net passive income (ENPI) if its passive investment income exceeds 25% of its gross receipts. The purpose of this requirement is to discourage a corporation with accumulated earnings and profits (E&P) from functioning as a holding company and gaining favorable tax treatment as an S corporation.

For this purpose, passive investment income includes interest, dividends, rents, and royalties. If income is generated in the ordinary course of business, it is non-passive, or active, income. The tax rate on excess net passive income is 35% and is applied against the lesser of:

- Excess net passive income, or
- Taxable income figured as though the corporation were a C corporation.

If the corporation has always been an S corporation, it would not have accumulated E&P and the ENPI tax would not apply.

If the corporation has accumulated E&P at the end of the tax year and has ENPI in excess of 25% of its gross receipts for three consecutive taxable years, the S election is terminated as of the beginning of the fourth year.

Example: For 2014, 2015, and 2016, Herzing Corporation, a calendar-year S corporation, earned passive investment income in excess of 25% of its gross receipts. If Herzing Corporation has accumulated E&P from earlier years in which it was a C corporation, its S election would be terminated as of January 1, 2017, and the corporation would be taxed as a C corporation as of January 1, 2017 (the beginning of the fourth year that it has ENPI in excess of 25%).

Example: Trailblazer Inc. is an S corporation with accumulated E&P from earlier years when it was a C corporation. In 2016, Trailblazer has gross receipts of $80,000, comprised as follows:

- Rental income: $25,000
- Interest income: $10,000
- Additional gross receipts from business operations: $45,000

Trailblazer's passive investment income for the year is $35,000, or 44% of its gross receipts. As this exceeds the 25% threshold, Trailblazer will be subject to the 35% excess net passive income tax on the lesser of its excess net passive income or its taxable income (calculated as if it were a C corporation).

Built-in Gains (BIG) Tax

When a C corporation elects to be taxed as an S corporation and has appreciated assets at that time, the appreciated gain in those assets can be taxed to the S corporation. These "unrealized" gains are called built-in gains. When these assets are later sold, the S corporation is forced to pay tax on the gains at the highest corporate tax rate of 35%.

This is why this tax is also referred to as the "BIG Tax." However, if the S corporation holds the assets long enough after the corporation has elected S-status, then this built-in gains tax does not apply. Instead, the gains would pass through to the shareholder and be taxed at the shareholder's normal capital gains rate.

Example: Deep-Sea Diver Corporation is a calendar-year C Corporation, as has been for several years. On May 1, 2016, Deep-Sea Corp. elects S-Corporation status. On December 15, 2016, the corporation sells a plot of land that it had held as an investment for several years. The S corporation recognizes a $10,000 long-term capital gain on the sale of the land. The entire capital gain is subject to tax, so there will be a $3,500 built-in gains tax ($10,000 gain X 35% BIG tax). If Deep-Sea had waited at least five years to sell the land, then there would not have been any built-in gains tax applied to the sale.

Note: *The Protecting Americans from Tax Hikes (PATH) Act*, which was signed into law in December 2015, made a number of favorable tax law changes impacting S corporations. One of these was the permanent reduction of the built-in gains period to five years (it was originally was 10 years).

The built-in gains (BIG) tax only applies to the following S corporations:

- An S corporation that was a C corporation before it elected to be an S corporation.
- An S corporation that acquired an asset with a basis determined by reference to its basis (or the basis of any other property) in the hands of a C corporation (a transferred-basis acquisition).

The S corporation pays tax on the recognized built-in gain at the highest corporate rate. The tax is reported on Form 1120S and is a deduction for the shareholders.

The built-in gains tax applies only to corporations that elected S status after 1986, and it only affects property dispositions during the five-year period beginning:

- On the first day of the first tax year in which the corporation is an S corporation, for an asset held when the S corporation was a C corporation, or
- On the date the asset was acquired by the S corporation, for an asset with a basis determined by reference to its basis in the hands of a C corporation.

Investment Credit Recapture

Business credit recapture is generally the responsibility of the entity that claims the credit. If a company is an S corporation when the credit originates, the credit passes through to the shareholders and they must report any subsequent recapture on Form 4255, *Recapture of Investment Credit*. However, if a C corporation claims the general business credit and then converts to S status, the S corporation itself may be responsible for the recapture.

LIFO Recapture Tax

A corporation that accounts for inventory using the last in, first out (LIFO) method is subject to a LIFO recapture tax in its final year as a C corporation after making an S corporation election.

This tax is intended to address built-in gains in inventory that might not otherwise be recognized. The taxable LIFO recapture amount is the amount by which the amount of inventory assets calculated under the first in, first out (FIFO) method exceeds the amount under the LIFO method. If the LIFO value is higher than the FIFO value, no negative adjustment is allowed.

Inventory assets include stock in trade of the corporation, or other property of a kind that would properly be included in the inventory of the corporation if on hand at the close of the taxable year.

The LIFO recapture tax is paid in four equal installments, beginning on the due date of the final C corporation return. The three subsequent installments are payable on the due dates of the first three S corporation returns.

The Accumulated Adjustments Account (AAA)

If a C corporation elects to become an S corporation, it may have an accumulated adjustments account (AAA). The AAA is a corporate account that does not relate to individual shareholders. The S corporation maintains the account to track undistributed income that has been taxed during the period its S election is in effect.

S corporations with accumulated E&P must maintain the AAA to determine the tax effect of distributions during S years and, if applicable, during the period after termination of an S election. It is not mandatory to track AAA if the S corporation does not have prior year C corporation E&P (IRC section 1368). Nevertheless, if an S corporation without accumulated E&P engages in certain transactions where an AAA account is required, such as a merger into an S corporation with accumulated E&P, the S corporation must be able to calculate its AAA at the time of the merger. Therefore, it is recommended that the AAA be maintained by all S corporations. The AAA may have a negative balance at year's end.

The ordering rules for distributions from an S corporation with accumulated E&P are as follows:

- First, from the AAA, tax-free to the shareholders and a reduction of each shareholder's basis.
- Second, from E&P, and taxable as dividends.
- Third, if applicable, from the corporation's Other Adjustments Account (OAA), which includes accumulated tax-exempt interest income that has not been distributed previously, and reduce basis.
- Additional distributions are considered return of capital, up to the amount of each shareholder's basis in his stock.
- Distributions in excess of a shareholder's basis in his stock are considered capital gains from the sale of property.

Termination of a Shareholder's Interest

If a shareholder sells or disposes of his stock interest in an S corporation, it is treated in the same manner as the sale of stock in a C corporation. The shareholder reports the sale of the stock on Schedule D. The gain or loss that is recognized by the shareholder is the difference between the shareholder's basis and the sale price of the stock.

If a shareholder in an S corporation terminates his interest in a corporation during the tax year, the corporation, with the consent of all affected shareholders (including those whose interest is terminated), may elect to allocate income and expenses as if the corporation's tax year consisted of two separate short tax years, the first of which ends on the date of the shareholder's termination.

To make this election, the corporation must attach a statement to a timely filed original or amended Form 1120S for the tax year for which the election is made and state that it is electing to treat the tax year as if it consisted of two separate tax years.

The statement must also explain how the shareholder's entire interest was terminated (e.g., sale or gift), and state that the corporation and each affected shareholder consented to the election. A single statement may be filed for all terminating elections made for the tax year.

If this election is made, "Section 1377(a)(2) Election Made" should be written at the top of each affected shareholder's Schedule K-1.

Reasonable Compensation

An S corporation may wish to pay little or no salary or wages to employees or officers who are also shareholders, as these amounts are subject to employment taxes, while distributions to shareholders are not.

However, if an S corporation is not paying a reasonable compensation to a shareholder-employee, distributions to him may be reclassified as wages subject to employment taxes. Therefore, an S corporation will be at risk if it attempts to avoid paying employment taxes by having its officers treat their compensation as cash distributions, payments of personal expenses, or loans rather than as wages.

Example: Leonard was the sole shareholder and employee of a professional corporation he elected to be taxed as an S corporation. He was an experienced accountant with a master's degree in business administration. His firm had annual revenues of $1.5 million. In 2016, Leonard paid himself an annual salary of $24,000 and received distributions from the firm of $200,000. The IRS concluded Leonard was deliberately paying himself a low salary to avoid employment taxes and required that $125,000 of the dividends be reclassified as salary. Additional employment taxes, penalties, and interest were assessed on the reclassified payments.

There are no specific guidelines in the IRC or in IRS regulations for what is considered reasonable compensation. Factors considered by the courts in determining reasonable compensation for employees or officers of an S corporation include:

- Training and experience
- Duties and responsibilities
- Time and effort devoted to the business
- Dividend history
- Payments to non-shareholder employees
- Timing and manner of paying bonuses to key people
- Amounts that comparable businesses pay for similar services
- Compensation agreements
- The use of a formula to determine compensation

The regulations provide an exception for an officer of a corporation who does not perform any services or performs only minor services and receives no compensation. Such an officer would not be considered an employee for tax purposes.

Health Insurance Premiums for Shareholders

Fringe benefits paid to employees who are not shareholders or who have ownership of less than 2% are generally deductible by the S corporation and tax-free to the employees. However, for shareholder-employees who have at least 2% ownership, health and accident insurance premiums paid on their behalf are deductible by the S corporation as fringe benefits and are reportable as wages for income tax withholding purposes on the shareholder-employees'

Forms W-2. The S corporation can exclude these health benefits from the wages subject to Social Security, Medicare, and FUTA taxes.

A 2% shareholder-employee is eligible for an AGI deduction for amounts paid during the year for health insurance premiums if the health insurance coverage is established by the S corporation. If the coverage plan is in the name of the shareholder rather than the name of the S corporation, the coverage can still be considered to be established by the S corporation if:

- The S corporation either paid or reimbursed the shareholder for the premiums, and
- It reported the premium payment as wages on the shareholder's Form W-2.

Neither Schedule K-1 (Form 1120S) nor Form 1099 can be used as an alternative to Form W-2 to report this additional compensation.

Example: Victory Energy Bars, an S corporation, provides health insurance coverage to its two owner-shareholders. Victory paid $5,000 of insurance premiums. The corporation treats the shareholders as having received the health insurance as additional compensation and reports the insurance premiums as W-2 wages.

An S corporation cannot take a deduction for amounts incurred during periods in which the shareholder-employee is eligible to participate in any subsidized health plan maintained by another employer (or the spouse's employer).

Example: Edward is the sole owner-shareholder in an S corporation. He pays the health insurance premiums for himself and his wife. His wife works full-time for an employer who has offered to provide family health coverage. Edward and his wife declined the coverage because they did not want to switch doctors. Because Edward had the option to participate in an employer plan through his wife, the health insurance premiums paid on his behalf by his S corporation are not deductible.

Termination of an S Election

Once the S election is made, it stays in effect until terminated. In addition to the ways already discussed, the election will terminate automatically in any of the following cases:

- The corporation no longer qualifies as a small business corporation.[114]
- For each of three consecutive tax years, the corporation
    - Has accumulated earnings and profits,[115] and
    - Derives more than 25% of its gross receipts from passive investment income.
- The corporation creates a second class of stock.
- The shareholders willingly revoke the S election.

Absent an automatic termination due to failure to meet the requirements of its S status, an S election can be revoked only with the consent of the majority shareholders (those holding more than 50% of the corporation's stock, including nonvoting stock). The corporation must file a statement of revocation with the IRS that is signed by each shareholder who consents.

A shareholder revocation may specify an effective revocation date that is on or after the day the revocation is filed. If no date is specified and the revocation is made on or before the fifteenth day of the third month of that tax year, the revocation is effective at the start of a tax year. If no date is specified and the revocation is made after the fifteenth day of the third month of the tax year, the revocation is effective at the start of the next tax year. A revocation may be rescinded before it takes effect.

---

[114] This termination of an election is effective as of the day the corporation no longer meets the definition of a small business corporation. A statement notifying the IRS of the termination and the date it occurred is attached to Form 1120S for the final year of the S corporation.

[115] This applies only to S corporations that were previously C corporations. An S corporation cannot accumulate earnings and profits as a C corporation can. However, it is possible for a C corporation to elect S corporation status and still have accumulated earnings and profits at the time of the election.

When an S election is terminated, two short tax years are created for the corporation. Income and loss must be allocated on a pro rata basis between the period the corporation operated as an S corporation and the period as a C corporation that was created when the S election was terminated.

The entity must file Form 1120S for the S corporation's short year by the due date (including extensions) of the C corporation's short year return.

Example: On May 1, 2016, Zander Corporation, a calendar-year S corporation, exceeded 100 shareholders. This will create two short tax years—one for the S corporation and one for the C corporation. Zander must file a Form 1120S and a Form 1120. The due date for the 1120S return, for the short year ending April 30, 2016, is July 15, 2016 (this would be the tax return for the S corporation that has terminated). The due date for the 1120 return, for the short year beginning May 1, 2016 and ending December 31, 2016, will be April 18, 2017 (this would be the tax return for the C corporation that is created upon the termination of the S corporation)..

If the IRS deems that a revocation was inadvertent (that the shareholders did not mean to revoke their S election or that the revocation was accidental), the corporation may be allowed to correct the error and retain its S election status.

Example: In 2016, Morrison Window Blinds, a calendar-year S corporation, inadvertently terminates its S status. The S corporation shareholders immediately correct the problem. Therefore, the S corporation status is considered to have been continuously in effect, and no termination is deemed to have occurred. Only a single S corporation tax return will need to be filed for tax year 2016.

A terminating event will be considered inadvertent if the event was not within the control of the corporation, and the shareholders did not plan to terminate the election. Further, all of the following must occur:

- The S election must have involuntarily terminated either because:
    - The corporation no longer qualified as a small business corporation, or
    - It had accumulated earnings and profits from past C corporation activities.
- The IRS must agree that the termination was inadvertent.
- The corporation must take reasonable and immediate steps to correct the issue.
- The shareholders and the corporation must agree to any adjustments proposed by the IRS.
- The corporation must request a private letter ruling from the IRS for any inadvertent termination relief.

Note: If the status of an S corporation is terminated, either because the shareholders elect to become a C corporation or because a terminating event has occurred, the S corporation cannot elect to become an S corporation within the next five years. However, the IRS may choose to waive the five-year restriction.

Unit 15: Study Questions

(Test yourself and then check the correct answers at the end of this section.)

1. Lydia transferred a residential rental building to an S corporation for stock, and immediately after the transfer, she owned 90% of the corporation. She received stock with a fair market value of $155,000 plus cash of $60,000. The corporation also assumed a $30,000 mortgage on the property for which Lydia was personally liable. Her basis in the transferred property was $175,000. What amount of gain must Lydia recognize, if any?

A. $70,000
B. $60,000
C. $30,000
D. $0

2. Greenhouse Gardens is an S corporation with four shareholders. The corporation has 10,000 shares outstanding. The shareholders have the following ownership:

Shareholder	Ownership
Jordan	4,500 shares
Mai	2,000 shares
Simon	2,000 shares
Nora	1,500 shares
Total	**10,000 shares**

Nora and Jordan wish to terminate the S election, but Mai and Simon do not. Which of the following statements is correct?

A. Jordan can elect to terminate the corporation's S status on his own.
B. All of the shareholders must agree to terminate the election.
C. Nora and Jordan have enough stock ownership to terminate the election.
D. At least 75% of the shareholders with active ownership must agree to the termination.

3. What is the total amount of the separately stated income items of this S corporation?

Gross Receipts	$700,000
Rental real estate income	300,000
Interest income	25,000
Royalty income	10,000
Section 1231 gain	20,000

A. $355,000
B. $345,000
C. $700,000
D. $720,000

4. What is the tax rate on excess net passive income?

A. 10%
B. 15%
C. 25%
D. 35%

5. Francisco is the sole employee-shareholder of an S corporation that has no accumulated earnings and profits. At the beginning of the year, his stock basis was $50,000. The corporation had no income in 2016. The corporation distributed property to Francisco with an FMV of $75,000 and an adjusted basis of $62,000. What is the treatment of the distribution?

A. $63,000 as a return of capital and $25,000 taxable capital gain
B. $50,000 as a return of capital and $12,000 taxable capital gain
C. $60,000 as a return of capital and $15,000 taxable capital gain
D. $62,000 as a return of capital and $0 taxable capital gain

6. Close family members can be treated as a single shareholder for S corporation purposes. A family member in this instance includes:

A. A nonresident alien spouse.
B. A first cousin.
C. The estate of a shareholder's deceased spouse.
D. A divorced spouse.

7. Which of the following events would cause the termination of an S corporation's status?

A. An S corporation that has an estate as a shareholder.
B. An S corporation that has a nonprofit corporation 501(c)(3) shareholder.
C. An S corporation that issues one share of stock to a C corporation.
D. An S corporation that owns one share of stock in a C corporation.

8. On January 1, 2016, Seth purchased 50% of the stock of Rancho Inc., an S corporation, for $100,000, and also loaned the corporation $20,000. At the end of 2016, Rancho Inc. incurred an ordinary loss of $180,000. How much of the loss can Seth deduct on his personal income tax return for 2016?

A. $90,000
B. $180,000
C. $0
D. $120,000

9. On December 31, 2015, Adrienne had a $2,000 basis in Liaison Corporation, an S corporation. She owns 50% of Liaison's outstanding stock. On January 3, 2016, Adrienne contributed a patent that she had acquired for $1,000 to Liaison. During 2016, Liaison Corporation received $5,000 of royalty income from licensing that patent. Liaison also had $2,500 of ordinary income and $500 of section 179 deductions. At the end of 2016, Liaison returned ownership of the patent, which now had a fair market value of $5,000, to Adrienne. What is Adrienne's basis in Liaison Corporation at the end of 2016?

A. $1,000
B. $3,500
C. $2,500
D. $5,000

10. In which circumstance is a C corporation unable to elect to become an S corporation?

A. The C corporation has 50 shareholders.
B. The C corporation is incorporated in Canada.
C. The C corporation has common stock with voting and nonvoting rights.
D. The C corporation is on a fiscal year with a legitimate business purpose.

11. Bettendorf Boating Company is a calendar-year C corporation that wishes to elect S corporation status in 2016. What is the latest date that Bettendorf Boating Company can elect S status for tax year 2016?

A. March 15, 2017
B. March 15, 2016
C. January 1, 2016
D. December 31, 2016

12. A calendar-year S corporation operating on the accrual basis has the following income items and expenses. What is the ordinary income of this S corporation, not counting the separately stated items?

Gross receipts	$300,000
Interest income	25,000
Royalty income	10,000
Salary paid to shareholder	20,000

A. $55,000
B. $280,000
C. $320,000
D. $345,000

13. Danielle is a 50% owner in Duo Software Corporation, an S corporation. Danielle's basis in her stock at the end of 2015 is $5,000. The following year, 2016, Duo Software reports $10,000 of ordinary income. In December 2016, the corporation makes a distribution to Danielle of appreciated property. It is a vintage motorcycle originally purchased for $1,000, but now worth $8,000. How much income must Danielle report on her individual tax return in connection with the property distribution?

A. $3,500
B. $1,000
C. $0
D. $8,000

14. An S corporation, regardless of when it became an S corporation, must use a permitted tax year. A permitted tax year is any of the following except:

A. The calendar year.
B. A tax year elected under section 444.
C. A fiscal tax year with a legitimate business purpose.
D. A short tax year.

15. S corporations are generally not subject to taxation and are primarily pass-through entities. But in certain cases, S corporations are subject to taxes. Which of the following taxes do not apply to S corporations?

A. Excess net passive investment income.
B. Built-in gains tax.
C. Self-employment tax.
D. LIFO recapture.

16. On January 1, 2016, Gloria, Kristin, and Nancy are all equal shareholders in Fairview Heights Corporation, a calendar-year C corporation that has been in existence for four years. On March 1, 2016, Gloria sells her entire stock interest in the corporation to an unrelated party, Irving. Irving immediately wants to convert the corporation to an S corporation effective January 1, 2016. Whose consent is required for Fairview to convert to S status?

A. Irving may convert the corporation into an S corporation so long as Kristin and Nancy consent.
B. Gloria must also consent to the election, along with Kristin and Nancy.
C. Irving may convert the corporation to an S corporation on his own.
D. The corporation cannot convert to S status until it has been in existence for five years.

17. In January 2016, Christopher and Eva are shareholders in Centex Company, a C corporation. Christopher owns 65% of the corporate stock and Eva owns the remainder. Christopher decides that he wants to convert Centex to an S corporation. Which of the following statements is correct regarding the conversion?

A. They must both consent to the conversion to the S corporation.
B. The election to become an S corporation is taken on Form 1120S.
C. Christopher may choose to convert the C corporation to an S corporation because he owns more than 50% of the stock.
D. They cannot elect S corporation status, because a C corporation cannot elect to become an S corporation.

18. A C corporation may not elect to become an S corporation if:

A. It is a domestic corporation.
B. It has voting and nonvoting stock.
C. It has two classes of stock.
D. It has common stock.

19. Which of the following will not terminate an S corporation's status?

A. The S corporation no longer qualifies as a small business corporation.
B. The S corporation, for each of three consecutive tax years, has accumulated earnings and profits, and derives more than 25% of its gross receipts from passive investment income.
C. The S corporation creates a second class of stock.
D. The S corporation earns the majority of its revenue from passive activities.

Unit 15: Answers

1. The answer is B. In an otherwise nontaxable section 351 exchange, a shareholder might have to recognize gain if she receives money or property other than the corporation's stock. The gain is limited to the total of money and the FMV of the other property received. If the corporation assumes the shareholder's liabilities, the assumption generally is not treated as if the shareholder received money or other property, unless:

- The liabilities the corporation assumes are more than the shareholder's adjusted basis in the property transferred, in which case gain is recognized up to the difference. However, if the liabilities assumed give rise to a deduction when paid, such as a trade account payable or interest, no gain is recognized.
- There is no good business reason for the corporation to assume the liabilities, or if the main purpose in the exchange is to avoid federal income tax.

The shareholder's basis in her stock must be reduced by the amount of the liabilities assumed by the corporation. Lydia receives a total of $245,000 ($155,000 stock + $60,000 cash + $30,000 debt relief) and has a $70,000 gain ($245,000 - $175,000 adjusted basis). As the liability assumed was less than Lydia's adjusted basis in the property and absent any indication the exchange was undertaken with the main purpose of avoiding federal income tax, the debt relief would not be considered in determining her recognized gain. Therefore, the gain is limited to the $60,000 of cash received.

2. The answer is C. An S election may be revoked if shareholders holding more than 50% of the stock consent. Since Nora and Jordan together own more than 50% of the outstanding stock, they can elect to revoke the S election.

3. The answer is A. All of the items, except for the gross receipts, must be separately stated on the S corporation's tax return.

4. The answer is D. Excess net passive income earned by S corporations is taxed at a rate of 35%.

5. The answer is A. Distributions from an S corporation with no accumulated E&P are generally treated as a nontaxable return of capital, up to the amount of the shareholder's adjusted stock basis. However, if an S corporation distributes appreciated property, the distribution is treated as a sale to the shareholder. To the extent the FMV of the property exceeds the corporation's basis, the corporation would recognize gain. The gain passes through to the shareholders and increases the basis of their stock.

Adjusted basis 1/1/2016:		$50,000
S corporation net income		$0
Gain related to distribution		$13,000
Adjusted basis 12/31/2016:		$63,000
Distribution:		
FMV of property:		$75,000
Minus shareholder's basis:		$63,000
Additional capital gain:	**$12,000**	

Francisco must report $25,000 of capital gain income on his tax return. This includes the gain of $13,000 recognized by the corporation and passed through to him. In addition, since the distribution reduces the basis of his stock to zero, the amount exceeding his basis ($12,000) is also treated as capital gain.

6. The answer is C. Spouses are automatically treated as a single shareholder, and when a shareholder dies, the deceased shareholder's spouse and the estate are still considered one shareholder for the purpose of the shareholder limit. A husband and wife cannot be considered a single shareholder if they divorce, or if the marriage is dissolved for any reason other than death. An S corporation cannot have a nonresident alien member, so a nonresident alien spouse would not qualify.

7. The answer is C. An S corporation may own stock in a C corporation, but it cannot have a C corporation as a shareholder. S corporation shareholders must generally be U.S. citizens or U.S. residents, and must be physical entities (persons), so corporate shareholders and partnerships are excluded. Certain estates, trusts, and tax-exempt corporations, including 501(c)(3) corporations, are also permitted to be shareholders.

8. The answer is A. An S corporation shareholder can deduct his share of the corporation's losses only to the extent of his stock and debt basis. Before consideration of Rancho Inc.'s 2016 loss, Seth's stock basis and debt basis were $100,000 and $20,000, respectively. Therefore, he can deduct his entire 50% share of the company's ordinary loss ($180,000 ÷ 2 = $90,000).

9. The answer is B. Adrienne's basis is calculated as follows:

Adrienne's stock basis at December 31, 2015	$2,000
Adrienne contributes the patent (January 3, 2016)	1,000
50% share of 2016 income:	
•Royalty income	2,500
•Ordinary income	1,250
Basis prior to consideration of distribution	6,750
50% share of gain related to patent	2,000
Distribution of a patent, at FMV	(5,000)
Subtotal	**$3,750**
50% share of section 179 deduction	(250)
Basis at December 31, 2016	**$3,500**

10. The answer is B. A C corporation can elect to become an S corporation if it otherwise qualifies. Only domestic U.S. corporations are allowed to elect S status. An S corporation can only have one class of stock, but differences in voting rights are allowed. An S corporation can have a fiscal year if it has a legitimate business purpose for doing so.

11. The answer is B. An eligible corporation must make an S election within two months and 15 days from the start of its tax year (or within 2.5 months of its inception). Since Bettendorf Boating is a calendar-year corporation, its tax year begins January 1 and ends on December 31. It must make the election on or before March 15, in order to be effective for that year.

12. The answer is B. Ordinary income would reflect the gross receipts of $300,000 minus the salary expense to the shareholder of $20,000, or $280,000. Interest income and royalty income would be separately stated items on Form 1120S, but would not be considered in determining ordinary income or loss. The amount is figured as follows: ($300,000 - $20,000 = $280,000).

13. The answer is C. If an S corporation distributes appreciated property, the distribution is treated as if the property had been sold to the shareholder. To the extent the FMV of the property exceeds the corporation's basis, the corporation would recognize gain. The gain passes through to the shareholders and increases the basis of their stock. In this case, the amount of the distribution ($8,000) is less than Danielle's adjusted stock basis after recognition of her share of the corporation's gain ($3,500). Therefore, she would reduce her basis by the distribution, but would recognize no additional income from the transaction:

Danielle's stock basis as of 1/1/2016:	$5,000
S corp. ordinary income × 50%:	5,000
Adjusted basis before distribution	10,000
Distribution:	
Gain on sale of $7,000 × 50%	3,500
Minus FMV of property distributed:	(8,000)
Adjusted basis as of 12/31/2016:	**$5,500**

14. The answer is D. A short tax year is only applicable when an S corporation is in its first year or its S status is terminated.

15. The answer is C. S corporations are not subject to self-employment tax. Self-employment tax applies only to individuals. The S corporation may have to pay tax due to:

- Excess net passive investment income
- Built-in gains
- Investment credit recapture
- LIFO recapture

16. The answer is B. In order for the election to be made, Gloria must also consent to the election, even though she has sold all of her shares to Irving. All the shareholders must consent to the election. If the S election is made during the corporation's tax year for which it first takes effect, any individual shareholder who holds stock at any time during the part of that year before the election is made must also consent to the election, even though the person may have sold or transferred his stock before the election is made.

17. The answer is A. All the shareholders must consent to an S election, so both shareholders would be required to consent to the change.

18. The answer is C. A corporation may not elect S corporation status if it has two classes of stock. A corporation may have both voting and nonvoting stock because they are not considered different classes of stock. A corporation must be a domestic corporation to qualify for S corporation status.

19. The answer is D. All of the following actions will terminate an S election:

- When the corporation no longer qualifies as a small business corporation.
- For each of three consecutive tax years, the corporation
  - Has accumulated earnings and profits, and
  - Derives more than 25% of its gross receipts from passive investment income.
- The S election may be willingly revoked by the shareholders.
- If the corporation creates a second class of stock (such as common and preferred stock).

Unit 16: Farming Businesses

More Reading:
Publication 225, *Farmer's Tax Guide*

Farming businesses may be engaged in activities such as crop production, animal production, or forestry and logging. They may include stock, dairy, poultry, fish, fruit, and tree farms, as well as plantations, ranches, timber farms, and orchards. The entity type does not matter; a business will be classified as a "farming business" as long as the business cultivates, operates, or manages a farm (or fishery) for profit.

A farming or fishing business operating as a sole proprietorship reports income and loss on Schedule F, *Profit or Loss from Farming*. A farmer is usually self-employed if he operates his own farm or rents farmland from others to engage in the business of farming. Self-employed farmers and fishermen must also complete Schedule SE.

Alternatively, a farming business may be organized as a partnership or a corporation. It is the nature of the activity that determines whether a business is classified as a "farming" business for tax purposes.

Not Classified as Farming Businesses: Certain associated businesses are not considered farming businesses and instead must file on Schedule C (if a sole proprietorship). Examples include:

- Veterinary businesses
- Businesses that only supply farm labor or farming equipment
- Businesses that only sell farm supplies, such as pesticides or herbicides
- Businesses that are only in the business of breeding, including those that raise or breed dogs, cats, or other household pets
- Businesses that provide agricultural services, such as soil preparation and fertilization, but do no actual farming of the land.

Not Classified as Farm Income: Certain types of income associated with farming businesses are not classified as farm income. Farm income does not include any of the following:

- Wages received as a farm employee
- Income received under a contract for grain harvesting with workers and machines furnished by the taxpayer
- Gains received from the sale of farmland and depreciable farm equipment
- Gains from the sale of securities, regardless of who owns the securities

Farming Rents

If a farmer rents his farmland for someone else to use, the related revenue is generally classified as rental income, not farming income. This also applies to crop shares, when a tenant farmer pays a proportion of crop harvest proceeds to the land owner for use of his farmland. This passive activity income is reported on Form 4835, *Farm Rental Income and Expenses*. This type of business activity is also called "sharecropping" or "cropping."

On the other hand, if a farmer simply rents his pasture or other farm real estate for a flat cash amount without providing services to the tenant, he will report the income as rent on Schedule E.

If a farmer *materially participates* in farming operations on the land he owns, the rent is considered farm income and is reported on Schedule F.

Example: Randall is a farmer who owns 200 acres of pastureland in Wyoming. Randall rents out his pasture to someone else who owns cattle. Randall also takes care of the cattle for a fee. Since Randall is actively involved in the activity by taking daily care of the livestock, the income is reported on his Schedule F as ordinary income.

Example: Garth also owns pastureland in Wyoming. Unlike Randall, he simply rents the pasture to other farmers for a flat cash amount. He does not provide any services or take care of the livestock in any way. Garth would report the income as rental income on Part I of Schedule E (Form 1040).

Example: Estelle owns a 90-acre farm in Montana. She generally rents out her land to a tenant farmer and does not do any of the planting herself. In 2016, Estelle rents the land to a sharecropper who grows organic beets. Estelle's contract with the tenant farmer requires the sharecropper to pay twenty-five percent of the crops harvested. Estelle reports her share of the income from the crops on Form 4835, which is attached to her Form 1040. Estelle's tenant farmer (the sharecropper) would be required to report *his* income on Schedule F as regular farming income, subject to self-employment tax.

Estimated Taxes

Special rules apply to the payment of estimated tax by qualified farmers and fishermen. If at least two-thirds of the individual's or business's gross income comes from farming or fishing activities, the following rules apply:

- The taxpayer does not have to pay estimated tax if he files his return and pays all the tax owed by the first day of the third month after the end of his tax year (usually this date is March 1).
- If the taxpayer must pay estimated tax, he is required to make only one estimated tax payment, called the required annual payment, by the fifteenth day after the end of his tax year. Usually, this date is January 15.

Accounting Methods for Farming

Farmers are allowed to use any accounting method that is available for other business types. In addition, there are a few special accounting methods that are applicable only to farming businesses. Farmers can use the following accounting methods:

- **Cash Method**
- **Accrual Method**
- **Combination (Hybrid) Method** (using two or more of the methods listed)
- **Special Methods, including the Crop Method:** The IRS allows a number of different special methods of accounting that apply to items such as depreciation, farm business expenses, or income. Among these is the crop method, which requires IRS approval and is allowed only for farming businesses. If crops are not harvested and disposed of in the same tax year they are planted, the farmer can capitalize the entire cost of producing the crop, including the expense of seed or young plants, and deduct them in the year income is realized.

Example: William is a self-employed farmer who uses the **accrual** method (not on the crop method). He keeps his books on a calendar-year basis. William sells grain in December 2016, but he is not paid until January 2017. He must include the sale on his 2016 tax return. He can also deduct the costs incurred in producing the grain on his 2016 return.

Example: Patrice is also a self-employed farmer who uses the **cash** method. Patrice sells beef cattle on December 15, 2016, but he is not paid until January 5, 2017. Since Patrice uses the cash method and there was no constructive receipt of the sale proceeds in 2016, Patrice includes the sale proceeds in income in 2017, the year he receives the payment.

Although the accrual method of accounting generally must be used when there is inventory, farmers are exempt from the usual requirements to maintain an inventory, and as a result, most farmers use the cash method. Inventory requirements do not apply to most crops.[116] Consequently, few farming operations are required to adopt the accrual method of accounting.

However, the following farming businesses must use the accrual method:

- A corporation (other than a "family farming corporation") that had gross receipts of more than $1 million for any tax year
- A family farming corporation that had gross receipts of more than $25 million for any tax year
- A partnership with a corporate partner
- A tax shelter (of any size or income)

To qualify as a "family farming corporation," the business must meet at least one of the following requirements:

- Members of the same family own at least 50% of the corporation's stock
- Members of two families have owned since October 1976, either directly or indirectly, at least 65% of the corporation's stock
- Members of three families have owned since October 1976, either directly or indirectly, at least 50% of the corporation's stock

Example: Dave and Raymond are brothers who operate and co-own a farm. They are the only shareholders of Da-Ray Farms Corporation, which is a qualified family farming corporation. Da-Ray Farms raises beef cattle, and in 2016, it has $20 million of gross receipts. Since Da-Ray is a qualified family farm, the entity is allowed to use the cash method of accounting.

Farming Inventory

Farm inventory includes all items that are held for sale, purchased for resale, and for use as feed or seed, such as the following:

- Eggs in the process of hatching.
- Harvested farm products held for sale, such as grain, cotton, hay, or tobacco.
- Supplies that become a physical part of an item held for sale, such as containers, wrappers, or other packaging. A business may expense the cost of supplies consumed in operations during the year.
- Any livestock held primarily for sale or purchased for resale.
- Purchased farm products that are being held for seed or feed.

If livestock was purchased primarily for draft, breeding, sport, or dairy purposes, the farmer can choose to depreciate it, or include the livestock in inventory. Regardless of the method chosen, it must be consistent from year to year.

Note: Farm inventory does not include real property, such as land or buildings, or depreciable equipment, such as tractors.

Farmers may use the same inventory methods that are available to other businesses, such as cost and lower of cost or market. However, there are two other inventory methods that are unique to farming businesses:

Farm-Price Method: Under the farm-price method, each item, whether raised or purchased, is valued at its market price minus the costs of disposition. The costs of disposition include broker's commissions, freight, hauling to market, and other marketing costs. If a

[116] Generally, growing crops are not required to be included in inventory unless they have a pre-productive period of more than two years. Plants with a pre-productive period of less than two years include many common crops such as corn and wheat. Plants with a pre-productive period of more than two years include many kinds of fruit and nut trees, grapes, and avocados, among others.

farming business chooses to use the farm-price method, it must use it for the entire inventory, except that livestock can be inventoried under the unit-livestock-price method.

Unit-Livestock-Price Method: The unit-livestock-price method is an easier inventory method that allows farmers to group livestock together, rather than track the costs of each individual animal. A farmer may classify livestock according to type and age and use a unit price for each animal within a class. The unit price must reasonably approximate the costs incurred in producing the animal.

If a farming business uses the unit-livestock-price method, it must include all raised livestock in inventory, regardless of whether they are held for sale or for draft, breeding, sport, or dairy purposes. This method accounts only for the costs incurred while raising an animal to maturity. It does not provide for any decrease in the animal's market value after it reaches maturity.

UNICAP for Farmers: Except for corporations, partnerships, and tax shelters that are required to use the accrual method, farming businesses are not required to apply the UNICAP rules to the costs of:

- Raising plants for which the pre-productive period is two years or less
- Animals
- Replanting certain plants lost or damaged due to casualty

If a farmer's crop has a pre-productive period of more than two years, the farmer can generally elect not to have the UNICAP rules apply, unless he is required to use the accrual method.

Example: Jane owns a peach orchard that produces an annual crop. The trees have a pre-productive period of more than two years. Jane must capitalize the direct costs of the orchard and an allocable part of indirect costs incurred due to the production of the trees. However, she is not required to capitalize the costs of producing the annual peach crop because its pre-productive period is two years or more.

For crops, pre-productive period costs include the costs of irrigation, pruning, spraying, and harvesting. For livestock, pre-productive costs include the costs of feed, maintaining pasture or pen areas, breeding, veterinary services, and bedding.

Sales of Farm Products and Farm Assets

When a self-employed farmer sells products raised on a farm, his entire proceeds are reported on Schedule F, in a manner similar to any other taxpayer who sells inventory and reports the sales proceeds on Schedule C. Gain on the sale of livestock raised on a farm is generally the gross sales price reduced by any expenses of the sale, such as commissions or freight charges. The basis of the animal sold is zero if the costs of raising it were deducted during the years the animal was being raised.

Example: In 2015, five piglets were born on Lisa's farm. She correctly deducted the cost of feed and other expenses of raising the animals on her 2015 tax return. In 2016, the now-adult hogs were hauled to a nearby town for auction, where they sold for a total of $2,500, with $75 of sales expenses to the auction house. Lisa will report income of $2,425 on her 2016 tax return ($2,500 - $75 = $2,425).

When a farmer sells farm products bought for resale, his profit or loss is the difference between his basis in the item (usually cost) and any payment received for it.

Example: Two years ago, Oscar bought 20 feeder calves for $6,000 for resale. He sold them in 2016 for $11,000. Oscar reports the $11,000 sales price, subtracts his $6,000 basis, and reports the resulting $5,000 gain on his Schedule F.

However, income reported on Schedule F does not include gains or losses from sales or other dispositions of the following farm assets:

- Land
- Depreciable farm equipment
- Buildings and structures
- Livestock held for draft, breeding, sport, or dairy purposes (unless held as inventory or held primarily for sale)

The sale of these assets is reported on Form 4797, *Sales of Business Property*, and may result in ordinary or capital gains or losses.

Like other businesses, when a farming business disposes of depreciable property (section 1245 property or section 1250 property) at a gain, the taxpayer may have to recognize ordinary income under the depreciation recapture rules. Any gain remaining after applying the depreciation recapture rules may be section 1231 gain, which may be taxed as capital gain.

Section 1245: Part or all of the gain of the sale of section 1245 property is treated as ordinary income under the rules of depreciation recapture. Buildings and structural components are not considered section 1245 assets. However, single purpose agricultural (livestock) or horticultural structures are section 1245 property. For example, a barn that houses different animals and is also used to store supplies would not be section 1245 property because it is not a single-purpose facility.

Example: A greenhouse that is used only to grow plants would be single purpose and thus section 1245 property. If a cash register is installed in the greenhouse so that a farmer can sell plants in addition to growing them there, the greenhouse would no longer be section 1245 property because it is no longer single-purpose.

Other examples of farming-related section 1245 property include a grain silo, fencing for the confinement of livestock, and wells for providing water to livestock.

Section 1231: Section 1231 assets include certain business (noncapital) assets that have been held for more than one year, as well as certain business and investment property disposed of in involuntary conversions.

Note: Section 1231 assets receive special tax treatment. If a taxpayer has a net loss from all section 1231 transactions, the loss is treated as ordinary loss. If the section 1231 transactions result in a net gain, the gain is generally treated as capital gain, with the exception of depreciation recapture and recapture under the five-year "look-back" rule, which is taxed as ordinary income.

Gain or loss on the following farm-related transactions is subject to section 1231 treatment:

1. Sale or exchange of cattle or horses held for draft, breeding, dairy, or sporting purposes and held for 24 months or longer.
2. Sale or exchange of other livestock held for draft, breeding, dairy, or sporting purposes and held for 12 months or longer. Other livestock includes hogs, mules, sheep, and goats, but does not include poultry.
3. Sale or exchange of depreciable property used in the farming business and held for longer than one year. Examples include farm machinery and trucks.
4. Sale or exchange of real estate used in the farming business and held for longer than one year. Examples are a farm or ranch, including barns and sheds.
5. Sale or exchange of unharvested crops.
6. Sale from cut timber.
7. The condemnation of business property held longer than one year. Condemnations of business property usually qualify for nonrecognition treatment if replacement

property is purchased within a certain time period, under the involuntary conversion rules.

Postponing Gain Due to Weather Conditions

There are special rules for farmers regarding the postponement of gain due to weather conditions. If a farmer sells or exchanges more livestock (including poultry), than he normally would in a year because of a drought, flood, or other weather-related conditions, he may postpone reporting the income from the additional animals until the following year.

The taxpayer must meet all the following conditions to qualify:

- The principal trade or business must be farming.
- The farmer must use the cash method of accounting.
- The farmer must be able to show that he would not have sold or exchanged the additional animals in that year except for the weather-related condition.
- The area must be designated as eligible for federal disaster assistance.

The livestock does not have to be raised or sold in the affected area. However, the sale must occur solely because the weather-related condition affected the water, grazing, or other requirements of the livestock. The farmer must figure the amount to be postponed separately for each generic class of animals, such as hogs, sheep, and cattle.

Example: Betsey is a calendar-year farmer, and she normally sells 100 head of beef cattle a year. As a result of a state-wide drought, Betsey sells 135 head during 2016 and realizes $70,200 from the sale. On November 9, 2016, because of drought, the affected area is declared a disaster area eligible for federal assistance. The income Betsey can postpone until 2017 is $18,200 ([$70,200 ÷ 135] × 35), which is the portion of the income attributed to the additional animals that she sold over her normal yearly amount.

To postpone gain, the farmer must attach a statement to his tax return for the year of the sale providing specific information about the weather conditions and circumstances that led to the postponement of gain for each class of livestock. For a sale that qualifies as an involuntary conversion, the farmer can file this statement at any time during the replacement period. The replacement period for the sale of livestock due to weather-related conditions is four years, and up to five years if the property is subject to an involuntary conversion in a federally-declared disaster area.

A weather-related sale or exchange of livestock held for draft, breeding, or dairy purposes (but in this case, not including poultry) may also qualify as an involuntary conversion.

Livestock that is sold or exchanged because of disease may not trigger taxable gain if the proceeds of the transaction are reinvested in replacement animals within two years of the close of the tax year in which the diseased animals were sold or exchanged.

Example: Paulo is a farmer who owns 3,000 head of cattle on two different farms. In 2016, his herd is struck by hoof-and-mouth disease, and he is forced to send 1,500 infected animals to slaughter. His insurance company reimburses his losses, and he promptly reinvests all the insurance proceeds into new livestock. This is treated as an involuntary conversion.

Crop Insurance and Government Payments

Insurance proceeds, including government disaster payments, may be received as a result of destruction or damage to crops or the inability to plant crops because of drought, flood, or another natural disaster. These payments are generally taxable in the year they are received.

However, a farmer can elect to postpone reporting the income until the following year if he meets all of these conditions:

- The farming business must use the cash method of accounting.
- Crop insurance proceeds were received in the same tax year the crops were damaged.

- Under normal business practices, the farming business would have reported income from the damaged crops in any tax year following the year the damage occurred.

A statement must be attached to the tax return indicating the specific crops that were damaged and the total insurance payment received. To make this election to postpone income, the farmer must be able to prove that the crops would have been harvested or otherwise sold in the following year.

If a farmer forgoes the planting of crops altogether and receives agricultural program payments from the government, payments are reported on Schedule F, and the full amount of the payment is subject to self-employment tax.

Other Unique Tax Rules for Farmers

There are many special rules that apply only to farming businesses. Other examples of tax rules unique to farmers include the following:

Car and Truck Expenses: Farmers can claim 75% of the use of a car or light truck as business use without any records (such as a mileage log) if the vehicle is used most of the business day in a farming business.

Soil Conservation: Farmers can choose to deduct as a business expense land-related expenses for soil or water conservation or for the prevention of erosion. Examples include leveling, eradication of brush, removal of trees, or planting of windbreaks. For most businesses, these would be considered capital expenses and would be added to the basis of the land.

Net Operating Losses: Farming losses qualify for longer carryback periods. The carryback period for farming losses is five years rather than the two-year carryback period that applies to other businesses.

Excise Tax Credits: Farmers may be eligible to claim a credit or a refund of federal excise taxes on fuel used on a farm.

Farm Income Averaging: Certain farmers that operate as sole proprietorships or partnerships may use Schedule J, *Income Averaging for Farmers and Fishermen,* to average all or some of their current year's farm income by allocating it to the three prior years. This may lower a farmer's current year tax liability if the current year is high and his taxable income from one or more of the three prior years was low. Income from the three previous years does not have to originate from farming or fishing activity.

Example: Jed is a citrus farmer in Florida. In 2016, he has a record crop with gross income nearly double that of 2014 and 2015, when a cold frost had damaged a large percentage of his crop. Jed elects to average his income by filing Schedule J. His taxable income for 2016 is averaged with the corresponding amounts for the three previous years, which significantly reduces his tax liability in the current year.

Unit 16: Study Questions

(Test yourself and then check the correct answers at the end of this section.)

1. With regards to farmers, what is Schedule J used for?

A. Schedule J is used to report farm-related casualty losses.
B. Schedule J allows a farmer to use income-averaging.
C. Schedule J allows a farmer to deduct his home office.
D. Schedule J allows a farmer report estimated payments.

2. William is a calendar-year, self-employed farmer who files on the cash basis. For purposes of the estimated tax for qualified farmers, all of the following statements are correct except:

A. William does not have to make any estimated payments if he files by April 15 and pays all the taxes with his return.
B. William is a qualified farmer if at least two-thirds of his previous year's gross income is from farming.
C. The required annual estimated tax payment for farmers is due on the fifteenth day after the close of their tax year.
D. The required annual payment is two-thirds of the current year's tax or 100% of the previous year's tax.

3. All of the following should be included in farming inventory except:

A. Farming equipment and machinery.
B. Livestock held primarily for sale.
C. Farm products held for feed or seed.
D. Supplies that become a physical part of items held for sale.

4. Joel is a qualified farmer who usually sells 500 beef cattle every year. However, because of a severe drought, he was forced to sell 800 beef cattle this year. Which of the following statements is correct?

A. Joel may choose to postpone all of the gain in this transaction.
B. Joel may choose to postpone a portion of his gain in this transaction.
C. Joel must use the accrual method in order to postpone gain.
D. Postponement of gain is not allowed.

5. Which of the following statements about farmers is correct?

A. Gross income from farming includes capital gains from the sale of equipment.
B. A farmer who is a sole proprietor may use income averaging to reduce his tax liability.
C. A farmer does not have to report income from crop insurance payments.
D. An individual who owns livestock as a hobby and grows a large garden can be considered a farmer for tax purposes.

6. Jon owns a dairy farming business and has income from the following sources:

Income from milk production	$50,000
Sale of old dairy cows no longer producing milk	20,000
Sale of feed	15,000
Sale of used machinery	4,000

What amount of income should be reported on Jon's Schedule F, *Profit or Loss from Farming?*

A. $50,000
B. $65,000
C. $74,000
D. $85,000

7. All of the following would be considered section 1245 property except:

A. A greenhouse.
B. A grain silo.
C. A wire chicken coop.
D. A barn that houses cows and horses, and also serves for the storage of supplies.

8. Oliver is a farmer who receives agricultural program payments after refraining from growing any crops in 2016. How should these payments be reported?

A. As "other income" on Oliver's individual Form 1040.
B. On Schedule E, *Supplemental Income and Loss*.
C. As farm income on Schedule F, not subject to self-employment tax.
D. As farm income on Schedule F, subject to self-employment tax.

9. Holly grows organic heirloom tomatoes and also raises goats on her 200-acre farm. Holly is an accrual-basis farmer who has the following income in the current year:

Rental of farmland in which she did not materially participate	$30,000
Sale of harvested tomatoes	145,000
Gain from sale of goats held primarily for breeding	85,000
Crop insurance payments	115,000

What amount of *farming* income must Holly report on Schedule F?

A. $145,000
B. $260,000
C. $290,000
D. $345,000

10. All of the following are acceptable methods for valuation of farm inventory except:

A. Cost method.
B. Harvest discount method.
C. Farm-price method.
D. Unit-livestock-price method.

11. Andy owns 150 acres of farmland that he rents to other farmers. His income from the rental is based on the productivity of the tenant-farmer. He does not actively participate in any of the farming activity. How should the income from this activity be reported?

A. As rental income on Form 4835.
B. As farming income on Schedule F.
C. As ordinary income on Schedule C.
D. As passive income on Schedule 4797.

12. The carryback period for farming losses is:

A. Two years.
B. Four years.
C. Five years.
D. Farmers are not allowed to carry back their losses.

13. Hope is a qualified farmer who grows soybeans. In 2016, her soybean crop was destroyed by flood. If the crop had not been destroyed, she would have harvested it in 2017. Hope receives federal disaster payments in 2016. Which of the following statements is correct?

A. Hope can choose to postpone the income from this disaster payment until 2017.
B. Disaster payments are not taxable income if they are treated as an involuntary conversion.
C. Hope must report the federal disaster payments on her 2016 return.
D. Hope may delay recognition of the federal disaster payments for two years.

14. Frank is a rancher in California who lives in an area that was declared a federal disaster area due to drought. The drought forced him to sell 50 head of cattle in 2016 that he would not have otherwise sold. Frank has _____________ to replace his livestock.

A. Two years.
B. Three years.
C. Four years.
D. Five years.

15. Farm income averaging is computed on Schedule J, which may be filed:

A. For the current year when a taxpayer files Schedule F showing a farm loss.
B. For the current year when a taxpayer files Schedule F showing net income from farming.
C. For the current year, along with Schedule C.
D. As an amended return showing the past three years of farming income.

16. To be eligible as a qualified farmer and not have to pay quarterly estimated taxes during the year, at least _____________ of a farmer's gross income must be from farming.

A. Half.
B. Two-thirds.
C. Three-quarters.
D. 80%.

17. What of the following conditions will force a farming business to use the accrual method?

A. A Family Farming Corporation that carries inventory, with gross receipts over $1 million.
B. A Family Farming Corporation that is also a tax shelter.
C. A farming business that files a Schedule F and has over 1 million in gross receipts.
D. A farming business that operates as a general partnership.

18. What is the Crop Method of accounting?

A. The crop method of accounting allows farmers to delay expense recognition for crops that they sell in the year after they are sown.
B. The crop method of accounting allows farmers to delay expense recognition for at least three years after they harvest their crops.
C. The crop method of accounting is an accrual-basis accounting method.
D. The crop method of accounting does not exist.

Unit 16: Answers

1. The answer is B. Schedule J, *Income Averaging for Farmers and Fishermen*, allows a farmer to average income over the prior three years to lower current-year tax liability.

2. The answer is A. If William waits until April 15 to file his return, he must pay estimated taxes just like any other business. If the taxpayer is a qualified farmer, he can either:

- Pay all the estimated tax by the fifteenth day after the end of the tax year (this date is usually January 15), or
- File his return and pay all the tax owed by the first day of the third month after the end of her tax year (usually March 1).

3. The answer is A. Farming equipment is a depreciable asset and therefore not included in inventory.

4. The answer is B. Joel may postpone a portion of his gain to the following year. If a farmer sells or exchanges more livestock, including poultry, than he normally would in a year because of a drought, flood, or other weather-related condition, he may postpone reporting the gain from the additional animals until the next year. The farmer must use the cash method of accounting in order to postpone gain in this manner.

5. The answer is B. Certain farmers may average all or some of their current year's farm income by allocating it to the three prior years. This may lower a farmer's current year tax if the current year is high and his taxable income from one or more of the three prior years was low. Income averaging is only available to farmers and fishermen who operate as sole proprietors or partnerships. It is reported on Schedule J, *Income Averaging for Farmers and Fishermen*.

6. The answer is B. The farming income reported is from milk production and sale of feed ($50,000 + $15,000 = $65,000). Gross income from farming activity is reported on Schedule F, and includes farm income, farm rental income, and gains from livestock that were raised specifically for sale on the farm, or purchased specifically for resale. The sale of old dairy cows and the sale of used machinery do not qualify. The sale of depreciable machinery and the sale of livestock used for dairy purposes are not reported on Schedule F. Instead, these amounts should be reported on Form 4797, *Sales of Business Property.*

7. The answer is D. Section 1245 typically excludes buildings and other structural components. However, there is an exception for single purpose agricultural or horticultural structures. A barn for cows and horses that also holds supplies is not a single purpose structure, so it would not be considered section 1245 property.

8. The answer is D. An agricultural program payment is reported on Schedule F, and the full amount of the payment is subject to self-employment tax.

9. The answer is B. The answer is calculated as follows: $145,000 sale of harvested crops + $115,000 of crop insurance payments = $260,000. If a farmer rents his farmland for someone else to use, the related revenue is generally considered rental income, rather than farm income. The gain from the sale of the livestock held for breeding would also not be reported on Schedule F. The insurance proceeds, (including government disaster payments), are generally taxable as ordinary income in the year they are received. A cash-basis farming business may elect to postpone reporting the income until the following year under certain conditions, but an accrual-basis business cannot. Income reported on Schedule F does not include gains or losses from sales or other dispositions of the following farm assets:

- Sale of land
- Depreciable farm equipment
- Buildings and structures
- Livestock held for draft, breeding, sport, or dairy purposes (unless held as inventory)

The sale of these assets is reported on Form 4797, *Sales of Business Property*, and may result in ordinary income or capital gains or losses.

10. The answer is B. The harvest discount method does not exist. All of the other inventory valuation methods listed are allowed for farming businesses.

11. The answer is A. The rent received for the use or rental of farmland is generally rental income, not farm income. If the farmer does not materially participate in operating the farm and the rental income is based on the productivity of the tenant-farmer, the income is reported on Form 4835, *Farm Rental Income and Expenses*, and the income is not subject to self-employment tax. However, if a farmer rents pasture or farmland out for a flat cash amount and does not provide any services to the tenant-farmer, then this rental income would be reported on schedule E.

12. The answer is C. The carryback period for farming losses is five years. Other businesses are allowed to carry back their losses only two years.

13. The answer is A. She can delay recognizing income on the federal disaster payments until 2017. Payments for disaster relief are taxable as ordinary income to farmers. These payments may be included in income in the tax year following the year in which they were awarded. In order to make this election, the farmer must be able to prove that the crops would have been harvested or otherwise sold in the following year.

14. The answer is D. Farmers generally have a four-year period to replace livestock sold due to weather conditions. However, in a federally-declared disaster area, a farmer can have up to five years to replace livestock.

15. The answer is B. If a farmer or fisherman elects income averaging, he must file Schedule J along with a Schedule F showing his net farming income.

16. The answer is B. An individual is a qualified farmer if at least two-thirds of his gross income from all sources was from farming.

17. The answer is B. Most farmers can use the cash method. However, all tax shelters must use an accrual method of accounting, regardless of the type of business activity. The following businesses, if engaged in farming, must use the accrual method of accounting.

- A corporation (other than a family farming corporation) that has $1 million or more in gross receipts
- A family farming corporation that had gross receipts of more than $25,000,000 for any tax year.
- A partnership with a corporation as a partner.
- A tax shelter.

18. The answer is A. Qualified farmers can, with approval of the Internal Revenue Service, use the crop method of accounting to delay expense recognition for crops. Farmers who do not harvest and sell their crop in the same year it is planted can capitalize the costs of production and deduct the entire cost of planting and producing the crop in the year they realize the income.

Unit 17: Exempt Organizations

More Reading:

Publication 4220, *Applying for 501(c)(3) Tax-Exempt Status*

Publication 557, *Tax-Exempt Status for Your Organization*

Publication 4221-PC, *Compliance Guide for 501(c)(3) Public Charities*

Publication 598, *Tax on Unrelated Business Income of Exempt Organizations*

Publication 1828, Tax Guide for Churches & Religious Organizations

Publication 1771, Charitable Contributions Substantiation and Disclosure Requirements

Nonprofit organizations are generally exempt from income tax and receive other favorable treatment under the tax law; however, certain income of an exempt organization may be subject to tax, such as income from an unrelated business activity. Despite their exempt status, nonprofit organizations are still subject to many filing and recordkeeping requirements under federal tax law.

IRC Section 501(c)(3)

The majority of nonprofit organizations qualify for tax-exempt status under section 501(c)(3) of the IRC. They are exempt from paying income tax in connection with their charitable activities, and they are eligible to receive tax-deductible charitable contributions. To qualify for these benefits, an organization must file an application with the IRS and must meet the following requirements:

- **Organization:** It must be organized as a corporation, a trust, or an unincorporated association, and its purpose must be limited to those described in section 501(c)(3). A nonprofit entity may not be organized as a partnership or sole proprietorship.
- **Exempt Purpose:** It must have one or more exempt purposes as listed under section 501(c)(3): charitable, educational, religious, scientific, literary, fostering national or international sports competition,[117] preventing cruelty to children or animals, and testing for public safety.
- **Operation:** A substantial portion of its activities must be related to its exempt purpose(s). Further, a 501(c)(3) organization must:
    - Refrain from participating in political campaigns of candidates
    - Restrict its lobbying activities to an "insubstantial" part of its total activities
    - Ensure that its earnings do not benefit any private shareholder or individual
    - Not operate for the benefit of private interests, such as those of its founder, the founder's family, or its shareholders
    - Not operate for the primary purpose of conducting a trade or business that is not related to its exempt purpose

Applying for 501(c)(3) Status

Before applying for tax-exempt status, an organization must be created by preparing an organizing document. This document must limit the organization's purposes to those set forth in section 501(c)(3) and must specify that the entity's assets will be permanently dedicated to the specified exempt purpose(s). The organizing document should also contain a provision for distributing funds if it dissolves.

To request exempt status under section 501(c)(3), an entity uses Form 1023, *Application for Recognition of Exemption*. An organization with annual gross receipts of no more than

[117] An example of a "sports-related" 501(c)(3) would be the Olympics and the Para Olympic Games. They are usually qualified amateur sports organizations, youth sports organizations, or sports organizations for the disabled.

$5,000 is not required to file Form 1023. However, it must file Form 1023 to request formal exemption within 90 days of the end of the year in which it exceeds this threshold.

Example: An animal rescue organization that was created five years ago did not exceed the $5,000 gross receipts threshold until its fiscal year ended September 30, 2016. The organization must file Form 1023 to request formal tax exemption by December 30, 2016, 90 days after reaching that threshold.

Note: A private foundation is *always* required to request formal tax exemption, regardless of the amount of its gross receipts.

Form 1023-EZ is designed for small tax-exempt organizations. The application is three pages long, compared to 26 pages for the traditional Form 1023. To qualify for the shorter form, an organization must have:

- Gross receipts of $50,000 or less, and
- Assets of $250,000 or less.

An organization must generally request exemption from the IRS by the end of the fifteenth month after it is created, with a 12-month extension available.

The IRS will review an organization's application and determine if it meets the requirements for exemption. If approved, the IRS will issue a letter recognizing the organization's exempt status and providing its public charity classification.

An organization that files its application before the deadline may be recognized as tax-exempt from the date of its creation. An organization that files an application after the deadline also may be recognized as tax-exempt from the date of the application by requesting exemption retroactive to the date of creation.

While an organization's Form 1023 is pending approval, the organization may operate as if it were tax-exempt. Donor contributions made while an application is pending would qualify, assuming the IRS later approves its 501(c)(3) status. If the application is not approved, these contributions would not qualify. The organization would also be liable for filing federal income tax returns unless its income is otherwise excluded from federal taxation.

Other Section 501(c) Organizations

Organizations that do not qualify for exemption under section 501(c)(3) may qualify for tax-exempt status by filing Form 1024, *Application for Recognition of Exemption Under Section 501(a).*

However, they may or may not qualify to receive contributions that are deductible by the donor. Examples include the following:

- 501(c)(4) Civic leagues and social welfare organizations
- 501(c)(5) Labor unions, agricultural, and horticultural organizations
- 501(c)(6) Business leagues (examples include local and state-level Chambers of Commerce).
- 501(c)(7) Social and recreation clubs (examples include: college fraternities and sororities; country clubs, and hobby clubs).
- 501(c)(8) and 501(c)(10) Fraternal beneficiary societies (examples include the Knights of Columbus, Sons of Norway, Freemasons and Odd Fellows).
- 501(c)(4), 501(c)(9), and 501(c)(17) Employees' associations
- 501(c)(12) Local benevolent life insurance associations
- 501(c)(13) Nonprofit cemetery companies
- 501(c)(14) Credit unions and other mutual financial organizations
- 501(c)(19) Veterans' organizations

Note: The PATH Act contained several provisions affecting tax-exempt organizations. New provisions require that all 501(c)(4)[118] organizations to file a notice of registration with the IRS within 60 days of the organization's formation. Any existing 501(c)(4) organizations that have not yet requested formal exemption or filed an annual information return (Form 990) must provide the notice required within 180 days of enactment of the PATH Act. In previous years, 501(c)(4) organizations were not required to submit an application (Form 1024) to the IRS to be recognized as a tax-exempt organization, but could self-declare exempt status, as long as the organization operated in a manner that was applicable to such organizations.

Public Charity or Private Foundation

Every organization that qualifies for tax-exempt status under section 501(c)(3) is further classified as either a public charity or a private foundation. Tax-exempt entities are presumed to be private foundations unless they fall into certain categories of organizations that are specifically excluded. Even if an organization falls into one of these excluded categories, it is presumed to be a private foundation unless it files a timely Form 1023 showing that it is not a private foundation.

The primary distinction between classification as a public charity or a private foundation is the organization's source of financial support. A public charity tends to have a broad base of support while a private foundation has more limited sources of support. Generally, an exempt organization will not be considered a private foundation if it receives more than one-third of its annual support from governmental units and/or the general public.

Example: Friedreich's Ataxia Research Alliance (FARA) is dedicated to finding a cure for a rare and disabling genetic disorder. The majority of its funding comes from individual donations from the public and various fundraising events that it sponsors, so FARA is classified as a public charity.

Example: Smithy Educational Ventures supports charter schools and 90% of its funding comes from members of the Smithy family, so it is classified as a private foundation.

The classification of public charity vs. private foundation is important because different tax rules apply: deductibility of contributions to a private foundation is more limited than deductibility of contributions to a public charity. Further, there is an excise tax on the net investment income of domestic private foundations. This excise tax must be paid annually or, if the total tax for the year is $500 or more, in quarterly estimated tax payments.

All private foundations must file Form 990-PF, *Return of Private Foundation*, every year, regardless of their income.

Filing Requirements

Every exempt organization must file an annual information return with the IRS, generally on Form 990, *Return of Organization Exempt from Income Tax*, unless it is specifically exempt from the filing requirement. The following organizations are not required to file:

- Churches and their affiliated organizations
- Government agencies

If an organization has gross receipts of less than $200,000 and total assets at the end of the year of less than $500,000, it can file Form 990-EZ. Tax-exempt organizations with gross receipts of $50,000 or less may file Form 990-N, *Electronic Notice for Tax-Exempt Organizations Not Required to File Form 990.* This form is also called an "e-postcard" because it is filed

[118] The 501(c)(4) exempt category is for politically active nonprofits. Examples include civic leagues and labor unions. While these organizations are required to have an exempt purpose, they are allowed to participate in political matters, as long as politics are not their primary focus.

electronically and is short. A small tax-exempt organization may voluntarily choose to file a long form (Form 990) instead.

An exempt entity may choose to file on a fiscal-year or a calendar-year basis. The applicable annual information return is due by the fifteenth day of the fifth month after the year ends. For a calendar-year entity, the due date is May 15. The extended due date for calendar year exempt entities is November 15.

Note: Starting with the 2016 tax year, exempt entities may request a six-month extension of time to file by filing Form 8868, *Application for Extension of Time to File an Exempt Organization Return*. In previous years, exempt entities would be required to request a 3-month extension, followed by an additional 3-month extension request.

Example: Friends of the Oak Knoll Library is a 501(c)(3) organization that operates on the calendar year. It had gross receipts of $20,000 in 2016. The organization must file Form 990-N, the e-postcard, by May 15, 2017.

If the organization has been dissolved, the return is due by the fifteenth day of the fifth month after the dissolution. An organization must file Form 990 electronically if it files at least 250 returns during the calendar year and has total assets of $10 million or more at the end of the tax year. A private foundation is required to file Form 990-PF electronically if it files at least 250 returns during the calendar year.

A section 501(c)(3) organization must make its application (Form 1023) and its three most recent annual returns (Form 990) available to the public. The IRS also makes these documents available for public inspection and copying.

Every tax-exempt entity must have an EIN, regardless of whether it has employees. Charitable organizations are required to provide a written disclosure to a donor who receives goods or services in exchange for a single payment in excess of $75.[119]

Penalties for Non-Filing

An exempt organization that fails to file a required return must pay a penalty of $20 a day for each day the return is late. The same penalty may apply if the organization provides incorrect information on the return. Generally, the maximum penalty is the smaller of:

- $10,000, or
- 5% of the organization's gross receipts for the year.[120]

The penalty applies on each day after the due date that the return isn't filed.

However, for an organization that has gross receipts of more than $1,020,000 for the year, the late filing penalty increased to $100 a day, up to a maximum of $51,000 (per return).[121]

An organization's exempt status may be revoked for failure to file. Failure to file an annual information return for three years in a row will result in the automatic revocation of exempt status. In this case, the organization would be required to reapply for exemption. However, no penalty will be imposed if reasonable cause for failure to timely file can be shown.

If an organization's tax-exempt status was automatically revoked for failing to file a return or notice for three consecutive years, it must apply to have its tax-exempt status reinstated by filing either Form 1023 or Form 1024 and paying the appropriate fee.

Note: Tax-exempt organizations that are required to file electronically, but do not, are deemed to have failed to file their return. This is true even if a paper return is submitted, unless the organization files by paper to report a name change.[122] Use of a paid preparer does not relieve the organization of its responsibility to electronically file their return if required to do so by law.

[119] See Publication 1771, *Charitable Contributions Substantiation and Disclosure Requirements.*

[120] IRC section 6652(c)(1)(A).

[121] These amounts are now indexed for inflation.

[122] See Form 990 instructions.

Exempt Entities with Employees

Just like other businesses, exempt organizations are subject to the basic requirements for tax and wage reporting compliance, calculating withholding, making deposits, and keeping tax and reporting records.

Even though some organizations (such as a church or other religious organization) are not required to file Forms 990, any entity with employees must withhold and remit income and Social Security and Medicare taxes on its employees' wages, and some exempt organizations are also responsible for Federal Unemployment Tax (FUTA).

Example: Trinity Methodist Church is not required to file an application for exemption in order to be recognized as tax-exempt by the IRS. Trinity applies for an EIN as an exempt entity and begins regular worship. In the same year, Trinity Church hires three employees: a part-time pastor, a Sunday child care worker, and a music leader. Although Trinity does not have to file Form 990, the church is still required to file employment tax returns and remit and collect employment taxes from its employees. In this way, an exempt organization is treated like every other employer.

Unrelated Business Income Tax (UBIT)

Although an exempt organization must be operated primarily for tax-exempt purposes, it may engage in income-producing activities that are unrelated to those purposes, so long as these activities are not a substantial part of the organization's regular activities. Income from unrelated business activities is subject to a federal tax called the *unrelated business income tax* (UBIT). For most organizations, an activity is considered an unrelated business activity and subject to UBIT if:

- It is a trade or business,
- It is regularly carried on, and
- It is not substantially related to furthering the exempt purpose(s) of the organization.

An exempt organization that has $1,000 or more of gross income from an unrelated business must file Form 990–T by the fifteenth day of the fifth month after the tax year ends. An exempt organization must make quarterly payments of estimated tax on unrelated business income if it expects its tax for the year to be $500 or more.

Example: A university enters into a multi-year contract with a company to be its exclusive provider of sports drinks for the athletic department and concessions. As part of the contract, the university agrees to perform various services for the company, such as guaranteeing that coaches make promotional appearances on behalf of the company. The university itself is a qualified nonprofit organization, but the income received from the exclusive contract is subject to UBIT. The university is therefore required to file Form 990-T.

Example: A college negotiates discounted rates for the soft drinks it purchases for its cafeterias in return for an exclusive provider arrangement. Generally, discounts are considered an adjustment to the purchase price and do not constitute gross income to the purchaser. Thus, the amount of the negotiated discount is not includable in UBIT. The college is not required to file Form 990-T.

Summary of Exempt Entity Requirements

Exempt Entities: Financial Activity	Annual Information Return Required
Gross receipts less than $50,000	Form 990-N (e-postcard)
Gross receipts less than $200,000 and total assets less than $500,000	Form 990-EZ or Form 990
Gross receipts more than $200,000, or total assets more than $500,000	Form 990
Unrelated business income of $1,000 or more	Form 990-T
Private foundation (must file every year, regardless of financial activity)	Form 990-PF
Churches and similar religious organizations	No annual information return filing requirement, but may be required to file payroll returns if the entity has employees

Unit 17: Study Questions

(Please test yourself and check the correct answers at the end of this section.)

1. Under streamlined application procedures, an exempt organization may use Form 1023-EZ if it has up to ___________ of gross receipts for the year.

A. $5,000
B. $25,000
C. $50,000
D. $250,000

2. Which of the following exempt organizations is not required to file an annual information return (Form 990)?

A. A church with gross donation receipts exceeding $250,000.
B. An exempt literary organization with $6,000 of gross receipts.
C. A Chamber of Commerce with $26,000 of gross receipts.
D. A private foundation with income of less than $5,000.

3. An organization will have its tax-exempt status revoked if it fails to file information returns for ________ years in a row.

A. Two.
B. Three.
C. Five.
D. Never. Once tax-exempt, an organization cannot have its status revoked.

4. A local Catholic church has two employees: Martha, who works as a secretary in the church rectory, and Jack, who is the church custodian. Which return(s) must the church file in order to fulfill its IRS reporting obligations?

A. Form 990.
B. Form 8300.
C. Employment tax returns.
D. Form 990-PF.

5. Child Rescue Inc. is a calendar-year nonprofit organization that helps prevent child abuse. It is required to file Form 990 in 2016. What is the due date of its tax return, not including extensions?

A. November 15
B. March 15
C. May 15
D. October 15

6. Most organizations seeking recognition of exemption from federal income tax must use specific application forms prescribed by the IRS. Which form must be filed in order to request recognition as a 501(c)(3) nonprofit organization by the IRS?

A. Form 1023.
B. Form 1024.
C. Form 1040.
D. Form 990.

7. What action does the IRS take if a nonprofit with $500,000 of gross receipts fails to file its required information returns or notices?

A. Nothing. Information returns are voluntary.
B. Impose a maximum penalty of up to the lesser of $10,000 or 5% of the organization's gross receipts for the year.
C. Automatic revocation of tax-exempt status if the organization fails to file returns or notices for three consecutive years.
D. Both B and C are correct.

8. Which of the following statements is correct?

A. If an exempt organization qualifies for tax-exempt status with the IRS, any contributions it receives are fully deductible by the donors.
B. A church is not required to file an annual information return (Form 990).
C. A religious entity does not have to file payroll tax returns if it has employees.
D. A church may be organized as a sole proprietorship.

9. Which of the following organizations does not qualify for tax-exempt status?

A. A charitable organization.
B. A religious organization.
C. A private foundation.
D. An educational partnership.

10. Which form does an organization that wishes to be recognized as a 501(c)(4) charity need to file with the IRS?

A. Form 990.
B. Form 990 and its organizing document.
C. Form 1024.
D. Form 1023, its organizing document, a listing of its board of directors, and its bylaws.

11. All of the organizations listed below would qualify for tax-exempt status under the Internal Revenue Code except:

A. A Christian church with only eight members.
B. A political action committee.
C. A trust for a college alumni association.
D. A local boys club.

12. A charitable organization has $2,000 in unrelated business income in the current year. How is this income reported?

A. The organization must file a business tax return for the unrelated business income.
B. The organization is required to file Form 990-T.
C. The organization will have its exempt status revoked.
D. The organization must file Schedule C to correctly report the business income.

13. Which kind of organization is allowed to file an e-postcard?

A. A private foundation.
B. A nonprofit with gross receipts of $250,000 or less.
C. A nonprofit with gross receipts of $50,000 or less.
D. A nonprofit with gross receipts of $100,000 or less.

14. Sierra Kids Sports is a calendar-year nonprofit organization that offers youth sports activities to impoverished children. Sierra Kids Sports is required to file Form 990 in 2016. What is the *extended* due date of its tax return?

A. November 15
B. March 15
C. May 15
D. October 15

Unit 17: Answers

1. The answer is C. The Form 1023-EZ is designed for small tax-exempt organizations that have gross receipts of $50,000 or less and assets of $250,000 or less.

2. The answer is A. Only the church would not be required to file a tax return. Tax-exempt organizations must file a Form 990 or Form 990-N (e-postcard) unless specifically exempt. Private foundations must file a Form 990-PF, regardless of income.

3. The answer is B. An organization's failure to file an annual information return for three years in a row will result in the automatic revocation of its exempt status. The organization would be required to reapply for exemption. The IRS has introduced new streamlined procedures for retroactive reinstatement of organizations eligible to file either Form 990-EZ or Form 990-N.

4. The answer is C. Exempt churches, their integrated auxiliaries, and conventions or associations of churches are not required to file information returns. However, every employer is responsible for filing employment tax returns.

5. The answer is C. Since Child Rescue is on a calendar year, its tax return is due May 15. Each tax-exempt organization is required to file by the fifteenth day of the fifth month after its fiscal year ends.

6. The answer is A. The form required by the IRS to apply for 501(c)(3) status is Form 1023, *Application for Recognition of Exemption Under Section 501(c)(3) of the Internal Revenue Code*. Form 1023-EZ may also be used by some small tax-exempt organizations.

7. The answer is D. Exempt organizations are subject to failure-to-file penalties and to automatic revocation if returns are not filed for three consecutive years. For exempt organizations with gross receipts up to $1.02 million for the year, the maximum penalty is up to $10,000 or 5% of the organization's gross receipts for the year (whichever is less). For exempt organizations with gross receipts of more than $1.02 million a year, the maximum penalty is increased to $51,000.

8. The answer is B. A religious organization is not required to file an annual information return.

9. The answer is D. A partnership does not qualify for exemption from income tax. A tax-exempt organization cannot be organized as a partnership or a sole proprietorship.

10. The answer is C. 501(c)(4) organizations are required to file Form 1024, *Application for Recognition of Exemption Under Section 501(a)* with the IRS, along with the entity's organizing document.

11. The answer is B. A political action committee would not qualify. In general, if a substantial part of an organization's activities includes attempting to influence legislation, the organization's exemption from federal income tax will be denied.

12. The answer is B. An exempt organization that has $1,000 or more of gross income from unrelated business activity must file Form 990–T.

13. The answer is C. A tax-exempt organization, other than a private foundation, with gross receipts of $50,000 or less may file the short "e-postcard" Form 990-N, *Electronic Notice for Tax-Exempt Organizations Not Required to File Form 990*, instead of the longer information return, Form 990, if it so chooses.

14. The answer is A. Since Sierra Kids Sports is on a calendar year, its normal tax return is due May 15. However, the *extended* due date of the organization's return would be November 15, six months after the regular due date.

Unit 18: Retirement Plans for Businesses

More Reading:
Publication 560, *Retirement Plans for Small Business*
Publication 590-A, *Contributions to Individual Retirement Arrangements*
Publication 590-B, *Distributions from Individual Retirement Arrangements*
Publication 3398, *Choosing a Retirement Solution for Your Small Business*

Employers may establish retirement plans as fringe benefits for their employees. Self-employed taxpayers are also allowed to set up retirement plans for themselves.

There are numerous forms of retirement plans that are available for small businesses: they include Simplified Employee Pension (SEP) plans, Savings Incentive Match Plan for Employees (SIMPLE) plans, and qualified plans.

Note: The term "**qualified** plan" refers to certain IRS requirements that the plan and the employer must adhere to in order to obtain tax-favored status. SEP and SIMPLE plans must also meet certain requirements, but the rules are much less complex than those that apply to qualified plans.

If retirement plans are structured and operated properly, businesses can deduct retirement contributions they make on behalf of their employees or, if self-employed, themselves. Both the contributions and the earnings are generally tax-free until distribution. The rules vary depending on the type of business. Any business, including a sole proprietorship or a partnership, can deduct retirement plan contributions made on behalf of employees, even if the business has a net operating loss for the year.

Example: Gemma is self-employed and reports her income and losses from her catering business on Schedule C. She has a retirement account set up for herself and her five employees. In 2016, Gemma's catering business showed a loss from operations on her Schedule C, and Gemma has no other source of taxable income. She made regular contributions to her employees' retirement accounts in 2016, and she can deduct these contributions as a regular business expense. However, Gemma cannot make a retirement contribution for herself in 2016 because she has no self-employment income. Since her business showed a loss, she has no qualifying income for purposes of her own retirement plan contribution.

In the case of a sole proprietorship or partnership, if the owners of the business contribute to their own retirement accounts, they may take the deduction on Form 1040, and only if they have self-employment income.

Self-employment income for the purpose of this deduction means net profits from Schedule C or Schedule F, or self-employment income from a partnership. Since an S corporation is a pass-through entity, certain shareholder-employees in an S corporation are also required to report these deductions on their individual returns.[123]

However, as a C corporation is not a pass-through entity, the corporation deducts the expense on Form 1120, *U.S. Corporation Income Tax Return,* whether the contributions are made for employee-shareholders, officers, or other employees.

[123] This rule applies to employee-shareholders who own more than 2% of the S corporation stock.

Retirement plans generally must adhere to certain nondiscrimination requirements intended to ensure they do not favor owners or executives of the sponsoring employer over other employees. Depending upon the type of plan, these requirements may include:

- Minimum coverage tests that limit elective deferral and employer contributions to highly compensated employees (HCEs) as percentages compared to the corresponding percentages for non-highly compensated employees.
- Prohibition of terms that favor HCEs' dollar amounts of contributions or benefits, or other rights.

Simplified Employee Pension (SEP) Plans

A SEP plan provides the simplest and least expensive method for employers to make contributions to a retirement plan for themselves and their employees.

An employer may establish a SEP as late as the due date (including extensions) of its income tax return and have it be effective for that year. The employer must also make its contribution to the plan by the due date (including extensions).

Example: Julie is a sole proprietor with two full-time employees. She plans to file her 2016 tax return on the extended due date of October 15, 2017. She has until the extended due date to establish and set up a SEP plan and make contributions for herself and her two employees.

With SEPs, there is no requirement for an official "plan document" such as those needed for qualified retirement plans. However, the employer must execute a written agreement[124] to provide benefits to all eligible employees under the SEP.

Except in certain circumstances, including when the employer also maintains a qualified plan, this can be done using Form 5305-SEP. Using this form will typically eliminate the need to file annual information returns with the IRS and the Department of Labor.

Contributions to a SEP can vary from year to year, so it is a very flexible option for small employers. A SEP can be set up for an individual person's business even if he participates in another employer's retirement plan.

Example: Mitch works full-time for the post office as a mail carrier, and also runs a profitable wedding photography business with his wife on the weekends. They have self-employment income from the photo business. Mitch may set up a SEP for himself and his wife through his photography business, even though he is already covered by a retirement plan through the post office.

Under a SEP, employers make contributions to an individual retirement arrangement (also called a SEP-IRA), which must be set up for each eligible employee. The SEP-IRA is owned and controlled by the employee, and the employer makes contributions to the financial institution where the SEP-IRA is maintained. SEP-IRAs are funded exclusively by contributions from the employer. A SEP does not require employer contributions every year, but it cannot discriminate in favor of HCEs. An eligible employee for SEP-IRA purposes is one who meets all the following requirements:

- Is at least 21 years old
- Has worked for the employer in at least three of the last five years
- Has received at least $600 of compensation in 2016

[124] Employers can satisfy the "written agreement" requirement by adopting an IRS model SEP using Form 5305-SEP.

An employer can use *less* restrictive participation requirements than those listed, but cannot use *more* restrictive ones. For example, an employer could choose to include all employees who are at least 18 years old, rather than at least 21 years old.

The following employees can be excluded from coverage under a SEP:

- Employees covered by a union agreement
- Nonresident alien employees who have received no U.S. source income from the employer

SEP Basic Rules

	Rules for Employers	Rules for Employees
Eligibility	Any business or self-employed individual may set up a SEP.	Employees aged 21 or older who have worked for the business for three of the last five years and earned at least $600 in 2016 are eligible.
Contributions	Vesting is immediate. Contributions under a SEP can be made to participants over age 70½.	Only employers and self-employed individuals can contribute to a SEP. Employees cannot contribute to a SEP.
Pros	Contributions can vary from year to year. Inexpensive to set up and administer.	Distributions from a SEP cannot be Prohibited by an employer, because vesting is immediate.
Drawbacks	A SEP must cover all qualifying employees. Only employers can contribute to the plan.	Employees cannot contribute.

Note: If an employer sets up a SEP, all eligible employees *must* participate in the plan, including part-time employees, seasonal employees, and employees who die or terminate employment during the year. This is true even if an employee does not want a retirement plan.

Contributions to a SEP must be made in cash; an employer cannot contribute property to a SEP. However, plan participants may be able to transfer or roll over certain property from another retirement plan account to a SEP-IRA. Each year an employer contributes to a SEP, it must contribute to the SEP-IRAs of all participants who had qualified compensation.

Example: Vazquez Company decides to establish a SEP for its employees. Vasquez has chosen a SEP because its industry is cyclical in nature. In good years, Vasquez can make larger contributions for its employees, and in down years, it can reduce or eliminate contributions. Vasquez knows that under a SEP, the contribution rate (whether large or small) must be uniform for all employees. The financial institution that Vasquez identifies to be the trustee for its SEP has several investment funds for employees to choose from. Individual employees have the opportunity to divide their employer's contributions to their SEP-IRAs among these fund options.

Employee salary reduction contributions cannot be made under a SEP. A SEP-IRA cannot be a Roth IRA. Employer contributions to a SEP-IRA do not affect the amount an individual can contribute to a Roth or traditional IRA. In other words, the IRS places no restrictions on contributing to both a SEP-IRA and a traditional IRA in the same year.

Example: Gary has a SEP-IRA through his employer. He also has a traditional IRA set up at his credit union. Gary's employer contributes $1,000 to his SEP-IRA in 2016. Gary may still contribute the maximum to his traditional IRA if he so chooses.

SEP Contribution Limits

With regard to SEP contribution limits, the maximum compensation limit that can be considered is $265,000 for 2016. In 2016, SEP contributions cannot exceed the lesser of:

- 25% of the employee's compensation, or
- $53,000.[125]

Employers cannot make contributions conditional, or require that any part of the contribution be kept in the employee's account after the business has made its contributions. SEPs generally are not required to file annual financial reports. SEP-IRA contributions are not included on the employee's Form W-2.

Example: Newhaven Grocery Store offers a SEP-IRA to its employees. Newhaven's bakery supervisor, Marie, earned $21,000 for 2016. The maximum contribution that Newhaven can make to her SEP-IRA is $5,250 (25% x $21,000). Marie cannot contribute to the plan. Only Newhaven, the employer, is allowed to contribute.

Note: Unlike a traditional IRA, contributions to a SEP can be made for participants over age 70½, as long as the taxpayer has qualifying earned income. However, participants age 70½ or over must still take required minimum distributions.

SEP Distributions and Withdrawals

Employees have control over their own SEP-IRAs, so employers cannot prohibit distributions from a SEP-IRA. Similar to traditional IRAs, money withdrawn from a SEP-IRA (if not rolled over to another qualified retirement plan) is subject to income tax for the year in which a distribution is received.

Participants cannot take loans from their SEP-IRAs. However, participants can make withdrawals at any time. These monies can be rolled over tax-free to another SEP-IRA, to another traditional IRA, or to another qualified retirement plan.

If an employee withdraws money from a SEP-IRA before age 59½, a 10% additional tax generally applies. A participant in a SEP-IRA must begin receiving required minimum distributions (RMDs) by April 1 of the year following the year the participant reaches age 70½.

SIMPLE Plans (SIMPLE IRA and SIMPLE 401(k))

A SIMPLE (Savings Incentive Match Plan for Employees) plan provides another simplified way for a business and its employees to contribute toward retirement. Like SEPs, SIMPLE plans have lower start-up and annual costs than most other types of retirement plans. A SIMPLE plan can be structured in one of two ways:

- as a **SIMPLE IRA** or
- as a **SIMPLE 401(k)** plan.

If a business has 100 or fewer employees who received $5,000 or more of compensation during the preceding year, it can establish a SIMPLE plan.[126] The business cannot maintain

[125] These limits increase to $270,000 and $54,000, respectively, in 2017.

another retirement plan unless the other plan is specifically for a union workforce (union employees are also called "collective bargaining employees" in IRS Publication 560).

The business must continue to meet the 100-employee limit each year. However, if a business maintains a SIMPLE plan and subsequently fails to meet the 100-employee limit, the business is allowed a two-year grace period to establish another retirement plan, with the business able to continue to maintain the SIMPLE plan during this 2-year grace period.

Another exception may apply if the business fails to meet the 100-employee limit as a result of an acquisition, disposition, or other similar transaction, so long as the coverage under the SIMPLE plan has not significantly changed during the grace period and the SIMPLE plan would have otherwise continued to qualify.

Example: Plunkett Financial is a check processing business with 90 employees. Plunkett offers a SIMPLE Plan to its entire staff. During the year, Plunkett Financial acquires a lucrative outside contract. Plunkett is forced to hire twenty additional employees in order to deal with the increased work volume. Since Plunkett Financial has exceeded the 100-employee limit (90 + 20 additional new hires = 110 employees), the company is required to establish another retirement plan. Plunkett has up to 2 years to establish a new retirement plan for its employees. The company is allowed to maintain its existing SIMPLE Plan during the 2-year grace period.

Employees can choose to make retirement plan contributions by allocating a portion of their salaries, and businesses can contribute matching or nonelective contributions. SIMPLE plans can only be maintained on a calendar-year basis.

SIMPLE IRAs

The SIMPLE IRA plan is less burdensome for an employer than other types of retirement plans. The employer has no requirement to make annual filings to the IRS.

Unlike a SEP-IRA, SIMPLE IRAs allow for employee contributions and also require employer contributions. Contributions to each employee's SIMPLE IRA are made up of their own salary reduction contributions and employer contributions.

A SIMPLE IRA must be set up for each eligible employee. An eligible employee is generally one who received at least $5,000 of compensation during any two years preceding the current calendar year and is reasonably expected to receive at least $5,000 in the current calendar year, except for:

- Employees covered by a union agreement.
- Nonresident alien employees who have received no U.S. source income.

Prior to an election period (generally 60 days) preceding the start of the calendar year, employees must receive formal notice of their rights to participate and make salary reduction contributions, and information regarding the employer's planned contributions.

Contributions to a SIMPLE IRA

During the election period, an employee may execute or modify a salary reduction agreement to defer a portion of his salary (up to $12,500 for 2016). The employer cannot place

[126] For purposes of the 100-employee limitation, all employees employed at any time during the year are taken into account, regardless of whether all of them are eligible to participate in the SIMPLE plan.

restrictions on the contribution amount (such as limiting the employee's contribution percentage), except to comply with the $12,500 limit for 2016.

Employees age 50 or over can also make a catch-up contribution of up to $3,000 in 2016. The salary reduction contributions under a SIMPLE IRA plan are elective deferrals that count toward an overall annual limit on elective deferrals an employee may make to this and other plans permitting elective deferrals.

Each year, the employer must choose to make either matching contributions or nonelective contributions to the employee's retirement plan. Employer matching of the employee's salary reduction contributions is generally required on a dollar-for-dollar basis up to 3% of the participant's compensation.

However, the employer may elect to make matching contributions at a rate of less than 3%, but at a rate of no lower than 1%, for no more than two years within a five-year period that ends with (and includes) the year the lower matching rate is effective. In addition, the employer must notify employees about the upcoming reduced matching rate for the upcoming year within a reasonable time before the 60-day period the employees have to enter into agreements to contribute to the SIMPLE plan for the year.

Instead of matching contributions, the employer may choose to make nonelective contributions of 2% of each eligible employee's compensation. An individual employee's compensation used for this contribution is limited to $265,000 in 2016.

Example: Elodie works for the Black Seal Tire Company, a small business with 75 employees. Black Seal decides to establish a SIMPLE IRA plan and will make a 2% nonelective contribution for each of its employees. Under this option, even if Elodie does not contribute to her own SIMPLE IRA, she would still receive an employer nonelective contribution to her SIMPLE IRA equal to 2% of her salary. Elodie has a yearly salary of $40,000 and has decided not to make a contribution to her SIMPLE IRA this year. Even though she does not make a contribution, Black Seal must make a nonelective contribution of $800 (2% of $40,000). The financial institution that Black Seal uses for the SIMPLE IRA has several investment options from which Elodie and the other plan participants can choose.

If the employer chooses to make nonelective contributions, it must make them for *all* eligible employees, regardless of whether they choose to make salary reduction contributions. The employer must notify employees of its choice to make nonelective contributions within a specified period prior to the employees' annual period for making their own salary reduction contribution elections.

An eligible employee may choose not to make salary reduction contributions for a given year. In this case, the employee would accrue no employer matching contributions, but would receive an employer nonelective contribution if the employer elects to make this type of contribution for the year.

Employee and employer contributions are 100% vested. This means that the money an employee has put aside plus employer contributions and net earnings from investments cannot be forfeited. The employee has the right to withdraw funds at any time, but those withdrawals may be subject to tax.

Definition: Vesting refers to a person's rights to receive some type of benefit, such as retirement benefits, or other employee benefits such as stock options. Vesting may occur on a gradual schedule, such as a certain percentage per year of employee service, or at a set time, such as five years after an employee has begun work for a company.

Example: Rockland Quarry Company is a small business with 50 employees. Rockland has decided to establish a SIMPLE IRA plan for all of its employees and will match its employees' contributions dollar-for-dollar up to 3% of each employee's salary. Under this option, if a Rockland employee does not contribute to his SIMPLE IRA, the employee does not receive any matching employer contributions. Elizabeth is an employee of Rockland Company. She has a yearly salary of $50,000 and decides to contribute 5% of her salary to her SIMPLE IRA. Elizabeth's yearly contribution is $2,500 (5% of $50,000). The Rockland matching contribution is $1,500 (3% of $50,000). Therefore, the total contribution to Elizabeth's SIMPLE IRA that year is $4,000 (her $2,500 contribution plus the $1,500 contribution from Rockland).

Salary reduction contributions must be deposited with the applicable financial institution within 30 days after the end of the month in which they would otherwise have been paid to the employee. Matching or nonelective contributions must be made by the due date (including extensions) for filing the company's income tax return for the year.

An employer can set up a SIMPLE IRA plan effective on any date from January 1 through October 1 of a year, provided the employer did not previously maintain another SIMPLE IRA plan. A new employer may set up a SIMPLE IRA plan as soon as administratively feasible after the business comes into existence.

An employer can deduct SIMPLE IRA contributions for a particular tax year if they are made for that tax year and are made by the due date (including extensions) of the federal income tax return for that year.

Example: Paul's Butcher Shop is a sole proprietorship with one employee. Paul reports his business income on Schedule C. Paul has one full-time employee, a bookkeeper named Nadine. In 2016, Paul sets up a SIMPLE IRA for himself and Nadine. Paul deducts contributions to his own SIMPLE IRA on line 28 of his Form 1040 as an adjustment to income (including contributions made in 2017 by April 18, 2017). The business' contributions to Nadine's SIMPLE IRA are deductible as a regular business expense on Schedule C.

A business cannot suspend its employer matching contributions mid-year or terminate its SIMPLE IRA plan mid-year. The business must maintain the plan for a full calendar year (except in the year the business first establishes the plan). The employer is required to make the contributions that were promised to the employees.

A SIMPLE IRA plan may not require a participant to be employed on a specific date to receive an employer contribution. If a participant terminates employment during the year after making a salary reduction contribution, he would still be entitled to an employer contribution.

SIMPLE IRA contributions are not included in the "Wages, tips, other compensation" box of Form W-2, *Wage and Tax Statement*. However, salary reduction contributions must be included in the boxes for Social Security and Medicare wages.

Distributions from a SIMPLE IRA

Distributions are subject to income tax in the year they are received. If a participant takes a withdrawal from a SIMPLE IRA before age 59½, an additional tax of 10% generally applies. If the withdrawal occurs within two years of beginning participation in the SIMPLE IRA plan, the additional tax is increased to 25%.

SIMPLE IRA contributions and earnings may be rolled over tax-free from one SIMPLE IRA to another. A rollover may also be made from a SIMPLE IRA to another type of IRA, but it will be tax-free only if it is made after two years of participation in the SIMPLE IRA plan.

Distributions from SIMPLE IRAs must occur eventually. A participant in a SIMPLE IRA plan must begin receiving required minimum distributions by April 1 of the year following the year the participant reaches age 70½.

Example: Bernadette turns 70½ in May of 2016. She decides to defer her first RMD until April 1, 2017. Her required minimum distribution is $4,000. She withdraws the amount on April 1, 2017. The distribution is taxable, but not subject to any penalty, because Bernadette is over the age of 59½.

SIMPLE-IRA Basic Rules		
	Rules for Employers	**Rules for Employees**
Eligibility	Any employer with 100 or fewer employees who received at least $5,000 in the preceding year. The employer cannot maintain another retirement plan in addition to the SIMPLE IRA.	Any employee who has earned at least $5,000 in any two prior years and who is expected to earn at least $5,000 in the current year.
Contribution Thresholds	Employers may choose to make either matching contributions at 1% to 3% of compensation for employees that make salary deferral contributions, or nonelective contributions at 2% of compensation for all eligible employees.	An employee can contribute up to $12,500 of his salary in 2016 (or self-employment earnings, for a self-employed owner), plus an additional $3,000 if age 50 or older.
Pros	Employees can make contributions. Vesting is immediate.	Employees can make contributions. Vesting is immediate.
Drawbacks	Employer matching is mandatory.	Employees with higher salaries may prefer a retirement plan option that allows them to contribute more.

SIMPLE 401(k) Plans

Under a SIMPLE 401(k) plan, an employee can elect to defer some of their compensation in to their retirement account. The employer is required to make either:

- A matching contribution up to 3% of each employee's pay, or
- A non-elective contribution of 2% of each eligible employee's pay.

No other contributions can be made. The employees are totally vested in any and all contributions. This means that the employee can withdraw from their SIMPLE 401(k) at any time. In order to establish a SIMPLE 401(k) plan, the business:

- Must have 100 or fewer employees.
- Cannot have any other retirement plans.
- Need to a Form 5500 annually.

A SIMPLE 401(k) plan can be adopted as part of a traditional 401(k) plan (see below) if the business meets the 100-employee limit discussed above for SIMPLE IRA plans and does not maintain another qualified retirement plan.

An employee can elect to make salary reduction contributions as a percentage of his compensation, but not more than $12,500 for 2016. An employee age 50 or over can also make a catch-up contribution of up to $3,000 in 2016.

SIMPLE 401(k) Basic Rules	
Pros	**Cons**
The plan is not subject to the discrimination rules that apply to traditional 401(k) plans.	No other retirement plans can be maintained if a business has a SIMPLE.
The plan may offer optional participant loans and hardship withdrawals to add flexibility for employees.	Withdrawal and loan flexibility adds an administrative burden for the employer.
Inexpensive to start.	Not available to larger employers with more than 100 employees.
Employees may contribute.	The plan must file Form 5500, *Annual Return/Report of Employee Benefit Plan*, annually.

Qualified Retirement Plans

There are two basic kinds of "qualified" retirement plans:

- **Defined contribution plans** (examples include a 401(k) or a 403(b)) and
- **Defined benefit plans** (often referred to as a pension plan or traditional pension)

Note: Most large companies offer some type of qualified plan to their employees. In general, an employee's contributions to a qualified plan are not taxed until they withdraw money from the plan.

Different rules apply to each. Defined **contribution** plans require the employee to fund their retirement account with their own money. A defined **benefit** plan is a type of retirement account for which the employer invests all the money and promises a set payout when the employee retires.

Defined benefit plans are more desirable for the employee, but they cost more money to administer and maintain. For that reason, defined benefit plans have become uncommon, except for those who work in government or public service.

Example: Denise earns $26,000 annually. She contributes $3,000 of her pay to her employer's 401(k) plan on a pretax basis. As a result, her taxable income is now $23,000. She isn't taxed on her contributions ($3,000), or any investment earnings, until she receives a distribution from the plan upon retirement. Her future benefits depend on the value of her retirement account. Denise has a "**defined contribution**" plan.

Example: Jethro worked as a custodian for his local public school district for over 25 years. The school district offers a traditional pension to all the employees who work for the district for at least two years. When Jethro retired in 2016 at age 65, he started receiving his monthly pension benefits. Jethro will receive lifetime monthly payments until his death. Jethro has a "**defined benefit**" plan.

An employer is allowed to have more than one type of qualified plan, but maximum contributions cannot exceed annual limits.

All qualified plans are subject to federal regulation under the Employee Retirement Income Security Act (ERISA). The federal government does not require an employer to establish a retirement plan, but it provides minimum federal standards for qualified plans.

ERISA covers qualified retirement plans, as well as health and welfare benefit plans. Among other requirements, ERISA specifies that individuals who manage plans (and other fiduciaries) meet certain standards of conduct. The law also contains detailed provisions for reporting to the government and for disclosure to participants. Further, there are provisions aimed at assuring plan funds are protected and participants receive their benefits. ERISA mandates minimum funding requirements to ensure that benefits will be available to employees when they retire. For defined benefit plans, it requires that plan funding be certified by an actuary.

ERISA also mandates that qualified plans meet specific requirements regarding eligibility, vesting, and communications with participants. The administrator of an employee benefit plan subject to ERISA must file an information return for the plan each year. Form 5500, *Annual Return/Report of Employee Benefit Plan*, must be filed by the last day of the seventh month after the plan year ends.

Defined Benefit Plans

A defined benefit plan (often called a traditional pension plan) promises a specified benefit amount or annuity after retirement. Most federal and state governments offer defined benefit plans to their employees. However, fewer companies now offer defined benefit plans because they are costly to administer and inflexible. The benefits in many defined benefit plans are protected by federal insurance.

Contributions to a defined benefit plan are not optional; a business is required to make them. They are typically based on actuarial calculations. Contributions for self-employed taxpayers are limited to 100% of compensation. If the business does not have any income for the year, no contribution can be made.

Defined Contribution Plans

A defined contribution plan provides an individual account for each participant in the plan. It provides benefits to the participant based on the amounts contributed to the participant's account, along with subsequent income, expenses, gains, losses, and, in some instances, allocations of forfeitures among participant accounts.

The participant, the employer, or sometimes both, may contribute to the individual participant accounts. The value of the account will fluctuate due to the changes in the value of investments that have been made with the amounts contributed. A participant's retirement benefits depend primarily on the amount of contributions made on his behalf, rather than upon his years of service with the employer or his earnings history. Examples of defined contribution plans include 401(k) plans, 403(b) plans, and 457 plans.

Traditional 401(k) Plans

A 401(k) plan is a defined contribution plan that allows each eligible employee to defer receiving a portion of his salary, which is instead contributed on his behalf to the 401(k) plan. Deferrals generally are made on a pretax basis, although some plans allow employees the option to make them on an after-tax basis.

Pre-tax deferrals are not subject to income tax withholding, and they are not included in taxable wages on the employee's Form W-2. However, they are subject to Social Security, Medicare, and federal unemployment taxes.

Sometimes the employer will make matching contributions. Employee deferrals and any employer matching contributions are accounted separately for each employee. Earnings on the retirement account grow tax-free until distribution.

401(k) plans can vary significantly in their complexity. However, many financial institutions administer 401(k) plans, which can lessen the administrative burden on individual employers of establishing and maintaining these plans.

Distributions from Qualified Plans

Generally, distributions cannot be made from a qualified plan until one of the following occurs:

- The employee retires, dies, becomes disabled, or otherwise terminates employment.
- The plan terminates.
- The employee reaches age 59½ or suffers financial hardship.

Unless a distribution is properly rolled over into another retirement plan or individual retirement account, it will be subject to income tax upon receipt. If a distribution is made to an employee before he reaches age 59½, the employee may have to pay a 10% additional tax on the distribution. This is often called an "early withdrawal penalty".

However, the additional 10% penalty may not apply in the following situations:

- Distributions are for the taxpayer's medical care, up to the amount allowed as a medical deduction.
- Disability or death.
- Distributions in the form of an annuity.

- Distributions are made because of an IRS levy on the plan.
- Distributions are made to a qualified reservist (an individual called up to active duty in the U.S. Armed Forces).

Even if these distributions are not subject to the additional 10% tax, they would be subject to tax at the taxpayer's applicable income tax rate. A distribution from a qualified plan must be reported on the employee's Form 1040.

Example: Lauren, age 43, takes a $5,000 distribution from her traditional IRA account. She does not meet any of the exceptions to the 10% additional tax, so the $5,000 is treated as an early distribution. Lauren must include the $5,000 in her gross income for the year the distribution is received and pay income tax on it. She must also pay an additional penalty of $500 (10% × $5,000).

Required Minimum Distributions from Qualified Plans

A participant in a qualified retirement plan must begin receiving distributions by April 1 of the first year following the later of:

- The calendar year in which he reaches age 70½
- The calendar year in which he retires from employment with the employer maintaining the plan

However, the plan may require distributions by April 1 of the year after the participant reaches age 70½, even if he has not retired. Further, if the participant is a 5% owner of the employer maintaining the plan, he must begin receiving distributions by April 1 of the year after the year he reaches age 70½.

Penalties for not taking required minimum distributions (RMDs) can be severe. Penalties are assessed if an account owner fails to withdraw an RMD, fails to withdraw the full amount of the RMD, or fails to withdraw the RMD by the applicable deadline. The penalty is 50% of the amount that is not withdrawn from the account when required.

Limits on Contributions and Benefits

The employer must ensure that contributions do not exceed certain limits. The limits differ depending on whether the plan is a defined contribution plan or a defined benefit plan.

- **Defined benefit plans:** For 2016, the annual benefit for a participant under a defined benefit plan cannot exceed the *lesser* of:
    - 100% of the participant's average compensation for his or her highest 3 consecutive calendar years, or
    - $210,000.
- **Defined contribution plans:** For 2016, a defined contribution plan's annual contributions to the account of a participant cannot exceed the lesser of:
    - 100% of the participant's compensation.
    - $53,000.

Penalties apply to excess contributions. An excise tax of 6% applies to excess amounts contributed by employees and self-employed individuals if these amounts and related earnings are not withdrawn by the due date of their returns (with or without extensions, depending upon the type of plan). An excise tax of 10% applies to excess employer contributions.

Prohibited Transactions

A prohibited transaction is a transaction between a retirement plan and a disqualified person that is prohibited by law. A disqualified person may include the following:

- A fiduciary of the plan
- A person providing services to the plan
- An employer, any of whose employees are covered by the plan
- An employee organization, any of whose members are covered by the plan
- An indirect or direct owner of 50% or more of the applicable employer or employee organization
- A member of the family of anyone described in the bullet points above
- A corporation, partnership, trust, or estate of which any direct or indirect owner described in the bullet points above holds a 50% or more interest
- An officer, director, 10% or more shareholder, or highly compensated employee of the entity administering the plan

An initial 15% tax is applied on the amount involved in a prohibited transaction for each year (or part of a year) in a taxable period. If the transaction is not corrected within the taxable period, an additional tax of 100% of the amount involved is imposed. These taxes are payable by any disqualified person who takes part in a prohibited transaction. If more than one person takes part, each can be jointly and severally liable for the entire amount of tax. Prohibited transactions include the following:

- A transfer of plan income or assets to, or use of plan income or assets for the benefit of, a disqualified person
- Any act of a fiduciary by which plan income or assets are used for his own benefit
- The receipt of money or property by a fiduciary for his own account from any party dealing with the plan in a transaction that involves plan income or assets
- The sale, exchange, or lease of property between a plan and a disqualified person
- Lending money between a plan and a disqualified person
- Furnishing goods or services between a plan and a disqualified person

Example: A plan fiduciary had a prohibited transaction by investing in a life insurance company's group annuity contract, resulting in a 10% commission paid to his company on the investment. This is a prohibited transaction between a plan fiduciary and a retirement plan.

If a prohibited transaction is not corrected during the taxable period, the taxpayer usually has an additional 90 days after the day the IRS mails a notice of deficiency to correct the transaction.

Comparison of Defined Benefit and Defined Contribution Plans		
Rule	**Defined Benefit Plan**	**Defined Contribution Plan**
Employer Contributions	Employer contributions are required based upon actuarial calculation of amounts needed to fund specified plan benefits.	The employer may choose to match a portion of employee contributions or to contribute without employee contributions.
Employee Contributions	Employees often do not contribute.	For many plans, employees are the primary contributors.
Managing the Investments	The employer must ensure that contributions to the plan plus investment earnings will be enough to pay the promised benefits.	The employee often is responsible for managing the investment of his account, choosing from investment options offered by the plan. For some plans, the plan administrator is responsible for investing the plan's assets.
Benefits Paid Upon Retirement	A promised benefit is based on a formula, often using a combination of the employee's age, years worked, and salary history.	The benefit depends on contributions made by the employee and/or the employer and investment earnings on the contributions.
Type of Retirement Benefit Payments	Traditionally, these plans pay the retiree monthly annuity payments that continue for life.	The retiree may transfer the account balance into an Individual Retirement Account (IRA) from which he may withdraw money. Some plans also offer monthly payments through an annuity.
Guarantee of Benefits	The government, through the Pension Benefit Guaranty Corporation (PBGC), may partially guarantee benefits.	No federal guarantee of benefits.

Unit 18: Study Questions

(Please test yourself and check the correct answers at the end of this section.)

1. Rudolph is a self-employed farmer who reports income on Schedule F. He earned $230,000 in net self-employment income for 2016. What is the maximum that Rudolph can contribute to his SEP-IRA in 2016?

A. $5,500
B. $53,000
C. $12,000
D. $57,500

2. Jensen Biomedical Corporation maintains a SIMPLE IRA for its employees and has elected to make 3% matching contributions. A former employee, Grace, quit her job on January 27, 2016, after the business had already deducted $75 from her wages based upon her election to contribute to its SIMPLE IRA plan. Grace had earned $2,000 of wages before she quit. How must Jensen Biomedical treat this $75 deduction from Grace's wages?

A. Jensen must return Grace's $75 salary reduction contribution.
B. Jensen must deposit Grace's salary reduction contribution in her SIMPLE IRA account. The company must also match Grace's salary reduction contributions up to 3% of her $2,000 compensation ($60).
C. Jensen must deposit Grace's salary reduction contribution in her SIMPLE IRA account. However, the company is not required to make a matching contribution for an employee who has terminated employment.
D. Jensen is required to remit the $75 to the U.S. Treasury.

3. "Prohibited transactions" are transactions between a retirement plan and a disqualified person. Which of the following is exempt from the prohibited transaction rules?

A. A fiduciary of the plan.
B. A person providing services to the plan.
C. An employer whose employees are covered by the plan.
D. A disqualified person who receives a benefit to which he is entitled as a plan participant.

4. What types of employers *cannot* establish a SEP?

A. A self-employed taxpayer without any employees.
B. A corporation with 90 employees.
C. A nonprofit entity with five employees.
D. All of the above can establish a SEP.

5. Ram is a sole proprietor whose tax year is the calendar year. He did not obtain an extension for his 2016 tax return. What is the latest date that he can contribute to his SEP for the 2016 tax year?

A. April 18, 2017.
B. December 31, 2016.
C. October 15, 2017.
D. May 15, 2017.

6. Huang Software, Inc. decides to establish a SEP for its employees. All of the following statements about Huang's retirement plan are correct *except*:

A. In good years, Huang can make larger contributions for its employees, and in down years, it can reduce the amount.
B. Individual employees have the opportunity to divide the employer's contributions to their SEP-IRAs among the funds made available to Huang employees.
C. Under a SEP, the contribution rate can be different for each employee, based on length of service and performance.
D. Only employers and self-employed individuals can make contributions to SEPs.

7. Maura, age 26, began participating in a SIMPLE IRA retirement account a year ago. She took an early distribution from the account on December 26, 2016. She does not qualify for any of the exceptions to the early withdrawal penalty. The distribution amount was $10,000. What is the penalty amount that Maura must pay on the early distribution?

A. $1,000
B. $1,500
C. $2,500
D. $3,000

8. The Bing Berry Company is a partnership with 150 employees. All of the following plans are available for Bing Berry except:

A. A qualified plan.
B. A defined benefit plan.
C. A SIMPLE IRA.
D. 401(k) Plan.

9. Can a SIMPLE IRA plan be maintained on a fiscal-year basis?

A. Yes, if the business is on a fiscal year.
B. Yes, even if the business uses a calendar year.
C. Yes, but only if the business requests a 444 election.
D. No, a calendar year must be used.

10. The Azalea Partnership has 15 employees and 3 general partners. The business contributes $3,000 to each employee's retirement account during the year. Identical contributions are made into each individual partner's retirement account. How is this transaction reported?

A. The business can take the deduction for the contribution to its employees' retirement accounts on Form 1065, *Partnership Income Tax Return*. Contributions made on behalf of the partners are passed through to each of them on Schedule K-1.
B. The partnership can deduct all the retirement contributions as an ordinary business expense directly on Form 1065.
C. The individual partners are allowed to deduct contributions to their employee retirement accounts on their individual returns.
D. Contributions made on behalf of the employees are deducted as regular wages on Form W-2. Contributions made on behalf of the partners are passed through to each of them on Schedule K-1.

11. Leah is a sole proprietor who establishes a SEP for her small coffee shop. The coffee shop has two employees. After figuring her deductions for the year, Leah has a net loss in 2016 on her Schedule C. Which of the following statements is correct?

A. Because the business shows a loss, she is prohibited from contributing to her retirement account, as well as the retirement accounts of her employees.
B. Because the business shows a loss, she is prohibited from contributing to her retirement account, but she can contribute to the retirement accounts of her employees.
C. Leah can make a retirement contribution to her own retirement account, as well as the accounts of her employees.
D. Leah can make a retirement contribution to her own retirement account, but not to the retirement accounts of her employees.

12. All of the following are requirements of ERISA (the Employee Retirement Income Security Act) except:

A. ERISA requires that employers file an annual report on Form 5500 for their sponsored retirement plans.
B. ERISA requires employers to set up retirement plans for their employees.
C. ERISA requires minimum funding standards for retirement plans.
D. ERISA requires certain communications with plan participants.

13. Under the rules for prohibited transactions, all of the following would be considered disqualified persons except:

A. A 5% shareholder of the entity administering the plan.
B. A fiduciary of the plan.
C. An employer whose employees are covered by the plan.
D. A person providing services to the plan.

14. Auburn Equipment is a small C corporation that maintains a SEP plan for its employees. Which of the following employees can be excluded from the retirement plan?

A. Stan, a 32-year-old part-time employee who has worked for Auburn Equipment for five years.
B. Aldo, a 42-year-old seasonal employee and U.S. resident alien who has worked for Auburn Equipment for three years.
C. Noel, a 21-year-old part-time employee who is also a union member.
D. Millie, a 55-year-old full-time employee who has worked for Auburn Equipment for four years.

15. Josie works full-time for the city of Las Vegas as parking enforcement officer. She participates in the city's pension plan. She also has her own tax preparation business which she works on the weekends. She reports her tax preparation income on Schedule C. Can Josie set up a SEP for her self-employment income, even though she is already participating in her employer's plan?

A. Yes, Josie can still set up a SEP for her Schedule C business.
B. No, Josie cannot set up a SEP because she is covered by an employer plan.
C. No, Josie cannot set up a SEP because she is a prohibited individual.
D. Josie can set up a SEP only if she incorporates. Sole-proprietorships cannot set up a SEP.

16. Which of the following statements regarding a SEP-IRA is correct?

A. Money can be withdrawn from a SEP-IRA by the employee at any time without tax or penalty.
B. Money can be withdrawn from a SEP-IRA by the employee at any time, but taxes may apply.
C. An employee must wait at least two years to withdraw money from a SEP-IRA.
D. An employee must wait at least three years to withdraw money from a SEP-IRA.

17. What are the penalties imposed on a disqualified person who takes part in a prohibited transaction?

A. 25% tax of the amount involved.
B. 50% tax of the amount involved.
C. An initial tax of 15% of the amount involved, and an additional tax of 100% if the transaction is not corrected within the taxable period.
D. An initial tax of 25% of the amount involved, and an additional tax of 100% if the transaction is not corrected within the taxable period.

18. What happens if an eligible employee entitled to a contribution is unwilling to set up a SIMPLE IRA?

A. Eligible employees may decline to participate in an employer's SIMPLE IRA.
B. Eligible employees may not opt out of a SIMPLE IRA.
C. Eligible employees may choose to set up a ROTH IRA in lieu of a SIMPLE IRA.
D. None of the above.

19. The Ellsworth Company has started a SEP plan for its employees. The company currently has four employees. Which of the following employees is the company not required to cover under the SEP plan?

A. Faye, age 45, a full-time employee for the last five years.
B. Bruno, age 25, a part-time employee for the last three years.
C. Randolph, age 20, a full-time employee for the last three years.
D. Mack, age 42, a seasonal employee for the last six years.

20. If an employer makes an excess contribution to a defined contribution plan, an excess tax of ________ will apply:

A. 6%
B. 10%
C. 25%
D. 50%

21. A 401(k) is a type of:

A. SEP-IRA.
B. Government pension plan.
C. Defined contribution plan.
D. Defined benefit plan.

Unit 18: Answers

1. The answer is B. The maximum amount for contribution to a SEP plan is the *lesser* of $53,000 or 25% of the participant's compensation. $230,000 x 25% =$57,500 (this exceeds the maximum dollar amount for 2016, so Rudolph is limited to $53,000).

2. The answer is B. Jensen Biomedical Corporation must deposit Grace's salary reduction contribution in her SIMPLE IRA account. The company must also match Grace's salary reduction contributions at 3% of her $2,000 compensation ($60). An employer cannot return a salary reduction contribution after it has already deducted it from wages as a SIMPLE IRA plan contribution. A SIMPLE IRA plan may not require a participant to be employed on a specific date to receive an employer contribution. If a participant terminates service during the year after making a salary reduction contribution, she would still be entitled to an employer contribution, regardless of whether it is matching or nonelective.

3. The answer is D. It is not a prohibited transaction if a disqualified person receives a benefit to which he is entitled as a plan participant or beneficiary.

4. The answer is D. Any employer or self-employed individual can establish a SEP.

5. The answer is A. Taxpayers can deduct contributions for a particular tax year if they are made by the due date (including extensions) of the federal income tax return for that year. Since Ram did not file an extension for his 2016 return, he could make deductible contributions until his regular due date of April 18, 2017, for his 2016 tax return.

6. The answer is C. Under a SEP, the contribution rate must be uniform for all employees. Employers may potentially contribute less when they have less income, but the plan cannot discriminate among employees.

7. The answer is C. Early withdrawals from an IRA generally are subject to an additional penalty tax of 10%. However, the additional tax is increased to 25% if funds are withdrawn within two years of beginning participation in a SIMPLE IRA. The answer is $10,000 × .25 = $2,500. The withdrawal would also be subject to income tax, in addition to the penalty.

8. The answer is C. Bing Berry cannot set up a SIMPLE IRA for its employees, because the company exceeds the 100-employee threshold, unless at least 50 of the employees earned less than $5,000 in the prior year.

9. The answer is D. A SIMPLE IRA plan may only be maintained on a calendar-year basis.

10. The answer is A. A partnership can deduct contributions to an employee's retirement plan, just as it would deduct any other ordinary business expense on Form 1065. However, the rules are different for contributions to the retirement accounts of the partners. Contributions made on behalf of the partners are passed through to each of them on Schedule K-1.

11. The answer is B. Leah is self-employed, so she must have compensation in order to contribute to her own retirement plan. However, she is not prohibited from contributing to her employees' retirement plan, even if the business has a loss.

12. The answer is B. The Employee Retirement Income Security Act of 1974 (ERISA) is a federal law that sets minimum standards for most pension and health plans. However, ERISA does not require that employers set up retirement plans for their employees. Retirement plans are always an optional benefit.

13. The answer is A. A 10% or more shareholder of the entity administering the plan would be a disqualified person under the rules for prohibited transactions. A 5% shareholder would not be a disqualified person.

14. The answer is C. Since Noel is covered by a union contract, he may be excluded. Employers may choose to exclude employees covered by a union agreement. Since Aldo is a resident alien (not a *nonresident* alien), he still qualifies to participate. Only nonresident aliens who do not have any U.S.-source income may be excluded.

15. The answer is A. Josie can set up a SEP for her sole-proprietorship. A SEP can be established for a person's independent business activity even if she participates in another employer's retirement plan.

16. The answer is B. Although income tax may apply, including an additional 10% tax for withdrawals prior to age 59½, participants are allowed to withdraw money from a SEP-IRA at any time. Withdrawals can be rolled over tax-free to another SEP-IRA, to another traditional IRA, or to another employer's qualified retirement plan.

17. The answer is C. An initial 15% tax is applied on the amount involved in a prohibited transaction for each year in a taxable period. If the transaction is not corrected within the taxable period, an additional tax of 100% of the amount involved is imposed. These taxes are payable by any disqualified person who takes part in a prohibited transaction.

18. The answer is B. An eligible employee may not opt out of participation. However, any eligible employee may choose not to make salary reduction contributions for a year. In that case, the employee would accrue no employer matching contributions for the year, but would still receive an employer nonelective contribution (if the plan provides for such contributions for the year).

19. The answer is C. Randolph is not automatically eligible because he is younger than 21 years old, so he may be excluded. For purposes of a SEP, an eligible employee is an individual who meets all the following requirements:

- Has reached age 21
- Has worked for the employer in at least three of the last five years
- Has received at least $600 of compensation

An employer can use less restrictive participation requirements than those listed (such as choosing to allow an employee younger than 21 to participate), but an employer cannot use more restrictive participation requirements.

20. The answer is B. An excise tax of 10% applies to excess employer contributions to a defined contribution plan. For employees and self-employed individuals, a penalty of 6% applies if excess contribution amounts and related earnings are not withdrawn by the due date of their returns (with or without extensions, depending upon the type of plan).

21. The answer is C. A 401(k) is a very common type of defined contribution plan in which employees contribute to their own accounts, generally on a pretax basis. Earnings grow tax-free until distribution. Employers often supplement or match employee contributions.

Unit 19: Trusts and Estates

More Reading:
Publication 559, *Survivors, Executors, and Administrators*
Publication 950, *Introduction to Estate and Gift Taxes*
Publication 536, *Net Operating Losses (NOLs) for Individuals, Estates, and Trusts*

Estates and trusts are separate legal entities that are defined by the assets they hold. An estate is created when a taxpayer dies and the estate tax may be imposed on the assets held by the estate.

A trust can be created while the taxpayer is alive, or by the taxpayer's last will. The trust can be structured to distribute income during the taxpayer's lifetime or after the taxpayer's death. A trust can hold title to property for the benefit of one or more persons or entities. An estate or trust is required to obtain an employer identification number (EIN), just like any other legal entity.

Note: For Part 2 of the EA exam, you must understand how estates and trusts function at the entity level. This includes their reporting requirements, filing due dates, and exemption thresholds. Part 1 of the EA exam focuses more on estates from the standpoint of the beneficiary, as well as how the distributions affect an individual taxpayer's returns.

Estates and trusts generally terminate when all of their assets and income have been distributed and all of their liabilities have been paid. If a trust or estate's existence is unnecessarily prolonged, the IRS can step in and terminate it after a reasonable period for completing the final administration. If an estate or trust has a loss in its final year, the loss can be passed through to the beneficiaries, allowing them deductions on their individual returns. Losses cannot be passed through to beneficiaries in a non-termination year.

Example: Gerardo died five years ago. He had two children, Daniella and Socorro, who are the only beneficiaries of his estate, which was worth $10 million at the time of his death. Daniella and Socorro immediately began to argue over the will and their late father's assets. While they are petitioning the court, Gerardo's estate continues to earn revenue from various assets, (stocks, rentals, and other investments). In this situation, Gerardo's estate will not terminate until an agreement is made between the beneficiaries and the estate assets are distributed.

Beneficiaries must generally treat estate items the same way on their individual returns as they are treated on the estate's return. Under new rules imposed by the Surface Transportation Act, the executor of any estate required to file an estate tax return must now furnish to IRS (and to each person acquiring any interest in property included in the decedent's gross estate) a statement identifying:

- The value of each interest in that property as reported on the estate tax return, and
- Any other information about the interest that the IRS might require.

This separate statement is required to be furnished no later than 30 days following the due date (including extensions) of the return, or the actual filing of the return, whichever is earlier. This new reporting requirement is designed to combat inconsistent basis reporting of property inherited with a stepped-up basis when a sale of the property is later reported by the beneficiary.

Note: The new Form 8971, *Information Regarding Beneficiaries Acquiring Property* from a Decedent is used to report the value of the property on an estate tax return. Executors who file estate tax returns will complete it and provide it to the IRS. Form 8971 includes a "Schedule A" which also must be filed with the IRS. Only the Schedule A is to be provided to the beneficiary.

Estates in General

For federal tax purposes, an estate is a separate legal entity created when a taxpayer dies. A person who inherits property directly from an estate is generally not taxed on the transfer. Instead, the estate itself is responsible for paying any applicable taxes before the property is distributed. However, if the estate's assets are distributed to beneficiaries before the taxes are paid, the beneficiaries can be held liable for the tax debt, up to the value of the assets distributed.

After a person dies, a personal representative, such as an executor named in the will or an administrator appointed by a court, will typically manage the estate and settle the decedent's financial affairs. If there is no executor or administrator, another person with possession of the decedent's property may act as the personal representative. The personal representative is responsible for filing the final income tax return and the estate tax return, if required.

Example: James was unmarried when he died on April 20, 2016. His only daughter, Lillian, was named as the executor of his estate. James earned $23,000 in wages during 2016 before his death, so a final tax return (Form 1040) is required for 2016. Lillian asks her accountant to help prepare her father's final Form 1040, which will include all the taxable income that James received in 2016 before his death. The accountant also helps Lillian with the valuation of her father's estate. After determining the fair market value of all her father's assets, they conclude that James's gross estate is valued at approximately $7 million. As this exceeds the threshold of $5.45 million for 2016, an estate tax return (Form 706) is also required to be filed. Lillian is the executor, so she is responsible for filing and signing both returns.

The personal representative is also responsible for determining any estate tax liability before the estate's assets are distributed to beneficiaries. Either the personal representative or a paid preparer must sign the appropriate line of each of the following tax returns that may need to be filed:

- The final income tax return (Form 1040) for the decedent (for income received before death);
- Fiduciary income tax returns (Form 1041) for the estate for the period of its administration; and
- The estate tax return (Form 706).

Note: The executor or "personal representative" must include fees paid to them from an estate in their gross income. If the executor is not in the trade or business of being an executor (for instance, the executor is a friend or family member of the deceased), these fees are reported on the executor's individual Form 1040, line 21. If the executor is in the "trade or business" of being an executor, they would report the fees received from the estate as self-employment income on Schedule C.

Example: Saul is an estate tax attorney. One of his long-time wealthy clients, Maribel, dies in 2016 after a long battle with cancer. Maribel names Saul as the executor of her estate in her will. The sole beneficiary of Maribel's estate is her son, Joaquin, who is 17 and still a minor. By the terms outlined in the will, Saul will manage the affairs of the estate until Joaquin turns 21. By law, the executor has the right to charge a fee for managing an estate. Maribel's will stipulated that the executor of her estate is entitled to 5% of the income of the estate. The remaining income will go to provide Joaquin's ongoing support and pay for his schooling. As the attorney, Saul would report the income that he earns as an executor on his Schedule C, subject to self-employment tax.

Final Income Tax Return (Form 1040)

The taxpayer's final income tax return is filed on the same form that would have been used if the taxpayer were still alive, but "deceased" is written after the taxpayer's name. The filing deadline is April 15 of the year following the taxpayer's death, the same deadline that applies for individual income tax returns.

The personal representative must file the final individual income tax return of the decedent for the year of death and any returns not filed for preceding years. If an individual died after the close of a tax year but before the return for that year was filed, the return for that year will not normally be the final return. The return for that year will be a regular return and the personal representative must file it.

Example: Milly dies suddenly on March 2, 2016. At the time of her death, she had not yet filed her 2015 tax return. She earned $51,000 of wages in 2015. She also earned $18,000 of wages between January 1, 2016, and her death on March 2, 2016. Therefore, Milly's 2015 *and* 2016 tax returns must be filed by her personal representative. The 2016 return would be her final individual tax return.

On a decedent's final tax return, the rules for personal exemptions and deductions are the same as those that apply for any individual taxpayer. The full amount of the applicable personal exemption (subject to any phase-out limitations based on income) may be claimed on the final tax return, regardless of how long the taxpayer was alive during the year.

Income in Respect of a Decedent (IRD)

Income in respect of a decedent (IRD) is any taxable income that was earned but not received by the decedent by the time of death. IRD is not taxed on the final return of the deceased taxpayer. IRD is reported on the tax return of the person (or entity) that receives the income. This could be the estate, in which case it would be reported on Form 1041, as described below. Otherwise, it could be the surviving spouse or another beneficiary, such as a child.

IRD retains the same tax nature that would have applied if the deceased taxpayer were still alive. For example, if the income would have been short-term capital gain, it is taxed the same way to the beneficiary. IRD can come from various sources, including:

- Unpaid salary, wages, or bonuses
- Distributions from traditional IRAs and employer-provided retirement plans
- Deferred compensation benefits
- Accrued but unpaid interest, dividends, and rent
- Accounts receivable of a sole proprietor who has died

Example: Carlos was owed $15,000 of wages when he died. The check for these wages was not remitted by his employer until three weeks later and was received by his daughter and sole beneficiary, Rosalie. The wages are considered IRD, and Rosalie must recognize the $15,000 as ordinary income, the same tax treatment that would have applied for Carlos.

Example: Beverly died on April 30. At the time of her death, she was owed (but had not yet received) $1,500 of interest on bonds and $2,000 of rental income. Beverly's beneficiary will include $3,500 of IRD in gross income when the interest and rent are received. The income retains its character as interest income and passive activity rental income.

IRD is included in the decedent's estate and may be subject to estate tax. If it is received by a beneficiary and subject to income tax on the beneficiary's return, the beneficiary can claim a deduction for estate tax paid on the IRD.

This deduction is taken as a miscellaneous itemized deduction on Schedule A and is not subject to the 2% floor.

Fiduciary Income Tax Return (Form 1041)

Form 1041 is a fiduciary return used to report the following items for a domestic decedent's estate, a trust, or a bankruptcy estate:

- Current income and deductions, including gains and losses from disposition of the entity's property and excluding certain items such as tax-exempt interest (collectively, *distributable net income* or DNI);
- A deduction for income that is either held for future distribution or distributed currently to the beneficiaries (income distribution deduction) that is limited to DNI; and
- Any income tax liability.

An estate or trust may exist as a taxable legal entity until all of its assets have been distributed. Current income of an estate may include IRD, if it was received by the estate rather than specific beneficiaries.

As investment assets will usually continue to earn income after a taxpayer has died, this income, such as rents, dividends and interest, must be reported. The expenses of administering an estate can be deducted either from the estate's income on Form 1041, in determining its income tax, or from the gross estate on Form 706, in determining the estate tax liability, but cannot be claimed for both purposes. Schedule K-1 is used to report any income that is distributed or distributable to each beneficiary and is filed with Form 1041, with a copy also given to the beneficiary.

The due date for Form 1041 is the fifteenth day of the fourth month following the end of the entity's tax year, but is subject to an automatic extension of five months if Form 7004 is filed.

The tax year of an estate may be either a calendar or a fiscal year, subject to the election made at the time the first return is filed. An election will also be made on the first return as to method (cash, accrual, or other) to report an estate's income. Form 1041 must be filed for any domestic estate that has gross income for the tax year of $600 or more, or a beneficiary who is a nonresident alien (with any amount of income).

Distributable Net Income

Taxable income earned by an estate or trust is taxable to either the entity or the beneficiaries, but not to both. Distributable net income (DNI) is income that is currently available for distribution. If the beneficiary receives a distribution in excess of DNI, only the DNI is taxed.

The income distribution deduction (IDD) is allowed to trusts and estates for amounts that are paid, credited, or required to be distributed to beneficiaries. The income distribution deduction is calculated on Schedule B (Form 1041) and is limited to the lesser of distributions minus any tax-exempt income or DNI minus any tax-exempt income.

Example: The Camden Family Trust has the following income in 2016: $25,000 of taxable interest and dividends; $35,000 of capital gains; and $10,000 of tax-exempt interest. The trust also incurred fiduciary and investment fees of $5,000. The trust document provides that capital gains are allocated to income, rather than the trust's corpus. The trust has DNI of $65,000 ($25,000 + $35,000 + $10,000 - $5,000). The trust makes distributions of $45,000 and an IDD of $35,000 may be claimed for the year. This amount represents the lesser of its DNI ($65,000) and its distributions ($45,000), minus its tax-exempt income.

Net Investment Income Tax (NIIT)

Estates and certain trusts are subject to the additional tax of 3.8% on net investment income. The provisions for this tax are generally similar to those for individuals, and it must be reported on Form 8960, *Net Investment Tax: Individuals, Estates, and Trusts.*

For trusts and estates, the tax applies to the lesser of undistributed net investment income or the excess of adjusted gross income over the threshold amount (For estates and trusts, the 2016 threshold is $12,400) at which the highest tax bracket begins. The tax does not apply to tax-exempt trusts or to grantor trusts. Net investment income that is subject to the tax includes:

- Interest
- Dividends
- Capital gains
- Rental and royalty income
- Non-qualified annuities
- Income from businesses involved in trading of financial instruments or commodities
- Income from businesses that are passive activities for the taxpayer

Form 706: The Estate Tax Return

An estate tax return is filed using Form 706, *United States Estate (and Generation-Skipping Transfer) Tax Return.* The estate tax applies to an individual's taxable estate, which is the gross estate less certain deductions.

After the taxable estate is computed, it is added to the value of taxable gifts made during the decedent's lifetime.

The applicable estate tax rate is applied to derive a tentative tax, from which any gift taxes paid or payable are subtracted to determine the gross estate tax. In 2016, each individual has the ability to transfer $5,450,000 to others, either in lifetime gifting or at death. The maximum estate tax rate is 40% in 2016.

All or a portion of the gross estate tax may be eliminated after consideration of the estate's available:

- **Basic Exclusion Amount:** This amount is adjusted for inflation each year and may be used to reduce or eliminate gift and/or estate taxes. For 2016, the basic estate tax exclusion amount is $5.45 million.
- **Deceased Spousal Unused Exclusion (DSUE):** This is the unused portion of the decedent's predeceased spouse's basic exclusion (the amount that was not used to offset gift or estate tax liabilities). The predeceased spouse must have died on or after January 1, 2011, and a portability election must be made to claim the DSUE on behalf of the surviving spouse's estate. This election can be made automatically by timely completion and filing of Form 706 for the estate of the predeceased spouse.

Only estates valued in excess of the sum of these amounts need to file a return and pay estate tax.

Essentially, this means that a surviving spouse's estate with value up to $10.9 million of estate value could be excluded from taxation if both spouses died during 2016, neither spouse had used any of his basic exclusion amount to offset gift tax liabilities, all of the assets from the first deceased spouse passed to the surviving spouse, and the portability election for DSUE was properly made on Form 706 for the first spouse's estate.

Example: Matt dies in early 2016 and leaves a gross estate valued at $9 million. His assets transfer to his wife, Leslie, and none are taxed because of the unlimited marital deduction. Thus, none of the $5.45 million basic exclusion amount available to Matt's estate is used (and none had been used to offset gift tax liabilities during his lifetime). Leslie dies later in the same year. Assuming Form 706 was timely filed for Matt's estate and Leslie had not used any of her basic exclusion amount, Matt's unused basic exclusion is added to Leslie's basic exclusion, for a total exclusion amount of $10.9 million ($5.45 million × 2).

Example: Marlene dies in 2016 and leaves an estate valued at $3 million. She had not previously used any of her basic exclusion amount to avoid paying gift taxes, so the entire exclusion amount of $5.45 million is available to her estate. As this amount exceeds the estate's value, no estate tax is owed and an estate tax return does not need to be filed.

Applicable Credit

The gross estate tax described above is reduced by the *applicable credit*, also referred to as the *unified credit,* which is a tax credit amount that corresponds with the basic exclusion amount and, if applicable, the DSUE available to a surviving spouse. In 2016, the applicable credit on the basic exclusion amount is $2,125,800 (exempting $5,450,000 from tax).

Just as with the basic exclusion amount, any portion of the applicable credit amount used to avoid payment of gift taxes reduces the amount of credit available in later years that can be used to offset gift or estate taxes. For example, if someone had used the full $2,125,800 applicable credit to avoid payment of gift taxes during his lifetime, he would have exhausted his entire $5.45 million basic exclusion. If he then died in 2016, his estate would be liable for tax on the taxable estate without further offset.

Example: Asher, who is single, dies in 2016 and leaves an estate valued at $20 million. During his lifetime, he had used $1 million of his basic exclusion to offset payments of gift tax. That reduces the amount his estate may exclude to $4.45 million, which is then subtracted from his $20 million taxable estate. That leaves a total of $15.55 million to be taxed at a 40% rate.

If required to be filed, the due date for Form 706 is nine months after the decedent's date of death. An automatic six-month extension may be requested by filing Form 4768. However, the tax is due by the due date and interest is accrued on any amounts owed that are not paid at that time. The assessment period for estate tax is three years after the due date for a timely filed estate tax return. The assessment period is four years for transfers from an estate.

The Gross Estate

The gross estate is based upon the fair market value of the decedent's property, which is not necessarily equal to his cost, and includes:

- The FMV of all tangible and intangible property owned by the decedent at the time of death.
- The full value of property held as joint tenants with the right of survivorship (unless the decedent and spouse were the only joint tenants)
- Life insurance proceeds payable to the estate, or payable to the heirs, for policies owned by the decedent.
- The value of certain annuities or survivor benefits payable to the heirs.
- The value of certain property that was transferred within three years before the decedent's death.

Example: Roger died in 2016. He was 98 years old when he died. At the time of his death, Roger owned several collectible baseball cards that he purchased during his childhood. The cards cost only pennies when he bought them, but now the cards are worth many thousands of dollars. For estate tax purposes, the baseball cards would be valued at their fair market value on the date of Roger's death.

The gross estate does not include property owned solely by the decedent's spouse or other individuals. Lifetime gifts that are complete (so that no control over the gifts was retained) are not included in the gross estate.

Deductions from the Gross Estate: Once the gross estate has been calculated, certain deductions (and in special circumstances, reductions to value) are allowed to determine the taxable estate. Deductions from the gross estate may include:

- Funeral expenses paid out of the estate.

- Administration expenses for the estate (if not deducted on Form 1041).
- Debts owed at the time of death.
- The marital deduction (generally, the value of the property that passes from the estate to a surviving spouse who is a U.S. citizen).
- The charitable deduction (generally, the value of the property that passes from the estate to qualifying charities).
- The state death tax deduction (generally, any inheritance or estate taxes paid to any state).

The following items are not deductible from the gross estate:

- Federal estate taxes paid.
- Alimony paid after the taxpayer's death. These payments would be treated as distributions to a beneficiary.

Property taxes are deductible only if they accrue under state law prior to the decedent's death.

> **Study Note:** For both Parts 1 and 2 of the EA exam, you should be familiar with what is included in the gross estate and the taxable estate.

The Marital Deduction: Transfers from one spouse to the other are typically tax-free. The marital deduction allows spouses to transfer an unlimited amount of property to one another during their lifetimes or at death without being subject to estate or gift taxes if the spouse is a U.S. citizen.

Decedent's Medical Expenses: Debts that were not paid before death, including medical expenses subsequently paid on behalf of the decedent, are liabilities of the estate and can be deducted from the gross estate on the estate tax return. However, if medical expenses for the decedent are paid out of the estate during the one-year period beginning with the day after death, the personal representative can alternatively elect to treat all or part of the expenses as paid by the decedent at the time they were incurred, and deduct them on the final tax return (1040) for the decedent.

Basis of Estate Property

The basis of property inherited from a decedent is generally one of the following:

- The FMV of the property on the date of death.
- The FMV on an alternate valuation date (which is normally the FMV of assets six months after the date of death, except for assets distributed to an heir after death but prior to six months after death, in which case the basis will be the FMV as of the date of distribution), if elected by the personal representative.
- The value under a special-use valuation method for real property used in farming or another closely-held business, if elected by the personal representative.
- The decedent's adjusted basis in land to the extent of the value excluded from the taxable estate as a qualified conservation easement.

Property that is jointly owned by a decedent and another person will be included in full in the decedent's gross estate unless it can be shown that the other person originally owned or otherwise contributed to the purchase price.

The surviving owner's new basis in property that was jointly owned is calculated by adding his original basis in the property to the value of the part of the property included in the decedent's estate. Any deductions for depreciation of the property allowed to the surviving owner are subtracted from the sum.

If property is jointly held between husband and wife as tenants by the entirety or as joint tenants with the right of survivorship (if they were the only joint tenants), one-half of the property's value is included in the gross estate, and there is a step-up in basis for that one-half.

If the decedent holds property in a community property state, half of the value of the community property will be included in the gross estate of the decedent, but the entire value of the community property will receive a step-up in basis.

Trusts in General

A trust is an entity created under the laws of the state in which it is formed. A trust may be created during an individual's life (an inter-vivos trust) or at the time of death under a will (a testamentary trust). A trust can be created to hold property for the benefit of other persons. It may be created for the benefit of a disabled individual, or it can be used to legally avoid certain taxes. The establishment of a trust creates a fiduciary relationship between three parties:

- **The Grantor:** The person who contributes property to the trust.
- **The Trustee (or Fiduciary):** The person or entity charged with the fiduciary duties associated with the trust.
- **The Beneficiary:** The person who is designated to receive the trust income or assets.

Example: AJ is having serious medical problems and decides to put her assets in a trust. She asks her attorney to create the trust and to manage the assets. The trust is structured so that it will pay AJ's living expenses, with the remainder of the assets going to her grandson after she dies. In this scenario, AJ is the **grantor**, the lawyer is the **trustee**, and AJ and her grandson are the **beneficiaries**.

Sometimes, a trust is used to transfer property in a controlled manner. For example, a parent may wish to transfer ownership of assets to his child, but does not want the child to waste the assets or spend them unwisely.

The assets could be transferred to a trust, with the parent as both the grantor and the trustee. The child would be the beneficiary. The parent still has control over the assets, and the child is prevented from using them all up.

The accounting period for a trust is generally the calendar year. The filing due date for a calendar-year trust is April 15. A trust must file Form 1041, *U.S. Income Tax Return for Estates and Trusts,* if it has:

- Any taxable income for the year (after subtracting the allowable exemption amount),
- Gross income of $600 or more (regardless of whether the income is taxable), or
- Any beneficiary who is a nonresident alien.

Example: The Prussic Family Trust has $400 of tax-exempt interest from municipal bonds during the year. There is no other income. Normally, the trust would not be required to file a tax return because the income earned by the trust is tax-exempt. However, the Prussic Family Trust has a beneficiary who is a nonresident alien. Therefore, the trust is required to file Form 1041.

A trust calculates its gross income in a manner similar to an individual taxpayer. Trusts are allowed an exemption, but the amount varies based on the type of trust. A trust that must distribute all of its income currently (a simple trust) is allowed an exemption of $300. Any other trust is allowed an exemption of $100 per year.

Most deductions and credits allowed to individuals are also allowed to trusts. However, there is one major distinction: a trust is a pass-through entity that is allowed a deduction for its distributions to beneficiaries. The beneficiaries (and not the trust) pay income tax on their distributive share of income. Schedule K-1 (Form 1041) is used to report income that a trust distributes to beneficiaries. The income must then be reported on the beneficiaries' income tax returns.

Simple and Complex Trusts

With regard to income distribution, there are two types of trusts: a simple trust and a complex trust. The IRC defines a **simple trust** as a trust that:

- Must distribute all of its income currently (in other words, it cannot accumulate income from year to year),
- Makes no distributions of principal, and
- Makes no distributions to charity.

Any trust that is not a simple trust is automatically classified as a complex trust. A complex trust:

- Is allowed to accumulate income,
- Can make discretionary distributions of income,
- Can make mandatory (or discretionary) distributions of principal, and
- Can make distributions to charity.

A trust may be a simple trust one year, and a complex trust in the following year. For example, if a simple trust fails to distribute all its income in the current year, it becomes a complex trust. Unlike an estate or a simple trust, a complex trust reports its accounting income, (which may differ from its taxable income and its DNI and may be more or less than distributions for the year), on Form 1041.

Study Note: For Part 2 of the EA exam, you should understand the differences between a simple trust and a complex trust and know the rules for how each distributes income.

Grantor Trusts

A grantor trust is a valid legal entity under state law, but it is not recognized as a separate entity for income tax purposes.

The grantor (also known as trustor, settlor, or creator) creates the trust relationship and retains control over the trust. In the eyes of the IRS, the grantor is the owner of the trust for income tax purposes. The grantor establishes the terms and provisions of the trust relationship between the grantor, the trustee, and the beneficiary. These will usually include the following:

- The rights, duties, and powers of the trustee,
- Distribution provisions,
- Ability of the grantor to amend, modify, revoke, or terminate the trust agreement,
- The designation of a trustee or successor trustees, and
- The designation of the state under which the trust agreement is to be governed.

Example: The Kenneth Chiang Trust is a grantor trust. Kenneth is the grantor. During the year, the trust sold 100 shares of ABC stock for $1,010 in which it had a basis of $10 and 200 shares of XYZ stock for $10 in which it had a $1,020 basis. The trust does not report these transactions on Form 1041 or issue Kenneth a Schedule K-1. Instead, a schedule is attached to Form 1041 showing each stock transaction separately and in the same detail as Kenneth (grantor and owner) will need to report these transactions on his Schedule D (Form 1040). The trust does not net the capital gains and losses to show a $10 long-term capital loss.

Revocable Trusts: Revocable trusts, including revocable living trusts, are grantor trusts in which the grantor retains the right to make changes or end the trust during his lifetime. The trust assets are subject to estate tax upon the grantor's death. The trust is generally created to manage and distribute property. Many taxpayers use this type of trust instead of, or in addition to, a will.

Non-Grantor Trusts

A non-grantor trust is any trust that is not a grantor trust. A non-grantor trust is considered a separate legal entity from the individual or organization that created it. The trust's income and deductions are reported on Form 1041.

If a non-grantor trust makes distributions to a beneficiary, in general those distributions carry any taxable income to the beneficiary. Examples include:

1. **Irrevocable Trusts**: An irrevocable trust is a trust that cannot be revoked after it is created. The transfer of assets into this type of trust is generally considered a "completed gift" subject to gift tax.
2. **Disability Trusts:** A qualified disability trust is a non-grantor trust created solely for the benefit of a disabled individual under age 65. A Qualified Disability Trust or QDT is allowed the same exemption as an individual ($4,050 in 2016). This is a specific exception to the regular exemption amount that applies to most trusts. A Qualified Disability Trust is a complex trust, because it is designed to hold income and assets for the future benefit of a disabled beneficiary.
3. **Charitable Trusts:** A charitable trust is a trust devoted to qualified charitable contribution purposes. Charitable trusts are irrevocable.

Example: Pamela creates a charitable trust. Its governing instrument provides that the Presbyterian Church (a qualified religious organization), and the SPCA (a 501(c)(3) charity) are each to receive 50% of the trust income for ten years. At the end of the ten-year period, the corpus will be distributed to the American Red Cross, also a 501(c)(3) organization. Pamela is allowed an income tax deduction for the value of the assets placed in the trust. This charitable trust is irrevocable, which means that the trust cannot be modified or terminated without the permission of the beneficiary (in this case, the beneficiaries are the charitable organizations themselves).

Abusive Trust Arrangements

Certain trust arrangements purport to reduce or eliminate federal taxes in ways that are not permitted under the law. These abusive or fraudulent trust arrangements may be used to hide the true ownership of assets and income or to disguise the substance of transactions.

They frequently involve more than one trust, each holding different assets of the taxpayer (for example, the taxpayer's business, business equipment, home, automobile, etc.).

Some trusts may hold interests in other trusts, purport to involve charities, or be foreign trusts. Participants and promoters of abusive trust schemes may be subject to civil or criminal penalties.

Abusive or fraudulent trust arrangements may promise such benefits as:

- Deductions for personal expenses paid by the trust
- Depreciation deductions for an owner's personal residence
- A stepped-up basis for property transferred to the trust
- The reduction or elimination of self-employment taxes
- The reduction or elimination of gift and estate taxes

Although these schemes give the appearance of separating responsibility and control from the benefits of ownership, as would be the case with legitimate trusts, the taxpayer in fact controls them.

When trusts are used for legitimate business, family, or estate planning purposes, either the trust, the beneficiary, or the grantor will pay the tax on the income generated by the trust.

Trusts cannot be used to transform a taxpayer's personal, living, or educational expenses into deductible items. A taxpayer cannot use a trust to avoid tax liability by ignoring either the true ownership of income and assets or the true substance of transactions.

Example: Hugo transfers his family residence and its furnishings to a trust, which rents the residence back to Hugo and his children. He deducts depreciation and the expenses of maintaining and operating the home, including landscaping, pool service, and utilities. Hugo's second trust transfers assets to the Edwards Charity Fund, which claims to be a charitable organization, but is not an IRS-qualified exempt organization. The trust pays for personal, education, and recreational expenses on behalf of Hugo and his family. The trust then claims the deductions on its tax returns. Both trusts Hugo created are fraudulent, and he would be subject to civil and criminal penalties.

Foreign Trusts

Foreign trusts are not always created to evade taxation. However, the IRS gives increased scrutiny to foreign trusts because of their growing popularity in foreign countries that provide financial secrecy and impose little or no tax on trusts. These are often in "tax haven" countries that are outside the jurisdiction of the U.S.

Typically, abusive foreign trust arrangements enable taxable funds to flow through several trusts or entities until the funds ultimately are distributed or made available to the original owner tax-free. Legally, however, the income from these arrangements is fully taxable.

Example: Shauna is a U.S. citizen with substantial business income. She forms an asset management company as a domestic trust, listing herself as the director and another individual as the trustee. She then forms a business trust, very similar to the domestic trust, with both intended to show she is not managing her own business. Next, Shauna forms a foreign trust in Bermuda, with the income from the business trust distributed to this foreign trust. Because the source of income is U.S.-based and there is a U.S. trustee, this foreign trust has filing requirements (discussed next). Her next step is to form a second foreign trust. The first foreign trust funnels all of its income to this second foreign trust, which has a foreigner as the trustee. Since the trustee and sources of income are now "foreign", Shauna claims there are no U.S. filing requirements. In actuality, she retains control of the income in this second foreign trust and has set up an elaborate scheme to evade U.S. tax laws. This is an abusive trust arrangement.

A trust is considered foreign unless a U.S. court supervises it and a U.S. fiduciary controls all substantial decisions.

U.S. taxpayers are required to file Form 3520, *Creation of or Transfer to Certain Foreign Trusts*, Form 3520-A, *Annual Return of Foreign Trust with U.S. Beneficiaries*, and Form 926, *Return by a Transferor of Property to a Foreign Estate or Trust*, when contributing property to a foreign trust. These trusts are usually U.S. tax neutral and are treated as grantor trusts with income taxable to the grantor that should be included on Form 1040.

Foreign Accounts: Both individuals and entities including trusts may be required to report their foreign accounts to the IRS by filing an electronic Financial Crimes Enforcement Network (FinCEN), Form 114, *Report of Foreign Bank and Financial Accounts* (FBAR). The FBAR report must be e-filed by April 15 (with an applicable six-month extension) if:

- The taxpayer had a financial interest in, or signature authority over, at least one financial account located outside of the United States, and
- The aggregate value of all foreign financial accounts exceeded $10,000 at any time during the calendar year to be reported.

Certain exceptions apply to the filing requirement. For example, if the foreign financial accounts are owned by a governmental entity, international financial institution, participants or beneficiaries of a qualified retirement plan, or IRA owners and beneficiaries, they are exempt from the FBAR filing requirements.

Unit 19: Study Questions

(Test yourself and then check the correct answers at the end of this section.)

1. Mulcher Trust had the following in 2016:

- Taxable interest: $4,000
- Capital gains: $12,000
- Fiduciary fee: $2,000

At the end of 2016, the fiduciary distributes $4,000. The trust instrument allocates capital gains to income. What is the distributable net income (DNI) of Mulcher Trust for 2016?

A. $12,000
B. $14,000
C. $16,000
D. $18,000

2. All of the following are characteristics of a simple trust except:

A. The trust may distribute assets to charity.
B. The trust must distribute all its income currently.
C. The trust makes no distributions of principal.
D. The trust makes no distributions to charity.

3. The calculation of the gross estate includes all of the following except:

A. Life insurance proceeds payable to the decedent's heirs.
B. The value of certain annuities payable to the estate.
C. Property owned solely by the decedent's spouse.
D. The value of certain property transferred within three years before the taxpayer's death.

4. Dominique, an American citizen, has a trust in Panama where she regularly deposits funds. Which of the following statements is correct regarding the trust?

A. Income deposited in the Panama trust is shielded from all U.S. taxes.
B. Dominique is not subject to any filing requirements in connection with her foreign trust.
C. Dominique may have to pay gift taxes on funds distributed from the trust, but will not owe income tax.
D. All income in Dominique's foreign trust is fully taxable.

5. The Chessmore estate is required to distribute all of its income currently and has distributable net income (DNI) of $20,000 on its 2016 return. The only distribution the executor made during the year was $5,000, paid to the decedent's son, Carlton. Accordingly to the terms of the will, Carlton is entitled to 50% of the estate's DNI. Which of the following statements is correct?

A. Carlton must pay tax on $10,000.
B. Carlton must pay tax on $20,000.
C. Carlton is not required to pay tax on the distribution, since it is an inheritance.
D. Carlton must pay tax on $5,000.

6. All of the following are examples of potentially abusive trusts except:

A. A taxpayer who claims charitable deductions from a charity trust he has created, without receiving an IRS exemption letter.
B. A taxpayer who forms a grantor trust and retains the power to control or direct the trust's income or assets.
C. A taxpayer who forms a foreign trust in a "tax haven" country so funds distributed will be outside the jurisdiction of the United States.
D. A taxpayer who transfers an ongoing business to a series of trusts to avoid taxation but continues to run the day-to-day activities of the business and control its income stream.

7. Roberto died on May 3, 2016. The estate's tax year ends on December 31, 2016. The estate had the following items of income during the year:

- Interest: $250
- Dividends: $150

The estate made no distributions during 2016. Based upon the information provided, which of the following statements is correct?

A. The estate is not required to file an income tax return.
B. The estate is required to file an income tax return.
C. The estate is required to file a return on Form 706.
D. Both B and C.

8. The terms of Regina's will required annual payments of $30,000 and $10,000 to her husband (the surviving spouse) and her son, respectively, out of her estate's income during each year of the administration. The estate's distributable net income (DNI) for 2016 was $20,000. What are the amounts of income that will be reported by the estate to each beneficiary on their 2016 Forms K-1?

A. Husband: $10,000; Son: $10,000.
B. Husband: $15,000; Son: $5,000.
C. Husband: $20,000; Son: $0.
D. Husband: $0; Son: $0.

9. Parker, a single taxpayer, died on June 6, 2016. Based on the following information, determine the value of his gross estate:

FMV on date of death	
Life insurance on Parker's life (payable to his estate)	$250,000
Parker's revocable grantor trust	700,000
Liabilities owed by Parker when he died	150,000

A. $250,000
B. $800,000
C. $950,000
D. $1.1 million

10. In 2016, an estate has distributable net income of $12,000, consisting of $6,000 of rents, $4,000 of dividends, and $2,000 of taxable interest. Connie and her three brothers are equal beneficiaries of the estate. The executor distributes the income under the provisions of the will, which includes a stipulation that allocates dividend income to Connie. How is the distribution to Connie characterized for tax purposes?

A. $0 rents; $3,000 dividends; $0 taxable interest.
B. $0 rents; $4,000 dividends; $0 taxable interest.
C. $2,000 rents; $1,333 dividends; $667 taxable interest.
D. $1,500 rents; $1,000 dividends, $1,000 taxable interest.

11. Who pays income tax on a trust's distributive share of income?

A. The trust.
B. The beneficiaries.
C. Income tax is split equally between the trust and its beneficiaries.
D. Income tax is not assessed on a trust's distributive share of income.

12. What is included in the gross estate?

A. The gross estate of the decedent includes everything the taxpayer owns at the date of death.
B. The gross estate of the decedent includes everything the taxpayer owns six months after the date of death.
C. The gross estate of the decedent includes everything the taxpayer owns at the date of death, including income that the taxpayer was owed but had not yet received.
D. The gross estate includes everything the decedent earned in the prior year, as well as income estimates for future years.

13. Georgiana died on March 1, 2016. The executor of her estate has elected to file the estate's income tax return on a calendar-year basis. No distributions have been made by the estate. Based on the following, what is the taxable income that will be reported on Form 1041 for the estate, for the 2016 tax year, before consideration of the estate's exemption amount?

Taxable interest	$2,000
Tax-exempt interest	1,000
Capital gain	3,000
Executor's fees	300

A. $5,700
B. $4,700
C. $5,100
D. $6,000

Unit 19: Answers

1. The answer is B. Distributable net income is income that is currently available for distribution. In this case, it is $14,000 ($4,000 taxable interest + $12,000 capital gains = $16,000 - $2,000 fiduciary fee).

2. The answer is A. The IRC defines a simple trust as one that distributes all its income currently, makes no distributions of principal, and makes no distributions to charity. Any trust that is not a simple trust is automatically a complex trust.

3. The answer is C. The gross estate does not include property owned solely by the decedent's spouse or other individuals.

4. The answer is D. Although foreign trusts are often established in certain countries in an effort to evade taxation, the income from such arrangements is fully taxable under U.S. law. Dominique would also be subject to an annual filing requirement, Form 3520-A, *Annual Return of Foreign Trust with U.S. Beneficiaries.*

5. The answer is A. The beneficiary of an estate required to distribute all its income currently must report his entire share of DNI, whether or not he actually received distributions for the full amount during his tax year. Thus, Carlton must report and pay tax related to his entire share of DNI, $10,000, (which is 50% of the estate's DNI) rather than the portion he received in distributions during the year.

6. The answer is B. A grantor trust is a legitimate form of trust. All of the other trusts described are potentially abusive. Trusts cannot be used to transform a taxpayer's personal, living, or educational expenses into deductible items. A taxpayer cannot use a trust to avoid tax liability by ignoring either the true ownership of income and assets or the true substance of transactions.

7. The answer is A. An income tax return (Form 1041) must be filed for any domestic estate that has gross income of more than $600 for the tax year, or a beneficiary who is a nonresident alien, regardless of the estate's gross income. Since the gross income is below the $600 exemption amount, an income tax return is not required to be filed for 2016.

8. The answer is B. The beneficiaries of an estate that is not required to distribute all its income currently must report all income required to be distributed to them currently (whether or not actually distributed), plus all other amounts paid, credited, or required to be distributed to them, up to their share of distributable net income. In this case, since DNI is lower than the total amounts required to be distributed, it forms the limit on the amounts that must be reported as income to each beneficiary. DNI is allocated to each beneficiary in proportion to the required annual payments he received, thus 75% ($30,000/$40,000), or $15,000, to Regina's husband and 25% ($10,000/$40,000), or $5,000, to her son.

9. The answer is C. Life insurance payable to a trust and assets held in a grantor trust are included in a decedent's gross estate. Liabilities of the decedent are not included in the gross estate. However, they are an allowable deduction from the gross estate in determining the taxable estate.

10. The answer is B. Based upon the stipulation that allocates dividend income to Connie, the full amount of dividends included in distributable net income ($4,000) is taxable to Connie.

11. The answer is B. A trust is a partial pass-through entity that is allowed a deduction for its distributions to beneficiaries. The beneficiaries pay income tax on their distributive share of income that is distributed to them. Schedule K-1 (Form 1041) is used to report income that a trust distributes to beneficiaries. The income must then be reported on the beneficiaries' income tax returns.

12. The answer is A. The gross estate of the decedent includes everything the taxpayer owns at the date of death.

13. The answer is B. Taxable income of $4,700 can be reported for the estate, determined as follows: taxable interest of $2,000 plus capital gain of $3,000, minus the executor's fees of $300. The expenses of administering an estate can be deducted either from the estate's income on Form 1041 in determining its income tax or from the gross estate on Form 706 in determining the estate tax liability, but cannot be claimed for both purposes. The tax-exempt interest retains the character that would have applied if it had been reported by the decedent. The estate would be eligible for an exemption amount of $600 in determining its actual taxable income.

PART 3: REPRESENTATION

New Tax Law for Part 3: Representation

ERPA program permanently suspended: Effective February 12, 2016, the IRS will no longer be offering the ERPA Special Enrollment Examination (ERPA SEE) to become an ERPA. Any current ERPAs will continue to hold the ERPA designation, allowing them to practice before the IRS.

Cash payment option: There is a new option for taxpayers whose only option is to pay their taxes in cash. Starting in 2016, the IRS now offers a cash payment option for taxpayers who do not have bank accounts. This is helpful for taxpayers who are not eligible for a bank account, or who work in industries that are ineligible for bank accounts. Participating retail stores provide a receipt after accepting the cash and the payment usually posts to the taxpayer's IRS account within two business days. There is a $1,000 payment limit per day and a $3.99 fee per payment.

Expanded Due Diligence Requirements for Refundable Credits: Starting in 2016, expanded due diligence requirements apply to the Child Tax Credit and American Opportunity credit. Increased penalties as well as potential bans are now possible for these credits.

- 2 Year limitation – reckless or intentional disregard
- 10 Year limitation – fraud

ACA Due Diligence: The IRS issued guidance on April 7, 2016 designed to help tax preparers resolve conflicting information between Form 1095-A and Form 1095-B, two common ACA forms.

Revised Power of Attorney Form 2848

- Form 2848 now provides space for the information and signatures of up to four representatives.
- A new, updated description and representation requirements has been added for unenrolled return preparers who have earned AFSPs
- The Registered Tax Return Preparer designation has been removed
- Prior versions of the form shall remain in effect until they are revoked by the taxpayer, or withdrawn by representative.

Starting in 2016, all unenrolled preparers must:

- Possess a valid and active PTIN
- For returns prepared in 2016, only unenrolled return preparers participating in the Annual Filing Season Record of Completion program may represent a taxpayer, and only with respect to returns prepared and signed by the preparer.

Definition of Marriage: the IRS issued final regulations in September 2016 regarding the definition of marriage after the landmark case of *Obergefell v. Hodges*. These regulations state that a marriage of two individuals is recognized for federal tax purposes if the marriage is recognized by the state, possession or territory of the United States in which the marriage is entered into, regardless of where the couple is living. This clarifies the law to include common law marriage as well as marriages performed in a foreign country.

Levels of Representation (Effective January 1, 2016)

- Unlimited Representation Rights: EAs, CPAs and Attorneys
- Limited Representation Rights: Annual Filing Season Program (AFSP) Participants
- No representation rights before IRS: Non-EA, CPA or Attorney PTIN holders who do not participate in the AFSP

Strengthening ID Verification on all Self-Prepared Returns

- Taxpayers must use prior-year AGI or prior year Self Select PIN to verify e-signature
- No changes to Practitioner PIN Method
- Electronic Filing PIN no longer an option for self-prepared returns

Taxpayer Assistance Center (TAC) Appointment-Service

- All Taxpayer Assistance Centers will provide in-person appointment service by the end of 2016.
- Many questions can be resolved online without visiting a TAC.
- TACs offer personal tax help when a taxpayer's tax issue cannot be handled online or by phone.

New IRS Acceptance Agent 2016 Program Changes

- The ITIN Acceptance Agent Certification process changes in 2016
- ITIN Acceptance Agent Applications are now accepted year round
- The IRS is actively recruiting IRS acceptance agents

Expanded due diligence requirements. The PATH Act also extended due diligence requirements to returns claiming the Child Tax Credit (CTC) and the American Opportunity Tax Credit (AOTC). Last year due diligence only applied to EITC. See "Paid Preparer Due Diligence Penalties" below for information on how IRS can assess penalties.

Paid Preparers Earned Income Credit Checklist: In previous years, the law required paid preparers to complete and submit the Form 8867 with every EITC claim. The form now includes the CTC and the AOTC. Beginning in 2017, paid preparers will need to complete and submit the Form 8867 with every electronic or paper return claiming EITC, CTC or AOTC or any claim for refund with one or more of these credits. The IRS can also assess penalties when the Form 8867 is not completed or not included with the tax return claiming one of the credits.

PATH Act Legislation and ITINs: Individual Taxpayer Identification Numbers may need renewal starting in 2016. Those who have not used their ITIN on a federal tax return at least once in the last three years will need to renew their ITIN. Also, all ITINs issued before 2013 will begin expiring in 2016. There are also new documentation requirements when applying for or renewing an ITIN for certain dependents. Renewals began in October 2016.

Paid Preparer Due Diligence Penalties Increased: The $500 penalty for each failure to meet your due diligence for one or more of the credits is now adjusted for inflation. The penalty for tax year 2016 is now $510. The penalty for 2017 will remain at $510. The penalty for failure to meet the due diligence requirements containing EITC, CTC or AOTC filed in 2017 is $510 per credit *per return*. The penalty will apply to each credit incorrectly submitted on a tax return and is now indexed for inflation. For example, if the preparer fails to meet due diligence for ALL THREE credits, the preparer's penalty would be $1,530 per return for 2016 returns.

Private Debt Collectors: The Internal Revenue Service plans to begin private collection of certain overdue federal tax debts in 2017 and has selected four contractors to implement the new program for the 2016 tax year. Under the new law (IRC §6306), the IRS is required to use private debt collection companies to collect debts that are classified as "inactive tax receivables."

AFSP Representation Rights Clarified: Beginning with the 2016 tax season, only Annual Filing Season Program participants have limited practice rights before the IRS. Unenrolled preparers who do not participate in this annual program will have no authority to represent clients before the IRS after December 31, 2015.

Annual Filing Season Program Record of Completion: Unenrolled tax preparers who wish to participate in the Annual Filing Season Program (AFSP) must complete the required continuing education from IRS-approved CPE providers by Dec. 31, 2016 in order to receive a 2017 Annual Filing Season Program Record of Completion.

Negotiation of taxpayer checks: The explicit recognition that a longstanding prohibition in Circular 230 against negotiation of Treasury "checks" issued to taxpayers likewise now applies to direct deposits and similar electronic forms of payment that are now commonplace.

Expedited suspensions from practice: Circular 230 expands and refines the process for suspension from practice on an expedited basis, which allows OPR to promptly suspend individuals in certain situations using a short form of administrative due process.

Random CPE Audits: Beginning in May 2016, the IRS will begin conducting random CPE audits of EAs with SSNs ending in 0, 1, 2, or 3 requesting copies of their continuing education certificates of completion for the past three years. Recipients of these letters will be asked to mail or fax the documents within 30 days.

PLR Fee Increase: Starting in February 2016, the fees for requesting a Private Letter Ruling are $10,000 and up (per request).

Unit 1: Legal Authority of the IRS

More Reading:
Circular 230, *Regulations Governing Practice Before the Internal Revenue Service*
Publication 947, *Practice Before the IRS and Power of Attorney*
Publication 1, *Your Rights as a Taxpayer*

Overview of SEE Part 3

Part 3 of the EA exam concerns the ethics, laws, and regulations that govern the tax profession: rules that tax practitioners must follow; standards that the tax profession is held to; who may represent taxpayers before the IRS; IRS procedures for assessment, collection, audit, and appeals; and penalties that tax preparers face if they violate the law.

Specifically, Part 3 of the exam is broken down into the following sections and corresponding percentage of questions: *Practice and Procedures*, 35%; *Representation before the IRS*, 30%; *Specific Types of Representation*, 30%; and *Completion of the Filing Process*, 5%.[127]

Issues of ethics, practice, and representation are dealt with in detail in Treasury Department Circular No. 230, *Regulations Governing Practice before the Internal Revenue Service*.[128] All practitioners who represent taxpayers before the IRS are subject to the rules and regulations set forth in Circular 230.

Federal Tax Law

The Internal Revenue Code (IRC) is the main body of tax law of the United States. The IRC is enacted by Congress and published as Title 26 of the United States Code. Other tax law is promulgated by individual states, cities, and municipalities. The IRS enrolled agent exam deals only with federal tax laws and not with the laws of any individual state or municipality.

Tax law is determined by all three branches of our federal government, although the legislative branch (Congress) has the primary function of originating tax laws. The executive branch (the president) is responsible for income tax regulations, revenue rulings, and revenue procedures. The judicial branch is responsible for court decisions.

The Internal Revenue Service is the federal agency that enforces tax law. It is the collection arm for the U.S. Treasury, which is responsible for paying various government expenses. The IRS takes the specifics of the laws enacted by Congress and translates them into the detailed regulations, rules, and procedures of the IRC. The IRS produces several kinds of documents that provide guidance to taxpayers, including the following:

1. Treasury regulations
2. Revenue rulings
3. Revenue procedures
4. Private letter rulings
5. Technical advice memoranda
6. IRS notices

Each of these has "substantial authority," which means the authority to serve as the basis for interpretation of current tax law and to establish precedents for the future.

---

[127]Specifications for tests administered during the prior year exam cycle.

[128]Regulations governing practice are set forth in Title 31, Code of Federal Regulations, Subtitle A, Part 10, and were published in pamphlet form as Treasury Department Circular No. 230 on June 12, 2014.

Definition: The Internal Revenue Code defines **substantial authority** as an "objective standard involving an analysis of the law and application of the law to relevant facts." The weight given an authority depends on its "relevance and persuasiveness," and the type of document providing the authority. For example, a "revenue ruling is accorded greater weight than a private letter ruling addressing the same issue." More recent documents also carry greater weight than older ones.

Under IRC §6662, sources of substantial authority include the following: provisions of the Internal Revenue Code, temporary and final regulations, court cases, administrative pronouncements, tax treaties, and Congressional intent as reflected in committee reports.

The list was later expanded to include proposed regulations, private letter rulings, technical advice memoranda, IRS information or press releases, notices, and any other similar documents published by the IRS in the Internal Revenue Bulletin.[129]

Treatises and articles in legal periodicals are not considered substantial authority under this statute.

Treasury Regulations

Treasury regulations are the U.S. Treasury Department's official interpretations of the Internal Revenue Code. The IRC authorizes the Secretary of the Treasury to "prescribe all needful rules and regulations for enforcement" of the code. All regulations are written by the IRS's Office of the Chief Counsel and approved by the Treasury secretary.

The courts give weight to Treasury regulations and will generally uphold the regulations so long as the IRS's interpretation is reasonable and does not contradict any provisions in the IRC.

Treasury regulations are published in the Federal Register.

Note: The IRS is bound by its regulations, but the courts are not. U.S. Treasury regulations are authorized by law, but U.S. courts are not obligated to follow administrative interpretations.

The three types of Treasury regulations are:

- **Legislative,**
- **Interpretative, and**
- **Procedural.**

Legislative regulations are created when Congress expressly delegates the authority to the Treasury secretary or the commissioner of the IRS to provide the requirements for a specific provision of the IRC. A legislative regulation has a higher degree of authority than an interpretative regulation. In general, legislative regulations carry the same authority as the law itself. However, a legislative regulation may be overturned if any of the following conflicts apply:

- It is outside the power delegated to the U.S. Treasury.
- It conflicts with a specific statute.
- It is deemed unreasonable by the courts.

Interpretive regulations are issued under the IRS's general authority to interpret the IRC. An interpretative regulation only explains the meaning of a portion of the code. Unlike a legislative regulation, there is no grant of authority for the promulgation of an interpretative regulation, so these regulations may be challenged on the grounds that they do not reflect Congress's intent.

Procedural regulations concern the administrative provisions of the code and are issued by the commissioner of the IRS and not the secretary of the Treasury. They often concern

[129] The Committee Report for the Revenue Reconciliation Act of 1989.

minor issues, such as when notices should be sent to employees or how to file certain IRS forms.

Classification of Treasury Regulations

Regulations are further classified as proposed, temporary, or final:

- **Proposed regulations** are open to commentary from the public. Various versions of proposed regulations may be issued and withdrawn before a final regulation is issued.
- **Temporary regulations** may remain in effect for three years. They are used to provide immediate guidance to the public and IRS employees prior to publishing final regulations.
- **Final regulations** are issued when a regulation becomes an official Treasury decision. They are the highest authority issued by Treasury Department.

Revenue Rulings and Revenue Procedures

The IRS issues revenue rulings and revenue procedures to inform and guide taxpayers. Neither has the force of Treasury Department regulations, but they may be used as precedents. A revenue ruling typically states the IRS position, while a revenue procedure provides instructions concerning that position.

Revenue rulings are intended to promote uniform application of the IRC. The national office of the IRS issues revenue rulings, which are published in the Internal Revenue Bulletin and the Federal Register. A revenue ruling is not binding in Tax Court or any other U.S. court. However, revenue rulings can be used by taxpayers as guidance to avoid certain accuracy-related IRS penalties.

The numbering system for revenue rulings corresponds to the year the ruling was issued. Thus, for example, revenue ruling 2016-1 was the first revenue ruling issued in 2016.

Revenue procedures are official IRS statements of procedure that affect the rights or duties of taxpayers under the IRC. A revenue procedure may be cited as precedent, but it does not have the force of law.

Example: A *revenue ruling* will announce that taxpayers may deduct certain automobile expenses. A *revenue procedure* will then explain how taxpayers must deduct, allocate, or compute these automobile expenses.

IRS Written Determinations

There are many types of official IRS correspondence and determinations. We will discuss the most common types in the following section.

Technical Advice Memorandum (TAM)

A TAM is written guidance furnished by the IRS Office of Chief Counsel upon the request of an IRS director. A TAM is issued in response to a technical or procedural question that develops during:

- The examination of a taxpayer's return
- Consideration of a taxpayer's claim for refund or credit
- A request for a determination letter
- Processing and considering non-docketed cases in an Appeals office

Technical advice memoranda are issued only on closed transactions and provide the interpretation of proper application of tax laws, tax treaties, regulations, revenue rulings, or other precedents.

The advice rendered represents the position of the IRS, but it only relates to the specific case in question.

Technical advice memoranda are made public after private information has been removed that could identify a particular taxpayer.

Private Letter Ruling (PLR)

A taxpayer who has a specific question regarding tax law may request a private letter ruling (PLR) from the IRS. A PLR is a written statement issued to a taxpayer that interprets and applies tax laws to the taxpayer's specific case. It is issued to communicate the tax consequences of a particular transaction before the transaction is consummated or before the taxpayer's return is filed.

A PLR is legally binding on the IRS, but only if the taxpayer fully and accurately described the proposed transaction in the request and carried out the transaction as described. In addition, it is only binding on the IRS for the particular taxpayer who requested the ruling.

PLRs are made public after the taxpayer's private, identifiable information has been redacted (removed or blacked out). A private letter ruling is not free. Starting in 2016, the current fees for a PLR range from $10,000 and up (per request).

Example: Joel, age 40, decides to roll over his IRA to another financial institution. However, his prior financial institution failed to institute the rollover and instead erroneously distributed the entire amount of his IRA into a regular savings account. By the time Joel discovered the error, it was past the 60-day required rollover window, and he is subject to IRS penalties and income tax on the distributed amount. Joel files a private letter ruling request to ask for a waiver to the normal 60-day rollover window. The IRS grants his formal request by issuing a private letter ruling.[130]

IRS Notices

An official IRS notice is a public pronouncement that may contain guidance involving substantive interpretations of the IRC or other provisions of the law. Information commonly published in IRS notices includes:

- Weighted average interest rate updates
- Inflation adjustment factors
- Changes to IRS regulations
- Tax provisions related to presidentially declared disaster areas
- IRS requests for public comments on changes to regulations, rulings, or procedures

Internal Revenue Bulletin

The Internal Revenue Bulletin is the authoritative source of official IRS tax guidance. It is a weekly collection of items of substantial interest to the professional tax community. The IRB announces official IRS rulings and publishes Treasury decisions, executive orders, tax conventions, significant legislation, and court decisions.

Anyone may search the IRS website, www.irs.gov, for past issues of the IRB. Issues are available in both HTML and PDF file formats.

The IRS often releases individual items in advance of their publication in the IRB. Tax professionals may subscribe to the IRS GuideWire service to receive automated email notifications about these items.

Internal Revenue Manual

The Internal Revenue Manual (IRM) is the single official compilation of policies, delegated authorities, procedures, instructions, and guidelines relating to the organization, functions, administration, and operations of the IRS. It is primarily used by IRS employees to guide them in all facets of operations.

As of early 2016, the manual has 39 separate parts, which include sections on the processing of tax submissions, examinations, collection, and appeals. Criminal investigations,

[130] This example is based on Private Letter Ruling 201204025.

legal advice, and litigation in the courts are also included in the manual. The IRM is public information and can be searched and read directly on the IRS website.

IRS Publications and Forms

Publications: The IRS disseminates information to both taxpayers and preparers through its publications. For example, Publication 17 covers the general rules for filing a federal income tax return for individuals. Publication 17 supplements information contained in the tax form instruction booklet and explains the law in more detail, so it is an important document for taxpayers who prepare their own income tax returns.

Although the information in publications is drawn from the Internal Revenue Code, Treasury regulations, and other primary sources of authority, publications themselves are not considered to have substantial authority. Taxpayers and preparers may not rely on guidance issued by IRS publications to avoid accuracy-related penalties.

Note: In 2014, a U.S. Tax Court judge declared, "taxpayers rely on IRS guidance at their own peril." [131] Judge Joseph W. Nega ruled against a married couple who used guidance from an IRS publication as the basis for their case disputing penalties imposed after an IRA withdrawal. The judge wrote that IRS guidance was not "binding precedent" or "sufficient authority" to excuse the couple from penalties. The IRS later revised the publication at issue.

Tax Forms and Schedules: IRS tax forms and schedules are used by taxpayers to report financial information to the IRS and calculate taxes to be paid or disclose other information as required by the Internal Revenue Code.

There are more than 800 forms and schedules in use. Many have accompanying instructions for taxpayers. Forms, schedules, and instructions are updated whenever necessary due to changes in the tax code.

All publications, forms, and instructions are listed and available for download on the IRS website at *www.irs.gov*, usually in both HTML and PDF file formats. Updated versions of publications are listed with the date revisions were made, so taxpayers can know they are using the most current information.

Many libraries and post offices offer free tax forms to taxpayers during the filing season, as do the more than 400 Taxpayer Assistance Centers across the country where the IRS offers face-to-face help to taxpayers. Taxpayers may also call the IRS to order current year tax forms, instructions, and publications by mail.

Due to the growth in electronic filing and the availability of free access to tax forms, the IRS no longer mails paper tax packages to taxpayers.

Case Law

Often, taxpayers and tax preparers will disagree with the IRS's interpretation of the IRC. In these cases, it is up to the courts to determine Congress's intent or the constitutionality of the tax law or IRS position that is being challenged. There are many instances where tax laws are either disputed or overturned. Court decisions then serve as guidance for future tax decisions.

In most instances, the IRS chooses whether or not to acquiesce to a court decision. This means that the IRS may decide to ignore the ruling of the court and continue with its regular policies regarding the litigated issue.

The IRS is not bound to change its regulations due to a loss in court. The only exception to this rule is the U.S. Supreme Court, whose decisions the IRS is obligated to follow.

The IRS does not announce acquiescence or non-acquiescence in every case. Sometimes its position is withheld. When it does announce its position, the IRS publishes its acquiescence or non-acquiescence first in the Internal Revenue Bulletin.

---

[131] *Bobrow v. Commissioner* of Internal Revenue

Study Note: The enrolled agent exam is based largely on IRS publications, and exam candidates will not be tested on court cases unless the law has already made its way into an IRS publication. Similarly, exam candidates will not be tested on any pending tax law or legislation; the exam is based on tax law from the prior year. However, EA candidates must understand the basics of tax law, the court system, and how it relates to the taxpayer and tax professional.

Freedom of Information Act Requests (FOIA)

The Freedom of Information Act (FOIA) is a law designed to ensure public access to U.S. government records.[132] Upon written request, federal agencies, including the IRS, are required to disclose requested records, unless they can be withheld under certain exceptions allowed in the FOIA. Under the terms of the act, agencies may charge reasonable fees for searching, reviewing, and copying records that have been requested.

The IRS may withhold a record that falls under one of the FOIA's nine exemptions and three exclusions.

The exemptions protect against the disclosure of information that would harm national security, the privacy of individuals, the proprietary interests of business, the functioning of the government, and other important recognized interests. Exclusions involve especially sensitive law enforcement records related to criminal, FBI, counterintelligence, and international terrorism investigations.

When a record contains some information that qualifies as exempt, the entire record is not necessarily exempt. Instead, the FOIA specifically provides that any portions of a record that can be set apart must be provided to a requester after deletion of the exempt portions.

The IRS generally has 20 business days to say whether it will comply with a FOIA request. When a request is denied, the IRS must give the reason for denial and explain the right to appeal to the head of the agency.

Note: There is a type of FOIA request specific to tax preparers, which is covered in Unit 3, *Authorizations and Disclosures*.

A taxpayer may contest the fees charged in the processing of a records request. The IRS will copy the requested records and send the taxpayer a bill for the fees. In most cases, there is no charge for the first 100 pages and the fee is 20 cents per page thereafter. A taxpayer may appeal other types of adverse determinations under the FOIA, such as the failure of the IRS to conduct an adequate search for requested documents.

A person whose request was granted in part and denied in part may appeal the part that was denied. If the IRS has agreed to disclose some but not all of the requested documents, the filing of an appeal does not affect the release of the documents that can be disclosed.

Taxpayer Bill of Rights

The IRS has a Taxpayer Bill of Rights. The program is designed to better communicate to taxpayers their existing statutory and administrative protections. The Taxpayer Bill of Rights groups the dozens of rights in the Internal Revenue Code, the IRS *Restructuring and Reform Act of 1998*, and the Internal Revenue Manual into ten fundamental rights to make them clear, understandable, and accessible both to taxpayers and IRS employees. These rights are detailed in IRS Publication 1. They are as follows:

1. **The Right to Be Informed:** Taxpayers have the right to know what they need to do to comply with the tax laws. They are entitled to clear explanations of the laws and IRS procedures in all tax forms, instructions, publications, notices, and correspondence. They

[132]For more information, see *The Freedom of Information Act Guide to Treasury Records* at www.treasury.gov and *Freedom of Information Act (FOIA) Guidelines* at www.IRS.gov.

have the right to be informed of IRS decisions about their tax accounts and to receive clear explanations of the outcomes.

Example: Certain notices must include the amount (if any) of the tax, interest and certain penalties the taxpayer owes and must explain why he owes these amounts (IRC §7522).[133]

2. **The Right to Quality Service:** Taxpayers have the right to receive prompt, courteous, and professional assistance in their dealings with the IRS, to be spoken to in a way they can easily understand, to receive clear and easily understandable communications from the IRS, and to speak to a supervisor about inadequate service.

Example: When collecting tax, the IRS should treat a taxpayer with courtesy. Generally, the IRS should only contact a taxpayer between 8 a.m. and 9 p.m. The IRS should not contact a taxpayer at his place of employment if the IRS knows, or has reason to know, that his employer does not allow this kind of contact (IRC §6304).

3. **The Right to Pay No More than the Correct Amount of Tax:** Taxpayers have the right to pay only the amount of tax legally due, including interest and penalties, and to have the IRS apply all tax payments properly.

Example: If a taxpayer believes he has overpaid his taxes, he can file a refund claim asking for the money back (IRC §6402).

4. **The Right to Challenge the IRS's Position and Be Heard:** Taxpayers have the right to raise objections and provide additional documentation in response to formal IRS actions or proposed actions, to expect that the IRS will consider their timely objections and documentation promptly and fairly, and to receive a response if the IRS does not agree with their position.

Example: If a taxpayer is notified his return has a mathematical or clerical error, he has 60 days to tell the IRS that he disagrees. If the IRS is not persuaded, it will issue a notice proposing a tax adjustment. The notice provides a taxpayer the right to challenge the proposed adjustment in Tax Court by filing a petition within 90 days of the date of the notice (IRC §6213(b)).

5. **The Right to Appeal an IRS Decision in an Independent Forum:** Taxpayers are entitled to a fair and impartial administrative appeal of most IRS decisions, including many penalties, and have the right to receive a written response regarding the Office of Appeals' decision. Taxpayers generally have the right to take their cases to court.

Example: If the IRS has sent a taxpayer a notice proposing additional tax, he may dispute the proposed adjustment in the U.S. Tax Court before he has to pay the tax (IRC §6213).

6. **The Right to Finality:** Taxpayers have the right to know the maximum amount of time they have to challenge the IRS's position, as well as the maximum amount of time the IRS has to audit a particular tax year or collect a tax debt. Taxpayers have the right to know when the IRS has finished an audit.

Example: The IRS generally has ten years from the assessment date to collect unpaid taxes from a taxpayer (IRC §6502).

7. **The Right to Privacy:** Taxpayers have the right to expect that any IRS inquiry, examination, or enforcement action will comply with the law and be no more intrusive than necessary, and will respect all due process rights, including search and seizure protections, and will provide, where applicable, a collection due process hearing.

Example: The IRS should not seek intrusive and extraneous information about a taxpayer's lifestyle during an audit if there is no reasonable indication that he has unreported income (IRC §7602(e)).

[133] Examples drawn from the Taxpayer Advocate Service's *What the Taxpayer Bill of Rights Means for You*.

8. **The Right to Confidentiality:** Taxpayers have the right to expect that any information they provide to the IRS will not be disclosed unless authorized by the taxpayer or by law. Taxpayers have the right to expect appropriate action will be taken against employees, return preparers, and others who wrongfully use or disclose taxpayer return information.

Example: In general, the IRS may not disclose a taxpayer's tax information to third parties unless he gives explicit permission (IRC §6103). There are exceptions for law enforcement and other limited scenarios.

9. **The Right to Retain Representation:** Taxpayers have the right to retain an authorized representative of their choice to represent them in their dealings with the IRS. Taxpayers have the right to seek assistance from a Low Income Taxpayer Clinic if they cannot afford representation.

Example: A taxpayer may select a qualified representative person to represent him in an interview with the IRS. The IRS cannot require that a taxpayer attend with his representative (IRC §7521(c)).

10. **The Right to a Fair and Just Tax System:** Taxpayers have the right to expect the tax system to consider facts and circumstances that might affect their underlying liabilities, ability to pay, or ability to provide information timely. Taxpayers have the right to request assistance from the Taxpayer Advocate Service if they are experiencing financial difficulty or if the IRS has not resolved their tax issues properly and timely through its normal channels.

Example: The IRS cannot levy (seize) all of a taxpayer's wages to collect his unpaid tax. A portion will be exempt from levy to allow payment of basic living expenses (IRC §6334).

IRS Divisions

The IRS has four main operating divisions. These are:

1. **Large Business & International Division:** This division serves corporations, including S corporations, and partnerships, with assets in excess of $10 million. This is the division of the IRS that audits large corporate taxpayers and partnerships, including publicly traded companies like Ford, Apple, Coca-Cola, etc.
2. **Small Business and Self-Employed Division**: This division serves corporations, and partnerships with assets less than $10 million; filers of gift, estate, excise, employment and fiduciary returns; individuals filing an individual Federal income tax return with accompanying Schedule C, Schedule E, Schedule F, Form 2106, *Employee Business Expenses*.
3. **Wage and Investment Division:** This division serves individuals with wage and investment income only (not including international tax returns) filing an individual Federal income tax return without accompanying Schedule C, E, or F, or Form 2106.
4. **Tax Exempt and Government Entities Division**: This division serves three distinct taxpayer segments: employee plans (including IRAs), exempt organizations, and government entities.

Taxpayer Advocate Service

The Taxpayer Advocate Service (TAS) is an independent organization within the IRS whose goal is to help taxpayers resolve problems with the IRS. A taxpayer may be eligible for TAS assistance when he is facing a number of different situations involving economic harm or significant delays in resolving a tax issue.

The Taxpayer Advocate Service is free and confidential, and is available for businesses as well as individuals. TAS has at least one office in every state, the District of Columbia, and Puerto Rico. There are local TAS offices where taxpayers can meet face-to-face with advocates, a video conferencing service for areas where there are no nearby offices, and toll-free telephone service. The quickest contact method is by fax, but a taxpayer may also submit Form 911, *Request for Taxpayer Advocate Service Assistance.* TAS may be able to help a taxpayer who is experiencing a problem with the IRS and:

- The problem with the IRS is causing financial difficulties for the taxpayer, his family, or his business;
- The taxpayer faces (or his business is facing) an immediate threat of adverse action; or
- The taxpayer has tried repeatedly to contact the IRS, but no one has responded, or the IRS has not responded by the date promised.

When the Taxpayer Advocate Service evaluates a taxpayer's request for assistance, it will use the following criteria to determine whether to intervene:

- The taxpayer is experiencing economic harm or is about to suffer economic harm.
- The taxpayer is facing an immediate threat of adverse action.
- The taxpayer will incur significant costs if relief is not granted (including fees for professional representation).
- The taxpayer will suffer irreparable injury or long-term adverse impact if relief is not granted.
- The taxpayer has experienced a delay of more than 30 days to resolve a tax account problem.
- The taxpayer did not receive a response or resolution to his problem or inquiry by the date promised.
- A system or procedure has either failed to operate as intended, or failed to resolve the taxpayer's problem or dispute within the IRS.
- The manner in which the tax laws are being administered raise considerations of equity, or have impaired or will impair the taxpayer's rights.
- The National Tax Advocate determines compelling public policy warrants assistance to an individual or group of taxpayers.

The Taxpayer Advocate Service will generally ask the IRS to stop certain collection activities while a taxpayer's request for assistance is pending (such as lien filings, levies, and seizures).

Example: Geraldine filed an amended tax return for 2016. She has an outstanding balance for the prior tax year and has been receiving IRS collection notices. Geraldine's expected refund would fully pay her balance due and leave her with a small refund. The official processing time for Form 1040X, *Amended U.S. Individual Tax Return*, is eight to twelve weeks. However, she has been waiting more than four months for her refund to be processed. She has contacted the IRS numerous times, but was never given a reason for the delay. Geraldine may request intervention from the Taxpayer Advocate Service.

Unit 1: Study Questions

(Test yourself and then check the correct answers at the end of this chapter.)

1. Which of the following would have the highest authority in establishing precedent for tax law for all taxpayers?

A. Private letter ruling.
B. Treasury regulation.
C. IRS publication.
D. Technical advice memorandum.

2. In matters of tax law, the IRS must acquiesce in all decisions rendered by the:

A. U.S. Tax Court.
B. U.S. Supreme Court.
C. U.S. Court of Appeals.
D. Both A and B.

3. Of the following situations, which is most likely to warrant intervention by the Taxpayer Advocate Service?

A. A taxpayer is experiencing financial difficulty. His home is in foreclosure and he is worried he will be unable to pay his federal income tax liability by the due date.
B. A taxpayer has experienced multiple, lengthy delays in trying to contact the IRS by telephone.
C. A taxpayer has waited for weeks for the IRS to discharge the lien on his property, which must be removed immediately or else the sale of the property will fall through.
D. A taxpayer has received an IRS Notice of Federal Tax Lien that his bank account will be subject to levy if he does not pay his federal tax liability.

4. Of the following choices, which does not meet the substantial authority test?

A. Proposed regulations.
B. Legal opinion printed in a law school journal.
C. Congressional intent as reflected in committee reports.
D. Information from an IRS press release.

5. Which of the following statements regarding revenue rulings is correct?

A. Revenue rulings cannot be used to avoid certain IRS penalties.
B. Revenue rulings can be used to avoid certain IRS penalties.
C. Revenue rulings are not official IRS guidance.
D. None of the above.

6. Which branch of government is the main source of tax law in the United States?

A. Legislative.
B. Executive.
C. Judicial.
D. All three branches contribute equally to the creation and adoption of tax law.

7. An IRS revenue officer has a question about a collection procedure involving a taxpayer. He should consult:

A. The Internal Revenue Manual.
B. The Internal Revenue Bulletin.
C. Publication 594, *The IRS Collection Process.*
D. The Congressional Record.

8. A private letter ruling is legally binding on the IRS if:

A. The taxpayer fully and accurately described the proposed transaction in his request and carried out the transaction as described.
B. The IRS is notified of any discrepancies on a taxpayer's return.
C. The taxpayer goes to the Tax Court and requests a formal decision.
D. None of the above.

9. Which has the highest level of authority with regards to IRS regulations?

A. Revenue regulations.
B. Procedural regulation.
C. Interpretative regulation.
D. Legislative regulation.

10. The IRS generally has __________ to say whether it will comply with a FOIA request.

A. 20 business days
B. Two weeks
C. 30 days
D. 90 Days

11. Treasury regulations are published in ________________.

A. The Congressional Notes.
B. The Federal Register.
C. The Office of Appeals.
D. The IRS Newswire.

Unit 1: Answers

1. The answer is B. A Treasury regulation is the Treasury Department's official interpretation of the Internal Revenue Code. It has substantial authority in establishing precedent for tax law.

2. The answer is B. The Internal Revenue Service is required to obey all decisions rendered by the highest court of the land, the U.S. Supreme Court. Although case law helps set precedent and will influence the IRS in its regulations, policies, and procedures, the IRS is not obligated to change its regulations in matters of tax law that are decided by other U.S. courts, including the U.S. Tax Court.

3. The answer is C. The Taxpayer Advocate Service is designed to attempt to resolve issues when a taxpayer has a serious problem with the IRS or has experienced a serious delay. There are specific criteria used to determine whether taxpayer assistance is warranted, and the example in the correct answer is drawn from an actual case. On Form 911, *Request for Taxpayer Advocate Service Assistance,* a taxpayer must indicate one or more of the following reasons he is asking for help:

- He is experiencing economic harm or is about to suffer economic harm.
- He is facing an immediate threat of adverse action.
- He will incur significant costs if relief is not granted (including fees for professional representation).
- He will suffer irreparable injury or long-term adverse impact if relief is not granted.
- He has experienced a delay of more than 30 days to resolve a tax account problem.
- He has not received a response or resolution to his problem or inquiry by the date promised.
- A system or procedure has either failed to operate as intended, or failed to resolve the taxpayer's problem or dispute with the IRS.
- The manner in which the tax laws are being administered raises concerns of equity, or has impaired or will impair the taxpayer's rights.

4. The answer is B. A legal opinion printed in a law journal does not have substantial authority. Sources of substantial authority are as follows: the Internal Revenue Code, temporary and final regulations, court cases, administrative pronouncements, tax treaties, Congressional intent as reflected in committee reports, proposed regulations, private letter rulings, technical advice memoranda, IRS information or press releases, IRS notices, and any other similar documents published by the IRS in the Internal Revenue Bulletin.

5. The answer is B. Revenue rulings can be used to avoid certain accuracy-related IRS penalties. Taxpayers may rely on revenue rulings as official IRS guidance on an issue to make a decision regarding taxable income, deductions, and how to avoid certain IRS penalties.

6. The answer is A. Although both the judicial and executive branches play important roles in interpreting, implementing, and enforcing tax laws, the legislative branch (Congress) is the main source of tax law in the United States. Congress is responsible for passing tax laws, which are published as the Internal Revenue Code, issued separately as Title 26 of the United States Code.

7. The answer is A. The Internal Revenue Manual (IRM) is the single official compilation of policies, delegated authorities, procedures, instructions, and guidelines relating to the organization, functions, administration, and operations of the IRS. It is the resource primarily used by IRS employees to guide them in all facets of operations.

8. The answer is A. A private letter ruling (PLR) is binding on the IRS if the taxpayer fully and accurately described the proposed transaction in his request and carried out the transaction as described.

9. The answer is D. A legislative regulation is authorized by Congress to provide the material requirements of a specific IRC provision. If written correctly, a legislative regulation carries the same authority as the Internal Revenue Code itself. It can only be overturned if it is outside the power delegated to the U.S. Treasury; it conflicts with a specific statute; or it is deemed unreasonable by the courts.

10. The answer is A. The IRS has 20 business days to say whether it will comply with an FOIA request. When a request is denied, the IRS must give the reason for denial and explain the right to appeal to the head of the agency.

11. The answer is B. Treasury regulations are published in the Federal Register.

Unit 2: Practice Before the IRS

More Reading:
Circular 230, *Regulations Governing Practice Before the Internal Revenue Service*
Publication 947, *Practice Before the IRS and Power of Attorney*
Publication 470, *Limited Practice Without Enrollment*

Practice before the IRS includes all matters connected with a presentation before the IRS, or relating to a taxpayer's rights, privileges, or liabilities under laws or regulations administered by the IRS. Representation, or "practice before the IRS," is defined in Publication 947, *Practice Before the IRS and Power of Attorney.*

Practice before the IRS includes:

- Corresponding and communicating with the IRS
- Representing a taxpayer at conferences, hearings, or meetings with the IRS
- Preparing and filing documents with the IRS
- Providing written advice that has a potential for tax avoidance or evasion

U.S. citizenship is not required to practice before the IRS.

Note: The IRS Office of Professional Responsibility (OPR) has responsibility for matters related to practitioner conduct, discipline, disciplinary proceedings and sanctions. The Return Preparer Office RPO) is responsible for the issuance of PTINs, acting on applications for enrollment and administering AFSP testing and continuing education for designated groups.

Note: In a significant loss for the IRS, the U.S. Court of Appeals for the District of Columbia upheld a lower court's decision that the IRS did not possess the legal authority to regulate tax return preparers when it created the registered tax return preparer (RTRP) program.[134] The issue centered on whether the "practice of representatives" included the mere preparation of tax returns. The appeals court ruled it did not, and the IRS chose not to appeal the decision. This means that tax return preparation, in and of itself, does not constitute "practice before the IRS" under current law.[135] Circular 230 has not yet been updated to include all the information for the IRS's new AFSP program, which is designed to replace the now-defunct RTRP program.

Enrolled Practitioners

The IRS defines *enrolled practitioners* as attorneys, CPAs, enrolled agents, enrolled retirement plan agents, or enrolled actuaries authorized to practice before the IRS. Other individuals may qualify to practice temporarily or engage in limited practice before the IRS. However, they are not referred to as practitioners.

The following individuals may represent taxpayers and practice before the IRS by virtue of their licensing, unless they are currently under suspension or disbarment:

Attorneys: An attorney who is a member in good standing of the bar of any state, possession, territory, commonwealth, or of the District of Columbia.

Certified Public Accountants (CPAs): A CPA who is duly qualified to practice as a CPA in any state, possession, territory, commonwealth, or the District of Columbia.

Enrolled Agents (EAs): An enrolled agent in active status may represent clients before any office of the IRS. Like attorneys and CPAs, EAs are unrestricted as to which taxpayers they can represent and what types of tax matters they can handle.

---

[134] *Loving,* No. 13-5061, D.C. Circuit Court of Appeals.

[135] The revised version of Circular 230 issued in June 2014 has not yet been updated to reflect the changes necessitated by the Loving v. IRS decision, including removal of the RTRP education and competency requirements. However, Publication 947 was updated in 2016, and now states that only unenrolled return preparers participating in the Annual Filing Season Record of Completion program may represent a taxpayer before the IRS, and only with respect to returns prepared and signed by the preparer. This rule went into effect in 2016 for all future tax returns.

Only attorneys, CPAs, and EAs have unlimited rights to represent taxpayers before the IRS.

Enrolled Actuaries: The practice of an individual enrolled as an actuary by the Joint Board for the Enrollment of Actuaries is limited to certain Internal Revenue Code sections that relate to his area of expertise, principally those sections governing employee retirement plans.

Enrolled Retirement Plan Agents (ERPAs): The practice of an enrolled retirement plan agent is limited to certain Internal Revenue Code sections that relate to his area of expertise, principally those sections governing employee retirement plans.

Annual Filing Season Program (AFSP)

The IRS replaced its now-defunct RTRP program with the voluntary Annual Filing Season Program (AFSP) program. Non-credentialed return preparers can elect to voluntarily demonstrate completion of basic 1040 filing season tax preparation and other tax law training by participating in the program.

The AFSP program is designed to encourage competence and education among unenrolled tax preparers. To receive an annual "record of completion," a preparer must normally have:

- A minimum of 18 hours[136] of continuing education from an IRS-approved continuing education provider, including a six-hour "Annual Federal Tax Refresher" (AFTR) course.[137]
- Passed a knowledge-based comprehension test administered by the CPE provider at the end of the AFTR course.
- A current preparer tax identification number (PTIN).
- Consented to the "duties and restrictions relating to practice before the IRS" in Circular 230. This consent gives the IRS the authority to regulate those individuals who receive the record of completion.

Certain individuals may obtain the AFSP Record of Completion without taking the annual refresher tax course and exam, assuming they took fifteen hours of continuing education courses in 2016. The following unenrolled preparers are exempt from the annual refresher course:

- **State-based return preparer program participants:** Return preparers who are active registrants of the Oregon Board of Tax Practitioners, California Tax Education Council, and/or Maryland State Board of Individual Tax Preparers.
- **SEE Part I Test-Passers:** Tax practitioners who have passed the Special Enrollment Exam Part I within the past two years.
- **VITA/TCPE volunteers:** VITA volunteers who are quality reviewers, instructors, and return preparers with active PTINs.
- **Other accredited tax-focused credential-holders:** The Accreditation Council for Accountancy and Taxation's Accredited Business Accountant/Advisor (ABA) and Accredited Tax Preparer (ATP) programs.

AFSP participants are included in a public, searchable database of tax return preparers on the IRS website.[138]

The *Directory of Federal Tax Return Preparers with Credentials and Select Qualifications* includes the name, city, state, zip code, and credentials of attorneys, CPAs, EAs, ERPAs, and

[136] Individuals who passed the now-defunct Registered Tax Return Preparer exam are exempt from the six hour federal tax law refresher course. They also only need 15 hours of continuing education each year to obtain an Annual Filing Season Program – Record of Completion.

[137] Individuals will need a total of 18 hours of continuing education hours. An AFTR course does not count toward enrolled agent continuing education requirements.

[138] The Directory of Federal Tax Return Preparers with Credentials and Select Qualifications is located here: *https://irs.treasury.gov/rpo/rpo.jsf*

enrolled actuaries with a valid PTIN, as well as AFSP Record of Completion holders. An individual may choose to opt out of being listed in the directory.

Example: Trina is a CPA. Her client, Samuel, has a large tax debt. Samuel does not wish to communicate directly with the IRS, but he wants to set up an installment agreement. Trina has Samuel sign Form 2848 giving her power of attorney and calls the IRS on his behalf to set up the installment agreement for him. This action is considered *practice before the IRS*.

Note: Beginning with the 2016 tax season, only Annual Filing Season Program participants have limited practice rights before the IRS. AFSP participants may only represent clients whose returns they prepared and signed, and only before revenue agents, customer service representatives and similar IRS employees, including the Taxpayer Advocate Service. Only unenrolled preparers that participate in IRS's Annual Filing Season Program (AFSP) will have limited representation rights. Unenrolled preparers who do not participate in this annual program will no longer have authority to represent clients before the IRS (Publication 947).

Unenrolled Tax Return Preparers

Individuals who prepare tax returns for other taxpayers but who are not EAs, CPAs, attorneys, ERPAs, or enrolled actuaries are called "unenrolled preparers." In general, unenrolled preparers have only limited practice rights before the IRS.

Only unenrolled tax return preparers that have current AFSP certificates may represent taxpayers and only during an IRS examination of the taxable year or period covered by the tax return or claim of refund they prepared and signed.

This representation may occur only before revenue agents, customer service representatives, or similar officers and employees of the IRS, including the Taxpayer Advocate Service. Unenrolled tax return preparers cannot do any of the following:

- Represent taxpayers before appeals officers, revenue officers, counsel, or similar officers or employees of the IRS or Department of Treasury
- Execute closing agreements
- Extend the statutory period for tax assessments or collection of tax
- Execute waivers
- Execute claims for refund
- Sign any document on behalf of a taxpayer

Unenrolled preparers who do <u>not</u> have an AFSP certificate are allowed to prepare tax returns for compensation, but they may not represent taxpayers before any level of the IRS, regardless of whether they prepared the return or not.[139]

Example: Louie is an unenrolled tax preparer. He does not hold any formal licensing or have an AFSP certificate. The IRS is conducting an audit of a client's income tax returns for the years 2013, 2014, and 2015 returns. Louie prepared all the tax returns under examination. However, since Louie is not an enrolled practitioner, he may not represent his client before the IRS.

Example: Antonella received her AFSP certificate in 2016. She has always prepared tax returns for her client, Isaac. In 2016, Isaac receives an audit notice from the IRS for his prior year return. Antonella is able to represent Isaac before the IRS as well as respond to the notice, because she has a current AFSP certificate and she prepared the return.[140]

[139] The IRS believes in a mandatory competency standard for federal tax return preparers. To this end, legislation continues to be their priority. In the interim, however, the AFSP program recognizes the efforts of unenrolled return preparers to improve their professional competency through continuing education. Anyone with a PTIN can prepare a federal tax return, but for those preparers with a PTIN who also work to ready themselves for the filing season through educational efforts, the AFSP program affords them a level of differentiation from the rest of the marketplace.

[140] Beginning January 1, 2016, only unenrolled return preparers who hold a record of completion for BOTH the tax return year (2015 or thereafter) under examination and the year the examination is conducted may represent under

Limited Practice Due to 'Special Relationship'

Other individuals who are not practitioners may represent taxpayers before the IRS because of a special relationship with the taxpayer, without having prepared the tax return in question.

An individual (self-representation): An individual may always represent himself before the IRS, provided he has appropriate identification, such as a driver's license. He does not have to file a written declaration of qualification and authority. Even a disbarred individual may represent himself before the IRS. Disbarred practitioners are also allowed to represent family members, or act as fiduciaries for an estate or trust, if they are appointed by the court.

Example: Gary was a tax attorney who was disbarred because of a felony embezzlement conviction. An individual who is disbarred is not eligible to represent other taxpayers before the IRS. Gary was audited by the IRS in 2016. Despite being disbarred, Gary may still represent himself before the IRS during the examination of his own return. Gary may also represent a close family member, like his son or his spouse.

A family member: An individual may represent members of his immediate family. Family members include a spouse, child, parent, brother, or sister of the individual.

Example: Jett's mother is being audited by the IRS. Jett is an accountant who works as a controller for a manufacturing firm. He does not normally prepare tax returns for the public or hold any type of state or federal licensing. Even though Jett is not enrolled to practice before the IRS, he is allowed to represent his mother because of the family relationship.

An officer: A bona fide officer of a corporation (including a parent, subsidiary, or affiliated corporation), association, organized group, or governmental agency may represent its corporation, association, organized group, or governmental agency before the IRS.

A partner: A general partner may represent the partnership before the IRS, but a limited partner may not.

An employee: A regular full-time employee can represent his employer. An employer can be an individual, partnership, corporation, association, trust, receivership, guardianship, estate, or organized group; or a governmental unit, agency, or authority.

Example: Angelique is a full-time bookkeeper for her employer, Valley Crest Landscaping. The IRS sent her employer a notice regarding some delinquent payroll tax returns. Angelique may file Form 2848, *Power of Attorney and Declaration of Representative*, and speak with the IRS on her employer's behalf. Even though Angelique is not an enrolled preparer, she may represent Valley Crest Landscaping before the IRS because of the employee-employer relationship.

A fiduciary: A fiduciary (trustee, executor, personal representative, administrator, receiver, or guardian) is considered to be the taxpayer and not a representative of the taxpayer.

Example: Tony was named the executor of his mother's estate after she passed away. He is allowed to represent his mother's estate before the IRS because he is the fiduciary for the estate.

Authorization for Special Appearances: In rare circumstances, the Commissioner of the IRS or a delegate will authorize a person who is not otherwise eligible to practice before the IRS to represent another person for a particular matter. The request is made to the Office of Professional Responsibility (OPR). If granted, the written consent will detail the specific circumstances related to the appearance.

---

the following conditions: Unenrolled return preparers may represent taxpayers only before revenue agents, customer service representatives, or similar officers and employees of the Internal Revenue Service (including the Taxpayer Advocate Service) and only during an examination of the taxable year or period covered by the tax returns they prepared and signed. (Pub 947)

Persons Ineligible to Practice Before the IRS

Individuals not previously described are generally not eligible to practice before the IRS. Corporations, associations, partnerships, and others that are not individuals also are not eligible to practice before the IRS. Even if named in a power of attorney as a representative, an individual will not be recognized if he has lost his eligibility to practice before the IRS.

Reasons for losing eligibility include suspension or disbarment by the OPR, being placed in inactive retirement status, and not meeting the requirements for renewal of enrollment, such as continuing professional education.

Actions That Are Not Practice Before the IRS

"Practice before the IRS" does not include:

- Representation of taxpayers before the U.S. Tax Court: The Tax Court has its own rules of practice and its own rules regarding admission to practice.
- Merely appearing as a witness for the taxpayer: In general, individuals who are not practitioners may appear before the IRS as witnesses—but they may not advocate for the taxpayer.

Tax Return Preparers

The IRS defines tax return preparers as individuals who participate in the preparation of tax returns for taxpayers for compensation. This includes preparers who are in business, casual or part-time preparers who receive fees for preparing tax returns, and certain e-file providers. Under Circular 230, the IRS requires the following:

- All paid tax return preparers must register with the IRS and obtain a preparer tax identification number (PTIN). Specifically, Circular 230 states that "any individual who for compensation prepares or assists with the preparation of all or substantially all of a tax return or claim for refund" must have a PTIN.
- Tax preparers who register for a PTIN must undergo a limited tax compliance check to ensure they have filed their own personal and business tax returns.

PTIN Requirements

The PTIN is a nine-digit number that preparers must use when they prepare and sign a tax return or claim for refund. The use of a PTIN is mandatory on all federal tax returns and claims for refund prepared by paid tax preparers.

The PTIN requirement applies to all enrolled agents and many attorneys and CPAs. Attorneys and CPAs do not need to obtain PTINs if they do not prepare federal tax returns.

Multiple individuals cannot share one PTIN. A PTIN is assigned to a single preparer to identify that he is the preparer of a particular return. A PTIN cannot be transferred to another preparer, even if the practice is later sold. As of the start of the filing season, more than 715,000 tax return preparers had active PTINs for 2016.

An applicant must be at least 18 years old to obtain a PTIN. Felony convictions and failure to meet federal tax obligations may affect an individual's ability to obtain a PTIN.

All paid preparers are required to pay a fee and renew their PTINs online each year between October 16 and December 31. Preparers who fail to list a valid PTIN on tax returns they sign are subject to penalties. Preparers may also be subject to disciplinary action by the Office of Professional Responsibility.[141]

---

[141] The IRS's loss in *Loving v. IRS* does not apply to the requirement that all paid tax preparers obtain PTINs. The judge ruled the PTIN program was valid and could be enforced by the IRS.

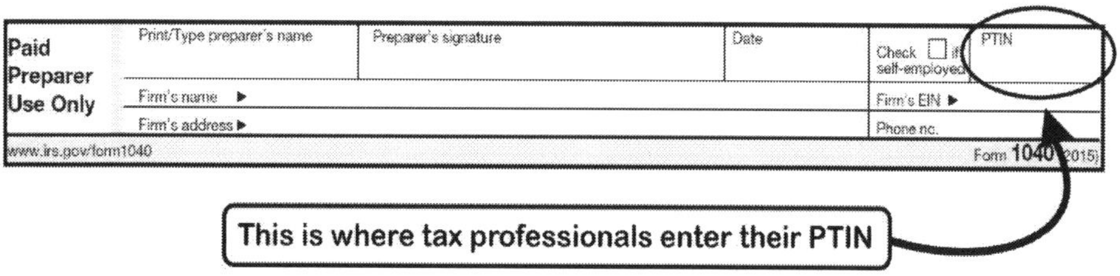

Supervised Preparers

Supervised preparers are also required to have PTINs. These are individuals who do not sign tax returns as paid return preparers but are:

- Employed by a law firm, EA office, or CPA practice; and
- Are directly supervised by an attorney, CPA, EA, ERPA, or enrolled actuary who signs the returns prepared by the supervised preparer as the paid tax return preparer.

Supervised preparers may not:

- Sign any tax return they prepare or assist in preparing.
- Represent taxpayers before the IRS in any capacity.
- Identify themselves as Circular 230 practitioners.

When applying for or renewing a PTIN, supervised preparers must provide the PTIN of their supervisor.

Exceptions to PTIN Requirements

An individual who prepares a tax return with no agreement for compensation is not considered a tax return preparer for IRS purposes. This is true even if the individual receives a gift or a favor in return. The agreement for compensation is the deciding factor as to whether the IRS considers an individual a tax return preparer.

Example: Terri is a retired CPA who only prepares tax returns for her close family members. She does not charge her family to prepare their tax returns. Sometimes, a family member will give Terri a gift in return. This year, her sister gave her home-baked cookies and her niece gave her a sweater. However, Terri did not ask for any presents or expect them. She is not a tax return preparer for IRS purposes, and she is not required to obtain a PTIN.

Example: Helen is a CPA who does audit and attest work. She works for a CPA firm with a tax division, but she does not prepare tax returns herself. Helen is not required to obtain a PTIN as long as she does not prepare tax returns. Lizeth is an enrolled agent who works for the same firm. She also does not prepare tax returns. Lizeth only does bookkeeping, and some occasional tax planning. Lizeth is required to have a PTIN, even though she does not prepare tax returns, because she is an enrolled agent.

An individual is not considered an income tax return preparer and would not be required to obtain a PTIN in the following instances:

- A person who gives an opinion about events that have not happened (such as tax advice for a business that has not been created).
- A person who furnishes typing, copying, or mechanical assistance.
- A person who prepares the return of his employer (or of an officer or employee of the employer) by whom the person is regularly and continuously employed.
- A fiduciary who prepares a tax return for a trust or estate.
- An unpaid volunteer who provides tax assistance under *Volunteer Income Tax Assistance* (VITA) or *Tax Counseling for the Elderly* (TCPE) programs.

- An employee of the IRS who performs official duties by preparing a tax return for a taxpayer who requests it.

Example: Thomas is a CPA. His neighbor, Ross, consults with Thomas about a business he is thinking about starting. Thomas gives Ross an opinion regarding the potential business and taxes. In this case, the IRS does not consider Thomas a tax return preparer. This is because Thomas is merely giving an opinion about events that have not yet happened.

Example: Ginny is a bookkeeper for Creative Candies Corporation. She is a full-time employee, and she prepares the payroll checks and payroll tax returns for all of the employees of Creative Candies. As a full-time employee, Ginny is not considered a tax return preparer since her employer is ultimately responsible for the accuracy of the payroll tax returns.

Example: Francisco is an EA who has a PTIN. He employs an administrative assistant, Claudia, who performs data entry during tax filing season. At times, clients call and provide Claudia with information, which she records in the system. Using the data Claudia has entered, Francisco meets with his clients and provides tax advice as needed. He then prepares and signs their returns. Claudia is not a tax return preparer and is not required to have a PTIN.

Example: Bob is a retired tax professional. He does not have a PTIN. Bob volunteers during the tax filing season at a VITA site, where he prepares individual tax returns for lower-income individuals for free. Bob is not a tax return preparer and is not required to have a PTIN.

Note: Do not confuse a PTIN with an EFIN, electronic filing identification number. An EFIN is a number issued by the IRS to individuals who have been approved as authorized IRS e-file providers. Although most tax preparers must use IRS e-file, some preparers are ineligible for the e-file program. Currently, the IRS e-file program does not accept foreign preparers without Social Security numbers who live and work abroad. These preparers must still obtain a PTIN, but they are not required to e-file their clients' returns since they are not eligible for an EFIN.

The "Substantial Portion" Rule

Only the person who prepares all or a "substantial portion" of a tax return is considered the preparer of the return. A person who merely gives advice on a portion or a single entry on a tax return is considered to have prepared only that portion. If more than one individual is involved in the preparation of a tax return, the person with the primary responsibility for the overall accuracy of the return is considered the preparer and must sign the return. In order to identify who is responsible for a substantial portion of the return, the following guidelines may be used.

A portion of a tax return is not typically considered to be substantial if it involves only amounts of gross income, amounts of deductions, or amounts on the basis of which credits are determined that are:

- Less than $10,000, or
- Less than $400,000 and less than 20% of the adjusted gross income on the return.

Usually, a single IRS schedule would not be considered a substantial portion of a tax return unless it represents a major portion of the income. One example of this may be a business taxpayer with a Schedule C that represents a majority of the income on the return.

Example: Greg and Eli are equal partners in a tax practice, where they both work as enrolled agents. In March, Eli finishes a few tax returns that Greg had started before he left on vacation. Later, one tax return comes up for audit, and it is determined that the return has a gross valuation misstatement for a large deduction. Greg prepared Schedule C on the return, and Eli prepared the rest of the return. Schedule C represents 95% of the income and expenses shown on the return. Therefore, for purposes of any potential preparer penalty, Greg is considered the preparer of this return, since he completed the schedule that represents the majority of the income and expenses on the return.

Enrolled Agent Licensing

As outlined in Circular 230, there are two tracks to becoming an enrolled agent. An individual may receive the designation by passing a three-part exam, or by virtue of past employment with the IRS.

1. Exam Track

For the first track, an EA candidate must apply for a PTIN and register to take the Special Enrollment Examination (SEE), also known as the EA exam, by filling out Form 2587, *Application for Special Enrollment Examination*. An applicant must be at least 18 years old. A candidate then must:

- Achieve passing scores on all three parts of the SEE.
- File Form 23, *Application for Enrollment to Practice before the Internal Revenue Service*, to apply for enrollment within one year from the date of passing the exam.[142] Form 23 can now be submitted online and the fee can be paid at *www.pay.gov.*
- Pass a background check conducted by the IRS. The tax compliance check makes sure the applicant has filed all necessary tax returns and has no outstanding tax liabilities. The suitability check determines whether an applicant has engaged in any conduct that would justify suspension or disbarment.

2. Previous Experience Track

For the second track, an EA candidate must possess a minimum of five years of past service with the IRS and technical experience as outlined in Circular 230. The application must be made within three years from the date the employee left the IRS. Factors considered with this second track are the length and scope of employment and the recommendation of the superior officer.

The applicant then must:

- Apply for enrollment on Form 23.
- Pass a background check, which includes a tax compliance and suitability check.

Former IRS employees who become enrolled agents without taking the EA exam may be granted limited or unlimited representation rights.

The IRS's Return Preparer Office (RPO) makes the determination on applications for enrollment to practice. The RPO provides oversight of competency testing, enrollment, renewal, and continuing education of enrolled agents.

> **Note:** Once an individual's application is approved, the RPO will issue an enrollment card, and enrollment becomes effective on that date.

Denial of Enrollment

Any individual who is involved in disreputable or criminal conduct is subject to disciplinary action or denial of enrollment. Disreputable acts alone may be grounds for denial of enrollment, even after the candidate has passed the EA exam. Failure to timely file tax returns or to pay one's taxes may also be grounds for the Return Preparer Office to deny any application for enrollment.

RPO must inform the applicant of the reason he or she is denied enrollment. The applicant may then file a written appeal to the Office of Professional Responsibility (OPR) within 30 days from the date of the notice. The appeal must be filed along with the candidate's reasoning why the enrollment application should be accepted.

[142] For successful examination candidates, the IRS goal is to have the application process completed within 90 days of receipt of Form 23. However, the applicant must pass a tax compliance check as well as a background check. The application for enrollment may be delayed if the Office of Professional responsibility finds any problems with either.

Example: Todd passed all three parts of the EA exam and filed Form 23, requesting enrollment. Because he had failed to file numerous tax returns in the past, his application was denied. Todd filed an appeal with the OPR, explaining he had failed to file on time because he had been seriously injured years ago. He attached supporting evidence, including copies of medical bills and a letter from his doctor. Todd also provided evidence that all his tax returns had been properly filed after his recovery. The OPR accepted Todd's appeal and granted him enrollment.

Renewal of Enrollment

Enrolled agents must renew their enrollment status every three years. To renew, an EA must file Form 8554, *Application for Renewal of Enrollment to Practice before the Internal Revenue Service*, and submit the required nonrefundable fee. If an EA does not renew his enrollment, he may not continue to practice before the IRS.

The three successive enrollment years preceding the effective date of renewal is referred to as the IRS enrollment cycle. Applications for renewal of enrollment must be submitted between November 1 and January 31 prior to April 1 of the year that the next enrollment cycle begins. The last digit of a practitioner's Social Security number determines when he must renew enrollment. If the candidate's SSN ends in:

- 7, 8, or 9 – This enrollment cycle began April 1, 2015.
- 0, 1, 2, or 3 –This enrollment cycle began April 1, 2016.
- 4, 5, or 6 – The next enrollment cycle begins April 1, 2017.

EAs who do not have an SSN must use the "7, 8, or 9" renewal schedule.

As part of the renewal process, the IRS will check the practitioner's filing history to verify that he has filed and paid all federal taxes on time. If the enrolled agent owns or has an interest in a business, the IRS will also check the tax compliance history of the business. In addition, the IRS will check that the EA has completed all necessary professional continuing education requirements.

The IRS sends a reminder notice when an EA is due for renewal. However, an enrolled agent is not excused from the obligation to renew if he does not receive the notice.

An EA must inform the Return Preparer Office of an address change within 60 days of a move.

Continuing Education for Enrolled Agents

During each three-year enrollment cycle, an EA must complete 72 hours of continuing education credit. A minimum of 16 hours, including two hours of ethics or professional conduct, must be completed during each enrollment year.

Note: Beginning in May 2016, the IRS will conduct random CPE audits of EAs with SSNs ending in 0, 1, 2, or 3 requesting copies of their continuing education certificates of completion for the past three years. Recipients of these letters will be asked to mail or fax the documents within 30 days.

For a new EA, the month of initial enrollment begins the CPE requirement. He must complete two hours of CPE for each month enrolled, and two hours of ethics for the enrollment year. Enrollment for any part of a month is considered enrollment for the entire month.

Note: The initial CPE Requirements for EAs in their *first* enrollment cycle are:

- 2 hours of CPE for every single month
- 2 hours of ethics annually (no exceptions)

When an EA's new three-year enrollment cycle begins, he will be required to satisfy the full 72-hour continuing education credit requirement.

Ethics courses must be taken every year. If a candidate takes more than two hours of ethics courses during a single year, the additional hours may count toward the overall requirements of 16 hours per year and 72 hours per cycle. However, an enrolled agent may not take additional ethics courses in the current year and neglect to take them in future years.

Example: Cammie became a new EA on September 30, 2016, which was the third year of the enrollment cycle based on her SSN. She is required to take two hours of CPE for each month before January 1, 2017, which equals eight hours for the period of September through December. Two of those hours must be on the topic of ethics. Since her initial enrollment came during the final year of the enrollment cycle, Cammie must renew her enrollment status in 2017 and will be subject to the full 72-hour CPE requirement during her subsequent renewal periods.

Exception: If an enrolled agent retakes and passes the SEE again since his last renewal, he is only required to take 16 hours of CPE, including two hours of ethics, during the last year of his current enrollment cycle.

CPE Providers: Individuals and companies who wish to offer continuing education to EAs must pay a registration fee and apply as providers. Providers are issued a provider number and may display a logo that says "IRS Approved Continuing Education Provider." Course providers must renew their status every year.

Approved Programs: Qualifying programs include traditional seminars and conferences, as well as correspondence or individual self-study programs on the Internet, so long as they are approved courses of study by approved providers. In order to qualify as CPE, a course must be designed to enhance professional knowledge in federal taxation or federal tax-related matters. Courses related to state taxation do not meet the IRS requirement unless at least 80% of the program material consists of a comparison of federal and state tax laws.

Contact Hours: Continuing education programs are measured in terms of contact hours. The shortest recognized program is one hour. In order for a course to qualify for CPE credit, it must feature at least 50 minutes of continuous participation. Individual segments at conferences and conventions are considered one total program. For example, two 90-minute segments (180 minutes) at a continuous conference count as three contact hours.

Example: Loretta is an enrolled agent who signs up for a half-day federal tax update class. The instructor starts the class promptly at 8 a.m. and lectures until 9:40 a.m., when the class takes a 20 minute break. The instructor resumes the class at 10 a.m. and it runs until 11:40 a.m., when the class is recessed. Loretta will receive four CPE credits because she completed four 50-minute segments of instruction, worth one contact hour each.

Instructor Credit: An enrolled agent may receive continuing education credit for serving as an instructor, discussion leader, or speaker on federal tax matters for approved educational programs. One hour of CPE credit is awarded for each contact hour completed. Two hours of CPE credit is awarded for actual subject preparation time for each contact hour completed as an instructor, discussion leader, or speaker at such programs. The maximum credit for instruction and preparation may not exceed six hours annually.

Verifying CPE Hours: After completing CPE coursework, an EA will receive a certificate from the course provider. The course provider will also report completed continuing education to the IRS, using the PTINs of the individual participants.

Tax preparers may check their online PTIN accounts to see a display of the CPE programs they have completed, as reported by providers. CPE hours completed prior to 2013 are not included. EAs are required to keep their own records related to continuing education hours for four years following the date of renewal.

CPE Waiver

An EA may request a full or partial waiver of CPE requirements from the RPO. Qualifying circumstances may include:

- Health issues
- Extended active military duty
- Absence from the United States for employment or other reasons
- Other reasons on a case-by-case basis

The request for a waiver must be accompanied by appropriate documentation, such as medical records or military paperwork. If the request is denied, the enrolled agent will be placed on the inactive roster. If the request is accepted, the EA will receive an updated enrollment card reflecting his renewal.

Example: Mario is an EA who is also an Army reservist. He was called to active duty in a combat zone for two years. During his deployment, Mario was unable to complete his CPE requirements for his enrolled agent license. Mario contacted RPO and requested a waiver based on his current active-duty military service. RPO grants the waiver. Mario later returns to the United States after an honorable discharge. Mario is free to begin preparing tax returns as an enrolled agent again.

Inactive and Terminated EAs

RPO notifies any EA who fails to comply with the requirements for eligibility for renewal of enrollment. A notice will be sent via first-class mail explaining the reason for noncompliance.

The notice further provides the preparer an opportunity to furnish the requested information, such as missing CPE credits, in writing. An EA has 60 days from the date of the notice to respond to this initial notice. If no response is received, the EA will move to inactive status as of April 1.

To be eligible for renewal after missing one full enrollment cycle, an EA must pay fees for both the prior and current renewal cycles and verify that the required CPE hours have been taken.

To have his termination status reconsidered, an EA must file a written protest within 30 days and provide a valid reason for not renewing on time. Reasons may include serious illness or extended travel out of the country.

Losing the Eligibility to Practice

Practitioners may lose their eligibility to practice before the IRS for the following reasons, among others:

- Failure to meet the yearly continuing education requirements for enrollment.
- Failure to renew a PTIN or pay required fees.
- Requesting to be placed on inactive/retirement status.
- Being disciplined by state regulatory agents. An attorney who has been disbarred from practice at the state level or a CPA whose license has been revoked or suspended at the state level is disbarred from practice at the federal level, and cannot practice before the IRS as long as his disbarment, revocation, or suspension is active.

Example: Wanda is an enrolled agent. In 2016, the Internal Revenue Service's Office of Professional Responsibility disbarred Wanda for stealing a client's tax payments and preparing tax returns with false deductions for multiple clients. Wanda's enrolled agent status is revoked for at least five years.

Unit 2: Study Questions

(Test yourself and then check the correct answers at the end of this chapter.)

1. "Practice before the IRS" does not include:

A. Communicating directly with the IRS on behalf of a taxpayer regarding his rights or liabilities.
B. Representing a taxpayer at an IRS examination.
C. Representing taxpayers before the IRS appeals division.
D. Representation of a taxpayer in the U.S. Tax Court.

2. Cameron is an enrolled agent who takes a continuing education class from an approved IRS provider. The class runs continuously from 9 a.m. until 11:45 a.m., when there is a break for lunch. How many CPE credits will Cameron receive for the morning session of the class?

A. One.
B. Two.
C. Three.
D. Four.

3. When does a new EA's enrollment take effect?

A. On the date he applies for enrollment with the IRS.
B. On the date listed on his enrollment card.
C. On the date he receives his enrollment card.
D. On the first day of January after he receives his enrollment card.

4. Denise and Gabriela are best friends. They are not family members. Gabriela must appear before the IRS for an examination. Denise wants to appear before the IRS on her friend's behalf, though she is not a practitioner. Which of the following statements is correct?

A. Denise may represent Gabriela before the IRS without Gabriela being present.
B. Denise may advocate for Gabriela to the best of her ability.
C. Denise may appear before the IRS as a witness and communicate information.
D. Denise may not appear before the IRS in any capacity.

5. Which of the following individuals is required to obtain a PTIN?

A. A CPA who does not prepare any tax returns.
B. An EA who works for a CPA firm, but does not sign any tax returns.
C. A tax attorney who only does representation of clients in the U.S. court system.
D. A retired accountant who prepares tax returns for free for his family.

6. Matthew is a full-time employee for Parkway Partnership. He is not an EA, attorney, or CPA. Parkway requests that Matthew represent the partnership in connection with an IRS audit. Which of the following statements is correct?

A. Matthew is allowed to represent the partnership before the IRS.
B. Matthew is not allowed to represent the partnership before the IRS.
C. Matthew is only allowed to represent individual partners before the IRS.
D. None of the above.

7. What is the enrollment cycle for enrolled agents?

A. The enrollment cycle is the year after the effective date of renewal.
B. The enrollment cycle means the three successive enrollment years preceding the effective date of renewal.
C. The enrollment cycle is the method by which the RPO approves EA exam candidates.
D. The enrollment cycle is the method Prometric uses to choose EA exam questions.

8. Which of the following individuals does not qualify as an enrolled practitioner?

A. Certified public accountant.
B. Enrolled actuary.
C. Registered tax return preparer.
D. All of the above are considered practitioners.

9. All of the following are potential grounds for denial of enrollment except:

A. Failure to timely file tax returns.
B. Failure to pay taxes.
C. Felony convictions.
D. A candidate who is only 18 years old.

10. Everett is an EA with a PTIN. His firm employs a bookkeeper named Fernanda. Fernanda gathers client receipts and invoices and organizes and records all information for Everett. She does not use Everett's professional tax return software, but she does use the firm's bookkeeping software. Everett then uses the information that his bookkeeper has compiled and prepares all the client tax returns. Which of the following statements is correct?

A. Fernanda needs to have a PTIN, and she is required to become an EA because she assists in the preparation of returns.
B. Fernanda needs to have a PTIN, but she is not required to become an EA.
C. Fernanda is not a tax return preparer and is not required to have a PTIN.
D. Fernanda is a supervised preparer and needs to have a PTIN.

11. The IRS's new public directory of tax return preparers includes listings for:

A. Practitioners with a current PTIN.
B. All current PTIN holders.
C. Enrolled agents and CPAs with a current PTIN.
D. All enrolled practitioners with a current PTIN as well as AFSP Record of Completion holders.

12. Which of the following is considered a tax return preparer under Circular 230 regulations?

A. A full-time bookkeeper working for an employer who prepares payroll tax returns.
B. A retired attorney who prepares tax returns under the VITA program.
C. A person who furnishes typing, reproducing, or mechanical assistance.
D. A full-time secretary who also prepares tax returns for pay part-time from home during tax season.

13. Enrolled agents must complete continuing education credits for renewed enrollment. Which of the following describes the credit requirements?

A. A minimum of 72 hours must be completed in each year of an enrollment cycle.
B. A minimum of 24 hours must be completed in each year of an enrollment cycle.
C. A minimum of 80 hours must be completed for the entire enrollment cycle.
D. A minimum of 16 hours must be completed in each year of the enrollment cycle, including two hours of ethics credits.

14. To determine which preparer is responsible for a "substantial portion" of a tax return, each of the following guidelines is used except:

A. Whoever has the primary responsibility for the accuracy of the return.
B. Whoever actually owns or manages the tax practice.
C. Whoever prepares the portion of the return that declares the greatest amount of adjusted gross income.
D. Amounts of gross income, amounts of deductions, or amounts on the basis of which credits are determined that are (1) under $10,000 or less or (2) less than $400,000 and less than 20% of the adjusted gross income on the return will not be considered a substantial portion.

15. Khan is a CPA who employs Amy, an accounting student, to assist in the preparation of tax returns. Khan signs all of the tax returns. Which of the following statements is correct?

A. Amy and Khan can share one PTIN.
B. Amy is required by law to sign the returns that she has prepared.
C. Amy is required to obtain a PTIN.
D. Amy cannot assist with the preparation of tax returns until she becomes a CPA.

16. Barry helps his friend, Jose, who does not speak English fluently. Barry appears before the IRS and translates for Jose at an IRS examination. Which of the following statements is correct?

A. Barry is practicing before the IRS.
B. Jose must sign a power of attorney form authorizing Barry to represent him.
C. Barry is not considered to be practicing before the IRS.
D. The IRS prohibits unrelated persons from being present at an IRS examination.

17. Andrea is an EA. Her records show that she had the following hours of qualified CPE in 2016:

- January 2016, seven hours: Federal tax CPE
- May 2016, one hour: Ethics
- December 2016, nine hours: Federal tax CPE

Has Andrea met her minimum yearly CPE requirements?

A. Yes, Andrea has met her minimum yearly CPE requirements.
B. No, Andrea has met her ethics requirement, but not the overall minimum requirement for the year.
C. No, Andrea has not met her ethics requirement.
D. None of the above.

18. All of the following are permitted to represent the taxpayer before the examination division of the IRS except:

A. The taxpayer's best friend who is an attorney licensed to practice law in the state where the taxpayer lives.
B. The taxpayer's brother who is not an attorney, CPA, or enrolled agent.
C. An unenrolled tax return preparer who did not prepare the taxpayer's return.
D. All of the above are permitted to represent the taxpayer before the IRS.

19. What action should an EA take if he chooses to appeal termination from enrollment?

A. Call the Office of Professional Responsibility to complain.
B. File a written protest within 30 days of the date of the notice of termination.
C. File a written protest within 60 days of the date of the notice of termination.
D. File a written protest within 90 days of the date of the notice of termination.

20. Stan is an EA with a PTIN. What must he do to retain his existing PTIN?

A. Nothing. Stan is allowed to retain his PTIN so long as he is current in his enrollment status.
B. Stan must renew his PTIN every three years when he renews his enrollment status.
C. Stan cannot retain his existing PTIN. He must apply for a new PTIN every year.
D. Stan must renew his existing PTIN each year and pay a required fee.

21. Enrolled agents who apply for renewal to practice before the IRS must retain information about continuing education hours completed. How long must this documentation be retained?

A. For one year following the enrollment renewal date.
B. For four years following the enrollment renewal date.
C. For five years if it is an initial enrollment.
D. The individual is not required to retain the education information if the CPE provider has agreed to retain it.

Unit 2: Answers

1. The answer is D. "Practice before the IRS" does not include the representation of clients in the U.S. Tax Court. The Tax Court is independent of the IRS and has its own rules of practice and its own regulations regarding admission to practice.

2. The answer is C. Continuing education program credits are measured in terms of contact hours, which must be at least 50 minutes long. The class ran for 165 minutes, which counts as three contact hours. If the class had run *continuously* until 12:20 p.m., it would have lasted 200 minutes, so it would have been worth four CPE hours.

3. The answer is B. An EA's enrollment becomes official on the date listed on his enrollment card, whether he has actually received the card or not.

4. The answer is C. Simply appearing as a witness before the IRS is allowed and not considered practice before the IRS. Individuals who are not practitioners may appear before the IRS as witnesses or communicate to the IRS on a taxpayer's behalf—but they may not advocate for the taxpayer.

5. The answer is B. All EAs are required to obtain PTINs as a condition of their licensing (the PTIN must be included on Form 23, which is the application form to become an enrolled agent). Attorneys and CPAs do not need to obtain a PTIN unless they prepare tax returns for compensation. Someone who prepares returns for free is not considered a tax return preparer by the IRS and does not need a PTIN.

6. The answer is A. Matthew is a full-time employee for Parkway Partnership, so in that capacity he may represent his employer before the IRS. A regular full-time employee of an individual employer may represent the employer.

7. The answer is B. The enrollment cycle means the three successive enrollment years preceding the effective date of renewal. After the initial enrollment period, regular renewal enrollments are required every three years. This is known as an enrollment cycle.

8. The answer is C. The registered tax return preparer designation is now defunct due to the IRS's loss in the *Loving v. Commissioner* case. An individual who passed the RTRP exam is considered an unenrolled preparer and not a practitioner; unenrolled preparers have limited rights of practice before the IRS. An unenrolled preparer may only represent a taxpayer for the tax return or claim of refund he personally prepared and signed. This representation may occur only before revenue agents and similar employees of the IRS, and not before appeals or revenue officers. An unenrolled preparer also may not sign any document on behalf of a taxpayer.

9. The answer is D. The minimum age for enrollment is 18, so anyone over 17 would not be denied enrollment based on his age. Failure to timely file tax returns or pay taxes, and felony convictions are all potential grounds for denying an application for enrollment. The Return Preparer Office will review all of the facts and circumstances to determine whether a denial of enrollment is warranted.

10. The answer is C. Fernanda is not a tax return preparer and is not required to have a PTIN. An individual who provides only typing, reproduction, or other mechanical assistance but does not actually prepare returns is not considered a tax return preparer by the IRS.

11. The answer is D. The Annual Filing Season Program is the IRS's new voluntary program to replace the registered tax return preparer program. Those who pass the program's education and testing requirements receive an AFSP Record of Completion for the year. Participants will be included in a public, searchable database of tax return preparers on the IRS website. The *Directory of Federal Tax Return Preparers with Credentials and Select Qualifications* includes the name, city, state, zip code, and credentials of all attorneys, CPAs, EAs, ERPAs, and enrolled actuaries with a valid PTIN, as well as all AFSP

Record of Completion holders. An individual may opt out of being listed in the directory. Unenrolled preparers with PTINs who are not Record of Completion holders are not listed in the directory.

12. The answer is D. A person who prepares tax returns for compensation is a tax return preparer, even if the activity is only part-time. A person who prepares and signs a tax return without compensation (such as for a family member or as a volunteer) is not considered a tax return preparer for purposes of preparer penalties. An employee who prepares a tax return for his employer or for another employee is not a preparer under Circular 230. The employer (or the individual with supervisory responsibility) has the responsibility for accuracy of the return.

13. The answer is D. A minimum of 16 hours of continuing education credit, including two hours of ethics credits, must be completed in each year of the enrollment cycle. An EA must complete a minimum of 72 hours of continuing education during each three-year period.

14. The answer is B. Ownership or management of a tax practice is immaterial in determining the substantial portion rule. The most important determination is whoever has the primary responsibility for the accuracy of the return. If several people are involved in preparing a return, the person who prepares the part of the return that declares the greatest amount of income would be considered the preparer who must sign the return.

15. The answer is C. Amy must obtain a PTIN. Every individual who prepares or assists in the preparation of a tax return or claim for refund for compensation must have her own PTIN.

16. The answer is C. Simply appearing as a witness or communicating information to the IRS does not constitute practice before the IRS. Barry is merely assisting with the exchange of information and is not advocating on Jose's behalf. An example of an individual assisting with information exchange but not practicing would be a taxpayer's friend serving as a translator when the taxpayer does not speak English.

17. The answer is C. The IRS requires a 16-hour minimum of CE per year, and requires two hours of ethics or professional conduct per year. Andrea has only completed one hour of ethics CE. She has met her annual general CE requirement, but she has not met the ethics requirement for the year, so her minimum requirements have not been met.

18. The answer is C. Unenrolled tax preparers are not permitted to represent a taxpayer except in the examination of a tax return they prepared. Even in that case, the taxpayer must be present during the examination. For returns prepared after January 1, 2016, only unenrolled return preparers participating in the Annual Filing Season Record of Completion (AFSP) program may represent a taxpayer, and only with respect to returns prepared and signed by the preparer.

19. The answer is B. An EA who has been terminated from enrollment should file a written protest within 30 days of the date of the notice. The protest must be filed with the Office of Professional Responsibility.

20. The answer is D. The IRS requires all paid preparers to have a preparer tax identification number (PTIN). Stan must pay a fee and renew his existing PTIN each year by the December 31 deadline. He may renew online at the IRS website or by mailing Form W-12 along with his payment.

21. The answer is B. Each individual applying for renewal must retain information about CE hours completed for four years following the enrollment renewal date.

Unit 3: Authorizations and Disclosures

More Reading:
Publication 947, *Practice Before the IRS and Power of Attorney*
Instructions for Form 2848
Publication 4019, *Third Party Authorization, Levels of Authority*
Publication 4557, *Safeguarding Taxpayer Data*
Publication 5199, *Tax Preparer Guide to Identity Theft*

Power of Attorney

A power of attorney (POA) is a taxpayer's written authorization for an individual to act on the taxpayer's behalf in tax matters. The power of attorney gives an eligible individual, which includes all practitioners, the ability to represent a taxpayer before the IRS. Often, this occurs when a taxpayer wants to be represented at a conference with the IRS or to have a written response prepared and filed with the IRS.

When a taxpayer wishes to use a representative, he should fill out and sign Form 2848, *Power of Attorney and Declaration of Representative*. In doing so, the taxpayer authorizes a specific individual or individuals to receive confidential tax information and to perform the actions detailed on the form. Up to four representatives can be authorized per form.

Note: In a recent revision to Form 2848, a representative must attest that he is subject to the regulations of Circular 230, as amended, governing practice before the IRS. This attestation gives the Office of Professional Responsibility authority to regulate unenrolled tax preparers.

On Form 2848, the taxpayer describes the tax matters the representative is authorized to handle, the time periods allowed, and the specific acts that are authorized or not authorized. A separate Form 2848 must be completed for each taxpayer who wishes representation; even joint filers must submit separate Forms 2848.

The types of tax and dates of a Form 2848 must be specific. The IRS will reject Forms 2848 with general references such as "all years" or "all taxes." In preparing the form, any tax years or periods that have already ended may be listed under "tax matters." For future tax periods, the period specified is limited to no later than three years after the date the POA is received by the IRS.

A representative must be eligible to practice before the IRS in order to sign Form 2848, and the duty may not be delegated to an employee. A practitioner must provide his PTIN and use his own name as the representative, rather than the name of his business.

Example: Rebecca operates Compass Tax Service Corporation. When she prepares Form 2848, she must represent her client as an individual. Rebecca is granted permission to represent her client, but her corporation and other members of her firm are not.

In filling out Form 2848, a representative must enter the designation under which he is authorized to practice before the IRS, and list the applicable jurisdiction. For example, an enrolled agent must list the IRS as the licensing jurisdiction. If a tax practitioner is disbarred or suspended, his power of attorney will not be recognized by the IRS.

Unenrolled individuals may also be authorized to represent a taxpayer under Form 2848, if specifically permitted in very limited circumstances (such as a family member representing a taxpayer, an executor representing an estate, or an unenrolled tax return preparer who prepared the specific tax return at issue).

Example: Danny Johnson is an unenrolled tax preparer. He does not participate in the IRS's Annual Season Filing Program. In most circumstances, Danny would not be able to represent a taxpayer before the IRS. However, his sister Bethany received an audit notice in 2016. Danny may file a Form 2848 and represent Bethany before all levels of the IRS. This is because of the exception for close family members.

Durable Power of Attorney

The IRS will accept a non-IRS power of attorney, such as a durable power of attorney, but it must contain all of the information included on a standard Form 2848.

A non-IRS power of attorney must contain the following information:

- The taxpayer's name, mailing address, and taxpayer identification number
- The name and mailing address of the representative
- The types of tax involved and the federal tax form number in question
- The specific periods or tax years involved
- For estate tax matters, the decedent's date of death
- A clear expression of the taxpayer's intention concerning the scope of authority granted to the representative
- The taxpayer's signature and date

A signed and dated statement made by the representative should also be attached to the non-IRS power of attorney. The statement is signed under penalties of perjury.

Example: Adara signs a durable power of attorney that names her best friend, Erik, as her representative. The durable power of attorney grants Erik the authority to perform all acts on Adara's behalf. However, it does not list specific information such as the types of tax covered. A year after Adara signs the power of attorney, she is declared incompetent due to Alzheimer's disease. Later, a tax matter arises concerning a prior year return filed by Adara. Erik attempts to represent Adara before the IRS, but he is rejected because the durable power of attorney does not contain required information. If Erik attaches a statement that the durable power of attorney is valid under the laws of the governing jurisdiction, he can sign a completed Form 2848 and submit it on Adara's behalf. If Erik is eligible to practice before the IRS, he can name himself as the representative on Form 2848.

Note: A durable power of attorney is not subject to a time limit and will continue in force after the incapacitation or incompetency of the individual. It is terminated upon the death of the individual. An ordinary power of attorney is automatically revoked if the person who made it is found to be incompetent, but a durable power of attorney can only be revoked by the person who made it, and while that person is mentally competent.

Unless a particular act is specifically not authorized by the taxpayer, a representative (with the exception of unenrolled tax return preparers) can generally perform the following acts:

- Represent a taxpayer before any office of the IRS
- Record an interview or meeting with the IRS
- Sign an offer or a waiver of restriction on assessment or collection of a tax deficiency, or a waiver of notice of disallowance of claim for credit or refund
- Sign consents to extend the statutory time period for assessment or collection of a tax
- Sign a closing agreement
- Receive (but never endorse or cash) a tax refund check

The rights of unenrolled tax return preparers are limited to representing taxpayers in examinations of the tax returns they prepared and signed.

A qualified representative can represent a taxpayer before the IRS without the taxpayer present, so long as the proper power of attorney is signed and submitted to the IRS.

Example: Delia is an enrolled agent with a signed Form 2848 for Mark, who is being audited by the IRS. Delia did not prepare Mark's tax return, but she is still eligible to represent him by virtue of her status as an EA. Mark does not have to appear at the examination hearing. If Delia were an unenrolled preparer, her representation rights would be restricted to the particular tax returns she had prepared for Mark that were under examination. She would be able to represent Mark only before IRS revenue agents and not revenue officers or appeals officers.

Revocation or Withdrawal of a POA

A power of attorney is valid until revoked by the taxpayer or until the representative withdraws from representation. If the taxpayer is revoking the power of attorney, he must write **"REVOKE"** across the top of the first page with his signature and the date below it. If the representative is withdrawing from representation, he must write **"WITHDRAW"** across the top of the first page with his signature and the date below it. The revocation or withdrawal must be mailed or faxed to the IRS. It must clearly indicate the applicable tax matters and periods.

Example: Nicola is an EA who had a power of attorney for her former client, Edwin. Nicola fired Edwin for nonpayment, but she continued to receive IRS notices on his behalf. Nicola writes "WITHDRAW" on the POA and submits it to the IRS, notifying the IRS that she no longer represents Edwin.

If a taxpayer or representative does not have a copy of the power of attorney, a statement of revocation or withdrawal must be sent to the IRS.

A newly-filed power of attorney concerning the same matter will revoke a previously-filed power of attorney. For example, if a taxpayer changes preparers and the second preparer files a power of attorney on behalf of the taxpayer, the old power of attorney on file will be rescinded. However, the taxpayer can specifically request that the old power of attorney remain active when a newer power of attorney is filed.

An IRS power of attorney is terminated if the taxpayer becomes incapacitated or incompetent.

Updating a Power of Attorney: Any update or modification to a power of attorney must be submitted in writing to the IRS. A recognized representative may substitute or delegate authority if the taxpayer has specifically given him the power to do so. The representative must file the following items with the IRS offices where the power of attorney was filed:

- A written notice of substitution or delegation signed by the recognized representative.
- A written declaration of representation made by the new representative.
- A copy of the power of attorney that specifically authorizes the substitution or delegation.

After a substitution is made, only the newly recognized representative will be considered the taxpayer's representative.

Power of Attorney Not Required: If a third party is not representing a taxpayer before the IRS, a power of attorney is not required. This would include preparation of a taxpayer's income tax return. The following situations also do not require a power of attorney:

- Providing information to the IRS
- Authorizing the disclosure of tax return information through Form 8821, *Tax Information Authorization*, or other written or oral disclosure consent
- Allowing the IRS to discuss return information with a third party via the checkbox provided on a tax return or other document
- Allowing a tax matters partner to perform acts for a partnership
- Allowing the IRS to discuss tax return information with a fiduciary

Representative Signing in Lieu of the Taxpayer

A representative named under a power of attorney is generally not permitted to sign a personal income tax return unless both of the following conditions are met:

- The signature is permitted under the Internal Revenue Code and the related regulations, and
- The taxpayer specifically grants signature authority on the power of attorney.

For example, IRS regulations permit a representative to sign a taxpayer's return if the taxpayer is unable to sign for any of the following reasons:

- Disease or injury (such as a taxpayer who is completely paralyzed or who has a debilitating injury)
- Continuous absence from the United States (including Puerto Rico) for a period of at least 60 days prior to the date required by law for filing the return
- Other good cause if specific permission is requested of and granted by the IRS

Example: Geoffrey is an EA with a client named Sally who travels extensively for business. She had signed Form 2848 specifically granting Geoffrey the right to sign her tax returns in her absence. Sally is currently traveling outside the U.S. for business and will not return until four months after the due date of her returns. Geoffrey is allowed to sign Sally's return.

When a tax return is signed by a representative, it must be accompanied by a copy of the power of attorney authorizing the representative to sign the return.

Tax Information Authorization, Form 8821

Form 8821, *Tax Information Authorization* (TIA), authorizes any individual, corporation, firm, organization, or partnership to inspect or receive confidential information for the type of tax and periods listed. Any third party may be designated to receive tax information.

Form 8821 is used by tax return preparers, employers, banks, and other institutions to receive financial information on behalf of an individual or a business. It is only a disclosure form, so it does not give an individual authority to represent a taxpayer before the IRS.

Similar to a POA form, Form 8821 requires the taxpayer to list the type of tax, the tax form number, the year or periods the authorization covers, and the specific tax matters that apply. Any prior tax years may be specified, but only future tax periods ending no later than three years after the date Form 8821 is received by the IRS are recognized.

Centralized Authorization File (CAF)

The centralized authorization file (CAF) is the IRS's computer database that contains information regarding the authorizations that taxpayers have given representatives for their accounts.

When a power of attorney or disclosure authorization document is submitted to the IRS, it is processed for inclusion in the CAF. A CAF number is assigned to a tax practitioner or other authorized individual when either a Form 2848 or Form 8821 is filed. It is a unique nine-digit number that is not the same as an individual's SSN, PTIN, or enrollment number.

Example: Josie is not a tax return preparer. In 2016, Josie's 21 year-old son, David, is audited by the IRS. David does not wish to speak directly with the IRS. Josie files a Form 2848 and becomes the authorized representative for her son. She is issued a CAF number.

Example: Mohammed is not an enrolled agent or a tax preparer. In 2016, his mother dies, and Mohammed is named as the executor of her estate. He files a Form 2848 and properly lists himself as the executor. He is issued a CAF number, and is allowed to represent his late mother's estate before all levels of the IRS.

Joint filers must complete and submit separate Forms 2848 to have the power of attorney recorded in the CAF. Alternative power of attorney forms, such as a durable power of attorney, will not be recorded in the CAF unless a Form 2848 is also attached.

The issuance of a CAF number does not indicate that a person is either recognized or authorized to practice before the IRS. It merely confirms that a centralized file has been established for the representative under that number.

Example: Darren is an EA who recently submitted Form 2848 to the IRS on behalf of his client, Jennifer. He later called the IRS to check the status of Jennifer's tax refund. The IRS employee requested Darren's CAF number, which he provided. The IRS employee found Jennifer's power of attorney information in the CAF system and gave Darren the information about his client's refund.

Having a CAF number also enables the IRS to automatically send copies of notices and other IRS communications to a representative.

Note: The revised Form 2848 instructions include an explanation of how practitioners can receive a list of their powers of attorney recorded on the CAF. A practitioner must make a FOIA request and ask the IRS to provide a copy of his CAF Representative/Client Listing. A sample letter and further instructions, including requirements to prove identity, are available on www.irs.gov by clicking on the "routine access to IRS records" link under the FOIA section.

Third Party Authorizations

A third party authorization is when a taxpayer authorizes an individual (usually his tax return preparer) to communicate with the IRS on his behalf. This authorization allows the IRS to discuss the processing of a taxpayer's current tax return, including the status of refunds, with whomever the taxpayer specifies. The authorization automatically expires on the due date of the next tax return.

A taxpayer can choose a third party designee by checking the "yes" box on his tax return, which is why it is known as "Check Box" authority. The taxpayer then enters the designee's name and phone number and a self-selected five-digit PIN, which the designee must confirm when requesting information from the IRS.

The designee can exchange verbal information with the IRS on return processing issues and on refunds and payments related to the return. The designee may also receive written account information including transcripts, upon request. A designee cannot receive a tax refund check on a client's behalf.

Example: Rashid named his EA, Patty, as his third party designee on his tax return. A few months after filing his return, Rashid still had not received his refund. He asked Patty if she could check the status of his refund. Patty called the IRS and was given the information over the phone, because she was listed as a third party designee on Rashid's return. No further authorization was necessary for Patty to receive this confidential taxpayer information.

The third party designee authorization is more limited than the authority given by Form 8821, *Tax Information Authorization* (TIA). Form 8821 can be used to allow discussions with third parties and disclosures of information to third parties on matters other than a taxpayer's current return.

Tax Return Copies and Transcripts

If a taxpayer needs an actual copy of his own tax return that has been filed and processed, he may use Form 4506, *Request for Copy of Tax Return.* Copies are generally available for the current year and the past six years. The IRS charges a fee for making the copy.[143]

A taxpayer can often receive all the information he needs by requesting a free transcript of a tax return, which is available immediately online via the IRS's "Get Transcript" tool, or by phone or mail.

Transcripts are available for the current year and the past three years. Form 4506-T, *Request for Transcript of Tax Return,* may be used when a taxpayer wants to authorize an individual or organization to receive or inspect confidential tax return information. This form is often used by financial institutions to verify tax compliance or income, such as when a taxpayer is applying for a mortgage. Form 4506-T does not authorize an individual to represent a taxpayer before the IRS.

The taxpayer must specify on the form what type of information is needed. If a "return transcript" is requested, the IRS will provide most of the line items of a filed tax return. A return transcript also includes items from any accompanying forms and schedules that were filed, but it does not reflect any changes made after the original return was filed.

If an "account transcript" is requested, the IRS will provide information on the financial status of the account, such as payments made and penalty assessments. Requesting a "record of account" produces the most detailed information as it combines the return transcript and account transcript information.

Privacy of Taxpayer Information (§7216)

The IRS has enacted strict privacy regulations designed to give taxpayers more control over their personal information and tax records. The regulations limit tax professionals' use and disclosure of client information, and explain precise and limited exceptions in which disclosure is permitted.

Note: Internal Revenue Code §7216 is a criminal tax provision enacted by Congress that prohibits tax return preparers from knowingly or recklessly disclosing or using tax return information. A preparer may be fined up to $1,000, imprisoned up to one year, or both, for each violation of §7216. There is also an additional civil penalty of $250 for improper disclosure or use of taxpayer information, outlined in IRC §6713. However, unlike §7216, this code section does not require that the disclosure be "knowing or reckless." This means that even an accidental disclosure of sensitive taxpayer information may cause the practitioner to be subject to a civil penalty.

Tax return preparers must generally obtain written consent from taxpayers before they can disclose information to a third party or use the information for any purpose other than the preparation of tax returns. The consent form must meet the following guidelines:

- Identify the purpose of the disclosure.
- Identify the recipient and describe the authorized information.
- Include the name of the preparer and the name of the taxpayer.

[143] The fee is currently $57 for each return requested and may be waived for taxpayers who live in a presidentially declared disaster area.

- Include mandatory language that informs the taxpayer that he is not required to sign the consent, and if he does sign the consent, he can set a time period for the duration of the consent.
- Include mandatory language that refers the taxpayer to the Treasury Inspector General for Tax Administration if he believes that his tax return information has been disclosed or used improperly.
- If applicable, inform the taxpayer that his tax return information may be disclosed to a tax return preparer located outside the U.S.
- Be signed and dated by the taxpayer. Electronic (online) consents must be in the same type as the website's standard text and contain the taxpayer's affirmative consent (as opposed to an opt-out clause).

Unless a specific time period is specified, the consent is valid for one year.

These privacy regulations apply to paid preparers, electronic return originators, tax software developers, and other persons or entities engaged in tax preparation. The regulations also apply to most volunteer tax return preparers, such as Volunteer Income Tax Assistance and Tax Counseling for the Elderly volunteers, and to employees and contractors employed by tax preparation companies in a support role.

Definition: These regulations pertain to the disclosure of **"tax return information,"** which is defined by law and very broad in scope. Tax return information is "all the information tax return preparers obtain from taxpayers or other sources in any form or matter that is used to prepare tax returns or is obtained in connection with the preparation of returns. It also includes all computations, worksheets, and printouts preparers create; correspondence from the IRS during the preparation, filing, and correction of returns; statistical compilations of tax return information; and tax return preparation software registration information."[144]

Allowable Disclosures

In certain circumstances, a preparer may disclose information to a second taxpayer who appears on a tax return. The preparer may disclose return information obtained from the first taxpayer if:

- The second taxpayer is related to the first taxpayer.
- The first taxpayer's interest is not adverse to the second taxpayer's interest.
- The first taxpayer has not prohibited the disclosure.

Example: Zach is an EA with two married clients, Serena and Tyler, who file jointly. Serena works long hours, so she is unavailable when Tyler meets with Zach to prepare their joint tax return. Later, Serena comes in alone to sign the return. She also has a question regarding the mortgage interest on the joint tax return. Zach is allowed to disclose return information to Serena because it is a joint return, Tyler has not prohibited any disclosures, and both Serena and Tyler's names are on the return.

A taxpayer is considered related to another taxpayer in any of the following relationships:

- A spouse of another
- Minor child and parent
- Grandchild and grandparent
- General partner in a partnership
- Trust or estate and the beneficiary

[144] "Tax return information" also includes the taxpayer's name, mailing address, and taxpayer identification number, including Social Security number or employer identification number; any information extracted from a return, including names of dependents or the location of a business; information on whether a return was, is being, or will be examined or subject to other investigation or processing; information contained on transcripts of accounts; the fact that a return was filed or examined; investigation or collection history; or tax balance due information.

- A corporation and shareholder
- Members of a controlled group of corporations

A tax return preparer may also disclose tax return information that was obtained from a first taxpayer in preparing a tax return of the second taxpayer, if the preparer has obtained written consent from the first taxpayer. For example, if an unmarried couple lives together and splits the mortgage interest, the preparer may use or disclose information from the first taxpayer to the second so long as the preparer has written consent.

Affordable Care Act Disclosures

§7216 prohibits tax return preparers, including those who offer services related to the Affordable Care Act, from using tax return information for unauthorized purposes. In addition to criminal penalties, a civil penalty of $250 for each unauthorized disclosure or use of tax return information by a tax return preparer is imposed by § 6713.

Current regulations allow preparers to use a list of client names, addresses, email addresses, and phone numbers to provide them general educational information, such as that related to the Affordable Care Act. However, a tax preparer must first obtain taxpayer consent before using tax return information to directly solicit clients for health care enrollment services or other services.

Example: Marcia is an enrolled agent who is also a health care "navigator" that helps enroll people in qualified ACA health care plans. She wants to contact clients to let them know that she is offering these services. Under the terms of §7216, she must first obtain written consent from her clients before she can solicit them.

This mandate also applies to VITA volunteers. Solicitation to offer health care enrollment services by all tax return preparers, including volunteer preparers, requires prior taxpayer consent.

Disclosure Consent Not Required

A tax return preparer is not required to obtain disclosure consent from a client if the disclosure is made for any of the following reasons:

- A court order or subpoena issued by any court of record, whether at the federal, state, or local level. The required information must be clearly identified in the document (subpoena or court order) in order for a preparer to disclose information.
- An administrative order, demand, summons, or subpoena that is issued by any federal agency (such as the IRS), state agency, or commission charged under the laws of the state with licensing, registration, or regulation of tax return preparers.
- To report a crime to proper authorities. Even if the preparer is mistaken and no crime has occurred, he will not be subject to sanctions if he makes the disclosure in good faith.
- For purposes of peer reviews.

A preparer may disclose private client information to his attorney or to an employee of the IRS, in connection with an IRS investigation of the preparer.

Example: The IRS is investigating a CPA named Harry for possible misconduct. Harry has an attorney who is assisting in his defense. As it turns out, Harry was a victim of embezzlement because his bookkeeper was stealing client checks. He only discovered the embezzlement when the IRS contacted him about client complaints. Harry may disclose confidential client information to his attorney in order to assist with his own defense. Harry may also disclose confidential client information to the IRS during the course of its investigation.

A preparer may disclose tax return information to a tax return processor. For example, if a preparer uses an electronic or tax return processing service, he may disclose tax return information to that service in order to prepare tax returns or compute tax liability.

Tax Practitioner Confidentiality Privilege

Under IRC §7525, enrolled practitioners and their clients are granted limited rights of confidentiality protection.[145] This Federally Authorized Tax Practitioner Confidentiality Privilege (FATP) applies to attorneys, CPAs, enrolled agents, enrolled actuaries, and certain other individuals allowed to practice before the IRS.

The confidentiality protection applies to communications that would be considered privileged if they were between the taxpayer and an attorney and that relate to:

- Noncriminal tax matters before the IRS, or
- Noncriminal tax proceedings brought in federal court by or against the United States.

This confidentiality privilege cannot be used with any agency other than the IRS. For example, an enrolled agent cannot assert the federal confidentiality privilege with any state taxing agency. The confidentiality privilege does not apply:

- In criminal tax matters
- To any written communications regarding the promotion of a tax shelter
- In state tax proceedings
- To the general preparation of tax returns

There is a long history of court decisions that deny confidentiality of information disclosed to an attorney for purposes of preparing tax returns. In a key 1983 ruling, the court stated that "information transmitted for the purpose of preparation of a tax return," though transmitted to an attorney, is not privileged information.

When information will be transmitted to a third party (in this case, on a tax return) such information is not confidential."[146] This restriction on the confidentiality privilege related to tax preparation applies to other practitioners besides attorneys, including enrolled agents and CPAs.

Identity Theft

Identity theft occurs when someone uses another individual's personally identifiable information, such as his name, Social Security number, or credit card number, without his permission to commit fraud or other crimes. Fraudulent refunds have become a major issue, and identity theft is considered one of the biggest challenges facing the IRS. Safeguarding taxpayer data has become a top priority for the IRS.

Innocent taxpayers are victimized by tax fraud because their refunds are subsequently delayed. The taxpayer may be unaware that this has happened until they attempt to e-file their own return and discover that a return had already been filed using their SSN. The IRS may also send the taxpayer a letter saying it has identified a suspicious return using someone else's SSN.

Employment-related identity theft occurs when someone other than the valid owner of an SSN, uses that SSN or other personal information for the purpose of obtaining employment. This type of fraudulent activity can affect both individuals and business entities.

If a taxpayer believes someone may have used his SSN fraudulently to file taxes, he should notify the IRS immediately. He will need to submit Form 14039, *Identity Theft Affidavit,* along with documentation to verify his identity.

---

[145] The "federally authorized tax practitioner privilege" is an amendment to the Internal Revenue Code made by the *Internal Revenue Service Restructuring and Reform Act of 1998.*

[146] *United States v. Lawless,* 709 F.2d 487 (7th Cir. 1983).

Warning Signs for Individual Clients

A client's SSN has been compromised when:

- A return is rejected and the IRS reject codes indicate the taxpayer's SSN already has been used.
- The client receives IRS notices regarding a tax return after all tax issues have been resolved, refund paid or account balances have been paid.
- An IRS notice indicates the client received wages from an employer unknown to them.

Note: a tax practitioner must have a valid power of attorney (Form 2848) on file and authenticate the taxpayer's identity before any IRS employee can provide the practitioner with any taxpayer information regarding a fraud issue.

Warning Signs for Business Entities

Business identity theft (also known as corporate or commercial identity theft) happens when someone creates or uses the identifying information of a business to obtain tax benefits. Business identity thieves file fraudulent business returns to receive refundable business credits or to perpetuate individual identity theft. Business identity theft is more complex than individual identity theft. Many of the same indicators that signify simple filing or processing errors also hint at business identity theft.

A client's EIN has been compromised when:

- The client's business return is accepted as an amended return, but the taxpayer has not filed an original return for that year.
- The business receives IRS notices about fictitious or non-existent employees.
- Your client notices activity related to or receives IRS notices regarding a defunct, closed or dissolved business entity.

Example: Harold is the sole shareholder of a C corporation in the State of California. In 2016, he receives a notice from the IRS about a large refund for an amended return that had been filed for his corporation. Harold never filed or signed an amended return. He later discovers that his former bookkeeper, who had worked for him in a prior year, had filed the return and directed the refund to her home address, intending to illegally cash the check using stolen documents that she took from the business. Harold immediately contacts the IRS to report the fraud.

The majority of tax-related identity theft is initiated online, by using fake or "spoofed" email accounts. The IRS does not initiate contact with taxpayers by email to request personal or financial information. This includes any type of electronic communication, such as text messages and social media channels.

Some of the individuals committing identity theft fraud are members of high-tech global rings engaged in organized criminal enterprises for stealing identities and profiting from that information.

Stolen Identity Refund Fraud (SIRF)

Tax refund fraud involving the use of stolen identities is referred to as SIRF, for Stolen Identity Refund Fraud.

This growing type of crime occurs when thieves file fraudulent refund claims using a legitimate taxpayer's identifying information, which they have stolen. In a recent IRS report, the IRS estimated that approximately $30 billion of identity theft-related refund fraud was attempted during the tax year, and approximately $5.8 billion was actually paid out (since some refund fraud remained undetected, the government's actual losses were actually even greater).[147]

Enforcement: The IRS has greatly expanded its identity theft enforcement efforts, with more than 3,000 employees now assigned to work on identity-theft related issues. In fiscal year 2016, the IRS started over 1,400 criminal investigations regarding taxpayer identity theft.

Theft Prevention

To help stop identity thieves, the IRS says it now has dozens of identity theft screening filters in place to protect tax refunds. To educate taxpayers, the IRS has added a guide to identity theft on its website.

Taxpayers are advised to be on the alert for possible identity theft if they receive an IRS notice or letter stating that any of the following has occurred:

- There was more than one tax return filed by the taxpayer.
- The taxpayer has a balance due, refund offset, or has had collection actions taken against him for a year in which he did not file a tax return.
- IRS records indicate the taxpayer received wages from an unknown employer.

The IRS will never seek financial or personal information by initiating contact with taxpayers by email. Many of these so-called "phishing" scams attempt to collect taxpayer Social Security numbers by contacting taxpayers using these methods. Phone scams with callers purporting to be from the IRS also have become widespread in recent years, with more than 190,000 reports of these calls in the last three years.

Clients may also be victims of identity theft not related to tax administration if they:

- Receive bills for business lines of credit or credit cards they do not have.
- Notice that a credit report indicates credit or other open accounts they did not authorize.
- See unexplained bank account withdrawals.
- Suddenly don't get their bills or other mail.
- Find unfamiliar accounts or charges on their credit report.

Even if the taxpayer has not been a victim of tax-related identity theft, but has been a victim of another type of fraud, it is still advisable for the taxpayer to fill out IRS Form 14039, *Identity Theft Affidavit,* in order to report the potential for future fraudulent activity.

Tax practitioners can also become targets of cyber-criminals. Online providers who experience a data breach are required to contact the IRS within one business day.

If the taxpayer's SSN is compromised, the IRS recommends the following steps:

- Get a notice that information was compromised by a data breach at a company where they do business or have an account.
- Complete IRS Form 14039, *Identity Theft Affidavit*, if the taxpayer's e-file return rejects because of a duplicate filing under the client's SSN.
- The taxpayer should continue to pay their taxes and file their tax return, even if they must do so by paper.
- If the taxpayer had previously contacted the IRS and did not receive a resolution, they may contact the IRS for specialized assistance at 1-800-908-4490.
- Respond immediately to any IRS notice; call the number provided or, if instructed, go to www.IDVerify.irs.gov.

[147] Internal Revenue Service Advisory Council 2016 Public Report.

IP PINs

As part of its crackdown on identity theft, the IRS is issuing an identity protection personal identification number (IP PIN) to certain taxpayers. A taxpayer is eligible if he:

- Reported to the IRS he has been the victim of identity theft and the IRS has resolved his case;
- Filed his federal tax return as a resident of Florida, Georgia, or the District of Columbia; or
- Received an IRS notice or letter asking him to voluntarily opt in to receive an IP PIN.

The IP PIN helps prevent the misuse of a taxpayer's Social Security number or taxpayer identification number. It is used on both paper and electronic returns. If the taxpayer attempts to file an electronic return without his IP PIN, the return will be rejected.

If it is missing on a paper return, there will likely be a delay in processing, as the IRS will have to validate the taxpayer's identity.

The IP PIN is only valid for a single year. A taxpayer will receive a new IP PIN every year for three years after reporting the identity theft incident to the IRS. If a spouse also has an IP PIN, only the person whose SSN appears first on the tax return needs to input his PIN.

Example: Leslie attempted to file her tax return electronically this year, but it was rejected. The IRS reject code stated that a tax return had already been filed for her. Leslie immediately contacted the IRS and reported the fraud. The IRS determined that she was a victim of refund fraud and placed an "identity theft indicator" on her account. Leslie is forced to file her return on paper this year, and the processing time for her return is increased. In December, the IRS will send her a CP01A Notice containing her IP PIN. Leslie will not be able to e-file her tax return without the IP PIN, which will help prevent refund fraud on her account in the future.

Direct Deposit Limits

A new IRS procedure limits the number of refunds electronically deposited into a single financial account or prepaid debit card to three. Any additional refunds will be converted to a paper refund check and mailed to the taxpayer.

The direct deposit limit is intended to prevent criminals from easily obtaining multiple tax refunds. It is also designed to protect taxpayers from unscrupulous tax preparers who obtain payment for their services by depositing part or all of their clients' refunds into their own bank accounts, an action that is prohibited under the IRC and subject to discipline under Circular 230.

Safeguarding Taxpayer Data

Since tax return preparers are required to obtain and store client information, they have an important role to play in keeping this information secure. To help prevent identity theft, the IRS suggests preparers confirm identities and taxpayer identification numbers of taxpayers, their spouses, and dependents on the returns to be prepared. TINs include Social Security numbers (SSNs), adopted taxpayer identification numbers (ATINs), and individual taxpayer identification numbers (ITINs).

To confirm identities, the preparer can request a picture ID showing the taxpayer's name and address, and Social Security cards or other documents providing the TINs for all other individuals to be listed on the return.[148] Additional steps practitioners can take to guard against identity theft include the following:

- File clients' returns early when possible.
- E-file returns, in order to be notified of duplicate return notices more quickly.

---

[148] A later unit, (*IRS E-File)*, covers new requirements to confirm clients' identities for tax preparers who e-file.

- Let clients know that refunds may take longer in future years as additional system security steps are taken.

Since tax return preparers are at risk of having their identities, and those of their clients, stolen, they should take special precautions to safeguard their clients' sensitive information. a tax practitioner must determine the appropriate security controls for their business. Security controls are the management, operational, and technical safeguards you may use to protect the confidentiality, integrity and availability of your customers' information. Examples of security controls are:

- Locking desk drawers and file cabinets.
- Locking doors to restrict access to paper and electronic files.
- Requiring passwords to restrict access to computer files
- Using encrypted flash drives and using other encrypted procedures in electronically transferring a client's information to a third party – including e-mails.
- Keeping a backup of electronic data for recovery purposes.
- Redacting or truncating SSNs and other personal information.
- Shredding paper containing taxpayer information before throwing it in the trash.
- Using couriers and certified mail to ensure that the correct person receives the correspondence.
- Installing and requiring antivirus and other security software on all of the firm's computers.
- Requiring that all outside contractors main the same level of security protocols as the preparer

Note: Taxpayer data is defined as any information that is obtained or used in the preparation of a tax return (e.g., income statements, bookkeeping records, information statements, tax organizers, etc.).

Unit 3: Study Questions

(Test yourself and then check the correct answers at the end of this chapter.)

1. Which designation or form gives the appointed person the greatest rights to represent a taxpayer?

A. Third party designee, also known as "Check Box" authority.
B. Form 8821, *Tax Information Authorization*.
C. Form 2848, *Power of Attorney and Declaration of Representative.*
D. Form 4506-T, *Request for Transcript of Tax Return.*

2. The maximum number of refunds that may be electronically deposited into a single financial account is:

A. One.
B. Two.
C. Three.
D. No limit.

3. In what situation is a preparer allowed to disclose information without first obtaining written permission from a client?

A. When he is issued a subpoena by a state agency that regulates tax return preparers.
B. When he is contacted by a newspaper reporter investigating a possible crime committed by his client.
C. When the information is requested by his client's uncle who helps support the client financially.
D. When the information is needed by a preparer who volunteers with VITA.

4. All of the following statements regarding the signature requirements for tax returns are correct except:

A. A preparer may sign a taxpayer's return in lieu of the taxpayer, if the taxpayer cannot sign his own tax return due to a physical disability.
B. A preparer may sign a taxpayer's return in lieu of the taxpayer, if the taxpayer cannot sign his own tax return due to an extended absence from the United States.
C. A preparer is allowed to copy a taxpayer's signature if he has a signed power of attorney.
D. A preparer must have a signed power of attorney in order to sign on the taxpayer's behalf.

5. A durable power of attorney remains in effect until an individual:

A. Gets divorced.
B. Becomes mentally incompetent or incapacitated.
C. Dies.
D. Both B and C.

6. For a taxpayer who wants someone to represent him at an examination by the IRS, all of the following statements are correct except:

A. The taxpayer must furnish that representative with written authorization on Form 2848, *Power of Attorney and Declaration of Representative*, or any other properly written authorization.
B. The representative can be an attorney, CPA, or EA.
C. The representative can be an unenrolled preparer who prepared the taxpayer's current year tax return, but not the year of the return under examination.
D. Even if the taxpayer appointed a representative, the taxpayer may choose to attend the examination or appeals conference and may act on his own behalf.

7. Which statement is correct regarding the privacy regulations of IRC §7216?

A. The regulations do not apply to e-file providers.
B. The improper disclosure must be "knowing or reckless" for criminal provisions to apply.
C. A practitioner may be fined up to $500 and imprisoned for up to one year for each violation of this code.
D. Practitioners must obtain oral consent from taxpayers before they can use information for anything other than the actual preparation of tax returns.

8. Form 8821, *Tax Information Authorization*, may be used to authorize the following:

A. Any individual, corporation, firm, organization, or partnership to receive confidential information for the type of tax and periods listed on Form 8821.
B. Any designated third party to receive tax information.
C. For unenrolled tax return preparers to indicate a representative relationship with a taxpayer and to authorize practice before the IRS.
D. Both A and B.

9. Which of the following is not necessary in connection with Form 2848?

A. For all signatures to be notarized.
B. For the form to be faxed or mailed to the IRS.
C. For the preparer to include his PTIN.
D. All of the above requirements are necessary in connection with Form 2848.

10. How long is a power of attorney authorization valid?

A. One year.
B. Three years.
C. Until it is revoked or superseded.
D. Until the due date of the next tax return.

11. Taxpayers are granted a limited confidentiality privilege with any federally authorized tax practitioner. Confidential communications include all of the following except:

A. Written tax advice.
B. A noncriminal tax proceeding in Federal court.
C. Participation in a tax shelter.
D. Noncriminal tax matters before the IRS.

12. If a practitioner no longer wishes to represent a taxpayer, he should take the following action:

A. Nothing. A taxpayer is the only one who can revoke power of attorney authorization.
B. Write the word "REVOKE" on the POA form and mail or fax it to the IRS.
C. Write the word "WITHDRAW" on the POA form and mail or email it to the IRS.
D. Write the word "WITHDRAW" on the POA form and mail or fax it to the IRS.

13. How many representatives can a taxpayer appoint using a single Form 2848?

A. One per form only.
B. Two.
C. Three.
D. Four.

14. The Centralized Authorization File (CAF) is:

A. An IRS computer database with information regarding the authority of individuals appointed under powers of attorney or designated under tax information authorizations.
B. A public, searchable database of federally authorized practitioners and certain other tax preparers with professional credentials.
C. An automated list of disbarred practitioners.
D. An automated file of taxpayer delinquencies.

15. Floyd is an unenrolled tax return preparer for a married couple. He is also licensed to sell securities. Floyd is not a practitioner. After preparing the couple's joint return, he was concerned that they were not saving adequately for retirement. Using information from their tax return, Floyd created a custom retirement plan for the couple. He had not obtained their consent. Which of the following statements is correct?

A. Because he is not a practitioner, Floyd is not subject to the rules of §7216.
B. Floyd is in violation of §7216.
C. Floyd is not in violation of §7216 because he used information from current clients; therefore, he was not required to obtain their consent.
D. Floyd is not in violation of §7216 because retirement planning is one of the exceptions listed as an allowable use of information.

16. For future tax periods, Form 2848 is valid for a period of no later than _____________ after the date the POA is received by the IRS.

A. One year.
B. Two years.
C. Three years.
D. Five years.

Unit 3: Answers

1. The answer is C. Only Form 2848, *Power of Attorney and Declaration of Representative,* allows a third party to represent a taxpayer before the IRS. The other consents are much more limited and only allow the third party to receive or inspect tax account information.

2. The answer is C. To combat identity theft, new IRS procedures limit the number of refunds that may be electronically deposited into a single financial account or prepaid debit card to three. Any additional refund(s) will be converted to a paper refund check and mailed to the taxpayer.

3. The answer is A. A tax return preparer who is issued a subpoena or court order, whether at the federal, state, or local level, is not required to obtain disclosure permission from a client. In all the other cases, disclosure is not allowed unless there has been prior written consent.

4. The answer is C. A tax return preparer is never allowed to copy a taxpayer's signature. A preparer may sign in lieu of the taxpayer in certain situations. For example, rules permit a representative to sign a taxpayer's return if he is unable to do so himself for any of the following reasons:

- Disease or injury
- Continuous absence from the United States for a period of at least 60 days prior to the date required by law for filing the return
- Other good cause if specific permission is requested of and granted by the IRS

When a return is signed by a representative, it must be accompanied by a power of attorney authorizing the representative to sign the return.

5. The answer is C. A durable power of attorney is not subject to a time limit. It remains in effect until the death of the individual, or until the individual revokes it.

6. The answer is C. Only persons eligible to practice before the IRS, including attorneys, CPAs, and EAs, have unlimited rights to represent taxpayers before the IRS. The representation rights of unenrolled preparers are much more limited. An unenrolled preparer who did not prepare and sign the specific tax return under examination would not be allowed to represent the taxpayer. Starting with the 2016 filing season, any unenrolled preparer who is not a participant in the IRS's voluntary Annual Filing Season Program will not be able to represent taxpayers before any level of the IRS.

7. The answer is B. IRC §7216 is a criminal code that limits tax professionals' use and disclosure of private client information. Answer B is correct because criminal penalties will apply only if the improper disclosure is "knowing or reckless," rather than simply negligent. The other answers are incorrect because the regulations do apply to e-file providers; a preparer may be fined up to $1,000, not $500, and imprisoned for up to a year for each violation; and written consent, not oral, is generally required before taxpayer information can be disclosed or used for other purposes.

8. The answer is D. Form 8821, *Tax Information Authorization*, authorizes any individual, corporation, firm, organization, or partnership to receive confidential information for the type of tax and periods listed on the form. Any third party may be designated by the taxpayer to receive confidential tax information. Form 8821 is only a disclosure form, so it will not give an individual any power to represent a taxpayer before the IRS. It may be used only to obtain information, such as copies of tax returns or tax return transcripts.

9. The answer is A. The signatures on Form 2848 are not required to be notarized.

10. The answer is C. A power of attorney is valid until revoked or superseded. It may be revoked by the taxpayer or withdrawn by the representative, or it may be superseded by the filing of a new power of attorney for the same tax and tax period.

11. The answer is C. The confidentiality privilege does not apply in the case of communications regarding the promotion of or participation in a tax shelter. A tax shelter is any entity, plan, or arrangement whose significant purpose is to avoid or evade income tax. Unlike the attorney–client privilege, the federally authorized tax practitioner privilege does not apply in criminal tax matters, and does not apply in state tax proceedings. The privilege may be asserted only in a "noncriminal tax matter before the Internal Revenue Service" and a "noncriminal tax proceeding in Federal court brought by or against the United States." The confidentiality privilege is also not extended to matters related to the general preparation of tax returns.

12. The answer is D. A preparer must write the word “WITHDRAW” on the first page of the POA form, include his signature and the date, and mail or fax the form to the IRS. Email is not an acceptable means of contact. The form must clearly indicate the applicable tax matters and periods. In contrast, if a taxpayer chooses to end a previously authorized power of attorney, he must write the word “REVOKE” on the form, include his signature and the date, and mail or fax the form to the IRS.

13. The answer is D. When a taxpayer wishes to use a representative, he should fill out and sign Form 2848, *Power of Attorney and Declaration of Representative.* By doing so, the taxpayer authorizes a specific individual or individuals to receive confidential tax information and to perform the actions detailed on the form. Up to four representatives can be authorized per form, an increase from the previous Form 2848 that allowed only three representatives to be designated.

14. The answer is A. The Centralized Authorization File, or “CAF,” contains information on third parties authorized to represent taxpayers before the IRS and receive and inspect confidential tax information on active tax accounts or those accounts currently under collection or examination by the IRS.

15. The answer is B. All paid tax return preparers are subject to the rules of §7216, a criminal statute. Floyd is in violation of §7216 because he did not obtain written consent from his clients prior to using their private information. A tax return preparer must generally obtain written consent from taxpayers before he can disclose information to a third party or use the information for any purpose other than the preparation of tax returns. Each violation of §7216 could mean a fine of up to $1,000, a prison term of up to one year, or both. There is also a separate civil penalty of $250 for improper disclosure or use of taxpayer information, as outlined in IRC §6713. However, unlike §7216, this code section does not require that the disclosure be “knowing or reckless”.

16. The answer is C. For future tax periods, the period specified is limited to no later than three years after the date the POA is received by the IRS. The types of tax and dates listed on Form 2848 must be specific. Tax years or periods that have already ended may be listed under “tax matters.”

Unit 4: Tax Practitioner Responsibilities

More Reading:
Circular No. 230, *Regulations Governing Practice Before the Internal Revenue Service*
Publication 947, *Practice Before the IRS and Power of Attorney*
Publication 216, *Conference and Practice Requirements*

The Treasury Department's Circular 230 sets forth regulations that govern all tax practitioners, including enrolled agents, CPAs, attorneys, and others who practice before the IRS. Circular 230 imposes professional standards and codes of conduct for practitioners and tax advisors. It prohibits certain actions, requires other actions, and details penalties for ethical violations and other misconduct by practitioners.

Circular 230 is broken into four subparts:

- Authority to practice
- Duties and restrictions relating to practice
- Sanctions for violations
- Disciplinary procedures

In the next two units, we will look closely at subpart 2 of Circular 230, which describes practitioner responsibilities and standards.

Diligence as to Accuracy §10.22

Central to the Circular 230 regulations is the mandate for practitioners to exercise due diligence when performing the following duties:

- Preparing or assisting in preparing, approving, and filing of returns, documents, affidavits, and other papers relating to IRS matters
- Determining the correctness of oral or written representations made to the Department of the Treasury
- Determining the correctness of oral or written representations made to clients related to any matter administered by the IRS

§10.22 does not state what due diligence entails, but there is more specific guidance in Circular 230 sections related to standards for written advice.

Reliance on Others: A practitioner will be presumed to have exercised due diligence if he relies on the work product of another person. That is assuming that the practitioner used "reasonable care" when he hired, supervised, trained, and evaluated that person or persons.

Example: Keisha is an enrolled agent. During the year, a new client, Leonardo, comes to her to prepare his return. Leonardo is self-employed. Keisha asks to see his prior year return, which she examines for accuracy. The return was prepared by another tax practitioner, and it includes a depreciation schedule for Leonardo's business assets. The schedule appears correct and the listed items are reasonable. Keisha may use the depreciation schedule as a reference, even though she did not prepare it herself.

Best Practices §10.33

Circular 230 explains the broad concept of *best practices*. Practitioners must provide clients with the highest quality representation concerning federal tax matters by adhering to best practices in providing advice and in preparing documents or information for the IRS.

Practitioners who oversee a firm's practice should take reasonable steps to ensure that the firm's procedures for all employees are consistent with best practices. Best practices include the following:

- Communicating clearly with the client regarding the terms of the engagement.

- Establishing the facts, determining which facts are relevant, evaluating the reasonableness of any assumptions, relating the applicable law to the relevant facts, and arriving at a conclusion supported by the law and the facts.
- Advising the client of the conclusions reached and the impact of the advice rendered; for example, advising whether a taxpayer may avoid accuracy-related penalties if he relies on the advice provided.
- Acting fairly and with integrity in practice before the IRS.

Note: The IRS has issued return preparer best practices related to the Affordable Care Act. Tax preparers are expected to resolve conflicting or contradictory statements from their clients, as they do for other items on a tax return. The IRS issued official guidance on April 7, 2016 to help tax preparers resolve conflicting information between Form 1095-A and Form 1095-B, two common ACA forms.

Competence §10.35

This provision states that a practitioner must be competent to engage in practice before the IRS. "Competence" is defined as having the appropriate level of knowledge, skill, thoroughness, and preparation for the specific matter related to a client's engagement.

Circular 230 says a practitioner can become competent in various ways, including consulting with experts in the relevant area or studying the relevant law.

Example: Aminta is an enrolled agent who has many years of experience in preparing partnership tax returns. In 2016, she takes continuing education classes related to changes in partnership law, and consults with another tax professional in her office on a particularly complex partnership return. Also in 2016, a longtime client whose mother has died asks Aminta to handle the estate tax returns for him. Aminta rarely handles estate tax matters and does not have time to research the law sufficiently to handle this case, so she refers the estate return to a tax attorney who specializes in estate tax law. Aminta has fulfilled her Circular 230 obligations related to §10.35.

Knowledge of Client's Omission §10.21

A practitioner who knows that his client has not complied with the revenue laws or who has made an error or omission on his tax return has the responsibility to advise the client promptly of the noncompliance, error, or omission, as well as its consequences.

The practitioner is not responsible for correcting the noncompliance once he has notified the client of the issue, or for notifying the IRS of a client's noncompliance.

Example: Jeremy is an EA with a new client, Monique, who has prepared her own returns in the past. Jeremy notices that Monique has been claiming head of household status on her tax returns, but she does not qualify for this status, because she does not have a qualifying dependent. Jeremy is required to promptly notify Monique of the error and tell her the consequences of not correcting the error. However, Jeremy is not required to amend Monique's prior year tax returns to correct the error. Nor is he required to notify the IRS of Monique's claim of incorrect status.

The §10.21 obligations are not limited to practitioners preparing returns, so the discovery of an error in the course of a tax consulting or advisory engagement will also trigger its requirements.

Example: Gina is an EA who takes over another tax return preparer's practice. She discovers that the previous preparer has been taking section 179 deductions on assets that do not qualify for this treatment. Gina must notify her clients of the errors and the consequences of not correcting the errors. She is not required to correct the errors.

Conflicts of Interest §10.29

Conflicts of interest are common, especially when it comes to divorce. There are special rules that apply to tax practitioners with regards to conflicts of interest between two clients. If there is a potential conflict of interest, the practitioner must disclose the conflict and be given the opportunity to disclose all material facts. A practitioner will have a conflict of interest if:

- The representation of one client will be directly adverse to another client; or
- There is a significant risk that the representation of one or more clients will be materially limited by the practitioner's responsibilities to another client, a former client, a third person, or by a personal interest of the practitioner.

A practitioner may represent a client when a conflict of interest exists if:

- The practitioner reasonably believes that he will be able to provide competent and diligent representation to each affected client;
- The representation is not prohibited by law; and
- Each affected client waives the conflict of interest and gives informed consent, confirmed in writing, within 30 days after giving any non-written informed consent to the tax practitioner.

IRS regulations allow the written consent to be made within a reasonable period after the informed consent, but not later than 30 days after the date on which the conflict is known by the practitioner.

Example: Andrew and Harry are business partners. Regina is an enrolled agent who prepares both their partnership return, as well as their individual returns. In 2016, Andrew and Harry have a major argument about the direction of the business. Andrew calls Regina and tells her that he is going to dissolve the partnership. Regina must prepare a conflict of interest waiver for Andrew and Harry, as well as the partnership itself, if she plans to keep them both as her clients.

The written consent must be retained for at least 36 months from the date representation ends, and must be given to any officer or employee of the IRS, if requested. At minimum, the consent should adequately describe the nature of the conflict and the parties the practitioner represents.

Example: Christa is an EA who prepares tax returns for Jana and Brett, a married couple. In 2016, Jana and Brett go through a contentious divorce, and Christa believes there is potential for conflict of interest relating to the services she would provide each of them. She prepares a written statement explaining the potential conflict of interest and reviews it with her clients. Jana and Brett still want Christa to prepare their returns, and Christa determines that she will be able to represent each fairly and competently. She has both Jana and Brett sign the statement that waives the conflict and gives their consent for her to prepare their individual tax returns. Christa must retain the record of their consent for at least 36 months after she last represents either party.

IRS Information Requests §10.20

Under Circular 230 §10.20, when the IRS requests information, a practitioner must comply and submit records promptly.

If the requested information or records are not in the practitioner's possession, he must promptly advise the requesting IRS officer and provide any information he has regarding the identity of the person who may have possession or control of the requested information or records. The practitioner must also make a "reasonable inquiry" of his client regarding the location of the requested records.

However, the practitioner is not required to make inquiry of any other person or to independently verify any information furnished by his client. Further, the practitioner is not required to contact any third party who might be in possession of the records.

A practitioner may not interfere with any lawful effort by the IRS to obtain any record or information unless he believes in good faith and on reasonable grounds that the record or information is privileged under IRC §7525. A practitioner can also be exempted from these rules if he believes in good faith that the request is of doubtful legality.

If the IRS's Office of Professional Responsibility requests information concerning possible violations of the regulations by other parties, such as other preparers, the practitioner must furnish the information and be prepared to testify in disbarment or suspension proceedings.

Example: An IRS revenue agent submitted a lawful records request to Randall, an EA, for accounting records relating to a former client who was under IRS investigation. However, earlier in the year, Randall had fired his client for nonpayment and returned his records. Randall promptly notified the IRS officer that he no longer had the records. He also attempted to contact his former client, but the phone number was disconnected. Randall is not required to contact any third parties to discover the location of the requested records. Therefore, Randall has fulfilled his obligations under §10.20.

Return of Client Records §10.28

A practitioner is required to return a client's original records upon request, whether or not his fees have been paid. Client records include:

- All documents a client provided to a practitioner that pre-existed their business engagement.
- Any materials that were prepared by the client or a third party that were provided to the practitioner relating to the subject matter of the representation.
- Any document prepared by the practitioner that was presented to the client relating to a prior representation if such document is necessary for the taxpayer to comply with his current federal tax obligations.

The practitioner must, at the request of a client, promptly return any and all records that are necessary for the client to comply with his federal tax obligations. Client records generally do not include the practitioner's work product. However, they may include any work product that the client has already paid for, such as a completed copy of a tax return. Client records do not include any return, claim for refund, schedule, affidavit, appraisal, or any other document prepared by the practitioner if he is withholding these documents pending the client's payment of fees.

Example: Leroy is an EA with a client, Samantha, who becomes upset after he tells her she owes money to the IRS. Samantha wants to get a second opinion, and she does not want to pay Leroy for his time. Leroy is required to hand over Samantha's original tax records, including copies of her W-2 forms and any other information she brought to his office. Leroy returns her original records, but he does not give her a copy of the tax return he prepared, since she did not pay his fee for the return.

Example: Clara's client, Alpine Corporation, has been slow to pay in the past, so she asks the owners to pay for the tax returns when they pick them up. The president of Alpine Corporation refuses to pay and demands the tax returns anyway. Clara must return the corporation's original records, but she is not required to give away any work product that the owners have not yet paid for.

A client must be given reasonable access to review and copy any additional records retained by the practitioner that are necessary for the client to comply with his federal tax obligations. The practitioner may retain copies of all the records returned to a client.

Copies of Tax Returns: IRC §6107

Under IRC §6107, tax return preparers are required to give a completed copy of a tax return or claim for refund no later than the time the return or claim is presented for the taxpayer's signature. The copy can be in any media, including electronic media.

Preparers are required to keep copies of all returns they have prepared or retain a list of clients and tax returns prepared. At a minimum, the list must contain the taxpayer's name, taxpayer identification number, tax year, and the type of return prepared. The copies of tax returns or the lists must be retained for at least three years after the close of the return period. The close of the return period is defined as June 30, meaning the three-year period to retain records begins July 1.

Note: In practice, most preparers keep scanned, digital, or hard copies of client tax returns rather than simply a list of the returns prepared.

Tax Return Preparer Employer Records (IRC §6060): The employer of tax return preparers must keep a record of all those employed and make it available for IRS inspection upon request. The records must include the name, taxpayer identification number, and place of work of each tax return preparer employed. Records must be retained for at least three years following the close of the return period.

Practitioner Fees §10.27

The IRS prohibits practitioners from charging "unconscionable fees." Although that term has not been defined, it is generally believed to refer to fees that the courts would consider grossly disproportionate in relation to the services provided.

The IRS has traditionally held that a practitioner may not charge a contingent fee (for example, a fee determined as a percentage of the taxpayer's refund) for preparing an original tax return. A contingent fee might also include a fee that is based on a percentage of the taxes saved or one that depends on a specific result.

However, in 2014, a U.S. district court ruled that the IRS lacked statutory authority to regulate contingent fee arrangements for the preparation and filing of ordinary refund claims (refund claims after the taxpayer has filed a return but before the IRS has started an audit of the return).[149]

The IRS chose not to appeal the decision, so this part of the Circular 230 prohibition on contingent fees is no longer in effect.

Note: At the time of this book's printing, the IRS had not issued a public comment on the issue of contingent fees specifically, so test-takers should be aware that if they encounter an exam question about the topic of contingent fees, they should proceed with caution.

It should also be noted that certain practitioners, such as certified public accountants, may still be subject to prohibitions against charging contingent fees under applicable state regulations.

Notwithstanding the general limitation that has applied to charging contingent fees, a practitioner has been allowed to charge a contingent fee in limited circumstances, including:

- Representation during the examination of an original tax return, or during the examination of an amended return or claim for refund, if the amended return or claim for refund was filed within 120 days of the taxpayer receiving a written notice of examination or a written challenge to the original tax return.

---

[149] The opinion in *Ridgely v. Lew* was issued in July 2014. Late in 2015, the IRS Advisory Council (IRSAC) issued a report recommending that legislation be enacted to overturn the results in Loving and Ridgely by expressly affirming the Treasury Department's authority under 31 U.S.C. §330 to regulate paid tax return preparers. At the time of this book's printing, no such legislation had been introduced. The IRS does not plan to appeal the decision, but they have not acquiesced to the case, either.

- Services rendered in connection with a refund claim for credit or a refund filed in conjunction with a penalty or interest charge assessed by the IRS.
- Services rendered in connection with any judicial proceeding arising under the IRC.

Advertising Restrictions §10.30

A practitioner may not use any form of advertising that contains false, deceptive, or coercive information, or that is in violation of IRS regulations. Practitioners who are authorized e-Service providers may use the IRS e-file logo.

> Note: Tax practitioners are **specifically prohibited** from using official IRS insignia, including the following logos (below):

Advertising Standards: Permissible Logos

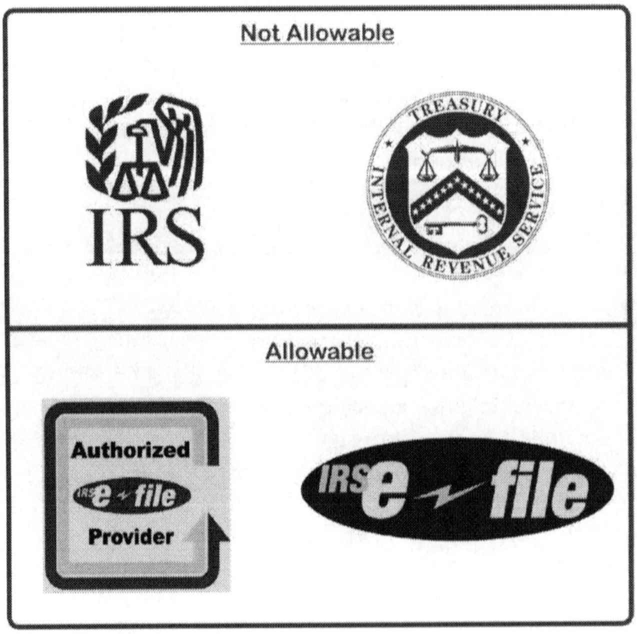

Acceptable Designation Terms

In describing their professional designation, enrolled agents may not use the term "certified" or imply any type of employment relationship with the IRS. Examples of acceptable descriptions for EAs are "enrolled to represent taxpayers before the Internal Revenue Service," "enrolled to practice before the Internal Revenue Service," and "admitted to practice before the Internal Revenue Service."

Solicitation Restrictions

A practitioner may, in certain circumstances, solicit his professional services. The solicitation may not violate federal or state law, or other applicable rules (such as attorneys who are bound to conduct guidelines in their particular states). A practitioner may not continue to contact a prospective client who has communicated that he does not wish to be solicited.

Mail Advertising: Mail advertising is allowed, but a solicitation must be clearly labeled as such and, if applicable, the source of information used in choosing the recipient must be identified. In the case of direct mail and e-commerce communications, the practitioner must retain a copy of the communication, along with a list of persons to whom the communication was mailed or distributed, for at least 36 months.

Practitioners may also send solicitations to other practitioners indicating their availability to provide professional services (such as bookkeeping or payroll services). The advertising and communications must not be misleading, deceptive, or in violation of IRS regulations.

Fee Information: A practitioner may publish and advertise a fee schedule. A practitioner must adhere to the published fee schedule for at least 30 calendar days after it is last published. Fee information may be published in newspapers, mailings, websites, email, or by any other method. A practitioner may charge based on the following:

- Fixed fees for specific routine services
- Hourly rates
- A range of fees for particular services
- A fee for an initial consultation

When advertising fees on radio or television, the broadcast must be recorded, and the practitioner must retain a copy of the recording for at least 36 months from the date of the last transmission or use.

Example: Gracie is an EA who publishes an advertisement in her local newspaper. The ad includes a published fee schedule for preparing certain tax return forms at deeply discounted rates. Gracie is inundated with calls and decides that the ad was a mistake. Regardless, she must adhere to the published fee schedule for at least 30 days after it was published.

Example: Travis is an EA who pays for a radio commercial about his services. It plays for four months during tax season. Travis is required to keep a copy of the radio commercial for at least 36 months from the last date that the commercial aired.

Negotiation of Taxpayer Refund Checks §10.31

A practitioner must not endorse or negotiate (cash) a refund check issued to the taxpayer. For example, a practitioner cannot use Form 8888, *Allocation of Refund (Including Savings Bond Purchases)*, to enter his own bank account in order to obtain payment for his tax preparation fee. Form 8888 instructions state that entering an account in someone else's name, such as a preparer's, will cause the direct deposit request to be rejected and the taxpayer to be sent a paper check instead. A preparer could also be subject to a penalty under IRC §6695(f).

In the latest Circular 230 revision, §10.31 clarifies that this provision applies to any practitioner, not just to one who prepares tax returns.

It also expands the scope of "endorse or otherwise negotiate any check" to state that negotiation of a taxpayer check includes accepting or directing payment by any method, including electronically or via direct deposit or wire transfer.

Example: Jeffrey is an enrolled agent with a new client who will receive a $500 refund on her tax return. The client has not yet paid Jeffrey's tax return preparation fee, so he enters his own bank account number, rather than his client's, on Form 8888. Jeffrey plans to take his $200 fee from the refund and give his client the remaining $300. However, this action is expressly forbidden, and Jeffrey could be subject to a preparer penalty for improper negotiation of a client's refund.

Other Duties and Prohibited Acts in Circular 230

No Delay Tactics Allowed §10.23: A practitioner must not unreasonably delay the prompt disposition of any matter before the IRS.

Example: Emory is an enrolled agent who is representing a client in an IRS examination. Emory has repeatedly rescheduled appointments with an IRS revenue agent in an attempt to delay proceedings. He has also delayed furnishing certain documents that the IRS has requested, and when he does provide them, the records are incomplete. Emory's actions are in violation of Circular 230.

No Employment of Disbarred or Suspended Persons §10.24: A practitioner may not knowingly employ a person or accept assistance from a person who has been disbarred or suspended from practice. This restriction applies even if the duties of the disbarred or suspended person would not include actual preparation of tax returns.

In addition, a practitioner may not accept assistance from a former government employee in matters in which the former employee personally and substantially participated in the particular matter while employed by the government.

Practice by Former Government Employees §10.25: A former government employee (and his partners and associates) cannot represent or knowingly assist a taxpayer if the representation would violate any law of the United States.

A government employee who personally and substantially participated in a particular matter cannot represent or assist a taxpayer in the same particular matter after leaving his government position. §10.25 also places other restrictions on former government employees, including former IRS workers, in order to avoid conflicts of interest during representation.

Performance as a Notary §10.26: A practitioner who is a notary public and is employed as counsel, attorney, or agent in a matter before the IRS or who has a material interest in the matter cannot engage in any notary activities related to that matter.

Signature Requirements for Tax Returns

Signature requirements for the preparation of tax returns are not spelled out in Circular 230, but instead are based on Treasury regulations. The requirements are as follows:

1. **Preparer Signature and PTIN:** A preparer is required by law to sign the tax return, include his PTIN, and fill out the preparer areas of the form. The preparer's declaration on signing the return states that the information contained in the return is true, correct, and complete based on all information he has. This statement is signed under penalties of perjury. The preparer must sign the return after it is completed but before it is presented to the taxpayer for signature. The preparer can sign original returns, amended returns, or requests for filing extensions by rubber stamp, mechanical device (such as a signature pen), or computer software program.
2. **Taxpayer Signature:** Regardless of whether a paid preparer or someone else has prepared a return, a taxpayer must sign his own return, affirming it is correct under penalties of perjury. A taxpayer is legally responsible for the accuracy of every item on the return. [150]
3. **More Than One Preparer:** If the original preparer is unavailable for signature, another preparer must review the entire preparation of the return or claim and then must manually sign it. For purposes of the signature requirement, the preparer with primary responsibility for the overall accuracy of the return or claim is considered the preparer, if more than one preparer is involved. The other preparers do not have to be disclosed on the return.

A preparer may sign on behalf of the taxpayer in the client's signature area only if certain standards are met (see Unit 3, under the section: *Representative Signing in Lieu of the Taxpayer*).

[150] Although the taxpayer is ultimately responsible for the items reported on the tax return, when a preparer e-files a taxpayer's return, the Form 8879 (IRS e-file Signature Authorization) must be completed by the preparer and signed by both the preparer and the taxpayer. The Form 8897 is signed under penalty of perjury by both parties.

Unit 4: Study Questions

1. If a practitioner knows that a client has filed an erroneous tax return, he is required to:

A. Correct the error.
B. Advise the client about the error and the consequences of not correcting the error.
C. Do nothing if he was not the one who prepared the erroneous return.
D. Inform the IRS about the error.

2. Which does not constitute a "best practice" for practitioners under Circular 230?

A. Consulting other professionals when questions arise about a particular tax issue.
B. Acting fairly and with integrity in practice before the IRS.
C. Communicating clearly with the client regarding the terms of the engagement.
D. Advising the client regarding the consequences of advice rendered.

3. Melanie is an EA who submits her clients' returns via IRS e-file. In order to save paper, she does not give a copy of the prepared tax return to her clients if they do not request it. Melanie allows her clients to have a copy of the return, so long as they pay a small fee. Which of the following statements is correct?

A. Melanie is not in violation of Circular 230.
B. Melanie is in violation of Circular 230.
C. Melanie is not in violation of Circular 230 if she gives clients the option of receiving a copy of their return for a small fee.
D. Melanie cannot offer a copy of the return to a client unless the client requests it.

4. Which of the following statements is correct regarding practitioners?

A. Practitioners cannot notarize documents of the clients they represent before the IRS.
B. Practitioners cannot be notaries.
C. Practitioners are required to be notaries.
D. A notary who is also a practitioner will not be eligible for the e-file program.

5. Which of the following statements is correct regarding a client's request for his original records in order to comply with his federal tax obligations?

A. The practitioner may choose not to return client records if there is a fee dispute.
B. A legal case relieves the practitioner of his responsibility to return a client's records.
C. The practitioner must, at the request of the client, promptly return a client's records, regardless of fee disputes.
D. The practitioner must, at the request of the client, return client records within one month of payment.

6. Dennis, an enrolled agent, wants to hire his friend, Brandon, who is also an enrolled agent. Brandon has been disbarred from practice by the IRS for misconduct. Brandon has appealed the disbarment, and it is currently under review. Which of the following statements is correct?

A. Dennis can still hire Brandon as a tax return preparer, provided Brandon does not represent any taxpayers.
B. Dennis can still hire Brandon, provided Brandon does not prepare or sign any tax returns.
C. Dennis cannot hire Brandon.
D. Dennis can hire Brandon while his appeal is pending.

7. How long must a practitioner retain records relating to clients who have provided their consent for representation in conflict-of-interest cases?

A. One year from the date representation ends.
B. Two years from the date representation ends.
C. Three years from the date representation ends.
D. Five years from the date representation ends.

8. If more than one tax return preparer is involved in preparing a return, who is required to sign?

A. All preparers involved in the preparation of the return.
B. Only the preparer with primary responsibility for the accuracy of the return; however, the other preparers must be disclosed on the return.
C. Only the preparer with primary responsibility for the accuracy of the return; the other preparers do not need to be disclosed on the return.
D. Only the taxpayer.

9. All of the following statements regarding a practitioner's responsibility to provide information requested by the IRS are correct except:

A. He must promptly turn over all records relating to the IRS request, no matter what the circumstances.
B. If the records are not in his possession, he must make a "reasonable inquiry" of his client about their whereabouts.
C. He is not legally obligated to contact any third party who might possess the requested records.
D. If he believes in good faith and on reasonable grounds that the requested material is legally privileged information, a practitioner may choose to decline a records request.

10. Sara, an enrolled agent, buys a practice owned by Mark, an EA who is retiring. As she reviews the records from Mark's practice, she learns he has been incorrectly claiming dependents for certain taxpayer clients. What should Sara do?

A. Notify the clients of the error and the consequences of not correcting the error.
B. Inform the clients that she will refuse to prepare their taxes if they do not file amended returns.
C. Contact the IRS to alert agents about the error and to request audits of those clients' prior year returns.
D. Inform Mark that he made mistakes on his clients' returns and advise him to notify them.

11. Whit is an EA who decides to advertise his fee schedule in the local newspaper. Which of the following fee arrangements is prohibited?

A. Hourly fee rates.
B. Fixed fees for tax preparation.
C. Contingent fees for original returns.
D. Flat fees for initial consultations.

12. Which of the following statements is correct?

A. Conflicts of interest apply only to attorneys and not to other tax professionals.
B. A practitioner may represent clients who have a conflict of interest under certain circumstances, but waivers to the conflict must be signed by both parties.
C. A practitioner may represent clients who have a conflict of interest if the practitioner receives a written confirmation of a waiver of the conflict of interest from the clients within 45 days of receiving any non-written, informed consent from the clients.
D. A practitioner may not represent clients who have a conflict of interest.

13. A new section in the revised Circular 230 relates to:

A. Covered opinions.
B. Due diligence.
C. Preparer penalties.
D. Competence.

14. Under IRC §6107, what is a tax return preparer required to keep for at least three years after the close of the return period?

A. A list of clients/tax returns prepared.
B. Copies of all tax returns prepared.
C. Both a list of clients/tax returns prepared and copies of all tax returns prepared.
D. Either A or B.

15. An employee of a tax accounting firm has spent hours constructing a spreadsheet used to determine a client's estimated tax payments. The client has yet to pay the firm for fees charged in connection with his tax return. Which of the following best describes the firm's responsibility regarding the client's request for a copy of the spreadsheet?

A. The firm is under no obligation to hand over the spreadsheet. It is also not required to give the client access to view or copy it.
B. The firm is required to hand over the spreadsheet.
C. The firm is not required to hand over the spreadsheet, but is required to allow the client access to view or copy it.
D. None of the above.

16. With the taxpayer's properly signed power of attorney, a practitioner may:

A. Receive a taxpayer's refund check, but not endorse or cash the check.
B. Receive and endorse a taxpayer's refund check and invest the proceeds in the taxpayer's own mutual fund.
C. Receive a taxpayer's refund check and endorse it, but only to pay tax preparation fees.
D. None of the above.

Unit 4: Answers

1. The answer is B. If a practitioner knows that a client has filed an erroneous tax return, he must advise the client to correct the error. The practitioner is not required to amend the return, but he must advise the client about the error and the consequences of not correcting the error. He is not required to notify the IRS about his client's error.

2. The answer is A. Although it may be a good idea to consult with other tax professionals when particular tax questions arise, this is not listed as one of the "best practices" in Circular 230.

3. The answer is B. Melanie is in violation of Circular 230. Tax return preparers must furnish copies of completed returns and claims for refund to all their clients. This must be done no later than when clients sign the original documents.

4. The answer is A. Practitioners cannot notarize documents of the clients they represent before the IRS. However, they are not prohibited from performing notary services for clients in connection with other financial or personal matters.

5. The answer is C. Client records must generally be returned promptly upon client demand, regardless of fee disputes. Client records are defined as any original records belonging to the client, including any work product that he has already paid for, such as a completed copy of a tax return. However, the practitioner is allowed to withhold the return of his own work papers or work product until the client has resolved any outstanding payment issues.

6. The answer is C. Dennis cannot knowingly hire a disbarred practitioner, regardless of whether that person would prepare tax returns. A practitioner may not knowingly employ a person or accept employment from a person who has been disbarred or suspended by the Office of Professional Responsibility, even if that person's case is under appeal.

7. The answer is C. In conflict of interest cases, a preparer must obtain a written consent signed by each party and retain the records for at least 36 months (three years) from the date representation ends.

8. The answer is C. Only the preparer with primary responsibility for the accuracy of the return is considered the preparer and is thus required to sign the return under penalties of perjury. The other preparers do not need to be disclosed on the return. The taxpayer is also required to sign the return, whether prepared by a preparer or not. The taxpayer is legally responsible for the accuracy of every item on his tax return.

9. The answer is A. Although Circular 230 dictates that a practitioner comply promptly with information and record requests, there are limited circumstances when records do not have to be turned over. A practitioner may decline to do so if he believes in good faith that the request is not legal or that the information is privileged. A practitioner also does not have to contact any third party to inquire about the records; he must simply make a reasonable inquiry of his client.

10. The answer is A. Under the rules of Circular 230, a practitioner has a duty to advise a client about issues of noncompliance, errors, or omissions, in addition to the consequences of the errors. However, the practitioner is not obligated to correct the error, inform the IRS of the error, or insist the client file an amended return. The duty to advise also applies when a practitioner discovers an error or omission in the course of tax consulting or an advisory engagement.

11. The answer is C. Circular 230 prohibits a practitioner from charging a contingent fee based on the refund amount for an original return. A practitioner may publish and advertise a fee schedule. All the other fee structures are acceptable (please note that the IRS currently lacks authority to regulate contingent fee arrangements for preparation of returns and refund claims due to the outcome of the Ridgely case in 2014, however, Circular 230 has not yet been updated to reflect this important court case).

12. The answer is B. Under certain circumstances, a practitioner can represent clients who have a conflict of interest. The practitioner must reasonably believe he will be able to provide competent and diligent representation to each affected client; the representation cannot be prohibited by law; and each affected client must be fully notified and sign a consent waiving the conflict of interest in writing. A practitioner must receive a written confirmation of a waiver of the conflict of interest from the clients within 30 days of receiving any non-written, informed consent from the clients.

13. The answer is D. The new Circular 230 §10.35 replaces the previous section detailing the covered opinion rules. It states that a practitioner must be competent to engage in practice before the IRS. "Competence" is defined as having the appropriate level of knowledge, skill, thoroughness, and preparation for the specific matter related to a client's engagement.

14. The answer is D. Under IRC §6107, a tax return preparer must keep copies of all returns he has prepared or a list of clients and tax returns prepared. The list must include the taxpayer's name, taxpayer identification number, tax year, and the type of tax return prepared. The copies or list must be kept for at least three years after the close of the return period.

15. The answer is A. The firm is under no obligation to hand over its own work product to a client who has not paid his fees. A tax return preparer is required only to return a client's original records. The client must also be given reasonable access to review and copy any additional records retained by the preparer that are necessary for the client to comply with his federal tax obligations. The spreadsheet is not necessary for the client to comply with his federal tax obligations.

16. The answer is A. With proper authorization, a practitioner may receive a refund check issued to the taxpayer. A practitioner is not allowed to negotiate taxpayer refunds under any circumstances, regardless of whether the client has given permission.

Unit 5: Practitioner Standards and Tax Advice

More Reading:
Circular 230, *Regulations Governing Practice Before the Internal Revenue Service*

Circular 230 outlines broad standards for practitioners when it comes to tax positions taken on income tax returns, as well as other forms of written advice they provide clients. Practitioners who fail to meet these standards are subject to penalties and other sanctions.

Requirements for Written Advice §10.37

§10.37 was extensively revised in the most recent version of Circular 230. It presents the due diligence requirements for practitioners to exercise when issuing written advice. The definition of "written advice" has been expanded to encompass almost anything in writing, including email, text, or any other type of electronic communication, on any federal tax matter.[151]

A practitioner must:

- Base the written advice on reasonable factual and legal assumptions.
- Consider all relevant facts and circumstances that he knows or reasonably should know.
- Use reasonable efforts to identify and ascertain the facts relevant to written advice on each federal tax matter.
- Not rely upon representations, statements, findings, or agreements of the taxpayer or any other person if reliance on them would be unreasonable.
- Relate applicable law and authority to facts.

In addition, when issuing written advice, a practitioner cannot take into consideration the chances that a tax return may or may not be audited, or that a particular matter may or may not be raised on audit.

Example: Knute is an enrolled agent. Knute's client, Veronica, asks him what the odds are that the IRS will audit certain deductions she wants to claim on her Schedule C. Knute responds that the IRS audits only about two percent of these types of tax returns, so the risk is worth taking, although the law is unsettled about whether the deductions are allowable. In the tax return he prepares, Knute includes the questionable deductions. Knute is playing "audit lottery," which is in violation of Circular 230. This type of practitioner advice is specifically prohibited by the IRS.

Similar to the provisions in §10.22, §10.37 has a paragraph that allows a practitioner to rely on the advice of another person, so long as the advice is reasonable and the reliance is in good faith. However, the section specifies that reliance is not reasonable when the practitioner knows or reasonably should know that:

- The opinion of the other person should not be relied on;
- The other person is not competent or lacks the necessary qualifications to provide the advice; or
- The other person has a conflict of interest in violation of the rules described in this part.

A "standard of review" paragraph was been added that establishes the basis by which the IRS will evaluate whether a practitioner has complied with the written advice rules of §10.37. It applies a "reasonable practitioner" standard, with all facts and circumstances to be taken into account. The scope of the engagement and the type and specificity of the advice sought by the client are also to be considered.

[151] There are two exceptions to what is considered written advice under §10.37: continuing education presentations on federal tax matters and government submissions on general policy are excluded.

Standards for Tax Returns and Documents (§10.34)

In addition to §10.37, Circular 230's §10.34 is vital to understanding a practitioner's responsibilities when it comes to providing written advice to a client.

The section directly ties back to IRC §6694, which describes tax return preparer penalties. §10.34 has four parts: positions taken on tax returns, positions taken on other documents or affidavits submitted to the IRS, advising clients on potential penalties, and relying on information furnished by clients.

Standards for Tax Returns: A practitioner may not willfully sign a tax return or claim for refund that he knows (or reasonably should know) contains a position that:

- Lacks a reasonable basis.
- Is an unreasonable position as described in IRC §6694(a)(2).[152]
- Is a willful attempt by the practitioner to understate the liability for tax or reflects a reckless or intentional disregard of rules or regulations.

In determining potential penalties, the IRS will take into account a pattern of conduct to assess whether a practitioner acted willfully, recklessly, or through gross incompetence.

Example: Itzel is an enrolled agent. She prepares a tax return for a self-employed client. A large deduction on the return did not have a reasonable basis and was not disclosed. Itzel can be liable for a substantial preparer penalty.

Tax Position Definitions
More Likely Than Not: There is a *greater than* 50% likelihood that the tax treatment will be upheld if the IRS challenges it. If a preparer is unsure that a position meets this standard, he may generally avoid penalties by disclosing the position on the return. However, a disclosure statement will not protect the preparer if the position is patently frivolous.[153] The "more likely than not" standard must be used for tax shelters and reportable transactions.
Reasonable Basis: This is the minimum standard for all tax advice and preparation of tax returns. The IRS defines it this way: "*Reasonable basis* is a relatively high standard of tax reporting that is significantly higher than not frivolous or not patently improper. The reasonable basis standard is not satisfied by a return position that is merely arguable". The precise likelihood that a reasonable basis position will be upheld on its merits is not defined in Circular 230. For purposes of avoiding §6694 penalties, the reasonable-basis standard applies only if the relevant tax position is disclosed on the return or document so that the IRS is aware of a potential issue.
Unreasonable Position: In general, this is an undisclosed position with no substantial authority.

Standards for Submission of Documents to the IRS: A practitioner may not advise a client to submit a document, affidavit, or other paper to the IRS:

- The purpose of which is to delay or impede the administration of the federal tax laws,
- That is frivolous, or
- That contains or omits information in a manner that demonstrates an intentional disregard of a rule or regulation, unless the practitioner also advises the client to submit a document that evidences a good faith challenge to the rule or regulation (such as a disclosure statement).

[152]Section 6694(a) imposes penalties on paid preparers who prepare returns reflecting an understatement of liability due to an unreasonable position if the preparer knew (or reasonably should have known) of the position. No penalty is imposed, however, if it is shown that there is reasonable cause for the understatement and the preparer acted in good faith.

[153] See Regulation 1.6694-2(a)(1) for more information.

A practitioner must not knowingly sign a frivolous return. A frivolous position is defined as one that the practitioner knows is in bad faith and is improper. A practitioner may sign a return with a tax position that meets at least one of two standards:

- The position is "more likely than not" to be sustained on its merits, or
- The position has a "reasonable basis."

Advising Clients on Potential Penalties

A practitioner is required to inform a client of any penalties that are reasonably likely to apply to a position taken on a tax return if:

- The practitioner advised the client with respect to the position, or
- The practitioner prepared or signed the tax return.

The practitioner also must inform the client of any opportunity to avoid penalties by disclosure of the position and of the requirements for adequate disclosure. This rule applies even if the practitioner is not subject to an IRC penalty related to the position, or to the document or tax return submitted.

Reliance on Information from Clients: When preparing income tax returns, a practitioner is not required to verify all the information furnished by his clients. In general, a practitioner:

- May rely in good faith without verification of information that a client provides.
- Should not ignore the implications of the information.
- Should make reasonable inquiries if the information appears to be incorrect, inconsistent, or incomplete.

Example: Jay is an EA who conducts an interview with his client, Barbara. She states she made a $50,000 charitable contribution of real estate during 2016. However, this is not true, and Jay fails to make reasonable inquiries to Barbara about the contribution. He does not ask about the existence of a qualified appraisal and he does not complete an IRS-required substantiation form. Jay includes the deduction for the charitable contribution on Barbara's tax return, which results in an understatement of tax liability. Barbara's return is later audited, and the charitable deduction is disallowed. Jay is in violation of §10.34 and would be subject to a preparer penalty for his negligence.

Example: Skye is an EA with a client who says he paid $100,000 of alimony during 2016. However, from his statement alone, Skye cannot know whether the $100,000 is indeed alimony. All or a portion of payments to a former spouse may be child support or family support, which are treated differently than alimony for federal tax purposes. It is Skye's responsibility to ask pertinent questions of her client in order to make the correct determination of whether or not the payment is actually alimony.

Disclosure Statements

Circular 230 §10.34 specifies the use of disclosure statements in certain instances. A tax return that requires a disclosure to the IRS must include Form 8275, *Disclosure Statement*, or Form 8275-R, *Regulation Disclosure Statement*.

Form 8275 is used by taxpayers and preparers to disclose items or positions on a tax return that are not otherwise adequately disclosed. It is primarily used to avoid accuracy-related penalties so long as the return position has a reasonable basis and the taxpayer (and preparer) acted in good faith in taking the position.

Form 8275 cannot be used to avoid the portion of the accuracy-related penalty attributable to certain types of misconduct, including the following:

- Negligence
- Disregard of regulations
- Any substantial understatement of income tax on a tax shelter item

A disclosure statement cannot be used by a preparer to avoid penalties if the position has no reasonable basis.

Form 8275 is normally used for most disclosure matters. Form 8275-R is only used in limited circumstances when a taxpayer takes a position that runs contrary to a specific Treasury regulation (or regulations).

Example: Amanda is an EA with a client who has a very complex tax situation. She notices that the IRS publications reflect one position, but there is a recent court case that may allow a more favorable position for her client. There are also two other similar cases being litigated, but the outcome of those cases is currently unknown. Amanda believes that the position has a 30% chance of prevailing on its merits. Amanda thinks that the client's position has a reasonable basis and decides to disclose the position on the tax return. Even though the position is contrary to the IRS's current position, Amanda may take the position on the return, so long as it is disclosed. She must file Form 8275 along with the tax return stating the position and referencing the court case or any other basis she has for the position.

Reporting Requirements for Tax Shelter Activities

There are certain types of tax shelter activities that must be reported to the IRS. A *reportable transaction*, also called a *listed transaction*, is one that the IRS has determined has the potential for tax avoidance or evasion.

The rules for reportable transactions apply to all individuals and entities (including trusts, estates, partnerships, and corporations). Form 8886, *Reportable Transaction Disclosure Statement*, must be attached to a taxpayer's return for any year that he participates in this type of tax shelter. A separate statement must be filed for each reportable transaction.

The fact that a tax shelter transaction must be reported on this form does not necessarily mean the IRS will disallow its tax benefits. If a reportable transaction is not disclosed and results in an understatement of tax, an additional penalty equal to 30% of the understatement may be assessed.

A taxpayer may request a ruling from the IRS to determine whether a transaction must be disclosed. In addition to the 30% understatement of tax penalty, a civil penalty of 75% of the reduction of tax associated with the reportable transaction may be imposed, with a minimum penalty of $10,000 ($5,000 if the taxpayer is an individual) and a maximum penalty as high as $200,000 ($100,000 if the taxpayer is an individual), pursuant to IRC section 6707A(b).[154]

Note about Covered Opinions

One of the most significant changes in the latest revision to Circular 230 was the elimination of the complex "covered opinion" rules in §10.35.[155] These rules had led practitioners to use blanket disclaimer statements on almost every piece of written communication, including emails. With the deletion of the covered opinion requirements, the IRS requests practitioners remove all such disclaimers that state they are required by the IRS, OPR, or Circular 230.

[154] In previous years, Form 8271, *Investor Reporting of Tax Shelter Registration Number*, was a required form. Before the enactment of the AJCA (the American Jobs Creation Act of 2004), section 6111 provided that tax shelter organizers were required to provide investors in tax shelters the registration number for the tax shelter. Form 8271 is no longer required. Because only a few investors must still file Form 8271 (for pre-AJCA section 6111 tax shelters) and because the IRS already is aware of these transactions, the Treasury Department has decided that investors are no longer required to file Forms 8271. The Form 8271 will be obsoleted. However, these final regulations continue to require that material advisors must provide the reportable transaction number to all taxpayers and material advisors. See Internal Revenue Bulletin: 2007-38

[155] Now replaced by the general "competence" standard.

Firm Compliance Procedures §10.36

§10.36 has been rewritten to address the measures a firm must take to ensure compliance with all provisions of Circular 230. A practitioner (or practitioners, if the duty is shared) who oversees a firm's practice must ensure adequate procedures are in place for every member, associate, or employee to comply with the requirements specified in Circular 230.

If a firm has not identified an individual with principal authority over the practice, the IRS may identify one or more practitioners who will be considered responsible for the §10.36 compliance requirements.

A practitioner who does not take reasonable steps to ensure the firm has adequate procedures in place to comply with Circular 230 requirements may face disciplinary action. He may also be subject to sanctions if he knows of other members of the firm who are engaging in a pattern of noncompliance, and he fails to take prompt action to correct the noncompliance.

Example: Erica is an enrolled agent working for a tax practice. Erica knows that her coworker is filing fraudulent EITC claims, but does nothing. Erica can be subject to sanctions, because she knew that other members of the firm were committing EITC fraud, and she did not report the illegal activity.

Unit 5: Study Questions

1. In the new "standard of review" section of Circular 230, the IRS will evaluate whether a practitioner has complied with the written advice rules of §10.37 by applying a _______________ standard:

A. "More likely than not"
B. "Substantial authority"
C. "Reasonable person"
D. "Reasonable practitioner"

2. Glen is a CPA who prepares income tax returns for his clients. One of his clients submits a list of expenses to be claimed on Schedule C of the return. Glen is required to do which one of the following?

A. Glen is required to independently verify the client's information.
B. Glen can ignore the implications of information known by him.
C. Glen does not have to make inquiry if the information appears to be incorrect or incomplete.
D. Glen must make appropriate inquiries to determine whether the client has substantiation for his Schedule C expenses.

3. When should a practitioner not rely on the advice of another person?

A. When the advice is reasonable and the reliance is in good faith.
B. When the person is competent in providing the advice.
C. When the person has a conflict of interest in the tax matter.
D. When the practitioner has a professional relationship with the other person.

4. Under Circular 230, what is the responsibility of a practitioner who oversees a firm's tax practice?

A. To ensure the firm has adequate procedures in place to ensure compliance with all provisions of Circular 230.
B. To appoint another practitioner in the firm to monitor compliance of other employees.
C. To review the personal tax filings of all employees of the firm to make sure they comply with Circular 230.
D. All of the above.

5. A practitioner is required to inform a client of penalties that are reasonably likely to apply to a position taken on a tax return if:

A. The taxpayer decides to self-prepare a return.
B. The practitioner gave the client professional advice on the position.
C. The IRS has the taxpayer under examination.
D. The taxpayer is deceased.

6. Ryan is an EA with a client named Hannah who has had significant income from a partnership for the past five years. However, Ryan did not see a Schedule K-1 from the partnership among the information Hannah provided to him this year. What do Circular 230 due diligence provisions require Ryan to do?

A. Attempt to estimate the amount that would be reported as income on the Schedule K-1 based on last year's Schedule K-1 and include that amount on Hannah's return.
B. Call Hannah's financial advisor and ask him about Hannah's investments.
C. Nothing, because Ryan is required to rely only on the information provided by his client, even if he has reason to believe the information may not be accurate.
D. Ask Hannah why she did not provide him with the partnership's Schedule K-1, as she had in previous years.

7. All of the following statements are correct about the new §10.37 of Circular 230 on written advice except:

A. An email to a client about a federal tax matter would be included in the definition of written advice.
B. A practitioner should advise a client of the chances his tax return will be chosen for audit.
C. A practitioner should base his written advice on reasonable factual and legal assumptions.
D. A practitioner should relate the applicable law and authority to the facts relevant to written advice issued on a federal tax matter.

8. A practitioner cannot sign:

A. A tax return for a family member.
B. A tax return that he prepares for free.
C. A tax return with a properly disclosed tax shelter position.
D. A frivolous tax return with a disclosure.

9. Bethany is an EA with a client, Dylan, who wishes to claim a deduction for a large business expense. However, there is a question about whether the expense is "ordinary and necessary" for his business. If the deduction were disallowed, there would be a substantial understatement of tax (over 10%). Bethany researches the issue and tells Dylan that the position should be disclosed. Dylan does not want to disclose the position on the return, because he is afraid that the IRS will disallow it. What are the repercussions for Bethany?

A. None. All the penalties apply to the client.
B. Bethany may be liable for preparer penalties.
C. Bethany will not be liable for preparer penalties so long as she explains the potential penalties to the client.
D. None of the above.

10. Which type of transaction must always be reported to the IRS?

A. Listed transaction.
B. Reliance opinion.
C. A loss from a Ponzi scheme.
D. A position with a more likely than not chance of being upheld.

Unit 5: Answers

1. The answer is D. In the most recent revision of Circular 230, a new "standard of review" paragraph was added that establishes the basis that the IRS will use to evaluate whether a practitioner has complied with the written advice rules of §10.37. It applies a "reasonable practitioner" standard, with all facts and circumstances taken into account. The scope of the engagement and the type and specificity of the advice sought by the client will also be considered.

2. The answer is D. A practitioner is not required to independently examine evidence of deductions. He may rely in good faith, without verification, upon information furnished by the taxpayer if it does not appear to be incorrect or incomplete. However, the practitioner must make reasonable inquiries about the validity of the information.

3. The answer is C. The revised §10.37 details the newest standards for written tax advice. Similar to the provisions in §10.22, §10.37 says a practitioner may rely on the advice of another person, so long as the advice is reasonable and the reliance is in good faith. However, reliance is not reasonable when the practitioner knows, or reasonably should know, that:

- The opinion of the other person should not be relied on,
- The other person is not competent, or lacks the necessary qualifications to provide the advice, or
- The other person has a conflict of interest in violation of the rules.

4. The answer is A. Under §10.36, a practitioner (or practitioners, if the duty is shared) who oversees a firm's practice must ensure adequate procedures are in place for every member, associate, or employee to comply with the requirements specified in Circular 230. A practitioner(s) who does not take reasonable steps to ensure the firm has adequate procedures in place may face disciplinary action or sanctions if he knows of other members of the firm who are engaging in a pattern of noncompliance, and he fails to take prompt action to correct the noncompliance.

5. The answer is B. A practitioner is required to inform a client of any penalties that are reasonably likely to apply to a position taken on a tax return if:

- The practitioner advised the client with respect to the position, or
- The practitioner prepared or signed the tax return.

6. The answer is D. Ryan must ask Hannah about the missing Schedule K-1 and ask pertinent questions to understand the facts of the situation. A practitioner who has reason to believe his client has not complied with the revenue laws or has made an error in or omission from any return, document, affidavit, or other required paper has the responsibility to advise the client promptly of the noncompliance, error, or omission.

7. The answer is B. §10.37 has been expanded to define written advice as almost anything in writing, including electronic communications, on any federal tax matter. When issuing written advice, a practitioner is expressly prohibited from taking into consideration the chances that a tax return may or may not be audited, or that a particular matter may or may not be raised on audit. A practitioner must:

- Base the written advice on reasonable factual and legal assumptions.
- Consider all relevant facts and circumstances that he knows or reasonably should know.
- Use reasonable efforts to identify and ascertain the facts relevant to written advice on each federal tax matter.

- Not rely upon representations, statements, findings, or agreements of the taxpayer or any other person if reliance on them would be unreasonable.
- Relate applicable law and authority to facts.

8. The answer is D. A tax return preparer cannot sign a frivolous tax return, even if the return has a disclosure. A frivolous position is defined as one that the preparer knows is in bad faith or is improper.

9. The answer is B. If the return does not adequately disclose the position and it is later examined by the IRS, Bethany may be subject to a preparer penalty. The disclosure form is filed to avoid the potential for penalties due to disregard of rules regarding the substantial understatement of income tax.

10. The answer is A. A listed transaction, also called a reportable transaction, is a type of tax shelter activity that must be reported to the IRS. Form 8886, *Reportable Transaction Disclosure Statement*, must be attached to a taxpayer's return for any year he participates in this type of tax shelter.

Unit 6: Due Diligence for Refundable Credits

More Reading:
www.eitc.irs.gov
Publication 596, *Earned Income Credit*
Publication 4687, *Refundable Credits Due Diligence*
Publication 3524, EITC Eligibility Checklist

Each year, tax preparers complete more than half of the tax returns claiming the Child Tax Credit (CTC), Additional Child Tax Credit (ACTC), Earned Income Credit (EITC) and/or the American Opportunity Tax Credit (AOTC). The IRS estimates that one in four of these claims are incorrect, which results in billions of dollars paid out in erroneous refunds each year.

The IRS recently updated their due diligence requirements to include the Child Tax Credit as well as the American Opportunity Credit. Starting with the 2016 tax year, the due diligence rules for these credits are more stringent than they were in previous years. This is because both the number of individuals claiming these refundable credits and the number of erroneous claims is high. Paid preparers must meet four additional due diligence requirements on returns with these claims or face possible penalties. Employers may also be penalized for an employee's failure to exercise due diligence.

New Knowledge Requirement for EITC, CTC/ACTC, and AOTC Returns

IRS regulations specify these due diligence requirements and set a performance standard for the *knowledge requirement:* what a reasonable and well-informed tax return preparer, knowledgeable in the law, would do.

Under the "knowledge requirement," a preparer must:

- Apply a common sense standard to the information provided by the client.
- Evaluate whether the information is complete and gather any missing facts.
- Determine if the information is consistent; recognize contradictory statements and statements the preparer knows are not true.
- Conduct a thorough, in-depth interview with every client, every year.
- Ask enough questions to reasonably know the return is correct and complete.
- Document in the file any questions he asked and his client's responses.

Example: Timothy is an enrolled agent. He has a new client named Karla. She is 18 years old with an infant son, named Joshua. Karla has a Form W-2 that shows $4,000 in wages and no other income. Karla states she and Joshua live with her parents. She wants to claim the infant as a qualifying child for the EITC and the Child Tax Credit. Timothy asks several probing questions. Karla admits that she does not pay rent and only used her wages to pay for her cellphone and some clothing. Timothy determines that Karla does not provide the majority of her own support—her parents are supporting her and her infant son. Since Karla is the qualifying child of her parents, she is not eligible to claim the EITC or the CTC.

Example: Esther is an EA. A new 28-year-old client, Charlie, wants to claim two sons, ages 14 and 15, as qualifying children for the EITC. Esther is concerned about the age of the children, since Charlie's age seems inconsistent with the ages of the children. Esther asks additional questions and discovers the boys are both adopted, which explains the age inconsistency. She completes the EITC Worksheet and Form 8867, and submits Form 8867 to the IRS. She retains copies of these records, as well as the adoption records that Charlie provides her and notes of her client interview, for a period of three years. Esther has complied with her due diligence requirements.

Example: Alonso is an EA. His client, Saskia, states that she is separated from her spouse. Her dependent son is 12 years old and lives with her. Saskia wants to claim the EITC and file as head of household. In reviewing his client's records, Alonso notes that Saskia earns a minimal income, which appears insufficient to support a household. As the preparer, Alonso must ask appropriate questions to determine Saskia's correct filing status, determine how long the child lived with each parent during the year, and probe for any additional sources of income. He must interview her thoroughly and document her answers. He must also fill out Form 8867, *Paid Preparer's Earned Income Credit Checklist*, and complete the EITC worksheet. After asking various questions, Saskia discloses that she receives substantial child support, which is not taxable or reportable on the return. She also receives food stamps and other public benefits, which also help support her son. Food stamps are also not taxable. Alonso notes this information in his work papers and is now more confident that he can prepare Saskia's return accurately.

Preparer Compliance Requirements

There are four mandatory "requirements" with regards to compliance. These have been updated to reflect the new tax law changes that came into effect in 2016. For the EA exam, you should memorize these four compliance requirements. It is possible that you will be asked several questions about this topic.

- **Requirement 1:** Completion and submission of Form 8867, *Paid Preparer's Due Diligence Checklist*
- **Requirement 2:** Completion of worksheet(s) and computation of the credit(s)
- **Requirement 3:** Knowledge
- **Requirement 4:** Record retention

The new due diligence requirements for preparers related are explained as follows:

1. **Complete and Submit Form 8867:** The preparer must complete Form 8867, *Paid Preparer's Due Diligence Checklist,* and submit this completed form to the IRS with every return with a EITC, CTC or AOTC. At the time of the interview, the preparer must document in their files the questions asked and the client's answers.
2. **Complete the worksheets and compute the Credit:** Most tax preparation software will compute these credits automatically on worksheets within the actual software program, but the IRS emphasizes that using software is not a substitute for knowledge of the law.
3. **Knowledge:** A preparer must not know (or have reason to know) that the information used to determine eligibility or to compute the amount of the credit is incorrect. A preparer must ask his client additional questions if the information furnished seems incorrect or incomplete.
4. **Retain Records:** A preparer must retain the following records for each claim:
    a. Form 8867, *Paid Preparer's Due Diligence Checklist*
    b. The applicable worksheet(s) for EITC, CTC/ACTC and AOTC claimed on the return
    c. Any documents or other written proof relied on to complete the Form 8867 or to determine eligibility
    d. A record of how, when, and from whom the information the preparer obtained to prepare the tax return as well as a record of any additional questions the preparer asked to determine eligibility for and the amount of the credits and the client's answers.
    e. All records should be kept for three years from the *latest* of:
        - The due date of the tax return.
        - The date the tax return was electronically filed.

- For a paper return, the date the return was presented to the client for signature.
- The date you gave the part of the return for which you are responsible to the signing tax return preparer, (if you are a non-signing tax return preparer).

f. The records must be retained in either paper or electronic format, and they must be produced on-demand if the IRS asks for them.

Form 8867 Documentation Requirements

Form 8867 includes several mandatory questions that preparers must ask taxpayers in order to comply with due diligence requirements.

Form 8867 is also used by a preparer to identify the documents that the taxpayer provided and that the preparer used to determine credit eligibility. In determining the residency of qualifying children, a preparer must specify whether he relied upon documents such as school, medical, or social service records. In determining the disability of a qualifying child, a preparer must indicate whether he relied upon documents such as a statement from a doctor, other health care provider, or social services agency.

Example: Judd is an EA. His new client, Fatima, 62, wants to take a dependency exemption for her son, Hamish, who is 32. She also wants to claim the Earned Income Tax Credit and the Dependent Care Credit for her son. Since Hamish is beyond the normal age limit for these credits, Judd makes reasonable inquiries and Fatima produces a doctor's statement that says Hamish is severely disabled and incapable of self-care. Therefore, Fatima may claim her son as a dependent, and the credits will be allowed regardless of Hamish's age. Judd has fulfilled his due diligence requirements by conducting a thorough interview with his client, asking enough questions to understand an individual tax situation, documenting the answers, and seeking appropriate supporting evidence. He completes his due diligence requirements by submitting Form 8867 to the IRS.

If Schedule C is included with the tax return, the preparer must specify whether he determined credit eligibility by relying upon any documents the taxpayer provided in connection with the business. These documents may include a business license, Forms 1099, records of gross receipts and expenses, or bank statements.

Example: Caleb is an EA. Mai is a new client who wants to claim the EITC as well as the AOTC. She has two qualifying children who both attend a local community college. Mai tells Caleb she had a Schedule C business and earned $12,500 in income, but had no expenses. This information appears incomplete because it would be unusual that someone who is self-employed has no business expenses. Caleb is required to ask reasonable questions to determine if the business exists and if the information about Mai's income and expenses is correct. Caleb must submit Form 8867 to the IRS and keep copies of any documents Mai provides for at least three years.

Common Errors on Refund Claims

There are certain types of errors that the IRS sees commonly on refund claims. Errors can delay the taxpayer's refund or can lead to a rejection of the credits listed on the return.

Note: Preparers are not always required to ask for documents to prove the relationship and residency of a qualifying child before completing a claim for a refundable credit, although a paid preparer may request those documents if the information provided by the client appears to be incorrect, inconsistent, or incomplete.

Most Common EITC Errors:

The three issues that account for most EITC errors are:

- Claiming EITC for a child who does not meet the qualifying child requirements
- Filing as single or head of household when married.
- Incorrectly reporting institution income or expenses.

A common method of EITC fraud is the "borrowing" of dependents. Unscrupulous tax preparers will "share" one taxpayer's qualifying child or children with another taxpayer in order to allow both to claim the EITC.

Any taxpayer who is claiming the EITC must have a Social Security number that is valid for employment purposes. Any qualifying child who is listed on an EITC return must also have a valid SSN (an ITIN or ATIN is not sufficient).

Example: Reggie has four children, but he only needs the first three children to receive the maximum EITC amount. The preparer lists the first three children on Reggie's return and lists the other child on another return. The preparer and Reggie are "selling" the dependents and will then split a fee or split the refund. This is an example of tax fraud that involves both the preparer and the taxpayer.

Most Common AOTC Errors

- **Claiming AOTC for a student who didn't attend an eligible educational institution.** The AOTC is for post-secondary education only, which may include education at a college, university or technical school. The AOTC cannot be claimed by graduate students.
- **Claiming AOTC for a student who didn't pay qualifying college expenses.** Educational expenses must be paid or considered paid by the client, the client's spouse or the dependent student claimed on the tax return.
- **Claiming AOTC for a student for too many years.** The AOTC is only available for the first four years of post-secondary education and your client can only claim it for four tax years per eligible student. This limitation includes any past years that the client may have claimed the Hope Credit.

Example: Penelope is an enrolled agent. In 2016, she interviews Patrick, a 26-year-old client who states that he's a full-time college student and would like to claim the AOTC. He provides a Form 1098-T, Tuition Statement, showing $6,000 paid for tuition at a qualifying institution. The Form 1098-T is a good indicator that Patrick is eligible for the AOTC but Penelope must ask more questions to determine eligibility. Patrick states that he does not have a bachelor's degree yet, because he switched majors last year. He has been an undergraduate student for five years. Since a taxpayer can only claim the AOTC for four tax years, this means that Patrick is ineligible to take the American Opportunity Credit on his 2016 return. He may still be eligible for the Lifetime Learning Credit.

The Most Common Child Tax Credit Errors

- **Claiming a child who does not meet the age requirement:** The child must be under the age of 17 at the end of the tax year. There are no exceptions to this rule.
- **Claiming a child who does not meet dependency requirements:** The child must be claimed as a dependent on your client's return and meet all the eligibility rules for a dependent.
- **Claiming the credit for a child who does not meet the residency requirement:** The child must be a U.S. citizen, U.S. national or a U.S. resident alien and the child must have lived with your client for more than half the year.

- **Children with an ITIN:** If the qualifying child uses an ITIN, *Individual Taxpayer Identification Number,* the child must meet the substantial presence test to qualify.

Since tax professionals prepare more than half of all returns claiming refundable credits, the quality of their work has a significant impact on reducing erroneous claims. Preparers who file high percentages of questionable claims or returns with a high risk of error may be subject to on-site audits. IRS agents will review preparer records to verify due diligence compliance, including whether they are meeting the knowledge requirement. Penalties may be assessed when noncompliance is identified.

In the previous year, the IRS sent more than 7,000 letters to preparers suspected of filing questionable refund claims. The letters detailed the critical issues identified on the returns and explained the consequences of filing inaccurate claims. The IRS warned these preparers that their future refund claims would be monitored closely and that their clients' returns may be audited.

The IRS says many of the claims were prepared using "do-it-yourself" tax software rather than professional tax software that requires Form 8867 to be submitted along with each applicable refund claim.

Penalties for Failure to Exercise Due Diligence

The penalties for preparers failing to exercise due diligence with refund claims can be severe. Taxpayers also face consequences for not complying with the due diligence rules. If the IRS examines a taxpayer's return and disallows all or part of an EITC, AOTC, or CTC/ACTC claim on a return, the taxpayer:

- Must pay back the amount in error with interest,
- May need to file Form 8862, *Information to Claim Earned Income Credit after Disallowance*, for the Earned Income Tax Credit[156]
- Cannot claim the credit for the next two years if the IRS determines the error is because of reckless or intentional disregard of the rules, or
- Cannot claim the credits for the next ten years if the IRS determines the error is because of fraud.

Further, if the IRS examines a taxpayer's claim and it is determined that the preparer did not meet all four due diligence requirements, he can be subject to penalties even beyond the usual penalty for each failure to comply.

If a preparer receives a return-related penalty, he may also face:

- Disciplinary action by the OPR
- Suspension or expulsion from IRS e-file
- Injunctions barring him from preparing tax returns

The IRS has streamlined procedures for faster referrals to the U.S. Department of Justice to try to prevent preparers from making fraudulent refund claims. These preparers could be permanently or temporarily barred from all types of federal tax preparation.

Note: In 2016, preparers face a penalty of $510[157] for each failure to comply with due diligence requirements. This penalty applies *per credit.* For example, if IRS finds a tax practitioner who has prepared 25 returns that fail to meet the EITC due diligence requirements, the penalty for tax year 2016 is $12,750. If those same returns also failed to meet the AOTC due diligence requirements, the penalty is increased to $38,250. There is no maximum dollar penalty amount.

[156] At the time of this book's printing, Form 8862 had not yet been updated to include reinstatements of the AOTC or CTC after disallowance. Since this is the first year that the 2-year and 10-year bans can apply to credits other than the EITC, the IRS will probably come out with either a modified 8862 or new forms at a later date.

[157] This penalty is now adjusted yearly for inflation.

Unit 6: Study Questions

1. Austin is an enrolled agent who submits a return for his client. The return claims the Earned Income Tax Credit, but Austin fails to submit Form 8867 for the return. What penalty does Austin potentially face?

A. None. Austin must keep a copy of each Form 8867, but the forms are not required to be submitted to the IRS.
B. $400
C. $510
D. $1,000

2. A client tells a tax return preparer:

- She has no Form 1099.
- She was self-employed cleaning houses.
- She earned $12,000.
- She had no expenses related to the cleaning business.
- She has three children who live with her, all three are under the age of 3.

The client says she would like to claim the Earned Income Tax Credit. What is the best course of action for the preparer in this case?

A. Refuse to prepare the return based on the client's information.
B. Ask probing questions to determine the correct facts and ask for proof of income or any expenses.
C. Accept the taxpayer's word so long as she fills out a legal liability release form.
D. Make the client swear to the truthfulness of her statements before an IRS officer.

3. All of the following are potential penalties for a preparer who files fraudulent refund claims *except*:

A. Suspension or expulsion from IRS e-file.
B. Criminal prosecution by the OPR.
C. A ban from preparing tax returns.
D. A preparer penalty.

4. When must a tax return preparer complete a client checklist for a client claiming the AOTC?

A. Every year.
B. For the first year preparing a return for a new client.
C. Every other year.
D. The client checklist is recommended, but is not required.

5. All of the following are due diligence requirements except:

A. To evaluate the information received from the client.
B. To apply a consistency and reasonableness standard to the information.
C. To verify the taxpayer's information with the appropriate third parties.
D. To make additional reasonable inquiries when the information appears to be incorrect, inconsistent, or incomplete.

6. The IRS can impose the following ban related to the AOTC, EITC, and/or CTC:

A. Ten-year ban for fraud.
B. Two-year ban for fraud.
C. Permanent ban for fraud.
D. The IRS cannot ban a taxpayer from claiming credits on future returns if the taxpayer otherwise qualifies for them.

7. Mack and Judy have valid ITINs. They have two children, both of whom have valid SSNs. Assuming they meet the income requirements, can Mack and Judy claim the EITC in 2016?

A. They can claim the EITC for themselves and their children.
B. They can claim the EITC for their children, but not for themselves.
C. They cannot claim the EITC, regardless of whether their children have valid SSNs.
D. Their children can claim the EITC, but only if they file separate returns.

8. All of the following are common errors taxpayers make in claiming the EITC except:

A. Incorrectly reporting income or expenses.
B. Incorrectly claiming a child who does not meet the specific EITC requirements.
C. Filing as head of household when married.
D. Listing earned income for the year.

9. Which of the following is not one of requirements for AOTC claims?

A. Reviewing the client's Social Security Card.
B. Making sure the client has qualifying educational expenses.
C. Completing and submitting the Form 8867.
D. Following the knowledge requirement.

10. All of the following are common errors taxpayers make in claiming the Child Tax Credit or Additional Child Tax Credit except:

A. Claiming the CTC/ACTC for a child who does not meet the age requirement.
B. Claiming the CTC/ACTC for a child who does not meet the dependency requirements.
C. Claiming the CTC/ACTC for a child who does not meet the educational requirements.
D. Claiming the CTC/ACTC for a child who does not meet the residency requirement.

Unit 6: Answers

1. The answer is C. Form 8867, *Paid Preparer's Earned Income Credit Checklist*, must be submitted for each client's return that claims the Earned Income Tax Credit, or the preparer will be in violation of his due diligence requirements. For tax year 2016, each failure can result in a penalty of $510. This penalty will remain at $510 for 2017.

2. The answer is B. The best course of action would be to ask probing questions and ask for proof of income and expenses. The tax return preparer must document the client's answers as part of his due diligence requirements. During the interview, a preparer must ask additional questions if the information appears incorrect, inconsistent, or incomplete.

3. The answer is B. The OPR may take disciplinary action against tax return preparers who violate rules related to fraudulent claims. However, the OPR never prosecutes criminal cases. Criminal cases are referred out to the proper authorities (the U.S. Justice Department).

4. The answer is A. For any client claiming the AOTC, a preparer must complete Form 8867 every year, even if the client is an existing client who has claimed the credit in the past. The preparer is required to keep a copy of the form in his records for at least three years.

5. The answer is C. A tax return preparer is not required to verify a taxpayer's answers with third parties. Due diligence requires a preparer to:

- Evaluate the information received from the client,
- Apply a consistency and reasonableness standard to the information,
- Make additional reasonable inquiries when the information appears to be incorrect, inconsistent, or incomplete, and
- Document additional inquiries and the client's response.

6. The answer is A. The IRS can impose the following types of bans related to refund claims of the AOTC, EITC, or CTC:

- Two-year ban for reckless or intentional disregard of due diligence rules, or
- Ten-year ban for fraud.

7. The answer is C. If a primary taxpayer, the spouse, or both have ITINs, they are ineligible to claim the Earned Income Tax Credit, even if their dependents have valid SSNs. A taxpayer (and his or her spouse, if married) must have valid Social Security numbers in order to claim the EITC. Qualifying children also must have valid SSNs.

8. The answer is D. To qualify for the EITC, a taxpayer must have earned income during the tax period. Assuming it is reported correctly, listing earned income is not an error made in claiming the EITC. The IRS cites the other three errors as common issues it sees with EITC claims.

9. The answer is A. Reviewing a client's Social Security cards is not a requirement but is a best practice, and recommended by the IRS (but not mandatory). If you do review a Social Security card, make sure you keep a copy of the card for your records.

10. The answer is C. The Child Tax Credit does not have an "educational" requirement. The IRS cites the other three errors as common issues with CTC/AOTC claims. For more information on this subject, see detailed instructions in Publication 4687, *Refundable Credits Due Diligence.*

Unit 7: Recordkeeping and Penalties

More Reading:
Publication 583, *Starting a Business and Keeping Records*
Publication 535, *Business Expenses*
Publication 552, *Recordkeeping for Individuals*
Publication 947, *Practice Before the IRS and Power of Attorney*

There are basic recordkeeping requirements for U.S. taxpayers that tax professionals need to be familiar with and make sure their clients understand. Recordkeeping requirements may be tested on all three parts of the EA exam, with Part 3 focusing primarily on substantiation and record retention for preparers.

Records that clearly demonstrate income, expenses, and basis should be retained, but tax law generally does not require that specific types of records be kept. Taxpayers may scan records and retain them electronically, as the IRS does not require a taxpayer to keep original paper records. A taxpayer must be able to store, preserve, retrieve, and reproduce electronic records when needed.

Supporting Documents

As an essential part of due diligence, it is a preparer's responsibility to request appropriate documentation from clients in order to prepare an accurate tax return. A preparer should review prior year tax returns to identify relevant issues, such as items that need to be carried forward to the current year and tax years going forward.

In addition, depending on the type of tax return being prepared, a preparer may need to see the following types of supporting documentation:

- **Financial documents:** Canceled checks, bank statements, credit card statements, receipts, brokerage records.
- **Legal documents:** Birth certificates, divorce decrees, lawsuit settlements.
- **Business entity supporting documents:** Partnership agreement, corporate bylaws, corporate minutes.
- **Expense records:** Mileage logs; receipts for business expenses such as travel, meals, entertainment, and lodging; and receipts and written acknowledgements from charitable organizations, particularly for non-cash contributions and expenses of $250 or more.

For a taxpayer to deduct travel, entertainment, gift, transportation, charitable, employee, and other expenses, he must be able to substantiate those expenses. A taxpayer cannot deduct amounts that are estimates.

A written record, including one prepared on a computer, generally is required to be considered adequate.

Example: A teacher tells her tax return preparer she had $23,000 in unreimbursed employee business expenses during the tax year. She provides no documentation, and her preparer does not ask to see any receipts. The IRS audits her return and disallows the expenses, which include an improper deduction for an $8,000 Mediterranean cruise. The preparer's failure to request receipts from his client shows a lack of due diligence.

Example: A taxpayer claims numerous deductions for her volunteer work in caring for feral cats. The U.S. Tax Court disallows expenses that were $250 or more because she failed to meet the substantiation requirement that required acknowledgement from the charitable organization. The taxpayer did not receive a contemporaneous, written acknowledgement from the organization, so her deduction was disallowed, even though she had proof of her expenses.

Business expenses claimed on a taxpayer's Schedule C must be both "ordinary and necessary." An ordinary expense is one that is common in the taxpayer's particular trade or business. A necessary expense is one that is helpful and appropriate in the taxpayer's trade or business, but it does not have to be indispensable in order for it to be deductible.

A taxpayer generally cannot deduct personal, family, or living expenses. If an expense is used partly for business and partly for personal purposes, only the business portion is deductible.

Example: Erin is a self-employed landscape architect who uses her van to visit clients and meet with suppliers and other subcontractors. She and her family also use the van for personal purposes. Erin keeps a mileage log that shows the business purpose, her business destination, and the date of each use of the car. Her records are adequate to substantiate that 75% of the car's use is for business purposes and 25% is for personal purposes, so she may deduct 75% of her auto expenses on her Schedule C.

Statute of Limitations for Records Retention

A taxpayer should keep all relevant records as long as they may be needed for the administration of any provision of the Internal Revenue Code. As a practical matter, this means a taxpayer must retain relevant records until the statute of limitations for each tax return expires. The responsibility to prove entries, deductions, and statements made on a taxpayer's tax return is known as the burden of proof. The taxpayers must meet their burden of proof by having the information and receipts for the expenses and deductions taken on the return.

For assessment of tax owed, this period is generally three years from the date a return was due or is filed, whichever is later.

For filing a claim for credit or refund, the period to make the claim is generally three years from the date the return was filed, or two years from the date the tax was paid, whichever is later.

If the return was filed prior to the original due date, the three-year statute of limitations starts as of the original due date of the return. If the return was filed on extension, the three-year period starts when the return was received by the IRS.

Example: Tatiana is a delinquent filer. In January 2017, she meets with a tax preparer who files her delinquent tax returns, 2011 through 2015. She is owed a refund for each year. However, she will receive refunds only for tax years 2013 through 2015, because they are the years still open under the three-year time statute. The claim for refund was due on April 15, 2015, for the 2011 return, and on April 15, 2016, for the 2012 return, so both of those refunds are now outside the statute of limitations. Tatiana will not receive refunds for those tax years.

Property Records: Records relating to the basis of property should be retained as long as they may be material to any tax return involving the property. The basis of property is material until the statute of limitations expires for the tax year an asset is sold or otherwise disposed. A taxpayer must keep these records to figure the asset's basis, as well as any depreciation, amortization, or depletion deductions.

Example: Cory sells a vacation home he has owned for eight years. He uses records relating to the purchase of the property and improvements made on it to compute the basis and his gain. He reports the sale on his 2016 tax return. He must retain the records relating to the sale until the statute of limitations for the tax return expires, usually three years from the original due date of the return.

Employment Tax Records: A business is required to retain payroll and employment tax records for at least four years after the tax becomes due or is paid, whichever is later. This rule also applies to businesses that employ other tax preparers.

Example: Joelle is an EA who employs five other tax preparers in her office. She is required to keep the employment tax records relating to her employees for at least four years.

Applicable employer tax records must be made available for IRS review upon request. These include:

- Employer identification numbers
- Amounts and dates of wages, annuity, and pension payments
- Amounts of tips reported
- Names, addresses, Social Security numbers, and occupations of employees
- Dates of active employment and sick leave
- Records of fringe benefits provided
- Forms W-4
- Dates and amounts of tax deposits
- and copies of all employment returns filed (this refers to payroll tax returns, such as Forms 940 and 941)

Statute of Limitations	
Type of Record/Return	**Applicable Statute or Retention Period**
Normal tax return	Three years after a return is due or filed, whichever is later
Omitted income that exceeds 25% of the gross income shown on the return	Six years from filing date
Fraudulent return	No limit
No return filed	No limit
A claim for credit or amended return	The later of three years from the due date of the original return or two years after tax was paid
A claim for a loss from worthless securities	Seven years
Employment and payroll tax records	The later of four years after tax becomes due or is paid
Fixed assets, real estate	Until the statute of limitations expires for the tax year in which the asset is disposed

Other Retention Periods

Longer record retention periods may apply in some cases. For example, if a taxpayer files a claim from a loss of worthless securities, the period to retain records related to the transaction is seven years. If a taxpayer fails to report income that exceeds 25% of the gross income shown on his return, the statute of limitations is six years from when the return is filed. The IRS has no time limit to assess tax if a taxpayer never files a return or if a taxpayer files a fraudulent return.

Tax Avoidance vs. Tax Evasion

The U.S. system of federal taxation operates on the concept of voluntary compliance; it is the taxpayer's responsibility to report all income. When a taxpayer fails to pay what officials say he owes, the IRS can collect back taxes and assess penalties. The Internal Revenue Code imposes many different kinds of penalties, ranging from civil fines to imprisonment for criminal tax evasion.

The term *tax avoidance* is not defined by the IRS, but it is commonly used to describe the legal reduction of taxable income, such as through deductions, credits, and adjustments to income. Most taxpayers use at least a few methods of tax avoidance in order to reduce their taxable income and therefore lower their tax liability.

Example: Darsha contributes to her employer-sponsored retirement plans with pretax funds. She also uses an employer-based flexible spending account for her medical expenses, which reduces her taxable income by making all of her medical expenses pretax. She owns a home and claims a deduction for interest she pays on her mortgage. All of these strategies lower her taxable income by using legal tax avoidance.

Tax evasion, on the other hand, is an illegal practice in which individuals or businesses intentionally avoid paying their true tax liabilities. Although most Americans comply with their tax obligations, the U.S. government estimates that 3% of taxpayers do not file tax returns at all. Tax evasion is a felony, and those caught evading taxes are subject to criminal charges and substantial penalties.

Note: For each year a taxpayer willfully does not file a tax return, the penalty can include a fine of up to $25,000 and a prison sentence of up to one year. If it can be demonstrated that the taxpayer deliberately did not file in an attempt to evade taxation, the IRS can pursue a felony conviction, which can include an additional fine of up to $100,000 and a maximum prison sentence of five years (IRC §7201).

Example: Eli owns a jewelry store. For several years, he failed to report cash he received from his stores. He often accepted large cash payments from his customers, but did not report the income. He also kept a separate accounting system for the cash receivables as a second set of books. In addition, Eli broke cash receipts greater than $10,000 into smaller receipts in order to evade federal cash reporting requirements. When he filed his tax report, Eli reported income of $27,000, while his actual taxable income was nearly $195,000. Eli was convicted of committing tax evasion, a felony.[158]

Penalties Imposed Upon Taxpayers

The IRS can assess penalties on individual taxpayers who fail to file, fail to pay, or both. The failure-to-file penalty is generally greater than the failure-to-pay penalty. If someone is unable to pay all the taxes he owes, he is better off filing on time and paying as much as he can, as the IRS will consider payment options with individual taxpayers.

A taxpayer will not have to pay either penalty if he shows he failed to file or pay on time because of reasonable cause and not willful neglect.

Penalties are payable upon notice and demand. They are generally assessed, collected, and paid in the same manner as taxes. The taxpayer will receive a notice that contains:

- The name of the penalty,
- The applicable code section, and
- How the penalty was computed.

Failure-to-File Penalty: The penalty for filing late is usually 5% of the unpaid taxes for each month or part of a month that a return is late, up to a maximum of 25% of the amount due. The penalty is based on the tax that is not paid by the due date, without regard to extensions.

If both the failure-to-file penalty and the failure-to-pay penalty apply in any month, the 5% failure-to-file penalty is reduced by the failure-to-pay penalty. However, if a taxpayer files his return more than 60 days after the due date or extended due date, the minimum penalty is the smaller of $205 or 100% of the unpaid tax.

If a taxpayer is owed a refund, he will not be assessed a failure-to-file penalty.

Failure-to-Pay Penalty: If a taxpayer does not pay his taxes by the due date, he will be subject to a failure-to-pay penalty of ½ of 1% (0.5%) of unpaid taxes for each month or part of a month after the due date that the taxes are not paid. This penalty can be as much as 25% of a taxpayer's unpaid taxes. If a taxpayer fails to file a tax return and it is determined that the

[158] Example is based on an actual case prosecuted by the IRS Criminal Enforcement division.

failure to do so is fraudulent, the maximum penalty is increased from the regular 25% penalty to 75% of the amount owed.

The failure-to-pay penalty rate increases to a full 1% per month for any tax that remains unpaid the day after a demand for immediate payment is issued, or ten days after notice of intent to levy certain assets is issued. For taxpayers who filed on time but are unable to pay their tax liabilities, the failure-to-pay penalty rate is reduced to ¼ of 1% (0.25%) per month during any month in which the taxpayer has a valid installment agreement with the IRS.[159] The taxpayer will also owe interest on the amount due. Interest accrues daily on any unpaid tax from the due date of the return until the taxpayer pays in full. The IRS may abate a taxpayer's penalties for filing and paying late if the taxpayer can show reasonable cause. There are exceptions in the law for the following situations:

- A member of the Armed Forces serving in a combat zone or contingency operation.
- A citizen or resident alien working abroad
- Victims in certain disaster situations. In those situations, the IRS has the legal authority to extend filing and payment deadlines.

Example: Stephanie was a victim of Hurricane Matthew that took place on October 4, 2016 in Georgia. The President declared a major disaster in the State of Georgia. Stephanie's business was destroyed and her house was severely damaged in the storm. The IRS postponed filing deadlines as well as deposit deadlines for employment taxes for people who were living in the affected region. Stephanie later receives a notice from the IRS. She calls the IRS disaster hotline to request tax relief, which is granted.

Other Penalties Imposed on the Taxpayer

IRC §6662 describes penalties for accuracy-related violations of underpaying income tax, including penalties for substantial understatement, substantial valuation misstatement, and negligence or disregard of rules or regulations. These penalties are calculated as a flat 20% of the net understatement of tax. In addition to other penalties, if the taxpayer provides fraudulent information on his tax return, he can be subject to a civil or criminal fraud penalty.

Penalty for Substantial Understatement: For individual taxpayers, an understatement is considered substantial if it is more than the larger of:

- 10% of the correct tax, or
- $5,000.

Penalty for Substantial Valuation Misstatement: This penalty applies when a taxpayer incorrectly reports an asset's value or its adjusted basis on a tax return; the value or basis is overstated by at least 150% of the correct value; which results in an underpayment of tax of at least $5,000 ($10,000 for most C corporations). However, the penalty jumps to 40% of the net understatement of tax if the taxpayer claims a value for property on a tax return that is 200% or more of the correct amount. This is known as a *gross valuation misstatement*.

Example: Damian donated a large parcel of land to a charitable foundation. He valued the donation at $9 million on his tax return and claimed a $3 million charitable deduction. The IRS examined his return and discovered that the land was significantly overvalued. The IRS adjusted the value of the land downward to $5 million, making Damian's true charitable deduction worth only $1.5 million. Damian is assessed a gross valuation misstatement penalty for overvaluing his property in order to receive an inflated deduction and pay less tax. The penalty rate would be 20% since the overstated amount of the land was greater than 150%, but less than 200%, of the land's correct value.

[159] Regardless of whether or not the taxpayer has the ability to pay, it is always better to file and pay what you can. The IRS will work with a taxpayer who makes the attempt to be compliant.

The valuation misstatement penalty also may apply if the price for any property or service claimed on a return is substantially less than the correct valuation.

Example: After a Pennsylvania woman died, the executor initially valued her estate's assets at $3.15 million when he filed Form 706, the estate tax return. He did not hire an appraiser to help determine the correct value. The IRS disputed the valuation, putting the estate's assets at $9.2 million. Since an estate is taxed on the values of its assets, a lower value could result in lower tax. The U.S. Tax Court ultimately ruled that $6.5 million was the correct value of the estate. The IRS imposed a substantial valuation misstatement penalty upon the estate, which the Tax Court upheld.

A taxpayer may avoid both the substantial understatement and the substantial overvaluation penalties if he has substantial authority for his position or the position has a reasonable basis and is adequately disclosed.

Failure to Comply with Information Reporting Requirements (§6723): If a taxpayer does not include a Social Security number or the SSN of another person where required on a return, statement, or other document, he is subject to a penalty of $50 for each failure. The taxpayer also faces the $50 penalty if he refuses to give the SSN to another person (such as a tax preparer) when it is required on a tax return.

Negligence and Disregard of the Rules and Regulations Penalty: IRC §6662 defines negligence as any failure to make a reasonable attempt to comply with the internal revenue laws. The penalty may be imposed on taxpayers who carelessly, recklessly, or intentionally disregard IRS rules and regulations by taking positions on their returns with little or no effort to determine whether the positions are correct, or who knowingly take positions that are incorrect.

Civil Fraud Penalty (§6663): If there is any underpayment of tax due to fraud, a penalty of 75% of the underpayment will be assessed against the taxpayer. In the case of a joint return, the penalty will apply to both spouses only if some part of the underpayment is due to the fraud of each spouse. Examples of tax fraud include:

- Filing a false tax return
- Hiding or transferring assets or income
- Claiming false deductions
- Keeping a second set of books
- Failure to deposit receipts to business accounts
- Covering up sources of receipts or deliberately omitting income

Definitions: Negligence or simple ignorance of the law does not constitute fraud. The IRS characterizes fraud as a deliberate action for the purpose of "deceit, subterfuge, camouflage, concealment, some attempt to color or obscure events, or make things seem other than what they are."

Criminal Fraud Penalty: In addition to being a civil offense, fraud may also be a criminal offense. A criminal offense must generally include an element of willfulness, meaning a voluntary and intentional violation of a known legal duty. If IRS examiners find evidence of criminal fraud in the course of an audit, they will refer the case to the IRS Criminal Investigation Division.

Frivolous Tax Return Penalty (§6702): A frivolous tax return is one that does not include enough information to figure the correct tax, or that contains information clearly showing that the tax reported is substantially incorrect.

A taxpayer faces a penalty of $5,000 ($10,000 if MFJ) if he files a frivolous tax return or other frivolous submissions. This penalty is in addition to any other penalties provided by law. Frivolous submissions include tax protester arguments, such as contentions that filing of a tax return or payment of income tax is voluntary; that only foreign-source income is taxable; or that a taxpayer is not a citizen of the United States and thus not subject to federal income tax. Frivolous submissions also include taxpayers who alter or strike out the preprinted language above the space provided for a signature. This declaration is called the jurat.

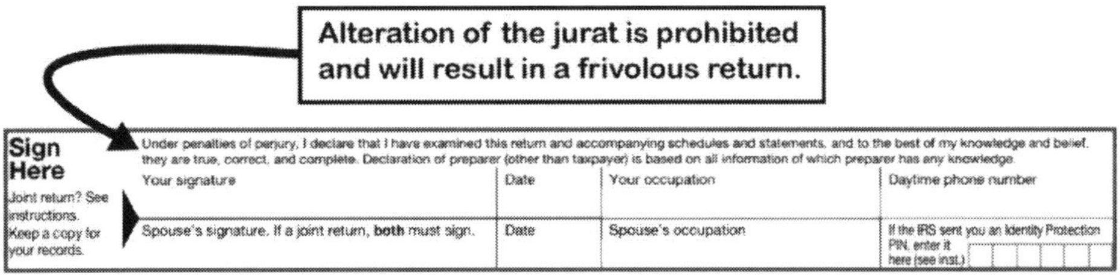

Civil penalties for altering a jurat may include:

- A $5,000 penalty imposed under §6702;
- Additional penalties for failure to file a return, failure to pay tax owed, and fraudulent failure to file a return under §6651; and
- A penalty of up to $25,000 under §6673 if the taxpayer makes frivolous arguments in the U.S. Tax Court.

Example: A taxpayer files Form 1040 for the 2016 tax year. The taxpayer signs the form, but crosses out the jurat on the return and writes the word "void" across it. This return is now considered frivolous and is subject to penalties.

Trust Fund Recovery Penalty (TFRP)

As authorized by IRC §6672, the trust fund recovery penalty involves the income and Social Security taxes an employer withholds from the wages of employees. These taxes are called trust fund taxes because they are held in trust on behalf of employees until they are remitted to the government. Sometimes, business owners neglect to remit these taxes to the IRS.

A trust fund recovery penalty equal to 100% of the amount of unpaid trust fund taxes can be assessed against anyone who is considered a "responsible person" in the business. This may include corporate officers, directors, stockholders, and rank-and-file employees. The IRS has assessed the penalty against accountants, bookkeepers, and even clerical staff, if they have authority to sign checks.

A person must be both "responsible" and "willful" to be liable for an employer's failure to collect or pay trust fund taxes. This means that he knew (or should have known) that the payroll taxes were not being remitted to the IRS, and that he also had the power to correct the problem.

Example: Shelly works for Smith Construction as a full-time bookkeeper and processes all the payroll tax forms. She also has check-signing authority, so she can pay the bills when her boss is working off-site. In 2016, her boss has a heart attack, and his wife, Dora, takes over the business in his absence. Dora cannot manage the business properly and Smith Construction is unable to meet its financial commitments. Dora tells Shelly to pay vendors first. The business continues to withhold payroll taxes from employee paychecks, but does not remit the amounts to the IRS. Eventually, the business declares bankruptcy. Dora disappears, and Shelly is contacted by the IRS. Even though Shelly was "just an employee" the IRS can assess the trust fund recovery penalty against her because she had check-signing authority, and she knew that the business was not remitting payroll taxes to the IRS as required.

Penalties Imposed on the Tax Practitioner

Just like taxpayers, tax professionals are also subject to penalties on improperly filed or fraudulent returns. Preparer fraud typically involves the preparation and filing of false income tax returns for clients. The returns may have inflated personal or business expenses, false deductions, unallowable credits, or excessive exemptions. Preparers may also manipulate income figures to obtain fraudulent tax credits, such as the Earned Income Tax Credit, for clients who are not eligible.

Sometimes a tax preparer will prepare a fraudulent return without the taxpayer being aware of the fraud. A preparer's clients may or may not know about the fraudulent items on their tax returns. Fraud may benefit preparers financially by:

- Diverting a portion of taxpayers' refunds for their own personal benefit,
- Increasing clientele by developing a reputation for obtaining large refunds; and/or
- Charging inflated fees for return preparation.

Example: Donny is a tax preparer. In 2016, he prepares a return for his client, Janice. He gives Janice a complete copy of the return, and she goes home. After Janice leaves his office, Donny adds fraudulent credits to her return, then adds his personal bank account to Janice's Form 8888, funneling a portion of the refund to himself.[160] Donny has committed tax fraud.

In the case of a tax professional who has committed tax fraud, or filed fraudulent returns, the IRS' Criminal Investigation Division works closely with the US Justice Department to prosecute the tax professionals who commit financial fraud.

Penalties for Substantial Understatement

If a tax return preparer willfully understates a client's tax liability, he is subject to penalties. Under IRS regulations, understatement of liability means:

- Understating net tax payable
- Overstating the net amount creditable or refundable

Under IRC §6694, there are two specific penalties when a tax preparer understates a taxpayer's liability.

- **IRC § 6694(a) – Understatement due to unreasonable position:** If there is an understatement on a tax return due to an unreasonable position, the penalty is the greater of:
    - $1,000 per tax return, or
    - 50% of the income the preparer received (or would have received) in income for preparing the tax return with the understatement.

  This penalty applies when a preparer knows, or reasonably should have known, that the position was unreasonable and would not have been sustained on its merits. Even if disclosure requirements are met, penalties may apply if the position is attributable to a tax shelter, if it is not properly substantiated, or if the taxpayer failed to keep adequate books and records to support the item or position. A preparer may be excused from the penalty if he acted in good faith and there was reasonable cause for the understatement.
- **IRC § 6694(b) – Understatement due to willful or reckless conduct:** If a tax return preparer shows negligent or willful disregard of IRS rules and regulations, and makes a willful or reckless attempt to understate tax liability, the penalty is the greater of:
    - $5,000 per tax return, or

[160] Example based on an actual criminal case. Criminal Case No. 14CR3658-JM.

- 75% of the income the preparer received (or would have received) in income for preparing the tax return with the understatement.[161]

Example: George prepares a tax return for a client, but ignores $50,000 of income that the client had told him about. George also reported five dependents on the return, when the client said he had only two dependents. George would be subject to a §6694 penalty.

If a tax return preparer is subject to a penalty for understatement of liability and this includes a change to the Earned Income Tax Credit, the preparer may be subject to additional penalties for failure to exercise due diligence while claiming the EITC.

IRC §6694 specifies that the understatement penalty will be abated if, under final judicial decision, it is found that there is no actual understatement of liability. Sometimes this occurs when a Tax Court case is decided in favor of the taxpayer.

Listing of Preparer Additional Penalties and Amounts

Exam Tip: Specific penalties that may be imposed on both preparers and taxpayers are frequently tested on Part 3 of the EA exam. Although it is not generally necessary to memorize the IRC section numbers, test-takers should be familiar with each of the penalties listed in this PassKey study guide.

IRC § 6695(a) – Failure to furnish copy to taxpayer: The penalty is $50 for each failure to furnish a copy of a completed return to a taxpayer. The maximum penalty is $25,000 a year.

IRC § 6695(b) – Failure to sign return: The penalty is $50 for each failure to sign a return. The maximum penalty imposed on any tax preparer is $25,000 a year.

IRC § 6695(c) – Failure to furnish identifying number: The penalty is $50 for each failure to furnish an identifying number (an SSN, ATIN, or ITIN, whichever applies) on a tax return. The maximum penalty is $25,000 a year.

IRC § 6695(d) – Failure to retain copy of the return (or list): The penalty is $50 for each failure to retain a copy (or list) of each completed return or claim. The maximum penalty is $25,000 a year.

IRC § 6695(e) – Failure to file correct information returns. The penalty is $50 for each failure to file correct information returns for a client (examples: Forms 1099 or other information returns). The maximum penalty is $25,000 a year.

IRC § 6695(f) – Negotiation of a taxpayer's refund check: The penalty is $500 for a tax return preparer who endorses or negotiates any check made in respect of taxes imposed by Title 26 which is issued to a taxpayer.

IRC § 6695(g) – Failure to exercise due diligence in determining eligibility for EITC, AOTC, or the CTC/ACTC: The penalty in 2016 is $510 for each failure to comply with the EITC, AOTC, or CTC due diligence requirements. This penalty is now adjusted for inflation.

IRC § 6700 – Promoting abusive tax shelters: The penalty is for a promoter of an abusive tax shelter is $1,000 for each organization or sale of an abusive plan or arrangement (or, if lesser, 100% of the income derived from the activity).

IRC § 6701 – Penalties for aiding and abetting understatement of tax liability: The penalty is $1000 ($10,000 if relating to a corporation's tax return) for aiding and abetting in an understatement of a tax liability. Any preparer subject to the penalty shall be penalized only once for documents relating to the same taxpayer for a single tax period or event.

IRC § 6713 – (Civil penalty) Disclosure or use of information by preparers of returns: The penalty is $250 for each unauthorized disclosure or use of information furnished for, or in connection with, the preparation of a return. The maximum penalty is $10,000 a year.

[161] IRC Sect. 6694(B)(1)(B)

IRC § 7216 – (Criminal provision) Disclosure or use of information by preparers of returns: Those found guilty of knowingly or recklessly disclosing information furnished in connection with a tax return or using such information for any purpose other than preparing or assisting in the preparation of such return. Upon conviction, a fine of up to $1,000, imprisonment for not more than 1 year, or both (together with the costs of prosecution).

IRC § 7206 – Fraud and false statements: Those found guilty of felony tax fraud, upon conviction, may be subject to a fine of up to $100,000 ($500,000 in the case of a corporation), jail time of up to 3 years, or both (together with the costs of prosecution).

IRC § 7207 – Filing a fraudulent return, statement, or other document: Any preparer who willfully files a false statement or document with the IRS may be convicted of a misdemeanor. And, upon conviction, a fine of up to $10,000 ($50,000 in the case of a corporation), plus imprisonment of not more than one year, or both.

IRC § 7407 – Action to enjoin tax return preparers: A federal district court may enjoin a tax return preparer from engaging in certain proscribed conduct, or in extreme cases, from continuing to act as a tax return preparer altogether.

IRC § 7408 – Action to enjoin specified conduct related to tax shelters and reportable transactions

A federal district court may enjoin a person from engaging in certain proscribed conduct (including any action, or failure to take action, which is in violation of Circular 230).

If a penalty is assessed against a tax preparer and he does not agree with the assessment, he may request a conference with the IRS officer or agent and explain why the penalty is not warranted. The preparer may also wait for the penalty to be assessed, pay the penalty within 30 days, and then file a claim for refund.

2016 Preparer Penalties Quick reference		
Type of Violation	**Penalty Per Violation**	**Calendar Year Maximum**
Failure to furnish a tax return copy to taxpayer (sec. 6695(a))	$50	$25,000
Failure to sign a taxpayer's return (sec. 6695(b))	$50	$25,000
Failure to furnish a PTIN on a return (sec. 6695(c))	$50	$25,000
Failure to retain copy or list of returns prepared (sec. 6695(d))	$50	$25,000
Failure to file correct information returns (sec. 6695(e))	$50	$25,000
Negotiation of a taxpayer's refund check (sec. 6695(f))	$510	No limit
Failure to be diligent in determining eligibility for Earned Income Tax Credit, American Opportunity Credit, or Child Tax Credit (sec. 6695(g))	$510	No limit

Other Preparer Penalties Quick reference		
IRC	**Violation**	**Penalty**
§6695	Failure to furnish a copy of return/claim for refund to taxpayer	$50 per failure/$25,000 maximum per year
	Failure to sign a return/claim for refund	$50 per failure/$25,000 maximum per year
	Failure to furnish a PTIN on a return	$50 per failure/$25,000 maximum per year
	Failure to retain a copy or list for a return/claim for refund	$50 per failure/$25,000 maximum per year
	Failure to file correct information returns	$50 per failure/$25,000 maximum per year
	Endorse, cash, or deposit taxpayer's refund check	$510 per failure/No maximum fine
	Failure to comply with EITC, CTC, or AOTC due diligence requirements	$510 per failure/No maximum fine
§6694	Understatement due to an unreasonable position	Greater of $1,000 per return or 50% of fees derived by preparer
	Understatement due to negligent/willful disregard	Greater of $5,000 per return or 75% of fees derived by preparer
§6700	Sells, organizes, or promotes abusive tax shelter	Lesser of $1,000 per activity, or 100% of gross income derived from activity
§6701	Aiding/abetting understatement of tax liability	$1,000 per individual return, $10,000 per corporate return
§6713	Unauthorized disclosure of client information (civil)	$250 per disclosure (not per return)/ $10,000 maximum per year
§7216	Unauthorized disclosure of client information (criminal)	$1,000 fine and/or up to one year in prison

Unit 7: Study Questions

1. Adele is a sole proprietor who files a Schedule C tax return. She meets with Carlos, her enrolled agent, and gives him a list of expenses she says she incurred for a home office, business mileage, travel, and business meals. She does not bring any receipts or other documentation to the meeting. What is Carlos required to do in order to prepare an accurate tax return for Adele?

A. Nothing further. Carlos can rely on the list of Adele's expenses without seeing any documentation.
B. Carlos must make appropriate inquiries of Adele about her list of expenses. However, he does not need to actually see any documentation if she tells him she did not retain any receipts or keep a mileage log.
C. Carlos must ask relevant and probing questions of Adele to help determine if the expenses are allowable. He must also ask if she has receipts to support the expenses.
D. Carlos must review all of Adele's receipts and her mileage log prior to preparing her tax return.

2. What penalty does a tax return preparer face for failing to include his PTIN on a client's return?

A. A warning letter from the IRS.
B. A fine of $50.
C. A fine of $100.
D. A fine of $500.

3. All of the following statements regarding the fraud penalty are correct except:

A. If there is any underpayment of tax due to fraud, a penalty of 75% of the underpayment will be assessed against the taxpayer.
B. The fraud penalty on a joint return will automatically apply to each spouse.
C. IRS examiners who find strong evidence of fraud may refer the case to the IRS Criminal Investigation Division for possible criminal prosecution.
D. Negligence or simple ignorance of the law does not constitute fraud.

4. What percentage of tax must a taxpayer pay if he is guilty of a substantial understatement penalty?

A. 5% of the net understatement of tax.
B. 10% of the net understatement of tax.
C. 20% of the net understatement of tax.
D. 25% of the net understatement of tax.

5. Which penalty is greater: the failure-to-file penalty or the failure-to-pay penalty?

A. The failure-to-file penalty.
B. The failure-to-pay penalty.
C. Both penalties are equal.
D. It depends on the taxpayer's individual facts and circumstances.

6. Siobhan hires a friend, Gus, to prepare her income tax returns. Gus has prepared returns for several years, but is not a CPA, an attorney, or an enrolled agent. Although he knows that Siobhan is single and childless, he prepares her tax return based on head of household filing status with two qualifying children so that Siobhan may qualify for the Earned Income Tax Credit, and thus a larger refund. Siobhan reviews a copy of the tax return and signs it. Gus also signs the return and submits it to the IRS for processing. If the IRS detects the fraudulent credit, which of the two, if either, will face potential penalties?

A. Gus only.
B. Siobhan only.
C. Both Gus and Siobhan.
D. Neither. Since Gus is not a CPA, attorney, or enrolled agent, he is not subject to penalties for paid tax return penalties. Siobhan is not responsible for any penalties because she relied upon Gus's professional advice in preparing her return.

7. Which of the following statements is correct?

A. Tax avoidance and tax evasion are always illegal.
B. Taxpayers who commit fraud are subject to civil penalties only.
C. The IRS will assess a failure-to-file penalty or a failure-to-pay penalty, but never both.
D. A felony conviction against a taxpayer who deliberately failed to file taxes could mean a fine of up to $100,000 and a prison sentence of up to five years.

8. What is the penalty a preparer faces for understating income on a tax return due to an unreasonable position?

A. $1,000 per tax return or 50% of the income the preparer received in fees for preparing the tax return with the understatement.
B. $5,000 per tax return.
C. 50% of the understatement.
D. No penalty, if the preparer failed to adequately disclose the position on the return.

9. All of the following statements about the trust fund recovery penalty are correct except:

A. The penalty is equal to 100% of the amount that was not properly paid.
B. The IRS primarily targets employees for this penalty.
C. The penalty involves payroll taxes withheld from the wages of employees.
D. The penalty can be assessed against anyone who is considered a responsible person and has failed to remit trust fund taxes to the U.S. government.

10. Corey recently discovered she missed a large education deduction that she was entitled to on her 2013 tax return, for which she had received an extension of time to file. She filed her return on October 12, 2014. What is the latest date she can file Form 1040X and make a claim for refund?

A. October 15, 2016.
B. April 15, 2016
C. October 12, 2017
D. October 15, 2016

11. What is the penalty for a taxpayer who has filed a return determined to be frivolous?

A. $500, plus any other penalty provided by law.
B. $1,000, plus any other penalty provided by law.
C. $5,000, plus any other penalty provided by law.
D. $10,000, plus any other penalty provided by law.

12. Which of the following statements is not correct?

A. If no other provisions apply, the statute of limitations for an IRS examination of a return is three years after the return was filed or the return was due, whichever is later.
B. If more than 25% of gross income has been omitted from the tax return, the statute of limitations is six years after the return was filed.
C. If a fraudulent return is filed, the statute of limitations is seven years.
D. If a tax return is not filed at all, there is no statute of limitations.

13. What is not considered a "badge of fraud" by the IRS?

A. Sloppy recordkeeping.
B. Taking improper credits.
C. All-cash businesses.
D. Deductions for foreign travel.

14. If there is substantial unreported income (over 25%), the IRS may audit tax returns for up to __________ after the filing date.

A. Three years.
B. Four years.
C. Six years.
D. Indefinitely.

15. All of the following statements regarding preparer penalties are correct except:

A. A preparer who has been assessed a penalty may request a conference with an IRS officer to dispute the fine.
B. A preparer who makes a willful or reckless attempt to understate tax liability faces a fine of $10,000 per return.
C. There may be additional penalties for understatement of income if the preparer has not exercised due diligence related to the EITC.
D. A preparer may avoid penalties if he relied on the advice of another preparer in good faith.

16. Accuracy-related penalties in IRC §6662 are imposed for substantial understatement of income tax and for:

A. Substantial misstatement of the value of assets.
B. Substantial overstatement of income tax.
C. Preparer fraud related to the Earned Income Tax Credit.
D. All of the above.

17. What is the minimum penalty for failing to file a tax return more than 60 days late (assuming the taxpayer is not owed a refund)?

A. 100% of the unpaid tax.
B. A fee of $135 or 90% of the unpaid tax, whichever is greater.
C. The smaller of $205 or 100% of the unpaid tax.
D. A minimum of 25% of a taxpayer's unpaid tax.

18. Colleen owns a business and has never filed a tax return. How long should she keep her records?

A. Three years if she owes additional tax.
B. Seven years if she files a claim for a loss from worthless securities.
C. For an unlimited period of time if she does not file a return.
D. None of the above.

19. What penalty does a tax return preparer face if he cashes a client's tax refund check?

A. Nothing. This is acceptable so long as the client has given written permission to do so.
B. A fine of $50 for each violation.
C. A fine of $100 for each violation.
D. A fine of $510 for each violation.

Unit 7: Answers

1. The answer is C. To prepare an accurate Schedule C return, a tax return preparer can generally rely in good faith, without verification, on information a client provides. However, a preparer cannot ignore the implications of the information. Carlos must make reasonable inquiries if the information appears to be incorrect, inconsistent, or incomplete. Since Adele may not fully understand the tax laws and may incorrectly believe she can claim deductions for non-qualifying expenses, Carlos must ask probing and relevant questions to help determine if the expenses are allowable. He must also ask if Adele has receipts to support the expenses, and further instruct her to keep the receipts in case the IRS requests supporting documentation.

2. The answer is B. IRC §6695 lists the penalties that may be assessed when it comes to the preparation of tax returns for other persons. The penalty is $50 for each violation of the following:

- Failure to furnish a copy of a return or claim to a taxpayer
- Failure to sign a return or claim for refund
- Failure to furnish an identifying number (PTIN) on a return
- Failure to retain a copy or list of a return or claim
- Failure to file correct information returns

Under the terms of IRC §6695, the maximum penalty imposed on any tax return preparer cannot exceed $25,000 in a calendar year for these specific violations. There is no annual dollar limit for the portion of IRC §6695 that deals with failures of EITC due diligence or with improper negotiation of client checks.

3. The answer is B. The fraud penalty on a joint return does not automatically apply to a spouse unless some part of the underpayment is due to the fraud committed by that spouse.

4. The answer is C. The substantial understatement penalty is calculated as a flat 20% of the net understatement of tax. A taxpayer may also face additional fraud-related penalties if he has provided false information on his tax return.

5. The answer is A. The penalty for filing late (or not filing at all) is usually 5% of the unpaid taxes for each month that a return is late. The penalty for not paying taxes by the due date is less: ½ of 1% (0.5%). The IRS advises that if someone is unable to pay all the taxes he owes, he is better off filing on time and paying as much as he can.

6. The answer is C. The taxpayer is ultimately responsible for the accuracy of her own return. However, a tax return preparer, whether officially licensed or not, also signs a tax return attesting to its accuracy under penalties of perjury. Both Gus and Siobhan could face penalties and other legal action in relation to the fraudulently claimed Earned Income Credit.

7. The answer is D. This is the maximum penalty and prison sentence in a tax evasion case. The other statements are false. Tax avoidance is not illegal. Taxpayers who commit fraud are subject to criminal penalties as well as civil. The IRS may assess both failure-to-file and failure-to-pay penalties.

8. The answer is A. A preparer faces an understatement penalty of $1,000 per tax return or 50% of the income the preparer received in fees for preparing the tax return with the understatement. If the position is adequately disclosed on the return, the penalty generally will not apply.

9. The answer is B. The trust fund recovery penalty is levied against employers, or other responsible persons, who have failed to pay the appropriate payroll taxes to the U.S. government.

10. The answer is C. For filing a claim for credit or refund, the period to make the claim is generally: three years from the date the original return was filed, or two years from the date the tax was paid, whichever is later. If the return was filed prior to the original due date, the three-year statute of limitations starts as of the original due date of the return. If the return was filed on extension, the three-year period starts that the return was received by the IRS. Since the original due date for Corey's return was April 15, 2013, but she filed on extension on October 12, 2014, she has three years from October 12, 2013, to file Form 1040X.

11. The answer is C. Any taxpayer who files a return found to be frivolous may be fined $5,000, in addition to any other penalties provided by law. This penalty may be doubled on a joint return.

12. The answer is C. If a fraudulent tax return is filed, there is no statute of limitations. Under federal law, a tax return is fraudulent if the taxpayer files it knowing that the return either omits taxable income or claims one or more deductions that are not allowable.

13. The answer is D. IRS auditors are trained to spot common types of deception and attempts to defraud on tax returns. These acts are known as badges of fraud and include deducting personal items as business expenses, the overstatement of deductions, and the understatement of income. Simply having deductions for foreign travel is not an indication of illegal behavior on the part of a taxpayer.

14. The answer is C. In most cases, tax returns can be audited for up to three years after filing. However, the IRS may audit for up to six years if there is substantial unreported income (over 25%).

15. The answer is B. A preparer who makes a willful or reckless attempt to understate tax liability faces a penalty of the greater of $5,000 per tax return, or 75% of the income upon which the penalty was imposed, whichever is greater.

16. The answer is A. IRC §6662 imposes penalties on taxpayers who misstate the value of assets in order to reap tax benefits. The penalty is 20% of the net understatement of tax for assets incorrectly valued at 150% or more than the correct amount of valuation or adjusted basis. The penalty increases to 40% of the net understatement of tax for assets incorrectly valued at 200% or more than the correct amount of valuation or adjusted basis.

17. The answer is C. Starting in 2016, the minimum penalty for filing a tax return more than 60 days late is now the smaller of $205 or 100% of the unpaid tax.

18. The answer is C. A taxpayer must keep records as long as they are needed for the administration of any provision of the IRC. Taxpayers must keep records that support an item of income or deduction on a tax return until the statute of limitations for that return runs out. If a tax return is not filed, there is no time limit.

19. The answer is D. It is illegal for tax return preparers to negotiate (cash) taxpayers' refund checks. A preparer faces a fine of $510 for each violation.

Unit 8: Practitioner Misconduct

More Reading:
Publication 947, *Practice Before the IRS and Power of Attorney*

The IRS's Office of Professional Responsibility (OPR) is responsible for interpreting and applying the provisions of Circular 230 to ensure that tax professionals follow the law. The office's oversight generally covers all individuals who interact with federal tax administration, whether in person, orally, in writing, or by the preparation and submission of documents.

The following are subject to Circular 230 jurisdiction, and thus to OPR oversight:

- State licensed attorneys and CPAs who interact with federal tax administration at any level and capacity.
- Enrolled agents, enrolled retirement plan agents, and enrolled actuaries.
- Persons providing appraisals used in connection with tax matters (such as valuing estate and gift assets).
- Unlicensed individuals who represent taxpayers before the IRS examination division, IRS customer service, and Taxpayer Advocate Service in connection with returns they prepared and signed.
- Licensed and unlicensed individuals who give written advice that has the potential for tax avoidance or evasion.
- Any person submitting a power of attorney in connection with limited representation or special authorization to practice before the IRS in a specific matter before the agency.

The OPR has authority in matters related to practitioner standards and exclusive authority in matters involving discipline and sanctions. This authority includes:

- Receiving and processing referrals regarding allegations of misconduct under Circular 230 and initiating disciplinary proceedings against individuals or entities relating to allegations or findings of practitioner misconduct consistent with the applicable disciplinary rules under Circular 230.
- Making final determinations on appeals regarding practitioner eligibility or suitability decisions and recommending and imposing sanctions for violations under Circular 230.
- Making determinations on whether to appeal administrative law judge decisions and reviewing and determining petitions from practitioners seeking reinstatement to practice.

Practitioner Misconduct

There are four broad categories of practitioner misconduct, all of which may be reasons for the OPR to initiate disciplinary action:

- Misconduct while representing a taxpayer
- Misconduct related to the practitioner's own return
- Giving a false opinion knowingly, recklessly, or through gross incompetence
- Misconduct not directly involving IRS representation (such as conviction of a criminal act)

Circular 230, §10.51 outlines many instances in which the OPR might sanction a practitioner for incompetence or disreputable conduct. These instances include, but are not limited to:

- Conviction of any criminal offense under federal tax laws.
- Conviction of any criminal offense involving dishonesty or breach of trust.

- Conviction of any felony under federal or state law in which the conduct renders the practitioner unfit to practice before the IRS.
- Giving false or misleading information, or participating in any way in the giving of false or misleading information to the Department of the Treasury.
- Soliciting employment as prohibited under Circular 230 or making false or misleading representations with intent to deceive a client.
- Willfully failing to file a federal tax return, or willfully evading any assessment or payment of any federal tax.
- Willfully assisting a client in violating any federal tax law, or knowingly counseling a client to evade federal taxes.
- Misappropriating funds received from a client for purposes of payment of taxes.
- Attempting to influence any IRS officer by the use of threats, false accusations, duress, coercion, or bribery.
- Disbarment or suspension from practice as a CPA, actuary or attorney.[162]
- Knowingly aiding and abetting another person to practice before the IRS during a period of suspension, disbarment, or ineligibility of such other person.
- Contemptuous conduct in connection with practice before the IRS, including the use of abusive language, knowingly making false accusations or statements, or circulating or publishing malicious or libelous matter.
- Willfully disclosing or using private tax return information.
- Willfully failing to sign a tax return.
- Willfully failing to e-file a return.
- Willfully signing a tax return without a valid PTIN.
- Willfully representing a taxpayer before the IRS without appropriate authorization.

Example: Beverly is an enrolled agent with a tax preparation business. In 2016, she was convicted of forgery because she forged her father's signature on several checks and cashed them. Although this was a case unrelated to her tax preparation firm, Beverly is guilty of disreputable conduct because she was convicted of any criminal offense involving dishonesty or breach of trust. The IRS can disbar her and strip her of her enrollment.

In addition, the most recent Circular 230 revision expands part of §10.51 that prohibits "giving a false opinion, knowingly, recklessly, or through gross incompetence." False opinions include those that reflect or result from:

- A knowing misstatement of fact or law.
- An assertion of a position known to be unwarranted under existing law.
- Counseling or assisting in conduct known to be illegal or fraudulent.
- Concealing matters required by law to be revealed.
- Consciously disregarding information indicating that material facts expressed in the opinion or offering material are false or misleading.

Definition: This rewritten paragraph of §10.51 defines **reckless conduct** in light of giving a false opinion as a "highly unreasonable omission or misrepresentation involving an **extreme departure from the standards of ordinary care that a practitioner should observe** under the circumstances."

The IRS will consider a practitioner's pattern of conduct to assess whether it reflects gross incompetence, meaning "gross indifference, preparation which is grossly inadequate under the circumstances, and a consistent failure to perform obligations to the client."

[162] For example, an attorney who is disbarred and loses his license at the state level would also be disbarred by the OPR at the federal level.

Referrals to the OPR

Most disciplinary cases opened by the OPR result from internal and external referrals. An IRS employee who believes a practitioner has violated any provision in Circular 230 is required to file a written report to the OPR. Referrals are also mandatory following the assessment of penalties for violations of §6694(b) (a willful attempt to understate the liability for tax).

A referral must also be made when there are penalties or sanctions imposed that relate to the promotion of abusive tax shelters (§6700), or aiding and abetting the understatement of a tax liability (§6701(a)).

The OPR says other common reasons for referral include:

- Inaccurate or unreasonable entries/omissions on tax returns
- A lack of due diligence exercised by the practitioner
- Cashing, diverting, or splitting a taxpayer's refund by electronic or other means
- Patterns of misconduct involving multiple years, multiple clients, or unprofessional conduct demonstrated to multiple IRS employees
- Potential conflict of interest situations, such as representation of both spouses who have a joint liability

A taxpayer may file a complaint against a tax return preparer by using Form 14157 and submitting it to the Return Preparer Office, which will undertake an initial investigation before referring a case to the OPR. The form allows identification of complaints within the following categories: theft of refund, e-file issues, preparer misconduct, PTIN issues, false items/documents, employment taxes, and other issues.

Anonymous complaints are allowed. However, if a taxpayer chooses to submit his name and other personal information when he files a complaint, the information will not be shared with the individual or business being reported.

A preparer who is reporting another preparer for misconduct involving a client should obtain the client's consent before sharing any protected tax information with the IRS.

Disciplinary Sanctions

The OPR may impose a wide range of sanctions upon practitioners and other preparers who are subject to Circular 230 jurisdiction:

Reprimand: A reprimand is the least severe sanction. It is a private letter from the director of the OPR, stating the practitioner has committed some kind of misconduct under Circular 230. Although the issuance of a reprimand is kept private, it stays on a practitioner's record.

Censure: Censure is a public reprimand, with the practitioner's name published in the Internal Revenue Bulletin. The facts of the case that triggered the censure are not published. Unlike disbarment or suspension, censure generally does not prevent a practitioner from representing taxpayers before the IRS. However, in certain situations, a censure may place conditions on a practitioner's future representations in order to promote high standards of conduct.

Suspension from Practice before the IRS: An individual who is suspended is not eligible to represent taxpayers before the IRS during the term of the suspension. Suspensions may be imposed for a period of one to 60 months (five years).

Disbarment from Practice before the IRS: An individual who is disbarred is not eligible to represent taxpayers before the IRS. Disbarment lasts a minimum of five years, and Circular 230 requires the practitioner to demonstrate that he has regained fitness to practice before the IRS before he may be reinstated.

As a result of suspension or disbarment, the practitioner will have the matter that caused the disbarment or suspension published in the Internal Revenue Bulletin.

Monetary Penalty: A monetary penalty may be imposed on an individual or a firm, or both, and can be in addition to any censure, suspension, or disbarment. The amount of the penalty may be up to the gross income derived, or to be derived, from the conduct that triggered the penalty.

Example: Tim is a CPA whose personal tax returns were audited by the IRS. The audit found he was improperly claiming personal expenses as business deductions and he had not timely filed his own tax returns. Even though no misconduct was discovered that related to his clients, Tim was suspended from practice by the OPR for a period of three years. The Internal Revenue Bulletin listed his name, length of time of the suspension, and personal tax compliance issues as the reasons for the disciplinary action.

OPR Complaint Process

The OPR's response to a complaint or other referral about possible misconduct will vary depending upon the seriousness of the allegation. The OPR will first investigate whether a violation has occurred, whether the violation is one that calls into question a practitioner's fitness to continue to practice, and if so, what an appropriate sanction might be.

When it has identified a violation following its preliminary investigation, the OPR will send a "Pre-Allegation Notice" to the practitioner regarding the alleged conduct. The notice gives the practitioner an opportunity to provide evidence or documentation in the case. The OPR will then determine the appropriate level of discipline warranted for the violation and try to reach agreement with the practitioner on a sanction. If agreement cannot be reached, the OPR will draft a complaint and refer the case to the Office of Chief Counsel, General Legal Services (GLS). The practitioner will have one final opportunity to resolve the matter before a formal disciplinary hearing.

When a formal complaint is issued against a practitioner, the complaint must:

- Name the respondent.
- Provide a clear and concise description of the facts.
- Be signed by the director of the OPR.
- Describe the type of sanction.

If suspension is sought, the duration must be specified. The complaint may be served to the practitioner in one of the following ways: certified mail; first-class mail if returned undelivered by certified mail; private delivery service; in person; or by leaving the complaint at the office of the practitioner. Electronic delivery, such as email, is not a valid means of serving a complaint.

The complaint must specify a date by which the practitioner is required to respond, which must be at least 30 days after it is served. Within ten days of serving the complaint, copies of the evidence against the practitioner must also be served.

When a practitioner responds to a complaint, he is expected to specifically admit or deny each allegation, or state that he does not have enough information to know whether it is true or false.

He cannot deny a material allegation in the complaint when he knows it to be true. If the practitioner fails to respond to a complaint, it constitutes an admission of guilt and sanctions may be imposed without a hearing.

After a practitioner responds to a complaint, a hearing will be scheduled for an administrative law judge to hear the evidence and decide whether the OPR has proven its case.

Note: To prevail in a disciplinary action involving suspension or disbarment, the OPR must prove by "clear and convincing evidence" that the practitioner willfully violated one or more provisions of Circular 230. "Willful" is defined as a voluntary, intentional violation of a known legal duty.

During a hearing, the practitioner may appear in person or be represented by an attorney or another practitioner. The OPR may be represented by a GLS attorney or by another IRS employee assigned to the case. Within 180 days of the conclusion of a hearing, the administrative law judge must enter a decision.

Example: The OPR receives a referral from another practitioner regarding Carolyn, an enrolled agent. After an investigation and preliminary discussions with Carolyn, the OPR drafts a complaint citing violations of Circular 230. The case is referred to the Office of Chief Counsel, which sends the complaint by certified mail alleging that Carolyn charged unconscionable fees, gave irresponsible advice to clients, and falsified documents. Thirty days later, Carolyn offers a response in writing. The case goes before an administrative judge, who listens to evidence presented by the OPR and by Carolyn's attorney. Within 180 days, the judge issues his ruling, which agrees with the OPR's recommendation that Carolyn be disbarred. She chooses not to appeal and is banned from practice before the IRS.

If there is no appeal, the decision by the administrative law judge becomes final. However, either party—the OPR or the practitioner—may appeal the judge's decision with the Treasury Appellate Authority within 30 days.

The Treasury Appellate Authority will receive briefs and render what is known as the "Final Agency Decision."

For the OPR, this decision is final, but the practitioner may contest the Final Agency Decision in a U.S. district court. The judge will review the findings from the administrative law hearing, but will only set aside the decision if it is considered arbitrary or capricious, contrary to law, or an abuse of discretion.

Note: A practitioner who has been disbarred may petition the OPR for reinstatement after five years. The OPR may reinstate the practitioner if it determines that his conduct is not likely to be in violation of regulations and if granting the reinstatement is not contrary to the public interest.

Note: Under a new provision in the latest revision to Circular 230, the OPR has the right to use expedited suspension procedures against a practitioner under certain circumstances. First, §10.82 allows for these procedures when an attorney or CPA has already had his license revoked for cause by any state licensing agency or board. Further, expedited procedures can be used when a practitioner has been convicted of a crime involving dishonesty or breach of trust, or when he has demonstrated a pattern of "willful disreputable conduct" by failing to comply with certain of his personal federal tax filing obligations. §10.82 gives the OPR the ability to move more quickly in sanctioning practitioners. If a practitioner fails to respond to a §10.82 complaint or does not appear at a §10.82 conference, the OPR can suspend the practitioner immediately.

Prohibited Actions during Suspension or Disbarment

During disbarment or suspension, a practitioner will not be allowed to practice in any capacity before the IRS (except to represent himself). A disbarred or suspended practitioner may not:

- Prepare or file documents or other correspondence with the IRS. The restriction applies regardless of whether the individual signs the documents and regardless of whether the individual personally files, or directs another person to file, documents with the IRS. However, as a result of the *Loving* case, disbarred and suspended practitioners are eligible to prepare and file tax returns for compensation.[163]
- Render written advice with respect to any entity, transaction, plan, or arrangement having the potential for tax avoidance or evasion.

[163] The Office of Professional Responsibility released an official statement on this matter (OPR Statement 20052314).

- Represent a client at conferences, hearings, and meetings.
- Execute waivers, consents, or closing agreements; receive a taxpayer's refund check; or sign a tax return on behalf of a taxpayer.
- File powers of attorney with the IRS.
- Accept assistance from another person (or request assistance) or assist another person (or offer assistance) if the assistance relates to a matter constituting practice before the IRS, or enlist another person for purposes of practicing before the IRS.
- State or imply that he is eligible to practice before the IRS.

However, a disbarred or suspended individual is still allowed to:

- Represent himself in any matter.
- As mentioned previously, prepare tax returns for clients for compensation (due to the outcome of the *Loving* case).
- Appear before the IRS as a trustee, receiver, guardian, administrator, executor, or other fiduciary if duly qualified/authorized under the law of the relevant jurisdiction.
- Appear as a witness for a taxpayer.
- Furnish information at the request of the IRS or any of its officers or employees.
- Receive IRS information pursuant to a valid tax information authorization. However, simply receiving this information does not entitle a disbarred or suspended preparer to practice before the IRS on behalf of that taxpayer.

Example: Xochitl is a CPA who prepares tax returns. In 2016, she hires an enrolled agent named Bernie. During the year, Bernie comes under investigation by the Office of Professional Responsibility. Bernie is later disbarred for financial fraud and loses his EA license. Xochitl must dismiss Bernie as her employee. She cannot accept assistance from, or employ, a disbarred practitioner.

Unit 8: Study Questions

1. Under the revised Circular 230, the OPR has the right to use expedited suspension procedures against a practitioner for "willful disreputable conduct" involving which of the following transgressions?

A. Violating due diligence procedures related to the Earned Income Tax Credit.
B. Failure to use a PTIN when filing clients' federal tax returns.
C. Failure to comply with his personal federal tax filing obligations.
D. Failure to abide by IRS standards related to advertising and fees.

2. A suspended or disbarred individual may:

A. Appear before the IRS as a trustee, receiver, guardian, administrator, executor, or other fiduciary, if duly authorized under the law of the relevant jurisdiction.
B. File documents on a taxpayer's behalf.
C. Represent a client at IRS conferences, hearings, and meetings.
D. Execute a closing agreement for a client, so long as the practitioner has a valid power of attorney.

3. The OPR receives a referral about a practitioner and launches its own investigation. The OPR then determines he has violated provisions of Circular 230. Which of the following best describes the due process procedures that occur when a practitioner faces a potential sanction?

A. Notification and settlement discussions with the practitioner; formal complaint is filed; disciplinary hearing is held with an administrative law judge presiding; either the OPR or the practitioner can appeal; a final decision is rendered by the Treasury Appellate Authority; the practitioner must sue in court to contest the decision.
B. Notification and settlement discussions with the practitioner; a disciplinary hearing is held with an administrative law judge presiding; only the practitioner can appeal; a final decision is rendered by the Treasury Appellate Authority; no further appeal is granted either side.
C. A formal complaint is filed; a disciplinary hearing is held with an administrative law judge presiding; a final decision is rendered by the judge; the practitioner must sue the Treasury Appellate Authority to contest the decision.
D. A formal complaint is filed; a disciplinary hearing is held with an administrative law judge presiding; a final decision is rendered by the Treasury Appellate Authority; either the practitioner or the OPR must sue in court to contest the decision.

4. Which of the following types of disciplinary actions allow a practitioner to continue practicing before the IRS?

A. Disbarment.
B. Suspension from practice.
C. Censure.
D. All of the disciplinary actions listed above prevent a practitioner from practicing before the IRS.

5. Following disbarment, a practitioner may petition the OPR for reinstatement after a period of:

A. One year.
B. Five years.
C. Ten years.
D. Never. Disbarment is always permanent.

6. Which of the following is not listed in Circular 230 as conduct that could cause a practitioner to be censured, suspended, or disbarred?

A. Abusive language in connection with practice before the IRS.
B. Willfully failing to sign a federal tax return.
C. Conviction of a felony charge.
D. Indictment on a criminal offense charge.

7. If a practitioner has been disbarred, which of the following actions is he not allowed to do?

A. Serve as a witness at a friend's examination before the IRS.
B. Furnish information to the IRS at the request of a revenue officer.
C. Act as a representative for a client for a fee in an IRS audit.
D. Prepare his own federal tax return.

8. What is the shortest period of suspension that will be imposed upon a practitioner who has been found to violate a provision of Circular 230?

A. One month.
B. Six months.
C. One year.
D. Two years.

Unit 8: Answers

1. The answer is C. Under the §10.82, the OPR may move quicker to sanction practitioners by using expedited procedures in certain circumstances, including when a practitioner has been convicted of a crime involving dishonesty or breach of trust. The procedures are also allowed when a practitioner has demonstrated a pattern of "willful disreputable conduct" involving the following:

- Failing to file his federal income tax returns in four of the five previous tax years
- Failing to file a return required more frequently than annually (such as an employment tax return) during five of the seven previous tax periods

2. The answer is A. A disbarred practitioner may appear before the IRS as a trustee, receiver, guardian, administrator, executor, or other fiduciary, if duly qualified or authorized under the laws of the relevant jurisdiction.

3. The answer is A. A practitioner who is subject to a possible sanction has the following due process rights available. After the OPR receives a referral and investigates whether a Circular 230 violation has occurred, it notifies the practitioner and attempts to reach agreement on a sanction. If agreement cannot be reached, a formal complaint is filed, with the practitioner expected to answer the specific charges in writing. An administrative law judge then holds a hearing, with both the OPR and the practitioner (or his representative) presenting evidence. The judge has 180 days to hand down his decision on possible sanctions. At that point, either the OPR or the practitioner can appeal to the Treasury Appellate Authority, which will issue the Final Agency Decision in the matter. If the practitioner does not agree with the decision, he can sue in a U.S. district court. However, the district court judge will only reverse the decision if it is considered arbitrary or capricious, contrary to law, or an abuse of discretion.

4. The answer is C. A practitioner who is censured by the OPR is still eligible to practice before the IRS. Censure is a public reprimand. Unlike disbarment or suspension, censure does not affect an individual's eligibility to represent taxpayers before the IRS, although the OPR may subject the individual's future representation of taxpayers to conditions designed to promote high standards of conduct.

5. The answer is B. A practitioner may petition the OPR for reinstatement after a period of five years.

6. The answer is D. Circular 230 §10.51 details a large number of violations related to incompetence or disreputable conduct for which a practitioner may face sanctions from the OPR. The statute specifically cites "conviction" of criminal offense or felony charges, rather than merely an indictment on criminal offense or felony charges. Circular 230 also does not specify that conviction of misdemeanor charges is a sanctionable offense. However, the statute warns that practitioners may be sanctioned for offenses that are not specifically listed.

7. The answer is C. A practitioner who has been disbarred (or suspended) may not represent a client in front of the IRS, sign a tax return on behalf of a taxpayer, file powers of attorney with the IRS, or any number of other actions that are considered practice before the IRS. The other actions listed are allowed, even for a practitioner who has been disbarred or suspended.

8. The answer is A. The OPR can suspend a practitioner who has violated the rules and regulations of Circular 230 for a period of one month to 60 months.

Unit 9: Tax Payments & IRS Collections

More Reading:
Publication 594, *The Collection Process*
Publication 1035, *Extending the Tax Assessment Period*
Publication 971, *Innocent Spouse Relief*
Publication 556, *Examination of Returns, Appeal Rights, and Claims for Refund*
Publication 1660, *Collection Appeal Rights*

Taxpayers generally have several options to make payments owed on their tax returns or for estimated taxes. The following methods of payments are currently accepted by the IRS:

1. **Direct debit** (note: this is not the same thing as "Direct Pay")
2. **Credit card**
3. **Personal check, cashier's check, or money order**
4. **Installment agreement requests**
5. **Electronic Federal Tax Payment System (EFTPS)**
6. **Electronic funds withdrawal**
7. **Federal Tax Application (same-day wire transfer)**
8. **Direct Pay**

Payments do not have to be sent at the same time an electronic return is transmitted. For example, the return may be transmitted in January and the taxpayer may mail a payment by check at a later date. As long as the payment is mailed by the due date of the return, it will be considered timely.

On all checks or money orders, the preparer should write the taxpayer's daytime phone number, EIN, TIN, or SSN; the type of tax return; and the tax year to which the payment applies.[164] The check or money order should be made payable to "United States Treasury."

Note: Recently, the IRS launched a free web-based payment option, Direct Pay. It allows individual taxpayers with a valid Social Security number to make IRS payments directly from their checking or savings accounts. Taxpayers may pay their tax bill or make an estimated tax payment using the service, and will receive instant confirmation that their payment was submitted.

Electronic Federal Tax Payment System (EFTPS)

For any type of payment due the IRS at any time of the year, taxpayers can use the Electronic Federal Tax Payment System (EFTPS). Taxpayers and businesses enroll in EFTPS by using an online application.

Businesses and individuals can pay all their federal taxes using EFTPS. Individuals can pay their quarterly estimated taxes, and they can make payments weekly, monthly, or quarterly. Businesses can schedule payments up to 120 days in advance of their tax due date.

Individuals can schedule payments up to 365 days in advance of their tax due date. Domestic corporations must deposit all income tax payments by the due date of the return.

Tax Refunds

Taxpayers have a number of options related to their tax refunds. They may:

- Apply a refund to next year's estimated tax.
- Receive the refund as a direct deposit.
- Receive the refund as a paper check.

[164] Per Form 1040-V instructions.

- Split the refund, with a portion applied to next year's estimated tax and the remainder received as direct deposit or a paper check, or split the refund between three different accounts.
- Use the refund (or part of it) to purchase U.S. Series I Savings Bonds. Taxpayers can purchase up to $5,000 in bonds for themselves or others.

The direct deposit option is the fastest way to receive refunds. Refunds may be designated for direct deposit to qualified accounts in the taxpayer's name. Qualified accounts include savings, checking, share draft, or retirement accounts (for example, IRA or money market accounts).

Direct deposits can be deposited into a *my*RA®, a starter retirement account offered by the Treasury Department. Direct deposits cannot be made to credit card accounts, but can be made to prepaid debit cards. Qualified accounts must be in financial institutions within the United States. The number of refunds electronically deposited into a single account is limited to three. A preparer is required to accept any direct deposit election to a qualified account at an eligible financial institution designated by the taxpayer. A preparer may not charge a separate fee for direct deposit.

A preparer must advise the taxpayer that a direct deposit election cannot be rescinded once a return is filed. In addition, changes cannot be made to routing numbers of financial institutions or to the taxpayer's account numbers after the IRS has accepted the return. A preparer should verify account and routing numbers with the taxpayer each year.

Example: Nikki filed her tax return on January 20, 2016. She e-filed and chose direct deposit for her refund. Three days later, her purse was stolen and she had to close her bank account to prevent fraud. The direct deposit information cannot be changed on her return after it has been e-filed. The IRS will attempt to deposit her tax refund, but once the bank declines her deposit, her refund will default to a paper check.

Tax Payment Options

If a taxpayer owes a balance after filing a return, the IRS will send him a bill for the amount due, including any penalties and interest, which must be paid within 30 days. If he agrees with the information on the bill but is unable to pay the full amount, he is advised to pay as much as he can, and contact the IRS immediately to explain his situation. For taxpayers who are unable to pay the tax they owe, options include extensions of time to pay, installment agreements, and offers in compromise.

Extension of Time for Payment (Form 1127): A taxpayer should file Form 1127, *Application for Extension of Time for Payment of Tax Due to Hardship*, by the due date of his return, or by the due date for the amount determined as a deficiency. The types of taxes covered by Form 1127 include income taxes, self-employment taxes, and gift taxes.

The term "undue hardship" does not mean a taxpayer will simply be inconvenienced by paying the tax. Rather, for the IRS to grant a Form 1127 request, a taxpayer must show he will sustain a substantial financial loss if he pays tax on the date it is due. In the request for extension, a taxpayer must:

- Enter the date he proposes to pay the tax,
- Provide a detailed explanation of the undue hardship that would result if he paid the tax on or before the due date, and
- Provide supporting documentation, including a statement of assets and liabilities and an itemized list of income and expenses for each of the three months prior to the due date of the tax.

Example: Luis has significant expenses in hospital bills in the prior year, which depleted his savings. To pay the $8,500 he owes in taxes, he would have to sell his car at a sacrifice price. Doing so would create an undue hardship because he would not have reliable transportation, which could cause him to lose his job. Prior to the April 15 tax deadline, Luis files Form 1127 to request an extension of time to pay tax owed because of an undue hardship. He provides a full explanation of his financial difficulties as well as the other required documentation.

The IRS generally will not grant an extension of more than six months to pay the tax shown on a return. An extension to pay an amount determined as a deficiency is generally limited to 18 months from the date payment is due, but an extension to pay a deficiency will not be granted at all if the deficiency is due to negligence, intentional disregard of rules and regulations, or fraud with intent to evade tax.

Installment Agreements

Installment agreements are arrangements in which the IRS allows taxpayers to pay liabilities over time. Before applying for any installment agreement, the taxpayer (or business) must file all required tax returns.

A taxpayer who files electronically may apply for an installment agreement once the return is processed and the tax is assessed. Taxpayers must either submit Form 9465, *Installment Agreement Request*, or apply online if they qualify.

The IRS charges a one-time user fee to set up an installment agreement. Almost all the fees are increasing in 2017 (these fees would apply for any tax returns that were filed after January 1, 2017). In 2017, the fees for applying online are lower than the fees for applying over the phone or by submitting the paper Form 9465.

An agreement will be granted only if it provides for full payment of the taxpayer's account. This means the taxpayer must agree to pay the full balance due; he cannot use an installment agreement to negotiate a lower tax liability. During the term of the installment agreement, penalties and interest continue to accrue. Future refunds are applied to the tax debt until it is paid in full.

Equal monthly payments are specified in the agreement, but the taxpayer may choose to pay more than the required monthly amount. The maximum period of time to pay is up to 72 months. Taxpayers may pay a variety of ways, including by check, credit card, payroll deduction, or direct debit.

Qualified taxpayers who owe $25,000 or less may have their Notice of Federal Tax Lien withdrawn after entering into a direct debit installment agreement.

A taxpayer who owes $10,000 or less in tax cannot be turned down for an installment agreement, assuming that the following apply:

- The taxpayer (and spouse, if married) has timely filed all income tax returns and paid all tax due during the past five years.
- The IRS has determined the taxpayer cannot pay the tax owed in full when it is due.
- The taxpayer agrees to pay the full amount he owes within three years.

Applying Online: Individuals must owe $50,000 or less in combined individual income tax, penalties and interest, and have filed all required returns in order to apply for an installment agreement online.

In the case of a business taxpayer with a payroll tax liability, the business must owe $25,000 or less in payroll taxes and must have filed all required returns.

Installment Agreements	2016 Fees	Increased Fee as of Jan 1, 2017
Regular installment agreement	$120	$225
Regular installment agreement with direct debit (DDIA)	$52	$107
Low income installment agreement (regular or DDIA)	$43	$43
Online payment agreement (regular installment agreement)	$120	$149
Online payment agreement (Direct debit installment agreement (DDIA))	$52	$31
Restructured/reinstated installment agreement	$50	$89
Restructured/reinstated low income installment agreement (new fee)	$0	$43

Example: Charlene owes $36,000 in taxes and is not able to pay the balance due. She is under the $50,000 threshold, so she is eligible to apply for an installment agreement online. She applies online, and her installment agreement is approved by the IRS. Charlene has $500 deducted from her checking account every month via direct debit. Under the terms of the agreement, she must pay the entire amount within 72 months.

If a taxpayer owes more than $50,000, he may still qualify for an installment agreement, but Form 433-A or Form 433-F, *Collection Information Statement*, must be submitted.

The IRS generally will not take collection actions:

- When an installment agreement is being considered.
- While an installment agreement is in effect.
- For 30 days after an agreement request is rejected.
- During the period the IRS evaluates an appeal of a rejected or terminated agreement.

If a taxpayer fails to make a payment on an installment agreement, an automatic 30-day notice is generated. The IRS typically charges a fee for reinstating an installment agreement that has gone into default.

IRS Collection Process

The IRS has wide powers when it comes to collecting unpaid taxes. If a taxpayer does not pay in full when filing his tax return, he will receive a bill from an IRS service center. The first notice explains the balance due and demands payment in full. It will include the amount of the unpaid tax balance plus any penalties and interest calculated from the date the tax was due. This first notice starts the collection process, which continues until the taxpayer's account is satisfied or until the IRS may no longer legally collect the tax, such as when the collection period has expired.

Note: The IRS generally has ten years from the date of assessment to collect a tax debt from a taxpayer.

However, the ten-year collection period can be suspended in the following cases:

- While the IRS and the Office of Appeals consider a request for an installment agreement or an offer in compromise

- From the date a taxpayer requests a collection due process (CDP) hearing
- While the taxpayer is residing outside the United States
- For tax periods included in a bankruptcy

The amount of time the suspension is in effect will be added to the time remaining in the ten-year period. For example, if the ten-year period is suspended for six months, the time left in the period the IRS has to collect will increase by six months. The IRS is required to notify the taxpayer that he may refuse to extend the statute of limitations.

Bankruptcy

A filing in bankruptcy court immediately stops all assessment and collection of tax. This is called an *automatic stay*, and it remains in effect until the bankruptcy court lifts the stay or discharges liabilities, meaning they are eliminated or no longer legally enforceable.

Income tax debt that may be forgiven in bankruptcy must meet the following conditions:

- The tax debt must be related to a return that was due at least three years before the taxpayer filed for bankruptcy.
- The tax return must have been filed at least two years ago.
- The tax assessment must be at least 240 days old.

The taxpayer cannot be guilty of tax evasion, and the tax return cannot be fraudulent or frivolous.

Taxpayer's Ability to Pay

When there is a delinquent tax liability or when the taxpayer makes a request for an installment agreement or an offer in compromise, the IRS may use a variety of methods to assess the taxpayer's ability to pay. The IRS may consider the taxpayer's general financial health, including factors such as cash flow and assets, lawsuits against the taxpayer, garnishments, and whether the taxpayer has filed bankruptcy. Third party research, such as property assessments, asset values, and state and local tax information, may also be used.

Collection Financial Standards: The IRS *Collection Financial Standards* are used to evaluate a taxpayer's ability to pay a delinquent tax liability. These standards help determine allowable living expenses that are necessary to provide for a taxpayer's (and his family's) health and welfare and/or production of income while his tax debt is being repaid.

Allowances for housing, utilities, and transportation vary by location, while standard amounts are allowed nationwide for food, clothing, out-of-pocket health care expenses, and other items. In most cases, the taxpayer is allowed the amount actually spent, or the local standard, whichever is less. For the items based on national standards, a taxpayer is allowed the total amounts applicable for his family size, without regard to the amounts actually spent. Generally, the number of persons for whom necessary living expenses are allowed is the same as the number of exemptions on the taxpayer's most recent income tax return.

The IRS uses these standards for taxpayers who do not qualify for streamlined installment agreements, which require little financial analysis or substantiation of expenses. If a taxpayer believes he needs a higher amount for basic living expenses than the *Collection Financial Standards* allow, he must provide documentation to explain why.

Collection Information Statements: The information described above regarding allowable living expenses may be used to prepare a *Collection Information Statement*, using Form 433-A, Form 433-B, or Form 433-F. This statement also contains detailed financial information about the taxpayer's income, his bank and retirement accounts, real estate and other assets, and his outstanding debts. Further, it may include information concerning the taxpayer's obligations for court-ordered payments, such as child support and alimony, since the taxpayer will generally have little flexibility regarding these obligations.

"Currently Not Collectible" Status: The IRS can declare a taxpayer to be *currently not collectible* if the agency has received evidence that a taxpayer has no ability to pay his tax debts. Generally, this action is taken only when other options, such as an offer in compromise, are not feasible because the taxpayer's financial situation is so bad he cannot even afford to make monthly payments.

Before this status will be declared, the IRS will require a taxpayer to submit Form 433-F in order to demonstrate that after paying necessary living expenses, he has no money left to make monthly payments to the IRS. Further, he must prove he has no assets that could be liquidated or sold to make a lump sum payment to the IRS.

Once a taxpayer is placed into currently not collectible status (also known as *Status 53),* the IRS must stop all collection activities, such as levies. A taxpayer is generally granted this status for at least one year, or until his income increases. While in currently not collectible status, penalties and interest continue to be added to the tax debt.

IRS Actions to Collect Unpaid Taxes

Congress has given the IRS broad powers to compel taxpayers to produce information it requires to determine tax liability or to collect tax. The IRS is permitted to do the following:

- Examine any books, papers, records, or other data;
- Summon a taxpayer or any other person, requiring the person to appear, to produce books and records, and to give testimony under oath; and
- Take testimony under oath.

These powers are most commonly used in connection with collection proceedings, such as when a taxpayer refuses to provide information voluntarily, and in IRS audits, referred to as *examinations.*[165]

IRS enforcement actions to collect unpaid taxes may include the following:

- Issuing a notice of levy on salary and other income, bank accounts, or property (legally seizing property to satisfy the tax debt)
- Filing a Notice of Federal Tax Lien
- Issuing a summons to secure information to prepare unfiled tax returns or determine the taxpayer's ability to pay. IRS employees will prepare *substitute returns* when taxpayers do not file voluntarily[166]
- Applying future federal tax refunds to any prior amount due
- Offsetting a taxpayer's refund.

Under the Federal government's Treasury Offset Program ("TOP") there is generally no limit on the period during which an offset may be initiated or taken, meaning debts that are years, or even decades, old may be repaid by a refund offset. Debts may include past-due federal income tax, other federal debts such as student loans, state income tax, child and spousal support payments, and state unemployment compensation debt. A state income tax refund may also be applied to a taxpayer's federal tax liability.

Example: RJ had been expecting a $2,000 refund from his federal tax return. However, RJ has past due child support payments and debt from a delinquent student loan totaling $3,000. The IRS notifies RJ that the entire $2,000 he had been anticipating as a refund will be used to offset these debts.

[165] Even though the IRS uses the term "examination" rather than "audit" the terms mean essentially the same thing.

[166] These substitute returns generally do not give credit for deductions and exemptions a taxpayer may be entitled to receive. Even if the IRS has already filed a substitute return, a taxpayer may still file his own return. The IRS will generally adjust the taxpayer's account to reflect the correct figures after they receive the filed returns from the taxpayer.

Federal Tax Lien

A federal tax lien is a legal claim against a taxpayer's property, including property that the taxpayer acquires after the lien is filed. By filing a Notice of Federal Tax Lien, the IRS establishes its interest in the taxpayer's property as a creditor and as security for his tax debt, and publicly notifies the taxpayer's other creditors of its claim.

A Notice of Federal Tax Lien may be filed only after:

- The IRS assesses the taxpayer's liability,
- The IRS sends a notice and demand for payment, and
- The taxpayer neglects to pay the debt.

Once these requirements are met, a lien is created for the amount of the taxpayer's debt. The lien attaches to all the taxpayer's property, such as a house or car, and to all the taxpayer's rights to property (such as accounts receivable, in the case of a business).

Under the IRS's Fresh Start program, the filing threshold for the amount taxpayers can owe before a Notice of Federal Tax Lien is issued has been increased from $5,000 to $10,000 in most cases.

Once a lien is filed, the IRS generally cannot release it until the taxes are paid in full or until the government may no longer legally collect the tax.

Notice of Levy

An IRS seizure is the legal act of confiscating a taxpayer's property to satisfy a tax debt, as authorized by an earlier filed tax lien. If a tax lien is the IRS's authorization to act by seizing property, then the IRS levy is the actual act of seizure. A levy allows the IRS to confiscate and sell property, which may include cars, boats, or real estate. The IRS may also levy wages, bank accounts, Social Security benefits, and retirement income.

There are special rules regarding IRS seizures. The IRS generally must wait at least 30 days from the date of the notice of intent to levy before it can make a seizure. However, if the IRS has determined that collection of tax is in jeopardy, it may immediately seize property without the normal waiting period.

Typically, the IRS may not seize property in the following circumstances:

- When there is a pending installment agreement
- While a taxpayer's appeal is pending
- During the consideration of an offer in compromise
- During a bankruptcy (unless the seizure is authorized by the bankruptcy court)
- If the taxpayer's liability is $5,000 or less in a seizure of real property
- While innocent spouse claims are pending

The IRS may not seize a main home without prior approval from the IRS district director or assistant district director; judicial approval is also generally required for seizure of a main home.

Further, the following items are exempt from IRS levy:

- Wearing apparel and school books.
- Fuel, provisions (food), furniture, personal effects in the taxpayer's household, arms for personal use, or livestock, up to $9,120 in value for tax year 2016.
- Books and tools necessary for the trade, business, or profession of the taxpayer, up to $4,560 in value for tax year 2016.[167]
- Undelivered mail.
- Unemployment benefits and amounts payable under the Job Training Partnership Act.
- Workers' compensation, including amounts payable to dependents.

---

[167] Rev. Proc. 2015-63

- Certain annuity or pension payments, but only if payable by the Army, Navy, Air Force, Coast Guard, or under the Railroad Retirement Act or Railroad Unemployment Insurance Act. Traditional and Roth IRAs are not exempt from levy.
- Judgments for the support of minor children (child support).
- Certain public assistance and welfare payments, and amounts payable for Supplemental Security Income for the aged, blind, and disabled under the Social Security Act. Regular Social Security payments are not exempt from levy.

If an IRS levy creates an immediate economic hardship, it may be released. A levy release does not mean the taxpayer is exempt from paying the balance due.

IRS Summons

If a taxpayer or other witness refuses to comply with requests for IRS records or other information, the IRS has the power to issue a summons. An IRS examiner may issue an administrative summons to the taxpayer (or other third parties). An administrative summons directs the person summoned to appear before the examiner and testify or produce information. IRC §7602 authorizes the IRS to issue summonses for the following purposes:

- To ascertain the correctness of any return,
- To prepare a return where none has been made,
- To determine the liability of a person for internal revenue tax,
- To determine the liability at law or in equity of a transferee or fiduciary of a person in respect of any internal revenue tax,
- To collect any internal revenue tax liability, or
- To inquire into any civil or criminal offense connected with the administration or enforcement of the internal revenue law.

A summons should require only that the witness appear on a given date to give testimony or produce existing books, paper, and records that "may be relevant or material." A summons cannot require a witness to prepare or create documents, including tax returns, which do not exist. A summons cannot be issued solely to harass a taxpayer or to pressure him into settling a dispute.

The IRS must follow precise procedures in serving a summons upon a taxpayer or third party. The summons must be delivered in person to the taxpayer or left at his last known residence. Third-party recordkeepers may also be served by certified or registered mail.

When a summons is served in person to a taxpayer or left at his home, the person serving the summons must sign a *certificate of service*. This certificate must include the date and time the summons was served, the manner in which it was served (such as the address and whether it was left with a person), the server's title, and the server's signature. The certificate of service certifies that the taxpayer has been properly served. The server must also sign a *certificate of notice* when he serves a summons on a third-party record keeper.

An individual has the right to contest a summons based on various technical, procedural, or Constitutional grounds. However, if a taxpayer or other witness fails to respond to a summons within the prescribed period, the IRS may seek judicial enforcement through a U.S. district court.

Collection Appeal Rights

A taxpayer may appeal an IRS collection action to the IRS Office of Appeals. The Office of Appeals is separate from and independent of the IRS Collection offices that initiate collection actions. The IRS ensures the independence of the Appeals office through a strict policy prohibiting *ex parte* communication with the IRS Collection office about the accuracy of the facts or the merits of each case.

Definition: An **ex parte communication** is one that takes place between any IRS Appeals employee and employees of other IRS functions, without the taxpayer or his representative being given a chance to participate in the communication, whether it is written, on the phone, or in person.

The two main ways that taxpayers use to appeal an IRS collection action are collection due process and the collection appeals program.

Collection Due Process Hearings (CDP)

A taxpayer who wants to protest an IRS collection notice may complete Form 12153, *Request for a Collection Due Process or Equivalent Hearing,* and submit it to the address listed on the IRS notice. CDP procedures are available to taxpayers who have received any of the following notices:

- Notice of Federal Tax Lien
- Notice of Intent to Levy

A collection notice will be mailed, given to the taxpayer, or left at his home or office. A taxpayer has 30 days from the date of a notice to request a CDP hearing. Before the hearing, the taxpayer may attempt to work out a solution with the Collection office that sent the notice. If the issue cannot be resolved, the case will be forwarded to Appeals for the taxpayer (or his representative) to schedule a conference with an Appeals officer. The conference may be by telephone, correspondence, or face-to-face for taxpayers who qualify.

Many taxpayers ignore IRS notices until they receive a final notice or a notice of intent to levy. Often, by the time this happens, it is too late to help the taxpayer solve these issues, and the IRS has already begun the collection process in earnest.

Issues that may be discussed during a collection due process hearing include:

- Whether or not the taxpayer paid all the tax owed
- Whether the IRS assessed tax and sent the levy notice when the taxpayer was in bankruptcy
- Whether the IRS made a procedural error in the assessment
- Whether the time to collect the tax (the statute of limitations) has expired
- Whether the taxpayer wishes to discuss collection options
- Whether the taxpayer wishes to make a spousal defense (innocent spouse relief)

In a CDP hearing, a taxpayer may request specific action regarding a lien against his property. For example, he may request a *lien withdrawal* on the grounds the IRS filed the Notice of Federal Tax Lien prematurely or did not follow established procedures. Alternatively. he may request a *lien discharge* that removes a federal tax lien from a specific property.

Example: The IRS placed a federal tax lien on Pete's vacation condo in Florida. Pete's attorney attends a CDP hearing and asks that the lien be discharged so Pete may sell the condo and use the sales proceeds to pay the tax he owes. The Appeals officer agrees and releases the lien so that the property may be sold. Pete uses the proceeds from the sale to pay his delinquent tax debt.

After a CDP hearing, the Appeals officer will issue a written determination letter. If the taxpayer disagrees with the determination, he can request judicial review by petitioning the U.S. Tax Court. The petition must be made within the time period specified in the Appeals' determination letter. The taxpayer cannot raise any issues with the Tax Court that he did not already raise during the appeals hearing.

If a taxpayer timely files a CDP hearing request, no collection action can be taken until a final determination is made following the hearing or a subsequent appeal to the Tax Court.

Equivalent Hearing: If a taxpayer misses the deadline for requesting a CDP hearing and still wants to meet with Appeals, he may request an equivalent hearing. A taxpayer must file Form

12153, *Request for a Collection Due Process or Equivalent Hearing*, by sending it to the address on the lien or levy notice.

Note: Unlike a CDP hearing, an equivalent hearing will not prohibit levy or suspend the 10-year period for collection. Also unlike a CDP hearing, a taxpayer cannot go to court to appeal the IRS's decision following an equivalent hearing.

Collection Appeals Program (CAP)

The collection appeals program (CAP) is generally quicker than a CDP hearing and available for a broader range of collection actions. However, as is the case with an equivalent hearing, the taxpayer cannot go to court to appeal if he disagrees with a CAP decision. Also, under CAP, the taxpayer may not contest the underlying tax liability.

CAP is available in the following instances:

- Before or after the IRS files a Notice of Federal Tax Lien
- Before or after the IRS levies or seizes a taxpayer's property
- After the termination of an installment agreement
- After the rejection of an installment agreement

To appeal an installment agreement that has been rejected or that the IRS is proposing be modified or terminated, the taxpayer should appeal by completing Form 9423, *Collection Appeal Request*. The form should be submitted within 30 days to the IRS office or revenue officer who took the action regarding the installment agreement.

Example: Wesley applied for an installment agreement in 2016. Later that year, he was a victim of bank fraud and his bank account was drained suddenly without his knowledge. It took Westley several months to correct the problem. In the meantime, he received notification that his installment agreement had been rescinded. Wesley wants to appeal the cancellation of his installment agreement. He files Form 9423, *Collection Appeal Request.* He will explain his circumstances to an IRS employee and request a reinstatement of his installment agreement.

Example: Thomas was paying his tax debt under an installment agreement and missed a few payments. The IRS sent a notice that the installment agreement was cancelled and he must now pay the full outstanding balance. Thomas can appeal the termination of the installment agreement by requesting an Appeal under the Collection Appeals program (CAP).

Form 9423, *Collection Appeal Request,* is also used in the cases of liens, levies, and seizures. Generally, the taxpayer would first try to resolve the disagreement by telephone with an IRS employee, manager, or revenue officer. If the issue cannot be resolved, the taxpayer would submit a written request for Appeals consideration by completing Form 9423. The taxpayer must explain why he disagrees with the collection action and how he proposes to resolve his tax problem.

In the appeals hearing, a taxpayer may represent himself, or he may appoint a qualified representative (attorney, CPA, EA, spouse, or other family member). In the case of a business, the entity may be represented by a regular full-time employee, a general partner, or a bona fide officer.

Once the IRS makes a determination under CAP, it is binding on both the taxpayer and the IRS. The determination is final and cannot be appealed to the Tax Court.

Abatement of Penalties and Interest

In certain cases, the IRS will waive or abate penalties and interest assessed a taxpayer.

Penalties: A taxpayer may qualify for penalty relief in the following circumstances:

- When the penalty is incurred due to a major disaster or emergency affecting a large number of taxpayers in a given geographical area. Relief is often provided in the form of extensions of time to file or pay.
- When the penalty is due to an IRS computation or assessment error.

- When the penalty is incurred as a result of the taxpayer relying on advice of a tax advisor. This generally involves accuracy-related penalties and is limited to issues that are considered highly technical or complicated.
- When the penalty is incurred as the result of erroneous written advice provided by an IRS employee.

Penalty relief may also be provided due to *reasonable cause*. This is when a taxpayer has established that, despite the "exercise of ordinary business care and prudence," he was assessed a penalty due to circumstances beyond his control.

Under a special program, the IRS will use the reasonable cause standard to consider abatement of a taxpayer's first-time penalty charge on a one-time basis. This penalty relief is only available for failure to file, failure to pay, and failure to deposit penalties. The IRS will consider this relief option only if the taxpayer has filed all returns and paid, or arranged to pay, all tax currently due.

Interest: Reasonable cause is not allowed as the basis for abatement of interest. Interest may be abated or waived in the following instances:

- When it is excessive, barred by statute, or erroneously or illegally assessed
- When it is assessed on an erroneous refund
- When it was incurred on an account while the taxpayer was in a combat zone or in a declared disaster area.

Further, the IRS will waive interest that is the result of certain errors or delays caused by an IRS employee. The IRS will abate the interest only if there was an unreasonable error or delay in performing a managerial or ministerial act (defined below). The taxpayer cannot have caused any significant aspect of the error or delay. The interest can be abated only if it relates to taxes for which a notice of deficiency is required, which includes income taxes and estate and gift taxes.

Definition: A **managerial act** is an administrative act that occurs during the processing of the taxpayer's case involving the temporary or permanent loss of records or the exercise of judgment or discretion relating to management of personnel.

Example: A revenue agent is examining Margaret's tax return. During the course of the examination, the agent is sent to an extended training course. The agent's supervisor decides not to reassign the case, so the examination is unreasonably delayed until the agent returns. Interest caused by the delay can be abated since the decision to send the agent to the training class and the decision not to reassign the case are both managerial acts.

Definition: A **ministerial act** is a procedural or mechanical act that does not involve the exercise of judgment or discretion and that occurs during the processing of the taxpayer's case.

Example: Calvin moves to another state before the IRS selects his tax return for examination. Notice of the examination was sent to his old address and then forwarded to his new address. When Calvin gets the letter, he responds with a request that the examination be transferred to the area office closest to his new address. The examination group manager approves his request. However, the original examination manager forgets about the transfer and fails to transfer the file for six months. The transfer is a ministerial act. The IRS can reduce the interest Calvin owes because of the unreasonable delay in transferring the case.

A taxpayer may request an abatement of interest on Form 843, *Claim for Refund and Request for Abatement.* The taxpayer should file the claim with the IRS service center where the examination was affected by the error or delay. If a request for abatement of interest is denied, an appeal can be made to the IRS Appeals office or the U.S. Tax Court. When a portion of interest is abated, the IRS must recalculate the amount of remaining interest the taxpayer owes.

Seeking Relief from Joint Liability

Married taxpayers often file jointly because of benefits this filing status affords. In the case of a joint return, both taxpayers are liable for the tax and any interest or penalties, even if they later separate or divorce. *Joint and several liability* means that each taxpayer is legally responsible for the entire liability. This is true even if only one spouse earned all the income, or if a divorce decree states that a former spouse is or is not responsible for any amounts due on previously filed joint returns.

In some cases, however, a spouse who filed joint returns can receive relief from joint and several liability:

Innocent Spouse Relief: Provides relief from additional tax if a spouse or former spouse failed to report income or claimed improper deductions.

Separation of Liability Relief: Provides for the allocation of additional tax owed between the taxpayer and his spouse or former spouse because an item was not reported properly on a joint return. The tax allocated to the taxpayer is the amount for which he is responsible.

Equitable Relief: May apply when a taxpayer does not qualify for innocent spouse relief or separation of liability relief for items not reported properly on a joint return and generally attributable to the taxpayer's spouse. A taxpayer may also qualify for equitable relief if the correct amount of tax was reported on his joint return but the tax remains unpaid.

Requesting Innocent Spouse Relief

The taxpayer must meet all of the following conditions in order to qualify for innocent spouse relief:

- The taxpayer filed a joint return that has an understatement of tax directly related to his spouse's erroneous items.
- The taxpayer establishes that, at the time he signed the joint return, he did not know and had no reason to know that there was an understatement of tax.
- Taking into account all the facts and circumstances, it would be unfair for the IRS to hold the taxpayer liable for the understatement.

In order to apply for innocent spouse relief, a taxpayer must submit Form 8857, *Request for Innocent Spouse Relief*, and sign it under penalty of perjury.

A request for innocent spouse relief will be denied if the IRS proves that property was transferred between the taxpayer and the spouse or former spouse as part of a fraudulent scheme to defraud the IRS or another third party. If a taxpayer requests innocent spouse relief, the IRS cannot enforce collection action while the request is pending, but interest and penalties continue to accrue.

Example: Nancy and Allen are married and file jointly. At the time Nancy signed their joint return, she was unaware her husband had a gambling problem. The IRS examined their return and determined that Allen's unreported gambling winnings were $25,000. Allen kept the gambling proceeds for himself and hid the bank statements from his wife. Nancy was able to prove that she did not know about, and had no reason to know about, the additional $25,000, because Allen had concealed his gambling winnings. The understatement of tax due to the $25,000 qualifies for innocent spouse relief.

Requesting Separation of Liability Relief

To qualify for separation of liability relief, the taxpayer must have filed a joint return and be no longer married (including a taxpayer who is widowed), legally separated, or living apart for the 12 months prior to the filing of a claim. Living apart does not include a spouse who is only temporarily absent from the household, in which case the taxpayer would not qualify for separation of liability relief.

The spouse or former spouse who is applying for separation of liability relief must not have known about the understatement of tax at the time of signing the return. An exception is made for spousal abuse or domestic violence, if the taxpayer had been afraid that failing to sign the return could result in harm or retaliation.

Example: Lenora and Martin have lived apart since 2014 and divorced in 2016. In the tax year before they separated, they filed a joint return showing Lenora's wages of $35,000 and Martin's self-employment income of $15,000. In an audit, the IRS found that Martin failed to report $25,000 of self-employment income, which resulted in a $7,500 understatement of tax. Since she is now divorced from Martin, Lenora filed Form 8857 to request relief by separation of liability. However, the IRS was able to prove that Lenora knew about the $25,000 of additional income because it was deposited into their joint bank account and she had use of the funds. She is not eligible for separation of liability relief, and the IRS denies her request.

Requesting Equitable Relief

A taxpayer who does not qualify for innocent spouse relief or separation of liability relief may qualify for equitable relief. The taxpayer must establish, based upon all the facts and circumstances, that it would be unfair to hold him liable for the understatement or underpayment of tax.

The IRS considers a taxpayer's current marital status, whether there is a legal obligation under a divorce decree to pay the tax, and whether he would suffer significant economic hardship if relief were not granted.

Example: Paula and Joshua were married in 2014 and filed a joint return that showed they owed $10,000. Paula had $5,000 of her own money and she took out a loan to pay the other $5,000. Paula gave Joshua the money to pay the $10,000 liability. Without telling Paula, Joshua spent $5,000 rather than paying the full tax liability. The couple divorced in 2016. Paula did not know at the time she signed the return that the tax would not be paid. These facts indicate to the IRS that it may be unfair to hold Paula liable for the $5,000 underpayment.

The following factors weigh in favor of equitable relief:

- Abuse by the spouse or former spouse
- Poor mental or physical health on the date the taxpayer signed the return or requested relief

The IRS has expanded the amount of time to request equitable relief. A taxpayer seeking relief from a balance due has up to ten years to file a request, the same period the IRS has to collect the tax. If the taxpayer is making a claim for a refund, he must file his request within the statute of limitations for refunds. More time may be allowed for taxpayers who are physically or mentally unable to manage their financial affairs or who live in federally-declared disaster areas.

Injured Spouse Claims

Innocent spouse relief should not be confused with an injured spouse claim. A taxpayer may qualify as an injured spouse if he filed a joint return and his share of the refund was applied against past due amounts owed by his spouse.

An injured spouse may be entitled to recoup only his share of a tax refund. When a joint return is filed and the refund is used to pay one spouse's past-due federal tax, state income tax, child support, spousal support, or federal nontax debt (such as a delinquent student loan), the other spouse may be considered an injured spouse. The injured spouse can request his share of the refund using Form 8379, *Injured Spouse Allocation*.

Example: Trudy and Brent marry and file jointly in 2016. Unknown to Trudy, Brent has unpaid child support and debt from a delinquent student loan. Their entire refund is retained to pay Brent's outstanding debts. Trudy may qualify for injured spouse treatment and recoup her share of the tax refund. The IRS will keep Brent's share of the refund to pay the delinquent debts.

Offer in Compromise Program

An offer in compromise (OIC) is an agreement between a taxpayer and the IRS that settles the taxpayer's tax liabilities for less than the full amount owed. Generally, the IRS will accept an offer if it represents the most the agency can expect to collect within a reasonable period of time. Absent special circumstances, an offer will not be accepted if the IRS believes that the liability can be paid in full as a lump sum or through a payment agreement. The IRS will consider each taxpayer's unique set of facts and circumstances in determining whether to grant an OIC, including his ability to pay, income, expenses, and asset equity.

To apply for an OIC on grounds of "doubt as to collectability" or "exceptional circumstances," a taxpayer must submit an application fee and initial nonrefundable payment along with Form 656, *Offer in Compromise*. Fees may be waived for low-income taxpayers. There is no fee or initial payment required to apply for an OIC on grounds of doubt as to liability and Form 656-L is used instead.

The taxpayer may appeal a rejected offer in compromise within 30 days. As part of its Fresh Start initiative, the IRS has expanded and streamlined the OIC program. The agency has more flexibility when analyzing a taxpayer's ability to pay, which makes the program available to a larger group of taxpayers. Taxpayers can use the OIC pre-qualifier tool at www.irs.gov to see if they may be eligible for an OIC. An offer in compromise can be applied to all taxes, including interest and penalties. A taxpayer may submit an OIC on three grounds:

Doubt as to Collectability
Doubt exists that the taxpayer could ever pay the full amount of tax liability owed within the remainder of the statutory period for collection.
Example: Elise owes $80,000 for unpaid tax liabilities and agrees that the tax she owes is correct. Elise is terminally ill and cannot work. She does not own any property and does not have the ability to fully pay the liability now or through monthly installment payments.
Doubt as to Liability
A legitimate doubt exists that the assessed tax liability is correct.
Example: Sofia was vice president of a corporation from 2006 to 2015. In late 2016, the corporation accrued unpaid payroll taxes and she was assessed a trust fund recovery penalty. However, by January 2016, Sofia had resigned from the corporation, prior to any of these delinquent payroll taxes accruing. Since there is legitimate doubt that the assessed tax liability is correct, she may apply for an OIC under doubt as to liability.
Exceptional Circumstances (Effective Tax Administration)
There is no doubt that the tax is correct and there is potential to collect the full amount of the tax owed, but an exceptional circumstance exists. A taxpayer must demonstrate that the collection of the tax would create serious economic hardship or would be unfair.
Example: Brad and Stacy Snyder have assets sufficient to satisfy their tax liability. However, they provide full-time care to their dependent child, who has a serious chronic illness. The unpaid taxes were a result of the Snyders providing necessary medical care for their sick child. They will need to continue to use their assets to provide for basic living expenses and ongoing care for the child. There is no doubt that the tax is correct, but to pay the tax would endanger the life of their child and would create a serious hardship.

Unit 9: Study Questions

1. What recourse does a taxpayer have if he misses the deadline to request a collection due process hearing with IRS Appeals?

A. None. He must pay the contested tax liability or enter into some other payment arrangement.
B. He may request an equivalent hearing.
C. Since he missed his deadline, he cannot use the IRS Appeals system. He must instead contest his liability in the U.S. Tax Court or sue for a refund in the U.S. court system.
D. There is no deadline to request a collection due process hearing, so he may pursue his case through IRS Appeals without any issue.

2. The statute of limitations on collection activity can be suspended in certain instances. The ten-year collection period may be suspended in each of the following instances except:

A. While the IRS and the Office of Appeals consider a request for an installment agreement or an offer in compromise.
B. From the date a taxpayer requests a collection due process (CDP) hearing.
C. While the taxpayer is in prison.
D. While the taxpayer lives outside the United States.

3. A taxpayer may qualify as an injured spouse if:

A. He files a joint return and his share of the refund is applied against past due amounts owed by a spouse.
B. He files a joint return and fails to report income.
C. He files a separate return and has the refund offset by past due student loan obligations.
D. He files for bankruptcy protection.

4. If the IRS rejects an offer in compromise, a taxpayer may appeal within:

A. 30 days.
B. 60 days.
C. 90 days.
D. There is no time limit to appeal an offer in compromise.

5. Belinda and Neil file jointly. They report $15,000 of income, but Belinda knows that Neil is not reporting $3,000 of dividends. The income is not hers, and she has no access to it since it is in Neil's bank account. She signs the joint return. The return is later chosen for examination, and penalties are assessed. Does Belinda qualify for innocent spouse relief?

A. No, because she knew about the understated income.
B. Yes, because she had no control over the income.
C. No, but she is eligible for injured spouse relief.
D. None of the above.

6. A levy allows the IRS to:

A. Publicly notify a taxpayer's creditors of a claim against his property.
B. Confiscate and sell property to satisfy a tax debt.
C. Collect tax beyond the statute of limitations.
D. Sell property on behalf of the taxpayer.

7. Art owes $55,000 to the IRS. He would like to set up an installment agreement. Which of the following statements regarding his payment options is correct?

A. Art may qualify for an installment agreement, but a *Collection Information Statement*, Form 433-F, must be completed.
B. Art does not qualify for an installment agreement because he owes more than $50,000.
C. Art may qualify for an installment agreement, but an offer in compromise must first be completed.
D. Art must enroll in EFTPS and have automatic withdrawals in order to have his installment agreement approved.

8. Lena owes $20,000 for unpaid federal tax liabilities. She agrees she owes the tax, but she has a serious medical problem and her monthly income does not meet her necessary living expenses. She does not own any real estate and does not have the ability to fully pay the liability now or through monthly installment payments. What type of offer in compromise may she qualify for?

A. Doubt as to collectability
B. Doubt as to liability
C. Effective tax administration
D. Collection advocate procedure

9. Which statement is correct regarding the process of a taxpayer appealing an IRS collection action?

A. The decision in a collection due process (CDP) hearing is final, and a taxpayer may not appeal even if he is unhappy with the determination.
B. A disposition in the collection appeals program is typically slower than in a CDP, but the taxpayer has the right to appeal if he is unhappy with a CAP determination.
C. Innocent spouse relief may not be discussed during a CDP hearing.
D. If a taxpayer disagrees with the Appeals office determination after a CDP hearing, he can appeal to the U.S. Tax Court.

10. By law, the IRS must sign a __________ when issuing a summons to a taxpayer.

A. Temporary restraining order
B. Federal notice of levy
C. Certificate of service
D. Federal notice of lien

11. Separation of liability relief does not apply to taxpayers who are:

A. Divorced.
B. Legally separated.
C. Widowed.
D. Single (never married).

12. How does the IRS begin the process of collections?

A. With an email to the taxpayer shortly after he files his tax return.
B. With a certified letter to the taxpayer immediately after a tax return is processed and flagged for audit.
C. With a written examination notice when the taxpayer is notified of the possibility of an audit.
D. A first notice will be sent, which is a letter that explains the balance due and demands payment in full.

13. Sheila and Dale were married in 2016. They are owed a refund on their joint return, but the refund is offset against Dale's past-due child support. Does Sheila have any recourse to recover her portion of the refund?

A. No. Since they filed jointly, Sheila's portion of the refund cannot be recovered.
B. Sheila may be eligible for injured spouse relief.
C. Sheila may be eligible for innocent spouse relief.
D. Both B and C.

14. The IRS may legally seize property in which of the following circumstances?

A. During the consideration of an offer in compromise.
B. If the collection of tax is in jeopardy.
C. If the taxpayer's liability is $5,000 or less in a seizure of real property (real estate).
D. While an innocent spouse claim is pending.

15. An installment agreement allows a taxpayer to do all of the following except:

A. Pay his tax debt in equal monthly payments over a period of time.
B. Negotiate with the IRS for a lower tax liability.
C. Pay his tax debt in variety of ways, such as by check, credit card, payroll deduction, or direct debit.
D. Avoid IRS collection actions, including levies.

16. All of the following statements about the IRS statute of limitations are correct except:

A. The IRS generally has ten years following an assessment to begin proceedings to collect the tax by levy or in a court proceeding.
B. The IRS is required to notify the taxpayer that he may refuse to extend the statute of limitations.
C. The IRS does not allow the taxpayer the right to extend the statute of limitations.
D. The statute of limitations on collection activity may be suspended in certain cases.

17. All of the following property is exempt from an IRS levy except:

A. Undelivered mail.
B. Child support payments.
C. Social Security payments.
D. Unemployment benefits.

18. The IRS may not generally pursue collection enforcement action against a taxpayer who has been placed in "currently not collectible" status for a minimum of:

A. Six months.
B. One year.
C. Two years.
D. No specified time limit.

19. All of the following statements regarding IRS installment agreements are correct except:

A. During the course of the installment agreement, penalties and interest continue to accrue.
B. A taxpayer who owes $10,000 or less in taxes will be automatically approved for an installment agreement.
C. An installment agreement allows a taxpayer to pay a set amount toward a tax liability on a monthly basis.
D. An IRS levy may be served during an installment agreement.

20. Which of the following amounts is the IRS least likely to challenge when evaluating a taxpayer's offer in compromise?

A. Rent
B. Prescription drugs
C. Child support
D. Food

21. Penalties and interest continue to accrue on a taxpayer's unpaid tax liability in which of the following instances?

A. When an installment agreement is in place.
B. When a taxpayer has been declared currently not collectible.
C. When a taxpayer requests innocent spouse relief.
D. All of the above.

22. How long may the IRS offset a taxpayer's past due federal tax liability by retaining his tax refund?

A. For three years.
B. For ten years.
C. Indefinitely.
D. Never. This action is prohibited.

23. If the IRS has filed a notice of seizure, how long must it wait before actually seizing a taxpayer's nonexempt property?

A. Immediately, with the exception of a taxpayer's home, which requires judicial approval.
B. Seven days.
C. 30 days.
D. 60 days.

24. Rosalyn is receiving a federal tax refund this year. Which of the following methods is not available for her to receive her refund?

A. She may apply the refund to next year's estimated tax.
B. She may receive the refund as a direct deposit to her retirement account.
C. She may use her refund to purchase U.S. Series I Savings Bonds.
D. She may direct deposit her refund to her credit card account.

25. How much extra time will the IRS grant for a taxpayer to pay his tax liability under the undue hardship extension?

A. Three months.
B. Six months.
C. One year.
D. 18 months.

Unit 9: Answers

1. The answer is B. If a taxpayer still wants a hearing with the IRS Appeals office after the deadline for requesting a timely collection due process (CDP) hearing has passed, he may request an equivalent hearing. A taxpayer must file Form 12153, *Request for a Collection Due Process or Equivalent Hearing*, and send it to the address on the lien or levy notice. However, an equivalent hearing has some disadvantages for the taxpayer. Unlike a CDP hearing, an equivalent hearing will not prohibit a levy or suspend the 10-year period for collection. Also, a taxpayer is not allowed to go to court to appeal the IRS's decision following an equivalent hearing. In a CDP hearing, a taxpayer does not give up his appeal rights if he loses.

2. The answer is C. The ten-year collection period is not suspended when a taxpayer is in prison. The ten-year collection period may be suspended in the following cases:

- While the IRS considers a request for an installment agreement or an offer in compromise
- From the date a taxpayer requests a collection due process (CDP) hearing
- For tax periods included in a bankruptcy
- While the taxpayer is residing outside the United States

3. The answer is A. A taxpayer may qualify as an injured spouse if he filed a joint return and his share of the refund was applied against past due amounts owed by a spouse. The injured spouse may be entitled to recoup only his share of a tax refund.

4. The answer is A. The IRS requires a taxpayer whose offer in compromise has been rejected to file an appeal within 30 days.

5. The answer is A. Belinda is not eligible for innocent spouse relief because she knew about the understated income. She signed the return knowing that the income was not included, so the IRS will not grant her relief.

6. The answer is B. A levy allows the IRS to confiscate and sell property to satisfy a tax debt. An IRS levy refers to the actual seizing of property authorized by an earlier filed tax lien. Answer A refers to a lien, which gives the IRS a legal claim to a taxpayer's property as security for his tax debt.

7. The answer is A. If a taxpayer owes more than $50,000, he may still qualify for an installment agreement, but the taxpayer will also need to complete Form 433-F, *Collection Information Statement*.

8. The answer is A. Lena may apply for an offer in compromise under doubt as to collectability. Doubt exists that she could ever pay the full amount of tax liability owed within the remainder of the statutory period for collection.

9. The answer is D. In an appeals hearing, the taxpayer retains the right to appeal to the Tax Court, unlike in the collection appeals program (CDP), where the determination is final.

10. The answer is C. When a taxpayer is served a summons in person or it is left at his home, the person serving the summons must sign a *certificate of service.* This certificate must include the date and time the summons was served, the manner in which it was served (such as the address and whether it was left with a person), the server's title, and the server's signature. The certificate of service certifies that the taxpayer has been properly served. The server must also sign a *certificate of notice* when he serves a summons on a third-party record keeper. The IRS can use its summons authority when a taxpayer or other witness refuses to comply with IRS requests for records or other information.

11. The answer is D. To qualify for separation of liability relief, the taxpayer must have filed a joint return, meaning the taxpayer must have been married at one time. Separation of liability applies to taxpayers who are no longer married (including a taxpayer who is widowed), legally separated, or living apart for the 12 months prior to the filing of a claim.

12. The answer is D. If a taxpayer does not pay in full when filing his tax return, he will receive a bill in the mail from an IRS service center. The first notice will explain the balance due and demand payment in full. It will include the amount of the tax plus any penalties and interest added to the taxpayer's unpaid balance from the date the tax was due. The IRS will never email a taxpayer a first notice about an unpaid liability.

13. The answer is B. Sheila can file Form 8379, *Injured Spouse Allocation*, and request injured spouse relief. If married taxpayers filed a joint return and the refund was offset, an injured spouse can file Form 8379 to request the portion of the refund attributed to him or her.

14. The answer is B. The IRS may seize or levy property if the collection of tax is in jeopardy, and may do so without the normal waiting period if a jeopardy assessment has been made. Typically, the IRS may not seize property in the following circumstances:

- When there is a pending installment agreement
- While a taxpayer's appeal is pending
- During the consideration of an offer in compromise
- During a bankruptcy (unless the seizure is authorized by the bankruptcy court)
- If the taxpayer's liability is $5,000 or less, in a seizure of real property
- While innocent spouse claims are pending

15. The answer is B. An installment agreement allows a taxpayer to pay his tax liability over a period of time if he cannot pay the amount when it is due. An installment agreement cannot be used to negotiate with the IRS for a lower tax bill. During the time an installment agreement is in place, penalties and interest continue to accrue.

16. The answer is C. The taxpayer may choose to extend the statute of limitations or he may refuse to extend the statute. If a taxpayer does not file a tax return, the statute of limitations does not expire. The statute of limitations on collection activity may also be suspended in certain instances. The amount of time the suspension is in effect will be added to the time remaining in the ten-year period.

17. The answer is C. Regular Social Security payments are not exempt from IRS levy.

18. The answer is B. If the IRS has determined a taxpayer's status is currently not collectible, it is generally prohibited from pursuing all collection activities for at least one year, or until the taxpayer's income has increased.

19. The answer is D. No levies may be served during installment agreements. During the course of an installment agreement, penalties and interest continue to accrue. A taxpayer who owes less than $10,000 in taxes will automatically be approved for an installment agreement under most circumstances.

20. The answer is C. The IRS *Collection Financial Standards* are used to evaluate a taxpayer's ability to pay a delinquent tax liability. These standards help determine allowable living expenses that are necessary to provide for a taxpayer's (and his family's) health and welfare and/or production of income while his tax debt is being repaid. Allowances for housing, utilities, and transportation vary by location, while standard amounts are allowed nationwide for food, clothing, out-of-pocket health care expenses, and other items. Consideration is also given to the taxpayer's income, his bank and retirement accounts, real estate and other assets, and his outstanding debts. Further, the taxpayer may have obligations for court-ordered payments, such as child support and alimony. Since the taxpayer will have little flexibility regarding these obligations, the IRS would be unlikely to challenge amounts that are supported by evidence the taxpayer provides.

21. The answer is D. The IRS will continue to assess penalties and interest on a taxpayer's unpaid tax liability in most circumstances, including during the period when an installment agreement is in place, when a taxpayer has been declared "currently not collectible", and when a taxpayer requests innocent spouse relief.

22. The answer is C. In most cases, the IRS may use a tax refund to offset a taxpayer's federal debts indefinitely. The regular 10-year collection statute does not apply. Debts may include past-due federal income tax; other federal debts such as student loans, state income tax, and child and spousal support payments; and state unemployment compensation debt.

23. The answer is C. After the IRS has filed a notice of intent to seize, it must wait 30 days before actually seizing a taxpayer's nonexempt property. It legally cannot seize items such as clothing, food, fuel, furniture, and personal effects up to a specified, inflation-adjusted amount. Undelivered mail and books and tools of the trade needed for the taxpayer's business are also exempt, up to a certain amount. Further, the IRS cannot seize unemployment benefits, worker's compensation, child support payments, and certain disability and public assistance payments. However, most Social Security benefits and retirement fund proceeds may be seized to fulfill a taxpayer's debt obligation. Before a taxpayer's home is seized, there generally must be judicial approval.

24. The answer is D. A taxpayer may not designate a credit card account for direct deposit of their federal tax refund. However, the IRS will deposit refunds onto a prepaid debit card.

25. The answer is B. The IRS generally will not grant an extension of more than six months to pay the tax due on a return. A taxpayer may file Form 1127, *Application for Extension of Time for Payment of Tax Due to Hardship*, to explain why he cannot pay the tax. He must provide a detailed explanation of the undue hardship that would result if he paid the tax when it is due and provide adequate documentation of his financial situation.

Unit 10: The IRS Examination Process

More Reading:
Publication 556, *Examination of Returns, Appeal Rights, and Claims for Refund*
Publication 1, *Your Rights as a Taxpayer*
Publication 3498, *The Examination Process*
Publication 3605, *Fast Track Mediation: A Process for Prompt Resolution of Tax Issues*

Overview of the IRS Audit Process

The IRS accepts most tax returns as they are filed, but selects a small percentage for examination.

Statistics: The IRS typically audits 1% of the total number of individual tax returns filed. Higher income earners were audited much more frequently than those who earned less. The IRS reports the audit rate for individual returns with total income of $1 million or more was 10.80%. Returns claiming refundable credits, such as the EITC, are also audited at a higher rate than normal returns. Of all the individual returns audited, more than a third were returns with Earned Income Tax Credit claims.[168]

An IRS examination is a review of the accounts and financial information supporting an organization or individual's income tax return. An examination evaluates whether information on the return is being reported correctly and according to the tax laws, and verifies that the amount of tax reported is accurate. Due to disclosure requirements, the IRS will always notify a taxpayer about an examination by mail, but never by email.

Filing an amended return does not affect the selection process for original returns. Amended returns go through a separate screening process and may be selected for audit.

Selecting a return for examination does not necessarily suggest that the taxpayer has made an error or has been dishonest. However, a taxpayer's responsibility to provide support for entries, deductions, and statements made on a tax return is known as the *burden of proof*. The taxpayer must be able to substantiate expenses in order to deduct them. Taxpayers can usually meet this burden of proof by having the receipts for the expenses.

After an examination, if any changes to a taxpayer's return are proposed, he can disagree with the changes and appeal the IRS's determination. This is done through the appeals process.

The IRS conducts most examinations entirely by mail. In these *correspondence audits*,[169] a taxpayer will receive a letter asking for additional information about certain items shown on the return, such as proof of income, expenses, and itemized deductions.

Correspondence audits typically occur when there is a minor issue that the IRS needs to clarify. For example, the IRS may have detected a math error or there may be a discrepancy between the tax return and the 1099 statements sent by brokers, banks, or mutual funds. Other times, the IRS simply requests evidence that a particular transaction has transpired as reported on the tax return.

Example: The IRS selects Anwen's return for examination. Anwen had claimed her older half-brother as a qualifying child based on his permanent disability, and she had also claimed head of household status. The IRS asks for proof of disability and residency, and Anwen provides copies of doctors' records and additional evidence that her brother lives with her full-time. The IRS accepts Anwen's documents and closes the case as a no-change audit. Anwen does not have to meet with the IRS auditor, as the entire audit is conducted by mail.

[168] Internal Revenue Service Data Book, 2013.
[169] IRS Data Book: In fiscal year 2013, 75% of all examinations were correspondence audits.

How Returns are Selected for Examination

The IRS examines a percentage of all federal tax returns to determine if income, expenses, and credits are being reported accurately. The IRS selects returns for examination using various methods which include random sampling, computerized screening, and comparison of information received by the IRS such as Forms W-2 and 1099 (this is also called "third-party" information).

When tax returns are filed, they are compared against the norms for similar returns. The IRS selects returns for examination using a variety of methods, including:

- **Potentially Abusive/Tax Avoidance Transactions:** Some returns are selected based on information obtained by the IRS through efforts to identify promoters of and participants in abusive tax avoidance transactions.
- **Computer Scoring/DIF Score:** Returns may be chosen on the basis of computer scoring. A computer program called the Discriminant Inventory Function System (DIF) assigns a numeric score to each individual and certain corporate tax returns after they have been processed.[170]
- **Information Matching:** Some returns are examined because third party reports, such as Forms W-2 or 1099, do not match the applicable amounts reported on the tax return.
- **Related Examinations:** Returns may be selected for audit when they involve transactions with or issues related to other taxpayers, such as business partners or investors, whose returns were selected for examination.
- **Third Party Information:** Returns may be selected as a result of information received from other third-party sources or individuals. Sources may include state and local law enforcement agencies, public records, and individuals. The information is evaluated for reliability and accuracy before it is used as the basis of an examination (or a possible criminal investigation).

A taxpayer's odds of being audited increase if his income is over $200,000, he is self-employed, or his itemized deductions were much higher than other taxpayers with similar incomes.

Other issues that may draw IRS attention include taking large charitable deductions; claiming the home office deduction; claiming rental losses; deducting business meals, travel, and entertainment; claiming 100% business use of a vehicle; deducting a loss for a hobby activity; running a cash business; failing to report a foreign bank account; and engaging in currency transactions.

Example: Perry is an EA with a client, Lila, who received an audit notice this year. Lila's tax return was selected because she had a large number of tax credits and very little taxable income. However, her tax return was prepared correctly. Lila had adopted four special-needs children in 2016 and was able to take a large Adoption Credit. Perry provided proof of the adoptions to the examining officer, which resulted in a positive outcome for Lila: a no-change audit.

---

[170] IRS computers automatically check tax returns and assign a Discriminant Inventory Function System (DIF) score based on the probability that the return contains errors, excessive tax deductions, or other issues. This does not necessarily mean that the return was prepared incorrectly. However, the screening is intended to identify aberrations and questionable items. If a taxpayer's return is assigned a high score under the DIF system, the return has a high probability of being chosen for audit. The IRS does not release information about how it calculates a taxpayer's DIF score.

Example: Van embezzled money from his employer and was arrested for felony embezzlement. The case was made public, and the police shared its information with the IRS. The IRS then contacted Van and proposed adjustments to his tax returns, assessing additional tax, interest, and penalties for fraud for failing to report the embezzled funds as income. This is an example of third party information that can trigger an IRS criminal investigation.

Taxpayer Examination Rights and Obligations

The IRS chooses to conduct some audits face-to-face, which are known as field audits. After notification of the planned audit, the taxpayer or the taxpayer's representative must make an appointment to meet with the IRS examiner. Either before or during an initial interview, the IRS examiner must explain the examination and collection process and the taxpayer's rights during the process. These rights include:

- A right to professional and courteous treatment by IRS employees
- A right to privacy and confidentiality about tax matters
- A right to know why the IRS is asking for information, how the IRS will use it, and what will happen if the requested information is not provided
- A right to representation, either by oneself or an authorized representative
- A right to appeal disagreements, both within the IRS and before the courts

During an examination, the IRS has the right to confirm every item on a taxpayer's return. Form 4564, *Information Document Request* (IDR), is used to request information from the taxpayer. The taxpayer must make available any documents the IRS requests, including providing access to computer files such as QuickBooks. If a taxpayer fails to produce requested documents, an examiner must determine whether to issue a summons to secure the documents.

The Taxpayer's Representative

A taxpayer may always represent himself during an examination. Alternatively, the taxpayer may use a qualified representative before the IRS. The taxpayer does not have to attend the audit if the representative has the proper power of attorney authorization and is an enrolled practitioner under Circular 230, a family member, or is an unenrolled preparer (and a participant in the IRS's AFSP program) who is providing representation solely in connection with an examination of a taxable year or period covered by a return he prepared.

Example: Emily is an EA. A taxpayer named Seth hires her to represent him before the IRS during the examination of his tax return. Seth does not want to attend the audit. He signs Form 2848 indicating that Emily is now his authorized representative for all his tax affairs. Emily attends the examination on Seth's behalf.

Example: DeShawn is an accounting student who is not a practitioner. The IRS is auditing his sister, who has designated DeShawn as her authorized representative via Form 2848. DeShawn may practice before the IRS in this limited circumstance because of the familial relationship with the taxpayer. His sister is not required to be present during the examination.

When a jointly filed tax return is selected for examination, either spouse may meet with the IRS, or the qualified representative may meet with the IRS without either spouse present. Without an administrative summons, the IRS cannot compel a taxpayer to accompany an authorized representative to an examination interview.

Just as a taxpayer is required to do, a representative is required to produce documents the IRS requests if he has them. If he does not have the requested documents, he must disclose what he knows about them. A representative cannot mislead the government, and he cannot allow his client to do so by presenting fraudulent documents or putting forth a frivolous argument. If a representative fails to promptly submit taxpayer records, fails to keep scheduled appointments, or fails to return phone calls or written correspondence, the examiner has the right to initiate procedures to bypass the representative and deal directly with the taxpayer.

Audit Location and Procedures

Field audits may take place at:

- The taxpayer's home or place of business
- An IRS office
- The office of the taxpayer's authorized representative

Most often, a taxpayer's return is examined in the area where he lives and where the books and records are located. But if the return can be examined more conveniently in another area, the taxpayer can request the audit be transferred to that area.

Example: Joyce runs a marketing business, and she travels frequently in order to meet with clients. She lives in Los Angeles; however, her CPA lives in Chicago, her old hometown. In 2016, Joyce's prior year tax return is selected for examination and she chooses to have her CPA represent her. Her CPA requests that the examination be transferred to Chicago where Joyce's records are located. The IRS grants the transfer.

IRS examiners are instructed to work out times, dates, and locations that are convenient for the taxpayer. However, the IRS retains the right to make the final determination of when, where, and how the examination will take place.

Regardless of where an examination takes place, an examiner has the right to visit the taxpayer's place of business or home to establish facts (such as information about inventory or verification of assets) that can only be accomplished by a direct visit.

The examination interview may be recorded by the taxpayer or his representative, or by the IRS, but whoever initiates the recording must notify the other party in writing ten days in advance. The taxpayer may request a copy of the IRS's recording.

If a taxpayer becomes uncomfortable during the audit and wishes to consult with a qualified representative, the IRS must suspend the interview and reschedule it.

Notice of IRS Contact of Third Parties

During the examination process, the IRS may contact third parties regarding a tax matter without the taxpayer's permission. Third parties may include neighbors, banks, employers, or employees. However, the IRS must give the taxpayer reasonable notice before contacting other persons about his individual tax matters.

The IRS must provide the taxpayer with a record of persons contacted, either on a periodic basis or upon the taxpayer's request. This requirement does not apply:

- To any pending criminal investigation.
- When providing notice would jeopardize collection of any tax liability.
- When providing notice may result in reprisal against any person.
- When the taxpayer has already authorized the contact.

Example: The IRS selects Max's tax return for audit because it suspects unreported income related to criminal drug activity. Max is also being investigated by the FBI. Because this is a pending criminal investigation, the IRS is not required to give Max notice before contacting third parties about his tax matters.

Revenue Agent Reports (RAR)

When the field work portion of an examination is completed, the revenue agent must prepare a detailed written report on his findings, known as a *revenue agent report* (RAR). A RAR is supposed to clearly state the amount of adjustments to a taxpayer's return and demonstrate how the tax liability was computed. Taxpayers have the right to disagree with a RAR and may choose to contest the agent's findings.

If the taxpayer agrees with the IRS's proposed changes in the report, he may immediately sign an agreement. The taxpayer is responsible for paying interest and penalties on any additional tax. If the taxpayer pays the additional tax owed when he signs the agreement, the interest and penalties are calculated from the due date of the tax return to the date of the payment.

If the taxpayer does not pay the additional amounts when he signs the agreement, he will receive a bill that includes interest and penalties. If the taxpayer pays the amounts due within ten business days of the billing date, he will not have to pay any more interest or penalties. This period is extended to 21 calendar days if the amount due is less than $100,000.

Audit Determinations

An audit can be closed in one of three ways:

- **No Change:** An audit in which the taxpayer has substantiated all of the items being reviewed and which results in no changes.
- **Agreed:** An audit in which the IRS proposes changes and the taxpayer understands and agrees with the changes.
- **Unagreed:** An audit in which the IRS proposes changes and the taxpayer understands, but disagrees with the changes. A conference with an IRS manager may be requested for further review of the issues. In addition, the taxpayer may request fast track mediation[171] or an appeal. A taxpayer does not have to file a written protest to request fast-track mediation. The taxpayer may also choose to go to court and contest the IRS determination.

The IRS will not typically reopen a closed examination case to make an unfavorable adjustment and assess additional tax unless:

- There was fraud or misrepresentation,
- There was a substantial error based on an established IRS position existing at the time of the examination, or
- Failure to reopen the case would be a serious administrative omission.

Audit Reconsideration

In certain cases, the IRS will reevaluate the results of a prior audit if additional tax was assessed and remains unpaid or a tax credit was reversed. A taxpayer may request reconsideration if he disagrees with an earlier audit assessment, but he must provide new information, with documentation, that was not considered during the original examination. The IRS may accept a taxpayer's reconsideration request if:

- Information that is submitted has not been considered previously.
- The taxpayer filed a return after the IRS completed a substitute return for him.
- The taxpayer believes the IRS made a computational or processing error in assessing his tax.
- The tax liability is unpaid or credits are denied.

In filing a request for reconsideration, the taxpayer must attach a copy of his examination report (Form 4549), if available, along with copies of any new documentation that supports his position.

[171] Fast Track Mediation (FTM) lets taxpayers resolve disputes at the earliest possible stage in the collection process. Once a FTM application is accepted, the goal is resolution within 40 days. With FTM, a trained mediator from the IRS Office of Appeals is assigned to help you and IRS Collection reach an agreement on the disputed issue(s).

Example: Michael is a sole proprietor who files on Schedule C. After an IRS examination, he was assessed $1,900 of additional taxes because he had lost the file with his receipts and other documentation supporting his business deductions. Michael disagrees with the findings of the examination, and a couple of weeks later he finds the missing file, which includes his original receipts. Michael requests an audit reconsideration due to the new documentation.

The IRS will not accept an audit reconsideration request if:

- The taxpayer previously agreed to pay the amount of tax owed by signing a closing agreement or compromise agreement.
- The amount of tax owed is the result of final partnership item adjustments related to a TEFRA partnership examination.
- The U.S. Tax Court, or another court, has issued a final determination on the tax liability.

The IRS will typically make a decision on an audit reconsideration within 30 days. The IRS is under no obligation to approve a request to reopen an audit. However, the taxpayer retains the right to appeal an IRS assessment.

Repeat Examinations

The IRS tries to avoid repeat examinations of the same items, but sometimes this happens. If a taxpayer's return was audited for the same items in the previous two years and no change was proposed to tax liability, the taxpayer may request the IRS discontinue the examination.

Example: Kelly donates a large percentage of her salary to her church. For the last two years, the IRS has selected Kelly's return for examination based on her large donations. In both instances, Kelly was able to substantiate her donations and no change was made to her tax liability. Her tax return is selected again for the same reason in 2016. Kelly contacts the IRS to request that the examination be discontinued, and the examining officer agrees to do so.

Example: Terrell's tax return has been selected for examination three years in a row. In 2014 and 2015, his tax return was selected to verify compliance with the EITC requirements. There was no change to his tax liability in either year. In 2016, Terrell's tax return is selected for audit again for the same issue. This time, the IRS is questioning his education deductions. Terrell cannot request that the examination be discontinued because it was selected for a different reason than in the previous two examinations.

Unit 10: Study Questions

1. For the IRS to consider accepting a taxpayer's audit reconsideration request:

A. The taxpayer must have already paid the contested additional tax.
B. The taxpayer must have filed a return after the IRS completed a substitute return for him.
C. The U.S. Tax Court must have already issued a ruling in the case.
D. The taxpayer must have signed a closing agreement agreeing to pay the contested additional tax.

2. Who may represent a taxpayer in an examination, assuming the proper power of attorney authorization is in place?

A. The taxpayer's sister.
B. The unenrolled preparer who prepared the tax return under audit and have completed the IRS's Annual Filing Season Program.
C. A tax attorney.
D. All of the above.

3. Cameron's federal income tax return has been under examination. After the revenue agent issues her report, Cameron must determine how to respond to its findings. Which of the following choices is not a term the IRS uses to classify a taxpayer's decision regarding the results of an examination?

A. No change.
B. Agreed.
C. Acknowledged.
D. Unagreed.

4. The IRS has begun an examination of Elaine's income tax return. The IRS would like to ask her neighbors questions related to the examination. There is no pending criminal investigation into the matter, and there is no evidence that this contact will result in reprisals against the neighbors or jeopardize collection of the tax liability. Before contacting the neighbors, the IRS must:

A. Provide Elaine with reasonable notice of the contacts.
B. Make an assessment of Elaine's tax liability.
C. Ask the court for a third-party subpoena.
D. Mail Elaine a Statutory Notice of Deficiency.

5. For a jointly filed tax return that has been selected for examination, which of the following statements is correct?

A. Both spouses must be present during an examination because both spouses signed the return.
B. Only one spouse must be present.
C. Each spouse must have his or her own representative.
D. Neither spouse may use a representative.

6. When do the IRS rules regarding notice of third parties not apply?

A. To any pending criminal investigation.
B. When providing notice would jeopardize collection of any tax liability.
C. When providing notice may result in reprisal against any person.
D. All of the above.

7. If a taxpayer or his representative wishes for an audit to be recorded, which of the following must he do?

A. Make a request the same day as the examination.
B. Notify the examiner ten days in advance, in writing.
C. Notify the examiner one week in advance, in writing.
D. Nothing. Examinations are automatically recorded by the IRS to ensure compliance.

8. What is a revenue agent report?

A. An agreement a taxpayer makes with the IRS after an examination.
B. A report detailing the in-person interview of a taxpayer or his representative.
C. A concluding report by a revenue agent that states the amount of adjustments to a taxpayer's return.
D. A preliminary report by a revenue agent that is made when a taxpayer's return is first flagged for audit.

9. Frank's tax return was chosen by the IRS for examination. He moved recently to another state, but the IRS notice says that his examination will be scheduled in the city where he used to live. Which of the following statements is correct?

A. Frank can request that his tax return examination be moved to another IRS service center since he has moved to another area.
B. Frank must schedule the examination in his former city of residence, but he can have a practitioner represent him there.
C. Frank is required to meet with the examiner at least once in person in order to move the examination to another location.
D. None of the above.

10. Only in rare circumstances will the IRS reopen a closed examination case and assess additional tax. Which of the following is not a reason that the IRS would reopen a closed audit case?

A. There was fraud or misrepresentation.
B. There was a substantial error based on an established IRS position existing at the time of the examination.
C. Failure to reopen the case would be a serious administrative omission.
D. The taxpayer filed a request for fast track mediation.

11. When a taxpayer is chosen for an IRS audit, which of the following statements is correct?

A. The taxpayer must appear before the IRS in person.
B. A taxpayer may choose to be represented by a federally-authorized practitioner and is not required to appear unless he chooses to do so.
C. An audit case may not be transferred to a different IRS office under any circumstances.
D. If a taxpayer feels that he is not being treated fairly during an IRS audit, he cannot appeal to the auditor's manager.

Unit 10: Answers

1. The answer is B. There are times the IRS will reevaluate the results of a prior audit if additional tax was assessed and remains unpaid or a tax credit was reversed. The IRS may accept a taxpayer's reconsideration request if:

- Information that is submitted has not been considered previously.
- The taxpayer filed a return after the IRS completed a substitute return for him.
- The taxpayer believes the IRS made a computational or processing error in assessing his tax.
- The tax liability is unpaid or credits are denied.

The IRS will not accept an audit reconsideration request if the taxpayer previously agreed to pay the amount of tax owed by signing a closing agreement or compromise agreement. The IRS also will not reconsider an audit if the Tax Court, or any other court, has already issued a decision in the case.

2. The answer is D. Family members and unenrolled preparers have limited rights of representation during the examination of a taxpayer's return. The taxpayer does not have to be present at the audit interview, (assuming a power of attorney is in place) for a qualified representative. Attorneys, CPAs, and enrolled agents have unlimited rights of representation before all offices of the IRS, not just the examination division.

3. The answer is C. An audit can be closed in one of three ways:

- **No change:** An audit in which the taxpayer has substantiated all of the items being reviewed and which results in no changes.
- **Agreed:** An audit in which the IRS proposes changes and the taxpayer understands and agrees with the changes.
- **Unagreed:** An audit in which the IRS proposes changes and the taxpayer understands, but disagrees with the changes. A conference with an IRS manager may be requested for further review of the issues. In addition, the taxpayer may request fast track mediation or an appeal. The taxpayer may also choose to go to court and contest the IRS determination.

4. The answer is A. Pursuant to IRC §7602(c), a third-party contact is made when an IRS employee initiates contact with a person other than the taxpayer. A third party may be contacted to obtain information about a specific taxpayer's federal tax liability, including the issuance of a levy or summons to someone other than the taxpayer. The IRS does not need permission to contact third parties, but it must generally notify the taxpayer that the contact with third parties will be made.

5. The answer is B. For taxpayers who file jointly, only one spouse is required to meet with the IRS. Alternatively, the taxpayers can use a qualified representative to represent them before the IRS. They could be present along with the representative, or they could choose not to be at the meeting.

6. The answer is D. During the examination process, the IRS must give the taxpayer reasonable notice before contacting other persons about his individual tax matters. This provision does not apply:

- To any pending criminal investigation.
- When providing notice would jeopardize collection of any tax liability.
- When providing notice may result in reprisal against any person.

7. The answer is B. If a taxpayer, his representative, or the IRS examiner wishes for an audit to be recorded, he must notify the other parties in writing ten days in advance. If the IRS records the interview, the taxpayer may request a copy.

8. The answer is C. An IRS examiner files a revenue agent report (RAR) after he has completed the field work part of an examination. The report should clearly state the amount of adjustments to be made to a taxpayer's return and demonstrate how the tax liability was computed. A taxpayer may agree with the RAR and pay any additional tax owed, or he may contest the agent's findings. He may appeal to the IRS or fight the tax in court.

9. The answer is A. If a taxpayer has moved or if his books and records are located in another area, he can request that the location of his audit be changed to another IRS service center. IRS examiners are instructed to work out times, dates, and locations that are convenient for the taxpayer. However, the IRS retains the right to make the final determination of when, where, and how the examination will take place.

10. The answer is D. Requesting fast track mediation during an examination is not a reason for the IRS to reopen a closed audit case. In general, the IRS will not reopen a closed examination case to make an unfavorable adjustment unless:

- There was fraud or misrepresentation,
- There was a substantial error based on an established IRS position existing at the time of the examination, or
- Failure to reopen the case would be a serious administrative omission.

11. The answer is B. The taxpayer is not required to be present during an IRS examination if he has provided written authorization, such as Form 2848, to a qualified representative per Circular 230.

Unit 11: The Appeals Process

More Reading:
Publication 5, *Your Appeal Rights & How to Prepare a Protest If You Don't Agree*
Publication 556, *Examination of Returns, Appeal Rights, and Claims for Refund*
Publication 4227, *Overview of the Appeals Process*
Publication 4167, *Appeals: Introduction to Alternative Dispute Resolution*

Because taxpayers often disagree with the IRS on tax matters, the IRS has an appeals process. The IRS Office of Appeals is independent of any other IRS office and serves as an informal administrative forum for any taxpayer who wishes to dispute an IRS determination.

IRS Appeals provides taxpayers an alternative to going to court to fight disagreements about the application of tax law. The role of Appeals is to resolve disputes on a fair and impartial basis that does not favor either the government or the taxpayer. Appeals officers are directed to give serious consideration to settlement offers by taxpayers or their representatives.[172]

The mission of the IRS Appeals Office is to resolve tax controversies without litigation. Appeals is a separate division and independent of IRS examinations and collections.

Appeal System Overview

A taxpayer has three choices when he wishes to protest an IRS determination on his taxes:

1. He may appeal either formally or informally within the IRS appeals system.
2. He may take his case directly to the U.S. Tax Court.
3. He may bypass both IRS Appeals and the Tax Court and take his case to the U.S. Court of Federal Claims or to a U.S. district court.

The contested tax does not have to be paid first if a taxpayer opts for either IRS Appeals or the Tax Court, but if the taxpayer goes directly to the Court of Federal Claims or a U.S. district court, he must pay the tax first and then sue the IRS for a refund.

An IRS appeal does not abate penalties and interest on the tax due. These continue to accumulate until one of two events occurs:

- The balance of the debt is paid, or
- The taxpayer wins his appeal and he is granted a no-change audit.

Reasons for an appeal must be supported by tax law. An appeal cannot be based solely on moral, religious, political, constitutional, conscientious, or similar grounds.

Appealing After an Examination

The 30-Day Letter: Within a few weeks after a taxpayer's closing conference with an IRS examiner, he will receive what is commonly called a 30-day letter. This letter includes:

- A notice explaining the taxpayer's right to appeal the proposed changes within 30 days
- A copy of the revenue agent report explaining the examiner's proposed changes
- An agreement or waiver form
- A copy of Publication 5, *Your Appeal Rights and How to Prepare a Protest If You Don't Agree*

The taxpayer has 30 days from the date of notice to accept or appeal the proposed changes.

[172] Internal Revenue Manual 1.2.17.7: "Appeals will ordinarily give serious consideration to an offer to settle a tax controversy on a basis which fairly reflects the relative merits of the opposing views in the light of the hazards which would exist if the case were litigated. However, no settlement will be made based upon nuisance value of the case to either party."

If the taxpayer chooses to appeal an examiner's decision through the IRS system, he can contact a local Appeals office, which is separate and independent of the IRS office that conducted the examination.

Conferences with Appeals office personnel may be conducted in person, through correspondence, or by telephone with the taxpayer or his authorized representative. Only practitioners are allowed to represent taxpayers before an IRS appeals hearing. The taxpayer does not need to attend if his representative has power of attorney authorization via a signed Form 2848 or any other properly-written POA authorization.

Note: An unenrolled tax return preparer may be a witness for a taxpayer at an appeals conference, but may not serve as an authorized representative for the taxpayer.

Filing a Formal Protest: A formal written protest is required in all cases to request an Appeals conference, unless the taxpayer qualifies for the small case request procedure. The protest statement must go into greater detail than the small case request. It must include the facts supporting the taxpayer's position and the law or authority that the taxpayer is relying upon in making his case. The protest is signed under penalties of perjury.

If an enrolled agent or other practitioner prepares and signs the protest for a taxpayer, he must substitute a declaration that states whether he knows personally that the facts in the protest and accompanying documents are true and correct.

Example: Carl is an enrolled agent who represents Sasha, a sole proprietor who runs a small restaurant. The IRS audited Shasha's business return and found discrepancies on her Schedule C. Sasha receives a 30-day letter stating that she owes an additional $32,000 in tax. Sasha disagrees with the amount, so Carl files a formal protest within 30 days with the Appeals office. In the protest, Carl details why the proposed assessment is incorrect and the legal basis for his argument. He also submits the required practitioner declaration. Carl then schedules a conference with an Appeals officer. When they meet, they discuss the matter and reach a settlement agreeable to each party. Since the IRS has a signed Form 2848 authorizing Carl to be Sasha's representative, she was not required to attend the appeals hearing.

The 90-Day Letter

If a taxpayer does not respond to a 30-day letter, or if he cannot reach an agreement with an Appeals officer, the IRS will send him a *Notice of Deficiency*, which is also known as the 90-day letter. A Notice of Deficiency is required by law and is used to advise the taxpayer of his appeal rights to the U.S. Tax Court.

A Notice of Deficiency must be issued before a taxpayer can go to the Tax Court. The taxpayer has 90 days (150 days if addressed to a taxpayer outside the United States) from the date of this notice to file a petition with the Tax Court.

If the taxpayer does not file the petition in time, the tax is due within ten days, and the taxpayer may not take his case to Tax Court. If the taxpayer does file a petition in time and the case is docketed before the Tax Court, his file will again go to an IRS Appeals office to see if it can be resolved before going to court. More than 90% of all tax cases are resolved before going to Tax Court.

U.S. Tax Court

The U.S. Tax Court is a federal court separate from the IRS where taxpayers may choose to contest their tax deficiencies without having to pay the disputed amount first. The court issues both regular and memorandum decisions. A regular decision is when the Tax Court rules on an issue for the first time. A memorandum decision is when the Tax Court has previously ruled on identical or similar issues.

The Tax Court has jurisdiction over the following tax disputes:

- Notices of deficiency
- Review of the failure to abate interest
- Notices of transferee liability
- Adjustment of partnership items
- Administrative costs
- Worker classification (employee versus independent contractor)
- Review of certain collection actions

The Tax Court has jurisdiction over the following types of tax:

- Income tax
- Estate tax and gift tax
- Certain excise taxes
- Re-determine transferee liability
- Worker classification
- Relief from joint and several liability on a joint return
- Whistleblower awards

Any individual taxpayer may represent himself before the U.S. Tax Court.

Note: Enrolled agents and CPAs must be admitted to practice before the Tax Court by first passing a separate exam specific to this purpose. Practice before the IRS does not include practice before the Tax Court. Licensed attorneys are the only practitioners who are not required to pass the Tax Court exam before practicing before the court.

Tax Court Small Tax Case Procedure

Small tax case procedures (also known as S-case procedures) in the Tax Court are one avenue to resolve disputes between taxpayers and the IRS. Small tax cases are handled under simpler, less formal procedures than regular cases. Often, decisions are handed down quicker than in other courts.

Within the IRS appeals system, a taxpayer may file a "small case request" if the total amount of tax, penalties, and interest for each tax period involved are under a certain threshold (explained below). To make a small case request, the taxpayer may use Form 12203, *Request for Appeals Review*, or prepare a brief written statement requesting an appeals conference. He must specify why he does not agree with the proposed tax assessment.[173]

The taxpayer and the Tax Court must both agree to proceed with the small case procedure. Generally, the Tax Court will agree with the taxpayer's S-case request if the taxpayer otherwise qualifies.

However, the Tax Court's decision in a small tax case cannot be appealed by the taxpayer. The decision is final, as the IRS is not allowed to appeal either if it loses the case. In contrast, either the taxpayer or the IRS can appeal a decision in a regular, non-S case to a U.S. Court of Appeals.

Dollar limits for the Tax Court Small Case Division vary:

- For a Notice of Deficiency: $50,000 is the maximum amount, including penalties and interest, for any year before the court.
- For a Notice of Determination: $50,000 is the maximum amount for all the years combined.
- For a Notice of Deficiency related to a request for relief from joint and several liability: $50,000 is the maximum amount of spousal relief for all the years combined.

[173] Employee retirement plans (Form 5500), exempt organizations, S corporations, and partnerships are not eligible for small case requests.

- For an IRS Notice of Determination of Worker Classification: The amount in the dispute cannot exceed $50,000 for any calendar quarter.

A decision entered in a small tax case is not treated as precedent for any other case and is not typically published.

Since the taxpayer cannot appeal a decision by the Small Tax Case Division, he must consider whether using the S-case procedure is worth the risk of not being able to contest an adverse decision in a higher court.

Delay Tactics are Prohibited

If a taxpayer unreasonably fails to pursue the internal IRS appeals system, if the case is filed primarily to cause a delay, or if the taxpayer's position is frivolous, the Tax Court may impose a penalty of up to $25,000.[174] Frivolous positions include those that contend that:

- The income tax is not valid,
- Payment of tax is voluntary,
- A person or a type of income is not subject to tax, or
- Espouse other arguments that the courts have previously rejected as baseless.

The Tax Court may also impose sanctions of up to $25,000 on those who misuse their right to a court review of IRS collection procedures merely to stall their tax payments. This rule is targeted at taxpayers who do not have a legitimate complaint and are instead using the Tax Court simply to delay collection action in their case.

Other Court Appeals

The vast majority of taxpayers who use the court system appeal their disputes in the Tax Court. However, a minority of taxpayers choose to challenge the IRS in a U.S. district court or Court of Federal Claims. In this case, a taxpayer must pay the contested tax deficiency first.

If either party loses at the trial court level, the court's decision may be appealed to a higher court.

Example: The IRS issues Peggy a notice of deficiency in the amount of $45,000. Peggy disagrees with the assessment and does not wish to contest the tax through the IRS Appeals office or the Tax Court. Instead, she wants to go straight to a U.S. district court. She must first pay the contested liability and then sue the IRS for a refund.

Note: Although enrolled agents have unlimited rights of representation before all levels and officers of the IRS, they cannot represent taxpayers in disputes with the IRS before U.S. district courts, bankruptcy courts, courts of appeal, or the U.S. Supreme Court. That authority is reserved only for licensed attorneys.

Taxpayer Rights to Bring Civil Action

The government cannot ask a taxpayer to waive his right to sue the United States or a government employee for any action taken in connection with the tax laws. However, a taxpayer can waive his right to sue if:

- He knowingly and voluntarily waives that right.
- The request to waive the right is made in writing to his attorney or other federally authorized practitioner.
- The request is made in person and his attorney or other representative is present.

---

[174] The IRS makes public the names and cases of taxpayers who have been assessed these §6673 penalties by the Tax Court. The cases are published on the IRS website as well as in the Tax Court Historical Opinion area.

Burden of Proof: In most cases, the burden of proof lies with the IRS during court proceedings, assuming the taxpayer has complied with all of the following issues:

- Adhered to IRS substantiation requirements.
- Maintained adequate records.
- Cooperated with reasonable requests for information from the IRS.
- Introduced credible evidence relating to the issue.
- In the case of a trust, corporation, or partnership, the taxpayer had net worth of $7 million or less and not more than 500 employees at the time of contested tax liability.

Recovering Court Costs

A taxpayer may be able to recover the expenses he incurred to defend his position while contesting tax assessed by the IRS. Under IRC §7430, the IRS is compelled to pay "reasonable litigation and administrative" costs incurred by a taxpayer in most administrative proceedings before the IRS and in court proceedings before most U.S. federal courts.

To recover court costs, the following general requirements must be met:

- The costs must be incurred in an administrative or court proceeding brought by or against the United States.
- The taxpayer must be the prevailing party.
- The taxpayer must have exhausted all administrative remedies within the IRS.
- The costs must be reasonable. They must have been incurred as a result of assessment, collection, or refund of tax, interest, or penalty imposed pursuant to the Internal Revenue Code.
- The taxpayer must not have unreasonably delayed any IRS proceeding.

Example: Phoebe is a registered nurse. During an examination, she disagreed with an IRS assessment that disallowed educational expenses she had claimed while pursuing an MBA degree for health professionals. After receiving a notice of deficiency, she took her case to the Tax Court and won. Phoebe is able to recover attorney fees and other court costs she incurred in her fight with the IRS.

The taxpayer will not be treated as the prevailing party if the IRS establishes that its position was substantially justified.

In order to request the recovery of litigation costs from the IRS, the taxpayer must meet certain net worth requirements:

- For individuals, net worth cannot exceed $2 million as of the filing date of the petition for review. Spouses filing a joint return are treated as separate individuals.
- For estates, net worth cannot exceed $2 million as of the date of the decedent's death.
- For exempt organizations and certain cooperatives, the entity cannot have more than 500 employees as of the filing date of the petition for review.
- For all other taxpayers, net worth cannot exceed $7 million and the entity must not have more than 500 employees as of the filing date of the petition for review.

Unit 11: Study Questions

1. An enrolled agent may NOT represent a taxpayer in a dispute before:

A. An IRS revenue agent.
B. An IRS revenue officer.
C. A U.S. district court judge.
D. The IRS appeals office.

2. The Statutory Notice of Deficiency is also known as:

A. A 30-day letter because the taxpayer generally has 30 days from the date of the notice to file a petition with the Tax Court.
B. A 90-day letter because the taxpayer generally has 90 days from the date of the notice to file a petition with the Tax Court.
C. An Information Document Request because the taxpayer is asked for information to support his position regarding his tax liability.
D. A federal tax lien.

3. Which of the following statements is correct about an IRS appeal?

A. An appeal does not abate the interest on a tax liability. Interest continues to accrue.
B. A taxpayer must pay the disputed tax before filing an appeal with the IRS.
C. The IRS is prohibited from filing a federal tax lien if the taxpayer is outside the U.S.
D. Taxpayers who disagree with the IRS changes may not appeal to the U.S. Tax Court.

4. Aaron wants to appeal the findings of an examination, but his tax return was prepared by an unenrolled preparer. Aaron does not wish to be present during the appeals process. What are his options?

A. Aaron must have a family member represent him.
B. Aaron may represent himself or hire a practitioner (CPA, attorney, or EA) to represent him at the appeals level.
C. Aaron may be represented by the unenrolled preparer, so long as the unenrolled preparer is the one who prepared the tax return at issue.
D. Aaron may ask an IRS employee to represent him at IRS Appeals.

5. Which of the following best states the purpose of the IRS Office of Appeals?

A. To help the taxpayer and the government settle their tax dispute and reach an equitable settlement.
B. To advocate for the taxpayer in connection with the taxpayer's disagreement with the collection or examination divisions of the IRS.
C. To advocate for the government and convince the taxpayer to pay his fair share before he pursues his case through the court system.
D. To look at the facts and circumstances of each case, and then take a side in the tax dispute.

6. Kevin and Javier are partners in a body shop business. Both had their individual returns examined and both disagreed with the IRS. Kevin decided to take his case to the IRS Appeals office. After the conference, he and the IRS still disagreed. Javier decided to bypass the Appeals office altogether and go directly to court. Which of the following statements is correct?

A. Neither may petition the Tax Court.
B. Both Kevin and Javier can take their cases to the following courts: U.S. Tax Court, U.S. Court of Federal Claims, or the U.S. District Court.
C. Only Kevin may petition the Tax Court, because he went through the IRS appeals process first.
D. Both can take their cases to the Tax Court, but not to other U.S. courts.

7. Alyssa disagrees with the IRS examiner regarding her income tax case. Her appeal rights are explained to her, and she decides to contest the tax by pursuing the case in the Tax Court. Which of the following statements is correct?

A. Alyssa must receive a Notice of Deficiency before she can go to the Tax Court.
B. Alyssa must wait for the IRS examiner to permanently close her audit case.
C. Alyssa must request a collection due process hearing before she can go to the Tax Court.
D. Alyssa cannot go to the Tax Court unless she agrees with the auditor's findings.

8. If a taxpayer wishes to challenge the IRS in a district court, the taxpayer must:

A. First attempt to resolve the contested tax with the IRS Appeals office.
B. Pay the contested liability first and then sue the IRS for a refund.
C. Pay a retainer to the IRS for a refund.
D. Go first to the U.S. Tax Court before appealing to a U.S. district court.

9. Danielle owes a substantial sum to the IRS. She files a petition with the U.S. Tax Court. Her case is later determined to be frivolous, wholly without merit, and merely to cause delay. As a repercussion to Danielle's action, the Tax Court may impose a penalty of:

A. Up to $10,000.
B. Up to $25,000.
C. Up to $50,000.
D. Up to $25,000 and one year in prison.

10. Which of the following statements is correct regarding a taxpayer's right to appeal a tax assessment?

A. A taxpayer must first pay the contested tax before he can appeal in the U.S. Tax Court, or U.S. district or federal courts.
B. A taxpayer has the right to appeal a tax assessment on the basis of religious, political, or constitutional grounds.
C. The IRS Appeals office is an arm of the IRS Collection division.
D. A taxpayer must first pay the contested tax before he can appeal in a U.S. district or federal court.

11. At the beginning of each examination, the IRS auditor must explain:

A. A taxpayer's appeal rights.
B. A taxpayer's right to a fair trial.
C. A taxpayer's right to remain silent.
D. A taxpayer's right to confidentiality.

Unit 11: Answers

1. The answer is C. An enrolled agent may represent taxpayers at all levels of the IRS, but does not have the same practice rights in the U.S. court system.

2. The answer is B. The Statutory Notice of Deficiency, or 90-day letter, gives the taxpayer 90 days to file a petition in the U.S. Tax Court challenging the proposed deficiency. However, a taxpayer is granted 150 days if the notice is addressed to a taxpayer outside the United States.

3. The answer is A. An IRS appeal does not abate the interest, which continues to accrue until the balance of the debt is paid, or until the taxpayer wins his appeal and he is granted a no-change audit. A no-change audit means the IRS has accepted the tax return as it was filed.

4. The answer is B. Aaron can appear before IRS Appeals by himself, or hire a qualified representative to appear on his behalf. If he wants to be represented by someone else, he must choose a person who is eligible to practice before the IRS. Only enrolled practitioners (attorneys, CPAs, and EAs) are allowed to represent taxpayers before an appeals hearing (unless a special exception applies, for example, an executor representing an estate or a parent representing their own minor child).

5. The answer is A. The Office of Appeals helps taxpayers resolve their tax disputes with the IRS without going to Tax Court. Appeals is an independent organization within the IRS. After the applicable IRS compliance division has made its decision, Appeals reviews a case and works to settle disagreements on a basis that is fair and impartial to both the government and the taxpayer.

6. The answer is B. Both Kevin and Javier can take their cases to court. A taxpayer is not required to use the IRS appeals process. If a taxpayer and the IRS still disagree after an appeals conference or a taxpayer decides to bypass the IRS appeals system altogether, the case may be taken to the U.S. Tax Court, the U.S. Court of Federal Claims, or a U.S. district court.

7. The answer is A. A Notice of Deficiency (90-day letter) must be issued before a taxpayer can go to Tax Court. A taxpayer has 90 days from the date of the notice to respond and file a petition with the court.

8. The answer is B. In order to appeal in district court, the taxpayer must first pay the contested liability and then sue the IRS for a refund. If either party loses at the trial court level, the court's decision may be appealed to a higher court.

9. The answer is B. If a taxpayer unreasonably fails to pursue the internal IRS appeals system, if the case is filed primarily to cause a delay, or if the taxpayer's position is frivolous, the Tax Court may impose a penalty of up to $25,000.

10. The answer is D. A taxpayer has the right to appeal a tax assessment through the IRS Appeals office, the U.S. Tax Court, or a U.S. District Court or the Court of Federal Claims. However, if the taxpayer opts to have his appeal heard in a district or Federal Claims court, he must first pay the contested tax and sue the IRS for a refund.

11. The answer is A. At the beginning of each examination, the IRS auditor must explain a taxpayer's appeal rights.

Unit 12: The IRS E-File Program

More Reading:
Publication 3112, *IRS e-file Application and Participation*
Publication 1345, *Handbook for Authorized IRS e-file Providers of Individual Income Tax Returns*

The IRS e-file program allows taxpayers to transmit their returns electronically. More than 84% of American taxpayers file their tax returns electronically. According to the IRS, the processing of e-file returns is not only quicker, but is also more accurate than the processing of paper returns. However, as with a paper return, the taxpayer is responsible for ensuring an e-filed return contains accurate information and is filed on time.

Paid preparers who prepare more than ten individual returns a year are required to e-file income tax returns.[175] The e-file mandate covers returns for individuals, trusts, and estates.

If that number is 11 or more for the calendar year, all preparers of a firm must e-file the returns they prepare and file. This is true even if, on an individual basis, a member prepares and files fewer than the threshold.[176]

Note: For the purposes of the e-file mandate, members of firms must count their returns *in the aggregate*. If the number of applicable income tax returns is 11 or more, then all members of the firm generally must e-file the returns they prepare and file. This is true even if an individual preparer expects to prepare and file fewer than 11 returns.

Example: Elena is an enrolled agent who works full-time for Hanover CPA firm. She also has a side business preparing tax returns from her home. Elena specializes in fiduciary and estate tax issues and does not prepare very many individual tax returns. For the coming tax year, Elena expects to prepare and file five Form 1041 returns (for estates and trusts) while working for the CPA firm. She also expects to prepare and file seven Form 1040 tax returns as a self-employed preparer. Since she expects to file 11 or more forms between her regular job and her side-business, Elena is required to e-file all of the returns.

Some preparers are exempt from the e-file mandate.[177] The IRS e-file does not accept foreign preparers without social security numbers into their e-file program, so those preparers are exempt. A tax preparer may request exemption from the e-file program by submitting Form 8944, *Preparer e-file Hardship Waiver Request,* to request a waiver.

Waivers are reviewed and approved in cases where the preparer demonstrates that complying would be an undue hardship. These exemptions are rare and considered only on a case-by-case basis.

Applying to the IRS E-File Program

To begin e-filing tax returns, a preparer must apply and be accepted as an authorized IRS e-file provider. There is no fee to apply, and the process takes up to 45 days. The first step is to create an IRS e-Services account by providing required personal information including a Social

[175] Individual taxpayers are not bound by this mandate. A taxpayer may always file on paper, if he chooses. The e-file mandate only applies to paid preparers. It does not apply to tax returns that are not prepared for compensation, such as a tax return that an enrolled agent files for a family member at no charge.

[176] Financial institutions and fiduciaries that file Forms 1041 as a trustee or fiduciary are not required to e-file and are not subject to the mandate. The e-file mandate also does not apply to payroll tax returns.

[177] A tax return preparer and a member of a recognized religious group that is conscientiously opposed to filing electronically is not required to apply for a waiver using Form 8944. Preparers who claim a religious exemption to e-filing must attach Form 8948, Preparer Explanation for Not Filing Electronically, to their clients' paper returns and check box 3.

Security number, an address where confirmation of the account will be mailed, and the preparer's adjusted gross income from the current or prior tax year.

After being approved for an e-services account, an applicant begins the comprehensive process to become an *IRS e-file provider*, which is an umbrella term for anyone authorized to participate in e-file, from software developers to transmitters. A preparer who wants to e-file for clients must be approved as an *electronic return originator* (ERO). The application must also identify a firm's principals and at least one responsible official.

Each person on an e-file provider application must:

- Be a United States citizen or a legal U.S. alien lawfully admitted for permanent residence,
- Be at least 18 years of age as of the date of application, and
- Meet applicable state and local licensing and/or bonding requirements for the preparation of tax returns.

If the principal or responsible official is someone who is certified or licensed (such as an attorney, CPA, or enrolled agent), he must enter current professional status information. All other individuals must be fingerprinted as part of the application process.

After the application is submitted, the IRS will conduct a suitability check on the firm and on each person listed on the application as either a principal or responsible official. Suitability checks may include the following:

- A criminal background check
- A credit history check
- A tax compliance check to ensure that the applicant's personal returns are filed and paid
- A check for prior noncompliance with IRS e-file requirements

It can take up to 45 days for the IRS to approve an e-file application. When a business is accepted to participate in IRS e-file, it is assigned an electronic filing identification number (EFIN). All preparers in a firm based in the same physical location are covered by the same number.

For example, a tax preparation business with ten employee-preparers in one location would all file using the same EFIN. Each preparer would then use his own PTIN on the returns that he individually prepares.[178]

Electronic Return Originators

An ERO is an authorized IRS e-file provider who originates the electronic submission of tax returns to the IRS.

Although an ERO may engage in tax return preparation, and many do, tax preparation is a distinct and separate activity from the electronic submission of tax returns to the IRS. An ERO submits a tax return only after the taxpayer has authorized the e-file transmission. The return must be either:

- Prepared by the ERO; or
- Collected from a taxpayer who has self-prepared his own return and is asking the ERO to e-file it for him.

An ERO is required to:

- Timely submit returns.
- Submit any required supporting paper documents to the IRS.
- Provide copies to taxpayers.
- Retain records and make records available to the IRS.
- Work with the taxpayer and/or the transmitter to correct a rejected return.

[178] The IRS requires firms with multiple physical locations to obtain separate EFINs for each location.

- Enter the preparer's identifying information (name, address, and PTIN).
- Be diligent in recognizing fraud and abuse, reporting it to the IRS and preventing it when possible.
- Cooperate with IRS investigations by making documents available to the IRS upon request.

An ERO who originates returns that he has not prepared, but only collected, becomes an income tax return preparer when he makes substantive changes to the tax return.

A non-substantive change is a correction limited to a transposition error, misplaced entry, spelling error, or arithmetic correction. The IRS considers all other changes substantive. As such, the ERO may be required to sign the return as the preparer.

Example: Diana is an ERO. A taxpayer brings a self-prepared tax return for Diana to e-file. She notices gross errors on the tax return and talks with the client about the mistakes. The taxpayer agrees to correct the return, and Diana makes the necessary adjustments in return for a small fee. Diana is now required to sign the return as the preparer.

Authorized Transmitters

After an ERO submits a tax return, it is sent to an authorized transmitter, which submits it to the IRS. Once received at the IRS, the return is automatically checked for errors. If it cannot be processed, it is sent back to the originating transmitter to clarify any necessary information.

After correction, the transmitter retransmits the return to the IRS. Within 48 hours of electronically sending the return, the IRS sends an acknowledgment to the transmitter stating the return is accepted for processing. This is called an electronic postmark, and it is the taxpayer's proof of filing and assurance that the IRS has the return.

Authorized e-file providers must retain a record of each electronic postmark until the end of the calendar year and provide the record to the IRS upon request. Most tax software packages automatically retain a record of the return transmission report and electronic postmark.

Example: Patrick is a paid preparer and an ERO who uses Ultra TaxPro software to prepare returns. Once he has completed a tax return, he gives a copy to the client, who gives signature authorization to e-file the return by completing Form 8879. Patrick transmits the return to Ultra TaxPro, which is an authorized transmitter. Ultra TaxPro then transmits the return to the IRS. Most tax practitioners use this method; all the major tax preparation software companies have e-file transmission options.

Electronic Signature Requirements

Electronically filed returns have signature requirements, just as paper tax returns do. For e-filed tax returns, both taxpayers and preparers must complete Form 8879, *IRS e-file Signature Authorization.* The IRS has issued recent guidance clarifying that taxpayers may sign Form 8879 with an electronic signature.

Form 8879 includes a taxpayer's consent to electronic filing; a declaration that the e-filed return is true, correct, and complete; and an indication of which method of signature authorization is used on the e-filed return. The form must be retained for three years from the return due date or the IRS received date, whichever is later. Unless the IRS requests to see the form, it is not submitted.

Example: Fred is an enrolled agent. He has a long-time client who comes to his office to consult with him about her tax return. Fred verifies her identity by inspecting her driver's license. Another long-term client lives in a different state. Fred uses an agency that provides identity verification services for this client. After confirming the identity of each client, Fred can allow each to sign Form 8879 with electronic signatures.

If an e-filed return does not have an appropriate electronic signature via a personal identification number (PIN), it will be rejected. This requirement also applies to volunteers at VITA and TCPE sites who provide free tax assistance and e-filing.

- The **self-select PIN** allows a taxpayer to electronically sign his e-filed return by selecting and entering a five-digit PIN as his signature. The IRS uses the taxpayer's prior year adjusted gross income or prior year PIN to validate the signature. The taxpayer may also authorize an ERO to enter or generate his PIN.
- The **practitioner PIN** is an 11-digit number that includes the ERO's six-digit EFIN and the preparer's five-digit self-selected PIN. The ERO uses the same practitioner PIN for the entire tax year.

Form 8453, *U.S. Individual Income Tax Transmittal for an IRS e-file Return*, is used to send any required paper forms or supporting documentation that may be needed with an e-filed return. Form 8453 must be mailed to the IRS within three business days after receiving acknowledgment that the IRS has accepted the electronically-filed return.

If the ERO is signing the tax return as a representative, Form 2848, *Power of Attorney and Declaration of Representative*, must be attached to Form 8453.

Example: Mitchell is an enrolled agent and ERO. He has power of attorney for a client, Al, who is working overseas for several months. Mitchell uses his practitioner PIN and signs Al's tax return on his behalf. He e-files the return and then mails Form 8453 to the IRS the next day. Mitchell attaches Form 2848 showing he is Al's authorized representative to sign his tax return.

New Verification Requirements: Practitioners who accept electronic signatures must take additional steps to authenticate the identity of the taxpayer. For in-person transactions, the preparer must inspect a valid government-issued picture ID, compare the picture to the applicant, and record the name, Social Security number, address, and date of birth. A credit check or other identity verification is optional. For remote transactions, the preparer must verify that the name, Social Security number, address, date of birth, and other personal information on record are consistent with the information provided through record checks with applicable agencies or institutions, or through credit bureaus or similar databases. The IRS has clarified that an electronic signature via remote transaction does not include handwritten signatures of Forms 8879 sent to the ERO by hand delivery, U.S. mail, private delivery service, fax, email, or an Internet website.

The verification of a client's identity[179] must be done every year; if a preparer cannot verify identity after three attempts, he must obtain a handwritten signature instead of an electronic one.

E-File Rejections

If the IRS rejects an e-filed return and the preparer cannot rectify the reason for the rejection, the preparer must inform the taxpayer of the rejection within 24 hours.

The preparer must provide the taxpayer with the IRS reject codes accompanied by an explanation. If the taxpayer chooses not to have the electronic return corrected and retransmitted to the IRS, or if the IRS cannot accept the return for processing, the taxpayer must file a paper return. The due dates for filing paper income tax returns also apply to

[179] Although no specific technology is required, the IRS gives the following examples of acceptable electronic signature methods: a handwritten signature input onto an electronic signature pad; a handwritten signature, mark, or command input on a display screen by means of a stylus device; a digitized image of a handwritten signature that is attached to an electronic record; a typed name (e.g., typed at the end of an electronic record or typed into a signature block on a website form by a signer); a shared secret code, password, or PIN used by a person to sign the electronic record; a digital signature; or a mark captured as a scalable graphic. The new guidance also applies to Form 8878, *IRS e-file Signature Authorization for Form 4868 or Form 2350*.

electronic returns, however, if an e-filed return is rejected, the taxpayer does have time to rectify the problem.

Paper Returns Submitted After an E-file Rejection

Sometimes, a taxpayer cannot correct the e-filed return, and is therefore forced to file a paper return. This happens in the case of identity theft. In order to timely file, the taxpayer must file the paper return by the later of:

- The due date of the return, or
- Ten calendar days after the date the IRS gives notification that it rejected the e-filed return. This is called the *ten-day transmission perfection period*; it is additional time the IRS gives a preparer and taxpayer to correct errors in the electronic filing and resubmit a tax return without a late filing penalty.

If a taxpayer files on paper after an e-file rejection, the following information must be included:

- An explanation of why the paper return is being filed after the due date
- A copy of the rejection notification
- A brief history of actions taken to correct the electronic return

The taxpayer should write in red at the top of the first page of the paper return:

"REJECTED ELECTRONIC RETURN-(DATE)"

The date should be the date of the first e-file rejection. The paper return must be signed by the taxpayer. The PIN that was used on the rejected e-filing may not be used as the signature on the paper return. If an e-file submission is rejected, a return can be corrected within the ten-day transmission period and not be subject to a late filing penalty, but this is not the case for a late payment penalty. If a return is rejected on the due date, an electronic payment should not be transmitted with the return, because a tax payment must still be submitted or postmarked by the due date.

Rejected individual e-filed returns can be corrected and retransmitted without new signatures or authorizations if the changes do not differ from the amount on the original electronic return by more than $50 to "total income" or "AGI," or more than $14 to "total tax," "federal income tax withheld," "refund," or "amount you owe."

Example: Russ is an EA who e-files a tax return for his client, Charita, on April 15. The next day, Russ receives an IRS notice that the return was rejected. Russ notifies Charita of the rejection within 24 hours. The issue cannot be corrected, so she must file a paper return. Russ mails the return on April 19, and gives Charita a copy. The tax return will be considered filed timely, because the paper return was filed within ten days of the rejection and the original e-filing of the return was attempted in a timely manner. If Charita had owed tax, she would have needed to send payment by the due date.

Safeguarding IRS e-File

Authorized IRS e-file providers are responsible for helping recognize and prevent fraud and abuse in IRS e-file. The IRS has mandated six security, privacy, and business standards to which providers must adhere, including the reporting of security incidents. Providers who e-file individual income tax returns must report incidents to the IRS as soon as possible, but no later than the next business day. Any unauthorized disclosure, misuse, modification, or destruction of taxpayer information is considered a reportable security incident.

Entity Electronic Filing Requirements

Certain corporations, partnerships, and tax-exempt organizations are required to file electronically. Corporate taxpayers, including tax-exempt organizations, with $10 million or more in assets and that file at least 250 returns (information returns and others, such as Forms 1099 and W-2) are required to file electronically via magnetic media. This requirement applies regardless of whether they use a paid preparer.

Definition: The term **magnetic media** means magnetic tape, tape cartridge, and diskette, as well as other media, such as electronic filing, which are specifically permitted by IRS regulations.

Example: The Clemmons Company is a calendar-year S corporation with assets of $11 million. In 2016, the company is required to file one Form 1120S, 105 Forms W-2, 145 Forms 1099-DIV, four Forms 941, and one Form 940. Since the Clemmons Company is required to file 256 returns during the calendar year, it is required to file its Form 1120S electronically via magnetic media.

Partnerships with more than 100 partners are also required to use magnetic media. Partnerships with 100 or fewer partners (Schedules K-1) may voluntarily file their returns electronically, but are not required to do so. A partnership has more than 100 partners if, over the course of the taxable year, the partnership had over 100 partners on any particular day in the year, regardless of whether a partner was a partner for the entire year.

A preparer's e-file application must be current and must list all the form types (1120, 1065, 990, etc.) that he will transmit to the IRS. If the preparer does not list a certain form on his application and later attempts to transmit that form, he will receive a rejection for the return type.

Example: Karen is an EA. When she first applied to be an e-file provider, she only prepared individual returns. In 2016, she prepares a partnership return. However, Karen forgets to update her e-file application. When she submits the partnership return online, it is rejected. Karen will have to update her e-file application in order to submit partnership returns electronically.

Paper Returns

A taxpayer may choose to file a paper return that has been prepared by a paid preparer. The taxpayer must mail the return himself and include a hand-signed and dated statement documenting his choice to file on paper. A preparer is required to attach Form 8948, *Preparer Explanation for Not Filing Electronically*, to a client's paper return.

A preparer may also request a hardship waiver from the IRS to be exempt from e-filing. The IRS says it will grant waivers only in rare cases and usually not for more than one calendar year. It will deny waivers if the request is made because the preparer does not have appropriate software or simply prefers not to e-file.

Some returns are impossible to e-file for various reasons and are therefore exempt from the e-file requirement. The following individual tax returns cannot be processed using IRS e-file:

- Amended tax returns
- Tax returns with fiscal year tax periods
- Returns containing forms or schedules that cannot be processed by IRS e-file
- Tax returns with taxpayer identification numbers within the range of 900-00-000 through 999-99-9999 (with the exception of certain ITIN and ATIN returns)
- Returns with rare or unusual processing conditions

The IRS also may grant administrative exemptions when technology issues prevent specified preparers from filing returns electronically.

Form W-2 Requirements for E-Filing

An e-file provider is prohibited from submitting electronic returns prior to the receipt of all Forms W-2, W-2G, and 1099-R from the taxpayer. A provider also cannot advertise that he can file a tax return using only pay stubs or earning statements.

Example: Autumn is a tax preparer. She advertises in her local newspaper that she will prepare a taxpayer's return "early" by using just their final earnings statement. This is prohibited.

If the taxpayer cannot provide a correct Form W-2, W-2G, or 1099R, the return may be electronically filed after Form 4852, *Substitute for Form W-2, Wage and Tax Statement*, or Form 1099-R, *Distributions from Pensions, Annuities, Retirement or Profit-Sharing Plans, IRAs, Insurance Contracts, etc.*, is completed. This is the only time information from pay stubs or leave and earnings statements is allowed.[180] The taxpayer must first make an attempt to obtain all the necessary forms from the employer. The Form 4852 should only be used as a last resort. Tax returns filed using Form 4852 cannot be e-filed. They must be filed on paper.

E-File Advertising Standards

Once accepted to participate in IRS e-file, a firm may represent itself as an "Authorized IRS e-file Provider." A practitioner must not use improper or misleading advertising in relation to IRS e-file, including promising a time frame for refunds.

Practitioners may not use the regular IRS logo (the eagle symbol) or IRS insignia in their advertising, or imply any type of relationship with the IRS. They may use the IRS e-file logo, but cannot combine the e-file logo with the IRS eagle symbol, the word "federal," or with other words or symbols that might suggest a special relationship with the IRS.

Advertising materials must not carry the FMS, IRS, or any other Treasury seals, but may use the IRS e-file logo. Use of any type of logo or insignia that copies of the IRS "eagle" logo is strictly prohibited.

If an e-file provider uses radio, television, Internet, signage, or other methods of advertising, the practitioner must keep a copy and provide it to the IRS upon request. Copies of any advertising must be retained until the end of the calendar year following the last transmission or use.

E-file Revocations and Sanctions

The IRS may revoke e-file privileges if a firm or individual is either:

- Prohibited or disbarred from filing returns by a court order, or
- Prohibited from filing returns by any federal or state legal action that forbids participation in e-file.

The IRS may also sanction any e-file provider who fails to comply with e-file regulations. Before sanctioning, the IRS may issue a warning letter that describes specific corrective action the provider must take.

The IRS categorizes the seriousness of infractions as Level One (the least serious), Level Two, and Level Three (the most serious). Sanctions may be a written reprimand, suspension, or expulsion from participation from IRS e-file. Suspended providers are generally not eligible to participate in e-filing for one to two years, depending on the seriousness of the infraction. If a principal or responsible official is suspended or expelled from participation in IRS e-file, every entity listed on the firm's e-file application may also be expelled.

Providers who are denied participation in IRS e-file usually have the right to an administrative review. In order to appeal, a provider must mail a written response within 30

[180] A leave and earning statement (LES) is a document given on a monthly basis to members of the U.S. military that documents their pay and leave status.

days addressing the IRS's reason for denial or revocation and include supporting documentation. During this administrative review process, the denial of participation remains in effect.

In certain circumstances, the IRS can immediately suspend or expel an authorized IRS e-file provider without prior notice.

Example: Reynaldo was a CPA who was convicted of felony embezzlement. He was also stripped of his license by his state accountancy board. The IRS revoked his e-file privileges without prior notice.

Unit 12: Study Questions

1. Which of the following tax return preparers would be subject to the mandate that requires preparers to e-file their clients' returns?

A. Dean, a bookkeeper who prepares a tax return for himself.
B. RJ, an EA who only prepares payroll tax returns for her employer.
C. Scott, who files six individual tax returns and seven estate returns for compensation.
D. Chon, a CPA who files 100 returns for the Volunteer Income Tax Assistance (VITA) program.

2. Which individual or business is not required to e-file their tax return?

A. A partnership with 100 partners.
B. A corporation with $8 million in assets that files more than 500 information returns.
C. An EA who prepares ten Forms 1040EZ through VITA, five Forms 1040 for a small fee for neighbors, and six Forms 1041 through the tax firm she works for.
D. All are required to e-file.

3. The IRS may sanction providers who fail to comply with e-file regulations. It uses a specific system of categorizing how serious infractions are. Which is the most serious?

A. Level One.
B. Level Two.
C. Level Three.
D. Level Four.

4. Katie is an EA subject to the e-file mandate. She has power of attorney authority for her client, Timothy, who is paralyzed and physically unable to sign the return himself. What must she do to e-file Timothy's return?

A. Use Form 8453 and submit Form 2848, *Power of Attorney and Declaration of Representative,* as an attachment.
B. Use Form 8879 and submit Form 2848, *Power of Attorney and Declaration of Representative,* as an attachment.
C. Use the Practitioner PIN method as her signature requirement.
D. Katie is not allowed to e-file Timothy's return in this instance. She must file it on paper.

5. If the IRS rejects an e-filed tax return for processing and the reason for the rejection cannot be rectified with the information already provided to the ERO, what is the ERO's responsibility at that point?

A. The ERO is not legally required to notify the taxpayer.
B. The ERO must attempt to notify the taxpayer within 24 hours and provide the taxpayer with the rejection code accompanied by an explanation.
C. The ERO is required to notify the taxpayer in writing within 72 hours.
D. The ERO is required to file the tax return on paper within 24 hours.

6. Electronic filing identification numbers (EFINs) are issued:

A. On a firm basis.
B. On a preparer basis.
C. On a client basis.
D. Only to foreign firms.

7. The IRS may excuse a preparer from the mandate to e-file in which of the following instances?

A. An administrative exemption due to technology issues.
B. An individual case of hardship documented by the preparer.
C. Lack of access to tax preparation software.
D. A preparer who does not like using a computer and prefers to fill out tax forms by hand.

8. Tammy is an enrolled agent who e-files a return for her client, Rick. However, Rick's e-filed return is rejected by the IRS. They cannot resolve the rejection issue, and the return must be filed on paper. In order to timely file Rick's tax return, what is the deadline for filing a paper return?

A. The due date of the return.
B. Ten calendar days after the date the IRS rejects the e-filed return.
C. Forty-eight hours after the date the IRS rejects the e-filed return.
D. The later of either A or B.

9. Which of the following statements is correct?

A. Separate fees may be charged for direct deposits.
B. An e-file provider cannot charge a contingent fee based on a percentage of the refund on an original return.
C. An e-file provider cannot charge a fee for paper returns.
D. An e-file provider cannot charge a fee for e-filing.

10. What is the first step of the process for an individual to become an authorized e-file provider?

A. Apply for a PTIN.
B. Be fingerprinted and undergo a background check by the IRS.
C. Become a federally authorized practitioner.
D. Create an authorized e-Services account online.

11. Which logo may a practitioner use in his advertising?

A. The official IRS logo.
B. The IRS e-file logo.
C. The official seal of the U.S. Treasury.
D. The IRS eagle symbol.

12. Under new verification requirements, what must a preparer who accepts electronic signatures do to authenticate the identity of a client he meets with in person?

A. Inspect the client's Social Security card, or other taxpayer identification document.
B. Perform a credit check or take other identity verification measures through a third party.
C. Inspect a valid government-issued picture ID, compare the picture to the applicant, and record the name, Social Security number, address, and date of birth.
D. Both B and C.

Unit 12: Answers

1. The answer is C. Any paid preparer who files 11 or more individual or trust returns in aggregate in a calendar year is required to e-file. There are limited exceptions, such as for returns that cannot be e-filed (returns that require paper attachments, nonresident returns, amended returns, etc.). The e-file mandate does not apply to payroll tax returns, volunteer preparers, or returns prepared under the Volunteer Income Tax Assistance (VITA) program.

2. The answer is D. A partnership with more than 100 partners must e-file. A partnership with 100 or fewer partners is not required to e-file, though it may choose to do so. A corporation with $10 million or more in assets must e-file if it files at least 250 returns of any type. The enrolled agent in Answer C is required to e-file because she prepares 11 tax returns for compensation, which is the minimum number that triggers the e-file mandate. VITA volunteers are not covered under the e-file mandate.

3. The answer is C. Under the IRS system of rating e-file infractions, Level One is the least serious, Level Two is moderately serious, and Level Three is the most serious. There is no Level Four infraction.

4. The answer is A. Since Katie is signing the return as Timothy's representative, she must use Form 8453, *U.S. Individual Income Tax Transmittal for an IRS e-file Return*, and also submit Form 2848, *Power of Attorney and Declaration of Representative,* as an attachment. Form 8879, *IRS e-file Signature Authorization,* is used by EROs, but only submitted to the IRS upon request.

5. The answer is B. If the IRS rejects an e-filed tax return for processing and the reason for the rejection cannot be rectified, the ERO must take reasonable steps to inform the taxpayer of the rejection within 24 hours. The ERO must provide the taxpayer with the rejection code(s) accompanied by an explanation. After receiving a rejection, the ERO is not required to file a tax return on paper. The ERO and the client should attempt to correct the e-file. However, if the return continues to be rejected, the taxpayer may be forced to file on paper.

6. The answer is A. Electronic filing identification numbers (EFINs) are issued on a firm basis. All tax return preparers in a firm with the same physical location are covered by a single EFIN. Providers need an EFIN to electronically file tax returns.

7. The answer is B. An individual preparer's dislike of using a computer or the fact that he does not have appropriate software are not considered legitimate reasons to grant a hardship waiver. The IRS will grant e-file waivers in cases when technology makes it impossible to file electronically. E-file waivers due to hardship will also be granted, but only on a rare case-by-case basis and typically only for a single year. The preparer must submit Form 8944, *Preparer e-file Hardship Waiver Request*, to request a waiver. Waivers are reviewed and approved in cases where the preparer demonstrates that complying would be an undue hardship.

8. The answer is D. In order to timely file a tax return, the taxpayer must file a paper return by the later of:

- The due date of the return, or
- Ten calendar days after the date the IRS gives notification that it rejected the e-filed return.

This is called the *Ten-Day Transmission Perfection Period*. This is not an extension of time to file; rather, this is additional time that the IRS gives a preparer and taxpayer to correct and resubmit a tax return without a late filing penalty.

9. The answer is B. Based on the current version of Circular 230, an e-file provider may not charge a contingent fee based on a percentage of the refund of an original tax return. Separate fees cannot be charged for direct deposits. However, a practitioner is allowed to charge a fee for e-filing. However, in 2014, in the landmark case of Ridgely v. Lew, the U.S. District Court issued a permanent injunction preventing the IRS from regulating contingent fee arrangements. At the time of this book's printing, the IRS has not yet made a public comment specifically about contingent fee arrangements or the outcome of the Ridgely case.

10. The answer is D. To become an authorized e-file provider, an individual must first register with the IRS by creating an IRS e-Services account online. The individual will need to provide personal information, including a Social Security number and an address where confirmation of the account will be mailed.

11. The answer is B. A practitioner may use the IRS e-file logo, but may not use the IRS logo or insignia in his advertising or imply a relationship with the IRS. A practitioner may not combine the e-file logo with the IRS eagle symbol, the word "federal", or with other words or symbols that suggest a special relationship between the IRS and the practitioner. Advertising materials must not carry the IRS or other Treasury seals.

12. The answer is C. For in-person transactions, the preparer must inspect a valid government-issued picture ID, compare the picture to the applicant, and record the name, Social Security number, address, and date of birth. A credit check or other identity verification measures are optional. For remote transactions, the preparer must verify that the name, Social Security number, address, date of birth, and other personal information on record are consistent with the information provided through record checks with applicable agencies or institutions, or through credit bureaus or similar databases.

INDEX

About the Authors

Richard Gramkow, EA, MST

Richard Gramkow is an Enrolled Agent with more than eighteen years of experience in various areas of taxation. He holds a master's degree in taxation from Rutgers University and is currently a tax manager for a publicly held Fortune 500 company in the New York metropolitan area.

Christy Pinheiro, EA, ABA®

Christy Pinheiro is an Enrolled Agent and an Accredited Business Accountant. Christy was an accountant for two private CPA firms and for the State of California before going into private practice.

Kolleen Wells, EA

Kolleen Wells is an Enrolled Agent and a Certified Bookkeeper who specializes in tax preparation for individuals and small businesses. She has worked in the accounting field for many years, including positions at a CPA office and at the county assessor's office.

Joel Busch, CPA, JD

Joel Busch is a professor of tax law at San Jose State University, where he teaches courses at both the graduate and undergraduate levels. Previously, he was in charge of tax audits, research and planning for one of the largest civil construction and mining companies in the United States.

69967362R00450

Made in the USA
Columbia, SC
26 April 2017